International Law and Economics

The world has been experiencing a long period of globalization. At the same time, ever more international law has been created to deal with the many consequences of globalization such as problems of coordination, spillover effects across countries, the protection of foreign direct investment or the prosecution of crimes against humanity. To date, the economic analysis of international law has been lagging behind this development. This series aims at changing this by contributing to the understanding of international law. It strives to be a forum for contributions on all aspects of the economic analysis of international law ranging from the analysis of the genesis of international law, its ratification, its effects on government behavior, the means to monitor compliance to sanctions against actors not complying with the law.

Ana Odorović

Overcoming Asymmetric Information in the Crowdfunding Market

A Law and Economics Approach

Springer

Ana Odorović
Institute of Law and Economics
Universität Hamburg
Hamburg, Germany

ISSN 2364-1851 ISSN 2364-186X (electronic)
International Law and Economics
ISBN 978-3-032-04117-3 ISBN 978-3-032-04118-0 (eBook)
https://doi.org/10.1007/978-3-032-04118-0

This Springer imprint is published by the registered company Springer Nature Switzerland AG
The registered company address is: Gewerbestrasse 11, 6330 Cham, Switzerland

Acknowledgements

This journey would not have come to fruition without the support and encouragement of many wonderful individuals and institutions.

First and foremost, I would like to express my deepest gratitude to my PhD supervisor, Wolf-Georg Ringe. Your guidance, insights, and patience have been invaluable. Thank you for helping me persevere.

Special thanks go to the members of my defence committee, Prof. Dr. Anne van Aaken and Prof. Dr. Roee Sarel, for their careful reading of my dissertation, insightful suggestions, and the stimulating discussion during the defence.

I am sincerely thankful for the intellectually stimulating, enriching, and joyful time at the University of Hamburg. It was an honour and privilege to be part of the Graduate School at the Institute of Law and Economics. My gratitude goes to the German Research Foundation and the University of Hamburg's merit scholarship programme for their financial support. I would like to thank Stephan Michel, Jerg Gutmann, and Marek Endrich for their valuable suggestions that helped me shape my research. I also appreciate the opportunity to interact with many other outstanding scholars during the weekly Law and Econ lectures and jour fixe events. Never before have I had the chance to be in such a wonderful group of kind and intelligent people as my peers at the Graduate School. In particular, I am deeply grateful to Julia Samwer, Nada Maamoun, Adriana Espés Pizarro, José Reis, and Hazal Basarik for their friendship and support when it mattered most. Thank you Oliver Englisch, Felicitas Eckebrecht, Fanny Schories, Martina Ferracane, Maximillian Mantei, Ilhan Ömer Kosar, Mohamad Fakhreddin, Karsten Kamps, and Oliver Hofmann for the great times we shared.

An invaluable milestone of this journey was my research stay at the University of Oxford. I would like to thank my mentor Luca Enriques, as well as John Armour, Nir Vulkan, John Vickers, and Frederick Tung for their helpful suggestions. Thanks to Katharina Hufgard for our beautiful Oxford experiences.

This research benefited greatly from collaboration with the Cambridge Centre for Alternative Finance and its associated researchers. Special thanks to my co-author Karsten Wenzlaff for his driving force in our projects. I deeply enjoyed working with Kieran Garvey, Tania Ziegler, Rotem Shneor, Grigory McKain, Dee

Allen, Philip Rowan, Bryan Zheng Zhang, and Emmanuel Schizas. Insightful exchanges with regulators and colleagues within the Cambridge Fintech and Regulatory Innovation programme were extremely helpful.

I appreciate the feedback from several academic conferences, including the 8e conference annuelle de l'Association Française d'Économie, European Alternative Finance Research Conference 2021, 17th Annual Conference of the German Law and Economics Association, 10th Annual Conference of the Spanish Law and Economics Association, the Workshop of the European Banking Institute (Young Researchers Group) at the University of Warsaw, the 2nd European Alternative Finance Conference, 16th Annual Conference of the German Law and Economics Association, 22nd Annual Conference of the Society for Institutional and Organizational Economics, and the EMLE Conference in Law and Economics.

My gratitude goes to the University of Belgrade, Faculty of Law, where I had the chance to start my academic career. I am thankful to Boris Begović for introducing me to the field of law and economics. I am truly grateful to Aleksandra Jovanović and Branko Radulović for their encouragement and support. I also thank my colleagues and friends Valerija Dabetić, Novak Vujičić, Bojana Todorović, Đorđe Marković, and Marija Vlajković for their kind words of reassurance.

I appreciate the support from my colleagues and friends at DNVG attorneys, Marina Nikolić, Srećko Vujaković, and Milorad Glavan, who generously shared their office with me during the final write-up stage.

I received much support from many dear friends. As always, my family was my anchor, encouraging me to take up this opportunity and hold on. Thanks to my brother Lav, my biggest support. Thanks to Damjan and Maksim for enduring the absences and distances, and for their love and understanding.

Competing Interests The author has no competing interests to declare that are relevant to the content of this manuscript.

Contents

List of Figures

List of Tables

Chapter 1
Introduction

1.1 The Context and Aims of the Study

The crowdfunding phenomenon is usually defined as an open call to the public to raise funds, which is made via a web-based platform. It provides individuals and small businesses with a new avenue of raising finances directly from many individuals who usually pledge small amounts. Praised for reducing the access to finance gap and democratising investment opportunities, some authors have even described crowdfunding as one of 'the most exciting financial innovations of the twenty-first century' (Rabbani et al., 2022). Many others have cautioned about the risks when retail investors bypass traditional financial intermediaries, which specialise in screening and monitoring fundraisers.

Various crowdfunding business models that emerged over time are usually distinguished based on the reward they generate for fund providers (backers, investors, or 'the crowd'). Models without a financial return or non-investment models (donation and reward-based crowdfunding) promise either an immaterial or tangible reward. Financial-return models are comprised of lending-based (peer-to-peer (P2P) lending, marketplace lending, debt-based crowdfunding) and equity-based models (investment-based crowdfunding, crowdinvesting). This study primarily addresses questions pertinent to financial-return models, as they involve distinctive promises and perils from their non-counterparts.

Financial-return crowdfunding is a new form of financial intermediation where contracts are concluded directly between fundraisers (individuals or SMEs) and investors. In contrast, the platform acts as a 'matchmaker' or an 'information intermediary', not taking any risk on its balance sheet. As part of a broader trend of disintermediation in financial services enabled thanks to the rise of new technologies (Adhami et al., 2023), crowdfunding is acclaimed for its ability to cut out the 'middleman' and thus make financial contracting more efficient (Lenz, 2016; Yum et al., 2012). Consequently, two features of crowdfunding platforms have been praised—their ability to reduce

A. Odorović, *Overcoming Asymmetric Information in the Crowdfunding Market*, International Law and Economics, https://doi.org/10.1007/978-3-032-04118-0_1

transaction costs and leverage the available information about fundraisers more efficiently (Estrin et al., 2022; Gomber et al., 2017; Liu et al., 2020).

For decades, information asymmetry has been one of the central themes in finance (Bebczuk, 2003) and used to explain the existence of traditional financial intermediaries such as banks or investment firms (Diamond, 1984; Leland & Pyle, 1977). Similarly, reducing information asymmetry has been a critical economic rationale for financial regulation, and ensuring investor protection is one of its most important goals (Armour et al., 2016, pp. 51–79). The crowdfunding market suffers from the same hidden information (adverse selection) and hidden action (agency costs) problems as traditional financial markets (Akerlof, 1970; Jensen & Meckling, 1976). They are likely to be even aggravated, given the characteristics of market participants. On the demand side, individuals and SMEs seeking funding often cannot get finances via traditional means, usually due to their thin track record of past performance. On the supply side, many unsophisticated investors pledge small amounts, reducing their screening and monitoring incentives.

At the onset of the crowdfunding phenomenon, regulators worldwide took distinctive approaches, largely unaware of the degree of market failures and promises and limitations of different regulatory tools that can be used to mitigate them. Even after a decade of law-making in this field, legal scholarship treating the question of optimal regulation of crowdfunding has remained primarily doctrinal, focusing either on the question of whether existing rules (banking or securities laws) can be applied to crowdfunding participants or employing a comparative law approach to studying crowdfunding-specific regimes. There is little theoretical account of whether and how the economic function of crowdfunding platforms corresponds to functions performed by traditional intermediaries in finance. Moreover, legal research has often neglected both theoretical and empirical contributions of economic theory in understanding the incentives of different market participants: fundraisers, investors, and, in particular, the platform. Similarly, little is known whether recent regulatory interventions have improved market outcomes by reducing information asymmetry and helping increase investor confidence in the market.

Consequently, this study aims to reduce the described gap by shedding light on several related issues. It starts by introducing the crowdfunding phenomenon and distinct services offered by crowdfunding platforms, comparing them to services of conventional (financial and information) intermediaries and traditional providers of entrepreneurial finance. Next, it discusses the promises and limitations of market-based mechanisms of mitigating information asymmetries by drawing on insights from information economics and empirical crowdfunding research. Moreover, this study provides a first account of self-regulation in the crowdfunding market by analysing rules that platforms conceived to govern their behaviour. In light of the above findings, this research discusses the residual role of the law in enabling well-functioning crowdfunding markets. Finally, the study empirically investigates the effects of introducing a bespoke crowdfunding regime on market outcomes, using evidence from the United Kingdom (UK). The equity crowdfunding market in the UK is one of the most significant equity crowdfunding markets worldwide and is also known for its 'light-handed' regulatory approach.

1.2 Motivation

Crowdfunding is a financing tool often used by individuals and small companies who either do not have access to traditional funding sources or face essential barriers in terms of costs and inconvenience. By targeting the underserved market segments, the most crucial merit of crowdfunding is reducing the financing gap (Pekmezovic & Walker, 2016). When individuals raise funds, crowdfunding can lead to greater financial inclusion. Moreover, when crowdfunding is used as a financing vehicle by SMEs, it promises to spur innovation and contribute to job creation and economic growth (Butticè & Vismara, 2021; Cumming & Hornuf, 2018). Besides providing finances, business fundraisers use a crowdfunding campaign to test the interest and potential demand for their products and receive valuable feedback on their business ideas through interaction with investors. Communication with many small investors occurs on the campaign page and social media. Thus, fundraisers receive helpful information on the promises of their products before they devote considerable resources, which contributes to allocative efficiency (Cumming et al., 2021). When it comes to retail investors, crowdfunding offers them an unprecedented opportunity to lend or invest directly pretty small amounts of money (sometimes as little as € 5), which can democratise access to risky investments, otherwise often reserved for professional or high-net-worth investors (Butticè & Vismara, 2021; Vismara, 2018).

The exponential growth of the crowdfunding market in recent years suggests that fundraisers and investors have been increasingly attracted to these promises. Namely, according to industry reports, the total amount raised via crowdfunding platforms reached approximately $113 billion (Ziegler et al., 2021). Financial-return models, in particular, loan-based crowdfunding, contributed the highest volumes. Nonetheless, the above-stated long-term benefits can only materialise if adequate investment returns support the market growth. Since crowdfunding is considered a high-risk investment, market outcomes will ultimately depend on the multifaceted interaction between market forces and regulatory intervention.

Regulators in different jurisdictions have struggled to balance investor protection and a moderate regulatory burden by platforms or fundraisers. This has resulted in the fragmentation of regulatory frameworks across various jurisdictions, which is partially due to ongoing experimentation of platforms with varying models of business, which often leads to a reintermediation of the crowdfunding market (Macchiavello & Sciarrone Alibrandi, 2021). Recent trends include the involvement of lead investors, governance through a nominee structure, platform participation in listed projects, operating a provision fund, offering credit risk pricing, automated bidding or portfolio management services, and operating secondary markets. Due to these reasons, even the European crowdfunding regulatory landscape remained fragmented for a long time, resulting in the recent adoption of the European

Crowdfunding Services Providers Regulation (ECSPR) (Regulation (EU), 2020).[1] While the number of crowdfunding bespoke regimes has considerably increased over time, not many jurisdictions outside Europe have comprehensive regulatory frameworks for both loan and equity-based crowdfunding. Many jurisdictions defer the adoption of a bespoke regulatory framework for fear that it will be perceived as regulators' endorsement and legitimisation of an industry whose risks to investors are still largely unknown. Thus, understanding how market-based and regulatory-based solutions to investor protection work and interact is crucial for market development and the confidence investors put in the financial system. While systematic risks of crowdfunding are still small, fragile investor trust can potentially produce spillover effects on other (more traditional) market segments.

1.3 Research Question and Methodology

The research on crowdfunding outside legal scholarship is fast growing. It encompasses a wide array of disciplines, notably economics, management (entrepreneurship), finance, but also psychology and computer science (information systems) (Mochkabadi & Volkmann, 2020; Rabbani et al., 2022). Most of the studies are country-specific and focus on a single crowdfunding model, while a few studies offer a cross-jurisdiction and cross-platform analysis (e.g., Battaglia et al., 2022; Hornuf, Schmitt, & Stenzhorn, 2018; Rossi et al., 2019, 2020). It is common to group crowdfunding research depending on whether it examines the behaviour of platforms, fundraisers, or investors. Studies examining investors' decisions to invest in individual campaigns are the most common,[2] while incentives and services of platforms are the least investigated (notable exceptions include, for instance, Cumming et al. (2019) and Rossi and Vismara (2018)). Two prominent books edited by Cumming and Hornuf (2018) and Shneor et al. (2020) have provided more systematic insights into the behaviour and incentives of different crowdfunding actors and mapped out recent trends in the industry.

A growing number of legal papers thoroughly describe crowdfunding-related regulatory changes in specific countries (e.g., Barrière, 2021; Klöhn et al., 2016; Paredes, 2015; Stemler, 2013; Yeoh, 2014), or provide a comparative law investigation (e.g., Butturini, 2016; Casas & Royo-Villanova, 2022; Cicchiello, 2019; Follak, 2016; Haniff et al., 2019; Juredieu & Mayoux, 2016; Klöhn, 2018; Li, 2022). Since the introduction of the ECSPR, two critical legal contributions have systematically

[1] The new European crowdfunding regime still leaves several open questions (Macchiavello, 2022b) and may evolve as the market matures and more data on market outcomes becomes available. Moreover, several crowdfunding models remain outside its scope either as a result of explicit or implicit exclusions in the text of the Regulation or Member States exercising considerable discretion concerning questions that are left unharmonised.

[2] For a literature review of factors driving investments and crowdfunding success, see, e.g., Shneor and Vik (2020) and Deng et al. (2022).

examined the cornerstones of the new regulation (Macchiavello, 2022a; Ortolani & Louisse, 2021). The goal of this research is to bridge the gap between these two strands of literature by:

- Providing an economics perspective on optimal regulation of financial-return crowdfunding.
- Assessing the effects of adopting bespoke crowdfunding rules.

The underlying hypothesis of this study is that market mechanisms can attenuate some but not all market failures due to information asymmetries. Thus, regulators should interfere when market safeguards are ineffective or insufficient. Moreover, when optimally designed, crowdfunding regulations are expected to foster market outcomes by ensuring better fundraisers appear on crowdfunding platforms and increasing investor confidence in the market.

A law and economics account of crowdfunding has been, thus far, primarily sporadic (e.g., Armour & Enriques, 2018; Cumming & Johan, 2013; Hornuf, Klöhn, & Schilling, 2018; Hornuf & Schwienbacher, 2017; Macchiavello & Sciarrone Alibrandi, 2021), although several contributions in economics and management (entrepreneurship) have important regulatory implications, as will be systematically discussed in this research. Moreover, a recent comprehensive publication by Schwartz (2023) has also focused on the interplay between market forces and regulatory intervention. However, notable differences exist concerning the scope of research, methods used, specific research questions, and main findings.

Based on the above, the overarching research question can be phrased as follows:

- How do market-based and regulatory-based mechanisms complement each other to reduce information asymmetry and ensure investor protection in the crowdfunding market?

The analysis will begin with an overview of how crowdfunding works and discuss its similarities and differences to traditional actors in financial markets (financial (balance sheet) intermediaries, information intermediaries (gatekeepers), and traditional providers of entrepreneurial finance). Next, the research will draw on the existing theoretical and empirical (economics) literature to understand the promises and limitations of measures adopted by fundraisers and platforms to mitigate information asymmetry. In adopting these measures, fundraisers are driven by the need to differentiate themselves from low-quality applications/projects, whereas platforms assume the role of gatekeepers. In other words, while seeking to maximise volumes raised on their portal, platforms tend to experiment with different reintermediation services, some of which raise new market failure concerns. This research will also provide an account of investors' apprehension of these mitigation measures to understand whether they are adequate and analyse how they can inform regulatory tools aiming to substitute market mechanisms (e.g., mandatory disclosure requirements). Thus, identified market failures will serve to discuss the residual role of the law and regulatory intervention. In addition to market-based mechanisms at the fundraiser and platform level, the analysis will also focus on self-regulation at the industry level, offering a systematic account of market failures from the lenses of platforms. Put differently, rules embedded in the codes of conduct of crowdfunding associations can be interpreted as an industry-wide consensus on areas that require regulatory intervention.

When discussing the residual role of the law, the research will examine how regulators in different jurisdictions approached the crowdfunding phenomenon. Their responses include the baseline scenario of no regulation, stretching the rules created for traditional services, allowing for experimentation through regulatory innovation initiatives (innovation offices and sandboxes), and adopting bespoke regulations. Furthermore, the research will discuss whether treating different crowdfunding models under one regulatory umbrella is optimal and which risk-related considerations call for a different regulatory treatment. Finally, drawing on the insights from the previous analysis, this research will discuss the critical aspects of crowdfunding regulations governing the behaviour of fundraisers, platforms, and investors.

Thus, the overarching research question can be subdivided into a set of more specific ones, including:

- What are the main crowdfunding business models, and how do they relate to traditional actors in financial markets? (Chap. 2).
- How do fundraisers communicate the quality of their ventures/loan applications, and how do investors perceive these measures? (Chap. 3).
- What do platforms do to reduce information asymmetry in their capacity as gatekeepers? Which additional risks emerge as platforms assume new reintermediation roles? (Chap. 3).
- Why do platforms adhere to industry-wide codes of conduct? How can the content of codes of conduct inform financial regulation theory in crowdfunding? (Chap. 4).
- Based on the above, what is the residual role of the law? What are (or should be) the critical approaches and principles in designing crowdfunding regulations? (Chap. 5).
- What is the value added of introducing a bespoke crowdfunding regime? What lessons can be learned from the UK equity-based crowdfunding market? (Chap. 6).

In addressing these questions, the research will primarily be jurisdiction-agnostic, drawing on empirical findings from different crowdfunding markets, models, and platforms. When discussing specific regulatory solutions, the review of relevant laws will involve early adopters of a tailored crowdfunding regime, primarily several European Member States, the UK, and the ECSPR. The goal is to discuss the principles of optimal financial regulation of crowdfunding while considering the risk implications of different business models. As a result, this research will neglect notable differences among jurisdictions that may be important due to legal origins, path dependence from regulations of traditional financial intermediaries, or different capacities of regulators to enforce specific rules.

It is also important to note that the central theme studied is information asymmetry and associated investor protection safeguards. Nevertheless, the crowdfunding phenomenon can also raise other regulatory concerns within or outside the regulatory perimeter of financial authorities, such as systematic risks, money laundering and terrorism financing (ML/TF), data breaches, and cybersecurity. These concerns and associated regulatory measures will not be discussed systematically either because they are (still) not pronounced (e.g., systematic risks)[3] or because they are not specific to crowdfunding (e.g., issues related to ML/TF, data protection, cybersecurity).[4]

As can be seen from how research subquestions are phrased, the study will comprise both positive (predominantly in Chaps. 2, 3, 4, and 6) and normative analysis (predominantly in Chap. 5). Several methods will be used to provide an interdisciplinary (law and economics) and systematic account of the issues mentioned above, depending on the nature of the question addressed (theoretical or empirical) and related subject matters.

In addressing the theoretical questions, the analysis will draw on the existing theory from information economics, touching upon some seminal discussions in law and finance and corporate governance, literature on platform economics (economics of two-sided markets), and existing (largely empirical) crowdfunding literature. The normative analysis of the optimal regulatory regime for crowdfunding (Chap. 5) may include elements of doctrinal legal research when reviewing existing regulatory solutions in different jurisdictions. Empirical questions will be explored using qualitative case studies (in the case of Chap. 4) and quantitative-econometric methods (in the case of Chap. 6).

1.4 Course of the Study

This study is organised into five core chapters. Chapter 2 introduces crowdfunding as a new means of direct finance. It explains the core issues in crowdfunding (asymmetric information and high coordination costs among fundraisers) and discusses them in the context of a broader financial system. Next, it reviews more precise definitions of crowdfunding, particularly financial-return crowdfunding, and provides an overview of core and auxiliary services offered by crowdfunding platforms in different stages. The scope of platform services is the key to understanding whether crowdfunding is truly a disintermediated funding mechanism. Therefore, the second part of this chapter discusses how the role of crowdfunding platforms relates to the role exercised by traditional financial intermediaries (banks and investment intermediaries) and information intermediaries in direct finance (gatekeepers). Finally, the last part compares crowdfunding to conventional forms of entrepreneurial finance.

[3] For a discussion on how a newly emerging trend of securitisation in P2P lending can potentially lead to systematic risk, see, e.g., Bavoso (2020).

[4] These risks have nevertheless been acknowledged and discussed in the crowdfunding context, see, e.g., Butarbutar (2020), Kjærgaard Sørensen and Steen (2022).

Chapter 3 draws on information economics and empirical crowdfunding literature to analyse market-based investor protection mechanisms in the crowdfunding market. They aim to reduce the information asymmetry gap between fundraisers and crowd investors. These mechanisms primarily include providing information and practices that reduce the costs of information verification and processing. The chapter begins by discussing the role of information in traditional financial markets and crowdfunding—mitigating adverse selection and agency problems or, conversely, enhancing investor confidence, inducing efficient capital allocation, and improving corporate governance. The chapter then explains information unravelling by fundraisers from a theoretical perspective, which occurs via information disclosure and signalling. This serves as a basis for a review of the existing empirical evidence on how fundraisers communicate the quality of their loan applications/ventures and how investors interpret them. In addition to signals originating directly from fundraisers, the chapter also discusses signals from other investors—'the crowd' (information cascades or herding) and professional (lead) investors. In reviewing the evidence, the chapter introduces an original framework aiming to disentangle different potential sources of market failure: incomplete information, limited attention or information processing, and lack of credibility of disclosed information or fundraisers' actions. The chapter also analyses investor protection mechanisms developed by platforms. In their role as gatekeepers, platforms offer several ex-ante and ex-post services. Ex-ante services include imposing disclosure rules on fundraisers, conducting due diligence and preselecting fundraisers, providing credit risk assessment and pricing, and enabling automatic investments. Ex-post services include delegated monitoring concerning loan contracts (debt collection and loss recovery), facilitating governance of funded companies, operating secondary markets, or provision funds. This chapter also discusses the variance in these practices and the new risks that emerge as the platform assumes the gatekeeping role.

Chapter 4 provides a theoretical and empirical account of the self-regulation of European crowdfunding markets. In the early years of crowdfunding in Europe, platforms in different jurisdictions joined crowdfunding associations, which created rules that govern platform behaviour (codes of conduct (CoCs)). Drawing on the economic theories of self-regulation, the chapter investigates why crowdfunding platforms adhere to CoCs and, more specifically, what their institutional characteristics can reveal about the underlying economic rationale. This chapter illustrates the differences in the regulatory context, inclusiveness, monitoring, and enforcement of CoCs. For this purpose, a comparative case study of nine CoCs in Europe is conducted. The chapter also offers the first systematic overview of substantial rules of CoCs in crowdfunding, showing the potential sources of market failure through the perspectives of platforms.

Chapter 5 draws on previous chapters' findings to discuss the law's residual role. It investigates several conceptual questions related to the regulation of financial-return crowdfunding. The first question relates to the regulatory 'tetralemma' in approaching the crowdfunding phenomenon. Namely, some jurisdictions left crowdfunding unregulated, or platforms designed their business models to escape regulatory oversight, which was deemed too burdensome. Other jurisdictions applied rules that govern the behaviour of traditional financial or information intermediaries (banks, investment firms, payment institutions, alternative investment funds managers, etc.) ('stretch-to-fit' approach). The third group of jurisdictions allowed a phase of learning and experimentation through the adoption of regulatory innovation initiatives (innovation offices and regulatory sandboxes). Finally, the fourth group of countries adopted crowdfunding-specific regimes. The second question addressed in this chapter is whether financial-return crowdfunding models should be put under the same regulatory umbrella and what should be the decisive criteria for a different regulatory treatment (the type of financial contracts, the type of fundraisers (consumers vs. businesses), or the scope of platform services). The last question addressed in this chapter is the fundamental principles in designing rules for fundraisers, platforms, and investors. More specifically, the chapter analyses the desirability of mandatory disclosure rules, rules that strengthen the gatekeeping functions of platforms, and specific retail investor safeguards.

Chapter 6 examines whether adopting a bespoke crowdfunding regulation in the UK affected market outcomes using data from equity platforms between 2012 and 2016. The UK regulator, the Financial Conduct Authority (FCA), introduced crowdfunding-specific rules in 2014 to provide more clarity on the obligations of platforms and introduced new regulatory safeguards for retail investors (Financial Conduct Authority, 2014). The question is whether this change influenced either one or both sides of the market—fundraisers and investors, and whether, as a result, the success of crowdfunding campaigns became more likely. As to the effect on the demand side of the market, the study examines whether crowdfunding regulation increased the legitimacy of this funding tool among potential fundraisers so that better quality projects appeared after 2014. If this were true, post-regulation projects would seek more significant amounts, retain more equity, and offer more voting rights to their investors than their pre-regulation counterparts.

Regarding the effect on the market's supply side, the question is whether regulation increased investors' participation, i.e. the number of investors per campaign and whether it affected average amounts pledged in a single campaign. Concerning individual investment amounts, the study also examines the behaviour of different types of investors: ordinary, sophisticated, high-net-worth, and investors receiving professional advice. In addition, the study further makes the difference between old investors—those who invested in crowdfunding even before the regulation, and new investors—those who appeared on crowdfunding platforms only after the regulation. Concerning this distinction, the study explores whether old investors changed their behaviour after the regulation and whether new investors are different from the old ones in terms of how much they invest. Finally, the study looks into campaign-level crowdfunding outcomes by examining whether campaigns that appeared after adopting a bespoke regime were more successful.

Chapter 6 summarises the main findings of the study and discusses its contributions, limitations, and avenues for future research.

References

Adhami, S., Gianfrate, G., & Johan, S. (2023). Risks and returns in crowdlending. *Eurasian Business Review, 13*(2), 309–340. https://doi.org/10.1007/s40821-022-00236-x

Akerlof, G. A. (1970). The market for 'lemons': Quality uncertainty and the market mechanism. *The Quarterly Journal of Economics, 84*(3), 488–500. https://doi.org/10.2307/1879431

Armour, J., Awrey, D., Davies, P. L., Enriques, L., Gordon, J. N., Mayer, C. P., & Payne, J. (2016). *Principles of financial regulation*. Oxford University Press. https://doi.org/10.1093/acprof:oso/9780198786474.001.0001

Armour, J., & Enriques, L. (2018). The promise and perils of crowdfunding: Between corporate finance and consumer contracts: The promise and perils of crowdfunding. *The Modern Law Review, 81*(1), 51–84. https://doi.org/10.1111/1468-2230.12316

Barrière, F. (2021). Le crowdfunding, ou l'adaptation du droit au service des investissements en France. In C. Kleiner (Ed.), *Legal aspects of crowdfunding* (pp. 303–319). Springer. https://doi.org/10.1007/978-3-030-79264-0_12

Battaglia, F., Busato, F., & Manganiello, M. (2022). A cross-platform analysis of the equity crowdfunding Italian context: The role of intellectual capital. *Electronic Commerce Research, 22*(2), 649–689. https://doi.org/10.1007/s10660-020-09453-w

Bavoso, V. (2020). The promise and perils of alternative market-based finance: The case of P2P lending in the UK. *Journal of Banking Regulation, 21*(4), 395–409. https://doi.org/10.1057/s41261-019-00118-9

Bebczuk, R. N. (2003). *Asymmetric information in financial markets: Introduction and applications*. Cambridge University Press.

Butarbutar, R. (2020). Personal data protection in P2P lending: What Indonesia should learn from Malaysia? *Pertanika Journal of Social Sciences and Humanities, 28*(3), 2295–2307. Retrieved from http://www.pertanika.upm.edu.my/resources/files/Pertanika%20PAPERS/JSSH%20Vol.%2028%20(3)%20Sep.%202020/39%20JSSH-5415-2019.pdf

Butticè, V., & Vismara, S. (2021). Inclusive digital finance: The industry of equity crowdfunding. *The Journal of Technology Transfer, 47*(4), 1224–1241. https://doi.org/10.1007/s10961-021-09875-0

Butturini, P. (2016). Financial crowdfunding regulation in EU countries. In R. Bottiglia & F. Pichler (Eds.), *Crowdfunding for SMEs: A European perspective* (pp. 185–210). Palgrave Macmillan. https://doi.org/10.1057/978-1-137-56021-6_8

Casas, M. C., & Royo-Villanova, S. Á. (2022). A comparative analysis of Spanish crowdfunding regulation and the ECSPR. In E. Macchiavello (Ed.), *Regulation on European crowdfunding service providers for business* (pp. 751–764). Edward Elgar Publishing. https://doi.org/10.4337/9781802209945.00062

Cicchiello, A. F. (2019). Harmonizing the crowdfunding regulation in Europe: Need, challenges, and risks. *Journal of Small Business & Entrepreneurship*. https://doi.org/10.1080/08276331.2019.1603945

Cumming, D., & Hornuf, L. (2018). *The economics of crowdfunding*. Springer.

Cumming, D., & Johan, S. (2013). Demand-driven securities regulation: Evidence from crowdfunding. *Venture Capital, 15*(4), 361–379. https://doi.org/10.1080/13691066.2013.847635

Cumming, D. J., Johan, S. A., & Zhang, Y. (2019). The role of due diligence in crowdfunding platforms. *Journal of Banking & Finance, 108*, 105661. https://doi.org/10.1016/j.jbankfin.2019.105661

Cumming, D. J., Vanacker, T., & Zahra, S. A. (2021). Equity crowdfunding and governance: Toward an integrative model and research agenda. *Academy of Management Perspectives, 35*(1), 69–95. https://doi.org/10.5465/amp.2017.0208

Deng, L., Ye, Q., Xu, D., Sun, W., & Jiang, G. (2022). A literature review and integrated framework for the determinants of crowdfunding success. *Financial Innovation, 8*(1), 41. https://doi.org/10.1186/s40854-022-00345-6

Diamond, D. W. (1984). Financial intermediation and delegated monitoring. *The Review of Economic Studies, 51*(3), 393–414. https://doi.org/10.2307/2297430

Estrin, S., Khavul, S., & Wright, M. (2022). Soft and hard information in equity crowdfunding: Network effects in the digitalization of entrepreneurial finance. *Small Business Economics, 58*(4), 1761–1781. https://doi.org/10.1007/s11187-021-00473-w

Financial Conduct Authority. (2014). *The FCA'S regulatory approach to crowdfunding over the internet, and the promotion of non-readily realisable securities by other media (policy statement PS14/4).* Financial Conduct Authority. Retrieved from https://www.fca.org.uk/publication/policy/ps14-04.pdf

Follak, K. P. (2016). Crowdfunding in international and National Regulatory Frameworks. *Banking & Finance Law Review, 32*(1), 167–181. Retrieved from https://www.proquest.com/openview/21884b7c643540edc10536fc68fba23c/1?pq-origsite=gscholar&cbl=44976

Gomber, P., Koch, J.-A., & Siering, M. (2017). Digital finance and FinTech: Current research and future research directions. *Journal of Business Economics, 87*(5), 537–580. https://doi.org/10.1007/s11573-017-0852-x

Haniff, W. A. A. W., Ab Halim, A. H., & Ismail, R. (2019). The regulation of equity crowdfunding in United Kingdom and Malaysia: A comparative study. *Academic Journal of Interdisciplinary Studies, 8*(3), 45–56. https://doi.org/10.36941/ajis-2019-0004

Hornuf, L., Klöhn, L., & Schilling, T. (2018). Financial contracting in crowdinvesting: Lessons from the German market. *German Law Journal, 19*(3), 509–578. https://doi.org/10.1017/S2071832200022781

Hornuf, L., Schmitt, M., & Stenzhorn, E. (2018). Equity crowdfunding in Germany and the United Kingdom: Follow-up funding and firm failure. *Corporate Governance: An International Review, 26*(5), 331–354. https://doi.org/10.1111/corg.12260

Hornuf, L., & Schwienbacher, A. (2017). Should securities regulation promote equity crowdfunding? *Small Business Economics, 49*(3), 579–593. https://doi.org/10.1007/s11187-017-9839-9

Jensen, M. C., & Meckling, W. H. (1976). Theory of the firm: Managerial behavior, agency costs and ownership structure. *Journal of Financial Economics, 3*(4), 305–360. https://doi.org/10.1016/0304-405X(76)90026-X

Juredieu, F., & Mayoux, S. (2016). Crowdfunding legal framework: An international analysis. In J. Méric, I. Maque, & J. Brabet (Eds.), *International perspectives on crowdfunding* (pp. 81–97). Emerald Group Publishing Limited.

Kjærgaard Sørensen, N., & Steen, U. (2022). The fundraiser's transfer of personal data from the European Union to the United States in context of crowdfunding activities. *Nordic Journal of Commercial Law, 2*, 117–136. https://doi.org/10.54337/ojs.njcl.2.7545

Klöhn, L. (2018). The regulation of crowdfunding in Europe. In D. Cumming & L. Hornuf (Eds.), *The economics of crowdfunding* (pp. 219–253). Palgrave Macmillan.

Klöhn, L., Hornuf, L., & Schilling, T. (2016). The regulation of crowdfunding in the German small investor protection act: Content, consequences, critique, suggestions. *European Company Law, 13*(2), 56–66. Retrieved from https://papers.ssrn.com/sol3/papers.cfm?abstract_id=2595773

Leland, H. E., & Pyle, D. H. (1977). Informational asymmetries, financial structure, and financial intermediation. *The Journal of Finance, 32*(2), 371–387. https://doi.org/10.2307/2326770

Lenz, R. (2016). Peer-to-peer lending: Opportunities and risks. *European Journal of Risk Regulation, 7*(4), 688–700. https://doi.org/10.1017/S1867299X00010126

Li, Y. (2022). The regulation of equity crowdfunding in the US: Remaining concerns and lessons from the UK. *Journal of Corporate Law Studies, 22*(1), 265–298. https://doi.org/10.1080/14735970.2022.2040815

Liu, Z., Shang, J., Wu, S., & Chen, P. (2020). Social collateral, soft information and online peer-to-peer lending: A theoretical model. *European Journal of Operational Research, 281*(2), 428–438. https://doi.org/10.1016/j.ejor.2019.08.038

Macchiavello, E. (Ed.). (2022a). *Regulation on European crowdfunding service providers for business: A commentary*. Edward Elgar Publishing.

Macchiavello, E. (2022b). The challenges awaiting the European crowdfunding services providers regulation: Ready for launch? *Nordic Journal of Commercial Law, 2*, 91–115. https://doi.org/10.54337/ojs.njcl.2.7544

Macchiavello, E., & Sciarrone Alibrandi, A. (2021). Marketplace lending as a new means of raising capital in the internal market: True disintermediation or reintermediation? In E. Avgouleas & H. Marjosola (Eds.), *Digital finance in Europe: Law, regulation, and governance* (pp. 37–86). De Gruyter. https://doi.org/10.1515/9783110749472-003

Mochkabadi, K., & Volkmann, C. K. (2020). Equity crowdfunding: A systematic review of the literature. *Small Business Economics, 54*(1), 75–118. https://doi.org/10.1007/s11187-018-0081-x

Ortolani, P., & Louisse, M. (2021). *The EU crowdfunding regulation*. Oxford University Press.

Paredes, T. (2015). JOBS act—The terrible twos-general solicitation and crowdfunding—The next frontier of securities regulation. *The Fordham Journal of Corporate & Financial Law, 299*, 293–347. Retrieved from https://ir.lawnet.fordham.edu/jcfl/vol20/iss2/7

Pekmezovic, A., & Walker, G. (2016). The global significance of crowdfunding: Solving the SME funding problem and democratizing access to capital. *William & Mary Business Law Review, 7*, 347–458. Retrieved from https://heinonline.org/HOL/LandingPage?handle=hein.journals/wmaybur7&div=14&id=&page

Rabbani, M. R., Bashar, A., Hawaldar, I. T., Shaik, M., & Selim, M. (2022). What do we know about crowdfunding and P2P lending research? A bibliometric review and meta-analysis. *Journal of Risk and Financial Management, 15*(10), 451. https://doi.org/10.3390/jrfm15100451

Regulation (EU). (2020). *2020/1503 of the European Parliament and of the Council of 7 October 2020 on European Crowdfunding Service Providers for Business, and Amending Regulation (EU) 2017/1129 and Directive (EU) 2019/1937*. Retrieved from https://eur-lex.europa.eu/legal-content/EN/TXT/PDF/?uri=CELEX:32020R1503

Rossi, A., Vanacker, T. R., & Vismara, S. (2020). Equity crowdfunding: New evidence from US and UK markets. *SSRN Electronic Journal*. https://doi.org/10.2139/ssrn.3752616

Rossi, A., & Vismara, S. (2018). What do crowdfunding platforms do? A comparison between investment-based platforms in Europe. *Eurasian Business Review, 8*(1), 93–118. https://doi.org/10.1007/s40821-017-0092-6

Rossi, A., Vismara, S., & Meoli, M. (2019). Voting rights delivery in investment-based crowdfunding: A cross-platform analysis. *Journal of Industrial and Business Economics, 46*(2), 251–281. https://doi.org/10.1007/s40812-018-0109-x

Schwartz, A. A. (2023). *Investment crowdfunding*. Oxford University Press.

Shneor, R., & Vik, A. A. (2020). Crowdfunding success: A systematic literature review 2010–2017. *Baltic Journal of Management, 15*(2), 149–182. https://doi.org/10.1108/BJM-04-2019-0148

Shneor, R., Zhao, L., & Flåten, B.-T. (2020). *Advances in crowdfunding: Research and practice*. Springer International Publishing. https://doi.org/10.1007/978-3-030-46309-0

Stemler, A. R. (2013). The JOBS act and crowdfunding: Harnessing the power—And money—Of the masses. *Business Horizons, 56*(3), 271–275. https://doi.org/10.1016/j.bushor.2013.01.007

Vismara, S. (2018). Signaling to overcome inefficiencies in crowdfunding markets. In D. Cumming & L. Hornuf (Eds.), *The economics of crowdfunding* (pp. 29–56). Palgrave Macmillan. https://doi.org/10.1007/978-3-319-66119-3_3

Yeoh, P. (2014). Implications of online funding regulations for small businesses. *Journal of Financial Regulation and Compliance, 22*(4), 349–364. https://doi.org/10.1108/JFRC-02-2014-0012

Yum, H., Lee, B., & Chae, M. (2012). From the wisdom of crowds to my own judgment in microfinance through online peer-to-peer lending platforms. *Electronic Commerce Research and Applications, 11*(5), 469–483. https://doi.org/10.1016/j.elerap.2012.05.003

Ziegler, T., Shneor, R., Wenzlaff, K., Suresh, K., Paes, F. F. C., Mammadova, L., Wanga, C., Kekre, N., Mutinda, S., & Wang, B. (2021). *The 2nd global alternative finance market benchmarking report*. Cambridge Centre for Alternative Finance. Retrieved from https://www.jbs.cam.ac.uk/faculty-research/centres/alternative-finance/publications/the-2nd-global-alternative-finance-market-benchmarking-report/

Chapter 2
Crowdfunding and 'Disintermediation'

2.1 Preliminaries

Before deep diving into the specifics of this study, it is helpful to put crowdfunding into a broader context and introduce some of the central concepts employed. A large-scale digital transformation of all sectors characterises the economy of the twenty-first century. Often described as a period of the 'fourth industrial revolution', technological innovations have no historical precedent regarding their velocity and scope (Schwab, 2017). Alongside breakthroughs in production processes, a radical shift has been brought about by new business models known as the 'platform economy' (Rodriguez de las Heras Ballell, 2019, p. 392). Platforms are defined as businesses that create opportunities for user interaction 'where non-organised marketplaces often have failed to properly solve coordination problems and the asymmetric information problem' (Belleflamme & Peitz, 2021, p. 2). From e-commerce to tourism, transportation, technology, and communications—platform business models have populated all kinds of industries. They contribute substantially to the world's GDP, whereas some of the largest companies worldwide were built thanks to platforms at the core of the value proposition.

The finance sector is no exception, with crowdfunding platforms being one prominent case.[1] The essential role of crowdfunding platforms is to connect the sources of capital (the crowd) with the uses of capital (fundraisers) (Cumming & Hornuf, 2022, p. 38). Often, those with capital to invest and those who need capital face high transaction costs to find each other and conclude and enforce contracts between them. These costs primarily stem from asymmetric information problems

[1] In addition to platform-based models, recent structural changes in the financial sector involve using distributed ledger technologies (DLT). In contrast to platforms, the latter system involves a decentralised and disintermediated system based on a trust widespread across many unknown users (Rodriguez de las Heras Ballell, 2019, pp. 392–397).

A. Odorović, *Overcoming Asymmetric Information in the Crowdfunding Market*, International Law and Economics, https://doi.org/10.1007/978-3-032-04118-0_2

since fundraisers are better informed than investors about their creditworthiness or projects' ability to generate future cash flows. Moreover, investors typically have limited capacity to monitor fundraisers ex-post, ensuring that fundraisers honour their promises. Ex-ante screening and ex-post monitoring costs are fixed and often disproportionately high compared to individual investments (Vismara, 2018, pp. 32–33). Investors' incentives to bear them individually are further reduced when they diversify their portfolios to mitigate the idiosyncratic risk of investments. Moreover, if all individual investors engaged in independent screening and monitoring, this would lead to unnecessary duplication of costs.

These issues could be overcome if they were able to coordinate their efforts to finance individual loans or projects jointly. However, coordination among investors is hindered by collective action problem that emerges when assessing the investment opportunity, negotiating contracts, monitoring the contract execution, and exercising different contractual rights, such as those associated with debt recovery or voting (Meoli et al., 2022, p. 8; Vismara, 2018, p. 30).[2] Most of these tasks have a public goods nature, which means that individual investors who decide to incur the necessary effort will appropriate only a fraction of the total benefit. Consequently, investors are prone to free-riding—they contribute insufficiently to activities in the joint interest of all investors, expecting others to perform instead. Consequently, their coordination is likely to fail.

Due to these reasons, traditional markets for direct finance only exist in instances where these market frictions are not that pronounced.[3] These include large companies raising funds via a public offering in primary financial markets (e.g., stock exchanges) or private companies seeking capital from institutional or professional investors (private equity and debt markets). In the case of public financial markets, issues of information asymmetry are also attenuated thanks to the operation of different information intermediaries (also known as gatekeepers), including the stock exchange, investment banks in their role of underwriters, credit rating agencies, investment brokers, securities analysts, lawyers, auditors, etc. Similarly, private markets are dominated by business angels and venture capitalists (VC) who have a long history of collective practice during which they developed different mechanisms for assessing investment quality and mitigating ex-post managerial opportunism (Estrin et al., 2022, p. 1763). Yet, it is worth noting that even traditional markets for direct finance have primarily taken off in developed countries (in particular, the US and UK).

In other instances, capital seekers and capital providers are compelled to interact through traditional financial intermediaries (depository institutions, investment

[2] The theory of collective action was first developed by Olson Jr (1965). For an overview of the theory, see Congleton (2015).

[3] The distinction between direct and indirect finance is based on whether the flow of funds between lenders/savers and borrowers/spenders goes through financial intermediaries (Mishkin, 2007, p. 24).

intermediaries, and contractual savings institutions).[4] In fact, according to the conventional theory of financial intermediation, the reduction of transaction costs and costs of asymmetric information is the underlying rationale for the existence of institutions of indirect finance (Allen & Santomero, 1997).[5] By internalising these costs and by specialising in information gathering and processing at a scale, financial intermediaries generate value for ultimate capital seekers and capital providers.[6] More recent theories of financial intermediation have also emphasised some other functions of intermediaries, particularly the value of risk management and risk transformation (Allen & Santomero, 1997; Scholtens & Van Wensveen, 2000). Namely, financial intermediaries can provide capital providers (e.g., depositors) with a comfortable level of credit, term, and liquidity risk while at the same time investing in longer-term, riskier, and less liquid assets.

The innovation of crowdfunding platforms is that they enable a market for direct finance that connects retail investors, on the one hand, with individual borrowers or SMEs, on the other, without at any point acting as a financial (balance sheet) intermediary. Retail investors actively and collectively decide which loans or enterprises to finance (Pur et al., 2023, p. 65). As a result, they gain access to a new (risky) asset class, which should also promise higher returns. Individual borrowers and SMEs are offered an additional financing channel, which is also expected to be more convenient in terms of accessibility, costs, and speed than traditional financing options. Another distinguishing feature of crowdfunding is that it stands between public and private markets. The participation of dispersed investors makes it similar to conventional (primary) financial markets. In contrast, the absence of (liquid) secondary markets for crowdfunding investment (debt or equity) brings it closer to investments in private firms. The 'non-mainstream' and illiquid nature of crowdfunding assets is

[4] According to Mishkin (2007, pp. 34–37), the distinction between intermediaries is based on what they use as the sources of funds (primary liabilities) and how they subsequently use the funds (primary assets). When it comes to the sources of funds, depositary institutions use deposits, investment intermediaries issue securities, while contractual savings institutions (e.g., insurance companies, pension funds) rely on insurance premiums and employment contributions.

[5] Diamond (1984) first emphasised the role of banks as delegated monitors, which use information production technology to minimise monitoring costs, while the costs of 'monitoring the monitor' are reduced thanks to diversification within financial intermediaries. Similarly, Leland and Pyle (1977, pp. 382–384) argued that intermediaries exist because sellers of information about certain assets face the appropriability and credibility problem. The former refers to a situation in which the seller of information cannot appropriate returns to their information gathering due to the public good nature of the information. The latter relates to the issue of buyers of information not being able to differentiate between the quality of information sold. The existence of intermediaries solves both problems because they sell and hold assets based on their own specialised information, which allows them to appropriate returns as well as signal the credibility of the information gathered.

[6] In a broader sense, this reasoning is aligned with the Coasian theory of the firm, which predicts that certain activities are organised within the firm (a hierarchy) as opposed to arms' length market transactions when transaction costs are higher than bureaucratic/managerial costs associated with coordinating many isolated activities (Coase, 1937).

why crowdfunding is considered a form of alternative finance (Farag & Johan, 2022, p. 1).[7]

The use of technology is at the core of the platform's value proposition. First, crowdfunding platforms exist only online, as opposed to 'brick-and-mortar' operations of traditional intermediaries such as banks. The driving factor of crowdfunding uptake is the development of a second generation of Internet offering ('Web 2.0 businesses'), which turned passive Internet users into active creators of web content who increasingly participate in digital interactions and disseminate information (Chaffee & Rapp, 2012, pp. 501–503; Pur et al., 2023, p. 64). This change coincided with or enabled an important shift in the behaviour of investors driven by new generations, which Ricci and Sautter (2021) denote as 'wireless investors'.[8] According to these authors, wireless investors are more accustomed to engaging in collective action, particularly if it also advances some social or environmental causes.[9] The rise of social media networks also underpinned these trends, allowing them to better harness information spread across many individual investors and facilitate the coordination of their efforts. Crowdfunding platforms also often rely on other technological advancements which facilitate their operation as two-sided marketplaces. Depending on their business model, these can include payment processing technologies, cloud computing, anti-fraud/digital identity technologies, and algorithms, particularly machine learning (ML) and artificial intelligence (AI), or distributed ledger technology (DLT).[10] When it comes to using algorithms of different complexity, their application in crowdfunding is diverse: anti-fraud/digital identity, credit scoring, creating content for campaigns, advertising, etc. In relation to this, crowdfunding platforms also sometimes leverage alternative data on fundraisers, which promises to make risk assessments more accurate.

In broadest terms, all these different technological developments enable a crowdfunding platform to offer an 'information production technology' that reduces market frictions associated with information asymmetries and the collective action

[7] The term 'alternative finance' is sometimes understood broadly to encompass investments that occur outside stock markets (Farag & Johan, 2022, p. 1), while sometimes it is used as a synonym for financial services offered by non-bank providers, usually leveraging financial technology (fintech) (e.g., Baeck et al., 2014; Bavoso, 2020; Zhang et al., 2016; Ziegler et al., 2020, 2021).

[8] These new generations are also sometimes referred to as 'tech-savvy and mobile consumers' (Brummer & Yadav, 2018, p. 276).

[9] Ricci and Sautter (2022) have argued that new investors can shift the rational apathy paradigm around retail investors' use of information and governance.

[10] The core platform information technology (IT) infrastructure can be secured via different means. According to Shneor et al. (2024), platforms can use a software-as-a-service solution (SaaS) (also known as white-label crowdfunding software), buy a proprietary software solution from an external vendor, and build the software in-house or with the help of an external team. These options differ regarding the degree to which they are customised to the needs of a specific platform, affecting the costs of acquisition as well as the costs of later software developments and adjustments. Interestingly, the study by Shneor et al. (2024) shows that, among European financial-return platforms (lending and equity crowdfunding models), about 60% built their core software in-house, in contrast to about 15%, which use white-label crowdfunding software.

problem, as explained earlier. It facilitates the participation of both sides of the market and reduces the costs of gathering, processing, and verifying information, which otherwise represent obstacles to concluding and executing financial contracts directly.

Crowdfunding is part of the broader fintech industry thanks to its technological underpinnings. With their user-friendly applications and greater focus on specific customer needs, fintech firms are often seen as threatening the banks' central role in the financial system. Namely, fintech innovations can contribute to the 'unbundling' or 'disintermediation' of banking services or 'decomposing' of the banking value chain (Adhami et al., 2023; Brummer & Yadav, 2018; Gibilaro & Mattarocci, 2018; Kaja et al., 2021; Macchiavello, 2021a; Macchiavello & Sciarrone Alibrandi, 2021). Put differently, they enable some of the typical banking services to be contracted out of banks and into technological firms or market transactions (Jackson, 2020, p. 11). As part of this broader disruption in the financial industry, crowdfunding platforms are also expected to shift the boundaries of traditional financial intermediaries (Tröger, 2021, pp. 93–94), potentially replacing some of the market segments these intermediaries serve[11] or to create a market that previously did not exist.

It should be emphasised that promises of creating a new market in which 'the middleman' is eliminated (Chaffee & Rapp, 2012, p. 492; Yum et al., 2012, p. 470) depend on active and engaged platforms. Despite not being exposed to financial risk, platforms take on several functions that reduce market imperfections inherent in direct financial markets. These may also include different degrees of screening, monitoring, and risk management on investors' behalf. Understanding platforms' core business model and variations in the services they offer is, thus, a starting point in the discussion of whether and how they should be regulated. In particular, avoiding a regulatory failure entails assessing whether platforms 'attenuate traditional justifications for government interventions' or they 'create new jeopardies for established policy goals' (Tröger, 2021, p. 94). With this perspective in mind, it is helpful to analyse first how platform services mirror those performed by traditional financial intermediaries, gatekeepers, and traditional providers of entrepreneurial capital.

To this aim, the following section takes a step back to define crowdfunding and its most important models (Sect. 2.2). Since this study focuses on crowdfunding with a financial return, particular emphasis is given to explaining its variations using different criteria adopted by scholars and financial regulators (Sect. 2.3). The next step introduces the core and auxiliary functions of crowdfunding platforms (Sect. 2.4). Concerning these functions, the last part of this chapter discusses how crowdfunding relates to actors in traditional finance, mainly financial and information intermediaries and conventional providers of entrepreneurial finance (Sect. 2.5). A summary of critical insights is provided at the end (Sect. 2.6).

[11] The idea that intermediaries could eventually become redundant with a reduction of information and transaction costs is not new. Yet, as witnessed in the last decades, despite the reduction of these costs, the relative importance of financial intermediaries even increased due to the greater sophistication of their functions (Scholtens & Van Wensveen, 2000, pp. 1243–1247).

2.2 Crowdfunding Definitions

There is no unique definition of crowdfunding, while key defining features mainly vary with specific crowdfunding models. It is also possible to differentiate between scholarly and statutory (legal) definitions. The latter type typically originates from regulatory authorities introducing crowdfunding-specific regulations, acknowledging the need for a tailored regulatory approach to the new phenomenon. Since financial regulators usually regulate specific business models, their definitions are generally narrow in scope.

The broadest definition of crowdfunding can be derived from its epistemology. It is a type of funding that originates from the crowd, i.e. many individuals who usually contribute a small amount (backers, funders, supporters, lenders, or investors). A closely related and more general (parent) term is crowdsourcing, which involves procuring any sort of support from the masses, including knowledge, ideas, or financial backing. For instance, Danmayr (2014, p. 4) describes crowdsourcing as 'using the crowd to obtain ideas, feedback and solutions in order to support corporate activities'. Similarly, Hazen (2011, p. 1736) defines crowdsourcing as 'mass collaboration efforts through large numbers of people [...]'.[12] In the same vein, Parhankangas et al. (2019, p. 1) emphasise that crowdsourcing allows the participation of the general public 'in the process of value creation'.

The broadest definition of crowdfunding indicates it is an old phenomenon. Often cited historical examples when a large number of people contributed small amounts to support a joint cause involve the translation of Homer's Iliad to English, Pulitzer's Statue of Liberty, or Mozart's piano concertos (Bouglet et al., 2022; Parhankangas et al., 2019; Short et al., 2017).

What makes crowdfunding a more recent concept is that the contributions are collected over the Internet. For instance, Morsy (2014, p. 1373) defines crowdfunding as the 'mechanism by which funds for projects are procured by appealing to the internet community'. Similarly, the European Commission describes crowdfunding as 'an open call via the Internet for the provision of funds by the public at large to support specific initiatives by typically small fundraisers' (European Commission, 2018, p. 7). The first documented case of an online fundraising campaign is the British rock band Marillion, which raised money for their tour abroad in 1997, according to Parhankangas et al. (2019, p. 2).

It is important to note that an open call for the collection of funds from the public is rarely made directly but rather through a designated platform which operates a website on which crowdfunding campaigns are listed (a crowdfunding intermediary, crowdfunding portal, or crowdfunding service provider). For example, Klöhn et al. (2016, p. 1, fn. 4) provide the following definition of crowdfunding: 'Collecting

[12] Crowdfunding usually involves relationships 'between previously unacquainted providers and consumers of capital'. In other words, the crowd is usually anonymous. Yet, as will be discussed later, early crowdfunding contributions often come from the fundraisers' closest circle, the so-called friends and family.

financial contributions from a multitude of persons to achieve a common goal through the use of a specialised internet platform'. The first online crowdfunding platform, ArtistShare, was launched in 2003, where artists could collect funds for their new albums while receiving a reward in return (e.g., the right to be among the first to download the album or to be mentioned in the album's booklet) (Zhao et al., 2019, p. 2). In the years to follow, and especially in the aftermath of the financial crisis, several online platforms started operating models in which backers received a financial reward, as will be discussed later.

Here, it is essential to emphasise that an online campaign is one of the defining features of crowdfunding, especially when funds are raised for business purposes. However, it is rarely mentioned in scholarly or legal definitions. A campaign usually involves a delicate and complex process with unique dynamics (Block et al., 2018; Dorfleitner et al., 2018; Hornuf & Schwienbacher, 2018; Nguyen et al., 2019). It starts by creating and publishing the pitch and campaign content, which serves as a basis for a rich and continuous interaction with the crowd through various channels. These include sending periodic updates, participating in online forums and on the Q&A page of the campaign, and engaging the crowd on social media, which also involves a solid social media presence. Leveraging the support from the existing social media networks, bringing influential backers on board, and attracting a critical mass of backers early on are essential to a successful fundraising process.

While all crowdfunding campaigns aim to obtain financial support from the crowd, campaigns differ regarding the reward backers gain by participating. The reward type is commonly used to delineate between different crowdfunding models. The most precise delineation between models is based on whether crowdfunding involves a financial (monetary) return.

Models without a financial return include donation-based crowdfunding (crowd-donating) and reward-based crowdfunding (crowd-supporting). They are sometimes called non-investment crowdfunding models (Belleflamme & Lambert, 2016). Backers in donation-based campaigns receive an immaterial (non-tangible) reward for supporting an important cause (social, environmental, cultural, economic, etc.). If they receive a tangible reward, it is usually of a negligible material value (e.g., a cap, cup or t-shirt). Backers in a reward-based campaign obtain a tangible reward generally consisting of a product or a service that will be created as a result of the project being financed. The relationship between backers and fundraisers is usually seen as a 'pre-sale' contract, in which the delivery of a product or service is postponed or made contingent on the completion of the project. Individual financial contribution, i.e. ticket size, is typically smaller than the retail price that will be charged once the product or service is produced. The discount often depends on the time between the contribution and the realisation of the project.

In contrast, financial-return crowdfunding models (sometimes called investment-based models) entail a future cash flow stream. Lenders or investors financially contribute to a crowdfunding campaign to gain a yield, i.e. an interest rate, a dividend, participation in future profits, future revenues, or a capital gain. Before examining financial-return models in greater detail, it is essential to explain some critical differences vis-à-vis donation and reward-based crowdfunding from backers' (investors') and fundraisers' perspectives.

Models without a financial return entail donation or consumption decisions, which fundamentally differ from investment decisions regarding incentive structures (Hervé et al., 2019, pp. 764–765). Backers in reward-based crowdfunding also face certain uncertainties regarding product development or delivery. Nonetheless, as the existing literature suggests, product production or delivery defaults are relatively rare, while delays are more frequent (Shneor, 2020, p. 32). In contrast, financial-return models can entail more complex issues, such as conflicts between shareholders and debt-holders or conflicts between majority and minority shareholders (company founders and the crowd), potentially leading to 'underinvestment, risk shifting, and asset stripping' (Farag & Johan, 2022, pp. 6–7).

From the (business) fundraisers' point of view, non-return models may be preferred as they do not require fundraisers to share their future revenues or returns (Armour & Enriques, 2018, p. 258) or relinquish a portion of control over their company. Moreover, reward-based crowdfunding also allows for collecting valuable information about the demand for the product or service since backers are usually the actual consumers. At the same time, this enables fundraisers to maximise their profits by price-discriminating between early backers, who are presumed to have a high willingness to pay and regular consumers who wait for the product or service to be offered on the market (Belleflamme & Lambert, 2016, p. 7). Reward-based campaigns are usually easier to launch, as financial-return platforms are more selective regarding project onboarding. Yet, non-financial models typically allow fundraisers to collect smaller sums, given that they are limited to actual consumers and unsuitable for projects oriented towards businesses or governments as customers (Shneor, 2020, pp. 32–37).

Overall, higher uncertainty and risks associated with financial-return models, stemming from both incentives of market participants and more considerable sums collected, brought them to the centre of regulatory attention. The analysis below explores these models in greater depth, outlying some of their decisive features.

2.3 Financial-Return Crowdfunding

Encompassing definitions of financial-return crowdfunding are rare since scholars and regulators tend to concentrate on specific crowdfunding models or model groups. Existing definitions are inconsistent in terms of crowdfunding models included in their scope. As mentioned earlier, the critical feature differentiating financial-return crowdfunding from donation and reward models is that individuals contribute to a crowdfunding campaign to gain monetary compensation. As put by Martínez-Climent et al. (2018, p. 529), individuals participating on financial-return crowdfunding platforms 'are urged by extrinsic or financial motivation'. Macchiavello (2021b, p. 2) provides an inclusive definition: 'Financial-return crowdfunding […] consists in the provision of small sums (individually considered) by a multitude of internet users (the "crowd") to other individuals or enterprises under the form of loans […] or equity investments […] and/or, more generally, other forms of investments […] through an online platform facilitating the operation'. Along these lines, other sources usually do not define financial-return crowdfunding but merely acknowledge that it is an umbrella term that encompasses 'peer-to-peer lending' and 'equity crowdfunding' (Kirby & Worner, 2014, p. 9), 'debt' and 'equity crowdfunding' (Polzin et al., 2018, p. 256), 'crowdlending' and 'crowdinvesting' (Leboeuf & Schwienbacher, 2018, p. 16).

Definitions focusing on specific models/model groups typically use one of the two resembling criteria. The first is whether crowdfunding entails debt (P2P lending, lending-based crowdfunding, marketplace lending) or equity (equity-based crowdfunding). For instance, the International Organization of Securities Commissions (IOSCO) defines P2P lending as 'the use of an online platform that matches lenders/investors with borrowers/issuers in order to provide unsecured loans' (Kirby & Worner, 2014, p. 9). Therefore, both loans to individuals and businesses, as well as debt securities, are assumed under the lending model. In contrast, equity crowdfunding is defined as 'many individuals investing in a business through the platform, gaining an equity stake' (Kirby & Worner, 2014, p. 9).

The second criterion used to define crowdfunding models distinguishes between loans (crowdlending) and investments (crowdinvesting). For instance, the European Banking Authority (EBA) and the European Securities and Markets Authority (ESMA) adopted this line of reasoning. EBA focuses on 'lending-based crowdfunding', which entails 'raising funds for a project or personal purposes, in the form of a loan agreement, with a promise to repay with (or in certain cases without) interest' (European Banking Authority, 2015, p. 8). Lending-based crowdfunding is seen as a funding alternative to the traditional credit market used by individuals and companies. In contrast, ESMA focuses on 'investment-based crowdfunding', which entails 'the people providing funds […] in return for a right to participate in a share of the revenues or profits of the project, or through the purchase of a debt, equity or other security' (European Securities and Markets Authority, 2014, p. 6). Thus, according to ESMA, investment models differ from models that use loan agreements despite acknowledging that securities to which investors subscribe (including debt securities) are not always transferable (European Securities and Markets Authority, 2014, p. 7).

One should note that the literature also uses the terms 'crowdequity' or 'equity crowdfunding' as a synonym for 'investment-based crowdfunding', including both equity and debt instruments (debt-based securities and mini-bonds) within its scope (Kleiner, 2021). This approach has also been adopted by the Cambridge Centre for Alternative Finance (CCAF), which has published the most comprehensive annual reports on the state of crowdfunding markets while also providing a detailed taxonomy of alternative finance models (Zhang et al., 2016; Ziegler et al., 2019, 2020, 2021; Ziegler, Johanson, King, et al., 2018; Ziegler, Johanson, Zhang, et al., 2018; Ziegler, Shneor, Garvey, et al., 2018). Under their taxonomy, real-estate crowdfunding, which involves investments in a property, also falls under the notion of equity crowdfunding.[13]

Moreover, in some jurisdictions (notably Germany), equity crowdfunding or crowdinvesting is used to refer to hybrid (mezzanine) instruments such as profit-participating loans or subordinated loans (Dorfleitner et al., 2018; Hornuf, Klöhn, & Schilling, 2018; Hornuf & Neuenkirch, 2017; Hornuf & Schwienbacher, 2018). Due to regulatory constraints, these instruments are commonly used as a substitute for issuing shares. They typically include a variable, performance-dependent component of the interest rate in addition to or instead of a fixed compensation (Tröger, 2021, p. 97). Thus, even if an instrument is debt-based, crowdinvesting assumes that 'the crowd participates in the uncertain cash flows', as opposed to crowdlending, where 'repayment by the borrowers starts immediately' (Cumming & Hornuf, 2018, pp. x–xi).

In contrast to these approaches, which assume that crowdfunding models are defined based on the form or the type of financial contracts used, it is also possible to draw the line between models based on who the fundraisers are (consumers or businesses). As a result, P2P consumer lending is considered separately from P2P business lending and various models that fall within investment-based crowdfunding. The assessment of the creditworthiness of business fundraisers tends to be more complex than that of individual borrowers. The latter category also raises a concern about whether they should enjoy additional consumer protections, as in traditional finance. For instance, competent bodies in the EU adopted this approach when drafting the ECSPR. The new regime is only applicable for business fundraising, including P2P business lending, crowdfunding involving the issuance of transferrable securities (both equity and debt), and the sale of shares in limited liability companies, if allowed under the rules of the Member States. However, one should note that P2P consumer lending is sometimes used by individuals who raise funds for their small businesses, making this distinction less neat.

[13] The rationale for treating real-estate crowdfunding under equity crowdfunding stems from the fact that investors often get an ownership of a property by holding securities in a special purpose vehicle (SPV), which juxtaposes between the real-estate project/property financed and investors. Another caveat of the CCAF taxonomy is that it refers to 'alternative finance', an umbrella term used to also include some models that do not fall within the narrow definition of crowdfunding. For instance, balance-sheet lending, which entails online platforms funding loans, is counted under debt models. Yet, as discussed earlier, crowdfunding is a form of direct (market-based) finance where the platform facilitates financial contracts between fundraisers and investors. Moreover, their taxonomy includes invoice trading. This model involves platforms facilitating the sale of account receivables at a discount by companies who want to gain liquidity. As argued by Shneor (2020, p. 26), this model is not really about fundraising but rather about companies better managing their cash flows.

2.4 Varieties in Business Models: What Do Platforms Do?

Definitions of crowdfunding merely acknowledge that funds are raised via crowdfunding platforms, rarely specifying services that platforms offer. This is partially because the scope of services varies across platforms, as well as the evolution of platform business models, which gradually assumed several roles which sometimes resemble those of traditional intermediaries.

It is indisputable that the vital functionality of platforms consists of matching the demand and supply of capital between fundraisers and investors, resulting in investors holding debt or ownership claims on the company, company proceeds, or income of individuals (European Commission, 2018, p. 7). As explained earlier, the platform matching process is expected to attenuate coordination and information asymmetry problems between the two sides of the market. Nonetheless, platforms do not internalise these issues by acting as a counterparty to a transaction to each side, as traditional financial intermediaries do, but rather act as a two-sided marketplace, generating revenue as the proportion of the total amount of funds collected.

The matching process begins by onboarding both sides and providing them with a virtual meeting space—a website where fundraisers can make an open call for funding (pre-campaign stage). Fundraisers have a page where they provide relevant information to prospective investors in various forms (a video, a campaign 'pitch', textual information, uploaded documents). Information remains available for the duration of the campaign, during which investors can express their interest—subscribe to the offer (campaign stage). Once the campaign is over, the platform provides the standardised financial contracts to be concluded between fundraisers and investors. It further facilitates the exchange of claims by enabling payments and transfer of legal titles (post-campaign stage) (Ahlers et al., 2015, p. 957).

It should be noted that, depending on the regulatory requirements in a given jurisdiction, platforms do not always handle their clients' money directly; instead, they sometimes partner with an authorised payment service provider (Fig. 2.1). Money handling involves temporarily holding investors' assets before allocating them to specific fundraisers or holding income from investments (e.g., loan repayments or dividends) before repaying to investors. When money handling is permissible, platforms manage cash flows through specific payment accounts, ensuring that their client's funds are separated from their own (Stefanelli et al., 2022, p. 6).

Within this broad setting, platforms' business models exhibit many variations. For the sake of clarity, it is possible to group them depending on whether they relate to (1) the pricing of a crowdfunding offer, (2) the scope of platform services (before, during, or after the crowdfunding campaign), (3) the involvement of a third party, or (4) the structure of platform fees. Naturally, some of these variations are interdependent. For instance, the scope of platform services usually relates to its fee structure.

In contrast to traditional intermediaries, crowdfunding investors typically decide which individual loan applications or projects they want to finance. However, platforms made different choices regarding who determines the terms of raising finance, i.e. the interest rate in debt-based finance and the price of shares (company

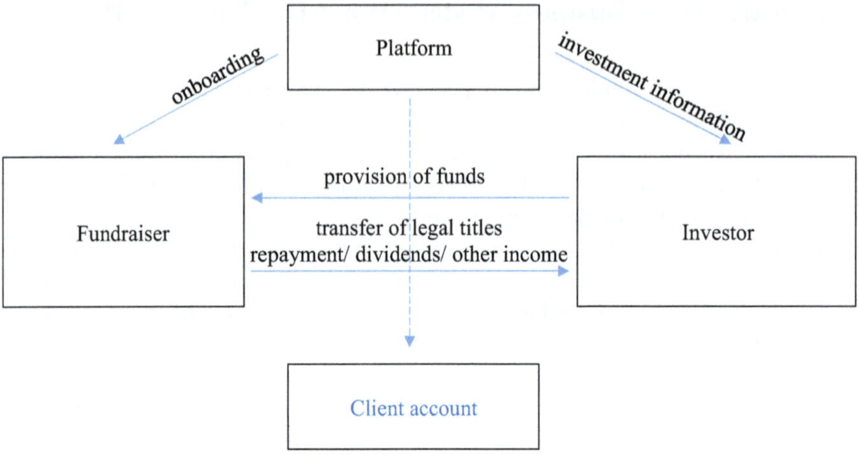

Fig. 2.1 A simplified crowdfunding scheme

valuation) in equity crowdfunding. Some platforms allow fundraisers to determine the terms of finance, which are non-negotiable for investors facing a 'take-it-or-leave-it' offer. Such pricing mechanism is known as the 'posted-price'. As will be discussed concerning variations in the scope of platform services, platforms can be involved in the pricing process to a different degree, ranging from no interference to imposing the price on fundraisers based on their estimates.

In contrast to the 'posted-price' mechanisms, investors can be directly involved in pricing on platforms that run auctions for each crowdfunding campaign. Auctions were commonly used by lending platforms in the early years of crowdfunding markets. In the Dutch auction, which is the preferred model in the crowdfunding context, the borrower sets the highest interest rate they are willing to pay. After that, investors bid by determining the chunk of loan they would like to finance and the interest rate they are willing to accept. Once the bidding is done, the loan is funded by investors who offer the most favourable terms, ensuring the entire loan amount is provided. Thus, the auction process is expected to aggregate all the public and private information of bidders about the borrower in the price. Here, platforms can also have a more active role in terms of using tools that help improve liquidity—the efficiency pain point of auctions beyond crowdfunding.[14]

Variations concerning the scope of platform services are the most numerous. Platforms continually innovate in different aspects of their business, allowing them to compete within non-price dimensions. Platform services can be grouped depending on whether they are provided before, during, or after the crowdfunding campaign.

[14] While markets with sporadic transactions are known for inefficient price discovery, technological advancements in the context of online auctions can also reverse the relationship between market liquidity and price efficiency. As shown by Kauffman et al. (2009), the presence of a greater number of bidders in online auctions can also lead to a greater participation of uninformed buyers who drive (up) prices away from their efficient levels.

Pre-campaign services can relate to the onboarding process of fundraisers, preparing information and materials to be showcased in a crowdfunding campaign, and enabling pre-fundraising. The fundraisers' onboarding procedure has two functions. One is preventing outright fraud by doing fundamental checks on the individual or company raising funds and their associated persons. Background checks can stem from requiring basic proof of identity and making sure that they do not have a criminal record to more complex inquiries, including on-site visits in some instances. The second function is filtering or preselection of the most promising applications or projects, which includes a deeper understanding of the intended use of proceeds, creditworthiness assessment, income/profit-generating capacity, the viability of a business idea from the market perspective, the soundness of financial projections, etc. As will be discussed later, the due diligence of fundraisers is sometimes outsourced to trusted third parties, professional (lead) investors, who leverage their reputation by selecting good investment opportunities that the crowd can take advantage of. One should note that the onboarding process happens behind closed doors, so investors only become acquainted with crowdfunding offers that went through the filtering mechanism. During the pre-campaign stage, platforms can collect substantial information on fundraisers. In the absence of regulatory requirements, platforms may specify the information that fundraisers should share with investors at the campaign stage. To this end, platforms typically provide a suitable form for sharing information (investment information sheet) and can also prescribe or advise specific information verification practices.

Before the campaign launch, platforms can also offer some specific services that help fundraisers with campaign preparation. They are usually more comprehensive in crowdfunding for businesses than P2P consumer lending, given that campaigns are more demanding in the former case. They can include assistance with a business plan, financial or feasibility analysis, financial projections, repayment plan, marketing and promotion materials, campaign pitch, and other communication strategies, and providing technical, strategic, and other types of guidance (Rossi & Vismara, 2018, p. 101). As to preparing financial information, it is noteworthy that some platforms also do their assessment and provide investors with an indicator of the quality or the risk level of fundraisers. This is usually done in lending-based models, where platforms assign credit grades to borrowers using different data sources. In relation to this, platforms can also influence the pricing of loans or shares. Platform interference can be consultative and often unknown to investors or binding when the platform directly defines terms of raising finance that fundraisers can agree to or not launch the campaign. Again, this is more common among lending platforms, where assigning risk grades to borrowers is often coupled with setting the interest rate borrowers commit to pay. Finally, platforms can enable a pre-fundraising round that occurs in a private mode, during which fundraisers attract funds from their closest circle of supporters or strategic (institutional, lead) investors to enable building momentum during the campaign stage (as will be discussed in relation to the potential involvement of a third party).

During the campaign stage, the focus is usually on the interaction between fundraisers and investors, while platform operations serve to smooth this process. As stated by Rossi and Vismara (2018, p. 101), platforms create a tailored space where interaction between two sides occurs (forum, Q&A section, email addresses, chat, etc.). Moreover, platforms can also engage to stimulate the interest of their existing investor base by sending promoting emails or via other channels, e.g. social media. In addition, an essential role of platforms is facilitating information exchange among investors (Belleflamme & Lambert, 2016, p. 11). Platform portals are typically designed to give prospective investors an overview of investments at any given moment, enabling information cascades from investors who have an information advantage due to their skills or proximity to fundraisers to less-informed investors. Some portals also make specific characteristics of investors visible (e.g., whether they are retail or accredited investors) as well as the amount they pledged. On some platforms, it is also possible for investors to disclose their complete profile (e.g., by linking their social media pages). The idea is to leverage the credibility of existing investors to attract new ones. In some instances, platforms also enable the creation of groups among fundraisers or investors (sometimes referred to as affinity groups). They serve as an additional channel of information exchange and a space for creating new or leveraging existing social networks.

Campaign dynamics are also affected by different platform rules. Platforms are usually grouped depending on whether they operate a 'keep-it-all' model or an 'all-or-nothing' model (also sometimes known as 'provision point mechanism') (Burtch et al., 2018). In the former case, fundraisers can appropriate all the funds they collect. In contrast, in the latter case, the total amount pledged must surpass a pre-defined funding goal for fundraisers to receive contributions. In the case of crowdfunding for business, the 'all-or-nothing' model ensures that the project collects sufficient funding for the investment to be viable and, thus, generate returns in the future. However, it is riskier from the fundraisers' perspective. Other rules can relate to what happens with the excess of funding (overfunding) when the total amount of contributions exceeds the funding goal. For instance, fundraisers can sometimes determine stretch goals in addition to their (original) target amount.

As mentioned earlier, autonomous investment decisions of the crowd are at the heart of a crowdfunding model. Some platforms facilitate the investment choice without interfering with this principle by allowing investors to filter the available crowdfunding offers based on specific objective criteria (e.g., industry, risk level, financial instruments offered). However, some platforms have also designed algorithmic systems for automatic investments (auto-bids, auto-investments, a portfolio builder tool). The platform allocates a certain amount of investors' funds to one or multiple crowdfunding offers in line with pre-defined parameters determined by investors, such as maturity, risk, and return preferences. This service is also called individual portfolio management (Minto & Legind, 2021). Automatic investments sometimes merely complement regular (manual) investments during a crowdfunding campaign. Yet, on some platforms, they have become a dominant feature, allowing platforms to create and manage individual portfolios on behalf of their investors (Cumming & Hornuf, 2022, p. 40). Platforms sometimes also advertise an annual target rate of return on investment (across the entire portfolio). Less frequently, this also allows them to actively manage loans before maturity, meaning that platforms are given the discretion to move some loans in and out of the portfolio. It should be noted, however, that the target rate of return does not amount to a guaranteed return, meaning that the platform guarantees with its balance sheet but merely promises to exercise its best effort. The automatic investment feature is more common among P2P lending than equity platforms.

Instead of making decisions on investors' behalf, some platforms also invest their funds into projects they list. Such a practice is not permissible in all jurisdictions. When not forbidden, platform co-investment is usually subject to additional rules to maintain the position of a neutral intermediary.

Finally, platforms can offer different services in the post-campaign stage with three distinct purposes. The first is facilitating the execution of financial contracts and collective decision-making in the funded company. P2P lending platforms typically overtake ex-post monitoring and administer the collection of loan repayments and loss recovery on investors' behalf (with or without the involvement of a third party, as mentioned earlier). Similarly, equity crowdfunding platforms often have arrangements to facilitate governance and exit in a funded company. One such practice is to establish an indirect investment structure such as a Special Purpose Vehicle (SPV) for each project, where investors hold shares in the SPV, which in turn enters into a financial contract with the funded company (Hornuf, Klöhn, & Schilling, 2018, p. 518). As a result, an SPV, instead of hundreds of individual investors, has a direct financial stake in the company. An alternative practice is mandatory contractual arrangements among crowd investors, such as a vote pooling agreement, which foresees collective voting on specific fundamental questions (Hornuf, Klöhn, & Schilling, 2018). The agreement also envisages the majority rule, which implies that the collective decision is binding for all investors and independent of their participation. Finally, some platforms offer a post-investment scheme known as the nominee structure. Instead of an SPV, the platform holds legal titles on investors' behalf and exercises their governance rights. The second purpose of post-campaign services is to minimise potential losses investors incur due to fundraisers' failures. This is done through provision (contingency) funds, which serve to partially compensate investors who suffered losses from their investments.[15] The third purpose of post-campaign services is to enable greater liquidity of crowdfunding investments by operating a secondary market. Secondary trading is usually simplified, resembling

---

[15] It should be noted that operating a provision fund that compensates investors for a portion of their losses does not amount to operating a 'guaranteed-return' crowdfunding model. This model was popularised in China before a regulatory prohibition, in which the platform promises a fixed return to crowd investors. It is described in the literature as a variant of balance-sheet crowdfunding since the platform ensures the returns are met with its own balance sheet, usually standing in between crowd investors and crowd lenders (Havrylchyk & Verdier, 2018; Kirby & Worner, 2014, p. 19; Macchiavello & Sciarrone Alibrandi, 2021, pp. 47–48). The regulatory intervention in China was driven by the practice of using the funds provided by new investors rather than repayments of existing loans to pay out the guaranteed return, that is, a Ponzi-like scheme (Nemoto et al., 2019, pp. 6–8). Given the misleading name, contradicting the very purpose of crowdfunding, all balance-sheet crowdfunding models, including the guaranteed return, do not fall within the scope of this study.

a bulletin board where investors list their interests in selling or buying securities rather than a regular multilateral trading venue (Fig. 2.2).

It is worth noting that platforms are not always completely transparent about the services they offer across different stages of the campaign process. This occurs more often with services involving various levels of effort and associated costs for the platform, making it difficult for investors to compare them. Nonetheless, their effort can sometimes be inferred ex-post if the funded individuals and entrepreneurs do not deliver on their commitments and if this information is observable by existing and prospective investors.

Platform business models also vary in reliance on a qualified third party to whom they outsource some services. Two types of outsourcing arrangements are prominent.[16] The first is engaging professional (lead) investors, such as institutional investors, business angels or VCs, to vet crowdfunding offers (Chen & Ma, 2023; Li et al., 2016; Zhang et al., 2023). This practice primarily exists on equity-based platforms. Professional investors are usually involved before the campaign's official launch (private launch) when they carefully screen loan applications or projects and select to participate in the most promising ones. They can also assume specific roles ex-post, such as monitoring the performance of individuals and companies that received funding and ensuring they deliver on their commitments. Platforms where

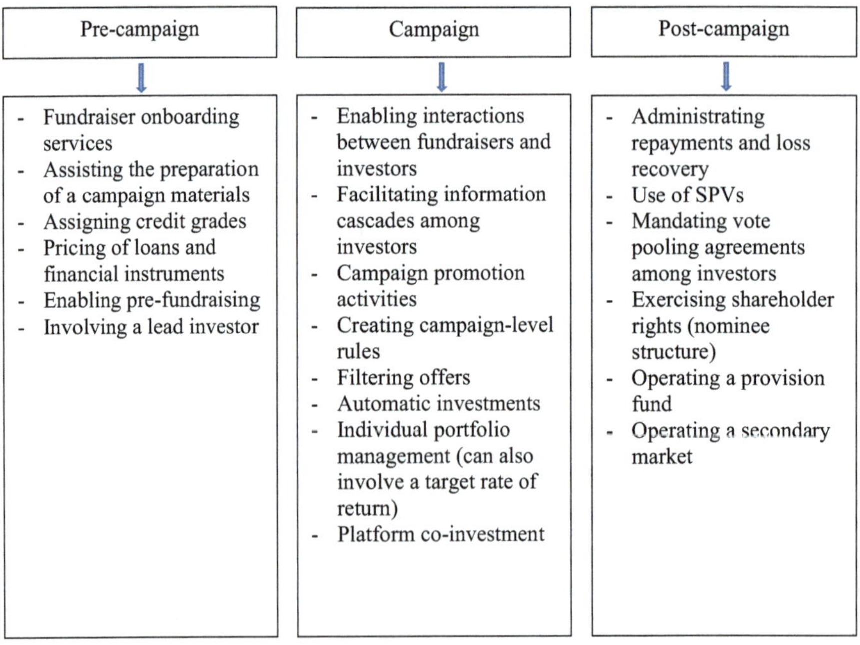

Fig. 2.2 Variations in platform services at different stages of crowdfunding

[16] Depending on the regulatory requirements, platforms can outsource some other services as well, such as payment services or custody of legal titles.

the involvement of a professional investor is a prerequisite for listing are sometimes referred to as investor-led platforms as opposed to entrepreneur-led platforms (Chen & Ma, 2023). Entrepreneurs sometimes bring professional investors, while in other cases, they work in partnership with a crowdfunding platform.

The second type of outsourcing arrangement is inherent in lending-based platforms, which outsource loan origination to an incumbent bank. Unlike the involvement of a professional investor, which has a material role, a bank's participation is usually driven by regulatory requirements in certain jurisdictions with restrictive laws on what falls under the exclusive prerogative of banks (e.g., Germany, Austria, and the US).[17] As a result, the bank has a more formal role, even though the simple crowdfunding scheme explained earlier is made more complex. The way in which the bank is involved differs between the US and Germany, for instance. In the US, once the bank originates the loan, all the claims against the borrower are passed on to the platform (or an SPV created for this purpose), which further issues notes (debt securities) to crowd investors. Platform repayments are contingent on collecting payments from crowd borrowers (Chaffee & Rapp, 2012, p. 493). Because of the issuance of notes, these platforms' business model is sometimes called the 'notary model' (Havrylchyk & Verdier, 2018, p. 119; Kirby & Worner, 2014, p. 18). In contrast, once the partnering bank originates the loan in Germany, all the claims against the borrower are assigned to crowd lenders (Käfer, 2018, pp. 5–6).

In relation to differences in pricing models, platform services, and reliance on third parties elaborated above, platforms can have different fee structures (Cogan et al., 2021, p. 35; Stefanelli et al., 2022, pp. 7–8). The fee is commonly paid upon completing a successful campaign, typically charged as a percentage of the funds raised from fundraisers (success fee). It is less common to charge success fees from investors. Thus, investors' participation is typically cross-subsidised by fundraisers, as the former group generates cross-size network effects for the latter.[18] A fixed fee can also be charged for mere listing on the platform portal, although this is less common (onboarding/listing fee). Platforms can charge an additional fee for other pre-campaign services, such as preparation of campaign materials and promotion and marketing. Platforms actively facilitating pre-financing from professional (lead) investors can sometimes earn a percentage of pre-funding arranged. During the campaign, investors can be charged a small fee per transaction or payment processing fees, which relates to outsourcing payment services to authorised providers. In the post-campaign stage, platforms can charge a fee from investors in case of administrating repayments (management fee), exercising shareholders' rights on investors' behalf (nominee fee), a successful transaction on secondary markets (secondary market fee), or an exit event (exit fee).

[17] The details of such regulatory requirements will be explained in Chap. 6.

[18] The operation of platforms is commonly studied through the lenses of network economics and industrial organisation, which treats platforms as two-sided (multisided) markets. In such markets, one side of the market (one group of users) is typically offered the service for free because the other side enjoys benefits from their participation and is willing to pay more.

Some platform services and associated business models that were concisely outlined here will be revisited in Chap. 3 when discussing market-based mechanisms of reducing information asymmetries. At this stage, it is essential to understand whether and how these services relate to those offered by traditional players in financial markets.

2.5 Is Crowdfunding Truly Disintermediated Finance?

Because of their distinctive set of services that facilitate financial transactions, crowdfunding platforms have some similarities to financial intermediaries, information intermediaries in direct finance (gatekeepers), and traditional providers of entrepreneurial finance. Understanding these similarities and critical features that differentiate them is paramount from both market and regulatory perspectives.[19]

2.5.1 Crowdfunding and Financial (Balance Sheet) Intermediaries

Financial intermediaries are institutions of indirect finance that receive or borrow funds from lenders-savers and then use these funds to make loans to or invest in borrowers-spenders (Mishkin, 2007, p. 29). They include banks and other depositary institutions, investment intermediaries, and contractual savings institutions (e.g., insurance companies and pension funds). A common feature of financial intermediaries is that the transfer of funds goes through their balance sheets, i.e. they act as a counterparty in a financial transaction to both capital seekers and capital providers. In relation to this, capital providers do not influence the choice of assets a financial intermediary holds. The financial intermediary exclusively screens investment opportunities and performs ex-post monitoring on behalf of all capital providers. Moreover, the way their money is used is typically not even visible to them (Havrylchyk & Verdier, 2018, p. 117; Vallee & Zeng, 2019, p. 1946). The resemblance of crowdfunding to financial intermediaries is based on the fact that they also connect people who have a surplus of funds to those who have a shortage of funds. Crowdfunding platforms also stand between capital seekers (fundraisers or

[19] It should be noted that this is not a closed list of actors in the financial system with which crowdfunding platforms share common features. As described earlier, platforms can sometimes offer some auxiliary services (e.g., payment services or custody services) which are traditionally provided by some other actors (non-bank payment institutions, custodians, etc.). Given that these services are not defining the crowdfunding model and that they are commonly outsourced to third-party providers, they are not included in the scope of the analysis in this section. Nonetheless, as will be explained in Chap. 5, there are instances in which regulators licensed crowdfunding platforms based on these auxiliary services.

borrowers) and capital providers (lenders or investors) and help transfer funds from one group to another.

(Lending-based) crowdfunding platforms are often compared to banks as a tool for providing an alternative source of credit for individuals and entrepreneurs or SMEs (Adhami et al., 2023; Buchak et al., 2018; De Roure et al., 2022; Jiang et al., 2018; Tang, 2019). This has raised concerns about whether they can be considered new 'shadow banks', usually defined as 'bank-like activities taking place outside of traditional deposit-taking institutions' (Buchak et al., 2018). Thus, they typically remain outside the regulatory oversight or are subject to light or insufficient regulation (Macchiavello, 2018, p. 709).[20]

As mentioned before, the core function of a bank consists of risk, maturity, and liquidity transformation—issuing liabilities (deposit claims) whose size, duration, and risks are different from those of its assets (loans). From the investor (depositor) perspective, the bank is 'pooling loans and issuing safe, information-insensitive claims' (Vallee & Zeng, 2019, p. 1939). Risk management stays with the bank, while depositors are not exposed to the risk of failure of individual loans, unless in extreme cases when the bank's financial stability is impaired. Even in such circumstances, depositors typically benefit from deposit insurance schemes up to a certain amount of funds deposited. Moreover, deposits are highly liquid as opposed to the underlying bank's assets.

In contrast, crowd investors are fully exposed to the risk of borrowers' default, and deposit/investment compensation schemes do not protect them. They are expected to screen individual loans independently or through some market-based mechanisms of information production and sharing among dispersed individual investors. Moreover, their financial stakes are typically illiquid. Against the backdrop, some additional platform services explained earlier can make crowdfunding resemble banking activities of screening, monitoring, performing risk management, and providing liquidity.

As recognised by several authors (Adhami et al., 2023, p. 3; Vallee & Zeng, 2019, p. 1940), the screening functions are increasingly split between the platform and crowd investors, whereas they jointly engage in producing the information and gauging riskiness of individual loans. In particular, platforms perform a large-scale prescreening of loan applications, sorting suitable borrowers in line with their predefined policy (e.g., accepting only applicants whose risk is below a certain level) and collect standardised information from them to be passed to prospective lenders.

[20] The concept of shadow banks gained prominence in the aftermath of the Financial Crisis of 2008, which was partially rooted in the activity of shadow banks, that is, unregulated financial institutions that facilitated the process of securitization (Adrian & Ashcraft, 2016). The latter involves pooling and trenching various financial instruments and issuing securities backed by the cash flows arising out of the underlying assets. As a result, risky long-term instruments are transformed into short-term and seemingly low-risk instruments (Adrian & Ashcraft, 2016, p. 15). The securitization further enabled the 'originate-to-distribute model' of traditional regulated banks, known as the process in which the bank originates loans to be later on sold to other intermediaries and investors, which decreases its level of scrutiny in screening potential borrowers and monitoring loan performance (Hildebrand et al., 2010, p. 2).

Platforms can enjoy an informational disadvantage compared to banks, in case they do not have access to credit histories and credit scores produced by credit bureaus (registries), which is the case in some countries, or proprietary information stemming from bank–client relationships.[21] Nonetheless, platforms often use non-conventional, alternative data sources, usually stemming from the applicant's online activity and reputation. Moreover, as explained earlier, based on the information gathered, P2P lending platforms often assign risk grades to each borrower application admitted for listing. Platform credit risk brackets can serve as guidance or even replace independent screening of borrowers when the size of investments undermines lenders' incentives to conduct their due diligence. The screening process is further appropriated by a crowdfunding platform when it also provides loan pricing, determining the interest rate to be charged between lenders and borrowers. Finally, in cases of automatic investments and platforms performing the service of individual portfolio management, screening by individual borrowers vanishes completely. In addition to ex-ante screening, platforms often provide services of ex-post monitoring, collecting repayments and ensuring loss recovery since crowd lenders have a small stake in individual loans, diversifying their investments across different crowdfunding offers.

In addition to screening and monitoring, some auxiliary services provided by P2P lending platforms resemble banks' risk management (Adhami et al., 2023, p. 3; Havrylchyk & Verdier, 2018, pp. 123–124). Platforms can use automatic investments (auto-bidding) to diversify the loan portfolio of crowd lenders—spreading the investment amount across many individual loans.[22] Moreover, platforms that operate provision (contingency) funds, which serve to partially compensate lenders in case of default, reduce some of the credit risk ultimately borne by lenders.

Finally, with liquidity being a pain point of crowdfunding investments, some platforms established secondary markets with more or less success, as will be discussed in Chap. 3. Havrylchyk and Verdier (2018, p. 122) have argued that operating a secondary market resembles providing liquidity services to fund providers.

Despite these similarities, the significant difference between P2P lending and banking persists. Investors remain exposed to the performance of individual assets and choose the risk/return level in line with their preferences (even in the case of auto-investing). This option does not exist for bank depositors.[23] Furthermore, none

[21] This idea is often known as relationship banking and relationship lending (Elyasiani & Goldberg, 2004). The information advantage of banks vis-à-vis alternative lenders is likely to considerably diminish with a wider adoption and implementation of open banking policies. They allow bank clients to share their banking data with third-party providers, purportedly allowing the provision of more convenient and affordable financial services. Successful examples of open banking initiatives include the EU, the UK, India, and Australia (Odorović, 2023).

[22] According to Macchiavello and Sciarrone Alibrandi (2021, p. 53, 62), these services are not sufficient to claim that lenders lose entirely their 'decisional power over the destination of the funds' as in banking, given that their funds are invested in line with objective criteria.

[23] As discussed earlier, quasi-crowdfunding models offering promised ex-ante returns (known as the guarantee-return model) are closer to balance-sheet intermediaries (Adhami et al., 2023, p. 2; Nemoto et al., 2019, pp. 6–8).

of the services mentioned above exposes lenders to the risk of a platform failure caused by bad fundamentals, as in the case of depositors' claims against the bank. Loan repayments should not, in principle, be affected as long as clients' assets are kept in a separate account and the platform has specific arrangements to ensure business continuity.[24] Unlike in the case of banks, credit risk is decentralised and spread across many crowd lenders, making the platform non-susceptible to runs (Adhami et al., 2023). For this reason, the financial stability of platforms is not an issue (Havrylchyk & Verdier, 2018, pp. 128–129). Similarly, platforms do not offer maturity transformation. Limited liquidity in some secondary markets does not amount to 'instant redemption rights', allowing routine withdrawal of investments (Macchiavello & Sciarrone Alibrandi, 2021, p. 53).

To sum up, the role of lending-based platforms in screening, monitoring, risk management, and providing liquidity does amount to performing bank functions of risk, maturity, and liquidity transformation. As a result, considering them as part of the shadow banking system would be misleading.

In its early days, crowdfunding was often associated with microfinance, given its focus on individuals and seed entrepreneurs who do not have access to traditional finance and its related social component. With the advent of the Internet and social media, many microfinance institutions started offering their services via online platforms, allowing the onboarding of both lenders and borrowers (Bruton et al., 2015, p. 11). In addition, as explained by Everett (2015, p. 16), microfinance can also involve borrowers acting as lenders to their peers within a closed group, allowing for better selection of borrowers and peer monitoring of loan repayment. This concept was also employed on some crowdfunding platforms, where lenders and borrowers can form groups to leverage the group's reputation, exercise peer pressure, and use other informal mechanisms to enforce loan repayment. Yet, microfinancing typically relies on a balance-sheet model of intermediation, where the institution originates all the loans and bears all the credit risk, as opposed to many crowd lenders directly funding a small portion of the target sum raised (Kirby & Worner, 2014, p. 8 fn. 2).

Mirroring the comparison between lending-based platforms and credit institutions, one can draw parallels between (equity) crowdfunding and investment intermediaries, notably collective investment structures such as mutual funds or alternative investment funds (AIF) and their managers. These intermediaries pool capital from many investors by selling them shares or other securities to make collective investments. Buying large volumes of diverse financial instruments allows one to minimise transaction costs (particularly brokerage fees) and hold a well-diversified portfolio (Mishkin, 2007, p. 297).

Like crowdfunding platforms, mutual funds are open to retail investors but typically invest in traditional financial instruments such as stocks and bonds of listed companies (instead of gaining a financial interest in small unlisted companies).

[24] This is not to say that lenders cannot be affected by platform malpractice and dysfunctionality (Adhami et al., 2023).

Alternative investment funds, in contrast, typically cater to sophisticated investors and invest in non-traditional financial instruments. Investors in mutual funds and alternative investment funds can choose the fund based on their risk tolerance level and the fund's investment strategy. As already discussed concerning banking, when crowd investors delegate the role of screening, monitoring, and risk management to a crowdfunding platform, the latter becomes more similar to investment intermediaries. As argued by Ferretti (2022, pp. 120–121), the similarity to collective asset management grows with the provision of the auto-investing feature. Even though individual investor portfolios are built based on a mandate provided by each investor (and thus best correspond to the service of portfolio management), the same platform can act on behalf of many individual investors with the same or similar risk/return preferences.

However, the fundamental difference from crowdfunding is that collective investment structures perform asset transformation. Investors in these funds have financial claims (securities on fund units) that differ from the underlying assets regarding risk, size, liquidity, and return. Instead of being exposed to the performance of individual assets, such as in crowdfunding, they are exposed to the overall performance of the fund, thus sharing the risk with all other investors. Moreover, investments in these collective investment structures are typically liquid, allowing investors to redeem or sell their financial interests on a regulated market (although liquidity is higher for mutual funds than alternative investment funds).

It should be noted, however, that similarities between described investment intermediaries and crowdfunding are seemingly more pronounced when crowdfunding investments use SPVs, which juxtapose crowd investors and fundraisers. Yet, even in such instances, SPVs are merely there to enable investments into indivisible assets (e.g., real estate), facilitate management of fundraising companies and further financing rounds so that a single SPV is created for each fundraising company or project. Thus, instead of pooling investments from many investors into a single fund, SPVs used in crowdfunding give exposure to only one underlying asset.

In sum, despite the different services used by crowdfunding portals to reintermediate the market, their economic function does not equate to the function(s) performed by financial intermediaries.

2.5.2 Crowdfunding and Information Intermediaries (Gatekeepers)

In the world of direct finance, financial transactions are concluded between capital seekers and capital providers (primary markets) and between capital providers (secondary markets). In other words, financial instruments are issued for the first time on primary markets, to be later freely traded on secondary markets. The market for direct finance would not exist or would exist with considerable friction if there were not for different information intermediaries, also known as gatekeepers. The role of gatekeepers is to ensure an additional layer of investor protection when dealing with securities issuers and other investors. As summarised by Moloney et al. (2015, pp. 255–257), there are two overlapping definitions of gatekeepers. They are sometimes seen as independent third parties that can prevent issuers' misconduct and deceit by refusing their cooperation or approval, which is necessary for accessing capital markets. A more comprehensive concept of gatekeepers implies trusted third parties who pledge their reputation to offer investors information verification and certification services.

Crowdfunding literature often refers to the gatekeeping function of crowdfunding platforms without always drawing parallels to a specific type of intermediary (Ande & Eroglu, 2021; Eisenbeiss et al., 2023; Hornuf, Klöhn, & Schilling, 2018; Löher, 2017; Schwartz, 2018). While different gatekeeping functions of platforms will be analysed in detail in Chap. 3, this section focuses on how platforms compare with varying types of traditional intermediaries. Crowdfunding has similarities to exchanges (capital markets), investment firms (brokers, portfolio managers, investment advisors, and underwriters), and credit rating agencies.

As discussed above, the core functionality of crowdfunding platforms consists of bringing together capital seekers and capital providers and enabling their financial transactions. The platform is a marketplace where the demand and supply of capital meet, just like other capital markets/exchanges. The particularity of a crowdfunding market is that it primarily serves as a primary market, enabling transactions between fundraisers and investors.

Traditional exchanges gatekeep the market by imposing listing requirements and trading rules. Listing requirements include that only firms with specific characteristics can be admitted for trading, as well as information that they need to disclose to prospective investors (at the time of offering and later on, on a continuous basis). This is how they ensure that only trusted issuers appear on the market. In setting the proper standards, exchanges balance the extra degree of protection against the need to generate sufficient volumes, which can also drop if the standards are set too high (Santos & Scheinkman, 2001).[25] The revenue of exchanges comes from listing fees and transaction fees related to secondary market trading.

Like traditional exchanges, crowdfunding platforms prescribe different standards for fundraiser onboarding (in terms of credit score, assets, revenues, or age (for companies) of fundraisers). Moreover, they typically verify some of the information provided by prospective fundraisers. In relation to this, in the absence of regulations, they are free to stipulate the information that fundraisers must disclose to investors, based on which the latter group decides whether to participate in a crowdfunding offer (Hornuf, Klöhn, & Schilling, 2018, p. 518; Li et al., 2016, p. 309). As described earlier, the platform's main fee is the success fee, which depends on whether the campaign reaches the funding target. In contrast, the listing fee, analogous to traditional exchanges, is less common.

[25] Even though the historical beginnings of stock exchanges are examples of self-regulating organisations, rules on securities markets are nowadays set in statutory regulations.

Against this backdrop, traditional stock exchanges and crowdfunding markets show substantial differences concerning the maturity of the fundraising firms they cater to. Companies listed on conventional exchanges are considerably bigger in size and revenue. The process of 'going public' is reserved for companies that have completed the expansion phase, in contrast to companies raising funds via crowdfunding, which are in one of the early stages of company growth (typically in a conception or seed phase) (as depicted in Fig. 2.3). However, it is worth noting that many stock exchanges, particularly in Europe, also organise a second-tier market (Alternative Investment Market) intending to list small firms, even though many did not prove successful (Vismara et al., 2012). By the very definition, they have lower listing requirements.

Moreover, the fundraising process on crowdfunding platforms is also different from an initial public offering (IPO) setting. The traditional way of raising funds from the public involves many different intermediaries such as underwriters, financial analysts, lawyers, accountants, and auditors whose purpose is to ensure transparency of public offerings and certify the quality of the fundraising company. No such intermediaries (or a few of them) operate in crowdfunding. However, the platform or an outsourcee (e.g., lead investor) can sometimes overtake some of their roles, as discussed below (Vismara, 2018, p. 44).

Another difference from stock exchanges is the means of market access. (Retail) investors in regulated markets must engage authorised brokers who execute transactions on their behalf. In contrast, investor access to the crowdfunding market is direct. It begins as soon as they complete the onboarding procedure, which usually involves the identification process, assigning investors into different categories (e.g., sophisticated, high-net-worth, retail investors, etc.) and passing specific tests (such as entry knowledge test) when required by the law.

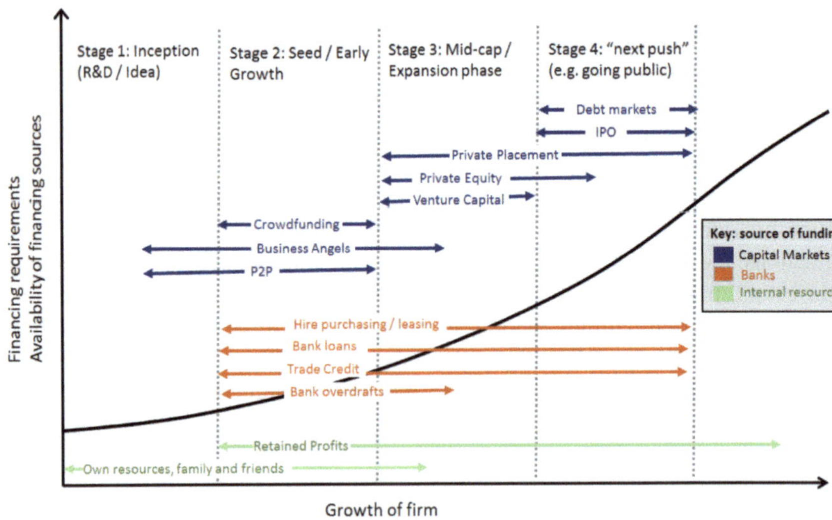

Fig. 2.3 Company growth and financing sources. (Source: European Commission (2018, p. 18))

The mere listing on a stock exchange also triggers some corporate law protections, which are usually unavailable without a listing on a regulated market. In most jurisdictions, corporate law standards are more flexible for non-listed companies and are often a matter of contractual negotiations between involved parties (Armour & Enriques, 2018, p. 263).

As mentioned earlier, crowdfunding markets mainly operate as primary markets. Operation of a secondary market is far from a universal practice, as will be elaborated in Chap. 3. (Presumed) low level of liquidity of crowdfunding investments also allowed platforms to intermediate the sale of assets other than (transferrable) securities—loans, hybrid (mezzanine) instruments, and shares in (private) limited liability companies. Trading these asset classes is sometimes limited by their lack of standardisation and restrictions to their transferability defined in the law. Furthermore, in relation to limited secondary market trading, platforms rarely foresee ongoing disclosure requirements that exist on traditional stock exchanges to ensure prices reflect all relevant information about fundraisers, as will be further stressed in Chap. 3. Moreover, platforms do not envisage secondary trading rules on market manipulation, insider trading, and or agency conflicts of brokers like traditional exchanges (Cumming et al., 2011). As argued by Cumming et al. (2021, pp. 69–70), the governance mechanisms of funded companies after the crowdfunding campaign are closer to private companies, as will be analysed in more depth in Chap. 3.

The core function of platforms, which consists of facilitating transactions and providing access to the market, also brings them closer to the role of brokers. As mentioned earlier, investor access to the crowdfunding market is direct, which means that the platform (which also serves as a marketplace) assumes the broker's role in primary markets. In particular, the crowdfunding platform receives the interest in selling/buying securities and other financial instruments from fundraisers and investors and passes their intention to transact to the other party. The second important broker service is executing clients' trading orders (in line with their instructions) in secondary markets. Therefore, it is not usually relevant to the crowdfunding context. Nonetheless, as mentioned by Macchiavello (2019, p. 15), the auto-bidding function provided by some platforms, where the investor predetermines some investment parameters and the platform allocates the funds on their behalf, resembles executing clients orders. Notably, setting investment parameters is similar to trade instructions made to a broker, which executes the transaction on the investor's behalf. The critical distinction is that the execution of orders takes place in the primary (crowdfunding) market.

As discussed before, crowdfunding presupposes that investors make their choices independently, meaning that they create and manage their crowdfunding portfolios. However, the service of auto-bidding also brings platforms close to the role of individual portfolio managers. In many instances, investors delegate all their investment decisions to the platform, which creates a portfolio of investments available on the portal, conforming to individual investors' risk appetite or a promised annual target rate of return. As argued by Ferretti (2022, p. 119), the only difference between individual portfolio management of crowdfunding platforms and portfolio management in traditional capital markets is the object of investment. Unlike conventional portfolio managers, who invest in financial instruments, platforms offering individual portfolio management usually do so with loans. One should note that (traditional) individual portfolio management can also include exercising shareholders' rights on the investor's behalf, which some platforms offer as an additional service in the post-campaign stage.

Relatedly, with their core function of creating a marketplace, platforms should present crowdfunding offers neutrally and not provide further guidance or recommendations on specific investments. However, services such as risk assessment (credit grading) and setting interest rates can include some elements of investment advice. While not giving investors clear recommendations on which loans to choose, investors can abandon their independent due diligence and follow the platform's risk and return metrics. Elements of investment advice can also hide behind the auto-investment service. In principle, platforms should exercise auto-bidding on a non-discretionary basis, in line with objective criteria (investors' parameters). Yet, the platform (the algorithm) assesses whether specific crowdfunding offers meet these criteria (e.g., a certain level of risk), possibly biasing the choice of one offer over another. It should be noted that crowdfunding services that resemble investment advice are, to some extent, in tension with the platform's neutrality in the intermediation process.

Similar to brokers, underwriters do not operate in the crowdfunding market. As a result, platforms sometimes offer additional services that serve a similar function, although with much less rigour and complexity. Underwriting is a complicated process whose core function is that a reputable intermediary helps the issuer structure the offering of securities, distribute them to the public, and curate their quality. Put differently, it lends its reputation as a repeated player in the market to a less-known issuer. By specialising in underwriting (such as investment banks do), they also bring the expertise necessary to evaluate the offers. Underwriting typically starts with bookbuilding, which entails price discovery, that is, understanding how much securities offered are worth. The reputable underwriter normally collects and aggregates price assessments of many sophisticated investors interested in the offer. As a second step, the underwriter places securities to the public with or without the commitment to buy a specific portion of the securities offered. Most crowdfunding platforms also have an essential role in preselecting offers, thus pledging their reputation that selected fundraisers are not fraudulent (trustworthy) and offering a valuable deal. Verifying information provided by the fundraiser and helping prepare campaign materials also resemble the advisory role of underwriters in framing and presenting the offer to the public. The underwriting function of platforms is even more pronounced when they assign credit rating and price crowdfunding offers (a service more common in lending-based crowdfunding). One should note that platform-co-investment also demonstrates that the platform has a 'skin in the game' analogously to underwriters committing to guarantee placement of securities. Yet, co-investment does not shift the risk of an IPO success to the platform, which always stays with the issuer in the case of crowdfunding. Crowdfunding also resembles underwriting in how fees are charged—rarely for curating (certifying) securities offerings but rather as a percentage of funds raised/proceeds from a sale of securities (Choi, 1997, p. 929). It should be noted that curating offers on a crowdfunding platform is sometimes outsourced to professional investors (sometimes assigned the role of the lead investor) who provide pre-financing. In such instances, it is possible to argue that those who provide pre-financing are effectively underwriting offers.

The resemblance of platforms to credit rating agencies stems from an increasingly widespread practice of providing credit grades. Platform credit grades often represent 'a black box' regarding the (alternative) data used and algorithms trained to discern borrowers' creditworthiness. Like credit rating agencies whose services are unavoidable in the case of debt securities offerings (Moloney et al., 2015, p. 256), crowdfunding platforms that rate borrowers do so systematically. To the extent that crowd investors prioritise platform ratings over conducting their due diligence (usually not having access to the same amount of information, among other reasons), platform estimates' accuracy is vital in maintaining a reputation in the long run.

In sum, the services of a crowdfunding platform can have similar functions as services offered by traditional gatekeepers. Generally, platforms can prevent or mitigate fraud and deception by withholding their consent for listing loan applications or projects. By the same token, they certify that crowdfunding offers are of a certain quality, and even more so when, in addition, they rate or price offers. The particularity of a crowdfunding market is that different gatekeeping services are simplified and usually consolidated in a single entity (except for models that out source certain gatekeeping functions to external investors). This contrasts the well-defined and delimited roles of gatekeepers in traditional capital markets. Moreover, the scope and depth of these services vary across different platforms, as will be further elaborated in Chap. 3.

2.5.3 Crowdfunding and Traditional Providers of Entrepreneurial Finance

Crowdfunding for businesses (in particular, equity-based models) belongs to entrepreneurial finance, which VCs and business angels have dominated for a long time. The most apparent similarity between crowdfunding and traditional providers of entrepreneurial capital is providing support for innovative, tech-based, high-risk companies (Fried & Ganor, 2006, p. 968; Sorenson et al., 2016). These companies often cannot obtain banking finance or collect funds on established public markets via an IPO due to a lack of track record of past performance or sizable revenues and collateral.

Nonetheless, it is not clear in the literature whether crowdfunding precedes financing from VCs and angel investors or whether they fill the access to finance gap of companies in a similar stage. On the one hand, it is not rare for traditional entrepreneurial finance providers to participate in a crowdfunding campaign (Coakley &

Lazos, 2021, p. 345). As mentioned briefly, some platforms mandate pre-financing from professional investors as a precondition for listing on their portal. On the other hand, the existing research also shows that running a successful crowdfunding campaign increases the chances of ensuring follow-up funding from VCs or business angels (Hornuf, Schmitt, & Stenzhorn, 2018). As Fig. 2.3 suggests, it seems that the stage of the company's growth determines whether crowdfunding will appear as a substitute or a complement to traditional external finance providers.

Another notable similarity to VC and business angel financing is that crowdfunding is a form of direct finance, requiring investors to perform their due diligence and monitor ex-post performance. However, screening and monitoring processes exhibit some significant differences when comparing the new and conventional types of entrepreneurial finance. VCs and business angels specialise in entrepreneurial investments, often focusing on a specific industry, thus gaining the necessary expertise and economies of scale in screening ventures. VCs, and less commonly business angels, also have a geographical focus, allowing them to understand market particularities of the local context better. Moreover, their sizable investments create a clear incentive to collect information, ensuring their veracity and engaging in company valuation. The screening process by traditional equity providers is 'formal, extensive and costly'—involving several activities such as hiring external consultants and physical meetings with the entrepreneurial team (Cumming et al., 2021, pp. 13–14).

While no such specialised skills and knowledge and clear incentives for screening ventures exist among most crowd investors, a few individuals may possess a superior information source. These can be professional investors participating in a crowdfunding campaign or individuals who have close personal ties to entrepreneurs and can trigger information cascades among crowd investors, as will be discussed in greater detail in Chap. 3. It is worth noting that the platform can also perform various degrees of due diligence (including offering additional services such as credit scoring, pricing of crowdfunding offers, and automatic investments), thus effectively complementing screening performed by the crowd. To some extent, platforms can leverage expertise similar to that of VCs and business angels, especially when they have a clear industry focus (e.g., clean energy). One should note that, from the ex-ante perspective, fundraisers can prefer traditional capital providers over running a crowdfunding campaign. As will be examined in more detail, entrepreneurs may fear revealing publicly details of a ground-breaking business idea, which competitors can potentially steal. In traditional venture financing, non-disclosure agreements with potential investors are a well-proven practice (Hornuf & Schwienbacher, 2016, pp. 10–11). Nonetheless, sharing their business idea with the general public can allow entrepreneurs to gain valuable knowledge about their viability. The interest in financing the company can serve as a form of market-testing. Crowd investors also sometimes provide direct feedback to entrepreneurs through discussions about project feasibility, financial projections, and other related aspects indicative of the likelihood of a venture's success (Cumming et al., 2021, p. 33).

In contrast, fundraisers would circumvent traditional providers if they fear the latter will exercise rigid monitoring ex-post, effectively constraining their managerial judgement and freedom of action (Armour & Enriques, 2018, pp. 259–260). Crowdfunding typically requires them to relinquish less control over the company than traditional providers, formally and informally. Concerning formal constraints, the VC industry is known for imposing strict financing terms on funded ventures. VC contracts typically foresee staged financing, convertible preferred stocks for VCs, often allowing the right to veto in certain circumstances as well as to serve on the board of directors (Fried & Ganor, 2006, pp. 970–971; Rossi et al., 2020, p. 10).[26] Moreover, VC contracts typically include strong anti-dilution protections and facilitate exit opportunities, such as tag-along and drag-along rights (Hornuf & Schwienbacher, 2016).

As discussed more thoroughly later, crowdfunding contracts do not always include similar shareholder protection mechanisms, sometimes not even granting voting rights. Moreover, even when certain protections are envisaged in financial contracts or company law, it is questionable to what extent dispersed investors exercise them. Thus, lack of control over company founders and managers can stem from the lack of informal mechanisms allowing to incite collective action among crowd investors necessary to monitor company performance, prevent misuses or inefficient uses of funds, and protect the crowd's position in the new financing round. Yet, as already discussed, platforms that offer governance services, such as those that operate nominee structures, can attenuate issues of ineffective ex-post control.

When the platform takes over screening investment opportunities and monitoring funded ventures, it shows some similarities to VC and business angel networks or syndication. Namely, VCs and angel investors sometimes form a network to facilitate joint investments. The syndicate is typically led by a syndicate lead, which performs specific tasks related to screening and monitoring, just like crowdfunding platforms do. Syndicates further benefit from risk sharing, portfolio diversification, and deal access (Manigart et al., 2006), which is also inherent in crowdfunding investments. Nonetheless, in the crowdfunding market, the syndicate would consist of all crowd investors investing in the same deal instead of closed networks of professional investors or wealthy individuals typical for traditional external equity providers (Schwartz, 2023, p. 92). Moreover, the platform usually does not have 'skin-in-the-game' like the syndicate lead, except for platforms that co-invest alongside crowd investors in deals listed on their portal. The resemblance to a syndicate model is also pronounced when the platform outsources screening (and monitoring) to a lead investor who invests a sizeable amount and vets the investment opportunity. Such crowdfunding schemes are sometimes referred to in the literature as syndicated equity crowdfunding (Coakley et al., 2024).

[26] Nonetheless, such governance interference can also contribute to the wealth creation of the company when external equity investors also bring along important industry knowledge and provide valuable coaching to the entrepreneurial team (Cumming et al., 2021; Fried & Ganor, 2006, p. 969).

2.6 Summary of Findings

As a new means of raising finance, crowdfunding offers an answer to the old issues between capital seekers and capital providers: coordination and asymmetric information costs. The novelty of crowdfunding lies in leveraging technology to provide financial services in a way that stands between direct and indirect finance. The scope of platform services evolved considerably over time, spanning different stages of the crowdfunding process (pre-campaign, campaign, and post-campaign stage). Yet, the defining feature has not changed—crowdfunding platforms are not parties in financial transactions but merely facilitate the conclusion of contracts between two sides of the market. As a result, they should not be treated as financial intermediaries whose core function consists of asset transformation. Nonetheless, given individual investors' limited abilities or incentives to screen investment opportunities and conduct ex-post monitoring and risk management, platforms often participate in these activities, similar to traditional financial intermediaries. The resemblance of platforms to information intermediaries in capital markets is perhaps even more substantial, with a particularity that platforms accumulate many functions performed by distinct gatekeepers (stock exchanges, brokers, underwriters, advisors, and credit rating agencies). The level of similarity varies considerably with different services offered throughout the crowdfunding process. The accumulation of different gatekeeping functions comes at the expense of the quality or depth of these services and can also create tension between them. (Business) crowdfunding also shares many common aspects with traditional providers of entrepreneurial finance (VC and angel investors), notably because of overlapping investment targets. While crowdfunding platforms usually do not act as investors in offers they list, they can perform several functions in the interest of investors, bringing them somewhat close to VC or angel investor syndicates.

References

Adhami, S., Gianfrate, G., & Johan, S. (2023). Risks and returns in crowdlending. *Eurasian Business Review, 13*(2), 309–340. https://doi.org/10.1007/s40821-022-00236-x

Adrian, T., & Ashcraft, A. B. (2016). Shadow banking: A review of the literature. In G. Jones (Ed.), *Banking crises: Perspectives from the new Palgrave dictionary* (pp. 282–315). Palgrave Macmillan. https://doi.org/10.1057/9781137553799_29

Ahlers, G. K. C., Cumming, D., Günther, C., & Schweizer, D. (2015). Signaling in equity crowdfunding. *Entrepreneurship Theory and Practice, 39*(4), 955–980. https://doi.org/10.1111/etap.12157

Allen, F., & Santomero, A. M. (1997). The theory of financial intermediation. *Journal of Banking & Finance, 21*(11–12), 1461–1485. https://doi.org/10.1016/S0378-4266(97)00032-0

Ande, J. A., & Eroglu, Z. K. (2021). Could New Zealand's equity crowdfunding regulations be the model for the developing world? *New Zealand Universities Law Review, 29*, 557–592. Retrieved from https://ssrn.com/abstract=3904063

Armour, J., & Enriques, L. (2018). Individual investors' access to Crowdinvesting: Two regulatory models. In D. Cumming & L. Hornuf (Eds.), *The economics of crowdfunding* (pp. 255–278). Palgrave Macmillan. https://doi.org/10.1007/978-3-319-66119-3_11

Baeck, P., Collins, L., & Zhang, B. (2014). Understanding alternative finance. In *The UK alternative finance industry report 2014* (pp. 1–95). University of Cambridge. Retrieved from https://media.nesta.org.uk/documents/understanding-alternative-finance-2014.pdf

Bavoso, V. (2020). The promise and perils of alternative market-based finance: The case of P2P lending in the UK. *Journal of Banking Regulation, 21*(4), 395–409. https://doi.org/10.1057/s41261-019-00118-9

Belleflamme, P., & Lambert, T. (2016). An industrial organization framework to understand the strategies of crowdfunding platforms. In J. Méric, I. Maque, & J. Brabet (Eds.), *International perspectives on crowdfunding* (pp. 1–19). Emerald Group Publishing Limited. https://doi.org/10.1108/978-1-78560-315-020151001

Belleflamme, P., & Peitz, M. (2021). *The economics of platforms*. Cambridge University Press.

Block, J., Hornuf, L., & Moritz, A. (2018). Which updates during an equity crowdfunding campaign increase crowd participation? *Small Business Economics, 50*(1), 3–27. https://doi.org/10.1007/s11187-017-9876-4

Bouglet, J., Garmilis, G., & Joffre, O. (2022). Protection of crowdfunders: A typology of equity crowdfunding platforms through governance mechanisms. *Revue de l'Entrepreneuriat, 20*, XXVI. https://doi.org/10.3917/entre1.pr.0006

Brummer, C., & Yadav, Y. (2018). Fintech and the innovation trilemma. *Georgetown Law Journal, 107*(2), 235–308. Retrieved from https://heinonline.org/HOL/LandingPage?handle=hein.journals/glj107&div=12&id=&page=

Bruton, G., Khavul, S., Siegel, D., & Wright, M. (2015). New financial alternatives in seeding entrepreneurship: Microfinance, crowdfunding, and peer–to–peer innovations. *Entrepreneurship Theory and Practice, 39*(1), 9–26. https://doi.org/10.1111/etap.12143

Buchak, G., Matvos, G., Piskorski, T., & Seru, A. (2018). Fintech, regulatory arbitrage, and the rise of shadow banks. *Journal of Financial Economics, 130*(3), 453–483. https://doi.org/10.1016/j.jfineco.2018.03.011

Burtch, G., Hong, Y., & Liu, D. (2018). The role of provision points in online crowdfunding. *Journal of Management Information Systems, 35*(1), 117–144. https://doi.org/10.1080/07421222.2018.1440764

Chaffee, E. C., & Rapp, G. C. (2012). Regulating Online peer-to-peer lending in the aftermath of Dodd–Frank: In search of an evolving regulatory regime for an evolving industry. *Washington and Lee Law Review, 69*(2), 485–533. Retrieved from https://heinonline.org/HOL/LandingPage?handle=hein.journals/waslee69&div=17&id=&page=

Chen, X., & Ma, L. (2023). Lead investors' insider ownership and crowd investors' agency concerns in investor-led equity crowdfunding. *Pacific-Basin Finance Journal, 78*, 101978. https://doi.org/10.1016/j.pacfin.2023.101978

Choi, S. (1997). Market lessons for gatekeepers. *Northwestern University Law Review, 92*(3), 916–966. Retrieved from https://heinonline.org/HOL/LandingPage?handle=hein.journals/illlr92&div=26&id=&page=

Coakley, J., Cumming, D. J., Lazos, A., & Vismara, S. (2024). Syndicated equity crowdfunding and the collective action problem. *European Corporate Governance Institute, 955*, 1–52. https://doi.org/10.2139/ssrn.4703001

Coakley, J., & Lazos, A. (2021). New developments in equity crowdfunding: A review. *Review of Corporate Finance, 1*(3-4), 341–405. https://doi.org/10.1561/114.00000008

Coase, R. H. (1937). The nature of the firm. *Economica, 4*(16), 386–405. https://doi.org/10.1111/j.1468-0335.1937.tb00002.x

Cogan, D., Odorović, A., Garvey, K., & Maffini, I. (2021). *Equity crowdfunding for energy access: Opportunities for scale-up?* (pp. 1–84). Energy4Impact. Retrieved from https://energy4impact.org/sites/default/files/crowdpower_equity_crowdfunding_for_energy_access_final.pdf

Congleton, R. D. (2015). The logic of collective action and beyond. *Public Choice, 164*(3-4), 217–234. https://doi.org/10.1007/s11127-015-0266-7
Cumming, D., & Hornuf, L. (2018). *The economics of crowdfunding*. Springer.
Cumming, D., & Hornuf, L. (2022). Marketplace lending of small- and medium-sized enterprises. *Strategic Entrepreneurship Journal, 16*(1), 32–66. https://doi.org/10.1002/sej.1411
Cumming, D., Johan, S., & Li, D. (2011). Exchange trading rules and stock market liquidity. *Journal of Financial Economics, 99*(3), 651–671. https://doi.org/10.1016/j.jfineco.2010.10.001
Cumming, D. J., Vanacker, T., & Zahra, S. A. (2021). Equity crowdfunding and governance: Toward an integrative model and research agenda. *Academy of Management Perspectives, 35*(1), 69–95. https://doi.org/10.5465/amp.2017.0208
Danmayr, F. (2014). *Archetypes of crowdfunding platforms: A multidimensional comparison*. Springer Science & Business Media. https://doi.org/10.1007/978-3-658-04559-3
De Roure, C., Pelizzon, L., & Thakor, A. (2022). P2P lenders versus banks: Cream skimming or bottom fishing? *The Review of Corporate Finance Studies, 11*(2), 213–262. https://doi.org/10.1093/rcfs/cfab026
Diamond, D. W. (1984). Financial intermediation and delegated monitoring. *The Review of Economic Studies, 51*(3), 393–414. https://doi.org/10.2307/2297430
Dorfleitner, G., Hornuf, L., & Weber, M. (2018). Dynamics of investor communication in equity crowdfunding. *Electronic Markets, 28*(4), 523–540. https://doi.org/10.1007/s12525-018-0294-5
Eisenbeiss, M., Hartmann, S. A., & Hornuf, L. (2023). Social media marketing for equity crowdfunding: Which posts trigger investment decisions? *Finance Research Letters, 52*, 103370. https://doi.org/10.1016/j.frl.2022.103370
Elyasiani, E., & Goldberg, L. G. (2004). Relationship lending: A survey of the literature. *Journal of Economics and Business, 56*(4), 315–330. https://doi.org/10.1016/j.jeconbus.2004.03.003
Estrin, S., Khavul, S., & Wright, M. (2022). Soft and hard information in equity crowdfunding: Network effects in the digitalization of entrepreneurial finance. *Small Business Economics, 58*(4), 1761–1781. https://doi.org/10.1007/s11187-021-00473-w
European Banking Authority. (2015). *Opinion of the European banking authority on lending-based crowdfunding (EBA-Op-2015-03)*. European Banking Authority. Retrieved from https://www.eba.europa.eu/sites/default/documents/files/documents/10180/983359/f6106173-dc94-4d22-ade8-d40fce724580/EBA-Op-2015-03%20%28EBA%20Opinion%20on%20lending%20based%20Crowdfunding%29.pdf?retry=1
European Commission. (2018). *Impact assessment accompanying the document proposal for a regulation of the European Parliament and of the Council on European crowdfunding service providers (ECSP) for business and proposal for a Directive of the European Parliament and of the Council amending directive 2014/65/EU on markets in financial instruments (COM(2018) 113 final)*. European Commission. Retrieved from https://eur-lex.europa.eu/legal-content/EN/TXT/HTML/?uri=CELEX%3A52018SC0056
European Securities and Markets Authority. (2014). *Opinion on investment-based crowdfunding (ESMA/2014/1378)*. European Securities and Markets Authority. Retrieved from https://www.esma.europa.eu/sites/default/files/library/2015/11/2014-1378_opinion_on_investment-based_crowdfunding.pdf
Everett, C. R. (2015). Group membership, relationship banking and loan default risk: The case of online social lending. *Banking and Finance Review, 7*(2), 1–54. https://doi.org/10.2139/ssrn.1114428
Farag, H., & Johan, S. (2022). How alternative finance informs central themes in corporate finance. *Journal of Corporate Finance, 77*, 102318. https://doi.org/10.1016/j.jcorpfin.2022.102318
Ferretti, R. (2022). Individual portfolio management of loans (art 6). In E. Macchiavello (Ed.), *Regulation on European crowdfunding service providers for business* (pp. 113–129). Edward Elgar Publishing.
Fried, J. M., & Ganor, M. (2006). Agency costs of venture capitalist control in startups. *NYU Law Review, 81*, 967–1025. Retrieved from https://heinonline.org/HOL/LandingPage?handle=hein.journals/nylr81&div=35&id=&page=

Gibilaro, L., & Mattarocci, G. (2018). Peer-to-peer lending and real estate mortgages: Evidence from United Kingdom. *Journal of European Real Estate Research, 11*(3), 319–334. https://doi.org/10.1108/JERER-12-2016-0048

Havrylchyk, O., & Verdier, M. (2018). The financial intermediation role of the P2P lending platforms. *Comparative Economic Studies, 60*(1), 115–130. https://doi.org/10.1057/s41294-017-0045-1

Hazen, T. L. (2011). Crowdfunding or fraudfunding-social networks and the securities laws-why the specially tailored exemption must be conditioned on meaningful disclosure. *NYU Law Review, 90*, 1735–1770. Retrieved from https://heinonline.org/HOL/LandingPage?handle=hein.journals/nclr90&div=50&id=&page

Hervé, F., Manthé, E., Sannajust, A., & Schwienbacher, A. (2019). Determinants of individual investment decisions in investment-based crowdfunding. *Journal of Business Finance & Accounting, 46*(5–6), 762–783. https://doi.org/10.1111/jbfa.12372

Hildebrand, T., Puri, M., & Rocholl, J. (2010). *Skin in the game: Evidence from the online social lending market*. Group. Retrieved from https://citeseerx.ist.psu.edu/document?repid=rep1&type=pdf&doi=bd9307a49d9c36ba529ad7a0cb9f64f4c4d7eb18

Hornuf, L., Klöhn, L., & Schilling, T. (2018). Financial contracting in crowdinvesting: Lessons from the German market. *German Law Journal, 19*(3), 509–578. https://doi.org/10.1017/S2071832200022781

Hornuf, L., & Neuenkirch, M. (2017). Pricing shares in equity crowdfunding. *Small Business Economics, 48*(4), 795–811. https://doi.org/10.1007/s11187-016-9807-9

Hornuf, L., Schmitt, M., & Stenzhorn, E. (2018). Equity crowdfunding in Germany and the United Kingdom: Follow-up funding and firm failure. *Corporate Governance: An International Review, 26*(5), 331–354. https://doi.org/10.1111/corg.12260

Hornuf, L., & Schwienbacher, A. (2016). Crowdinvesting: Angel investing for the masses? In H. Landström & C. Mason (Eds.), *Handbook of research on business angels* (pp. 381–398). Edward Elgar Publishing. Retrieved from https://www.elgaronline.com/edcollchap/edcoll/9781783471713/9781783471713.00024.xml

Hornuf, L., & Schwienbacher, A. (2018). Market mechanisms and funding dynamics in equity crowdfunding. *Journal of Corporate Finance*. https://doi.org/10.1016/j.jcorpfin.2017.08.009

Jackson, H. E. (2020). The nature of the Fintech firm. *Washington University Journal of Law and Policy, 61*, 9–24. Retrieved from https://heinonline.org/HOL/LandingPage?handle=hein.journals/wajlp61&div=5&id=&page=

Jiang, C., Wang, Z., Wang, R., & Ding, Y. (2018). Loan default prediction by combining soft information extracted from descriptive text in online peer-to-peer lending. *Annals of Operations Research, 266*(1–2), 511–529. https://doi.org/10.1007/s10479-017-2668-z

Käfer, B. (2018). Peer-to-peer lending—A (financial stability) risk perspective. *Review of Economics, 69*(1), 1–25. https://doi.org/10.1515/roe-2017-0020

Kaja, F., Martino, E. D., & Pacces, A. M. (2021). Fintech and the law and economics of disintermediation. In I. Chiu & G. Deipenbrock (Eds.), *Routledge handbook of financial technology and law* (pp. 78–95). Routledge.

Kauffman, R. J., Spaulding, T. J., & Wood, C. A. (2009). Are online auction markets efficient? An empirical study of market liquidity and abnormal returns. *Decision Support Systems, 48*(1), 3–13. https://doi.org/10.1016/j.dss.2009.05.009

Kirby, E., & Worner, S. (2014). *Crowd-funding: An infant industry growing fast*. IOSCO Research Department. 2014, 1–63.

Kleiner, C. (2021). General report: The legal regulation of crowdfunding. In C. Kleiner (Ed.), *Legal aspects of crowdfunding* (Vol. 55, pp. 49–89). Springer.

Klöhn, L., Hornuf, L., & Schilling, T. (2016). The regulation of crowdfunding in the German small investor protection act: Content, consequences, critique, suggestions. *European Company Law, 13*(2), 56–66. Retrieved from https://papers.ssrn.com/sol3/papers.cfm?abstract_id=2595773

Leboeuf, G., & Schwienbacher, A. (2018). Crowdfunding as a new financing tool. In D. Cumming & L. Hornuf (Eds.), *The economics of crowdfunding* (pp. 11–28). Palgrave Macmillan.

Leland, H. E., & Pyle, D. H. (1977). Informational asymmetries, financial structure, and financial intermediation. *The Journal of Finance, 32*(2), 371–387. https://doi.org/10.2307/2326770

Li, X., Tang, Y., Yang, N., Ren, R., Zheng, H., & Zhou, H. (2016). The value of information disclosure and lead investor in equity-based crowdfunding: An exploratory empirical study. *Nankai Business Review International, 7*(3), 301–321. https://doi.org/10.1108/NBRI-01-2016-0002

Löher, J. (2017). The interaction of equity crowdfunding platforms and ventures: An analysis of the preselection process. *Venture Capital, 19*(1–2), 51–74. https://doi.org/10.1080/13691066.2016.1252510

Macchiavello, E. (2018). Financial-return crowdfunding and regulatory approaches in the shadow banking, FinTech and collaborative finance era. *European Company and Financial Law Review, 14*(4), 662–722. https://doi.org/10.1515/ecfr-2017-0030

Macchiavello, E. (2019). 'What to expect when you are expecting' a European crowdfunding regulation: The current 'Bermuda triangle' and future scenarios for marketplace lending and investing in Europe. *European Banking Institute Working Paper Series, 55*, 1–47. https://doi.org/10.2139/ssrn.3493688

Macchiavello, E. (2021a). Disintermediation in fund-raising: Marketplace investing platforms and EU financial regulation. In I. Chiu & G. Deipenbrock (Eds.), *Routledge handbook of financial technology and law* (pp. 291–306). Routledge.

Macchiavello, E. (2021b). The European crowdfunding service providers regulation: The future of marketplace lending and investing in Europe and the 'crowdfunding Nature'Dilemma. *European Business Law Review, 32*(3), 557–608.

Macchiavello, E., & Sciarrone Alibrandi, A. (2021). Marketplace lending as a new means of raising Capital in the Internal Market: True disintermediation or reintermediation? In E. Avgouleas & H. Marjosola (Eds.), *Digital finance in Europe: Law, regulation, and governance* (pp. 37–86). De Gruyter. https://doi.org/10.1515/9783110749472-003

Manigart, S., Lockett, A., Meuleman, M., Landstrom, H., Bruining, H., Desbrières, P., & Hommel, U. (2006). Venture capitalists' decision to syndicate. *Entrepreneurship Theory and Practice, 30*, 131–153. https://doi.org/10.1111/j.1540-6520.2006.00115.x

Martínez-Climent, C., Zorio-Grima, A., & Ribeiro-Soriano, D. (2018). Financial return crowdfunding: Literature review and bibliometric analysis. *International Entrepreneurship and Management Journal, 14*(3), 527–553. https://doi.org/10.1007/s11365-018-0511-x

Meoli, M., Rossi, A., & Vismara, S. (2022). Financial literacy and security-based crowdfunding. *Corporate Governance: An International Review, 30*(1), 27–54. https://doi.org/10.1111/corg.12355

Minto, A., & Legind, N. D. (2021). Zooming in on the "individual portfolio management of loans" in the ambit of the regulation on European crowdfunding service providers. *Law and Economics Yearly Review, 10*, 142–162. Retrieved from https://hdl.handle.net/10278/3745553

Mishkin, F. S. (2007). *The economics of money, banking, and financial markets*. Pearson Education.

Moloney, N., Ferran, E., Payne, J., & Payne, J. (2015). The role of gatekeepers. In N. Moloney, E. Ferran, & J. Payne (Eds.), *The Oxford handbook of financial regulation* (pp. 254–278). Oxford University Press. https://doi.org/10.1093/oxfordhb/9780199687206.013.11

Morsy, S. (2014). The JOBS act and crowdfunding: How narrowing the secondary market handicaps fraud plaintiffs. *Brooklyn Law Review, 79*(3), 1373–1405. Retrieved from https://heinonline.org/HOL/LandingPage?handle=hein.journals/brklr79&div=52&id=&page=

Nemoto, N., Huang, B., & Storey, D. J. (2019). Optimal regulation of P2P lending for small and medium-sized enterprises. *SSRN Electronic Journal*. https://doi.org/10.2139/ssrn.3313999

Nguyen, T., Cox, J., & Rich, J. (2019). Invest or regret? An empirical investigation into funding dynamics during the final days of equity crowdfunding campaigns. *Journal of Corporate Finance, 58*, 784–803. https://doi.org/10.1016/j.jcorpfin.2019.07.011

Odorović, A. (2023). Open banking: Between cooperation and competition. *Annals of the Faculty of Law in Belgrade, 71*(1), 65–91. https://doi.org/10.51204/Anali_PFBU_23102A

Olson, M., Jr. (1965). *The logic of collective action: Public goods and the theory of groups*. Harvard University Press.

Parhankangas, A., Mason, C., & Landström, H. (2019). Crowdfunding: An introduction. In H. Landström, A. Parhankangas, & C. Mason (Eds.), *Handbook of research on crowdfunding* (pp. 1–21). Edward Elgar Publishing. https://doi.org/10.4337/9781788117210.00005

Polzin, F., Toxopeus, H., & Stam, E. (2018). The wisdom of the crowd in funding: Information heterogeneity and social networks of crowdfunders. *Small Business Economics, 50*(2), 251–273. https://doi.org/10.1007/s11187-016-9829-3

Pur, S., Huesig, S., & Schmidhammer, C. (2023). Towards a theory on dominant business model emergence of marketplace lending in Germany. *Credit and Capital Markets, 56*(1), 63–102. https://doi.org/10.3790/ccm.56.1.63

Ricci, S. A., & Sautter, C. M. (2021). Corporate governance gaming: The collective power of retail investors. *Nevada Law Journal, 22*, 51–97. https://doi.org/10.1017/err.2020.8

Ricci, S. A. G., & Sautter, C. M. (2022). Wireless investors & apathy obsolescence. *Washington University Law Review, 100*, 1653–1686. Retrieved from https://heinonline.org/hol-cgi-bin/get_pdf.cgi?handle=hein.journals/walq100&section=49

Rodriguez de las Heras Ballell, T. (2019). The layers of digital financial innovation: Charting a regulatory response. *Fordham Journal of Corporate & Financial Law, 25*, 381–421. Retrieved from https://heinonline.org/HOL/LandingPage?handle=hein.journals/fjcf25&div=16&id=&page=

Rossi, A., Vanacker, T. R., & Vismara, S. (2020). Equity crowdfunding: New evidence from US and UK markets. *SSRN Electronic Journal*. https://doi.org/10.2139/ssrn.3752616

Rossi, A., & Vismara, S. (2018). What do crowdfunding platforms do? A comparison between investment-based platforms in Europe. *Eurasian Business Review, 8*(1), 93–118. https://doi.org/10.1007/s40821-017-0092-6

Santos, T., & Scheinkman, J. A. (2001). Competition among exchanges. *The Quarterly Journal of Economics, 116*(3), 1027–1061. https://doi.org/10.1162/00335530152466304

Scholtens, B., & Van Wensveen, D. (2000). A critique on the theory of financial intermediation. *Journal of Banking & Finance, 24*(8), 1243–1251. https://doi.org/10.1016/S0378-4266(99)00085-0

Schwab, K. (2017). *The fourth industrial revolution*. Crown Currency.

Schwartz, A. A. (2018). The gatekeepers of crowdfunding. *Washington University Law Review, 75*, 885–955. Retrieved from https://heinonline.org/HOL/LandingPage?handle=hein.journals/waslee75&div=21&id=&page=

Schwartz, A. A. (2023). *Investment crowdfunding*. Oxford University Press.

Shneor, R. (2020). Crowdfunding models, strategies, and choices between them. In R. Shneor, L. Zhao, & B.-T. Flåten (Eds.), *Advances in crowdfunding* (pp. 21–42). Springer International Publishing. https://doi.org/10.1007/978-3-030-46309-0_2

Shneor, R., Wenzlaff, K., Boyko, K., Baah-Peprah, P., Odorović, A., & Okhrimenko, O. (2024). *The European crowdfunding market report 2023*. University of Agder- Crowdfunding Research Center. Retrieved from https://papers.ssrn.com/sol3/papers.cfm?abstract_id=4713135

Short, J., Ketchen, D., Mckenny, A., Allison, T., & Ireland, R. (2017). Research on crowdfunding: Reviewing the (very recent) past and celebrating the present. *Entrepreneurship Theory and Practice, 41*, 149–160. https://doi.org/10.1111/etap.12270

Sorenson, O., Assenova, V., Li, G.-C., Boada, J., & Fleming, L. (2016). Expand innovation finance via crowdfunding. *Science, 354*(6319), 1526–1528. https://doi.org/10.1126/science.aaf6989

Stefanelli, V., Ferilli, G. B., & Boscia, V. (2022). Exploring the lending business crowdfunding to support SMEs' financing decisions. *Journal of Innovation & Knowledge, 7*(4), 100278. https://doi.org/10.1016/j.jik.2022.100278

Tang, H. (2019). Peer-to-peer lenders versus banks: Substitutes or complements? *The Review of Financial Studies, 32*(5), 1900–1938. https://doi.org/10.1093/rfs/hhy137

Tröger, T. H. (2021). Regulation of crowdfunding in Germany. In C. Kleiner (Ed.), *Legal aspects of crowdfunding* (Vol. 55, pp. 93–125). Springer. https://doi.org/10.1007/978-3-030-79264-0_3

Vallee, B., & Zeng, Y. (2019). Marketplace lending: A new banking paradigm? *The Review of Financial Studies, 32*(5), 1939–1982. https://doi.org/10.1093/rfs/hhy100

Vismara, S. (2018). Signaling to overcome inefficiencies in crowdfunding markets. In D. Cumming & L. Hornuf (Eds.), *The economics of crowdfunding* (pp. 29–56). Palgrave Macmillan. https://doi.org/10.1007/978-3-319-66119-3_3

Vismara, S., Paleari, S., & Ritter, J. R. (2012). Europe's second markets for small companies. *European Financial Management, 18*(3), 352–388. https://doi.org/10.1111/j.1468-036X.2012.00641.x

Yum, H., Lee, B., & Chae, M. (2012). From the wisdom of crowds to my own judgment in microfinance through online peer-to-peer lending platforms. *Electronic Commerce Research and Applications, 11*(5), 469–483. https://doi.org/10.1016/j.elerap.2012.05.003

Zhang, B., Wardrop, R., Ziegler, T., Lui, A., Burton, J., James, A., & Garvey, K. (2016). *Sustaining momentum: The 2nd European alternative finance industry report.* Cambridge Centre for Alternative Finance. Retrieved from https://www.jbs.cam.ac.uk/faculty-research/centres/alternative-finance/publications/sustaining-momentum/

Zhang, Y., Hughes, M., Fu, K., Scholes, L., & Tang, F. (2023). The effect of lead investors' trustworthiness on funding performance: The moderating effect of investment-specific human capital. *Technology in Society, 73*, 102222. https://doi.org/10.1016/j.techsoc.2023.102222

Zhao, Y., Harris, P., & Lam, W. (2019). Crowdfunding industry—History, development, policies, and potential issues. *Journal of Public Affairs, 19*(1), e1921. https://doi.org/10.1002/pa.1921

Ziegler, T., Johanson, D., King, M., Zhang, B., Mammadova, L., Ferri, F., Trappe, R., Suresh, K., Hao, R., & Ryll, L. (2018). *Reaching new heights: The 3rd Americas alternative finance industry report.* Cambridge Centre for Alternative Finance. Retrieved from https://www.jbs.cam.ac.uk/wp-content/uploads/2020/08/2019-05-ccaf-3rd-americas-alternative-finance-industry-report.pdf

Ziegler, T., Johanson, D., Zhang, B., Ben, S., Wang, W., Mammadova, L., Hao, R., Luo, D., Wang, Z., & Chen, H. (2018). *The 3rd Asia Pacific region alternative finance industry report.* Cambridge Centre for Alternative Finance. Retrieved from https://www.jbs.cam.ac.uk/faculty-research/centres/alternative-finance/publications/3rd-asia-pacific-region-alternative-finance-industry-report/

Ziegler, T., Shneor, R., Garvey, K., Wenzlaff, K., Yerolemou, N., Rui, H., & Zhang, B. (2018). *Expanding horizons: The 3rd European alternative finance industry report.* Cambridge Centre for Alternative Finance. Retrieved from https://www.jbs.cam.ac.uk/wp-content/uploads/2020/08/2018-02-ccaf-exp-horizons.pdf

Ziegler, T., Shneor, R., Wenzlaff, K., Odorović, A., Johanson, D., Hao, R., & Ryll, L. (2019). *Shifting paradigms: The 4th European alternative finance benchmarking report.* Cambridge Centre for Alternative Finance. Retrieved from https://www.jbs.cam.ac.uk/faculty-research/centres/alternative-finance/publications/shifting-paradigms/

Ziegler, T., Shneor, R., Wenzlaff, K., Suresh, K., Paes, F. F. C., Mammadova, L., Wanga, C., Kekre, N., Mutinda, S., & Wang, B. (2021). *The 2nd global alternative finance market benchmarking report.* Cambridge Centre for Alternative Finance. Retrieved from https://www.jbs.cam.ac.uk/faculty-research/centres/alternative-finance/publications/the-2nd-global-alternative-finance-market-benchmarking-report/

Ziegler, T., Shneor, R., Wenzlaff, K., Wang, B., Kim, J., Paes, F. F. C., Suresh, K., Zhang, B. Z., Mammadova, L., & Adams, N. (2020). *The global alternative finance market benchmarking report.* Cambridge Centre for Alternative Finance. Retrieved from https://www.jbs.cam.ac.uk/faculty-research/centres/alternative-finance/publications/the-global-alternative-finance-market-benchmarking-report/

Chapter 3
Promises and Limitations of Market-Based Mechanisms in Crowdfunding

3.1 Introduction

Information asymmetry remains one of the central issues in finance and one of the main rationales for financial regulation. Despite the rising complexities of (traditional) financial markets, securities regulations have not changed much regarding their core components: protections against fraud and disclosure requirements at the time of the securities offering and thereafter. They have been supplemented by anti-manipulation provisions concerning securities trading, including rules on insider trading, which prohibit trading based on information that was not previously disclosed. In traditional financial markets, regulators have mostly refrained from substantive regulations, such as banning certain financial products or price interventions. The basic premise is that, as long as the market is provided with the right information in a timely manner, anyone 'can sell or buy whatever he wants at whatever price the market will sustain' (Easterbrook & Fischel, 1991, p. 670).[1] In addition, financial regulations have regulated the operation of financial and information intermediaries, recognising the importance of their role in information production, verification, and processing.

Discussions on how to regulate crowdfunding (particularly crowdfunding for businesses) usually mirror these considerations, with particular attention paid to the need to introduce special safeguards for small retail investors. The key debates

[1] Some limitations to this basic premise are embedded in rules regulating the institutional context of securities trading (Kahan, 1991, pp. 984–985). These include rules on circuit breakers (forcing markets to close when securities prices exhibit extraordinary volatility), margin requirements (limiting the amount of credit that can be used for buying securities), and market makers (charged with the role of trading securities to maintain orderly functioning of markets). However, their purpose is also concerned with ensuring that securities prices are accurate and reflect all relevant information.

A. Odorović, *Overcoming Asymmetric Information in the Crowdfunding Market*, International Law and Economics, https://doi.org/10.1007/978-3-032-04118-0_3

relate to the necessity of introducing a lighter mandatory disclosure regime on fundraisers and designing a regulatory framework for crowdfunding intermediaries that reflects the scope and depth of services they provide. Given the particularities of crowdfunding, most of the regulatory solutions considered or adopted reflect the regulators' fear of not intervening and the fear of not intervening too much. However, policy-making in the field often lacks systematic account of the source and the degree of market failure.

With a view of better understanding the issue of information asymmetry in crowdfunding, which can point to the desired direction of the regulatory intervention, this chapter discusses promises and limitations of market-driven solutions. They can originate from fundraisers or the crowdfunding intermediary, as briefly discussed in Chap. 2. The analysis draws on theoretical considerations in information economics and law and finance literature and transfers them to the realm of crowdfunding. Furthermore, the chapter reviews and systematises growing empirical crowdfunding literature that provides evidence on the behaviour of fundraisers, investors, and platforms.

The analysis begins by discussing why information asymmetry is the key consideration in crowdfunding (Sect. 3.2) and whether information plays the same functions as in traditional financial markets (Sect. 3.3). As a next step, it explores whether and how fundraisers unravel information about their quality (Sect. 3.4), using voluntary disclosures (Sect. 3.4.1) or signalling (Sect. 3.4.2). The last part investigates different gatekeeping services of crowdfunding platforms in depth (Sect. 3.5). For the sake of clarity, the summary of findings is provided at the end of each relevant section or subsection.

3.2 Information Asymmetry and Why It Matters in Crowdfunding

It is conventional wisdom that truthful and sufficient information about individuals or firms raising funds and their subsequent (entrepreneurial) activities is fundamental for well-functioning financial markets and their existence. The crowdfunding market is no exception. To explain this causal relationship, it is helpful to depicture a scenario in which information asymmetries between fundraisers and investors are paramount, meaning that investors have prohibitively high costs of acquiring the information about the fundraiser's quality before and their actions after committing funds.

The starting premise is that a firm issuing securities or raising funds via other means promises to invest these funds into risky assets that will pay an uncertain cash flow in the future. In addition to the uncertainty inherent in any economic endeavour, external investors do not possess information that is private to the fundraising firm, its managers and employees. Such information encompasses knowledge about different external contingencies that affect the firm's prospects and internal capacity to cope with them. In addition to private information about managers' and staff's skills, capabilities, and efforts they intend to invest, external investors lack information about their readiness to divert the funds raised to themselves.

The willingness of potential investors to commit funds critically depends on their ability to estimate the expected returns, that is, to distinguish between high-quality and low-quality fundraisers. If the costs of acquiring information are prohibitively high, some potential investors can decide not to accept high-risk exposure. Other investors can be willing to commit funds but under terms that are unfavourable for high-quality (low-risk) firms. In other words, investors are ready to offer a lower price for securities that will compensate them for the additional risk taken. The price provided corresponds to the average expected quality for the entire pool of fundraisers. This means that the high-quality fundraisers would have to sell more securities to raise the funds needed to carry on their projects. As a result, the costs of raising funds are higher (such as when paying higher interest or dividends or giving up a higher equity stake), which can divert high-quality fundraisers from raising external funds.[2] The more high-quality projects are out of the market, the lower the average expected quality investors face. If this reasoning is applied consistently, in the end, only the lowest quality or riskiest fundraisers are willing to accept the market price for their securities, diverting the economy's scarce resources from promising projects. The seminal article by George Akerlof, explaining the phenomenon of adverse selection (Akerlof, 1970), was further developed by Myers and Majluf, describing why firms may pass up valuable investment opportunities or rely on internal sources of funds (Myers & Majluf, 1984). This will be the case if the cost of issuing shares outweighs the project's net present value.

It is straightforward to argue that, at the outset, ex-ante information asymmetry in crowdfunding is significantly more pronounced than in traditional finance. Similar to 'truly new securities' in conventional markets, investors in crowdfunding cannot rely on the market price of the previously listed securities that are currently trading as guidance of the firm's value (Fox, 2016, pp. 683–684). Beyond this, firms behind crowdfunding offerings have little or no track record of their past performance. Small innovative firms have often not generated any income yet, and some still do not have a product ready to market.

While information asymmetry can prevent channelling society's scarce savings into what appears to be their most productive use ex-ante, it can also undermine fundraiser's incentives to pursue successful implementation of their projects ex-post. Agency costs theory, starting with the seminar article of Jensen and Meckling, shows that the entrepreneur or manager of the firm, which is not its sole owner, has limited incentives to undertake activities that would maximise the firm's value (Jensen & Meckling, 1976). The reason is that the entrepreneur who does not own

---

[2] The costs of raising equity (costs of capital) decrease in the price of shares sold via public offering. Capital infusion is determined by the price of shares and the number of shares sold. For a given amount of a desired cash infusion, the lower the price of shares achieved, the greater the dilution of stakes of existing stakeholders.

a 100% of claims on the firm (its assets and cash flows) bears only a fraction of costs stemming from activities that also generate personal benefits (Jensen & Meckling, 1976, pp. 312–313). Thus, dispersed investors bear costs in monitoring whether entrepreneurs or managers are investing enough effort into the project or whether they use 'corporate assets for self-interested purposes' (Mahoney, 1995, p. 1042). Yet, these costs can be prohibitively high. External investors sometimes cannot discern whether the firm's performance can be attributed to entrepreneurial activities and, consequently, cannot effectively limit the entrepreneur in pursuing self-interest. As a result, they may be reluctant to provide funding in the first place.

The agency problem is also likely to be more severe for firms that raised funds via crowdfunding when compared to large corporations, in relation to which agency costs theory was initially developed. Monitoring costs increase in the dispersion of ownership, whereas the very definition of crowdfunding implies financing from a large number of retail investors each pledging a small amount. Moreover, since fundraisers in crowdfunding are usually innovative early-stage companies, external contingencies affecting a firm's performance outnumber those faced by more established firms, making it even harder to understand entrepreneurs' contributions to certain (un) favourable events.

3.3 The Role of Information in Traditional Financial Markets and Crowdfunding

If one were to assume that the issue of information asymmetry can be resolved or significantly alleviated (by market forces as discussed in the sections that follow, or by a regulatory intervention), it is worth questioning whether information can perform the same functions in crowdfunding as in traditional financial markets. This becomes pertinent in light of some fundamental differences: the prevalence of unsophisticated (retail) investors, lack of information intermediaries (e.g., underwriters, auditors, financial analysts), and inexistence of operational secondary markets.

The provision of accurate, complete, and timely information in traditional markets enables (1) investor confidence in the market, (2) efficient pricing of securities and capital allocation, and (3) efficient corporate governance mechanisms (Enriques & Gilotta, 2014, pp. 513–520). While the first two functions are achieved by providing information both ex-ante and ex-post, the third function is primarily enabled through ongoing disclosures after securities offerings.[3]

The idea that more information leads to greater protection of investors and, consequently, investor confidence is readily comprehensible. In principle, when

[3] A notable exception includes providing detailed information about managers' compensation or any transactions concluded between them and the company at the time of the offering, with the view of shareholders being able to constrain managers' self-interested behaviour ex-post (Mahoney, 1995, p. 1051).

provided with adequate information, investors are empowered to make competent investment decisions and choose financial products best tailored to their needs, including their risk-return appetite. In other words, as the risk of individual projects is easily identifiable, investors opt for a risk-retention level necessary to pursue financial returns (Kingsford-Smith & Dixon, 2015). The risk is discerned from information on the issuer, securities issued, attached rights, etc.[4] Equal access to information is also expected to create an even playing field among different market players. It protects retail investors from being exploited by professional investors and insiders (initial shareholders, i.e. founders or managers), although this argument has been largely contested in the literature (Enriques & Gilotta, 2014, pp. 6–7). Rising investor confidence facilitated through financial information may also contribute to the depth and liquidity of financial markets, as some empirical evidence suggests outside the crowdfunding context (e.g., Maham & Safikhani, 2014). The interdependence between provision of information and investor confidence should, in principle, also exist in crowdfunding, to the extent that the level of sophistication of retail investors allows them to draw better inferences from more information.

Information disclosure also enables prices to fully reflect all relevant information at a given moment.[5] Such prices are also known as efficient prices, while markets where such prices exist at any time are called efficient markets (Fama, 1970, p. 383).[6] Efficient prices are assumed to approximate the intrinsic (fundamental) value of securities offered.[7] The price accuracy allows financial markets to perform their essential role of allocating scarce resources in the economy through their effect on the cost of capital. When deciding on the issuance of new securities, existing shareholders (entrepreneurs) aim to maximise the value of their shares (Kahan, 1991, pp. 1006–1008). If the company and the new investment opportunity are

[4] In a seminal article on the Capital Assets Pricing Model (CAPM), Sharpe (1964) explains the relationship between risk and expected returns and offers a market equilibrium theory of asset prices.

[5] Nevertheless, the response to new information is not instantaneous, as otherwise professional investors and analysts would not have the incentive to invest resources to obtain information, as Grossman and Stiglitz (1980) first argued. Instead, the new information is reflected in market prices as more investors become informed and trade in their pursuit of returns. Put differently, 'the market will remain efficient only if most market participants believe it is not' (Gordon & Kornhauser, 1985, p. 786).

[6] It is common to distinguish between three forms of efficient market hypotheses: a weak form, in which prices reflect historical data; a semi-strong form, in which prices reflect all information that is publicly available; and a strong form, in which prices reflect both public and private information (when some 'investors or groups have monopolistic access to any information') (Fama, 1970, p. 383). While the efficient market hypothesis in its different forms is commonly associated with Eugene Fama, it was formulated in the mid-1960s. For early contributions to the discussion, see Gordon and Kornhauser (1985, p. 762, fn. 1).

[7] The fundamental value of a security represents the net present value of future cash flows that the security will generate. The extent to which prices reflect the fundamental value of securities depends on 'the availability of value-relevant information and market mechanisms that cause that information to be reflected in security prices' (Gilson & Kraakman, 2014).

assessed correctly, meaning that the prices of the new securities are efficient, all the profits and losses from undertaking the investment will accrue proportionately to existing shareholders. As a result, they will only undertake welfare-maximising projects, i.e. projects with positive net present value. If new securities are undervalued, the cost of issuing new securities borne by existing shareholders can outweigh the gains from undertaking a profitable project. Alternatively, if new securities are overpriced, existing shareholders' gains may exceed the losses generated by an investment project. In both scenarios of securities mispricing, decisions regarding raising external finance and undertaking real investments can be suboptimal from a social welfare perspective.[8] Thus, the availability of information and market mechanisms that enable that information to be aggregated in market prices are indispensable for inducing socially optimal decisions on issuing new securities and making investments.[9]

The interlinkage between the existence of information ex-ante, cost of capital, and allocative function of financial markets exists both in traditional (primary) markets and crowdfunding. There are two notable caveats. Firstly, this interlinkage relies on the assumption that investors can verify and process the available information at relatively low cost, which is less likely satisfied in crowdfunding. This is due to a small portion of professional investors and the absence of traditional intermediaries (e.g., underwriters). Secondly, information alone is likely insufficient to induce efficient securities pricing in crowdfunding due to expected liquidity restrictions after the financing round. Namely, the inexistence or underdevelopment of secondary markets makes crowdfunding investments largely illiquid, affecting the price investors are willing to pay at the time of the offering. This line of reasoning is supported by existing research concerning traditional primary markets, which shows that restricted securities that can be sold only after some time or otherwise

[8] It is worth noting that lack of information will generally lead to underpricing of securities, i.e. high cost of capital, as explained above when discussing adverse selection. The expectation is that uninformed investors are 'always holding too much of stocks with bad news, and too little of stocks with good news' (Easley & O'hara, 2004, p. 1554).

[9] Nevertheless, underpricing is common in traditional primary markets. Finance literature provided several competing hypotheses on what leads to higher post-IPO prices. Rock (1986) contends that the underlying cause is asymmetric information regarding an issuer's value among different investors. Given that uninformed investors face the risk of adverse selection, i.e. purchasing a large portion of overpriced securities compared to privileged investors, they are willing to submit their purchase orders only if securities are underpriced. Building on this premise, Ritter (1987) explains how underpricing depends on the investment bank's role in offering securities (a best-effort offer vs. a firm commitment). Benveniste and Spindt (1989) also underline the role of underwriters to argue that underpricing results from underwriters' efforts to induce better-informed investors to reveal positive information they hold about the issuer during the process of soliciting indications of interest. Because withholding information until after the offering would benefit informed investors as it would lead to a lower offer price, the investment bank has to compensate them during presales. Welch (1992) develops the concept of information cascades in which later investors can infer information from the purchase decisions of early investors and follow their investment decision. Because the demand of early investors is so essential for an issuer's total proceeds, he will underprice securities to ensure early investors have an incentive to invest.

have low liquidity are sold at a discount (e.g., Ghaidarov, 2021; Silber, 1991). While the described caveats concern the pricing of a new securities offering, the price efficiency after issuing securities is significantly more challenging to achieve in crowdfunding than in traditional markets, as explained in the following analysis concerning corporate governance. The underlying causes of ex-ante and ex-post inefficiencies are common, nevertheless.

The production of information after the financing round can improve corporate governance through direct or indirect channels that influence monitoring costs (Fox, 1999, pp. 116–123). One direct channel is that investors who are better informed about a firm's performance can more efficiently exercise their voting rights, thus curtailing managerial opportunism. Examples include shareholders voting on the board of directors, managerial compensation, approval of transactions, etc. (Enriques & Gilotta, 2014, p. 8). Another direct channel is that information facilitates managers' compliance with their fiduciary duties, such as rules on conflict of interest. Simply put, because situations in which a conflict of interest arises are known, managers either try to avoid them or ensure that the terms of a transaction leading to a conflict of interest are not detrimental to the shareholders' value. Again, if one assumes low information-processing costs and low costs of bringing action against managers in a breach of fiduciary duties, the described channels should work both in traditional markets and crowdfunding.

Indirect channels, which assume that information affects corporate governance through its effect on prices of securities, seem even more critical in traditional markets. They primarily include the market for corporate control, share-price-based managerial compensation, and the cost of capital (Fox, 1999, pp. 120–123). The market for corporate control enables takeovers of underperforming companies, i.e., whose value can be increased by resolving mismanagement issues. An efficient market price of securities enabled by public information serves as primary guidance in assessing underachieving companies by potential acquirers. A takeover threat further imposes discipline on managers, thus aligning their interests with the interests of investors. Share-price-based managerial compensation works in a similar manner. Managers' incentives to act in the best interest of shareholders are fostered by entrenching their personal payoff in the company's value. Again, public information about the company increases the accuracy of securities prices, making management deceit less likely.[10] Finally, an example of how market scrutiny facilitated by public information guides managerial choices is the cost of capital. Existing prices of listed securities affect the terms of raising new capital via debt or equity (securities markets or bank loans). The cost of (new) capital, in turn, affects

---

[10] Increasing the amount of information available through disclosure practises can lead to increased managerial compensation, independently from share-price-based managerial compensation. Hermalin and Weisbach (2012) argue that increased production of information adversely affects managers who ask for a compensating differential. Moreover, managers with a certain level of bargaining power can capture a portion of a firm's profits that increase as a result of better monitoring. Consequently, they conclude that there exists a point beyond which additional disclosure reduces benefits to shareholders.

the selection of new investment projects. As explained earlier (concerning the importance of efficient prices for capital allocation when issuing securities for the first time), raising finance under efficient terms curtails managers' incentives to undertake unprofitable projects or pass up profitable projects in their pursuit of self-interest.[11]

It is important to emphasise that, unlike direct channels of influence of information on corporate governance, all the indirect channels depend on the existence and well-functioning secondary markets.[12] One cannot expect markets to respond to new information without active trading (Gilson & Kraakman, 2014, p. 325). Trading activity is the primary mechanism that enables information to be reflected in securities prices. Fama (1970, p. 387) originally examined market conditions that could hinder efficient adjustments of securities prices and concluded that high transaction costs in trading securities are a potential source of market inefficiency. Therefore, one can expect that the inexistence of operational or liquid secondary markets in crowdfunding raises transaction costs in trading securities and thus impairs indirect channels through which information production can mitigate managerial opportunism. Consequently, crowdfunding often develops corporate governance mechanisms that are closer to those that exist in private markets, as will be discussed below.

In sum, information production performs similar functions in traditional markets and crowdfunding—mitigating adverse selection and agency problems or, conversely, enhancing investor confidence, inducing efficient capital allocation, and improving corporate governance. However, mechanisms through which these functions are enabled are sometimes absent or weakened in crowdfunding, especially with regard to ex-post information asymmetry.

The rest of this chapter analyses different ways fundraisers' superior information can be effectively conveyed to crowd investors. In other words, it explores different market-based solutions to information asymmetry, originating from fundraisers or crowdfunding platforms.

[11] It is worth noting that the relationship between the cost of capital and corporate governance is characterised by reversed causality. Namely, the quality of corporate governance also impacts the price of capital, given its ability to influence a firm value through reducing agency costs (e.g., Chen et al., 2009; Zhu, 2014).

[12] One can argue that the existence of secondary markets can also affect direct channels of influence of information on corporate governance. This is because firms gain increased visibility and are usually subject to ongoing disclosure requirements mandated by exchanges or securities regulations. Consequently, they are put under scrutiny, which should reduce the risk of ex-post expropriation of managers or company founders (Armour & Enriques, 2018, p. 263).

3.4 Information Unravelling by Fundraisers

Information asymmetry characterises almost any market to a larger or smaller extent. Nevertheless, most markets outside the financial sector are not regulated, while market forces drive information production necessary for their functioning without significant frictions. This has spurred the law and finance literature debate on whether similar voluntary mechanisms of overcoming information asymmetries could work in financial markets. In reconsidering the discussion over the effectiveness of voluntary mechanisms, this section provides a closer look into factors pertinent to crowdfunding.

The starting point in analysing voluntary mechanisms is the premise that high-quality sellers or fundraisers suffer losses from adverse selection and agency costs. They cannot raise finances under terms that correspond to real prospects of projects they intend to carry.[13] It is worth noting that agency costs can also affect firms' ability to raise finance ex-ante, as investors will price in the risk inherent in their inability to effectively monitor entrepreneurs' actions and countervail their incentives to deceit. In other words, investors will ask for higher returns to hold securities with 'greater private (and correspondingly less public) information' (Easley & O'hara, 2004, p. 1554). The higher cost of capital arises because the increased estimation risk is usually non-diversifiable (Botosan, 1997, p. 324).[14] Consequently, high-quality fundraisers should, in principle, have incentives to distinguish themselves from low-quality fundraisers. The information unravelling by fundraisers can occur via voluntary disclosures and signalling.

Before examining these two mechanisms, it is worth noting that information unravelling by fundraisers provides important advantages over investors' independent acquisition of information. It leads to savings in real resources devoted to information gathering and prevents socially wasteful duplications of costs when two or more investors engage in similar types of information acquisition activities (Coffee, 1984, pp. 733–734). Moreover, information unravelling by fundraisers should result in homogenous estimations of securities prices by individual investors, thus improving risk-sharing among investors (Diamond, 1985, p. 1073). Most importantly, crowdfunding investors have significant limitations in gathering information independently. The reasoning in the literature examining traditional financial markets appears even more grounded in the crowdfunding context. Goshen and Parchomovsky (2005, p. 738) argue that the costs of independent collection of

[13] Verrecchia (2001, p. 94) coined the term 'information asymmetry component of the cost of capital'. He defines the cost of capital as 'the percentage of the firm an entrepreneur must sell to raise a fixed amount of capital' (Verrecchia, 2001, p. 103).

[14] The estimation risk arises from assessing unknown parameters of the firm's value distribution. Botosan (1997) documents a negative association between voluntary disclosures and the cost of equity capital in stock markets. Similarly, Sengupta (1998) finds that higher disclosure ratings lead to lower interest costs of issuing debt. A more recent study by DeBoskey and Gillett (2013) looks into more comprehensive corporate transparency measures and finds that different kinds of corporate disclosures lead to better credit ratings and lower costs of both debt and equity.

information are prohibitive even for professional investors and analysts (information traders), who, as outsiders, do not have access to the knowledge shared among the firm's management, which is generated as a by-product of their regular activities.

It is even less reasonable to assume that crowdfunding investors, with their small stakes in a crowdfunding offer, would be willing to incur such costs individually. Evidence from some platforms suggests that investors typically bid the minimum allowed amount to diversify their portfolio (Herzenstein, Sonenshein, & Dholakia, 2011, p. 6). Theoretically, investors could split the search costs so that each investor would gather specific pieces of information. However, the public good nature of information will likely undermine search efforts. Namely, the inability to exclude investors who did not contribute to information gathering will undermine everyone's incentives to exert effort and encourage free-riding behaviour (Coffee, 1984, pp. 725–727).

Moreover, the characteristics of crowdfunding projects further undermine the purpose of independent information gathering. Namely, most crowdfunding offers intend to promote an innovative product, the technical details of which are hardly understandable by a broad audience of retail investors who are not industry experts. It is thus hard for investors to even identify all the information that needs to be collected to evaluate the crowdfunding offer.[15]

3.4.1 *Voluntary Disclosures*

Theoretical Considerations

Voluntary disclosures imply that an issuer of securities (entrepreneurs or company founders in the crowdfunding context) deliberately reveals all the information necessary for assessing the quality of an offering and making an informed investment decision. While it is reasonable to assume that entrepreneurs will have incentives to reveal all the information that will help them create an optimistic estimate of the firm's value, their incentives to disclose unfavourable information are more ambiguous. While a large body of theoretical work has identified conditions under which competitive unravelling occurs both in consumer and financial markets, it is necessary to examine them in the realm of crowdfunding.

The basic premise is that high-quality sellers operating in competitive markets want to separate themselves from low-quality sellers and thereby disclose all relevant features of their products, including their risks and limitations (Grossman & Hart, 1980; Milgrom, 1981). The rationale for full disclosure is that they face

[15] While this argument applies to the investors on general-purpose crowdfunding platforms, it is less relevant to industry-specific crowdfunding platforms (e.g. platforms specializing in fundraising in green energy), as many investors may be professionally inclined towards this industry and well-informed about technical aspects of the offer.

rational buyers who infer that withheld information or shrouded attributes are unfavourable about the quality of the product. In other words, buyers discount the product's value until it is in the seller's best interest to disclose all the information. All the sellers except for the seller of the lowest quality product follow the unravelling strategy since it allows them to demonstrate the superiority of their product to the product of their competitors and charge a higher price.

Subsequent research into the conditions that make disclosure privately optimal changed some of the assumptions of the early information unravelling models to show that there exist equilibria that do not imply full disclosure of information.[16] These assumptions include: (1) negligible costs of transferring information, (2) buyers know that the seller has some information about the quality or how much information is available to her, (3) 'lying is illegal and does not occur' (Grossman & Hart, 1980, pp. 323–324).

The assumption about costless disclosure or information transmission is often violated in real markets due to direct and indirect disclosure costs. Direct costs imply expenses incurred to make credible announcements about specific characteristics based on which one can infer the quality. Direct costs stem from the fact that disclosed information often has to be proven by verified documents or by engaging third-party certifiers, which entails accounting, audit, and publication costs (Huddart et al., 1999, pp. 255–256). Direct costs of disclosure are certainly non-negligible for crowdfunding issuers. One might argue that firms with project quality above a certain threshold would have more incentives to disclose under such circumstances since the expected value of their future profits is higher. However, seed-stage crowdfunding firms have little resources in the first place to finance such costs before the fundraising process is completed. They may be discouraged from starting a crowdfunding campaign in light of uncertainty about its success and the fact that disclosure costs are sunk.

Indirect costs of disclosure are likely to be even more prominent in crowdfunding. These imply the costs of revealing proprietary information (Dye, 1986). Proprietary information 'is defined as information whose disclosure reduces the present value of cash flows of the firm endowed with the information' (Dye, 1986, p. 331).[17] New and innovative businesses tend to dominate crowdfunding markets, whereas the value of many of them still mainly consists of an idea (Agrawal et al., 2014, p. 92). Revealing detailed information about their existing operations and profitability increases the likelihood of their idea being stolen by competitors (Donovan, 2021, p. 7218). This, in turn, reduces the expected present value of future cash flows. For this reason, many innovative crowdfunding firms may be reluctant to opt for a complete disclosure strategy. Hornuf and Schwienbacher

[16] For a comprehensive literature review on factors driving and hindering voluntary disclosures, see Verrecchia (2001).

[17] In addition to information that is strategically valuable, it includes information that can trigger 'regulatory action, create potential legal liabilities, reduce consumer demand for its products, induce labour unions or other suppliers to renegotiate contracts, or cause revisions in the firm's credit standing' (Dye, 1985, p. 123).

(2016, pp. 10–11) have argued that high indirect costs of disclosure may even divert many firms from using crowdfunding, leaving this funding mechanism to firms whose ideas are either difficult to copy or not worth replicating.[18]

The decision to withhold information can also be driven by buyers' uncertainty about whether the seller possesses complete and private information about its product quality (Dye, 1985; Jung & Kwon, 1988). Namely, for buyers to create rational expectations that withheld information is unfavourable and, consequently, discount the product's value, they must be able to conclude that the seller's disclosures are flawed. If buyers pay little attention to all available information or face difficulties understanding the details of disclosed content, a seller's strategy to hide unfavourable information will likely go unnoticed. Such an outcome is not necessarily incompatible with the rational behaviour of investors if detecting flaws in disseminating information is costly for buyers.[19]

Therefore, a failure of voluntary disclosures in crowdfunding markets can also occur because of investors' perception of how fundraising firms behave and their disclosure strategies. Entrepreneurs are, by very definition, better acquainted with firm and industry-specific factors that influence the project's feasibility. The innovation aspect of crowdfunding projects further undermines investors' ability to assess whether entrepreneurs are endowed with certain information, either because the information is very technical or there are few similar firms to compare. The larger the amount of information investors have to process and the smaller the benefits of detection, the higher the costs of detecting issues in information unravelling. Given that individual investments in crowdfunding are relatively small, it may be rational for investors not to invest time and effort to question the disclosure strategy of a firm. In such circumstances, shrouding unfavourable information may be optimal for entrepreneurs.

A third factor hindering the competitive unravelling of information with implications for the crowdfunding market is the possibility of untruthful reporting. As already mentioned, early literature examining voluntary disclosure largely rules out that sellers make false or misleading statements because deceit generates costs. They stem from general anti-fraud laws that prohibit providing false or misleading

[18] Proprietary costs of crowdfunding issuers depend on the level of innovation, the product, production process, industry characteristics, and a fundraiser's specific knowledge and personality, which affect how difficult it is for competitors to replicate the business idea. Such costs are less pronounced in traditional forms of financing, such as angel investing, where potential investors are subject to non-disclosure agreements (NDA) as well as concerned with the reputational effects of possible leakage of sensitive information (Hornuf & Schwienbacher, 2016, p. 10).

Intellectual property law, particularly when certain rights are recognised before initiating a crowdfunding campaign (e.g. a company owning patents), reduces proprietary costs and increases a firm's incentives for more detailed disclosures. However, intellectual property may also signal a firm's quality, thus reducing the need for full disclosure, as will be discussed in greater detail in the following section.

[19] However, financial literature provides abundant evidence that ordinary investors suffer from behavioural biases when making financial decisions. See Kingsford-Smith and Dixon (2015, pp. 712–715) for an overview.

information, resulting in a risk of litigation and an erosion of the human capital of managers (Verrecchia, 2001, p. 63). Here, it is helpful to distinguish between hard (objective and verifiable) information and soft (subjective and unverifiable) information. Hard information usually entails 'facts about which there is a general agreement' [...], whereas 'soft information is open to debate or alternative interpretations of its implications' (Estrin et al., 2022, p. 1763). Soft information is unverifiable because it requires 'a personal assessment and depends upon its context, neither of which can be easily captured and communicated' (Liberti & Petersen, 2019, p. 4).[20]

Information economics primarily deals with voluntary disclosures of hard information. In principle, market participants should only base their decisions on information that can be independently verified since it allows them to distinguish quality disclosures from broader marketing efforts, which are intended to create only a favourable image of a product (Dranove & Jin, 2010, p. 935).

Regarding hard information disclosed by fundraisers, an important question is whether the information is indeed verified and by whom, either before or after the crowdfunding campaign. This appears necessary for the risk of litigation and human capital loss to materialise and deter inaccurate disclosures. The ability of crowdfunding investors to conduct large-scale systematic checks on information provided by different fundraisers is impaired for the same reason that prevents their independent collection of information—the cost of collective action. Put differently, the public good nature of due diligence will undermine individual efforts to verify information (Chen et al., 2016, p. 2). Nevertheless, some authors, such as Estrin et al. (2022, p. 1764), contend that the mere fact that large numbers of potential investors will scrutinise disclosed information induces accuracy.

Similarly, Keel et al. (2021, pp. 27–28) argue that when information is distributed via the Internet, its verification is easier compared to an offline fundraising process. One reason is the number of different actors involved in (re)posting content about an offer (videos, discussions, analysis), including internet media, which indirectly lend their reputation to the fundraiser.[21] Additionally, interested parties other than investors, such as customers, suppliers, or employees in the case of business crowdfunding, can also verify information they can access from alternative

[20] As will be shown from the discussion that follows, criteria for differentiating between hard and soft information is not common in the literature. Scholars sometimes consider hard information as verified and soft information as unverified. In other instances, hard information is understood as data that can have a numerical value, whereas soft information is subjective, ambiguous, and often incomparable (Pötzsch & Böhme, 2010, p. 383). Indeed, soft information is usually available in a textual format (Liberti & Petersen, 2019, p. 3). Nevertheless, the criterion of information being (un)quantifiable is inadequate, given that there are examples of soft (unverifiable) information that is quantifiable, such as when information is forward-looking (e.g. 'projected financial statements, or intangible and difficult to value such as brands and patents') (Estrin et al., 2022, p. 1763).

[21] In an IPO setting in the Internet era, information flows from the issuer to potential investors are increasingly intermediated via media, sometimes called 'infomediaries' (Keel et al., 2021, p. 29). Because crowdfunding offers are small, they rarely receive comprehensive media coverage. For this reason, this verification mechanism is not often available in crowdfunding.

sources. Moreover, the Internet serves as 'a long-term repository for one's statements', making subsequent deletion or edits close to impossible (Keel et al., 2021, p. 28).

Similar to a typical IPO, fundraisers on crowdfunding platforms could ensure the credibility of information by obtaining third-party certification, e.g., from auditors, credit rating agencies, or financial analysts. However, in most instances, such accuracy seals are too costly for them. For example, an empirical study by Donovan (2021) on equity crowdfunding in the UK reveals that only a single firm in the sample provided audited financial statements (income statement, balance sheet, and statement of cash flows). On some lending platforms, verification of information is facilitated by allowing borrowers to join an affinity group voluntarily. These groups are created based on common characteristics of their members such as geography, profession, university they attended, etc. A group leader manages the group and verifies the borrower's personal and financial information against an interest (Herzenstein et al., 2008, p. 7). Finally, verification of hard information can be delegated to the platform. This may result from competition between platforms along non-price dimensions of their services, such as due diligence or a regulatory intervention.

It is possible to argue that a mere threat of litigation, independent of whether the information provided is verified or not, deters untruthful reporting. This would mean that after a fundraising firm fails, a borrower defaults or another unfavourable event occurs, it is possible to establish that false or misleading information was the cause of it, allowing investors to claim damages. Regarding investment-based crowdfunding, damage claims do not have a high probability of success given the time gap and the number of factors affecting the success of early-stage and growth companies. When it comes to individual loans, borrowers on some platforms are not even individually known by lenders, whereas all debt collection efforts are delegated to the platform (Michels, 2012, p. 1390). For all types of crowdfunding, it appears that bringing an action against fundraisers for false or misleading information would have to be delegated to the platform or another organisation to minimise the costs of collective action.

In addition to hard information, there are instances in which soft (unverifiable) information is vital for estimating a product's quality, a firm's value, or a borrower's creditworthiness. In the context of primary financial markets, this will typically be the case when traditional quantitative information is lacking (e.g., limited track record of profits and sales) or is unable to capture investments in intangible assets (e.g., human capital or customer satisfaction), or when a company valuation is highly uncertain due to a novel and disruptive business model of the issuing firm (Edmans et al., 2016, p. 2152; Keel et al., 2021, p. 24). In the latter case, even some preliminary analysis, such as defining the industry and understanding who the competitors and customers are, can be challenging (Keel et al., 2021, p. 29). Consequently, investors must also price forward-looking information provided by the firm's management (Verrecchia, 2001, p. 63). This includes, for instance, earning claims or financial projections made by fundraisers (Michael, 2009).

Soft information is particularly relevant to investment-based crowdfunding. Fundraisers are usually seed or growth-stage companies whose valuation depends on their expected growth and the realisation of future investments. Traditional accounting standards do not permit 'capitalisation of uncertain future growth', and therefore, disclosure of financials alone does not allow for adequate company valuations (Donovan, 2021, p. 7214).[22] Estrin et al. (2022) argue that soft information represents the critical component of information asymmetries that hinder the ability of early-stage ventures to raise finance. In their view, the role of crowdfunding platforms is to reduce the transaction costs of collecting, disseminating, and interpreting soft information (Estrin et al., 2022, p. 1762). Similarly, Agrawal et al. (2016, p. 111) contend that the success of early-stage ventures depends on tacit information, which can only be 'shared through socialisation' and which is 'difficult to transfer to others by writing it down'. The examples they use are founders' personalities and relationships, which are often central to the survival of early-stage companies. The lack of face-to-face interactions makes it difficult for entrepreneurs to convey these characteristics.

It is important to note that disclosure of soft information can also bear importance for real efficiency, that is, employing resources in their most productive uses (Edmans et al., 2016). As mentioned above, investments in intangible assets (e.g., human capital or customer satisfaction) are usually only captured by soft data, such as projections of future earnings. If disclosure of such data is not allowed, or if soft data is crowded out by hard data that investors assign greater value to (e.g., current earnings), entrepreneurs may diminish their investments into assets that would increase the company's value in the long run. This may, in turn, lead to a loss in real efficiency.

Soft information can also be informative when assessing the creditworthiness of individual borrowers. The relevance of soft information is likely higher for borrowers of lower credit quality, given the limited value of hard information such as credit score (Cornée, 2019; Iyer et al., 2016), or in countries where credit scores are not available for large parts of the population (Chen et al., 2022).[23] For instance, by revealing personal information, borrowers create interpersonal cues that allow lenders to discern borrowers' social background and their social proximity (Pötzsch & Böhme, 2010, p. 383). Such cues can help them assess informal norms influencing borrowers' behaviour ex-post. Similarly, forward-looking and unverifiable information, such as the intended use of proceeds, can directly impact the riskiness of individual borrowers. Namely, loan purposes such as debt consolidation and

[22] Some authors (e.g., Michels, 2012, p. 1390) argue that managers' forecasts are not unverifiable, given that it is possible to verify them ex-post when accounting reports for a given period become available. Such a view has two significant limitations that are particularly pertinent to crowdfunding. Firstly, they are unverifiable at the time of the investment decision. Secondly, it is disputable whether and to what extent an individual can be held liable if their subjective estimates turn out to be inaccurate ex-post unless it is possible to prove bad faith.

[23] In the context of social banking, Cornée (2019) shows that the value of soft vis-à-vis hard information in predicting defaults increases the more opaque the borrower is.

credit card repayment can increase the ability to repay through their effect on revolving credit utilisation (Carmichael, 2014, p. 16). Some authors, like Liu et al. (2020), even argue that P2P lending represents an innovation in screening through its ability to leverage soft information.

In information economics, claims that entail costless and unverifiable information are referred to as cheap talk (Farrell, 1995; Farrell & Gibbons, 1989). This suggests that credibility is at the heart of discussions about whether the uninformed party is (or should be) guided by soft information when making a decision. Information economics literature identified specific conditions that can lead to trustworthy soft claims. For instance, Farrell and Gibbons (1989, pp. 1216–1217) show that claims that are otherwise uninformative when made in private become credible when made in public. A talk directed to one audience (e.g., capital market) can be disciplined by the presence of another audience (e.g., a rival firm contemplating entry). The idea is that what is in the best interest of the informed party to claim before one audience contradicts the interest in communication with the other audience. In the example the authors use, inflating favourable earnings prospects may also potentially lead to the undesired entry of uninformed potential rivals, thus creating incentives for truthful reporting. As the example shows, credibility depends on how strong the incentives to lie to each audience are.

To some extent, a similar argument was made by Gigler (1994), who contends that the proprietary costs of certain claims (e.g., revealing strategic information to third parties) make otherwise unverifiable claims trustworthy. In the crowdfunding context, if entrepreneurs do not fear the entry of rivals or disclosing sensitive information to other interested audiences (employees, suppliers, tax authorities, etc.), they will not be disciplined in their (soft) claims made to potential investors. In contrast, one can conjecture that the higher the level of innovation of a crowdfunding project, and the easier it is for potential competitors to copy the business idea, the more credible the soft claims made by their entrepreneurs.

Independently of the existence of different audiences, Stocken (2000) shows that managers' reputational concerns are likely to lead to truthful disclosures of unverifiable information (e.g., forecasts) to investors in what is called a 'repeated cheap-talk game'. In his model, trustworthy disclosure is driven by repetitive interactions between an issuer and investors. Namely, subsequent accounting reports allow investors to verify managers' voluntary claims and decide whether to provide the firm with the next financing round. Suppose one were to apply this reasoning to crowdfunding. In that case, it seems that fundraisers' incentives for honest reporting will likely depend on their long-term perspective of using crowdfunding as a funding mechanism more than once. In the alternative, accurate, voluntary (soft) disclosures in crowdfunding can enhance the probability of raising additional finance via other means, e.g., venture capital. The issue with this argument is that most crowdfunding listings originate from 'the first-time' fundraisers on a crowdfunding platform, meaning that investors cannot rely on their existing reputation for honesty. Overall, despite the importance of soft information for investment decisions, it appears that a restrictive set of conditions for soft claims to be credible is not often met. The economic theory predicts that, in such instances, the rational, uninformed party should treat such claims as if there were no communication and rely on hard data (Forsythe et al., 1999, p. 483).

To better understand whether voluntary disclosures of both hard and soft information contribute to mitigating information asymmetry in the crowdfunding market in light of the above considerations, it is necessary to examine the existing empirical evidence critically. By integrating findings from different empirical settings, the following section will provide a more comprehensive account of the effectiveness of voluntary disclosures in crowdfunding.

Review of the Empirical Evidence on Crowdfunding

Empirical crowdfunding literature has grown substantially in recent years, cross-cutting different disciplines. The most common issue studied is fundraisers' characteristics or actions that attract individual campaign volumes or determine ex-post campaign outcomes (e.g., default and survival rates). Several studies have focused on voluntary disclosures of information. These studies examine either investors' responsiveness to the difference in the disclosure level of fundraisers or how investors apprehend the information voluntarily conveyed. Some of them also investigate whether voluntary disclosures are predictive of the post-campaign success of fundraisers.

One should note that the focus of the existing studies is ex-ante disclosures, that is, communication made before and during the crowdfunding campaign. The empirical literature largely neglects fundraisers' communication with investors in the post-campaign stage, which can attenuate ex-post information asymmetries.

This section systematically examines empirical crowdfunding literature from a market failure perspective, focusing on ex-ante information asymmetries. As discussed above, economic theory on voluntary disclosures suggests that they are ineffective for preventing market failure when disclosures are incomplete, when investors fail to consider all the available information when making an investment decision, or when disclosed information is not credible (truthful). Here, it is helpful to summarise the reasons behind the three potential sources of market failure, as they can offer a roadmap for analysing the existing empirical evidence.

Information incompleteness occurs when investors are unable to notice differences in disclosure levels of different fundraisers and, consequently, punish those that withhold information (either by not investing or by investing under unfavourable terms for fundraisers, e.g., by accepting only high interest rates).[24] Moreover, investors' failure to analyse all available information, notably hard financial data, can be attributed to high information-processing costs. Finally, a lack of credibility

[24] As discussed above, information incompleteness also occurs when fundraisers bear high (proprietary and non-proprietary) costs of disclosure. However, as long as investors are sensitive to differences in the disclosure level among fundraisers, those that do not reveal information will likely be considered untrustworthy, as investors have high costs discerning the reasons behind hidden information.

in information happens due to investors not having the means to verify hard data or being unable to discern cheap talk from trustworthy (soft) claims.

Thus, this section reviews empirical studies in crowdfunding to provide answers to three different questions. Firstly, it explores whether crowd investors are responsive to differences in disclosure levels, indicating whether incomplete information is the source of market failure (Q1). Secondly, it sheds some light on investors' usage of soft and hard (financial) data, which is relevant to the question of whether a potential source of market failure lies in information-processing costs (Q2). Thirdly, this section examines whether differences in disclosure levels convey valid information about fundraisers' quality. Put differently, it analyses whether those fundraisers that disclose more information are more trustworthy (Q3). This allows one to understand better whether the source of market failure lies in information credibility.

From a methodological point of view, this section uses a combination of qualitative systematic and integrative literature reviews (Snyder, 2019; Torraco, 2005). It is systematic as it offers a comprehensive review of evidence on the effect of disclosures on campaign-level indicators and post-campaign outcomes, which bears important regulatory implications, as will be discussed in Chap. 5. To this end, relevant sources are collected using the Social Science Citation Index (SSCI), the Web of Science, and Google Scholar databases.[25] Sources are further filtered in line with pre-defined criteria, which include using quantitative (econometric) methods, focusing on financial-return models, individual campaigns as a unit of analysis, and information pertinent to risk-return assessment.[26] The total number of relevant sources is 34.

The integrative approach of the review is embedded in a novel conceptual framework that draws on the three potential sources of market failure: incomplete information, limited attention (potentially leading to inaccurate judgements), and non-credible information. It should be stressed that empirical studies reviewed do not make such a distinction while implicitly offering answers to one or more questions identified. The empirical evidence is also clustered based on the

[25] Relevant literature was identified up until 30 March 2023 using the following keywords: voluntary disclosures in crowdfunding, reporting in crowdfunding, information asymmetry in crowdfunding, soft information in crowdfunding, financial information in crowdfunding, disclosures and crowdfunding success, disclosures and defaults in crowdfunding, disclosures and survival in crowdfunding, disclosures and performance in crowdfunding.

[26] It is worth noting that filtering relevant sources in line with pre-defined criteria led to the exclusion of studies that provide comparable findings in related research areas—non-financial return crowdfunding and traditional financial markets. The importance of voluntary disclosures of (soft) information is documented in numerous studies that look into donation and reward crowdfunding (Allison, 2017; Anglin, Short, et al., 2018; Anglin, Wolfe, et al., 2018; Bachrach et al., 2022; Ferreira et al., 2022; Madsen & McMullin, 2018; Parhankangas & Renko, 2017; Wuillaume & Janssen, 2020; Yang et al., 2020; Zhou et al., 2018). Similarly, in the context of financial markets, for instance, Leone et al. (2007) evidence that more specific disclosure of the intended use of proceeds is associated with lower IPO underpricing. The reasoning is that investors are willing to pay higher prices when there is less ex-ante uncertainty.

Table 3.1 Conceptual framework for analysing the empirical evidence on voluntary disclosures

Contextual information			Questions addressed
Crowdfunding business model	Jurisdiction and platform name	Disclosure level indicator/information type (hard, soft, mixture)	Q1: Investors' responsiveness to the disclosure level (positive/negative/unresponsive/ambiguous)
			Q2: Investors' responsiveness to hard (financial) data (positive/negative/unresponsive/ambiguous)
			Q3: Ex-post credibility of disclosed information (credible, non-credible, misleading)

crowdfunding model, jurisdiction, and platform, allowing some context-specific considerations to be drawn. Existing studies also exhibit a great variety regarding the disclosure indicator used. While most studies focus on disclosures of soft information, they choose different data points. Moreover, some studies often treat unverified hard data as soft information. This review also accounts for these differences. The conceptual framework is depicted in Table 3.1.

The following analysis discusses in depth the findings of the empirical literature on P2P lending and equity-based crowdfunding. For clarity, findings are presented separately for the two overarching models. The analysis summary for all financial-return models is given in Annex 3A.

P2P Lending

Studies on P2P lending that answer the first question have looked into the effect of differences in disclosures on bidding activity, funding success, and interest rates. The underlying hypothesis is that lenders observe these differences, so borrowers who disclose more information induce a higher bidding activity are more likely to reach their funding goal and pay lower interest rates. As noted earlier, the emphasis is on voluntary disclosure of soft information. The reason is that sometimes regulators, but even more frequently, platforms impose certain disclosure obligations on borrowers, which usually relate to hard data. It should be stressed that disclosures of soft information are not always the result of a deliberate fundraiser choice. As shown in several studies under review, some soft information can be unearthed from the funding application containing implicit cues about certain fundraisers' characteristics (e.g., spelling errors, narrative tone, text readability, the appearance of trustworthiness based on a photo, etc.).[27] Studies on P2P lending that aim to answer the second question, whether lenders use specific information disclosed, are rarer. Lenders' responsiveness to specific soft and hard data is usually examined in the same studies that aim to shed light on the first question, often by including them as control variables. Therefore, it is worth combining the analysis for the first two questions while offering a more concise summary of each one in Annex 3A.

Several studies that examine the influence of voluntary disclosures on loan funding outcomes used evidence from Prosper, one of the leading US P2P lending platforms (Duarte et al., 2012; Gao et al., 2018; Herzenstein et al., 2008; Herzenstein, Sonenshein, & Dholakia, 2011; Iyer et al., 2016; Kgoroeadira et al., 2019; Michels, 2012). The platform used to operate a Dutch auction process in which the borrower sets the maximum interest rate he is willing to pay, while lenders bid on parts of loans by setting the minimum interest rate they would accept and the amount of loan they intend to fund.[28] According to Herzenstein et al. (2008, p. 10), platform rules mandate borrowers to disclose income, existing debt, and homeownership, and the platform verifies this information.[29] In addition, borrowers could voluntarily disclose personal information such as demographics[30] and other personal descriptive information (such as personal history, current income, reasons for requesting a loan, etc.). To account for the difference in the level of disclosure, the authors created a variable that classifies borrowers into three groups (no personal information, general personal information, and specific personal information, although differences are much more nuanced).[31] Herzenstein et al. (2008) find that financial strength measured by hard data and personal descriptive information affects funding success, while the effects of demographics are very small compared to the first two categories.

Herzenstein, Dholakia, and Andrews (2011) use a more nuanced measure of voluntary disclosures, which they call the number of identity claims, and examine their effect on loan funding and the final interest rate set in the auction

[27] Some of these implicit clues are expected to negatively affect loan outcomes, such as when they are seen as a characteristic of untrustworthy borrowers. These clues are often difficult to falsify, making them more credible than typical disclosures of soft information. In some cases, they can even be considered costly signals.

[28] Prosper changed its business model after the intervention of the US Securities Commission (SEC), which required platforms 'to register their securities and make loans through a bank' (Carmichael, 2014, p. 2). Under the new model, the credit grade and the loan price are determined by Prosper, with a diminished role of lenders in screening borrowers autonomously.

[29] Based on this data, the platform publishes a credit grade, debt-to-income ratio and homeownership status for each loan listed.

[30] Borrowers can decide to disclose age, gender, marital status, whether they have children and religion.

[31] According to the study, in extreme cases, borrowers describe 'their personal history, reasons for the loan, current income, detailed current budget, and an action plan for paying off the loan. They may also upload pictures of themselves, their family members, and other information (such as a product they designed). Finally, borrowers may even explain negative aspects of their profile such as a low credit grade or past delinquencies' (Herzenstein et al., 2008, p. 13).

process. The authors define identity claims as 'the ways that individuals describe themselves for others', where each borrower can provide up to six different identity claims: 'trustworthy, economic hardship, hardworking, successful, moral, and religious' (Herzenstein, Sonenshein, & Dholakia, 2011, p. 5, 7). While the authors treat such narratives as purely subjective (soft) information, they often include reporting of hard (verifiable) but unverifiable information, such as education or monthly expenses. The results indicate that lenders are reactive to the overall level of disclosure—the number of narratives, which positively affect loan funding and lead to a reduction in interest rates. However, claims of trustworthiness and success have a greater relative influence than other claims.

Michels (2012) also studies the effects of costless and voluntary disclosures on bidding activity and the cost of debt on Prosper. Michels (2012) finds that more significant disclosures are associated with increased bidding activity and lower interest rates. The indicator used in this study differs from that used by Herzenstein, Dholakia, and Andrews (2011). It is constructed as a sum of points assigned for each specific piece of information reported by the borrower without interpreting the impression the borrower intended to create.[32] The author's explanation of a significant variation in the amount of voluntary and unverifiable disclosures is that some borrowers are unaware of the effect of disclosures on the cost of debt or have an aversion to lying (Michels, 2012, p. 1388). What Michels does not consider is a distinction between hard but unverified information and soft (unverifiable) information, but instead measures the total effect of voluntary disclosures when the two types of information are bundled.[33] The author also controls for some hard financial information and finds that lenders sometimes fail to consider it. For instance, having a loan on the same platform on which the borrower defaulted or is late with payments is not associated with worse campaign outcomes.

While all of the above studies focus on the disclosure of information in a textual form, Duarte et al. (2012) assess the effects of borrowers' decision to upload a photograph as part of their loan request. More specifically, they examine how the appearance of trustworthiness inferred from a photograph affects the probability of successful loan funding and interest rates.[34] Their findings imply that borrowers who appear more trustworthy have a higher likelihood of obtaining a loan and getting lower interest rates.[35]

[32] Items considered are 'the purpose of the loan, income amount, income source, education, amount of other debt, interest rate on other debt, explanation for poor credit grade, listing of monthly expenses, and a picture of a person' (Michels, 2012, p. 1393).

[33] Among the items included in the disclosure indicator, only 'the purpose of the loan' and, to some extent, 'explanation for poor credit grade' are soft (unverifiable) information. Other items are (hard) verifiable data but unverified at the time of a loan listing.

[34] The appearance of trustworthiness is based on assessment from 25 independent reviewers.

[35] Many papers study whether borrowers with specific personal characteristics (age, race, ethnicity, gender, attractiveness, sexual orientation) are more likely to get their loans funded (e.g., Pope &

Iyer et al. (2016) test the relative importance of standard (financial) information, quantifiable nonstandard (soft) information, and nonquantifiable soft information for lenders' inferences in the P2P lending market.[36] Interestingly, they assume to capture nonquantifiable soft information by unexplained variance (residuals) of interest rates that borrowers obtain as a result of the auction process. Their results suggest that all three categories of information influence lenders' decisions, while standard financial information has the most significant impact. Among quantifiable soft information, the interest rate borrowers are willing to accept is the strongest predictor of interest rates. Nevertheless, the authors also acknowledge that this is not soft information but rather a costly signal.[37] They also find that soft information (both quantifiable and unquantifiable) is relatively more important for inferring the creditworthiness of borrowers with the lowest credit scores, as the marginal contribution of standard financial data drops for such borrowers.

Building on this work, Gao et al. (2018) offer another comprehensive analysis of the effects of soft information by further quantifying information contained in 'an optional written description of the borrower's financial situation and purpose of the loan' (Gao et al., 2018, p. 2).[38] They construct variables for specific soft clues: the level of text readability, positivity, and deception cues on funding outcomes.[39] Their results indicate that loan applications that are more readable and have a more positive tone are associated with more bidding activity and lower interest rates. On the contrary, deception cues are related to less favourable loan outcomes, which is economically justifiable. In contrast to some other studies, Gao et al. (2018) also

Sydnor, 2011; Ravina, 2019). While such data can often be considered hard non-financial information, it should not influence on the decision of lenders who are interested in risk-return optimisation unless belonging to a specific group affects the borrower's creditworthiness (known as statistical theory of discrimination (e.g., Phelps, 1972)). Belonging to a particular group can also affect market outcomes in crowdfunding if investors are driven by non-monetary (intrinsic) motivations, which can be either favourable or discriminatory towards that group (known as taste-based discrimination).

[36] A large number of variables are characterised as soft/nonstandard variables such as borrower maximum interest rate, loan duration, loan purpose category, bank draft annual fee, city of residence, photo availability, variables related to text length, orthography, number endorsements by friends, etc. (Iyer et al., 2016, p. 44). It is worth noting that many of the variables are, by their nature, verifiable (hard) non-financial data.

[37] Borrowers have an incentive to disclose their (close to) reservation price given that posting an interest rate that is too low creates a risk of not getting funding. Still, it is costlier for lower-quality borrowers to obtain a loan from a bank or other sources (Iyer et al., 2016, p. 4). In addition, this information is always disclosed as part of the loan application process and is, thus, less relevant for the discussion of voluntary disclosures.

[38] Similar to the work of Iyer et al. (2016), they also account for 'easily quantifiable soft information (e.g., maximum rate the borrower is willing to pay)' (Iyer et al., 2016, p. 2).

[39] The readability indicator is constructed based on spelling errors, grammatical errors, and lexical complexity of a loan description. Deception cues are based on psychology research that finds that 'deceivers tend to use more motion words, third-person pronouns, and negative emotion words, but fewer exclusion words and first-person pronouns' (Gao et al., 2018, p. 14).

control for both verified (e.g., credit grade) and unverified hard data (e.g., employment status), with a clear distinction between them. However, they do not report results on investors' responsiveness to hard information on borrowers.

It is worth noting that Prosper also intermediates P2P business loans. However, evidence on the impact of disclosures on campaign outcomes for business borrowers is scarce, with a notable exception of research by Kgoroeadira et al. (2019). They examine determinants of success of small firm unsecured loan applications. Their results indicate that a business owner's personal characteristics matter more than a firm's business characteristics. Nevertheless, their evidence shows that only hard information about the business owner (e.g., homeownership or personal credit score) predicts the probability of funding and interest rates. In contrast, the quantity of narratives in the loan description is not statistically significant. When it comes to the firm's characteristics, the authors also show that investors are not always responsive to some important hard data, such as previous failures (delinquencies or judgements against the firm).

Another study that looks into disclosures of business lenders in the P2P market in the US uses data from the platform Lending Club (Nowak et al., 2018).[40] The operating model of this platform is very different from Prosper[41] since it is the platform that assigns a credit grade and interest rate to each borrower and not the lenders who only get to choose whether to invest.[42] In addition to standard indicators of creditworthiness,[43] investors have access to the self-reported purpose of the loan and a description of the project. Interestingly, Nowak et al. (2018, p. 322, fn. 14) report that (hard) verifiable data contained in the project description is verified by the platform ex-post upon the successful completion of a funding campaign and before passing on the funds to the borrower, which should deter them from lying.[44]

[40] While the study focuses on small business loans, Lending Club also intermediates loans to individuals with various (consumer) purposes (e.g. car, credit card, debt consolidation, educational loans, moving, vacation, etc.).

[41] The difference primarily applies to the business model of Prosper up until 2008, the period covered by previously cited studies. The regulatory intervention of the SEC made the models of the two US platforms much more aligned.

[42] The exact method that the platform uses for assigning credit grades is not known. According to Polena and Regner (2018, p. 4), the credit grade partially reflects the FICO score, that is, the traditional credit score used by banks and credit providers which is based on a personal credit report generated by credit bureaus in the US. 'The FICO score is a function of a borrower's loan repayment history, number of open credit accounts, number of credit applications, and total amount of borrowing across all lines of open credit'(Nowak et al., 2018, p. 319, fn. 3). In addition to the FICO score, the platform uses the self-reported personal information on the borrower (annual income, home situation, employment length, the loan purpose and a loan description) to assign credit grades. The platform uses same information to generate a more nuanced measure of borrowers' creditworthiness—a subcategory of credit grade (Polena & Regner, 2018, p. 4).

[43] These indicators include the FICO score, debt-to-income ratio, income, employer, duration of employment, and location (Nowak et al., 2018, p. 323).

[44] According to another study that also uses data from Lending Club, the platform occasionally verifies self-reported income ex-ante, while the verification status is also available on the platform (Carmichael, 2014, p. 7).

Similar to Gao et al. (2018), the study's results have indicated that lenders award borrowers whose listings have fewer spelling errors and a greater lexical diversity. The authors' interpretation is that richer communication is more readable and informative (Nowak et al., 2018, p. 329). The results concerning the length of the project description, which is assumed to proxy the level of disclosures, require a more nuanced analysis. Namely, the study reveals that lenders react positively to both very long and very short descriptions. While very long descriptions are deemed informative, very short descriptions can protect borrowers from revealing negative information (Nowak et al., 2018, p. 329). This finding contradicts the assumption in some of the early information economics models that rational investors infer that withheld information is unfavourable.

Chen et al. (2022), Li et al. (2020), and Yao et al. (2019) examine the phenomenon of voluntary disclosures in the Chinese P2P consumer market. The study of Yao et al. (2019) is narrow in scope as it only explores whether indicating loan purpose in the loan title on the Renrendai platform is a good predictor of borrowing success. Their findings suggest that loans with an ambiguous purpose in the title have lower chances of success. In addition, lenders are more likely to fund loans for investment and entrepreneurship-related purposes and are less likely to fund loans intended for a car purchase. The authors also report that lenders are responsive to some hard indicators (e.g., the total amount of delinquent payments and overdue time).

The other two studies on the Chinese market test the effects of much broader disclosure indicators, which combine objective (verifiable) and subjective (unverifiable) information. Their findings are consistent in that voluntary disclosures matter for loan funding outcomes despite using evidence from different platforms. Chen et al. (2022) find that borrowers who disclose more information on the Renrendai platform have a higher probability of obtaining a loan, while the effect is particularly strong for borrowers with a lower credit rating. Even though most items that borrowers can disclose are verifiable data, the authors state that only a few items are verified by the platform.[45] Nevertheless, they find that voluntary disclosure of verified information matters more than disclosure of unverified information. Li et al. (2020) examine whether cheap talk by repetitive borrowers matters more than disclosures made by first-time borrowers using data from the Ppdai lending platform. Consistent with the economic theory (Stocken, 2000), the information provided by borrowers with a borrowing history on the platform is considered more credible. Namely, the positive relationship between disclosures and funding success is stronger for such borrowers, even more so when they had a successful borrowing experience. Nevertheless, this result only applies to loan listings without

[45] The information that borrowers can voluntarily reveal includes nine items that are accounted for in the information disclosure index: education, working experience, income, marital status, place of living, firm size, the purpose of borrowing, industry, and a position in a workplace (Chen et al., 2022, p. 4).

a personal guarantee.[46] This suggests that borrowers have lower incentives to screen voluntary disclosure of borrowers when their credit risk is reduced thanks to a credit guarantee. In the next step, Li et al. (2020) also differentiate between the impact of objective (verifiable) and subjective (unverifiable) information and find that both types of disclosures have an impact on funding success, while the borrowing history amplifies the effect of subjective information only when the past borrowing experience was successful.

In contrast to crowdfunding markets in the US and China, evidence from German platforms suggests a more complex relationship between voluntary disclosures of soft data and loan funding outcomes, which primarily depends on the availability of hard data. Pötzsch and Böhme (2010) look into the effect of soft information on interest rates based on the evidence from a German P2P lending platform, Smava. The platform model allows potential borrowers to determine loan conditions (the amount, maturity, and interest rate) while lenders decide whether they are willing to invest and how much. The authors include voluntary disclosures of personal data[47] and appeals to social behaviour[48] in the definition of soft information. Disclosed personal data is not verified by the platform even when verifiable, in contrast to other available hard data (e.g., credit score).[49] The study results show that, generally, disclosing personal data does not influence interest rates. However, specific categories such as education, profession, and qualifications lead to a statistically significant but marginal decline in interest rates. Similarly, appeals to social behaviour are not generally found to influence interest rates. Still, specific categories are found to be statistically significant, such as emotional statements, which, contrary to the authors' expectations, are associated with higher interest rates.

In a later study on the P2P market in Germany, Dorfleitner et al. (2016) use a short text describing the loan's purpose and the personal situation of the potential borrower as a predictor of funding success. The evidence they provide comes

---

[46] The voluntary disclosure variable is an aggregate score that accounts for the presence of objective and subjective indicators. Objective indicators include the number of words in the personal statement, expressions related to the purpose of raising funds (consumption, operation or none), expressions related to revenue, and expressions associated with being an online seller. Subjective indicators include expressions that reflect credibility, stability, family, quality, enterprise, and morality (Li et al., 2020, pp. 6–9).

[47] Personal data voluntarily disclosed by borrowers include 'the borrower's name, contact information (address, phone, e-mail, etc.), financial situation, education, profession, further special skills or knowledge, housing situation, health, hobbies, and information about close relatives (children or partner)' (Pötzsch & Böhme, 2010, p. 387). Personal data is collected from the textual descriptions of the project, the optional fields of the borrower profile page, and disclosed pictures.

[48] This variable refers to emotional statements, direct appeals for help, and claims indicating reciprocity (such as stating that the borrower helped others in the past or intends to do so in the future) (Pötzsch & Böhme, 2010, p. 386).

[49] More specifically, Smava verifies borrowers' identity and other (hard) information, which is compulsory according to its own rules (e.g. demographics such as age, gender, or self-employed status). The platform also obtains the credit score (SCHUFA) and calculates the debt-to-income ratio (Pötzsch & Böhme, 2010, p. 386).

from two German P2P lending platforms, Smava and Auxmoney, which both operate a model in which the borrower suggests the interest rate in the loan application. However, the two platforms differ in terms of some other design features. Smava only allows loan applications from borrowers with a minimum pre-defined credit score, while providing a credit score is not compulsory on Auxmoney.[50] As a result, borrowers provide much less soft information on Smava than on Auxmoney. Consistent with the findings of Pötzsch and Böhme (2010), soft information plays a minor role in funding probability on Smava but is a good predictor of a funding success on Auxmoney. More specifically, the study finds that spelling errors, text length, and the use of keywords evoking positive emotions matter for funding outcomes on Auxmoney.[51] The contrasting evidence from the two platforms suggests that the importance of soft information increases with a lack of hard data or when hard data is not indicative of creditworthiness.

Another study on the P2P lending market in Germany is worth attention despite the fact information disclosures are not voluntary, as it sheds light on the importance of fine-grade financial information for lenders' decisions (Cumming & Hornuf, 2022). The only soft information captured in this study is the reasons for raising external capital. Cumming and Hornuf (2022) use data from Zencap, a P2P lending platform intermediating loans to SMEs.[52] In contrast to Smava and Auxmoney, the platform assigns a credit grade to each borrower and determines the interest rate on the loan.[53] The credit grade aggregates information beyond entrepreneurs' financial information, while the exact metric of the algorithm is unknown. The results of the study show that, in the presence of a platform-generated credit grade, peculiar financial information on the borrower (e.g., net income, assets, or liabilities) does not significantly affect lenders' decisions to pledge. The authors explain that the value of (hard) information disclosure is reduced as unsophisticated investors do not use quantitative credit risk models typically applied by professional lenders when creating loan

[50] Another difference between the two platforms is that Smava also provided a bidding assistant during the study period. The bidding assistant allows investors to make automated investments based on the credit score and loan duration (Dorfleitner et al., 2016, p. 172).

[51] Here, one can also question the authors' decision to present orthography and emotional keywords as soft information. Orthography can also be seen as a credible (costly) signal since it is more difficult for less trustworthy borrowers (because they are less educated or because they are more likely to have 'poor cognitive skills' as the authors suggest (Dorfleitner et al., 2016, p. 171)) to mimic this information trait. Lenders' reactions to emotional keywords can also indicate that they are driven by intrinsic motivations unrelated to the pursuit of financial return, as many other studies in crowdfunding show.

[52] The platform subsequently merged with Funding Circle. The data used in the study refer to the period before the merger.

[53] In this regard, the operating model of the platform is similar to Lending Club, as previously explained in the review of the study by Nowak et al. (2018). Another difference to Smava and Auxmoney is that Zencap does not reject almost any loan application (Cumming & Hornuf, 2022, p. 41). Thus, the preselection process is very different across these platforms.

portfolios. Different reasons for borrowing are not found to be statistically significant.

In summary, it appears that P2P lenders are mainly responsive to differences in disclosure levels, implying that incomplete information is not likely to be a source of market failure. Nevertheless, some evidence also suggests that lenders put more weight on differences in disclosures when disclosed information is verified, when borrowers have a borrowing history on the platform, and when standard hard data such as credit scores are unavailable. Moreover, lenders can be less responsive to disclosure disparities when a platform provides credit ratings for each loan application. While evidence on the second question is insufficient and inconclusive, a few studies show that lenders fail to account for some hard (financial) information in their investment decisions or that their responsiveness to it drops for borrowers with lower credit scores. Consequently, this can suggest that their limited attention or high information-processing costs are a potential source of market failure.

Since the evidence predominantly indicates that investors are sensitive to the differences in disclosures, the third question is what type of borrowers (high-quality vs. low-quality) disclose more (soft) information. In other words, it is vital to understand whether such disclosures are informative about borrowers' creditworthiness. Studies that shed light on this issue have employed different types of analysis.

The first type of analysis looks into the association of credit scores as a traditional measure of borrowers' creditworthiness and voluntary disclosures. The underlying hypothesis is that if disclosures are credible, borrowers with higher credit scores should disclose more information. Alternatively, if disclosures are non-credible, there should be no difference in the disclosure level among borrowers with different risk levels. In other words, disclosures should not create a 'separating equilibrium' between borrowers. Finally, if disclosures are misleading, borrowers with lower credit scores should disclose more to obfuscate bad credit records. For instance, Herzenstein, Dholakia, and Andrews (2011) analyse individual loans on the US P2P lending platform Prosper and find that borrowers with lower credit scores provide more voluntary disclosures of unverified data, which is captured by the number of (positive) identity claims they make in their loan description. In the same vein, Polena and Regner (2018) show that lenders in the 'very high risk' category, as captured by their credit grade, write the lengthiest loan descriptions on average.

The limitation of this type of analysis is that disclosures (especially revealing soft information) potentially have different importance for borrowers with various credit scores. In particular, borrowers with low credit scores can have stronger incentives to disclose additional (non-financial hard and soft) information to demonstrate their creditworthiness by other means. Assuming that an individual credit score is an imperfect or inaccurate indicator of one's quality, borrowers may want to create a more complete image of themselves.

The second type of analysis examines the relationship between voluntary disclosures and ex-post defaults. Similarly to the reasoning above, this relationship depends on the credibility of disclosed information. If disclosures are credible, borrowers who disclose more are less likely to default. In contrast, if disclosures are non-credible, there should be no significant relationship between disclosures and ex-post outcomes of loans. Finally, if disclosures are misleading, low-quality borrowers are more likely to disclose in their attempt to mimic good-quality borrowers.[54]

Several studies on the US market employed this type of analysis, providing evidence from platforms such as Prosper or Lending Club. In the abovementioned study on Prosper, Herzenstein, Dholakia, and Andrews (2011) conduct further analysis to explain the relation between unverified disclosures (the number of identities claimed) and loan performance. They find that, as the number of identity claims increases, borrowers have a higher probability of default than paying late and a higher probability of paying late than paying on time. However, they also find that not all soft claims are equally predictive of a loan performance. Namely, borrowers claiming to be trustworthy or successful are less likely to default than those claiming to be moral or in economic hardship.

Interestingly, other studies provide contrasting evidence using data from the same platform, Prosper. Research by Michels (2012) reveals a strong negative relationship between disclosure levels and loan defaults. Differences in obtained results can be explained by the fact that the disclosure indicator used in this study also captures disclosures of unverified hard data, which is costlier and riskier to falsify. Yet, two other studies specifically examining the impact of soft information further support a negative relationship between disclosures and default probabilities. Duarte et al. (2012) find that borrowers whose photographs appear more trustworthy have a lower likelihood of default. Consistent evidence was found by Gao et al. (2018) who report that borrowers' writing style is informative about default probabilities. They indicate that spelling errors and positive tone are associated with lower default probabilities, in contrast to deception clues, which are frequent in the loan applications of risky borrowers.

Three related studies examine the importance of disclosures for predicting defaults using data from the US platform Lending Club (Carmichael, 2014; Nowak et al., 2018; Polena & Regner, 2018). As explained above, this platform assigns a credit grade and interest rate to each borrower, which is available to lenders before they make an investment decision. The three studies use optional loan descriptions in borrowers' applications to construct soft indicators.[55]

[54] Similar to the examination of the first question, here it is also helpful to understand the usability of certain soft clues contained in the loan descriptions for predicting loan defaults (those that are not always the result of deliberate disclosures by the borrower).

[55] Soft information provided by borrowers is not a core variable of interest in these studies. Instead, they have aimed at modelling defaults in the P2P lending market using a comprehensive set of hard data indicators in addition to a credit grade determined by the platform. Some hard data are sourced from the borrower's credit report and are thus verified, while some are self-reported (annual income, home situation, employment length). As mentioned before, the platform occasionally verifies self-reported income ex-ante (Carmichael, 2014, p. 7), while it performs more comprehensive verification after the successful completion of a campaign (Nowak et al., 2018, p. 322, fn. 14).

Carmichael (2014) finds that borrower's self-claimed creditworthiness is negatively associated with default probabilities, suggesting that such claims are believable. He also points out that a loan description lacking a full stop increases the chances of default.[56] Similarly, Polena and Regner (2018) document that creditworthy borrowers write longer loan descriptions than borrowers who defaulted. However, surprisingly, the length of loan description is a good predictor of defaults only in low-risk classes. Both Carmichael (2014) and Polena and Regner (2018) point out that ex-ante unverifiable claims, such as the intended use of borrowed funds, influence default probabilities. For instance, both studies find that loan purposes of credit card repayment and debt consolidation are related to fewer defaults.

The study of Nowak et al. (2018) differs from the two aforementioned studies for focusing exclusively on loans for small businesses. Moreover, the study first conducts a textual analysis to identify words and phrases that predict loan funding. In the next step, these are used as possible predictors of loan performance.[57] The advantage of this approach is that it uses soft indicators that lenders are found to be driven by when making an investment decision. Their findings reveal that soft information from loan descriptions decreases the expected odds of defaults, indicating that investors' interpretations of soft claims are adequate. Moreover, another significant result is that such claims have the strongest impact on the loan performance of borrowers with low credit scores, again pointing out that soft claims can complement standard measures for riskier loan classes.[58]

The evidence from the Chinese market is mixed. The recent paper by Chen et al. (2022) shows that the level of disclosure is positively associated with default probabilities. They explain that the lack of verification incentivises low-quality borrowers to mimic good-quality borrowers by disclosing a large amount of manipulated data. Given that they also show that lenders are sensitive to the number of

---

[56] Claims about creditworthiness are captured by screening the loan description for some keywords that are typically associated with positive claims about oneself: responsible, trustworthy, always pay, etc. (Carmichael, 2014, p. 9).

[57] Specific phrases commonly associated with loan funding (either positively or negatively, e.g. debt free, recently purchased, business grow, etc.) are used to form an index that is used as a predictor of loan performance.

[58] As discussed before, the issue of (voluntary) disclosures is inseparable from the question of the veracity of disclosed information, as self-reported information by borrowers is usually unverified by the platform or third parties.

Three studies examine whether unverified or misreported information has an influence on loan performance using data from Lending Club (Eid et al., 2016; Gallo, 2021; Pursiainen, 2023). As explained above, Lending Club does not always ask borrowers to provide a source for disclosed hard data before listing on the platform, and the verification status is visible to lenders. Gallo (2021) finds that unverified status on information about annual income or employment length is a significant predictor of low recovery rates of non-performing loans. Similarly, Eid et al. (2016) and Pursiainen (2023) point out that information misreporting is associated with a greater probability of defaults. Information misreporting in these studies is presumably captured by income rounding or the inconsistency of the loan amount with outstanding credit balance when a crowdfunding loan is taken with the purpose of credit card repayment or debt consolidation.

disclosures, the authors acknowledge that, other than being misled, investors may be attracted by the high yields these loans promise to generate (Chen et al., 2022, pp. 11–12).[59] Research by Jiang, Wang, et al. (2018) and Li et al. (2020) provide, to some extent, contrasting and more nuanced results. Li et al. (2020) aim to understand the value of disclosures in a repeated game (for borrowers with a borrowing history on the platform) and report different results for experienced and new borrowers. Experienced borrowers who disclose more information are less likely to default, suggesting their disclosures are credible. However, the level of disclosures for first-time borrowers is not indicative of default probability. The study by Jiang, Xu, et al. (2018) is specific for focusing on P2P business lending. By aiming to propose a default prediction method for P2P lending, they test for the significance of soft indicators in predicting default on the Chinese P2P lending platform Eloan.[60] Business borrowers with lengthier loan descriptions are less likely to default, although mentioning specific phrases influences default probability differently. Descriptions relating to family, work, and income positively affect loan defaults, unlike descriptions of assets, business, and agriculture, which reduce default probabilities.[61] In contrast to some other studies reviewed above, Jiang, Wang, et al. (2018) do not look into whether crowdfunding lenders use soft information relevant to defaults.[62]

Dorfleitner et al. (2016) examine the relationship between individual disclosures and defaults in the German P2P lending market. The study shows that soft information embedded in spelling errors, loan description length, and use of specific keywords is not predictive of loan performance on either of the two platforms examined (Smava and Auxmoney). However, the authors have also compared

[59] What this study does not reveal clearly, though, is whether pricing is inefficient in terms of risk-return trade-off so that voluntary disclosures increase the risk of default for which borrowers are not compensated by an increase in the interest rate.

[60] The platform primarily serves individual businesses, small micro-owners and farmers (Jiang, Wang, et al., 2018, p. 514).

[61] As the study is meant to offer a comprehensive default prediction model, all the usual hard information is included in the analysis as control variables.

[62] With the emergence of research that aims to develop default prediction models for the P2P lending market, some other studies have also considered (ex-ante unverifiable) soft information. For instance, Xu et al. (2021) have looked into factors determining default probabilities on Funding Circle, a major UK crowdfunding platform for SMEs. They find that loan purpose for capital needs is associated with higher default probabilities than other purposes (e.g. refinancing a loan, tax liability, etc.).

It is important to note that studies under review here use a traditional (manual) approach to identifying text characteristics that can help discern borrower quality, in contrast to newly available deep learning and natural language processing techniques of extracting soft information from P2P loan descriptions (Fitzpatrick & Mues, 2021; Kriebel & Stitz, 2022; Stevenson et al., 2021). The reason is that a typical individual lender can only rely on soft information that has well-established links with the borrower's behaviour, which is based on common sense or more advanced knowledge of psychology and finance. In contrast, different natural language processing techniques recognise patterns that are not necessarily based on existing knowledge and, thus, are not used by individual borrowers.

annual rates of return on two platforms. As discussed before, since hard data is more readily available on Smava than on Auxmoney, soft data plays a more critical role in screening borrowers on the latter platform. The findings show that the annual rates of return are higher, and accompanying defaults are lower on Auxmoney than on Smava. This brings indirect evidence that soft data can attenuate information asymmetries compared to the almost exclusive use of hard information.

The third approach, which is the rarest, entails exploring whether loan pricing based on lenders' assessment of both hard and soft information available is efficient. In other words, the question examined is whether interest rates are a good predictor of loan defaults. If that is the case, then voluntarily disclosed (soft) information is truthful, or investors interpret the credibility of disclosed information correctly.

Iyer et al. (2016) evaluate the screening practices of lenders on the US platform Prosper. The study documents that lenders rely on standard (financial) and nonstandard information to assess the borrower's quality. However, lenders only have access to the borrower's aggregate credit category but not the exact credit score. This enables the relative efficiency of lenders' default predictions, primarily based on soft data, to be compared to the default predictions based on a credit score. Lenders' screening ability is embedded in interest rates they were willing to accept, as determined in the auction process. The study finds that lenders can predict default with 45% higher accuracy than default predictions that merely use the borrower's credit score.[63] In addition, soft information appears more valuable in the screening process of low-quality borrowers.[64] In a related study on the same platform, Gao et al. (2018) also provide evidence that certain soft factors help predict defaults and that investors do account for them in their funding decisions. Namely, they find that borrowers whose loan description is less readable, less positive, and has more deception cues are more likely to default and that they obtain higher interest rates as a consequence. Nevertheless, their results show that lenders fail to incorporate soft clues fully. The evidence suggests that, on average, the interest rate is not high enough to compensate lenders for the additional default risk entirely. This, in turn, indicates that pricing in the P2P market is not fully efficient.[65]

---

[63] To reach such a conclusion, they conduct two regressions with a default rate as the dependent variable. The explanatory variable in the first regression was the interest rate determined in the auction process, whereas the explanatory variable in the second regression was the credit score. The higher adjusted R^2 in the first regression was used as evidence of the higher explanatory power of soft information embedded in interest rates compared to the credit score.

[64] In contrast to other related research, this study does not exploit the variation in the level or type of voluntary disclosures among different borrowers but rather relies on the overall perception of lenders inferred from interest rates they were willing to accept. Such an approach is helpful if investors' interpretation of voluntary disclosures in crowdfunding does not always follow the simplistic logic that the quantity of (soft) information provided determines the borrower's quality, as well as in situations when soft data cannot be coded.

[65] They conclude this based on a regression analysis in which soft clues are statistically significant variables in explaining default rates after controlling for interest rates. This shows that soft clues

The UK P2P lending market exhibits similar patterns. Using data from Lending Club while still operating an auction mechanism, Franks et al. (2021) employ a similar empirical strategy to Iyer et al. (2016) to estimate an increase in price efficiency by relying on nonstandard (soft) data. They find that interest rates determined in an auction process are a statistically significant predictor of defaults, even after controlling for the credit score. Again, this suggests that screening borrowers beyond credit ratings increases price efficiency. In addition to soft information provided by borrowers, Franks et al. (2021, p. 19) acknowledge that individual investors can also have private information about borrowers aggregated in the loan price through an auction. However, they do not find support for an efficient market hypothesis in this market, while the leading cause of deviations is attributed to liquidity shocks.[66]

In summary of the third question, the prevailing evidence suggests that voluntary disclosures of (soft) information and some less deliberate soft clues can facilitate the screening process in P2P lending, particularly for borrowers with lower credit scores. However, such disclosures are not always credible, and lenders sometimes fail to give them the appropriate weight in their investment decisions. Information non-credibility as a source of market failure can also depend on other factors, such as whether borrowers are first-time or repeated borrowers on the platform, whether some of the information disclosed is hard but unverified data, and whether a platform provides credit grades or assigns interest rates that complement borrowers' voluntary disclosures and soft clues.

Equity Crowdfunding

Empirical literature examining the role of information disclosures in equity crowdfunding is more recent and less comprehensive than the literature on P2P (consumer) lending, with existing studies also covering different jurisdictions. Nevertheless, this section reviews existing studies on equity crowdfunding using the same structure as before, which is based on the market failure perspective. Thus, the first question is whether investors in equity crowdfunding are responsive to the differences in disclosure levels, which can shed light on whether incomplete information is the source of market failure. The second question is whether investors give sufficient weight to specific hard (financial) information. This can suggest

are informative about defaults beyond what lenders already processed and incorporated in interest rates they were willing to accept. Put differently, their results demonstrate that lenders failed to give soft information sufficient weight when deciding on interest rates.

[66] Deviations from price efficiency are captured by the explanatory power of some other variables included in the regression explaining defaults, in addition to interest rates (e.g. credit score, proxies for liquidity shocks). Franks et al. (2021, p. 20) contend that the efficient market hypothesis implies that interest rates absorb all relevant information while other variables should lose explanatory power. As they find deviations from the efficiency benchmark increased over time, they argue that liquidity issues were at the heart of Lending Club's decision to abandon auctions in favour of the posted price mechanism in 2017.

whether the source of inefficiency stems from investors' limited attention or high information-processing costs. As with the empirical evidence on P2P lending, relevant studies on equity crowdfunding often intertwine the analysis of the two questions. Therefore, this section will discuss the two questions together while offering a more concise summary for each question in Table 3–1.

Several studies provide evidence on the UK equity crowdfunding market (Donovan, 2021; Estrin et al., 2022; Jo & Yang, 2021). They examine market behaviour on Crowdcube, one of the world's first and biggest equity crowdfunding platforms.

Donovan (2021) investigates how disclosing unverified financials affects campaign success. He finds that the availability of financials is associated with a greater percentage of funds raised and a greater probability of reaching the funding goal. An interesting fact reported in the study is that 67% of all firms disclosed financials despite the absence of a regulatory obligation to do so (Donovan, 2021, p. 7219). Yet, disclosing financials does not seem to be equally important for all firms. The study results suggest that financials matter primarily for firms with a longer history of operations. In contrast, for startups, 'expected growth opportunities provide the majority of the firm's value' (Donovan, 2021, p. 7228). Moreover, financials also play a greater role for firms that provide more contextual information by disclosing the shareholders' agreement, which adds credibility to unverified financials. In the author's view, the costs of revealing proprietary information can also contribute to the perception of credibility of financial disclosures, which is in line with the theoretical model of Gigler (1994).

Estrin et al. (2022) test the importance of soft (unverifiable) information and hard (verifiable) information on funding success. In contrast to Donovan (2021), they do not account for voluntary disclosures of financials but look at the effects of specific soft and hard data available for each campaign.[67] Their results show that soft information is more important for the likelihood of funding success than hard information. Furthermore, the effect of soft information is strengthened the larger the size of the investor network on the platform. The explanation is that the size of the pool of potential investors increases the experience and knowledge shared among them necessary for interpreting soft information (Estrin et al., 2022, p. 1768). The caveat of the study is that the hard data they account for does not include any financial information that firms could have voluntarily disclosed.

[67] The study treats as hard data and tests the statistical significance of the following information: the entrepreneur's demographics, the firm's age, size, location, and industry, information on whether the firm had a previously successful equity crowdfunding raise on the platform, and information on whether the firm had received early investments before the pitch started (Estrin et al., 2022, p. 1768). Information characterised as soft includes firm evaluation, growth prospects, and revaluation change (if, during the campaign, there has been a revaluation of the firm's equity). In addition, the authors treat as soft some information that does not originate from entrepreneurs directly but rather from other investors on the platform, that is, the largest amount invested as a proportion of the funding goal and number of followers of the campaign pitch (Estrin et al., 2022, p. 1768).

In a closely related study, Jo and Yang (2021) take a more nuanced approach to examining the effects of specific soft information—financial forecasts on funding outcomes. They exploit the requirement imposed by Crowdcube that all projects of certain maturity provide investors with forecasted financial statements (Jo & Yang, 2021, p. 724). More specifically, they examine whether investors' decisions are driven by entrepreneurs' forecasts of sales, sales growth, earnings, profit margin, assets, leverage, capital expenditure, dividends, and equity financing. While they do not control for a firm's decision to disclose historical financial statements, they account for the total value of assets before launching a crowdfunding campaign.[68] The findings show that investors react selectively to certain soft information. More specifically, investors' decisions are driven by forecasts of sales, equity and debt financing, and lack of dividend payouts, while projections of profitability are not found to have an influence. As to investors' responsiveness to past financial information, the total value of prior assets increases the probability of reaching the fundraising target.

Several studies examine the impact of different types of information disclosures on campaign outcomes in the US (Aland, 2023; Johan & Zhang, 2020; Knyazeva & Ivanov, 2017). The existing studies use aggregated data from all platforms that operated in the chosen observation period.[69] The US context is specific because Regulation Crowdfunding requires all fundraising firms to file electronically their offerings with the SEC in Form C. This entails mandatory disclosure of hard (financial) data, in contrast to voluntary disclosures of unverified hard data captured by other studies.

Knyazeva and Ivanov (2017) investigate the importance of hard and soft information in equity crowdfunding in the first year following the introduction of crowdfunding regulation in the US.[70] They find that hard data has only a marginal, usually insignificant, impact on funding success, while soft information is a significant predictor of crowdfunding outcomes. They offer three possible explanations for such findings (Knyazeva & Ivanov, 2017, p. 4, 13). Firstly, crowdfunding firms can have limited assets and a short operating history, which makes their value a function of their growth prospects. Secondly, investors might face limitations in interpreting historical disclosures of early-stage firms. Thirdly, investors might factor in non-financial preferences in their investment decisions. An important caveat of this study in the context of discussions in this section is that the authors have not analysed disclosures of soft information by issuers but instead use a proxy—social media coverage of a crowdfunding campaign. They reason that social media

[68] The information on the value of assets is either found in disclosed financial statements or in the latest filings on Companies House before the crowdfunding campaign (Jo & Yang, 2021, p. 746).

[69] The data on the US market encompasses all operating platforms thanks to regulatory requirements to publish campaign-level data, unlike in other jurisdictions where researchers had to collect data themselves from specific platforms.

[70] Hard data variables used in the study include the size of assets, the firm's age, the issuer's net income, and the executive team size (Knyazeva & Ivanov, 2017, p. 20).

reporting reflects 'unobservable buzz about the issuer among customers, prospective investors and other followers' (Knyazeva & Ivanov, 2017, p. 4).[71]

In a related study, Johan and Zhang (2020) test the impact of qualitative business information on campaign success indicators using data on crowdfunding campaigns both before and after the regulatory change. The authors define as qualitative information that 'reflects entrepreneurs' self-evaluation on the business and can be hardly verified' (Johan & Zhang, 2020, p. 2).[72] Qualitative information is captured by the length of the business description and the use of promotional words. Interestingly, the authors use the length of the business description as a proxy for a level of disclosure. In contrast, they use promotional words as a proxy for entrepreneurs' overstatement of a firm's quality. Consequently, their findings suggest that the length of qualitative disclosures is associated with higher funding success, while the percentage of promotional words is associated with lower funding success. This study also sheds light on how unsophisticated investors use qualitative (soft) information. Namely, the study reveals that the introduction of the crowdfunding regulation in the US, which allowed unsophisticated (retail) investors access to crowdfunding platforms for the first time, moderated the effect of qualitative information on campaign outcomes. With retail investors entering the market, the positive impact of the length of disclosures becomes stronger, and the negative effect of promotional words becomes weaker and even insignificant.[73]

Disclosures in the US equity crowdfunding market are further examined by Aland (2023), who uses evidence from all campaigns launched in the first 18 months following the regulatory change introducing the crowdfunding regime (Jumpstart Our Business Startups Act, 2012). The design of this study is unique because it looks not only into the effects of specific financials on funding outcomes (whose disclosure is mandated by regulation)[74] but also into two types of voluntary disclosures available on the crowdfunding offering page. The first type involves specific financial information, which, although available in the regulatory Form C, can be additionally emphasised elsewhere on the offering page to reduce investors' processing costs or to make it more salient (Aland, 2023,

[71] While it is likely that social media following partially captures soft information not measured directly in this study, it also reflects the size of entrepreneurs' social network, which is considered a (costly) signal, as will be discussed below. The study also uses two other proxies for soft information that originate from entrepreneurs: the number of frequently asked questions and the number of responses to investors' questions. Only the latter was found to be statistically significant.

[72] Under qualitative business information, the authors include 'entrepreneurs' introduction on the business model, competitive strategy, product market, drivers and barriers for product/service adoption and business milestones' (Johan & Zhang, 2020, p. 2).

[73] This study also captures the effects of quantitative business information on the campaign success. Hard data that was controlled for include variables on 'financial statements in previous years, management educational background and years of relevant industry experience, number of employees, estimated product market size, etc.' (Johan & Zhang, 2020, p. 2).

[74] Firm financial variables controlled for in the study include size, age, revenue, net income, debt, and employees.

pp. 4–5).[75] The second type includes what the author calls non-financial information that helps tell the company's story (Aland, 2023, p. 30).[76] The study does not reveal a consistent relation between voluntary disclosure of financials and offering success, indicating that the salience of (positive) financial information does not improve campaign outcomes. The total investment and percentage of funds raised are more closely associated with non-financial disclosures on the offering page. The authors find that discussions on the intended use of raised funds, the company's history, frequently asked questions, and various audio-visual elements matter for reaching the funding goal. Some hard (financial) data in the regulatory form C were also included as controls. The findings suggest that investors are responsive to issuers' level of debt but unresponsive to some other financials (e.g., firm's size, revenue, net income, firm's age).

Two studies examine voluntary disclosures in the Australian equity crowdfunding market, providing evidence from the platform ASSOB (Ahlers et al., 2015; Pattanapanyasat, 2021). The earlier study by Ahlers et al. (2015) focuses on costly signals but has also brought evidence that some non-verifiable, forward-looking information matters for campaign outcomes. They find that providing financial forecasts or at least a disclaimer explaining that the lack of forecasts is due to legal reasons improves funding prospects.[77] They also control for the effects of other forward-looking variables such as proposed exit channel (e.g., trade sale as compared to IPO) and estimated time horizon until planned exit. While an IPO as a planned exit channel attracts more investors, it does not increase the overall funding. Similarly, the study results suggest that crowdfunding investors treat the estimated time until exit as cheap talk. Overall, equity crowdfunding investors seem to assign different credibility to different types of soft information.

Pattanapanyasat (2021) investigates the effects of voluntary disclosures by looking into hard but unverified data (unaudited financial statements) and soft information embedded in the tone of entrepreneurs' narratives. Her findings imply that disclosing financials is associated with greater funding. In addition, her study examines how disclosing financials affects investors' reactions to soft information embedded in the tone, that is, the use of positive words on the

[75] Voluntary disclosed financial variables examined include income, revenue, and expenses. The study also accounts for a number of associated variables related to the place and the format of voluntary reported financial information.

[76] The company's history, intended use of proceeds, frequently asked questions, audio-visual elements, financial projections, etc. fall under this type of information in this study. What the author characterises as non-financial information largely corresponds to soft information, as defined in other studies.

[77] Financial forecasts include information on future sales, net earnings, EBITDA, and EBIT (Ahlers et al., 2015, p. 969). While Australian regulations at the time provided flexibility regarding the choice of financial forecast indicators and the form of presenting them, investors could also submit a disclaimer for not including any financial projections or forecasts. Such a disclaimer is used to indicate that future earnings are difficult to predict due to uncertainty regarding the company's operations (Ahlers et al., 2015, p. 969, fn. 9).

campaign page. Pattanapanyasat (2021) reveals a negative association between the (positive) tone of the campaign and investors' contributions, which is amplified when financials are disclosed. In other words, disclosing financials further decreases the credibility of soft claims. Her interpretation is that (optimistic) narratives are balanced against information contained in financials (Pattanapanyasat, 2021, p. 2).

Only one study examining voluntary disclosures in equity crowdfunding in China is identified in this review. Li et al. (2016) provide evidence from Dajiatou, the first platform in China that introduced a set of standardised forms of information disclosure for entrepreneurs to fill out (Li et al., 2016, p. 307). Nevertheless, the variation in the level of disclosures comes from the possibility of uploading a video, the length of the project introduction, and the length and frequency of updates during the campaign. The study finds that project updates and videos are significant in explaining campaign outcomes, suggesting that they can reveal additional details about the project that investors praise in their investment decisions.

The study by Lukkarinen et al. (2016) provides evidence of the value of disclosures on the equity platform Invesdor, which operates in several European jurisdictions.[78] The platform offers a template for disclosing financials, thus making it easier for investors to compare projects. Yet, the results show that investors are not responsive to the provision of financials, such as revenues or EBITDA. Moreover, investors are not sensitive to the actual information in financial disclosures valued by traditional investors in early-stage companies, VCs, and angel investors (e.g., EBITDA margin and sales growth).

The communication behaviour of fundraisers on crowdinvesting platforms in Germany has been examined in several studies (Block et al., 2018; Dorfleitner et al., 2018; Goethner et al., 2021; Hornuf & Schwienbacher, 2018b). Similar to the prevailing evidence in other jurisdictions, Goethner et al. (2021) demonstrate that investors on the platform Companisto value the information embedded in financial projections. They also document that the effect of financial projections on investor behaviour differs among different investor types, which they categorise into casual investors, crowd enthusiasts, and sophisticated investors.[79] More specifically, crowd enthusiasts are the least responsive to this type of disclosure, notably because they put less emphasis on future payoffs than other types (Goethner et al., 2021, p. 914).

Other studies examining disclosure practices in the German crowdfunding market focus on voluntary communication during the crowdfunding campaign through

[78] While the authors only indicate that Invesdor is a Nordic platform, the company website suggests that its countries of operation are Finland, Austria, and Germany (Invesdor, 2024).

[79] Casual investors are the biggest group comprised of individuals who invest small amounts. They are not particularly concerned with the project's innovativeness but rather making profits. Crowd enthusiasts invest primarily in innovative projects and are likely to be driven by pro-social and community considerations. Sophisticated investors pledge the highest amounts and are the most involved in the project development, as indicated by the number of comments they make on the platform (Goethner et al., 2021, pp. 911–912).

updates (Block et al., 2018; Dorfleitner et al., 2018; Hornuf & Schwienbacher, 2018b). The form and the content of updates are not regulated, while platforms often do not verify the disclosed information (Dorfleitner et al., 2018, p. 538). Therefore, updates allow entrepreneurs to provide additional information about the project and the team more flexibly (Block et al., 2018, p. 6). Although updates are meant to inform investors about business aspects that were unknown at the time of the campaign launch (e.g., new business developments, collaborations, and external financing), they are often used to captivate investors' attention (Reichenbach & Walther, 2021, p. 9). The evidence from the three studies is consistent that posting updates improves the success of a campaign, measured by the number of investments, percentage, or the total amount raised.[80] Block et al. (2018) further examine whether investors perceive updates with certain characteristics as more informative using evidence from equity crowdfunding platforms Seedmatch and Companisto.[81] Their results suggest that an easier language of updates matters for their influence on investors, unlike the length of updates. Similarly, updates with verifiable information about new business and campaign developments are found to have a positive relationship with campaign success, unlike, for instance, information about the team, business model, or promotional activities.[82] An important related question is whether communication through updates can be used strategically by entrepreneurs to create a buzz that inflates investors' expectations. Evidence from a traditional IPO setting shows that a 'substantial amount of online discussion' affects the valuation of securities (Keel et al., 2021). Similarly, Dorfleitner et al. (2018) capture in their study that entrepreneurs on equity crowdfunding platforms Seedmatch and Companisto use updates strategically. They post more updates during the crowdfunding campaign than after they receive funding. This also refers to using linguistic techniques to boost the group's identity and cohesion and inform the crowd about recent business developments.[83] Moreover, the authors have documented that the competition from other popular campaigns on the platform intensifies the use of updates.

In summary, the prevailing evidence suggests that investors on equity crowdfunding platforms are responsive to the level of disclosures. Similarly to findings on P2P lending, this can indicate that incomplete information is not likely to be the source of market failure. While investors pay much attention to disclosures of soft data, such as financial projections, they often fail to process past

[80] Consistent evidence was also found in studies on reward-based crowdfunding, although the data comes from Kickstarter in the US (Li et al., 2018; Mollick, 2014; Moradi & Dass, 2019; Xu et al., 2014).

[81] The platforms do not intermediate investments in equity but rather hybrid instruments due to a requirement to involve a costly notary when transferring equity (Block et al., 2018, p. 10).

[82] Put differently, investors do not seem to be reactive to information that already existed at the start of the campaign.

[83] The linguistic techniques used to strengthen the group's identity and cohesion are proxied by the use of first-person plural and the number of emotional words in an update (Dorfleitner et al., 2018, p. 525).

financial information. Again, similarly to the evidence on P2P lending, this may indicate that their limited attention is a potential source of market failure. However, it is also worth noting that for some early-stage companies, the existing financial record can have limited value compared to forward-looking information.

Since investors are responsive to differences in disclosures and rely on soft information, it is vital to understand how they relate to firms' characteristics and ex-post performance. A few studies in equity crowdfunding shed light on these issues.

Aland (2023) examines the association between firms' characteristics and the tendency to disclose soft information and discuss financial information on the offering page. More specifically, the author tests whether discussions about the intended use of proceeds, the company's history, frequently asked questions, and multimedia content correlate with financial information on the company, which firms must disclose by the law. Since no consistent relation is found, the author concludes that non-financial disclosures are not motivated by the need to hide a poor or limited financial record (Aland, 2023, p. 5). However, such disclosures also do not indicate a superior ex-ante financial record. When it comes to the discussion of hard financial data on the offering page, the results are more informative. According to this study, firms that have generated prior revenues are more likely to discuss their financial information on the offerings page.

Research that examines the association between information disclosures during an equity crowdfunding campaign and firms' ex-post performance is still nascent. Existing studies have contrasting findings, often depending on whether they examine the disclosure of hard or soft information.

Donovan (2021) examines the effects of voluntary disclosure of unverified financials on ex-post firm performance of firms raising finances on the UK platform Crowdcube. Ex-post performance is proxied by whether the firm is subsequently liquidated or insolvent[84] and growth in total assets in the fiscal year following the crowdfunding campaign. The results show that disclosing financials reduces the likelihood of a firm's failure directly and indirectly through the percentage of capital raised, which is also positively associated with firms' survival rates. While the study finds no direct effect of disclosing financials on the subsequent growth in total assets, it has captured an indirect effect through the percentage of funds raised. Namely, the success of a crowdfunding campaign affects subsequent asset growth.

On the contrary, evidence on the effects of disclosures of soft information on ex-post success is mixed (Jo & Yang, 2021; Pattanapanyasat, 2021; Reichenbach & Walther, 2021). Like Donovan (2021), Jo and Yang (2021) examine the behaviour of fundraisers on the UK platform Crowdcube. According to their research, entrepreneurs systematically overestimate sales, earnings, profit margin, and total assets

[84] The authors assume that firms failed if liquidated or insolvent 3 years following the crowdfunding campaign.

and underestimate leverage. Interestingly, even though investors are attracted by some of these forecasts, as discussed earlier, firms with the most optimistic forecasts (when considering their subsequent realisation) attract fewer funds and investors. In contrast, they find no evidence that forecasts information that investors are responsive to is a good predictor of a firm's survival ex-post. In other words, forecasts are not indicative of entrepreneurial ability. This holds independently of the level of (optimism) bias in forecasts.

In Australia, Pattanapanyasat (2021) finds that successfully funded firms with greater use of (positive) tone in their narratives have poor performance ex-post. Nevertheless, since the same study shows a negative association between the (positive) narratives and investor funding, no evidence suggests that investors are misled in their assessments.

Reichenbach and Walther (2021) examine the importance of voluntary disclosures in the form of updates for the ex-post performance on ventures financed via a German crowdfunding platform, Companisto. While the overall number of updates during a campaign is not predictive of the company's survival, updates which were found to have a greater influence on the success of funding (Block et al., 2018) are also generally associated with a lower risk of default. However, this does not hold for all types of updates. Reichenbach and Walther (2021) provide evidence that the crowd is attracted by some updates associated with a lower likelihood of survival, such as campaign developments.[85]

Lastly, the evidence on the credibility of voluntary disclosures in equity crowdfunding is insufficient. Scarce research indicates that voluntary disclosures of hard data are credible, while the findings on disclosures of soft information generate mixed results.

Summary of Findings on Voluntary Disclosures

When information economics theory is applied to the context of crowdfunding markets, one can argue that voluntary disclosures are likely to be an ineffective mechanism for overcoming information asymmetries. Firstly, disclosures are incomplete when disclosures are costly for fundraisers, and this is likely for business fundraisers when they need to reveal proprietary information. Secondly, this market mechanism is impaired when investors have reduced incentives to detect flaws in disclosed content. With their small stakes, crowdfunding investors are expected to have limited capacities to check information completeness. Thirdly, the effectiveness of voluntary disclosures depends on the truthfulness of disclosed content. Here, it is important to distinguish between hard (verifiable) and soft (unverifiable) data. Again, it is costly for small fundraisers to provide external certification of hard data and even more costly for many uncoordinated retail investors to verify

[85] Since campaign updates primarily serve to sensitise prospective investors about the existing level of funding, their effect can be confounded with signals originating from other investors, which will be discussed in the next section.

information independently. Soft information disclosure reduces information asymmetry in a very limited set of circumstances, and it is questionable whether crowd investors can discern when they merely represent cheap talk.

However, the review of empirical evidence provides more nuanced results on the effectiveness of this market mechanism in the crowdfunding context. Investors in both P2P lending and equity crowdfunding are mostly responsive to the level of disclosure. Fundraisers who do not reveal enough information are usually less successful in crowdfunding campaigns. Therefore, they have reduced incentives to try to attract investors by selectively providing the most favourable information to their image. Consequently, incomplete information is not likely to be the source of market failure.

Nevertheless, there are certain caveats to these findings. Firstly, most studies examine variations in the disclosures of soft information, not least because platforms often prescribe the disclosure standards for offerings on their portals. Secondly, empirical findings indicating that investors can capture differences in disclosure level do not amount to a conclusion that a full disclosure occurs in every crowdfunding campaign. Notably, there can be idiosyncratic circumstances or facts pertinent to a single or few campaigns, which investors are usually unaware of. Finally, the fact that investors are reluctant to invest when certain information is missing can deter fundraisers with the highest proprietary costs from using this funding mechanism. As discussed earlier, these are companies whose products are easy to copy or products that have the greatest innovative potential, which fear that disclosing too much information would reduce their earnings potential.

While crowd investors appear to be able to detect information obscuring, at least regarding the comparable information across different projects, sporadic evidence suggests that they do not always use all the available information. In particular, some hard (financial) information is often neglected in the investment decisions of the crowd. Consequently, the limited attention of crowd investors can be a source of market failure. Nevertheless, as found in some studies, hard financial information can have a reduced value for fundraisers with thin records of past performance or fundraisers whose value primarily consists in their growth potential, while soft, forward-looking information, as well as soft clues, also become significant in assessing their future earnings.

In relation to this, empirical evidence further shows that crowd investors put much weight on soft disclosures, which are not always credible, as captured by their ability to predict post-campaign performance. Consequently, information credibility can be a source of market failure in addition to investors' limited attention to hard data.

An incidental insight from the review of empirical evidence in crowdfunding is that the online information exchange channel can affect disclosure practices. In contrast to a more traditional setting of public offerings, disclosures are not limited to the offerings page at the beginning of a crowdfunding campaign. Instead, an important source of information exchange is updates and discussions during the campaign, which are less structured and rarely subject to external oversight by the platform or the regulator. Similarly, much of the information exchange happens on related web pages and social networks ('online buzz'), whose influence is yet sufficiently examined in the existing empirical studies. Here, information can be distributed from persons related to fundraisers, who can increase the salience of facts and figures that help create a more favourable image of fundraisers. In contrast to these perils of the online information exchange, it is possible to argue that online disclosures reduce the costs of detecting distortion of verifiable (hard) data. While no empirical evidence on this has been gathered, it would mean a reduced need to verify information formally or engage third-party certifiers.

3.4.2 Signalling

Theoretical Considerations

Disclosure of information is not the only way fundraisers can attenuate information asymmetries. Instead, or in addition to disclosure, they can use signalling to obtain better terms of financing (higher valuations or lower interest rates). Signals are observable actions or attributes of the informed party used to convey their unobservable quality to the uninformed party (Ahlers et al., 2015, p. 959).[86] Fundraisers' potential to generate future cash flows or ensure the company's growth is the unobservable quality that investors are interested in.

Signals are alterable attributes of individuals or companies that they have an influence on, that is, that they can manipulate (Spence, 1973, p. 357).[87] For signals to be credible, it must be costly for low-quality sellers (borrowers or issuers) to imitate them. Put differently, the difference in the cost of signalling between the high-quality and low-quality fundraisers should be such that signalling becomes a profitable strategy only for the former type ('a separating equilibrium'). A more nuanced approach implies differentiating between signals of different strengths, whereas the strength of a signal depends on the level of correlation between a signal and unobservable quality (Bafera & Kleinert, 2022, p. 2). It is worth noting that signalling cost differential for good-quality and bad-quality fundraisers does not have to appear ex-ante. However, for the signal to be credible, the low-quality type should be unable to recover the signalling investments ex-post, such as when hiring

---

[86] Signalling theory is usually associated with the seminal article on signalling in the job market by Spence (1973), which compares the hiring of employees to an investment decision. Such a decision involves interpreting signals such as education that reveal the unobserved quality of job applicants, that is, their productive capability. Signals enable distinguishing between the quality of job applicants since signalling costs (time, money, and psychic costs) are negatively associated with their productive capability. In the context of firms raising external finance, Leland and Pyle (1977) and Downes and Heinkel (1982) explained how the fraction of equity retained by entrepreneurs and their dividend policy can reveal the firm value.

[87] This stands in contrast to immutable attributes (e.g., sex, gender), over which individuals do not have influence (Spence, 1973, p. 357).

an auditor reveals that there are certain misrepresentations in the financial statements.[88]

In the context of raising external finance, 'signalling becomes a substitute for disclosure, undertaken to convey information about the firm's earnings 'generating power without divulging the information itself' (Dye, 1986, p. 332, fn. 4). Dye (1986, p. 332, fn. 4) explains that, when both disclosure and signalling are possible, the choice between them 'depends on a comparison of the efficiency of the signal in communicating the information and the cost of the information's disclosure'. Disclosures and signals can also be seen as complements where 'disclosure provides more precise and comparable information' (Dranove & Jin, 2010, p. 939), while signals act as quality assurance mechanisms with greater credibility. According to Spence (1973, p. 356), information is transferred via signalling when incentives for veracity in disclosed information are weak.

In the crowdfunding context, both scenarios are possible—when signalling is used as a substitute or complement to full disclosure. One can conjecture that, in the absence of mandatory rules, small firms significantly burdened with direct costs of disclosure will use signalling instead. Similarly, highly innovative firms that incur high proprietary costs associated with divulging critical aspects of their innovation are also more likely to opt for signalling. If strong signals are available, savings on direct or indirect disclosure costs are an optimal strategy from both the fundraising firm's and social welfare perspective. Investors would also be better off if entrepreneurs used signals instead of full disclosure because releasing proprietary information reduces expected future cash flows and their expected return on investment. While proprietary and non-proprietary information is relevant to the market estimates of the firm value, strong signals can convey necessary information without inducing future profit loss.

In contrast, as discussed above, much of the information that fundraisers want to disclose relevant to investment decisions is non-verified or soft (forward-looking or non-verifiable). In such cases, signalling complements disclosures by adding the necessary credibility. As Leland and Pyle (1977, p. 371) argued, 'there may be substantial rewards for exaggerating positive qualities', while it may be costly or impossible for outside investors to verify the true characteristics of borrowers and entrepreneurial projects. Similarly, Vismara (2018b, p. 32) has contended that signals are widely used in crowdfunding because it is difficult for fundraisers to convey the quality of their venture to investors via other means.

One should note that the effectiveness of a signal also depends on the investors' ability to observe the signal and extract information from it (Vismara, 2018b, p. 30). An equally important question is whether investors' high information-processing costs allow them to grasp signalling credibility. In relation to this, investors should be able to discern practices of signal manipulation when they occur. The following section sheds light on these issues by reviewing existing literature on signalling mechanisms in crowdfunding.

[88] Vismara (2018b, p. 33) uses the term 'penalty costs' to refer to a situation in which the sender of a signal faces the same ex-ante signalling costs independently of their type, but only the low-quality type receives negative feedback afterwards.

Review of the Empirical Evidence on Crowdfunding

Similar to research looking into the effects of voluntary disclosures, signalling literature in crowdfunding has focused on campaign outcomes and, to a lesser extent, the ex-post performance of fundraisers that received finances. Put differently, these studies examine which fundraisers' characteristics or actions are important for investor decision-making and whether they effectively convey the quality of fundraisers. The research has mainly been conducted in equity crowdfunding and, to a lesser extent, P2P lending. This may be because the most important signals in P2P lending are contained in credit information (Ahlers et al., 2015, p. 957). Yet, as discussed above, such information is often unavailable for the underprivileged, that is, unbankable individuals (Yum et al., 2012, p. 470). Likewise, startups raising debt finance frequently lack credit histories.

This section conducts a qualitative systematic review of existing empirical studies in P2P lending and equity crowdfunding. To this end, relevant sources are collected using the Social Science Citation Index (SSCI), the Web of Science, and Google Scholar databases.[89] Analogously to the analysis of voluntary disclosures, sources are then filtered in line with pre-defined criteria, which include the use of econometric methods, focus on financial-return crowdfunding models, individual campaigns as a unit of analysis,[90] and examination of fundraisers' actions or attributes that can be regarded as signals.[91] The total number of identified sources is 59.

As in the case of voluntary disclosures, the theoretical lenses of the review are sources of market failure. The first question examined is whether investors are responsive to signals that traditional providers of entrepreneurial finance usually

Table 3.2 Conceptual framework for analysing the empirical evidence on signalling

Contextual information				Questions addressed
Signal group	Signal type	Crowdfunding business model	Jurisdiction and platform name	Q1: Investors' responsiveness to signal (positive/negative/unresponsive/ambiguous)
				Q2: Ex-post credibility of signal (credible, non-credible, misleading)

[89] Relevant literature was identified until 30 March 2023, searching for the following keywords: signals/signalling in crowdfunding/P2P lending, determinants/factor/drivers of crowdfunding success, determinants/factors/drivers of defaults/survival in crowdfunding, investor motivation in crowdfunding/P2P lending.

[90] Studies that look at the success factors of platforms, even when including some fundraisers' characteristics, are filtered out from the analysis.

[91] Fundraisers' immutable attributes (e.g., sex, gender), attributes that are unrelated to their professional capabilities (e.g., volunteering experience), as well as some campaign characteristics that fundraisers do not always have a direct influence on (e.g., campaign duration, geographical distance of investors), are not covered in this literature review even when they are tested alongside signals in some of the studies analysed. Similarly, studies focusing on investors' characteristics are not covered in this study.

consider (Q1). This allows one to understand better whether signals are observable by crowd investors and whether they can interpret them accurately. The second question investigated is whether characteristics or actions investors are attracted to are indicative of the ex-post performance of fundraisers, that is, whether signals are credible (Q2).

Existing studies differ regarding fundraisers' characteristics or actions that they treat as signals. Some studies merely test for the significance of different indicators observable on offering pages without using the theoretical lenses of signalling. To this end, signals of various types are assigned to several groups: (1) providing assurance of disclosed information; (2) fundraisers' characteristics (human and social capital, as well as social media activities); (3) venture characteristics (portion of retained equity, intellectual property, and shareholders rights); (4) signals emanating from other investors, that is, the number and the identity of current investors—the crowd (information cascades), or the involvement of a reputable (lead) investor. The empirical evidence is further clustered based on the crowdfunding model, jurisdiction, and platform to identify some context-specific variations.

The conceptual framework of the analysis is depicted in Table 3.2. The summary of findings using the proposed conceptual framework is presented in Annex 3B.

Assurance of Disclosed Information

As explained earlier, it is typical for crowdfunding fundraisers to provide (hard) information that is unverified, even though it is verifiable. Unlike the traditional IPO setting, where the regulatory agency vets the disclosed documents (prospectuses), no such formal procedure exists in most jurisdictions with regard to crowdfunding. Certification of disclosed information by a trusted third party is not a standard regulatory requirement. When it exists, low-cost alternatives are usually allowed to minimise the burden on the fundraisers.

In such instances, the deliberate decision of fundraisers to provide an assurance of disclosed information is, by definition, a credible signal, given that it is both easily observable and costly for the fundraiser. Such costs are direct when engaging a third-party certifier or indirect as any misrepresentation or an overstatement of a potential fundraiser is presumably revealed. Assuring the accuracy of disclosed information is a straightforward example of how signals can complement disclosures. The existing studies in P2P lending and equity crowdfunding demonstrate that investors attach value to information-assurance mechanisms when deciding which project to invest in, while the evidence on the credibility of this signal group is scarce.

Talavera and Xu (2018) look into the verification practices by crowdfunding borrowers and their effects on funding success, borrowing costs, and delinquency rates. The evidence they provide comes from the Chinese P2P lending platform Renrendai, which makes the verification of some information optional (such as income, asset ownership, educational background, or credit report). Still, it clearly shows investors the verification status for each item disclosed. Borrowers provide information assurance by disclosing the necessary documentation.[92] Unsurprisingly, the results indicate that loans with a higher verification level are more likely to get funded and obtain lower interest rates while being less likely to default. The paper also looks into the effects of the verification status of different information, suggesting that investors care more about the truthfulness of certain pieces of information than others.[93] Similar findings have been reported by Yum et al. (2012) for the behaviour of lenders on the South Korean platform, Popfunding. Information with a certified status increases borrowing prospects. The authors have not examined the effect of certification on ex-post outcomes.

Similar signals were examined by Bogdani et al. (2022) in the context of equity crowdfunding in the US. Their study examines practices of certifying financial statements with a different degree of credibility using encompassing data for all equity campaigns run during 2016 and 2017. The US regulations allow for financial statements to be simply verified by management for offerings below a certain threshold to minimise the direct costs of disclosure borne by the issuer. Nevertheless, the issuer can also opt for a review by an independent accountant or an audit, presumed to signal greater impartiality and veracity of disclosed information.[94] The results of the study imply that investors are sensitive to these signals. Firms with audited financial statements or financial statements reviewed by an independent accountant are more likely to reach their funding goal, raise larger amounts, and attract more investors than firms whose financial statements were certified by management. Even though assurance by an audit is greater in scope and more detailed than a review by an independent accountant, investors do not seem to favour the former assurance mechanism.

Fundraisers' Characteristics

Human and social capital of fundraisers (entrepreneurs or venture founders) are among the least disputable signalling devices, as their effect on funding success and entrepreneurial performance has been documented in numerous studies outside the crowdfunding context.[95] Human capital is a combination of an individual's

---

[92] Nevertheless, some supporting documents are mandatory according to platform rules (e.g., identity cards) (Talavera & Xu, 2018, p. 11).

[93] For instance, bringing evidence on income, employment status and credit report affects funding probability, whereas verification of social media and education matters for interest rates and delinquency rates (Talavera & Xu, 2018, p. 17).

[94] According to US regulations, offerings below $107,000 within a 12-month period can be certified by the principal executive officer, while issuers can voluntarily choose to provide an assurance of a higher level. Offerings between $107,000 and $535,000 and first-time offerings between $535,000 and $1,070,000 must be certified by an independent accountant or audit. Second-time offerings above $535,000 are required to have an audit (Bogdani et al., 2022, p. 4).

[95] The importance of human capital as a signal is documented in related literature on angel investors and VC funding (e.g., Hsu et al., 2014). Human capital has been identified as one of the most consistent factors predicting entrepreneurial success (e.g., Unger et al., 2011).

knowledge, experience, skills, and abilities that contribute to their productivity and earnings potential (Becker, 1993; Schultz, 1961). As discussed earlier, the signalling role of education dates back to the seminal article by Spence (1973). Better-educated individuals demonstrate their productive capability relevant to the job market as well as the success of their ventures by investing time and incurring high psychic and monetary costs.

Crowdfunding literature has provided predominantly consistent evidence on the value of human capital for campaign success, although different indicators have been used. Ahlers et al. (2015) find that the share of directors holding an MBA degree increases the chances of success of ventures raising funds on the Australian equity platform ASSOB. They have opted for this proxy of human capital as it captures not only costly investments in education but also certain levels of qualification and prior professional experience (Ahlers et al., 2015, p. 968). Similarly, Kleinert et al. (2020) find that ventures in which one of the founders holds an MBA or PhD degree are more successful in raising funds on the UK platform Crowdcube. In the same vein, Goethner et al. (2021) document that ventures listed on the German platform Companisto are more likely to obtain financing if one of the project creators has a PhD degree. However, the effect depends on the investor type. Casual investors, crowd enthusiasts, and sophisticated investors (as explained above) are not equally responsive to the human capital of creators. Unsurprisingly, the likelihood of pledging if one of the project creators has a PhD is the smallest for casual investors, although they also perceive this signal as credible.

As an alternative, Nitani and Riding (2017) opt for a more easily attainable but less specific indicator of education—whether the primary owner has a graduate degree while using prior startup experience as an additional indicator of human capital. Both indicators influence the success of campaigns listed on four European platforms (Crowdcube, Companisto, Invesdor, and FundedbyMe).[96] However, they report that the effect of the startup experience is more significant than education.

Two studies demonstrate that human capital is perceived as a quality signal in equity crowdfunding campaigns in Italy (Battaglia et al., 2022; Piva & Rossi-Lamastra, 2018). Piva and Rossi-Lamastra (2018) have taken a more comprehensive approach by studying the influence of various human capital signals of entrepreneurs using data from the Italian equity-based platform SiamoSoci. They have contended that business and industry-related education are more readily associated with unobserved startup quality than education in other areas. Similarly, they have argued that entrepreneurial experience and industry-related work experience should have a greater influence on investor behaviour than other types of work experience. Nevertheless, their empirical analysis demonstrates that investors only react to fundraisers' business education and previous entrepreneurial experiences. In contrast, other characteristics, such as industry-specific education and work experience, do not matter for funding outcomes. They explain that crowd investors

[96] The four platforms are based in the UK, Germany, Finland, and Sweden, respectively.

have more difficulty inferring the value of these characteristics for the startup performance (Piva & Rossi-Lamastra, 2018, pp. 2–3).

While all of the above studies have focused on the human capital of individual founders, several studies have attempted to capture the effect of the overall quality of the entrepreneurial team on the fundraising performance (Ahlers et al., 2015; Barbi & Mattioli, 2019; Lukkarinen et al., 2016; Vismara, 2016, 2019). For instance, Barbi and Mattioli (2019) show that investors' investments in campaigns listed on the UK platform Crowdcube increase with each new team member holding a graduate degree. In parallel, Li et al. (2016) test the importance of various team characteristics (e.g., the number of staff, average working experience of entrepreneurs, and the number of board members) for investment behaviour on the Chinese platform Dajiatou. Their findings suggest that investors care about the total number of staff and the ratio of full-time staff, which likely captures their expected devotion to the project's realisation rather than human capital per se. In contrast to this approach, Lukkarinen et al. (2016) rate each campaign run on the Nordic platform Invesdor based on the team's overall quality, considering a comprehensive list of objective and subjective characteristics.[97] Interestingly, they find that the overall assessment of the team's quality does not predict campaign success.

In contrast to a large number of studies examining the effect of human capital on investor behaviour, little is known about the credibility of this signal type. Reichenbach and Walther (2021) have contributed to this discussion by examining the survival of companies raising funds on the German equity platform Companisto. They find some evidence that ventures in which a CEO holds a university degree are less likely to fail following a successful crowdfunding campaign, albeit the effect is not significant across different model specifications. Similarly, the industry experience of a CEO is found to be relevant for the post-campaign performance of a venture. Regarding the overall quality of the entrepreneurial team, Hornuf, Klöhn, and Schilling (2018) investigate whether the number of senior managers improves ex-post outcomes of firms using various equity portals in the UK and Germany. Their results indicate that firms with more senior managers are more likely to ensure follow-up funding while being less likely to fail.

The social capital of fundraisers is a measure of their relations with other individuals that facilitate fundraisers' productive activities (Coleman, 1988, p. 100). The 'goodwill' they benefit from is usually captured by the size of an individual's social network and participation in different communities (Giudici et al., 2013, p. 4). Interpersonal relations and networks have proven crucial to both financing and ex-post performance of early-stage firms (Hochberg et al., 2007; Shane & Cable, 2002). There are different paths through which social capital can facilitate the fundraising process on a crowdfunding platform. Fundraisers' social networks represent the most proximate group of potential investors (Morse, 2015, pp. 9–10).

[97] Team rating is based on the following characteristics: 'industry expertise, track record, educational background, experience, balance between team members' skill sets, as well as perceived motivation, drive, passion, commitment, and honesty' (Lukkarinen et al., 2016, p. 33).

Interpersonal trust makes information asymmetries less pronounced, encouraging contributions from within the network (Alharbey & Van Hemmen, 2021). For this reason, pledges from one's private network typically constitute a large portion of funding raised in the first days of a crowdfunding campaign. Some platforms have even made this part of the campaign hidden from the public (Lukkarinen et al., 2016, p. 29). Moreover, social capital can act as a quality assurance mechanism that enables information transmission to prospective investors outside the fundraiser's social network. It helps increase the project's visibility and spread 'word-of-mouth familiarity' (Vismara, 2016, p. 583). In relation to this, early pledges from one's private network can trigger information cascades, as will be discussed later (Xu et al., 2014, p. 592). Furthermore, social capital can even reduce moral hazard ex-post by imposing a reputational (stigma) cost on fundraisers who fail to meet their promises (Lin et al., 2013, p. 18; Morse, 2015, pp. 20–21). Finally, other benefits of crowdfunding, such as offering new marketing channels or an environment for market testing, depend on the social capital of fundraisers (Nitani & Riding, 2017, p. 10). These other benefits, in turn, affect the project's future payoffs and, thus, potentially investors' interest in the campaign. It is worth noting that crowdfunding platforms can also facilitate the creation of social capital thanks to their different design features, as will be discussed below.

Numerous empirical studies examine the relationship between social capital and the success of crowdfunding campaigns in both P2P lending and equity crowdfunding. Existing research has provided mostly consistent evidence that social capital plays a significant role in crowdfunding dynamics. The evidence covers different jurisdictions and platforms, including the US (Prosper, Lending Club), Italy (multiple platforms), the UK (Crowdcube and Seedrs), Germany (Companisto, Innovestment), Finland (Invesdor), Sweden (FundedbyMe), France (WiSeed), China (Renrendai), and Australia (Assob). However, studies rarely distinguish between the investments from and outside the fundraiser's network. In other words, it is not entirely clear which path of influence described earlier the existing studies have captured, nor what their relative importance is. Moreover, studies less frequently provide evidence of whether this signal is indicative of ex-post performance.

The most commonly used proxy of fundraisers's social capital is the number of connections/followers on different social media networks (e.g., Facebook, LinkedIn) (Battaglia et al., 2022; Giudici et al., 2013; Graziano et al., 2023; Hervé et al., 2019; Nitani & Riding, 2017; Piva & Rossi-Lamastra, 2018; Troise et al., 2020; Vismara, 2016). This appears justifiable as fundraisers describe social media as the most critical channel for reaching potential investors (Baeck et al., 2014, p. 72). Moreover, the size of the social media network is often known to prospective investors as fundraisers link their offerings page to their accounts on social media.[98]

---

[98] Nevertheless, linking the offerings page to social media websites does not seem to be the universal practice. For instance, Hornuf and Schwienbacher (2018a, p. 569) have noted that this has not been the case in any German platforms used in their study.

As to the size of social media networks, a few studies examine whether the level of activity on social media or social media presence has a positive effect on campaign outcomes in different jurisdictions (Eisenbeiss et al., 2023; Graziano et al., 2023; Lukkarinen et al., 2016; Nevin et al., 2017; Nitani & Riding, 2017). While the evidence has predominantly shown a positive effect, it is worth exploring the mechanism behind it. Posting campaign details on the company's social media page or fundraisers can be a channel for leveraging the investments from their existing network. In addition, it can stimulate interactions with prospective investors from outside fundraisers' networks. The question arises as to whether social media marketing can entail effective signals. If posts are informative so that they convey the information that can otherwise appear on the crowdfunding platform, they may simply increase the observability of existing signals. Consequently, investors become better informed before making an investment decision.

However, persuasive posts, which do not convey specific information about the crowdfunding campaign but rather intend to shape investors' preferences, are also found to influence crowdfunding investments in Germany (Eisenbeiss et al., 2023).[99] Eisenbeiss et al. (2023, p. 2) explain that persuasive posts on social media are influential due to heuristic clues, which investors use to make inferences when systematic information processing is costly.[100] Alternatively, social media activity can also signal fundraisers' confidence in the success of a campaign. The latter explanation presupposes that a campaign failure that becomes visible to existing customers and other members of the fundraisers' social network will likely generate reputational costs for the company (Lukkarinen et al., 2016, p. 35).[101] When it comes to the issue of credibility, most studies have not examined whether social media activity is predictive of the ex-post success of funded firms. Nonetheless, Graziano et al. (2023) show that a higher level of managers' activity on LinkedIn is associated with a higher innovative capacity.

The stock of existing social capital has also been proxied by the presence of non-executive board members (Guenther et al., 2018; Kleinert et al., 2020). Signori and Vismara (2018) test whether the reliance on this indicator of social capital is sensible from the ex-post perspective, using evidence from the UK platform Crowdcube. They find that non-executive board members increase the chances of

[99] The study has provided evidence from three major German investment-based platforms (Companisto, Innovestment, and Seedmatch).

[100] For instance, media posts about the existing number of investors (selling history) can act as a 'social validation' for the crowdfunding campaign (Eisenbeiss et al., 2023, p. 2). The argument the authors have made can, to some extent, be interpreted as investors' reliance on signals originating from other investors, as discussed below.

[101] Diffusion of information via social media does not only occur on fundraisers' social media pages. Recent research has also shown that platforms play a central role in spreading the news about crowdfunding campaigns (Battisti et al., 2021). Moreover, information about crowdfunding offers can also be featured in traditional media (magazines, newspapers, TV shows). Barbi and Mattioli (2019) show that featuring campaigns in traditional media increases campaign success on the UK platform Crowdcube.

an SEO/M&A following a crowdfunding campaign, while they do not significantly influence a firm's likelihood of failure.

Some studies have even investigated regional social capital instead of individual social capital of fundraisers (Hasan et al., 2022; Lu et al., 2020). Interestingly, the latter studies have also revealed that the size of regional social capital matters for default likelihood on P2P lending platforms in the US and China.

As mentioned earlier, crowdfunding platforms have also experimented with various design features that enable the creation of social connections and networks on their portals. Such connections and networks are sometimes called internal social capital (Buttice et al., 2017; Colombo et al., 2015). For instance, the US P2P lending platform Prosper has allowed borrowers to create a friendship network by inviting their real-world connections to join them as either borrowers or lenders.[102] The size of the borrowers' network is then prominently displayed as part of the loan application. In addition, friends can assume several roles, making their connection to borrowers more robust and credible. Lin et al. (2013) have explored this platform feature by distinguishing between friends who belong to borrowers and lenders, as well as between lender-friends with and without a lending history on the platform. Furthermore, they have accounted for whether lender-friends bid on the loan in question. The authors have argued that the credibility of borrowers' connections should influence the signalling value of friends' networks. The empirical evidence has supported their predictions. Lenders are sensitive to the hierarchy of relationships on the platform, so borrowers with more credible connections are more successful in funding their loans and less likely to default. In a related study on the same platform, Freedman and Jin (2017) show that loans with friend endorsements perform better, but only if actual bids follow endorsements. In contrast, friend endorsements without bids perform worse than other loans. While lenders account for these differences, they are not fully reflected in their bidding decisions.[103]

In addition to social capital that is based on (verified) real-world connections, some lending-based platforms have allowed for the creation of affinity groups where borrowers (and lenders) self-select based on a shared affiliation with other members (such as profession, geography, university attended, military affiliation, ethnicity, etc.). Social ties between often anonymous group members do not necessarily exist outside the online environment (Ribeiro-Navarrete et al., 2022, p. 2389). Nevertheless, groups are expected to screen their members before they list their loan applications on the platform. Besides being asked to verify certain information (e.g., employment status), borrowers are expected to reveal additional soft information through closer interactions with other group members (Käfer, 2018, p. 17). The signalling role of affinity groups is not limited to ex-ante information

[102] Friendship connections on the platform are established via an email invitation, whereas individuals have to mutually recognise each other as friends (Freedman & Jin, 2017, p. 193).

[103] The authors calculate an internal rate of return (IRR) based on the interest rate determined in the auction process and ex-post defaults. They demonstrate that loans with friend endorsements without bids have lower IRRs, while loans with friend endorsements and bids have higher IRRs, compared to other loans (Freedman & Jin, 2017, pp. 202–203).

gathering and verification. As there might be some reputational spillovers within the group, borrowers are likely subject to peer pressure to repay the loan (Freedman & Jin, 2017, p. 186; Herzenstein et al., 2008, p. 13). According to Everett (2015, p. 19), groups are subject to star ratings, which drop if some of their members default, reducing their attractiveness to new members and the borrowing prospects of existing borrowers. Put differently, costly signals can be produced by 'embedding individual reputations within a community reputation' (Collier & Hampshire, 2010, p. 197).

Another important feature is that affinity groups are managed by a group lead who provides additional vetting (Herzenstein et al., 2008, p. 7). For instance, the lead verifies personal and financial information provided by the borrower, helps them prepare the loan application, and stimulates interest among prospective investors.[104] Given these roles, one can argue that the group is overtaking the role of a new intermediary, enabling a sort of relationship lending, typical in banking, instead of arm's length contracting that happens outside affinity groups (Everett, 2015, p. 25). In the early days of crowdfunding, the lead used to receive a reward for each new loan funded. Members of the affinity group and the group lead can additionally endorse borrowers by posting a message on their page or pledging their funds, which is visible to other lenders on the platform (Freedman & Jin, 2017, p. 186).

Four interrelated studies examine the signalling value of membership in affinity groups using data from the US P2P lending platform Prosper while still running the auction mechanism (Faia & Paiella, 2017; Freedman & Jin, 2017; Herzenstein et al., 2008; Hildebrand et al., 2010). Their evidence consistently finds a significant and positive effect of belonging to an affinity group on the likelihood of loan funding or obtaining a lower interest rate. Freedman and Jin (2017) and Hildebrand et al. (2010) have additionally looked into the credibility of this signal type under different circumstances, providing contrasting evidence.

An early study by Hildebrand et al. (2010) shows that borrowers belonging to an affinity group have lower default probabilities. However, when the group lead is compensated for their engagement, participation in a group does not always warrant the desirable ex-post performance, and investors seem to recognise that the signal is weakened in such instances. Groups in which the lead is rewarded are less likely to succeed, pay higher interest rates, and are more likely to default than groups without rewards.[105] Interestingly, even in groups where a lead earns a reward, bidding their resources has a countervailing effect on the probability of default. The study shows that having 'skin in the game' improves screening incentives of a group lead and reduces default likelihood.

[104] Since the group lead is expected to know the potential borrower from other contexts, he has additional means of collecting information relevant to the repayment ability (e.g., interviews, on-site visits, contacting the employer, etc.) (Freedman & Jin, 2017, p. 193).

[105] According to the study, Prosper introduced the change to a non-reward system in late 2007 (Hildebrand et al., 2010, p. 3).

In contrast to these results, a later study by Freedman and Jin (2017) demonstrates that group membership is associated with worse loan outcomes, even though groups in which the lead is not rewarded performed significantly better. Moreover, groups have significant heterogeneity regarding their ability to screen and monitor borrowers. Smaller groups, groups with a higher portion of lenders as opposed to borrowers, and groups with stronger offline connections have a lower likelihood of default. Still, these characteristics are not fully priced when bidding on the interest rate. In other words, while some groups appear to bring additional information about borrowers' creditworthiness, lenders do not appear to be able to identify such groups.

Overall, crowd investors are predominantly responsive to fundraisers' characteristics: individual and the team's human and social capital. It is worth emphasising that different studies show that social networks play a vital role in signalling fundraisers' quality. Crowdfunding platforms have designed different mechanisms that make them noticeable to the crowd, while some social networks do not even exist outside crowdfunding portals. Yet, the credibility of signals embedded in fundraisers' characteristics is rarely tested. Some limited evidence suggests that social networks that do not necessarily exist in the 'offline world' are not always credible and can even be misleading. At the same time, investors' ability to recognise it is not warranted.

Venture Characteristics

Signals in crowdfunding exist beyond the characteristics of fundraisers and can be directly attributed to the characteristics of a venture in crowdfunding for businesses. The most important signals examined in the crowdfunding literature include the percentage of retained equity, intellectual property, and shareholder rights.

The percentage of equity retained by company founders is considered one of the most well-known signals in entrepreneurial finance (Leland & Pyle, 1977).[106] The idea is that founders' high equity share indicates that they have positive private information about the quality of a project. Moreover, their financial commitment creates incentives to hold on to their declared intent to perform well. In contrast, founders offering a large portion of equity might attempt to shift the risk of potential losses to external investors (Ralcheva & Roosenboom, 2020, pp. 41–42). Evidence from equity crowdfunding literature primarily suggests that investors praise ventures with high equity stakes of their founders in Australia, Italy, and the UK (Ahlers et al., 2015; Battaglia et al., 2022; Cumming, Johan, & Zhang, 2019; Nitani & Riding, 2017; Pattanapanyasat, 2021; Ralcheva & Roosenboom, 2020; Vismara, 2016, 2019).

Studies examining the credibility of this quality signal provide mixed findings. Evidence is not consistent across two studies examining the performance of

[106] An equivalent indicator used in empirical studies is the percentage of equity offered.

ventures raising funds on the UK platform Crowdcube (Cumming, Meoli, & Vismara, 2019; Signori & Vismara, 2018). Signori and Vismara (2018) document that retaining more equity does not significantly influence the pursuit of an SEO/ M&A nor the probability of failure of crowdfunding firms. In contrast, Cumming, Meoli, and Vismara (2019) show that equity retention increases the prospects of long-run success and reduces the chances of failure.[107] Evidence from the German platform Companisto has even indicated that equity retention can be a misleading signal. According to Reichenbach and Walther (2021), firms that offer more equity have a higher probability of survival. However, the authors have argued that this is likely because instruments intermediated on German platforms are not plain equity shares but rather participatory loans (*partiarische Darlehen*), which do not affect the voting rights of founders (Reichenbach & Walther, 2021, p. 19).

The importance of intellectual property (IP) signals, similar to retained equity, stems from the fact that (equity) crowdfunding is primarily used as a means of financing corporate growth and innovation (Hornuf & Schwienbacher, 2016, p. 382). However, as discussed above, disclosing details of a groundbreaking idea can impose proprietary costs on fundraisers. Moreover, investors on crowdfunding platforms can face high information-processing costs concerning the technical aspects of a project that has yet to be realised. For this reason, entrepreneurs have to demonstrate their innovative capacity via other means. The most commonly used proxy of intellectual property is whether a venture holds patents or trademarks. Formally recognised IP rights are expected to signal a venture's innovation potential and protect the idea from misappropriation when disclosed to many anonymous individuals (Ralcheva & Roosenboom, 2020, p. 42). IP rights are also expected to generate a sustainable competitive advantage that can be exploited in the development of the commercial value of a product.[108] The existing studies on crowdfunding have also used other proxies of IP (e.g., awards, grants, and expenditures on research and development (R&D)).

However, the evidence is inconsistent on whether IP indicators are perceived as signals of venture quality. Two related studies examining investor behaviour on the Australian platform ASSOB have not found a statistically significant influence of awards, grants, or granted patents on the success prospects of campaigns (Ahlers et al., 2015; Guenther et al., 2018). Similarly, investors on various German platforms are predominantly unresponsive to IP rights, as documented by Hornuf and Schwienbacher (2018a, 2018b).

Evidence from the UK market is mixed. Patents and trademarks are not found to be a significant predictor of campaign success in several studies examining data from platforms Crowdcube and Seedrs (Cumming, Johan, & Zhang, 2019; Kleinert

[107] The long-run success is captured by a proxy indicating whether the venture attracted further funding or offered an exit opportunity to crowd investors via an IPO or M&A following a successful crowdfunding campaign (Cumming, Johan, & Zhang, 2019, p. 6).

[108] Existing literature has pointed out the challenge of disentangling the signalling function of IP rights from their economic function when studying their influence on VC investments (e.g., Hoenen et al., 2014).

et al., 2020; Ralcheva & Roosenboom, 2020; Vismara, 2018a). A study by Vismara (2018a) finds that, while patents are not related to campaign success, they attract sophisticated investors, that is, those who invest early in a campaign. In relation to this, Rossi et al. (2020) examine the role of platforms on three UK platforms: Syndicate Room, Crowdcube, and Seedrs. They find that patents only affect the campaign success on Syndicate Room. In contrast, consistent with other studies, patents do not attract pledges on Seedrs and Crowdcube. As discussed in greater detail below, Syndicate Room differs from the latter two platforms by requiring ventures to find a lead investor among VCs or business angels before launching a crowdfunding campaign (a so-called investor-led platform as opposed to an entrepreneur-led platform). Such a condition leads to the self-selection of ventures at the later stage of development. In the authors' view, this is the reason for contrasting findings. Patents are expected to play a more significant role in the capital raising of more mature firms (Rossi et al., 2020, p. 6).[109] Interestingly, the same study also examines evidence from the US market and finds no impact of patents on campaign success. The US data covers all equity platforms operating during the period under study.

In contrast, studies examining success drivers on Italian equity platforms show a positive influence of patents and R&D expenditures (Battaglia et al., 2022; Piva & Rossi-Lamastra, 2018).

Block et al. (2018, p. 14) contend that the lack of consistent evidence on the importance of IP rights for crowdfunding success has to do with the dubious nature of this signal. Namely, investors may be questioning why firms with granted IP rights have not secured financing via other (more traditional) means.[110] An alternative explanation is that the company value already reflects the market value of patents, whereas crowd investors may search for undervalued companies. Additionally, Hornuf, Schmitt, and Stenzhorn (2018, p. 340) have pointed out that companies hold patents of varying quality, whereas they differ in the capacity to explore and commercialise patents. In the authors' view, these features are not captured in the existing empirical research.

Three studies test the validity of IP signals in the UK and German markets. Two studies examining the post-offering performance of ventures raising funds on Crowdcube have provided inconsistent findings. While Signori and Vismara (2018) document that patents are associated with a higher likelihood of a post-campaign SEO/M&A, Cumming, Johan, and Zhang (2019) report that patents are not predictive of either long-run success or probability of failure. In a more comprehensive

[109] In sharp contrast to this view, Hoenen et al. (2014) have argued that the signalling value of patents should be the greatest for early-stage firms, exhibiting a diminishing marginal influence as firms become more mature. They have dealt with this issue in the context of VC financing.

[110] While Block et al. (2018) have not tested the effects of a firm holding IP rights on campaign prospects, they examine whether updates with specific content increase the chances of reaching the funding target. Interestingly, they find that updates about external certification (including, for instance, news about awards, patent applications, and patent approvals) negatively affect the success probability.

study covering both UK and German platforms, Hornuf, Klöhn, and Schilling (2018) found that IP rights (patents and trademarks) do not significantly influence the probability of failure.

Another signal group worth examining is the quality of corporate governance. As discussed before, asymmetric information in the crowdfunding market is also likely to give rise to agency problems in the relationship between investors and fundraisers (company founders and managers) (Jensen & Meckling, 1976). Absent adequate controls, investors are exposed to the risk of appropriation, self-dealing, and other means entrepreneurs can use to extract private benefits. Corporate governance theory studies how investors 'assure themselves of getting a return on their investment' (Shleifer & Vishny, 1997, p. 737). Put differently, it explains mechanisms that finance suppliers have at their disposal to discipline the company managers to act in their interest. The variation in the corporate governance mechanisms of crowdfunding firms primarily originates from platform-level rules, which will be studied in greater detail in the next chapter. Here, it is vital to understand whether investors perceive corporate governance protections as a signal of venture quality when fundraisers can choose between different corporate governance arrangements.[111]

The investigation of this issue is complex as it is poorly understood which governance mechanisms lead to selecting the most promising ventures. This is due to the fact that crowdfunding has features of both public and private markets, as discussed earlier (Cumming et al., 2021, p. 70). Moreover, from an entrepreneurial perspective, one of the main benefits of crowdfunding is that they do not relinquish as much control as with other forms of entrepreneurial finance (Hornuf et al., 2021, p. 1). Two necessary safeguards inherent in VC financing are missing in the crowdfunding context: staged financing and sitting on the board of directors of a financed company (Lin, 2017, p. 337). Staged financing incentivises both VCs to closely monitor the financial company and company founders to perform well and secure subsequent funding. The right to appoint one or more company directors also ensures tighter supervision and the ability to influence important decisions.[112] The lack of these safeguards exposes crowd investors to an even greater risk of post-campaign opportunism (Armour & Enriques, 2018, p. 264).

Investors' control over managerial decisions is typically exercised thanks to voting rights attached to their equity share and some special rights included in investment contracts (e.g., information rights, anti-dilution rights, rights in cases of follow-up funding, etc.). It is necessary to understand whether crowd investors appreciate these control rights when making an investment decision. Investors can perceive sound corporate governance mechanisms as a signalling device even though a dispersed ownership structure coupled with collective action problems

[111] One should note that fundraisers' selection of a particular platform which mandates governance rules can also be a self-selection mechanism signalling their intention to align their decisions with the interest of investors.

[112] VCs' rights to control over the investee company are often disproportionate to their equity stake (Lin, 2017, p. 337).

can prevent them from effectively monitoring managers (Cumming, Meoli, & Vismara, 2019, p. 2). Alternatively, investors may be unresponsive to a higher level of control rights, knowing that they will remain largely unused (Hornuf et al., 2021, p. 2).

Four studies have shed light on the importance of control and cash-flow rights in the context of crowdfunding in the UK and Germany (Cumming, Johan, & Zhang, 2019; Hornuf et al., 2021; Kleinert & Volkmann, 2019).

The study by Cumming, Meoli, and Vismara (2019) is unique in exploring a specific design feature of the UK platform Crowdcube. Fundraisers can opt for shares with or without voting rights (class A and class B shares), as well as for dual-class shares where there is an investment threshold below which no voting rights are assigned to prospective investors (Cumming, Meoli, & Vismara, 2019, p. 2). The authors examine the responsiveness of both retail and qualified investors to the separation between ownership and control, which is proxied by the ratio of voting to cash-flow rights of the controlling shareholder.[113] The difference between the two investor categories is that retail investors with their small investment tickets would usually fall below the threshold. In contrast, professional investors can pledge below or above the threshold, depending on the value they attach to corporate control. The study results have revealed that investors are sensitive to governance concerns. A higher separation between ownership and control lowers the probability of a campaign success. Moreover, a significant portion of professional investors pledge just above the threshold, suggesting that they particularly value the ability to exercise corporate control. The study by Kleinert and Volkmann (2019) points to a similar conclusion. They investigate the relevance of discussion boards and their different topics for campaign outcomes on Crowdcube. The authors report that discussions about shareholder rights and concerns about the possible dilution of shares undermine the prospects of successful funding.

Contrasting evidence has been documented in the German market, characterised by another unique feature. As mentioned, crowdfunding platforms typically intermediate investments in hybrid instruments such as profit-participating loans due to costly notary requirements associated with common equity transfers. While, by the very definition, no voting rights are attached to such instruments, additional control rights can be granted via contractual clauses. Hornuf et al. (2021, p. 5) point out that these may include 'information rights, rights relating to follow-on funding and dilution rights, and protection against opportunistic behaviour'. Their study covering campaigns run on 19 different German platforms also examines exit rights as a stand-alone category. The latter allows investors to force an exit or grant them a

[113] Voting rights of fundraisers, which remain the controlling shareholder, depend on how much voting rights they give away by setting the threshold above which investors are entitled to voting rights shares. Cash flow rights are determined by the percentage of equity offered in the campaign. The underlying assumption is that the greater the divergence between voting and cash-flow rights, the stronger the potential corporate governance concerns (Cumming, Meoli, & Vismara, 2019, p. 4).

higher priority in the event of a liquidation.[114] Neither control nor exit rights are found to significantly affect the campaign success rate.[115] The authors interpret these results as investors' awareness that they will remain largely unused. An alternative explanation is that most crowd investors in Germany benefit from a redemption clause, allowing them to sell back their securities to entrepreneurs before the company's remaining value is lost. This strong disciplining tool makes other control and exit rights less important (Hornuf et al., 2021, p. 12).

It is also important to investigate whether control rights predict the ex-post performance of funded companies. The analysis is more complex as two plausible explanations exist for this relationship. As stated above, the first explanation is that providing investors with a higher level of control serves as a credible signal of fundraisers' claimed intentions to maximise shareholder value. The second one is that investors effectively exercise their rights, so there is little room for managerial opportunism. Alternatively, it can be the mere threat of using control rights that disciplines managers not to pursue their self-interest. From an empirical point of view, it is challenging to delineate which of the two mechanisms is captured. Existing studies have generated mixed results.

Two studies that use evidence from the UK platform Crowdcube provide conflicting findings, although using different indicators. An earlier study by Signori and Vismara (2018) merely distinguishes between class shares with and without voting rights, notwithstanding the case of dual-class shares. Their findings indicate that voting rights are a misleading signal. Offering voting rights (which corresponds to three-fourths of companies in the sample) is associated with a lower likelihood of SEO/M&As and a higher likelihood of a firm's failure. As explained earlier, the above study by Cumming, Johan, and Zhang (2019) uses a more subtle indicator of separation between ownership and control which captures the degree of divergence from the one share one vote rule. Their results indicate that lower levels of separation lead to greater post-offering long-run success.[116]

In Germany, investors' unresponsiveness to the level of control rights appears justified when examining ex-post performance. Hornuf et al. (2021) have not found evidence that these rights predict the likelihood of failure. Nevertheless, greater exit rights are found to negatively affect the survival rates of financed companies, even though they do not significantly affect investors' pledging

[114] More specifically, the authors examine variations in 'rights related to redemption, transferability, and insolvency' (Hornuf et al., 2021, p. 5).

[115] Interestingly, the authors find that contractual rights impact how entrepreneurs value their offerings. While exit rights increase the price of offerings, control rights are associated with lower offering price. In contrast to the conjecture that control rights signal fundraisers' determination to act in the interest of shareholders, the authors contend that higher control rights signal a higher degree of agency concerns in ventures (Hornuf et al., 2021, p. 9).

[116] The long-run success of a venture is captured by whether a firm failed following the crowdfunding offering (e.g., in case of insolvency or liquidation), as well as whether it attracted further equity capital or offered an exit opportunity to crowd investors via an IPO or M&A (Cumming, Johan, & Zhang, 2019, p. 3).

behaviour. The explanation is that exit rights allow investors to force repayment in their own interest, even if it undermines the company's long-term perspective (Hornuf et al., 2021, p. 10).

Overall, the evidence on the effects of venture characteristics generates mixed results regarding investors' responsiveness to them and their credibility as signals. Retained equity is a signal that investors are mainly responsive to. However, its credibility is not granted, given the conflicting findings in the existing research on its relationship with the long-run success of funded firms. Signals related to IP weakly attract crowd investors in Australia, the UK, the US, and Germany, in contrast to investors on Italian platforms. Interestingly, similarly to retained equity, current studies do not provide enough evidence that this signal should be trusted in terms of its influence on the survival prospects of a funded company. Signals related to the quality of corporate governance are specific because it is not entirely clear which corporate governance arrangements work best in crowdfunding. Investors may not appreciate a stronger level of corporate rights if they think they will remain largely unused. Nevertheless, empirical research shows that investors in the UK market are responsive to corporate governance safeguards. Conversely, German investors are not attracted to a higher level of protection in investment contracts, which can also be due to the hybrid nature of instruments sold, which do not grant voting rights. As to the other two signal types examined, no consistent evidence exists that corporate governance rights boost post-offering outcomes.

Signals Emanating from Other Investors

While previous signals originated from fundraisers, crowdfunding literature has also investigated signals from other investors (third-party signals). Put simply, the pledging behaviour of other investors is sometimes an effective means of disseminating private information about a venture or the personal characteristics of fundraisers. Other than possessing a private source of information, other investors can have superior knowledge and skill sets to estimate an investment opportunity. Information economics literature often refers to third-party signalling as certification, which entails that a third party bears costs if the 'certifying target', an individual or a venture, is of a low quality (Booth & Smith, 1986; Kleinert et al., 2020, p. 342). The costs of a certifier can stem from low returns or the loss of reputation when affiliating with dubious fundraisers.[117]

[117] Since ensuring quality that passes the criteria of a certifier should also be costly for fundraisers, it is worthwhile examining investors' signalling under the conceptual umbrella of information unravelling by fundraisers. The costs of third-party signalling for the fundraiser sometimes entail selling financial instruments at a discount. The concept of certification was first developed in financial markets to describe the role of underwriters in ensuring that the price of offerings reflects available inside information (Booth & Smith, 1986).

Third-party signals in crowdfunding sometimes emanate from successive investments of a group of often anonymous individuals (known as information cascades, herding, 'following the crowd' phenomenon, or the 'bandwagon effect') or a significant pledge made by one or a few knowledgeable and skilled individuals. In the latter case, such investors are sometimes formally assigned the role of a lead investor.

Information Cascades (Herding)

Information cascades explain why, in sequential decision-making such as crowdfunding investments, individuals tend to rely on prior investments as guidance for their own investment decisions. Therein, they possibly ignore their own information or do not interpret fundraisers' signals (Bikhchandani et al., 1992).[118] Imitating other people's behaviour can mean 'drawing rational inferences from limited information' (Easley & Kleinberg, 2010, p. 484). Put differently, even though subsequent investors cannot directly observe the private information of early investors, they can assume that early investors possess such information based on their decision to pledge.[119] The operation of crowdfunding platforms and social media has

[118] Information cascades should not be confused with the notion of 'wisdom of the crowd', which refers to collective wisdom achieved through a statistical aggregation of many dispersed opinions. Surowiecki (2005) coined this term to describe independent decision-making by many individuals who jointly possess greater knowledge than any person does individually. Consequently, under certain conditions, the outcomes of such collective intelligence can be superior to a choice or estimates made by any given individual (Budescu & Chen, 2015). Information cascades, or herding, imply precisely the opposite: 'abandonment of screening' by individual investors and reliance on the judgement of others (Käfer, 2018, p. 20). If one were to assume that information cascades do not occur in crowdfunding, it is questionable whether pooling many individual judgements into an aggregate estimate would generate 'crowds' wisdom'. One limiting factor, as identified outside the crowdfunding context (Palley & Soll, 2019), is when much information is shared among individual decision-makers, which is inherent in crowdfunding.

Interestingly, one South Korean P2P lending platform, Popfunding, experimented with its design to trigger a statistical aggregation of opinions from different lenders. According to Yum et al. (2012), the platform introduced a voting feature where lenders provide their estimate of whether each borrower will repay the loan. The answers to such a probabilistic question are then aggregated and made available to all lenders as additional guidance in their decision to pledge. The authors have provided evidence that the outcomes of the voting process are predictive of loan funding success. However, their results are not indicative of whether they are also predictable of loan defaults.

Information cascades or 'intentional herding' in crowdfunding also differ from what is usually called 'spurious herding'. The latter phenomenon is typically observed in stock markets where individuals make concurrent and similar investments based on the same information (e.g., reacting to company announcements indicating changes in fundamentals) (Zhang & Chen, 2017, pp. 45–46).

[119] The theory of herding was first developed by Banerjee (1992), who shows that decision-makers rationally rely on choices of those before them as they can reflect the information only available to first-comers. Yet, even rational herding can lead to inefficient outcomes if decision-makers systematically ignore the information that they possess. Welch (1992) further developed this idea in the context of IPOs, explaining how the favourable inclination of early investors can lead to the success of the offering of overpriced shares and vice versa. However, these models judge the effi-

fostered the occurrence of information cascades by enabling digital visibility of prior investors and their behaviour (Kim & Viswanathan, 2018, p. 3).[120] For this reason, investors in a crowdfunding campaign typically have more information about previous bids than investors in a traditional IPO setting, where they can simply distinguish between institutional and retail investors (Vismara, 2022, p. 1633). Similar to other e-commerce websites, some platforms have even provided a sorting option for existing campaigns based on popularity (Lee & Lee, 2012, pp. 495–496; Vismara, 2015, p. 3). Clearly, many crowdfunding investors also herd to minimise the costs of information acquisition and analysis (Luo & Lin, 2013).

'Following the crowd' or herding phenomenon can generate both efficient and inefficient outcomes, depending on the information set of early investors and the ability of subsequent investors to assess the quality of judgements of the former group. Herding can be efficient if those whose pledges trigger the cascade possess information otherwise unavailable to other ordinary investors or have stronger incentives or a greater ability to screen crowdfunding offers. If these conditions do not hold, especially if first bids are manipulated strategically (Käfer, 2018, p. 20, fn. 29), herding can generate inferior outcomes compared to every individual screening on their own.

Given that there are no professional analysts or underwriters on crowdfunding platforms similar to those on stock exchanges, some authors have even questioned the existence of a superior source of information among the crowd (Lee & Lee, 2012, p. 496). Others emphasise that it is the 'proximate knowledge' of investors gained through 'real-world connections' that is transferred to others when their investments are visible (Morse, 2015, p. 3). As mentioned earlier, social media networks and activity allow better visibility of such proximate knowledge.

Numerous studies examining individual campaign dynamics document that early investments are considered signals in both lending based (Caglayan et al., 2021; Ceyhan et al., 2011; Chen et al., 2015; Herzenstein, Dholakia, & Andrews, 2011; Jiang, Xu, et al., 2018; Kim, 2019; Lee & Lee, 2012; Zhang & Chen, 2017; Zhang & Liu, 2012) and equity-based crowdfunding (Agrawal et al., 2015; Astebro et al., 2019; Goethner et al., 2021; Hornuf & Schwienbacher, 2018b; Kim & Viswanathan, 2018; Lukkarinen et al., 2016; Meoli & Vismara, 2021;Vismara,

ciency of herding by comparing it to a perfect aggregation of judgements by individual investors or even their joint assessment. Yet, in crowdfunding, it is questionable to what extent individual investors would systematically use the information they own, even if they could not rely on decisions of prior investors. As discussed earlier, information acquisition and information processing costs are likely to restrain their efforts to do their own valuations. For a review of the theory of herding in financial economics, see Devenow and Welch (1996).

[120] Information cascades are not the only rational reason individuals can decide to follow the behaviour of the crowd. Another is when one receives a direct benefit from aligning their behaviour with the behaviour of others (network effects) (Easley & Kleinberg, 2010, p. 485). In crowdfunding, this can occur, for instance, when investors want to invest in projects for which they are confident they will reach their funding goal. Ceyhan et al. (2011) find evidence of a concentration in bids in P2P lending campaigns towards the end, suggesting that lenders care about the loan being fully funded.

2018a; Vulkan et al., 2016). Empirical evidence from various jurisdictions is consistent: campaigns that attract bids early have higher chances of reaching their target amount or obtaining lower interest rates in P2P lending with an auction mechanism. Early contributions are associated with better campaign outcomes even when happening 'behind closed doors', in a hidden campaign phase during which fundraisers collect contributions from their private networks (Lukkarinen et al., 2016). Interestingly, one study has also found that herding is even more pronounced among investors with more experience on the platform, which the authors interpret as investors' learning about how to use social information about fundraisers (Caglayan et al., 2021, p. 35).

Nevertheless, the evidence on the credibility of signals emanating from crowd investors is mixed, while studies have used at least four different approaches. The first approach entails testing directly whether crowd participation in a campaign is associated with better ex-post performance of fundraisers. An early study by Herzenstein, Dholakia, and Andrews (2011) examines strategic herding in the US P2P market using data from Prosper.[121] They show that loan applications with more bids also perform better ex-post. Contrasting evidence is found in the Chinese P2P lending market. Chen et al. (2015) conduct an early study on herding on one of the biggest Chinese platforms, Ppdai. They show that the total number of bids is associated with an increased default rate, suggesting this signal is misleading. In a later study, Kim (2019) criticises using the total number of bids as an overly simplistic indicator of herding[122] and proposes using bidding momentum as a more appropriate approach.[123] Using data from one of the leading P2P platforms in South Korea, Moneyauction, the authors show that bidding momentum is negatively related to default rates.

The other three approaches investigate whether the herding of crowd investors is rational depending on whom the signal originates from, campaign listing attributes, and campaign dynamics. These studies also bring evidence of the credibility of a signal embedded in early investments, given that the two concepts are closely intertwined. While pledging behaviour at the beginning of a campaign can be informative about fundraisers' quality, follow-on investors must be able to identify a superior source of information among the crowd. Rational herding implies that investors can differentiate between credible, non-credible, or misleading signals embedded in early investments. Consequently, their accuracy in

[121] They use the term strategic as their results show that the existing number of bids increases the chances of receiving additional bids up to the point the loan is fully funded. This suggests that subsequent investors are unwilling to offer a lower interest rate to win the auction (Herzenstein, Dholakia, & Andrews, 2011, p. 28).

[122] The argument is that the variable number of bidders mediates the effect of other borrower's characteristics, such as credit scores and the amount requested (Kim, 2019, p. 129).

[123] Bidding momentum is an indicator of an 'accelerating bidding pattern over time', and it depends on the bidding time of each lender, the number of cumulative lenders preceding the bidding decision, and the total number of investors at the end of a campaign (Kim, 2019, p. 128).

selecting good from bad fundraisers is improved (Dambanemuya et al., 2023, p. 2).

The second approach is based on the premise that herding is rational when triggered by pledges of knowledgeable and skilled individuals. As it has been argued outside the crowdfunding context, the quality of statistical aggregation of opinions within a group depends on the relative contribution of experts to the group's performance (Budescu & Chen, 2015). In other words, the crowd will outperform individuals if investors who take the lead and influence the collective decision-making also have superior knowledge and skills to assess an investment opportunity.

It is, thus, necessary for such knowledge and skills to become visible to subsequent investors. For this reason, two studies on the UK equity crowdfunding market have explored a feature allowing (early) investors to decide to make their profiles public in a crowdfunding campaign (Vismara, 2018a; Vulkan et al., 2016). These public profiles can include investors' locations, short biographies, the amounts invested in previous campaigns, and links to their social media and other relevant pages (Vulkan et al., 2016, p. 40). Based on the evidence from the platform Seedrs, Vulkan et al. (2016) do not find that the share of investors with public profiles significantly influences campaign success. However, they find that participation of investors who fall within 1% of the biggest investors on the platform, as captured by the average value of their pledges in previous campaigns, increases campaign prospects. These investors are expected to be more sophisticated than other investors in the crowd. The study by Vismara (2018a) provides a more profound investigation of the importance of early investors' expertise on the platform Crowdcube. Instead of controlling for the share of investors with public profiles, the authors have compared the influence of investors with and without a public profile on individual campaign dynamics. The study results reveal that investors with a known identity strongly influence early pledges, which, in turn, attract subsequent ones. In addition, investors with revealed profiles are also found to be better educated, have more industry-related experience, and have more experience investing on the platform than an average investor. Thus, crowd investors appear to be mindful of the screening capacities of investors whose behaviour they mimic on the platform, supporting the idea of rational herding.[124]

In a related study, Kim and Viswanathan (2018) examine the rationality of herding by identifying the presence of 'the experts in the crowd' on the US platform Appbackr. The platform has specialised in funding the development of mobile applications, either in their conceptual stage of development or once they have already gone live.[125] The authors investigate whether experts among the crowd

[124] However, the authors acknowledge that making one's profile public by posting links to social networks can act as a marketing channel for a crowdfunding campaign. It can increase the pool of prospective investors besides triggering information cascades (Vismara, 2018a, p. 5).

[125] The platform intermediates hybrid instruments that resemble revenue sharing. Investors get a fixed proportion of the revenue generated by selling the application that they previously financed, conditional on the application being sold (Kim & Viswanathan, 2018, p. 14).

disproportionately influence subsequent pledges of other investors compared to 'non-experts'. In addition, they examine whether experts' investments have a superior ex-post performance. In contrast to traditional financial markets, experts in crowdfunding are usually not individuals with specific educational backgrounds or those affiliated with reputed employers or organisations. Instead, the authors have identified two groups of uncertified experts—those with application development expertise who are thought to know the product well and those with investment expertise who are expected to assess market developments well. Their results indicate that not only does the crowd follow the lead of expert investors, but it also differentiates between the two types of expertise. Namely, the application development expertise of early investors serves as an important signal when it comes to applications in the conceptual stage. In contrast, their investment expertise primarily influences the financing of applications that have already gone live. Similarly, the results have revealed that early investments of experts are a credible signal of venture quality ex-post since it is positively associated with subsequent sales of applications.

Instead of differentiating between experts and non-experts in the crowd, two studies have explored the design feature of the Chinese P2P lending platform Renrendai, which provides for both manual and automated bids (Jiang, Xu, et al., 2018; Zhang & Chen, 2017). The platform system automatically allocates a certain amount of funds to loans that meet the investor's pre-determined investment criteria. The type of previous bids for each loan (manual or automated) is visible to prospective lenders. The underlying assumption of both studies is that only manual bids can be based on superior private information, suggesting that rational lenders should only mimic investments made by manual bidders. The study by Jiang, Xu, et al. (2018) documents that automatic bidding reduced the herding effect overall, suggesting that herding is rational. The study by Zhang and Chen (2017) has revealed more nuanced results. It shows that investors follow both manual and automated bids, indicating a mixture of rational and irrational behaviour. Interestingly, rational herding becomes more frequent than irrational when loans have poor credit grades, possibly indicating that, in the eyes of crowdfunding investors, private information plays a greater role in such loans. Put differently, early bids by humans are considered a more robust signal when conventional credit information is lacking.

Some limited evidence on the rationality of herding in the German crowdfunding market can be found in the study by Goethner et al. (2021). One particularity of this study is that the authors do not question the rationality of herding but rather examine whether different investor types exhibit differences in their investment behaviour. Nevertheless, they implicitly assume the rationality of herding by only testing the investors' response to pledges of sophisticated investors. In contrast to prevailing evidence, they find that (rational) herding does not occur on the platform Companisto. One possible interpretation of such results is that the platform runs a 'first-come, first-served' model in which investments are not allowed once the total amount collected surpasses a pre-defined limit.[126] Consequently, investors who free-ride on the due diligence of others can miss out on some investment opportunities. However, they also find that one investor type—crowd enthusiasts are prone to (rational) herding. The authors offer two plausible explanations (Goethner et al., 2021, p. 914). The first one is that crowd enthusiasts tend to invest in the most innovative projects, which are highly uncertain and where the judgement of sophisticated investors matters the most. The second contrasting one is that, rather than appreciating the information embedded in earlier pledges, crowd enthusiasts potentially want to become part of a larger community.

A third approach involves investigating whether campaign listing attributes moderate herding. Zhang and Liu (2012) argue that rational herding implies that, instead of passively mimicking the behaviour of others on the platform, investors also consider observable borrowers' characteristics. In the authors' view, 'active observational learning' assumes that the stronger the apparent weaknesses of the borrower's application (e.g., poor credit rates, high debt-to-income ratio), the stronger the effect of the current funding on subsequent investments. The explanation is that prospective investors infer that early investors who pledged despite borrowers' unfavourable characteristics possess positive private information about them. In contrast, the stronger the apparent signs of creditworthiness (e.g., friends' endorsements), the weaker the attraction of prior investments. Again, the intuition is that early investments were driven by publicly observable positive characteristics, thus reducing their informativeness for prospective lenders. Using data from the US platform Prosper, Zhang and Liu (2012) provide support for their hypothesis that borrowers' traits moderate the herding effect. Moreover, well-funded projects are also found to have a lower likelihood of default, suggesting that herding is efficient in the P2P lending market.[127]

A fourth approach proposed by Astebro et al. (2019) assumes that the fundamental difference between irrational and rational herding is whether investors react only to the cumulative amount invested before they decide to pledge or, instead, consider the size of the most recent (individual) pledge and the time elapsed since the most recent pledge. Therefore, the authors are critical of the view that cumulative investment amounts can be used as an indicator of rational herding. Instead, they contend that naive investors only pay attention to cumulative amounts or a very good campaign start, ignoring any subsequent campaign dynamics and

[126] The funding limit is typically higher than the target limit, but it prevents fundraisers from collecting additional funds even in response to excess supply (Goethner et al., 2021, p. 908).

[127] Interestingly, the authors compare the outcomes of rational herding, which is in line with their theoretical predictions, with hypothetical irrational herding. The latter is a counterfactual funding outcome that would have occurred had the lenders ignored observable borrowers' characteristics when interpreting the importance of prior accumulated funding. This analysis shows that irrational herding is also informative about borrowers' default rates, but its predictive power is reduced compared to rational herding (Zhang & Liu, 2012, p. 29).

information being transmitted. In contrast, rational investors are reactive to the most recent pledge, which is assumed to capture all prior investment history for a given campaign (Astebro et al., 2019, p. 6). Using data from the UK equity platform Seedrs, they show that the last pledge matters for the next investor even after controlling for cumulated amounts previously invested, thus supporting the rational herding hypotheses. Hornuf and Schwienbacher (2018a) find similar evidence in the German equity crowdfunding market, using data from four major platforms (Companisto, Innovestment, United Equity, and Seedmatch). According to their study, investors' participation is driven by the size of prior individual investments. Investors tend to participate more when they observe significant individual pledges, notably because they are associated with more thorough due diligence (Hornuf & Schwienbacher, 2018b, p. 561). Moreover, investors are also influenced by campaign comments posted by other investors, which are likely to increase the salience of a campaign.

Despite prevalent evidence favouring rational herding, one specific feature of crowdfunding investments calls for greater caution, as Meoli and Vismara (2021) show in their study.[128] Investors on crowdfunding platforms typically benefit from withdrawal rights that allow them to cancel their participation in securities offerings or a loan agreement within a certain period, usually until the end of a campaign. The 'cooling-off period' is generally regulated by consumer law and applicable to all distance contracting. While withdrawal rights provide an additional reflection period during which investors can reconsider their decisions, it also leaves space for a strategic manipulation of early contributions. Meoli and Vismara (2021) examine to what extent these rights are exercised in light of a possible misuse of the information cascade mechanism. They find that a surprisingly large portion of pledges are withdrawn before the end of a campaign (around 10%), while this behaviour is particularly prominent among platform members.[129] The latter invested in about 60% of campaigns while withdrawing from 30%. Interestingly, pledges originating from platform members are found to have a substantial influence on subsequent investments. The authors have also documented that investments that were later withdrawn tend to concentrate among riskier offerings, which they interpret as a clue of strategic behaviour that aims to encourage the dynamics of otherwise unattractive ('cold') campaigns (Meoli & Vismara, 2021, p. 16).

Moreover, information cascades or herding are found to trigger another potentially undesired consequence in equity crowdfunding, that is, overfunding (Li et al.,

[128] The study reveals neither the platform nor the country which was used as a data source, presumably due to reputational concerns of the platform.

[129] Platform members include the management and the employees of the funding platform. The authors assume that platform members' interests are aligned with those of the platform, which earns revenues in the form of percentage fees of the total amount raised (Meoli & Vismara, 2021, p. 5).

2022).[130] The latter refers to a situation where the total amount of investments surpasses the funding target, but the fundraisers decide to keep all funds raised. Li et al. (2022, p. 2) have argued that overfunding is inefficient from both the investors' and society perspectives. They have raised concerns that entrepreneurs are unlikely to efficiently invest the funding surplus as it has not been foreseen in the original business plan. Moreover, the initial 'buzz' about some campaigns leading to overfunding also deprives some other promising but less salient projects of the necessary funding, leading to the inefficient allocation of resources. The evidence from their study focusing on the UK market has revealed that different features of herding, such as immaturity, intensity, and persistency, intensify the effect of the initial herd on overfunding.[131]

Overall, the signalling value of crowd participation must be taken with caution regarding potential manipulations, particularly those originating from platform members. Moreover, its positive effects on reducing information asymmetry should be weighed against possible allocative inefficiencies when herding also leads to overfunding.[132]

Lead Investors

Another related signal widely discussed in the equity crowdfunding literature is the involvement of a lead investor. It is worth noting that neither crowdfunding literature nor platforms always distinguish between the formal role of a lead investor and the co-investment of business angels or VCs alongside the crowd. For the analysis here, the notion of a lead investor will be understood broadly and encompasses the co-investments of sophisticated investors when crowd investors perceive them as professional endorsements that demonstrate venture quality.[133]

---

[130] The data source for the study is not revealed, other than mentioning that the equity crowdfunding platform is based in the UK.

[131] Immaturity entails that the initial herd develops in the earlier stages of a campaign. Intensity involves the number of investors mobilised during the herding's peak. Finally, persistency explains whether there has been consistent progress towards reaching the funding goal (Li et al., 2022, pp. 4–5).

[132] It is worth noting that interaction among investors does not boil down to the imitation of the investment behaviour of those thought to have a superior source of information. On the contrary, several studies document that the transmission of information among investors happens through an intensive exchange within investors' social networks, on social media pages, as well as on discussion boards of crowdfunding platforms (Freedman & Jin, 2017; Hervé et al., 2019; Kleinert & Volkmann, 2019). Some of the results indicate that investors are not simply attracted by the 'buzz' around certain campaigns but rather process the actual content of discussions.

[133] If one were to separate the notion of lead investors from (simple) co-investments by business angels and VC, key elements of distinction would include the size and the stage of investment, the number of different roles assumed, and compensation earned. For instance, Coakley and Lazos (2021, p. 375) have argued that the lead investor model is a more advanced version of a co-investment model. A standard co-investment model implies that professional investors invest at any stage of the campaign, typically pledge limited amounts and act as passive investors in the post-campaign stage. As shown above, pledges from knowledgeable and experienced individuals, when

The most common role of a lead investor is information vetting. In addition, a lead investor typically conducts business due diligence and assesses the investment opportunity on behalf of other investors. In some instances, a lead investor assumes several roles after the financing round to attenuate agency concerns or facilitate future financing rounds. These may include, for example, monitoring the progress of the project, providing investors with updates, or providing help to project founders as an external expert, which is typical for traditional angel investors or VC financing (e.g., business advice, networking opportunities, etc.). A lead investor with the most comprehensive role is the one who groups all investors into a syndicate, usually through an SPV, which invests directly in the venture. The lead investor then acts as a syndicate manager. The investor syndicate 'stands behind one powerful vote', representing all crowdfunding investments (Deschler, 2013, p. 1185). Overall, the scope of the lead investor's activities, the stage at which he gets involved, and whether he receives compensation largely depend on the platform's business model. In all cases, the size of the lead investor's contribution to the project affects the credibility of the signal.

In the UK, the participation of the lead investor is typically ensured before the campaign goes public. On so-called entrepreneur-led platforms (e.g., Seedrs and Crowdcube), entrepreneurs independently determine the conditions for raising finance (e.g., share price). After being admitted to the platform, their campaign operates in a private mode for a certain period, during which it is desirable to bring a lead investor on board. Their participation is seen as necessary to 'build momentum', 'raise the profile' of the campaign and 'provide validation' (Crowdcube) (Crowdcube, n.d.). In contrast, on platforms commonly denoted as investment-led platforms (e.g., Syndicate Room), the involvement of a lead investor is a prerequisite for a campaign listing. The role of a lead investor in these platforms is encompassing. That is, he directly negotiates the valuation of the company and other investment terms with entrepreneurs. The terms agreed between the fundraiser and the lead investors are mandatory for subsequent investments by the crowd.[134]

Ralcheva and Roosenboom (2020) and Kleinert et al. (2020) examine whether the fact that a firm secured external finance before launching a crowdfunding campaign increases crowdfunding success. Their definition of prior financing is broad enough to include investor types that are not formally assigned the role of a lead investor but can nevertheless 'send a strong signal of legitimacy and financial viability' of the venture (Ralcheva & Roosenboom, 2020, p. 42).[135] Using data from

recognised as such by the crowd, are found to drive campaign dynamics and trigger information cascades or herding.

[134] It is worth noting that this was not always the case. According to Coakley and Lazos (2021, p. 375), lead investors on Syndicate Room originally invested on preferential terms, but the platform changed this rule in November 2015, when all investments from a single campaign were pooled into an investment vehicle (nominee account), thus providing all investors with equal rights.

[135] The definition of external finance in the first study includes 'grants, business angels, angel networks, family offices, corporate investors, venture capital and/or private equity' (Ralcheva & Roosenboom, 2020, p. 44). In addition to these investor types, the second study includes prior

major entrepreneur-led platforms in the UK, Seeders and Crowdcube, their findings are consistent in that prior financing serves as a 'stamp of approval' that propels crowdfunding investments.[136] Yet, Kleinert et al. (2020, p. 342) acknowledge that, in addition to signalling, affiliation with some investors can bring benefits such as business advice or networking that could drive crowdfunding volumes. To delineate the two effects, the authors test whether the impact of prior financing changes with the venture's uncertainty level. By showing that prior financing matters more for less established (seed) companies, the authors have intended to ascertain that the signalling effect prevails in the crowdfunding market.[137]

Evidence from a related study by Wang et al. (2019) also indicates that there are considerable information flows between angel investors and the crowd, as well as among angel investors on an entrepreneur-led platform in the UK.[138] The study examines business angels who invest alongside crowd investors during a crowdfunding campaign and, thus, cannot be considered lead investors in the strict sense. A spike in angels' contributions during a crowdfunding campaign is associated with greater funding from both the crowd and other angels. This study also finds that angels' pledges have a higher effect on the investment behaviour of others in larger than in smaller campaigns. The explanation is that angels' high-concentration pledges in larger campaigns are more credible signals than their pledges in smaller campaigns. This is because such pledges are, by very definition, of more significant size and because it is harder for larger projects to reach their funding goal, thus generating higher opportunity costs for angels (Wang et al., 2019, p. 3).

The study by Rossi et al. (2020) is more encompassing in the sense that it compares fundraisers that appear on entrepreneur-led and investor-led platform models in the UK. They show that larger and more mature ventures self-select into the investor-led platform Syndicate Room, most probably due to the difficulty of ensuring the early participation of an angel investor or a VC. This study also finds that the average success rate of this platform is higher than that of its competitors running an entrepreneur-led model (Seedrs and Crowdcube).

Similarly to the UK, in China, a lead investor's involvement model depends much on the platform design. For instance, on some platforms, the lead investor

crowdfunding campaigns as a potential source of (external) entrepreneurial finance (Kleinert et al., 2020, p. 342).

[136] Given that equity crowdfunding is often used by startups, Ralcheva and Roosenboom (2020) have also documented that accelerator attendance is associated with campaign success. This is because accelerators are often founded and led by VCs and angel investors, who not only pre-select promising projects but also provide them with valuable guidance.

[137] Another interesting finding by Kleinert et al. (2020) is that investors praise the most when external financing originates from various investor types as well as when a company has successfully run a crowdfunding campaign.

[138] The name of the platform is not disclosed in the article due to a non-disclosure agreement, but the authors highlight that the platform runs a nominee structure (Wang et al., 2019, p. 3), which was first developed by Seedrs.

is selected from the crowd after the project is posted on the portal, conditional on being registered as an accredited (professional) investor (Chen et al., 2016, p. 4, 5). On such platforms, investors following the lead do not pay the lead a carry (Shen et al., 2020, p. 632),[139] and the lead investor decides independently on the level of engagement with the crowd. Li et al. (2016) explore the variation in the level of services the lead investor provides using data from the platform Dajiatou. Their results show that not only does the presence of a lead investor increase the likelihood of campaign success, but also their characteristics (e.g., providing identity information, investment experience) and behaviour (e.g., percentage of funds pledged, the number of comments on the project being financed made available to potential followers). Consistent evidence is found by Shen et al. (2020), who explore the data from the same platform. They also demonstrate that a lead investor's experience and proportion of funding committed positively affect the probability of reaching the funding goal, while the help offered to project founders (as self-reported by the lead) does not have an influence.

In contrast to the above studies, Chen and Ma (2023) put into question the assumption that the interests of the lead and crowd investors are always aligned. Their research context is different from other studies on the Chinese market as they study an investment-led platform, JD.com, where a lead investor assumes several functions concerning delegated monitoring. The participation of a lead investor is secured before a crowdfunding campaign. After the successful completion of a crowdfunding campaign, investments of all investors are pooled together into a fund, which is managed by the lead investor (Chen & Ma, 2023, p. 3). This study highlights that the relationship between lead and crowd investors can give rise to agency problems that investors may be aware of. The concentration of ownership in the hands of a lead investor can lead to insider ownership issues, in addition to typical agency problems between investors and company founders (managers). These include negotiating a better deal for themselves than what crowd investors get in case of follow-on investments, having an information advantage over others and the capacity to act upon it in their own interest, mispresenting company information ex-post to earn higher carried interests, etc. (Chen & Ma, 2023, p. 4). Concentration of ownership in the hands of the lead implies insufficient bargaining power of the crowd to negotiate contract terms that would limit their misconduct (Chen & Ma, 2023, p. 5). Contrary to other studies on the Chinese market, the results of this study show a negative association between a lead investor's ownership stake and crowd investors' daily and total contributions. Thus, they indicate that crowd investors perceive large pledges from a lead investor as a potential insider ownership threat. However, crowd investors' concerns seem attenuated when a lead investor has a

[139] Carried interest is a portion of profits earned by other investors following the lead (usually formally members of a syndicate of investors).

reputation[140] and a track record of competence.[141] Moreover, after the Chinese authorities had provided more regulatory clarity on a lead investor's fiduciary duties in 2015,[142] the negative effect of the lead's concentrated ownership on investors' pledges decreased.

In the US, a lead investor typically introduces the project to the platform. In one of the early studies on US equity crowdfunding, Agrawal et al. (2016, pp. 116–122) provide details on the role of lead investors on the platform AngelList, described as the biggest equity platform in the country. Like a typical VC financing, the lead—typically an angel investor—forms a syndicate of co-investors, allowing them to share the risk, diversify their portfolios, and invest under the same contract terms. Investors who follow the lead and whom the lead accepts to become part of the syndicate (known as backers) commit to investing in multiple deals selected by the lead.[143] As a reward for selecting ventures, their due diligence, and ongoing monitoring efforts, the lead investor charges a carry to their backers. In addition to 'skin in the game', the alignment of interests between the lead and its backers is facilitated through the platform's rules. Namely, the platform ensures that investors have access to standardised and verified information on the lead's reputation and past performance and introduces rules that mitigate the potential for a conflict of interest. The specifics of this research context are that only accredited investors were allowed to become backers on AngelList, while not all projects were syndicated. Drawing on insights from a traditional VC industry, Agrawal et al. (2016) assume that the more (physically) distant the investors are, the greater the information asymmetry. Consequently, they contend that the fact that distant investors are more frequently attracted to syndicated than to non-syndicated projects is evidence of the lead investor signalling.

Building on this work, Zhang, Hughes, et al. (2023) question whether a lead investor's human capital and reputation affect the syndicate's success in raising funds. In other words, they are interested in whether the credibility of lead investor's signalling depends on their personal characteristics. Using data from the same platform, AngelList, the authors demonstrate that a lead investor's specialised human capital (e.g., experience in investments, entrepreneurship, and advisory) is associated with better fundraising performance for their syndicate. In contrast, more general human capital (e.g., education and work experience) of a lead does not contribute to attracting

[140] Reputation and trustworthiness were proxied with a dummy variable indicating whether the lead investor 'is awarded 50 Best Venture Capital Firms in China' (Chen & Ma, 2023, p. 9).

[141] Competence was proxied with a dummy variable indicating whether the lead investor had successful exits with previous investments and a dummy variable indicating whether their expertise and prior investment experience belong to the same industry as the crowdfunding project (Chen & Ma, 2023, p. 9).

[142] The China Securities Regulatory Commission issued a Notice clarifying the regulatory framework applicable to equity crowdfunding, specifically, that a lead investor would be subject to private investment fund rules (Chen & Ma, 2023, p. 9).

[143] Nevertheless, individual investors keep the right to opt out from investments in specific ventures (Agrawal et al., 2016, p. 114).

funds. The study results also reveal that a lead investor's reputation mediates the effect of specialised human capital on funding success.[144] Zhang, Scholes, et al. (2023) contend that this is because it is easier for entrepreneurs with high human capital to gain a reputation on the platform.

In Germany, the involvement of a lead investor is not a common practice on crowdfunding platforms. However, fundraisers can provide information about support received from traditional resource providers—VCs and angel investors before running a crowdfunding campaign. Goethner et al. (2021) test whether advertising business or social ties to a VC or an angel investor on a project page affects investment decisions by different investor types (casual investors, crowd enthusiasts, and sophisticated investors). Using data from Companisto, they show that pledges of casual investors are positively affected by observing such information. In contrast, preexisting ties to a VC or an angel investor appear to discourage investments of sophisticated investors and crowd enthusiasts. Goethner et al. (2021, p. 913) argue that this is because sophisticated investors do their own due diligence and, thus, do not depend on the judgement of traditional investors, while crowd enthusiasts are more driven by supporting a project or a cause than making profits.[145]

The validity of a signal embedded in prior funding from traditional resource providers (including lead investors) has not been sufficiently tested. Scarce research has provided conflicting findings. Signori and Vismara (2018) demonstrate that none of the companies that initially received funds from qualified investors (angel investors or VCs) on the UK platform Crowdcube failed afterwards. In contrast to these findings, Hornuf, Klöhn, and Schilling (2018) report that the number of initial VC investors increases the likelihood of a firm failure, as shown in their study on both the German and UK markets. Surprisingly, they have also documented that the number of initial VC investors increases the chances of receiving follow-up funding from business angels or VCs. Following these studies, Reichenbach and Walther (2021) examine the post-offering success of companies raising funds on the German platform Companisto. They do not find a significant effect of the reputable investors' support.

In sum, the involvement of a lead investor is considered a strong signal across different jurisdictions and platforms, even though the meaning of a lead investor and their roles vary considerably. The validity of this signal has not been sufficiently tested, while rare studies on this matter generate contrasting results. As a side insight, the involvement of a lead raises the question of whether they invest under the same terms as crowd investors, as well as whether their high stake in a company can raise insider ownership issues.

---

[144] The lead investor's reputation is proxied by the number of limited partners that the lead investor co-invested with on the platform in the past (Zhang, Scholes, et al., 2023, p. 23).

[145] This explanation would be more plausible if investments of traditional resource providers had no effect on crowd enthusiasts and sophisticated investors, while it appears insufficient to explain the negative relationship found in their study.

Summary of Findings on Signalling

Signals play an essential role in communicating the quality of fundraisers in crowdfunding, serving either as substitutes or complements of full disclosures. They can sometimes replace full disclosures when disclosures are costly for fundraisers (such as when information is proprietary) or when investors have high information-processing costs when it comes to a high level of detail, as shown with regard to granular financial data. Alternatively, signals can strengthen the validity of disclosures when ex-ante verification is costly or impossible, such as in the case of soft information disclosures.

The investigation of signalling mechanisms in this section has focused more on equity crowdfunding than P2P lending, given that the evidence on the latter model is scarce. The focus of existing studies suggests that signalling plays a more significant role in entrepreneurial financing than in lending to individuals. The rationale lies in the indirect costs of disclosures for fundraisers, information-processing costs of investors, and soft, forward-looking information, which may be less relevant in the case of (individual) loans.[146]

The review of existing research shows that several unique features characterise the crowdfunding market. Firstly, crowd investors do not always appreciate characteristics that are considered well-established signals in traditional entrepreneurial finance. Sometimes, this may be because crowd investors do not always pay attention to nuances in signal strength (e.g., when they do not appreciate the value of industry-specific education or experience). In some instances, their unresponsiveness to signals appears justified when looking into the long-run prospects of funded firms. This is, surprisingly, the case with indicators of IP (e.g., patents, trademarks), which are not associated with better post-offering outcomes.

Secondly, in some instances, there is still uncertainty about what the credible signal is. As shown when discussing corporate governance protections, it is unclear whether class A shares and associated rights should be appreciated if crowd investors envisage that they would not be exercised.

Lastly, it has been shown that reliance on some signals has become almost a defining feature of crowdfunding investments. These include social capital, social media activity, and information cascades. As to social capital, the operation of crowdfunding markets appears to be highly intertwined with other segments of the platform economy, such as social networks (media). The size of fundraisers' social media networks and their social media activity can leverage additional (private) information about fundraisers or bring credibility to public information. Interestingly, crowdfunding platforms are places where additional social capital is created through various channels (e.g., affinity groups, running several crowdfunding campaigns, or acting as investors in campaigns run by other fundraisers). Social capital has been shown as an important signalling device across different crowdfunding models, including P2P lending. While

146 The lack of evidence on signalling in P2P business loans is likely a research gap.

the credibility of signals embedded in social capital has been insufficiently researched, some studies caution about social capital that does not exist in the 'offline world'.

Information cascades or herding are closely intertwined with social capital. They serve as a means of leveraging proximity knowledge about potential fundraisers. Contrary to a widely held view, existing research shows that information cascades in crowdfunding are usually beneficial in reducing information asymmetry. Several studies capture that investors can identify a superior source of information among the crowd. Nonetheless, in some instances, this signal has also been manipulated in relation to the right of investment withdrawal (cooling-off period).

3.5 Platforms as Gatekeepers

As discussed earlier, crowdfunding is often described as a form of disintermediated finance, that is, a marketplace allowing for a direct (almost automatic) matching of the funding interest between the two sides of the market. Nevertheless, platforms have devised several gatekeeping mechanisms to reduce information asymmetry between prospective contracting parties in their pursuit of market share. These mechanisms sometimes entail internalising screening, monitoring, and risk management functions that typically fall on investors. In other instances, platforms create rules for market participants, primarily fundraisers, which induce them to (credibly) reveal information or act in the interest of investors. Lastly, some platform mechanisms are intended to attenuate the consequences of information asymmetry. It is important to note that the mechanisms described in this section fall under private ordering or self-regulation (Katz, 1996; Ogus, 1995; Stefanadis, 2003).[147] In other words, platforms can deliberately decide to offer services above and beyond responsibilities prescribed by the regulator, thus self-regulating their behaviour (Ande & Eroglu, 2021, p. 559), as well as imposing rules on market participants.

From the lens of platform economics theory, platform gatekeeping can be understood as platform design features that allow for non-price competition on the market (Belleflamme & Peitz, 2021, pp. 125–130). Platforms are typically defined as two-sided markets in which the benefits enjoyed by one group or one side (investors, fundraisers) depend on the number and the quality of the other group or the other side (cross-side network effects) (Evans et al., 2011). Fundraisers value the platform more if there are higher chances of reaching their funding goal. Investors are attracted to those platforms that onboard high-quality fundraisers (Belleflamme & Lambert, 2016; Viotto da Cruz, 2015). Thus, to increase the strength of cross-side network effects, the platform has incentives to design features which alleviate

[147] It should be noted that private ordering or self-regulation sometimes has a narrower sense, i.e. the members of the same organisation or industry (e.g., sellers operating in the same industry or members of the same profession) jointly create rules to govern their behaviour. This type of private ordering or self-regulation in the context of crowdfunding is described in Chap. 4.

asymmetric information (hidden information and hidden action). Certain platform measures (such as prescribing a minimum quality standard or providing insurance against certain risks) can also benefit the selling side of the market (the fundraisers) since those that meet the quality standard can expect to sell their product under better terms (Belleflamme & Peitz, 2021, pp. 128–129).

From the lens of the theory of financial regulation, as already discussed in Chap. 2, gatekeepers are intermediaries that stand between issuers and investors. They control issuers' access to the market and protect investors by certifying or verifying issuers' information or quality (Moloney et al., 2015, pp. 256–259). On a general level, the use of a crowdfunding portal to raise funds from the public is a legal requirement in most jurisdictions that regulate crowdfunding. Nevertheless, crowdfunding platforms often independently determine rules that fundraisers need to adhere to if they want to be admitted for listing on their portal. These rules can entail not only providing credible information before the crowdfunding campaign but also governing fundraisers' behaviour ex-post (for instance, through the design of loan agreements or investment contracts). Fundraisers' unwillingness to comply with such rules typically results in platforms' refusal to list their campaigns. Platforms' role in evaluating and certifying fundraisers' quality often exceeds a simple decision to onboard, such as when the platform performs credit risk assessment or even makes investment decisions on investors' behalf.[148]

Yet, similar to traditional gatekeepers, the incentives and abilities of crowdfunding platforms to protect investors are not granted.[149] It is unknown whether the platform competition along non-price dimensions will lead to a 'race to the top', 'race to the bottom', or 'nowhere in particular' (Hornuf, Klöhn, & Schilling, 2018, pp. 520–522). In the absence of a gatekeeper liability, such as when gatekeeping obligations are imposed by regulations (Kraakman, 1986, p. 53), it is the platform's reputation that ensures that investors are protected from illicit or unpromising crowdfunding offers. Reputation capital of repeated players in the market is considered a necessary condition for gatekeepers to perform their tasks well.[150] Loss of

---

[148] The concept of gatekeepers summarised by Moloney et al. (2015) is sufficiently broad to encompass the variety of mechanisms platforms employ to reduce information asymmetry, which will be discussed in greater detail below. Yet, from the point of view of some other authors, not all services provided by the platform qualify as gatekeeping. For instance, Hornuf, Klöhn, and Schilling (2018, p. 511) have argued that crowdfunding platforms 'simultaneously serve as gatekeepers, information intermediaries, and drafters of contracts'. However, when channelling information from fundraisers to investors and mandating the contract terms between them, platforms effectively gatekeep the market from those fundraisers who don't want to disclose enough information or legally constrain the room for their misconduct ex-post. Thus, the term 'gatekeeper' in this section is used in the all-embracing sense proposed by (Moloney et al., 2015, pp. 256–259).

[149] The most well-known cases of corporate failures, such as Enron, are often attributed to the role of gatekeepers who failed to identify or expose financial irregularities and management misconduct. Similarly, inflated credit ratings of financial products such as mortgage-backed securities (MBS) provided by CRA are often deemed as one of the key factors leading to the global financial crisis (Moloney et al., 2015, pp. 260–261).

[150] In addition to reputation, gatekeepers can perform well when facing a litigation threat (Moloney et al., 2015, pp. 272–274). However, since gatekeeping obligations of crowdfunding platforms are

reputation has been proven ineffective in incentivising gatekeepers to perform well when there is a lack of competition in the market. The competition in the crowdfunding market might be constrained in the long run due to cross-side network effects explained earlier, which often lead to market concentration. Even without these factors, newly established crowdfunding platforms have yet to build a reputation. In other words, a possible erosion of reputation might not be an important factor for new or short-term oriented platforms. Finally, the quality of gatekeeping functions can be undermined in case of conflict of interest or agency costs (and moral hazard) (Moloney et al., 2015, pp. 260–275).

This section provides an overview of platform gatekeeping mechanisms, describing their variations across platforms and empirical evidence capturing their influence on crowdfunding market outcomes. It draws on the existing empirical literature, which is much less abundant than the literature on market-based mechanisms originating from fundraisers (as discussed in the previous section).

The discussion in this section will follow a chronological order in which gatekeeping services are performed. Some services are performed ex-ante, comprising due diligence, mandating disclosure requirements for fundraisers, credit assessment and pricing, and automated investments. Other services are performed ex-post, including delegated monitoring (repayments and loss recovery), designing and facilitating governance mechanisms for funded firms, operating secondary markets or provision funds. It is worth noting that some of these functionalities exist both in lending-based and equity-based crowdfunding, while others are, for the time being, at least, reserved for only one of the model types.

3.5.1 Due Diligence and Pre-selection of Fundraisers

External financing typically presupposes extensive due diligence to attenuate adverse selection. Due diligence involves a combination of information collection, verification, and assessment. Agrawal et al. (2016, p. 112) argue that due diligence costs may be sufficiently high even for angel investors and VCs, so 'many potentially value-creating deals never happen'. As discussed earlier, the costs of due diligence do not vary with the size of the investment, reducing incentives for many individual crowd investors to do it independently. The need to create a diversified portfolio and regulations that prescribe the maximum investment amount per crowdfunding offer can further attenuate investors' screening efforts. Moreover, the costs of collective action undermine investors' ability to share the effort necessary to evaluate different investment opportunities.

seldom fully defined in their contracts with investors, litigation is not an effective alternative for inducing platforms to prevent fundraisers' deception or misconduct. In addition, the probability of litigation against the platform is reduced due to a collective action problem among many crowd investors.

For this reason, financial-return platforms always perform some degree of screening of loans or projects to be listed on their websites. In doing so, platforms usually allow only a subset of fundraisers to start a crowdfunding campaign (platform pre-selection or onboarding). Platform due diligence can vary from merely ensuring that borrowers and entrepreneurs are not fraudulent, preventing high-risk loans or unpromising projects ('lemons') from being listed to picking only a subset of high-quality applications.[151] Equity-based platforms are known for being more selective than loan-based platforms when it comes to onboarding (Ziegler et al., 2019, pp. 38–39), as some lenders prefer high-risk/high-return investment opportunities.[152] However, there are important disparities among platforms belonging to each model. For instance, Schwartz (2018, pp. 932–934) has illustrated contrasting examples of two equity platforms in New Zealand. The platform Snowball Effect accepts only 2% of all applications. In contrast, the platform PledgeMe does not prevent any company from listing, subject to attending a multi-week course before the campaign launch.[153] Similarly, according to Cumming and Hornuf (2022, p. 41), German P2P business lending platform Zencap did not reject any loan applications during the observation period.[154] In contrast, some other lending platforms are very transparent about their listing requirements, rejecting borrowers whose credit score, debt-to-income ratio, and credit history do not meet pre-defined criteria.[155]

In conducting due diligence, platforms are driven primarily by their reputational concerns. As contended by Cumming, Johan, and Zhang (2019, p. 3), in their pursuit of revenue maximisation, platforms differentiate among themselves along three most important dimensions: fee structures, due diligence, and industry focus. Vismara (2022, p. 1631) has argued that platforms' selection of fundraisers is, to some extent, comparable to due diligence conducted by stock exchanges. Alternatively, the literature has noted that the platforms' role is to provide a certification effect similar to that of underwriters in traditional IPOs (Knyazeva & Ivanov, 2017, p. 14). However, platforms are usually not entirely free in their choice of an

[151] Vallee and Zeng (2019, p. 1945) denote these activities as prescreening on the extensive margin. In contrast, prescreening on the intensive margin assumes that fundraisers (borrowers) are assigned risk grades and subgrades, as will be discussed in greater detail below.

[152] As to platforms operating in Europe, Ziegler et al. (2019, pp. 38–39) have documented that the onboarding rate among equity platforms is 6%, while the campaign success rate is 83%. P2P business lending platforms are also selective, with onboarding and funding success rates of 17% and 83%, respectively. P2P consumer lending platforms accept 22% of all loan applications, with 29% being successfully funded.

[153] Nevertheless, only about half of all applications complete the course, allowing the platform to reconcile the principle of inclusiveness with project curation (Schwartz, 2018, pp. 933–934).

[154] In 2015, Zencap merged with the US-based platform Funding Circle, becoming a worldwide leading P2P lending platform focusing on SMEs in the UK, US, Germany, Spain, and the Netherlands (Cumming & Hornuf, 2022, p. 33).

[155] For instance, according to Gallo (2021, pp. 10–11), one of the leading US P2P lending platforms, Lending Club, does not accept loans from applicants with a FICO score below 600 and a debt-to-income ratio above 40% and a credit history of less than 3 years.

adequate due diligence level. Regulators sometimes impose on platforms the duty to perform some checks on the fundraisers and safeguard against fraud and ML/FT risks. Understanding the actual level of platform due diligence is one of the critical issues in crowdfunding since the mismatch between investors' expectations and platforms' efforts can pose a serious concern.

Moreover, it is important to understand whether investors are responsive to the platform's due diligence. The evidence on this question is scarce. The study by Cumming, Meoli, and Vismara (2019) has examined the disparity in screening efforts among 51 crowdfunding platforms in Canada between 2013–2017. The uniqueness of this study is that the sample encompasses crowdfunding with and without financial return (equity-based, loan-based, and reward-based crowdfunding). It should be mentioned that crowdfunding regulations mandate disclosure requirements for fundraisers and require crowdfunding platforms to vet all the documents before posting them on their portals (Cumming, Johan, & Zhang, 2019, p. 2). Yet, the authors have captured platform differences concerning 'background checks, site visits, credit checks, cross-checks, account monitoring, and third-party proof' (Cumming, Meoli, & Vismara, 2019, p. 3). They aimed to understand the factors driving these differences and investors' responsiveness to this kind of platform gatekeeping. Their results have indicated that larger platforms, as captured by the number of fundraisers and employees, and financial-return crowdfunding platforms (equity and lending) apply more encompassing due diligence. Due diligence efforts also increased following the legislative change. Moreover, the results have suggested that investors perceive more thorough due diligence as a desirable platform design feature. More specifically, a higher level of platform due diligence is associated with a higher probability of campaign success and higher overall amounts raised at the platform level.[156]

It is worth mentioning that some platforms leverage investor participation in the due diligence process before the project is admitted for listing or before the start of the campaign. For instance, the French platform WiSEED asks investors to disclose their non-binding interest in investing in a specific company. Their engagement with the company founders before the campaign allows them to provide feedback and rate projects. In their study on services provided by crowdfunding platforms in Europe, Rossi, and Vismara (2018, p. 101) denote the process of collecting 'pre-fundraising consensus by potential investors' as crowd-sourcing. However, their study has not found that platforms that offer this service are more likely to be successful, as measured by the total amount of funds raised annually.

[156] In a related paper, Rossi and Vismara (2018) investigate which platform services offered to fundraisers increase platform success. The authors have distinguished between pre-launch services, ongoing campaign services, and post-campaign services offered by investment-based platforms in Europe. While these services are aimed at fundraisers, some of the pre-launch services, such as helping prepare financial analysis, can qualify as due diligence in a broader sense. Interestingly, the overall level of pre-launch services offered to fundraisers does not contribute to platform success, in contrast to post-campaign services. Nevertheless, some individual pre-campaign services, such as helping fundraisers with financial analysis, increase the total amount of funds raised annually.

In addition, as discussed earlier, a more common practice of outsourcing due diligence occurs on investor-led platforms, which entails the formal involvement of a lead investor before the public campaign. Despite the significant advantages of this model that come with professional investors' expertise in screening, it is unclear whether lead investors are penalised in cases where they intentionally mislead investors or perform due diligence poorly (Chen et al., 2016, p. 15). Factors such as compensation scheme, the size of their investments, and their reputational capital are expected to affect the alignment of interests with crowd investors.

In sum, platform due diligence and pre-selection exhibit significant differences across platforms, including within the same models or model groups. The extent to which investors are responsive to this platform (reintermediation) service is under-researched, which may also depend on the regulatory context (for instance, whether there is an obligation to publish due diligence procedures or whether the regulator checks the adherence to promised due diligence standards). Due diligence standards may further vary when platforms design different outsourcing mechanisms, such as when engaging a professional (lead) investor.

3.5.2 *Imposing Disclosure Rules on Fundraisers*

As Meoli et al. (2022, p. 4) explain, 'platforms are responsible for the quality of information exchanged between entrepreneurs and investors'. Several other scholars emphasised that crowdfunding portals act as 'information intermediaries', providing investors with standardised information necessary to choose individual investment opportunities (Hornuf, Klöhn, & Schilling, 2018, p. 511; Vallee & Zeng, 2019, p. 1946).

Before discussing the scope of information provided to investors, it is vital to understand how information on fundraisers' characteristics and their loans or projects is produced in the first place, assuming that this is not regulated. Depending on the scope of their prescreening activities, platforms collect information from fundraisers and other sources to later distribute (a subset of) it to investors, or they mandate disclosure requirements for fundraisers. The latter involves specifying data points and the format in which they must be made public on a campaign webpage. For more sophisticated investors who develop their own algorithms to analyse crowdfunding offers, information is sometimes available via Application Programming Interfaces (APIs) (Vallee & Zeng, 2019, p. 1946).

The critical question is what level of information disclosure platforms choose when no disclosure duties stem from relevant regulations. This will typically be when issuers' disclosures are exempt from securities regulations, and no additional requirements are introduced by crowdfunding bespoke rules (such as the case in the UK or New Zealand). It should be noted that the question of information disclosures is equally relevant to lending-based platforms, even though it has rarely been discussed in the (legal) literature, as loans are not securities and thus often not within the remit of securities regulators.

The analysis of market-based practices in previous sections has illustrated that disclosure standards vary across different platforms. Different studies have shown that platforms also leave some room for fundraisers to decide on the level of information they reveal to prospective investors. Nonetheless, as discussed earlier, most studies have examined the variation in soft disclosures because platform-level rules often standardise the provision of hard information. However, crowdfunding literature has not yet provided a cross-platform comparison of platform disclosure requirements for fundraisers and how they affect platform success. In other words, it is unclear whether platforms tend to choose high or low disclosure standards (whether the selected level is efficient from a social welfare perspective) nor how they affect fundraisers' and investors' willingness to opt for a specific platform.

Therefore, some theoretical considerations can provide more clearance. As mentioned above, platforms are two-sided markets that use price and non-price strategies to bring both sides on board. Competition among platforms incentivises them to design disclosure rules to maximise the joint surplus of both sides of the market, as they earn a fixed fee from the total amount of funds raised (Belleflamme & Lambert, 2016; Viotto da Cruz, 2015). In this respect, platforms resemble traditional exchanges, which create and enforce listing and other requirements for issuers and traders (Santos & Scheinkman, 2001).[157] Yet, contrary to arguments by Mäschle (2012), platforms are not likely to maximise investor protection. The disclosure level will depend on direct and indirect fundraiser costs and the net benefits of higher disclosure standards for investors. The latter is contingent on increased (price) efficiency from more information and information-processing costs. While marginal costs of fundraisers increase with higher disclosure standards, net marginal benefits of investors decrease. As discussed earlier, if investors could coordinate or join their screening efforts, their information-processing costs would be lower, and thus, their net benefits from additional disclosures would be higher.[158] Presuming this is not the case (due to a collective action problem), the platform chooses the disclosure level where the marginal costs for fundraisers equal marginal net benefits for investors. This is not a socially optimal level of disclosure, but it is the 'second-best' solution without adequate mechanisms for investors to screen investment opportunities collectively. An illustration of the above analysis is provided in the Fig. 3.1.

The above analysis is based on the premise that platforms' rules are observable by market participants (Santos & Scheinkman, 2001, p. 1028), that platforms are neutral intermediaries, and that they incur no costs from additional disclosures. Yet, this is not always the case, particularly with respect to their due diligence

[157] Santos and Scheinkman (2001, p. 1028) argue that, when the quality of exchanges is observable, the competition induces them to choose the optimal amount of (margin) requirements, where the reduced risk of default is balanced against the higher costs incurred to ensure an extra layer of protection.

[158] If investors were able to coordinate their efforts, they would split due diligence efforts. Thus, the level of costs incurred by an individual investor would be lower than in a situation in which all of the costs of due diligence are incurred by each.

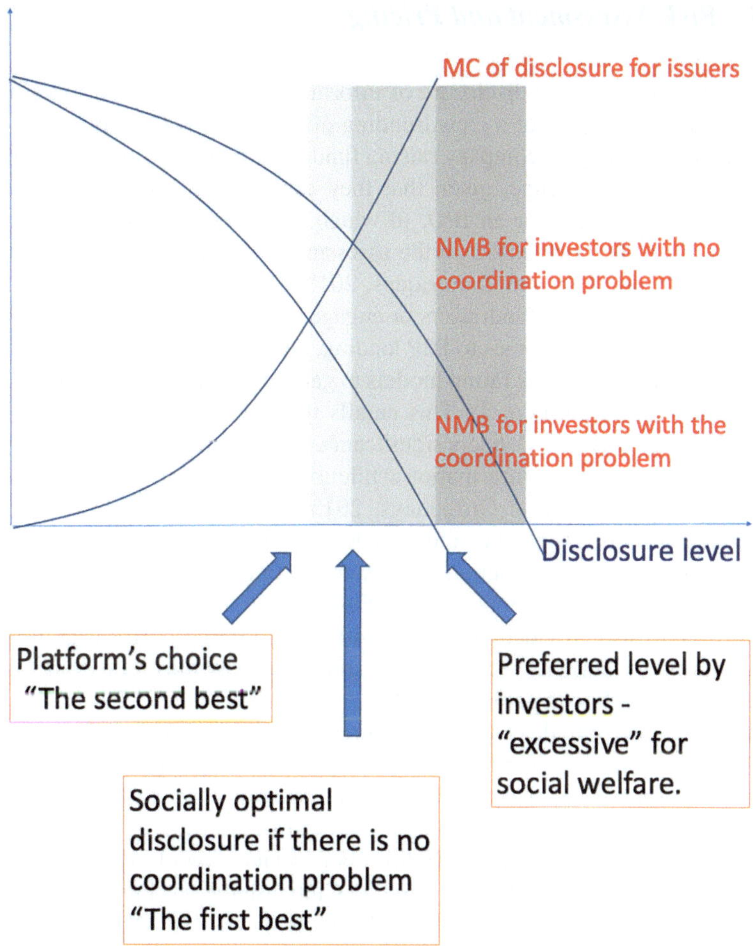

Fig. 3.1 The platform's choice of disclosure standards for fundraisers

(information verification) efforts. Thus, regulations that impose high information verification requirements on platforms can reduce their incentives to opt for an adequate level of disclosure.

Moreover, even in the absence of platform-related costs, it is unlikely that disclosure standards will be uniform across platforms. As explained earlier, the divergence of standards can be related to different fundraisers and investors appearing on platforms (e.g., firms of varying size, a higher/lower portion of sophisticated investors, and industry focus) and platform prescreening. Yet, given these differences, one may contend that universal disclosure standards are not necessarily optimal.

3.5.3 Risk Assessment and Pricing

Due diligence process and disclosure of information ultimately lead to estimating the risk and opportunities of a crowdfunding offer, which essentially means credit pricing and evaluating the company raising funds. For retail investors, price discovery is the biggest challenge, given that they cannot take advantage of a book-building process typical for an IPO, in which the investment bank acting as an underwriter sets the price based on the assessment of informed investors of what securities are worth (Armour & Enriques, 2018, pp. 261–262). Instead, investors face a fixed price offer by fundraisers or engage in the auction process.

Nevertheless, when it comes to P2P lending, an increasing number of platforms have introduced internal risk rating models to gauge the riskiness of individual loan applications (Gallo, 2021, p. 2). This entails that each loan is assigned a credit grade. Evidently, this saves lenders significant costs emerging from the necessity to process a large amount of information while giving sufficient weight to both soft and hard factors (Böhme & Grossklags, 2013, p. 71). In some instances, even though the platform assigns the credit grade, interest rates are still determined by borrowers or lenders in an auction. For example, Franks et al. (2021) have documented that the UK P2P lending platform Funding Circle, which used to operate an auction system, also provided borrowers with credit ratings.[159] However, it is even more common for platforms to determine simultaneously the credit grade and the interest rate for each loan application.[160]

When the platform determines risk grades and loan prices, they are non-negotiable for borrowers and lenders. Borrowers can simply refuse to raise funds under terms proposed by the platform. It is worth noting that risk buckets (grades or subgrades) are not necessarily comparable across platforms, as platforms developed their own systems of categorisation. For instance, two leading P2P lending competitors in the US, Prosper and Lending Club, use the scoring system of 7 and 35 risk (sub) categories, respectively (Vallee & Zeng, 2019, p. 1945).

It is important to emphasise that platform credit pricing can exist on platforms where lenders manually choose loans and on platforms that provide automated (passive) investments, as discussed below. Three interrelated questions arise when the platform assigns risk grades while investors independently decide which loans to invest in. The first question is whether platforms assign accurate risk grades. When pricing credit, platforms may be subject to agency costs. As pointed out by Cumming and Hornuf (2022, p. 39), such costs arise when platforms assign higher risk grades than what borrowers' financial information would suggest to attract more listings on the portal.

[159] According to the authors, the rating system of the Funding Circle was based on Experian credit ratings, the credit history of the borrower, and disclosed financial statements while allowing the platform's employees also to exercise a certain degree of discretion (Franks et al., 2021, p. 2325).

[160] As explained earlier, Vallee and Zeng (2019, p. 1945) denote such platform activities as screening on the intensive margin.

Platform risk grades differ from traditional credit scores from credit bureaus (e.g., FICO in the US, SCHUFA in Germany, or Experian in the UK, etc.) both concerning the volume and sources of information they use as well as the technology behind data analysis and data aggregation. When it comes to data sources, digital platforms are known for using alternative sources of data, which include both 'non-credit, financial data' [...] and 'non-credit, non-financial data' (Aggarwal, 2018, p. 2). The approach known as 'all data is credit data' assumes that different information points extracted from borrowers' online and offline behaviour can be used to improve estimates of their creditworthiness (Hurley & Adebayo, 2016, p. 151). Examples of alternative data include granular bank transaction history, rent payments, utility bills, mobile phone location and data, insurance claims, details on the fundraiser's employment or education, social media activity, spending habits, online consumer preferences, etc. (Hurley & Adebayo, 2016, p. 148; Jagtiani & Lemieux, 2019, p. 1010).

In the absence of agency costs, alternative data is expected to provide a more accurate credit quality assessment, especially for individuals and companies with limited credit history. Some borrowers can be deemed more creditworthy than traditional credit scores imply. Additionally, platforms have built proprietary algorithms for risk assessment, sometimes relying on novel technologies such as machine learning or artificial intelligence (AI). Hence, the often-used term 'algorithmic credit scoring' is praised for its ability to establish patterns in large amounts of unstructured and anonymised data and constantly improve its performance as new training data becomes available (Aggarwal, 2018, pp. 2–3). The code of algorithms is seldom transparent and can even be treated as a trade secret in some jurisdictions.[161]

Several empirical studies have estimated the efficiency of platforms' credit risk estimates. In an early account of the market, Serrano-Cinca et al. (2015) examined factors predicting loan defaults using data from the US P2P platform Lending Club. Their results have suggested that platform risk grades are the strongest predictor of loan performance, even though some other financial information (e.g., borrower's debt level) is found to have explanatory power beyond and above credit grades, suggesting that the accuracy of platform grading can be improved. Using data from the same platform, a later study by Jagtiani and Lemieux (2019) also found a strong correlation between risk grades and loan outcomes. Yet, the authors have also captured that the platform's internal credit rating system evolved to rely more on alternative data. Namely, they have documented that the importance of the conventional credit score (FICO) in explaining the variation in risk grades dropped considerably towards the end of the observation period.[162] The departure from the traditional metrics has proven

[161] For instance, as reported by Serrano-Cinca et al. (2015, p. 8), the US-based platform Lending Club merely mentions that the formula for assigning the credit grade is based on the borrower's FICO score, credit information, and some other data provided as part of the application process.

[162] The authors have reported that the correlation between FICO and risk grades dropped from 80% in 2007 to 35% in 2015 (Jagtiani & Lemieux, 2019, p. 1015).

beneficial for predicting loan defaults of borrowers that are considered subprime according to FICO scores. It allowed Lending Club to better identify creditworthy borrowers among them. In relation to these findings, Vallee and Zeng (2019) have captured that the screening intensity of platforms Lending Club and Prosper increased over time, resulting in better accuracy of their risk assessment. However, the authors have also documented that sophisticated investors using their proprietary algorithms to predict loan defaults could consistently outperform the platform.

Studies examining the P2P business lending market have reported more alarming findings. Cumming and Hornuf (2022) have investigated risk grades provided on the German platform Zencap. Instead of looking into the likelihood of default like the above studies, the authors have examined whether traditional financial information predicts platform risk grades.[163] Surprisingly, the results have shown insignificant or weak relationships between fine-grained financial data and the platform's risk brackets. While such results can suggest an increasing reliance on alternative data, as suggested by Jagtiani and Lemieux (2019), the authors of the study interpret them as evidence of agency costs in risk ratings. In a related study, Adhami et al. (2023) ran a cross-platform analysis encompassing 73 European platforms intermediating P2P business loans.[164] They have found that promised returns (stated interest rates) of crowdfunding loans do not correspond to the risk borne by lenders. Counterintuitively, they have documented that promised returns are negatively associated with the riskiness of loans, suggesting a severe degree of credit mispricing in this market. Yet, the limitation of their study is that they do not estimate the risk of individual loans but instead use a proxy that corresponds to the average risk of the industry in which the borrower operates.[165]

If platform risk assessment is not to be trusted (absolutely), the second question is whether platforms' credit grading affects the amount of information available to investors to screen loans independently. In the already mentioned study by Vallee and Zeng (2019), it has been shown that, as the accuracy of platform screening improved over time, less information became available to investors to do their own assessments. More specifically, the authors have reported that Lending Club decided to reduce about 50 out of more than 100 borrowers' characteristics provided to lenders. The authors interpret this change as the platform effort to create a more even playing field between sophisticated

[163] Fine-grained hard information used in the study includes indicators such as total assets, the ratio of current assets to liabilities, the ratio of liabilities to the sum of liabilities and assets, and the company's net income (Cumming & Hornuf, 2022, p. 46).

[164] The study sample includes P2P business loans of different seniority (senior, subordinated, hybrid) and bonds.

[165] More specifically, the risk is captured by the volatility of equity indexes of the relevant industry (Adhami et al., 2023, p. 17). Another caveat is that the metrics the authors use to capture the promised returns of hybrid loans (for which at least one return component depends on the firm's performance, i.e. revenues or profits) are unclear.

and retail investors, as the former type consistently outperformed the latter in terms of returns when provided with a high level of information disclosure (Vallee & Zeng, 2019, p. 1941). More specifically, the platform's efforts to protect retail investors are motivated by the fact that the overall volumes drop when sophisticated investors can choose first the most promising investments. The reason is that retail investors are more exposed to adverse selection, asking for higher interest rates, which, in turn, attract fewer loan applicants.

The third question is whether investors use the information provided in addition to platforms' credit grades. Again, as mentioned before, Vallee and Zeng (2019) have demonstrated a significant disparity in screening efforts between retail and sophisticated investors in the US P2P lending market, resulting in superior performance of portfolios of the latter group. In a related study already mentioned above, D. Cumming and Hornuf (2022) have examined whether hard financial data is predictive of loan application success, once controlling for credit ratings of platforms. The evidence from the German market suggests that crowd investors base their decisions on the platforms' risk gradings, while they usually neglect granular financial data.

In contrast to (pure) loan-based platforms, equity-based platforms predominantly do not formally evaluate the companies listed on their portals, at least not in a way that would entice investors to believe that a platform claims the accuracy of security prices. Instead, fundraisers directly target crowd investors by providing them with self-produced evaluations (Armour & Enriques, 2018, p. 262). However, in many instances, platforms negotiate company evaluations behind closed doors as part of the pre-selection and due diligence process. In a qualitative study of the German crowdinvesting market, Löher (2017) has examined how company valuations are set. The study results have revealed that entrepreneurs usually propose company evaluations, whereas the platform ensures that the proposition follows one of the established valuation methods.[166] Sometimes, this process also involves hiring an external accountant or using an auction (Löher, 2017, p. 19).[167]

Similarly, Cumming, Johan, and Zhang (2019) have investigated the pre-selection practices of 51 Canadian platforms. They have found that 28.6% of platforms in their sample provided ventures with pre-evaluation before listing. Similarly, according to Ferretti et al. (2021, p. 5), equity crowdfunding platforms in Italy typically estimate the company's value before the campaign. As discussed in the context of fundraisers' signalling and platform due diligence, company evaluations can also be negotiated between entrepreneurs and the lead investor on investor-led platforms.

[166] It is worth noting that traditional valuation methods exhibit limitations when applied to equity crowdfunding companies (Jegeleviciute & Valanciene, 2014).

[167] The study does not provide the details of the auction process (e.g., who the bidders are and their relationship with the platform or crowd investors).

3.5.4 Automated Investments and Diversification

In addition to pricing, many platforms offer passive investment tools (automated investment, auto-bidding, portfolio builder, autolend). By definition, such tools minimise investors' efforts in choosing investment opportunities while offering automatic diversification. They are far more widespread in lending-based than in equity-based crowdfunding. When it comes to lending models, automated investment tools can be optional to direct investment ('lender choice model') or can be an exclusive means of investing for retail investors ('diffused model') (Stefanelli et al., 2022, p. 4).

Automated investments as an optional tool can exist in both 'posted price' and auction models. For instance, according to Pötzsch and Böhme (2010, p. 387), borrowers on the German-based P2P lending platform Smava suggest the interest rate they are willing to accept, while lenders decide whether to lend money under such terms. However, since 2009, lenders have also used a trading agent (bidding assistant) offered by the platform, which places bids across different credit projects on their behalf. According to the authors, at least 50% of the pledged amount must originate from manual bids. Similarly, both manual and automated bids are available on the German P2P lending platform Zencap, with the difference from Smava that the loan interest rate is set by the platform (Cumming & Hornuf, 2022). A portfolio builder tool automatically allocates a certain amount of funds to different loans that meet the investor's pre-set investment criteria. A similar alternative was offered to investors on the Chinese P2P lending platform Renrendai, where manual bids are expected to come from investors who have private information about the borrower (Zhang & Chen, 2017).

Auto-bids as an optional (complementary) investment strategy have also been identified on platforms operating an auction system. For instance, Franks et al. (2021) have described credit pricing on one of the leading UK-based P2P business lending platforms, Funding Circle. The platform allows passive investors to use the algorithmic autobid instead of direct participation in the auction, placing orders on their behalf. Thus, the platform chooses a diversified portfolio that matches investors' preferences regarding borrowers' risk profiles, presumably based on platform credit grades. As the authors explain (Franks et al., 2021, p. 5, 17), the idea behind auto-bidding is to provide the market with necessary liquidity, protecting it against liquidity shocks similar to market makers in stock markets. Furthermore, automated investments are expected to integrate the information contained in the funding flows from other (manual) investments, not interfering with the price discovery mechanism. Similarly, the French P2P business lending platform Unilend, which operates an auction mechanism, introduced a bidding agent called Autolend (Darmon et al., 2022, pp. 3–4). The auto-bidding functionality comes in simple and advanced mode, which differs regarding investors' ability to give more detailed instructions to the bidding agent regarding combinations of credit rating, interest rates, and loan maturity.

When automated investments are offered in addition to direct investments, an important question is whether there is an interaction between the two investment means, as well as whether market outcomes are superior as a result. Several empirical studies have shed some light on these issues, using data from posted-price and auction models. Regarding posted-price models, early research by Böhme and Grossklags (2013) revealed that introducing the (automated) trading agent affected the information disclosure level on the German platform Smava. More specifically, the authors have documented that the amount of soft information available to lenders was reduced due to the new investment tool.[168] The intuition is that borrowers are aware that the trading agent does not consider soft information when pledging funds on lenders' behalf, which gradually reduces the expectations among market participants regarding the optimal level of disclosure (Böhme & Grossklags, 2013, pp. 71–73).[169] In other words, manual bidders also have access to less information as a result of automated investments. In a related but more comprehensive study, Chen et al. (2021) investigated whether the introduction of an automated investment tool affected herding behaviour, the average duration of a campaign, and the return on investment (ROI). The data comes from the Chinese P2P lending platform Renrendai, which operates a posted-price model. The platform also assigns a credit rating to each borrower, which is one of the criteria lenders use to instruct the automated investment system on how to place their investments. Interestingly, the authors have reported that the auto-bidding functionality reduced herding behaviour. Their interpretation is that many investors stopped investing manually, whereas other investors could see whether previous pledges originated from manual investors or the automated tool. As a result, manual investors were less likely to infer the existence of an information cascade (Chen et al., 2021, pp. 15–16). Another finding of this study is that the average bidding duration, which is supposed to approximate the efficiency of a crowdfunding platform, did not change following the introduction of automated investments. The authors argue that this is because most automated pledges correspond to low-risk loans, whereas investments into high-risk loans became less frequent, increasing the average bidding duration (Chen et al., 2021, pp. 16–17). Finally, the study revealed that ROI did not improve with greater platform interference with investment decisions. The authors have contended that the automated investment tool failed to consider valuable soft

[168] The study uses two proxies for the amount of soft information revealed by borrowers: the length of unverified descriptions in their loan applications and whether or not borrowers uploaded custom photos (Böhme & Grossklags, 2013, p. 74).

[169] It is worth noting that such an effect is not merely the consequence of introducing a lenders' trading agent (bidding assistant) but another design feature introduced soon after. The authors explain that the platform also offered an automated agent that helps borrowers determine their interest rate. The borrowers' automated agent is calibrated so that the loan application is matched with parameters determined by the lenders' trading agent. As a result, borrowers can get a loan much faster (Böhme & Grossklags, 2013, pp. 73–74). However, this also means that borrowers know that their loan application will not be assessed by manual bidders. However, in the authors' view, borrowers' choices regarding the level of detail in their loan application affect the general expectations for all loans.

information that investors bidding manually would typically internalise in their investment decisions (Chen et al., 2021, p. 17).

Combining manual and automated bids can also affect (price) efficiency on auction-based platforms. In line with the above study, Jiang, Wang, et al. (2018) have also found evidence that automated bids weakened herding behaviour in auctions on the Chinese P2P lending platform PaiPaiDai. However, the authors have not investigated the behaviour of manual bidders; instead, they have investigated whether the overall herding was reduced because automatic bids are not affected by previous pledges. Some positive developments resulting from automated lending (Autolend) have also been documented by Darmon et al. (2022), examining auction outcomes on the French platform Uniland. The authors have reported that the automated agent improved the platform's efficiency in different aspects. It increased the number of bids and lenders per loan application, as well as shortened the average campaign duration, suggesting the ability of this automated investment tool to save screening costs. Moreover, loans falling within low-risk brackets were assigned lower interest rates following the introduction of Autolend. However, the study has not captured whether this also implies more efficient pricing in terms of the accuracy of estimating the default probability. The only research focusing on price efficiency is the study mentioned earlier by Franks et al. (2021). The authors have reported that the auto-bidding model on the UK platform Funding Circle was not well calibrated. Hence, the price efficiency of auctions even dropped after this investment tool became available. The reason is that it often failed to incorporate information contained in the funding flows from manual investments, misinterpreting lack of demand driven by higher default probability as a liquidity shortage (Franks et al., 2021, pp. 2320–2321).

It is important to emphasise that some platforms eventually abolished the lender choice model in favour of the exclusive use of automated investments (diffused model). This has become increasingly common in the UK market. For instance, according to Ofir and Sadeh (2019, pp. 693–694), the P2P business platform Funding Circle started offering two different auto-bidding tools, which, depending on the risk preferences of lenders, invest only in low-risk loans or diversify investor funds across different borrower types.

Interestingly, automated investment tools can also be offered by third-party providers, which are independent of the platform. Vallee and Zeng (2019, p. 1947) have provided examples of firms specialising in the provision of algorithmic tools for screening and automated execution of orders that operate in the US P2P lending market.[170]

While passive investment strategies are slowly becoming a dominant model in P2P lending, at least in some markets, such as the UK, there have been only a few similar developments in equity-based crowdfunding. Coakley and Lazos (2021, p. 358) have described passive funds developed on UK platforms Crowdcube and

[170] According to Vallee and Zeng (2019, p. 1947), some firms such as LendingRobot or NSR Invest, target retail investors, while others such as Orchard cater to institutional investors.

Seedrs. The latter was the innovator in this respect, introducing the Twenty8 passive fund in 2016. The idea was that the fund mimics the investment activity of sophisticated investors on the platform by diversifying investments across 28 crowdfunding campaigns eligible for EIS tax relief. According to these authors, Seedrs has followed suit with the Seedrs EIS100 fund, which targets a hundred companies across different sectors that satisfy specific criteria (e.g., reaching 70% of the target amount, attracting 100 investors, being eligible for tax relief, etc.).

3.5.5 Delegated Monitoring, Debt Collection, and Loss Recovery

Even though platforms' revenues usually depend on fees charged upon successfully completing a crowdfunding campaign, platforms assume several gatekeeping roles post-investment. It is a common practice of P2P lending platforms to act on lenders' behalf in exercising rights stemming from the loan agreement. Platforms service the loan by collecting and distributing payments (interest and redemption of principal) until maturity. In addition, platforms typically recover the outstanding debt in case of loan delinquency. In the latter case, platforms are expected to negotiate with borrowers a prompt payment, arrange a new payment plan, or hire an external collection agency to recover the loan (Havrylchyk & Verdier, 2018, p. 121).[171] Alternatively, some platforms have introduced automated litigation processes (Lenz, 2016, p. 8). P2P loans (consumer or business) are often unsecured. However, when a personal guarantee or physical collateral is pledged, platforms also claim the personal guarantee or liquidate the collateral to recover the unpaid loan balance on behalf of lenders.

By assuming this role, platforms effectively engage in ex-post monitoring and reduce moral hazard in the relationship between lenders and borrowers. As crowd investors have a credit claim that usually refers to only a small portion of a loan, the involvement of a platform is also necessary to reduce transaction costs and the costs of collective action inherent in coordinating efforts of many small investors. Nevertheless, by delegating the monitoring role to the platform, the lenders become dependent on the best efforts exercised by platforms, with new agency costs arising from their relationship. Particularly problematic is a potential platform failure, when lenders depend on platforms' arrangements to ensure the continuation of loan repayments. Such arrangements are usually mandated by crowdfunding regulations.

---

[171] According to Havrylchyk and Verdier (2018, p. 121), in some countries, the involvement of platforms is inevitable as consumer protection provisions ban direct contact between lenders and individual borrowers in case of default.

3.5.6 Governance Mechanisms

In their capacity as gatekeepers, platforms have developed different corporate governance mechanisms to mitigate agency costs between investors and fundraisers on equity (and equity alike) crowdfunding platforms. Even though fundraisers, in some instances, have the freedom to decide on the degree of control rights they want to allocate to their investors (e.g., by issuing particular type of financial instruments), as discussed in the context of signalling, most governance mechanisms stem from customary solutions required under the platform's terms and conditions, which also designs the boilerplate contract to be signed with prospective investors.

A large variety of corporate control tools used in crowdfunding stems from three different factors. Firstly, as argued by Cumming et al. (2021, pp. 69–70), corporate governance issues of firms financed via crowdfunding are peculiar for their mixed characteristics of both public and private firms. Their similarity to public firms lies in many (small) external investors, while the concentration of ownership in the hands of company founders or managers makes them resemble private entrepreneurial ventures. Consequently, the typical separation of ownership and control of large public corporations does not really exist in these firms as both are concentrated in the hands of founders.[172] For instance, Vismara (2016) has documented that the average percentage of equity offered in a crowdfunding campaign is approximately 13%. Nevertheless, agency conflicts between controlling and minority shareholders (principal-principal conflicts), with the former also typically acting as company managers, are present (Cumming, Johan, & Zhang, 2019, p. 2; Rossi et al., 2019, p. 262). Secondly, as shown above, allocating certain control rights to crowd investors is not limited to the intermediation of straight equity. In the case of hybrid instruments sold on some crowdfunding platforms (e.g., platforms brokering profit-participating loans in Germany), the subordination of claims exposes investors to a similar type of ex-post risks as if they purchased an equity stake. As a result, several different contract-based solutions emerged to substitute for the lack of voting rights when hybrid instruments are issued. Finally, unlike the campaign stage of the crowdfunding process, which is often regulated and supervised by competent financial authorities, the post-campaign stage is largely left free from any specific regulatory requirements, leaving the platforms and fundraisers with much more room for experimentation with market-based mechanisms.

Most governance mechanisms in crowdfunding are more closely aligned with controls in privately held firms despite a dispersed ownership structure, which largely undermines direct monitoring by investors. The reason is that mechanisms inherent in public firms are mostly unavailable due to a lack of operational secondary markets and different information intermediaries that oversee managers' decisions and firm performance (financial analysts and dedicated media) (Cumming

[172] As Fama and Jensen (1983, p. 304) put it, agency problems arise 'when the decision managers who initiate and implement important decisions are not the major residual claimants and therefore do not bear a major share of the wealth effects of their decisions'.

et al., 2021, p. 76). As a result, there is not enough information on managerial opportunism and wrong decision-making. Moreover, investors lack adequate means of exercising their market discipline on managers by selling their shares, causing a price plunge. Similarly, as Cumming et al. (2021, p. 76) have also pointed out, even hostile takeovers are usually unavailable since it is typical for fundraisers, which generally also act as managers, to keep the controlling share of the company.

When it comes to crowdfunding platforms intermediating (pure) equity investments, two principal models of governance have been identified: the direct shareholder model ('direct ownership structure' or 'club membership model') and the nominee account model ('nominee structure' or 'holding model') (Bouglet et al., 2022; Coakley et al., 2021; Rossi et al., 2019). In the direct shareholder model, crowdfunding investors become the legal owners of shares in the company they invested in. The platform does not play any role in intermediating the relationship between investors and fundraisers after the completion of the campaign. Under this model, corporate governance practices depend on the scope of investor rights stipulated in the investment contract and investors' incentives and ability to exercise them.

Regarding the scope, platforms differ in the design of the investment contracts. Most importantly, crowdfunding offerings do not always offer voting shares, potentially raising the issue of separation of ownership (cash-flow rights) and control. Moreover, crowd investors may or may not benefit from pre-emption rights, tag-along and drag-along rights, which are important when a new majority shareholder, such as a VC or an angel investor, is interested in acquiring the firm. Pre-emption rights provide existing investors with the right of first refusal. That is, they have a priority in acquiring shares in case of new issuances to prevent dilution of their shareholdings. Tag-along rights allow minority shareholders to sell shares under the same terms as those offered to the majority shareholder if they wish to sell their stake. Thus, they enable crowd investors to get favourable terms of sale that would be difficult to negotiate individually. Drag-along rights allow the majority shareholder to force minority shareholders to sell their shares. Nevertheless, drag-along rights can also protect minority shareholders against other minority shareholders threatening to undermine the exit opportunity. As discussed above, fundraisers are sometimes given the possibility to discriminate against small investors so that only investors who pledge above a certain threshold are provided with some of these safeguards. For instance, the UK platform Crowdcube permits fundraisers to set the investment limit that is used to delineate between investors with and without voting and pre-emption rights (Cumming, Meoli, & Vismara, 2019).

As discussed in relation to the signalling value of governance mechanisms, effective control over managers' decision-making in the direct shareholder model presupposes active investors. Yet, the lack of monitoring incentives among small crowd investors and high coordination costs can undermine the effectiveness of governance tools provided in investment contracts. This may be part of why some platforms offering direct shareholder models have experimented with co-investments of institutional investors, business angels, or the platform itself. Bouglet et al. (2022, pp. 22–23) have documented that several platforms in France offer a direct shareholder model in which the platform participates in funding the company or sits on the board of directors or the supervisory board of the funded company. Considerable discretion in the action course of managers could have incentivised some platforms to permit fundraisers to choose between the direct shareholder and the nominee model of governance (e.g., UK-based Crowdcube).

In the nominee account model, as originally introduced by the UK platform Seedrs, investments from all investors are pooled into a single account, which is legally owned and managed by a nominee or trustee. The nominee becomes the legal shareholder in the company's shareholder register, exercising rights for all crowdfunding investors who remain beneficial owners. Sometimes, the platform acts as a nominee; in other instances, it delegates this role to an external entity (Rossi et al., 2019, p. 263). Thus, the platform assumes an active role in corporate governance. It reduces coordination costs associated with direct monitoring and voting by hundreds of individual shareholders. Investors are up to date with the project's progress thanks to regular reporting by the platform (Bouglet et al., 2022, p. 6). In the case of major events for the company, such as the issuance of new shares, the platform organises digital voting. Such a governance scheme also relieves the administrative burden for the managers when dealing with many small investors and facilitates exit opportunities. As Coakley et al. (2021, p. 6) pointed out, in the event of a takeover, the new investor can conveniently deal with the nominee representing all shareholders. They have also contended that the nominee structure resembles more traditional VCs and business angels syndicate investments, with a notable difference that investors do not pay carry fees in addition to the nominal fee paid to the platform allowing them to invest in a crowdfunding campaign (Coakley et al., 2021, p. 2). In some instances, as documented in France, the platform reintermediation goes beyond the role of a trustee. Namely, Bouglet et al. (2022, pp. 23–24) have identified platforms which combine the nominee account model with direct investments or platforms sitting on the board of directors or the supervisory board of the funded company. Alternatively, co-investment under the nominee structure comes from institutional investors or business angels.

It is worth noting that an increased role of the platform in corporate governance under the nominee account model may also give rise to a conflict of interest or moral hazard. Namely, the interests of the platform may not be fully aligned with the interests of crowd investors. Moreover, without the carry fees or co-investment, the platform does not have 'skin in the game', which is often considered necessary for effective and informed monitoring (Farag & Johan, 2022, p. 5). Bouglet et al. (2022, p. 7) argue that limited resources and techniques available to the platform undermine the effectiveness of its monitoring. However, reputation concerns of platforms as repeated players in the market can make these issues less pronounced (Rossi et al., 2019, p. 263).

Another problem with the nominee structure is that investors remain dependent on the platform operations as long as they hold their shares in the company. The risk of a platform failure is attenuated by the nominee feature that if the platform ceases its operations, shares held by the nominee are transferred to crowd investors as beneficial owners who thus become direct shareholders (SyndicateRoom, n.d.).

In addition to the two governance models described, Rossi et al. (2019) have argued that investor-led platforms, which they denote as 'syndicate-like platforms' (e.g., Syndicate Room in the UK, JD.com in China or ASSOB in Australia), have their own governance mechanisms. Such platforms require the involvement of a lead investor as a precondition for the project to be listed, assuming that the lead would overtake much of the monitoring duties. However, the question arises of whether the presence of large investors merely enhances the control over management or creates agency problems in the relationship between the lead and crowd investors. As already discussed above, in the context of signalling, the concern is that the lead investor can benefit at the expense of crowd investors (e.g., negotiating a better deal for herself, having an information advantage, etc.) (Chen & Ma, 2023). Interestingly, investor-led platforms can also use a nominee structure, with only one legal shareholder representing all investments via the platform. This has been the case for UK-based Syndicate Room since 2015. As Coakley and Lazos (2021, p. 391) have pointed out, the interests of the lead and the crowd can be better aligned if all of the investments are structured under the nominee scheme.

As already mentioned, questions of control also arise with platforms brokering hybrid instruments. As discussed above, crowdfunding platforms in Germany predominantly facilitate the offer of profit-participating loans. These instruments usually allow investors to cumulatively gain a fixed interest, a variable interest (which depends on the profit of the venture), and sometimes a bonus interest payment at the end of the investment, which represents a share in the increased value of the company (Hornuf, Klöhn, & Schilling, 2018, pp. 538–554). The bonus interest payment is a contractual solution meant to imitate gains from (pure) equity holdings. Both the variable interest payment and the bonus interest payment are calculated based on the investment ratio, that is, a virtual share of an investor in a company recognised by the investment contract but not by the contract law (Hornuf, Klöhn, & Schilling, 2018, p. 543).[173] The claims of crowd investors have a priority over (residual) claims of company shareholders but are subordinated to claims of other debt holders. Thus, the lack of voting rights, on the one hand, and the subordination of claims, on the other, raises the need for specific contractual safeguards against the misconduct of company managers and founders.

In a comprehensive study covering 18 investment-based platforms and campaigns in Germany, Hornuf, Klöhn, and Schilling (2018) have mapped out the dominant contractual design of governance mechanisms and how they evolved. The authors grouped them into rights related to protection against dilution and follow-up financing, control rights, and information rights. Protection against dilution plays a role, given that investors' participation in proceeds depends on the investment ratio, which needs to change with follow-up investments. While proportionate dilution of their virtual shares is necessary to attract funds from new investors, investment contracts typically contain clauses that protect

[173] Similar to equity holders, profit-participating loans also typically provide investors with exit rights, that is, participation in the value increase of the company realised in the event of an exit (Hornuf, Klöhn, & Schilling, 2018, pp. 554–558).

investors against company undervaluation, notably in case of a down round.[174] Regarding control rights, the authors have documented that contracts have evolved. While early contracts granted investors veto powers concerning certain managerial decisions, more recent contracts do not contain such clauses allowing investors to influence how the company is managed. In contrast, ample information rights are stipulated in investment contracts of different platforms (e.g., quarterly reporting, annual financial statements, cash-flow statements, etc.), as well as penalties in case of breaching information duties.

Interestingly, analogously to the nominee account model that exists on platforms intermediating (pure) equity, Hornuf, Klöhn, and Schilling (2018, p. 532) have identified one German platform (Innovestment) offering an indirect financing structure using an SPV. The SPV acts as a direct shareholder in the funded company, while investors provide profit-participating loans to the SPV. Alternatively, some platforms intermediating direct investments also allow investors to conclude a pooling agreement, which facilitates the collective decision-making of crowd investors. Given that investors in hybrid instruments do not have voting rights, such mechanisms are limited to specific decisions, such as the purchase of their investments by a third party or amendments to the existing investment contract (Hornuf, Klöhn, & Schilling, 2018, pp. 572–574).

Several empirical studies have intended to shed light on the effects of different governance mechanisms in the crowdfunding market, primarily focusing on (pure) equity investments. They usually distinguish between the direct shareholder and nominee account models, while some studies have treated the investor-led model separately. A few studies have investigated the effects of governance models on individual campaign success rates or platform success (captured by the number of successful offerings or their survival rates). These studies have intended to capture how investors perceive the effectiveness of specific governance models. Other studies have examined the relationship between governance mechanisms and ex-post campaign outcomes, such as firms' performance, innovation capacity, or the ability to attract follow-on funding. The underlying assumption is that certain governance tools are more effective than others in disciplining the management, generating more favourable post-campaign outcomes.

Using evidence from the UK platforms Seedrs and Crowdcube, Coakley et al. (2021) have demonstrated that, from the investors' perspective, the nominee structure is a more desirable corporate governance model than direct ownership. Their results suggest that ventures raising finance under the former model run more successful crowdfunding campaigns.[175] Rossi et al. (2019) have provided related findings in a large study comprising 185 platforms in different

[174] A down round refers to a situation when a company raises new capital at a lower price than in a previous financing round.

[175] Interestingly, the results of the study hold even after Crowdcube, which originally offered only direct ownership, allowed fundraisers to opt for the nominee account model. Put differently, the effect they capture cannot be attributed to other differentiating features of the two platforms.

countries.[176] The direct ownership model (denoted as 'delivering individual voting rights') is associated with fewer successful offerings per platform. In contrast, the nominee model (denoted as 'delivering pooled voting rights') does not influence the number of successful offerings per platform. Interestingly, they have also examined syndicate-like platforms as a stand-alone model and found that fewer successful offerings are related to this model.[177] It is important to note that investors' perception of the effectiveness of certain governance mechanisms may depend on investor financial literacy. For instance, in a study comprising 432 platforms in 37 OECD countries, Meoli et al. (2022) demonstrated that financial literacy positively affects platform survival rates. In addition, this relationship is stronger when voting rights are delivered. The interpretation is that better-educated investors are more aware of the importance of voting rights for mitigating agency concerns. Thus, in countries with higher financial literacy rates, platforms are more likely to survive if ventures offer voting rights to investors.[178]

Several studies have explored the variation in the ex-post outcomes of successfully funded firms under different governance rules introduced by platforms. The research by Walthoff-Borm et al. (2018) was the first to explore the effects of the two main governance models by looking at the survival rates of equity crowdfunding firms as well as their innovation capacity. The results have indicated a nominee account model is associated with fewer ex-post failures, but it lags behind the direct ownership model regarding the number of patent applications.

Governance structure also appears to matter for subsequent financing rounds, as Butticè et al. (2020) have shown in the UK context. Their results suggest that crowdfunding firms are more likely to receive follow-on VC investments than firms that did not receive any external seed financing. The effect is particularly strong for firms with a nominee shareholder structure. Interestingly, such firms outperform even angel-backed firms when looking into their attractiveness to VCs. Besides lowering agency conflicts, the nominee model can also relieve the administrative burden of change in the ownership structure.

Further evidence supporting the efficiency of the nominee account model is brought by Coakley et al. (2021). Their results suggest that ventures raising

---

[176] Platforms examined in the study by Rossi et al. (2019) are based in the following countries: Australia, Austria, Canada, France, Germany, Italy, New Zealand, the UK, and the US.

[177] A limitation of this study is that it does not consider the fact that investor-led and entrepreneur-led platforms are likely to attract different types of ventures due to the requirement to engage professional investors before the campaign launch. For instance, Coakley et al. (2022) have shown that investor-led platforms attract larger and more heterogeneous founder teams. Thus, it seems inadequate to argue that the difference in the number of successful campaigns per platform can only be attributed to the difference in governance mechanisms.

[178] Interestingly, the same study provides limited support for the negative moderating effect of the requirement to ensure the co-investment of an accredited investor before the campaign launch (mainly corresponding to investor-led platforms). The interpretation is that financial literacy matters less for platform survival when accredited investors perform their due diligence and monitoring, thus alleviating some informational concerns (Meoli et al., 2022, p. 4).

finance under a nominee structure are more likely to conduct seasoned equity crowdfunding offerings. However, in contrast to findings by Walthoff-Borm et al. (2018), the difference in the governance model is not significant for the post-campaign survival rates of financed ventures.

3.5.7 Secondary Markets

The core functionality of well-functioning secondary markets in crowdfunding investments is ensuring liquidity. When secondary markets are viewed as a viable exit route by crowd investors, demand for this type of investment rises, affecting the cost of capital for fundraisers. Namely, investors no longer have to use a high discount rate in company valuations or ask for a liquidity premium in interest rates to offset the liquidity risk (Lukkarinen & Schwienbacher, 2023, p. 2; Reher, 2014, pp. 14–15). In addition to ensuring liquidity, secondary markets can be essential in reducing post-campaign information asymmetry and enhancing corporate governance. As discussed earlier, secondary markets can affect both direct and indirect channels of influence of information on corporate governance. Listed companies are under greater scrutiny due to increased visibility and ongoing disclosure requirements, which facilitate exercising control over company managers (Armour & Enriques, 2018, p. 263).

Moreover, secondary markets with sufficient depth enable critical information to be reflected in securities prices. The latter has an important disciplining effect on company managers, revealing instances of their opportunism or unsound business decisions. In relation to this, secondary markets may even enable information dissemination, as those who possess new (publicly unavailable) information on the company engage in trading, which, in turn, drives prices. Another critical function of secondary markets and securities prices is that they provide a benchmark for any future sale of securities, reducing the risk of dilution (Armour & Enriques, 2018, p. 264).

It is important to note that, unlike most other gatekeeping functionalities of platforms, the development of secondary markets has been limited, particularly on equity-based platforms.[179] As discussed, the lack of operational secondary markets has led many platforms to develop governance mechanisms closer to controls in privately held firms. Interestingly, in the UK, for instance, the term that the regulator (FCA) uses to denote equity crowdfunding instruments is 'non-readily realisable securities', which implies 'securities for which no liquid

[179] Secondary markets or some of its functions are more commonly offered on loan-based than equity-based platforms. As contended by Lukkarinen and Schwienbacher (2023, p. 2), part of the reason is that P2P loans have a maturity (typically less than 2 years), unlike equity investments, which have a much longer investment horizon. As R&D accounts for a significant portion of company investments, it is expected that a company will start generating profits only in the long run. The longer investment horizon can also explain lower primary market volumes of equity crowdfunding compared to P2P lending, which in turn affects secondary market volumes.

secondary market exists' (Armour & Enriques, 2018, p. 232). In the US, the resale of crowdfunding securities is not even allowed in the first year of ownership, with a few exceptions (Morsy, 2014).

In most countries, operating a trading venue requires the platform to hold a special licence.[180] Thus, regulations have typically limited activities that platforms can perform to reduce transaction costs associated with finding a potential counterparty to a transaction, obtaining relevant information about the asset being traded, and executing the transaction (Gargantini, 2022, pp. 360–365). A service such as running an internal matching system that executes clients' orders with respect to buying and selling securities usually falls within the definition of a (regulated) trading venue.

As a result, some platforms have established cooperation with licensed institutions. For instance, US-based Lending Club and Prosper in 2008 and 2009 were the first lending platforms to offer secondary markets. Both platforms enabled secondary trading in cooperation with a licensed brokerage firm, FolioFN (Reher, 2014, p. 13). When it comes to equity crowdfunding, allegedly, the first secondary market was established in 2014 as a result of cooperation between Finish platform Invesdor and Privanet, a broker already operating a secondary market for shares in privately held companies (Lukkarinen & Schwienbacher, 2023, p. 2). The market subsequently allowed listings of companies financed via four different equity crowdfunding platforms. In addition to publishing investors' buying and selling interests, the market operator matches orders and executes transactions in accordance with the best available price and the order of arrival (Lukkarinen & Schwienbacher, 2023, p. 4).

A far more common approach of platforms is to offer only some secondary market functionalities, which fall outside the regulatory perimeter (so-called bulletin boards). An early initiative of this kind appeared on the UK equity platform Seedrs. Its secondary market allows both potential buyers and buyers to express, that is, advertise their interest in trading, but the platform does not provide matching services. The market opens on the first Tuesday of each month and lasts a week. According to Coakley and Lazos (2021, pp. 357–358), only existing shareholders and authorised Seedrs members were allowed to trade at first, while this rule was abolished in 2018 so that anyone interested could join the market. The platform provides an indicative valuation for each company listed following its valuation policy. Yet, the seller can request a sale at any price they deem appropriate, at a discount or premium of the value determined by the platform, subject to a few restrictions.[181]

---

[180] Platforms operating a secondary market in Europe may fall under provisions of the Markets in Financial Instruments Directive (MiFID) (Directive, 2014) and the Markets in Financial Instruments Regulation (MiFIR) (Regulation (EU), 2014) governing the operation of regulated markets, multilateral trading facilities (MTF), or organised trading facilities (OTF). Similarly, a secondary market in the US may be qualified as an alternative trading system.

[181] The platform sets the minimum and maximum limits for the share price: £0.01/share and 500% of the current valuation share price, respectively. Moreover, the platform can consider some shares ineligible for trading following pre-specified criteria and thus refuse the sell offer to be listed (Secondary Market Terms & Conditions, 2024).

Less frequently, platforms obtain a stand-alone licence for operating a trading venue. For instance, the US-based platform StartEngine, which began operating an alternative trading system in 2020 (regulated by the SEC), currently lists securities of only one company (*Buy and Sell Shares in Startups*, 2024). Another example is the Estonian platform Funderbeam, whose marketplace has been recognised as an authorised market operator under the laws of the Republic of Singapore and regulated by the Monetary Authority of Singapore. The platform for secondary trading runs a matching engine that automatically matches buy and sell orders from two investors. As with other regulated markets for secondary trading, the platform has strict rules on issuers whose investments are to be admitted to trading and their ongoing disclosure requirements, trading members who act as intermediaries for executing trade orders for their clients (non-accredited investors), and accredited or professional investors who have direct access to trading (Funderbeam, 2022).

Several (equity) platforms have also announced the introduction of a secondary market (e.g., Crowdcube, StartEngine, FundedByMe, and Invesdor). Still, only a few among them have eventually done so (Lukkarinen & Schwienbacher, 2023, p. 2, fn. 2). Some secondary markets also ceased to operate after some time, such has been the case with the lending platform Prosper, which ended up its secondary trading facility due to low trading volumes (Holden et al., 2020). Similarly, UK-based equity platform Crowdcube has decided to gradually abolish its trading facility as of 2021 (Lukkarinen & Schwienbacher, 2023, p. 2, fn. 2).[182] Even for those platforms with active secondary markets, liquidity remains an important concern, not least because there are no (sufficient) informed traders and securities analysts.

Empirical studies on secondary markets for crowdfunding investments are still scarce. The key question addressed is how investors perceive the importance of secondary markets and, thus, what their effect is on (primary) crowdfunding market outcomes. It is worth noting that crowd investors are likely to be driven by prospects of greater liquidity of their investments rather than thinking about possible implications for ex-post information asymmetry and corporate governance.

In an early study of the US-based platform Lending Club, Reher (2014) investigated the effects of introducing the secondary market on investor demand for securities in the primary market and, consequently, interest rates. His findings indicate that while the promise of a new exit route stimulates the demand for P2P lending loans, its effect on interest rates is ambiguous. As the author contends (Reher, 2014, pp. 15–21), the existence of the secondary market can reduce the liquidity premium and thus lead to a decrease in interest rates. However, lenders who are given the possibility of exit before default or maturity can also decide to turn to riskier loans as a result. The idea is that incentives to select good borrowers in the

[182] Interestingly, some equity-based platforms, such as Sweden-based FundedByMe, openly nudge their clients against secondary market trading, especially before fundraisers have had a chance to deliver on the promises pitched in the campaign (Gargantini, 2022, p. 354, fn. 14). The reasoning is that divesting goes against the purpose of crowdfunding, which is about participating in the company growth.

primary market are weaker when loans can be sold prematurely, thus increasing the risk premium. The empirical results have shown that while the overall interest rates fell after the introduction of secondary trading, investors holding safer loans turned to riskier loans, generating a higher interest rate. Another study examining the effects of secondary trading on P2P lending campaigns was conducted by Holden et al. (2020), who exploited the fact that the US-based platform Prosper ceased its secondary market operations in 2016. Their findings also support the hypothesis that lenders are less likely to invest when secondary trading is unavailable. The closure of the secondary market reduced primary market liquidity, as captured by the time needed to fund loans, the percentage of the loans financed, and funding costs. In addition, the authors have reported some positive spillover effects for the primary market of Prosper's main competitor, Lending Club. It is important to note that, despite the importance of the secondary market for primary market outcomes, Prosper decided to shut it down precisely because 'very few investors are using the secondary market' (Holden et al., 2020, p. 7).

Similarly, Lukkarinen and Schwienbacher (2023) found evidence that prospects of secondary market trading are valued by investors in the equity crowdfunding market but conditional on secondary market liquidity. More specifically, the authors have tested whether a plan to list on the secondary market affects individual campaign outcomes, as stated during an equity crowdfunding campaign. Thus, their setting is unique as the crowdfunding firm must opt in for secondary market trading. Their data comes from Invesdor, which, as explained above, cooperates with an established secondary market for private companies—Privanet. The authors have found that ventures that promised this exit route run more successful crowdfunding campaigns, as captured by the overall amounts raised, the number of investors, and the size of individual pledges. Nevertheless, they have also documented that these effects diminish or disappear 2 years after introducing the secondary market. The authors have contended that this is because, with more time passing, investors generally become aware that these markets are primarily illiquid. Moreover, even the initial effect of plans to list on a secondary market has been found to exist only among 'regular' investors. 'Legal entity' investors or 'key' investors do not change their behaviour in response to the operation of the secondary market, implying that they expect the market to suffer from liquidity shocks (Lukkarinen & Schwienbacher, 2023, p. 2).[183]

In addition to and in relation to liquidity, another relevant question that can be explored empirically is pricing efficiency. As discussed before, secondary markets reduce post-campaign information asymmetry and enhance corporate governance practices primarily via (efficient) asset prices. Limited empirical evidence on secondary markets for P2P loans suggests that there are many instances of asset mispricing. Caglayan et al. (2020) have investigated whether

[183] Invesdor distinguishes between different investor statuses, whereas the status of a 'key' investor is earned by cumulative pledges exceeding € 10,000. While 'key' investors sometimes receive news about new projects ahead of regular investors, they invest on the same terms and are equal in their shareholder rights (Lukkarinen & Schwienbacher, 2023, p. 3).

secondary market outcomes, that is, the success of a loan resale, diverge from what asset fundamentals and terms of sale would suggest. The data used comes from the Estonia-based platform Bondora, which allows the participation of investors from Continental Europe.[184] According to the authors, the secondary market was established in 2013, allowing P2P lending primary market investors to list their loans for sale at a premium/discount within 30 days. To measure asset mispricing, Caglayan et al. (2020) have compared the estimated sale probability of an asset with the actual outcome on the secondary market (sold or unsold).[185] Their findings have indicated that two types of mispricing errors are present. Some assets do not get sold despite being adequately priced by the seller. In contrast, transactions in assets with a lower likelihood of being sold are often successfully completed. The authors interpret their finding as evidence of dispersed beliefs on asset pricing among P2P lending investors rather than ex-post information asymmetry, as the platform makes a substantial amount of relevant information available to all investors (Caglayan et al., 2020, pp. 2–3).

In sum, existing empirical studies suggest that the existence of secondary markets is usually valued by investors as a means of reducing liquidity risk, even though achieving sufficient transaction volumes remains a challenge. As shown in another study by Ölvedi (2021), even performing loans are sold with a significant discount, suggesting that liquidity comes with a considerable cost for sellers in secondary markets.

The role of secondary markets in reducing ex-post information asymmetry and enhancing corporate governance in funded firms is limited, even though empirical evidence is still lacking. As pointed out above, secondary markets for securities issued via crowdfunding sometimes require the funded company to decide on the listing, implying that the company managers choose to be put under close scrutiny.[186] Moreover, companies whose securities are listed on a secondary market are not always subject to ongoing disclosure requirements that would give external investors equal access to information compared to existing investors (Lukkarinen & Schwienbacher, 2023, p. 20). These two factors, together with the issue of liquidity, put into question the assumption of efficient asset prices on crowdfunding secondary markets. Overall, one can expect that these caveats, taken together, significantly diminish secondary markets' effects on ex-post information asymmetry and sound corporate governance.

[184] More specifically, investors can be citizens of the EU, Switzerland, Norway, or a country approved by Bondora. The study sample covers loans obtained from three countries: Estonia, Spain, and Finland (Caglayan et al., 2020, p. 2, 5).

[185] The sale probability of a loan is calculated based on how close is the asset valuation by the seller to its fundamental value. Consequently, a low probability of sale is predicted when the asset is overvalued (Caglayan et al., 2020, pp. 9–11).

[186] Lukkarinen and Schwienbacher (2023, p. 20) have argued that crowdfunding companies may not want their securities to be listed on a secondary market as low liquidity, high volatility, or low prices can affect their ability to raise follow-up capital.

Despite this, it is worth noting that a great variety of services are offered in secondary markets, depending on the regulatory constraints of the jurisdiction in which the platform operates. It would be helpful to understand better how secondary market characteristics affect liquidity and pricing efficiency.

3.5.8 Provision Funds

Some platforms create contingency or provision funds to absorb the first losses investors incur. Provision funds are more common on loan-based than on equity-based platforms due to the fixed return and maturity of loans as opposed to equity. There are two ways in which they can be financed (Havrylchyk, 2018, p. 13). Sometimes, they are created thanks to risk-adjusted contributions from borrowers who raise funds on the platform. In other instances, it is the platform which contributes its capital. Platforms ensure that the fund is kept separate from other platform's asset classes.[187] Provision funds differ regarding their size and the associated coverage ratio. For instance, some platforms, such as Ppdai in China, determine the target size of the provision fund so that the ratio of the contingency fund to the total value of intermediated loans always has to exceed the historical loan default ratio (Nisar et al., 2020, p. 360). Provision funds also have different rules on when investors are entitled to recover losses (e.g., when a borrower misses a payment, a few months after the payment has been overdue or after all the recovery attempts have failed) (Faulkner, 2015).

It is worth noting that many regulatory regimes prohibit platforms from establishing such funds to ensure that platforms remain neutral (non-balance sheet) intermediaries, not being exposed to any credit risk. Provision funds have been a notable feature of lending-based platforms operating in the UK and China (Nisar et al., 2020, p. 360).

It is self-understood that the key function of provision funds is mitigating the consequences of information asymmetry—losses investors are exposed to because of a loan default or project failure. However, provision funds financed by platforms can also indirectly reduce ex-ante information asymmetry, increasing platforms' incentives to perform other gatekeeping roles, notably due diligence and credit risk assessment. The higher the likelihood of a loan default or project failure, the greater the platform's 'skin in the game'. The described mechanism is likely stronger when the provision fund is financed by platforms' capital instead of financing from fundraisers. Consequently, provision funds can lead to a better alignment of interests between the platform and investors without the platform investing in crowdfunding offers alongside retail investors.[188]

[187] For instance, the oldest P2P lending platform, Zopa, manages a Safeguard fund, a trust that stays with a not-for-profit organization (Chishti, 2016, p. 58).

[188] Platform co-investments in loans or projects listed on their website are prohibited in many jurisdictions as they raise the issue of conflict of interest and the possibility for platforms to cherry-pick the most promising offers (Havrylchyk, 2018, p. 37).

Nevertheless, there are two inherent risks associated with this platform gatekeeping function. Firstly, there is a question of transparency as to the size of the fund, the percentage of losses covered, as well as how platforms exercise their discretion in case the fund is insufficient to compensate all investors. It is essential that investors do not perceive the provision fund as a guarantee of expected return. As argued by Chishti (2016, p. 62), provision funds accompanied by a low default track record of a platform can misguide investors to believe that P2P generates higher returns when compared to banks without incurring additional risk.

Secondly, provision funds effectively reinforce the reintermediation function of platforms. This may, in turn, reduce investors' incentives to conduct due diligence and make sound investment decisions even when provided with enough information.

3.5.9 Summary of Findings on Platform Gatekeeping

The analysis of this chapter provided insights into platform reintermediation or gatekeeping services that can attenuate the information asymmetry between fundraisers and investors. Some services are provided before or during the crowdfunding campaign, while others are offered after a successful fundraising round. Ex-ante services help with issues arising from hidden information, mitigating the costs of screening and pre-selecting investment opportunities (due diligence, disclosure rules for platforms, credit assessment and pricing, and automatic investments). Ex-post services help with issues arising from hidden action, reducing agency costs or moral hazard of fundraisers (administering loan repayments and loss recovery, services related to governance, operating secondary markets or provision funds). It should be noted, however, that secondary markets offered by some platforms have a limited role in reducing ex-post information asymmetry (in contrast to traditional secondary markets) because of insufficient liquidity, low frequency of trading, and lack of professional analysts and traders analysing corporate disclosures. Moreover, contingency funds (despite their function of mitigating the risks stemming from information asymmetry once they materialise) can potentially reduce ex-ante information asymmetry if the platform contributes its assets to the fund and thus has stronger incentives to prescreen fundraisers.

The analysis in this chapter showed that the scope and depth of platform gatekeeping services vary considerably across platforms. While empirical evidence is not always available or sufficient (e.g., regarding platform disclosure requirements for issuers), it is evident that there is little market consolidation concerning almost all services. One exception is administering loan repayments and loss recovery on behalf of lenders, which lies at the heart of the lending-based crowdfunding model. Moreover, some services emerged due to market maturing, e.g. pricing and or individual loan portfolio management, and thus, are not necessarily present in less developed markets. In relation to this, pricing and individual portfolio management are currently captured only in lending models. However, it is not difficult to imagine that similar services will become available for investment-based models in the future (if they are allowed under relevant regulatory frameworks).

One crucial issue that requires further research is to what extent market participants are responsive to these services or their quality and whether they perceive them as desirable platform features. The response to this question is important from a regulatory point of view, as it can influence regulators' choice concerning the scope of permissible services as well as the choice between different regulatory tools (e.g., whether regulations should provide greater transparency or mandate quality standards).

In connection to this, it was discussed that some platform services, such as credit scoring or pricing, automatic investments, and operating provision funds, can interfere with other market-based mechanisms, notably herding, information production by fundraisers, and investors' incentives to conduct their due diligence.

Relatedly, it is not entirely clear what the optimal level of platform interference or reintermediation is or whether the choices made on behalf of market participants are efficient. For instance, regarding the design of investment contracts, particularly governance-related issues, it is often indefinite what works best in the crowdfunding context. Moreover, services that involve platform screening, monitoring, and risk management can produce superior outcomes for investors only if platforms adhere to high standards. However, this is not granted for the reasons described in relation to traditional gatekeepers (e.g., conflict of interest, agency costs). Moreover, platform services with regard to which no specific regulatory requirements exist raise the concern of investors' overreliance on them and false perceptions about their scope and depth. As discussed in greater detail in Chap. 5, platform services shift the source of risks from fundraisers to platforms, requiring a different regulatory approach.

References

Adhami, S., Gianfrate, G., & Johan, S. (2023). Risks and returns in crowdlending. *Eurasian Business Review, 13*(2), 309–340. https://doi.org/10.1007/s40821-022-00236-x

Aggarwal, N. (2018). Machine learning, big data and the regulation of consumer credit markets: The case of algorithmic credit scoring. In N. Aggarwal, H. Eidenmüller, L. Enriques, J. Payne, & K. Van Zwieten (Eds.), *Autonomous systems and the law* (pp. 1–6). SSRN Library. https://ssrn.com/abstract=3309244

Agrawal, A., Catalini, C., & Goldfarb, A. (2014). Some simple economics of crowdfunding. *Innovation Policy and the Economy, 14*(1), 63–97. https://doi.org/10.1086/674021

Agrawal, A., Catalini, C., & Goldfarb, A. (2015). Crowdfunding: Geography, social networks, and the timing of investment decisions. *Journal of Economics and Management Strategy, 24*(2), 253–274. https://doi.org/10.1111/jems.12093

Agrawal, A., Catalini, C., & Goldfarb, A. (2016). Are syndicates the killer app of equity crowdfunding? *California Management Review, 58*(2), 111–124. https://doi.org/10.1525/cmr.2016.58.2.111

Ahlers, G. K. C., Cumming, D., Günther, C., & Schweizer, D. (2015). Signaling in equity crowdfunding. *Entrepreneurship Theory and Practice, 39*(4), 955–980. https://doi.org/10.1111/etap.12157

Akerlof, G. A. (1970). The market for 'lemons': Quality uncertainty and the market mechanism. *The Quarterly Journal of Economics, 84*(3), 488–500. https://doi.org/10.2307/1879431

Aland, J. M. (2023). Equity crowdfunding and offering page disclosure. *Journal of Financial Reporting, 8*(2), 25–53. https://doi.org/10.2308/JFR-2021-011

Alharbey, M., & Van Hemmen, S. (2021). Investor intention in equity crowdfunding. Does trust matter? *Journal of Risk and Financial Management, 14*(2), 53–72. https://doi.org/10.3390/jrfm14020053

Allison, T. H. (2017). Persuasion in crowdfunding: An elaboration likelihood model of crowdfunding performance. *Journal of Business Venturing, 32*(6), 707–725. https://doi.org/10.1016/j.jbusvent.2017.09.002

Ande, J. A., & Eroglu, Z. K. (2021). Could New Zealand's equity crowdfunding regulations be the model for the developing world? *New Zealand Universities Law Review, 29*, 557–592. Retrieved from https://ssrn.com/abstract=3904063

Anglin, A. H., Short, J. C., Drover, W., Stevenson, R. M., McKenny, A. F., & Allison, T. H. (2018). The power of positivity? The influence of positive psychological capital language on crowdfunding performance. *Journal of Business Venturing, 33*(4), 470–492. https://doi.org/10.1016/j.jbusvent.2018.03.003

Anglin, A. H., Wolfe, M. T., Short, J. C., McKenny, A. F., & Pidduck, R. J. (2018). Narcissistic rhetoric and crowdfunding performance: A social role theory perspective. *Journal of Business Venturing, 33*(6), 780–812. https://doi.org/10.1016/j.jbusvent.2018.04.004

Armour, J., & Enriques, L. (2018). Individual investors' access to crowdinvesting: Two regulatory models. In D. Cumming & L. Hornuf (Eds.), *The economics of crowdfunding* (pp. 255–278). Palgrave Macmillan. https://doi.org/10.1007/978-3-319-66119-3_11

Astebro, T. B., Fernández Sierra, M., Lovo, S., & Vulkan, N. (2019). Herding in equity crowdfunding. *RAND Journal of Economics*. https://doi.org/10.2139/ssrn.3084140

Bachrach, Y., Lev, O., & Shemesh, J. (2022). The role of soft information in crowdfunding: Evidence from crowdsourced data. *SSRN Electronic Journal*. https://doi.org/10.2139/ssrn.4173548

Baeck, P., Collins, L., & Zhang, B. (2014). Understanding alternative finance. In *The UK alternative finance industry report 2014* (pp. 1–95). University of Cambridge. Retrieved from https://media.nesta.org.uk/documents/understanding-alternative-finance-2014.pdf

Bafera, J., & Kleinert, S. (2022). Signaling theory in entrepreneurship research: A systematic review and research agenda. *Entrepreneurship Theory and Practice*. https://doi.org/10.1177/10422587221138489

Banerjee, A. V. (1992). A simple model of herd behavior. *The Quarterly Journal of Economics, 107*(3), 797–817. https://doi.org/10.2307/2118364

Barbi, M., & Mattioli, S. (2019). Human capital, investor trust, and equity crowdfunding. *Research in International Business and Finance, 49*, 1–12. https://doi.org/10.1016/j.ribaf.2019.02.005

Battaglia, F., Busato, F., & Manganiello, M. (2022). A cross-platform analysis of the equity crowdfunding Italian context: The role of intellectual capital. *Electronic Commerce Research, 22*(2), 649–689. https://doi.org/10.1007/s10660-020-09453-w

Battisti, E., Graziano, E. A., & Christofi, M. (2021). Equity crowdfunding platforms and social media: A Twitter analysis. *International Journal of Entrepreneurial Behavior & Research, 28*(5), 1206–1221. https://doi.org/10.1108/IJEBR-01-2021-0081

Becker, G. S. (1993). *Human capital: A theoretical and empirical analysis, with special reference to education* (3rd ed.). The University of Chicago Press.

Belleflamme, P., & Lambert, T. (2016). An industrial organization framework to understand the strategies of crowdfunding platforms. In J. Méric, I. Maque, & J. Brabet (Eds.), *International perspectives on crowdfunding* (pp. 1–19). Emerald Group Publishing Limited. https://doi.org/10.1108/978-1-78560-315-020151001

Belleflamme, P., & Peitz, M. (2021). *The economics of platforms*. Cambridge University Press.

Benveniste, L. M., & Spindt, P. A. (1989). How investment bankers determine the offer price and allocation of new issues. *Journal of Financial Economics, 24*(2), 343–361. https://doi.org/10.1016/0304-405X(89)90051-2

Bikhchandani, S., Hirshleifer, D., & Welch, I. (1992). A theory of fads, fashion, custom, and cultural change as informational cascades. *Journal of Political Economy, 100*(5), 992–1026. https://doi.org/10.1086/261849

Block, J., Hornuf, L., & Moritz, A. (2018). Which updates during an equity crowdfunding campaign increase crowd participation? *Small Business Economics, 50*(1), 3–27. https://doi.org/10.1007/s11187-017-9876-4

Bogdani, E., Causholli, M., & Knechel, W. R. (2022). The role of assurance in equity crowdfunding. *The Accounting Review, 97*(2), 51–76. https://doi.org/10.2308/TAR-2019-0427

Böhme, R., & Grossklags, J. (2013). Trading agent kills market information: Evidence from online social lending. In Y. Chen & N. Immorlica (Eds.), *Web and internet economics (WINE 2013)* (pp. 68–81). Springer.

Booth, J. R., & Smith, R. L. (1986). Capital raising, underwriting and the certification hypothesis. *Journal of Financial Economics, 15*(1–2), 261–281. https://doi.org/10.1016/0304-405X(86)90057-7

Botosan, C. A. (1997). Disclosure level and the cost of equity capital. *The Accounting Review, 72*(3), 323–349. Retrieved from https://www.jstor.org/stable/248475

Bouglet, J., Garmilis, G., & Joffre, O. (2022). Protection of crowdfunders: A typology of equity crowdfunding platforms through governance mechanisms. *Revue de l'Entrepreneuriat, 20*, 26. https://doi.org/10.3917/entre1.pr.0006

Budescu, D. V., & Chen, E. (2015). Identifying expertise to extract the wisdom of crowds. *Management Science, 61*(2), 267–280. https://doi.org/10.1287/mnsc.2014.1909

Buttice, V., Colombo, M. G., & Wright, M. (2017). Serial crowdfunding, social capital, and project success. *Entrepreneurship Theory and Practice, 41*(2), 183–207. https://doi.org/10.1111/etap.12271

Butticè, V., Di Pietro, F., & Tenca, F. (2020). Is equity crowdfunding always good? Deal structure and the attraction of venture capital investors. *Journal of Corporate Finance, 65*, 101773. https://doi.org/10.1016/j.jcorpfin.2020.101773

Caglayan, M., Pham, T., Talavera, O., & Xiong, X. (2020). Asset mispricing in peer-to-peer loan secondary markets. *Journal of Corporate Finance, 65*, 101769. https://doi.org/10.1016/j.jcorpfin.2020.101769

Caglayan, M., Talavera, O., & Zhang, W. (2021). Herding behaviour in P2P lending markets. *Journal of Empirical Finance, 63*, 27–41. https://doi.org/10.1016/j.jempfin.2021.05.005

Carmichael, D. (2014). Modeling default for peer-to-peer loans. *SSRN Electronic Journal*. https://doi.org/10.2139/ssrn.2529240

Ceyhan, S., Shi, X., & Leskovec, J. (2011). Dynamics of bidding in a P2P lending service: Effects of herding and predicting loan success. In *Proceedings of the 20th international conference on world wide web* (pp. 547–556). ACM. https://doi.org/10.1145/1963405.1963483

Chen, C., Li, G., Fan, L., & Qin, J. (2021). The impact of automated investment on peer-to-peer lending: Investment behavior and platform efficiency. *Journal of Global Information Management, 29*(6), 1–22. https://doi.org/10.4018/JGIM.20211101.oa36

Chen, D., Hu, H., Lou, H., & Yong, W. (2015). Herding behavior in online microloan markets: Evidence from China. In *WHICEB 2015 proceedings* (pp. 215–218). Retrieved from https://aisel.aisnet.org/whiceb2015/84

Chen, K. C. W., Chen, Z., & Wei, K. C. J. (2009). Legal protection of investors, corporate governance, and the cost of equity capital. *Journal of Corporate Finance, 15*(3), 273–289. https://doi.org/10.1016/j.jcorpfin.2009.01.001

Chen, L., Huang, Z., & Liu, D. (2016). Pure and hybrid crowds in crowdfunding markets. *Financial Innovation, 2*(1), 1–18. https://doi.org/10.1186/s40854-016-0038-5

Chen, X., Huang, B., & Shaban, M. (2022). Naïve or sophisticated? Information disclosure and investment decisions in peer to peer lending. *Journal of Corporate Finance, 77*, 101805. https://doi.org/10.1016/j.jcorpfin.2020.101805

Chen, X., & Ma, L. (2023). Lead investors' insider ownership and crowd investors' agency concerns in investor-led equity crowdfunding. *Pacific-Basin Finance Journal, 78*, 101978. https://doi.org/10.1016/j.pacfin.2023.101978

Chishti, S. (2016). How peer to peer lending and crowdfunding drive the fintech revolution in the UK. In P. Tasca, T. Aste, L. Pelizzon, & N. Perony (Eds.), *Banking beyond banks and money: A guide to banking services in the twenty-first century* (pp. 55–68). Springer. https://doi.org/10.1007/978-3-319-42448-4_4

Coakley, J., Cumming, D. J., Lazos, A., & Vismara, S. (2021). Enfranchising the crowd: Nominee account equity crowdfunding. *CFS Working Paper Series, 664*, 1–45. https://doi.org/10.2139/ssrn.3830741

Coakley, J., & Lazos, A. (2021). New developments in equity crowdfunding: A review. *Review of Corporate Finance, 1*(3-4), 341–405. https://doi.org/10.1561/114.00000008

Coakley, J., Lazos, A., & Liñares-Zegarra, J. (2022). Strategic entrepreneurial choice between competing crowdfunding platforms. *The Journal of Technology Transfer, 47*(6), 1794–1824. https://doi.org/10.1007/s10961-021-09891-0

Coffee, J. C. (1984). Market failure and the economic case for a mandatory disclosure system. *Virginia Law Review, 70*(4), 717–753. https://doi.org/10.2307/1073083

Coleman, J. S. (1988). Social capital in the creation of human capital. *American Journal of Sociology, 94*, S95–S120. https://doi.org/10.1086/228943

Collier, B. C., & Hampshire, R. (2010). Sending mixed signals: Multilevel reputation effects in peer-to-peer lending markets. In *Proceedings of the 2010 ACM conference on computer supported cooperative work* (pp. 197–206). ACM. https://doi.org/10.1145/1718918.1718955

Colombo, M. G., Franzoni, C., & Rossi-Lamastra, C. (2015). Internal social capital and the attraction of early contributions in crowdfunding. *Entrepreneurship Theory and Practice, 39*(1), 75–100. https://doi.org/10.1111/etap.12118

Cornée, S. (2019). The relevance of soft information for predicting small business credit default: Evidence from a social bank. *Journal of Small Business Management, 57*(3), 699–719. https://doi.org/10.1111/jsbm.12318

Crowdcube. (n.d.). *How can I secure lead investment?* Retrieved from https://help.crowdcube.com/hc/en-us/articles/360012450280-How-can-I-secure-lead-investment

Cumming, D., & Hornuf, L. (2022). Marketplace lending of small- and medium-sized enterprises. *Strategic Entrepreneurship Journal, 16*(1), 32–66. https://doi.org/10.1002/sej.1411

Cumming, D., Meoli, M., & Vismara, S. (2019). Investors' choices between cash and voting rights: Evidence from dual-class equity crowdfunding. *Research Policy, 48*(8), 103740. https://doi.org/10.1016/j.respol.2019.01.014

Cumming, D. J., Johan, S. A., & Zhang, Y. (2019). The role of due diligence in crowdfunding platforms. *Journal of Banking & Finance, 108*, 105661. https://doi.org/10.1016/j.jbankfin.2019.105661

Cumming, D. J., Vanacker, T., & Zahra, S. A. (2021). Equity crowdfunding and governance: Toward an integrative model and research agenda. *Academy of Management Perspectives, 35*(1), 69–95. https://doi.org/10.5465/amp.2017.0208

Dambanemuya, H. K., Wachs, J., & Horvát, E.-Á. (2023). Understanding (Ir)rational herding online. In *Proceedings of the ACM collective intelligence conference* (pp. 79–88). ACM. https://doi.org/10.1145/3582269.3615598

Darmon, E., Oriol, N., & Rufini, A. (2022). Bids for speed: An empirical study of investment strategy automation in a peer-to-business lending platform. *Decision Support Systems, 156*, 113732. https://doi.org/10.1016/j.dss.2022.113732

DeBoskey, D. G., & Gillett, P. R. (2013). The impact of multi-dimensional corporate transparency on us firms' credit ratings and cost of capital. *Review of Quantitative Finance and Accounting, 40*(1), 101–134. https://doi.org/10.1007/s11156-011-0266-8

Deschler, G. D. (2013). Wisdom of the intermediary crowd: What the proposed rules mean for ambitious crowdfunding intermediaries. *Saint Louis University Law Journal, 58*, 1145–1188. Retrieved from https://heinonline.org/HOL/LandingPage?handle=hein.journals/stlulj58&div=59&id=&page

Devenow, A., & Welch, I. (1996). Rational herding in financial economics. *European Economic Review, 40*(3-5), 603–615. https://doi.org/10.1016/0014-2921(95)00073-9

Diamond, D. W. (1985). Optimal release of information by firms. *The Journal of Finance, 40*(4), 1071–1094. https://doi.org/10.1111/j.1540-6261.1985.tb02364.x

Directive. (2014). *2014/65/EU of the European Parliament and of the Council of 15 May 2014 on Markets in Financial Instruments and Amending Directive 2002/92/EC and Directive 2011/61/EU*. Retrieved from https://eur-lex.europa.eu/legal-content/EN/TXT/PDF/?uri=CELEX:32014L0065

Donovan, J. (2021). Financial reporting and entrepreneurial finance: Evidence from equity crowdfunding. *Management Science, 67*(11), 7214–7237. https://doi.org/10.1287/mnsc.2020.3810

Dorfleitner, G., Hornuf, L., & Weber, M. (2018). Dynamics of investor communication in equity crowdfunding. *Electronic Markets, 28*(4), 523–540. https://doi.org/10.1007/s12525-018-0294-5

Dorfleitner, G., Priberny, C., Schuster, S., Stoiber, J., Weber, M., de Castro, I., & Kammler, J. (2016). Description-text related soft information in peer-to-peer lending—Evidence from two leading European platforms. *Journal of Banking & Finance, 64*, 169–187. https://doi.org/10.1016/j.jbankfin.2015.11.009

Downes, D. H., & Heinkel, R. (1982). Signaling and the valuation of unseasoned new issues. *The Journal of Finance, 37*(1), 1–10. https://doi.org/10.1111/j.1540-6261.1982.tb01091.x

Dranove, D., & Jin, G. Z. (2010). Quality disclosure and certification: Theory and practice. *Journal of Economic Literature, 48*(4), 935–963. https://doi.org/10.1257/jel.48.4.935

Duarte, J., Siegel, S., & Young, L. (2012). Trust and credit: The role of appearance in peer-to-peer lending. *Review of Financial Studies, 25*(8), 2455–2484. https://doi.org/10.1093/rfs/hhs071

Dye, R. A. (1985). Disclosure of nonproprietary information. *Journal of Accounting Research, 23*, 123–145. https://doi.org/10.2307/2490910

Dye, R. A. (1986). Proprietary and nonproprietary disclosures. *The Journal of Business, 59*(2), 331–366. Retrieved from http://www.jstor.org/stable/2353023

Easley, D., & Kleinberg, J. (2010). *Networks, crowds, and markets: Reasoning about a highly connected world*. Cambridge University Press.

Easley, D., & O'hara, M. (2004). Information and the cost of capital. *The Journal of Finance, 59*(4), 1553–1583. https://doi.org/10.1111/j.1540-6261.2004.00672.x

Easterbrook, F. H., & Fischel, D. R. (1991). *The economic structure of corporate law*. Harvard University Press.

Edmans, A., Heinle, M. S., & Huang, C. (2016). The real costs of financial efficiency when some information is soft. *Review of Finance, 20*(6), 2151–2182. https://doi.org/10.1093/rof/rfw030

Eid, N., Maltby, J., & Talavera, O. (2016). Income rounding and loan performance in the peer-to-peer market. *SSRN Electronic Journal*. https://doi.org/10.2139/ssrn.2848372

Eisenbeiss, M., Hartmann, S. A., & Hornuf, L. (2023). Social media marketing for equity crowdfunding: Which posts trigger investment decisions? *Finance Research Letters, 52*, 103370. https://doi.org/10.1016/j.frl.2022.103370

Enriques, L., & Gilotta, S. (2014). Disclosure and financial market regulation. In E. Ferran, N. Moloney, & J. Payne (Eds.), *The Oxford handbook on financial regulation* (pp. 511–536). Oxford University Press.

Estrin, S., Khavul, S., & Wright, M. (2022). Soft and hard information in equity crowdfunding: Network effects in the digitalization of entrepreneurial finance. *Small Business Economics, 58*(4), 1761–1781. https://doi.org/10.1007/s11187-021-00473-w

Evans, D. S., Schmalensee, R., Noel, M. D., Chang, H. H., & Garcia-Swartz, D. D. (2011). *Platform economics: Essays on multi-sided businesses*. Competition Policy International. Retrieved from https://ssrn.com/abstract=1974020

Everett, C. R. (2015). Group membership, relationship banking and loan default risk: The case of online social lending. *Banking and Finance Review, 7*(2), 1–54. https://doi.org/10.2139/ssrn.1114428

Faia, E., & Paiella, M. (2017). *P2P lending: Information externalities, social networks and loans' substitution*. CEPR Discussion Paper No. DP12235 (pp. 1–68). Retrieved from https://ssrn.com/abstract=3028601

Fama, E. F. (1970). Efficient capital markets: A review of theory and empirical work. *The Journal of Finance, 25*(2), 383–417.
Fama, E. F., & Jensen, M. C. (1983). Separation of ownership and control. *Journal of Law and Economics, 26*, 301–325. https://doi.org/10.1086/467037
Farag, H., & Johan, S. (2022). How alternative finance informs central themes in corporate finance. *Journal of Corporate Finance, 77*, 102318. https://doi.org/10.1016/j.jcorpfin.2022.102318
Farrell, J. (1995). Talk is cheap. *The American Economic Review, 85*(2), 186–190. Retrieved from https://www.jstor.org/stable/2117916
Farrell, J., & Gibbons, R. (1989). Cheap talk with two audiences. *The American Economic Review, 79*(5), 1214–1223. Retrieved from https://www.jstor.org/stable/1831447
Faulkner, N. (2015). *How the P2P lending provision funds compare*. 4thway. Retrieved from https://www.4thway.co.uk/candid-opinion/p2p-lending-provision-funds-compare/
Ferreira, V., Papaoikonomou, E., & Terceño, A. (2022). Unpeel the layers of trust! A comparative analysis of crowdfunding platforms and what they do to generate trust. *Business Horizons, 65*(1), 7–19. https://doi.org/10.1016/j.bushor.2021.08.004
Ferretti, R., Venturelli, V., & Pedrazzoli, A. (2021). Do multiple competing offerings on a crowdfunding platform influence investment behavior? *Journal of Behavioral and Experimental Finance, 30*, 100506. https://doi.org/10.1016/j.jbef.2021.100506
Fitzpatrick, T., & Mues, C. (2021). How can lenders prosper? Comparing machine learning approaches to identify profitable peer-to-peer loan investments. *European Journal of Operational Research, 294*(2), 711–722. https://doi.org/10.1016/j.ejor.2021.01.047
Forsythe, R., Lundholm, R., & Rietz, T. (1999). Cheap talk, fraud, and adverse selection in financial markets: Some experimental evidence. *The Review of Financial Studies, 12*(3), 481–518. https://doi.org/10.1093/revfin/12.3.0481
Fox, M. B. (1999). Required disclosure and corporate governance. *Law and Contemporary Problems, 62*(3), 113–127. Retrieved from https://heinonline.org/HOL/LandingPage?handle=hein.journals/lcp62&div=31&id=&page
Fox, M. B. (2016). Regulating public offerings of truly new securities: First principles. *Duke Law Journal, 66*, 673–727. Retrieved from https://heinonline.org/HOL/LandingPage?handle=hein.journals/duklr66&div=24&id=&page=
Franks, J., Serrano-Velarde, N., & Sussman, O. (2021). Marketplace lending, information aggregation, and liquidity. *The Review of Financial Studies, 34*(5), 2318–2361. https://doi.org/10.1093/rfs/hhaa101
Freedman, S., & Jin, G. Z. (2017). The information value of online social networks: Lessons from peer-to-peer lending. *International Journal of Industrial Organization, 51*, 185–222. https://doi.org/10.1016/j.ijindorg.2016.09.002
Funderbeam. (2022). *Trading rules*. Retrieved from https://www.funderbeam.com/fbmsg/trading-rules
Gallo, S. (2021). Fintech platforms: Lax or careful borrowers' screening? *Financial Innovation, 7*(1), 7–58. https://doi.org/10.1186/s40854-021-00272-y
Gao, Q., Lin, M., & Sias, R. W. (2018). Words matter: The role of texts in online credit markets. *Journal of Financial and Quantitative Analysis*. https://doi.org/10.2139/ssrn.2446114
Gargantini, M. (2022). Secondary markets for crowdfunding: Bulletin boards (Art 25). In E. Macchiavello (Ed.), *Regulation on European Crowdfunding Service Providers for Business* (pp. 350–366). Edward Elgar Publishing. https://doi.org/10.4337/9781802209945.00034
Ghaidarov, S. (2021). Price discounts for unlisted equity securities with random or indefinite liquidity horizons. *The Journal of Investing, 30*(3), 92–107. https://doi.org/10.3905/joi.2021.1.171
Gigler, F. (1994). Self-enforcing voluntary disclosures. *Journal of Accounting Research, 32*(2), 224–240. https://doi.org/10.2307/2491283
Gilson, R. J., & Kraakman, R. (2014). Market efficiency after the financial crisis: It's still a matter of information costs. *Virginia Law Review, 100*, 313–375. Retrieved from https://heinonline.org/HOL/LandingPage?handle=hein.journals/valr100&div=12&id=&page

Giudici, G., Guerini, M., & Rossi Lamastra, C. (2013). Why crowdfunding projects can succeed: The role of proponents' individual and territorial social capital. *SSRN Electronic Journal*. https://doi.org/10.2139/ssrn.2255944

Goethner, M., Luettig, S., & Regner, T. (2021). Crowdinvesting in entrepreneurial projects: Disentangling patterns of investor behavior. *Small Business Economics, 57*(2), 905–926. https://doi.org/10.1007/s11187-020-00332-0

Gordon, J. N., & Kornhauser, L. A. (1985). Efficient markets, costly information, and securities research. *New York University Law Review, 60*, 761–849. Retrieved from https://heinonline.org/HOL/LandingPage?handle=hein.journals/nylr60&div=34&id=&page

Goshen, Z., & Parchomovsky, G. (2005). The essential role of securities regulation. *Duke Law Journal, 55*, 711–782. Retrieved from https://heinonline.org/HOL/LandingPage?handle=hein.journals/duklr55&div=27&id=&page

Graziano, E. A., Fattobene, L., Giovando, G., & Pellicelli, A. (2023). Contacts on LinkedIn: Equity crowdfunding platforms' networks and creators' innovation performance. *European Journal of Innovation Management*. https://doi.org/10.1108/EJIM-03-2022-0125

Grossman, S. J., & Hart, O. D. (1980). Disclosure laws and takeover bids. *The Journal of Finance, 35*(2), 323–334. https://doi.org/10.1111/j.1540-6261.1980.tb02161.x

Grossman, S. J., & Stiglitz, J. E. (1980). On the impossibility of informationally efficient markets. *The American Economic Review, 70*(3), 393–408. Retrieved from https://www.jstor.org/stable/1805228

Guenther, C., Johan, S., & Schweizer, D. (2018). Is the crowd sensitive to distance?—How investment decisions differ by investor type. *Small Business Economics, 50*, 289–305. https://doi.org/10.1007/s11187-016-9834-6

Hasan, I., He, Q., & Lu, H. (2022). Social capital, trusting, and trustworthiness: Evidence from peer-to-peer lending. *Journal of Financial and Quantitative Analysis, 57*(4), 1409–1453.

Havrylchyk, O. (2018). *Regulatory framework for the loan-based crowdfunding platforms (OECD Economics Department Working Papers 1513)* (pp. 1–56). OECD. https://doi.org/10.1787/24ad924a-en

Havrylchyk, O., & Verdier, M. (2018). The financial intermediation role of the P2P lending platforms. *Comparative Economic Studies, 60*(1), 115–130. https://doi.org/10.1057/s41294-017-0045-1

Hermalin, B. E., & Weisbach, M. S. (2012). Information disclosure and corporate governance. *The Journal of Finance, 67*(1), 195–233. https://doi.org/10.1111/j.1540-6261.2011.01710.x

Hervé, F., Manthé, E., Sannajust, A., & Schwienbacher, A. (2019). Determinants of individual investment decisions in investment-based crowdfunding. *Journal of Business Finance & Accounting, 46*(5-6), 762–783. https://doi.org/10.1111/jbfa.12372

Herzenstein, M., Andrews, R. L., Dholakia, U. M., & Lyandres, E. (2008). The democratization of personal consumer loans? Determinants of success in online peer-to-peer lending communities. *Boston University School of Management Research Paper, 14*(6), 1–36. Retrieved from https://citeseerx.ist.psu.edu/document?repid=rep1&type=pdf&doi=8127f26bef3e11191f84ccbb2f768c6abc37b095

Herzenstein, M., Dholakia, U. M., & Andrews, R. L. (2011). Strategic herding behavior in peer-to-peer loan auctions. *Journal of Interactive Marketing, 25*(1), 27–36. https://doi.org/10.1016/j.intmar.2010.07.001

Herzenstein, M., Sonenshein, S., & Dholakia, U. M. (2011). Tell me a good story and I may lend you money: The role of narratives in peer-to-peer lending decisions. *Journal of Marketing Research, 48*, S138–S149. https://doi.org/10.1509/jmkr.48.SPL.S138

Hildebrand, T., Puri, M., & Rocholl, J. (2010). *Skin in the game: Evidence from the online Social Lending Market Group*. Retrieved from https://citeseerx.ist.psu.edu/document?repid=rep1&type=pdf&doi=bd9307a49d9c36ba529ad7a0cb9f64f4c4d7eb18

Hochberg, Y. V., Ljungqvist, A., & Lu, Y. (2007). Whom you know matters: Venture capital networks and investment performance. *The Journal of Finance, 62*(1), 251–301. https://doi.org/10.1111/j.1540-6261.2007.01207.x

Hoenen, S., Kolympiris, C., Schoenmakers, W., & Kalaitzandonakes, N. (2014). The diminishing signaling value of patents between early rounds of venture capital financing. *Research Policy, 43*(6), 956–989. https://doi.org/10.1016/j.respol.2014.01.006

Holden, C. W., Lin, M., Lu, K., Wei, Z., & Yang, J. (2020). The effect of secondary market existence on primary market liquidity: Theory and evidence from a natural experiment in peer-to-peer lending. *SSRN Electronic Journal*. https://doi.org/10.2139/ssrn.3502006

Hornuf, L., Klöhn, L., & Schilling, T. (2018). Financial contracting in crowdinvesting: Lessons from the German market. *German Law Journal, 19*(3), 509–578. https://doi.org/10.1017/S2071832200022781

Hornuf, L., Schilling, T., & Schwienbacher, A. (2021). The relevance of investor rights in crowdinvesting. *Journal of Corporate Finance, 77*, 101927. https://doi.org/10.1016/j.jcorpfin.2021.101927

Hornuf, L., Schmitt, M., & Stenzhorn, E. (2018). Equity crowdfunding in Germany and the United Kingdom: Follow-up funding and firm failure. *Corporate Governance: An International Review, 26*(5), 331–354. https://doi.org/10.1111/corg.12260

Hornuf, L., & Schwienbacher, A. (2016). Crowdinvesting: Angel investing for the masses? In H. Landström & C. Mason (Eds.), *Handbook of research on business angels* (pp. 381–398). Edward Elgar Publishing. Retrieved from https://www.elgaronline.com/edcollchap/edcoll/9781783471713/9781783471713.00024.xml

Hornuf, L., & Schwienbacher, A. (2018a). Internet-based entrepreneurial finance: Lessons from Germany. *California Management Review, 60*(2), 150–175. https://doi.org/10.1177/0008125617741126

Hornuf, L., & Schwienbacher, A. (2018b). Market mechanisms and funding dynamics in equity crowdfunding. *Journal of Corporate Finance, 8*, 556–574. https://doi.org/10.1016/j.jcorpfin.2017.08.009

Hsu, D. K., Haynie, J. M., Simmons, S. A., & McKelvie, A. (2014). What matters, matters differently: A conjoint analysis of the decision policies of angel and venture capital investors. *Venture Capital, 16*(1), 1–25. https://doi.org/10.1080/13691066.2013.825527

Huddart, S., Hughes, J. S., & Brunnermeier, M. (1999). Disclosure requirements and stock exchange listing choice in an international context. *Journal of Accounting and Economics, 26, 237–269*. https://doi.org/10.1016/S0165-4101(98)00034-2

Hurley, M., & Adebayo, J. (2016). Credit scoring in the era of big data. *Yale Journal of Law & Technology, 18*, 148–216. Retrieved from https://heinonline.org/HOL/LandingPage?handle=hein.journals/yjolt18&div=6&id=&page=

Invesdor. (2024). *Invesdor*. Retrieved from https://www.invesdor.com/#/

Iyer, R., Khwaja, A. I., Luttmer, E. F., & Shue, K. (2016). Screening peers softly: Inferring the quality of small borrowers. *Management Science, 62*(6), 1554–1577. https://doi.org/10.1287/mnsc.2015.2181

Jagtiani, J., & Lemieux, C. (2019). The roles of alternative data and machine learning in fintech lending: Evidence from the LendingClub consumer platform. *Financial Management, 48*(4), 1009–1029. https://doi.org/10.1111/fima.12295

Jegeleviciute, S., & Valanciene, L. (2014). Crowdfunding: An overview of valuation problems. In *European conference on innovation and entrepreneurship* (pp. 246–251). Retrieved from https://www.proquest.com/openview/48497fa55558eccf41d4da06b6c6db10/1?pq-origsite=gscholar&cbl=396494

Jensen, M. C., & Meckling, W. H. (1976). Theory of the firm: Managerial behavior, agency costs and ownership structure. *Journal of Financial Economics, 3*(4), 305–360. https://doi.org/10.1016/0304-405X(76)90026-X

Jiang, C., Wang, Z., Wang, R., & Ding, Y. (2018). Loan default prediction by combining soft information extracted from descriptive text in online peer-to-peer lending. *Annals of Operations Research, 266*(1-2), 511–529. https://doi.org/10.1007/s10479-017-2668-z

Jiang, C., Xu, Q., Zhang, W., Li, M., & Yang, S. (2018). Does automatic bidding mechanism affect herding behavior? Evidence from online P2P lending in China. *Journal of Behavioral and Experimental Finance, 20*, 39–44. https://doi.org/10.1016/j.jbef.2018.07.001

Jo, K. M., & Yang, S. (2021). Is there crowd wisdom in accounting? Evidence from forecasts in equity-based crowdfunding. *Journal of Accounting, Auditing and Finance, 36*(4), 723–749. https://doi.org/10.1177/0148558X20912100

Johan, S., & Zhang, Y. (2020). Quality revealing versus overstating in equity crowdfunding. *Journal of Corporate Finance, 65*, 101741. https://doi.org/10.1016/j.jcorpfin.2020.101741

Jumpstart Our Business Startups Act. (2012). *Pub. L. No. 112-106, U.S. Congress*. Retrieved from https://www.govinfo.gov/content/pkg/BILLS-112hr3606enr/pdf/BILLS-112hr3606enr.pdf

Jung, W.-O., & Kwon, Y. K. (1988). Disclosure when the market is unsure of information endowment of managers. *Journal of Accounting Research, 26*, 146–153. https://doi.org/10.2307/2491118

Käfer, B. (2018). Peer-to-peer lending—A (financial stability) risk perspective. *Review of Economics, 69*(1), 1–25. https://doi.org/10.1515/roe-2017-0020

Kahan, M. (1991). Securities laws and the social costs of inaccurate stock prices. *Duke Law Journal, 41*, 977–1044. Retrieved from https://heinonline.org/HOL/LandingPage?handle=hein.journals/duklr41&div=37&id=&page=

Katz, A. (1996). Taking private ordering seriously. *University of Pennsylvania Law Review, 144*(5), 1745–1763. https://doi.org/10.2307/3312638

Keel, A. L., Lending, C. E., & Marshall, B. (2021). The impact of online buzz on internet IPO valuation. *Journal of Strategic Marketing, 29*(1), 24–46. https://doi.org/10.1080/0965254X.2019.1593222

Kgoroeadira, R., Burke, A., & van Stel, A. (2019). Small business online loan crowdfunding: Who gets funded and what determines the rate of interest? *Small Business Economics, 52*(1), 67–87. https://doi.org/10.1007/s11187-017-9986-z

Kim, D. (2019). The importance of detailed patterns of herding behaviour in a P2P lending market. *Applied Economics Letters, 27*, 1–4. https://doi.org/10.1080/13504851.2019.1610698

Kim, K., & Viswanathan, S. (2018). The 'Experts' in the crowd: The role of experienced investors in a crowdfunding market. *SSRN Electronic Journal*. https://doi.org/10.2139/ssrn.2258243

Kingsford-Smith, D., & Dixon, O. (2015). The consumer interest and the financial markets. In N. Moloney, E. Ferran, & J. Payne (Eds.), *The Oxford handbook of financial regulation* (pp. 695–735). Oxford University Press.

Kleinert, S., & Volkmann, C. (2019). Equity crowdfunding and the role of investor discussion boards. *Venture Capital, 21*(4), 327–352. https://doi.org/10.1080/13691066.2019.1569853

Kleinert, S., Volkmann, C., & Grünhagen, M. (2020). Third-party signals in equity crowdfunding: The role of prior financing. *Small Business Economics, 54*(1), 341–365. https://doi.org/10.1007/s11187-018-0125-2

Knyazeva, A., & Ivanov, V. I. (2017). Soft and hard information and signal extraction in securities crowdfunding. *SSRN Electronic Journal*. https://doi.org/10.2139/ssrn.3051380

Kraakman, R. H. (1986). Gatekeepers: The anatomy of a third-party enforcement strategy. *The Journal of Law, Economics, and Organization, 2*(1), 53–104. https://doi.org/10.1093/oxfordjournals.jleo.a036906

Kriebel, J., & Stitz, L. (2022). Credit default prediction from user-generated text in peer-to-peer lending using deep learning. *European Journal of Operational Research, 302*(1), 309–323. https://doi.org/10.1016/j.ejor.2021.12.024

Lee, E., & Lee, B. (2012). Herding behavior in online P2P lending: An empirical investigation. *Electronic Commerce Research and Applications, 11*(5), 495–503. https://doi.org/10.1016/j.elerap.2012.02.001

Leland, H. E., & Pyle, D. H. (1977). Informational asymmetries, financial structure, and financial intermediation. *The Journal of Finance, 32*(2), 371–387. https://doi.org/10.2307/2326770

Lenz, R. (2016). Peer-to-peer lending: Opportunities and risks. *European Journal of Risk Regulation, 7*(4), 688–700. https://doi.org/10.1017/S1867299X00010126

Leone, A. J., Rock, S., & Willenborg, M. (2007). Disclosure of intended use of proceeds and underpricing in initial public offerings. *Journal of Accounting Research, 45*(1), 111–153. https://doi.org/10.1111/j.1475-679X.2006.00229.x

Li, X., Tang, Y., Yang, N., Ren, R., Zheng, H., & Zhou, H. (2016). The value of information disclosure and lead investor in equity-based crowdfunding: An exploratory empirical study. *Nankai Business Review International, 7*(3), 301–321. https://doi.org/10.1108/NBRI-01-2016-0002

Li, Y., Fan, W., Liu, F., Lim, E., & Liu, Y. (2018). *Exploring the nudging and counter-nudging effects of campaign updates in crowdfunding*. Retrieved from https://core.ac.uk/download/pdf/301376052.pdf

Li, Y., Li, C., & Gao, Y. (2020). Voluntary disclosures and peer-to-peer lending decisions: Evidence from the repeated game. *Frontiers of Business Research in China, 14*(7), 1–26. https://doi.org/10.1186/s11782-020-00075-5

Li, Y., Liu, F., Fan, W., Lim, E. T. K., & Liu, Y. (2022). Exploring the impact of initial herd on overfunding in equity crowdfunding. *Information & Management, 59*(3), 103269. https://doi.org/10.1016/j.im.2020.103269

Liberti, J. M., & Petersen, M. A. (2019). Information: Hard and soft. *The Review of Corporate Finance Studies, 8*(1), 1–41. https://doi.org/10.1093/rcfs/cfy009

Lin, L. (2017). Managing the risks of equity crowdfunding: Lessons from China. *Journal of Corporate Law Studies, 17*(2), 327–366. https://doi.org/10.1080/14735970.2017.1296217

Lin, M., Prabhala, N. R., & Viswanathan, S. (2013). Judging borrowers by the company they keep: Friendship networks and information asymmetry in online peer-to-peer lending. *Management Science, 59*(1), 17–35. https://doi.org/10.1287/mnsc.1120.1560

Liu, Z., Shang, J., Wu, S., & Chen, P. (2020). Social collateral, soft information and online peer-to-peer lending: A theoretical model. *European Journal of Operational Research, 281*(2), 428–438. https://doi.org/10.1016/j.ejor.2019.08.038

Löher, J. (2017). The interaction of equity crowdfunding platforms and ventures: An analysis of the preselection process. *Venture Capital, 19*(1-2), 51–74. https://doi.org/10.1080/13691066.2016.1252510

Lukkarinen, A., & Schwienbacher, A. (2023). Secondary market listings in equity crowdfunding: The missing link? *Research Policy, 52*(1), 104648. https://doi.org/10.1016/j.respol.2022.104648

Lukkarinen, A., Teich, J. E., Wallenius, H., & Wallenius, J. (2016). Success drivers of online equity crowdfunding campaigns. *Decision Support Systems, 87*, 26–38. https://doi.org/10.1016/j.dss.2016.04.006

Luo, B., & Lin, Z. (2013). A decision tree model for herd behavior and empirical evidence from the online P2P lending market. *Information Systems and e-Business Management, 11*(1), 141–160. https://doi.org/10.1007/s10257-011-0182-4

Lu, H., Wang, B., Wang, H., & Zhao, T. (2020). Does social capital matter for peer-to-peer-lending? *Empirical evidence. Pacific-Basin Finance Journal, 61*, 101338.

Madsen, J., & McMullin, J. L. (2018). Economic consequences of risk and ability disclosures: Evidence from crowdfunding. *SSRN Electronic Journal*. https://doi.org/10.2139/ssrn.3202453

Maham, K., & Safikhani, F. (2014). Quality of financial information and liquidity. *Management Science Letters, 4*(8), 1619–1624. https://doi.org/10.5267/j.msl.2014.7.026

Mahoney, P. G. (1995). Mandatory disclosure as a solution to agency problems. *The University of Chicago Law Review, 62*(3), 1047–1112. https://doi.org/10.2307/1600055

Mäschle, O. (2012). Which information should entrepreneurs on German crowdinvesting-platforms disclose? *Thünen-Series of Applied Economic Theory, 127*, 1–25. Retrieved from https://www.econstor.eu/bitstream/10419/74650/1/719822912.pdf

Meoli, M., Rossi, A., & Vismara, S. (2022). Financial literacy and security-based crowdfunding. *Corporate Governance: An International Review, 30*(1), 27–54. https://doi.org/10.1111/corg.12355

Meoli, M., & Vismara, S. (2021). Information manipulation in equity crowdfunding markets. *Journal of Corporate Finance, 67*, 101866. https://doi.org/10.1016/j.jcorpfin.2020.101866

Michael, S. C. (2009). Entrepreneurial signaling to attract resources: The case of franchising. *Managerial and Decision Economics, 30*(6), 405–422. https://doi.org/10.1002/mde.1460

Michels, J. (2012). Do unverifiable disclosures matter? Evidence from peer-to-peer lending. *The Accounting Review, 87*(4), 1385–1413. https://doi.org/10.2308/accr-50159

Milgrom, P. R. (1981). Good news and bad news: Representation theorems and applications. *The Bell Journal of Economics, 12*, 380–391. https://doi.org/10.2307/3003562

Mollick, E. (2014). The dynamics of crowdfunding: An exploratory study. *Journal of Business Venturing, 29*(1), 1–16. https://doi.org/10.1016/j.jbusvent.2013.06.005

Moloney, N., Ferran, E., Payne, J., & Payne, J. (2015). The role of gatekeepers. In N. Moloney, E. Ferran, & J. Payne (Eds.), *The Oxford handbook of financial regulation* (pp. 254–278). Oxford University Press. https://doi.org/10.1093/oxfordhb/9780199687206.013.11

Moradi, M., & Dass, M. (2019). An investigation into the effects of message framing on crowdfunding funding level. *Journal of Electronic Commerce Research, 20*(4), 238–254. Retrieved from https://www.researchgate.net/profile/Masoud-Moradi-10/publication/352705869_An_Investigation_into_the_Effects_of_Message_Framing_on_Crowdfunding_Funding_Level/links/60d433c492851c8f7995f49e/An-Investigation-into-the-Effects-of-Message-Framing-on-Crowdfunding-Funding-Level.pdf

Morse, A. (2015). Peer-to-peer crowdfunding: Information and the potential for disruption in consumer lending. *Annual Review of Financial Economics, 7*, 463–482. https://doi.org/10.1146/annurev-financial-111914-041939

Morsy, S. (2014). The JOBS act and crowdfunding: How narrowing the secondary market handicaps fraud plaintiffs. *Brooklyn Law Review, 79*(3), 1373–1405. Retrieved from https://heinonline.org/HOL/LandingPage?handle=hein.journals/brklr79&div=52&id=&page=

Myers, S. C., & Majluf, N. S. (1984). Corporate financing and investment decisions when firms have information that investors do not have. *Journal of Financial Economics, 13*(2), 187–221. https://doi.org/10.1016/0304-405X(84)90023-0

Nevin, S., Gleasure, R., O'Reilly, P., Feller, J., Li, S., & Cristoforo, J. (2017). Social identity and social media activities in equity crowdfunding. In *Proceedings of the 13th international symposium on open collaboration* (pp. 1–8). https://doi.org/10.1145/3125433.3125461

Nisar, T. M., Prabhakar, G., & Torchia, M. (2020). Crowdfunding innovations in emerging economies: Risk and credit control in peer-to-peer lending network platforms. *Strategic Change, 29*(3), 355–361. https://doi.org/10.1002/jsc.2334

Nitani, M., & Riding, A. (2017). On crowdfunding success: Firm and owner attributes and social networking. In *2017 emerging trends in entrepreneurial finance conference* (pp. 1–40). https://doi.org/10.2139/ssrn.2945081

Nowak, A., Ross, A., & Yencha, C. (2018). Small business borrowing and peer-to-peer lending: Evidence from Lending Club. *Contemporary Economic Policy, 36*(2), 318–336. https://doi.org/10.1111/coep.12252

Ofir, M., & Sadeh, I. (2019). A revolution in progress: Regulating P2P lending platforms. *NYU Journal of Law & Business, 16*, 683–748. Retrieved from https://heinonline.org/HOL/LandingPage?handle=hein.journals/nyujolbu16&div=22&id=&page=

Ogus, A. (1995). Rethinking self-regulation. *Oxford Journal of Legal Studies, 15*, 97–108. Retrieved from https://heinonline.org/HOL/LandingPage?handle=hein.journals/oxfjls15&div=14&id=&page=

Ölvedi, T. (2021). The liquidity aspects of peer-to-peer lending. *Studies in Economics and Finance, 39*(1), 45–62. https://doi.org/10.1108/SEF-09-2020-0376

Palley, A. B., & Soll, J. B. (2019). Extracting the wisdom of crowds when information is shared. *Management Science, 65*(5), 2291–2309. https://doi.org/10.1287/mnsc.2018.3047

Parhankangas, A., & Renko, M. (2017). Linguistic style and crowdfunding success among social and commercial entrepreneurs. *Journal of Business Venturing, 32*(2), 215–236. https://doi.org/10.1016/j.jbusvent.2016.11.001

Pattanapanyasat, R.-P. (2021). Do conventional financial disclosures matter in alternative financing? Evidence from equity crowdfunding. *Journal of Accounting and Public Policy, 40*(3), 106799. https://doi.org/10.1016/j.jaccpubpol.2020.106799

Phelps, E. S. (1972). The statistical theory of racism and sexism. *The American Economic Review, 62*(4), 659–661. Retrieved from https://www.jstor.org/stable/1806107

Piva, E., & Rossi-Lamastra, C. (2018). Human capital signals and entrepreneurs' success in equity crowdfunding. *Small Business Economics, 51*(3), 667–686. https://doi.org/10.1007/s11187-017-9950-y

Polena, M., & Regner, T. (2018). Determinants of borrowers' default in P2P lending under consideration of the loan risk class. *Games, 9*(4), 1–17. https://doi.org/10.3390/g9040082

Pope, D. G., & Sydnor, J. R. (2011). What's in a picture? Evidence of discrimination from Prosper.com. *Journal of Human Resources, 46*(1), 53–92. https://doi.org/10.3368/jhr.46.1.53

Pötzsch, S., & Böhme, R. (2010). The role of soft information in trust building: Evidence from online social lending. In *Trust and trustworthy computing. Trust 2010. Lecture notes in computer science* (Vol. 6101, pp. 381–395). Springer. https://doi.org/10.1007/978-3-642-13869-0_28

Pursiainen, V. (2023). Borrower misreporting and credit risk: Evidence from marketplace loans. *SSRN Electronic Journal*. Retrieved from https://ssrn.com/abstract=3326588

Ralcheva, A., & Roosenboom, P. (2020). Forecasting success in equity crowdfunding. *Small Business Economics, 55*(1), 39–56. https://doi.org/10.1007/s11187-019-00144-x

Ravina, E. (2019). Love & loans: The effect of beauty and personal characteristics in credit markets. *SSRN Electronic Journal*. https://doi.org/10.2139/ssrn.1101647

Regulation (EU). (2014). *No 600/2014 of the European Parliament and of the Council of 15 May 2014 on Markets in Financial Instruments and Amending Regulation (EU) No 648/2012 Text with EEA Relevance*. Retrieved from https://eur-lex.europa.eu/legal-content/EN/TXT/PDF/?uri=CELEX:32014R0600

Reher, M. (2014). Do de novo secondary markets affect primary market interest rates? A case study of peer-to-peer lending. *Michigan Journal of Business, 7*(1), 11–54. Retrieved from https://citeseerx.ist.psu.edu/document?repid=rep1&type=pdf&doi=216e5efa77a3e9ffd22fdd0df7e1b248a5ef4034

Reichenbach, F., & Walther, M. (2021). Signals in equity-based crowdfunding and risk of failure. *Financial Innovation, 7*(1), 54–83. https://doi.org/10.1186/s40854-021-00270-0

Ribeiro-Navarrete, S., Piñeiro-Chousa, J., López-Cabarcos, M. Á., & Palacios-Marqués, D. (2022). Crowdlending: Mapping the core literature and research frontiers. *Review of Managerial Science, 16*(8), 2381–2411. https://doi.org/10.1007/s11846-021-00491-8

Ritter, J. R. (1987). The costs of going public. *Journal of Financial Economics, 19*(2), 269–281. https://doi.org/10.1016/0304-405X(87)90005-5

Rock, K. (1986). Why new issues are underpriced. *Journal of Financial Economics, 15*(1–2), 187–212. https://doi.org/10.1016/0304-405X(86)90054-1

Rossi, A., Vanacker, T. R., & Vismara, S. (2020). Equity crowdfunding: New evidence from US and UK markets. *SSRN Electronic Journal*. https://doi.org/10.2139/ssrn.3752616

Rossi, A., & Vismara, S. (2018). What do crowdfunding platforms do? A comparison between investment-based platforms in Europe. *Eurasian Business Review, 8*(1), 93–118. https://doi.org/10.1007/s40821-017-0092-6

Rossi, A., Vismara, S., & Meoli, M. (2019). Voting rights delivery in investment-based crowdfunding: A cross-platform analysis. *Journal of Industrial and Business Economics, 46*(2), 251–281. https://doi.org/10.1007/s40812-018-0109-x

Santos, T., & Scheinkman, J. A. (2001). Competition among exchanges. *The Quarterly Journal of Economics, 116*(3), 1027–1061. https://doi.org/10.1162/00335530152466304

Schultz, T. W. (1961). Investment in human capital. *The American Economic Review, 51*(1), 1–17. Retrieved from https://www.jstor.org/stable/1818907

Schwartz, A. A. (2018). The gatekeepers of crowdfunding. *Washington and Lee Law Review, 75*, 885–955. Retrieved from https://heinonline.org/HOL/LandingPage?handle=hein.journals/waslee75&div=21&id=&page

Secondary Market Terms & Conditions. (2024). *Seedrs*. Retrieved from https://www.seedrs.com/pages/secondary-market-terms

Sengupta, P. (1998). Corporate disclosure quality and the cost of debt. *Accounting Review, 73*, 459–474. Retrieved from https://www.jstor.org/stable/248186

Serrano-Cinca, C., Gutiérrez-Nieto, B., & López-Palacios, L. (2015). Determinants of default in P2P lending. *PLoS ONE, 10*(10), e0139427. https://doi.org/10.1371/journal.pone.0139427

Shane, S., & Cable, D. (2002). Network ties, reputation, and the financing of new ventures. *Management Science, 48*(3), 364–381. https://doi.org/10.1287/mnsc.48.3.364.7731

Sharpe, W. F. (1964). Capital asset prices: A theory of market equilibrium under conditions of risk. *The Journal of Finance, 19*(3), 425–442. https://doi.org/10.1111/j.1540-6261.1964.tb02865.x

Shen, T., Ma, J., Zhang, B., Huang, W., & Fan, F. (2020). "I invest by following lead investors!" The role of lead investors in fundraising performance of equity crowdfunding. *Frontiers in Psychology, 11*, 1–9. https://doi.org/10.3389/fpsyg.2020.00632

Shleifer, A., & Vishny, R. W. (1997). A survey of corporate governance. *The Journal of Finance, 52*(2), 737–783. https://doi.org/10.1111/j.1540-6261.1997.tb04820.x

Signori, A., & Vismara, S. (2018). Does success bring success? The post-offering lives of equity-crowdfunded firms. *Journal of Corporate Finance, 50*, 575–591. https://doi.org/10.1016/j.jcorpfin.2017.10.018

Silber, W. L. (1991). Discounts on restricted stock: The impact of illiquidity on stock prices. *Financial Analysts Journal, 47*(4), 60–64. https://doi.org/10.2469/faj.v47.n4.60

Snyder, H. (2019). Literature review as a research methodology: An overview and guidelines. *Journal of Business Research, 104*, 333–339. https://doi.org/10.1016/j.jbusres.2019.07.039

Spence, M. (1973). Job market signaling. *The Quarterly Journal of Economics, 87*(3), 281–306. https://doi.org/10.2307/1882010

Stefanadis, C. (2003). Self-regulation, innovation, and the financial industry. *Journal of Regulatory Economics, 23*(1), 5–25. https://doi.org/10.1023/A:1021858812744

Stefanelli, V., Ferilli, G. B., & Boscia, V. (2022). Exploring the lending business crowdfunding to support SMEs' financing decisions. *Journal of Innovation & Knowledge, 7*(4), 100278. https://doi.org/10.1016/j.jik.2022.100278

Stevenson, M., Mues, C., & Bravo, C. (2021). The value of text for small business default prediction: A deep learning approach. *European Journal of Operational Research, 295*(2), 758–771. https://doi.org/10.1016/j.ejor.2021.03.008

Stocken, P. C. (2000). Credibility of voluntary disclosure. *The Rand Journal of Economics, 31*(2), 359–374. https://doi.org/10.2307/2601045

Surowiecki, J. (2005). *The wisdom of crowds*. Anchor.

SyndicateRoom. (n.d.). *Our most common questions from companies and investors*. Retrieved June 24, 2024, from https://www.syndicateroom.com/faqs

Talavera, O., & Xu, H. (2018). *Role of verification in peer-to-peer lending*. Swansea University. Retrieved from https://rahwebdav.swan.ac.uk/repec/pdf/WP2018-25.pdf

Torraco, R. J. (2005). Writing integrative literature reviews: Guidelines and examples. *Human Resource Development Review, 4*(3), 356–367. https://doi.org/10.1177/1534484305278283

Troise, C., Tani, M., & Jones, P. (2020). Investigating the impact of multidimensional social capital on equity crowdfunding performance. *International Journal of Information Management, 55*, 102230. https://doi.org/10.1016/j.ijinfomgt.2020.102230

Unger, J. M., Rauch, A., Frese, M., & Rosenbusch, N. (2011). Human capital and entrepreneurial success: A meta-analytical review. *Journal of Business Venturing, 26*(3), 341–358. https://doi.org/10.1016/j.jbusvent.2009.09.004

Vallee, B., & Zeng, Y. (2019). Marketplace lending: A new banking paradigm? *The Review of Financial Studies, 32*(5), 1939–1982. https://doi.org/10.1093/rfs/hhy100

Verrecchia, R. E. (2001). Essays on disclosure. *Journal of Accounting and Economics, 32*(1–3), 97–180. https://doi.org/10.1016/S0165-4101(01)00025-8

Viotto da Cruz, J. (2015). Competition and regulation of crowdfunding platforms: A two-sided market approach. *Communications and Strategies, 99*, 33–50. Retrieved from https://papers.ssrn.com/sol3/papers.cfm?abstract_id=2741883

Vismara, S. (2015). Information cascades among investors in equity crowdfunding. *Academy of Management Proceedings, 2015*(1), 11519. https://doi.org/10.5465/ambpp.2015.11519abstract

Vismara, S. (2016). Equity retention and social network theory in equity crowdfunding. *Small Business Economics, 46*(4), 579–590. https://doi.org/10.1007/s11187-016-9710-4

Vismara, S. (2018a). Information cascades among investors in equity crowdfunding. *Entrepreneurship Theory and Practice, 42*(3), 467–497. https://doi.org/10.1111/etap.12261

Vismara, S. (2018b). Signaling to overcome inefficiencies in crowdfunding markets. In D. Cumming & L. Hornuf (Eds.), *The economics of crowdfunding* (pp. 29–56). Palgrave Macmillan. https://doi.org/10.1007/978-3-319-66119-3_3

Vismara, S. (2019). Sustainability in equity crowdfunding. *Technological Forecasting and Social Change, 141*, 98–106. https://doi.org/10.1016/j.techfore.2018.07.014

Vismara, S. (2022). Expanding corporate finance perspectives to equity crowdfunding. *The Journal of Technology Transfer, 47*(6), 1629–1639. https://doi.org/10.1007/s10961-021-09903-z

Vulkan, N., Åstebro, T., & Sierra, M. F. (2016). Equity crowdfunding: A new phenomena. *Journal of Business Venturing Insights, 5*, 37–49. https://doi.org/10.1016/j.jbvi.2016.02.001

Walthoff-Borm, X., Vanacker, T., & Collewaert, V. (2018). Equity crowdfunding, shareholder structures, and firm performance. *Corporate Governance: An International Review, 26*(5), 314–330. https://doi.org/10.1111/corg.12259

Wang, W., Mahmood, A., Sismeiro, C., & Vulkan, N. (2019). The evolution of equity crowdfunding: Insights from co-investments of angels and the crowd. *Research Policy, 48*(8), 103727. https://doi.org/10.1016/j.respol.2019.01.003

Welch, I. (1992). Sequential sales, learning, and cascades. *The Journal of Finance, 47*(2), 695–732. https://doi.org/10.1111/j.1540-6261.1992.tb04406.x

Wuillaume, A., & Janssen, F. (2020). Legitimacy in crowdfunding: Some surprising patterns. *International Review of Entrepreneurship, 18*(4), 611–640. Retrieved from https://dial.uclouvain.be/downloader/downloader.php?pid=boreal%3A245799&datastream=PDF_01&disclaimer=8c5adb140105cb8cd4fb165e429ece0e3e3d48bbd5131e5c6b959989199db907

Xu, A., Yang, X., Rao, H., Fu, W.-T., Huang, S.-W., & Bailey, B. P. (2014). Show me the money! An analysis of project updates during crowdfunding campaigns. In *Proceedings of the SIGCHI conference on human factors in computing systems* (pp. 591–600). ACM. https://doi.org/10.1145/2556288.2557045

Xu, B., Su, Z., & Celler, J. (2021). Evaluating default risk and loan performance in UK peer-to-peer lending: Evidence from funding circle. *Journal of Advanced Computational Intelligence and Intelligent Informatics, 25*(5), 530–538. https://doi.org/10.20965/jaciii.2021.p0530

Yang, J., Li, Y., Calic, G., & Shevchenko, A. (2020). How multimedia shape crowdfunding outcomes: The overshadowing effect of images and videos on text in campaign information. *Journal of Business Research, 117*, 6–18. https://doi.org/10.1016/j.jbusres.2020.05.008

Yao, J., Chen, J., Wei, J., Chen, Y., & Yang, S. (2019). The relationship between soft information in loan titles and online peer-to-peer lending: Evidence from RenRenDai platform. *Electronic Commerce Research, 19*(1), 111–129. https://doi.org/10.1007/s10660-018-9293-z

Yum, H., Lee, B., & Chae, M. (2012). From the wisdom of crowds to my own judgment in microfinance through online peer-to-peer lending platforms. *Electronic Commerce Research and Applications, 11*(5), 469–483. https://doi.org/10.1016/j.elerap.2012.05.003

Zhang, J., & Liu, P. (2012). Rational herding in microloan markets. *Management Science, 58*(5), 892–912. https://doi.org/10.1287/mnsc.1110.1459

Zhang, K., & Chen, X. (2017). Herding in a P2P lending market: Rational inference OR irrational trust? *Electronic Commerce Research and Applications, 23*, 45–53. https://doi.org/10.1016/j.elerap.2017.04.001

Zhang, Y., Hughes, M., Fu, K., Scholes, L., & Tang, F. (2023). The effect of lead investors' trustworthiness on funding performance: The moderating effect of investment-specific human capital. *Technology in Society, 73*, 102222. https://doi.org/10.1016/j.techsoc.2023.102222

Zhang, Y., Scholes, L., Fu, K., Hughes, M., & Tang, F. (2023). Equity crowdfunding syndicates and fundraising performance: The effect of human capital and lead investor reputation. *Journal of Small Business and Enterprise Development, 30*, 645–666. https://doi.org/10.1108/JSBED-06-2022-0282

Zhou, M., Lu, B., Fan, W., & Wang, G. A. (2018). Project description and crowdfunding success: An exploratory study. *Information Systems Frontiers, 20*(2), 259–274. https://doi.org/10.1007/s10796-016-9723-1

Zhu, F. (2014). Corporate governance and the cost of capital: An international study. *International Review of Finance, 14*(3), 393–429. https://doi.org/10.1111/irfi.12034

Ziegler, T., Shneor, R., Wenzlaff, K., Odorović, A., Johanson, D., Hao, R., & Ryll, L. (2019). *Shifting paradigms: The 4th European alternative finance benchmarking report*. Cambridge Centre for Alternative Finance. Retrieved from https://www.jbs.cam.ac.uk/faculty-research/centres/alternative-finance/publications/shifting-paradigms/

Chapter 4
Self-Regulation in European Crowdfunding Markets

4.1 Introduction

The analysis in the previous chapter showed that crowdfunding platforms exhibit important differences regarding the scope and the quality of (gatekeeping) services they offer. Crowdfunding platforms often started to operate in unregulated or lightly regulated environments, and their regulatory obligations raised a number of ambiguities for all parties involved: platforms, fundraisers, and investors. This was because 'the promise and perils of crowdfunding' (Armour & Enriques, 2018) were not entirely known to regulators, who struggled to balance investor protection and the sector's growth. Regulatory issues that remained unaddressed led to uncertainty in the market, which could stifle the development of an emerging industry. To prevent this, crowdfunding associations across Europe have created Codes of Conduct (CoC). These CoCs complement existing rules by clarifying how regulations should be implemented and introducing new standards of behaviour for crowdfunding platforms. The practice of drafting and implementing codes of conduct is commonly denoted in the literature of law and economics as private ordering (Schwarcz, 2002). The voluntary association of firms to control their collective behaviour is also known in the social science literature as industry self-regulation (Bowen, 2019; Williams, 2004).[1]

This chapter is based on an earlier version previously published (Odorović & Wenzlaff, 2020).

[1] Literature on private ordering and self-regulation has mainly focused on private ordering of professions, such as lawyers and accountants (Dingwall & Fenn, 1987; Philipsen, 2012; Van den Bergh, 2004), voluntary environmental codes (Howard et al., 2000; Prakash & Potoski, 2007), voluntary corporate governance standards (Black, 1996), international accountability standards (Gilbert et al., 2011), self-regulation in banking (Stefanadis, 2003), and the ethics of industry self-regulation (Bowen, 2019).

A. Odorović, *Overcoming Asymmetric Information in the Crowdfunding Market*, International Law and Economics, https://doi.org/10.1007/978-3-032-04118-0_4

The study of crowdfunding CoCs adds a new dimension to understanding market-based solutions to information asymmetries. While market mechanisms examined in the previous chapter originate from fundraisers, investors, and individual platforms, rules embedded in industry CoCs are created jointly by all (or many) platforms in a given market to govern their behaviour. Thus, this chapter aims to answer what motivates crowdfunding platforms to enact the rules of CoCs. Drawing on the economic theory of self-regulation and the theory of clubs, it outlines a theoretical framework for the study of CoCs in crowdfunding, focusing on the context of their emergence and various institutional dimensions.

Moreover, a comparative case study highlights common features and diversity in the institutional design of CoCs in different European countries. It further relates the institutional design of CoCs to specific solutions to the collective action problem among platforms. Finally, the case study provides an overview of substantial rules contained in CoCs in Europe, which are important to understand the potential sources of market failure from the platform perspective.[2]

This chapter is structured in the following way. The second section discusses existing theories of self-regulation and characteristics of the crowdfunding market that prompt self-regulation. It also proposes a theoretical framework for studying the institutional design of CoCs of crowdfunding associations. The third section explains the methodology used to identify the case studies in Europe and cluster substantial provisions in CoCs. The fourth section analyses CoCs in light of the self-regulation theory and discusses variations in institutional features of CoCs across Europe. It also systematises substantial provisions of CoCs, highlighting the regulatory issues the platforms find the most pertinent. The fifth section concludes and provides directions for further research.

---

[2] Previous literature on self-regulation in the crowdfunding sector is very scarce. Schwienbacher (2014) briefly explains the merits of a CoC in crowdfunding. He argues that a CoC sets the basis for the platforms' behaviour and provides recommendations for the interaction between platforms, investors, and projects. Jegelevičiūtė and Valančienė (2015) make a brief reference to the CoCs of the UK Crowdfunding Association, the Financement Participatif France, and the European Crowdfunding Network as one of the means to promote the crowdfunding industry. Turan (2015) briefly refers to the CoC discussions in the European Crowdfunding Stakeholder Forum in 2014, where the ECN CoC and the Peer to Peer Finance Associations Principles were discussed as part of discussions on the regulatory framework in Europe. Wenzlaff (2019) discusses the maturity of crowdfunding ecosystems and proposes that CoCs emerge only in the later stages of crowdfunding market development.

4.2 Theoretical Framework for Self-Regulation in Crowdfunding

4.2.1 Literature Review of the Theory of Self-Regulation

In the legal scholarship and the scholarship of law and economics, self-regulation is understood as collective rules of conduct which do not originate from the government. These rules are meant to produce market outcomes which would not have been achieved if market participants were left to market forces alone (Ogus, 1995). Self-regulation is taken to imply 'the situation of a group of persons or bodies, acting together, performing a regulatory function in respect of themselves and others who accept their authority' (Black, 1996, p. 27). It helps achieve 'public policy objectives at a lower cost than government regulation' because of the information advantage which industry representatives have over regulators (Bowen, 2019, p.257). As opposed to formal institutions of the state, self-regulation belongs to informal, private, and social institutions, which may also facilitate the search for information by members of society (Dixit, 2009). Self-regulating institutions can imply one or several functions: formulation of rules and their interpretation, resolving disputes among group members and enforcement, which usually includes some form of sanctions (Black, 1996).

However, self-regulation does not necessarily imply an absence of government. Four ways in which state actors can relate to self-regulatory groups and bodies are (Black, 1996, p. 27):

- Mandated self-regulation: The government delegates regulatory powers to a self-regulatory group.
- Sanctioned self-regulation: The government approves rules drafted by a self-regulatory group.
- Coerced self-regulation: As a response to a rising threat of government regulation not tailed to industry's needs, a self-regulatory group creates standards.
- Voluntary self-regulation: Without government engagement of any kind, industry or a profession's members create common standards for the behaviour of market participants.

Rules formulated by self-regulatory groups can be legally binding or non-binding (Ogus, 1995, p. 100). The breach of legally binding rules leads to private or public law consequences. Violating non-binding rules leads to the deprivation of certain rights within a group or association, such as ostracism. Sometimes, non-binding regimes allow group members to opt out from certain norms as long as more appropriate behaviour can be demonstrated. Self-regulatory rules formulated as recommendations lead to no sanctions in case of non-compliance.

The question of the advantages and disadvantages of self-regulation is central in discussing the effectiveness of such a framework. Van den Bergh (2004, pp. 3–8) argues that self-regulation is desired in industries where market participants possess information advantage over regulators. This information advantage allows the creation of more suitable rules and achieves cost savings in relation to the enforcement of the rules. On the other hand, industry members lack the democratic legitimacy to create and enforce regulations. A lack of governmental oversight might lead to abusing self-regulatory powers to restrict competition.

The emergence of self-regulatory organisations depends on their advantages for the companies bound by the self-regulatory framework. Similar to government regulation, self-regulation results from a market failure in the form of information asymmetries, externalities, or public goods. On the assumption of unconstrained competition among firms, which internalise all the costs of their activities, and well-informed consumers, who can choose the supplier with the best quality, regulatory rules would not be necessary. Under this assumption, firms that opt for low-quality standards would be forced to leave the market.

Self-regulation, as was described in relation to the emergence of law in primitive societies (Benson, 1988; Posner, 1980), is based on voluntary reciprocal arrangements. Members of an industry or a profession are willing to comply with self-regulatory norms if they can expect that other members will also adhere to such norms. The adherence to and sustainability of self-regulatory regimes depend on the ability of the group to enforce rules. The most common enforcement mechanisms are the threat of expulsion of the non-compliant member or temporary suspension of membership rights.

Theories explaining the emergence of private ordering emphasise either the 'coerced' or the 'voluntary' nature of self-regulatory institutions (both are discussed below). One strand of economic literature emphasises that self-regulatory rules and organisations emerge because of a threat of government regulation. Maxwell et al. (2000) argue that firms are willing to reduce their harmful behaviour to save on political transaction costs associated with government regulations. These costs stem from organising themselves to influence policy-makers once they enter a political process (Maxwell et al., 2000, p. 586). Stefanadis (2003) develops a model that explains the emergence of self-regulation in an innovative industry in which new products are developed. Self-regulatory organisations can be regarded as a 'club owned by industry participants' (Stefanadis, 2003, p. 5). Their incentive to introduce self-regulatory standards is to prevent the bureaucratic delays associated with ex-ante approval of new products in the system of statutory regulations. The advantage of an industry club formulating and enforcing regulatory rules is its superior knowledge of new technologies, which allows the club members to save on the costs of delaying new products.

The other strand of economic literature assumes that self-regulation emerges voluntarily and independently of government intervention to expand or complement existing regulation. Due to information asymmetries, consumers cannot distinguish between the product qualities of firms whose products typically represent credence or experience goods.[3] It might be profitable for a firm to offer higher standards, yet

---

[3] Credence goods or credence qualities are 'those which, although worthwhile, cannot be evaluated in normal use' (Darby & Karni, 1973, p. 69). They differ from search qualities, which can be evalu-

it might as well be prohibitively costly to produce credible signals of quality. Under conditions of uncertainty, adverse selection emerges (Akerlof, 1970). Gehrig and Jost (1995) explain that self-regulation of industry members serves as a signal of quality to outsiders. Industry members have strong incentives to enforce and punish any member that deviates, given that a failure to comply with industry standards weakens the signal of the entire club.

Prakash and Potoski (2007) explain why companies adhere to voluntary rules whose purpose is to reduce negative externalities. Industry members who pursue voluntary programmes create a club as an 'institution that supplies impure public goods' (Prakash & Potoski, 2007, p. 776). Impure public or club goods are used within the meaning of the Buchanan theory (Buchanan, 1965) as goods that the members of a club use exclusively in a non-rivalrous way. In this context, club goods are the 'affiliation with the club positive brand reputation' (Prakash & Potoski, 2007, p. 777) and are only available to those industry members who incur the costs of producing positive (reducing negative) externalities. Both Gehrig and Jost (1995) and Prakash and Potoski (2007) emphasise that self-regulation overcomes the free-rider problem of public goods by introducing mechanisms of exclusion of those club members who do not incur the costs of protecting the club's reputation.

Gorton and Mullineaux (1987) and Yue and Ingram (2012) argue that the reputations of different firms in the same industry are interrelated. Non-compliance by one member breaking consumers' trust harms the industry's reputation. Adherence to high-quality standards by competitors creates a positive image of the industry, splitting rewards among all members. Yue and Ingram (2012) claim that 'reputation commons' cause the emergence of self-regulation in sectors where 'outsiders are not equipped with specialised knowledge to distinguish between the behaviours of the industry's individual members' (Yue & Ingram, 2012, p. 6). It is in the self-interest of market participants to cooperate concerning setting and enforcing rules. Cooperation among industry members allows for mutual benefits that market forces could not attain.

The above theories were developed outside the crowdfunding context in relation to different financial and non-financial industries. They are nevertheless relevant to the crowdfunding market in Europe, given that a self-regulatory regime has governed this industry since a few years after its emergence. Platforms in various countries have adopted Codes of Conduct (CoCs), which were drafted and promoted by crowdfunding associations. Self-regulatory regimes emerged in very different regulatory contexts, sometimes in anticipation of a crowdfunding-specific regulation and in other instances after or as a reaction to it. A widespread practice of adopting CoCs in crowdfunding markets in different European jurisdictions raises the question of which of the above theories best explains their purpose. The answer to this question has multiple implications for the regulators in these countries, given that

ated before a purchase, and experience qualities, which can be assessed after the purchase. The distinction between search and experience goods was made originally by Nelson (1970).

the motivation behind this phenomenon is likely to affect the outcomes in these markets. Moreover, the content of self-regulatory rules is informative about which aspects of the crowdfunding business are a potential source of market failure.

The subsection below discusses crowdfunding market characteristics that support competing self-regulation theories. The following subsection outlines a theoretical framework for understanding the purpose of CoCs in the crowdfunding markets and examines the motivation to focus on the institutional design of the CoCs.

4.2.2 *Characteristics of the Crowdfunding Market and the Theory of Self-Regulation*

In an attempt to discern the motivation behind the widespread practice of adopting CoCs in different European jurisdictions, it is informative to look at some of the characteristics of the crowdfunding industry.

Several features support the theory of 'coerced self-regulation'. Crowdfunding platforms, which act as financial intermediaries between projects and investors, are part of the digital transformation of businesses and profit from the widespread use of social media (Cumming & Hornuf, 2018, p. 12). The novelty of this industry consists of providing new channels of communication and new ways to gather information, allowing investors to assess projects' viability better. Technological tools to estimate the risk of projects and match it with investors' risk preferences are commonly used. From the point of view of projects, the participation of many investors also generates information about their individual preferences for the goods or services they offer. This is commonly denoted as the 'wisdom of crowds' (Surowiecki, 2005). Crowdfunding platforms have been experimenting with different business models and products, including various financial instruments and tools to pre-select projects and govern investments after the completion of a campaign. Regulatory delays in approving new business models and products may stifle these innovative efforts. This incentivises industry members to develop self-regulatory rules in the form of CoC, which are more flexible and quickly revised, allowing them to keep pace with industry developments. In line with Stefanadis (2003, p. 5), self-regulation in crowdfunding, which pre-empts government regulations, can be attributed to continuous technological change in this industry and the requirement to ask for ex-ante permission from the regulator to introduce new products and services.[4]

Support for 'voluntary self-regulation' theories comes from the nature of platforms' services, which can be characterised as 'credence goods' (Darby & Karni,

[4] In the last years, crowdfunding markets have seen substantial technological change, especially concerning the set-up and business models of the platforms. For instance, crowdfunding platforms have introduced new mechanisms for determining the prices of assets and creating secondary markets. Platforms have also introduced new technologies, such as blockchain-based mechanisms of intermediation through Initial Coin Offerings (ICOs) and Security Token Offerings (STOs). All of these changes have triggered much regulatory uncertainty.

1973, p. 69; Nelson, 1970). Investors are often unable to judge the quality of platforms' services before or right after their experience on the platform. Crowdfunding platforms have a specific 'look and feel', which makes them indistinguishable from other platforms at first sight. The presentation of projects on a platform often includes a pitch video, a project description, a team section, and a bar graph displaying the volume funded by the crowd.[5] The similarity of the websites' designs across the industry stems from the interaction between competitors, duplicating successful website layouts. Market players increase the likelihood of investment by providing user interfaces known to potential investors, thus reducing the switching costs between platforms. The layout can be replicated at a low cost by a new entrant. Thus, setting up the platform is not a credible signal of quality. The recognisable design increases the costs for an investor to infer the quality of platforms' services, which are relevant for selecting a platform, such as fees, due diligence of projects, operational infrastructure, data protection standards, and post-campaign services. The 'credence' nature of these services is reinforced by the fact that retail investors typically pledge small amounts of money, which do not justify the high costs of platforms' comparison. As a result, platforms offering high-quality services cannot distinguish themselves from low-quality ones. In addition, they are likely to experience negative reputational spillovers from platforms that deceive investors (Akerlof, 1970).

In line with the voluntary self-regulation theory of Gehrig and Jost (1995) and Prakash and Potoski (2007), crowdfunding platforms are incentivised to coordinate their behaviour and create club-like institutions that enforce rules for high-quality service.[6] Such institutions are embedded in CoCs, which stipulate substantial rules of platforms' behaviour and procedural rules of enforcement. Through the mechanism of a threat of exclusion of those platforms unwilling to adhere to the high standards, platforms ensure that high service standards are achieved and benefits enjoyed by complying members. Enforcement can also be achieved by withdrawing specific rights, such as the right to make their membership in the club-like institution public.

The emergence of CoCs in the early stages of industry development underpins an argument that it is a means to protect 'reputation commons'. When CoCs were introduced in different European countries, the crowdfunding industry was going through a legitimisation process with a cognitive and socio-political component (Aldrich & Fiol, 1994, p. 648). Cognitive legitimisation refers to public knowledge about crowdfunding activity, whereas socio-political legitimisation implies public acceptance of the industry as appropriate and economically viable. As shown by

---

[5] Reward-based crowdfunding platforms like Kickstarter and Indiegogo have popularised this website layout. It can also be found on many equity- and lending-based crowdfunding platforms. This 'look and feel' of Crowdfunding platforms is not governed by a standard set by market players. The study does not aim to explain the emergence of a technological standard. Yet, as seen in the list of provisions discussed below, the CoCs do not mention the website design.

[6] The introduction of CoCs as a club good can also serve as a means to restrict competition by increasing barriers to market entry.

Jegelevičiūtė and Valančienė (2015), CoCs are one of the tools through which the crowdfunding sector is promoted by its members. The interdependence between the individual reputation of platforms and the reputation of the crowdfunding industry has been highlighted in several surveys. Platform operators rank the risk of a failure of a prominent competitor as very high (Ziegler et al., 2018), suggesting that 'reputation commons' are threatened.[7]

Different characteristics of the crowdfunding market underpin both 'coerced' and 'voluntary' theories of self-regulation and explain the widespread reliance on CoCs. Unlike in traditional financial markets, many aspects of crowdfunding activity are left to platforms to choose from, even in jurisdictions which have adopted a bespoke crowdfunding regime. This is either a result of incompleteness of existing regulations, uncertainty regarding inherent risks, or platforms' innovative efforts, which can result in circumvention of applicable rules. In many instances, the applicability of specific laws that are not crowdfunding-specific is subject to ambiguous interpretations.

In the following subsection, the study will discuss how the institutional design of CoCs can explain the emergence of self-regulation in crowdfunding markets.

4.2.3 Institutional Design of Codes of Conduct and the Theory of Self-Regulation

Mere features of the crowdfunding industry do not provide a definite answer as to which theoretical explanations are the most plausible. In contrast, the institutional design of the chosen self-regulatory regime provides better guidance. In the rest of the section, the study argues that if the CoC is rationally designed, some institutional features can reveal the rationale for its adoption. In relation to this, the study outlines a simple theoretical framework for the study of CoCs in the crowdfunding industry, which builds upon competing theories of self-regulation discussed above.

Each of the three theories of self-regulation ('coerced theory', 'club theory', and 'reputation common theory') emphasises a different economic problem that market players are trying to solve when adopting and adhering to self-regulatory rules. Consequently, the institutional design of CoCs is expected to reflect the underlying rationale for their adoption.

The 'coerced theory' of self-regulation emphasises the threat of government regulation. As discussed above, either savings on 'political costs' or 'costs of delaying the introduction of new products' motivate market participants to introduce a self-regulatory regime. For the industry to succeed at pre-empting or deferring government regulation, the adopted self-regulatory framework must emulate the

[7] Since separate CoCs for P2P lending and equity-based crowdfunding in the UK exist, the fear of failure does not necessarily transcend the business models of crowdfunding. Equity-based crowdfunding platforms might not be afraid of the failure of a lending platform and vice versa.

framework a government would create. Deferring state regulation implies that CoCs are introduced before crowdfunding-specific regimes. However, it is conceivable that 'coerced CoCs' also intend to defer further revisions of the crowdfunding-specific regime.

Given that government regulations would be mandatory for all industry members, 'coerced CoCs' are likely to be open for signing by all platforms (that operate a particular business model, in line with a perceived scope of the regulation). Given that government regulations rely on centralised monitoring by the regulator and robust enforcement mechanisms, 'coerced CoCs' are expected to have a similar institutional design. For instance, a crowdfunding association will likely take over the monitoring and enforcement role in a 'coerced CoC'. As to the content of substantial rules of CoCs, a 'coerced CoC' would create new obligations for platforms. Such a CoC would not emphasise rules already written in laws and regulations, as the regulator already enforces these.

Proposition 1
Platforms creating CoCs to stifle government regulation, following the 'coerced theory', are more likely to opt for rules which:

1. Precede the introduction of crowdfunding-specific regulatory regime.
2. Target all market participants (inclusive membership).
3. Create strong and centralised monitoring by the crowdfunding association.
4. Introduce robust enforcement mechanisms.
5. Do not restate obligations that are already required by existing laws and regulations.

Voluntary theories of self-regulation deny that self-regulation is primarily a result of a threat of government regulation. Instead, voluntary theories of self-regulation propose that it is in the best interest of market participants to create rules which would help them resolve the collective action problem inherent in public goods or the issue of overuse of commons. 'Club goods' theories assume that self-regulation resolves the problem of free-riding in relation to industry reputation by creating a club of close-knit market participants. These market participants comply with self-regulatory rules to benefit from a credible quality signal. For the signal to be credible, the institutional design of the self-regulatory regime has to solve the issue of excludability of non-compliant industry members.

In the crowdfunding context, the 'club good' rationale for CoCs entails that a membership will be limited to a few platforms willing to adhere to high-quality standards, which will be distinguishable from the rest of the industry. A right to display a logo or other label associated with a CoC is likely to be envisaged. Unlike 'coerced CoCs', which are likely to appear before state regulations, CoCs that create a club of quality platforms are likely to be adopted either before or after state regulations. A self-regulatory club can also emerge in a regulated environment because incomplete or unclear rules can be insufficient for market participants aiming to provide high-quality services. For exclusion to be a credible threat, such CoCs will likely introduce strong monitoring and enforcement mechanisms.

However, unlike 'coerced CoCs', decentralised monitoring, in which platforms supervise each other's compliance, is likely to be introduced. This is because a small membership base leads to reduced monitoring costs. Since excludability lies in the definition of a club, CoCs that serve as a club-like institution are expected to have strong enforcement mechanisms to ensure compliance. Moreover, given that self-regulatory clubs serve as a quality signal, this signal might also be used to demonstrate compliance with existing state regulations. As such, substantial CoC rules are likely to restate platforms' obligations already provided in existing laws and regulations.

Proposition 2
Platforms creating CoCs to signal their quality, following the 'club good theory', are more likely to opt for rules which:

1. Precede the introduction of the crowdfunding-specific regulatory regime or follow and complement an existing one.
2. Target a limited number of market participants (exclusive membership).
3. Create strong centralised and/or decentralised monitoring.
4. Introduce strong enforcement mechanisms.
5. Create new rules and/or restate obligations already provided in existing laws and regulations.

'Reputation commons' theory considers self-regulation as a means to overcome the issue of overuse of commons. In the crowdfunding market, industry reputation is being 'overused' because platforms cannot internalise all the costs they create for the industry reputation when lowering the quality of their service. Low-quality platform service creates spillover effects for the entire industry, given the interconnectedness of the reputation of all industry members. Consequently, CoCs are likely to create rules that will help get all market participants' on board' by increasing the benefits of cooperation or the costs of deviation. Similarly to other voluntary theories of self-regulation, the adoption of CoCs is independent of the time of introducing state regulations in a particular jurisdiction. Inclusive membership of such CoCs also dictates monitoring and enforcement mechanisms. Due to the large number of members, monitoring will likely be delegated to a crowdfunding association or another designated body. However, their monitoring powers might be weak due to the resistance of smaller platforms to more intrusive methods of detecting non-compliance. As a result of a compromise of a large number of actors, rules are likely to reflect the common ground among them. Consequentially, weak monitoring is often accompanied by weak enforcement. Regarding the content of CoCs' substantial provisions, new rules and references to state regulations are likely to be included since industry reputation is equally at stake when existing rules are not adequately implemented.

Proposition 3
Platforms creating CoCs to protect industry reputation, following the 'reputation commons theory', are more likely to opt for rules which:

Table 4.1 The theoretical framework for crowdfunding CoCs

Institutional dimension	Coerced theory	Voluntary theory	
		Club goods	Reputation commons
Origin	Anticipating state regulations	Anticipating or reacting to existing state regulations	Anticipating or reacting to existing state regulations
Inclusiveness	Inclusive membership	Exclusive membership	Inclusive membership
Enforcement and monitoring	Strong and centralised	Strong and centralised/ decentralised	Weak and centralised
Content	Creating new rules	Creating new rules and/or restating existing rules	Creating new rules and/or restating existing rules

1. Precede the introduction of the crowdfunding-specific regulatory regime or follow and complement an existing one.
2. Target all market participants (inclusive membership).
3. Create weak/centralised monitoring.
4. Introduce weak enforcement mechanisms.
5. Create new rules and/or restate obligations already required by existing laws and regulations.

Table 4.1 summarises the theoretical framework outlined above, emphasising common institutional dimensions between existing theories and their distinctive dimensions.

In conclusion, the three competing theories share many institutional characteristics. The main elements of distinction between 'coerced' and 'club goods' theories are exclusive membership, decentralised enforcement, and reference to existing laws, which are more likely to appear in relation to club-like institutions. Self-regulatory regimes that emerge as a response to a threat of government intervention are also unlikely to have weak monitoring and enforcement mechanisms, which are inherent in CoCs that aim to protect reputation commons. Finally, the difference between the two voluntary theories of self-regulation lies in the inclusiveness of membership and the efficacy of monitoring and enforcement mechanisms.

The rest of the study relies on this theoretical framework to discuss what the institutional design of CoCs adopted in different European jurisdictions suggests about the economic rationale for self-regulation in crowdfunding.

4.3 Methodology of Case Studies

This research conducts a comparative case study of existing CoCs in European crowdfunding markets (Yin, 2014). In line with crowdfunding literature (Belleflamme et al., 2014; Blohm et al., 2013; Haas et al., 2014; Hemer et al., 2011), the study uses the term 'crowdfunding' to denote all four business models (donation-based, reward-based, equity-based, and lending-based crowdfunding). The use of this term does not necessarily coincide with its narrower use in some CoCs.

This study focuses on CoCs in European crowdfunding markets since comparable legal frameworks regulate platforms headquartered in the EU.[8] The focus is on CoCs adopted by crowdfunding associations. Association-wide CoCs do not prevent platforms from having their own CoCs. Desk-based research of the most significant crowdfunding platforms found that platforms describe the relationship with their users in specific terms, which are part of the contractual arrangements between platforms and investors. The duties imposed by the CoCs of associations shape the contractual arrangements on a platform. For instance, the German Crowdfunding Association requests projects to report regularly to investors. Members of the German Crowdfunding Association have to implement these reporting standards into their terms.[9]

Desk-based research was conducted to assess if and where CoCs exist in Europe. The first step was to create a list of associations of crowdfunding platforms and download and translate the CoCs found on their websites. Furthermore, representatives of the crowdfunding associations were contacted to verify any unclear details, such as the year of adoption of the CoC. In addition, standard search engines were used to search terms such as ‘Code of Conduct Crowdfunding’ and ‘Best Practice Guidelines Crowdfunding’. The term ‘Crowdfunding’ was exchanged with more specific terms such as ‘Crowdinvesting’, ‘Equity-based Crowdfunding’, ‘Peer-to-Peer-Lending’, or ‘Lending-based Crowdfunding’.

The Internet search might not have captured all existing CoCs since the term ‘Code of Conduct’ was not always used. For instance, the Austrian CoC is published under the name ‘Standesregeln’ (rules of the branch). Therefore, some crowdfunding experts and representatives of crowdfunding associations were contacted to verify the existence and details of CoCs.[10] If the statutes of the association referred to the CoC, statutes were also included in the analysis. Still, this study might not have captured all rules related to the behaviour of members inside associations. For instance, the German Crowdfunding Association has a separate document that organises the mandate of the board (Vorstands-Geschäftsordnung), which has not been published. Thus, the analysis of all statutes is beyond the scope of this study.

The sample did not include all found CoCs. The website www.crowdsourcing.org developed the Crowdfunding Accreditation for Platform Standards (CAPS). Crowdsourcing.org also created the first global market reports (Adjakou, 2015). The CAPS programme was active between 2010 and 2012 and accredited mostly Anglo-American platforms. The standards developed by Crowdsourcing.org are no

[8] The data collection process was conducted between April and July 2019.

[9] The implementation of the association-wide CoCs in platforms' terms and conditions is beyond the scope of this study.

[10] They were contracted through the Cambridge Centre for Alternative Finance, the European Alternative Finance Research Network, and the Interreg Central Europe Project, CrowdFundPort.

longer available for analysis. The impact of the CAPS programme on CoCs in the UK cannot be assessed. The Spanish Crowdfunding Association released a CoC for investors (CrowdfundPort, 2016), which outlines the tax provisions for supporters and investors. Since this CoC does not regulate platform or project owner behaviour, it was not included in the analysis. The EU-financed project CrowdFundPort included three equity-based crowdfunding platforms which were asked to create a CoC for crowdfunding platforms in Germany, Austria, Italy, Hungary, Czech Republic, Slovakia, Poland, Slovenia, and Croatia (CrowdfundPort, 2016).[11] The Austrian and German CoC existed before the publication of the CrowdfundPort recommendations. No crowdfunding association exists in Italy, Hungary, Czech Republic, Slovakia, Poland, Slovenia, or Croatia. Therefore, it was concluded that no crowdfunding association had implemented the recommendations and did not include this document in the analysis.

In total, 12 CoCs drafted by associations of platforms or platform consortiums were identified. The sample includes nine of these twelve CoCs. Two CoCs are transnational (European CoC and Nordic CoC), while the remaining seven are country-specific CoCs (Table 4.2).

A preliminary analysis from this sampling suggests a predominance of CoCs drafted for financial-return models, equity-based and lending-based platforms. The business model focus of the CoC is captured firstly from a specific mention of equity- and lending-based crowdfunding in the CoC, secondly, from the content analysis of the provisions which apply only to financial-return models, or thirdly, from the membership structure of the association. The focus of CoCs on financial-return models can be explained by the more prevailing fear of market failure, as discussed in the previous section (Ziegler et al., 2018, 2019).

Identified CoCs and their provisions are analysed along several dimensions: (1) the origin; (2) inclusiveness and membership criteria; (3) monitoring, enforcement, and dispute-resolution mechanisms; and (4) the content (substantial provisions). Provisions were clustered and systematised using the method of grounded theory

Table 4.2 Overview of CoCs identified

	Internet search (7)	Outreach to associations (5)
Included in the sample (9)	UK crowdfunding CoC UK lending CoC Dutch CoC European CoC Nordic CoC	Austrian CoC German CoC French CoC Estonian CoC
Not included in the sample (3)	CAPS CoC CrowdfundPort CoC	Spanish CoC

[11]The recommendations are structured along the following categories: Fair Competition, Transparency, Treatment of Investor Funds, Data Protection, Crime Prevention, Information and Information Quality, Risk Warnings and Statements, Consumer Protection and Advertising Behaviour, Conflicts of Interest and Remuneration System.

Table 4.3 The methodology of clustering substantial provisions in CoCs

Level 1 Provision purpose	Level 2 Provision context	Level 3 Provision duty	Provision text and translated text (example taken from the French CoC)
Investor protection	Post-investment	Label *Limitation of losses* Reformulated text *Investors' losses are limited to their original investment*	Original text §6 [...] *En tout état de cause, le financeur ne peut subir de pertes sur une platforme au-delà de son investissement initial.* [...] Translation §6 [...] *In any event, the funder may not incur losses on a platform beyond its initial investment.* [...]

and open coding (Corbin & Strauss, 2015). The study uses a three-tier structure for the analysis of CoC provisions. Table 4.3 illustrates the methodology used.

The clustering of different provisions was based on common themes and subthemes. The first-level clustering involves four themes:

- Provisions pertaining to the relationship between the association and the platform (framework).
- Provisions pertaining to transparency either of the platform or the project.
- Provisions pertaining to investor protection.
- Provisions pertaining to the business conduct of the platform.

The last three themes are tightly intertwined, and drawing a sharp line between them is difficult. In particular, the theme of investor protection is used to accommodate different rules relevant to the status and protection of investors beyond transparency requirements and business conduct rules for platforms. Table 4.4 illustrates the second-level clustering and associated subthemes of CoCs provisions.

The following analysis is based on systematisation and clustering of provisions of CoCs in line with the described method. It has two main aims. The provisions that fall under the theme 'framework' are used to discern the economic rationale for adopting CoCs in different countries. Notably, the purpose of CoCs, inclusiveness, and rules governing monitoring and enforcement can provide insights into platforms' incentives to design such a framework. The analysis of substantial provisions that fall under the remaining three categories (transparency, investor protection, and business conduct) can help understand regulatory issues from the platforms' perspective.

4.4 A Comparative Study of European Codes of Conduct

This section analyses CoCs in crowdfunding markets in Europe and discusses their institutional characteristics in relation to economic theories explaining the purpose of self-regulation, as examined above. The first part of this section examines the origin of CoCs in relation to the existence of a bespoke crowdfunding regime in a

Table 4.4 First-level and second-level clustering of provisions in CoCs

First-level clustering	Second-level clustering
Framework	Purpose
	Inclusiveness
	Monitoring and enforcement
Transparency	Platform-specific transparency (pre-investment)
	Platform-specific transparency (post-investment)
	Project-specific transparency (pre-investment)
	Project-specific transparency (post-investment)
Investor protection	Investor protection (pre-investment)
	Investor protection (post-investment)
Business conduct	Good governance
	Conflict of interest
	Detection of unlawful behaviour
	Transactions
	Data security and IT
	Cease of operation
	Competition

given jurisdiction.[12] The second part considers the inclusiveness and membership criteria of different CoCs. The third part examines the efficacy of different CoCs as a regulatory tool based on their monitoring, enforcement, and dispute-resolution mechanisms. The last part provides an overview of the substantial provisions in CoCs, indicating the issues of transparency, investor protection, and good governance that arise in crowdfunding from the lenses of platforms.

4.4.1 Origins of Codes of Conduct

Most crowdfunding markets in Europe emerged before a bespoke national crowdfunding regime. Existing rules tailored to traditional intermediaries are not necessarily applicable and suitable to this nascent industry. Yet, as discussed in Chaps. 2 and 3, crowdfunding markets face the same issues that led to extensive capital markets and banking regulations. The magnitude of these issues is unknown to policymakers. Some countries deferred the adoption of a crowdfunding-specific regulatory

[12] A bespoke crowdfunding regime is a regulatory framework designed specifically for crowdfunding activities, platforms, and other market participants (such as issuers/borrowers and investors/lenders). Bespoke regimes can differ regarding the scope and depth of tailored rules.

regime until the industry reached a particular stage of maturity (Wenzlaff, 2019). In some other countries, regulators introduced bespoke crowdfunding regimes to stimulate its development. In either case, some of the relevant questions often remained unaddressed by regulations or gave rise to ambiguities in interpretation.

Consequently, crowdfunding platforms in different countries, usually under the auspices of national or transnational crowdfunding associations, introduced a self-regulatory regime in the form of CoC. Table 4.5 provides an overview of the association, the country of origin, the CoC and its denotation in this study,[13] the year of adoption of the CoC and the year of adoption of the respective crowdfunding regulatory framework.[14]

Table 4.5 Overview of existing CoCs and crowdfunding regulations

Name of the association	Country	Code of conduct and the denotation in this study	Year of adoption	Crowdfunding regulatory framework
UK Crowdfunding Association (UKCFA)	United Kingdom	UK Crowdfunding CoC	2013	1 April 2014
Peer2Peer Finance Association (P2PFA)	United Kingdom	UK Lending CoC	2013	1 April 2014 (revised rules applicable as of 9 December 2019)
Financement Participatif France (FPF)	France	French CoC	2014	1 October 2014
Bundesverband Crowdfunding (BVCF)	Germany	German CoC	2016	10 July 2015
Wirtschaftskammer Österreich—Fachverband Finanzdienstleister—Arbeitsgruppe Crowdfunding (WKO)	Austria	Austrian CoC	2016	14 August 2015
Nederlands Crowdfunding (NF)	Netherlands	Dutch CoC	2017	1 April 2016
Finance Estonia (FE)	Estonia	Estonian CoC	2016	X
European Crowdfunding Network (ECN)	Europe	European CoC	2015	20 October 2020 (ECSPR)
Nordic Crowdfunding Alliance (NCA)	Norway, Sweden, Denmark, Finland, Iceland	Nordic CoC	2017	1 September 2016 (only in Finland)

[13] The list of CoCs can be found in Annex 4A.

[14] Under the crowdfunding regulatory framework, the study considers only laws and regulations tailored to crowdfunding activity (bespoke regimes), notwithstanding that crowdfunding can trigger the application of other rules in relation to the provision of financial services.

As mentioned earlier, the study identified nine relevant CoCs in crowdfunding markets in Europe, as listed in the Table 4.5. Two CoCs are transnational (European CoC and Nordic CoC), while the remaining seven are country-specific.[15] Some CoCs are explicit about the possibility of foreign-based platforms operating in that country joining the crowdfunding association and adhering to the CoC (for instance, UK Crowdfunding CoC and UK Lending CoC). The UK is the only country where two CoCs were identified (lending- and equity-based crowdfunding).

CoCs in most jurisdictions were adopted under the umbrella of crowdfunding associations at the national or transnational level. In two countries, the CoC was published by an organisation whose membership is open to companies other than crowdfunding platforms. In Estonia, the CoC was issued by Finance Estonia, an organisation that gathers members from various fintech industries. In Austria, the CoC was issued by a subsection of the Austrian Chamber of Commerce (Wirtschaftskammer Österreich)—financial intermediary (Fachverband Finanzdienstleister), which established a working group on crowdfunding (Arbeitsgruppe Crowdfunding).

CoCs have appeared in countries with the most developed crowdfunding markets, either in terms of total volumes (UK, France, Germany, Netherlands, Nordic Countries, Austria) or volumes per capita (Estonia) (Ziegler et al., 2018, 2019). The relationship between the maturity of a crowdfunding market and the existence of CoCs and crowdfunding associations is twofold. The costs of operating a crowdfunding association and enforcing the rules of CoCs become more justifiable in a consolidated market. CoCs might also facilitate the industry's growth by creating trust among stakeholders. Given the number of factors that affect the development of the crowdfunding industry (Rau, 2020), the question of reverse causality between self-regulation and market development would merit further research beyond the scope of this study.

The CoCs in different European countries originated between 2013 and 2017. Most crowdfunding markets were still nascent yet facing strong growth. CoCs were either anticipatory or reactionary with respect to crowdfunding regulations. Five of the eleven national markets covered in this study, including Nordic countries, did not operate under a crowdfunding-specific regulatory regime (Estonia, Norway, Sweden, Denmark, and Iceland).[16] Among the jurisdictions with tailored crowdfunding regulations, the UK saw the emergence of the two CoCs before adopting statutory regulations. Similarly, the European CoC was created in anticipation of the ECSPR. The UK lending-based crowdfunding market is specific in that a bespoke crowdfunding regime was also revised after the two revisions of the UK Lending CoC in 2019. Therefore, this market features very dynamic interactions between self-regulatory and statutory regimes.

---

[15] The European CoC explicitly states that it does not constitute a court-enforceable regulation and does not overrule national CoCs' provisions. No such provisions can be found in the Nordic CoC.

[16] The information refers to the status prior to the adoption of the ECSPR, which became directly applicable in all Member States when it entered into force (10 November 2021).

In France, Germany, Netherlands, Austria, and Finland, CoCs were created following the adoption of Crowdfunding regulations. In several instances, the CoCs were also revised. As mentioned above, the UK Lending CoC was revised twice in 2015 and 2018. The French CoC was revised in 2016. In Germany, the CoC published in 2016 was complemented by the Reporting Guidelines in 2017. In addition to the Guidelines, in 2019, the German Crowdfunding Association produced a list of criteria for receiving a 'transparency certificate' or 'label' of the association.

The timing of the emergence of CoCs in relation to crowdfunding bespoke regimes may point to the economic rationale for self-regulation in crowdfunding. However, this relationship is complex. By the very definition of anticipatory self-regulatory regimes, it is meant to prevent the forthcoming government intervention. Given that four out of nine CoCs were introduced or revised after crowdfunding-specific regulations, voluntary theories of self-regulation cannot be ruled out. However, as seen in the UK lending-based crowdfunding market, it is also possible that a CoC precedes revisions of the existing crowdfunding regulation. In other words, reactionary CoCs suggest that voluntary theories will likely prevail in countries where revisions of bespoke regimes are not 'on the horizon'. Further analysis of the institutional design of different CoCs is necessary to discuss which of the theories of self-regulation is the most convincing in crowdfunding.

4.4.2 Inclusiveness of Codes of Conduct

This section examines features of national and transnational CoCs that determine how inclusive the membership in self-regulatory institutions is. Inclusiveness in this study refers to the scope of business models covered by CoCs, preconditions for becoming a member, and the right to display a logo for those platforms that fulfil specific criteria. Although crowdfunding can refer to different business models, the CoCs covered in the analysis of this study make an explicit or implicit reference to the business model addressed.

The study identified three types of CoCs in relation to the business models covered:

1. CoCs aimed at all business models (Nordic CoC).
2. CoCs aimed at and restricted to only one business model (UK Lending CoC, Austrian CoC).
3. CoCs aimed at all business models, yet provisions are mainly appropriate for financial-return business models (European CoC, UK Crowdfunding CoC, Estonian CoC, Dutch CoC, German CoC, and French CoC).

The UK Lending CoC is the only example of self-regulation restricted to lending-based platforms. The restrictiveness to lending models can only be inferred indirectly, given that Art. 4 of the Rules of Association stipulates that 'any legal entity that operates a platform is eligible for membership of the Association provided that entity does substantive business in the UK and meets the Membership criteria published by the Board and amended from time to time'. The Membership criteria lay down credit risk and operational risk management procedures and rules on a sound and responsible business model, many of which are meaningless for non-lending platforms. At the time of data collection, the UK Lending Association was the only association for P2P lending platforms in Europe. However, some lending platforms have joined industry associations in the banking sector and thus have to adhere to the CoCs of these organisations.[17] Similarly, the Austrian CoCs is limited to 'operators of crowdinvesting platforms [...] within the meaning of § 2 no. 5 AltFG', which essentially limits the scope of the CoC to equity-based crowdfunding since the bespoke crowdfunding regime in Austria covers this model.

All other CoCs are open to signing by any crowdfunding platform independent of the business model. For instance, provisions of the Nordic CoC are very general and aimed at all crowdfunding models. The transnational character of the association makes it primarily a tool to foster awareness and legitimise crowdfunding activity. Since members of the Nordic CoC face different regulatory regimes in their home jurisdictions, a more detailed CoC would not be sensible. In contrast to the Nordic CoC, all remaining CoCs (European CoC, UK Crowdfunding CoC, Estonian CoC, Dutch CoC, German CoC, and French CoC) contain provisions which indicate that they primarily target financial-return models, in particular, equity-based crowdfunding platforms. For instance, the Reporting Guidelines and the Transparency Certificate of the German CoC contain provisions which are only relevant for equity-based crowdfunding. Thus, it is not surprising that their signatories are overwhelmingly equity-based platforms.

The fact that provisions of CoCs are often more tailored to financial-return crowdfunding (lending- and equity-based crowdfunding) and address donation and reward-based crowdfunding only in general terms does not indicate that CoCs are meant to constraint membership, in line with 'club goods' theories of self-regulation. In the case of donation-based and reward-based crowdfunding, the risks of market failures are simply less pronounced. Consequently, both the threat of government regulation and reputation spillovers are more likely in relation to financial-return models.

Similarly, the existence of separate CoCs for lending and equity-based platforms in the UK might also indicate that reputation spillovers between lending and equity crowdfunding are limited. This is in line with arguments in the literature that reputation externalities are less intense 'the more numerous, distant, and heterogenous are the members' (Barnett, 2006, p. 1763). Alternatively, the limitation of a CoC to a specific business model, such as in the UK and Austria, may mirror separate regulatory regimes at the state level. In sum, neither explicit nor implicit restrictions of CoCs to a specific business model are enough to conclude that CoCs are driven by an intention to create a club-like institution. However, such limitations indicate that potential market failures are not universal across different models.

[17] For instance, in Germany, the Banking Association expanded its membership criteria to include Lending Platforms. In the Netherlands, the Corporate Finance Association opened its membership to platforms that sign the Code of Conduct.

In addition to business models, CoCs differ regarding which platforms can join a self-regulatory regime. The study identified three ways in which CoCs restrict who can become their signatory:

1. Only members of the crowdfunding association.[18]
2. Only platforms licensed by the state supervisory authority.
3. Only platforms that fulfil certain criteria (such as annual volumes invested in the platform).[19]

Seven out of nine CoCs apply exclusively to the members of the crowdfunding association (European CoC, UK Lending CoC, French CoC, German CoC, Nordic CoC, Dutch CoC, UK Crowdfunding CoC, and UK Lending CoC). In Austria, all crowdfunding platforms are required by law to join the Chamber of Commerce, making access to CoCs inseparable from membership in the association. The only true exception is the Estonian CoC (Best Practice Guidelines). It is not necessary to be a member of Finance Estonia to receive the label of the Best Practice Guidelines but to follow the Guidelines and report it to Finance Estonia, which conducts checks on an annual basis and decides whether to renew the label.

In essence, restricting access to CoCs to members of the crowdfunding association is not indicative that platforms were aiming at creating club-like institutions. In the case of a large number of platforms, decentralised monitoring and enforcement are too costly to implement. The implementation of CoCs critically depends on the operation of a crowdfunding association, which receives monitoring and enforcement powers from the members. Linking adherence to CoCs to adherence to crowdfunding associations is simply a way to cover the costs of implementing a self-regulatory regime.

In two cases, only platforms with a state license are allowed to join a CoC. The Austrian CoC restricts access to platforms licensed under Austria's bespoke crowdfunding regime (*Alternativfinanzierungsgesetz*). The rules for joining the Nordic Crowdfunding Association require prospective members to provide a statement of authorisation in their home market. In contrast, the UK Crowdfunding CoC states explicitly that its rules apply to platforms regardless of whether the state authority authorises them.

The Dutch CoC is the only example of restricting membership to existing platforms that fulfil specific requirements. The Dutch CoC stipulates that platforms must have at least five projects and have raised at least € 500,000 to become a

[18] Some crowdfunding associations (in the United Kingdom, Germany, France, Netherlands, and Nordic Countries) allow the associated membership of companies which are not platforms, such as law firms, payment providers, banks, or universities. However, CoCs do not apply to the associated members. In contrast, the French CoC, for instance, states specifically that White-label-Software Providers are also covered by CoCs.

[19] If adherence to the CoC is subject to becoming a member of the crowdfunding association, and vice versa, then different ways of restricting access to CoCs become tightly intertwined.

member.[20] The rationale for limiting the membership to platforms that fulfil specific criteria is to intensify the quality signal of the club-like institutions. The more constrained the membership, the smaller the costs associated with effective enforcement and, thus, the stronger the signal.

Overall, in relation to the precondition for platforms to adhere to a self-regulatory regime, restricting membership is an exception rather than a rule. This indicates that, with regard to this criterion, there is more support for the 'coerced theory' and 'reputation commons theory' than for the 'club goods theory' of self-regulation.

However, there are three cases in which a specific right is conferred only to platforms that fulfil additional requirements in terms of the quality of their service. This right refers to a logo display upon verification by the association that the platform meets additional criteria.[21] As described above, the label of the Best Practice Guidelines in the Estonian crowdfunding market is only available to those platforms that regularly report to Finance Estonia, which conducts checks on an annual basis and decides whether to renew the label. Similarly, the Transparency certificate (logo) of the German crowdfunding association is only available to members who comply with additional transparency requirements and provide various information to the association once per year, which enables the association to check compliance. The German case example is specific for explicitly distinguishing between standard members and those who also adhere to higher transparency standards. Finally, the European CoC goes one step further in establishing quality signals for a limited number of platforms. Art. 2.4 grants rights to ECN to deliver an independent ranking on compliance performance by association members. However, these rankings can be published on the ECN website subject to a member's prior acceptance. The ECN has not yet implemented the compliance rating system. While disclosing members' compliance would allow some of them to capture 'ability rents' (Gorton & Mullineaux, 1987, p. 461), it would deter many platforms from joining the association.

Another interesting provision differentiating platforms is known as 'comply or explain'. Only two of nine CoCs (the UK Lending CoC and the Estonian CoC) contain this provision. The 'comply-or-explain'-procedure can be found in Art. 4 of the Operating Principles of the UK Lending CoC, stipulating that waivers must be approved by the Association's board members and are published on the association's website. In contrast, the 'comply-or-explain'-procedure found in the Reporting Form for Compliance in the Estonian CoC forces the platform to publish a deviation

[20] Beyond CoCs, some statutes of crowdfunding associations foresee similar membership criteria. For instance, the statute of the German association requires a platform to have been in operation for at least 1 year, to have a minimum of five crowdfunding projects, and to have raised at least € 500,000 in total.

[21] Display of a crowdfunding association logo, which is not subject to the fulfilment of any specific criteria verified by the association, is a common practice in various countries. Sometimes, this right is explicitly mentioned in the CoC (European CoC, UK Crowdfunding CoC, German CoC, Estonian CoC). Some other associations nevertheless provide a logo to display to their members, even though this is not referenced explicitly in the CoC.

from the CoC on its platform. In contrast to the right of a logo, this provision exemplifies a non-complying platform, thus preventing attempts to undermine the quality signal of other members.

In conclusion, developing specific preconditions for membership and conferring certain rights only to a subsample of crowdfunding platforms are not widespread. Most CoCs opted for a large and unrestricted membership base supporting the argument of either 'coerced' or 'reputation commons' theory. However, those few exceptional examples described above indicate that club-like self-regulatory institutions also emerge in certain crowdfunding markets. The case of the German crowdfunding association reconciles both the 'club' theory and 'reputation commons' theory perspective since it ensures minimum standards for all industry members while at the same time allowing a stronger quality signal from a subsample of platforms. The findings of this section suggest that the rationale for CoCs might not be universal across different markets.

4.4.3 *Monitoring and Enforcement of Codes of Conduct*

This section discusses how associations monitor and enforce rules created through CoCs. As to monitoring, which serves to detect platforms that fail to comply with self-regulatory rules, the study identified three types of obligations borne by platforms:

1. Information Duty—Platforms are required to provide the association with information about their compliance.
2. Denouncing Obligation—Platforms are required to notify the association about unlawful behaviour of other platforms (including non-compliance with CoC).
3. Audits—Platforms are required to allow audits and reviews by the association.

Table 4.6 provides an overview of monitoring tools in different CoCs. The monitoring mechanisms are put in order according to how strong (efficient) they are, from the weakest (none) to the strongest (audits). It is possible to distinguish between centralised (information duty and audits) and decentralised forms of monitoring (denouncing duty). A distinction should also be made between information duty and auditing, on the one hand, and denouncing the breach of CoCs by other platforms, on the other. The former mechanisms entail centralised monitoring by the self-regulatory organisation, whereas the latter involves decentralised monitoring by other industry members. Decentralised monitoring is expected to produce efficient outcomes in detecting a breach only in close-knit communities with limited membership. Both the costs of monitoring and a free-riding problem increase with a broad membership.

French, Dutch, and Nordic CoCs do not foresee any monitoring mechanisms. This does not exclude the possibility that such a mechanism is foreseen in other association rules, such as statutes. Only the German CoC foresees the information duty. Art. 4 of the Transparency Certificate Guidelines of the German CoC requires

Table 4.6 Overview of monitoring mechanisms in CoCs

CoC	None	Information duty	Denouncing duty	Audits
European CoC				x
UK Crowdfunding CoC			x	x
UK Lending CoC			x	x
French CoC	x			
Austrian CoC			X	
German CoC		x		
Dutch CoC	x			
Estonian CoC				x
Nordic CoC	x			

the platforms to provide information about the owners, the latest auditors report, the data security officer, and procedures in case of platform insolvency. This information is shared with a designated officer in the association, but it is not published externally or shared among the platforms.[22]

Three CoCs foresee an obligation to denounce unlawful behaviour and non-compliance with the CoC. Art. 15 of the UK Crowdfunding CoC describes and limits the denouncing obligation at the same time. This article states that the ability of platforms to denounce negative behaviour is restricted by the obligation of confidentiality. Similarly, the Austrian CoC in Art. 14 ensures that deviations from the CoC are being brought to the attention of the Subcommittee of the Financial Intermediaries in the Chamber of Commerce. Since the Subcommittee of Financial Intermediaries is higher in the hierarchy than the Working Group for Crowdfunding Platforms in Austria, this provision poses a severe threat to the platform that breaches the CoC.

Audits are usually done by the associations themselves or by external agents. Four CoC (European CoC, UK Crowdfunding CoC, UK Lending CoC, Estonian CoC) foresee audits and require the platform members to agree to be audited. The UK Lending CoC in Art. 7 stipulates that a formal inquiry can result in an audit through the association—the audit is the consequence of an earlier notification of misconduct submitted by a competitor of the platform. The Estonian CoC in Art. 11 of the Best Practices Guidelines stipulates that the label is reviewed once per year. The same is true for the Transparency Certificate of the German Crowdfunding Association.

In sum, monitoring mechanisms are very diverse across crowdfunding markets. Crowdfunding associations, except for the Austrian CoC, opted for centralised or mixed systems (in the UK). This is in line with the broad membership discussed above. Audits, as the most intrusive monitoring mechanism, are foreseen in a few markets. It is worth noting that the European CoC, German Transparency Certificate, UK lending CoC, and Estonian CoC are also self-regulatory regimes with exclusive

[22] The obligation to inform the association can also be a part of the association's statutes, which was outside the scope of this study.

membership, as discussed in Subsection B. This correlation suggests that, in a few cases, self-regulatory regimes are meant to serve as club signals. Other cases of weak monitoring support the 'reputation commons' theory.

Rules on enforcement are another critical component of CoCs. As Buchanan, 1965, p. 1965 points out, 'the theory of clubs is [...] a theory of optimal exclusion'. The exclusion devices must be in place to ensure that no one can benefit from club goods created through self-regulation without contributing as a club member. Clubs without means to withdraw or suspend membership are inefficient in enforcing the rules. Similarly, the 'coerced' theory assumes that the association can impose sanctions on non-complying industry members.

The study finds that four (UK Crowdfunding CoC, UK Lending CoC, French CoC, and Estonian CoC) of nine CoCs contain withdrawal or suspension clauses.[23] The procedures for a suspension or withdrawal of membership are pretty diverse. The UK Crowdfunding CoC in Art. 16 delegates the authority to the association's directors. The UK Lending CoC in Art 7 allows for the suspension of the membership only after a formal inquiry and hearing of the member. The Estonian CoC in Art.11 (2) foresees the expulsion of members if they do not comply with the best practice guidelines and that no compensation can be retrieved from the association. It is important to note that enforcement of the rules is more vigorous if it entails a label that can be withdrawn, making the expulsion from an association also visible to investors.

Another related mechanism of enforcement is a dispute-resolution mechanism. A dispute can arise either between members and the association or between members. Four (European CoC, UK Lending CoC, French CoC, and Estonian CoC) out of nine CoCs foresee dispute-resolution mechanisms. The European CoC in Art. 2 (5) describes the mechanism for a dispute resolution between members, motivating that 'parties will always seek a negotiated solution'. The members of the European Association can also appoint an external mediator. The UK Lending CoC Art. 7 of the Rules outlines a similar complaint procedure. Complaints by members can be resolved without a formal inquiry. Still, if a significant breach is detected, a formal investigation will be launched, which can result in expulsion from the association. The French CoC in Art. 11 is unique because it stipulates that the French Association can mediate disputes between platforms and between platforms and investors or platforms and projects. Art. 10 of the Best Practice Guidelines of the Estonian CoC stipulates that the association will publish dispute cases.

Overall, strong enforcement mechanisms are foreseen in less than half of the CoCs discussed. Similar to findings of the prevalence of inclusive membership and weak monitoring in previous subsections, the 'reputation commons' theory has the most explanatory power. However, case examples like the Estonian CoC and UK Lending CoC, with their strong enforcement mechanisms accompanying the restrictive membership and robust monitoring, bring evidence for the 'club goods' theory.

[23] Withdrawal or suspension of membership.

4.4.4 Content of Codes of Conduct

The following overview of substantial rules contained in European CoCs and the coherent systematisation of provisions may facilitate future in-depth study and cross-country comparisons. Due to many provisions appearing under different wording and sporadically in several CoCs, this section does not indicate where provisions appear and how they differ. Such an extensive analysis merits a deeper reflection on the underlying regulation in each country, which is beyond the framework of this study. As explained earlier, the study identified three broad themes of substantial provisions in CoCs:

1. Provisions related to the transparency of platforms' behaviour.
2. Provisions related to the business conduct of platforms.
3. Provisions related to the protection of Investors (beyond transparency).

Even though transparency, business conduct, and investor protection relate to each other in manifold ways, the list of provisions in the following Tables 4.7 and 4.8 allows a first glimpse of the topics covered in CoC. The main concern of regulators and industry participants is potential market failures due to information asymmetries. Platforms compete not only in terms of fees but also in terms of the quality of their service.

As discussed before, customers often find essential aspects of platforms' services unobservable. Screening and selection of projects are frequently not made transparent. Contracts between platforms and project owners are not made public. The outcome of platforms' due diligence of financial documents and the corporate structure of project owners is not always published. Management of conflicts of interest is not easily discerned for individual investors. Investors cannot easily identify services offered in the post-investment stage and assess the overall performance of projects.

All CoCs contain a mixture of rules that increase transparency and rules that establish service quality standards. The systematisation of provisions contained in CoCs sheds light on services with which platforms choose to compete. For instance, greater transparency is often required concerning fees, project selection criteria, and platforms' due diligence. From the platforms' point of view, the information remedy is sufficient for these services. On the contrary, platforms choose to regulate directly the quality of other services. For instance, rules of business conduct are of this type. Some of the provisions of CoCs, such as anti-money laundering or data security, are already required by the law. The rationale for including them in a CoC is to provide additional monitoring and enforcing mechanisms.

While the primary purpose of CoCs is to reduce information asymmetries between platforms and their clients, many of the provisions of CoCs indirectly reduce the information advantage of project owners over investors. This is done by mandating that platforms have a mechanism that induces greater disclosure by project owners. Trust in the platforms then translates into trust in the projects.

Table 4.7 Transparency and investor protection provisions in CoCs

Transparency	Platform-specific transparency (pre-investment)	Clear information	Terms and conditions are written in a clear way
		Project selection criteria	Platforms state their selection criteria
		Disclosure requirements	Platforms state which information they require from project owners to disclose
		Due diligence/ verification of information	Platforms state how they verify the information from projects Platforms publish their role in the verification of data
		Fees and charges	Platforms state how they are remunerated
	Platform-specific transparency (post-investment)	Statistics and market development	Platforms provide data about their activity
		Full list of investment projects Full loan book	Platforms provide a complete overview of all projects on their platform. Platforms do not hide unsuccessful projects
	Project-specific transparency (pre-investment)	Clear and unbiased information	Projects display potential returns and risks of projects in a clear manner
		Mandatory disclosure of project information	Project owners provide the minimum information to investors (mandated by the platform, law, and/or association) Platforms publish their information disclosure requirements for project owners
	Project-specific transparency (post-investment)	Scenario analysis	Platforms test the performance of their investment/loan portfolio under adverse scenarios
		Individual portfolio analysis	Platforms analyse how the portfolio of an individual investor behaves and inform them about it
		Ongoing disclosure of projects	Projects report about their activities after the campaign
		Individual investor's fund information	Platforms provide information to investors on where their funds are at each moment

(continued)

Table 4.7 (continued)

Investor Protection	Investor protection (pre-investment)	Risk warnings	Platforms provide risk warnings to investors
		Tax regime information	Platforms give information about the applicable tax treatment
	Investor protection (post-investment)	Cooling-off-period	Investors can withdraw their investment during the funding period
		Limitation of losses	Investors losses are limited to their original investment
		Dispute resolution	Platforms maintain a mechanism for solving conflicts between projects and investors and between platforms and investors

The content analysis of the provisions of CoCs does not allow one to decide whether 'coerced' theories are more plausible than 'voluntary' theories. The provisions which restate the obligation to comply with state laws and regulations already in place support the explanatory power of 'voluntary' self-regulation theories since 'coerced CoCs' would focus on new provisions to defer or stifle regulation.

4.5 Summary of Findings and Implications for Further Research

This chapter has discussed the emergence of self-regulation in European crowd funding markets. Based on a systematic overview of CoCs in different European jurisdictions, including transnational efforts, the analysis reveals that CoCs are a common form of coordination and cooperation between competing platforms. The question of what explains the prevalence of self-regulation in the crowdfunding market must be addressed by looking at existing economic theories on self-regulation developed for different industries. The study in this chapter has built upon existing theories of self-regulation to provide a theoretical framework for the comparative analysis of CoCs in crowdfunding markets. In particular, the study elaborated on how the institutional design of CoCs can help understand their economic purpose.

At the outset, different characteristics of crowdfunding markets can support two competing theoretical frameworks for the emergence of self-regulation: theories of 'coerced' and 'voluntary' self-regulation. Within 'voluntary' theories of self-regulation, the study distinguished between self-regulation serving as a club-like institution to signal quality and self-regulation providing 'reputation commons' to industry members.

Table 4.8 Business conduct provisions in CoCs

Business conduct	Good governance	Permitted activities	Platforms do not act as an investment firm or bank and do not offer investment advice unless authorised
		Operation of platform	Platforms ensure that they are operated in a reliable manner
		Staff and management	Platforms hire competent staff
	Conflict of interest	Conflict of interest management	Platforms manage conflict of interest between platform staff and investors, the platform as an entity and investors. Platforms publish conflicts of interest if they occur
		Non-discrimination of investors	Platforms treat all investors equally
		Non-discrimination of projects	Platforms treat all projects equally
		Project owners information	Projects have the right to be informed about rejection or acceptance Project owners have no right to be accepted on a platform
	Detection of unlawful behaviour	Detection of fraud	Platforms have a mechanism to detect fraud
		Anti-money-laundering activities	Platforms have a mechanism to detect money laundering practices
	Transactions	Segregation of funds	Platforms ensure that the funds of investors are separate from the operational accounts of the respective platform
		Security of transactions	Platforms ensure that the funds of the investor reach the desired project
		Transfer of funds	Platforms transfer funds to projects after rules of investment are triggered
	Data security and IT structure	Security of user information	Platforms ensure that user information is kept safe
		Security of it system	Platforms ensure that the security of the IT system is guaranteed
		Security of project data	Platforms ensure that commercially sensitive information of projects is secure and remains confidential
	Cease of operation	Process for winding down operations	Platforms have a process for winding down their operation
		Ownership of investments	Platforms ensure that investors retain ownership of their investments
	Competition	Fair marketing	Platforms ensure that sales and marketing activity complies with existing laws and regulation
		Healthy competition	Platforms promote healthy competition; unfair competitive practices are not accepted
		Competitors' trademarks	Platforms do not compete on competitors' trademarks in marketing

Institutional design features of CoCs analysed in subsequent sections mainly support one of the 'voluntary' theories of self-regulation. The findings on the inclusiveness of CoCs illustrate that most CoCs opted for a broad membership. The weak monitoring and enforcement mechanisms found in several CoCs indicate that platforms are mainly concerned with the minimum standards that all industry members would adhere to, thus ensuring that 'reputation commons' are protected. It is worth noting that platforms joining CoCs often group around business models, which implies that reputation spillovers are not significant between different types of crowdfunding from the platforms' perspective. In contrast, institutional features of a few CoCs, the most prominent Estonian example, clearly indicate club-like features of some self-regulatory regimes.

The study in this chapter also provided a first systematic overview of substantial rules of CoCs in crowdfunding. Provisions of CoCs are surprisingly elaborate and detailed, suggesting that self-regulatory efforts in crowdfunding go far beyond general principles found in CoCs of other industries. All the provisions found in different CoCs were grouped into three categories: rules related to transparency, investor protection, and business conduct. The analysis revealed that platforms emphasised provisions related to transparency. While this can underpin the argument that platforms try to pre-empt government from regulating quality standards ('Coerced' self-regulation), a more detailed analysis showed that many provisions simply reinforce some of the existing regulations, adding a second level of enforcement. These provisions provide further support for 'voluntary' theories of self-regulation. The overview of substantial rules of CoCs also illuminated potential sources of market failure in the crowdfunding market through the lenses of platforms.

Although the study provided the most support for the theory of 'reputation commons', it does not imply that 'coerced' theories of self-regulation should be entirely abandoned. For one reason, crowdfunding markets' regulatory, economic, and social environments can create different incentives for different platforms. These factors are also likely to bear importance for the institutional design of CoCs beyond the overarching purpose of self-regulation discussed in this study.

To deepen this analysis, further research would be necessary to analyse in detail the regulatory frameworks in each country and discuss the interaction between statutory provisions and those contained in CoCs. Concerning the observed practice of revising CoCs, further research is needed to assess whether and to what extent the content of CoCs affects the choice of rules of subsequent statutory regulations. Other country-specific factors, particularly the depth and liquidity of financial markets and other institutional factors, are expected to strongly influence the development of the crowdfunding industry and the dynamics of self-regulatory rules. In some instances, crowdfunding CoCs developed with the help of associations of conventional financial industries, potentially creating path dependence in terms of the institutional design of CoCs. Finally, further research should assess patterns of diffusion of CoC provisions across different jurisdictions since some anecdotal evidence suggests that a few crowdfunding associations found inspiration for their CoC in ready-made solutions in other jurisdictions.

Another significant extension of this study would be assessing the actual implementation of CoCs. Since many of the provisions are very specific and partially verifiable, checking whether platforms implement and follow these rules is necessary. Such findings bear important implications for regulators worldwide struggling to find an optimal level of regulatory intervention. In connection with this, at the macro level, further research is needed to estimate the effect of self-regulation on the level of trust in the crowdfunding industry and market developments.

The discussion of CoCs in this study can be informative for crowdfunding associations worldwide. The summary of substantial provisions supports crowdfunding associations planning to introduce a self-regulatory regime. The study provides guidance on which areas of self-regulation and specific regulatory solutions are important to the crowdfunding industry. The study highlights the necessity to align the institutional design and the content of the CoC. Depending on the goal of a CoC, the institutional design and the content of the CoC should mirror each other. Principle-based provisions are better tailored to a more inclusive CoC, whereas specific CoC obligations can be effectively enforced through a more club-like institutional design of a CoC.

References

Adjakou, O. J. L. (2015). *The crowdfunding industry report 2015. Massolution*. Retrieved from http://reports.crowdsourcing.org/index.php?route=product/product&product_id=54

Akerlof, G. A. (1970). The market for 'lemons': Quality uncertainty and the market mechanism. *The Quarterly Journal of Economics, 84*(3), 488–500. https://doi.org/10.2307/1879431

Aldrich, H. E., & Fiol, C. M. (1994). Fools rush in? The institutional context of industry creation. *Academy of Management Review, 19*(4), 645–670. https://doi.org/10.5465/amr.1994.9412190214

Armour, J., & Enriques, L. (2018). The promise and perils of crowdfunding: Between corporate finance and consumer contracts: The promise and perils of crowdfunding. *The Modern Law Review, 81*(1), 51–84. https://doi.org/10.1111/1468-2230.12316

Barnett, M. L. (2006). Finding a working balance between competitive and communal strategies. *Journal of Management Studies, 43*(8), 1753–1773. https://doi.org/10.1111/j.1467-6486.2006.00661.x

Belleflamme, P., Lambert, T., & Schwienbacher, A. (2014). Crowdfunding: Tapping the right crowd. *Journal of Business Venturing, 29*(5), 585–609. https://doi.org/10.1016/j.jbusvent.2013.07.003

Benson, B. L. (1988). Legal evolution in primitive societies. *Journal of Institutional and Theoretical Economics (JITE), 144*(5), 772–788. Retrieved from https://www.jstor.org/stable/40751135

Black, J. (1996). Constitutionalising self-regulation. *The Modern Law Review, 59*(1), 24–55. https://doi.org/10.1111/j.1468-2230.1996.tb02064.x

Blohm, I., Leimeister, J. M., Wenzlaff, K., & Gebert, M. (2013). *Crowdfunding-studie 2013/2014: Analyse, Perspektiven und Erfolgsfaktoren innovativer Unternehmens- und Projektfinanzierungsformen*. Epubli. Retrieved from https://www.alexandria.unisg.ch/handle/20.500.14171/88407

Bowen, F. (2019). Marking their own homework: The pragmatic and moral legitimacy of industry self-regulation. *Journal of Business Ethics, 156*(1), 257–272. https://doi.org/10.1007/s10551-017-3635-y

Buchanan, J. M. (1965). An economic theory of clubs. *Economica, 32*(125), 1–14. https://doi.org/10.2307/2552442

Corbin, J. M., & Strauss, A. L. (2015). *Basics of qualitative research: Techniques and procedures for developing grounded theory* (4th ed.).

CrowdfundPort. (2016). *Code of conduct. CrowdfundPort, Interreg Central Europe*. Retrieved from https://www.interreg-central.eu/Content.Node/CROWD-FUND-PORT/CFP-D.T1.1.2-Code-of-conduct.pdf

Cumming, D., & Hornuf, L. (2018). *The economics of crowdfunding*. Springer.

Darby, M. R., & Karni, E. (1973). Free competition and the optimal amount of fraud. *The Journal of Law and Economics, 16*(1), 67–88. https://doi.org/10.1086/466756

Dingwall, R., & Fenn, P. (1987). "A respectable profession"? Sociological and economic perspectives on the regulation of professional services. *International Review of Law and Economics, 7*(1), 51–64. Retrieved from https://d1wqtxts1xzle7.cloudfront.net/76918681/0144-8188_2887_2990006-820211220-18905-1r109se-libre.pdf?1640044578=&response-content-disposition=inline%3B+filename%3DA_respectable_profession_Sociological_a.pdf&Expires=1719927704&Signature=Rb8hZ~fZsla6m88TIlvpzaaJ3d9fUQ30jHOGP6T7-78S5Urm~wh69BAuaBukq5h5vne03GKaCm~LqB2n~AC7doom70rfW57649sQ11gwyTvEC3L-M~d0Imd1XAhCA-chhSXr5HleAS5xDVvFHkk~24Y3qOLdmR2Mb7ysyunyGFGAkIgN4hGb0IYr1JKjwNT2jd2vMU79y~NyJv9hkIbBnESSneTDyYEv5XCSIGHrE5zhLIeKZsHKD6CTW6U8iHAxwd~pgsZ7HJB2h1BluuGo9TiVWJbYEIzKTGyw9AX09Gt5SjiA~ny33VdA2eNOBNuwFIqyZQA9sODSwttS-AvOCxg__&Key-Pair-Id=APKAJLOHF5GGSLRBV4ZA

Dixit, A. (2009). Governance institutions and economic activity. *American Economic Review, 99*(1), 5–24. https://doi.org/10.1257/aer.99.1.5

Gehrig, T., & Jost, P.-J. (1995). Quacks, lemons, and self regulation: A welfare analysis. *Journal of Regulatory Economics, 7*(3), 309–325. https://doi.org/10.1007/BF01067100

Gilbert, D. U., Rasche, A., & Waddock, S. (2011). Accountability in a global economy: The emergence of international accountability standards. *Business Ethics Quarterly, 21*(01), 23–44. https://doi.org/10.5840/beq20112112

Gorton, G., & Mullineaux, D. J. (1987). The joint production of confidence: Endogenous regulation and nineteenth century commercial-bank clearinghouses. *Journal of Money, Credit and Banking, 19*(4), 457–468. https://doi.org/10.2307/1992614

Haas, P., Blohm, I., & Leimeister, J. M. (2014). *An empirical taxonomy of crowdfunding intermediaries*. International Conference on Information Systems. Retrieved from http://aisel.aisnet.org/icis2014/proceedings/SocialMedia/13/

Hemer, J., Schneider, U., Dornbusch, F., & Frey, S. (2011). *Crowdfunding und andere Formen informeller Mikrofinanzierung in der Projekt-und Innovationsfinanzierung*. Fraunhofer Verlag.

Howard, J., Nash, J., & Ehrenfeld, J. (2000). Standard or smokescreen? Implementation of a voluntary environmental code. *California Management Review, 42*(2), 63–82. https://doi.org/10.2307/41166033

Jegelevičiūtė, S., & Valančienė, L. (2015). Comparative analysis of the ways crowdfunding is promoted. *Procedia - Social and Behavioral Sciences, 213*, 268–274. https://doi.org/10.1016/j.sbspro.2015.11.536

Maxwell, J. W., Lyon, T. P., & Hackett, S. C. (2000). Self-regulation and social welfare: The political economy of corporate environmentalism. *The Journal of Law and Economics, 43*(2), 583–618. https://doi.org/10.1086/467466

Nelson, P. (1970). Information and consumer behavior. *Journal of Political Economy, 78*(2), 311–329. https://doi.org/10.1086/259630

Odorović, A., & Wenzlaff, K. (2020). The joint production of confidence–self-regulation in European crowdfunding markets. *Baltic Journal of Management, 15*(2), 303–331. https://doi.org/10.1108/BJM-04-2019-0119

Ogus, A. (1995). Rethinking self-regulation. *Oxford: The Journal of Legal Studies, 15*, 97–108. Retrieved from https://heinonline.org/HOL/LandingPage?handle=hein.journals/oxfjls15&div=14&id=&page=

Philipsen, N. J. (2012). Regulation of accountants. In R. Van den Bergh & A. M. Pacces (Eds.), *Encyclopedia of law and economics* (pp. 715–742). Edward Elgar Publishing.

Posner, R. A. (1980). A theory of primitive society, with special reference to law. *The Journal of Law and Economics, 23*(1), 1–53. https://doi.org/10.1086/466951

Prakash, A., & Potoski, M. (2007). Collective action through voluntary environmental programs: A club theory perspective: Prakash/Potoski: Collective action through voluntary environmental programs. *Policy Studies Journal, 35*(4), 773–792. https://doi.org/10.1111/j.1541-0072.2007.00247.x

Rau, P. R. (2020). Law, trust, and the development of crowdfunding. *SSRN Electronic Journal*. https://doi.org/10.2139/ssrn.2989056

Schwarcz, S. L. (2002). Private ordering. *Northwestern University Law Review, 97*, 319–350. Retrieved from https://heinonline.org/hol-cgi-bin/get_pdf.cgi?handle=hein.journals/illlr97&section=12

Schwienbacher, A. (2014). *Crowdinvesting in The Netherlands: Market analysis, securities regulation and policy options* (pp. 1–20). Duisenberg School of Finance.

Stefanadis, C. (2003). Self-regulation, innovation, and the financial industry. *Journal of Regulatory Economics, 23*(1), 5–25. https://doi.org/10.1023/A:1021858812744

Surowiecki, J. (2005). *The wisdom of crowds*. Anchor.

Turan, S. S. (2015). Financial innovation - Crowdfunding: Friend or Foe? *Procedia - Social and Behavioral Sciences, 195*, 353–362. https://doi.org/10.1016/j.sbspro.2015.06.334

Van den Bergh, R. (2004). Towards efficient self-regulation in markets for professional services. *European Competition Law Annual, 2006*, 1–24. Retrieved from https://citeseerx.ist.psu.edu/document?repid=rep1&type=pdf&doi=580b1d532e676c3641696e0c894c3ecf7f66e3c4

Wenzlaff, K. (2019). Developing a policy framework for emerging crowdfunding ecosystems. *ORF Policy Briefs, 302*, 12.

Williams, A. D. (2004). *An economic theory of self-regulation* (pp. 1–24). Retrieved from http://anthonydwilliams.com/wp-content/uploads/2006/08/An_Economic_Theory_of_Self-Regulation.pdf

Yin, R. K. (2014). *Case study research: Design and methods* (5th ed.). Sage.

Yue, L. Q., & Ingram, P. (2012). *Industry self-regulation as a solution to the reputation commons problem: The case of the New York Clearing House Association*. Oxford University Press. https://doi.org/10.1093/oxfordhb/9780199596706.013.0014

Ziegler, T., Shneor, R., Garvey, K., Wenzlaff, K., Yerolemou, N., Rui, H., & Zhang, B. (2018). *Expanding horizons: The 3rd European alternative finance industry report*. Cambridge Centre for Alternative Finance. Retrieved from https://www.jbs.cam.ac.uk/wp-content/uploads/2020/08/2018-02-ccaf-exp-horizons.pdf

Ziegler, T., Shneor, R., Wenzlaff, K., Odorović, A., Johanson, D., Hao, R., & Ryll, L. (2019). *Shifting paradigms: The 4th European alternative finance benchmarking report*. Cambridge Centre for Alternative Finance. Retrieved from https://www.jbs.cam.ac.uk/faculty-research/centres/alternative-finance/publications/shifting-paradigms/

Chapter 5
The Residual Role of the Law: A Normative Approach to Crowdfunding Regulation

5.1 Introduction

This chapter discusses the residual role of the law in the crowdfunding market. The aim is to offer responses to some universal regulatory concerns and dilemmas in this market instead of proposing a specific regulatory reform in any jurisdiction. However, some guiding principles elaborated in this chapter can serve as a basis for designing crowdfunding regulations in countries that have not yet adopted a crowdfunding-specific regime and countries aiming to ameliorate existing rules.

The insights in this chapter draw on the findings from previous chapters, which are juxtaposed with prominent regulatory solutions from different jurisdictions. In line with Chap. 2, the regulatory recommendations are guided by some defining features of the crowdfunding market: many small contributions from unsophisticated investors, small (unsophisticated) fundraisers, and platforms that act as information rather than financial intermediaries. However, the regulatory treatment must also accommodate the diversity of platform-business models. While crowdfunding is a channel for direct finance, some platforms assume several different roles, allowing them to reintermediate the market without taking any risk on their balance sheets.

Moreover, the regulatory intervention should be based on promises and limitations of market mechanisms, as thoroughly discussed in Chap. 3. This primarily relates to potential sources of market failure arising from information asymmetry between fundraisers and investors. However, platform gatekeeping roles can also create an information gap between them and investors, giving rise to agency problems.

Finally, regulatory recommendations should also consider the platforms' perspective on the scope of necessary regulatory intervention. Industry codes of conduct investigated in Chap. 4 provide a basis for identifying key issues where market forces, driven by platform competition, cannot yield sufficient protection for investors.

A. Odorović, *Overcoming Asymmetric Information in the Crowdfunding Market*, International Law and Economics, https://doi.org/10.1007/978-3-032-04118-0_5

This chapter begins by discussing early regulatory responses to crowdfunding phenomena (Sect. 5.1). They range from no regulation, stretching existing financial regulations to accommodate new models and experimentation through regulatory innovation initiatives (also known as innovation facilitators), to adopting bespoke crowdfunding rules. Next, this chapter explores the economic rationale for a different regulatory treatment of crowdfunding models based on the following criteria: the type of instruments intermediated, parties to a transaction, and services offered by the platform (Sect. 5.2). After discussing these overarching questions, it then proceeds to discuss the residual role of the law in light of its subtle interplay with market-based mechanisms (Sect. 5.3). Particular attention is paid to the merits of mandatory disclosures for fundraisers, rules that reinforce the gatekeeping roles of platforms, and retail investor protections. The last section summarises the main findings (Sect. 5.4).

5.2 The Regulatory 'Tetralemma' in Approaching the Crowdfunding Phenomenon

Before diving deep into the specifics of crowdfunding regulations, explaining the merits of four different regulatory paths or approaches is helpful. They represent a theoretical interpretation of what regulators have done in response to the emergence of crowdfunding platforms. The first approach or the baseline scenario is the absence of regulation. The second approach entails applying the rules conceived for traditional (financial) intermediaries to crowdfunding platforms. The third approach involves learning and experimentation for both platforms and regulators through innovation offices and regulatory sandboxes. The fourth, the most complex, approach consists in creating bespoke crowdfunding regulations.

It is worth noting that the four approaches are not necessarily unique to crowdfunding. On the contrary, they largely reflect broader regulatory challenges of dealing with financial technology, specifically in the new era of startup-led financial innovations (Arner et al., 2015; Brummer & Yadav, 2018).[1] These challenges require regulators to abandon the conventional 'entity-based' regulation, where only a predefined list of institutions falls under their regulatory remit (Jackson, 2020, pp. 12–15). The 'entity-based' approach assumes that regulated activities align with specific (traditional) entities instead of recognising that discrete parts of a regulated

[1] Brummer and Yadav (2018) argue that the fintech policy trilemma consists of (1) maintaining market integrity, (2) providing clear, simple rules, and (3) encouraging financial innovation, while regulators can achieve, at best, two out of three objectives. The regulatory responses to this trilemma, as seen by these authors, have some overlapping elements with the approach developed in this section. They include: (1) Informal guidance; (2) Pilots; (3) Licences; (4) Regulatory sandboxes (Brummer & Yadav, 2018, pp. 282–297).

activity can be split among different entities in the fintech era (Levitin, 2021, p. 329). Moreover, regulators should discern a regulated activity behind the use of new technologies and communication channels or embrace a 'technology-neutral' approach (Benlala, 2023, p. 252). Against this backdrop, as Restoy (2019, pp. 7–8) argues, the same activity performed by different entities can also pose distinct risks. Additionally, some risks are inherent in the very use of new technologies. Finally, technology can enable the emergence of new services that interfere with regulatory goals and, thus, deserve special regulatory treatment. In particular, companies operating platform-business models often do not provide financial services directly but merely enable their users to interact and sometimes carry out such services themselves (Rodriguez de las Heras Ballell, 2019, p. 396).

For the purpose of this chapter, the proposed theoretical framework will be discussed solely with respect to regulatory responses to crowdfunding in different jurisdictions. It is worth noting that regulatory approaches are often interrelated and evolving due to the challenges described above. It is common for regulators and policymakers to apply two or more approaches consecutively. Naturally, bespoke regulations often follow a period in which crowdfunding was left unregulated. Alternatively, they can result from applying overly strict or inadequate regulations aimed at traditional financial services and institutions (e.g., banks, investment intermediaries, investment firms (brokers), and payment institutions). Also, a bespoke regime can be adopted following a learning and experimentation phase by interacting with platforms within innovation offices and regulatory sandboxes. In other words, the latter two regulatory innovation initiatives can act as policy enablers (Restoy, 2019, pp. 5–6). Interestingly, regulatory innovation initiatives can coexist with bespoke crowdfunding regulations, allowing crowdfunding platforms to test their business model before obtaining a full licence.

It is essential to mention that regulators can adopt different approaches to different crowdfunding models, treating, for instance, lending-based crowdfunding under existing regulations and creating a bespoke regime for equity-based crowdfunding or vice versa (Fig. 5.1).

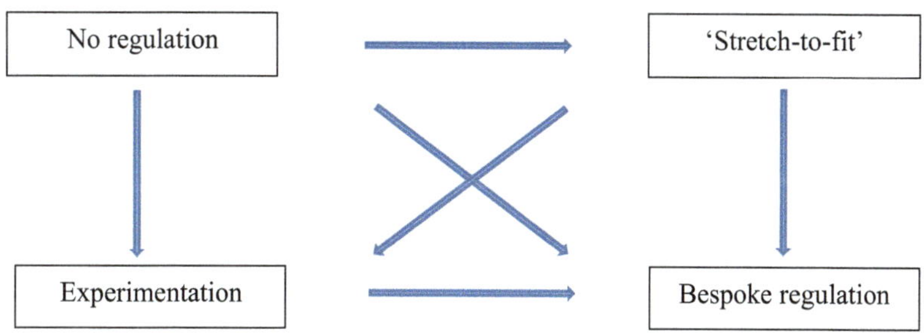

Fig. 5.1 The regulatory 'tetralemma' in approaching the crowdfunding phenomenon

5.2.1 Baseline Scenario: No Regulation

At the outset of crowdfunding, it was common for regulators worldwide to take a passive approach ('wait-and-see'), allowing some or all crowdfunding business models to escape regulatory oversight entirely. Such an approach was only available to regulators where existing regulations for traditional intermediaries were not broad enough to easily extend the regulatory remit to new market entrants (as discussed below under 'stretch-to-fit-approach'). It should be emphasised that the notion of 'no regulation' embraced here refers to a situation where platforms are not subject to regulatory oversight by a financial authority. Their relationships with fundraisers and investors are inevitably governed by their contracts, which are supplemented by statutory provisions of the contract or corporate laws. Moreover, their behaviour may still be subject to other statutory rules and regulations not inherent to the financial sector (e.g., data protection, cybersecurity, tax rules) or licensing and oversight by non-financial regulators. In addition, as discussed below, the lack of regulations applicable to the crowdfunding intermediary can coexist with financial regulations applicable to fundraisers and investors.

Before evaluating the possible implications of the baseline scenario, it is helpful to understand its rationale. In many instances, the lack of regulations is not a deliberate choice of policymakers but rather the consequence of a fast-paced development of financial technology when the rule-making process always lags behind. In that sense, crowdfunding is not different from other fintech innovations, or financial innovations in the broadest terms, which always forced regulators to retroactively adapt to the new challenges posed (also known as the 'pacing problem') (Ruof, 2023, pp. 77–79).

In many jurisdictions, limited volumes, particularly in equity crowdfunding, created a perception that crowdfunding was still 'too-small-to-care' (Anagnostopoulos, 2018, p. 17; Arner et al., 2015, pp. 1309–1310). It is an often-held view that regulations should intervene only when a particular phenomenon becomes sufficiently widespread or poses risks to financial stability. In the aftermath of the 2008 Global financial crisis, when crowdfunding started emerging in different countries, systematic risks were at the heart of regulators' concerns (Benoit et al., 2017; Brummer & Yadav, 2018, p. 262). Even nowadays, when the crowdfunding market matured in some jurisdictions, it often remains modest compared to traditional finance, with little interdependencies between the two sectors, posing no or limited systematic risk.

The 'wait-and-see approach' is also sometimes justified by the fact that regulatory objectives multiplied over time (Brummer, 2015, pp. 1037–1038). Regulatory authorities no longer see their function as limited to protecting the financial system's stability and ensuring investor safeguards; they are also increasingly promoting innovation and competition in financial markets, as well as financial inclusion.[2]

[2] According to Brummer and Yadav (2018, p. 262), financial inclusion was first formally acknowledged as a regulatory goal in the US in the GrammLeach-Bliley Act and the Commodity Futures

In many jurisdictions, regulatory authorities embraced these objectives as part of their formal mandate. Enabling greater access to finance for SMEs and reducing the associated regulatory costs have also been on policymakers' agendas following the rationing of bank lending after the Financial crisis. For instance, the European Parliament resolution of 9 July 2015 on Building a Capital Markets Union acknowledged that 'the lack of access to finance for SMEs is one of the greatest obstacles to growth in the EU' (European Parliament, 2015, para. 21). It also stressed out the need to promote the growth of non-bank financing (European Parliament, 2015, para. 47), which makes part of a broader 'CMU Action plan objective to mobilise capital and channel it to all companies, including SMEs' (European Commission, 2017, p. 14).

This shift in regulatory objectives and strategies sometimes coincided with the emergence of fintech, which is praised for its consumer-oriented approach and the ability to offer more affordable services to a broader range of consumers. Thus, a 'laisser-faire' approach to crowdfunding regulation, being part of broader attitudes towards fintech, was also motivated by the fear of stifling innovation and deterring the entry of new players in different segments of financial markets (Brummer & Yadav, 2018, p. 263; Omarova, 2020). New players are seen as a potential solution to issues in the traditional sector, such as insufficient competition, legacy systems, and high regulatory compliance costs, due to which large market segments often remain underserved. Early regulatory intervention in the fintech market was also seen as undesired or a potential waste of resources, as not every new technological innovation becomes a widespread market product or service, often taking time to evolve and find its definite applicability (Arner et al., 2015, p. 1307). Instead, some regulators' stance was to enable the unconstrained discovery of best practices in the market, leaving some space for 'trial-end-error'. Similarly, allowing regulators to observe and learn from market developments reduces the risk of a regulatory failure of under-regulating or over-regulating the market in the light of an important information deficit of regulators (Ringe & Ruof, 2020, p. 605; Ruof, 2023, pp. 43–67).

While motivations behind the baseline approach of no regulation are diverse, including pro-innovation perspectives, it prevented crowdfunding from emerging or stifled its growth in some jurisdictions. This was due to two sets of reasons. Firstly, in many jurisdictions, crowdfunding activity was prohibited (or expensive to conduct) without a tailored regulatory regime due to restrictive rules applicable to fundraisers or investors.[3]

Limitations on P2P lending usually involve an extensive interpretation of what falls under the banking monopoly. In Europe, for instance, it is common for banking regulations in Member States to require licensing from anyone raising (repayable)

Modernization Act, as part of a broader deregulation trends in the 1990s. As opposed to financial inclusion, some authors are critical of embracing financial innovation as a regulatory goal due to potential harm to consumer protection and financial stability (Allen, 2019; Lumpkin, 2010).

[3] The application of existing rules to fundraisers or investors differs from regulating crowdfunding platforms by means of extending regulations created for traditional intermediaries, as will be discussed in the next section.

funds from the public or providing credit to a certain number of individuals when certain conditions are met. Thus, there are instances in which crowd borrowers or lenders would be considered breaking the banking monopoly if engaged in a crowdfunding activity.[4]

In 2007, the former Belgian financial regulator (Commission Bancaire, Financière et des Assurances—CBFA) declared that the project owner, that is, a potential borrower, would violate the existing Belgian Bank Act by announcing their credit needs on a crowdfunding platform since this involves making an appeal to more than 50 persons (Colaert, 2016, pp. 183–184). Conversely, in France and Austria, private lenders were potential infringers of banking regulations. Before adopting the French bespoke crowdfunding regime, even the second act of lending was deemed to fall under the notion of habitual lending (*à titre habituel*), thus triggering licensing requirements (Capdeville, 2015, pp. 4–5). An even stricter interpretation of the banking monopoly came from the Austrian Financial Market Authority (FMA). As elaborated by Raschauer and Muller (2016, p. 222), private lenders are potential infringers of banking regulations in Austria as long as they 'act with an intention to repeat the action and offers to be available on the market'.

Interestingly, in Germany, the activity of both borrowers and lenders could qualify as the activity of a credit institution. As Raschauer and Muller (2016, pp. 3–4) explained, the banking business involves a regulated lending activity and/or the taking of deposits. If crowd lenders act commercially, whereas the interpretation of this term by the German regulator (BaFin) is relatively broad (including even an intention to carry out several transactions, similar to Austria), they may be required to obtain a banking licence. Likewise, if crowd borrowers accept funds from more than 25 individuals, which is typically the case in the crowdfunding context, they would also be performing a regulated activity of taking deposits.

Limitations on equity (investment-based) crowdfunding are typically provided in securities laws regulating public securities offerings. In most jurisdictions, such offerings require publishing a prospectus that has to be registered with/approved by the regulatory authority, which is disproportionately costly for crowdfunding issuers. Securities laws often set out a certain number of exemptions, which may be unsuitable for crowdfunding offerings. Exemptions are typically foreseen if the offer targets only a limited number of persons or accredited (qualified) investors only, as well as when the offering amount is below a certain threshold set in the law.

Before the adoption of the JOBS Act in the US (Jumpstart Our Business Startups Act, Pub. L. No. 112-106, U.S. Congress, 2012), none of the existing exemptions

[4] It should be noted, however, that the EBA's interpretation of what falls under the perimeter of a credit institution under the Capital Requirements Regulation and Directive (CRR/CRD) (Directive, 2013; Regulation, 2013) excludes all crowdfunding market participants (platforms, borrowers, and lenders). In an early report on the crowdfunding industry, the EBA underlines that the definition of a credit institution includes two cumulative elements: accepting deposits or other repayable funds and granting credits (European Banking Authority, 2015, para 89). In other words, undertaking a business that consists only of one of the two elements does not bring the entity within the purview of the CRR/CRD.

from registration requirements could have been used by fundraisers on a crowdfunding platform (Bradford, 2012, pp. 44–48; Wang, 2023, pp. 246–249). This is because most of the available exemptions either limit the offerings of securities to accredited investors, prohibit general solicitations, or impose both of these limitations.[5] Evidently, they go against the very purpose of crowdfunding, which assumes advertising securities offering to many anonymous retail investors. One exemption that allows general solicitations from non-accredited investors (Regulation A) requires issuers to pursue a 'mini-registration', a simplified disclosure procedure, if the total offering amount is below $5 million. This was, nevertheless, considered an expensive alternative for very small offerings typical for crowdfunding. As a result, until the adoption of the JOBS Act, the 'market for speculative business investments' via internet platforms remained limited to wealthy, accredited investors (Schwartz, 2013, pp. 44–45). Title III of the JOBS Act created a new exemption from registration requirements when offering securities to the 'crowd'.[6]

Another interesting case is the Chinese market. Even though securities regulations are clear that securities offered to the public must be registered with the China Securities Regulatory Authority (as long as there are more than 200 investors), the latter was lenient about a crowdfunding market practice that circumvented these rules for several years (Wang, 2023, pp. 284–292). As explained by Wang (2023, pp. 284–292), equity platforms structured investments so that a structure resembling an SPV (so-called limited partnership enterprise) juxtaposed between retail investors and the company raising finances.[7] Retail investors and company founders would merely hold quasi-shares in this investment structure, which were not treated as securities and thus not subject to regulatory oversight. The limited partnership enterprise would have ownership over the fundraising company. As a result, crowdfunding investors participated in the distribution of profits but were deprived of control over a fundraising company. However, in 2015, the Chinese regulator issued a notice clarifying that the equity crowdfunding market did fall under securities regulation, leading to a market crackdown.

In some other jurisdictions, notably EU Member States, public offers of securities are not subject to prospectus requirements if they are deemed small issuances, that is when the fundraising amount is below a certain threshold. The EU Prospectus Directive, which was in force until 2017, allowed Member States to set the threshold below which an offer does not require a prospectus, as long as it is below €5

[5] This applies to exemptions under Rule 504, 505, and 506 of Regulation D and Sect. 4(5) of the Securities Act (Securities Act of 1933, 1933). For more details on the exact conditions for the application of these exemptions and possible implications for the crowdfunding market, see Bradford (2012, pp. 44–48).

[6] Title III of the JOBS Act became effective on 16 May 2016. However, according to Johan and Zhang (2020, p. 3), even before the adoption of the JOBS Act, a few state securities regulators created crowdfunding exemptions at the state level. Still, most of them were again limited to accredited investors. The effects of these regulations were further limited by the fact that both issuers and investors had to be established/have a residency in a given state.

[7] Such a practice was pioneered by the platform Renrentou (Wang, 2023, p. 287).

million over 12 months (Directive, 2003; Directive, 2010). The threshold varied significantly among Member States. In some cases, it was set so low that it made issuing securities to the public via a crowdfunding platform unappealing to either fundraisers or platforms. The European Crowdfunding Network (2017) states that several Member States set the fundraising limit at a minimum of €100,000 (e.g., Bulgaria, Estonia, Germany, Latvia, etc.). Yet, in many countries, specific financial instruments were not considered transferrable securities and, thus, not subject to prospectus requirements independently of the issuing amount (e.g., silent partnerships in Germany, shares in limited liability companies in Estonia), allowing crowdfunding fundraisers to avoid costly prospectus requirements. With the adoption of the EU Prospectus Regulation, the minimum exemption threshold was increased to €1 million, whereas Member States have the discretion to set it higher as long as it is less than €8 million when publishing a prospectus becomes mandatory (Regulation, 2017).

Securities regulations can constrain crowdfunding activity even when the prospectus exemption threshold is set high, as in the case of Greece before law amendments that regulated crowdfunding (Wang, 2023, pp. 284–292). Offerings between €100,000 and €5 million were subject to simplified disclosure requirements, which involved a mandatory approval procedure by the competent authority. The requirement of approval was deemed too burdensome for crowdfunding firms.

High regulatory uncertainty is the second reason the crowdfunding market can stagnate when crowdfunding platforms remain outside the regulatory remit. As discussed in Chap. 6, regulatory uncertainty can negatively affect all three market participants. Platforms incur high costs of scoping and interpreting existing regulations, making sure that none of their activities infringe regulatory requirements. Investors can fear that they are not sufficiently protected as regulatory authorities supervise neither the operation of platforms nor the behaviour of fundraisers. Fundraisers can also question how the unregulated environment affects the terms of raising finance and the overall viability of this funding mechanism. As a result, one or both sides of the market can shy away from this financing/investing opportunity.

Nevertheless, as discussed in Chap. 4, there are instances in which the lack of supervision by the public authority can be substituted with industry self-regulation. In small, growing markets, industry members sometimes have incentives to create rules to preempt overly strict statutory regulations, signal their quality to the market, or ensure that all industry members adhere to some minimum standards to minimise negative reputational spillovers. As mentioned earlier, a successful example of such an initiative is FinanceEstonia's. A set of well-balanced self-regulatory rules, known as the Crowdfunding Best Practice, appeared sufficient for the Estonian crowdfunding market to rank second in Europe in total volumes per capita (Laub, 2021).

It is important to note that the passive approach towards platform regulation can become a regulatory failure even if it enables a booming crowdfunding market. Market forces alone cannot always ensure all the necessary investor protection safeguards, such as that client funds are clearly separated, including from the platform's funds. This is particularly important when investors do not benefit from deposit guarantees or investment compensation schemes, as in the case of regulated financial services (Kleiner, 2021, p. 36). An example of a crowdfunding market where the lenient approach of regulators led to a large-scale misuse of investor funds is China. As explained by Nemoto et al. (2019, pp. 6–8), some Chinese P2P lending platforms started operating a guaranteed-return model, which implies that a fixed return is promised to investors. If crowdfunding investments did not generate the guaranteed return, investors had a claim against the platform balance sheet. It was not uncommon for Chinese platforms to use pledges from new investors to reimburse the old ones (a Ponzi-like scheme), leading to misappropriation of investor funds or platform collapse. This has resulted in a regulatory intervention, which banned the guaranteed-return model and mandated holding clients' money in segregated bank accounts. Since then, several problematic platforms have left the market.

It should be mentioned that the duration of this baseline scenario of no regulation varies significantly between countries. Where the market growth was unconstrained, crowdfunding often reached a point where it was no longer 'as small as to be neglected' (Anagnostopoulos, 2018, p. 15). In countries where the sector did not take off, regulators increasingly considered it as an unused opportunity. Both of these outcomes often incentivised regulators to apply one of the three remaining approaches.

5.2.2 Extending Regulations Conceived for Traditional Financial Services

As elaborated in Chap. 2, the operation of crowdfunding platforms shares some similarities with traditional financial system actors, notably financial and information intermediaries. As a result, another widespread practice among regulators is to extend the interpretation of existing regulations developed for conventional financial services to account for risks emerging from new models.

Bringing the operation of crowdfunding platforms within the purview of existing rules can be described as 'stretch-to-fit'. The rationale behind it is a concern that some of the critical goals of financial regulation will not be achieved with these new market entrants. Such a concern was widespread in the years following the Financial Crisis, whose roots were often found in deregulatory measures in the financial sector (Born, 2011; Morsy, 2014, p. 1376), as well as entities and activities escaping regulatory supervision (often referred to as shadow banks) (Lysandrou & Nesvetailova, 2015).[8] With the increased regulatory burden imposed on traditional banks, new technology-driven non-deposit institutions were expected to develop and fill some of the gaps left by incumbents (Buchak et al., 2018).

Against this backdrop, crowdfunding platforms were often required to hold one of the licences conceived for traditional entities providing financial services.

[8] The analysis in Chap. 2 has shown that crowdfunding platforms do not perform asset transformation and, as a result, should not be treated as new 'shadow banks'.

Depending on the model, crowdfunding platforms needed to have a licence for a deposit/credit institution (bank), a credit intermediary (credit broker), a payment service provider, an investment firm (investment broker), or an alternative investment fund manager (AIFM). One should note that all of the examples used in this section refer to the regulatory treatment of platforms before adopting bespoke regimes in different countries (or at the European level), which introduced a new type of licence for crowdfunding intermediaries.[9]

The 'stretch-to-fit' approach usually followed a traditional division between the banking business and capital markets, where loan-based crowdfunding was assimilated with the former and equity-based crowdfunding with the latter. A clear division of the regulatory remit of banking and capital markets regulators in some jurisdictions also supported such reasoning.

Extending banking regulations to loan-based platforms is based on the premise that they, while not acting as creditors, collect funds from the public (Macchiavello, 2018, p. 683), which potentially qualifies them as deposit-taking institutions in some countries. In Switzerland, taking deposits on a commercial basis is considered an exclusive prerogative of banks. Deposit-taking activity is considered broad enough to encompass 'all sorts of debts on one's own account' (Troxler, 2021, p. 430). As explained by Troxler (2021, pp. 434–435), even the fact that platforms collected funds from investors temporarily to be later passed on to fundraisers would mean that platforms engaged in a banking business. The existence of repayable funds could be even more firmly established in cases where the campaign did not reach the funding target and the funds collected from investors were odd to be repaid to investors.[10] Similarly, in Austria, a P2P lending platform is required to either hold a licence under the Austrian Banking Act (BWG) or to partner with a licensed credit institution, which collects all the funds intermediated over the course of a crowdfunding transaction on its own account (Raschauer & Muller, 2016, p. 222). In the latter case, the platform must only hold a loan broker licence, regulated under the Austrian Industrial Code (GewO) and issued by a local trade authority (a non-financial regulator).

Other cases in which P2P lending platforms were treated as credit brokers (intermediaries) but subject to financial regulators' supervision are France and the Netherlands. The treatment of loan-based platforms in France before the adoption of a bespoke crowdfunding regime is specific since crowd lenders were the ones that could infringe on the banking monopoly, as explained earlier. Thus, crowdfunding activity could only be performed with the involvement of a bank that extends credit. Nonetheless, platforms were also required to hold a special licence for intermediation in relation to banking and payment services (*L'intermédiation en opérations de*

[9] However, it should be acknowledged that bespoke crowdfunding regimes, including the EU-level texts, usually do not cover all crowdfunding models. As a result, some of the licences for traditional providers of financial services may still be relevant to models falling outside the scope of new regimes.

[10] A requirement for a crowdfunding platform to hold a banking licence was subsequently abolished (FINMA, 2020).

banque et en services de paiement (IOBSP)) (Autorité de Contrôle Prudentiel, 2013, pp. 5–6). Such a licence imposed fewer onerous regulatory requirements than a banking licence. Yet, an IOBSP was only allowed to facilitate the conclusion of contracts within the domain of banks and payment institutions without being involved in any capacity to make decisions on granting credits. Selecting borrowers was considered an exclusive prerogative of banks, whereas crowd lenders could only express their preferences, which were not binding for the bank (Autorité de Contrôle Prudentiel, 2013, p. 6).

Similarly, P2P consumer lending platforms in the Netherlands were authorised as offerors of consumer credit (Ortolani & Louisse, 2021, pp. 11–12). The Dutch regulator intended to ensure consumer protection safeguards are in place regarding borrowers. The licence of an offeror of consumer credit required platforms to comply with regulations stemming from the Dutch implementation of the European Consumer Credit Directive (CCD) (Directive, 2008) and some additional consumer protection requirements provided in the Dutch law (Ortolani & Louisse, 2021, pp. 11–12). Treating P2P platforms as credit intermediaries instead of creditors is also more in line with the EBA's interpretation of the relevant provisions of the CCD (letter (f) of Article 3).[11] According to EBA (European Banking Authority, 2015, pp. 31–32, fn. 27), the credit intermediary status of a platform triggers the application of some pre-contractual information requirements and some additional information requirements regarding intermediation.

Regulators on other continents have also sought suitable alternatives to a banking licence for P2P lending platforms. For instance, in India, banking regulations provide for the licensing of non-bank entities engaged in financial activity, with the decisive element being whether the majority of a firm's income relates to the financial sector (Minupuri, 2018, pp. 442–447). As a result, P2P lending platforms are subject to strict prudential and governance requirements.

Alternatively, loan-based and equity-based platforms are sometimes required to hold a licence for a payment service provider to cover payment-related aspects of their business. As explained in Chap. 2, platforms sometimes provide money transfer services. Therefore, crowdfunding platforms must have protections to safeguard clients' assets, protecting them from possible misappropriation. This is primarily done by segregating their client's assets from the platform's assets. In addition, the security of money transfers and the continuity of payment services in case of a platform failure are essential risks for both fundraisers and investors. For these reasons, unless platforms outsource money handling to an authorised payment service provider, they are often required to hold a payment institution or another payment

[11] The EBA is clear that most crowdfunding platforms would not qualify as creditors under the CCD since they do not grant or promise to grant credit directly (European Banking Authority, 2015, pp. 31–32, fn. 27). Yet, a platform can be qualified as a credit intermediary, if it performs one of the following activities defined in letter (f) of Article 3: (1) presents or offers credit agreements to consumers; (2) assists consumers by undertaking preparatory work in respect of credit agreements other than as referred to in (1); or (3) concludes credit agreements with consumers on, behalf of a creditor.

service provider licence. For instance, in the Opinion of the European Banking Authority on lending-based crowdfunding, it is explicitly held that platforms should obtain their own licence in the absence of an outsourcing arrangement with a licensed institution (European Banking Authority, 2015, p. 26–27). The Italian Banking Authority followed the same reasoning when authorising the first P2P platforms as payment institutions (Macchiavello, 2018, p. 683). A recent study examining P2P business lending in Italy also documented that six out of nine platforms in the sample were authorised as 'payment entities' or 'agents of payment entities' (Stefanelli et al., 2022, p. 5). One should note that such a licence merely addresses the risks arising from money handling, an auxiliary crowdfunding service. Neither the protection of borrowers in the case of P2P consumer lending nor the safeguards to investors across different crowdfunding models are ensured if the platform is merely authorised as a payment institution.

Extending the application of existing regulations is even more common regarding equity-based platforms. For instance, in 2015, ESMA inquired into the regulatory treatment of such platforms in Europe (European Securities and Markets Authority, 2015, p. 2). 18 out of 46 regulated platforms acted as investment firms under the Markets in Financial Instruments Directive (MiFID) (Directive, 2014).[12] One should note that the licence of an investment firm under MiFID corresponds to several types of information intermediaries discussed in Chap. 2 (notably, brokers, portfolio managers, investment advisors, and underwriters). However, the text does not use these terms; it distinguishes between different services and activities undertaken.[13] According to the ESMA analysis, regulators in various Member States typically qualified crowdfunding services as one of the following: (1) reception and transmission of orders in relation to one or more financial instruments, (2) and/or placing of financial instruments without a firm commitment basis. The first service consists of matching funding interests of both sides of the market, including communication with market participants and passing their interest in transacting to their counterparty. Tröger (2021, p. 109) explains that it is a widely held view that, for such a service to be performed, it does not matter whether the transactions occur on primary or secondary markets.[14] The second service is often deemed invisible since the distribution of crowdfunding offers is embedded in the existence of a web-based

[12] This directive is also commonly referred to as MiFID II since it replaced the original MiFID (Directive, 2004).

[13] The services and activities of investment firms are provided in ANNEX I Section A of MiFID (Directive, 2014).

[14] It is worth noting that activities of loan-based crowdfunding platforms could also have fallen under the definition of investment firms if MiFID had not been limited to intermediation of financial instruments. As will be discussed in more detail below, the treatment of P2P loans as financial instruments is questionable, and European regulators have seldom qualified them as such (Macchiavello & Sciarrone Alibrandi, 2021, p. 53).

platform (European Commission, 2018, p. 34). Nonetheless, some platforms actively promote crowdfunding offers depending on the regulatory constraints.[15]

In France, in addition to the status of an investment firm under MiFID (*prestataire de services d'investissement*), platforms could also apply for a licence of a financial advisor (*conseiller en investissements financiers*) (Autorité de Contrôle Prudentiel, 2013, pp. 8–11). Even though this regime was lighter and therefore preferred among crowdfunding platforms operating at the time, the scope of services they were allowed to perform was not entirely clear. The regulatory agencies explicitly stated that the licence of a financial advisor could be used for offering advice but not for any other service reserved for investment firms, such as placement with a firm commitment basis or reception and transmission of orders with respect to financial instruments other than units in collective investment schemes (Autorité de Contrôle Prudentiel, 2013, pp. 10–11).

Similar to some European regulators, before the adoption of the JOBS Act, platforms in the US could also fall under the definition of brokers or investment advisors, subject to regulations of the Exchange Act and the Investment Advisers Act, respectively (Investment Advisers Act of 1940, P.L. 117–263, U.S. Congress, 1940; Securities Exchange Act of 1934, 1934).[16] According to Bradford (2012, pp. 51–67), even though none of the platforms were actually registered as brokers, the existing case law suggests that the SEC's interpretation of what constitutes a broker is broad enough to include crowdfunding platforms that facilitate the sale of securities. Similarly, Bradford (2012, pp. 67–81) argues that many crowdfunding websites could fall under the definition of an investment advisor, even though the guidance in the existing case law is less clear than in the case of brokers.

Regulators less often chose to qualify crowdfunding platforms as AIFM. As elaborated in Chap. 2, AIFM is an investment intermediary that pools capital from many investors and buys assets in line with a defined investment policy for investor benefit. In contrast, crowdfunding does not assume a collective investment structure. Nonetheless, in some countries, such as the Netherlands, platforms can be confronted with licensing requirements for AIFM, in addition to a more common approach of treating them as investment firms under MiFID (Ortolani & Louisse, 2021, p. 11).

Interestingly, in Greece, the 'stretch-to-fit' approach was further ascertained by amendments to the existing law that recognised crowdfunding services. The law specified that crowdfunding services can be provided by entities holding one of the three existing licences: credit institution, investment firm, or AIFM (Matthaiou, 2021, pp. 323–324).

While applying existing regulations can overcome some limitations of the baseline scenario, in which new market participants are simply not recognised by

[15] Crowdfunding platforms were less frequently deemed to offer other MiFID services, such as investment advice (e.g., France), individual portfolio management, execution of orders on behalf of clients, or operating trading venues (in relation to the service of operating a secondary market).

[16] As discussed earlier, crowdfunding was illegal in the US before the adoption of the JOBS Act due to restrictions on public offerings.

regulators, several issues emerge. Most notably, it is likely that existing regulations are not flexible or broad enough to put all crowdfunding models under the regulatory remit. The UK, which has well-developed lending- and equity-based crowdfunding markets, is a good example. UK platform Zopa is considered the oldest P2P lending platform, established in 2005 (Havrylchyk, 2018, p. 15; Xu et al., 2021, p. 531). However, in the wake of crowdfunding, only equity-based platforms were under the regulatory remit of the FCA and authorised on an ad hoc basis. Offer of shares and other securities would fall under a regulated activity under the Financial Services and Markets Act 2000 (Financial Services and Markets Act 2000, 2000), such as arranging deals in investments and communication of a financial promotion. In contrast, P2P lending platforms were outside the FCA's regulatory oversight. Only in 2014, with the adoption of new rules (Financial Conduct Authority, 2014), did the FCA introduce a new regulated activity—operating an electronic system in relation to lending—to accommodate the P2P lending model.[17]

Secondly, as discussed in Chap. 2, despite some standard features, the differences between crowdfunding and traditional (financial) intermediaries are substantial. Therefore, existing financial regulations are often ill-fitted and can impose a disproportionate regulatory burden on platforms (and/or fundraisers). Responding to high compliance costs, some platforms have intentionally designed their business model to circumvent them. A prominent example is investment-based crowdfunding in Germany. Platforms that facilitate the offering of financial instruments—securities or investment products (*Vermögensanlagen*)—would be considered to provide financial services under the German Banking Act (Gesetz Über Das Kreditwesen (Kreditwesengesetz - KWG), BGBl. I S. 2776, 1998; Aschenbeck-Florange et al., 2013, p. 10; Tröger, 2021, pp. 109–110). This is because they usually perform one of the regulated activities of investment firms under the MiFID framework in relation to these instruments, as discussed earlier. As a result, they would need to obtain a licence from the German financial regulator (*Bundesanstalt für Finanzdienstleistungsaufsicht—BaFin*). However, hybrid instruments, subordinated loans (*Nachrangdarlehen*), and profit-participating loans (*partiarisches Darlehen*) were originally not regulated under the German Investment Products Act (Gesetz Über Vermögensanlagen (Vermögensanlagengesetz - VermAnlG), BGBl. I S. 2481, 2011; Aschenbeck-Florange et al., 2013, p. 11). This means that platforms brokering these types of contracts were not considered to carry out a regulated activity requiring a licence from BaFin but a simple licence under the German Trade, Commerce and Industry Regulation Act (Gewerbeordnung - GewO, 1999). With law amendments that recognised the crowdfunding activity for the first time in 2015 (Small Investor Protection Act) (Kleinanlegerschutzgesetz, 2015), the aforementioned hybrid instruments were included in the definition of investment products, but platforms could nevertheless benefit from an exemption from licensing as an

[17] It is worth noting that, even before the FCA extended its regulatory remit over P2P lending platforms, some platforms intermediating P2P consumer loans were regulated by the Office of Fair Trading (OFT). The regulatory remit of OFT only concerned consumer credit (borrowing side), whereas there was little regulatory protection for investors (Financial Conduct Authority, 2013).

investment firm if certain conditions are met (European Crowdfunding Network, 2017, pp. 245–246).[18]

Alternatively, in response to the 'stretch-to-fit' approach, crowdfunding platforms have partnered with a licensed entity (usually a bank or an investment firm). This practice, known as 'rent-a-charter', has occurred in many fintech industries (Bomberger, 2021, p. 9; Enriques & Ringe, 2020; Jackson, 2020, p. 13; Levitin, 2021).[19] The partnership between a P2P lending platform and a bank involves a bank formally originating all loans, which are then transferred to crowd lenders who ultimately hold all the credit risk. For instance, this has been the case with P2P lending in the US. As Chaffee and Rapp (2012, p. 493) describe, the process begins with a platform matching the lending and borrowing interests of the two sides. Lenders' funds are transferred to the partnering bank, which originates a consumer loan and sells it to the crowdfunding platform. The platform issues a note (debt security) to crowd lenders, whose return on investment is contingent on borrowers' repayments.[20] Namely, the platform collects borrowers' repayments and passes them to lenders. However, such an arrangement effectively means that lenders become creditors of the platform, exposing them to additional risk of a platform failure (Käfer, 2018, p. 21; Nemoto et al., 2019, p. 4). Interestingly, this solution leads to a parallel application of banking and securities regulations in the US. Banking regulations protect borrowers in their relationship with the bank. At the same time, P2P lending platforms are treated as issuers of securities when they offer and sell notes or investment contracts to the public (Chaffee & Rapp, 2012, pp. 523–524).[21] Thus, they have to comply with registration requirements under relevant securities acts.[22] Accordingly, the regulatory remit is split between different regulatory authorities.[23]

The involvement of a bank is also a well-established practice in P2P consumer lending in Germany. However, as discussed earlier, it is not the operation of platforms that can fall under the German Banking Act (Gesetz Über Das Kreditwesen

[18] For a detailed overview of the regulatory treatment of investment-based crowdfunding in Germany, and how existing practices are affected by the adoption of the ECSPR, see Wenzlaff and Odorović (2022).

[19] Jackson (2020, p. 13) argues that this practice has become possible thanks to technological developments that allowed some activities to be contracted out of hierarchical institutions, expanding the domain of market-based activities in the sense of the Coasian theory of the firm.

[20] As mentioned in Chap. 2, this kind of cooperation between a platform and a bank is sometimes considered a specific crowdfunding model known as the 'notary model'.

[21] The treatment of notes on P2P lending websites as securities was clarified in an order that the SEC issued against Prosper Marketplace on 24 November 2008 (Order Instituting Cease-And-Desist Proceedings against Prosper Marketplace, Inc., Securities Act Release No. 8984, 94 SEC Docket 1913). The SEC alleged that the relevant securities regulations were violated as the P2P lending platform neither registered a sale of securities nor had an exemption from registration (Chaffee & Rapp, 2012, p. 517).

[22] In the US, these include the Securities Act and Exchange Act.

[23] Notably, the Consumer Financial Protection Bureau (CFPB) and the Federal Trade Commission (FCT) oversee the borrowing side, while the SEC oversees the investment side of the P2P lending model (Nemoto et al., 2019, p. 4).

(Kreditwesengesetz - KWG), BGBl. I S. 2776, 1998), but rather the activity of lenders and/or borrowers. To avoid the risk of such a regulatory treatment, P2P lending platforms rely on a bank as an intermediary while merely acting as credit brokers. Once the partnering bank extends the loan, all the claims are assigned to individual lenders upon paying the price—their loan share (Käfer, 2018, pp. 5–6). Thus, a notable difference from the US model is that lenders have a direct claim against borrowers instead of against the platform (Käfer, 2018, p. 5). Yet, similar to the US, protections vis-à-vis borrowers fall on the bank since platforms are not subject to financial regulations; instead, they need to obtain a credit broker licence under the German Trade, Commerce and Industry Regulation Act (Gewerbeordnung - GewO, 1999).

Analogously, equity crowdfunding platforms have often partnered with licensed investment firms. In the European context, the MiFID framework explicitly provides for the concept of 'tied agents' (Directive, 2014), which allows the outsourcee (the platform) to conduct the regulated activity under the regulatory umbrella of the licensed investment firm.[24] The regulated firm remains fully responsible for any breach or misconduct by the partnering platform. In the abovementioned early analysis on the regulatory status of investment platforms conducted by ESMA (notably before 2015), 12 out of 46 regulated platforms acted as tied agents of investment firms (European Securities and Markets Authority, 2015, p. 2).

Besides being complex, the above-described partnerships between platforms and licensed entities raise different regulatory concerns. In the case of lending-based models, the regulated part of the crowdfunding activity (e.g., loan origination/borrowing) is outsourced to the bank. In contrast, the remaining parts (e.g., onboarding, channelling information to investors, defining contract terms, and loan servicing) do not fall under the purview of the banking regulator. Thus, the bank does not have to oversee the regulatory compliance of a crowdfunding platform. Another relevant issue is whether the bank, which formally originates the loan, can delegate the choice of borrowers to crowd lenders (Enriques & Ringe, 2020, p. 10), which lies at the heart of crowdfunding.[25] In contrast, an equity platform acting as an investment firm's tied agent while alleviating some of the regulatory burdens—notably concerning licensing (e.g., capital or indemnity insurance requirements)—is still subject to organisational or conduct rules governing its activities. The investment firm acting as a principal oversees the platform's compliance. The issue with this type of partnership is that the rules that the platform needs to comply with may still be disproportionate or difficult to adapt in the crowdfunding context. As discussed earlier, platforms perform only a subset of services of investment firms under the MiFID

[24] As explained by Enriques and Ringe (2020, pp. 20–22), an analogous concept in the UK is known as the 'appointed representative'.

[25] Interestingly, in this case, the outsourcing goes in the opposite direction—the bank outsources the borrowing decision to the crowd. As discussed by Enriques and Ringe (2020, p. 10), regulations in many jurisdictions impose limits on delegating activities that refer to the core of the banking business.

framework.[26] In all cases of partnerships, platforms remain dependent on traditional players, which may be reluctant to contract with them in the first place. On the contrary, if traditional players are not selective enough, any instability in the crowdfunding market can produce negative spillovers, impairing the trust in the conventional financial system (Enriques & Ringe, 2020, pp. 14–16; Macchiavello, 2018, p. 686).

Overall, the 'stretch-to-fit' approach resulted in diverse regulatory responses across jurisdictions and crowdfunding models. This is unsurprising. As discussed in Chap. 2, the economic function of platforms, on the one hand, does not neatly fit any of the traditional providers of financial services. On the other hand, it shares some features with several of them. As a result, the regulatory treatment of platforms was often over-inclusive while at the same time neglecting some specific risks of crowdfunding.

5.2.3 Learning and Experimentation

Many regulators soon acknowledged the shortcomings of the first two approaches. One of the underlying issues with both approaches is the information deficit of both crowdfunding platforms and regulators. Platforms face regulatory uncertainty as to whether they fall under the regulatory remit of competent authorities, particularly when they are also experimenting with different services or financial instruments. In relation to the 'stretch-to-fit' approach, they often struggle to understand how specific regulatory obligations would apply to their business practice.

Likewise, both the regulatory void and the all-embracing interpretation of the scope of existing regulations are often the result of regulators' lack of understanding of crowdfunding business models. In addition, crowdfunding represented just a subset of financial innovations interfering with traditional finance. With fintech burgeoning in various financial sectors, regulatory organisations need a more systematic way of dealing with financial innovation, allowing them and market players to learn from each other and test out possible regulatory/business solutions.

As a result, many regulators worldwide have responded to financial innovation by embracing regulatory and supervisory innovation within their organisations (Allen, 2022). To date, three initiatives have gained importance: innovation office, regulatory sandbox, and supervisory technology (SupTech). All three initiatives represent organisational and structural changes inside regulatory authorities, with potential implications across different fintech verticals, with crowdfunding being just one.

---

[26] Moreover, as considered in a broader context of fintech, outsourcing arrangements of this type raise several questions regarding effective enforcement and supervision, including the allocation of responsibilities between the regulated entity and the outsource, their joint liability, and the scope of supervisory powers (Enriques & Ringe, 2020).

Innovation Offices

Innovation offices facilitate the information exchange and engagement between regulators and innovative firms that provide or aim to provide financial services (e.g., a crowdfunding platform) (Zhang et al., 2019). Introducing an innovation office within a regulator also signals a supportive attitude towards financial innovation instead of a conventional—rigid, conservative attitude of aversion towards new practices that do not align with well-established products and institutions.

Innovation offices support a steep learning curve for both industry members and regulators. Helping industry members navigate through complex financial regulations lies at the heart of this regulatory innovation initiative (Zhang et al., 2019, p. 19). Regulatory enquiries are typically received by new and prospective market entrants in need of guidance on licensing requirements and licensed entities considering introducing new and innovative products or services. Innovation offices usually require several incremental changes within the internal organisation of the regulator.

Innovation offices commonly open up new communication channels that fintech companies, such as crowdfunding platforms, can use to obtain regulatory information (e.g., dedicated office hours, telephone lines, or email) (Zhang et al., 2019, p. 20). Even though they are not envisaged to replace comprehensive legal support from external compliance experts, innovation offices can be the first point of contact with a regulatory agency. In particular, when crowdfunding platforms and other fintechs doubt whether their activities are permitted under the existing framework and which laws and regulations apply to them, innovation offices can provide valuable assistance. Yet, certain innovation offices, such as the Innovation Hub at the FCA in the UK, prescribe criteria against which applicants are chosen for receiving formal support (Financial Conduct Authority, n.d.). Fintech firms need to demonstrate that they offer genuine innovation that promises to generate benefits for consumers and that they have done the necessary background research showing that they do not easily fit the existing regulations.

Secondly, the operation of innovation offices creates new interlinkages between different departments of a regulatory agency. The operation of crowdfunding platforms and other new business models often transcends the competence of a single department. This has to do with the fact that the internal organisation of regulatory agencies usually reflects or aligns with traditional financial intermediaries and the different risks they pose (e.g., consumer protection financial risks). For this reason, innovation offices typically consist of staff from various departments to provide a more comprehensive interpretation of relevant rules. Staff can be allocated to an innovation office permanently, or more commonly, they meet on dedicated dates to exchange information and identify regulatory issues pertinent to specific fintech solutions.

Thirdly, innovation offices often issue non-binding opinions as a response to enquiries from industry members. When regulators take a clear stance on the regulatory treatment of a particular fintech model, they may also publish guidance relevant to all prospective firms with similar concerns. Regulators can also opt for shorter formats by publishing a section with commonly asked questions about fintech activities.

Besides helping existing and prospective providers of financial services, innovation offices are also meant to improve the efficiency and decision-making of the regulator. As mentioned earlier, the regulatory lag is often caused by fast-paced technological developments that regulators struggle to keep up with. A closer engagement with the industry improves the regulator's understanding of technology solutions embraced by new market entrants. Innovation offices can serve as a means of collecting comprehensive data on fintech business models, including crowdfunding, which is paramount to better supervision, as well as future regulatory initiatives. Regulator's interaction with the fintech industry allows them to set priorities regarding future regulatory changes and design tailored regulatory responses. In relation to this, crowdfunding and other emerging fintech models can sometimes fall within the regulatory remit of different regulatory agencies. Innovation offices can also facilitate interagency cooperation.

Regulatory Sandboxes

The second regulatory innovation initiative is meant to enable learning, testing, and experimentation for market participants and regulators (Ringe & Ruof, 2020). Regulatory sandboxes allow innovative companies to test their financial products and services under a lighter regulatory regime before applying for a (full-blown) licence (Allen, 2019; Bromberg et al., 2017; Ringe & Ruof, 2020).[27] During time spent in a sandbox, fintechs are temporarily exempt from licensing when one of the existing licences would otherwise apply to them. This allows them to test the viability of their solutions by working with real customers in a 'controlled environment' (Omarova, 2020, p. 37) without requiring all licensing costs upfront. Thus, they have lower barriers to entry, allowing them to potentially compete with larger incumbent institutions (Allen, 2019). Sandboxes are also an essential learning tool for regulators, given that they closely monitor the operation of admitted firms, collecting valuable data that catalyse any future regulatory reforms (e.g., creating a bespoke crowdfunding regime).

Admission to a sandbox is usually conceived as a formal process during which a company needs to demonstrate that it satisfies eligibility criteria. As mentioned concerning innovation hubs, these typically include demonstrating innovation potential, potential benefits to consumers (e.g., increased accessibility, affordability,

[27] The concept of a regulatory sandbox was pioneered by the UK FCA in 2016 (Regulatory Sandbox, 2022). Since then, an increasingly large number of countries followed suit. According to the World Bank Group (2021), 111 out of 198 jurisdictions examined had in place at least one regulatory innovation initiative—innovation facilitators (innovation office, regulatory sandbox, or a regtech (suptech) lab).

quality, or security in the provision of financial services), and identifying a regulatory gap or a related regulatory issue. Thus, eligibility criteria are usually defined broadly to accommodate different types of financial innovation.[28] However, sometimes regulators want to encourage the testing of specific products or services and, thus, create thematic sandboxes. As a result, eligibility criteria are more specific to the operation and needs of a particular fintech industry. Several sandboxes worldwide have focused on crowdfunding (including Vietnam (Kim & Chang, 2022), Thailand (Moody's Analytics, n.d.), Namibia (Regulatory Sandbox|NAMFISA, 2024), Eastern Caribbean states (ECSRC Launches Regulatory Sandbox, 2023), etc.).[29]

Less commonly, regulators encourage testing of specific business models or innovations by making the admission to a sandbox automatic. For instance, since 2016, the sandbox of the Australian Securities and Investments Commission (ASIC) has envisaged one such regime suitable for P2P lending platforms (firms acting as an intermediary or providing credit assistance in relation to specific credit contracts) (Bromberg et al., 2017, pp. 6–8). The formal admission procedure to the sandbox is replaced with a simple notice to the regulator. Yet, to be automatically eligible for the sandbox, firms must comply with some additional conditions (e.g., credit contract is limited to AUD25,000, the maximum annual cost rate is 24%, etc.) (Everhart, 2020, p. 71). It is worth noting that such an industry-wide exemption from licensing existed in parallel with a more common sandbox approach based on individual application processes and individual licensing exemptions (Bromberg et al., 2017, pp. 6–8).[30]

It should be noted that a licensing waiver while being in a sandbox does not (and should not) imply a regulatory void and a form of deregulation (Allen, 2019, p. 583). On the contrary, regulators typically prescribe certain restrictions (operation parameters) to contain potential risks to consumers and the financial system. In the crowdfunding context, these can include services that platforms are permitted to provide, as well as different thresholds (such as the maximum number of customers, individual investor threshold limits, the maximum loan amount per borrower, or the maximum issuance amount). Depending on the fintech industry, these parameters

---

[28] In some jurisdictions, sandboxes are only available for unlicensed entities; in others, they also accept licensed entities wanting to test out new products or services (Ringe & Ruof, 2020).

[29] Eligibility criteria are at the heart of any criticism towards regulatory sandboxes as a policy initiative. In particular, regulatory sandboxes raise the question of whether fintech services are truly innovative to deserve special regulatory treatment (also in relation to creating an even playing field for all market participants), how to measure the benefit they generate (private vs. public benefit), as well as whether regulatory agencies are left too much of a discretionary power to decide which market entrants to admit to this experimental environment (Omarova, 2020).

[30] It should be noted that ASIC introduced some important amendments to the operation of its sandbox in 2020, which, among other things, expanded the scope of services eligible for automatic admission to the sandbox but also introduced some new obligations for the market entrants. (Australian Securities and Investments Commission, 2020).

are sometimes found in existing regulations or determined on an ad hoc basis by the regulator if no pertinent regulations are yet in place. In non-thematic sandboxes, operation parameters are often determined on a case-by-case basis. In contrast, in thematic sandboxes, they are frequently defined in advance, applying the same terms to all industry members.

Operation in a sandbox is limited in time (typically between 6 months and 2 years). Upon exit, companies are required to obtain a formal licence. Yet, time spent in a sandbox also allows regulators to understand better how licensing requirements should be applied to specific financial innovation and, if needed, adjust the licensing standards or even create a bespoke (crowdfunding) regime.[31] Two examples of the latter scenario are Mauritius and Kenya. A P2P lending platform, Fundkiss was admitted to a sandbox operated by the Financial Services Commission (FSC) when a licensing regime for their business model was not yet in place. While operating in the sandbox, crowdfunding-specific rules were enacted in 2021, allowing this platform to transition into a fully licensed entity at the end of the sandbox period (Rapaport, 2021). Similarly, a crowdfunding platform, Pezesha Limited, was admitted to the Regulatory Sandbox of the Capital Markets Authority (CMA) in Kenya in 2019 to intermediate the sale of loan notes to SMEs. As a result of a close engagement of the CMA with this platform within the sandbox, Kenya adopted rules for investment-based crowdfunding in 2022 (Legamart, 2022).

It should be noted that regulatory sandboxes are also sometimes used by crowdfunding platforms in countries where bespoke crowdfunding rules are already in place. For instance, the Austrian Financial Market Authority (FMA) announced in 2022 that four crowdfunding platforms would test their services before obtaining a licence under the ECSPR (Plank-Bachselten, 2022). Interestingly, in some countries like Kazakhstan, participation in a sandbox is mandatory before applying for a full-blown crowdfunding licence.

In sum, a regulatory sandbox represents a helpful regulatory facility to mitigate the shortcomings of the first two approaches: lack of regulations or regulatory uncertainty regarding how existing laws apply to crowdfunding platforms. The core challenge lies in implementing the application process and operation parameters to balance the time to the market and necessary investor protection safeguards. When carefully designed, a regulatory sandbox can be a valuable instrument to bridge the gap between the first two approaches and the bespoke crowdfunding regime, which takes time to develop carefully. Moreover, it can also smooth the implementation of newly adopted crowdfunding regulations, such as enabling the adoption of bylaws. Nonetheless, as an experimental policy instrument, it offers only temporary relief for regulators to take a clear stance on the scope and depth of regulatory obligations for a given (crowdfunding) market practice.

---

[31] Regulatory sandboxes used to evaluate specific rules or test the desirability of certain regulatory changes are sometimes referred to as 'policy testing sandboxes' (Zhang et al., 2019).

SupTech

While innovation offices and sandboxes are regulatory initiatives, SupTech represents technology-enabled supervision of market developments and operation of entities that fall within the regulator's remit. As such, it promises to revolutionise various segments of supervisory work: licensing, reporting, behavioural and conduct analysis, sanctioning regulatory breaches, etc. (Chirulli, 2021, p. 455). The underlying rationale of SupTech is that the only way regulators can keep up with a fast-paced innovation embraced by market players is to increasingly employ technological tools as well (such as big data, machine learning, AI, or natural language processing (NLP)) (Allen, 2022; Chirulli, 2021, p. 455). With a growing number of financial products becoming technologically sophisticated and data-intensive, regulators started introducing innovative means of monitoring the compliance process of regulated entities and broader market developments that can interfere with regulatory goals.[32] Creating and maintaining data repositories on different segments of financial markets lies at the heart of any SupTech solution. For these data repositories to be used, it is necessary to be able to extract structured data and put them into a machine-readable form. As the next step, SupTech involves creating and training data processing programmes and validating their results against well-established traditional supervisory methods.

SupTech technologies rarely focus on specific segments of financial markets, such as crowdfunding, but instead, aim at systematically reforming how the regulatory agency exercises oversight over different regulated entities.[33] Moreover, as a supervisory tool, SupTech does not directly affect the choice of regulatory rules in any area of financial regulation. Hypothetically, more efficient monitoring allows for easier detection of deficiencies in the way how current rules are formulated. Yet, given the slow uptake of SupTech practices in most jurisdictions, including the UK or EU (McCarthy, 2022), no such case has been identified up to date with the implications for crowdfunding regulations.

5.2.4 *Bespoke Regulations*

Bespoke crowdfunding regulations do not have a clear meaning in the literature, nor is there always consensus among (legal) scholars and practitioners on whether a specific jurisdiction has a bespoke regime. Sometimes, it is also referred to as an ad

[32] These can include, for instance, risks to market integrity caused by collusive behaviour or market manipulation in regulated markets. With the increased use of AI in trading, some authors have argued that regulators need to leverage parallel technologies to improve their supervisory capabilities, subject to the availability of training data (Azzutti et al., 2021, pp. 131–132).

[33] The exception is when a SupTech solution is first introduced by choosing one use case. Nonetheless, such a use case typically involves market segments with a longer history (as opposed to new segments, such as crowdfunding), so enough data can be gathered to train the algorithm.

hoc regime (Macchiavello, 2018). A narrow definition would imply adopting rules tailored to the needs of a crowdfunding market and bringing crowdfunding platforms within the purview of financial authorities by introducing a new licence type. A broader definition includes explicitly recognising crowdfunding as a financial service in the existing legal framework (by making amendments to the texts), even if platforms are not subject to a particular licensing regime. For clarity, the latter situation can also be referred to as a 'semi-bespoke' regime.[34]

The first bespoke regime was introduced in Italy in 2013 and only applied to innovative startups and small firms raising finance via Internet portals (Regolamento Sulla Raccolta Di Capitali Tramite Portali On-Line, 2013). Many European countries followed suit. Notably, the UK (2014), France (2014), Spain (2015), Germany (2015), Austria (2015), Portugal (2016), Finland (2016), Lithuania (2016), and Belgium (2017) explicitly recognised crowdfunding in their legal texts (European Commission, 2018, pp. 75–93). The new regulations applied to either lending-based or investment-based crowdfunding or both. In the years to follow, a pan-European crowdfunding regime was created—the ECSPR. The harmonised framework aimed to mitigate the shortcomings of fragmented regulatory regimes across Member States and create a pan-European crowdfunding market for business fundraisers.[35] The ECSPR went into force on 10 November 2021, while platforms holding a licence under national bespoke rules were required to obtain the new licence to continue their operations until 10 November 2023.

Bespoke regulations also spread across other continents. Notable examples include US (2016) and Canada (2021) in Northern Europe, Brazil (2017), Argentina (2018) and Mexico (2018) in Latin America, Malaysia (2015), Indonesia (2016), and China (2016) in Asia, and New Zealand (2014) and Australia (2017). As in the case of European jurisdictions, some of these frameworks only apply to lending or investment models. The last available data on fintech regimes worldwide collected by the World Bank in 2021 captures the existence of crowdfunding regulations in 85 out of 198 jurisdictions (World Bank Group, 2021).[36] It should be noted that bespoke regulatory regimes in several countries have evolved over time for reasons such as the need to include additional models or financial contracts within their scope, novel services offered by platforms, and reassessment of market risks as captured by periodic regulatory reviews.

[34] Some notable examples include investment-based crowdfunding in Germany and Greece. In both instances, legal texts acknowledged crowdfunding activities without introducing a special licence for crowdfunding platforms.

[35] Certain financial contracts brokered on established crowdfunding platforms (e.g. profit-participating loans in Germany) remain outside the scope of the ECSPR, together with P2P consumer lending.

[36] It should be noted that the explanation of data does not make it clear whether these figures only refer to bespoke regulations ('regulated under framework created for this activity') or they also include extending existing regulations to accommodate crowdfunding models ('regulated under pre-existing framework').

Bespoke regulations came about as a result of two distinct considerations among regulators and policymakers. The first one is recognising the potential benefits of crowdfunding as an alternative financing tool for individuals and SMEs and an investment opportunity for retail investors. An illustrative example of this is the words of Barack Obama, who signed into law the JOBS Act:

> And for startups and small businesses, this bill is a potential game changer. Right now, you can only turn to a limited group of investors—including banks and wealthy individuals—to get funding. Laws that are nearly eight decades old make it impossible for others to invest. But a lot has changed in 80 years, and it's time our laws did as well. Because of this bill, startups and small businesses will now have access to a big, new pool of potential investors—namely, the American people. For the first time, ordinary Americans will be able to go online and invest in entrepreneurs that they believe in. (Remarks by the President at Whitehouse.gov, 2012).

The second consideration behind bespoke regulations is acknowledging the limitations of alternative three regulatory approaches. As discussed in previous sections, they can potentially stifle the industry's growth or inadequately address its risks. In relation to the latter, some regulators were more cautious. As put by the Reserve Bank of India (RBI) in its Consultation Paper on Peer-to-Peer Lending:

> This industry has the potential to disrupt the financial sector and throw a surprise. A sound regulatory framework will prevent such surprises. (Minupuri, 2018, p. 434).

It should be recognised, however, that alternative regulatory approaches also allow some regulators to better grasp the desired direction of the regulatory change (in particular through regulatory innovation initiatives). In jurisdictions where sufficient time has elapsed between the emergence of the crowdfunding market and the change in the regulatory approach, market practices have also had a chance to consolidate.

In line with regulators' considerations driving their adoption, bespoke regimes have as an objective (1) eliminating regulatory hurdles that create prohibitively high costs for market participants; (2) regulating the operation of platforms, ensuring truthful disclosures by fundraisers, and introducing additional investor protection safeguards. In most jurisdictions, bespoke regimes embrace a combination of these objectives, with a stronger inclination towards one or another.

Regarding the first objective, most bespoke regimes were created by carving out exemptions from the existing regimes. As discussed earlier, P2P lending in many jurisdictions was constrained by over-inclusive rules on banking monopoly, which applied to activities of fundraisers, investors, or platforms. Thus, bespoke crowdfunding regulations in some of these countries focus on limiting the exclusive domain of the banking business. Similarly, rigid rules on offering securities to the public often limit investment-based crowdfunding. Therefore, crowdfunding-specific regulations created a new exemption from these rules, typically increasing the threshold below which prospectus requirements do not apply and allowing retail investors to participate in such offerings. Finally, in jurisdictions where crowdfunding platforms would fall under the licensing regimes for traditional providers of financial services, crowdfunding exemptions often involve introducing a new licence type. The idea is to acknowledge that the scope of platform services and associated risks differ from services provided by traditional financial or information intermediaries.

Regarding the second objective, new crowdfunding regulations specified the services crowdfunding platforms are allowed to perform, ensuring that they are not used to mask deposit-taking activities, collective investment schemes, or other services for which stricter licences were required. In relation to permissible activities of platforms, regulations usually prescribe clear prudential, organisational, and business conduct rules. It should be noted that regulations governing the behaviour of P2P consumer lending platforms less frequently also included specific provisions aiming to protect borrowers. Moreover, in line with the second objective, crowdfunding rules often seek to mitigate fraud and information misrepresentations or omissions by fundraisers. To this end, the obligation to provide investors with fair, clear, and not misleading information (defined in abstract terms or by specifying disclosure requirements) fell on fundraisers, platforms, or both. Lastly, crowdfunding regulations often envisage different rules that aim to mitigate investors' risk exposure since crowdfunding involves many small, unsophisticated investors who choose to invest in high-risk opportunities. These rules include risk warnings, entry knowledge tests, and more paternalistic regulatory measures such as individual investment limits.

Even though drafters of bespoke regulations in different jurisdictions were driven by similar considerations and often focused on similar aspects of crowdfunding, the exact rules exhibit notable differences. Before discussing these differences in the sections that follow, it should be noted that they have led to a new (third) consideration for introducing crowdfunding-specific rules—the need to reduce the resulting fragmentation in regulatory frameworks of jurisdictions with close cultural and economic ties. As mentioned earlier, the ECSPR in Europe was created with the objective of harmonising rules applicable to crowdfunding for businesses in different Member States. This would, in turn, allow platforms authorised in one Member State to passport their services to other Member States without incurring additional regulatory costs. Internationalisation of platform operations would allow the most successful ones to scale and boost cross-border crowdfunding activity (Wenzlaff et al., 2020, p. 381). Before the full implementation of the ECSPR, cross-border activity, as captured by different indicators, was not significant (Shneor et al., 2024, pp. 45–48).[37] Surprisingly, some early data on platform authorisation under the ECSPR suggests that only a small subset of platforms intend to operate outside their home jurisdiction (Wenzlaff & Odorović, 2024). While it is too early to draw conclusions, this can suggest that the merits of a supranational bespoke regime cannot countervail other factors hindering platform internationisation, such as platforms'

[37] According to the most recent data, 82.6% of European platforms operated in a single jurisdiction in 2022. International flows accounted for about 12% of the total flows in lending and 5.4% in equity-based crowdfunding in 2022 (Shneor et al., 2024).

limited resources and knowledge of local conditions in foreign markets, as well as investors' home bias.[38]

Reverting to the main differences in bespoke crowdfunding regimes, one can analyse them using two dimensions: horizontal and vertical. The horizontal dimension refers to the scope of regulations. More specifically, crowdfunding regimes can apply to different financial contracts intermediated via crowdfunding platforms and various market participants (parties to a transaction) and allow for and regulate different activities of crowdfunding platforms. In contrast, the vertical dimension entails the type or depth of obligations or limitations imposed on fundraisers, platforms, and investors. The analysis that follows discusses the optimal regulatory approach along these two dimensions. Therefore, the first question that needs to be addressed is whether there is an economic rationale for putting different financial-return models under one regulatory umbrella or which criteria should be used to delineate different regulatory treatments. The second question of relevance involves defining the fundamental rules to govern the behaviour of fundraisers, platforms, and investors. In answering the second question, the key insights are drawn from findings on market-based mechanisms in Chap. 3 and self-regulatory regimes discussed in Chap. 4.

5.3 Should Different Financial-Return Models Be Put Under One Regulatory Umbrella?

As elaborated in different parts of this study, crowdfunding is far from a homogeneous and universal practice across platforms and jurisdictions. Platforms can broker different investment contracts, cater to consumer or business fundraisers, and offer various services. Given that these differences affect the level of (financial) risks investors and fundraisers are exposed to, the question arises whether different crowdfunding models should be put under one regulatory umbrella. In other words, bespoke regimes can apply the same (or similar) set of rules to different crowdfunding models or can aim to reflect the difference in risks stemming from the crowdfunding activity. The latter implies grouping models with a similar level of risk under a distinctive regulatory regime (e.g., by designing separate regulatory frameworks for P2P lending and equity crowdfunding, consumer and business fundraising, etc.).

As mentioned before, the specifics of crowdfunding are that different factors affect the risk that this activity generates (the type of financial contract intermediated, type of fundraisers, and specific services provided by platforms). Thus, the

[38] Home or local bias is the investors' tendency to provide funds to local fundraisers on local platforms despite other appealing conditions when investing abroad. It has been documented in numerous studies in crowdfunding (e.g., Hornuf et al., 2020; Li et al., 2024; Niemand et al., 2018). While this bias primarily refers to the behaviour of investors, it can also undermine platforms' incentives to offer their services cross-borders.

first goal of this section is to discuss different risk categories that can trigger the difference in regulatory treatment. In relation to these risk categories, it is also helpful to analyse whether the scope of some of the existing bespoke regimes aligns with them. However, it should be noted that such an alignment can be (and often is) accidental. Put differently, it does not mean regulators and policymakers intentionally designed bespoke regimes to reflect distinct risk levels. Specific risk categories can also overlap with the regulatory remit of different financial authorities. Moreover, regulators and policymakers often aim to regulate the crowdfunding practice, which is the most widespread in their jurisdiction, or crowdfunding models currently escaping regulatory oversight. Finally, this section discusses which risk-related categories (investment contract types, consumer vs. business fundraisers, and platform services) should be prioritised, given that regulations with many granular regimes can be overly complex and thus costly to implement.

Section 5.3.1 discusses different types of financial contracts in line with the above. Section 5.3.2 analyses the risk stemming from providing loans to individual borrowers. Section 5.3.3 discusses different services offered by platforms.

5.3.1 *The Type of Financial Contracts*

The crowdfunding market has seen a proliferation of different financial contracts used between fundraisers and investors (such as loans to consumers, loans to businesses, stocks, bonds, shares in private limited liability companies, silent partnerships, profit-participating loans, SAFE instruments,[39] etc.). Market participants opted for a particular contract type, sometimes following their economic needs, while in other cases, they were influenced by its regulatory treatment. In relation to this, one of the issues where jurisdictions exhibit the most significant difference in their bespoke regimes is the types of financial contracts that can be concluded on crowdfunding platforms. Sometimes, only specific financial contracts are permitted or brought within the scope of bespoke regulations, while in other cases, separate regimes are created for distinct contract types. As mentioned above, the economic justification for the difference in the regulatory treatment can be found in the risks they create for investors. In relation to this, it is possible to differentiate financial contracts along several risk-related dimensions.

Firstly, the risk to investors can depend on whether financial contracts are concluded with consumers or businesses. Presumably, information asymmetry is more

[39] SAFE stands for the Simple Agreement for Future Equity, and it has been commonly used on US crowdfunding platforms. It is a financial instrument that grants its holder the right to acquire equity under pre-defined terms sometime in the future when a triggering event occurs. The latter often involves a company exit, such as via an IPO or new financing round. The idea behind SAFE is that the valuation of the company is deferred until the triggering event when the company matures, and more information becomes available. Holders of SAFE can acquire shares at the same price as future investors, but more often, they receive a certain percentage discount.

pronounced concerning businesses than individual borrowers. As discussed in Chap. 3, not only is the amount of hard (verifiable) information that investors need to consider greater in the case of business fundraising, but also the amount of soft (unverifiable) information and financial projections. Moreover, economic activity, particularly for SMEs, always involves a certain level of uncertainty, which is also driven by factors beyond managers' control. The level of uncertainty grows with the novelty of technology being used. Crowdfunding is typically used by small and innovative firms. Thus, it should be more challenging to estimate the creditworthiness (or business prospects) of a venture than of an individual. Moreover, business fundraising per se assumes the limited liability of company founders, while crowdfunding firms typically have restricted assets to settle unsecured creditors. This makes crowdfunding for businesses particularly risky. Thus, regulators driven by this concern would apply a distinct set of rules to crowdfunding for businesses (P2P business lending, equity and debt securities, etc.) as opposed to P2P consumer lending.

Secondly, the risk to investors depends on whether financial contracts generate a fixed or variable return. By definition, financial return in debt contracts does not depend on the company's performance, as opposed to equities and other contracts with variable returns (e.g., profit-sharing agreements). Moreover, debt claims are a priority over equity claims in insolvency cases. Thus, regulators that take this as a decisive criterion would treat differently all pure debt contracts (independently who the fundraisers are—P2P consumer lending, P2P business lending, and debt securities) from other financial contracts (equity, royalties, profit-sharing agreements, etc.).

Thirdly, the difference in risk can also stem from the level of complexity of financial contracts. Small retail investors have high information costs concerning understanding complex instruments, which add to the high costs associated with assessing the quality of fundraisers. While it is difficult to draw a clear line between simple and complex instruments, it is possible to argue that loans, equity (ordinary shares), and bonds, commonly used in traditional finance, qualify as simple contracts.

Finally, financial contracts in crowdfunding can also involve different liquidity risks (rather than credit risk, as discussed earlier). The notion of financial instruments (and securities as their most common type), in contrast to loan contracts, implies that these are easily transferrable and commonly traded on (traditional) secondary markets. However, this distinction has limited value in the crowdfunding context. Both loan agreements (or creditors' claims arising out of them) and securities (stocks and bonds) can be sold on crowdfunding secondary markets, even though the liquidity of these markets is still low, and thus, liquidity risk remains high for all contract types. It is possible to argue that the liquidity risk is lower for all contracts with fixed maturity, as opposed to equity investments.[40] However, it is essential to note that the distinction between loans and financial instruments (securities) closely aligns with the split in the regulatory remit between banking and

[40] It should be noted that certain instruments, such as profit-participating loans, have a maturity date, but the interest rate is dependent on the company's profits.

securities regulators in most jurisdictions. Namely, all lending-related matters fall under the competence of banking authorities, as opposed to the capital markets authorities, which traditionally oversee the issuance and trading of financial instruments. Thus, the difference in the regulatory treatment along these lines can mask the regulatory remit or competence issues rather than concerns related to liquidity risk.

Against this backdrop, it is helpful to analyse regulatory choices in different jurisdictions and discuss whether and how they align with the risk-related considerations just explained. It should be noted that all examples from the EU Member States refer to national regulations before the adoption of the ECSPR. As a result, they may no longer be in force to the extent that their scope overlaps with the European framework.[41]

Some jurisdictions do not account for the abovementioned differences in risk levels in financial contracts. Notable examples include crowdfunding frameworks in Spain, Mexico, and the UK. They put securities and loans under one regulatory umbrella, including loans to consumers and businesses. In the UK, the treatment of lending-based and securities-based crowdfunding is not entirely the same, but differences are mainly driven by distinct services offered by platforms. Moreover, consumer borrowers are also subject to additional consumer protection safeguards, as will be discussed in more detail later.

Surprisingly, among jurisdictions that appear to account for differences in risks stemming from contract types, it is rare to find jurisdictions with two distinct bespoke regulatory frameworks governing crowdfunding activity. Examples include Indonesia and Argentina, which have a unique set of rules for P2P lending (both consumer and business) and securities-based crowdfunding. Similarly, a bespoke crowdfunding framework was created in China for P2P lending (both consumer and business), while securities-based crowdfunding is no longer permitted. As mentioned earlier, such a distinction most accurately reflects the differences in (potential) liquidity risk of financial contracts; however, it also closely aligns with the competence of distinct regulatory authorities.

Jurisdictions that introduced only one bespoke regulatory regime typically focus on crowdfunding for business (usually referred to as investment-based crowdfunding). This can indicate that regulators were concerned about a higher risk stemming from business than consumer fundraising. However, there are two caveats to such an assumption. Firstly, in many jurisdictions that regulate only crowdfunding for business, P2P consumer lending can still fall under existing (banking) regulations. Therefore, it is not granted that the bespoke regime for investment-based crowdfunding is stricter or that the level of investor protection is higher when compared to

---

[41] The regulatory information is based on the data collected by the European Commission and publishes as part of the Impact Assessment (European Commission, 2018). Meanwhile, some additional Member States could have adopted bespoke regulatory frameworks, but for the sake of time consistency, they are not included in the analysis. Also, any subsequent amendments to existing bespoke regulations are not accounted for unless explicitly mentioned.

P2P consumer lending. Secondly, regulations of investment-based crowdfunding differ regarding the scope of investment contracts included within their scope.

Some frameworks are indeed all-encompassing. A notable example is the US, whose framework for crowdfunding under the JOBS Act applies to all investment contracts used by businesses to raise capital. Investment contracts have an extensive interpretation under the US case law. A similar approach was adopted by the Monetary Authority of Singapore (Ang & Kwek, 2020). Among European jurisdictions, Belgium, Finland, and Lithuania introduced a tailored framework for securities and business lending. Similarly, Portugal covered both securities and business lending under the same regime but surprisingly included non-financial return models (donation and reward). The scope of the ECSPR was aligned with the logic in these jurisdictions, covering securities, business loans, and admitted instruments for crowdfunding purposes (basically, shares in private limited liability companies when the laws of a Member State allow so).

In contrast, investment-based crowdfunding regimes in some other jurisdictions apply only to a subset of financial contracts potentially used by business fundraisers. This suggests that some other risk-related factors or political or regulatory considerations drove regulators' decisions on the scope. For instance, the choice of instruments in crowdfunding regulations in France and Italy (before the ECSPR) and Australia and New Zealand could have also been motivated by the need to offer only simple instruments to crowdfunding investors. The French regime had initially allowed only (simple) loans to businesses, ordinary shares, and plain vanilla fixed-rate bonds to be brokered on crowdfunding platforms.[42] The Italian bespoke regime was limited to equity instruments, while Australia and New Zealand only permitted ordinary shares (stocks) to be offered to crowd investors.

In contrast, the choice of instruments in investment-based crowdfunding frameworks of Austria and Germany appears to be almost detached from risk-related concerns. Namely, in Austria, in addition to different securities (both equity and debt), platforms were also allowed to broker other 'alternative financial instruments' such as participation rights, silent partnerships, and subordinated loans. Yet, simple (unconditional) business loans were not included in the special crowdfunding regime, which has to do with the fact that traditional lending remained under the purview of the banking regulator. The choice of instruments for crowdfunding purposes is further constrained under the German Small Investor Protection Act (Kleinanlegerschutzgesetz, 2015), allowing only profit-participating loans, subordinated loans, and other investment products (thus excluding the use of transferrable securities).[43]

[42] There are some caveats regarding the French crowdfunding framework. While it is predominantly a regime for business crowdfunding, consumer loans for educational purposes were also included within its scope. Moreover, platforms brokering securities and business loans were subject to distinct licences. Furthermore, subsequent amendments to the regulatory framework also allowed for more complex products to be offered.

[43] It should be noted that the bespoke framework governing these hybrid instruments remains in force even after the adoption of the ECSPR. It is yet to be seen whether German platforms, predominantly brokering the sale of these instruments, will find the economic interest to bring their operations within the scope of the ECSPR or continue operating under the national regime.

In sum, while investment contracts concluded on crowdfunding platforms can entail different risk levels for investors, bespoke regulations do not always account for them or often do so unintentionally, such as when the scope of crowdfunding regulations overlaps with the remit of regulatory authorities. Moreover, as some risk-related considerations are interrelated, regulators find it difficult to draw a line consistently. For instance, it is difficult to argue that there is a clear difference in risks when comparing P2P business loans and debt securities or equity and some hybrid instruments (e.g., profit-participating loans).

Yet, neglecting risk considerations concerning contract types can also be justified on different grounds. Firstly, treating all crowdfunding models in the same or similar manner can allow crowdfunding regulations to systematically address more fundamental risks that are common across different crowdfunding models. These include risks stemming from the operation of platforms and services they offer and the very participation of many retail investors. It is also possible to argue that risks related to the behaviour of different market participants (platforms, fundraisers, and investors), as opposed to risks associated with the type of financial contracts, are something that regulators can have an impact on. For instance, regulations can mandate disclosure requirements for fundraisers or business conduct rules for platforms or enforce investment limits. Still, it is difficult to mitigate risks arising from different financial contracts other than by banning their use in the crowdfunding market. Treating all financial contracts in the same manner should also be favoured when there is a risk of regulatory arbitrage (e.g., leaving out some financial instruments would allow platforms or fundraises to escape regulatory oversight—as discussed in relation to the baseline scenario in the previous section).

Moreover, an encompassing approach also allows market forces to find optimal instruments, which are far from straightforward given the uniqueness of the crowdfunding market (small fundraisers, unsophisticated investors, lack of liquid secondary markets, and traditional intermediaries). For instance, as discussed in Chap. 3 regarding corporate governance of funded firms, granting voting rights to crowd investors can provide limited benefits if they do not effectively exercise them. Nonetheless, there are instances in which corporate laws or other idiosyncratic factors in a given jurisdiction do not favour the use of specific contracts in the crowdfunding market (e.g., when a notary form is required to transfer shares in private limited liability companies, making it incompatible with the digital nature of crowdfunding services). Therefore, the above discussion can serve as a guiding principle rather than being followed in absolute terms.

5.3.2 *The Type of Fundraisers: Consumers Vs. Businesses*

The above discussion deals with the difference in the regulatory treatment of P2P consumer lending and investment-based crowdfunding from the angle of risks to investors. However, a more pertinent concern is whether these models should be regulated separately from the borrowers' perspective. By definition, borrowers in

P2P consumer lending, as opposed to debt-based investment models (P2P business lending and debt securities), are consumers.[44] Individual (consumer) borrowers in traditional finance, notably in their relationship with a bank, benefit from an array of additional consumer protection measures.[45]

Their economic rationale lies in preventing the harm borrowers can suffer due to an information asymmetry in favour of a bank (Armour et al., 2016, pp. 55–57). Namely, as a result of greater expertise (dealing in the course of business) and economic power more generally, a bank is in a position to offer (detrimental) contract terms that borrowers are willing to accept despite not fully understanding the actual costs of borrowing (or precisely because of it). While contract terms with a bank cannot be negotiated (they fall under standard form contracts), borrowers could 'shop around'—compare contract terms of different banks, and, thus, induce competition among banks along this dimension (Bakos et al., 2014). However, information asymmetry between borrowers and banks prevents market forces from eliminating harmful contractual practices. An alternative (additional) economic rationale for consumer protection in banking relates to insights from behavioural economics (Armour et al., 2016, p. 64; Bar-Gill, 2012, pp. 51–115). Even when presented with all the relevant information (in contract terms and complementary terms and conditions of a bank), borrowers have issues processing available information—they are boundedly rational and suffer from several biases. These include, for instance, short-sightedness (myopia), focus on instant gratification, optimism bias, anchoring, etc., leading to underestimation of the cost of borrowing and overestimation of their ability to repay the loan in the future (Odorović, 2017, pp. 144–148; Odorović, 2018, pp. 158–165). This, in turn, can lead to their financial distress or over-indebtedness. Theoretically, the same considerations are perhaps relevant in the crowdfunding context.

It should be noted, however, that the focus of this study thus far has been the information asymmetry between fundraisers or the crowdfunding platform, on the one hand, and crowd investors, on the other. Nonetheless, it is also possible to reverse this discussion by arguing that individual borrowers can suffer harm from being a less well-informed party in their relationship with lenders or, even more importantly, with the platform. Borrowers can underestimate the total borrowing costs, consisting of the interest rate, different platform fees, and some other contingent claims on them (early repayment fees, late payment fees, exorbitant costs associated with loss recovery practices, etc.). Thus, information asymmetry can induce them to enter into suboptimal contracts, that is, agreements that they would not have concluded had they known the actual costs of borrowing or otherwise accepting some onerous contract clauses for which they are not compensated by paying a more favourable interest rate.

[44] The term consumer has different meanings. As explained by Armour et al. (2016, p. 64), it can refer to all situations in which individuals act outside the course of their business. Nonetheless, in financial regulation (particularly in the US and EU), it is usually used in the context of consumer credit, where consumers are a synonym for borrowers.

[45] For instance, these include rules on advertising and transparency, the creditworthiness obligation, requirements regarding the form and content of loan agreements, rules on withdrawal and early repayments, etc. (Morello, 2023, p. 864).

Despite these risks, consumer protection safeguards vis-à-vis borrowers are rarely applied in the crowdfunding market. The critical challenge in introducing them in the regulatory practice (or bespoke regimes) is that loan agreements are concluded directly with crowd lenders. Since crowd lenders are also individuals acting outside the course of business (also not always being better off economically and contributing only a portion of the entire loan amount), it is difficult to argue why information asymmetry would exist in the first place. Even from a practical perspective, imposing consumer protection obligations on crowd lenders, sometimes hundreds of them in a single campaign, appears impossible.

Yet, as known from the crowdfunding practice (as discussed in Chaps. 2 and 3), platforms typically define terms of loan agreements, unilaterally set their fees, and engage in debt collection practices (alone or by outsourcing it to a third-party provider). Thus, if the protection of borrowers is necessary, it has to be framed as the obligation of platforms. These obligations can include greater transparency (mandating platform-level disclosure requirements) or banning certain practices.[46]

Without a bespoke regulatory framework for P2P consumer lending, regulators in many jurisdictions struggle to find grounds to extend such obligations to platforms. For instance, in the EU, it was not clear whether the obligations under the CCD could be stretched to accommodate crowdfunding platforms. The EBA's interpretation was that the protection of borrowers under CCD falls on credit institutions, while neither fundraisers nor platforms qualify as such (European Banking Authority, 2015, pp. 31–32, fn. 27). This has not prevented some jurisdictions, such as the Netherlands, to nevertheless, extend the consumer protection obligations to platforms in their national laws implementing the directive, as mentioned above. Some legal scholars have also argued in favour of applying the CCD in the crowdfunding context. They have contended that an extensive interpretation should replace a literal one given the pivotal role of platforms in determining key terms of loan agreements, and even more so concerning platforms that provide the service of automated investments (Alibrandi & Grossule, 2022, pp. 597–598; Ebers et al., 2021, pp. 11–13). Interestingly, the new Proposal for the CCD also ultimately missed the opportunity to regulate P2P consumer lending platforms similarly to fully-fledged lenders, despite such explicit intentions in an earlier version of the text (European Commission, 2021). As argued by Morello (2023, pp. 864–865), this appears reasonable in light of the peculiarities of crowdfunding, where platforms do not act as genuine creditors.

It should be noted that the challenge of introducing consumer protection safeguards for borrowers is less of a concern in jurisdictions where crowdfunding is subject to banking regulations, that is, when banks originate all loans financed by crowd lenders. As mentioned, in the US, Germany, or Austria, the bank must comply with all relevant consumer protection measures vis-à-vis borrowers. Yet, the

[46] The choice between transparency and limiting the scope of permissible market practices depends on whether it is reasonable to assume that consumers will rely on available disclosures—which has proven to be problematic from an empirical point of view as documented in other markets (Bakos et al., 2014; Bar-Gill & Board, 2012).

costs arising from borrowers' relationship with the platform, notably platform fees, are not brought within the compliance duties of a bank and depend on the regulatory status of the platform and its associated information duties.[47]

Bespoke regimes focusing primarily on P2P consumer lending are surprisingly uncommon (compared to those applicable to P2P business lending and investment-based crowdfunding), as discussed above. Even when they exist, such as in China, they often focus on investor protection rather than borrower protection. As documented by Ofir and Sadeh (2019, p. 736), the protection of borrowers boils down to preventing privacy threats and applying complementary laws that limit the maximum interest rate that can be charged.[48]

One regime with ample protection for borrowers in the crowdfunding market is the UK. Despite designing a common regime for diverse financial-return models, P2P consumer lending platforms have been subject to the existing Consumer Credit sourcebook, with some parts being explicitly dedicated to the crowdfunding market. To minimise the risk of financial distress, platforms in the UK are required to assess the borrower's ability to repay the loan in light of their wider financial situation, to explain clearly the contract terms, and to send reminders in case of late payments or default (Ofir & Sadeh, 2019, p. 730).

In sum, this study has not focused on information asymmetry where fundraisers are the less informed party (but instead examined the opposite scenario). However, such a situation should not be ruled out when borrowers are consumers. Nonetheless, in reality, the information asymmetry arises in their relationship with the platform (rather than with lenders), which often has a decisive influence on borrowing terms. Regulators and policymakers drafting bespoke regulations that focus on or include P2P consumer lending within their scope should consider consumer protection safeguards for borrowers. The scope and depth of such safeguards would inevitably depend on similar protections that already exist in traditional finance, notwithstanding that the role of platforms is not as substantial as that of credit institutions.

5.3.3 *The Scope of Platform Services*

Thus far, it has been argued that a coherent and encompassing approach to crowdfunding regulation should be favoured—covering different crowdfunding models under one regulatory umbrella (with the exception of some special provisions

[47] As explained by Ofir and Sadeh (2019, p. 726), in the US, the platform also has the status of a lender. Namely, after the bank originates the loan, the platform juxtaposes between borrowers and crowd lenders by holding claims against borrowers and issuing debt securities to crowd lenders. As a result, the platform has to conform to the duty of fair and clear disclosures of contract terms, explain why some loan applications were rejected, and prevent abusive debt collection practices (Ofir & Sadeh, 2019, p. 726).

[48] This should not come as a surprise, given that P2P lending in China is primarily used as a financing vehicle for small businesses (Huang, 2018, p. 69).

ensuring consumer protection vis a vis individual borrowers). Nonetheless, one additional risk category needs closer attention—different platform services. As shown through various parts of this study, platforms offer a wide array of services that span different stages of the campaign process (before, during, or after a crowdfunding campaign). Services that deserve special regulatory attention are services that bring crowdfunding platforms closer to financial and information intermediaries in traditional finance, as discussed in Chap. 2 (notably those that correspond to screening, monitoring, and risk management). Yet, as illustrated in Chap. 3, crowdfunding platforms show significant varieties regarding the scope and depth of these services, affecting investors' risk. Moreover, some of these services are more frequently exercised in relation to specific crowdfunding models—lending or equity.

It is important to emphasise that it is difficult to assess whether the level of risk for investors decreases or increases due to platforms reintermediating the market. It is the source of risk that changes, which should be acknowledged in bespoke crowdfunding regulations. As already discussed apropos platform gatekeeping roles (Chap. 3), as investors delegate screening, monitoring, and risk management to platforms, the importance of information asymmetry between them and fundraisers diminishes. In contrast, the information asymmetry between investors and the platform becomes a critical source of risk. In the agency relationship created between them, similar to traditional indirect finance, investors as the principal have high costs of monitoring the platform that acts as their agent. At the same time, their interests are not always aligned. Put differently, the platform does not always have proper incentives to act in the best interest of investors, particularly when providing a high-quality service is costly, and investors have no means to establish its direct influence on the quality of outcomes—the success or failure of crowdfunding projects (or repayment or default of loans) or even more remote consequences (such as exit opportunities and protection of their interests in the relationship with founders and new investors).

It is possible to distinguish between 'reintermediation' services exercised by all platforms (or all platforms offering specific financial contracts, e.g., loans) and 'auxiliary' services that some platforms offer as their competitive advantage. An example of the first category of services is platform onboarding and due diligence (screening) or administering loan repayments in lending-based platforms (monitoring). An example of the second category of services is platform pricing (setting the interest rate of loans or company valuations), which is only offered by a subset of (lending) platforms. It should be noted, however, that the distinction between these two categories is not set once for all. It can depend on the prevailing market practices in a given jurisdiction, which evolve over time.

Yet, these two categories of services raise different regulatory issues. Services exercised across different crowdfunding models (albeit to a different degree), by their very definition, do not affect the scope of crowdfunding regulations. Regulatory concerns relate to their quality. Here, the regulatory dilemma is whether to prescribe a specific performance standard and supervise its implementation, let platforms compete along these non-price dimensions, or use the combination of the two. For instance, when it comes to platform onboarding and due diligence practices, regulation can mandate the exact information to be collected on fundraisers, information verification procedures, and onboarding criteria (e.g., minimum credit grade) or merely mandate platforms to prevent fraudulent fundraisers while leaving the rest to the platform discretion.

The 'auxiliary' reintermediation services directly interfere with the scope of crowdfunding regulations, as the first question regulators and policymakers need to address is whether to include them.[49] The concern is that these services can mark a departure from crowdfunding as a means of direct finance for individuals and SMEs and bring crowdfunding closer to well-known and tightly regulated services in traditional finance. The second question regarding these services is if included, whether they should trigger a different regulatory treatment since they lead to an increased risk for investors or the source of the risk shifts, as explained above. In light of these considerations, it is helpful to sketch a taxonomy of crowdfunding models based on services offered by the platform first. The taxonomy is derived from the analysis of platform gatekeeping functions in Chap. 3 and focuses on auxiliary services offered ex-ante (before and during a crowdfunding campaign). Ex-post services are analysed separately in order not to make the possible combination of crowdfunding models too complicated, as well as because crowdfunding regulations typically put greater emphasis on the fundraising process than post-campaign activities.

Crowdfunding models differ along two key dimensions (and associated services offered by platforms):

1. Who makes the investment decision (investors, the platform, or both concurrently)?
2. Who estimates the risk and provides pricing (investors, the platform, or jointly)?

As to the first dimension, the default crowdfunding model entails that investors make independent decisions on which crowdfunding offers to support. They choose every loan or project they contribute their money to, creating a more or less diversified portfolio, depending on their preferences. While acknowledging investors' limitations in choosing good investment opportunities and building a well-diversified portfolio, some platforms offer auto-investing services (auto-bidding, bidding assistant, portfolio builder). These services can be provided as an alternative to manual investments (meaning that investor and platform decisions are made concurrently) or entirely replace manual bidding. In the latter situation, the platform makes all

[49] The term 'including within the scope' of crowdfunding regulations can have different meanings depending on how these services relate to services regulated under the existing rules (as discussed in relation to the 'stretch-to-fit' approach above). If these services already qualify as one of the services reserved for traditional intermediaries, bringing them within the scope would entail introducing a new exemption. In the alternative, crowdfunding regulations can specify that crowdfunding activity does not allow the provision of such services. If auxiliary services do not qualify as one of the services reserved for traditional intermediaries (e.g., because the regulated services are limited to certain financial instruments and not those intermediated on crowdfunding platforms), crowdfunding regulations can explicitly regulate them or prohibit them.

investment decisions for each investor separately, based on the mandate that the investor explicitly provided (regarding characteristics of investment offers that the platform can allocate funds to on the investor's behalf).

Regarding the second dimension, the default (early) crowdfunding practice assumes that investors make (credit) risk assessments and price crowdfunding offers based on ample information available on the platform. As mentioned earlier, pricing can refer to setting the interest rate or pricing shares (evaluating the company). It should be noted, however, that it is only the auction model, in which investors' bids also carry a price suggestion (the interest rate that they are willing to accept for a given loan). In other instances (posted-price model), it is the fundraiser that sets the price, but investors are expected to assess its accuracy and decide whether to invest based on their estimates. If the platform has some influence on the price set by fundraisers, this process happens behind closed doors, and investors do not rely (or should not) on these estimates mindlessly. In some instances, although rare, the platform makes a credit risk assessment by assigning credit grades to each (loan) application, while pricing is still left to market participants (via an auction or posted-price mechanism, as explained earlier). For the purpose of differentiating between crowdfunding models, this situation is referred to as a joint assessment. Finally, the platform can provide both credit assessment (risk grading) and pricing services. While in such instances, investors can still question the quality of platform estimates, many of them will likely have reduced incentives to do so.

When combining these two dimensions, it is possible to create a taxonomy of crowdfunding models that depends on platform services, where each model corresponds to a unique risk level for investors. For clarity, different models are depicted in Table 5.1.

Models A, B, and C are models in which investment decision lies with the investor (investor choice models). The difference between them is to what extent they rely on credit risk assessment and pricing provided by the platform.

Model A is the most straightforward since the platform provides no auxiliary services. Investors are expected to assess risks and pricing accuracy and allocate their funds to different campaigns. It is commonly used among equity-based platforms, although the platform can still help with company valuations (e.g., by preventing the listing of companies with inflated valuations). However, the extent to which the platform stands behind pricing is often unknown to investors.

Model B departures from model A as the platform provides risk grades, while pricing is left to market participants. Platform risk grades are an anchor, though investors are still expected to consider all information provided by fundraisers or spread by other investors. For instance, as captured by Franks et al. (2021), this model had been operated by the UK platform Funding Circle while still offering an auction-based pricing mechanism, which was eventually abolished.

Model C is a natural consequence of the fact that risk grading is almost inseparable from pricing. Thus, platforms offering risk grading set the interest rate as well. Yet, this feature can lead to an overreliance on platform assessment, ignoring other available information, including both financial data and soft, proximate knowledge

Table 5.1 Taxonomy of crowdfunding models by type of ex-ante platform services

Assessment Investment decision	Investor	Jointly	Platform
Investor	A. Investors choose offers based on their own assessment	B. Investors choose offers based on their own assessment of price accuracy but are assisted by platform credit grades	C. Investors choose offers based on credit grades and pricing provided by the platform
Concurrently	D. Investors choose offers based on their own assessment. Alternatively, the platform invests on investors' behalf, mimicking the choice of other investors	E. Investors choose offers based on their own assessment of price accuracy but are assisted by platform credit grades. Alternatively, the platform chooses offers on their behalf, combining platform credit grades and prior investor choices	F. Investors choose offers based on credit grades and pricing provided by the platform. Alternatively, the platform invests on investors' behalf
Platform			G. Platforms create individual investor portfolios based on platform credit grades and pricing

(Cumming & Hornuf, 2022). As discussed in Chap. 3, the accuracy of platform pricing is not granted, making it a critical regulatory concern regarding all models where the platform offers this service.

Models D, E, and F are models in which platforms combine investor decision-making with platform decision-making (concurrent-choice models). In other words, these models assume that platforms offer auto-investment service alongside manual bids. There are three important considerations to these models, as captured by empirical studies and presented in Chap. 3.

Firstly, auto-investments can generate different risk levels depending on the information that the platform algorithm uses. Model D is seemingly the most benign among models that offer auto-investment features, even though platforms sometimes refer to this service as investing into a fund. As explained in Chap. 3, some equity platforms offer their investors an option to automatically allocate their funds across different crowdfunding offers available on their portal, which pre-satisfy specific criteria defined by the platform (e.g., that offers are funded by sophisticated investors or a certain number of all investors, that they are close to reaching the funding target, etc.) (Coakley & Lazos, 2021, p. 358). At first, given that the fund is created based on criteria set by the platform, this service resembles collective management schemes. Yet, unlike these schemes (in particular AIF), no asset transformation is involved (investors are still exposed to individual projects). The platform has no discretion in choosing underlying assets but merely mimics the choice of other investors on the platform. To the extent that the platform respects pre-defined investment criteria, this service resembles platform-enabled herding (presumably rational, given that the investment criteria are supposed to imitate the choice of informed investors) and diversification.

Model E assumes that automatic investments are based on a combination of platform risk grades and choices of previous investors. As illustrated in Chap. 3, the UK platform Funding Circle, the French platform Unilend, and the Chinese platform PaiPaiDai also enabled automatic bids alongside manual bids in the auction process. Automatic bids apparently combine risk parameters defined by investors (corresponding to platform risk grades) and funding flows from other investors (Darmon et al., 2022, pp. 3–4; Franks et al., 2021).

Model F is substantially different from previous auto-investment models as the platform allocates the funds only based on its own estimates of credit risk and pricing. Thus, the platform is given the greatest discretion regarding the choice of underlying assets and meeting the mandate given by each investor (regarding the desired risk exposure, returns, and maturity). From a risk perspective, a particularly problematic issue is when investors are promised an annual target rate of return on investment, which the platform is expected to achieve by combining loans of different risk levels.

The second consideration regarding concurrent-choice models is that the existence of automatic bids can impact the quality of investment decisions of those investing manually. A common thread across different empirical studies discussed in Chap. 3 is that auto-bids interfere with market-based mechanisms of overcoming information asymmetry. They can reduce the amount of (soft) information fundraisers disclose to investors (presumably because platform algorithms do not use this information) (Böhme & Grossklags, 2013) or reduce herding (Chen et al., 2021; Jiang et al., 2018). As discussed before, depending on whether herding originates from investors with a superior source of information or skill set, reduced herding can lead to better or worse outcomes for individuals investing manually.

The third consideration regarding concurrent-choice models is that they raise a question of investors self-selecting into manual and automatic bids. Presumably, those with private information about fundraisers or those with a superior skill set to estimate crowdfunding offers would opt for manual pledges, as opposed to all others who minimise their screening efforts by delegating the choice of investments to the platform. This should not be problematic as long as sophisticated investors bidding manually cannot crowd out less sophisticated investors using the auto-investment feature from the best-quality offers on the platform. Yet, as captured by Vallee and Zeng (2019), the latter concern could have led many retail investors to leave the market, which incentivised one US P2P lending platform to reduce the amount of information available to all investors.

Finally, model G marks the most significant departure from crowdfunding as a concept, given that investors are deprived of both assessing the risks and promises of different opportunities and choosing independently which of them to invest in (platform-choice model). This model is also known as individual portfolio management due to its close resemblance to portfolio management in traditional markets. As mentioned in Chap. 2, the critical difference is that only loans, not financial instruments (e.g., securities), have been used in crowdfunding so far (Ferretti, 2022, p. 119). As already discussed in relation to its predecessor, Model F, the platform is given the greatest discretion regarding the choice of underlying assets, particularly when a target rate of return on investment is promised. In addition, 'the wisdom of the crowd' vanishes completely, as investors are not allowed to invest directly.

It should be noted again that risk assessment and pricing services are typically provided by P2P lending platforms and investment platforms intermediating hybrid instruments. As explained before, equity-based platforms assist with company valuations in a way that is not clearly visible to investors. In other words, they typically correspond to models A and D, while lending-based models can correspond to any of the models described above. This creates an important yet unexpected consequence—lending-based crowdfunding can be riskier than equity-based crowdfunding if platform risk assessment and pricing are inferior to investors' assessments relying on market-based forces, as discussed in Chap. 3. Even without making a final call on whether investors' or the platform's assessment is superior (which can depend on many factors), it is reasonable to conclude that the source of risks in these models is different. Therefore, if introduced, the difference in the regulatory treatment of lending and equity models should be driven by these risk concerns.

Regarding ex-post 'reintermediation' services, they can relate to monitoring—when the platform administers loan repayments or governance arrangements, or risk management—when the platform operates a provision (contingency) fund. As mentioned in relation to ex-ante services, here it is also possible to distinguish between services that have become an industry standard (and are, thus, exercised by all platforms) and those offered as an auxiliary feature aiming to create a competitive advantage over other platforms.

P2P lending platforms routinely administer loan repayments. This is because crowdfunding assumes that individual borrowers enter into bilateral relationships with many investors, each contributing a small amount. Consequently, neither individual investors' administration of the loan agreement nor their coordinated effort is a viable alternative to a platform centralising the process of debt collection and loss recovery. The risk that regulators should address relates to the quality of this service and, more importantly, ensuring its continuity in case of a platform failure.

In contrast, the operation of a provision fund is an auxiliary service offered by some (P2P lending) platforms. As discussed in Chap. 3, a provision fund financed from the platform's resources can strengthen the platform's incentives to perform well other gatekeeping roles. On the contrary, it can diminish investors' incentives to conduct due diligence, driven by a false sense of security that their returns are guaranteed. Therefore, regulators need to decide whether to allow this service. If the answer is positive, it is reasonable to argue that a particular set of rules should govern the operation of these platforms. Notably, bespoke regulations need to restrict how the provision fund is advertised to investors and the platform's discretionary powers in relation to its use.

Similarly, as seen in Chap. 3, platform services related to the governance of firms that raised funds via investment-based platforms are not universal. Platforms have been experimenting with many different governance arrangements, which often depend on the type of financial interest in the funded company. Given the importance of mitigating moral hazard, it is unquestionable that such governance arrangements can have a decisive significance on investor's returns, notwithstanding the lack of liquid secondary markets. As shown in some studies discussed in Chap. 3 (Butticè et al., 2020; Coakley et al., 2021; Walthoff-Borm et al., 2018), models of delegated monitoring, such as the nominee structure, have been shown to be efficient. Yet, it is not granted that the platform always puts the necessary effort in exercising shareholder rights on the investor's behalf, nor that it sufficiently protects investors from a dilutive issuance of new shares. While crowdfunding regimes seldom regulate the activity of platforms ex-post, delegated monitoring can create a new source of risks for investors.

Additionally, it should be noted that some platform auxiliary services do not involve market 'reintermediation' but can nevertheless have an essential influence on the risk level borne by investors. These are, for instance, co-investment schemes. Platforms can invest alongside crowd investors or involve a reputable (lead) investor who vets crowdfunding offers. In both cases, investors do not formally delegate assessment of investment opportunities and investment choices to the platform or the lead investor, but their presence can stir investors' decisions. Again, the question is whether to permit such services under the bespoke framework and whether a particular set of rules should apply to these platforms. The co-investment of a platform is problematic as it potentially impairs its role as a neutral (information) intermediary. It has to be ensured that the platform does not have a conflict of interests. As to the role of a lead investor, as shown in Chap. 3, a potential concern is that a lead negotiates a better deal for themselves, that they have an information privilege or that other insider ownership issues arise as a result of their considerable financial stake in the funded company (Chen & Ma, 2023, pp. 4–5). Thus, the regulatory issue here is whether it is possible to extend the regulatory purview to lead investors, such as to ensure they comply with their fiduciary duties. Alternatively, regulators can require platforms to ensure that the lead participates in crowdfunding deals on the same terms as the crowd.

In sum, auxiliary crowdfunding services, particularly those that bring crowdfunding platforms closer to intermediaries in traditional finance, raise important questions regarding the scope of a bespoke crowdfunding regime. Different crowdfunding services and their unique combinations (as discussed in relation to ex-ante 'reintermediation' services) generate distinct risks for investors. With each new service allowed under the bespoke framework, the sophistication of crowdfunding models rises, posing a clear trade-off for policymakers and regulators. This trade-off implies choosing between a granular risk-based approach (where the regulatory treatment depends on the risk associated with a specific model or a service) and an increasingly complex regulatory framework. The complexity of rules is desired neither by platforms that need to navigate them (often small tech firms) nor by regulatory agencies with limited resources to supervise their implementation.

Nonetheless, some risk-related considerations elaborated above should be addressed, and one way to do this is to prioritise certain regulatory obligations while relaxing some others, depending on the model. The following section provides some recommendations in this regard while discussing some key rules that govern the behaviour of fundraisers, platforms, and investors (as seen in jurisdictions with bespoke crowdfunding regimes).

5.4 The Residual Role of the Law: The Subtle Interplay with Market-Based Mechanisms

While previous sections have focused on some overarching regulatory questions in crowdfunding, this section provides a closer look into specific regulatory issues in bespoke crowdfunding regulations. The structure of the section reflects the fact that crowdfunding regulations typically introduce specific rules for fundraisers, platforms, and (retail) investors. As in previous sections, the aim is to address the most disputed issues from a comparative perspective, drawing on the insights on market practices scattered throughout this study. The frame of reference is the information asymmetry between market participants, notwithstanding that bespoke crowdfunding regimes can also aim to address other important regulatory concerns (e.g., ML/TF). It should be noted that examples from different jurisdictions are invoked to illustrate some prominent regulatory solutions rather than to provide a detailed comparative legal analysis.

5.4.1 Regulating Fundraisers: On the Merits of Mandatory Disclosures

As already explained, crowdfunding is a special kind of public fundraising via designated web portals. Raising funds from an undefined number of unrelated and unsophisticated investors has been governed by securities laws, often several decades or almost a century old. The core of securities regulations concerns the requirement to publish a prospectus (registration statement for an IPO), a mandatory disclosure document whose content, length, form, and registration with the competent authority are well-defined. The purpose of a prospectus is clear. It is meant to ensure an informed-decision making of investors.

Bespoke crowdfunding regulations introduce new or rely on existing exemptions from prospectus requirements. The idea that small innovative firms cannot bear the high burden of regulatory compliance embedded in rules on public securities offerings is seldom contested. Instead, little consensus exists on two related matters. Firstly, it is disputable what the appropriate exemption threshold is, and relatedly, whether only firms of a specific size or other characteristics (e.g., level of innovativeness) should be given access to the crowdfunding market. Secondly, the question arises of whether prospectus requirements should be replaced with laxer disclosure rules, which should strike the right balance between providing investors with sufficient information and not imposing an unduly burden on fundraisers.

The debate around the exemption threshold cannot be settled without considering circumstances in a given jurisdiction, most notably the (direct) costs of prospectuses (which depend on lawyers', auditors', notaries' fees, access to public registries, etc.), access to finance gap among fundraisers, as well as the size distribution of companies that are likely to use crowdfunding. For instance, in Europe, existing solutions have ranged from €100,000 in the early days of crowdfunding to €8 million. Given that this study has not shed light on any of the factors mentioned above, no further recommendations can be provided at this point. The same refers to the characteristics of firms that can rely on crowdfunding exemption. Yet, some solutions seen in comparative crowdfunding laws appear to serve the same purpose as an exemption threshold or are challenging to implement. For instance, crowdfunding regulations in Brazil only allow fundraising by companies with gross annual revenue under 10 million Reais. Given that raising a limited amount of funds is only meaningful for companies of modest size and that the very purpose of crowdfunding is that retail investors support companies still in the seed or growth stage, it seems that such a requirement brings little additional value. Theoretically, the crowdfunding threshold can be abused by several consecutive offerings by large firms. Still, this is impossible in practice as the threshold typically applies to the total amount of funds raised within 12 months. In relation to this, requirements related to the level of innovativeness of crowdfunding companies, for instance, in the early Italian law on crowdfunding (and eventually abolished), turned out to be too complicated and arbitrary for the competent authorities.

A more substantial debate concerns whether crowdfunding regulations should introduce a light disclosure regime. Mandatory disclosure regimes, in general, are based on two premises. Firstly, information plays a material role in the functioning of financial markets, stirring scarce resources to their most productive uses, as explained in detail in Chap. 3. Secondly, voluntary disclosures by those seeking funds are likely to fail. This can happen because of the high costs of disclosure for fundraisers and the inability of (retail) investors to identify omissions in disclosure practices or to verify the accuracy of disclosed information, as discussed earlier. Simply put, mandatory disclosures are there to mitigate the source of a potential market failure. While crowdfunding regulations cannot aim at detailed disclosures (such as in prospectuses), they can strive to provide investors with the most substantial information at reasonable costs for fundraisers. Moreover, light-handed mandatory disclosures are expected to standardise the format for presenting information, facilitating the comparison of crowdfunding offers.

In contrast to this straightforward reasoning, several arguments suggest that introducing mandatory disclosures is inappropriate in crowdfunding. Some stem from economic theory, and some are substantiated by specific evidence on market-based practices in crowdfunding, as thoroughly discussed in Chap. 3. Theoretically, one can contend that the costs of mandatory disclosures can be greater than the benefit generated to investors. Interestingly, arguments substantiating this claim are closely related to arguments that can explain the failure of voluntary disclosure in the first place. As discussed in Chap. 3, the costs of disclosure include direct costs of credibly revealing information and indirect costs of divulging the critical aspect of business innovation. Such costs are unavoidable under a mandatory disclosure regime, although the design of rules can substantially affect their size. In principle, the direct and indirect disclosure costs increase in the amount of information required to be revealed and/or certified. If such costs are deemed too high, a fund-raiser considering crowdfunding as a funding mechanism may decide not to run a crowdfunding campaign. The question is, what are the implications for the problem of adverse selection? Which types of fundraisers are more likely to sidestep crowd-funding as a result? The direct costs are sunk costs that cannot be recovered if the target amount is not reached by the end of a crowdfunding campaign. This means that, in principle, better-quality projects or loan applications whose owners are more confident about the campaign's success are more likely to use this funding mechanism. In other words, rules on mandatory disclosures can enable a self-selection mechanism for good-quality projects. A caveat to this conjecture is that the direct costs of disclosure create a different burden for businesses of varying sizes or stages of development, and these characteristics are not necessarily correlated with their project quality. The opposite effect may stem from the indirect costs of disclosure, that is, the costs of disclosing proprietary information. As discussed before, these can increase with the innovation level, implying that a mandatory disclosure regime can potentially steer away the most innovative projects. Such projects are likely to generate higher expected returns but can also be riskier.[50] Secondly, retail investors who incur high costs in detecting flaws in voluntary disclosure practises may analogously pay little attention to the disclosed content.[51] As mentioned numerous times, it may be rational for investors with a small stake in a crowdfunding offer to minimise their due diligence efforts and rely on other information clues, notably different quality signals.[52] Lastly, mandatory disclosures predominantly focus on hard (verifiable data), while some valuable information is also contained in soft clues, particularly regarding fundraisers with thin track records. Legal requirements that

[50] It should be noted, however, that the proprietary costs also depend on the easiness of appropriating the innovation or the existence of alternative ways to exercise protection against appropriators (e.g., on the existence and enforcement of IP rights), as mentioned in Chap. 3.

[51] In addition to the rational minimisation of information processing costs, investors can fail to process disclosed information as a result of their bounder rationality or behavioural biases, as captured in ample finance literature (Statman, 2017).

[52] A counterargument can be that, even in traditional markets, mandatory disclosures are only formally there to protect retail investors, while their real value lies in informing sophisticated investors ('informed traders'), whose activity drives prices to efficient levels (Georgakopoulos, 1996). If analogously applied to the crowdfunding context, this would imply that mandatory disclosures are important to attract sophisticated investors, while retail investors free-ride on their efforts by imitating their choice of crowdfunding offers. However, sophisticated investors are in a good position to detect flaws in voluntary disclosure practices. Moreover, different channels of direct communication with fundraisers allow them to ask for all the missing data without imposing unnecessary proprietary costs on fundraisers.

mandate fundraisers to disclose some soft information (e.g., risks) do not necessarily increase their credibility. Consequently, mandatory disclosures can generate limited value to investors.

More importantly, as the review of empirical evidence in Chap. 3 suggests, the central concern of the crowdfunding market is not the amount of information available to investors but somewhat limited attention to hard data and overreliance on unverifiable claims, which are often non-credible or even misleading. More specifically, it has been shown that investors are mainly responsive to the level of voluntary disclosures and that fundraisers selectively providing information are usually less successful in their offerings. While the examined studies have predominantly focused on voluntary disclosure of soft clues, this is a direct consequence of the fact that disclosure of verifiable, hard data is often mandated by platform-level rules (in the absence of regulatory requirements). Even though investors seem to notice the difference in disclosure levels, this does not amount to the conclusion that they apprehend the disclosed content. Some limited evidence also suggests that investors do not always use all the available information in their investment decisions. Finally, existing studies have predominantly captured that investors put much weight on (unverifiable) soft data, which can be informative, for instance, when individual fundraisers lack credit scores or regarding early-stage businesses whose value primarily lies in their growth potential. Yet, soft information is not always predictive of post-campaign outcomes or can even be misleading. In sum, mandatory disclosures do not adequately respond to the most probable causes of market failure in crowdfunding.

Comparative regulatory solutions show sharp differences regarding mandatory disclosures in crowdfunding, which align with the opposing considerations elaborated above. They range from extensive disclosure requirements (e.g., US, China) to a concise key investor information sheet (e.g., the ECSPR) and a lack of any disclosure requirements (e.g., UK and New Zealand). Disclosure requirements in the US are considerably downsized when compared to traditional securities offerings. However, as argued by Schwartz (2023, pp. 105–114), they still appear disproportionate when comparing the typical issuance amount in an IPO and crowdfunding. They include more than 25 different themes (many of which include further subthemes), often requiring the assistance of lawyers and accountants to fill out.[53] Nevertheless, when it comes to certifying financial statements, the US regulator acknowledged that offerings of modest size do not merit the same level of certification reliability as large crowdfunding offerings. Thus, depending on the offering amount, financial statements must be certified by the principal executive officer, an independent accountant or an audit (Bogdani et al., 2022, p. 4; Schwartz, 2023, p. 111).

The solution embraced in the ECSPR differs from the US solution, not only regarding the level of detail of the disclosure document (known as the KIIS) but also

[53] As further discussed by Schwartz (2023, p. 106), only eight categories were foreseen originally in the JOBS Act, but the SEC subsequently made use of its mandate to add additional information items to the list of Regulation Crowdfunding.

the platform's position. As to the content, the KIIS includes various themes (Regulation, 2020, Annex I), with many overlapping with disclosure requirements under the JOBS Act and Crowdfunding Regulation in the US, with a notable difference in the level of conciseness—the KIIS is supposed to be six pages long (Regulation, 2020). Moreover, the provision of the KIIS is an obligation that falls on the platform, even though the document is to be drawn by the project owner. Namely, platforms must apply procedures that ensure completeness, correctness, and clarity of disclosed information (Regulation, 2020).

In the UK and New Zealand, the regulator also requires the platform to ensure investors are sufficiently informed to make sound investment decisions. Yet, instead of prescribing specific data points to be revealed, platforms in the UK must ensure that financial promotions on their portals are 'fair, clear, and not misleading', as well as that they provide 'sufficient detail' for investors to obtain 'a balanced indication of the benefits and the risk involved' (Financial Conduct Authority, 2014, p. 42). Similarly, crowdfunding regulations in New Zealand require platforms to introduce specific internal standards and processes to ensure that investors are provided with 'timely and understandable information to assist [them] to decide whether to acquire the shares' (Schwartz, 2023, p. 163). Thus, UK and New Zealand platforms can decide on the form and the exact content of disclosures.

Interestingly, mandatory disclosures are usually introduced in securities (or investment-based) crowdfunding, while they are seldom discussed with respect to P2P lending platforms. The reason is that mandatory disclosures are considered a simplified version of prospectus (registration) requirements that exist when securities are issued to the public, as explained above. Nonetheless, one could contend that arguments against mandatory disclosures are weaker regarding P2P (consumer) lending. Most importantly, individual fundraisers do not incur proprietary costs when revealing specific information about themselves. Moreover, screening individual borrowers boils down to less information that investors need to digest; thus, disclosures generate more significant benefits to investors. Finally, soft, forward-looking information, while beneficial for assessing the creditworthiness of borrowers with no credit history, is not as crucial as in estimating the growth potential of young companies. China is an example of a jurisdiction with ample mandatory disclosures in P2P lending. Similar to the EU, UK, and New Zealand, disclosures are seen as an obligation of the platform. According to Huang (2018, pp. 75–76), they represent the central piece of the Chinese bespoke regime (The 2016 Interim Measures on Online Lending), originally consisting of 96 items, which combine information about borrowers and information about the platform. Several implementation rules and guidelines that followed further operationalised regulatory expectations in this regard.

In sum, while significant variations in bespoke regulatory regimes may suggest no clear answer to the debate on mandatory disclosures in crowdfunding, a systematic review of empirical evidence in this study speaks against them. Mandatory disclosures do not resolve the issue of fundraisers not sufficiently using available hard information (they can potentially even worsen it in case investors find disclosures overwhelming), nor do they help increase the credibility of soft information that investors heavily rely on. The platforms seem better positioned than regulators to assess the appropriate level of disclosures, including experimenting with different disclosure practices over time. The prerequisite is that platforms see themselves as repeated players in the market with a reputation to build and maintain. This is something rules on crowdfunding can further support, as will be discussed later in relation to platform gatekeeping. Another argument against uniform disclosure rules is that different platforms can attract different types of fundraisers, for instance, catering to companies in different stages, with varying levels of innovation, or operating in specific industries. Furthermore, different financial contracts brokered on crowdfunding platforms may require companies to reveal different information. All these factors influence the variety of information investors need to assess different crowdfunding offers comprehensively. While the truthfulness of soft information remains an issue even under platform-level rules, different signalling mechanisms reviewed in Chap. 3 may be used to strengthen their credibility. As seen in Chap. 3, signals can substitute for detailed (complete) disclosures when disclosures are costly or can complement them when some information disclosed cannot be verified.

A counterargument can be that a safe harbour for regulators is to create disclosure rules that correspond to the minimum of (general-purpose) information like the intention was with summary disclosure documents (the KIIS in the ECSPR, for instance). At the outset, this appears like a regulatory intervention that cannot harm. After all, platforms can always require companies to disclose beyond regulatory requirements, including details specific to the type of projects the platform specialises in. Other than questioning whether such (minimum) disclosures serve their purpose (to enable informed decision-making), the peril is that they can anchor participants' expectations regarding the optimal level of disclosure. In other words, it may be difficult for platforms to move away from this (potentially inefficient) equilibrium. The platform would need to bargain over additional requirements with every prospective fundraiser, while different disclosure forms to be filled out and analysed can add complexity and confusion among market participants.

Furthermore, it should be mentioned that the online nature of this fundraising mechanism and its close interconnectedness with social media networks further reduce the value of any formal legal disclosures. Notably, information exchange on crowdfunding platforms is not limited to data provided at the beginning of the crowdfunding campaign but rather continues through updates and discussions during the campaign, as well as on related social media networks. The way information is framed in these additional channels of communication (which is likely to be unbalanced and biased if it originates from persons related to fundraisers) creates a greater risk of distorted decision-making than insufficient disclosures. Against this backdrop, as already mentioned, the online nature of disclosures facilitates verification of disclosed (hard) information (or increases the costs of misrepresentation for fundraisers), further reducing the need for formal certification of information inherent in disclosures mandated by the law. While platforms may not be able to resolve the issue of biased information available through these additional channels of communication, the design of portals may create a more convenient way to frame the most critical information in a way that is salient to investors (compared to formal mandatory disclosure forms).

A related question is whether trade-offs associated with mandatory disclosures change as the platform assumes some additional (ex-ante) reintermediation roles. It is straightforward to argue that the platform-choice model (Model F) makes information disclosures on the fundraiser level completely redundant. Investors delegate the choice of investment opportunities to the platform precisely because they do not want to invest resources into processing information independently. In contrast, the need for comprehensive information is greater in relation to investor choice models (Models A, B, C). Yet, in cases where the platform provides credit assessment and pricing, investors' reliance on these estimates reduces the benefit they generate from disclosed content.[54] Finally, concurrent-choice models, where the choice of investments is split between investors and the platforms (auto-investments), are likely to lead to a self-selection of investors, as explained earlier. The value of disclosures for manual investors can increase if sophisticated investors dominate this group, while disclosures may be of little use if manual investors primarily consist of individuals from the fundraiser's social network (as they rely on their proximate knowledge).

As a final remark, it should be emphasised that arguments against mandatory disclosures used here primarily relate to ex-ante disclosures since crowdfunding serves as a primary market. Crowdfunding regimes with mandatory regimes also focus on pre-investment information. A notable exception is the US, where fundraisers are also subject to ongoing disclosures after the financing round (Schwartz, 2023, pp. 114–116). Although no systematic evidence has been gathered yet in crowdfunding, one can contend that market-based mechanisms of information disclosures are likely to be considerably weaker ex-post, increasing the risk of moral hazard. This is a direct consequence of fundraisers not having proper incentives to disclose information voluntarily, as they no longer need to attract funds from investors. Platform incentives to impose ongoing disclosure standards are also undermined since they primarily earn fees as a percentage of total amounts raised (as discussed in Chap. 2, carry and exit fees are less common). Nonetheless, platforms that care about their long-term reputation and are, thus, interested in the long-term success of funded firms can introduce information duties in investment contracts, as captured by Hornuf et al. (2018). The key question again is whether investors make use of ongoing disclosures, which relates to their high costs of independent monitoring and the costs of collective action. Arguably, platforms that exercise investor rights ex-post internalise the monitoring function, making ongoing disclosures more meaningful. In sum, while mandatory disclosures ex-post seem more justified than ex-ante disclosures from the market failure perspective, it is questionable whether they would be used to discipline the management effectively. Their effects

[54] It should be noted, however, that these services are more common on lending-based platforms, where, as mentioned earlier, the costs of disclosures for consumer borrowers are fewer compared to business fundraisers.

are undoubtedly incomparable to ongoing disclosures in traditional markets, with numerous informed traders and financial analysts who make their earnings by acting upon them.

5.4.2 Regulating the Platform: Reinforcing the Gatekeeping Role

As pointed out, bespoke regimes typically create a new licence type for crowdfunding platforms and regulate their activity. The preliminary question is how to define the 'crowdfunding activity' and the scope of permissible services. In relation to these services, the regulatory dilemma is whether to mandate specific performance standards or merely require platforms to be transparent about how they perform them, allowing platforms to compete along these non-pricing dimensions.

The analysis throughout this study has shown that platforms voluntarily take on several different roles that bring them close to intermediaries in traditional finance. In exercising these roles, the danger is that they depart from what crowdfunding is supposed to represent: a mechanism of direct finance for individuals and SMEs. Therefore, the first role of crowdfunding regulations is to ensure that platforms operate within clear boundaries of the 'crowdfunding activity' and do not embark into the territory of financial intermediaries. This is something commonly observed in crowdfunding bespoke regimes. Regulations often define crowdfunding activity in terms of both permissible and forbidden services. In other words, they also determine what crowdfunding platforms are not allowed to do and what falls under the exclusive prerogatives of traditional institutions, such as banks or alternative investment funds.

For instance, the ECSPR provides that crowdfunding service providers should be prohibited from taking deposits or other repayable funds from the public unless they are also authorised as a credit institution (Regulation, 2020, recital 9). Similarly, it was explicitly stated that the authorisation obtained under [the ECSPR] should not grant crowdfunding service providers the right to provide individual or collective asset management services (Regulation, 2020, recital 19). Similar provisions are found in the Chinese crowdfunding rules.

While not necessarily incompatible with the core crowdfunding activity, some other platform services may unduly complicate the crowdfunding model and thus generate additional risks for market participants. These include, for instance, money handling and payment-related services or custody services. For this reason, some jurisdictions, notably the EU, ask platforms that do not hold specific licences to outsource these services to a licensed institution.

The more challenging part is delineating the crowdfunding activity from activities typically performed by traditional information intermediaries (gatekeepers), as discussed in Chaps. 2 and 3. If policymakers and regulators aim to create a 'neat' crowdfunding licence, allowing services that are clearly distinctive from services performed under traditional licences, then crowdfunding platforms would merely act as facilitators of online transactions between fundraisers and investors. Their activity would be limited to organising a neutral marketplace that enables information exchange and execution of contracts (in instances where the involvement of a platform is indispensable, such as when administering repayment of loans).

The key risks stemming from the operation of platforms relate to their neutrality as intermediaries, operational risks, and risks of a platform failure. Platform neutrality implies that neither the platform nor its related persons are affiliated with one of the fundraisers, incentivising them to create an advantageous position for these fundraisers vis-à-vis other offers. Yet, given that the platform has no role in pre-selecting offers nor presenting the information that fundraisers disclose to investors, the means by which any potential conflict of interest can materialise are limited (other than, for instance, manipulating the order in which offers are presented to investors). The neutrality of platforms can also be impaired if the platform or its related persons act as investors in offers listed on the portal, with the ability to 'cherry-pick' the most promising offers. These risks can be addressed by rules on conflict of interest, which can include different levels of precaution, notably disclosing the potential conflict of interest, managing the conflict of interest (if it occurs), or having procedures in place to prevent the occurrence of conflict of interest.

In addition, crowdfunding participants can be exposed to operational risks of platforms, such as 'delay or mistake in the information flow, processing, safekeeping, or administration (e.g., computer breakdown, mistake)' (European Commission, 2018, p. 14). To address these issues, crowdfunding regulations can mandate organisational requirements that prescribe internal procedures and processes that mitigate the probability for such risks to materialise. Moreover, the risk of a platform failure can prevent crowdfunding participants from collecting their funds during or after a crowdfunding campaign. This is an essential concern for platforms providing services of money handling and lending platforms that administer loan repayments and loss recovery. It is vital to ensure that these platforms have business continuity plans that ensure the ongoing provision of these services in case of a failure.

Overall, typical licensing requirements for the simplest model of crowdfunding platforms imply that they demonstrate their capacity to adhere to the above-described standards. They often include some light prudential requirements (minimum capital or insurance). In addition to the risks of platform operations, regulations can require platforms to implement different investor protection measures, as will be discussed in the next section.

Yet, such a narrow concept of a crowdfunding activity, treating platforms as websites where fundraising offers are listed, is unproductive. Foremost, it ignores several reintermediation services that emerged as a result of market forces, which can be material for reducing the information asymmetry between fundraisers and investors. As discussed in the previous section, it is possible to distinguish between reintermediation services that became an established market practice and 'auxiliary' services that are compatible with some models and not universally adopted. Concerning the first category of services, all platforms exercise some screening on investors' behalf, including due diligence (information collection and verification) and pre-selection of crowdfunding offers (platform onboarding), as discussed in Chaps. 2 and 3. Arguably, platforms are in a better position than individual investors to conduct these activities, not least because of gathered expertise and economies of scale, and they can save on unnecessary duplication costs. Consequently, there is no debate that such reintermediation services should be allowed despite an evident resemblance to traditional information intermediaries. A more contentious issue is whether platform due diligence and pre-selection practices should be mandated or encouraged by crowdfunding regulations, given that their quality varies across platforms (as discussed in Chap. 3). There are several important considerations. Platforms that aim to build and maintain a good reputation can induce a 'race to the top' regarding screening practices, which can support the argument that no intervention is necessary. Yet, due diligence services must be salient to investors for this to hold. Consequently, crowdfunding regulations can mandate platform transparency regarding prescreening activities, with the view of inducing market participants to choose the optimal level of platform prescreening and costs imposed on them (It is reasonable to assume that fees charged to fundraisers and less commonly to investors increase in the level of platform due diligence.). Moreover, a 'race to the top' scenario is unlikely if investors cannot verify whether platforms adhere to their declared screening efforts and pre-selection criteria. The issue is that long-term outcomes in crowdfunding (loan repayments, project success and exit in case of equity crowdfunding) take time to observe, and sometimes it is hard to link them to the ex-ante due diligence of platforms (or the lack thereof). As a result, crowdfunding regulations can require platforms to demonstrate their internal capacity to adhere to these standards as part of the licensing procedure or make them subject to ex-post supervision by regulators.

Even if the 'race to the top' regarding platform screening is arguably likely to emerge, this does not mean all platforms would be part of this race. Without strict prudential (capital) requirements, which would increase barriers to entry (and thus sunk costs of a crowdfunding activity), some new platforms can be short-term oriented, exercising little prescreening efforts. While they will not be able to compete with platforms that exercise more robust screening, their activity can cause harm to investors while still in business. Such concerns have motivated several scholars to argue for precise and robust gatekeeping duties of platforms (Ande & Eroglu, 2021, p. 559; Schwartz, 2018). Nonetheless, mandating platform gatekeeping responsibilities can vary from introducing minimal anti-fraud provisions to requiring more comprehensive checks. The latter involves ensuring the completeness, consistency, or even accuracy of information disclosed to investors (in particular when there are mandatory disclosure rules for fundraisers) or applying specific pre-selection criteria, which are more in the domain of investment choice (e.g., assessing the viability of a business plan or financial projections, accepting loan applications with predefined credit scores).

As seen from a comparative perspective, regulators' expectations are divergent. Some jurisdictions, like the UK, encourage 'the race to the top' scenario without prescribing minimum due diligence efforts. Namely, in its Policy Statement on crowdfunding, the FCA explicitly clarified that no due diligence standards are set, allowing platforms to 'determine risks present in their business models and to develop appropriate processes to deal with them' (Financial Conduct Authority, 2014, p. 15). Yet, the FCA also requires platforms to be transparent about 'whether or not any due diligence has been carried out on an investee company, the extent of the due diligence, and the outcome of any analysis' (Financial Conduct Authority, 2014, p. 42). Similarly, in relation to P2P lending platforms, the rules require the platform to describe 'its role in facilitating P2P agreements', including 'the nature and extent of due diligence the [platform] undertakes in respect of borrowers' (Financial Conduct Authority, 2019, 18.12.24). It should be noted, however, that the apparent hands-off approach to due diligence of the UK regulator should not be taken for granted. The rules also require platforms to ensure that all financial promotions are 'fair, clear, and not misleading' (Financial Conduct Authority, 2014, p. 42), which would suggest that platforms are nevertheless required to verify the accuracy of information contained in fundraisers' disclosures. Before the ECSPR, several EU Member States (Belgium, Italy, and Lithuania) also prescribed no minimum due diligence requirements but required platforms to disclose procedures and criteria for selecting fundraisers (European Commission, 2018, p. 85). While transparency requirements are intended to make the due diligence process more salient, the limitation of the solution in the jurisdictions mentioned above is that investors are also expected to assess whether platforms adhere to promised standards, which is not always plausible.

A more common approach among regulators is explicitly prescribing some minimum due diligence requirements while allowing platforms to carry out more extensive prescreening at their discretion. A notable example is New Zealand. Platforms must exclude 'companies that they discover have been engaging in deceptive conduct, or which have made a false, misleading, or unsubstantiated representation' (Ande & Eroglu, 2021, p. 578).

In addition, platforms need to disclose their eligibility criteria, the scope of checks and assessments conducted, including a description of information collected on each fundraiser and its related persons (e.g., directors or managers) (Ande & Eroglu, 2021, p. 579). It is worthwhile mentioning that platforms are also required to demonstrate their capacity to adhere to the announced pre-selection criteria as part of the licensing process, avoiding the need for investors to carry out such an assessment (Ande & Eroglu, 2021, p. 586).

In some instances, instead of allowing for platform competition, regulations mandate high due diligence standards. A noteworthy example is the ECSPR. The way due diligence is defined in the text, it appears that the requirements are minimal. Platforms must bring 'evidence that the project owner has no criminal record regarding infringements of national commercial law [...]' and that 'the project owner that seeks to be funded through the crowdfunding platform is not established in a non-cooperative jurisdiction [...]' (Regulation, 2020, Art. 5). However, a more burdensome screening requirement exists for the KIIS. Platforms are required to 'have in place and apply adequate procedures to verify the completeness, correctness, and clarity of the information contained in the [KIIS]' (Regulation, 2020, Art.

23 (11)).[55] In drafting this requirement, the European legislator abandoned a common solution among EU Member States (e.g., Austria, Spain, France), which only required platforms to check the completeness and consistency of disclosure documents and not to verify their accuracy. Interestingly, the ECSPR does not require platforms to disclose procedures and criteria used for selecting project owners, which would allow for an easier comparison of any additional prescreening activities of platforms.

In sum, some minimum due diligence requirements (such as ensuring that fundraisers are not fraudulent) are necessary to spur investor confidence in the market and prevent small and unknown platforms from exploiting the mismatch in investor expectations and their practices. Regarding other due diligence and pre-selection activities, regulations encouraging platform competition are preferable over high due diligence standards. The reason is that a platform's high screening intensity is not necessarily optimal. It can generate high operating costs for platforms, which ultimately pass them on to market participants, undermining the idea of crowdfunding as a cost-effective means of raising finance. Even if such expenses are only passed on to fundraisers and not investors, some good-quality fundraisers can leave the market, thus harming investors as well.

Mandating platforms to verify the accuracy of all information fundraisers disclose to investors has one additional caveat in jurisdictions where no mandatory disclosure regime exists (which is the preferred option in line with arguments brought in this study). Platforms introducing their own rules on disclosure can reduce the amount of information available to investors, fearing that they can be liable for any misstatements that are costly to verify. Overall, suppose instead of mandating high standards, regulations aim to spur competition on the quality of screening practices. In that case, it is nevertheless vital to make due diligence practices transparent and easy to compare and for regulators to check whether platforms comply with their claims. As illustrated above, the bespoke crowdfunding regime in New Zealand appears to be an excellent example of such an approach.[56]

A final remark on screening relates to the involvement of a lead investor. As mentioned throughout this study, the role of lead investors can be substantial, yet their recognition in crowdfunding regulations is rare. While the reputation of lead investors should warrant the quality of their screening, platforms can nevertheless be required to ensure that the same conduct or transparency standards apply to them.

---

[55] ESMA subsequently clarified that the responsibility of platforms in relation to the KIIS is limited to 'having adequate procedures to verify the completeness, correctness, and clarity of the information' and not the actual content of the KIIS (European Securities and Markets Authority, 2023, p. 24).

[56] Arguably, the same approach should be applied to disclosure rules for fundraisers mandated by platforms. As contended before, regulations should not mandate disclosures since platforms are better positioned to set these standards, balancing the costs to fundraisers and benefits to investors. Nonetheless, regulations can induce competition on the design of disclosure requirements at the platform level, by requiring platforms to publish clearly their disclosure requirements.

As discussed in the previous section, some other (ex-ante) reintermediation services (credit assessment, pricing, and auto-investments) are not universally adopted, and their different combinations can lead to varying risks for investors. As also pointed out earlier, regulators must decide whether to allow them in the first place, given the risk of creating an uneven playing field for similar services provided by crowdfunding platforms and traditional gatekeepers. Moreover, as the source of information asymmetry shifts from fundraisers to platforms, the decision should also be based on estimates of whether it is possible to assure a certain level of service quality so that investors are ultimately better off.

The quality of all three service types depends on mitigating the risk of conflict of interest and the risk related to the technology employed. Credit risk assessment, pricing, and auto-investments are all services which create room for platform discretion, making them more susceptible to conflict of interest. In other words, they increase the likelihood that platforms will unduly stir investors' money into funding individuals or projects related to the platform or its associated persons. Thus, their provision potentially undermines the ability to act as a neutral intermediary, which is fundamental to the crowdfunding concept. This issue is not new. Finding optimal ways of mitigating conflict of interest has been at the heart of regulators' concerns with respect to traditional gatekeepers (Moloney et al., 2015). Therefore, if allowed, the auxiliary reintermediation services in crowdfunding should trigger more stringent rules on conflict of interest.

Regarding the technology-related risk, the difference should be made between credit risk assessment and pricing, on the one hand, and auto-investments, on the other. Credit risk assessment and pricing are two sides of the same coin. The critical issue is whether platforms' algorithms (using machine learning, AI, or other data processing techniques) use appropriate data and whether they are calibrated to render their estimates accurately. Yet, as seen in Chap. 2 and further discussed in the previous section, some platforms offer the service of risk grading while leaving the pricing decision to market participants. This was more common in developed P2P lending markets a few years ago but can be a timely issue in newly emerging markets. Platforms may decide not to assess the interest rate directly because they know their credit assessment is not as sophisticated as it should be (for instance, because the programme has been recently introduced and requires further training or adjustment). They want to allow investors to price in other valuable information, including their soft (proximate) knowledge about fundraisers. Thus, platform risk grades are used more as anchors than precise credit risk estimates. To allow platforms more flexibility in designing their programmes and improving their performance over time (such has been the case with two leading P2P platforms in the US (Vallee & Zeng, 2019)), regulations should not be overly prescriptive regarding the quality of credit assessment on these platforms. Yet, it should be noted that relaxing quality standards is only justified when investors make decisions themselves and, thus, use the additional information on borrowers (Model B), but not when platforms are also allowed to invest on their behalf (Model E), as will be discussed later.

In contrast, platforms providing both credit grades (and subgrades) and setting interest rates, which are non-negotiable for market participants, undermine the incentives for investors to make their estimates, further reducing the value of any adjacent information provided on borrowers (Models C, F, and G). Thus, the standards regarding the quality of technology employed by these platforms should be high. The question is how to ensure that these high standards are met. Mandating transparency regarding the data sources, methodology, or technical details of algorithms, arguably increasing competition among platforms along this dimension, is unlikely to generate desirable results. In contrast to platform due diligence and preselection criteria, which are easily digestible by investors, technical details of algorithms are difficult to understand for most investors, let alone compare their predictive capacity across different platforms or assess whether described procedures and standards were respected in practice. While long-term oriented platforms can have incentives to adhere to the highest level of quality available at the time as investors will be able to perceive it ex-post, as already discussed, such accountability requires a substantial amount of time during which low-quality platforms can harm investors. Moreover, many credit risk algorithms are proprietary—revealing too many details on how exactly they work can undermine platforms' competitive advantage, reducing their incentives to invest further in research and development. Thus, these arguments speak in favour of more prescriptive regulations. The caveat is that regulators often lack the necessary expertise to set the appropriate standards and, more importantly, to update legal texts as the technology advances regularly. Thus, the regulatory lag is likely to be significant. As an alternative, a more appropriate solution would be to delegate this task to the industry self regulatory organisations (as seen in Chap. 5).[57] Depending on the powers of the industry organisation, the adherence to these standards can be checked by associations (or an independent third party they hire) or the regulator.

For platforms offering the service of automatic investments, the question of conflict of interest and technology are intertwined. The critical concern here is to minimise the room for platform discretion, which should make investment choices strictly following the mandate provided by individual investors (regarding the risk, interest rate, industry, or other characteristics of loans). In other words, it is vital to ensure that the platform invests investors' funds in the same manner they would have done themselves had they had the same information and the information processing capacity in their best interest. Thus, the first regulatory issue is ensuring that the mandate is clearly (and narrowly) defined. The second regulatory issue is providing that the platform strictly follows this mandate. This entails ensuring that the platform algorithm has no technological flaws that would cause undue mistakes and is not intentionally calibrated to favour specific borrowers over others. These two regulatory issues are pertinent to all auto-investment models (Models D, E, F, G).

Presuming that issues regarding the individual investor mandate are absent, the ultimate outcome for investors will depend on the information used by the platform algorithm to allocate the funds, as mentioned in the previous section. Put

[57] Delegating the task of setting standards has also been observed in some other areas of fintech, such as APIs and open banking (Odorović, 2023).

differently, the auto-bidding functionality will be as good as the information it relies upon—investor choices of other investors or credit assessment/credit pricing provided by the platform. If the automatic investment tool merely mimics the choices of other investors (Model D), no additional regulatory requirements are needed. Yet, if the platform uses its own estimates (credit assessment/and pricing) to allocate investors' assets (Models E, F, G), the quality of technology employed becomes paramount for investment outcomes. Thus, a pertinent question is whether rules governing these models should go beyond what is already prescribed when platform credit assessment/and pricing are available to investors who make their own decisions (Models B and C). As has already been argued, in all instances when the platform provides both credit assessment and pricing, regulations should ensure that high technology standards are met. Therefore, no additional requirements regarding the technology employed should be required merely because the auto-investment service is combined with platform pricing. Yet, regarding platform models where only credit rating but not pricing is offered, it has been contended that regulatory standards should not be overly prescriptive since investors can also use other information to assess loan applications. However, this reasoning does not hold if the platform relies on these indicative (and potentially imprecise) estimates to allocate investors' funds. In such instances, high-quality credit assessments should be ensured (analogous to what has been proposed concerning platform pricing).

The final remark regarding platform reintermediation services relates to concurrent-choice models (D, E, F), where both manual and automatic bids are enabled. As already discussed, these models raise the issue of whether manual investors are harmed because of automatic bids (e.g., because there is less information available or because mechanisms of rational herding are weakened). One way to mitigate the potential source of harm is to set the maximum percentage of funds originating from auto-investments for each offer, as some platforms have experimented with. Yet, another issue with concurrent models may require precisely the opposite regulatory intervention. As seen before, concurrent models raise an issue that manual bidders are chosen by well-informed (sophisticated) investors who outperform the platform algorithm and, thus, can crowd out from best offers investors who rely on auto-investment tools (presumably, retail investors). Therefore, if regulators care about this concern, they should consider prescribing the maximum percentage of funds originating from manual bids. Yet, it should be noted that neither of the two considerations provides any indication of what this percentage threshold should be. Its arbitrability can potentially prevent some offers from reaching their funding target, and it should be chosen carefully (Table 5.2).

Overall, the proposed regulatory model aims to propose a tailored response to distinct risk levels inherent in crowdfunding reintermediation services and their combinations. As mentioned, regulators and policymakers should decide whether to allow each of these models and whether there is a need to apply a unique set of rules to them, bearing in mind the prevailing market practice is their jurisdiction.

Table 5.2 Proposed regulatory requirements for platforms providing reintermediation services

Requirements Model	Strict rules on conflict of interest	High-quality technology employed	Rules on defining and respecting individual investor mandate	Rules on the percentage of funds originating from automatic/manual investments
Investor choice (B)	✓			
Investor choice (C)	✓	✓		
Concurrent choice (D)	✓		✓	✓
Concurrent choice (E)	✓	✓	✓	✓
Concurrent choice (F)	✓	✓	✓	✓
Platform choice (G)	✓	✓	✓	

5.4.3 *Investor Paternalism: Tailoring Retail-Investor Safeguards*

While this study has devoted much attention to the regulation of fundraisers and platforms, investor paternalism has been one of the defining features of bespoke crowdfunding regimes worldwide. Investor paternalism can be understood as different rules aiming to protect investors by interfering with their freedom of choice. It resides on the idea that investors' decisions should be guided (nudged) in the direction that is presumably in their best interest or even constrained when they threaten to cause them significant harm. It is easy to understand why bespoke crowdfunding regulations include an array of solutions whose purpose is to limit investors' risk exposure or even dissuade them from using crowdfunding in the first place. As discussed earlier, the uniqueness of crowdfunding is that it enables direct investments of small retail investors into asset classes that have been reserved for professional investors and affluent individuals since the emergence of entrepreneurship (or the concept of limited liability companies). Regulators and policymakers, being sceptical about the efficiency of market-based mechanisms of investor protection (as discussed throughout this study) and their own regulatory tools constraining the behaviour of fundraisers and platforms, thought the best approach would be to directly regulate the behaviour of investors. It should be mentioned, however, that rules that regulate investor behaviour are often phrased as obligations of platforms because they are required to ensure that specific (retail) investor protection safeguards are met. Another aspect to keep in mind is that similar investor protections are standard in the domain of consumer finance, which presumes that retail investors are concluding contracts with persons acting in their professional capacity (specialising in the provision of financial services) rather than other individuals or startups and SMEs (as already discussed in relation to protection of borrowers, albeit from an opposite perspective).

Regulatory solutions typically include three distinct measures—risk warnings, investment limits, and appropriateness tests. They differ in whether they are meant to make certain risks more salient to investors (recommendation-based, imposing soft investor limits) or effectively limit investor choice (constraint-based, imposing hard investor limits).

The first measure is warnings about how crowdfunding works and the risks involved. In particular, they are meant to draw investor attention to the fact that they may not receive any return and that even all of the capital invested is at risk (and that investors should not be investing more than what they can afford to lose as usual banking deposit or investment compensation schemes are not applicable). Risk warnings are sometimes provided before an investor can see specific crowdfunding offers or before investing. In some jurisdictions, risk warnings are more tailored to particular models, such as when the platform has to warn investors about risks inherent in the financial contract intermediated (or any associated investor rights). Moreover, these risk warnings are sometimes used to inform investors about the exact role that the platform has in the crowdfunding process and investor rights stemming from crowdfunding regulations (e.g., cooling-off period during which investors can withdraw their offers). Investors are usually asked to acknowledge that they have understood these warnings. Given that they are neither costly to implement nor limitative, including risk warnings in bespoke regimes is seldom contested. A more critical issue is how to frame them so that they do not represent mere box-ticking but rather induce prospective investors to process the information contained in them.

Other paternalistic measures can be designed as both constraint-based and recommendation-based, and comparative regulatory practice provides numerous examples of both types. Most jurisdictions with bespoke regulations have introduced retail investor limits (one notable exception is New Zealand (Ande & Eroglu, 2021, p. 580)). They are meant to directly constrain retail investor risk exposure to specific crowdfunding offers or crowdfunding as a highly risky asset class. Put differently, investor limits can be designed as the relative or absolute amount of funds an investor is allowed (or recommended) to invest in a single crowdfunding offer or across all crowdfunding offers, typically in 12 months.

An example of a hard investor cap that applies to all crowdfunding offers as an asset class is the US. The JOBS Act introduced several retail investor limits that increase with an investor's annual income or net worth. The limit is set at USD 2000 or 5% of the investor's annual income or net worth if that is less than USD 100,000, or at 10% if the annual income or net worth is above USD 100,000 (Ande & Eroglu, 2021, p. 584). An example of a hard investor cap that applies to a single crowdfunding offer is Australia, although the threshold is set relatively high, at AUD 10,000 (Ande & Eroglu, 2021, p. 584).

An example of a soft investor cap that applies to all crowdfunding offers is the UK. According to the FCA rules, retail investors need to certify that they will not invest more than 10% of their net investible assets in non-readily realisable securities (Financial Conduct Authority, 2019, 4.7.10). An example of a soft investor cap that applies to both the total amount of funds invested in crowdfunding offers and individual offers is the ECSPR. It provides that retail investors must simulate their ability to bear losses (calculated as 10% of their net worth) (Regulation, 2020, Art. 21(5)) and that the platform explicitly advises them not to invest above this amount (Regulation, 2020, Art. 23, (6) (c)). Moreover, every time investors accept an individual offer, investing an amount that exceeds the higher of either EUR 1000 or 5% of their net worth, they receive an additional warning, after which they must provide consent for an investment to be made (Regulation, 2020, Art. 21(7)).

In a close connection to this, platforms are sometimes required to conduct some kind of an appropriateness test (in MiFID terms), whose role is to ensure that investors have the adequate knowledge and experience relevant to investing via a crowdfunding platform. Again, rules can be framed as constraints or recommendations. For instance, the UK framework mandates platforms to check investors' knowledge and experience to understand the risks involved before providing them access to investment opportunities, that is, communicating direct offer financial promotion (Financial Conduct Authority, 2019, 4.7.7). In contrast, the appropriateness test in the ESCPR is more flexible, requiring platforms to only issue a warning to clients who did not demonstrate sufficient knowledge and experience and further require such clients to consent to a form in which they acknowledge having understood the consequences (Regulation, 2020, Art. 21(4)).

Several arguments support the view that recommendation-based rather than constraint-based rules are preferred in the crowdfunding context. The first one is not specific to crowdfunding, and it is based on the premise that there are many domains outside finance where individuals enjoy greater freedom of choice that are potentially far more harmful (e.g., gambling). The conventional counterargument is that the difference from these domains is the general perception of them as dangerous, as opposed to certain market segments in finance (such as crowdfunding), which are considered legitimate or safe. Nonetheless, such safety perception bias can be mitigated by adequate risk warnings while not limiting the investor's freedom of choice. The second, more pragmatic argument is that it is costly for platforms to enforce some of these rules, such as when investor limits apply to crowdfunding instruments as an asset class, and the platform has almost no means to verify the amounts investors have pledged on other platforms. Another issue is that investors trying to circumvent hard limits can misstate facts to portray their situation as more favourable. Regulations can mandate platforms to require investors to bring evidence of their income or wealth, but this appears too costly for young tech firms with limited human resources.

Regarding specific paternalistic measures, an investment limit on the total amount of crowdfunding investments should be a preferred option over an investment limit on individual offers. In investor choice and concurrent models where investors make their own investment decisions, caps that apply to individual offers can unduly reduce investors' incentives to conduct their due diligence. In other words, such limits can reinforce what is considered one of the main weaknesses of crowdfunding. In auto-investment models, caps on individual offers appear meaningless since the algorithm automatically diversifies the investor portfolio across many offers.

The way knowledge tests are designed in practice reduces their value for actual investment outcomes. They are typically conceptualised in a way that checks investors' understanding of risks in crowdfunding (and the consequences of, for instance, holding an undiversified portfolio). They do not necessarily check investors' ability to make reasonable estimates of the risks and opportunities of individual offers. As such, they are appropriate for auto-investment models but not necessarily for investor choice models. The rationale for not providing a more stringent test can lie in different market-based mechanisms of overcoming information asymmetry, which do not require investors to comprehensively assess each offer (as discussed, these include proximate knowledge, various signals, and platform prescreening).

5.5 Summary of Findings

This chapter provided an analysis of different regulatory approaches to crowdfunding and their role in underpinning market-based mechanisms of overcoming asymmetric information. It started by analysing early and more recent responses under the framework described as the 'regulatory tetralemma in regulating crowdfunding'. The framework includes four approaches: no regulation, extending the rules conceived for traditional financial services, learning and experimentation, and bespoke regulations. The baseline scenario of no regulations applicable to crowdfunding platforms allows crowdfunding to emerge and develop only if other market participants (fundraisers and investors) are not subject to restrictive rules governing banking monopoly and offering securities and financial instruments to the public. Platforms escaping regulatory oversight can create legal uncertainty for all market participants and potentially perform services reserved for financial intermediaries.

As an alternative, many jurisdictions extended rules for traditional financial services (banking, payments, investment firms, AIFM, and credit intermediaries) to crowdfunding platforms. Given that crowdfunding services do not neatly fit any of the existing licences, this approach has caused several issues, including regulatory arbitrage, the necessity to rent a licence or partner with an established institution, and neglecting some crowdfunding-specific risks.

Some regulators have acknowledged the weaknesses of the first two approaches and adopted regulatory innovation initiatives to deal with fintech innovation more generally (in particular, innovation offices and regulatory sandboxes). The idea behind these structural changes within the regulatory agency is to spur learning and experimentation for market participants and the regulator while ensuring that the most critical consumer safeguards are met. In particular, several regulatory sandboxes worldwide have had a crowdfunding-thematic focus, allowing regulators and policymakers to create a tailored regulatory response.

Finally, many jurisdictions adopted bespoke crowdfunding frameworks, often driven by opposing considerations. Bespoke rules are typically based on the exemptions from rules applicable to banking, public offerings of securities, and licensing of investment firms. They also usually include a unique set of rules that govern the behaviour of fundraisers, platforms, and investors.

The diversity of crowdfunding regulations raises the question of what optimal rules should be in light of findings on market-based mechanisms explored in previous chapters. Consequently, the analysis in this chapter further explored which crowdfunding models should be included within the scope of bespoke regulations, given the differences in risk they generate for market participants. It was shown that the crowdfunding models could be differentiated along three risk categories—the type of financial contracts brokered on crowdfunding platforms (e.g., loans vs. securities), the type of fundraisers, and reintermediation services exercised by some crowdfunding platforms. It was argued that the type of crowdfunding contract should not drive a substantial difference in the regulatory approach unless it also coincides with the differences in services offered by platforms. Put differently, more inclusive regulatory frameworks (such as in the UK and to a lesser extent in the EU) should be favoured as opposed to frameworks focusing on a subset of financial contracts in crowdfunding (not least because some of the existing national frameworks suggest that the scope was determined based on the split in the regulatory remit between regulatory agencies rather than risk-related considerations).

In contrast, special provisions governing P2P consumer lending can be justified on the grounds that borrowers should also benefit from consumer protection safeguards analogously to those existing in traditional finance. It was further discussed why such an approach was not often embraced. While putting different crowdfunding models under one regulatory umbrella appears sensible, the analysis further supports the view that a unique set of rules should govern the provision of some auxiliary crowdfunding services. Drawing on findings in Chaps. 2 and 3, these services allow crowdfunding platforms to reintermediate the market, shifting the source of information asymmetry from fundraisers to platforms. Particular attention should be paid to ex-ante reintermediation services, notably credit assessment, pricing, and auto-investments. It was shown that the unique combinations of these services lead to eight different crowdfunding models, each corresponding to a distinct risk level and associated threats to investor protection.

Drawing on these considerations, as well as other findings on market-based mechanisms discussed in previous chapters, the analysis further explores some critical issues in regulating the behaviour of fundraisers, platforms, and investors. It was contended that crowdfunding rules should not impose 'lighter' mandatory disclosures on fundraisers, as they are not expected to resolve the potential source of market failure, as shown in Chap. 3. Notably, the previous analysis showed that, while investors are responsive to differences in the level of disclosures, they often fail to apprehend all the available hard data and put much emphasis on soft (unverifiable) data, which is often non-credible or even misleading. It was contended that platforms are in a better position to choose the optimal level of disclosures for fundraisers, not least because of the differences in the type of fundraisers, financial contracts, and other areas of platform specialisation. Mandatory disclosures are an even less sensible approach vis-à-vis crowdfunding models where platforms offer reintermediation services.

Nonetheless, ex-post (ongoing) mandatory disclosures deserve more thoughtful consideration, given that market-based mechanisms are weaker after the completion of a financing round. In contrast, platform-level rules should reinforce the platform gatekeeping role. This implies delineating the platform role from financial intermediaries, defining essential rules applicable to all crowdfunding platforms, and deciding on the scope and rules governing the provision of auxiliary reintermediation services (also taking into consideration their similarities to services offered by traditional information intermediaries). One of the central questions is how to regulate platform prescreening (due diligence and platform selection criteria), given the differences in the quality of this service across platforms. The prescriptive approach is only reasonable concerning the minimum level of investor protection (e.g., anti-fraud provisions). At the same time, other prescreening services should be left to platform competition while ensuring that such competition does take place (by mandating platforms' transparency vis-à-vis services they offer and regulatory checks that promised standards are met). As to the auxiliary reintermediation services, it was argued that additional rules are required to govern their provision, introducing a risk-based approach to crowdfunding regulation. A proposed framework includes several additional platform obligations, which apply selectively to distinct crowdfunding models, depending on the combination of reintermediation services that platforms provide. Lastly, the analysis discussed different measures of investor paternalism in crowdfunding regulations, arguing in favour of a recommendation-based rather than a constraint-based approach.

References

Alibrandi, A. S., & Grossule, E. (2022). Crowdfunding and consumer credit protection in the EU. In E. Macchiavello (Ed.), *Regulation on European crowdfunding service providers for business* (pp. 591–606). Edward Elgar Publishing. https://doi.org/10.4337/9781802209945.00052

Allen, H. J. (2019). Regulatory sandboxes. *George Washington Law Review, 87*, 579–645. https://doi.org/10.2139/ssrn.3056993

Allen, H. J. (2022). Regulatory innovation and permission to fail: The case of suptech. *New York University Journal of Law & Business, 19*, 237–308. https://doi.org/10.2139/ssrn.4239079

Anagnostopoulos, I. (2018). Fintech and regtech: Impact on regulators and banks. *Journal of Economics and Business, 100*, 7–25. https://doi.org/10.1016/j.jeconbus.2018.07.003

Ande, J. A., & Eroglu, Z. K. (2021). Could New Zealand's equity crowdfunding regulations be the model for the developing world? *New Zealand Universities Law Review, 29*, 557–592. Retrieved from https://ssrn.com/abstract=3904063

Ang, A., & Kwek, S. (2020). Regulation of crowdfunding in Singapore. *Business Law International, 21*(1), 59–68. Retrieved from https://heinonline.org/HOL/LandingPage?handle=hein.journals/blawintnl21&div=9&id=&page=

Armour, J., Awrey, D., Davies, P. L., Enriques, L., Gordon, J. N., Mayer, C. P., & Payne, J. (2016). *Principles of financial regulation*. Oxford University Press. https://doi.org/10.1093/acprof:oso/9780198786474.001.0001

Arner, D. W., Barberis, J., & Buckley, R. P. (2015). The evolution of Fintech: A new post-crisis paradigm. *Georgetown Journal of International Law, 47*, 1271–1319. Retrieved from https://heinonline.org/HOL/LandingPage?handle=hein.journals/geojintl47&div=41&id=&page=

Aschenbeck-Florange, T., Blair, D., Beltran, J., Garcia, A., Nagel, T., Piattelli, U., Quintavalla, L., & Gajda, O. (2013). *Regulation of crowdfunding in Germany, the UK, Spain and Italy and the impact of the European single market*. European Crowdfunding Network. Retrieved from https://www.taxlawplanet.it/wp-content/uploads/20130610_Regulation_of_Crowdfunding_ECN_OC.pdf

Australian Securities and Investments Commission. (2020). *Comparison of key features of the ASIC sandbox and the Australian Government's enhanced regulatory sandbox*. Retrieved from https://download.asic.gov.au/media/5763135/comparison-asic-sandbox-enhanced-regulatory-sandbox-published-25-august-2020.pdf

Autorité de Contrôle Prudentiel. (2013). *Autorité des marchés financiers, & Autorité de contrôle prudentiel. Guide du financement participatif (crowdfunding) à destination des plates-formes et des porteurs de projet. Autorité des marchés financiers*. Retrieved from https://www.amf--france.org/sites/institutionnel/files/contenu_simple/guide/guide_professionnel/Guide%20du%20financement%20participatif%20%28Crowdfunding%29%20a%20destination%20des%20plates-formes%20et%20des%20porteurs%20de%20projet.pdf

Azzutti, A., Ringe, W.-G., & Stiehl, H. S. (2021). Machine learning, market manipulation, and collusion on capital markets: Why the "black box" matters. *University of Pennsylvania Journal of International Law, 43*, 79–135. Retrieved from https://heinonline.org/HOL/LandingPage?handle=hein.journals/upjiel43&div=6&id=&page=

Bakos, Y., Marotta-Wurgler, F., & Trossen, D. R. (2014). Does anyone read the fine print? Consumer attention to standard-form contracts. *The Journal of Legal Studies, 43*(1), 1–35. https://doi.org/10.1086/674424

Bar-Gill, O. (2012). *Seduction by contract: Law, economics, and psychology in consumer markets*. Oxford University Press. https://doi.org/10.1093/acprof:oso/9780199663361.001.0001

Bar-Gill, O., & Board, O. (2012). Product-use information and the limits of voluntary disclosure. *American Law and Economics Review, 14*(1), 235–270. https://doi.org/10.1093/aler/ahr021

Benlala, M. A. (2023). Exploring risks and issues related to policy making and regulation in FinTech. *Perspectives of Law and Public Administration, 12*, 249–255. Retrieved from https://heinonline.org/HOL/Page?public=true&handle=hein.journals/perbularna12&div=32&start_page=249&collection=journals&set_as_cursor=0&men_tab=srchresults

Benoit, S., Colliard, J.-E., Hurlin, C., & Pérignon, C. (2017). Where the risks lie: A survey on systemic risk. *Review of Finance, 21*(1), 109–152. https://doi.org/10.1093/rof/rfw026

Bogdani, E., Causholli, M., & Knechel, W. R. (2022). The role of assurance in equity crowdfunding. *The Accounting Review, 97*(2), 51–76. https://doi.org/10.2308/TAR-2019-0427

Böhme, R., & Grossklags, J. (2013). Trading agent kills market information: Evidence from online social lending. In Y. Chen & N. Immorlica (Eds.), *Web and internet economics (WINE 2013)* (pp. 68–81). Springer.

Bomberger, L. (2021). The OCC FinTech charter and the bank holding company act. *University of Miami Business Law Review, 29*(2), 1–30. Retrieved from https://heinonline.org/HOL/LandingPage?handle=hein.journals/umblr29&div=13&id=&page=

Born, B. (2011). Deregulation: A major cause of the financial crisis. *Harvard Law & Policy Review, 5*(231), 242–243. Retrieved from https://heinonline.org/HOL/LandingPage?handle=hein.journals/harlpolrv5&div=17&id=&page=

Bradford, C. S. (2012). Crowdfunding and the federal securities laws. *Columbia Business Law Review, 1*, 1–150. Retrieved from https://heinonline.org/HOL/LandingPage?handle=hein.journals/colb2012&div=4&id=&page=

Bromberg, L., Godwin, A., & Ramsay, I. (2017). Fintech sandboxes: Achieving a balance between regulation and innovation. *Journal of Banking and Finance Law and Practice, 28*(4), 314–336. Retrieved from https://papers.ssrn.com/sol3/papers.cfm?abstract_id=3090844#

Brummer, C. (2015). Disruptive technology and securities regulation. *Fordham Law Review, 84*(3), 977–1052. Retrieved from https://heinonline.org/HOL/LandingPage?handle=hein.journals/flr84&div=44&id=&page=

Brummer, C., & Yadav, Y. (2018). Fintech and the innovation trilemma. *Georgetown Law Journal, 107*(2), 235–308. Retrieved from https://heinonline.org/HOL/LandingPage?handle=hein.journals/glj107&div=12&id=&page=

Buchak, G., Matvos, G., Piskorski, T., & Seru, A. (2018). Fintech, regulatory arbitrage, and the rise of shadow banks. *Journal of Financial Economics, 130*(3), 453–483. https://doi.org/10.1016/j.jfineco.2018.03.011

Butticè, V., Di Pietro, F., & Tenca, F. (2020). Is equity crowdfunding always good? Deal structure and the attraction of venture capital investors. *Journal of Corporate Finance, 65*, 101773. https://doi.org/10.1016/j.jcorpfin.2020.101773

Capdeville, J. L. (2015). La réforme du crowdfunding en droit français: Les aspects du droit bancaire. *Revue Générale Du Droit, 4*, 1–10. Retrieved from https://www.revuegeneraledudroit.eu/wp-content/uploads/ER2015_4.pdf

Chaffee, E. C., & Rapp, G. C. (2012). Regulating online peer-to-peer lending in the aftermath of Dodd–frank: In search of an evolving regulatory regime for an evolving industry. *Washington and Lee Law Review, 69*(2), 485–533. Retrieved from https://heinonline.org/HOL/LandingPage?handle=hein.journals/waslee69&div=17&id=&page=

Chen, C., Li, G., Fan, L., & Qin, J. (2021). The impact of automated investment on peer-to-peer lending: Investment behavior and platform efficiency. *Journal of Global Information Management, 29*(6), 1–22. https://doi.org/10.4018/JGIM.20211101.oa36

Chen, X., & Ma, L. (2023). Lead investors' insider ownership and crowd investors' agency concerns in investor-led equity crowdfunding. *Pacific-Basin Finance Journal, 78*, 101978. https://doi.org/10.1016/j.pacfin.2023.101978

Chirulli, P. (2021). FinTech, RegTech and SupTech: Institutional challenges to the supervisory architecture of the financial markets. In I. Chiu & G. Deipenbrock (Eds.), *Routledge handbook of financial technology and law* (pp. 447–464). Routledge. Retrieved from https://www.taylorfrancis.com/chapters/edit/10.4324/9780429325670-24/fintech-regtech-suptech-paola-chirulli

Coakley, J., Cumming, D. J., Lazos, A., & Vismara, S. (2021). Enfranchising the crowd: Nominee account equity crowdfunding. *CFS Working Paper Series, 664*, 1–45. https://doi.org/10.2139/ssrn.3830741

Coakley, J., & Lazos, A. (2021). New developments in equity crowdfunding: A review. *Review of Corporate Finance, 1*(3-4), 341–405. https://doi.org/10.1561/114.00000008

Colaert, V. (2016). On the absence of peer-to-peer lending in Belgium. *Journal of European Consumer and Market Law, 5*, 182–189. Retrieved from https://heinonline.org/HOL/LandingPage?handle=hein.kluwer/jeucml0005&div=46&id=&page

Cumming, D., & Hornuf, L. (2022). Marketplace lending of small- and medium-sized enterprises. *Strategic Entrepreneurship Journal, 16*(1), 32–66. https://doi.org/10.1002/sej.1411

Darmon, E., Oriol, N., & Rufini, A. (2022). Bids for speed: An empirical study of investment strategy automation in a peer-to-business lending platform. *Decision Support Systems, 156*, 113732. https://doi.org/10.1016/j.dss.2022.113732

Directive. (2003). *2003/71/EC of the European Parliament and of the Council of 4 November 2003 on the Prospectus to Be Published When Securities Are Offered to the Public or Admitted to Trading and Amending Directive 2001/34/EC*. Retrieved from https://eur-lex.europa.eu/legal-content/EN/TXT/PDF/?uri=CELEX:32003L0071

Directive. (2004). *2004/39/EC of the European Parliament and of the Council of 21 April 2004 on Markets in Financial Instruments Amending Council Directives 85/611/EEC and 93/6/EEC and Directive 2000/12/EC of the European Parliament and of the Council and Repealing Council Directive 93/22/EEC*. Retrieved from https://eur-lex.europa.eu/legal-content/EN/TXT/PDF/?uri=CELEX:32004L0039

Directive. (2008). *2008/48/EC of the European Parliament and of the Council of 23 April 2008 on Credit Agreements for Consumers and Repealing Council Directive 87/102/EEC*. Retrieved from https://eur-lex.europa.eu/legal-content/EN/TXT/PDF/?uri=CELEX:32008L0048

Directive. (2010). *2010/73/EU of the European Parliament and of the Council of 24 November 2010 Amending Directives 2003/71/EC on the Prospectus to Be Published When Securities Are Offered to the Public or Admitted to Trading and 2004/109/EC on the Harmonisation of Transparency Requirements in Relation to Information about Issuers Whose Securities*

Are Admitted to Trading on a Regulated Market. Retrieved from https://eur-lex.europa.eu/legal-content/EN/TXT/PDF/?uri=CELEX:32010L0073

Directive. (2013). *2013/36/EU of the European Parliament and of the Council of 26 June 2013 on Access to the Activity of Credit Institutions and the Prudential Supervision of Credit Institutions and Investment Firms, Amending Directive 2002/87/EC and Repealing Directives 2006/48/EC and 2006/49/ECText with EEA Relevance*. Retrieved from https://eur-lex.europa.eu/legal-content/EN/TXT/PDF/?uri=CELEX:32013L0036

Directive. (2014). *2014/65/EU of the European Parliament and of the Council of 15 May 2014 on Markets in Financial Instruments and Amending Directive 2002/92/EC and Directive 2011/61/EU*. Retrieved from https://eur-lex.europa.eu/legal-content/EN/TXT/PDF/?uri=CELEX:32014L0065

Ebers, M., Quarch, B. M., & Busch, D. (2021). EU consumer law and the boundaries of the crowdfunding regulation. In P. Ortolani, M. Louisse, P. Ortolani, & M. Louisse (Eds.), *The EU crowdfunding regulation* (pp. 83–112). Oxford University Press.

ECSRC Launches Regulatory Sandbox. (2023). *Invitation for applications from prospective equity crowdfunding intermediaries/platforms*. Winnmediaskn. Retrieved from https://www.winnmediaskn.com/ecsrc-launches-regulatory-sandbox-invitation-for-applications-from-prospective-equity-crowdfunding-intermediaries-platforms/

Enriques, L., & Ringe, W.-G. (2020). Bank–fintech partnerships, outsourcing arrangements and the case for a mentorship regime. *Capital Markets Law Journal, 15*(4), 374–397. https://doi.org/10.1093/cmlj/kmaa019

European Banking Authority. (2015). *Opinion of the European banking authority on lending-based crowdfunding (EBA-Op-2015-03)*. European Banking Authority. Retrieved from https://www.eba.europa.eu/sites/default/documents/files/documents/10180/983359/f6106173-dc94-4d22-ade8-d40fce724580/EBA-Op-2015-03%20%28EBA%20Opinion%20on%20lending%20based%20Crowdfunding%29.pdf?retry=1

European Commission. (2017). *Identifying market and regulatory obstacles to cross-border development of crowdfunding in the EU*. European Commission. Retrieved from https://data.europa.eu/doi/10.2874/65957

European Commission. (2018). *Impact assessment accompanying the document proposal for a regulation of the European Parliament and of the council on European crowdfunding service providers (ECSP) for business and proposal for a directive of the European Parliament and of the council amending directive 2014/65/EU on markets in financial instruments (COM(2018) 113 final)*. European Commission. Retrieved from https://eur-lex.europa.eu/legal-content/EN/TXT/HTML/?uri=CELEX%3A52018SC0056

European Commission. (2021). *Proposal for a directive of the European Parliament and of the council on consumer credits (2021/0171 (COD))*. European Commission. Retrieved from https://eur-lex.europa.eu/resource.html?uri=cellar:2df39e27-da3e-11eb-895a-01aa75ed71a1.0001.02/DOC_1&format=PDF

European Crowdfunding Network. (2017). *Review of crowdfunding regulation 2017. Interpretations of existing regulation concerning crowdfunding in Europe, North America and Israel*. The European Crowdfunding Network. Retrieved from https://eurocrowd.org/wp--content/uploads/2022/02/ECN_Review_of_Crowdfunding_Regulation_2017.pdf

European Parliament. (2015). *European Parliament resolution of 9 July 2015 on building a capital markets union (2015/2634(RSP))*. European Parliament. Retrieved from https://www.europarl.europa.eu/doceo/document/TA-8-2015-0268_EN.pdf

European Securities and Markets Authority. (2015). *Investment-based crowdfunding insights from regulators in the EU (ESMA/2015/856 Ann 1)*. European Securities and Markets Authority. Retrieved from https://www.esma.europa.eu/sites/default/files/library/2015/11/esma-2015-856_ann_1_esma_response_to_ec_green_paper_on_cmu_-_crowdfunding_survey.pdf

European Securities and Markets Authority. (2023). *Questions and answers on the European crowdfunding service providers for business Regulation.* Retrieved from https://www.esma.europa.eu/sites/default/files/library/esma35-42-1088_qas_crowdfunding_ecspr.pdf

Everhart, J. R. (2020). The FinTech sandbox: An overview of regulatory sandbox regimes. *Southern Journal of Business and Ethics, 12*, 64–73. Retrieved from https://sjbe.s3.us-east-2.amazonaws.com/SJBE_Volume_12_2020.pdf#page=64

Ferretti, R. (2022). Individual portfolio management of loans (art 6). In E. Macchiavello (Ed.), *Regulation on European crowdfunding service providers for business* (pp. 113–129). Edward Elgar Publishing.

Financial Conduct Authority. (2013). *The FCA'S regulatory approach to crowdfunding (and similar activities) (consultation paper CP13/13).* Financial Conduct Authority. Retrieved from https://www.fca.org.uk/publication/consultation/cp13-13.pdf

Financial Conduct Authority. (2014). *The FCA'S regulatory approach to crowdfunding over the internet, and the promotion of non-readily realisable securities by other media (policy statement PS14/4).* Financial Conduct Authority. Retrieved from https://www.fca.org.uk/publication/policy/ps14-04.pdf

Financial Conduct Authority. (2019). *Loan-based ('peer-to-peer') and investment-based crowdfunding platforms: Feedback to CP18/20 and final rules (PS19/14).* Financial Conduct Authority. Retrieved from https://www.fca.org.uk/publication/policy/ps19-14.pdf

Financial Conduct Authority. (n.d.). *Project innovate: Criteria for support.* Retrieved 24 June 2024, from https://www.fca.org.uk/publication/forms/project-innovate-criteria.pdf

Financial Services and Markets Act 2000. (2000). Retrieved from https://www.legislation.gov.uk/ukpga/2000/8/contents

FINMA. (2020). *Fact sheet: Crowdfunding.* FINMA. Retrieved from https://www.finma.ch/en/~/media/finma/dokumente/dokumentencenter/myfinma/faktenblaetter/faktenblatt-crowdfunding.pdf?sc_lang=en&hash=9F1D272EB2A44AC08B6869C0AB7C3B64

Franks, J., Serrano-Velarde, N., & Sussman, O. (2021). Marketplace lending, information aggregation, and liquidity. *The Review of Financial Studies, 34*(5), 2318–2361. https://doi.org/10.1093/rfs/hhaa101

Georgakopoulos, N. L. (1996). Why should disclosure rules subsidize informed traders? *International Review of Law and Economics, 16*(4), 417–431. https://doi.org/10.1016/S0144-8188(96)00035-X

Gesetz Über Das Kreditwesen (Kreditwesengesetz - KWG), BGBl. I S. 2776. (1998). Retrieved from https://www.gesetze-im-internet.de/kredwg/KWG.pdf

Gesetz Über Vermögensanlagen (Vermögensanlagengesetz - VermAnlG), BGBl. I S. 2481. (2011). Retrieved from https://www.gesetze-im-internet.de/vermanlg/VermAnlG.pdf

Gewerbeordnung - GewO. (1999). *BGBl. I S. 202.* Retrieved from https://www.gesetze-im-internet.de/gewo/GewO.pdf

Havrylchyk, O. (2018). *Regulatory framework for the loan-based crowdfunding platforms (OECD economics department working papers)* (Vol. 1513, pp. 1–56). OECD. https://doi.org/10.1787/24ad924a-en

Hornuf, L., Klöhn, L., & Schilling, T. (2018). Financial contracting in crowdinvesting: Lessons from the German market. *German Law Journal, 19*(3), 509–578. https://doi.org/10.1017/S2071832200022781

Hornuf, L., Schmitt, M., & Stenzhorn, E. (2020). Does a local bias exist in equity crowdfunding? *Max Planck Institute for Innovation & Competition Research Paper, 16*, 1–86. Retrieved from https://papers.ssrn.com/sol3/papers.cfm?abstract_id=3555581

Huang, R. H. (2018). Online P2P lending and regulatory responses in China: Opportunities and challenges. *European Business Organization Law Review, 19*(1), 63–92. https://doi.org/10.1007/s40804-018-0100-z

Investment Advisers Act of 1940, P.L. 117–263, U.S. Congress. (1940). Retrieved from https://www.govinfo.gov/content/pkg/COMPS-1878/pdf/COMPS-1878.pdf

Jackson, H. E. (2020). The nature of the Fintech firm. *Washington University Journal of Law and Policy, 61*, 9–24. Retrieved from https://heinonline.org/HOL/LandingPage?handle=hein.journals/wajlp61&div=5&id=&page=

Jiang, C., Xu, Q., Zhang, W., Li, M., & Yang, S. (2018). Does automatic bidding mechanism affect herding behavior? Evidence from online P2P lending in China. *Journal of Behavioral and Experimental Finance, 20*, 39–44. https://doi.org/10.1016/j.jbef.2018.07.001

Johan, S., & Zhang, Y. (2020). Quality revealing versus overstating in equity crowdfunding. *Journal of Corporate Finance, 65*, 101741. https://doi.org/10.1016/j.jcorpfin.2020.101741

Jumpstart Our Business Startups Act, Pub. L. No. 112–106, U.S. Congress. (2012). Retrieved from https://www.govinfo.gov/content/pkg/BILLS-112hr3606enr/pdf/BILLS-112hr3606enr.pdf

Käfer, B. (2018). Peer-to-peer lending—A (financial stability) risk perspective. *Review of Economics, 69*(1), 1–25. https://doi.org/10.1515/roe-2017-0020

Kim & Chang. (2022). *Summary of 2nd draft decree on Fintech regulatory sandbox in Vietnam*. Retrieved from https://www.kimchang.com/en/insights/detail.kc?sch_section=4&idx=24982

Kleinanlegerschutzgesetz. (2015). *BGBl. I S. 1114*. Retrieved from https://www.bgbl.de/xaver/bgbl/text.xav?SID=&tf=xaver.component.Text_0&tocf=&qmf=&hlf=xaver.component.Hitlist_0&bk=bgbl&start=%2F%2F*%5B%40node_id%3D%27944486%27%5D&skin=pdf&tlevel=-2&nohist=1&sinst=32224405

Kleiner, C. (2021). Rapport Général sur la régulation juridique du crowdfunding. In C. Kleiner (Ed.), *Legal aspects of crowdfunding* (Vol. 55, pp. 3–47). Springer.

Laub, G. (2021). Legal regulation of crowdfunding in Estonia. In C. Kleiner (Ed.), *Legal aspects of crowdfunding* (Vol. 55, pp. 255–269). Springer.

Legamart. (2022). *Overview of the Investment Crowdfunding Regulations in Kenya—Legamart*. Retrieved from https://legamart.com/articles/investment-crowdfunding-regulations-in-kenya/

Levitin, A. J. (2021). Rent-a-Bank: Bank partnerships and the evasion of usury laws. *Duke Law Journal, 71*, 329–417. Retrieved from https://heinonline.org/HOL/LandingPage?handle=hein.journals/duklr71&div=9&id=&page=

Li, J., Zhou, Y., Hu, J., & Guo, F. (2024). Local bias versus home bias: Evidence from debt-based crowdfunding. *Applied Economics, 56*(23), 2705–2719. https://doi.org/10.1080/00036846.2023.2200230

Lumpkin, S. (2010). Regulatory issues related to financial innovation. *OECD Journal: Financial Market Trends, 2*, 1–31. https://doi.org/10.1787/fmt-v2009-art14-en

Lysandrou, P., & Nesvetailova, A. (2015). The role of shadow banking entities in the financial crisis: A disaggregated view. *Review of International Political Economy, 22*(2), 257–279. https://doi.org/10.1080/09692290.2014.896269

Macchiavello, E. (2018). Financial-return crowdfunding and regulatory approaches in the shadow banking, FinTech and collaborative finance era. *European Company and Financial Law Review, 14*(4), 662–722. https://doi.org/10.1515/ecfr-2017-0030

Macchiavello, E., & Sciarrone Alibrandi, A. (2021). Marketplace lending as a new means of raising capital in the internal market: True disintermediation or reintermediation? In E. Avgouleas & H. Marjosola (Eds.), *Digital finance in Europe: Law, regulation, and governance* (pp. 37–86). De Gruyter. https://doi.org/10.1515/9783110749472-003

Matthaiou, E. (2021). Legal regulation of crowdfunding in Greece. In C. Kleiner (Ed.), *Legal aspects of crowdfunding* (Vol. 55, pp. 321–330). Springer.

McCarthy, J. (2022). The regulation of RegTech and SupTech in finance: Ensuring consistency in principle and in practice. *Journal of Financial Regulation and Compliance, 31*(2), 186–199. https://doi.org/10.1108/JFRC-01-2022-0004

Minupuri, N. (2018). Rushing to regulate: Rethinking the RBI's directives on peer-to-peer regulations in India. *Mory International Law Review, 33*, 433–458. Retrieved from https://heinonline.org/HOL/LandingPage?handle=hein.journals/emint33&div=20&id=&page=

Moloney, N., Ferran, E., Payne, J., & Payne, J. (2015). The role of gatekeepers. In N. Moloney, E. Ferran, & J. Payne (Eds.), *The Oxford handbook of financial regulation* (pp. 254–278). Oxford University Press. https://doi.org/10.1093/oxfordhb/9780199687206.013.11

Moody's Analytics. (n.d.). *BOT launched testing for peer-to-peer (P2P) lending platform under the regulatory sandbox*. Retrieved from https://www.moodysanalytics.com/regulatory-news/jun-05-20-bot-launches-testing-for-p2p-lending-platform-under-regulatory-sandbox

Morello, F. (2023). From consumer credit to consumer credits? Merits and flaws of the 2008/48/EC directive's reform proposal. *European Review of Private Law/Revue Européenne de Droit Privé/Europäische Zeitschrift Für Privatrecht, 31*, 845–870. https://doi.org/10.54648/ERPL2023036

Morsy, S. (2014). The JOBS act and crowdfunding: How narrowing the secondary market handicaps fraud plaintiffs. *Brooklyn Law Review, 79*(3), 1373–1405. Retrieved from https://heinonline.org/HOL/LandingPage?handle=hein.journals/brklr79&div=52&id=&page=

Nemoto, N., Huang, B., & Storey, D. J. (2019). Optimal regulation of P2P lending for small and medium-sized enterprises. *SSRN Electronic Journal*. https://doi.org/10.2139/ssrn.3313999

Niemand, T., Angerer, M., Thies, F., Kraus, S., & Hebenstreit, R. (2018). Equity crowdfunding across borders: A conjoint experiment. *International Journal of Entrepreneurial Behavior & Research, 24*(4), 911–932. https://doi.org/10.1108/IJEBR-07-2017-0256

Odorović, A. (2017). Why do borrowers choose suboptimal mortgage contracts? A behavioral economics approach. *Annals of the Faculty of Law in Belgrade, 65*(4), 135–152. https://doi.org/10.5937/AnaliPFB1704135O

Odorović, A. (2018). The "new" paternalism in consumer credit regulation: When, why, and how? *Annals of the Faculty of Law in Belgrade, 66*(4), 156–176. https://doi.org/10.5937/AnaliPFB1804156O

Odorović, A. (2023). Open banking: Between cooperation and competition. *Annals of the Faculty of Law in Belgrade, 71*(1), 65–91. https://doi.org/10.51204/Anali_PFBU_23102A

Ofir, M., & Sadeh, I. (2019). A revolution in progress: Regulating P2P lending platforms. *NYU Journal of Law & Business, 16*, 683–748. Retrieved from https://heinonline.org/HOL/LandingPage?handle=hein.journals/nyujolbu16&div=22&id=&page=

Omarova, S. T. (2020). Dealing with disruption: Emerging approaches to fintech regulation. *Washington University Journal of Law and Policy, 61*, 25–54. Retrieved from https://heinonline.org/HOL/LandingPage?handle=hein.journals/wajlp61&div=6&id=&page=

Ortolani, P., & Louisse, M. (2021). Introduction. Keep calm and continue crowdfunding. In P. Ortolani & M. Louisse (Eds.), *The EU crowdfunding regulation* (pp. 3–24). Oxford University Press.

Plank-Bachselten, A. (2022). *FMA admits four crowdfunding platform providers to the regulatory Sandbox. Now seven FinTechs already in the sandbox. First participant obtained licence.* FMA Österreich. Retrieved from https://www.fma.gv.at/en/fma-admits-four-crowdfunding-platform-providers-to-the-regulatory-sandbox-now-seven-fintechs-already-in-the-sandbox-first-participant-obtained-licence/

Rapaport, E. (2021). *Regulatory sandboxes in Africa. Empower Africa*. Retrieved from https://empowerafrica.com/regulatory-sandboxes-in-africa/

Raschauer, N., & Muller, T. (2016). Peer-to-peer lending in Austria. *Journal of European Consumer and Market Law, 5*, 222–223. Retrieved from https://heinonline.org/HOL/LandingPage?handle=hein.kluwer/jeucml0005&div=57&id=&page=

Regolamento Sulla Raccolta Di Capitali Tramite Portali On-Line. (2013). *Adottato Con Delibera n. 18592Del26Giugno2013*. Retrieved from https://www.consob.it/documents/1912911/1950567/reg_consob_2013_18592.pdf/9b1d415a-577a-e33d-4d7d-aa2af3a09f53

Regulation. (2013). *(EU) No 575/2013 of the European Parliament and of the Council of 26 June 2013 on prudential requirements for credit institutions and investment firms and amending regulation (EU) No 648/2012*. Retrieved from https://eur-lex.europa.eu/legal-content/EN/TXT/PDF/?uri=CELEX:32013R0575

Regulation. (2017). *(EU) 2017/1129 of the European Parliament and of the Council of 14 June 2017 on the Prospectus to Be Published When Securities Are Offered to the Public or Admitted to Trading on a Regulated Market, and Repealing Directive 2003/71*. Retrieved from https://eur-lex.europa.eu/legal-content/EN/TXT/PDF/?uri=CELEX:32017R1129

Regulation. (2020). *(EU) 2020/1503 of the European Parliament and of the Council of 7 October 2020 on European Crowdfunding Service Providers for Business, and Amending Regulation (EU) 2017/1129 and Directive (EU) 2019/1937*. Retrieved from https://eur-lex.europa.eu/legal-content/EN/TXT/PDF/?uri=CELEX:32020R1503

Regulatory Sandbox. (2022). *Financial Conduct Authority*. Retrieved from https://www.fca.org.uk/firms/innovation/regulatory-sandbox

Regulatory Sandbox|NAMFISA. (2024). *Namibia financial institutions supervisory authority*. Retrieved from https://www.namfisa.com.na/regulatory-sandbox/

Restoy, F. (2019). *Regulating fintech: What is going on, and where are the challenges* (pp. 1–7). Bank for International Settlements. Retrieved from https://www.suerf.org/wp-content/uploads/2023/12/f_a97f6e2fedcabc887911dc9b5fd3ccc3_10355_suerf.pdf

Ringe, W.-G., & Ruof, C. (2020). Regulating Fintech in the EU: The case for a guided sandbox. *European Journal of Risk Regulation, 11*(3), 604–629. https://doi.org/10.1017/err.2020.8

Rodriguez de las Heras Ballell, T. (2019). The layers of digital financial innovation: Charting a regulatory response. *Fordham Journal of Corporate & Financial Law, 25*, 381–421. Retrieved from https://heinonline.org/HOL/LandingPage?handle=hein.journals/fjcf25&div=16&id=&page=

Ruof, C. (2023). *Regulating financial innovation: Fintech and the information deficit*. Springer Nature Switzerland. https://doi.org/10.1007/978-3-031-32971-5

Schwartz, A. A. (2013). Keep it light, chairman white: SEC rulemaking under the crowdfund act. *Vanderbilt Law Review En Banc, 66*, 43–62. Retrieved from https://heinonline.org/HOL/LandingPage?handle=hein.journals/valewenb66&div=5&id=&page=

Schwartz, A. A. (2018). The gatekeepers of crowdfunding. *Washington and Lee Law Review, 75*, 885–955. Retrieved from https://heinonline.org/HOL/LandingPage?handle=hein.journals/waslee75&div=21&id=&page=

Schwartz, A. A. (2023). *Investment crowdfunding*. Oxford University Press.

Securities Act of 1933. (1933). *P.L. 117–263, U.S. Congress*. Retrieved from https://www.govinfo.gov/content/pkg/COMPS-1884/pdf/COMPS-1884.pdf

Securities Exchange Act of 1934. (1934). *P.L. 117–328, U.S. Congress*. Retrieved from https://www.govinfo.gov/content/pkg/COMPS-1885/pdf/COMPS-1885.pdf

Shneor, R., Wenzlaff, K., Boyko, K., Baah-Peprah, P., Odorović, A., & Okhrimenko, O. (2024). *The European crowdfunding market report 2023*. University of Agder-Crowdfunding Research Center. Retrieved from https://papers.ssrn.com/sol3/papers.cfm?abstract_id=4713135

Statman, M. (2017). *Finance for normal people: How investors and markets behave*. Oxford University Press.

Stefanelli, V., Ferilli, G. B., & Boscia, V. (2022). Exploring the lending business crowdfunding to support SMEs' financing decisions. *Journal of Innovation & Knowledge, 7*(4), 100278. https://doi.org/10.1016/j.jik.2022.100278

Tröger, T. H. (2021). Regulation of crowdfunding in Germany. In C. Kleiner (Ed.), *Legal aspects of crowdfunding* (Vol. 55, pp. 93–125). Springer. https://doi.org/10.1007/978-3-030-79264-0_3

Troxler, T. (2021). Crowdfunding in Switzerland. In C. Kleiner (Ed.), *Legal aspects of crowdfunding* (Vol. 55, pp. 421–449). Springer. https://doi.org/10.1007/978-3-030-79264-0_19

Vallee, B., & Zeng, Y. (2019). Marketplace lending: A new banking paradigm? *The Review of Financial Studies, 32*(5), 1939–1982. https://doi.org/10.1093/rfs/hhy100

Walthoff-Borm, X., Vanacker, T., & Collewaert, V. (2018). Equity crowdfunding, shareholder structures, and firm performance. *Corporate Governance: An International Review, 26*(5), 314–330. https://doi.org/10.1111/corg.12259

Wang, C. (2023). The way to revive crowdfunding in China: Based on the rules and practices in the US. *UC Davis Business Law Journal, 23*, 240–305. Retrieved from https://heinonline.org/HOL/LandingPage?handle=hein.journals/ucdbulj23&div=9&id=&page

Wenzlaff, K., & Odorović, A. (2022). The crowdfunding regulation in Germany-on the path to self-isolation? In E. Macchiavello (Ed.), *Regulation on European crowdfunding service providers for business* (pp. 673–693). Edward Elgar Publishing. https://doi.org/10.4337/9781802209945.00058

Wenzlaff, K., & Odorović, A. (2024). Into the unknown –monitoring how European digital finance platforms adapt to the new European crowdfunding service provider regime (ECSP-R). *SSRN Electronic Journal*. https://doi.org/10.2139/ssrn.4740433

Wenzlaff, K., Odorović, A., Ziegler, T., & Shneor, R. (2020). Crowdfunding in Europe: Between fragmentation and harmonization. In R. Shneor, L. Zhao, & B.-T. Flåten (Eds.), *Advances in crowdfunding: Research and practice* (pp. 373–390). Springer International Publishing. https://doi.org/10.1007/978-3-030-46309-0_16

Whitehouse.gov. (2012). *Remarks by the president at JOBS act bill signing*. Retrieved from https://obamawhitehouse.archives.gov/the-press-office/2012/04/05/remarks-president-jobs-act-bill-signing

World Bank Group. (2021). *Global Fintech-enabling regulations database*. Retrieved from https://www.worldbank.org/en/topic/fintech/brief/global-fintech-enabling-regulations-database

Xu, B., Su, Z., & Celler, J. (2021). Evaluating default risk and loan performance in UK peer-to-peer lending: Evidence from funding circle. *Journal of Advanced Computational Intelligence and Intelligent Informatics, 25*(5), 530–538. https://doi.org/10.20965/jaciii.2021.p0530

Zhang, B. Z., Rowan, P., Duff, S., Homer, M., Schizas, E., Soriano, M., Cloud, K., Umer, Z., Garvey, K., & Ziegler, T. (2019). *Early lessons on regulatory innovation to enable inclusive FinTech: Innovation offices, regulatory sandboxes and RegTech*. Cambridge Centre for Alternative Finance. Retrieved from https://www.jbs.cam.ac.uk/wp-content/uploads/2020/08/2019-early-lessons-regulatory-innovations-enable-inclusive-fintech.pdf

Chapter 6
Does a Bespoke Regulation Matter for Market Outcomes? Evidence from Equity Platforms in the UK

6.1 Introduction

Since its emergence, the crowdfunding market has grown at various paces in different countries. The growth is likely to be affected by the regulation in place. As seen in Chap. 5, the question of optimal regulatory response has led regulators to embrace different regulatory approaches. Some regulators embraced a 'wait-and-see' strategy, allowing the industry to emerge in a hardly regulated environment. In other jurisdictions, regulators tried to extend the application of regulations tailored to traditional financial services. A few countries were eager to adopt a bespoke regime for crowdfunding intermediaries early on, introducing different regulatory solutions. Little is known about the added value of a crowdfunding-specific regulation.

Existing empirical studies considering the relationship between formal rules and crowdfunding primarily explore cross-country variations in the number of platforms and aggregate crowdfunding volumes (Di Pietro & Butticè, 2020; Dushnitsky et al., 2016; Rau, 2020, 2021). This chapter offers one of the first insights into the effects of crowdfunding-specific regulations on micro-level outcomes in a crowdfunding market (Goethner, Hornuf et al., 2021; Johan & Zhang, 2020). The focus of the study is the equity crowdfunding market in the UK. Equity crowdfunding has received the most regulatory attention among all crowdfunding models even though its size in global terms is still small compared to loan-based crowdfunding.

The UK market seems like a suitable environment for testing the effects of bespoke regulations, as being the most significant European equity crowdfunding market, with an average annual growth of 53% from 2014 to 2017 (Zhang et al., 2018). Crowdfunding regulations were introduced in 2014, a few years following the opening of the first platform (2011), allowing the market to operate under general securities laws and interim permissions for the operation of crowdfunding platforms.

A. Odorović, *Overcoming Asymmetric Information in the Crowdfunding Market*, International Law and Economics, https://doi.org/10.1007/978-3-032-04118-0_6

The data used in this study is collected by the Cambridge Centre for Alternative Finance and includes both campaign-level and investor-level data from February 2012 until June 2016. The sample consists of 201 crowdfunding campaigns run on different equity crowdfunding platforms and more than 30,000 investor-level observations made by more than 16,000 investors. The study aims to explore the potential effect of crowdfunding regulations on the behaviour of fundraisers and investors and overall market outcomes as captured by campaign success. The study is divided into five main parts. By way of introduction, it seems appropriate to provide a research context, describing the equity crowdfunding market in the UK and the aim and the scope of the crowdfunding bespoke regime (Sect. 6.2). The second part of the study defines the hypotheses, focusing on the demand side, supply side, and market outcome effects of crowdfunding regulations (Sect. 6.3). This is followed by an explanation of the data and methods used (Sect. 6.4). The fourth part contains the main analysis and discusses the results (Sect. 6.5). The last part summarises the most important findings and discusses the limitations of the study (Sect. 6.6).

6.2 Research Context

6.2.1 Equity Crowdfunding in the UK

In the aftermath of the financial crisis, equity crowdfunding emerged in the UK as a response to the rising difficulties of entrepreneurs who lack stable cash flows and collateral to get finances for their innovative business ideas. Since 2011, the UK equity alternative finance market has grown exponentially, reaching $870.19 million in 2018 (Ziegler et al., 2020, p. 41). This places the UK as the largest equity market in Europe and third in the world, after China and the USA. According to the CCAF methodology, equity models include equity crowdfunding, real-estate crowdfunding, revenue-sharing, and community shares—pure equity crowdfunding accounts for 56% of all equity activity, reaching $484.7 m in 2018. For comparison, the second and third largest European equity crowdfunding markets are Finland and Spain, with 67.9 m and 48.4 m in volumes, respectively (Ziegler et al., 2020, p. 82).

The development of the equity alternative market in the UK correlates with the satisfaction of platforms with the regulatory regime in place. According to the CCAF study, 84% of the platforms in the UK perceive existing regulations as adequate and appropriate for their platform's activities (Ziegler et al., 2020, p. 70). Apart from crowdfunding regulation, which is the focus of this study, several other factors underpin the development of crowdfunding for businesses in the UK. The crowdfunding association in the UK was established in 2013 to promote the industry's interests and design and monitor the implementation of a code of conduct for platforms before the bespoke regime was enacted. Other crowdfunding success factors are pertinent to entrepreneurial finance in the broadest terms. According to the Venture Capital & Private Equity Country Attractiveness Index (Groh et al., 2023), these factors include economic activity, depth of capital market, size and liquidity of the stock market, volume and the number of IPOs, tax incentives, and investor protection and corporate governance, among others. As Vismara (2016, p. 580) points out, the UK ranks fourth worldwide and ahead of all other European countries in terms of the Depth of Capital Markets Index. The importance of the London Stock Exchange, London's Alternative Investment Market, and the VC market is likely to have significant spillover effects on crowdfunding listings. There are even instances in which companies simultaneously went public on the Alternative Investment Market targeting institutional investors and on a crowdfunding platform catering to retail investors (Vismara, 2016, p. 580).

The first and, up to date, the most significant equity crowdfunding platform in terms of total volumes in the UK, Crowdcube, opened its doors in 2011. The first platform to be registered by the British regulator, FSA at the time, was Seedrs in 2012. While ranking second in total volumes, Seedrs facilitated the greatest number of equity investments among crowdfunding platforms in the UK in 2019 (Beauhurst, 2020, p. 30). Today, about 30 equity crowdfunding platforms are operating in the UK (CrowdSpace, 2024). Syndicate Room is the third largest UK platform, founded in 2013. This platform requires at least 25% of the amount sought to be committed by business angels and professional investors before the campaign is launched (Signori & Vismara, 2018, p. 581). Among the first market entrants is Venture Founders, another platform allowing crowd investors to co-invest with VCs and business angels.

Despite some differences in their business model, equity crowdfunding platforms across the UK share several common features. Typically, entrepreneurs seeking to raise funds approach the platform through an online form provided on the website. In some instances, entrepreneurs are recruited through business development managers. The platform then screens projects, checks the accuracy of the statements in the campaign, and preselects projects that correspond to the platform's eligibility criteria. Compared to other crowdfunding models, equity crowdfunding entails stricter rules for listing. In the next stage, entrepreneurs prepare the campaign video, which typically features their business, team, and current investors. Marketing materials are also prepared at this stage, whereas the platform often offers some guidance to entrepreneurs. The platform ensures that video and marketing materials are standardised, allowing investors to compare investment opportunities easily. Before the campaign goes public, it goes through a private launch. During this stage, founders of the company, customers and their network have the exclusive opportunity to invest in the project. Investments during the private launch are considered an important signal to external investors without ties to the project or entrepreneurs.

The campaign is then published on the platform's website alongside some critical information, such as the amount they aim to raise and the proportion of shares they offer in return for investment. The campaign is listed on the website for a certain number of days (up to 40). During this time, entrepreneurs and the platform promote the campaign via social media to increase its salience to the general public. UK equity platforms usually allow investments of as little as £10, even though platforms often require investing an exact multiple of the share price. After making an investment, investors may share the campaign on their social networks to attract the attention of other potential investors. Investors are entitled to cancel their investment before the investment round closes, as well as to withdraw any funds they hold on a designated account for the purpose of investing on a given platform.[1]

All of the investments pledged during the campaign are conditional on campaigns reaching their target amount within a given time (a so-called 'all-or-nothing-rule', as opposed to 'keep-it-all' (Cumming, Johan, & Zhang, 2019)). All investors receive their money back if the target amount is not attained. If the target amount is reached before the campaign duration period expires, overfunding is allowed if entrepreneurs choose to accept additional amounts. However, entrepreneurs can accept additional investment subject to giving additional equity in return. Before transferring funds to entrepreneurs, the platform completes the legal due diligence, prepares documentation, and charges its commission fee. In a subsequent stage, investors receive an electronic share certificate and guidance on how to follow the progress of the business in the post-investment stage.

6.2.2 *Regulatory Approach*

The UK legislator did not introduce a tailored regulatory regime in the wake of the crowdfunding phenomenon. Nevertheless, crowdfunding activity would fall within the existing national regime, transposing the regulatory framework for the issuance of securities and financial intermediaries at the EU level, the Prospectus Directive and MiFID. The Prospectus Directive allowed member states to exempt from prospectus requirements offerings of securities amounting to less than €five million by a single firm in 12 months (Directive, 2003). The Financial Services and Markets Act (FSMA) implemented this option, introducing the highest exemption threshold allowed at the time (Financial Services and Markets Act, 2000, Section 85(5) (a), Schedule 11A, para 9). This has led to significant savings in compliance costs for issuing firms (Armour & Enriques, 2018b).

Conversely, FSMA provisions governing regulated activities grounded in MiFID were directly applicable to equity-based crowdfunding platforms. The offer of shares and other securities on a crowdfunding platform would generally amount to a communication of a financial promotion or arranging deals in investments, which constituted a regulated activity in the UK (Financial Conduct Authority, 2013, p. 4).

As a result, a financial promotion to retail investors was only allowed if it was communicated or approved by a firm that holds an FCA authorisation. In other words, a platform was supposed to either have a licence or rely on an FCA-licensed firm to approve the promotion unless it benefits from an exemption from the

[1] Crowdcube also offers a cooling-off period after the financing round is closed, during which investors can consider their investment.

financial promotion regime. Carrying out regulated activities implies that platforms are subject to the requirements of the Conduct of Business Sourcebook (COBS). In addition to these rules, the FCA's approach was to apply other restrictions on individual platforms on a case-by-case basis at the authorisation stage to protect consumers (Financial Conduct Authority, 2013, p. 36).[2]

Since authorisation requirements can be costly and administratively burdensome, some platforms managed to ensure that their promotions fall under one of the existing exemptions (Gajda et al., 2013, p. 183; Ridley, 2016, p. 62). The first exemption entails offerings of securities to existing shareholders. To benefit from it, the platform would create a shareholder relationship with all investors and a parent relationship with firms raising funds. The second exemption involves offering shares to sophisticated, high net worth, and other professional investors, where investors certify their own net worth or investment experience. Moreover, there were instances in which some firms that were running crowdfunding platforms did not hold the required regulatory permissions and might not have met the regulatory standards (Financial Conduct Authority, 2014, p. 15).

In light of the perils that some platforms may escape the regulatory oversight and the need to clarify the regulator's approach to crowdfunding, a bespoke regime was announced in March 2014 (Financial Conduct Authority, 2014). The bespoke regime for equity-based crowdfunding was part of a larger regulatory initiative concerning crowdfunding, which started with a consultation paper in October 2013 (Financial Conduct Authority, 2013). In the consultation paper, the FCA intended to clarify the scope of existing rules, distinguishing between regulated, unregulated, and exempt activities performed by crowdfunding platforms. In their own words, 'It is not always clear when crowdfunding activities fall or will fall, within the scope of FCA regulation' (Financial Conduct Authority, 2013, p. 10). Platforms operating lending-based models were not under the regulatory perimeter of the FCA at the time. Consequently, the major change to the crowdfunding ecosystem was subjecting lending-based platforms to existing rules of financial regulation. For this purpose, a new regulated activity was introduced—'operating an electronic system in relation to lending' (i.e. operating a lending-based crowdfunding platform). The idea was to treat investments on lending platforms similarly to other investments since many risks are shared across different financial-return crowdfunding models. In the view of the UK regulator, the difference between the underlying instruments should not drive the difference in prudential requirements for lending and equity platforms (Financial Conduct Authority, 2013, p. 19).

The UK regulator acknowledged that while investment-based crowdfunding platforms fell within the scope of existing rules before the bespoke regime, such rules were not designed with crowdfunding in mind. Consequently, there was a need for 'a revised approach to regulating firms that operate investment-based

[2] Ten firms were authorised to operate an investment-based crowdfunding platform in the UK before the new regulatory regime. Moreover, eleven appointed representatives of authorised firms operated a platform, and a number of firms were in the process of authorisation when the consultation stage in relation to new rules was initiated (Financial Conduct Authority, 2013, p. 40).

crowdfunding platforms or market unlisted equity or debt securities' (Financial Conduct Authority, 2013, p. 4). Alternatives to a bespoke regime, soon abandoned by the regulator, were to continue with the existing approach of restricting firms on a case-by-case basis at the authorisation stage or limit investment-based crowdfunding only to professional, sophisticated, and high-net-worth retail investors.[3]

The scope of the bespoke regulation covers all investment-based crowdfunding platforms, including firms on which consumers can buy unlisted shares, debt securities and units in an unregulated collective investment scheme. The regulator introduced the term 'non-readily realisable security' to cover investments that are 'difficult to value' and 'illiquid' (Financial Conduct Authority, 2014, p. 7). Consequently, liquid and traded securities for which there is a recognised secondary market, such as Alternative Investment Market (AIM), do not fall under the bespoke crowdfunding regime. However, the UK regulator did not distinguish between securities with differing investment risks inherent in the underlying asset. For instance, securities that are secured or asset-backed securities (by real-estate or renewable energy installations) or securities issued by more established companies received the same regulatory treatment. The rationale was that most of the crowdfunding risks are independent of the type of security being issued, such as the risk of a capital loss when investors are unable to do proper due diligence or when the business value is overstated, or similarly, the risk of dilution of shareholder value (Financial Conduct Authority, 2014, p. 38).

The regulator's aim is that 'investment opportunities are available to more retail investors than currently, but with appropriate safeguards to check that investors are able to understand and bear the risks involved' (Financial Conduct Authority, 2013, p. 5). The new rules were meant to reconcile two regulatory objectives of the FCA: promoting effective competition and securing consumer protection. As such, they were not intended to affect corporate finance and VC businesses when they communicate with their professional contacts, nor retail investors when they receive regulated advice or investment management services in relation to their investments.

Given that investing in early-stage companies entails a high probability of failure and a capital loss can amount to 100%, the core of the new regulatory approach is restrictions on who can become an investor on investment-based platforms. In principle, platforms are allowed to offer financial promotions to the following categories of retail clients: (1) retail clients who are certified or self-certify as sophisticated investors; (2) retail clients who are certified as high net worth investors; (3) retail clients who confirm before a promotion is made that they will receive regulated investment advice or investment management services from an authorised person; or (4) retail clients who certify that they will not invest more than 10% of their net

[3] In the consultation stage, some stakeholders argued against introducing a bespoke regime for investment-based crowdfunding. The main argument was that crowd investors often play a more active role in projects being financed, and, as a result, they have a better understanding of their risks and benefits than traditional financial products. Similarly, investors may have emotional or rational ties to the project, for which they are not merely interested in the financial return (Financial Conduct Authority, 2014, p. 45).

investible portfolio in unlisted shares or unlisted debt securities (Financial Conduct Authority, 2014). In light of the concern that retail investors do not have the knowledge and experience to understand the risks involved, the new rules introduced the appropriateness test for investors. The test's original purpose was to limit access to investment opportunities only to those who demonstrate the minimum level of knowledge and experience in investing in risky assets. In practice, such a test boils down to automated systems incorporated into platforms' websites, which are one of the necessary steps to register on the platform.

The bespoke crowdfunding regime did not change rules for issuing shares on crowdfunding platforms. The exemption from requirements to publish a prospectus was not supplemented by a simplified mandatory disclosure regime for issuers, such as in other jurisdictions, notably the US. The concern that investors may not have enough information to make informed investment decisions is attenuated by obligations on platforms concerning financial promotions. Platforms that communicate or approve financial promotions must ensure that the promotion is fair, clear, and not misleading. This assumes that platforms verify that investors have not only accurate but also sufficient information and give a balanced indication of potential benefits and risks inherent in specific investment opportunities (Financial Conduct Authority, 2014, p. 42). In relation to this, the UK regulator embraced a principle-based approach regarding the due diligence of platforms. No minimum due diligence standards were prescribed for platforms to meet regulatory requirements. However, the FCA indicated that platforms are expected to disclose whether and to what extent they have performed due diligence on issuers and the outcome of such an analysis (Financial Conduct Authority, 2014, p. 42).

The new rules for investment-based crowdfunding went into force on 1 April 2014. However, a transition period was foreseen. Firms that already held an authorisation could either start complying with the new rules immediately or abide by the old ones until 1 October 2014 and then implement the new ones (Financial Conduct Authority, 2014, p. 12). The expectations of the UK regulator concerning the effects of the new rules were twofold. Firstly, given that some restrictions on the type of investor that may invest were relaxed, the FCA expected the investor base to increase. However, the size of this change was expected to be 'minimal' (Financial Conduct Authority, 2013, p. 60). The explanation was that the same groups of investors would be targeted. Secondly, 'investors' appetite' was expected to increase, leading to an overall increase in investment in crowdfunding due to increased confidence in the crowdfunding market (Financial Conduct Authority, 2013, p. 60). In the consultation paper, FCA made hardly any reference to their expectations regarding direct effects on the demand side of the market. When analysing whether compliance costs would lead to an increase in operating costs of platforms, which would then be passed to their clients (investors and issuers), the regulator estimated that such costs are likely to be minimal in relation to investment-based crowdfunding (Financial Conduct Authority, 2013, p. 61). However, in the policy paper outlining the new regime, the regulator stated that one aim is to provide more clarity to individuals and businesses seeking to raise money on investment-based crowdfunding platforms (Financial Conduct Authority, 2014, p. 35).

6.3 Literature Review

When seeking to understand the importance of a bespoke crowdfunding regulation for market outcomes, it is worth considering the existing theoretical and empirical literature which looks into the effects of institutions, particularly capital market institutions, on the emergence and development of capital markets and entrepreneurial finance. As crowdfunding is a tool used by entrepreneurs and early-stage ventures to raise finance, both strands of literature provide helpful insights into possible mechanisms through which a new regulation can affect the behaviour of all three types of market participants: issuers, investors, and platform intermediaries.

Institutions, commonly referred to as 'manly devised constraints that structure political, economic, and social interaction', are considered a key device societies use to reduce the uncertainty of economic exchange (North, 1991, p. 97). When transactions are not repeated, when there is a large number of parties and information on the other parties is lacking, cooperative behaviour cannot be upheld without substantial transaction costs. According to North (1991, p. 98), the role of institutions is to increase the benefits of cooperation and costs of defection, thus raising the feasibility and profitability of economic interactions. Nevertheless, the choice of institutional design necessarily involves selecting between imperfect alternatives describing the 'institutional possibility frontier' (Djankov et al., 2003, pp. 598–604). Such a choice presumes to identify the domain of market failure and harmful conduct from market participants and determine the desirable scope of state intervention. As we move towards more regulation, the reduction of social costs of private expropriation is offset by social losses inherent in state expropriation. Even rules that are a result of an efficient social choice raise a question of the adequate degree of vagueness. Strict regulations intended to mitigate the room for loopholes cause some market participants to underinvest in economic activity (Ferguson & Peters, 2000). Moreover, a set of rules governing private conduct raises the question of whether the enforcement should be left to the parties in a transaction or delegated to a public agency (Shleifer, 2005).

Prior research demonstrates that the existence and choice of institutions matter for the development of financial markets. Several studies have looked into the effect of broad political and economic institutions in a country on financial market outcomes (see, e.g., Blau (2017), Boubakri et al. (2014), Eleswarapu and Venkataraman (2006), Hearn et al. (2017), Lakshmi et al. (2021)). This study is more closely aligned with the literature examining the importance of corporate laws and securities regulations.

Modigliani and Perotti (1997) show that the level of development of corporate governance laws determines the relative importance of security markets vis-à-vis bank finance. They argue that, while excessive government regulation can be an obstacle to the growth of capital markets, so can the lack of basic rules. 'The importance of an adequate legal framework and its reliable enforcement for the development of security markets is perhaps best appreciated when it is missing' (Modigliani & Perotti, 1997, p. 520). Securities are 'arms-length contracts' deprived of a mechanism of private enforcement (Modigliani & Perotti, 1997, p. 519). Consequently, they depend on the scope and the enforcement of their associated rights, typically contained in complementary regulatory rules. If such rules are lacking, a firm's ability to raise external equity is impaired, while financial transactions tend to concentrate among banking institutions and agents with long-term relationships.

In a cross-country setting, La Porta et al. (1998) find that the concentration of ownership of shares in large public companies is negatively associated with investor protection, supporting the hypothesis that the readiness of small diversified investors to finance firms critically depends on their ability to exercise their rights. In a related study, they show the size of capital markets, both equity and debt, is also affected by the level of investor protection against expropriation by insiders in a given country (La Porta et al., 1997). Inadequacy of legal rules and poor law enforcement can result in inferior opportunities for obtaining external finance, both in terms of the valuation of the securities and the number of firms that have access to it. Consistent with these arguments, there is mounting evidence that legal protection for minority investors is positively associated with equity valuations and negatively related to the costs of accessing capital markets (Doidge et al., 2007; Dyck & Zingales, 2004). Moreover, the effect of firm-level corporate governance on the cost of equity capital appears to be influenced by country-level investor protection, with existing evidence suggesting that the two can be considered substitutes (Chen et al., 2009).

Several studies ask whether securities market regulation enhances investors' confidence and improves stock market outcomes. Securities market regulations usually encompass rules on securities offerings, market manipulation, insider trading, mandatory disclosure, and takeover bids, complemented by rules on financial services and accounting law (Enriques & Gatti, 2008, p. 46). Existing empirical studies typically focus on the effect of rules governing secondary markets, including stock exchange trading rules, on market liquidity (see, e.g., Christensen et al. (2016), Cumming and Johan (2019), Cumming, Johan, and Zhang (2019)) while the crowdfunding rules are most closely aligned with, or created on the basis of exemption from, rules on securities offerings and rules on financial services (Klöhn, 2018, p. 222).

The evidence of the effect of rules on security offerings in financial markets is mixed. La Porta et al. (2006) find that laws governing the issuance of new securities to the public matter for stock market development. They argue that the importance of laws governing initial public offerings stems from the fact that reputational, contractual, and tort law consequences of omissions or misrepresentation of relevant information by issuers are insufficient. The reason is that issuers' payoff from opportunistic behaviour is high, while the costs of private litigation deter investors from pursuing enforcement. The standardisation of a contractual framework between issuers and investors through securities law can take the form of mandating disclosure of information and specifying the liability standards for both issuers and intermediaries in case of material omissions. Increasing the liability standards for issuers essentially entails lowering the standard of proof for investors aiming to recover damages. The study by La Porta et al. (2006) supports the hypothesis that both forms of contract standardisation determine the development of stock markets. In contrast to this study, which highlights the importance of private enforcement mechanisms, Jackson and Roe (2009) find support that enforcement of securities laws by public agencies is the factor driving the differences in the development of financial markets. The primary reason why the private enforcement system is often inefficacious in the case of securities is that it is subject to the problem of collective action, with strong free-riding incentives among dispersed shareholders. Other pitfalls of private lawsuits include lawyers' rent-seeking, slow and ill-informed judiciaries, and a lack of high financial penalties imposed on issuers and intermediaries.

Apart from financial market development, rules on the issuance of new securities can affect the cost of equity capital (Hail & Leuz, 2006). The basic idea is that rules on disclosure reduce uncertainty and consequently lead to a reduction of non-diversifiable risk for outside investors. As a result, monitoring costs they bear are reduced, and they are likely to ask for smaller price compensation for their equity investments. Similarly, reducing uncertainty leads to a broader recognition of the securities market among investors, thus increasing the investor base and enhancing risk-sharing.

Equity crowdfunding differs from traditional capital markets in many aspects, the most important being the financing stage, the degree of information asymmetries and the level of investors' expertise (Di Pietro & Butticè, 2020, p. 1). Its role in promoting entrepreneurship makes it more closely aligned with early-stage angel investing and VC financing (Ahlers et al., 2015). In fact, it is not uncommon for angel investors and VCs to invest via crowdfunding platforms attracted by the convenience of easiness of the online investment process and diversification opportunities (Lukkarinen, 2020; Wang et al., 2019). Previous literature demonstrates that formal institutions also influence VC activity (Grilli et al., 2018; Li & Zahra, 2012; Stenholm et al., 2013). Similarly, prior research indicates that the number of nascent entrepreneurs in a country is determined by a broad set of legal rules (Klapper et al., 2006; Levie & Autio, 2011).

Much empirical research in the domain of crowdfunding has focused on determinants of campaign success and the importance of signals (e.g., Ahlers et al., 2015; Hornuf & Neuenkirch, 2017; Piva & Rossi-Lamastra, 2018), funding dynamics (Hornuf & Schwienbacher, 2018), and investor motivations (e.g., Estrin et al., 2018; Goethner, Luettig, & Regner, 2021; Hornuf & Schmitt, 2016). Less attention has been devoted to how broader institutional and macro-level factors influence successful crowdfunding practices (Shneor & Vik, 2020).

A few recent studies have investigated the importance of contractual institutions for crowdfunding outcomes, which govern the relationship either between investors and the platform or between investors and the project owners. Rossi and Vismara (2018) investigate which platform-level services are most valuable to investors by examining 127 platforms in France, Italy, Germany, and the UK. They find that post-campaign services, e.g., exit assistance, periodic updates, or advisory for further funding, affect the number of successful campaigns at the platform level. In contrast, their findings suggest that services offered before and during crowdfunding campaigns do not attract more campaigns to the platforms.

Equity crowdfunding is praised as a convenient solution for entrepreneurs unwilling to relinquish the same levels of control that VCs and angel investors would typically demand (Estrin et al., 2018, p. 431). Existing evidence is inconclusive as to whether investors value the quality of corporate governance mechanisms of equity crowdfunding issuers. Cumming, Meoli, and Vismara (2019) examine whether the divergence from the one-vote-one-share ownership structure lowers the probability of offering success. They examine crowdfunding offerings on the UK platform Crowdcube, where project owners can offer A shares, B shares, or dual-class shares, i.e. when voting rights are only allocated to investors whose contributions are above a certain threshold. Their study finds that the separation between ownership and control reduces the likelihood of campaign success. The research of Rossi et al. (2019) and Hornuf et al. (2019) contradicts these findings. By examining platform-level data from nine countries, the study by Rossi et al. (2019) does not find that the delivery of voting rights has an impact on the number of annual successful offerings on a platform, and even find that individual voting rights, which are not exercised through a nominee structure, have a negative effect on the number of successful offerings. Hornuf et al. (2019) examine the impact of different sets of rights (including cash-flow rights, control rights, and exit rights) offered by entrepreneurs when they launch a crowdfunding campaign on 19 different investment-based crowdfunding platforms in Germany. Their findings indicate that investors pay higher prices if they receive more cash-flow[4] and exit rights. In contrast, they document a negative correlation between control rights and investors' willingness to pay, suggesting that crowd investors are passive due to a free-riding problem associated with dispersed ownership or lack of knowledge to exercise control rights. Similarly, control rights do not affect the campaign's likelihood of success.

There has been relatively little economic literature published on the importance of state-level institutions, particularly crowdfunding-specific regulation, for the development of crowdfunding markets. Hornuf and Schwienbacher (2017) developed a theoretical model that explores the optimal regulation of equity crowdfunding in relation to the availability of alternative early-stage financing mechanisms. They argue that bespoke regulation, which relies on exemptions in securities regulation, is more necessary in countries where VC and angel finance are underdeveloped. In line with these arguments, Kshetri (2018 p. 43) argues crowdfunding can be considered a substitute for other sources of early-stage financing. In their view, institutions are likely to legitimise crowdfunding practices among all stakeholders, increasing entrepreneurs' propensity to engage in efforts to raise funds via this funding option and the investors' propensity to invest. In a related research, Kshetri

[4] Variation in cash flow rights is specific for German investment-based platforms on which investors do not issue pure equity but hybrid financial instruments between debt and equity. Hornuf et al. (2021, p. 4) distinguish between the following cash flow rights: a fixed interest payment, profit participation, share in the enterprise value, participation in exit proceeds, no loss participation, and no additional funding obligation.

(2015, p. 107) hypothesises that the success of entrepreneurs in equity crowdfunding campaigns is positively related to the 'existence of a clear crowdfunding-related regulatory framework that balances the interest of entrepreneurs and investors'. Cai et al. (2020) further develop these theoretical considerations by emphasising various channels through which crowdfunding regulations can affect the performance of individual campaigns. Apart from a direct effect, legal institutions increase trust (social capital) in projects and fundraisers, which plays a vital role in investors' decision-making. They also highlight that regulations on crowdfunding affect the quality of platforms, which in turn mediate the effect of crowdfunding regulations by ensuring the legal requirements for the issues are complied with.

Existing empirical studies considering the relationship between formal institutions and crowdfunding primarily explore cross-country variations in the number of platforms and aggregate crowdfunding amounts. Dushnitsky et al. (2016) have examined the factors that drive the creation of platforms across 15 European countries. They find that the strength of legal rights positively affects the creation of lending-based platforms and negatively affects the creation of equity- and reward-based platforms.

Rau (2020) examines how country characteristics influence crowdfunding volumes and finds that the quality of regulation, financial development, and access to the Internet are the main factors driving differences in the size of crowdfunding markets. In a related study examining the effect of explicit crowdfunding regulation, Rau (2021) finds that both the publication of regulation and the level of detail in the regulation have a significant positive impact on crowdfunding volumes at the country level. His research also finds that the rule of law and banking efficiency factors are related to cross-country variation in crowdfunding volumes. Similarly, Di Pietro and Butticè (2020) show that the crowdfunding market is larger in countries characterised by a business-friendly legal environment and well-developed financial market in the case of lending crowdfunding.

None of the above studies, however, empirically examines how the creation of a bespoke crowdfunding regime influences campaigns' characteristics, campaigns' success, and individual investor behaviour. In contrast, two existing studies investigate how the crowdfunding regulatory regime affects micro-level outcomes. Goethner, Hornuf, and Regner (2021) explore how the single-issuer limit (1000 EUR) introduced by German crowdfunding regulation affects the investment decisions of individual investors. They also examine the effect of the rule in Germany that investments over 10,000 EUR can only be made through corporate entities. Their study finds that, following the introduction of the crowdfunding act, large investments became less frequent, suggesting that sophisticated investors have left the market. In contrast, medium investments have become more frequent. Johan and Zhang (2020) study the impact of qualitative business information on the campaign success of projects listed on equity-based platforms in the US. They also examine the effect of introducing crowdfunding bespoke regulation (Title III of the JOBS Act) on campaign success. The results of this study suggest that while introducing the bespoke regulation reduced the percentage of successful fundraisings, it increased the effect of (unverifiable) qualitative business information on crowdfunding success.

This study also aims to improve the understanding of the effects of a bespoke regime on micro-level outcomes in crowdfunding using UK data. Its scope is somewhat broader than the studies mentioned above since the study examines separately the potential effects of new regulations on the behaviour of fundraisers, investors, and overall market outcomes. In contrast to previous research, the study first explores whether the bespoke regulation in the UK has affected the demand side of the equity crowdfunding market. To this end, the study investigates whether the projects that appear on equity crowdfunding platforms after the UK bespoke regime differ in their characteristics that might be perceived as quality signals. Moreover, similarly to Goethner, Hornuf, and Regner (2021), the study seeks to explain whether and how the bespoke regulation affected individual investment decisions (captured by the amount they invested in a single crowdfunding campaign). In contrast to Goethner, Hornuf et al. (2021), differences in project characteristics after the regulatory change are also accounted for, allowing one to examine whether there is an independent effect of regulations on investor behaviour, i.e., the effect unrelated to the quality of investment opportunities. The present study is also similar to the research by Goethner, Hornuf, and Regner (2021) in aiming to identify the heterogeneous effect among different investor types. However, unlike the mentioned study, in which the authors create investor groups using a clustering analysis, this study uses more precise investor categories captured by crowdfunding platforms (relying on a methodology determined by regulations). Furthermore, the purpose of this study is to assess the influence of crowdfunding regulations on campaign success, similar to Johan and Zhang (2020). Yet, in contrast to the mentioned study, this research also seeks to account for the interaction effects between market signals and crowdfunding regulation (instead of (unverifiable) qualitative business information).

6.4 Hypotheses Development

Crowdfunding regulations can have an effect on fundraisers, investors (their participation rates and amounts pledged), or the overall success of crowdfunding campaigns. Following this distinction, hypothesis development is divided into three subsections: demand side effects, supply side effects, and market outcomes.

6.4.1 *Demand Side Effects*

According to the pecking-order theory, self-finance as a source of entrepreneurial capital has an advantage over external finance since entrepreneurs contributing their own money do not face costs related to information asymmetries (Myers & Majluf, 1984). However, entrepreneurs' own funds are seldom sufficient for the company's growth, so they turn to the most cost-effective financing alternative. The cost of external funds depends on the ability of firms to effectively signal the quality of the venture, as comprehensive and reliable information on the actual and projected performance of the company is lacking. The higher the information asymmetry, the greater the cost of external finance, as providers of capital are likely to price in the uncertainty around firms' prospects. Therefore, the firm's decision to raise external funding depends on whether it can expect the market's favourable valuation (Vismara, 2018b, p. 47).

Regarding funding options, debt finance is often considered inadequate for early-stage innovative firms characterised by high information asymmetry (Stiglitz & Weiss, 1981). However, growing empirical evidence suggests that this type of firms often rely on bank finance (Cosh et al., 2009; Robb & Robinson, 2014), while new forms of debt finance are becoming available for early-stage companies including mini-bonds and P2P business lending.

As to equity capital, small and innovative firms typically rely on angel investors and VCs. It is often conjectured that crowdfunding is used by firms of inferior quality, which cannot obtain financing from these more traditional capital suppliers (Capizzi & Carluccio, 2016; Walthoff-Borm et al., 2018). Walthoff-Borm et al. (2018) show that firms that are less profitable and have limited debt capacity, measured by debt levels and value of intangible assets, are more likely to opt for equity crowdfunding. Conversely, there are several reasons why entrepreneurs may prefer equity crowdfunding over receiving finance from angel investors and VCs (Armour & Enriques, 2018a, pp. 259–260). The first group of reasons relates to the freedom of action and governance of the firm after the investment. Unlike the concentrated ownership structure in the case of angel investors and VCs, equity crowdfunding assumes that ownership is dispersed among a large pool of small investors with limited capacity to exercise their governance rights. Moreover, VC firms are known for negotiating several contractual terms that allow them to have close control over entrepreneurs' course of action, including staged financing. While professional investors often provide business guidance to the firms they finance, this may translate into a higher cost of capital for the entrepreneurs as compared to equity crowdfunding. The second group of reasons equity crowdfunding may be preferred over other funding options are marketing considerations and 'testing the waters' with crowd investors who are often final users. Equity crowdfunding allows one to leverage the firm's existing customer base, advertise the product, and estimate the demand (Estrin et al., 2018). Equity crowdfunding may be a good substitute for VC financing, particularly for early-stage investments, since VCs tend to focus on expansion-stage ventures (Kshetri, 2018, p. 35). One empirical study shows that market validation, ability to demonstrate their potential to professional investors, and retaining a maximum level of governance autonomy are the primary rationale for opting for this financing tool (Di Pietro, 2021). As a result, one may expect that a certain portion of good-quality ventures seek capital via equity crowdfunding rather than through more traditional means if they estimate that they can effectively convey their project's quality to crowd investors, leading to a successful raise under favourable terms.

As in traditional financial markets (Dyck & Zingales, 2004; Hail & Leuz, 2006; La Porta et al., 1997), the level of investor protection in the equity crowdfunding market is likely to affect the terms of raising finance, such as equity valuations and the number of firms that successfully raise funds. The aim of a tailored crowdfunding regime, such as the one adopted in the UK, is to enhance regulatory safeguards by strengthening the role of crowdfunding platforms as gatekeepers (Ande & Eroglu, 2021; Klöhn, 2018, p. 238; Schwartz, 2018) and limiting investors' risk exposure. As a result, entrepreneurs might expect the bespoke regulation to reduce non-diversifiable investment risk in this asset class, reassuring more investors to participate in the crowdfunding market. Such developments may, in turn, reduce the gap between companies' valuations and the underlying expected cash flows caused by regulatory uncertainty.[5]

In addition to more favourable terms for raising equity, a tailored bespoke regulation may affect the direct transaction costs of entrepreneurs opting for this funding mechanism. It is often neglected that there are costs associated with scoping and interpreting applicable rules for issuers, especially when they do not fall under one 'legislative umbrella' but rather dispersed in a number of statutes and regulations (Ridley, 2016, p. 63). These include rules on securities issuances, such as conditions for the exemption from prospectus requirements for small offerings, company law provisions, AML rules, etc. Without a tailored regime, these costs may be prohibitively high for early-stage firms with limited resources devoted to regulatory compliance.

Consequently, one may assume that good-quality firms would welcome the introduction of a bespoke regulation and opt for equity crowdfunding more frequently than before. These may include firms with access to other funding sources (debt or equity) and firms with limited financing alternatives but unwilling to raise funds under unfavourable terms due to low levels of investor protection and regulatory uncertainty. This aligns with the argument that crowdfunding-friendly legislation leads to the institutionalisation of equity crowdfunding, increasing entrepreneurs' efforts to raise funds via this means (Kshetri, 2018, p. 37).

Nevertheless, it is arguable that bespoke crowdfunding regulations would equally incentivise low-quality firms to seek funds via equity crowdfunding, especially when they do not impose a heavy regulatory burden on the issuers, such as in the UK.[6] Nevertheless, platforms that can choose from a large pool of heterogeneous projects will likely list those that promise high returns and strengthen their reputation. As early evidence suggests, equity crowdfunding platforms admit only a small

---

[5] As discussed earlier, companies raising funds via equity crowdfunding are typically free to set their company valuations and the price of shares alone, in consultation with the platform. In other words, investors are confronted with the take-it-or-leave-it price of shares (Klöhn, 2018, p. 243). Nevertheless, investors may not be willing to invest in shares whose price does not reflect the assumed risk to a sufficient degree. This risk may include both project-specific risk and the risk stemming from regulatory uncertainty.

[6] As discussed earlier, the UK's approach is in sharp contrast to the US's, which imposes burdensome disclosures on crowdfunding offerings.

percentage of projects to be listed on their website (Hornuf & Schwienbacher, 2018; Löher, 2017). This means that if favourable regulations can attract both good and bad quality ventures, the former group is likely to crowd out a certain portion of the latter group. As a result, one may conjecture that a greater number of good-quality ventures appear on crowdfunding platforms after the regulation.

While the quality of crowdfunding projects is not directly observable, the strength of signals of post-regulation campaigns can be indicative in this regard. As discussed in detail in Chap. 3, there has been growing literature examining the importance of signals in the equity crowdfunding market (e.g., Ahlers et al., 2015; Courtney et al., 2017; Hornuf & Neuenkirch, 2017; Ralcheva & Roosenboom, 2016; Vismara, 2016, 2018a). As already explained, signals in the crowdfunding context can be defined as observable and alterable characteristics or activities of fundraisers, their projects or crowdfunding campaigns, which are used to convey information about the unobserved quality of the investment credibly.[7] One of the most well-known signals in entrepreneurial literature is retained equity, i.e. the fraction of the equity in the project retained by entrepreneurs (Leland & Pyle, 1977). The argument is that entrepreneurs who know more than potential investors about expected cash flows are likely to retain high ownership interest only if they are confident that the project will earn high returns. The underlying assumption is that by retaining a high equity stake in their own project, entrepreneurs forgo the opportunity to diversify their portfolios, which is costly if expected returns do not offer adequate compensation for risk exposure (Downes & Heinkel, 1982, p. 3). As discussed in Chap. 3, the signalling value of retained equity has also been examined in crowdfunding with prevailing evidence of its positive influence on campaign success (e.g., Ahlers et al., 2015; Battaglia et al., 2022; Ralcheva & Roosenboom, 2016; Reichenbach & Walther, 2021; Rossi et al., 2019).

The target amount in a crowdfunding campaign can also serve as a quality signal in combination with the 'all-or-nothing rule', which has become the industry standard. The rule entails that entrepreneurs whose projects do not reach the target amount cannot appropriate any of the investors' contributions. As a result, entrepreneurs are expected to seek higher amounts if, based on their superior knowledge about the project, they are confident they will attract enough interest from investors. Similarly, it has been argued that company valuations, as determined by entrepreneurs, are both an observable and costly signal since the campaign might receive no funding if perceived as too high by investors (Hornuf & Neuenkirch, 2017).[8] Lastly,

[7] As already discussed, in line with signalling theory (Spence, 1973, p. 358), the costs of these characteristics or activities need to be inversely related to the unobserved quality to create a separating equilibrium between good and bad projects. Investors rely on signals when making their investment decisions, as they cannot expect entrepreneurs to be entirely sincere about their projects, given the 'substantial rewards for exaggerating positive qualities' (Leland & Pyle, 1977, p. 371). In a broader sense, signals may also include penalty costs, which are not borne by entrepreneurs' ex-ante, but once the signal is known to be false.

[8] This is consistent with theoretical models in the market for goods, where price signals product quality (Daughety & Reinganum, 2008, p. 975). The effect of company valuations on campaign

entrepreneurs' choice of corporate governance mechanisms should also indicate the degree of future agency costs arising between them and investors. Investors in equity crowdfunding become minority shareholders, which raises standard concerns arising from the separation of ownership and control (Vismara, 2015, p. 8). Divergence from one-share-one-vote further increases the possibility for entrepreneurs to extract private benefits from the firm at the expense of crowd investors (Cumming, Meoli, & Vismara, 2019, p. 2). As a result, one may expect that more credible founders offer more voting rights to their prospective investors as a commitment device.[9]

In sum, if higher-quality firms are more likely to appear on crowdfunding platforms after the introduction of the crowdfunding regime, they are also expected to have stronger quality signals than their pre-regulation counterparts.

Hypothesis 1: Post-regulation campaigns are launched by more valuable SMEs, which seek to raise higher amounts, retain more equity, and offer more voting rights to their potential investors as compared to their pre-regulation counterparts.

6.4.2 Supply Side Effects

Investor Participation

While the bespoke crowdfunding regime can encourage greater participation of promising quality ventures, it primarily aims to reduce regulatory uncertainty that could have turned away potential investors (Ridley, 2016, p. 63). Therefore, one might conjecture that new or more refined investor protections directly affect investors, independently of the quality distribution of projects appearing on crowdfunding platforms.

Crowdfunding investments are arm's length transactions in which issuers of securities are seldom repeated players in the market. As young companies, they rarely have well-established reputations in other markets. Their payoffs from opportunistic behaviour—omissions or misrepresentations of material information ex-ante or extracting private benefits ex-post, may be high when regulatory oversight is missing or unclear. The expected costs from opportunistic behaviour may be even lower than in traditional financial markets, given the highly dispersed investor base, which has high coordination costs to pursue a private (contract or tort) litigation (La Porta et al., 2006). Unlike in traditional financial markets, crowdfunding investors cannot rely on signals of well-reputable intermediaries such as investment banks as

outcomes can also have an opposite impact since higher valuations mean a smaller share in future cash flows for individual investors (Hornuf & Neuenkirch, 2017, p. 801).

[9] While the choice of governance structure is usually left to entrepreneurs, platforms may influence their decisions in line with an established practice. Also, some platforms exercise voting rights on behalf of investors via a nominee structure instead of voting rights, which are exercised individually (Rossi et al., 2019).

underwriters who vet the investment deals and price shares before they are offered to the public (Anand, 2014, p. 216; Butticè & Vismara, 2021, p. 3; Ralcheva & Roosenboom, 2016, p. 6). Investors are required to conduct their own due diligence or may free-ride on the screening efforts of others, may it be the 'crowd' (Astebro et al., 2019; Li et al., 2020; Vismara, 2015) or a reputable (lead) investor (Kim & Viswanathan, 2018; Ralcheva & Roosenboom, 2016). The contractual and market-based safeguards of equity crowdfunding might not be sufficient for some investors who, despite being interested in this asset class, would pass up the investment opportunities without being provided with additional investor protections.

Bespoke crowdfunding regulation, such as the one adopted in the UK, is likely to attenuate some of the investors' concerns. The rationale for the new regime was to introduce specific investor protection rules for equity crowdfunding platforms (Armour & Enriques, 2018b, p. 65). As mentioned above, one of the cornerstones of the bespoke regulation was to specify the conduct of business obligations for crowdfunding intermediaries similar to the MiFID regime. The focus of these rules is to ensure that financial promotions include balanced information on risks and opportunities and to establish the veracity of claims made on the platform. As a result, the responsibility for complete and accurate disclosures is de facto shifted from issuers, which are exempt from prospectus requirements, to licensed crowdfunding platforms, which are subject to regulatory oversight (Klöhn, 2018, p. 232). This may reduce instances of fraud but also attenuate information asymmetries exacerbated by the fact that everyday (retail) investors, as a predominant investor type, have limited capacity and resources to verify fundraisers' statements. The UK regulation does not prescribe the exact due diligence process to be conducted by equity platforms, as explained above. Nevertheless, investors may have higher expectations regarding platforms' screening efforts after the adoption of the bespoke regime due to higher regulatory scrutiny. The latter is likely to increase following the adoption of new regulations not only because the business conduct rules were made more specific but also because their greater publicness may increase the accountability of regulators (Sale & Thompson, 2015, p. 494).

The evidence from another jurisdiction suggests that investors are sensitive to platforms' due diligence checks, which are found to be positively correlated with the percentage of successful campaigns, number of investors, and overall amount of capital raised on platforms (Cumming, Johan, & Zhang, 2019). While major equity crowdfunding platforms in the UK were authorised and regulated on an ad hoc basis before introducing a crowdfunding regime, adopting new rules is likely to have increased the salience of their supervision under the FCA and the scope of their legal obligations for investors. It has been documented in a broader economic context that individuals solely 'consider information which is right in front of them' (Enke, 2020, p. 1363), while recent literature has also shown that the salience of an issue matters in investment decisions, even more for individual than for professional investors (Chaudary, 2019; Koehler & Mercer, 2009; Yalcin et al., 2016).

Independent of the specifics of bespoke crowdfunding regulations, their most direct, though often unintended consequence, is an implicit legitimisation of the crowdfunding practice (Kshetri, 2015, p. 102; Kshetri, 2018, p. 33). Before the new regime was introduced, some experts in the UK had described equity crowdfunding as 'a scandal waiting to happen' in their urge for a clear regulatory framework (Loveless, 2013). Therefore, the new regime could have been understood as an implicit endorsement by the regulator, changing the public's perception of the viability of this model of financial intermediation. Consequently, one can expect the overall trust in fundraisers to increase (Cai et al., 2020, pp. 191–193). It should be noted, however, that the legitimisation of the industry might not have been the intention of regulators, who, quite the opposite, aimed to alert potential investors about the risks arising from the crowdfunding activity.

Hypothesis 2: Ceteris paribus, *campaigns that were launched after the bespoke regulation attract a larger number of investors.*

Investment Amounts

Besides a wider recognition of the crowdfunding practice, the bespoke regime can influence the amount contributed by individual investors to a single campaign. Following the same reasoning above, one can presume that, with reduced regulatory uncertainty about the scope of investor safeguards, investors feel better protected overall and invest more significant amounts.

Hypothesis 3: Ceteris paribus, *individual pledges are higher after the bespoke regulation.*

Several considerations point out that Hypothesis 3 is not evident and is worth subjecting to empirical testing. The new rules can produce the opposite or no effect, depending on the population of investors participating in crowdfunding campaigns. For this reason, several investor categories will be considered separately.

First, one may distinguish between *Old Investors*—who registered as investors on crowdfunding platforms before the bespoke regime and *New Investors*—who registered only after. *Old Investors* were eager to invest even without additional investor safeguards, which may suggest that they relied on general rules applicable in the absence of the bespoke regime. Similarly, they could have trusted market-based mechanisms of investor protection, as discussed in Chap. 3. As a result, it is plausible that the new regime did not change their investment patterns.

However, both an increase and decrease in their investment amounts are also plausible scenarios. Some *Old Investors* could have joined the crowdfunding market with high precautions before bespoke regulations, investing only limited amounts that 'they can afford to lose'. After they had been reassured with additional regulatory safeguards, they started investing more.

In contrast, some *Old Investors* could have joined the crowdfunding market without relying on platforms' screening but instead conducted thorough due diligence on each project by themselves. This is more likely to be true for professional investors than everyday investors (Butticè & Vismara, 2021, p. 4). Since a detailed screening process involved high fixed costs, there could have been an investment threshold below which it was unprofitable to conduct due diligence. If, after the adoption of the bespoke regime, *Old Investors* started relying more on the platform's due diligence and, hence, reduced their screening efforts, the investment threshold was likely to drop. This may incentivise them to further diversify their portfolio of crowdfunding investments, resulting in smaller contributions to individual projects. Similarly, there could have been an additional return on due diligence conducted before the bespoke regime (information premium for discovering the best deals), which was reduced with the increased role of platforms in ensuring comprehensive and accurate information is disclosed to all investors. Again, this could have led to a drop in investment amounts.[10] Finally, the bespoke regulation could have indirectly affected the amounts pledged by *Old Investors*, such as when a greater pool of good-quality projects to invest in (Hypothesis 1) incentivised investors to diversify their portfolio further.[11]

Hypothesis 3a: Ceteris paribus, *individual pledges of Old Investors increase/ decrease after the bespoke regulation.*

As for the *New Investors* (those that registered on the platform following the adoption of the bespoke regime), it is impossible to observe counterfactuals. Since new investors did not participate in the crowdfunding market before the bespoke regime, it is worthwhile exploring whether their investment behaviour differs from the behaviour of *Old Investors*. The differences in pledges between the two groups can result from some paternalistic investor protection measures, but even more so, the heterogeneity of investors appearing on crowdfunding platforms before and after adopting the new regime.

As explained before, one of the regulatory aims was to caution everyday investors about the risks inherent in crowdfunding through mandatory risk warnings, as well as to contain their risk exposure through aggregate investment limits.[12] These paternalistic solutions can incentivise *New Everyday Investors* to diversify their portfolio further and pledge only small amounts. Risk warnings may do so by increasing the salience of potential losses (Bordalo et al., 2012; Montford et al., 2019), while aggregate limits may indirectly restrict investment amounts on a project level for investors who are interested in supporting various projects. However, the practical consequences of such provisions are likely to be limited. As evidence suggests in other areas of consumer protection, 'warnings that simply serve as reminders' bear little importance for consumer decision-making (Viscusi, 1999, p. 228). Also, crowdfunding platforms do not have to verify investors' claims on their income and wealth, so investors may simply misstate the amount of their investable assets to surpass investment limits (Klöhn, 2018, p. 233).

Consequently, the difference in individual pledges between *Old Investors* and *New Investors* is more likely to be driven by the characteristics of these two groups.

---

[10] For an overview of literature examining excess return in relation to 'narrowly available information', see (Statman, 2017, pp. 297–303).

[11] For instance, it has been shown that the number of active (competing) campaigns on a crowdfunding website negatively affects investor participation (Nguyen et al., 2019), as well as funding percentage and probability of campaign success (Vismara, 2015).

[12] As explained above, everyday investors need to certify that they will not invest more than 10% of their net investible portfolio in unlisted securities as an asset class.

Firstly, the bespoke regulation or its lack thereof could have led to the self-selection of investors based on their level of risk aversion. The fact that *New Investors* waited for greater regulatory certainty to invest in crowdfunding projects indicates that they have a higher level of risk aversion on average. As a result, they might invest smaller amounts than *Old Investors* when provided with similar investment opportunities. This may hold for both everyday and professional investors.

Apart from the risk tolerance level of *New Investors*, the bespoke regime could have influenced the income/wealth distribution of investors and their level of financial sophistication. It has been argued above that bespoke regulations could have encouraged the participation of a greater number of (everyday) investors (Hypothesis 2). This is consistent with the view that the willingness of individual investors to engage in this type of activity critically depends on their crowdfunding awareness (Vaznyte et al., 2020), which is likely to increase with regulatory changes. A broader recognition of crowdfunding practice among everyday investors is expected to result in greater financial inclusion, bringing less sophisticated and less well-off individuals on board. One commonly held opinion is that the merits of crowdfunding lie in its inclusionary nature and its potential to democratise access to investment opportunities (Anand, 2014; Butticè & Vismara, 2021, pp. 7–8; Meoli et al., 2022, p. 1).[13] Accordingly, a greater participation of small and less sophisticated investors may lead to a drop in investment amounts compared to old everyday investors.[14] A greater financial inclusion may also make personal ties between fundraisers and investors less common, potentially causing a decrease in average pledges.

Conversely, legitimising crowdfunding among professional investors due to new regulations could have had the opposite effect, attracting more reputable investors. After all, securities regulations have always been about creating and promoting a competitive market for professional investors and analysts (information traders), even when nominally protecting ordinary investors (Goshen & Parchomovsky, 2005, p. 714). Therefore, some professional investors had been possibly reluctant to join the market before the regulatory treatment of platforms and issuers was clearly defined.[15] Unless they can profit from an informational advantage in an environment

---

[13] One may argue that the participation of a larger number of everyday investors could have equally shifted the mean of income/wealth and financial sophistication distribution towards the right tail. This is primarily because the new regime introduced the appropriateness test, which requires platforms to ensure that investors are able to understand and bear the risks involved. Such a test originates from the suitability doctrine, which implies that the responsibility for wrong investment decisions is shifted from investors to platforms (Statman, 2017, p. 242).

However, as mentioned before, this regulatory requirement boils down to a simple automated test on the nature and risks of crowdfunding investments (Armour & Enriques, 2018b, p. 65). Moreover, one may expect that early investors in crowdfunding were above-average informed or that they were part of the entrepreneur's social network.

[14] The reason why less well-off individuals are likely to invest smaller amounts can be explained by their budgetary constraints, but also higher (absolute) risk aversion levels, even though the relationship between income/wealth and risk tolerance is complex.

[15] Anecdotal evidence suggests that some professional investors followed this line of reasoning. For instance, the head of financial planning at Hargreaves Lansdown Danny Cox said about crowd-

with regulatory uncertainty, professional investors are expected to be more cautious about the level of investor protection. For instance, existing evidence suggests that they are more sensitive to the attribution of voting rights than everyday investors (Cumming, Meoli, & Vismara, 2019). If more reputable professional investors joined the market after the bespoke regime, they are expected to pledge higher amounts than their pre-regulation counterparts.

To sum up, *New Investors* are likely to pledge lower amounts than *Old Investors* if paternalistic investor protection measures (risk warnings and investment limits) produce an effect, if *New Investors* are more risk averse, or if crowdfunding regulations lead to a greater financial inclusion on the investment side (with investors of lower income/wealth joining the market). Conversely, *New Investors* are likely to pledge higher amounts than *Old Investors* if bespoke regulations attract more prominent professional (sophisticated and high net worth) investors who invest large sums.

Hypothesis 3b: Ceteris paribus, *individual pledges of New Investors are higher/lower than pledges of Old Investors.*

6.4.3 Market Outcomes

Campaign Success

The promise of crowdfunding ultimately lies in filling the funding gap for early-stage companies (Leboeuf & Schwienbacher, 2018; Walthoff-Borm et al., 2018). The impact of a bespoke regime should be assessed in light of its ability to enable access to finance while ensuring investor protection standards are met. Therefore, one may ask whether crowdfunding campaigns launched after the adoption of the bespoke regime were more successful than their pre-regulation counterparts.

While crowdfunding regulations could have improved the quality of projects appearing on crowdfunding platforms (Hypothesis 1), it is worth testing whether there is an independent effect on the success of crowdfunding campaigns, as captured by the *Achieved Funding Ratio* (the ratio of amount raised and amount sought). This will depend on the number of investors participating (Hypothesis 2) and the size of individual contributions (Hypothesis 3). However, it is also plausible that, due to differences in projects appearing before and after the regulatory change (Hypothesis 1), competition among good-quality projects increases, making it harder for individual projects to reach the target amount. Thus, increased competition among fundraisers can offset or even reverse the positive effect of regulations on the market's supply side.

Hypothesis 4: Campaigns launched after the adoption of the bespoke regime are more successful, ceteris paribus.

---

funding: 'It is something we are keeping an eye on. Once it becomes regulated we will probably see better products with better protection for investors. Until we have regulation, this market is still too immature and risky' (Yarker, 2013).

The Moderating Role of Signals

Investors' decision to participate in the market and their willingness to contribute a certain amount may depend on the regulatory environment and the strength of market signals of crowdfunding projects. The question arises whether there is an interaction between the two effects, that is, whether the importance of market signals changes after the adoption of the bespoke regime. From a different angle, one may ask whether the effect of crowdfunding regulations is different for projects with varying signal strengths.

Extant law and finance literature considered the question of to what extent financial regulations and market-based mechanisms are substitutes or complementary (e.g., Benston, 1973; Einhorn, 2005; Stigler, 1964). As explained above, the crowdfunding context is unique in the scarcity of credible information on projects' prospects. In the absence of regulation, credible voluntary disclosure of all the relevant information may be inefficient for fundraisers as most investors in crowdfunding cannot independently verify their claims (Dranove & Jin, 2010, p. 936), nor can they rely on verification, certification, or rating of independent agencies (Janssen & Roy, 2015).

When credible disclosure is costly, firms are expected to use signalling instead (Daughety & Reinganum, 2008). The very definition of market signals implies that their senders incur costs if they are false (Connelly et al., 2011; Spence, 1973). Consequently, unlike other information provided during the crowdfunding campaign, the information revealed through signals does not have to be verified by investors or a third party.

In contrast, crowdfunding regulations increase the credibility of other information disclosed by increasing the accountability of either issuers or platforms for any misstatements or omissions.

In principle, these two investor protection mechanisms can be independent, where regulations equally spur investments in all projects, notwithstanding the strength of signals. However, it seems more plausible that there is a certain degree of interaction (substitutability) between signals and regulation. In a less regulated environment, with a low credibility of voluntary disclosures, the importance of market signals is likely to be high. In contrast, if one can rely more on fundraisers' claims after adopting the bespoke regime, the relevance of some market signals is expected to diminish. This may be particularly true for rudimentary signals, such as target amount or retained equity. In addition, if the bespoke regime increases the number of projects with stronger market signals (Hypothesis 1), higher competition among them can further reduce their effect on investors. Thus far, it has been assumed that bespoke regulations can moderate the impact of signals on campaign success.

However, from a different angle, signals can moderate the effect of regulations on campaign outcomes. The bespoke regime is likely to spur more investments in projects with weaker market signals. The reason is that the minimum level of investor protection, including fraud prevention, is ensured through the gatekeeping (certifying) role of regulated platforms. Conversely, crowdfunding regulations are expected to matter less for investments into projects with stronger signals. This is because platforms' screening efforts may not substitute for an assessment of investment opportunities, which goes beyond simple fact-checking.

Hypothesis 4a: Ceteris paribus, *there is a negative interaction effect between market signals and crowdfunding regulations on campaign success.*

6.5 Data and Methods

6.5.1 Data

The data were collected by the Cambridge Centre for Alternative Finance. They included campaign-level and investor-level observations for the equity crowdfunding market in the UK, covering the period from February 2012 until June 2016. The sample data disclose 201 equity crowdfunding campaigns run on one of the three major crowdfunding platforms (Seedrs, Crowdcube, and SyndicateRoom) and 30,708 individual investments made by 16,857 investors.[16]

Campaign-level data is used to test hypotheses on the effect of the regulatory change on campaign characteristics (Hypothesis 1), investor participation (Hypothesis 2), and market outcomes (Hypotheses 4 and 4a). Campaign-level data includes pooled cross-section data on campaign and fundraisers' characteristics, number of investors participating, and campaign outcomes. While specific platforms on which campaigns were run cannot be identified in the sample, all of them ran the 'all-or-nothing' model, in which fundraisers can keep the capital raised if they reach the target amount. Only two campaigns in the sample raised funds in EUR, indicating that their fundraisers were based outside the UK. Eighteen fundraisers in the sample ran more than one campaign, of which two fundraisers ran three campaigns.[17]

Investor-level data is used to test hypotheses on how the adoption of the bespoke regime affected the amount pledged by individual investors (Hypotheses 3, 3a, and 3b). Investor-level data, which includes the amount investors contributed to a single campaign and investors' characteristics, is complemented with campaign-level data as controls. 42.7% of investors in the sample appear only once, suggesting they possibly invested in only one campaign. 57.29% of investors invested in between 2 and 100 different campaigns. Similar to Goethner, Hornuf, and Regner (2021), a panel dataset is constructed from these data. A unit of analysis is the amount pledged in a single campaign, with a particular investor as a cross-sectional dimension and the

[16] This corresponds to approximately 20% of the market in the covered period. Since data collected from different platforms are not interconnected, one may not exclude that some investors invested on various platforms. This would not be captured in this dataset.

[17] As explained above, one may not exclude the possibility that some fundraisers ran two or more campaigns on different platforms, which this dataset would not capture.

time of investments (funds committed date) as a time dimension.[18] The difference from Goethner, Hornuf et al. (2021) is that the focus is on individual amounts invested for the entire duration of a campaign instead of aggregate amounts invested in a single campaign on a given day.[19]

The date when the bespoke regime went into force, which is 1 April 2014, is the change whose effects we aim to explore. As a result, both campaign-level and investor-level observations are split into two periods, depending on whether the campaign was launched or the investment was made before or after the regulatory change. The sample comprises 79 campaigns launched before and 122 after the regulatory change. Likewise, 7, 283 investments were made before, and 23,425 investments were made after the adoption of the new regime. In addition, the sample includes 13,911 investments made by *Old Investors* (those who registered on a platform before 1 April 2014) and 16,797 investments made by *New Investors*.

Similar to the research of Nguyen et al. (2019) and Hornuf and Neuenkirch (2017), crowdfunding data provided by the Cambridge Centre for Alternative Finance is complemented with data on standard deviation of FTSE returns (FTSE 100 VIX) (Investing.Com, n.d.). In addition, for investor-level regressions, data on some macroeconomic indicators (interest rates and money supply) provided by the Bank of England are included, to account for economic trends.

Outcome Variables

To investigate whether the characteristics of individual campaigns changed after the regulatory change (Hypothesis 1), the study uses four variables that may be considered as market signals: *SME Value*, *Amount Sought*, *Retained Equity*, and *Voting Rights*. *SME Value* is the pre-money valuation of the firm estimated by fundraisers, usually in consultation with the platform, which is disclosed at the campaign launch. The *Amount Sought* is the target fundraising amount, which needs to be reached for fundraisers to keep any funds. In line with the literature (e.g., Johan & Zhang, 2020), both variables are log transformed to adjust for lack of normality (Annexes 6B and 6C). Retaining equity is another campaign characteristic that might have changed after adopting the bespoke regime. As explained above, *retained equity* is one of the most widely researched signals in entrepreneurial finance, and equity crowdfunding in particular, which denotes the percentage of equity kept by its founders (Ahlers et al., 2015; Cumming, Meoli, & Vismara, 2021; Ralcheva & Roosenboom, 2016; Vismara, 2016). Lastly, the study constructs the variable *Voting Rights*, a dummy variable equal to 0 if only Class B shares (no voting shares) are

[18] More precisely, the 'funds committed date' is used to construct the variable 'the number of investments', which allows for the random investor-specific effect to be accounted for.

[19] In cases in which a particular investor invested several times in the same campaign, these amounts were summed up because the focus of this study is not on the investment dynamics within a single campaign, such as in the study by Goethner, Hornuf, and Regner (2021), but rather on changes in the behaviour of individual investors due to the bespoke regime.

offered. The dummy variable takes 1 if a campaign offers dual-class shares. This entails that both B shares (no voting shares) and A shares (voting shares) are offered, while investors need to invest above a certain threshold to be able to receive A shares. It is worth noting that in the case of dual-class shares, investors pay the same price for different asset classes (Cumming, Meoli, & Vismara, 2019, p. 2). Finally, the dummy variable equals 2, if only voting shares are offered to all investors. All four variables are later used as control variables when testing other hypotheses.

Furthermore, the study uses the *Number of investors* contributing to a given campaign as a dependent variable to test whether the regulatory change encouraged a greater participation of investors (Hypothesis 2). The number of investors is often considered an alternative indicator of campaign success, given that equity crowdfunding usually serves the purpose of market validation (Cumming, Johan, & Zhang, 2019; Cumming, Vanacker, & Zahra, 2021; Ralcheva & Roosenboom, 2016; Vismara, 2016).

To investigate Hypotheses 3, 3a, and 3b, the study uses the *Amount invested per project* as a dependent variable. To normalise the distribution of this variable, the study uses log values instead (Annex 6D).

Finally, the ratio of the amount raised and the amount sought in a given campaign (*Achieved Funding Ratio*) is used as a dependent variable to explore the effect of regulation on market outcomes (Hypotheses 4 and 4a). It is widely held in the literature that this indicator is a more fine-tuned measure of campaign success as compared to binary indicators of whether the campaign reached its funding goal (Ralcheva & Roosenboom, 2016; Vismara, 2015, 2016). It shows how close the project was to reaching its target amount, as well as how much capital was raised above the amount sought, as overfunding is a common practice in equity crowdfunding (Li et al., 2020).

Explanatory Variables

Given that the study investigates the effect of the regulatory change, two dummy variables are constructed. *PostregCampaign* is a dummy variable that equals 1, if the campaign was launched after the adoption of the bespoke regulation, and 0 otherwise. More precisely, this dummy variable is constructed based on a campaign request date provided in the sample. It is particularly suitable for testing Hypothesis 1, given that it reflects the date when the fundraising decision was made and the process initiated. The same explanatory variable is used for testing hypotheses 2, 4, and 4a. To explore whether the regulatory change affected individual pledges (Hypotheses 3, 3a, and 3b), the study uses a dummy variable *Postreg,* which is equal to 1 if the funds committed date is after 1 April 2014 and 0 otherwise.

Similar to the research by Goethner, Hornuf et al. (2021), this study also explores the differences in investing behaviour between *Old Investors*, who registered on a crowdfunding platform before the regulatory change, and *New Investors*, who appeared only after. For this purpose, the study uses *PostregInvestor*, a dummy variable equal to 1 if the investor registered on the platform after 1 April 2014 and 0 otherwise.

Control Variables

As mentioned above, some of the critical determinants of investor participation, their pledging intentions, and the overall success of a campaign may also be affected by the regulation (Hypothesis 1). These include *SME Value*, *Amount Sought*, *Retained Equity,* and *Voting Rights*. Their inclusion in models testing other hypotheses is necessary to reduce the unexplained variation in the dependent variable and investigate whether the bespoke regime produced an independent effect on investors. Put differently, it is essential to discern whether campaign outcomes and individual investment decisions changed as a result of factors unrelated to the differences in projects appearing on crowdfunding platforms after the regulatory change.

While all four variables considered independently are expected to positively affect investor participation, individual pledges, and campaign success, it is unclear whether their positive effect remains when they are all included in the model. For instance, risk-loving investors are likely to prefer when small firms undertake ambitious projects, in which case the sign of *SME Value* would be negative, and the sign of *Amount Sought* would be positive. Conversely, more risk-averse investors are likely to prefer small-scale projects undertaken by already established firms. Preference for smaller firms, after controlling for the *Amount Sought*, can also relate to the risk of overvaluation of companies raising funds.

The study also accounts for whether share issues qualify for the Enterprise Investment Scheme (*EIS*) and Seed Enterprise Investment Scheme (*SEIS*) tax incentives.[20] Both tax incentives are expected to encourage investments. However, SEIS also signals that firms are still in the seed stage, which may have the opposite effect. In the absence of data on firm age, the *SEIS* dummy may serve as a proxy for very young firms.

Given that some fundraisers in the sample launched more than one campaign, the study further controls for the *Prior_Campaigns* experience—a dummy variable equal to 1 if the fundraiser had run another campaign before and 0 otherwise. Running two or more consecutive campaigns allows one to gain valuable experience, leverage the existing investor base, and demonstrate the capacity to lead or successfully complete a project. Thus, it is expected to have a positive effect on outcome variables.

The study also controls for *fundraiser_age*. It has been argued that age discrimination may lower the chances of older people becoming entrepreneurs (Butticè & Vismara, 2021). One study also finds that firms with younger top management teams are more likely to launch an equity crowdfunding campaign and complete it successfully (Cumming, Meoli, & Vismara, 2021).

[20] EIS gives investors initial tax relief of up to 30% on investments up to £1 million per tax year. SEIS offers investors the possibility of receiving initial tax relief of up to 50% on investments up to £100,000 per tax year. Further, investors in both EIS and SEIS shares are exempt from Capital Gains Tax if shares are held for at least 3 years; they are also entitled to loss relief if the shares are disposed of at a loss (Crowdcube, n.d.-a).

Campaign duration is also included in all models, although its influence may work both ways. Shorter campaigns may suggest that the funding amount was reached fast, especially in the light of frequent herding behaviour (Astebro et al., 2019; Li et al., 2020), while prolonged duration increases the chance of receiving additional funding (Vismara, 2015).

To account for unobserved heterogeneity among different industries, the study includes *Campaign_sector*, a dummy variable equal to 1 for each campaign sector and 0 otherwise. Due to the limited number of observations at the campaign level, the study also uses the *Tech_sector* dummy as the alternative. In line with previous literature (Nguyen et al., 2019; Ralcheva & Roosenboom, 2016), the dummy equals 1 if the campaign is launched within the tech sector and 0 otherwise.

For testing Hypothesis 3, 3a, and 3b, in addition to all controls outlined above, the study includes some investor characteristics. Besides investor age, the study controls for the *Number_of_investments* into different campaigns, similar to the study by Hornuf and Neuenkirch (2017). The idea is to account for the difference in the pledges of investors supporting only one project, possibly due to personal ties to its founders, and investors that follow a diversification strategy and possibly participate in the crowdfunding market over a longer period. Another question of interest is whether the effect of regulation depends on the investor's level of sophistication. The data allow one to identify *everyday investors*, *sophisticated investors*, *high net-worth individuals*, and *advised investors*. As explained above, most investors qualify as everyday investors, which, according to the new regulations, should invest less than 10% of their net assets each year in securities that are not listed on an exchange. Self-certified sophisticated investors include those who have invested in more than one unlisted company in the last 2 years, or been a director of a company with an annual turnover of at least £1 million, or been a member of a business angels' network or worked in the private equity sector for at least the last 6 months. High-worth individuals include investors earning more than £100,000 per year or holding net assets of at least £250,000. Advised investors have an FCA-regulated advisor advising them about each investment on a crowdfunding platform.[21] For each of these investor types, the study constructs a dummy variable equal to 1 if the investor is of a particular type or 0 otherwise. Similar to the study by Goethner, Luettig, and Regner (2021), the study creates the reference group for investments for which no investor type is identified in the data.

Finally, the last set of controls refers to macroeconomic variables, which may reflect economic trends and affect investors' choice of equity crowdfunding over other available investment opportunities. Following the study of Nguyen et al. (2019) and Hornuf and Neuenkirch (2017), the study constructs an indicator of volatility in a traditional financial market by measuring the standard deviation of FTSE returns over a rolling 30-day window preceding the launch of each campaign or preceding each investment. Based on the findings in previous studies, one may

[21] Definitions of investor types can be found in applicable regulations and are also available, with slight differences, on crowdfunding websites (Seedrs Help Centre, n.d.; Crowdcube, n.d.-b).

expect that investors consider stocks and equity crowdfunding as substitutes and invest in equity crowdfunding more during times of stress in the financial market. Alternatively, one may also conjecture that equity crowdfunding attracts risk-loving investors who choose this investment alternative in times of low volatility of the financial market when high-risk-high-return investment opportunities are limited. The study also includes quarterly *Interest_rate*, expecting it to be negatively correlated with equity crowdfunding investments.[22] Similarly, the study includes a measure of quarterly money supply (M2).[23] Annex 6A provides an overview of all the variables and their description.[24]

6.5.2 Descriptive Statistics

Annex 6E provides a summary of key descriptive statistics for observations on the campaign level. A representative campaign[25] in the data is launched by a company with an estimated approximate value of £950,000, which seeks to raise £140,000 by offering around 90% of A-class shares. The company is outside the tech sector and qualifies for EIS tax incentives for its investors. The company's main fundraiser is 38 years old and has no prior equity crowdfunding experience. The campaign lasts for 53 days and is overfunded, reaching 130% of the target amount and attracting 121 investors. Annex 6F provides a summary of key descriptive statistics for observations on the investor level. A representative investor[26] is 37 years old and has invested in only one campaign in the sample, about £150.

To gain some initial insights into the development of the crowdfunding market before and after the regulatory change, the study first conducts a univariate analysis by comparing campaigns launched before and after the bespoke regime went into force. A similar comparison of individual investment decisions is made by dividing the sample based on whether the investment was made before or after the change. Finally, the study explores whether investors who appeared on crowdfunding platforms after the change (*New Investors*) have different investment patterns than those who appeared before (*Old Investors*). In the next step, the study turns to a more

[22] More precisely, the variable measures the Quarterly average Sterling 3 month mean interbank lending rate and was obtained from the Bank of England database (Bank of England, n.d.-a).

[23] More precisely, the variable measures Quarterly amounts outstanding of monetary financial institutions' sterling and all foreign currency M2 (UK estimate of EMU aggregate) liabilities to private and public sectors (in sterling millions) seasonally adjusted and was obtained from the Bank of England database (Bank of England, n.d.-b).

[24] M2 is included as additional controls only in investor-level regressions where there is a large number of observations (for testing Hypotheses 3, 3a, and 3b).

[25] A representative campaign exhibits median values for variables included in the summary statistic table for campaign-level data.

[26] A representative investor exhibits median values for variables included in the summary statistic table for investor-level data.

comprehensive multivariate analysis, which accounts for the simultaneous effect of various campaign and investor characteristics.

Table 6.1 provides t-test statistics at the campaign level. It shows that campaigns launched after the bespoke regime were more successful using different indicators. Post-regulation campaigns attracted more investors, raised higher amounts, and had a higher *Achieved Funding Ratio* (ratio of the amount raised and the amount sought), and these differences are highly statistically significant. There is little consensus when the sample size is large enough so that *the t-test* provides unbiased estimates of the difference in means for non-normally distributed data, in line with the Central Limit Theorem. For this reason, the study also performs the Mann-Whitney U test to compare differences between pre-regulation and post-regulation campaigns. This is done for outcome variables which are non-normally distributed according to the Kolmogorov–Smirnov Test (*Number of Investors*, *Achieved Funding Ratio* and *Amount Raised*). The results of the Mann-Whitney U test show a statistical difference in means between campaigns launched before and after the bespoke regime concerning the *Number of Investors*, *Achieved Funding Ratio*, and *Amount Raised* ($P < 0.01$). Given that the Mann-Whitney U test does not capture the size of the difference, the study also performs a set of quantile regressions. Quantile regression provides the test for the equality of medians, and it is considered an equivalent of the *t-test* for medians (Conroy, 2012, p. 187). The results of quantile regressions show that the difference in median *Number of Investors* before and after the regulatory change is 72 (at 1% level of significance), and the difference in median *Achieved Funding Ratio* is 36.8% (at 1% level of significance). The difference in median *Amount Raised* is £79,850 (at 5% level of significance).

However, in support of Hypothesis 1, it is also indicative that post-regulation campaigns differ with respect to several characteristics, which may be considered quality signals. They are launched by more valuable SMEs, which seek to raise higher amounts, retain more equity, and give more voting rights to their investors at high statistical significance. In line with the considerations above, the study also performs the Mann-Whitney U test and quantile regressions for campaign characteristics with non-normally distributed data (*SME Value*, *Amount Sought*, and *Retained Equity*). The results of the Mann-Whitney U test show a statistical difference between campaigns launched before and after the bespoke regime concerning *SME Value*, *Amount Sought*, and *Retained Equity* at 1% significance. The results of the quantile regressions show that the difference in median *SME Value* before and after the regulatory change is £583,690, the difference in median *Amount Sought* is £50,000 (at 5% level of significance), and the difference in *Retained Equity* 4% (at 1% level of significance).

Among other campaign characteristics, the only statistically significant difference exists with regard to campaigns in the technology sector, which have become less frequent. Regarding macroeconomic variables of interest, it is worth noting that the FTSE volatility increased in the post-regulation period by 0.1% (at 5% level of significance).

To gain further insights into the dynamics of change in campaign characteristics over time in line with Hypothesis 1, Fig. 6.1 presents the scatterplot of campaign

Table 6.1 Difference in means between pre-regulation and post-regulation campaigns

	Pre-regulation		Post-regulation		Diff	
	Mean	s.d.	Mean	s.d.	*b*	*t*
Outcome variables						
Number of investors	110.316	98.822	199.910	165.799	−89.593***	(−4.796)
Achieved funding ratio	1.328	0.499	1.662	1.084	−0.334**	(−2.954)
Amount raised	194,206.190	240,890.970	392,303.527	417,219.011	−198,097.338***	(−4.261)
Control variables						
SME value	1,064,345.430	1,275,032.153	3,140,786.509	9,357,725.269	−2,076,441.079*	(−2.417)
Amount sought	145,260.886	141,766.765	253,909.125	294,145.371	−108,648.239***	(−3.500)
Retained equity	0.840	0.126	0.892	0.055	−0.053***	(−3.473)
Voting rights	1.101	0.612	1.680	0.502	−0.579***	(−7.019)
Prior campaigns	0.076	0.267	0.115	0.320	−0.039	(−0.930)
Campaign duration	55.649	37.184	48.287	29.367	7.362	(1.472)
EIS approved	0.633	0.485	0.598	0.492	0.035	(0.490)
SEIS approved	0.316	0.468	0.336	0.474	−0.020	(−0.289)
Fundraiser age	39.915	10.954	39.708	11.000	0.207	(0.109)
Tech sector	0.354	0.481	0.148	0.356	0.207**	(3.282)
FTSE volatility	0.007	0.002	0.008	0.003	−0.001**	(−2.832)
Interest rate	0.568	0.171	0.547	0.014	0.021	(1.103)
N	79		122		201	

This table shows summary statistics at the campaign level for pre-regulation and post-regulation campaigns. The last column provides test statistics for the pre- and post-regulation comparison

***p 0.01, **p 0.05, *p 0.1

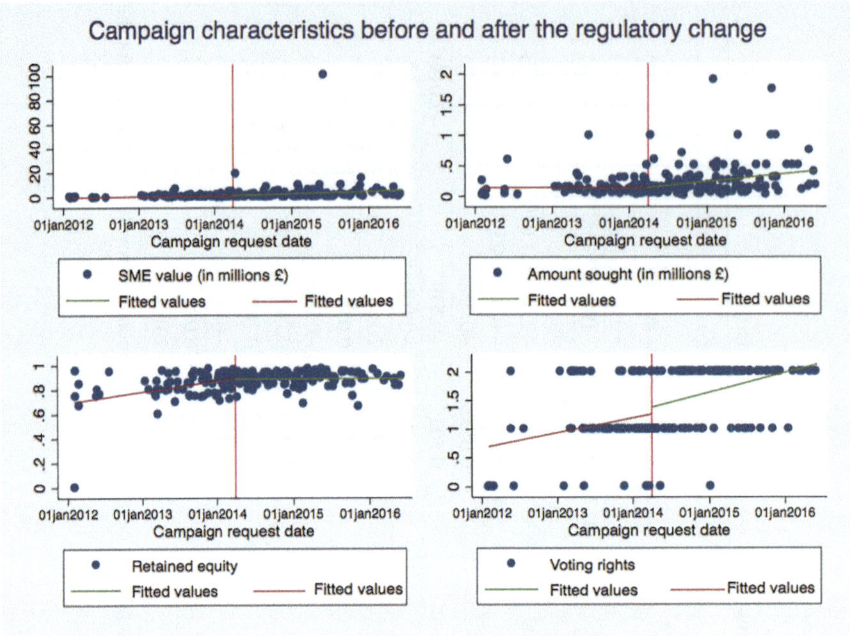

Fig. 6.1 Scatter plot of certain campaign characteristics over time with a fitted regression line before and after the regulatory change

characteristics with a fitted regression line before and after the regulatory change. One can observe that the change in different campaign characteristics did not follow the same pattern. *SME Value* did not change much over time, neither in the period before nor after the regulatory change. However, SMEs with relatively high valuations appeared only after the adoption of the bespoke regime. Regarding the target amount, there seems to be no growth in the *Amount Sought* over time in the period before the regulatory change. After the change, the increase in the target amount was gradual, suggesting that the regulatory change possibly enabled the market to mature over time rather than causing a sharp change in this campaign characteristic. The change in *Retained Equity* over time stands in sharp contrast. While a gradual increase in *Retained Equity* happened before the regulatory change, most crowdfunding campaigns in the post-regulation period are characterised by high values of this quality signal. This can suggest that higher competition among better-quality projects after the regulatory change allowed platforms to list projects with a high percentage of *Retained Equity* primarily. Finally, concerning *Voting Rights*, one can observe a shift in the values of this variable around the adoption of the bespoke regime, with fewer firms offering only B shares and more firms providing only A shares. In contrast, many firms offer dual-class shares both before and after the adoption of the new regime.

Table 6.2 shows the difference in the mean amount of individual investments per project made before and after the adoption of the bespoke regime. Univariate

Table 6.2 Difference in means between pre-regulation and post-regulation individual investments

	Pre-regulation		Post-regulation		Diff	
	Mean	s.d.	Mean	s.d.	*b*	*t*
Amount invested per project	1721.172	6595.865	1604.840	12,458.385	116.332	(1.036)
SME value	1,429,429.366	1,802,328.491	4,249,647.991	12,048,297.590	−2,820,218.625***	(−34.602)
Amount sought	238,615.874	269,918.963	334,007.597	342,158.204	−95,391.723***	(−24.629)
Retained equity	0.843	0.103	0.888	0.063	−0.046***	(−35.836)
Voting rights	1.129	0.619	1.696	0.484	−0.567***	(−71.678)
Prior campaigns	0.991	0.094	0.995	0.070	−0.004***	(−3.328)
Campaign duration	59.513	40.608	46.563	29.680	12.950***	(24.928)
EIS approved	0.764	0.425	0.673	0.469	0.091***	(15.578)
SEIS approved	0.231	0.422	0.273	0.446	−0.042***	(−7.267)
Fundraiser age	41.391	9.813	39.858	10.164	1.534***	(9.592)
Tech sector	0.359	0.480	0.157	0.364	0.201***	(32.999)
FTSE volatility	0.007	0.002	0.009	0.003	−0.002***	(−52.680)
Interest rate	0.557	0.149	0.549	0.016	0.007***	(4.153)
M2	2,077,835.504	17,505.467	2,112,345.977	52,754.218	−34,510.474***	(−86.040)
Investor age	41.860	12.541	38.616	12.860	3.244***	(18.610)
Reference group	0.253	0.435	0.173	0.379	0.080***	(14.048)
Everyday investor	0.370	0.483	0.467	0.499	−0.098***	(−14.990)
Sophisticated investor	0.251	0.434	0.182	0.385	0.069***	(12.244)
High net worth	0.123	0.329	0.174	0.379	−0.050***	(−10.979)
Advised investor	0.003	0.055	0.004	0.062	−0.001	(−1.136)
Number of investments	3.438	4.917	4.311	8.027	−0.873***	(−11.207)
N	7283		23,425		30,708	

This table shows summary statistics at the investor level for investments made before and after the regulatory change. The last column provides test statistics for the comparison of pre-regulation and post-regulation investments

***p 0.01, **p 0.05, *p 0.1

analysis indicates that post-regulation investments are smaller, but the mean difference is not statistically significant. Given the highly skewed distribution of the variable *Amount Invested Per Project*, the study also performs the Mann-Whitney U test and a quantile regression. The results of the Mann-Whitney U test indicate that the pre-regulation and post-regulation investments are statistically different. The quantile regression shows a decrease in the median *Amount Invested Per Project* after the regulatory change, equal to £195 (statistically significant at 1%). This potentially suggests that the new regime has encouraged even smaller investors to join the equity crowdfunding market. However, the effect may differ for various investor types, which will be examined in the subsequent analysis.

As with campaign-level observations, post-regulation investments are made in more valuable companies, which seek larger amounts, retain more equity, and offer more voting rights as compared to pre-regulation investments (at 1% level of significance). However, the difference in some other variables becomes significant as well when the unit of analysis is individual investments.[27] Post-regulation investments are made in campaigns that last shorter and are more frequently launched by younger fundraisers who have previous fundraising experience. Moreover, investments are also made in campaigns that are less likely to be in the technology sector, with more frequent SEIS approvals and less frequent EIS approvals. As to the macroeconomic indicators, post-regulation investments are made in times of higher volatility of the stock market, lower interest rates, and an increase in money supply in the economy.

The mean investor age decreases after the regulatory change. Everyday investors and high-net-worth individuals are more frequent in the sample in the post-regulation period. In contrast, sophisticated investors and the investors in the reference group (for which no investor type can be determined) are less frequent. Unsurprisingly, crowdfunding investment experience increases after the regulatory change, with the mean number of investments made by an individual investor being statistically higher.

Slightly different results are obtained when comparing *Old* and *New Investors*, as shown in Annex 6G. The results of the *t*-test statistics show that *New Investors* invest higher mean amounts than *Old Investors*. The results of quantile regressions show that the difference in median investment per project between Old and New investors is £99 ($P < 0.01$). In other words, median investment amount of *New Investors* is smaller than thc medium investment amount of *Old Investors*. New investors are also younger on average, and, unsurprisingly, they also have less crowdfunding investment experience, measured by the number of crowdfunding

---

[27] The main reason for the higher statistical significance of other control variables at the investor level is a considerably greater number of observations. However, other reasons may also include the fact that campaigns with a higher *Number of Investors* are given more weight as they appear more often in the sample. Moreover, the moment in time used for dividing the sample into the pre-regulation and the post-regulation period is not the same for campaign-level and investor-level observations. In the former case, the campaign request date is used, while in the latter case, the time of individual investment decisions is used.

investments made in the sample. New investors are also more frequently one-time investors in the sample.

The univariate analysis is not conclusive, as it does not control for possible confounding factors. The following multivariate regression analysis investigates regulatory effects in greater detail for all the hypotheses except Hypotheses 1.

6.5.3 Empirical Method

To test the hypotheses, the study uses different empirical methods depending on the unit of observation. It first conducts a multivariate regression analysis to test hypotheses 2, 4, and 4a, for which campaign-level data is used. One of the challenges in the identification strategy lies in the fact that the regulatory change might have simultaneously affected project characteristics (Hypothesis 1) and the outcome variables: *Number of Investors* participating (Hypothesis 2) and investment amounts (Hypothesis 3). In order to test whether the bespoke regime has had an independent (direct) effect on investors, the study needs to consider that investment opportunities after the regulatory change likely improved as well. In other words, crowdfunding projects that appear before and after this change are not randomly assigned. This raises the question of whether pre-regulation campaigns offer a proper counterfactual for estimating the treatment effect on the treated (ATT). In this context, ATT represents the difference in the outcome of post-regulation campaigns and their counterfactual outcome, that is, the outcome of these campaigns if the bespoke regime had not been in place.

The study employs a matching approach to mitigate the described self-selection problem. The idea of matching is to mimic the randomisation of treatment assignment by creating a control group which is as similar as possible to the treatment group. In this study, the purpose of the matching exercise is to create a control group consisting of pre-regulation campaigns, which resembles the treatment group with regard to observable campaign characteristics, that are (a) likely affected by crowdfunding regulations and, at the same time, (b) influence the outcome variable.[28]

The chosen matching technique is entropy balancing, which was developed by Hainmueller (2012). The technique consists of two stages. In the first stage, weights are assigned to units not subject to the treatment, that is, to crowdfunding campaigns launched before the regulatory change. Weights are chosen to comply with pre-determined constraints, which assume that the treatment and the control group have equal means of covariates. In the framework of this study, weights are chosen so that the control group of pre-regulation campaigns resembles, as much as possible, the treatment group of post-regulation campaigns in terms of characteristics that could have been affected by the regulatory change. Based on theoretical

[28] The inspiration for employing this method was found in an unrelated study by Gutmann et al. (2021).

considerations and results of t-test statistics elaborated above, entropy balancing is done based on the following covariates: *SME_value*, *amount_sought*, *retained_equity*, and *voting_rights*. Descriptive statistics of these covariates before and after the entropy balancing can be found in Annex 6H.

In the second stage, the weights assigned in the first stage are used in a weighted regression analysis, in which the regulatory change is the explanatory variable. The weighted regression also includes as controls the covariates that were used for matching in the first stage. The main advantage of using entropy balancing in combination with a regression analysis over a simple regression analysis is that the functional form assumption does not have to be satisfied to yield unbiased estimates (Gutmann et al., 2021, p. 10). Entropy balancing is also superior to other matching techniques in small samples, given that, instead of matching each treated unit with one similar untreated unit, a high covariate balance is achieved between the treatment and a control group as a whole (Gutmann et al., 2021, pp. 10–11). Nevertheless, in terms of causal interpretation of the results, this method is subject to the same identification assumption as OLS, that is, selection on observables.

Testing Hypotheses 3, 3a, and 3b, for which investor-level data is used, requires a different empirical approach. This is due to a panel structure of the data, in which the same individuals appear several times if they make more than one investment. The study performs Random-effects GLS regression for all model specifications, as results of the Breusch and Pagan LM test indicate that random effects are present. Random-effects GLS regression cannot be combined with entropy balancing.

6.6 Results

The results of the study are grouped based on the data sample used (campaign-level vs. investor-level data) and the chosen empirical method. As a result, the presentation of results does not follow the order of hypotheses. Instead, results on Hypotheses 2, 4, and 4a are presented first, using campaign-level data (Sect. 6.4.1), and results on Hypotheses 3, 3a, and 3b are presented second, using investor-level data (Sect. 6.4.2).

6.6.1 Investor Participation and Campaign Outcomes

For the analysis of the impact of bespoke crowdfunding regulations on investor participation (Hypothesis 2), the basic model specifications follow.

1. *Number of Investors* = *Constant* + $\beta 1$ * *Postreg Campaign Dummy* + $\beta 2$ **SME Value* + $\beta 3$ * *Amount Sought* + $\beta 4$ * *Retained Equity* + $\beta 5$ * *Voting Rights* + $\beta 6$ * *Controls* + *Residuals*.

For Model I and Model II, the study estimates a negative binomial regression to account for the fact that the dependent variable is a non-negative integer or count variable (Ahlers et al., 2015; Block et al., 2018; Nguyen et al., 2019). The difference between the two models is that the first uses a Technology dummy instead of a full set of sector dummy variables due to a limited number of observations at the campaign level, as in some other studies (e.g., Ralcheva & Roosenboom, 2016). Model III and IV are the main specifications for which the study performs entropy balancing combined with OLS regression on the natural log of the *Number of Investors*. Using the log-transformation can also be justified by the non-normal distribution of the variable. Model III and IV also differ with respect to whether only the technology dummy or a full set of sector dummies are used as controls.

	Model I	Model II	Model III	Model IV
	Number of investors (negative binomial)	Number of investors (negative binomial)	Ln number of investors (matching and OLS)	Ln number of investors (matching and OLS)
Postreg campaign	0.0221	−0.00635	−0.0137	−0.0116
	(0.160)	(0.152)	(0.148)	(0.162)
SME value (log transformed)	0.0556	0.0681	0.139	0.207
	(0.144)	(0.154)	(0.156)	(0.177)
Amount sought (log transformed)	0.388**	0.399**	0.316*	0.261
	(0.161)	(0.170)	(0.171)	(0.193)
Retained equity	0.900	1.039	0.702	0.223
	(1.388)	(1.470)	(1.608)	(1.803)
Voting rights	0.211*	0.183	0.108	0.0722
	(0.118)	(0.140)	(0.116)	(0.141)
Prior campaigns	0.178	0.423*	0.234	0.353
	(0.227)	(0.235)	(0.236)	(0.250)
Campaign duration	−0.00291*	−0.00206	−0.00446**	−0.00267
	(0.00170)	(0.00165)	(0.00173)	(0.00178)
Fundraiser age	−0.00283	−0.00951**	−0.0105**	−0.0148***
	(0.00465)	(0.00444)	(0.00450)	(0.00465)
EIS approved	0.215	0.122	0.340***	0.0697
	(0.138)	(0.121)	(0.127)	(0.137)
SEIS approved	0.246*	0.0920	0.201	−0.0138
	(0.141)	(0.127)	(0.150)	(0.157)
		(0.345)		(0.394)
FTSE volatility	36.41*	−2.729	34.40*	5.489
	(19.53)	(20.71)	(20.05)	(22.31)
Interest rate	0.390	0.0699	−3.638	1.313
	(3.417)	(3.358)	(3.513)	(3.860)
Sector dummies included	No	Yes	No	Yes

	Model I	Model II	Model III	Model IV
	Number of investors (negative binomial)	Number of investors (negative binomial)	Ln number of investors (matching and OLS)	Ln number of investors (matching and OLS)
Tech	−0.170		−0.205	
	(0.131)		(0.132)	
Constant	−1.861	−0.432	0.582	−0.915
	(2.098)	(2.094)	(2.428)	(2.552)
Observations	157	140	157	140
R-squared			0.420	0.606

Standard errors in parentheses
***$p < 0.01$, **$p < 0.05$, *$p < 0.1$

The findings across different model specifications are consistent with regard to the effect of the independent variable. The study finds no support for Hypothesis 2. In contrast to univariate analysis, post-regulation campaigns do not attract a greater *Number of Investors* when campaign characteristics are controlled for. This may suggest that the difference in the mean *Number of Investors* per campaign before and after the regulatory change is driven by differences in project characteristics, while the regulatory change does not produce an independent effect on investor participation. The study finds that investors are attracted to campaigns with a higher target amount, which are launched by younger fundraisers. Also, campaigns that last shorter spur greater investor participation, although the effect is not robust to the inclusion of sector dummies.

For the analysis about the impact of bespoke crowdfunding regulations on the campaign outcomes measured by the *Achieved Funding Ratio* (Hypothesis 4), the basic model specifications follow

1. *Achieved Funding Ratio* = *Constant* + $\beta 1$ * *Postreg Campaign Dummy* + $\beta 2$ **SME Value* + $\beta 3$ * *Amount Sought* + $\beta 4$ * *Retained Equity* + $\beta 5$ * *Voting Rights* + $\beta 6$ * *Controls* + *Residuals.*

For the analysis about the interaction effect between market signals and crowdfunding regulations on campaign success (Hypothesis 4a), the basic model specifications follow

2. *Achieved Funding Ratio* = *Constant* + $\beta 1$ * *Postreg Campaign Dummy* + $\beta 2$ **SME Value* + $\beta 3$ * *Amount Sought* + $\beta 4$ * *Retained Equity* + $\beta 5$ * *Voting Rights* + $\beta 6$ * *Interaction Variables* + $\beta 7$ * *Controls* + *Residuals.*

Models I, II, III, and IV are used for testing Hypothesis 4. For Model I and II, the study conducts an OLS regression on the Achieved Funding Ratio, with the only difference being that the latter model uses a full set of sector control dummies as controls. Model III and IV are the main specifications for testing Hypothesis 4, for which the study performs entropy balancing combined with OLS regression on the Achieved Funding Ratio. Model III and IV differ with respect to whether only the technology dummy or a full set of sector dummies as controls.

Model V is the main specification for testing Hypothesis 4a, for which the study also performs entropy balancing combined with OLS regression on the Achieved Funding Ratio (Table 6.3). The difference from previous models is that the study adds three interaction terms to test whether the effect of a bespoke regime depends

Table 6.3 Regression analysis: the effect of bespoke regulations on achieved funding ratio

	Model I	Model II	Model III	Model IV	Model V
	Achieved funding ratio (OLS)	Achieved funding ratio (OLS)	Achieved funding ratio (matching and OLS)	Achieved funding ratio (matching and OLS)	Achieved funding ratio (matching and OLS)
Postreg campaign	0.0106	−0.191	−0.102	−0.246	6.722
	(0.246)	(0.243)	(0.227)	(0.239)	(4.232)
SME value (log transformed)	−0.651***	−0.429*	−0.675***	−0.479*	−0.539**
	(0.227)	(0.250)	(0.240)	(0.262)	(0.265)
Amount sought (log transformed)	0.510**	0.251	0.567**	0.323	0.501
	(0.254)	(0.278)	(0.263)	(0.286)	(0.330)
Retained equity	7.921***	5.903**	8.293***	6.524**	10.18***
	(2.220)	(2.414)	(2.468)	(2.668)	(3.639)
Voting rights	0.327*	0.441**	0.444**	0.720***	0.871***
	(0.183)	(0.220)	(0.178)	(0.209)	(0.288)
Postreg campaign# amount sought					−0.169
					(0.247)
Postreg campaign# retained equity					−5.159
					(3.335)
Postreg campaign# voting rights					−0.254
					(0.410)
Prior campaigns	−0.579*	−0.0541	−0.607*	−0.0907	−0.0183
	(0.348)	(0.361)	(0.362)	(0.370)	(0.383)
Campaign duration	−0.00663**	−0.00143	−0.00478*	−0.000195	−0.000879
	(0.00262)	(0.00263)	(0.00265)	(0.00263)	(0.00270)
Fundraiser age	−0.00177	−0.00845	−0.00152	−0.00781	−0.0101
	(0.00705)	(0.00726)	(0.00690)	(0.00688)	(0.00712)
EIS approved	0.500**	0.397**	0.343*	0.386*	0.453**
	(0.201)	(0.197)	(0.196)	(0.202)	(0.207)
SEIS approved	−0.00308	0.0596	−0.0760	0.109	0.168
	(0.204)	(0.201)	(0.230)	(0.233)	(0.235)

(continued)

Table 6.3 (continued)

	Model I	Model II	Model III	Model IV	Model V
	Achieved funding ratio (OLS)	Achieved funding ratio (OLS)	Achieved funding ratio (matching and OLS)	Achieved funding ratio (matching and OLS)	Achieved funding ratio (matching and OLS)
FTSE volatility	33.60	−25.62	37.12	−23.51	−17.78
	(30.02)	(32.14)	(30.79)	(33.01)	(33.43)
Interest rate	−4.192	0.0619	−4.331	−0.211	−1.493
	(5.331)	(5.467)	(5.394)	(5.712)	(6.012)
Sector dummies included	No	Yes	No	Yes	Yes
Tech	−0.0115		0.112		
	(0.203)		(0.203)		
Constant	−0.711	−0.607	−1.412	−1.758	−5.816
	(3.387)	(3.451)	(3.728)	(3.776)	(4.832)
Observations	157	140	157	140	140
R-squared	0.200	0.434	0.181	0.446	0.465

Standard errors in parentheses
$^{***}p < 0.01$, $^{**}p < 0.05$, $^{*}p < 0.1$

on the strength of the market signal, i.e. the *Amount Sought*, *Retained Equity,* and *Voting Rights*.

Different specifications are consistent in providing no support for Hypothesis 4. Contrary to the results of univariate analysis, post-regulation campaigns do not raise a higher percentage of the target amount once the study controls for a set of campaign characteristics. The study also finds that the *SME Value* has a negative impact on campaign success once the target amount is controlled for, possibly suggesting that investors are reluctant to invest in companies that they find overvalued or they prefer risky investments when smaller companies seek financing for large projects. *Retained Equity* and *Voting Rights* both have a positive impact on the percentage raised, and these findings are robust across different model specifications. The study also finds that EIS tax incentives have a positive and statistically significant effect on the fundraising outcome.

None of the interaction effects in Model V is significant, suggesting the study cannot provide support for Hypothesis 4a.[29]

[29] The interaction effects of different signals and the post-regulation variable on the amount invested per campaign were also tested using investor-level data. Results were not statistically significant and, thus, were not presented in this chapter.

6.6.2 Investment Amounts

For the analysis about the impact of the bespoke regime on individual amounts invested in a given campaign (Hypothesis 3), the basic model specifications follow

1. *Ln Amount Invested per Project* = *Constant* + *β1* * *Postreg Dummy* + *β2* **Campaign Characteristics* + *β3* * *Investor Characteristics* + *β4* * *Controls* + *Residuals.*

For both Model I and Model II, the study performs Random-effects GLS regression, in which the dependent variable is the *Amount Invested Per Project* (log transformed). The explanatory variable of interest is *Postreg*, a dummy variable equal to 1 if the investment was made after the regulatory change and 0 otherwise. In Model II, the study also tests for the heterogeneity effect, distinguishing between everyday investors, sophisticated investors, high-net-worth individuals, and advised investors. Investors for which no investor type is identifiable in the sample are in the reference group (Table 6.4).

Table 6.4 Regression analysis: the effect of bespoke regulations on amount invested per project

	Model I	Model II
	Amount invested per project	Amount invested per project
postreg	−0.0894**	−0.390***
	(0.0393)	(0.0778)
everyday_investor		−0.152**
		(0.0725)
sophisticated_investor		0.542***
		(0.0884)
high_net_worth		1.349***
		(0.108)
advised_investor		−0.291
		(0.266)
1.everyday_investor#1.postreg		0.244***
		(0.0801)
1.sophisticated_investor#1.postreg		0.400***
		(0.0883)
1.high_net_worth#1.postreg		0.358***
		(0.109)
1.advised_investor#1.postreg		0.989***
		(0.134)
lnSME_value	−0.137***	−0.135***
	(0.0338)	(0.0335)
lnamount_sought	0.239***	0.243***
	(0.0358)	(0.0356)

(continued)

Table 6.4 (continued)

	Model I	Model II
	Amount invested per project	Amount invested per project
retained_equity	0.977***	0.855***
	(0.304)	(0.301)
voting_rights	−0.00341	−0.00994
	(0.0239)	(0.0240)
prior_campaigns	−0.188**	−0.128*
	(0.0747)	(0.0755)
fundraiser_age	0.00180**	0.00256***
	(0.000827)	(0.000822)
campaign_duration	−0.00115***	−0.00114***
	(0.000272)	(0.000270)
eis_approved	0.0287	0.0145
	(0.0219)	(0.0218)
seis_approved	−0.0669***	−0.0672***
	(0.0216)	(0.0215)
Sector dummies included	Yes	Yes
investor_age	0.0470***	0.0412***
	(0.00115)	(0.00112)
lnnumber_of_investments	−0.0271*	−0.0694***
	(0.0145)	(0.0146)
FTSE volatility	−15.13***	−12.80***
	(3.219)	(3.175)
interest_rate	−2.239***	−1.577**
	(0.780)	(0.776)
M2	−1.29e-06***	−1.26e-06***
	(2.99e-07)	(2.95e-07)
Constant	5.658***	5.335***
	(0.639)	(0.629)
Observations	23,664	23,664
Number of investors	13,884	13,884

Robust standard errors in parentheses
***$p < 0.01$, **$p < 0.05$, *$p < 0.1$

Contrary to predictions of Hypothesis 3, individual investment amounts are statistically lower after the regulatory change. The finding is robust even when controlling for the variable number of investments made by an individual investor, which shows that the investment amount tends to decrease with the number of investments made in equity crowdfunding projects.

As elaborated in the theory section above, such a decrease in individual investment amounts may be due to different reasons. Theoretically, investors can be sensitive to risk warnings introduced by the bespoke regime. More importantly, there might exist differences in the wealth and income distribution of new investors who joined the equity crowdfunding market after the regulatory change, as well as their risk aversion. Alternatively, it can be that an increased role of crowdfunding platforms after the regulatory change spurred greater diversification across different crowdfunding projects, or such an effect may be a consequence of higher competition among projects post-regulation, in line with Hypothesis 1. In Model II, the study tests whether the effect is homogenous across different investor types. For this purpose, similar to the study of Goethner, Hornuf, and Regner (2021, p. 12), the study jointly tests the effect of explanatory variables and the *Postreg* dummy using Wald tests. Figure 6.2 shows the average marginal effects of the *Postreg* dummy on the *Amount Invested per Project* by different investor types.

The study finds that the change in investment amounts after the adoption of the bespoke regime exhibits sharp contrast across different investor types. As in the case of the reference group, everyday investors pledge lower amounts in the post-regulatory period. Everyday investors decrease their investments by approximately 15% at 1% level of significance. There is no statistically significant difference in the amount pledged by high-net-worth individuals and sophisticated investors, while the only group that increases pledges in the post-regulation period are advised investors. Their amounts are increased by approximately 60% at 1% level of significance. As a next step, it is helpful to investigate whether the difference in the amount pledged per project originates from *Old Investors* or *New Investors*.

For the analysis about the impact of the bespoke regime on individual pledges of Old investors (Hypothesis 3a), the basic model specifications follow.

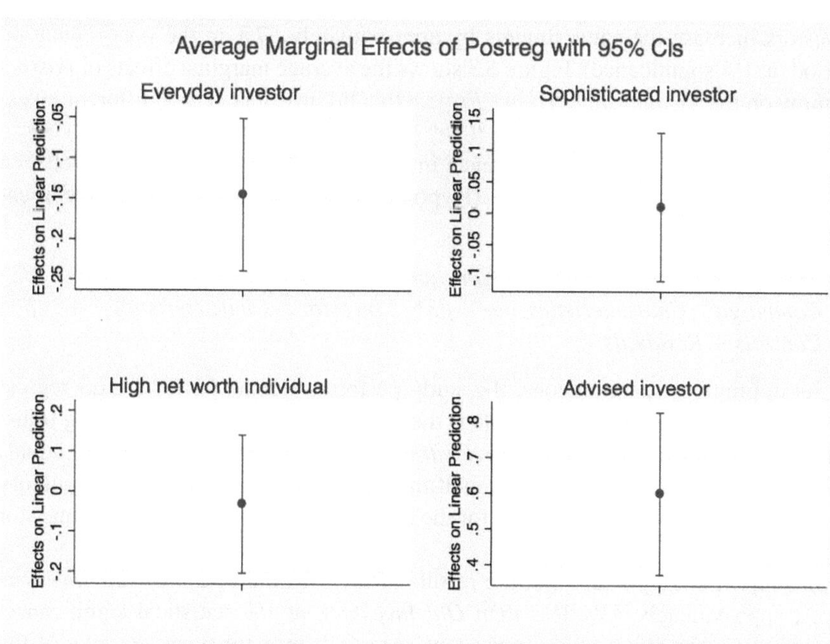

Fig. 6.2 Average marginal effects of postreg dummy across different investor types

2. *Amount Invested per Project = Constant + β1 * Postreg Dummy + β2*Postreg Investor Dummy + β3*Campaign Characteristics + β4* Investor Characteristics + β5 * Controls + Residuals.*

To test the effect of the bespoke regime on *Old Investors*, that is, those who registered on a crowdfunding platform before the regulatory change, the study includes two dummy variables, *Postreg* dummy and P*ostreg Investor* dummy. The interpretation of the *Postreg* dummy changes from previous specifications to now account for the difference in amounts invested by *Old Investors* before and after the regulatory change (that is, the difference in amounts pledged before and after the regulatory change when *Postreg Investor* dummy equals 0). The *Postreg* Investor dummy shows the difference in investment amounts of *New Investors* and investment amounts of Old Investors before the regulatory change (that is when *Postreg* dummy equals 0). As before, for both Model I and Model II, the study performs Random-effects GLS regression, in which the dependent variable is the *Amount Invested per Project* (log transformed). In Model II, the study tests for the heterogeneity effect on different investor types (Table 6.5).

Contrary to Hypothesis 3a, the study finds no evidence that the bespoke regime affected the investment behaviour of Old Investors. However, in line with some theoretical considerations, this finding is not robust across different investor types. As before, the study performs the Wald test to jointly test the effect of explanatory variables and the *Postreg* dummy. Old Everyday Investors reduce their investments by approximately 11% at 5% level of significance. While high-net-worth individuals and sophisticated investors do not change the amount of their pledges, advised investors increase their investments by approximately 57% in the post-regulation period (at 1% significance). Figure 6.3 shows the average marginal effects of *Postreg* dummy on the *Amount Invested per Project* by Old investors across different investor types.

For the analysis about the difference in individual investment amounts between *Old Investors* and *New Investors* (Hypothesis 3b), the basic model specifications follow.

3. *Amount Invested Per Project = Constant + β1 * Postreg Investor Dummy + β2* Campaign Characteristics + β3* Investor Characteristics + β4* Controls + Residuals.*

As in previous specifications, the study performs Random-effects GLS regression, in which the dependent variable is the *Amount Invested per Project* (log transformed). The independent variable is *Postreg Investor*, a dummy variable that equals 1 if the investor registered on a crowdfunding platform only after the regulatory change. In Model II, the study tests for the heterogeneity effect on different investor types (Table 6.6).

In support of Hypothesis 3b, the results of Model I indicate that *New Investors* invest approximately 33% less than *Old Investors*, at 1% statistical significance. Nevertheless, the effect is not consistent across all investor types. Results of the Wald test suggest that only *New Investors* in the reference group and everyday investors invest smaller amounts than *Old Investors*. New everyday investors invest

Table 6.5 Regression analysis: the effect of bespoke regulations on the amount invested per project by old investors

	Model I	Model II
	Amount invested per project	Amount invested per project
Postreg	−0.0308	−0.0935
	(0.0407)	(0.114)
Postreg investor	−0.325***	−0.412***
	(0.0439)	(0.116)
1.everyday_investor		−0.104
		(0.0752)
1.postreg#1.everyday_investor		-0.0164
		(0.118)
1.sophisticated_investor		0.427***
		(0.0944)
1.postreg#1.sophisticated_investor		0.0885
		(0.122)
1.high_net_worth		1.236***
		(0.116)
1.postreg#1.high_net_worth		0.0381
		(0.140)
1.advised_investor		-0.464
		(0.565)
1.postreg#1.advised_investor		0.666***
		(0.178)
1.postregInvestor#1.everyday_investor		0.237*
		(0.125)
1.postregInvestor#1. sophisticated_investor		0.554***
		(0.149)
1.postregInvestor#1.high_net_worth		0.525***
		(0.151)
1.postregInvestor#1.advised_investor		0.612
		(0.733)
lnSME_value	−0.145***	−0.139***
	(0.0338)	(0.0335)
lnamount_sought	0.251***	0.248***
	(0.0359)	(0.0356)
retained_equity	1.025***	0.879***
	(0.303)	(0.301)
voting_rights	−0.00233	−0.00869
	(0.0238)	(0.0239)

(continued)

Table 6.5 (continued)

	Model I	Model II
	Amount invested per project	Amount invested per project
prior_campaigns	−0.164**	−0.130*
	(0.0745)	(0.0759)
fundraiser_age	0.00189**	0.00257***
	(0.000827)	(0.000821)
campaign_duration	−0.00115***	−0.00113***
	(0.000272)	(0.000270)
eis_approved	0.0288	0.0145
	(0.0219)	(0.0218)
seis_approved	−0.0631***	−0.0661***
	(0.0216)	(0.0215)
Sector dummies included	Yes	Yes
investor_age	0.0468***	0.0411***
	(0.00115)	(0.00112)
lnnumber_of_investments	−0.0548***	−0.0754***
	(0.0152)	(0.0151)
FTSE volatility	−14.10***	−12.50***
	(3.216)	(3.177)
interest_rate	−1.616**	−1.398*
	(0.787)	(0.779)
M2	−1.10e-06***	−1.21e-06***
	(3.00e-07)	(2.96e-07)
Constant	5.048***	5.205***
	(0.644)	(0.636)
Observations	23,664	23,664
Number of investors	13,884	13,884

Robust standard errors in parentheses
***$p < 0.01$, **$p < 0.05$, *$p < 0.1$

approximately 22% less than the Old everyday investors. There is no statistically significant difference in pledges between New and Old sophisticated investors, high-net-worth individuals, and advised investors. Figure 6.4 shows the average marginal effects of the *Postreg Investor* dummy on the *Amount Invested per Project* across different investor types.

6.7 Summary of Findings

This empirical analysis conducted in this chapter tested whether the equity crowdfunding market in the UK changed after the adoption of the bespoke crowdfunding regime on April 1, 2014. As previous literature in law and finance suggests,

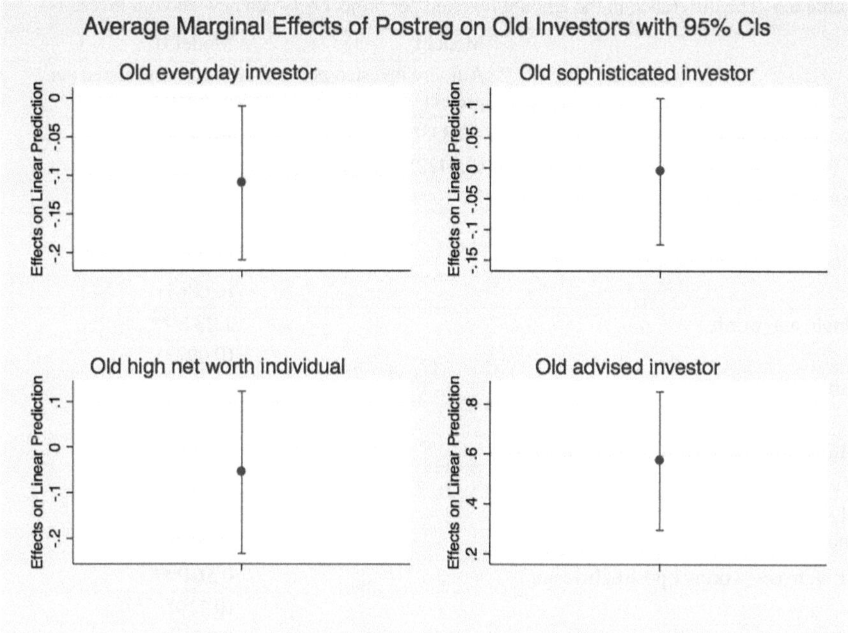

Fig. 6.3 Average marginal effects of postreg dummy on old investors across different investor types

adequately tailored rules that increase investor protection are expected to spur investor trust in the market, lower the costs of capital for fundraisers, and consequently improve market outcomes. The UK equity market is a suitable environment for testing the effect of a bespoke crowdfunding regime, given that the market is well-developed and lightly compared to some other regimes (which often replicate rules that exist in traditional capital markets, such as by mandating disclosure requirements for fundraisers). Yet, the specifics of the UK bespoke regime is that, according to the FCA, equity platforms had already been subject to licensing requirements, even though the exact scope of rules applicable to them was determined on an ad hoc basis and it was not known to market participants. The new bespoke regime introduced further clarity on the obligations of platforms, particularly their duty to ensure that all crowdfunding offers (financial promotions of non-readily realisable securities) are fair, clear, and not misleading, thus strengthening the gatekeeping role of platforms. Moreover, it strengthened investor protection safeguards, ensuring that retail investors cannot participate in crowdfunding campaigns before receiving adequate risk warnings, passing an appropriateness (entry knowledge) test, and certifying that they will not invest more than 10% of their net investable assets. The consultation process preceding the adoption of the new rules and discussions around their publication increased the saliency of the rules to market participants. It could also have been understood as regulators' legitimisation of otherwise contentious and risky crowdfunding practices.

Table 6.6 The difference in the amount invested per project between new and old investors

	Model I	Model II
	Amount invested per project	Amount invested per project
postregInvestor	−0.333***	−0.460***
	(0.0422)	(0.0757)
everyday_investor		−0.130*
		(0.0706)
sophisticated_investor		0.456***
		(0.0867)
high_net_worth		1.232***
		(0.0973)
advised_investor		−0.0474
		(0.635)
1.everyday_investor#1.postregInvestor		0.243***
		(0.0822)
1.sophisticated_investor#1.postregInvestor		0.612***
		(0.117)
1.high_net_worth#1.postregInvestor		0.564***
		(0.119)
1.advised_investor#1.postregInvestor		0.856
		(0.708)
lnSME_value	−0.142***	−0.132***
	(0.0334)	(0.0332)
lnamount_sought	0.246***	0.239***
	(0.0354)	(0.0352)
retained_equity	0.982***	0.794***
	(0.299)	(0.297)
voting_rights	−0.00290	−0.00969
	(0.0238)	(0.0238)
prior_campaigns	−0.165**	−0.134*
	(0.0745)	(0.0759)
fundraiser_age	0.00185**	0.00253***
	(0.000822)	(0.000816)
campaign_duration	−0.00116***	−0.00115***
	(0.000271)	(0.000269)
eis_approved	0.0278	0.0135
	(0.0218)	(0.0217)
seis_approved	−0.0642***	−0.0675***
	(0.0215)	(0.0215)
Sector dummies included	Yes	Yes

(continued)

Table 6.6 (continued)

	Model I	Model II
	Amount invested per project	Amount invested per project
lnnumber_of_investments	−0.0566***	−0.0786***
	(0.0148)	(0.0147)
FTSE volatility	−13.62***	−11.65***
	(3.145)	(3.098)
interest_rate	−1.932***	−1.971***
	(0.666)	(0.661)
M2	−1.01e-06***	−1.05e-06***
	(2.82e-07)	(2.78e-07)
Constant	5.053***	5.214***
	(0.644)	(0.635)
Observations	23,664	23,664
Number of investors	13,884	13,884

Robust standard errors in parentheses
***$p < 0.01$, **$p < 0.05$, *$p < 0.1$

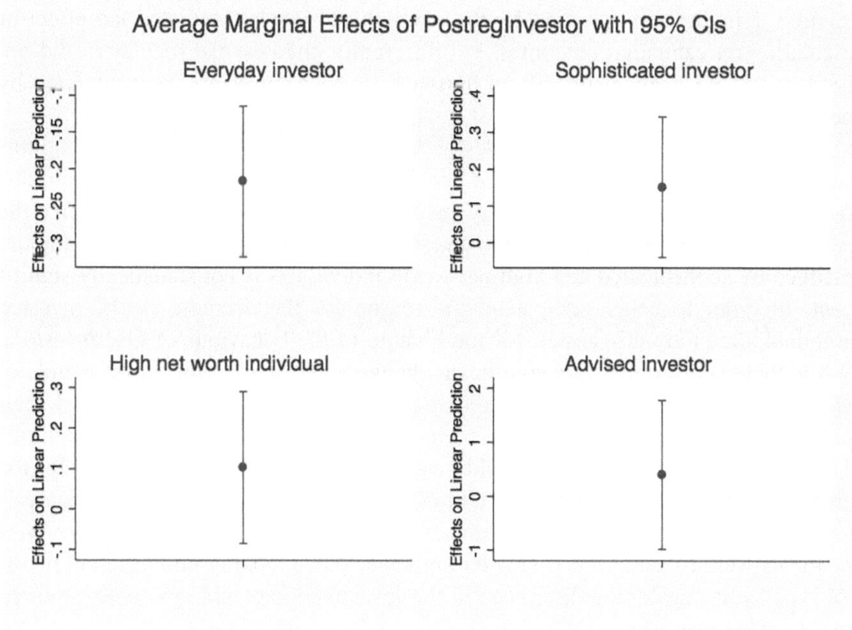

Fig. 6.4 Average marginal effects of postreg investor dummy across different investor types

This study tested the potential effects of bespoke regulations on the demand side (fundraisers), supply side (investors), and market outcomes (campaign success). On the demand side, it tested whether the quality of fundraisers, as captured by the strength of their signals, improved following the regulatory change. On the supply side, the study tested whether more investors participated in crowdfunding campaigns post-regulation. Furthermore, it tested whether the amount of an individual pledge per campaign changed, also differentiating between different investor types (everyday, sophisticated, high net worth, and advised investors). The study also accounted for the differences in individual investment amounts of old and new investors (depending on whether they registered on the platform before or after the regulatory change), as well as whether old investors behaved differently post-regulation. Finally, the study explored whether the likelihood of a campaign's success increased as a result of all of the above potential mechanisms of influence.

The results of the univariate analysis showed that post-regulation campaigns attracted projects with stronger signals (as captured by *Retained Equity*, *Amount Sought*, *SME Value*, and *Voting Rights*), attracted a higher *Number of Investors*, and were more successful. Yet, regression analysis did not find that post-regulation campaigns attracted more investors or achieved a higher funding ratio once all project characteristics were controlled. A plausible interpretation of the results is that the quality of fundraisers (proxied by the strength of signals) mediated the effect of regulation on campaign outcomes. Put differently, the bespoke regulation did not produce an independent impact on investors; instead, investors were attracted by better-quality projects appearing post-regulation.

When looking into individual investor data, the study found a statistically significant decrease in the *Amount Invested per Project*. However, when looking into different investor types, only everyday investors pledge smaller amounts after the regulatory change. Advised investors invest more, while the difference in the amount pledged by sophisticated and high-net-worth individuals is not statistically significant. In order to better understand the reason for the decrease in the invested amounts, the study also tested for the change in the behaviour of *Old Investors*. While there is no statistically significant change at the level of the entire sample of *Old Investors*, again, it was captured that Old everyday investors reduced their pledges. In contrast, Old advised investors increased their pledges post-regulations. Thus, the heterogeneity effect on Old investors mirrors the results obtained for the entire sample (including both *Old* and *New Investors*). Furthermore, the analysis tested for the difference in the investment amounts of *New* and *Old Investors*. *New Investors* were found to invest smaller amounts. When looking into different investor types, once again, the difference in the investment amounts was only captured for everyday investors.

There are several plausible interpretations of these findings. Risk warnings and investment limits introduced by the bespoke regime could have affected the investment amounts per project of both Old and New Investors. Alternatively, better-quality projects appearing on the platform or a higher level of due diligence performed by platforms could have incentivised everyday investors to diversify their portfolios further (as they also potentially reduced their own due diligence).

Finally, the fact that New everyday investors invest less than Old everyday investors indicates that the bespoke regime legitimised crowdfunding as an investment tool among individuals with lower income/wealth levels, who pledge smaller amounts accordingly.

Surprisingly, the study does not find that professional (sophisticated and high net worth) investors invested higher amounts following the regulatory change, suggesting that it did not attract more reputable investors to invest in this asset class. Alternatively, it could be that their presence is not visible if they also diversify their portfolios further, thanks to better-quality projects appearing on the platform. Overall, this study does not intend to make causal claims. Its main limitation stems from the fact that it is impossible to separate the effect of the crowdfunding market maturing over time and crowdfunding regulations. In fact, these two factors are mutually reinforcing. The main task of future research is to use an identification strategy that would allow for causal inference, such as by using data from comparable markets that were not affected by the legislative change (at least not at the same time) as a control group.

References

Ahlers, G. K. C., Cumming, D., Günther, C., & Schweizer, D. (2015). Signaling in equity crowdfunding. *Entrepreneurship Theory and Practice, 39*(4), 955–980. https://doi.org/10.1111/etap.12157

Anand, A. (2014). Is crowdfunding bad for investors. *Canadian Business Law Journal, 55*, 215–230.

Ande, J. A., & Eroglu, Z. K. (2021). Could New Zealand's equity crowdfunding regulations be the model for the developing world?'. *New Zealand Universities Law Review, 29*, 557–592. Retrieved from https://ssrn.com/abstract=3904063

Armour, J., & Enriques, L. (2018a). Individual investors' access to Crowdinvesting: Two regulatory models. In D. Cumming & L. Hornuf (Eds.), *The economics of crowdfunding* (pp. 255–278). Palgrave Macmillan. https://doi.org/10.1007/978-3-319-66119-3_11

Armour, J., & Enriques, L. (2018b). The promise and perils of crowdfunding: Between corporate finance and consumer contracts: The promise and perils of crowdfunding. *The Modern Law Review, 81*(1), 51–84. https://doi.org/10.1111/1468-2230.12316

Astebro, T. B., Fernández Sierra, M., Lovo, S., & Vulkan, N. (2019). Herding in equity crowdfunding. *RAND Journal of Economics*. https://doi.org/10.2139/ssrn.3084140

Bank of England. (n.d.-a). *Interbank lending rate 3 month mean*. Retrieved from https://www.bankofengland.co.uk/boeapps/database/FromShowColumns.asp?Travel=NIxAZxI3x&FromCategoryList=Yes&NewMeaningId=RILR3M&CategId=6&HighlightCatValueDisplay=Interbank%20lending%20rate%20%203%20month%20mean

Bank of England. (n.d.-b). *Monthly changes of monetary financial institutions' sterling and all foreign currency M2 (UK estimate of EMU aggregate) liabilities to private and public sectors (in sterling millions) residual between seasonally adjusted total and instrument breakdown*. Retrieved from https://www.bankofengland.co.uk/boeapps/database/_iadb-FromShowColumns.asp?Travel=NIxSCx&ShadowPage=1&SearchText=m2&SearchExclude=&SearchTextFields=TC&Thes=&SearchType=&Cats=&ActualResNumPerPage=21X41X&TotalNumResults=47&XNotes=Y&C=11P&ShowData.x=47&ShowData.y=13&XNotes2=Y

Battaglia, F., Busato, F., & Manganiello, M. (2022). A cross-platform analysis of the equity crowdfunding Italian context: The role of intellectual capital. *Electronic Commerce Research, 22*(2), 649–689. https://doi.org/10.1007/s10660-020-09453-w

Beauhurst (2020). The state of UK equity crowdfunding. https://www.beauhurst.com/blog/uk-equity-crowdfunding/

Benston, G. J. (1973). Required disclosure and the stock market: An evaluation of the securities exchange act of 1934. *The American Economic Review, 63*(1), 132–155. Retrieved from https://www.jstor.org/stable/1803131

Blau, B. M. (2017). Economic freedom and crashes in financial markets. *Journal of International Financial Markets, Institutions and Money, 47*, 33–46. https://doi.org/10.1016/j.intfin.2016.11.010

Block, J., Hornuf, L., & Moritz, A. (2018). Which updates during an equity crowdfunding campaign increase crowd participation? *Small Business Economics, 50*(1), 3–27. https://doi.org/10.1007/s11187-017-9876-4

Bordalo, P., Gennaioli, N., & Shleifer, A. (2012). Salience theory of choice under risk. *The Quarterly Journal of Economics, 127*(3), 1243–1285. https://doi.org/10.1093/qje/qjs018

Boubakri, N., El Ghoul, S., & Saffar, W. (2014). Political rights and equity pricing. *Journal of Corporate Finance, 27*, 326–344. https://doi.org/10.1016/j.jcorpfin.2014.05.009

Butticè, V., & Vismara, S. (2021). Inclusive digital finance: The industry of equity crowdfunding. *The Journal of Technology Transfer, 47*(4), 1224–1241. https://doi.org/10.1007/s10961-021-09875-0

Cai, W., Polzin, F., & Stam, E. (2020). Legal institutions, social capital, and financial crowdfunding: A multilevel perspective. In R. Shneor, L. Zhao, & B.-T. Flåten (Eds.), *Advances in crowdfunding* (pp. 183–205). Springer International Publishing. https://doi.org/10.1007/978-3-030-46309-0_9

Capizzi, V., & Carluccio, E. M. (2016). Competitive frontiers in equity crowdfunding: The role of venture capitalists and business angels in the early-stage financing industry. In R. Bottiglia & F. Pichler (Eds.), *Crowdfunding for SMEs* (pp. 117–157). Palgrave Macmillan. https://doi.org/10.1057/978-1-137-56021-6_6

Chaudary, S. (2019). Does salience matter in investment decision? Differences between individual and professional investors. *Kybernetes, 48*(8), 1894–1912. https://doi.org/10.1108/K-09-2018-0490

Chen, K. C. W., Chen, Z., & Wei, K. C. J. (2009). Legal protection of investors, corporate governance, and the cost of equity capital. *Journal of Corporate Finance, 15*(3), 273–289. https://doi.org/10.1016/j.jcorpfin.2009.01.001

Christensen, H. B., Hail, L., & Leuz, C. (2016). Capital-market effects of securities regulation: Prior conditions, implementation, and enforcement. *Review of Financial Studies, 29*(11), 2885–2924. https://doi.org/10.1093/rfs/hhw055

Connelly, B. L., Certo, S. T., Ireland, R. D., & Reutzel, C. R. (2011). Signaling theory: A review and assessment. *Journal of Management, 37*(1), 39–67. https://doi.org/10.1177/0149206310388419

Conroy, R. M. (2012). What hypotheses do "nonparametric" two-group tests actually test? *The Stata Journal: Promoting Communications on Statistics and Stata, 12*(2), 182–190. https://doi.org/10.1177/1536867X1201200202

Cosh, A., Cumming, D., & Hughes, A. (2009). Outside enterpreneurial capital. *The Economic Journal, 119*(540), 1494–1533. https://doi.org/10.1111/j.1468-0297.2009.02270.x

Courtney, C., Dutta, S., & Li, Y. (2017). Resolving information asymmetry: Signaling, endorsement, and crowdfunding success. *Entrepreneurship Theory and Practice, 41*(2), 265–290. https://doi.org/10.1111/etap.12267

Crowdcube. (n.d.-a). *Investing & tax relief: What you need to know*. Retrieved from https://www.crowdcube.com/explore/investing/tax-relief

Crowdcube. (n.d.-b). *Investor categories*. Retrieved from https://www.crowdcube.eu/explore/investor-categories

CrowdSpace. (2024). *Equity crowdfunding platforms in United Kingdom*. Retrieved from https://thecrowdspace.com/directory/equity-crowdfunding-platforms-in-uk/

Cumming, D., & Johan, S. (2019). Capital-market effects of securities regulation: Prior conditions, implementation, and enforcement revisited. *Finance Research Letters, 31*, S1544612318307402. https://doi.org/10.1016/j.frl.2018.12.013

Cumming, D., Meoli, M., & Vismara, S. (2019). Investors' choices between cash and voting rights: Evidence from dual-class equity crowdfunding. *Research Policy, 48*(8), 103740. https://doi.org/10.1016/j.respol.2019.01.014

Cumming, D., Meoli, M., & Vismara, S. (2021). Does equity crowdfunding democratize entrepreneurial finance? *Small Business Economics, 56*(2), 533–552. https://doi.org/10.1007/s11187-019-00188-z

Cumming, D. J., Johan, S. A., & Zhang, Y. (2019). The role of due diligence in crowdfunding platforms. *Journal of Banking & Finance, 108*, 105661. https://doi.org/10.1016/j.jbankfin.2019.105661

Cumming, D. J., Vanacker, T., & Zahra, S. A. (2021). Equity crowdfunding and governance: Toward an integrative model and research agenda. *Academy of Management Perspectives, 35*(1), 69–95. https://doi.org/10.5465/amp.2017.0208

Daughety, A. F., & Reinganum, J. F. (2008). Communicating quality: A unified model of disclosure and signalling. *The Rand Journal of Economics, 39*(4), 973–989. https://doi.org/10.1111/j.1756-2171.2008.00046.x

Di Pietro, F. (2021). The rationale for listing on equity crowdfunding: Actual and expected benefits for companies. *Journal of Industrial and Business Economics, 48*, 527–549. https://doi.org/10.1007/s40812-021-00188-9

Di Pietro, F., & Butticè, V. (2020). Institutional characteristics and the development of crowdfunding across countries. *International Review of Financial Analysis, 71*, 101543. https://doi.org/10.1016/j.irfa.2020.101543

Directive. (2003). *2003/71/EC of the European Parliament and of the Council of 4 November 2003 on the prospectus to be published when securities are offered to the public or admitted to trading and amending directive 2001/34/EC*. Retrieved from https://eur-lex.europa.eu/legal-content/EN/TXT/PDF/?uri=CELEX:32003L0071

Djankov, S., Glaeser, E., La Porta, R., Lopez-de-Silanes, F., & Shleifer, A. (2003). The new comparative economics. *Journal of Comparative Economics, 31*(4), 595–619. https://doi.org/10.1016/j.jce.2003.08.005

Doidge, C., Karolyi, G. A., & Stulz, R. M. (2007). Why do countries matter so much for corporate governance? *Journal of Financial Economics, 86*, 1–39. https://doi.org/10.1016/j.jfineco.2006.09.002

Downes, D. H., & Heinkel, R. (1982). Signaling and the valuation of unseasoned new issues. *The Journal of Finance, 37*(1), 1–10. https://doi.org/10.1111/j.1540-6261.1982.tb01091.x

Dranove, D., & Jin, G. Z. (2010). Quality disclosure and certification: Theory and practice. *Journal of Economic Literature, 48*(4), 935–963. https://doi.org/10.1257/jel.48.4.935

Dushnitsky, G., Guerini, M., Piva, E., & Rossi-Lamastra, C. (2016). Crowdfunding in Europe: Determinants of platform creation across countries. *California Management Review, 58*(2), 44–71. https://doi.org/10.1525/cmr.2016.58.2.44

Dyck, A., & Zingales, L. (2004). Private benefits of control: An international comparison. *The Journal of Finance, 59*(2), 537–600. https://doi.org/10.1111/j.1540-6261.2004.00642.x

Einhorn, E. (2005). The nature of the interaction between mandatory and voluntary disclosures. *Journal of Accounting Research, 43*(4), 593–621. https://doi.org/10.1111/j.1475-679X.2005.00183.x

Eleswarapu, V. R., & Venkataraman, K. (2006). The impact of legal and political institutions on equity trading costs: A cross-country analysis. *Review of Financial Studies, 19*(3), 1081–1111. https://doi.org/10.1093/rfs/hhj026

Enke, B. (2020). What you see is all there is. *The Quarterly Journal of Economics, 135*(3), 1363–1398. https://doi.org/10.1093/qje/qjaa012

Enriques, L., & Gatti, M. (2008). Is there a uniform EU securities law after the financial services action plan. *Stanford Journal of Law, Business & Finance, 14*, 43–82. Retrieved from https://heinonline.org/HOL/LandingPage?handle=hein.journals/stabf14&div=5&id=&page=

Estrin, S., Gozman, D., & Khavul, S. (2018). The evolution and adoption of equity crowdfunding: Entrepreneur and investor entry into a new market. *Small Business Economics, 51*(2), 425–439. https://doi.org/10.1007/s11187-018-0009-5

Ferguson, M. F., & Peters, S. R. (2000). But I know it when I see it: An economic analysis of vague rules. *SSRN Electronic Journal*. https://doi.org/10.2139/ssrn.218968

Financial Conduct Authority. (2013). *The FCA'S regulatory approach to crowdfunding (and similar activities) (consultation paper CP13/13)*. Financial Conduct Authority. Retrieved from https://www.fca.org.uk/publication/consultation/cp13-13.pdf

Financial Conduct Authority. (2014). *The FCA'S regulatory approach to crowdfunding over the internet, and the promotion of non-readily realisable securities by other media (policy statement PS14/4)*. Financial Conduct Authority. Retrieved from https://www.fca.org.uk/publication/policy/ps14-04.pdf

Financial Services and Markets Act. (2000). Retrieved from https://www.legislation.gov.uk/ukpga/2000/8/contents

Gajda, O., Aschenbeck-Florange, T., & Nagel, T. (2013). Crowdfunding regulation. In *Interpretations of existing regulation concerning crowdfunding in Europe, North America and Israel* (pp. 1–246). European Crowdfunding Network. Retrieved from http://www.europecrowdfunding.org/2013/10/review-crowdfunding-regulation-2013/

Goethner, M., Hornuf, L., & Regner, T. (2021). Protecting investors in equity crowdfunding: An empirical analysis of the small investor protection act. *Technological Forecasting and Social Change, 162*, 120352. https://doi.org/10.1016/j.techfore.2020.120352

Goethner, M., Luettig, S., & Regner, T. (2021). Crowdinvesting in entrepreneurial projects: Disentangling patterns of investor behavior. *Small Business Economics, 57*(2), 905–926. https://doi.org/10.1007/s11187-020-00332-0

Goshen, Z., & Parchomovsky, G. (2005). The essential role of securities regulation. *Duke Law Journal, 55*, 711–782. Retrieved from https://heinonline.org/HOL/LandingPage?handle=hein.journals/duklr55&div=27&id=&page=

Grilli, L., Mrkajic, B., & Latifi, G. (2018). Venture capital in Europe: Social capital, formal institutions and mediation effects. *Small Business Economics, 51*(2), 393–410. https://doi.org/10.1007/s11187-018-0007-7

Groh, A., Liechtenstein, H., Lieser, K., & Biesinger, M. (2023). *The venture capital & private equity country attractiveness index*. Retrieved from https://blog.iese.edu/vcpeindex/

Gutmann, J., Neuenkirch, M., & Neumeier, F. (2021). Sanctioned to death? The impact of economic sanctions on life expectancy and its gender gap. *The Journal of Development Studies, 57*(1), 139–162. https://doi.org/10.1080/00220388.2020.1746277

Hail, L., & Leuz, C. (2006). International differences in the cost of equity capital: Do legal institutions and securities regulation matter? *Journal of Accounting Research, 44*(3), 485–531. https://doi.org/10.1111/j.1475-679X.2006.00209.x

Hainmueller, J. (2012). Entropy balancing for causal effects: A multivariate reweighting method to produce balanced samples in observational studies. *Political Analysis, 20*(1), 25–46. https://doi.org/10.1093/pan/mpr025

Hearn, B., Phylaktis, K., & Piesse, J. (2017). Expropriation risk by block holders, institutional quality and expected stock returns. *Journal of Corporate Finance, 45*, 122–149. https://doi.org/10.1016/j.jcorpfin.2017.04.016

Hornuf, L., & Neuenkirch, M. (2017). Pricing shares in equity crowdfunding. *Small Business Economics, 48*(4), 795–811. https://doi.org/10.1007/s11187-016-9807-9

Hornuf, L., Schilling, T., & Schwienbacher, A. (2019). *Are equity crowdfunding investors active investors?* CESifo Working Paper, No. 7884, 1–41. Retrieved from http://hdl.handle.net/10419/207275

Hornuf, L., Schilling, T., & Schwienbacher, A. (2021). The relevance of investor rights in crowdinvesting. *Journal of Corporate Finance, 77*, 101927. https://doi.org/10.1016/j.jcorpfin.2021.101927

Hornuf, L., & Schmitt, M. (2016). Success and failure in equity crowdfunding. *CESifo DICE Report, 14*(2), 16–22. Retrieved from https://www.econstor.eu/bitstream/10419/167259/1/ifo-dice-report-v14-y2016-i2-p16-22.pdf

Hornuf, L., & Schwienbacher, A. (2017). Should securities regulation promote equity crowdfunding? *Small Business Economics, 49*(3), 579–593. https://doi.org/10.1007/s11187-017-9839-9

Hornuf, L., & Schwienbacher, A. (2018). Internet-based entrepreneurial finance: Lessons from Germany. *California Management Review, 60*(2), 150–175. https://doi.org/10.1177/0008125617741126

Investing.Com. (n.d.). *FTSE 100 VIX historical data*. Retrieved from https://www.investing.com/indices/ftse-100-vix-historical-data

Jackson, H. E., & Roe, M. J. (2009). Public and private enforcement of securities laws resource-based evidence. *Journal of Financial Economics, 93*, 207–238. https://doi.org/10.1016/j.jfineco.2008.08.006

Janssen, M. C. W., & Roy, S. (2015). Competition, disclosure and signalling. *The Economic Journal, 125*(582), 86–114. https://doi.org/10.1111/ecoj.12110

Johan, S., & Zhang, Y. (2020). Quality revealing versus overstating in equity crowdfunding. *Journal of Corporate Finance, 65*, 101741. https://doi.org/10.1016/j.jcorpfin.2020.101741

Kim, K., & Viswanathan, S. (2018). The 'Experts' in the crowd: The role of experienced investors in a crowdfunding market. *SSRN Electronic Journal*. https://doi.org/10.2139/ssrn.2258243

Klapper, L., Laeven, L., & Rajan, R. (2006). Entry regulation as a barrier to entrepreneurship. *Journal of Financial Economics, 82*, 591–629. https://doi.org/10.1016/j.jfineco.2005.09.006

Klöhn, L. (2018). The regulation of crowdfunding in Europe. In D. Cumming & L. Hornuf (Eds.), *The economics of crowdfunding* (pp. 219–253). Palgrave Macmillan.

Koehler, J. J., & Mercer, M. (2009). Selection neglect in mutual fund advertisements. *Management Science, 55*(7), 1107–1121. https://doi.org/10.1287/mnsc.1090.1013

Kshetri, N. (2015). Success of crowd-based online technology in fundraising: An institutional perspective. *Journal of International Management, 21*(2), 100–116. https://doi.org/10.1016/j.intman.2015.03.004

Kshetri, N. (2018). Informal institutions and internet-based equity crowdfunding. *Journal of International Management, 24*(1), 33–51. https://doi.org/10.1016/j.intman.2017.07.001

La Porta, R., Lopez-de-Silanes, F., & Shleifer, A. (2006). What works in securities laws? *The Journal of Finance, 61*(1), 1–32. https://doi.org/10.1111/j.1540-6261.2006.00828.x

La Porta, R., Lopez-De-Silanes, F., Shleifer, A., & Vishny, R. W. (1997). Legal determinants of external finance. *The Journal of Finance, 52*(3), 1131–1150. https://doi.org/10.1111/j.1540-6261.1997.tb02727.x

La Porta, R., Lopez-de-Silanes, F., Shleifer, A., & Vishny, R. W. (1998). Law and finance. *Journal of Political Economy, 106*(6), 1113–1155. https://doi.org/10.1086/250042

Lakshmi, G., Saha, S., & Bhattarai, K. (2021). Does corruption matter for stock markets? The role of heterogeneous institutions. *Economic Modelling, 94*, 386–400. https://doi.org/10.1016/j.econmod.2020.10.011

Leboeuf, G., & Schwienbacher, A. (2018). Crowdfunding as a new financing tool. In D. Cumming & L. Hornuf (Eds.), *The economics of crowdfunding* (pp. 11–28). Palgrave Macmillan.

Leland, H. E., & Pyle, D. H. (1977). Informational asymmetries, financial structure, and financial intermediation. *The Journal of Finance, 32*(2), 371–387. https://doi.org/10.2307/2326770

Levie, J., & Autio, E. (2011). Regulatory burden, rule of law, and entry of strategic entrepreneurs: An international panel study: Regulation, rule of law, and entrepreneurial entry. *Journal of Management Studies, 48*(6), 1392–1419. https://doi.org/10.1111/j.1467-6486.2010.01006.x

Li, Y., Liu, F., Fan, W., Lim, E. T. K., & Liu, Y. (2020). Exploring the impact of initial herd on overfunding in equity crowdfunding. *Information & Management, 59*, 103269. https://doi.org/10.1016/j.im.2020.103269

Li, Y., & Zahra, S. A. (2012). Formal institutions, culture, and venture capital activity: A cross-country analysis. *Journal of Business Venturing, 27*(1), 95–111. https://doi.org/10.1016/j.jbusvent.2010.06.003

Löher, J. (2017). The interaction of equity crowdfunding platforms and ventures: An analysis of the preselection process. *Venture Capital, 19*(1-2), 51–74. https://doi.org/10.1080/13691066.2016.1252510

Loveless, H. (2013). *Is equity crowdfunding a scandal waiting to happen? Experts warn lack of regulation leaves door open to rogue firms. This is money*. Retrieved from https://www.thisismoney.co.uk/money/smallbusiness/article-2342291/Is-equity-crowdfunding-scandal-waiting-happen-Experts-warn-lack-regulation-leaves-door-open-rogue-firms.html

Lukkarinen, A. (2020). Equity crowdfunding: Principles and investor behaviour. In R. Shneor, L. Zhao, & B.-T. Flåten (Eds.), *Advances in crowdfunding* (pp. 93–118). Springer International Publishing. https://doi.org/10.1007/978-3-030-46309-0_5

Meoli, M., Rossi, A., & Vismara, S. (2022). Financial literacy and security-based crowdfunding. *Corporate Governance: An International Review, 30*(1), 27–54. https://doi.org/10.1111/corg.12355

Modigliani, F., & Perotti, E. (1997). Protection of minority interest and the development of security markets. *Managerial and Decision Economics, 18*(7-8), 519–528. https://doi.org/10.1002/(SICI)1099-1468(199711/12)18:7/8<519::AID-MDE857>3.0.CO;2-M

Montford, W. J., Leary, R. B., & Nagel, D. M. (2019). The impact of implicit self-theories and loss salience on financial risk. *Journal of Business Research, 99*, 1–11. https://doi.org/10.1016/j.jbusres.2019.02.015

Myers, S. C., & Majluf, N. S. (1984). Corporate financing and investment decisions when firms have information that investors do not have. *Journal of Financial Economics, 13*(2), 187–221. https://doi.org/10.1016/0304-405X(84)90023-0

Nguyen, T., Cox, J., & Rich, J. (2019). Invest or regret? An empirical investigation into funding dynamics during the final days of equity crowdfunding campaigns. *Journal of Corporate Finance, 58*, 784–803. https://doi.org/10.1016/j.jcorpfin.2019.07.011

North, D. C. (1991). Institutions. *The Journal of Economic Perspectives, 5*(1), 97–112. Retrieved from http://www.jstor.org/stable/1942704

Piva, E., & Rossi-Lamastra, C. (2018). Human capital signals and entrepreneurs' success in equity crowdfunding. *Small Business Economics, 51*(3), 667–686. https://doi.org/10.1007/s11187-017-9950-y

Ralcheva, A., & Roosenboom, P. (2016). On the road to success in equity crowdfunding. *SSRN Electronic Journal*. https://doi.org/10.2139/ssrn.2727742

Rau, P. R. (2020). Law, trust, and the development of crowdfunding. *SSRN Electronic Journal*. https://doi.org/10.2139/ssrn.2989056

Rau, P. R. (2021). Sometimes, always, never: Regulatory clarity and the development of crowdfunding. *SSRN Electronic Journal*. https://doi.org/10.2139/ssrn.3797886

Reichenbach, F., & Walther, M. (2021). Signals in equity-based crowdfunding and risk of failure. *Financial Innovation, 7*(1), 54–83. https://doi.org/10.1186/s40854-021-00270-0

Ridley, D. (2016). Will new regulation on crowdfunding in the United Kingdom and United States have a positive impact and lead to crowdfunding becoming an established financing technique? *Statute Law Review, 37*(1), 57–76. https://doi.org/10.1093/slr/hmv026

Robb, A. M., & Robinson, D. T. (2014). The capital structure decisions of new firms. *Review of Financial Studies, 27*(1), 153–179. https://doi.org/10.1093/rfs/hhs072

Rossi, A., & Vismara, S. (2018). What do crowdfunding platforms do? A comparison between investment-based platforms in Europe. *Eurasian Business Review, 8*(1), 93–118. https://doi.org/10.1007/s40821-017-0092-6

Rossi, A., Vismara, S., & Meoli, M. (2019). Voting rights delivery in investment-based crowdfunding: A cross-platform analysis. *Journal of Industrial and Business Economics, 46*(2), 251–281. https://doi.org/10.1007/s40812-018-0109-x

Sale, H. A., & Thompson, R. B. (2015). Market intermediation, publicness, and securities class actions. *Washington University Law Review, 93*, 487–552. Retrieved from https://heinonline.org/HOL/LandingPage?handle=hein.journals/walq93&div=20&id=&page=

Schwartz, A. A. (2018). The gatekeepers of crowdfunding. *Washington and Lee Law Review, 75*, 885–955. Retrieved from https://heinonline.org/HOL/LandingPage?handle=hein.journals/waslee75&div=21&id=&page=

Seedrs Help Centre. (n.d.). *Create your individual investor account*. Seedrs. http://help.seedrs.com/en/articles/4269569-create-your-individual-investor-account

Shleifer, A. (2005). Understanding regulation. *European Financial Management, 11*(4), 439–451. https://doi.org/10.1111/j.1354-7798.2005.00291.x

Shneor, R., & Vik, A. A. (2020). Crowdfunding success: A systematic literature review 2010–2017. *Baltic Journal of Management, 15*(2), 149–182. https://doi.org/10.1108/BJM-04-2019-0148

Signori, A., & Vismara, S. (2018). Does success bring success? The post-offering lives of equity-crowdfunded firms. *Journal of Corporate Finance, 50*, 575–591. https://doi.org/10.1016/j.jcorpfin.2017.10.018

Spence, M. (1973). Job market signaling. *The Quarterly Journal of Economics, 87*(3), 281–306. https://doi.org/10.2307/1882010

Statman, M. (2017). *Finance for normal people: How investors and markets behave*. Oxford University Press.

Stenholm, P., Acs, Z. J., & Wuebker, R. (2013). Exploring country level institutional arrangements on the rate and type of entrepreneurial activity. *Journal of Business Venturing, 28*(1), 176–193. https://doi.org/10.1016/j.jbusvent.2011.11.002

Stigler, G. J. (1964). Public regulation of the securities markets. *The Journal of Business, 37*(2), 117–142. https://doi.org/10.1086/294677

Stiglitz, J. E., & Weiss, A. (1981). Credit rationing in markets with imperfect information. *The American Economic Review, 71*(3), 393–410. Retrieved from https://www.jstor.org/stable/1802787

Vaznyte, E., Andries, P., & Manigart, S. (2020). Are you part of the crowd? The role of sex and environmental characteristics for crowdfunding awareness. *Journal of Small Business Management*. https://doi.org/10.1080/00472778.2020.1831808

Viscusi, W. K. (1999). Using warnings to extend the boundaries of consumer sovereignty. *Harvard Journal of Law & Public Policy, 23*, 211–232. Retrieved from https://heinonline.org/HOL/LandingPage?handle=hein.journals/hjlpp23&div=29&id=&page=

Vismara, S. (2015). Information cascades among investors in equity crowdfunding. *Academy of Management Proceedings, 2015*(1), 11519. https://doi.org/10.5465/ambpp.2015.11519abstract

Vismara, S. (2016). Equity retention and social network theory in equity crowdfunding. *Small Business Economics, 46*(4), 579–590. https://doi.org/10.1007/s11187-016-9710-4

Vismara, S. (2018a). Information cascades among investors in equity crowdfunding. *Entrepreneurship Theory and Practice, 42*(3), 467–497. https://doi.org/10.1111/etap.12261

Vismara, S. (2018b). Signaling to overcome inefficiencies in crowdfunding markets. In D. Cumming & L. Hornuf (Eds.), *The economics of crowdfunding* (pp. 29–56). Palgrave Macmillan. https://doi.org/10.1007/978-3-319-66119-3_3

Walthoff-Borm, X., Schwienbacher, A., & Vanacker, T. (2018). Equity crowdfunding: First resort or last resort? *Journal of Business Venturing, 33*(4), 513–533. https://doi.org/10.1016/j.jbusvent.2018.04.001

Wang, W., Mahmood, A., Sismeiro, C., & Vulkan, N. (2019). The evolution of equity crowdfunding: Insights from co-investments of angels and the crowd. *Research Policy, 48*(8), 103727. https://doi.org/10.1016/j.respol.2019.01.003

Yalcin, K. C., Tatoglu, E., & Zaim, S. (2016). Developing an instrument for measuring the effects of heuristics on investment decisions. *Kybernetes, 45*(7), 1052–1071. https://doi.org/10.1108/K-05-2015-0130

Yarker, J. (2013). *Is crowdfunding the best way to access start-up investments? Money Marketing*. Retrieved from https://www.moneymarketing.co.uk/analysis/is-crowdfunding-the-best-way-to-access-start-up-investments/

Zhang, B., Ziegler, T., Mammadova, L., Johanson, D., Gray, M., & Yerolemou, N. (2018). *The 5th UK alternative finance industry report*. Cambridge Centre for Alternative Finance. Retrieved from https://www.jbs.cam.ac.uk/faculty-research/centres/alternative-finance/publications/5th-uk-alternative-finance-industry-report/

Ziegler, T., Shneor, R., Wenzlaff, K., Wang, B., Kim, J., Paes, F. F. de C., Suresh, K., Zhang, B. Z., Mammadova, L., & Adams, N. (2020). The Global Alternative Finance Market Benchmarking Report. *Cambridge Center for Alternative Finance*. https://www.jbs.cam.ac.uk/faculty-research/centres/alternative-finance/publications/the-global-alternative-finance-marketbenchmarking-report/

Chapter 7
Conclusion

Crowdfunding represents a new form of direct finance in which individuals, start-ups, and SMEs raise funding from many small (retail) investors via web-based platforms. The central question of this new funding source and investment channel is whether and how it provides new solutions to the old problems: the information asymmetry and collective action issues that arise in relation to selecting the most promising fundraisers and monitoring their performance. Crowdfunding platforms often emerged in unregulated or lightly regulated environments, allowing them to experiment with market-based mechanisms for mitigating information asymmetry. These mechanisms can originate from fundraisers, other investors, or platforms. Driven by reputational concerns and competitive pressure, platforms have created rules at three distinct levels: rules that govern the behaviour of fundraisers, rules that govern their own behaviour, and rules at the level of crowdfunding associations aiming to introduce industry-wide standards. Thus, this study explored these market-based mechanisms and derived regulatory implications. The fundamental premise is that crowdfunding regulations should complement and reinforce market-based mechanisms, mainly because fundraisers and crowdfunding intermediaries (the 'usual suspects' for a heavy regulatory burden) are typically small companies that cannot bear the high costs of regulatory compliance. Additionally, this study sheds light on the value of introducing a 'light-handed' crowdfunding bespoke regime by empirically testing whether and how market outcomes in the UK have changed.

Chapter 2 illustrated the core and auxiliary crowdfunding services and discussed how they relate to services performed by different actors in traditional finance. It was shown that platforms often deviate from the standard disintermediation model, meaning they merely offer a marketplace where different offers are listed. Instead, platforms assume several reintermediation roles that bring them closer to traditional financial or information gatekeepers or syndicate leads in entrepreneurial finance. The platform's role most closely aligns with the role of information intermediaries

A. Odorović, *Overcoming Asymmetric Information in the Crowdfunding Market*, International Law and Economics, https://doi.org/10.1007/978-3-032-04118-0_7

(gatekeepers) with particularity that they simultaneously assume many different functions spread across different gatekeepers in traditional finance.

Chapter 3 provided an in-depth analysis of promises and limitations of market-based mechanisms of mitigating information asymmetry, drawing on the existing empirical literature and theoretical insights from information economics and the economics of platforms. In relation to the unravelling of information by fundraisers, disclosures and signalling practices were reviewed using a framework that distinguishes between different sources of market failure (incomplete information, limited attention, and lack of credibility of disclosed information). Concerning fundraisers' disclosures, the analysis showed that while investors are usually responsive to differences in the level of disclosure, they sometimes fail to process the available information and rely on soft (unverifiable) claims that are non-credible. Regarding signalling practices, the analysis revealed that some well-known signals in entrepreneurial finance do not always attract investors' attention. At the same time, social media networks intertwined with information cascades represent an effective mechanism through which soft information and information from well-informed investors stir the crowd's decisions. The limitations of this mechanism are also discussed. An equally important investor protection mechanism is enabled through platform gatekeeping services, which can take place ex-ante or ex-post. It was shown that these services' scope and depth vary considerably across platforms while potentially shifting the source of information asymmetry from fundraisers to platforms.

Chapter 4 further explored market-based solutions, focusing on rules embedded in codes of conduct adopted by European crowdfunding associations. To test which of the existing theories of self-regulation is the most appropriate to explain the self-regulation of crowdfunding platforms, a new theoretical framework was proposed. This framework connects the institutional traits of codes of conduct (origin, inclusiveness, monitoring, and enforcement) with different economic rationales for adoption. A case study of nine European codes of conduct was conducted in the next step using the proposed framework. The results revealed that self-regulation in crowdfunding could be best explained by voluntary theories, particularly the theory of reputation commons, even though codes adopted by some associations also have prominent features of the club theory.

Chapter 5 discussed different regulatory issues in crowdfunding, drawing on the insights from previous chapters. It explained four different approaches embraced by regulators worldwide in treating the crowdfunding phenomenon. After elaborating on their advantages and shortcomings, the analysis focused on bespoke crowdfunding regimes. In particular, it was argued that an encompassing regulatory framework is preferred over a narrow, model-specific regime. Yet, the analysis showed that introducing a specific set of rules is justified in the case of consumer borrowing and different reintermediation services of platforms. A risk-based approach was proposed for platform regulation, focusing on distinct risk levels stemming from various combinations of platform services. Moreover, it was contended that the regulation regime focusing on platform gatekeeping was preferred over mandatory disclosure rules for fundraisers.

Chapter 6 investigated the effects of introducing a bespoke regime on equity crowdfunding market developments in the UK. Using campaign and investor-level data, the analysis explored the potential impact of new rules on fundraisers, investors, and the success of crowdfunding campaigns. The results revealed that post-regulation campaigns are launched by fundraisers with stronger quality signals, potentially indicating that bespoke rules incentivised better quality fundraisers to use this funding mechanism. While the number of investors per campaign and campaign success increased in the post-regulation phase, these developments can only be attributed to fundraisers' characteristics. Thus, contrary to the regulator's expectation, the bespoke regime's potential effect lies in the market's demand side. The analysis further revealed that individual investment amounts decreased following the regulatory change, allowing for several competing interpretations. The most plausible one is that the regulatory change legimitised the crowdfunding model and spurred trust among a wider investor population, thus shifting the income and wealth distribution of the investor base towards the left tail.

The overarching contribution of this study is a systematic account of a subtle interplay between market-based and regulatory-based solutions to information asymmetry in the crowdfunding market. Its findings span across three strands of literature. Firstly, the study sheds light on long-standing discussions in law and economics literature on the limits of markets and the desirable level of legal intervention by exploring a unique setting of the crowdfunding market, where largely unrestricted market forces were able to shape market outcomes. It was shown that standard regulatory tools (such as mandatory disclosures) are not always an adequate response to the limitations of market-based mechanisms. As already pointed out, in the crowdfunding context, such limitations stem from fundraisers not using all the available hard information and overly relying on soft information, which is sometimes non-credible or misleading. Instead, other market-based mechanisms, such as signalling (by fundraisers or other investors), as well as platform-based screening, monitoring, and risk management services, are better suited to mitigate the potential sources of market failure.

Nonetheless, the law is central in reinforcing the gatekeeping role of crowdfunding platforms, whose delicate system of controls should be adapted to different crowdfunding services. The viability of the crowdfunding mechanism still needs to endure the test of time, and one issue where neither market-based nor regulatory-based solutions seem adequate is ex-post information asymmetry. This issue is more pronounced in investment-based crowdfunding (including different mezzanine instruments such as profit-sharing loans). Market incentives for fundraisers to disclose sufficient information and those of investors to act upon it to mitigate agency costs are questionable. Fundraisers no longer have to attract funding, and investors suffer from a collective action problem in exercising their (shareholder) rights. Whether platforms' reintermediation services in the form of delegated monitoring (such as through a nominee structure) will mitigate these issues is yet to be ascertained.

In relation to this, the findings of this study also relate to law and finance literature, exploring the question of the emergence, performance, and optimal regulation of different intermediaries in finance. The crowdfunding phenomenon is unique for standing at the intersection of direct and indirect finance, where, as argued before, financial contracts are concluded directly, even though the platform typically internalises many screening, monitoring, and risk management tasks. Relatedly, crowdfunding connects the provision of credit, traditionally in the banking domain, and the issuance of securities, in the domain of (primary) capital markets. Finally, the particularity of crowdfunding relates to its mixed features of public and private markets for direct finance. The fundraising process is more akin to traditional IPOs (although without traditional gatekeepers). At the same time, the post-investment control, in the absence of operational secondary markets, better aligns with private markets. The study explores in detail these peculiar aspects of crowdfunding by (1) analysing the resemblance of crowdfunding platforms to financial intermediaries, information intermediaries, and traditional providers of entrepreneurial finance, and different regulatory (licensing) approaches; (2) discussing the intersection of P2P lending and investment-based crowdfunding and the question of putting them under one regulatory umbrella; (3) investigating different aspects of investor protection before and after a crowdfunding campaign, by looking into market-based and regulatory measures.

Lastly, the findings of this study contribute to the relatively new, fast-growing and interdisciplinary literature on fintech, alternative finance and crowdfunding as one of its most prominent segments. An essential part of this study (Chap. 3) draws on existing empirical research examining disclosures and signalling practices in the crowdfunding market. The study conducted an integrative literature review by applying a novel conceptual framework. The empirical evidence is systematised and analysed along three potential sources of market failure: incomplete information, limited attention, and non-credible information (and an analogous framework for signalling mechanisms), which can also guide future research on the topic. Moreover, for the first time, this study examined self-regulation practices in crowdfunding by looking into the economic rationale, content, and enforcement of industry codes of conduct in Europe. Finally, this study represents one of the first attempts to assess the effects of fintech regulations on market outcomes by providing evidence from the equity crowdfunding market in the UK.

The multifaceted and interdisciplinary approach of this study, as well as the fast-paced changes in the crowdfunding market, lead to several limitations in the findings. Firstly, the review of empirical evidence in Chap. 3 relies on research focusing on various jurisdictions, crowdfunding models, and platforms. This is a direct consequence of the fact that despite its exponential growth, crowdfunding literature on many essential questions is still scarce. Thus, despite the attempt to group some existing evidence along the categories mentioned above (jurisdiction, model, platform), most conclusions are generalised. Generalisation, especially when based on a limited number of studies, such as the case here, raises the question of (external) validity. Thus, future research should reassess the findings on market-based mechanisms in light of new empirical evidence. While this limitation primarily relates to disclosures and signalling practices of fundraisers and their use by investors, the same applies to platform services. The study aimed to provide a comprehensive review of platform services, independent of how common they are and their geographical distribution. Yet, some crowdfunding models explored in this study are dominant in certain markets while non-existent in others. Some services were also eventually abolished on platforms in relation to which they were described in the literature. This can potentially undermine the relevance of some parts of the analysis in Chap. 5, where the regulatory implications of different reintermediation services are explained with equal importance. Another caveat to examining platform services is that they are limited to services identified in the crowdfunding literature, which often lags behind market practices. Thus, the framework for models with distinct risk levels developed in this study and discussions on their optimal regulatory treatment should be re-examined in light of new findings on platform services.

The limitation stemming from the dynamics of the crowdfunding market is perhaps even more important in Chap. 4, examining the codes of conduct of crowdfunding associations in Europe. As argued in this study, self-regulatory frameworks, like crowdfunding regulations, evolve over time and even directly interact with one another. Since the data collection process and analysis, some self-regulatory frameworks have been changed, and some have lost their importance with adopting new crowdfunding regulations. Nevertheless, it would be interesting to examine in the future whether and how they influenced new rules and whether any new self-regulatory initiatives could potentially signal the emergence of new risks stemming from the crowdfunding activity.

The main limitation of the analysis in Chap. 5 stems from the fact its goal was to discuss some general principles of regulating crowdfunding, drawing on the findings on promises and limitations of market-based mechanisms. Legal scholars can see the abstract and jurisdiction-agnostic way of approaching specific regulatory issues as inappropriate. Notably, it is plausible that some of the proposed solutions cannot find their application in particular jurisdictions because they are not consistent with the regulatory powers of different competent authorities, the structure and internal logic of financial regulations in a given legal system, or different constraints related to the way certain regulated activities, financial instruments, and intermediaries are defined in statutes. This is particularly pertinent to supranational lawmaking (e.g., at the European level), which is further constrained by the competence or regulatory mandate of supranational institutions. Moreover, examples from different crowdfunding regimes worldwide were invoked in this study to illustrate a specific regulatory solution instead of providing a comparative law analysis. Therefore, legal scholars can build on the analysis provided in this study to examine whether and how some of the proposed solutions can be adopted in a given jurisdiction or conduct a systematic comparative legal exercise on specific points raised.

Lastly, the empirical study on the effects of bespoke crowdfunding regimes on market outcomes has two main limitations. The first one is its external validity. The bespoke crowdfunding regime in the UK is specific for not introducing many new rules for market participants. Still, it clarifies the regulator's approach to crowdfunding and the rules governing the operation of platforms (making them more salient to the public). In line with findings in Chap. 5, many jurisdictions followed a different regulatory path and adopted more stringent bespoke regulations.

Consequently, further research is needed to examine the effects of crowdfunding rules in other market and regulatory contexts. Another limitation is that the study does not make causal claims, given the absence of an identification strategy to mitigate potential omitted variable bias. Future research using the data from two or more comparable crowdfunding markets, in which regulations were introduced at different points, would potentially allow for a causal inference.

This study has several practical implications. It is primarily relevant to policymakers and regulators struggling to understand the risks inherent in crowdfunding and the role of financial regulations in mitigating those risks. Different regulatory approaches and associated trade-offs explained in this study (the 'regulatory tetralemma') can help them choose the one optimal for their local context and existing regulations. Moreover, this study also sheds light on risks stemming from different crowdfunding models, providing policymakers and regulators with insights relevant to determining the scope of crowdfunding bespoke regimes. Lastly, the discussion on rules governing the behaviour of fundraisers, platforms, and investors portrays different regulatory solutions and their interplay with market-based solutions for information asymmetries.

Annexes

Annex 3A: Overview of Empirical Evidence on Fundraisers' Disclosures

Q1: Are investors responsive to the differences in the level of disclosure of (soft) information?
Q2: Are investors responsive to hard (financial) information?
Q3: Are differences in disclosure levels indicative of ex-post outcomes (are voluntary disclosures credible)?

A. Odorović, *Overcoming Asymmetric Information in the Crowdfunding Market*, International Law and Economics, https://doi.org/10.1007/978-3-032-04118-0

Numbering	Study	Crowdfunding business model	Jurisdiction and platform name	Disclosure level indicator/information type (hard, soft, mixture)[a]	Q1: Investors' responsiveness to the disclosure level (Positive/negative/ unresponsive/ ambiguous)[b]	Q2: Investors' responsiveness to hard (financial) data[c]	Q3: Ex-post credibility (credible, non-credible, misleading)[d]
1.	Herzenstein et al. (2008)	P2P consumer lending (auction)	US, prosper	Demographics, personal information (no personal information, general personal information, and specific personal information)/mixture	Positive	Positive	n.a.
2.	Herzenstein, Sonenshein, et al. (2011)	P2P consumer lending (auction)	US, prosper	The number of identity claims (trustworthy, economic hardship, hardworking, successful, moral, and religious)/mixture	Positive	n.a.	Misleading (borrowers with a lower credit score make a higher number of identity claims. As the number of identity claims increase, borrowers have a higher probability of default as compared to paying late, as well as higher probability of paying late as compared to paying on time)
3.	Michels (2012)	P2P consumer lending (auction)	US, prosper	A sum of points assigned for each specific information reported/mixture	Positive	Positive and unresponsive (having a loan on the same platform on which the borrower either defaulted or is late with payments)	Credible

4.	Duarte et al. (2012)	P2P consumer lending (auction)	US, prosper	Decision to upload a photograph/the appearance of trustworthiness/soft	Positive	n.a.	Credible
5.	Iyer et al. (2016)	P2P consumer lending (auction)	US, prosper	Standard (financial) information, quantifiable nonstandard (soft) information, and nonquantifiable soft information/mixture	Positive for all three information categories (the relative influence of standard financial information is the greatest)	Positive (the marginal effect of hard data drops for borrowers with lowest credit scores)	Credible (soft information appears more valuable in the screening process of low-quality borrowers)
6.	Gao et al. (2018)	P2P consumer lending (auction)	US, prosper	The level of text readability, positivity, and deception cues in the optional written description of the borrower's financial situation and loan purpose/soft	Positive (readability, positivity), negative (deception clues)	n.a.	Credible (prices are not efficient; on average, the interest rate is not high enough to compensate lenders for the additional risk)
7.	Kgoroeadira et al. (2019)	P2P business loans (auction)	US, prosper	Personal characteristics of a business owner (hard information and the quantity of narratives)/ mixture	Positive (hard information), unresponsive (the quantity of narratives)	Positive and unresponsive (e.g., previous failures such as delinquencies or judgements, firm's attributes not always significant)	n.a.

(continued)

Numbering	Study	Crowdfunding business model	Jurisdiction and platform name	Disclosure level indicator/information type (hard, soft, mixture)[a]	Q1: Investors' responsiveness to the disclosure level (Positive/negative/ unresponsive/ ambiguous)[b]	Q2: Investors' responsiveness to hard (financial) data[c]	Q3: Ex-post credibility (credible, non-credible, misleading)[d]
8.	Nowak et al. (2018)	P2P lending (posted price, grade and interest rate determined by the platform)	US, lending club	The number of spelling errors, lexical diversity, and the text length/soft	Negative (spelling errors) Positive (lexical diversity) Ambiguous (text length—lenders' response is positive to both very long and very short descriptions)	n.a.	n.a.
9.	Nowak et al. (2018)	P2P lending (posted price, grade and interest rate determined by the platform)	US, lending club	Specific words and phrases that the textual analysis identified as predictors of investors' funding decisions/soft	n.a.	n.a.	Credible (the impact on loan performance is the strongest for borrowers in the lowest quartile of credit scores)
10.	Carmichael (2014)	P2P lending (posted price, grade and interest rate determined by the platform)	US, lending club	Claims about creditworthiness captured by screening the loan description for some keywords that are typically associated with positive claims about oneself; loan description lacking full stop/soft	n.a.	n.a.	Credible

11.	Polena and Regner (2018)	P2P lending (posted price, grade and interest rate determined by the platform)	US, lending club	Length of loan descriptions/soft	n.a.	n.a.	Credible (creditworthy borrowers write longer loan descriptions than borrowers who defaulted. However, when looking into different risk categories, the length of disclosures is only significant in low-risk category)
12.	Yao et al. (2019)	P2P consumer lending	China, Renrendai	Stating loan purpose (investment and entrepreneurship, or car purchase)/soft	Positive (loans for investment and entrepreneurship more likely to be funded than loans for car purchase)	Positive	n.a.
13.	Chen et al. (2022)	P2P consumer lending	China, Renrendai	Amount of information disclosed/mixed	Positive (verified information matters more)	n.a.	Misleading
14.	Li et al. (2020)	P2P consumer lending	China, Ppdai	Amount of voluntary disclosure of objective (verifiable) and subjective (unverifiable) information)/mixture	Positive (stronger for borrowers with a borrowing history)	n.a.	Credible (repeated borrowers) Non-credible (first-time borrowers)
15.	Jiang et al. (2018)	P2P business lending	China, Eloan	Length of loan descriptions; descriptions relating to family, work, income, assets, business, and agriculture/mixture	n.a.	n.a.	Credible and mixed (mentioning of specific phrases has different influence on default probability, suggesting that not all soft information is credible)

(continued)

Numbering	Study	Crowdfunding business model	Jurisdiction and platform name	Disclosure level indicator/information type (hard, soft, mixture)[a]	Q1: Investors' responsiveness to the disclosure level (Positive/negative/ unresponsive/ ambiguous)[b]	Q2: Investors' responsiveness to hard (financial) data[c]	Q3: Ex-post credibility (credible, non-credible, misleading)[d]
16.	Pötzsch and Böhme (2010)	P2P consumer lending platform	Germany, Smava	Disclosures of personal data and appeals to social behaviour/Mixture	Unresponsive (with the exception of education, profession, and qualifications, which have a positive influence)	n.a.	n.a.
17.	Dorfleitner et al. (2016)	P2P consumer lending platform	Germany, Smava and Auxmoney	Spelling errors, text length, and the use of keywords evoking positive emotions in the applicant's description of the loan's purpose and the personal situation/soft	Unresponsive (Smava) Positive (Auxmoney)	n.a.	Non-credible, however, the annual rates of return are higher and accompanying defaults are lower on Auxmoney than on Smava, thus providing indirect support that the use of soft data is helpful in assessing borrowers' creditworthiness
18.	Cumming and Hornuf (2022)	P2P business loans (posted price by the platform)	Germany, Zencap	Financial information and reasons for raising external capital/ mixture	Unresponsive (reasons for raising external capital)	Unresponsive (granular financial information when presented with platform's credit ratings)	n.a.

19.	Franks et al. (2021)	P2P business loans (auction)	UK, funding circle	n.a.	n.a.	n.a.	Credible (interest rates determined in an auction process are a statistically significant predictor of defaults, even after controlling for credit scores; however, prices are not efficient)
20.	Donovan (2021)	Equity crowdfunding	UK, crowdcube	Disclosure of unverified financials and contextual information in the shareholder agreement/hard	Positive (disclosure of unverified financials matters more for firms with credit history; the effect is stronger when contextual information is also provided)	n.a.	Credible
21.	Estrin et al. (2022)	Equity crowdfunding	UK, crowdcube	Specific soft and hard data/mixture	Positive (soft data important than hard data, the effect of soft increases in the size of the fundraisers' social network)	Unresponsive (the majority of hard variables included do not significantly affect the probability of success)	n.a.
22.	Jo and Yang (2021)	Equity crowdfunding	UK, crowdcube	Financial forecasts/ soft	Positive (with the exception of forecasts of profitability)	Positive (value of assets)	Non-credible

(continued)

Numbering	Study	Crowdfunding business model	Jurisdiction and platform name	Disclosure level indicator/information type (hard, soft, mixture)[a]	Q1: Investors' responsiveness to the disclosure level (Positive/negative/unresponsive/ambiguous)[b]	Q2: Investors' responsiveness to hard (financial) data[c]	Q3: Ex-post credibility (credible, non-credible, misleading)[d]
23.	Knyazeva and Ivanov (2017)	Equity crowdfunding	US, all platforms	Hard and soft data (social media coverage)/mixture	Positive (soft data more important than hard data)	Unresponsive (profitability, asset size, and the age of the issuer are positively but insignificantly associated with campaign success)	n.a.
24.	Johan and Zhang (2020)	Equity crowdfunding	US, all platforms	Qualitative business information (the length of business description, and the use of promotional words)/soft	Positive (the length of business description) Negative (percentage of promotional words, but the effect is weakened or insignificant once retail investors were allowed to enter the market)	Positive	n.a.

25.	Aland (2023)	Equity crowdfunding	US, all platforms	Financial information emphasised on the offering page, non-financial information (the intended use of raised funds, a history of the company, frequently asked questions, etc.)/ mixture	Positive (non-financial information) Unresponsive (financial information emphasised on the offering page)	Positive (debt) and unresponsive (results not consistent across different specifications, but the firm's size, revenue, net income, and age are not statistically significant)	Credible (prior revenues are strongly associated with the discussion of financial information on the offerings page) non-credible (no statistically significant relationship between the tendency to disclose soft-information and firm's ex-ante characteristics)
26.	Ahlers et al. (2015)	Equity crowdfunding	Australia, ASSOB	Providing financial forecasts or a disclaimer; disclosing other forecasts (proposed exit channel and estimated time horizon until planned exit)/soft	Positive (financial forecasts or a disclaimer, IPO as a planned exit channel) Unresponsive (estimated time horizon until planned exit)	n.a.	n.a.
27.	Pattanapanyasat (2021)	Equity crowdfunding	Australia, ASSOB	Unaudited financial statements and the tone of entrepreneurs' narratives/mixture	Positive (financials) Negative (positive tone)	n.a.	Misleading (positive tone is associated with poor post-campaign performance, although investors respond negatively to such disclosures, and therefore, are not really mislead)

(continued)

Numbering	Study	Crowdfunding business model	Jurisdiction and platform name	Disclosure level indicator/information type (hard, soft, mixture)[a]	Q1: Investors' responsiveness to the disclosure level (Positive/negative/unresponsive/ambiguous)[b]	Q2: Investors' responsiveness to hard (financial) data[c]	Q3: Ex-post credibility (credible, non-credible, misleading)[d]
28.	Li et al. (2016)	Equity crowdfunding	China, Dajiatou	The possibility to upload a video, length of project introduction, and the length and frequency of updates during the campaign/soft	Positive	n.a.	n.a.
29.	Lukkarinen et al. (2016)	Equity crowdfunding	Nordic countries, Invesdor	Provision of financials, actual information contained in financial disclosures/hard	Unresponsive (both provision of financials and actual financial information valued by angel investors and VCs)	Unresponsive	n.a.
30.	Goethner et al. (2021)	Equity crowdfunding	Germany, Companisto	Information contained in financial projections/soft	Positive (the effect varies among different investor types)	n.a.	n.a.
31.	Block et al. (2018)	Equity crowdfunding	Germany, seedmatch and companisto	Updates during a campaign/mixture	Positive	n.a.	n.a.
32.	Dorfleitner et al. (2018)	Equity crowdfunding	Germany, seedmatch and companisto	Updates during a campaign/mixture	Positive	n.a.	n.a.

33.	Hornuf and Schwienbacher (2018)	Equity crowdfunding	Germany, seedmatch, innovestment, companisto, and united equity	Updates during a campaign/mixture	Positive	n.a.	n.a.
34.	Reichenbach and Walther (2021)	Equity crowdfunding	Germany, companisto	Updates during a campaign/mixture	n.a.	n.a.	Non-credible (the number of updates), Credible (specific updates that were found to have a greater influence on the success of funding by Block et al. (2018)

[a] The distinction between hard and soft data is whether it is verifiable or non-verifiable, independent of how authors denote it. A mixture means that the study tests the effect of hard and soft data separately or as one indicator that aggregates different data points

[b] Investors' responsiveness to disclosure is positive when greater disclosure (or disclosure of specific information) is associated with a higher number of investors contributing, higher amount pledged per individual investor, higher amount raised per campaign, higher likelihood of a campaign success, or lower interest rates. On the contrary, negative responsiveness assumes that greater disclosure (or disclosure of specific information) is associated with a lower number of investors contributing, lower amount pledged per individual investor, lower amount raised per campaign, lower likelihood of campaign success, or higher interest rates. Investors are unresponsive when greater disclosure (or disclosure of specific information) does not have a significant effect on the indicators of campaign success mentioned above. Investors' response is deemed ambiguous if the effect varies depending on the level of disclosures or specific fundraiser's characteristics (e.g., credit score)

[c] The distinction between positive, negative, unresponsive, and ambiguous reactions to hard financial data is analogous to the explanation above. Evidence on investors' responsiveness to specific hard information is seldom systematic and presented clearly in empirical studies. Instead, hard data indicators are usually merely included as controls

[d] Disclosures are considered credible if they are associated with better ex-ante fundraisers' characteristics (e.g., credit scores) or ex-post outcomes, as captured by the survival rate, default probabilities, or paying on time vs. paying late. Disclosures are deemed non-credible if no statistically significant relationship exists between disclosures and ex-ante characteristics or ex-post outcomes. Disclosures are treated as misleading if they are associated with worse ex-ante characteristics or ex-post outcomes. Alternatively, disclosures are considered credible if they are proven to increase pricing efficiency

Annex 3B: Overview of Empirical Evidence on Signalling

Q1: Are investors responsive to different signals? Q2: Are signals credible?

Signal group	Signal type	Studies	Crowdfunding business model	Jurisdiction and platform	Q1: Investors' responsiveness to signal (positive/negative/unresponsive)[a]	Q2: Ex-post credibility of signal (credible, non-credible, misleading)[b]
Assurance of disclosed information	Verification	Talavera and Xu (2018)	P2P consumer lending	China, Renrendai	Positive	Credible
		Yum et al. (2012)	P2P consumer lending	South Korean platform popfunding	Positive	n.a.
	Certified financial statement	Bogdani et al. (2022)	Equity crowdfunding	US, all crowdfunding platforms	Positive (however, assurance by an audit is not preferred over a review by an independent accountant)	n.a.
Fundraiser's characteristics	Human capital	Ahlers et al. (2015)	Equity crowdfunding	Australia, ASSOB	Positive	n.a.
		Kleinert et al. (2020)	Equity crowdfunding	UK, Crowdcube	Positive	n.a.
		Nitani and Riding (2017)	Equity crowdfunding	UK, Crowdcube, Germany, Companisto, Finland, Invesdor, and Sweden, FundedbyMe	Positive	n.a.
		Goethner et al. (2021)	Equity crowdfunding	Germany, Companisto	Positive (the effect is the weakest for casual investors)	n.a.
		Reichenbach and Walther (2021)	Equity crowdfunding	Germany, Companisto	n.a.	Credible (CEO with a university degree or relevant industry experience)

		Piva and Rossi-Lamastra (2018)	Equity crowdfunding	Italy, SiamoSoci	Positive (fundraisers' business education and previous entrepreneurial experiences) Unresponsive (industry-specific education and work experience)	n.a.
		Battaglia et al. (2022)	Equity crowdfunding	Italy, many different platforms	Positive	n.a.
	Team quality	Barbi and Mattioli (2019)	Equity crowdfunding	UK, Crowdcube	Positive	n.a.
		Vismara (2016)	Equity crowdfunding	UK, Crowdcube and Seedrs	Positive	n.a.
		Vismara (2018a)	Equity crowdfunding	UK, Crowdcube	Positive	n.a.
		Li et al. (2016)	Equity crowdfunding	China, Dajiatou	Positive	n.a.
		Lukkarinen et al. (2016)	Equity crowdfunding	Finland, Austria, and Germany, invesdor	Unresponsive	n.a.
		Hornuf et al. (2018)	Equity crowdfunding	UK and Germany, 13 different portals	n.a.	Credible (the number of senior managers is associated with higher probability of follow-up funding and lower probability of failure)
	Social capital and social media coverage	Lin et al. (2013)	P2P lending	US, prosper	Positive (the size of fundraiser's network on the crowdfunding platform)	Credible (borrowers with more credible connections are less likely to default)
		Freedman and Jin (2017)	P2P lending	US, prosper	Positive (the size of fundraiser's network on the crowdfunding platform)	Credible (friend endorsements followed by actual bids) Misleading (friend endorsements without bids)
		Faia and Paiella (2017)	P2P lending	US, prosper	Positive (affinity group membership)	n.a.

(continued)

Signal group	Signal type	Studies	Crowdfunding business model	Jurisdiction and platform	Q1: Investors' responsiveness to signal (positive/negative/unresponsive)[a]	Q2: Ex-post credibility of signal (credible, non-credible, misleading)[b]
		Freedman and Jin (2017)	P2P lending	US, prosper	Positive (affinity group membership)	Misleading
		Herzenstein et al. (2008)	P2P lending	US, prosper	Positive (affinity group membership)	n.a.
		Hildebrand et al. (2010)	P2P lending	US, prosper	Positive (affinity group membership)	Credible (however, when the group lead earns compensation credibility is reduced)
		Lu et al. (2020)	P2P lending	US, lending club	Positive (the size of regional social capital)	Credible
		Hasan et al. (2022)	P2P lending	China, renrendai	Positive (the size of regional social capital; the effect is stronger for low-quality borrowers)	Credible
		Giudici et al. (2013)	Equity crowdfunding	Italy, eleven platforms	Positive (the size of the fundraiser's social media network)	n.a.
		Piva and Rossi-Lamastra (2018)	Equity crowdfunding	Italy, SiamoSoci	Positive (the size of the fundraiser's social media network)	n.a.
		Troise et al. (2020)	Equity crowdfunding	Italy, eleven platforms	Positive (the size of the fundraiser's social media network)	n.a.
		Battaglia et al. (2022)	Equity crowdfunding	Italy, many different platforms	Positive (the size of the fundraiser's social media network)	n.a.
		Graziano et al. (2023)	Equity crowdfunding	Italy, many different platforms	Positive (the size of the fundraiser's social media network and intensity of interactions)	Credible (innovation performance)
		Vismara (2016)	Equity crowdfunding	UK, Crowdcube and Seedrs	Positive (the size of the fundraiser's social media network)	n.a.

		Kleinert et al. (2020)	Equity crowdfunding	UK, Crowdcube	Unresponsive (the presence of non-executive board members)	n.a.
		Nevin et al. (2017)	Equity crowdfunding	UK, Crowdcube	Positive (Social media activity)	n.a.
		Barbi and Mattioli (2019)	Equity crowdfunding	UK, Crowdcube	Unresponsive (social media presence)	n.a.
		Signori and Vismara (2018)	Equity crowdfunding	UK, Crowdcube	n.a.	Credible (the presence of non-executive board members increases the chances of SEO/M&A) Non-credible (probability of failure)
		(Guenther et al. (2018)	Equity crowdfunding	Australia, Assob	Positive (the presence of non-executive board members; the effect is not consistent across different model specifications)	n.a.
		Hervé et al. (2019)	Equity crowdfunding	France, WiSeed	Positive (the size of the fundraiser's social media network)	n.a.
		Eisenbeiss et al. (2023)	Equity crowdfunding	Germany, Companisto, Innovestment, and Seedmatch	Positive (social media activity)	n.a.
		Lukkarinen et al. (2016)	Equity crowdfunding	Finland, Austria, and Germany, Invesdor	Positive (social media activity)	n.a.
		Nitani and Riding (2017)	Equity crowdfunding	UK, Crowdcube, Germany, Companisto, Finland, Invesdor, and Sweden, FundedbyMe	Positive (the size of the fundraiser's social media network)	n.a.
		Ahlers et al. (2015)	Equity crowdfunding	Australia, Assob	Positive	n.a.

(continued)

Signal group	Signal type	Studies	Crowdfunding business model	Jurisdiction and platform	Q1: Investors' responsiveness to signal (positive/negative/unresponsive)[a]	Q2: Ex-post credibility of signal (credible, non-credible, misleading)[b]
Venture characteristics	Retained equity	Pattanapanyasat (2021)	Equity crowdfunding	Australia, Assob	Positive	n.a.
		Battaglia et al. (2022)	Equity crowdfunding	Italy, many different platforms	Positive	n.a.
		Ralcheva and Roosenboom (2020)	Equity crowdfunding	UK, Crowdcube and Seedrs	Positive	n.a.
		Vismara (2016)	Equity crowdfunding	UK, Crowdcube and Seedrs	Positive	n.a.
		Vismara (2018a)	Equity crowdfunding	UK, Crowdcube	Unresponsive	n.a.
		Vismara (2019)	Equity crowdfunding	UK, Crowdcube and Seedrs	Positive	n.a.
		Kleinert et al. (2020)	Equity crowdfunding	UK, Crowdcube	Unresponsive	n.a.
		Signori and Vismara (2018)	Equity crowdfunding	UK, Crowdcube	n.a.	Non-credible
		Cumming et al. (2019)	Equity crowdfunding	UK, Crowdcube	Positive	Credible (more likely to experience long-run success and less likely to experience a failure)
		Nitani and Riding (2017)	Equity crowdfunding	UK, Crowdcube, Germany, Companisto, Finland, Invesdor and Sweden, FundedbyMe	Mixed (results differ across different model specifications)	n.a.
		Reichenbach and Walther (2021)	Equity crowdfunding	Germany, Companisto	n.a.	Misleading
	Intellectual property	Ahlers et al. (2015)	Equity crowdfunding	Australia, Assob	Unresponsive (awards, grants, or granted patents)	n.a.

		Guenther et al. (2018)	Equity crowdfunding	Australia, Assob	Unresponsive (granted patent)	n.a.
		Hornuf and Schwienbacher (2018)	Equity crowdfunding	Germany, all equity platforms operating in the observed period	Positive (number of patents, not significant across all model specifications)	n.a.
		Hornuf and Schwienbacher (2018)	Equity crowdfunding	Germany, Companisto, United Equity, seedmatch and innovestment	Unresponsive (number of patents)	n.a.
		Vismara (2018a)	Equity crowdfunding	UK, Crowdcube	Unresponsive (patents; however, they do attract sophisticated investors)	n.a.
		Ralcheva and Roosenboom (2020)	Equity crowdfunding	UK, Crowdcube and Seedrs	Unresponsive (intellectual property rights: the number of patents and trademarks)	n.a.
		Kleinert et al. (2020)	Equity crowdfunding	UK, Crowdcube	Unresponsive (patent) Positive (grant; not consistent across different model specifications)	n.a.
		Rossi et al. (2020)	Equity crowdfunding	UK, Crowdcube, Seedrs, and SyndicateRoom	Positive (patents, investor-led platform SyndicateRoom) Unresponsive (entrepreneur-led platforms Crowdcube and Seedrs)	n.a.
		Signori and Vismara (2018)	Equity crowdfunding	UK, Crowdcube	n.a.	Credible (patents are associated with higher likelihood of a post-campaign SEO/M&A)
		Cumming et al. (2019)	Equity crowdfunding	UK, Crowdcube	Unresponsive (firm owns or is filing patent application)	Non-credible (long-run success or probability of failure)
		Hornuf et al. (2018)	Equity crowdfunding	UK and Germany, 13 different portals	n.a.	Non-credible (number of granted or filed patents, the number of granted trademarks)

(continued)

Signal group	Signal type	Studies	Crowdfunding business model	Jurisdiction and platform	Q1: Investors' responsiveness to signal (positive/negative/unresponsive)[a]	Q2: Ex-post credibility of signal (credible, non-credible, misleading)[b]
		Rossi et al. (2020)	Equity crowdfunding	US, all platforms	Unresponsive (patents)	n.a.
		Piva and Rossi-Lamastra (2018)	Equity crowdfunding	Italy, SiamoSoci	Positive (holding a patent or having filed or aiming to file a patent application)	n.a.
		Battaglia et al. (2022)	Equity crowdfunding	Italy, many different platforms	Positive (patents and R&D)	n.a.
	Corporate governance	Cumming et al. (2019)	Equity crowdfunding	UK, Crowdcube	Positive (separation between ownership and control lowers the likelihood of success)	Credible
		Kleinert and Volkmann (2019)	Equity crowdfunding	UK, Crowdcube	Negative (discussions about shareholders rights and concerns about possible dilution of shares)	n.a.
		Signori and Vismara (2018)	Equity crowdfunding	UK, Crowdcube	n.a.	Misleading (offering voting rights reduces the likelihood of SEO/M&As and increases the likelihood of a firm's failure)
		Hornuf et al. (2021)	Equity crowdfunding	Germany, 19 different platforms	Unresponsive (control and exit rights)	Non-credible (control rights) Misleading (exit rights)
Signals from other investors	Investments from the crowd	Ceyhan et al. (2011)	P2P lending	US, prosper	Positive	n.a.
		Herzenstein, Dholakia, et al. (2011)	P2P lending	US, prosper	Positive	Credible (herding is positively associated with borrowers paying on time)

		Zhang and Liu (2012)	P2P lending	US, prosper	Positive	Credible (herding depends on campaign listing attributes—well-funded projects have a lower likelihood of default)
		Chen et al. (2015)	P2P lending	China, PPdai	Positive	Misleading (herding is associated with a higher default rate)
		Zhang and Chen (2017)	P2P lending	China, Renrendai	Positive	Mixed (investors follow both manual and automatic bids)
		Jiang et al. (2018)	P2P lending	China, PaiPaiDai,	Positive	Credible (automatic bidding weakened herding effect)
		Caglayan et al. (2021)	P2P lending	China, Renrendai	Positive (the effect is stronger for more experienced investors on the platform)	n.a.
		Lee and Lee (2012)	P2P lending	South Korea, Popfunding	Positive	n.a.
		Kim (2019)	P2P lending	South Korea, Moneyauction	Positive	Credible (accelerating bidding over time is positively associated with loan repayment)
		Agrawal et al. (2015)	Equity crowdfunding (revenue-sharing)	Netherlands, Sellaband	Positive (the effect is weaker for local investors as opposed to distant investors)	n.a.
		Vulkan et al. (2016)	Equity crowdfunding	UK, Seedrs	n.a.	Non-credible (share of public pledges) Credible (following investors in top 1% regarding the average value of their pledges in previous campaigns)

(continued)

Signal group	Signal type	Studies	Crowdfunding business model	Jurisdiction and platform	Q1: Investors' responsiveness to signal (positive/negative/unresponsive)[a]	Q2: Ex-post credibility of signal (credible, non-credible, misleading)[b]
		Vismara (2018a).	Equity crowdfunding	UK, Crowdcube	Positive	Credible (influence of investors with a known identity on subsequent investments is stronger, such investors are also better educated and have more industry-related experience)
		Astebro et al. (2019)	Equity crowdfunding	UK, Seedrs	Positive	Credible (investors' rationality stems from their responsiveness to the size of the last pledge in addition to cumulative amount invested)
		Li et al. (2022)	Equity crowdfunding	UK, platform unknown	Positive	n.a.
		Kim and Viswanathan (2018)	Equity crowdfunding	US, Appbackr	Positive	Credible (investors follow the experts in the crowd)
		Jiang et al. (2018)	Equity crowdfunding	China, Renrendai	Positive	Credible (automatic bidding reduced herding effect)
		Zhang and Chen (2017)	Equity crowdfunding	China, Renrendai	Positive	Mixed (investors follow both manual and automated bids; rational herding becomes more frequent when loans have poor credit grades)
		Hornuf and Schwienbacher (2018)	Equity crowdfunding	Germany, Companisto, United Equity, seedmatch and innovestment	Positive	Credible (investors are responsive to large individual pledges)

		Goethner et al. (2021)	Equity crowdfunding	Germany, Companisto	n.a.	Non-credible (investors are unresponsive to pledges of sophisticated investors, except for crowd enthusiasts)
	Prior financing/ lead investors	Ralcheva and Roosenboom (2020)	Equity crowdfunding	UK, Seeders and Crowdcube	Positive (securing external financing before launching a crowdfunding campaign)	n.a.
		Kleinert et al. (2020)	Equity crowdfunding	UK, Seeders and Crowdcube	Positive (securing external financing before launching a crowdfunding campaign)	n.a.
		Wang et al. (2019)	Equity crowdfunding	UK, n.a.	Positive (business angels who invest alongside crowd investors during a campaign)	n.a.
		Rossi et al. (2020)	Equity crowdfunding	UK, Syndicate Room, Seedrs and Crowdcube	Positive (the average success rate of Syndicate room, where the involvement of a lead investor is a prerequisite for a campaign listing, is higher than that of its competitors)	n.a.
		X. Li et al. (2016)	Equity crowdfunding	China, Dajiatou	Positive (presence of a lead, their characteristics and behaviour increase the likelihood of campaign success)	n.a.
		Shen et al. (2020)	Equity crowdfunding	China, Dajiatou	Positive (lead investor's experience and proportion of funding committed positively affect the probability of reaching the funding goal, while the help offered to project founders does not have an influence)	n.a.
		Chen and Ma (2023)	Equity crowdfunding	China, JD.com	Negative (a lead investor's ownership stake; the effect is weaker when a lead investor has a reputation and a track record of competence)	n.a.

(continued)

		Agrawal et al. (2016)	Equity crowdfunding	US, AngelList	Positive (distant investors are more frequently attracted to syndicated than to non-syndicated projects)	n.a.
		Zhang et al. (2023)	Equity crowdfunding	US, AngelList	Positive (a lead investor's specialised human capital; more general human capital has no effect)	n.a.
		Goethner et al. (2021)	Equity crowdfunding	Germany, Companisto	Positive (advertising business or social ties to a VC or an angel investor on a project page increases investments of casual investors) Negative (sophisticated investors and crowd enthusiasts)	n.a.
		Signori and Vismara (2018)	Equity crowdfunding	UK, Crowdcube	n.a.	Credible (receiving initial financing from angel investors or VCs)
		Hornuf et al. (2018)	Equity crowdfunding	UK and Germany, 13 platforms	n.a.	Misleading (the number of initial VC investors increases the likelihood of a firm failure) Credible (the number of initial VC investors increases the chances of receiving follow-up funding)
		Reichenbach and Walther (2021)	Equity crowdfunding	Germany, Companisto	n.a.	Non-credible (reputable investor backing)

[a] Investors' responsiveness to signals is positive when the existence of a signal (or its strength) is associated with a higher number of investors contributing, higher amount pledged per individual investor, higher amount raised per campaign, higher likelihood of a campaign success, or lower interest rates. On the contrary, negative responsiveness assumes that the existence of a signal (or its strength) is associated with a lower number of investors contributing, lower amount pledged per individual investor, lower amount raised per campaign, lower likelihood of campaign success, or higher interest rates. Investors are unresponsive when the existence of a signal (or its strength) does not have a significant effect on the indicators of campaign success mentioned above

[b] Signals are considered credible if they are associated with better ex-post outcomes, as captured by the survival rate, default probabilities, paying on time vs. paying late, having a post-campaign SEO/M&A (or receiving other follow-up funding) and innovation performance. Signals are deemed non-credible if no statistically significant relationship exists between signals and ex-post outcomes. Signals are treated as misleading if they are associated with worse ex-post outcomes. In the case of third-party signals (investments from the crowd), credibility is analysed through the lenses of rational vs. irrational herding

Annex 4A: The List of Codes of Conducts

Asociación Espanola de Crowdfunding. (2018). *Guía de Buenas Prácticas.* Retrieved from http://www.spaincrowdfunding.org/wa_files/Guia-de-buenas-pra_CC_81cticas.pdf

Bundesverband Crowdfunding. (2016a). *Reporting Guidelines für Crowdfunding-Plattformen im Bundesverband Crowdfunding e.V.* Retrieved from https://www.bundesverband-crowdfunding.de/reporting-guidelines-fuer-crowdfunding-plattformen-im-bundesverband-crowdfunding-e-v/

Bundesverband Crowdfunding. (2016b). *Verhaltenskodex für Crowdfunding-Plattformen.* Retrieved from https://www.bundesverband-crowdfunding.de/verhaltenskodex-fuer-crowdfunding-plattformen-im-bundesverband-crowdfunding-e-v/

Bundesverband Crowdfunding. (2019). *Transparenzsiegel.* Retrieved from https://www.bundesverband-crowdfunding.de/transparenzsiegel/

CrowdfundPort, I. C. E. (2016). *Code of Conduct.* Retrieved from https://www.interreg-central.eu/Content.Node/CROWD-FUND-PORT/CFP-D.T1.1.2-Code-of-conduct.pdf

European Crowdfunding Network. (2015, July 1). *Code of Conduct.* Retrieved from https://eurocrowd.org/membership/code-of-conduct/

Finance Estonia, & Deloitte Legal Estonia. (2016, February). *Finance Estonia - Best Practice for Crowdfunding Platforms.* Retrieved from http://www.financeestonia.eu/wp-content/uploads/2016/02/Crowdfunding-Best-Practice.pdf

Financement Participatif France. (2014, April). *Code de déontologie.* Retrieved from http://financeparticipative.org/wp-content/uploads/2015/03/FPF-Code-déontologie-_-Avril_2014.pdf

Financement Participatif France. (2016, July 4). *Code de déontologie.* Retrieved from http://financeparticipative.org/wp-content/uploads/2016/04/FPF-Code-déontologic_avril-2016.pdf

Nederland Crowdfunding. (2017). *Gedragscode.* Retrieved from http://startcrowdfunding.nl/about

Nordic Crowdfunding Association. (2017). *Code of Ethics.* Retrieved from http://www.nordic-crowdfunding.com/about.php#anchor3

Peer-to-Peer Finance Association. (2013). *Operating Principles.* Retrieved from http://p2pfa.info/wp-content/uploads/2014/05/P2PFA-Operating-PrinciplesV020713.pdf

Peer-to-Peer Finance Association. (2015). *Operating Principles.* Retrieved from http://p2pfa.info/wp-content/uploads/2015/09/Operating-Principals-vfinal.pdf

Peer-to-Peer Finance Association. (2018). *Operating Principles.* Retrieved from https://p2pfa.org.uk/wp-content/uploads/2018/06/2018.06.27-Operating-Principles-1.pdf

UK Crowdfunding Association. (2018). *Operating Principles.* Retrieved from https://www.ukcfa.org.uk/join-us/code-of-conduct/

WKÖ Wirtschaftskammer Österreich, F. F. (2016). *Standesregeln für Crowdfunding Plattform*. Retrieved from https://www.wko.at/branchen/sbg/information-consulting/finanzdienstleister/standes-und-ausuebungsregeln-ci.html

Annex 6A: Variable Description

Variable	Description
Outcome variables	
Number_of_investors	The number of investors at the end of the campaign
Amount_invested_per_project (log transformed)	Amount invested by the individual investor in the given campaign (in £)
Achieved funding ratio	Percentage raised or the ratio of the total amount raised at the end of the campaign and the target amount
Amount raised (log transformed)	The total amount raised at the end of the campaign (in £)
Independent variables	
PostregCampaign	Dummy variable that equals 1, if the campaign request date was after the regulation came into force (April 1, 2014), and 0 otherwise
Postreg	Dummy variable that equals 1, if the date of investing funds by the individual investor was after the regulation came into force (April 1, 2014), and 0 otherwise
PostregInvestor	Dummy variable that equals 1, if the date of registering on the platform by the individual investor was after the regulation came into force (April 1, 2014), and 0 otherwise
Control variables	
SME value (log transformed)	Valuation of the company raising funds (pre-money)
Retained equity	The percentage of equity retained by the founders of the company (1 – equity offered)
Amount sought (log transformed)	Target capital to be raised
Voting rights	Dummy variable that equals 1, if dual-class shares are offered or that equals 2 if only voting shares are offered, and 0 otherwise (if only non-voting shares are offered)
Campaign duration	Duration of the campaign measured at the end of the pitch
EIS approved	Dummy variable that equals 1, if the Enterprise Investment Scheme (EIS) tax relief is available for investors, and 0 otherwise
SEIS approved	Dummy variable that equals 1, if the Seed Enterprise Investment Scheme (SEIS) tax relief is available for investors, and 0 otherwise
Prior campaigns	Dummy variable is equal to 1 if the fundraiser had run another campaign before, and 0 otherwise
Fundraiser age	The age of fundraiser
Campaign sector	Set of dummy variables controlling for different industries
Tech sector	Dummy variable is equal to 1 if the campaign belongs to the technology sector, and 0 otherwise

Variable	Description
Investor age	The age of investor
Number of investments	Number of campaigns that the individual investor contributed to
Reference group	Dummy variable that equals 1, if no investor type is identified in the data, and 0 otherwise
Everyday investor	Dummy variable that equals 1, if the investor type is everyday (restricted) investor, and 0 otherwise
High Net Worth Individual	Dummy variable that equals 1, if the investor type is high net worth individual, and 0 otherwise.
Sophisticated investor	Dummy variable that equals 1, if the investor type is sophisticated investor, and 0 otherwise
Advised investor	Dummy variable that equals 1, if the investor type is advised investor, and 0 otherwise
FTSE volatility	The standard deviation of FTSE returns over a rolling 30-day period up to the campaign request date, or up to the date of investment
Interest rate	Quarterly average Sterling 3 month mean interbank lending rate
M2	Quarterly amounts outstanding of monetary financial institutions' sterling and all foreign currency M2 (UK estimate of EMU aggregate) liabilities to private and public sectors (in sterling millions) seasonally adjusted

Annex 6B: Log-Transformation of the Variable SME Value

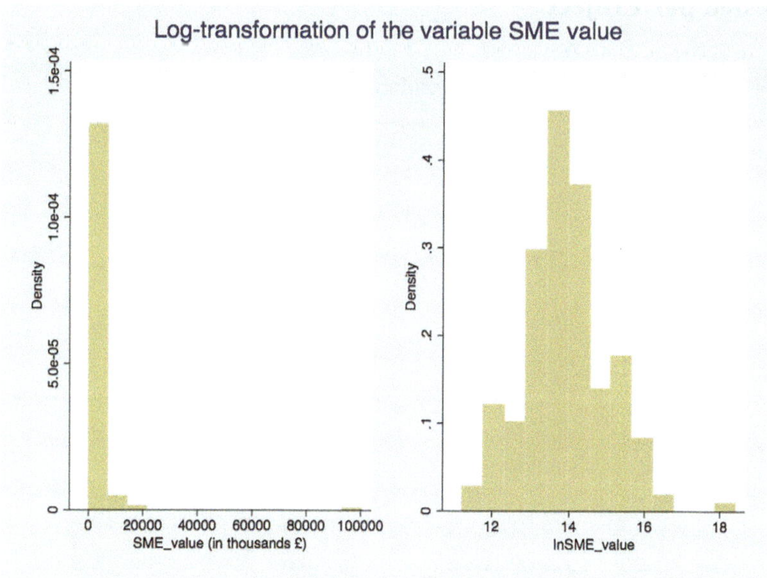

Annex 6C: Log-Transformation of the Variable Amount Sought

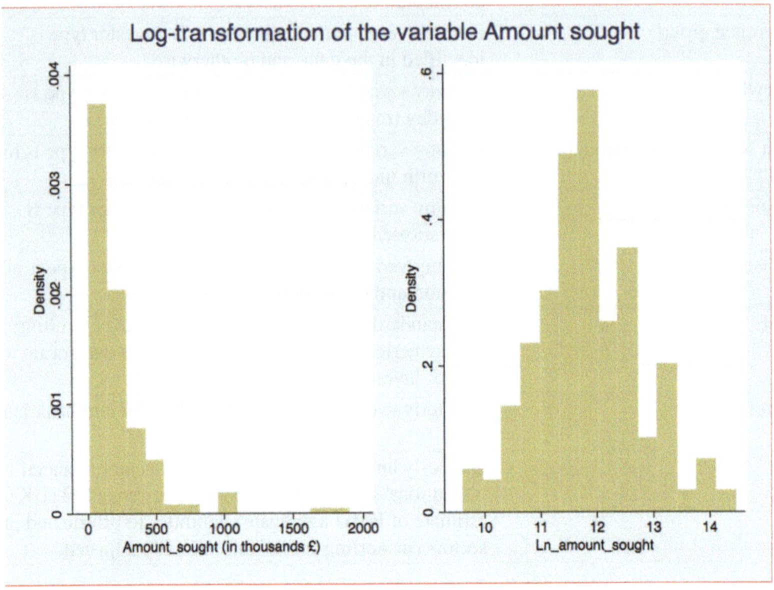

Annex 6D: Log-Transformation of the Variable Amount Invested per Project

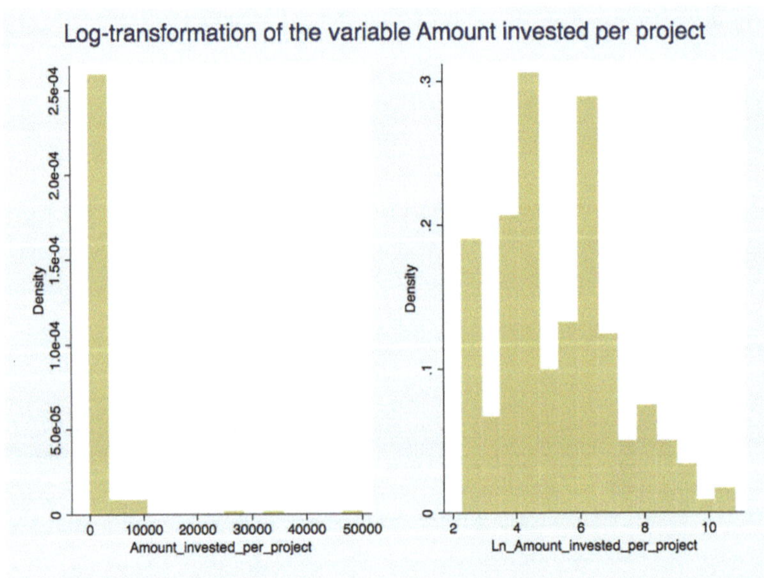

Annex 6E: Descriptive Statistics for Campaign-Level Data

Variable	Obs	Mean	Std. Dev.	Min	Max
Number of investors	201	164.697	149.546	1	1248
Amount raised	201	314,444.38	370,611.56	2670	2,163,300
Achieved funding ratio	201	1.531	0.914	0	9.197
Postreg campaign	201	0.607	0.49	0	1
SME value	201	2,324,672.9	7,392,278.9	0	1.005e+08
Amount sought	201	211,206.58	251,025.46	15,000	1,900,000.8
Retained equity	193	0.871	0.095	0	0.974
Voting rights	201	1.453	0.616	0	2
Prior campaigns	201	0.1	0.3	0	1
Campaign duration	199	51.136	32.721	0	209
EIS approved	201	0.612	0.489	0	1
SEIS approved	201	0.328	0.471	0	1
Fundraiser age	167	39.766	10.954	19	69
Tech sector	201	0.229	0.421	0	1
FTSE volatility	201	0.008	0.003	0.004	0.017
Interest rate	201	0.555	0.108	0.485	1.093

Annex 6F: Descriptive Statistics for Investor-Level Data

Variable	Obs	Mean	Std. Dev.	Min	Max
Amount invested per project	30,708	1632.431	11,345.408	0	1,000,022.2
Postreg	30,708	0.763	0.425	0	1
SME value	30,708	3,580,778.2	10,627,410	0	1.005e+08
Amount sought	30,708	311,383.59	328,982.05	15,000	1,900,000.8
Retained equity	29,357	0.877	0.077	0	0.974
Voting rights	30,708	1.562	0.572	0	2
Prior campaigns	30,708	0.994	0.077	0	1
Campaign duration	30,524	49.575	33.007	0	209
EIS approved	30,708	0.694	0.461	0	1
SEIS approved	30,708	0.263	0.44	0	1
Fundraiser age	27,722	40.11	10.123	19	69
Tech sector	30,708	0.205	0.404	0	1
FTSE volatility	30,708	0.009	0.003	0.004	0.02
Interest rate	30,708	0.551	0.074	0.485	1.093
M2	30,708	2,104,161.1	49,102.856	2,022,915	2,245,967
Investor age	29,755	39.355	12.86	1	96
Reference group	30,708	0.192	0.394	0	1

Variable	Obs	Mean	Std. Dev.	Min	Max
Everyday investor	30,708	0.444	0.497	0	1
Sophisticated investor	30,708	0.198	0.399	0	1
High net worth individual	30,708	0.162	0.368	0	1
Advised investor	30,708	0.004	0.061	0	1
Number of investments	30708	4.104	7.418	1	99

Annex 6G: Difference in Means Between Investments Made by Old Investors and New Investors

	Old investors		New investors		Differences	
	Mean	s.d.	Mean	s.d.	*b*	*t*
Amount invested per project	1456.312	6506.976	1778.289	14,149.720	−321.976**	(−2.632)
SME value	2,721,583.735	8,589,608.948	4,292,349.045	12,010,929.908	−1,570,765.310***	(−13.327)
Amount sought	264,411.524	292,374.051	350,285.090	351,756.958	−85,873.567***	(−23.362)
Retained equity	0.866	0.088	0.886	0.065	−0.020***	(−21.495)
Voting rights	1.361	0.627	1.728	0.462	−0.366***	(−57.284)
Prior campaigns	0.989	0.104	0.998	0.041	−0.009***	(−9.941)
Campaign duration	52.604	36.710	47.100	29.409	5.504***	(14.227)
EIS approved	0.713	0.452	0.678	0.467	0.035***	(6.637)
SEIS approved	0.253	0.435	0.271	0.445	−0.018***	(−3.516)
Fundraiser age	39.956	10.109	40.213	10.131	−0.257*	(−2.068)
Tech sector	0.269	0.444	0.151	0.358	0.118***	(25.294)
FTSE volatility	0.008	0.002	0.009	0.003	−0.001***	(−47.119)
Interest rate	0.551	0.108	0.551	0.016	0.000	(0.344)
M2	2085505.265	31627.350	2119611.641	55250.613	−34106.376***	(−67.721)
Investor age	40.715	12.257	38.241	13.230	2.474***	(16.715)
Reference group	0.155	0.362	0.223	0.416	−0.068***	(−15.258)
Everyday investor	0.359	0.480	0.515	0.500	−0.156***	(−27.915)
Sophisticated investor	0.297	0.457	0.116	0.320	0.182***	(39.562)

	Old investors		New investors		Differences	
	Mean	s.d.	Mean	s.d.	*b*	*t*
High net worth individual	0.185	0.389	0.142	0.349	0.044***	(10.230)
Advised investor	0.003	0.056	0.004	0.064	−0.001	(−1.572)
Number of investments	6.025	9.451	2.513	4.585	3.512***	(40.095)
N	13,911		16,797		30,708	

This table shows summary statistics at the investor level for investments made by Old Investors and New Investors. Old investors registered on crowdfunding portals before the regulatory change, while New Investors registered after. The last column provides test statistics for the comparison of investments made by Old Investors and New Investors
***p 0.01, **p 0.05, *p 0.1

Appendix 6H: Descriptive Statistics of Chosen Covariates Before and After Entropy Balancing for the Dependent Variable Postreg Campaign

	Mean	Treat variance	Skewness	Mean	Control variance	Skewness
Before: without weighting						
lnSME_value	14.09	0.9189	0.3972	13.49	1.019	−0.04348
lnamount_s~t	11.94	0.8705	0.2378	11.64	0.4851	0.1471
retained_e~y	0.8921	0.003069	−1.472	0.8387	0.01693	3.835
voting_rig~s	1.658	0.2625	−1.058	1.139	0.3466	−0.0311
After: w_postregCampaign as the weighting variable						
lnSME_value	14.09	0.9189	0.3972	14.09	0.7898	−0.1861
lnamount_s~t	11.94	0.8705	0.2378	11.94	0.494	0.3585
retained_e~y	0.8921	0.003069	−1.472	0.8919	0.003758	−0.8527
voting_rig~s	1.658	0.2625	−1.058	1.657	0.243	−0.8427

FSC
www.fsc.org
MIX
Papier aus verantwortungsvollen Quellen
Paper from responsible sources
FSC® C105338

If you have any concerns about our products,
you can contact us on
ProductSafety@springernature.com

In case Publisher is established outside the EU,
the EU authorized representative is:
Springer Nature Customer Service Center GmbH
Europaplatz 3, 69115 Heidelberg, Germany

Printed by Libri Plureos GmbH
in Hamburg, Germany

Judi Neal
Editor

Personal, Educational and Organizational Transformation

Leading During Times of Metacrisis

Springer

Editor
Judi Neal
Edgewalkers International
Fayetteville, AR, USA

ISSN 2662-2467 ISSN 2662-2475 (electronic)
Future of Business and Finance
ISBN 978-3-031-29252-1 ISBN 978-3-031-29253-8 (eBook)
https://doi.org/10.1007/978-3-031-29253-8

This Springer imprint is published by the registered company Springer Nature Switzerland AG
The registered company address is: Gewerbestrasse 11, 6330 Cham, Switzerland

I dedicate this book to my friend Paul Kwiecinski who keeps me on the path of accomplishing what I set out to do, to my husband Ralph Ellis, who is the wind beneath my wings, and to my children, grandchildren, and future great-grandchildren. May we collectively find ways to leave you a better world.

Preface

We live in a time of metacrisis, defined as an era when several major crises occur at the same time. As this book goes to publication, we are still in the midst of a global pandemic, political polarization, an increase in autocratic leadership and threats to democracy, a war in Ukraine that has led to energy and food shortages, severe weather, and no clear path to collectively responding to these individual and collective crises. Our old leadership and educational models no longer work in this unpredictable and complex environment. This is not the time for business as usual. What worked in the past is not working in the present, as we witness systems breaking down, from healthcare to education to business.

Times like these historically have offered opportunities for breakthrough and transformation. What does work in times of turmoil is the ability to envision and enact new models, new systems, and new forms of leadership. One must have the optimism and the vision to see the possibilities of a new era for humanity, where all people and the planet can flourish.

The chapter authors in this volume offer models, ideas, and processes for transformation in three domains: Personal Transformation, Educational Transformation, and Organizational Transformation. We begin with an exploration of personal transformation because you cannot have systems transformation without personal transformation. The three chapters in this section are written by professional change agents who have each developed systems to support individuals in their personal and professional journeys. They each provide very practical steps on ways change agents can support the growth and development of their clients.

The second section of this book focuses on innovative and cutting-edge approaches to creating transformation in the lives of students. The role of education is to prepare students for careers and for life after graduation. Most educational institutions focus on developing specialized skills that would have worked in the stable environment of the past, but we are now learning that the traditional curriculum is not enough to prepare students who will face continued metacrises. Not only do they need traditional work skills, students need to be able to think differently and to be able to respond in creative ways to opportunities and challenges that never existed before. Many of us in the management field are coming to see that education must not only be of the mind, it must also be of the body, emotions, and spirit. The chapters in this section provide inspirational examples of ways in which education, particularly management education, are being transformed.

The final section of this book provides multiple lenses in which to view organizational transformation. The metacrisis that faces humanity requires systems thinking, great courage, a willingness to do what has never been done before, and a new level of consciousness that is committed to the greater good. Each of the chapters in this section provides concrete examples of organizational transformation, from multiple perspectives. There are examples from different cultures, different types of businesses such as corporations, non-profits, and family businesses, and from diverse points of view including gender issues and religious perspectives.

It is our hope that the readers of this book will come away with a broader perspective on how transformation takes place across different domains, as well as some practical steps that can be implemented in various situations. These times call for rapid transformation, radical experimentation, quick learning, and resilience when things don't work out as predicted. It's helpful to accept that transformation efforts won't work out as predicted, but that the models, examples, and tools provided here will help change agents to quickly adapt and to embrace and enhance whatever emerges. Each of these chapters provide individual perspectives on what kind of transformation is needed for a new era to emerge. Taken together, they provide a roadmap to a more positive future for all.

Fayetteville, AR, USA Judi Neal
September 12, 2022

Contents

About the Author

Judi Neal, Ph.D., is currently the Executive Director of the Global Consciousness Institute, affiliated with George Washington University and Case Western Reserve University. She is an author, scholar, speaker, and consultant. Her primary research focus is on workplace spirituality, transformation, and global consciousness. After receiving her Ph.D. in Organizational Behavior from Yale University, she served as an internal consultant to Honeywell for 8 years. Judi then taught management at the University of New Haven for 17 years. Her research was on business leaders who have a strong commitment to their spirituality, and she researched the ways in which they bridged the invisible world of spirituality and the material world of business. Dr. Neal was Founding Director of the Tyson Center for Faith and Spirituality in the Workplace at the University of Arkansas. She was a cofounder and former Chair of the Management, Spirituality and Religion (MSR) Interest group and has served on the MSR Executive Committee. She chairs the MSR Scholarship Committee and was founder of the MSR Flamekeeper Committee. She also serves on the boards of the AITIA Institute and INDICA Academy, and was a founding board member of the Conscious Leadership Guild. As one of the founding editors of the *Journal of Management, Spirituality and Religion* (JMSR), she is on the journal's editorial board and is also on the board of the journal's parent organization – the International Association of Management, Spirituality, and Religion (IAMSR). Dr. Neal is the author of nine books on workplace spirituality and transformation and is the President of Edgewalkers International, a workplace spirituality community. She has published *Handbook*

of Faith and Spirituality in the Workplace, *Handbook of Personal and Organizational Transformation*, and seven other books on workplace spirituality, transformation, and global consciousness.

Part I

Personal Transformation

The Hero and the Sherpa: Your Guide Through Life's Challenges

1

Brian Gorman

Abstract

Joseph Campbell got it right. There is one universal path that leads through all of life's challenges. In *The Hero with a Thousand Faces* (Campbell, The hero with a thousand faces. New World Library, Novato, 1949), he introduces The Hero's Journey. For five decades I have been a catalyst for social, organizational, and personal change, and I have been a change Sherpa. For much of that time, I have also been a student of the human dynamics of change. In this chapter I share the most important lessons on change I have learned through The Universal Change Journey, a transformation framework I have created based on The Hero's Journey. This chapter can serve as your personal Sherpa as you create your change story, prepare for the journey, plan for the journey, take the journey, and live the new reality; it can also serve as a guide as you support others through their transformations.

Keywords

Hero's journey · Sherpa · Sherpas · The hero's journey · The universal change journey

Introduction

Simply defined, change is a disruption in expectations. The bigger the disruption, the bigger the change. This definition leads to one of the two most important lessons you can learn about change: *all change is personal.* Societies don't change unless

B. Gorman (✉)
TransformingLives.Coach, Newark, NJ, USA
e-mail: Brian@TransformingLives.Coach

J. Neal (ed.), *Personal, Educational and Organizational Transformation*, Future of Business and Finance, https://doi.org/10.1007/978-3-031-29253-8_1

the people in them change. Organizations don't change unless the people in them change. People change, and through their changes they change the institutions—and the people—they engage with.

Not only is all change personal; how we react to a particular change is personal as well. Two people facing the same change may respond to it very differently. One may see it as positive, the other as negative. One may see it as slightly disruptive, the other as causing major disruption. Having been a change practitioner at the organizational and societal levels, I know that all too often, that lesson is forgotten. The focus is on "stakeholders" or "constituents" or "shareholders" or "communities." The stakeholder, the constituent, the shareholder, and the person down the block become a demographic.

In the following pages, I offer an approach to change based on the understanding that all change is personal. This brings us to the second of the important lessons I have learned along the way. While the catalysts for change are too many to be counted, in truth *there is only one universal path through all change*. In *The Hero with a Thousand Faces* (Joseph Campbell 1949), Joseph Campbell introduces that path; he calls it The Hero's Journey.

> Looking back at what had promised to be our own unique, unpredictable, and dangerous adventure, all we find in the end is such a series of standard metamorphoses as men and women have undergone in every quarter of the world, in all recorded centuries, and under every odd disguise of civilization. (p. 8)

I have been an intentional change catalyst and Sherpa for more than five decades. As a freshman at Syracuse University in 1967, I attempted to convince the administration that the university mascot (at the time, the Saltine Warrior, dressed in a breech cloth, running around waving a tomahawk and letting out war whoops) was denigrating to Native Americans. I failed. (The nearby Onondaga Nation was successful at bringing about a change in the University's mascot a decade later.) For 4 years I was a Basic Military Training Instructor ("drill sergeant") in the Air Force, working with over 1500 young men as they underwent transformational change from civilian to military life. I was hired by one university to establish a living learning center in what had been a dormitory. Another hired me to turn around a moribund annual giving program. I consulted on college and university mergers; developed a "human due diligence template" for a tech firm that was growing through acquisition; and was hired by a nascent AIDS organization to build an administrative infrastructure that would support—without becoming burdensome—their efforts to provide permanent housing and services to homeless people living with AIDS. I was a social activist during the Vietnam era, and I was an AIDS activist in the 1980s and 1990s. I have consulted on global corporate transformations. And now I coach individuals on their own personal and professional transformations.

Throughout my own journey, I have learned many lessons. I have benefited from the coaching, mentoring, and teaching of others, as well as from my own experience. I have developed a framework for what I have learned that is based on The Hero's Journey. The Universal Change Journey consists of five distinct but interrelated phases: create your change story, prepare for the journey, plan for the journey, take the journey, and live the new reality. I apply this framework in my coaching practice. Those who are facing and moving through transformation are the heroes. If you are the coach, therapist, mentor, or any other form of change practitioner, you are the Sherpa. I invite you to consider how the framework—and/or the lessons that it contains—may benefit your own practice. It can be applied as presented here when working one-on-one and adapted for work at the organizational and social change levels.

If you are facing your own change journey, I invite you to consider the following as well. Understanding and following The Universal Change Journey cannot guarantee success; it can help you to be better prepared and help make your change journeys less difficult. On your change journeys, you are your hero. This chapter, and The Universal Change Journey can by your Sherpa.

As you read this chapter, I invite you to reflect on your history with change. How does what you are reading resonate with your own change experience? Are their lessons you can draw from your past? How might your experiences have been different had you been intentionally following the path that is laid out here, using The Universal Change Journey as your Sherpa?

Let's see what lessons The Universal Change Journey has to offer!

Create Your Change Story

The more faithfully you listen to the voice within you, the better you will hear what is sounding outside. And only he who listens can speak. Is this the starting point towards the union of your two dreams—to be allowed in clarity of mind to mirror life and in purity of heart to mold it? (Markings, Dag Hammarskjöld 2003, p. 13).

There are many versions of The Hero's Journey. In his book *The Art of Pilgrimage: The Seeker's Guide to Making Travel Sacred* (1998), Phil Cousineau offers his. Phil, whose mentors included Joseph Campbell, writes, "Questions tune the soul. The purpose behind questions is to initiate the quest" (p. 24). The fundamental question before you begin any change journey is "What is your destination?" The philosopher Seneca put it this way. "When a man does not know what harbor he is making for, no wind is the right wind."

There will be times when you will know the harbor you are heading for. Even then, I invite you to question. How was the harbor chosen? Who chose it? What do you feel when you think about entering that harbor? Where do you feel it? All too often, we let our harbors be chosen for us. "Everyone in my family except me has a PhD." "For generations all the men in my family have been lawyers." "The aptitude tests said I would be a good salesman." In my coaching experience, over and over, I have heard reasons such as these as rationale for the paths my clients are on. All too often, they regretted heading to the harbor chosen for them by others.

The Three Brains

It is interesting to note that Phil Cousineau wrote "Questions tune the soul," not "Questions tune the mind." Knowing your destination is not strictly a mental exercise. Neuroscience tells us that in fact we have three brains. In addition to the brain that we typically think of, there is a heart brain and a gut brain. These communicate upward more than our cranial brain communicates down to them. This means that following your heart and listening to your gut are not just intuitive responses. I invite my clients to connect with all three brains as they consider their destination. One client quite literally says, "What does my head brain say?" "What does my heart brain say?" "What does my gut brain say?" If they are all in agreement, he is clear about his decision. If they are not, we will explore misalignments; sometimes they get resolved, and other times they don't. At that point he makes an intentional decision to follow his head, or his heart, or his gut with awareness of what all three are telling him.

When faced with determining the destination of a major change, one of the most important questions that I ask my clients is "What would make your heart sing?" "As you consider all the possible career choices you could pursue, what would make your heart sing?" "As you think of retiring to someplace warm, what would make your heart sing?" "As you reflect on finding your life partner, what would make your heart sing?" There will be plenty of time to get into the head brain later. That is not where passion resides. And as you will see in this chapter, there are many reasons to ensure that passion is at the heart of determining your destination.

Sometimes, circumstances inform the destination. Perhaps it is the loss of a job or a loved one that is driving the transformation. Perhaps it is being diagnosed with a serious illness yourself. What is important in these situations is that you not become the victim of the change. When I was a young boy, my grandfather taught me how to play pinochle; in doing so he offered me a life lesson that I call upon to this day. "You can't control the hand you are dealt," he said. "But you can always choose how to play it." When I was working in an AIDS organization, our clients were all homeless. Homeless and living with AIDS is not a situation anyone would choose. But these clients still did make choices. Some chose to see themselves as living with AIDS; others saw themselves as dying of AIDS. Not surprisingly, even in the early 1990s when treatment options were limited and often experimental, the health, well-being, and lifespan of the former were significantly greater than those who viewed themselves as victims. When a client comes to me with a change catalyst that would allow—or even invite—the victim role, I still ask the same question. "Given this circumstance, what would make your heart sing?"

All too often, we are the impediments to what is possible in our lives. Each of us has those things that prevent us from living fully into what is possible. Some people refer to them as their gremlins, or saboteurs. They are limiting beliefs. "I'm not good enough." "I'm not worthy." "I'm not smart enough." "I'm too old (or too young, or too something)." "I can't." And again, I return to the question. "If you could put all of those constraints aside, what would make your heart sing?"

Here is why I always ask, "What would make your heart sing?" As humans, our beings are self-regulating. While we may want to go back to school for an advanced degree, or to return to dating after a tough breakup, or to leave an abusive relationship, or to find a new career, we have programmed our neural networks and muscle memory to maintain the status quo. The idiom "It's better the devil you know than the devil you don't" is one that I often hear when I challenge my clients to think more broadly, more creatively, more deeply within themselves. If they aren't going to be able to let go of the devil they know to become something different, then their journey will not take them very far from who they are now; it will certainly not be one of transformation.

"What makes your heart sing?"

Sometimes a client lights up at hearing the question, and the answer comes pouring out. However, this isn't always an easy question to answer. Unfortunately, many people wall off their passions to live the lives that they believe they are supposed to be living. For them, the question brings discomfort, uncertainty. I see them looking away, searching wistfully for the answer. Some clients will find the answer during our time together. For others, reflecting on the question becomes a key component of their action plan as we end our session.

"What makes your heart sing?"

Be a Storyteller

Once you know the destination, it is time to write your change story. While most people don't think of themselves as such, we are all powerful storytellers. After all, what are those saboteurs and gremlins than stories we tell ourselves? We tell ourselves the story of the meeting we are going to have with our boss over and over again. We tell ourselves the story of the vacation we are going to take. We tell ourselves the story of the disagreement we had with our spouse. We tell ourselves the story about not being good at taking advice, or not being able to live with another person, or of living in a world of scarcity, or, or, or. We tell ourselves stories. And we believe them.

The change story is a story written from the future; it is not written about the future. A story about the future taps into the head brain. A story written from the future, when well crafted, reaches the head brain, heart brain, and gut brain, along with all of our emotions. Which do you find more powerful? "I can picture myself retiring 5 years from now, moving to Costa Rica, and living near the beach." Or "This morning I woke up for the first time in my own bed in Costa Rica. The ocean breeze is blowing through my windows and the monkeys are chattering in the trees. Every cell in my body is smiling! I did it!"

Neuroscience tells us that the brain responds to a well-told story in the same way as it does to an actual event. Remember that scene near the end of *The Sixth Sense* when you found out why the young boy who was the main character can "see dead people?" The hair on my arms stood on end just now as I wrote that sentence; yours may have as you read it! Well-filmed movies, well-written books, and skilled storytellers all have the power to bring us into the moment and to touch us. That is the story that you write about your change. It is told from the future. It engages each of your brains, all of your emotions. It reflects on some of the major milestones along the way that let you know you are truly making progress; some of the major obstacles you overcome; some of the saboteurs replaced by sages; some of the victories achieved; and the success of reaching your destination.

Who are the people in your story? Who are the ones that made the journey with you? Who are the ones that you left behind? What can you say about the new people who have joined you along the way? You may not know their names. That's okay. One of my clients has "Dear Beloved," a future partner, in his story. Dear Beloved doesn't yet have a name, but his essence is so vividly described in the story that if you met him, you would know it was Dear Beloved immediately.

Does your story involve a physical relocation of any type? If so, research it. Get to know it. Visit it if possible. What does it look like, sound like, smell like, and feel like? What are the local tastes that you love best? Experience the new commute you will have. Where does the sun rise? What path does it take across the sky? Where does it set? If you are not relocating, what has changed? Perhaps there is new furniture, or different art on the walls. Maybe it is just the energy that has changed. It is different.

Your story will serve many purposes, including becoming the foundation for your preparation and planning. What will it need to include in order for you to make the journey successfully? Is there education involved? Are new skills developed? Have you learned a new language?

While I keep on referring to "writing your story," it may not contain any words when you are done. It should be written in your language. Perhaps that is music, or water colors, or clay. First and foremost you are writing your story for you. Create the story that makes your heart sing. You may need to talk through an art-based story for others, but if art is your medium, start there, not with words. Your words will come from the art much more successfully than the art would come from your words.

Recently I had a client ask me how you can write a story from the future. "Things change," she said. Yes they do. And if they do, you can edit the story. After all, you are the author. "Dear Beloved" may become "Kevin." The oceanfront of Costa Rica may become the cloud forest. You may decide that your home office should be replaced by an office on Main Street. The fact that things change doesn't invalidate the power of story, and doesn't invalidate the story itself. Edit the story and move on.

CREATE YOUR CHANGE STORY

Listen to your three brains.

What makes your heart sing?

Be a storyteller.

Write your story from the future; engage the three brains and the emotions.

Write your story in your language.

Prepare for the Journey

The imaginary lines with which we connect the dots are the bars of our imaginary prison. When we let them fall away, what remains is freedom. (Zen Commandments, Dean Sluyter 2001, p. 161).

The next step in The Universal Change Journey is preparation. I work with my clients in preparation for their journeys before they start planning. There are a couple of reasons for this. First, we plan based on what we are aware of. If this is going to be a significant change, there are inevitably things that you haven't thought of, those "imaginary lines" that "are the bars of our imaginary prison." Beginning an intentional preparation process will call these to mind so that addressing them can be included in the planning. Second, the preparation process helps to make more concrete the realities of what it will take to leave your present life and move into the transformational future you have written about. It can help temper the uninformed optimism that may still be with you as you sit with your story. It can help increase your belief in yourself—and your story—as you think more concretely about your preparations. And it can help you reconsider whether the story you have created is one that you are willing to do the hard work to achieve.

Anchors

I usually start preparation with an anchors inventory. When you think of anchors, it is likely that you think of those heavy metal objects that rest on the floor of a body of water. They keep the boat or ship that they are connected to from drifting away. If the line connecting the anchor to the vessel is of sufficient strength and appropriate length, the boat can rise and fall with the tide, and turn with the current. It will be safe.

We all have anchors in our lives. Those things that hold us in place, that keep us from drifting too far from the path we are on. They help keep us focused and feeling somewhat secure. They give us a sense of identity. Anchors are personal. What has meaning to one person is meaningless to another. Your neighbor's car might be his most-prized possession, an anchor in his life. To you, a car may be nothing more than a necessity.

Unfortunately, by doing what they are supposed to do, anchors sometimes fail the vessels they are intended to protect. I live in Hoboken, New Jersey, directly across the Hudson River from New York City. Our elevation averages 16 feet above sea level; much of the city is only a few feet above. There are two inlets off the Hudson, one on the northern border and one at the south end. During Superstorm Sandy we experienced a 6.5-foot storm surge at high tide. The results were devastating. Streets, homes, offices, stores, garages, etc. were flooded. In some parts of the city, it took more than 48 h for the water to recede. We were without electricity for more than a week, without phone service even longer.

Once I could get out of the apartment, I walked around town, surveying and photographing the damage. As I reached the north end, I spotted a sailboat resting atop the railing along the river, maybe a half mile from where it had been anchored. Clearly, the line between the anchor and the vessel was not strong enough to withstand the pressure that Sandy put on it. Approaching the inlet I saw several boats bobbing on the surface of the water as if nothing unusual had occurred. And, a few masts were protruding from the surface. The anchors on those vessels were attached too tightly for them to rise with the rising water. By doing what they were intended to do most of the time, they failed the boats they were meant to protect.

When my clients are clear on their destinations, I invite them to conduct an anchor's inventory. It's important to not limit this inventory to the area of life in which the change is located. For example, don't just look at professional anchors when facing a job or career change. The walls between personal and professional are artificial. Any highly disruptive change is highly disruptive; it isn't just disruptive personally or disruptive professionally. It is also important to not limit the inventory to "anchors that have to stay," or "anchors that can sink the change."

Among the things that are almost always identified as anchors are as follows:

- Family.
- Friends.
- Colleagues.
- Profession.
- Professional titles (Dr., Professor, etc.)
- Home.
- Geographic location.
- Religious or spiritual practice.
- Finances (income, savings, retirement, etc.)

Less frequently people might include the following:

- Education (degrees, licenses, certifications, etc.)
- Pets.
- Vehicles.
- Second homes.
- Boats.
- Internet presence.
- Publications.
- Exercise (working out, playing sports, biking, running, etc.)

What people often fail to call out are their beliefs, other than those that are religious or spiritual. It is important that they identify their affirming beliefs (e.g., "Anything is possible.") as well as their limiting beliefs (e.g., "Nobody wants to hire someone my age."). These, too, are anchors.

For each anchor, the client is asked a series of one or more questions.

- Does your relationship to this anchor have to change in some way if you are going to reach your future as told in your story?
- If yes, how does it have to change?
- If yes, when does it have to change?
- If yes, what actions do you need to take to make this change happen?
- If yes, what permission do you need to give yourself to make this happen?

I often find it easiest to explain the meaning of this last question through an example. Perhaps you are a perfectionist. You believe that until you are prepared to get it right, you should continue preparing, rather than taking action. You know that this is an anchor you need to let go if, since you are stepping into uncharted territory in your life, and know that you can't do so perfectly. You give yourself permission to take risks and to make mistakes.

Once my clients have completed their anchor inventories, I ask them to go back in and identify their sea anchors. Sea anchors are used by vessels on open water where they cannot be secured to the sea bed. These anchors are designed to float under the surface. The function of a sea anchor is to keep the vessel facing into the turbulence so that it doesn't capsize. When facing turbulent change, it is important to know what your sea anchors are, what is going to keep the change from overwhelming you, what is going to prevent you—when the going gets tough—from just giving up.

It is often the case that the relationship with a sea anchor will need to be changed during a transformational change, or it will fail to do what it is intended to. For example, sometimes clients will strengthen their religious or spiritual practice. Or perhaps the sea anchor needs to be let out further. After one workshop a participant came up to me. "I wish someone had introduced me to anchors before now," he said." My love for my sport and for my family have always been my sea anchors. When I was recruited by colleges for athletic scholarships, I selected the college in my home town. When I was recruited to play ball professionally, I signed to play with the team in my home town. When my team went to trade me across the country, I stopped playing. I thought I had to decide between my two sea anchors. I didn't realize I could continue to play my sport by changing how I was connected to my family!"

What are the anchors that are holding you in place?

Avoiding

We all avoid things. Perhaps it is things that scare us. It may be things we don't like doing. Possibly it is things that we find really hard to do, or that bring back disturbing memories. Sometimes we are conscious of the fact that this is what we are doing; sometimes our avoidance has deep roots in our unconscious. When preparing for a really big change, it is time to call out the avoidance: to bring it to the surface if it isn't already there, make it conscious, and decide how to address it. Otherwise, avoidance becomes another saboteur, and may well cause the failure of the change even well after it is underway.

One of the things that I find clients frequently avoid are difficult conversations. Whether it is with a colleague, a boss, a family member, a friend, or even with those of us who are there in one capacity or another to serve as Sherpas on their change journeys, stating the difficult things is difficult. There are innumerable reasons found for delaying the conversation. Efforts are made to finesse the language so that it won't feel so harsh. All too often, when the conversation is then had, it misses the mark; in finding language that feels better in the saying, the client has found language that fails to fully convey the message that has to be heard. Playing out these tough conversations in advance with a trusted confidant always proves helpful.

Difficult actions are, likewise, something that is often avoided—stopping an aging parent from driving when they are putting their own and other lives at risk; meeting with the divorce lawyer; leaving the abusive relationship. The time comes when action is essential, or the story from the future will remain nothing more than a story unfulfilled.

When preparing for the change, it is important to identify what you avoid, and to determine whether that avoidance will affect the likelihood of success. If it will, you need to plan for how and when you overcome the avoidance to move your change forward.

What tough conversations are you avoiding?

What difficult actions are you avoiding?

Be Eye-to-Eye with Yourself

As you move closer to actually starting the change journey, you will have to start telling your story to others. Before you do, you will need to tell it to yourself. You will need to tell it to yourself over and over and over. It came from your head and your heart and your gut. It drew from your emotions. It needs to be told the same way. The best way I know how to prepare yourself is to be eye-to-eye with your change. And the best way that I know how to do that is to be eye-to-eye with yourself in the mirror.

I was first introduced to this practice at a retreat several years ago. I had expressed a limiting belief earlier in the week that I wanted to tackle. That afternoon, the facilitator introduced us to this simple, powerful practice by inviting me to work with him on the limiting belief I wanted to overcome. When I agreed, he asked me to stand facing a full length mirror, and began asking me a series of questions. "What is the belief that is getting in your way?" "How is it preventing you from making the progress you want?" What will happen if you do not move beyond this belief?" "What is an affirming belief that could replace this limiting one?" "What is required to replace the old belief with this new one?" "Who do you need to be to make this happen?"

The questions were hard. The answers didn't come easy. There was a lot of "dead air." And, throughout the time, he insisted that I keep looking at myself in the mirror. Not the "I'm brushing my teeth" look; not the "How do I look today" look. Really look at, and see, myself. It was tough! Even more difficult was the process of seeing myself, talking to myself, and hearing—truly hearing—myself. It was difficult. And it was powerful!

When I came home, I added being eye-to-eye with myself to my morning practice. It continued to be difficult for some time. But it became easier, more natural as I did it. For myself, and for my clients, I recommend this practice as you work to embody your story. Tell yourself the story; see yourself telling the story, hear yourself telling the story, and see your response to it. But I also recommend this approach to the everyday work of your change. "Today I am fully committed to completing my anchors inventory." "I can have this tough conversation, and achieve what I am setting out to achieve by doing so." Say it. See yourself saying it. Hear yourself saying it. Believe it.

I also use this practice to help me recognize my achievements and to hold me accountable when I mess something up. "Way to go! I was right that Tom wasn't going to be happy with what I was telling him. But I was able to avoid getting emotionally dragged into his drama, and brought the talk to a satisfactory conclusion." "I really found ways to waste time today, despite everything that I had committed to doing. I think I am pushing myself too hard every day. Tomorrow, schedule in some self-care time and see whether that helps bring my productivity back up."

Where Are You Now?

Most of us spend much of our time in a different place in our minds than we are in our bodies. It may be revisiting the conversation with the boss that didn't go too well. Or the phone call with the recruiter that went better than expected. Perhaps it is planning a well-deserved night out, or even thinking about the next vacation. But do you remember the feel of the water as you took your shower today? Or the smell of the air as you stepped outside? What do you remember about your commute to work?

If you are taking on a big change, being present with yourself and your interactions with your environment is critical. Quite simply, change requires your presence. You can't change while operating automatically. You need to be aware of what triggers those thoughts and actions you are going to change; then you need to be conscious of them being triggered. At this point you don't need to know what those changes are going to be. But now is the time to begin preparing for greater presence. Presence takes time to develop.

Cultivate Mind Presence

You probably know people who are always present. When you are with them, there is nothing else in their world but you. They are not distracted by external noise. Their thoughts don't drift. They are fully present with you. If you are such a person—or even close—you can skip to the next section. But for most of us, myself included, cultivating mind presence is essential. Here is one approach.

Your breathing is always with you. And, it can be a great tool to use in bringing you into the present. If you are not experienced in using breath for presence, I encourage you to begin this practice in a quiet space, free from distraction. Sit or lie down in a comfortable position. Set a timer so you don't have to "be someplace else," looking at your watch. Begin this practice by allowing yourself 5 or 10 min. Once you have settled in, start to observe your breath. Don't try to control it; just observe it. When you inhale, think to yourself "breathing in." When you exhale, think "breathing out." That's all—"breathing in" and "breathing out."

Your mind will wander. Random thoughts will come up. You may find yourself becoming critical of your difficulty staying focused on your breath. Acknowledge the thoughts as they arise, and let them go. One of my teachers put it this way. "Your thoughts are like trains pulling into the station as you stand on the platform. You don't have to get on them; you can chose to let them pull out again." When you are present, you can chose to let your thoughts go, and not be taken for a ride even when you are not "breathing in" and "breathing out."

As you become more practiced with using your breath to become present, you will find that you can do this at any time, in any circumstance, and that in a few breaths, you will be fully present.

Cultivate Body Presence

How often are you present in your body?

If you think about your change, you know that changing your thinking will not be enough to get you where you want to go. You need to change what you do and/or how you do it as well. This requires reprogramming your muscle memory. Developing body presence is as important to the success of your change as developing mind presence.

To develop body presence I recommend a practice called centering. An online search will present you with countless variations. The one that I offer here works well for my clients; it is based on a centering practice of Mind Tools (www.mindtools.com).

Step 1: Focus on Your Breathing.

Your centering breath is different than your mind presence breath. When centering, you want to take long, slow, deep breaths, filling your lungs. If you are not familiar with deep breathing, practice lying down. Place a hand on your stomach. As you breathe in, your shoulders should remain stationary and you should feel your hand rising. As you breathe out, your stomach and hand should sink again. As you continue your deep breathing, let go of any tension in the body. Scan your body, starting with your feet. Stop scanning when you reach anyplace you are feeling tense. Relax the tense muscles by tightening them, and then releasing; then continue scanning.

Step 2: Find Your Center.

Locate your physical "center of gravity." In centering, this is a point about 2 inches below your naval. Become familiar with where your center is, and remember what it feels like—you'll probably find that you feel grounded and stabilized by focusing your mind on this part of your body. When you begin to feel stressed, turn your attention to your center to remind yourself that you have balance and control. Once you've found it, breathe in and out deeply at least five times. Continue to concentrate on your center, and feel the sensation of being stabilized and on the ground.

Step 3: Redirect Your Energy.

Imagine all of the energy in your body flowing into your center. Find some imagery that works for you; for example, picture this energy as a glowing ball, or perhaps a balloon. Visualize putting all of your negative thoughts into the ball or balloon and then releasing it. As you inhale, say "1 let" and as you exhale, say "go." If you picture your energy as a ball, imagine throwing it far into the distance. If you see it as a balloon, imagine it floating away above your head. Let go of everything that is causing you to feel stressed. Imagine your center filled with calm.

On your next inhalation, think about what you want to achieve, and focus on thinking positively. Use affirmations like "The job is mine," or "I give great presentations," while letting your tensions go. You could even repeat one word to yourself, such as "success" or "confidence."

As with any practice, the more you do it, the better at it you become. As you learn to center, it becomes a practice that you can apply at any time, in any place. You don't need to be lying down. You can be sitting or standing, walking, standing in the subway, or stuck in traffic. Healthcare workers often center as they stop in the hallway briefly between hospital rooms. Practice your centering often.

Cultivate Heart Presence

Whatever the change is that you are undertaking, if it is a big one, your heart has to be in it and to stay in it. Cultivating and sustaining heart presence will be critical. So how do you cultivate it?

The first practice is quite simple. With repetition you can learn to complete it without those around you even knowing you are doing it if that is important to you. It's simply about touching your heart, not thinking about touching your heart, not thinking about other things as you touch your heart—simply touching your heart. When you begin this practice, it is best done in a quiet place, alone. After all, it is a practice. Find a comfortable place to sit. Close your eyes. Center yourself. Now reach to the upper center of your chest, and touch your heart. Smile. And wait. At first, you may or may not feel anything. That's okay. Remember, it is a practice. When you do feel, let the feeling grow. Let your heart grow. Cultivate presence in your heart. Over time, much like some of the earlier practices, you will be able to cultivate heart presence in any situation, at any time.

I learned the next practice when I was a child. I have forgotten and relearned it more than once along the way. There are numerous forms of this saying; here is one.

Before you judge someone, walk a mile in their shoes.

This is a lesson in nonjudgment and gratitude. It is a lesson in cultivating heart presence. Make it more than an intellectual lesson; make it a practice in cultivating compassion. The next time you find yourself being judgmental, step into the other person's life: their situation, their body, their mind, and their heart. Feel what they feel as that voice that sounds like yours says what it is saying. Feel what they feel as that body that looks like yours shows its repulsion for them. Feel what they feel as that heart that is your heart shuts them out. Then step back into your shoes. Open your heart, and smile.

One of the important things to know about heart presence is that it can lead you to a different place than mind presence. We all know this; we all have experienced it. The new person in your life that has all the right boxes checked on your list; the new job that meets all the criteria that you were looking for. Yet there is that nagging *I'm not really feeling it in my heart.* Pay attention to what your heart is telling you. What is in your heart is part of who you are? Cultivating heart presence helps you live in integrity. It can help to define the change(s) you want to make. And, it will provide guidance as you prepare for, plan for, and take your change journey, and live your new reality.

Don't Focus on Breaking Bad Habits

Habits often show themselves unconsciously. As a young man, I was a smoker; I began in my mid-teens and smoked for over 20 years. When I was finally able to quit, the physiology of quitting came relatively easy to me. The psychology of quitting took much more work! Everything that I did as an adult had a relationship to smoking. After meals I reached for a cigarette. When I got into my car, I reached for a cigarette. When I answered the phone, I reached for a cigarette. When I stopped smoking, I continued to reach for my cigarettes every time one of my "cigarette triggers" was activated. For me, quitting smoking wasn't about breaking one bad habit. It was learning countless new habits. I had to learn to end meals without a cigarette. I had to learn how to drive without cigarette. I had to learn to talk on the phone without a cigarette, etc.

Don't focus on breaking bad habits. Focus on creating new ones.

What are the new habits that your change journey will require? You may have identified some of them when you did your anchors inventory. What old habits will get in the way on your journey? What new habits will you replace them with? Spend time inventorying your habits in much the same way that you did your anchors. Don't attempt to change every bad habit; only focus on those that will put your change at risk and work on them over time.

It is important that you become conscious of the triggers that activate your bad habits. You can do this by creating a "habits journal." Identify three or four times a day when you will intentionally write down any of the habits to change that were triggered since you last journaled. Record what the triggers were. As you continue your journaling, you will discover that you are becoming aware each time the triggers are set off. When you notice a trigger, you can make a choice, and take the new action that will become a new habit.

The old habits will continue to show themselves for a while. As with my smoking, they may appear in situations that you have not had the opportunity to replace them in before. Stress can trigger old behaviors even after new ones are learned. Over time, the new habits will be firmly rooted; as you develop your new habits, don't fault yourself when the old ones pop up. Reattune yourself to the triggers and the new habits you want to develop. Recruit those around you whom you trust and can confide in to help you in the process of creating your new habits; their support will go a long way to helping lock the new habits in.

How Are Your Beliefs Serving You?

Our beliefs are our truths. They are the way things are. They are "facts." Much like those truths in the Declaration of Independence, we hold our truths to be "self-evident." They are unquestioned. They are what we believe. They are Truth with a capital T.

But are they really truth everlasting? Are they really facts? Are they the way things are, to remain unquestioned? Or are they open to examination? Our beliefs are among our strongest anchors. I certainly wouldn't recommend throwing them to the wind, cutting ourselves lose from them without careful reflection. But when you are facing change, when you are moving from a past into a future in an intentional way, I do encourage you to ask the question, *How well are my beliefs serving me?*

It isn't necessary to ask of every belief. But it is worth asking of those that may, in fact, not be serving you well. Here is a short list of some of the beliefs that I have found clients holding that were preventing them from moving forward successfully with their changes.

- I can do it all.
- I can't do anything right.
- I can't say no.
- I'm no good with technology (or languages, or math, or writing, etc.).
- I can do this in X time (while always underestimating by orders of magnitude).
- I'm no good at (fill in the blank).
- I'm too shy to network.
- I have too many years invested to change now.
- I'm a workaholic by nature.
- I can't fail.
- I never succeed.
- I'm too old.
- I'm too young.

- I would have to start all over again, and I'm not in a position to do that.
- They need to change; I don't.
- I know what I am doing; I don't need any help.

It's easy to see how each of these beliefs could work against successfully completing a transformational change. They are the invisible lines that form our prisons, trapping us where we are.

So what do you do if you have a belief (or beliefs) that are not serving you well? The first question you have to ask yourself is whether the belief or the change that it will be preventing is more important. If you can't have both your belief and successful change, which are you going to let go of? If the answer is that you are going to let go of the change, acknowledge to yourself that this is a choice you are making, and move on. The change may have been a bad idea anyway; or perhaps it was a good idea. *If it is essential, you aren't going to let it go.*

If your decision is that you need to move forward with the change, you are going to have to confront your belief to change it, or to let it go completely. This takes courage, and it takes discipline. it takes learning new ways of seeing things and thinking about them; it takes new ways of acting. It takes falling down and getting back up again. It is best accomplished with the support of others. Perhaps it is a coach, a mentor, a therapist, family members, co-workers, or friends. Find those who have a commitment to your success, and recruit them to cheer you on, to lift you up, to stand by you, to hold you accountable, and to call you out when you let up.

It's likely you will want to let up. Challenging beliefs is not for the faint at heart. You have every right to change your decision. There is a price to pay for challenging our beliefs, and a price to pay for standing by them. Just don't pay the price blindly. Ask, and answer, the question, *How well are my beliefs serving me?*

Pack Your Change Journey Toolbox

Change, even at the personal level, requires a toolbox. Organizational change practitioners use assessment tools, but that is not what I am talking about here. I am addressing those things that are inside of you that help or hinder you as you navigate change.

What do you do like breathing?

What an important question to ask as you think about your change toolkit! *What do you do like breathing?* What is it that comes so naturally to you that you don't even know that it is there? We all have things that we are unconsciously competent about. One challenge of unconscious competence is that you can't call on it when you need it. Either it works, or it doesn't. On a bad day, it doesn't. If you raise it to the level of consciousness, you can intentionally apply it when it is needed. What you do like breathing belongs in your toolbox.

Below are some of the other significant "tools" in a strong change toolbox. Some you may "do like breathing," others you may be okay at, and others you may not do well at all. You definitely want to know your strengths, and be prepared to apply them. Use this as a checklist for determining what is in your toolbox, what you need to strengthen, and what you have to add. Remember the old adage, *If all you have is a hammer, everything looks like a nail*. You definitely need more than a proverbial hammer for a major change journey!

- **Accountability:** If you do not hold yourself personally accountable for how it unfolds, your change is unlikely to go well. Accountability has to be an ongoing activity, not just an end of the journey check-in. Call on those whom you trust and who will support you on the journey to serve as accountability buddies. This may include professionals (e.g., coach, therapist, spiritual advisor) as well as colleagues, family, and/or friends.
- **Ambiguity:** Whatever your change, if it is big, you will be dealing with a great deal of ambiguity. Get used to it. You need incredible clarity on where you are going. You need incredible clarity on how you will know you are making progress, and how you will know when you have achieved success. And along the way, you need the ability to move through ambiguity. If you need "all your ducks in a row," or to "know what's waiting around the corner," undertaking a transformational change is not for you.
- **Big picture; little details:** You need to be able to see the big picture. Where is the change going? What will the journey be like? What is required to achieve success? How will you know you we have gotten there? And, you need to be able to define and execute all of the infinite number of steps required to successfully complete your change.
- **Boundaries:** Know when to work, and when to step away, when to let others in, and when not to. Know who to let in and who not to.
- **Courage:** Transformational changes are not for the timid; you will be stepping into the unknown over and over again. There are risks, many of which can be preempted if you "know the patterns" (below); but they are real, and they can be scary!
- **Decisiveness:** Engaging in big change, you need to be able to make decisions, and act on them. And, you need to be able to do so even when the information available to you is insufficient.
- **Hold on; let go:** If you are to succeed, no matter what the change, you need to know what to hold onto and what to let go of. And you need to know when to hold on and when to let go (also, see Mistakes).
- **Know the patterns:** This tool is fundamental to all the rest; in some ways it is "Tool # 1." There are clear patterns that underlie the human response to change; this chapter lays out many of them for you. If you know the patterns, you can apply the other tools to help you successfully navigate your way through them. If you don't, you are "flying blind." You have tools, and you may be applying them, but you don't really understand what is going on.

- **Mindfulness:** Are you one of those people who remembers getting into the car in the driveway, and then finds yourself parking it at the office? Never assume anything about your change is so routine that you can do it on autopilot; you need to be mindfully attentive every time you touch it.
- **Mistakes:** You will make mistakes along the way. Success requires recognizing them, admitting them (which may mean admitting them to more than yourself), learning from them, applying the lessons learned, and moving on.
- **Pay the price:** Big change isn't cheap, no matter what. There are some changes that may not cost a lot of money, but they still require an incredible investment of time, energy, personal power, etc. You cannot avoid paying the price, so it is better to pay it in prevention than in healing.
- **Presence:** In additional to mindfulness, you will be well served by cultivating your body and heart presence.
- **Reflection:** Step back and think about your change periodically. Have things shifted in the environment that require adjustments to the plan, or even to the desired end state? What is going well, and what isn't? How effectively are you executing the change, and what do you need to do differently?
- **Reframing:** How many lenses do you have in your toolbox? Can you reframe how you see things? Can you reframe them so that others see them differently?
- **Resilience:** How well, and how quickly, can you recalibrate to changes in expectations?
- **Resolve:** It may be that this is the best idea you ever had. It may be that you lose sleep every night over it. It may be that you "can't afford to fail." All of that may be, but in the absence of resolve, your transformation will fail. Big change means a difficult journey; you will need resolve to get through it successfully.
- **Storytelling:** You need to be able to move your own and other people's hearts and guts, not just heads. All the logic in the world cannot accomplish that. Storytelling can.
- **Teamwork:** You can't do it alone. Even the most personal of changes, if it is major, requires skills and insights beyond what you possess. Day to day you may pride yourself on being an independent spirit. But when it is time for change, you can't be independent; you can't be siloed. It takes a team.
- **Trust:** You need to be able to trust, and you need to be trustworthy.
- **What you need to hear:** Some people surround themselves with others who tell them what they want to hear. We all like to have cheerleaders. But you also need to seek counsel from those who will tell you what you need to hear, even when you don't want to hear it.

Prepare to Choose

It's your choice.
How do I choose?
I don't have a choice.

When it comes to choice, all too often we approach the situation with a fundamental misperception. We think "choice" means selecting between good and bad, right and wrong, and easy and difficult. Sometimes it does. But sometimes it doesn't.

Sometimes choice is between bad and bad, between right and right, between difficult and difficult. In the Old Testament, we have the story of Abraham being commanded to offer his son Isaac as a sacrifice. More recently, we have the work of fiction, *Sophie's Choice*, in which Sophie is forced to select which of her children is gassed to death in the concentration camp. Choices are not always good, or easy. There is still a choice.

Daryl Conner tells the story of Andy Mochan, the Piper Alpha oil rig worker who jumped 150 feet into burning oil in the North Sea after the rig had exploded. When interviewed on Nightline, Andy stated that he had *chosen probable death over certain death.* Andy made a choice—not an easy one by any stretch of the imagination—and lived to tell his story. One hundred sixty-six of his fellow workers on the rig died (*Managing at the Speed of Change*, Daryl Conner 1993, p. 92).

Daryl uses this story as a metaphor for the resolve that we each need when we are facing difficult changes. In taking your change journey, it is likely that there will be choices that are easy to make along the way. These are the "god/bad," "right/wrong" kind. But there will also be agonizing, difficult choices to be made, ones for which you are ill-prepared, for which you want more time and/or information; ones for which you shudder at the possible consequences of any decision you make. These, too, are choices. Prepare to make tough choices.

Know Your Boundaries

Whatever boundaries you have in your life right now will likely have to change as you move forward. Your change journey is going to require time, attention, focus, physical-spiritual-mental-emotional energy, money, and more. Planning for the change will help you figure out where these things are coming from. At this point, you have to know where your boundaries are so that you can know what boundaries you will need to change to ensure the resources you need are available when you need them. And, you will know what boundaries you want to maintain as they are.

As you think about your boundaries, consider whether they are too rigid. If so, you will make it difficult, and uncomfortable, for others to join you on the journey. On the other hand, if they are too loose, you will never be able to live into your future story. Note that we are talking about boundaries here, not walls. Boundaries can move; walls cannot. There may be times when you need to adjust your boundaries along the way. Ensure you have boundaries, not walls.

Strengthen Your Time Management

Momentum is important in any change. While there are some things for which the timing may be pre-determined (e.g., earning a certificate or degree), you are going to have a great deal of control over the length of time, and how you use your time, as you travel through your transformation. Here are four questions to help strengthen your time management.

1. **What is the next step?** We all have our own ways of keeping track of things we need to do. You may keep a list, or use sticky notes. There may be a white board or a large calendar on the wall. I use a productivity journal. Each of these can be effective if you work at it. All too often, however, things get missed along the way. I have found this works for me; each time I complete a task, I ask myself, "What is the next step?" The next step then gets added to my productivity journal.
2. **How important is this?** As seen in Fig. 1.1, think of things in terms of urgency and importance. Our tendency is to respond to urgency. The result is that we are often doing things that are urgent, but unimportant (Priority 3). Things that are important but not urgent. (Priority 2) gets set aside again and again and again. Focus on importance. Give priority to urgent and important (Priority 1). Set time aside for important but not urgent (Priority 2). I invite my clients to treat important but not urgent time as sacred. Put it on the calendar. Set boundaries on how far you can move these times, and stick to them. Handling things that are important when they are not urgent gives you a better opportunity to handle them well. Priority 3 (urgent and not important) and Priority 4 (not urgent and not important) should receive much less of your attention, if any at all.

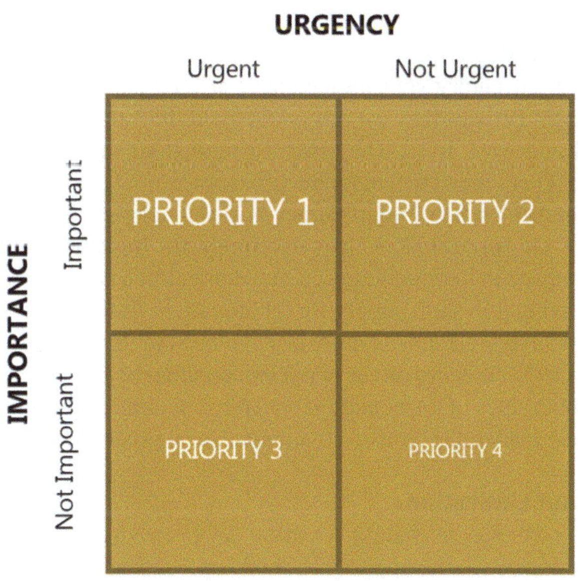

Fig. 1.1 Important vs. Urgent Matrix

3. **Am I being productive, or am I just being busy?** This ties in with the previous question. Regularly look at the work you are doing to prepare for, plan, and take your change journey. Is it contributing to reaching your storied future? If not, you may be busy but you aren't being productive.
4. **Am I inventing things to do in order to avoid the truly important?** The important stuff is also often the hard stuff. It is often the stuff we want to avoid. The difficult conversation we are going to have to have. The irreversible action we are going to have to take. The unfathomable challenge we have to solve. Inventing things to do is often the solution that "justifies" avoidance. When you identify things to do, run them through these questions. What is it the next thing to do on behalf of this change? How important is this thing to be doing? Is it a productive use of my time? Am I using this to avoid something that I really should be doing?

Paying attention to these questions can make a significant impact on your change journey.

Limitations

We all have them. As you prepare to begin your change journey, it is important that you know what yours are. Knowing—and challenging—your limitations, as well as working with them, are key factors in living into your future story.

Know Your Limitations

It is important to inventory your limitations at an early stage of defining and planning your change. Perhaps they are resource-based: time, money, and the balance of your personal and work lives. They may be limitations of skills and abilities, or understanding. There may be geographic limitations.

As the desired end state of your journey begins to take shape, think: *What will it take to achieve, and sustain this?* Not surprisingly, the limitations inventory should be made in comparison to those things; if you don't need a particular thing at all, not having it, or having it in short supply isn't a limitation. At the early stages, you will be working at a high level; this is not when you need to think about "dotting the i's and crossing the t's." It is important to remember, though, that you are working at a high level on both sides of the equation: both the requirements for the possible limitations and their availability. If there is an imbalance, proceed to the next step.

Challenge Your Limitations

Too often when it comes to change, we make one of two major mistakes at the outset: we set out to achieve the impossible, thinking that somehow "it will work out." Or, we aim too low, "settling" for what we think is possible without any sort of stress-testing to see if we can go further. Stress-testing your limitations may allow you to discover that the goal that you have set could be raised significantly.

So how do you go about stress-testing your limitations? Begin by challenging the underlying beliefs and assumptions. (Yes, that is hard to do!) How strongly is the limitation anchored in fact vs. perspective? Most of us are not good at challenging our limitations on our own; we can't see what we can't see. The most effective challenges to your limitations will come through someone who (1) is committed to supporting your success and (2) can remain objective about your change and what is required to succeed. This may be a coach, a mentor, a friend, a family member, or another trusted advisor. It has to be someone who can be brutally honest with you when necessary; who can empathize with your struggles and yet will not let you take the easy path out; and who will unconditionally 100% support you once you have made your decisions. This is neither someone who tells you what you want to hear, nor someone who undermines you when your decisions are different than the ones that they would have made.

There is something paradoxical about some limitations as well. We think about them as holding us back in some way, and they can if we let them. But, we also think that challenging them means moving beyond them. In fact, in some cases, we are best served going in the other direction. Bringing an "essentialism" mindset to your limitations may well prove to break many of them wide open. "(Essentialism) is about making the wisest possible investment of your time and energy in order to operate at your highest point of contribution by doing only what is essential" (*Essentialism,* Doug McKeown 2014, p. 5).

Steve Jobs is one of the best-known essentialists; he said "no" to an incredible number of ideas, many of which could have succeeded in the marketplace, in order to say "yes" to a small handful that have changed everything from how we buy and listen to music, to how we buy and read books, to how we communicate, and more. In the process he built perhaps the most widely known brand (and one of the most successful) in the world. He addressed limitations of time and creative focus not by seeking to do more, but by bringing a laser focus to the few select things that made Apple what it is today.

When you look at your limitations, what can you say "no" to that will redefine the degree to which they limit you? What limitations should you seek to further tighten, rather than loosen?

Work with Your Limitations

If you have sincerely challenged your limitations, it is now time to work with them. Begin by updating your limitations inventory against your identified needs. Should you redefine your desired outcome to accommodate your limitations? What limitations have now become assets that you can apply to the change journey, much as Steve Jobs used principles of essentialism to provide Apple with laser focus in developing its new products? Which remain limitations?

Don't look at your limitations as negatives; they are the reality in which you need to move forward. In fact, some of the greatest progress can be made in constrained environments. For example, think of your own cycle of growth and development from those early days out on your own until now. It is likely that initial economic constraints kept you focused on work and growth that while living in what you now (and perhaps then) perceive as a constrained environment, you were able to make some our your most profound discoveries about yourself and your place in the world.

In her book *Big Magic* (2015), author Elizabeth Gilbert talks about working within constraints. While she sought to write every day, she also "always had a day job"; she had successfully published three books, all of which were reviewed by *The New York Times*, and one of which was nominated for a National Book Award. She kept writing, and kept her day jobs. She was a waitress; she worked on a ranch out west; and she kept writing. She kept her day jobs until the success of *Eat, Pray, Love* allowed her to know that she could support her creativity without placing financial demands on it. She knew that depending on her art for income would place an unnecessary—and most likely destructive—limitation on her creativity, and removed that limitation by working day jobs.

Know your limitations, and work with them.

Prepare Yourself and Others

It feels good when people agree with you. If feels even better when they say supportive things and offer their encouragement. But when it comes time to carry out a really tough change, are they actually helping?

The answer is it depends. It depends on whether they are saying what they think you want to hear or are telling you what you need to hear in order to be successful. Some people set themselves up for failure, surrounding themselves with head-shakers, yes-sayers, and make-me-feel-gooders. Those who dare to speak up and say "The emperor has no clothes" are quickly silenced. We see it with business leaders, with politicians, and even with our family and friends. Inevitably the train goes off the tracks; unfortunately, they are not the only ones who suffer in the process.

Most of us are more open to the truth, even when it contains bad news. After all, you don't want a doctor giving you a clean bill of health because he doesn't want you to be upset about the illness he has diagnosed. Unfortunately, all too often, friends, family, and peers are less candid. Perhaps they don't want to upset you, to hurt your feelings, to dim your enthusiasm. But, in their absence of candor, they are not helping. Rather, they are putting the change you are working on at risk.

Tell people that you want them to challenge you, and mean it.

Tell them to give you the bad news as well as the good, and don't shoot the messenger.

Have candid conversations.

Ask tough questions.

Be vulnerable.

Acknowledge your mistakes, and learn from them.

Learn from the mistakes that others have made.

Surround yourself with people who want to help you by being truthful with you. Then encourage them to do so. When you hear the good news, be encouraged. When you hear what you need to hear in order to course-correct, to stay on track, and to succeed, listen.

Know What It Takes to Get the Commitment You Will Need

How long have you been thinking about this change? Analyzing it? Considering the pros and cons? Shaping it in your mind? Assessing what it will take, and how likely that it will work? Maybe you've talked it over with a few people, a spouse or best friend. You've decided to move forward. You're committed!

Or are you?

And what about the people who have to make this journey with you?

Let's take a look at a few key things about commitment.

For as much time as you have spent with this important change maturing in your head, it's likely that you don't know what you don't know. Every big change, whether positively or negatively perceived, has a "honeymoon." You don't know what you don't know. The road ahead has unforeseen obstacles. The dream, the fantasy, and the "ideal future" aren't as easy to obtain or to sustain as you imagine it to be. Even if others have told you to expect the surprises, chances are you will still be surprised.

As you learn more, you will be challenged to continue forward—to continue deepening your commitment—or to let go of the change. There will be periods of pessimism as the inevitable challenges surface. There will be mistakes, and some really big mistakes, that will drain resources, confidence, and time. If you are prone to believing in your own infallibility—or even to just projecting that image to others—your self-confidence, and the confidence others have in you, is likely to wane.

Commitment to something new means uncommitting to something old. And, if the change is big, it often means uncommitting to something that you have been strongly committed to. Committing to a serious monogamous relationship or marriage? It means letting go of those free-wheeling days (and nights); letting go of the dishes in the sink, books in the oven, Chinese take-out in the fridge; letting go of the open toothpaste squeezed from the middle; and letting go of the dirty clothes strewn around the apartment or the laundry basket overflowing. It may mean letting go of friendships, or professional relationships. It can even mean letting go of family.

As you get older, commitment to something new often means uncommitting to something that you have invested significantly in creating and/or sustaining. In your personal life, it may be your lifestyle, your friends, your leisure activities, or your home. It may mean letting go of the job you have spent much of your career working toward, or the colleagues whose own careers have supported the growth of yours. It may mean letting go of a long-term relationship or letting go of health and entering a life of chronic illness.

Commitment requires deep understanding. Each time you learn more, commitment is tested. If it passes the test, the commitment is strengthened. If the new learning breaks the commitment-building cycle, it is time to work at either rebuilding, or to "cut loose."

Commitment comes in different forms.

Compliance is one way to express commitment. You wear your seatbelt because you don't want to get a ticket. You "follow orders" because you need the job, or you don't want to get into a conflict with your boss. You perform your job "by the book" since you've seen how that gets others bonuses and promotions. You attend religious services regularly "to keep the peace." You host the family Thanksgiving dinner because "it's become a tradition." Commitment at this level is externally driven; remove the external driver and you would be doing something different.

Internalized commitment is much stronger. It is self-motivated, self-powered, and self-reinforcing. It is also much more difficult to achieve, especially when the change is not one that you have initiated. For this reason, always consider whether the commitment needed for success can be a commitment of compliance, or whether it has to be internalized.

As difficult as commitment is to achieve, it always baffles me how many people assume that others will instantly commit when introduced to a change. In our personal lives, people come to us with changes they have been contemplating (or working on) for extended periods of time; the expectation is that we will "jump on board." We, in turn, do the same with others. There are all sorts of rationales given for avoiding earlier conversations. "I wanted to make sure that I was committed myself"; "I had to do the research so I could answer questions"; "I wasn't sure how people would respond," etc. While these may be valid reasons for waiting to enter the conversation, they do not overcome the reality about commitment. It doesn't just happen. If you get expressions of commitment when you first introduce the new idea, remember, it is only commitment to the idea. Time will tell whether it can and will develop into commitment to the reality.

Complete Your Inventories

You have inventoried your anchors, your habits, your beliefs, and your limitations. You have identified how you need to work with these to complete your transformational journey. There are two more inventories to complete before you move fully into planning.

- **Create a resources inventory.** As with everything, this will not be comprehensive at the outset. But, what are the resources that you can identify will be required in order to live into your future story? Many of these may already appear in your anchors or limitations inventories; it is not necessary to record them again. Once you have identified any additional resources you will need, estimate how much will be required, and when. Compare that with what you already need. If there is a gap, how large is it? Closing that resource gap will need to be part of your planning.
- **Create a change inventory.** Your transformation isn't a single change. It is a myriad of changes. Brainstorm a list of what they are. Again, there's no need to repeat those changes that appear in the other inventories; they will all be brought together as you move more fully into planning.

PREPARE FOR THE JOURJNEY

Know what your anchors are, and prepare to adjust them.

Identify your sea anchors.

Prepare to stop avoiding.

Be eye-to-eye with yourself.

Cultivate mind presence.

Cultivate body presence.

Cultivate heart presence.

Don't focus on breaking old habits; focus on creating new ones.

How are your beliefs serving you?

Pack your change journey toolbox.

Prepare to choose.

Know your boundaries.

Strengthen your time management.

Know, challenge, and prepare to work with your limitations.

Prepare yourself and others.

Know what it takes to get the commitment you need.

Complete your inventories.

Plan the Journey

Man plans, and the gods laugh.

There is a lot that solid planning can do, and much that it cannot. Here are some of the key things that I have learned about change planning over the years. Remember, you have your change story. You have early elements of preparation: you've inventoried your anchors, your habits, your beliefs, and your limitations. You've inventoried resource needs and projected gaps. You've brainstormed the changes you will need to make. You have developed an initial set of milestones as part of your future story. All of these serve as inputs to your planning.

Plan for What You Don't Want!

One of the big mistakes we often make when planning a change is that we fail to think about what we don't want to happen. Sometimes we catch the absence of this planning when we come face-to-face with an "Oh, No!" And, sometimes we only discover it after the fact.

The best way to plan for what you don't want is to ask the question, *What could happen that I don't want to happen?* Then plan in a way that ensures—or at least limits—the possibility of it occurring. Don't get carried away. You will never be able to think of, or plan for, every contingency; but you can significantly lower the likelihood of going off track by planning for what you don't want. One client I worked with knew that the decision he had made concerning the next step in his career path would not sit well with his parents. Although he was in his late 30 s, they—and their opinions and moral support—were still extremely important to them. He didn't rush off to tell them of his decision, nor did he wait as long as possible to share it. Rather, he sat down and looked at the path they had encouraged him to take. He wrote down all of the reasons they wanted him to take that path. And then he looked at the path he had chosen, and constructed a narrative that compared his path to theirs, factoring in both what was important to him about the choice he made and how that choice aligned with what was important to them. After the three of them had a conversation, his parents became fully supportive of his decision.

Plan for Results and Plan to Keep a Focus on Your Desired Outcomes

All too often we are wooed into a change for the results that it promises. Then, the planning focuses not on the results, but on the "things" that need to be put in place. Several years ago I created an e-Book for a client. *Painting the Room Blue* communicated this concept simply. If all you want is a blue room, then just paint the room blue. But if what you are seeking to do is to create a calmer environment, or a more tranquil customer experience, etc., then painting the room blue may be necessary, but it is not sufficient.

What shifts in mindsets need to happen? What shifts in behaviors are required? What relationships (including but not limited to relationships with anchors) have to change, and in what ways?

Don't try to "cross every 't' and dot every 'i'." If you do, you will be planning for years to come. Plan the near-term; create a roadmap for the longer-term. Depending on the scope of the change, near-term may be 4–6 weeks, or 6 months. But remember, the further out you are planning, the more likely things will change and your plan will need to change. You have done a lot in your preparation, so you are not "blind to" or "ignoring" the full journey; you are acknowledging the reality that it will be filled with unexpected surprises, detours, and mistakes and that detailed longer-range planning is likely filled with inaccuracies. Typically my clients will create a "start-to-finish roadmap" that sets target dates for meeting key milestones and identifies the major things that they will need to do to be successful in achieving those milestones. Then they prepare a rolling 4- to 6-week plan, updating it on a weekly or bi-weekly basis. The plan contains the milestones as well as action, helping ensure they are doing more than keeping busy; they are making progress toward their goals.

Plan for periodic status checks; find someone beyond yourself who you will "report in to," someone who can help you be accountable.

Don't Overload

One of the biggest mistakes that gets made when it comes to change is thinking that the importance of the change, or the risk of not changing, or the reward of changing will be enough to carry the change to a successful conclusion.

Wrong!

We each have a limited capacity for change. A limited capacity for all the change we are experiencing. It could be personal change. It could include professional change. There might be social changes—in our spiritual or religious institutions, in our communities, or nationally—that are having an effect on us. There aren't separate buckets inside of us in which to put each of these changes. Their impact is cumulative.

And when we exceed our change capacity, every change suffers. When the proverbial "straw broke the camel's back," it wasn't the last straw that fell to the ground; it was all of them, as well as the camel! So, one of the important steps to take when planning is to ask *What other change demands are there, either currently or in the foreseeable future?* For each of these changes, determine how essential it is. If it is not essential, either put a halt to it, or be prepared to put a halt to it when change demand requires. If it is essential, there are several ways to reduce its change demand. You may intentionally decide to just put the key elements in place now ("paint the room blue"), while delaying the other elements of the change required for it to deliver its full benefit. You may choose to delay it; or you may extend the timeline.

Note, however, this monitoring of change demand and capacity is not "once and done." Other demands will continue to come along. For this reason, it is important to plan on routinely monitoring for symptoms of overload.

Plan to Put Your Support "Infrastructure" in Place

It is likely that you don't have everything in place that you will need to get you through a major change. Your change may require budget management that wasn't needed before. It may call for carefully laying out and adhering to a daily and weekly schedule. It may call for reinforcing some anchors, while changing your relationship to (or cutting free) others. It may call for a physical relocation or physical alterations in your space. It may call for new sources of income. All of the "infrastructure" that you need to succeed with the change should be planned for.

Plan for the Unexpected

There is an important place for planning when approaching and moving through change. But, things happen. The lesson is simple. Yes, plan. And then do it. Know that your plan is incomplete. Know that you will have to make some of it up as you go along. Know that you will make mistakes. Know that at some point your change will go off course. If you are too dependent on the plan, you will too.

Plan, and then be prepared for the unexpected. It is inevitable. And, don't wait for every line of your plan to be written. The opportunity that you are pursuing may pass you by; the course you are attempting to correct will veer even further astray. Move forward. And don't be surprised by the surprises.

Plan for Resistance

Resistance happens.

Whether you want to take this change journey or not, if it is a big change, you will find yourself resisting.

Whether it was your idea or not, if it is a big change, you will find yourself resisting. Whether you see this as a negative change, or as a positive one, if it is a big change, you will find yourself resisting. Ditto for those around you who are affected by the change. And, sometimes our strongest resistance (often expressed as "I can't") arises with the changes that are most important to us. The truth is resistance happens. It is a part of the change journey.

While it can take many forms—from gossip to failing to acknowledge a change, from subterfuge to immobilization—at its root, resistance is the result of unwillingness and/or inability.

It is easy to understand resistance when you (and/or others) see the change as negative. But why do we resist changes that we initiate, that we think are good ideas or even true imperatives? The answer is actually pretty simple. At some point we begin to resist because we find out what the cost of the change is really going to be. (The cost might be financial, but it is generally much more. It might include a cost in prestige, in relationships that have anchored us for years, time, in having to let go of other things we want to do, in paying attention to things that we really don't want to pay attention to, etc.) When I first began training in change many years ago, Daryl Conner provided important guidance that I still use today. *The cost of the status quo must be significantly greater than the cost of the transition, or you will start the change journey but will not complete it.*

With this in mind, it is critical that as you prepare for your change, you not only look at the opportunities that it offers if you are successful. You also need to be very honest with yourself and others about the cost of making the transition and the cost of not doing so!

All too often, we see resistance as a sign of something going wrong. It isn't. Resistance during a major change journey is inevitable. Surfacing resistance, and being clear about the willingness and/or ability causes that underlie it, will help you to continue to move the change forward. Ignoring it, treating it as a distraction, or responding to it negatively will leave you short of achieving the change you have set for yourself.

Plan for Catharsis

Your change journey is most likely be an emotional roller-coaster ride. It can be extremely exciting at one moment and incredibly scary at another. It may bring you unbounded joy and mournful sorrow.

Even if this is the most positive change you believe you will ever experience, plan for catharsis. Change doesn't just mean moving forward to something new; *it also means letting go of something(s) old.* Sometimes it means letting go of friendships, or relationships. Sometimes it means letting go of places or things that mean a great deal to you. Sometimes it even means letting go of beliefs that have been with you for as long as you can remember.

Know that your change will likely require catharsis, and plan for it. Often I will work with my clients to create rituals that acknowledge and honor those things they are letting go of. These may be accompanied by other rituals celebrating that which is coming into being as a result of the letting go.

Plan to Monitor Your Progress

How do you measure success? What are the milestones along the way that let you know that you are—or are not—making progress?

Throughout this section I will use the example of a major career change. You are leaving your financial services career on Wall Street to become an actor; it is a passion that has burned inside you as long as you can remember, and you are going to make your dream come true. Your intent is to feel secure in your ability to support yourself as an actor.

Installation is achieved when things are put in place. Installation metrics may include getting accepted to acting school; submitting your resignation; commencing training; completing your training; being selected for your first part; and completing your first acting assignment.

Realization is achieved when the promise of the change is fully delivered. For you, realization will be achieved when you feel secure in your ability to support yourself as an actor—no more waiting tables, valet parking cars, or serving hors d'oeuvres at catered parties.

All too often, when we plan a major change for ourselves, we start with the passion that is in our heart as our desired future state, and then we plan as if installation will get us there. Unfortunately, installation only gets us installation; it doesn't get us realization. Nor can you start thinking about "what else do I need to do" once you have achieved installation. It is important to plan on, and move toward, realization from the outset.

If it is a big change, start by thinking through and listing out all of the major adjustments you are going to have to make not only in what you do, but in how you think. Perhaps while on Wall Street, the thinking was "eating out is convenient, and I can afford it." It may still be just as convenient but may be much less affordable as you work your way through acting school, auditions, and your early parts as an extra or a member of the chorus. So, not only will you have to change how you spend money, you most likely have to change how you think about money. You will also probably need to make changes in where you live; your wardrobe will be different; how you spend your time—including both working and non-working time—will change, as might when you get up and when you go to bed. They call it "major change" for a reason!

What about the people in your life? The colleagues who used to drink martinis with you before a late dinner out may be less excited about downing a beer after the final curtain call. The friends who loved getting invited to your beach house may find they have less excitement about a picnic in the park. And the family that worked and sacrificed to help you and your siblings through college so you could have a better life, perhaps they will be less than enamored with your new-found enthusiasm for what they see as a less professional, less lucrative, and less secure career path.

We touched on this in the discussion on anchors, but it bears repeating here. In planning a major change, you are going to have to consider those around you. What role do they play in your life now? What role do they need to play in the transition? What role will they play when you achieve your desired future state? Which ones will be the same, which ones will be different, and which people will you need to end your relationship with in order to succeed? What other anchor changes do you need to make?

Once you've listed all of the changes in thinking and behavior you can come up with, grab some sticky notes and a pen or pencil. Gather your inventories. Put each change on a separate piece of paper, and put it up on the wall (or white board or closet door or window). You may want to use different colors for mindsets and behaviors or for different aspects of the change (e.g., leaving the old job; training; redefining relationships with people).

Now you can begin to group these together. Use your story to help you think this part through. Think of these groups as "work streams"; each stream consists of the changes that you have to make in order to achieve some aspect of your intent.

Let's go back to your intent. *I feel secure in my ability to support myself as an actor!*

Begin by defining your realization indicators. What will make you feel secure? Be specific; be sure it is measurable. You may already have some measures among the sticky notes you have posted; you might need to develop others. Position your notes in a relative sequence within your work streams. In the example below, the first two of the bulleted indicators may be targeted for attainment near the end of the change, as you approach full realization. The third one you might decide to position earlier in the process.

These may be some of your metrics.

- I have $X in the bank, of which $Y has been made as an actor.
- For the past 18 months, I have had a positive cash flow, all of it as an actor.
- I have re-framed my lifestyle so that I am comfortable in my studio apartment.

Now think through your installation indicators. Again, many of these may come from the sticky notes you have already developed. What do you have to put in place in order to achieve each of the realization indicators? For example, what will it take for you to move out of your three-bedroom apartment and feel comfortable in a studio?

- I have identified the characteristics of a living space in which I can be comfortable (a more open plan vs. individual rooms, whether a view is needed, etc.).
- I have pared down my possessions so that I have what I can comfortably live with inside the new apartment.
- I have a plan in place for ensuring that I don't begin to clutter my space.
- I have defined the type of neighborhood in which I will be comfortable.
- I have found, leased, and moved into my new apartment.

Look at the sticky notes that you first put on the wall and that have not become either realization or installation indicators or changes that allow you to achieve those indicators. Ask yourself two questions.

- Have I identified an indicator that this contributes to achieving?
- If not, am I missing an indicator, or is this change unnecessary?

You should end up with a series of "work streams" made up of change projects or activities, as well as installation and realization indicators. Finally, review your work streams. If you achieve all of the indicators in each of the work streams, will you be able to look at yourself in the mirror and say, *I feel secure in my ability to support myself as an actor?*

Keep a record of what you have on the wall. It will change over time. You don't have all the answers now; you don't even know all the questions. Things will change around you. So, your indicators will have to change as well. Nonetheless, you are well on your way to planning and preparing to launch a very big, and important, change in your life.

Plan to Celebrate

Yes, you may want to celebrate the start of your change journey, and the successful conclusion. But don't stop there. Most of us spend much of our lives doing. We complete one thing and pick up the next thing in the pile, the next task in the plan, and the next item on the list. We often fail to even see the milestone we are passing as we move toward the next. We create our change story, plan for the change, prepare for the journey, and move on through it, failing to acknowledge along the way what we (or we and others) are achieving. Check. Check. Check. Whether literal or figurative, we check things off as we complete them; and we keep on rolling along.

Celebration is a way to acknowledge our own accomplishments, and those of others. It is a way to acknowledge the significant achievements we can (and deserve to, and should) claim along the way. Remember this old adage? It applies to each of us. "All work and no play makes (your name here) a dull (your sexual identity here)." Celebrations are a way to bring more balance to our life, to take time away from the climb in order to "play." Yes, there should be a huge celebration at the successful completion of your change journey. This will be the brass band, balloons and fireworks, noisemakers, and dancing-until-dawn celebration. But other, smaller celebrations along the way can serve to honor the steps you have taken, the progress you have made. They can re-energize you and encourage you to continue on the journey.

What comprises a celebration? That's simple. Whatever you say is a celebration for you and others that are celebrating with you. What is important about a celebration is that it isn't part of your routine. For someone who strives for 6 h of sleep a night, an extra hour or two can be a celebration. Perhaps it is a massage, or a manicure and pedicure, or a special bottle of wine at dinner, or a walk on the beach, or "playing hooky" for an afternoon, or going to a museum or a gallery or a play, or sitting down with a coloring book for an hour. For one friend, celebration is sushi.

PLAN THE JOURNEY

Plan for what you don't want.

Plan for results, and plan to keep a focus on your desired outcomes.

Don't overload.

Plan to put your support infrastructure in place.

Plan for the unexpected.

Plan for resistance.

Plan for catharsis.

Plan to monitor your progress.

Plan to celebrate.

Take the Change Journey

Not knowing does not mean giving up on the question. It means not settling for an easy answer. Live the question. Feel it in your core. Who are you in truth? This question is the great work. (Chasing Rumi, Roger Housden 2002, p. 63).

Begin with the End in Mind; Keep the End in Mind

Remember, you began by creating the change story for a reason. A clearly articulated end state that you can work toward is critical to success. As you prepared and planned, some of the uncertainties were answered. But many remain. As you take your transformation journey, live your story from the future; that is where you are now heading! As you take your transformation journey, live the question *What makes my heart sing?*

"Bright, shiny objects" might offer easy answers, or just distract you from the tough work of the journey. Your closest friend may ask you to join his bowling team. Maybe it's an article in a journal, or a documentary you just saw that drives a shift in focus. "Crises of the moment" also have the ability to easily distract us.

Every day, ask "What am I doing today to move this change forward?" Every day, ask those who are supporting you in the change; "What are you doing today to move this change forward?"

When a bright shiny thing appears, ask yourself, "How will this help us move forward with the change?" If it won't, don't pursue it.

When those crises arise, ask yourself, "How will this affect progress toward the goal?" All too often, supposed crises appear urgent, and yet they are unimportant in the context of your change, or even your broader life. Don't let unimportant crises distract you from the important work that you are doing on your change.

Continue to tell yourself and others your change story. Keep the end in mind.

Don't Forget the World Is Changing Too

I live in a former slide rule factory. If you are not familiar with slide rules, they were the mechanical precursor to any form of electronic calculator. I learned how to program a computer on punch cards. When I entered the workforce, the expectation was that you would get a job out of college, stay with that employer, advance (or not), and ultimately retire from the same employer.

The point here is the world keeps changing. In a recent study, 91% of millennials reported that they expect to stay in their current job less than 3 years. The slide rule was replaced by the electronic calculator and was replaced by the app on the smart phone. Eighty-eight percent of the Fortune 500 companies of 1955 are gone.

Keep your eye on the destination of your change journey. But also keep your eye on the changes going on around you. Any one of them could signal the need for a change in the route you are taking, *or the need to stop and rethink the destination itself.*

Monitor Progress and Risks

Monitor progress toward your milestones. As was discussed earlier, don't just monitor "installation"; ensure that you are tracking progress toward the actual outcomes you want to achieve ("realization"). Monitor risks. Watch for early warning signs. The sooner you see a risk, the greater the opportunity to do something about it before it grows and does significant damage to your progress.

"C" Is for Courage

Change is hard. Big change is really hard.

And it is scary. If you have done your homework, your intent is clear; but, no matter how well you plan or prepare, the path forward is littered with uncertainty.

It takes courage to step into change. It takes letting go of what is familiar.

Think about it. How often, for how long, have you stayed in less-than-comfortable situations because the thought of what it would take to change them, what you might have to let go of, the risk involved, whatever, kept you from acting?

Sometimes change means stepping "out of the frying pan and into the fire," even though you are not sure that the suit you are wearing is fireproof. It is not doing so foolishly, but doing so with forethought, commitment, and courage.

Change takes the courage to let go of your ego. You will make mistakes. There will be times that you will look and feel foolish. People will call you everything under the sun—behind your back and/or to your face—for even considering the change.

Change takes the courage to fail and the courage to succeed. Any big change is going to present you with a whole new set of challenges, some of which you will be prepared for and some of which may seem overwhelming.

Change takes the courage to risk, to explore, and to make really tough decisions without the information that you would like to have. It takes the courage to say no to some really important things in life so that you have the ability and the resources required to remain focused on the change.

Change takes courage. There will be times when your courage waivers. When mine does I remind myself, *I would rather look back and know that my best wasn't good enough, than look back and know I didn't try as hard as I could.*

Change takes courage.

"D" Is for Discipline

For more than a decade, I have periodically assisted at a workshop for men. Over the course of 2 days, the participants develop a deeper connection to themselves as they explore a number of aspects of their lives. For me, these weekends are meaningful both for the service I am able to provide to others and for the reflection they foster in me.

Many of the topics we address draw different responses from me at different workshops. One consistently draws the same answer. The instruction is to discuss the gifts you received from your father. While there are many, *the one that is always at the fore for me is self-discipline.*

Both of my parents worked. By the time I was in junior high school, I worked after school as a bicycle delivery boy; while I kept my tips, my earnings ($0.35 for in-town deliveries, $0.50 for out-of-town) went directly into a college fund. I began working at a Boy Scout camp when I was 14. My siblings and I shared chores at home: dishes, garbage, walking the dog, housecleaning, and taking care of the yard. There was homework, Boy Scouts, church, and acolyte service on Sundays.

This isn't to say I didn't have time to play, or to have fun, when growing up. I certainly did. But it underscores the important lesson that I learned. You need to work in order to achieve your goals. And, doing the work that needs to be done requires a great deal of self-discipline. It is a lesson that I carry with me to this day.

Big changes are tough. They take a great deal of self-discipline. They don't happen overnight. Other important things come up, calling for your time and attention. They require physical, mental, and emotional energy, sometimes every ounce that you can muster. They require the discipline to say "No" to some things so that you can say "Yes" to this one. They require the discipline to make hard choices, difficult decisions. They require the discipline (along with the courage) to take difficult action. They require the discipline to get up each time you fall down, to draw the lesson from each mistake, and to continue to forge forward.

They also require the discipline of self-care, of setting boundaries, of avoiding burnout. They require the discipline of celebrating progress along the way, of sharing successes. They require the discipline of reflection. They require the discipline of making time to have fun. And, they require the discipline of getting "back to the task at hand."

Discipline 2.0

We have talked about some of the key elements of succeeding when faced with a major life change: start with what's in your heart; whether or not you initiated the change, take charge of how you respond to it; know your anchors, and your relationship to them; focus on what is important, not what is urgent; maintain your equanimity.

Now I want to address another key to success: *Discipline 2.0.*

Working with my clients, I find that some have very little discipline when it comes to actually taking action. Often—though not always—these are the more creative types. They are great at generating ideas, conceiving of new things, and envisioning exciting and different futures. However, they never quite get started on the change journey. They come to me with some sense of the change they want to make, though they may be struggling to articulate it. They may know some of the steps they have to take, though they have done little to prepare for—or actually take—them.

This situation surfaces one of the two aspects of discipline I want to address here. It is the part of discipline that we tend to think of most often. *He (or she) just doesn't have the discipline to do what needs to get done.*

The second aspect of discipline that I want to discuss is no less common, but it is much less often recognized. It is the discipline of honoring our boundaries, maintaining a focus on ensuring that we keep a balance in our lives.

I see this lack of discipline in many ways. I have one client who for years thought she had to be available to her employer 24/7. Her energy was consumed in waiting. Another came to me complaining about the lack of support provided by loved ones who were, in turn, complaining about the fact that he worked day and night, 7 days a week. There are those who take pride in "burning the midnight oil" or in having "not taken a vacation in years."

If your change is a significant one, these approaches won't lead to a successful result. In the first instance, you will find yourself in a constant launch, re-launch, re-launch cycle. In the second, you will end up losing your passion, then disliking, and then perhaps even hating the very intent that drove you to initiate the change in the first place.

In both circumstances, the most effective approach is to find and work with an "accountability buddy." In my experience, this role is best filled by someone who is far enough removed to be objective, and someone whom you trust to be direct and honest with you. You want someone who can be supportive of you; who can guide you through the planning process so that you define real action steps if that is what is needed; a person who can work with you to clarify the boundaries if your challenge relates to not honoring them; someone who can help you set realistic goals (whether around moving forward or honoring boundaries); and someone who will—on an agreed-upon cycle—check back in and hold you accountable.

When faced with any important change in your life, Discipline 2.0 is vital: discipline to take the steps necessary to succeed and discipline to ensure that you maintain the equanimity required to keep you from burning out over the long haul.

Balance Is More Than Not Falling Down

Be open to action and to reflection.

Be open to holding on and to letting go.

Be open to knowing and to not knowing.

Be open to doing and to not doing.

In 2007, I took a Himalayan pilgrimage. Over the 8 months before I left, I invested in preparing myself for the experience. While those preparations began in the gym, I soon realized that this journey would require more than physical training; it would require mental and spiritual preparation as well. One day early in my preparations, I met a friend for dinner at a Chinese restaurant. When the check came, I opened my fortune cookie. It read, *Balance is more than not falling down.*

Wherever you are on your change journey, there is an important lesson here. It is a lesson that applies in so many ways that one could probably write books on it. Just as my pilgrimage required me to call on my physical, spiritual, and mental energy, each change journey makes its own unique energetic demands on us. It may challenge long-held beliefs and practices. It may require us to re-frame our relationship to others, or to work, or to religious or spiritual or political beliefs. Whatever the change, it is likely that successfully completing the journey will not be possible with one shift; multiple shifts will be required.

Perhaps you are still committed to that New Year's resolution that resulted in a new gym membership. While the gym may be an important element in losing weight and developing the body that you want, it cannot be the only one if you are to succeed. Doing so may also require you to change your relationship to your body: how you see it, what you expect of it, and/or how you treat it. That's why I have never understood those people who walk out of the gym and light up a cigarette, or the ones who spend their entire workout telling their buddies about how much they drank over the weekend. It's not just about the workout.

Balance is more than not falling down.

"Play to your strengths." There is one theory of change that suggests this is exactly the way to go; build on strengths rather than focus on weaknesses. Another suggests that you should focus on your vulnerabilities, or they will undermine your success; manage them as risks, or risk failing. Who is right? In my experience, both are. When the going gets tough, we each tend to play to our strong suit. Perhaps you're known for making decisions, or taking action, or planning, or anticipating problems. And, sometimes your strong suit is exactly what is needed at that point in time.

But sometimes, what is needed is the opposite; sometimes what is needed is your weakness. Perhaps you are strong on reflecting, on finding the solution through a long and deep contemplative process; but circumstances necessitate quick decisions and action. Maybe you are known for holding on to things that have had meaning in the past, sustaining traditions or heirlooms, or beliefs; but circumstances call for letting go of these things before the door closes on the opportunity to complete the change. *Balance is more than not falling down.*

Do you know your strengths, and your vulnerabilities? Do you consciously choose when to call on each? Are you at the action gym, or the reflection gym, or the decision gym, becoming the ever-more-masterful exerciser of your strengths? Or, are you at the action gym, or the reflection gym, or the decision gym, working on your vulnerabilities to bring them more into balance with your strengths? Balance is *both* leveraging your strengths *and* strengthening your weaknesses. It is knowing the full range of resources that you have available to you and calling on each when appropriate. Balance is being open to action and to reflection. Balance is being open to holding on and to letting go. Balance is being open to knowing and to not knowing. Balance is being open to doing and to not doing.

Balance is more than not falling down.

Plateaus on Your Journey

Plateaus are inherent in the change journey. They can be exactly what we need. And, they can undermine our journey to success. Plateaus allow us to stabilize, to strengthen our commitment. They allow us to prepare to go deeper, further, higher than we have been able to go before. They are a place to rest in our weariness and to launch our ascent to the next level.

Too often, however, a plateau can become the final destination. It can be the place where we plant the flag of victory, even though we haven't reached our intended future. (We make the decision okay, proclaiming *I never thought I would make it this far.*) It can be the place where we stop until we answer all of the "what ifs" that lie ahead. (Of course, they will never all be answered.) It can be the place where our self-doubt takes hold, stopping us from moving forward again.

When you are planning your change journey, include your plateaus. Plan them as places to stabilize, to strengthen your commitment. Plan them as places where you prepare to go deeper, further, higher than you have been able to go before. Plan them as places to rest in your weariness and to launch your ascent to the next level. On your journey use them in the way that they are intended. Don't take up permanent residence on the plateau. It is not the destination.

Stuck Happens

If your change is big, it is only a matter of time before you'll be stuck. It may be early on. Or, things may seem to be on track and moving along when suddenly they start going awry. Or, you may be moving toward the finish line when progress slows to a crawl, just stops, or even begins a backslide. Stuck happens.

So, if stuck happens, what do you do to get unstuck?

What you shouldn't do is panic or start pointing fingers and finding blame.

When stuck happens, don't jump into action. At best, you may fix some symptoms. Start with some thoughtful reflection. What is it that is telling you that the change is stuck? Is it a feeling? Are there symptoms that you can call out, put your finger on? Are there actual metrics? You may want to write the symptoms down, white board them, or put them on stickies. But don't jump up and try to fix them. Remember, what you are seeing are symptoms, not the "thing" or "things" that are actually threatening change success.

What you need to uncover is the root cause. This may require you to look at the symptoms through a variety of lenses. Is it that the intent of the change isn't clear, and different people that you are counting on to support you are—in fact—working on different versions of the same change? Is it that those on the journey with you are shaking their heads *Yes* while waiting for the change to go away; they are not truly committed to it? Is it that the change is a really, really good idea, but you and/or others don't see it as imperative? Is it that people you need to take this journey with you just don't have the capacity for yet one more change? Is it that they have put all of the things that are needed in place, but haven't planned for—or worked on—the needed changes in thinking and acting that will actually deliver the benefits of the change?

Ask questions. Dig deeper. If it will help, find someone who is not invested in the success of the change to help you explore the reasons you are stuck.

What you are really digging for are not the behaviors that have brought the change to the point of "stuck," but the mindsets that are driving those behaviors. Stuck is the result of how you and/or others are thinking about the change, and what is being done (or not) as a result of that thinking! If you only work to change the behaviors, you will find yourself stuck again, perhaps even more deeply than you are now.

Once you understand why the change has become stuck, you can figure out a path to getting it back on track. You may need to go back to the beginning and develop greater clarity about the destination. It may mean that you need to let go of things, or people, that you have been holding onto for many years. It may mean any number of changes in thinking and action are required of you for the change to become unstuck.

Whatever it means, plan it. Then do it. If the change is really that important, then as difficult as it may be to get unstuck, you are going to have to take the necessary action. Even though the cost of doing so may be high, the cost of not doing so will be even higher.

Stuck happens. Becoming unstuck is up to you.

Work Your Plan 1 Week at a Time

Undertaking a big change is daunting; it can seem overwhelming. In general, my recommendation is to work your plan 1 week at a time. Momentum is important during change. Move too fast and you may get all of the pieces in place, but never achieve the actual outcomes that you are seeking. Move too slow, and your change is likely to grind to a halt.

Taking a week-by-week approach with your installation and realization milestones in mind helps to maintain momentum. Think about it. *In the next month, I am going to update my resume* doesn't quite drive action the same way as *This week I am going to make 15 networking calls.*

You may or may not have any realization milestones that you plan to meet each week; you should definitely have installation milestones for yourself. Quoting from Wikipedia, "A milestone is one of a series of numbered markers placed along a road or boundary. Milestones are constructed to provide reference points along the road. This can be used to reassure travelers that the proper path is being followed, and to indicate either distance traveled or the remaining distance to a destination" (www.wikipedia.org).

Using milestones on a weekly basis allows you to know not only that you are actively doing things but that you are on "the proper path." So why not create milestones for every day? Generally, unless you are in a position to control virtually every aspect of your day, daily milestones become burdensome; it's too easy to not achieve them as other day-to-day things come up; and, the discouragement of not achieving them can drain energy and actually get in the way of forward momentum.

That being said, I will sometimes work with a client to create "buckets of activity," with the goal of accomplishing something out of each bucket on a daily basis. For example, someone who is looking to build a brand presence using social media might have one bucket for Twitter, one for LinkedIn, one for their business's Facebook page, etc. Rather than spending every spare minute for a week strengthening their LinkedIn presence—and losing connection with their followers on the other media—my recommendation is to ensure that they do at least one thing out of each of the other buckets every day as well.

Your weekly milestones allow you flexibility over when you undertake your change-related tasks. If today is lost to unexpected overtime at work or unanticipated disruptions at home, you still have the remainder of the week to complete the work that you have set out for yourself.

What happens if, week after week, you are not meeting your milestones? If you find yourself in this situation, it is likely that one of two things is going on.

1. You are setting your weekly expectations too aggressively relative to what you are able to deliver. You either need to re-calibrate your expectations of what you can get done in a week, or you need to look at what you can take off the plate so that you can meet your targets. Then, you need to actually take things off the plate!

2. Your change is a good idea, but not imperative. The other things in your life that are taking your time, energy, focus, etc. away from this change outweigh the importance of the change you are working on. It is time to either lower your expectations for this change or to put it aside.

If, on the other hand, you are completing everything you have set out to achieve mid-week each week, you should be accelerating your plan. You are not setting your weekly goals high enough. They should be both challenging and achievable.

There is another reason to work your plan 1 week at a time. Things don't always go as planned. I recently worked with a client whose "buckets" included addressing certain aspects of his health. When he encountered an unanticipated delay in a planned surgery, he had two choices: push his entire plan back by months or accelerate other aspects of the plan to fill in the intervening weeks. My encouragement is whenever possible to maintain the forward momentum.

Finally, working your plan 1 week at a time helps you maintain your boundaries. It tells you when to take a break and rest for the next week; it helps you to avoid burnout. When the only thing that we have in mind is the desired end state, the urge to be constantly working can drive you in unhealthy ways. Being able to say *I have accomplished what I set out to do this week. I am proud of myself, and can see the progress. Now I deserve a break (and perhaps even a small celebration)* is a much healthier approach.

TAKE THE JOURNEY

Begin with the end in mind; keep the end in mind.

Don't forget the world is changing too.

Monitor progress and risks.

"C" is for courage.

"D" is for (self) discipline.

Discipline 2.0: the discipline to take action, and the discipline to honor your boundaries.

Balance is more than not falling down.

The plateaus on your journey are important, but they aren't your destination.

Stuck happens.

Work your plan one week at a time.

Live the New Reality

The end of our explorations will be to arrive where we started and know the place for the first time. (T.S. Eliot).

Each change journey comes to an end. If it has been successful, you will be living the new reality that you defined when you created your change story. In *The Art of Pilgrimage*, Phil Cousineau wrote, "The challenge is to learn how to carry over the quality of the journey into your everyday life. The art of pilgrimage is the craft of taking time seriously, elegantly" (p. 227). As this chapter nears the end, I pass on some of the ways I have learned to carry those lessons over.

"Returning Home"

If this was a big change, you and those who accompanied you have learned a lot. Your thinking has shifted. Most likely you have cut loose some old anchors, redefined your connection to other anchors, and established new ones. You have developed new skills. Priorities have shifted. It's likely that you are acting, thinking, and perhaps even looking, different. Don't be surprised that life is different now. Even if your physical "home" (whether home or workplace for the journey) is the same, you are not. You are living a new normal.

Reflection

Take time to reflect. Catalog what those changes are and how they occurred. As different as every change is, the underlying patterns are the same. What can you discern from this journey that may be of use on your next one?

Intention

If this was a big change and it was successful, there was a clear intent from the start, and there was a concerted effort to remain true to it throughout the journey. Your success required, as quoted above, "taking time seriously, elegantly." Now that the journey is over, what is your intention? You need to identify it, to declare it, and to commit to it if you are to "carry over the quality of the journey into your everyday life."

What You Passed By

"How long the road is. But, for all the time the journey has already taken, how you have needed every second of it in order to learn what the road passes by" (*Markings*, Dag Hammarskjöld 2003, p. 81). What did you pass by in order to take this journey?

Of all those things, which are best left "passed by?" Which are worth now attending to?

Stop, Start, Continue

The end of the change journey is a "stop." It could be that the stop came slowly, as you maneuvered your way along the path and overcame the obstacles that awaited you. Or it could be that it came surprisingly quickly as synchronicity helped move you over the threshold. Either way, don't let the mental, physical, and psychological energy that you were investing in the journey be eaten by all the urgencies that now arise. Many of them will be of the "urgent and unimportant" variety. Pay attention to what is *now* important; invest there. Now that you have reached a "stop," you have the ability to intentionally make another "start."

Celebrate

This is special. Treat it as such. Find a way to honor yourself, along with all of those who made the journey with you. In the business world, research says that only about 30% of organizational change initiatives deliver on their promise. At the personal level, we may do better. But whatever the statistics are, if you were in it and "win it," celebrate!

At the End of Your Change Journey

"What we call the beginning is often the end. And to make an end is to make a beginning. The end is where we start from" (T.S. Eliot). If you look at this quote, the message is really quite simple. New things come out of the old. Some thing or things have to end for others to begin. Starting a transformational journey, whether at the personal, organizational, or even the societal level, means letting go of something that has served as an anchor in the past. Beginnings can't happen without endings.

There is great power in metaphors, analogies, and stories, ways of communicating that move deeply inside of us, rather than just firing neurons in our brains. One of the greatest teachers of this message was Joseph Campbell. There are several important things that I have learned about change journeys from Campbell over the years; I want to share a few more of those lessons here.

Joseph Campbell's Hero's Journey provides a powerfully wise road map to what your transformational journey is (and/or will be) like. First, as Campbell makes clear, it is important to know that there are really two journeys needed if you are to achieve your desired outcomes. There is the outer journey: the new career choice, the new relationship, the new home, etc. But, there is also the inner journey: the new way of seeing yourself and your role in relation to others, for example. And, there are new ways of behaving (outer) as a result of the new ways of thinking (inner). The hero cannot make the journey successfully to the end without addressing both the inner and the outer.

The next important lesson that Campbell offers is the answer to the question *Who is the hero?*

As someone who has been a change practitioner all of his life, the unfortunate truth is that all too often those who support others on their journeys (coaches, change agents, mentors, trusted advisers, counselors, therapists, leaders of varying types, etc.) see ourselves as the heroes. We are not. We are simply the guides, the Sherpas. We may do our jobs well, or poorly. We may offer exquisite guidance and profound insights, or we may mislead those who are taking the journey. We may walk alongside them, or serve as Sherpas carrying the weight of guide and counselor. But we are not the heroes. Hopefully, we apply every bit of wisdom we have; we offer the truth even when it is uncomfortable; we support the decisions, even when we disagree; we learn and grow; and we share our deepening wisdom with others so that those we are supporting and our professions continue to advance. But, none of that makes us heroes of the change journey. The heroes are those who make the journey.

Now That Your Change Is Done

"This is a great moment, when you see, however, distant, the goal of your wondering. The thing which has been living in your imagination suddenly becomes a part of the tangible world," Freya Stark (*The Art of Pilgrimage*, Phil Cousineau 1998, p. 159).

Let's assume for a minute that you have successfully completed that really big change. It may have taken months, years, or more. Let out a sigh. Celebrate! Really celebrate! But what else is important at the end of the change journey? Here are a few things I have learned along the way.

Wake up to your surroundings and to what you have accomplished.

Remember why you set out on this transformation. What motivated you; what you were seeking; what you hoped to achieve.

Be in awe. Once this was a dream, a vision, an intention. It was not tangible, not real. You brought it to life. You transformed! Take time to focus your thoughts, to cherish where you are, and to honor yourself for the journey you have made. Down the road it will most likely become routine. Don't let that begin here, now.

Be present. Open each and all of your senses to it.

Reflect on the differences from "back then" until "now." Reflect also on the lessons the journey has given you. If you haven't already, record them. Keep them where you can reference them down the line; they may help to better prepare you for your next big change.

Consider the new perspectives and the new insights you have gained. Perhaps it has shifted your priorities, or who and what you value, or even more fundamentally how you want to live your life going forward. *Wow! That is one amazing powerful transformation journey!*

Know that you—and the others who made the journey with you—have invested deeply to reach a satisfactory conclusion.

Follow the counsel of Joseph Campbell. In *Myths to Live By* he wrote, "The ultimate aim of the quest, if one is to return, must be neither release nor ecstasy for oneself, but the wisdom and the power to serve others" (*The Art of Pilgrimage,* Phil Cousineau, 1998, p. 217). How will you use this journey—the wisdom and power that it gave to you—to serve others?

Whether you have sown the seed or others have, know that another change journey awaits you. Perhaps it will be a series of minor shifts as you attune to your new reality. Perhaps small adjustments as the world outside the new reality continues to change. And, in this turbulent and dynamic world of ours, the time will come to set out again on another transformation. Until then, cherish your time living your new reality. Live it fully. Live it deeply. Stay awake to it as long as you can. Live the new reality, fully, in presence.

LIVE THE NEW REALITY

"Returning home" you have been transformed.

Reflect. What have you learned that can help you better prepare for the next journey?

What is your intention now that this journey is over?

What should you attend to that you passed by on the journey? What should you leave behind?

Stop, start, and continue. With the end of this journey, what do you start?

Celebrate.

At the end of your change journey, know that another change awaits you.

References

Books

Campbell J (1949) The hero with a thousand faces. New World Library, Novato

Conner D (1993) Managing at the speed of change. Villard Books, New York

Cousineau P (1998) The art of pilgrimage: the seeker's guide to making travel sacred. Conari Press, Berkeley

Gilbert E (2015) Big magic: creative living beyond fear. Riverhead Books, New York

Hammarskjold D (2003) Markings. Alfred A. Knopf, New York

Housden R (2002) Chasing Rumi: a fable about finding the heart's true desire. Harper Collins, San Francisco

McKeown G (2014) Essentialism: the disciplined pursuit of less. Crown Business, Random House, New York
Sluyter D (2001) The Zen commandments: Ten suggestions for a life of inner freedom. Penguin Putnam, New York

Photograph

Copyright 2016, Brian Gorman. While taken more recently than the storm, this is one of the sailboats that sank during Superstorm Sandy

Creating Space for Personal Transformation

2

Michele Austin

Abstract

The art of facilitating and embodying the essence of transformation is a life-long pursuit of growth and reawakening. As facilitators of transformation, we are hopefully, in our successes and failures, learning and transforming ourselves at the same time as we are holding the space for transformation of others. Our growth as facilitators, teachers, and leaders is dependent upon our willingness to flow, move, and create a safe space with the collective needs and capabilities of the participants that we are working with in mind. Our ability to facilitate great change is equal to our own understanding of these shifts within ourselves. In this chapter, I explore the qualities of a facilitator, the principles of transformation, and the skills necessary to facilitate transformation for a group or individual. Most of the concepts that are explored are applicable to both the facilitator and the participants. My own life research into the art of transformation has suggested that there is no beginning or ending, no facilitator or participant, but an infinite flow of growth and exchange as both parties embody and understand what has to be let go of or embraced for transformation to occur.

Keywords

Compassion · Faith · Judgment · Mindfulness · Perspective · Presence · Trust · Intuition · Receiving · Boundaries

---

M. Austin (✉)
Lomilife, LLC, Fayetteville, AR, USA

J. Neal (ed.), *Personal, Educational and Organizational Transformation*, Future of Business and Finance, https://doi.org/10.1007/978-3-031-29253-8_2

Introduction

Personal Transformation

Eckhart Tolle says in his book *The Power of Now*, "You cannot transform yourself and you certainly cannot transform your partner or anybody else. All you can do is create a space for transformation, for grace and love to enter" (1997: 158).

In this chapter, I will review the elements that are necessary for personal transformation and creating this space of "grace and love." Many of these elements can be applied to organizational transformation and may need to be modified in language or structure, but nevertheless are effective and integral to the transformational experience.

Transformation can come in many different forms. I have a client who feels that transformation only happens when we are willing to navigate pain and painful experiences. When I look back on my own transformation in life, I have to agree that pain is the major catalyst for transformation. When we are taken to the edge of our reality, or get in touch with our deepest, buried pain, we are more apt to move, break down the layers of our internal resistance, and get to the source.

My most recent experience with this began on a beautiful sunny day when Bill, my husband, and I were going on a motorcycle ride. We stopped at a gas station on our way and fueled up. We had been riding together for more than 20 years, and I always rode in front with Bill bringing up the rear. For some unknown reason, on this day, Bill pulled out of the gas station in front of me. About five miles down the road we entered into a construction zone on a bridge. There was a truck coming toward us in the opposite lane with a king size mattress and box spring on the bed rails of his truck. The mattress started to billow up as the truck approached. Both Bill and I saw it and I slowed way down. Bill being much closer to the truck had no choice but to speed up and try to get past the vehicle before the mattress came off the truck. He was unsuccessful in his attempt, and the mattress broadsided him at 55 miles per hour. The bike went in one direction, and Bill went flying through the air in another direction. When I arrived on the scene, I remember being very efficient and unemotional. The bike was leaking gas so I went and turned off the ignition first, asked someone to call 911, and had people stand over Bill and shade him from the sweltering summer sun. I got down on the ground and he laid back in my lap. As soon as he did, his eyes bulged white, blood poured out of his mouth, and he slumped over onto me. He was dying. He was going toward the light, not hearing a word while I am screaming my head off in fear, grief, and shock. I don't know how long this went on, but it seemed an eternity before the fireman came and took him out of my arms, put him on a stretcher, and moved him to the shade. They were able to resuscitate him, and within 30 min we were taking our first ambulance ride to the hospital. I remember that his white beard was pink from all the blood and he was talking crazy about one Halloween that I made him an energizer bunny costume and he sprayed his beard pink. The colorant didn't wash out for weeks. The EMT asked me if this was normal behavior, and I assured her that if he was talking, he would be just fine!

The coming weeks, months, and years were very challenging for both of us. I was dealing with a certain amount of PTSD and having to work double time as we lost 50% of our income in 1 day. At the age of 65, Bill's determination to get his body back and heal was unsurpassed although a 3-year process. Many of our friends found the length of rehabilitation exhausting and moved on from our lives. I was overwhelmed with the responsibility of properties, work, and being a full-time caregiver.

This event was a complete life overhaul for both my husband and me. We definitely received the gift of a new perspective. We are much more aware and engaging with each other. We eat at the dining table versus in front of the TV. We support each other unconditionally and have more patience. We have better boundaries with friends and family and take care of ourselves in emotional ways that were never part of our previous lexicon. I personally understand grief on a deeper, more meaningful level. Just that 5-min wait for the ambulance has allowed me to connect with my client's suffering from loss on deeper, more personal, present, and more engaging ways and my ability to empathize has enhanced my ability to facilitate. This experienced transformed my life in ways I cannot articulate. And I know that I am a better person.

Most of the time, the need for transformation comes from deep traumatic episodes or disfunction. That being said, the solution to healing, in my estimation, can only be achieved with love and grace.

As a transformational workshop facilitator, life coach, massage therapist, and loved one, I have had the honor of witnessing thousands of individuals experience transformational change. Each individual and group absorbs information differently and allows shifting at different rates, but there are necessary components that, from my experience, are required to create the space for grace and love that sets the stage for transformation to happen. Mindfulness, faith, holding space, presence, perspective, acceptance of diversity, trust, compassion, and a sense of safety are just a few of the components that enhance the road to personal transformation.

I participate regularly in transformational workshops. Whenever I feel like I need a bump of inspiration in life, I find a workshop that I feel can provide a new sense of passion and purpose in my daily life. Transformation can happen without a guide through meditation and more solo disciplines, but in my experience, facilitated transformational experiences are more effective in one's quest to evolve. It is my belief that we cannot heal ourselves no matter how amazing we are. We need a guide, therapist, doctor, or a healer, and even as leaders we need someone to help us see, expand, and be better bosses. After Bill's motorcycle accident, we both participated in various types of therapy in order to move through our own processes. And I am thankful to the people who were there to help us along our way.

This chapter is broken down into three sections. The first addresses the inner qualities or mindset of the person who is facilitating transformation. The second section describes core principles that I have found support sustainable transformation in clients. The third section describes specific transformational skills that can be learned and practiced to increase professional development for mental health professionals, coaches, healers, massage therapists, and consultants. The chapter concludes with a summary of my understanding of how individual transformation takes place and some helpful ideas of self-care and integration for us, as facilitators. I have studied, tested, and incorporated all of these ideas into my work and my personal life as a way to flexibly transcend from one reality to another; to a way of being that is appropriate in the now and in our ever-changing world.

Inner Qualities of a Transformation Facilitator

The four key inner qualities to becoming an effective transformational facilitator are presence, willingness, perspective, and intuition. I will explore each of these independently, although they all work together in concert to provide a foundation of truth for facilitation (Fig. 2.1).

Presence

I teach Lomi Lomi (Hawaiian massage) to massage therapists. The reason I chose this practice is because Lomi Lomi is much more than a massage modality. It teaches us a way of being and walking in the world that is more connective and present. Lomi Lomi envelops Aloha. The concept is that we are connected to everything around us and have a symbiotic relationship not only to people but the air and the water, plants, and trees through love. It reflects a lifestyle and teaches us how to not only hold a safe space for another but also for ourselves.

One of my biggest challenges is teaching students how to create this safe container to allow transformation to take place. I think it is important to start by defining presence. What does it mean to be present and to achieve being completely present in this moment?

Being present is not something we inherently know how to do. It must be learned, cultivated, and mastered. Telling someone or yourself to be present is akin to telling someone to relax. Unless you have practiced and experienced what it feels like to be present for someone else or to have someone truly present for you, presence is a

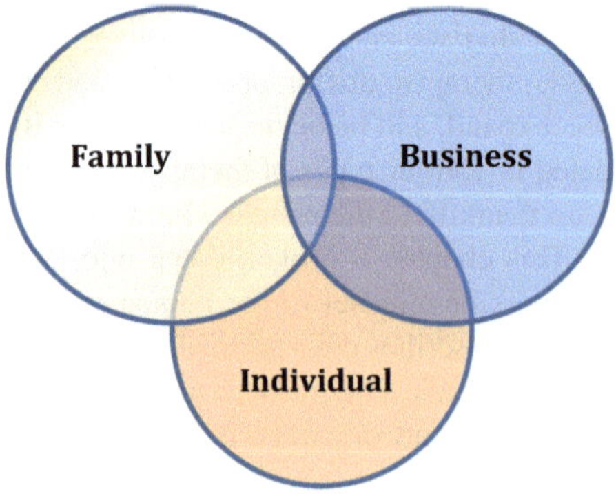

Fig. 2.1 The interrelatedness of family, business and individual systems

state of mind that most people are not connected to. My teaching partner, Lisa, likes to say "If you have one foot in the past and one foot in the future, you are pissing on the present moment." Most of the time, we are unaware of how we move through this world, constantly questioning, thinking, and experiencing in space without seeing, hearing, and feeling in that moment. Maybe we spend an inordinate amount of time in a state of self-criticism, which is just a state of lamenting the past or worrying about performance in the future. Embodying presence requires one to be aware. To recognize when you are participating in self-judgment and criticism or even spaced out and unawake is essential to being able to be completely present with the person or group that you are facilitating. The obstacles to presence very often come in the form of performance issues, self-consciousness, or boredom. Because the massage I am teaching is such a completely different modality than most therapists have ever experienced, even the highly skilled find it frustrating to start something that, in the beginning, they may struggle with proficiency. And I often witness a breaking away from self-limitation in order to allow a shift to take place.

Transformation happens when we have the ability to induce a trance state. This state slows the brain waves and allows us to connect into the wisdom of our bodies while quieting the chatter of our ego and mind. Facilitators who are very adept at what they do can often get trapped into a cycle of comfort, and when we push ourselves out of our comfort zone, learn how to be comfortable in the midst of our discomfort, we can create space in our life to be in each and every moment as they are transpiring. Our internal discomfort often is the source of our inability to live in the present moment or be present for others.

One of the ways I teach presence and help people achieve this trance state is through movement. Just imagine yourself focusing on your heart and breath as if to start a meditation. Start moving around the room and allow your focus to go to each of your body parts. Move and feel your neck, your toes, and your hands. Allow yourself to recognize how each part of your body feels. Recognize the resistance or the fluidity in each part of your body. This can be an even more powerful exercise when you share it with others and culminate the exercise with shared dance. I know of very few things that make people feel more self-conscious than dancing—especially sober. When we create an environment to facilitate the release of feeling self-conscious, we have the opportunity to experience an elevated awareness and a breakthrough in one's own self-identification. Gabrielle Roth, a master dancer, has identified the five universal rhythms that are elemental when any human being explores dance. Gabrielle Roth created a whole transformational movement based on these "five rhythms."

1. The flowing rhythm is a teacher of fluidity and grace.
2. The staccato rhythm is the teacher of definition and refinement.
3. The rhythm of chaos is an announcement of creativity seeking form.
4. The lyrical rhythm is the teacher of syntheses and integration.
5. The rhythm of stillness is the teacher of contentment and peace. (Roth 1998)

In her wisdom, Gabrielle Roth used dance as the vehicle for transformation.

When we allow our bodies to move in the way that we want to express ourselves versus what we think is the socially acceptable way, we allow ourselves to connect with those parts of our being that have very possibly been buried in order to fit in or even are ingrained in our bodies through our ancestry. My personal experience with the "five rhythms" allowed me to take the learned wisdom and the essence of the five rhythms and apply them to many more aspects of life, relationship, and facilitation. In essence, the experience was a catalyst for transformation in my facilitation style and my awareness of myself.

Years ago, I was working with a client that had lived with extreme anxiety and tension for most of her life and realized her life seeking answers through therapy and transformational workshops. We had just finished experiencing a Gabrielle Roth "five rhythms" workshop together, and she wanted to pursue her feeling of an imminent breakthrough with Lomi Lomi. One of the Lomi Lomi sessions that she received, she was able to effectively identify that the anxiety that she lives with came to her directly from her mother while in her mother's womb. Her parents survived the concentration camps and became pregnant with her in the first year that they were liberated. The intensity of this realization was that her anxiety was not her own, but something passed down to her in the womb that she had adopted as her own. The power of bringing that memory and realization from the wisdom of her body into her conscious self allowed her to start integrating into a healing process of transformation!

> Start gathering info from the inside versus the outside.
> The trash is the only thing competing against this moment. NOW
> The journey brings us happiness, not the destination. *The Way of The Peaceful Warrior* (Millman 1980)

I have had the honor of coaching many dedicated professionals, professionals who are passionate about transforming their businesses and personal relationships. My awareness was piqued by one such client that exhibited the desire to bring more presence and mutual connection to her work environment, but needed help understanding and embodying presence within herself. She inspired me to emphasize an exercise to help her understand what being present requires within herself. Basically, she could talk the talk, but hadn't embodied the tools to walk the walk. I joined her in an exercise where we sat looking into each other's eyes and without words, absorbed the nuance and familiarity in each other's faces. The question that we answered for ourselves while silently looking at each other was "What do I see in your eyes, in your face, that I recognize in myself?" When we ask the question and in the stillness of the moment receive an answer, we can connect on a level of understanding that allows us to be more present and accepting of ourselves and others. The exercise gives us a starting point of connection. By seeing a part of ourselves in another, we create a focal point to build on. This focal point becomes the foundation for being present with others. It allows us to embody the tools necessary to lead in a transformational setting. The ability to connect and feel the person in front of us allows us, as facilitators, the opportunity to connect more deeply and genuinely.

A few weeks later, I took this same exercise and introduced it to a classroom environment. Most of the people didn't know each other, and we moved through the room, changing partners and connecting silently on this level. The feedback from the students suggested that they were able to connect with people more easily on their recognized similarities through this silent observation versus their original preconceptions of another. And the students also reported feeling less confused and more in alignment with the concept of what "being present" means to them. The end result made for a much more intimate and genuine environment with less confusion from the participants, many of whom had never contemplated the subject matter.

Willingness

Like many of the elements in this chapter, willingness is an element of transformation applicable to both the facilitator and the recipient. I believe that transformation happens with both parties coming together in a place of mutual understanding. There is a prevalent idea that the facilitator is separate than the recipient and that only one will be engaged in the transformation. I disagree. As a teacher, I walk away from each class with new ways of seeing and believing that are the direct gifts of my students. The same is true when I work one on one with clients. When I, as the facilitator, am willing to allow for an experience to unfold in a way that is organic or right for the recipient and myself, we both shift in ways that are integral to our core.

There are many roads that are effective in creating transformation in our lives. None of them are wrong or right except if they are right for you, as a facilitator and your recipient. I have known people to have visions and great shifts in life with everything from shamanic drumming, transformational bodywork, Ayahuasca, mushrooms, drugs, dancing, prayer, meditation, being in nature, extraordinary circumstances of trauma, parenthood, prison sentences, leadership roles, passionate teachers, weekend retreats, self-help classes, church, etc., and the list goes on. Each one of us is uniquely different and gravitates to different paths and sources. I believe that there are many attributes necessary for creating a transformative opportunity that are incorporated in grace. So what is grace and what does it look like? How do we manifest it in our lives? It is a lofty word. The first thing I think of is *willingness*. We have to be willing to relinquish control and feel, hear and see ourselves, before we can be present. We have to be willing to trust the people around us with our vulnerability and our desire to change our perspectives. Our willingness to be seekers of our own truths and to see ourselves as ever-changing beautiful beings is at the core of transformation. These are truths to embody whether one is facilitating or participating in the experience.

Some people never allow themselves to open up to the uncertainty of transforming their lives, to trusting someone else enough to hold their hand and walk down a path that may disrupt the entire way one sees the world, or to venture forth and embody the willingness to set one's ego aside in order to hold space for a person to have their moment—whatever it may be. The challenge is to the experience and the possibility of walking down a path that takes us into a quieter shift, and believing that we can hold the grace and space for someone else's greater change. The unknown is unsettling for most people, including myself, although some chase it with gusto. I have been a person that in the past has held on to my ideas and perceptions very closely until I started on my transformational path in the early 2000s. Today, I am willing to give up my own ideology that has been based on my life experience in order to see the gifts and new ways of being that are presented to me. I realize that every human being in my midst has something to offer me and teach me, if I am willing to let go of those ways of thinking I am so attached to and open myself up to the teachings of life that come to us from every angle and every unsuspecting source. Much of my truth is based on my life experience, but I have found that when I am willing to listen and question the relevance of those past truths in the life stage of today, I learn and continue to grow exponentially.

Perspective

Each individual has a completely different perspective and expectation of what is transformative. I have often wondered how this affects what we recognize as transformation and how we can become more sensitive to those shifts that are not explosive, but just suggestions. I find myself wanting a big bang of new ideas and new ways of being.

Transformation is not always a big spanking; sometimes it is a whisper waiting to be integrated into our life of habitual patterns of behavior like the perfect icing on the cake.

I recently was asked by a friend to facilitate a session using a therapeutic dose of psilocybin mushrooms. She was scared and unsure and had never had a "transformational" experience to her knowledge. We spent about 6 h together before the session talking about what she wanted out of the experience and what her intention was for herself. I wanted deeply to be able to facilitate this experience for her, but had my own misgivings that I needed to address before I could completely hold the space for her without my own fears entering into the experience. The day of, she showed up at my home with her drugs in hand, scared and determined. We talked about intention and safety and buzzwords that manifested feelings of safety for her. We delved into her fears and concerns and created a safe container for her to let go in whatever way she needed. I set her up with tactile stimulation that could calm her, set flowers by her chair, and listened to her needs. I made her the tea that she drank, and within an hour, she was lying back in a recliner with an eye mask on and soothing music in her ears. Five hours later she came out of the experience and I took her outside. It took her at least an hour to speak about her experience, and even then her words were not fully developed. I gently helped her understand that the workshop has officially begun. The integration of what she had experience would be the defining moment of the experience. I suggested that in the next weeks or months, she would be reminded of images and experiences that she might not remember now in this moment.

The immediate conscious experience of transformation is a rush of adrenaline. The integration of these kinds of experiences are much more solo and introspective. It is a time to embrace yourself and be kind and allow the shift to happen with self-love and the grace of practice and imperfection.

After a few weeks, when I later reconnected with my friend, she said one thing that struck me as wise truth. She said, "It is funny. I see the world completely differently, but I am still me." Transformation does not remove us from our true nature, but from the perceptions that bind us in realities that aren't useful to our present moment awareness. We let go of the old in order to make more space in our beings for new light and information to come in. Or we can just let go and embrace a lightness of being!

Intuition and the Power of the Collective

Much of the time, staying present, aware, and mindful as a facilitator is enhanced when we have faith in listening to our own intuition—watching, listening, seeing the body language and verbal language of the client, and trusting our own knowing can lead us, as facilitators, to take unexpected but appropriate action in the moment with a client. When we come from our egotistical way of thinking of our own ideology and our way of seeing the world is the only way we can do damage. When we stop worrying about how much we know and stay humble in the face of facilitation, we can help the shift. Trust yourself. You will know what the right action is when you come from a container of love and allow your intuition to guide you. I have found that when I show up in a completely present way, embracing not only myself but also the person I am holding space for, I am able to intuitively know what to do for them even when I find myself in uncharted territory, which often happens due to each of our very individual experiences. Trusting in myself seems to convey an energetic safety to my clients. When I am able to completely lean into my own magnificence and intuition, I am able to participate fully in creating a spacc of grace and love for the client to let go of their old paradigms in order to make space for new ways of being!

One of the tools in presence that I use is conscious intention. As an NLP master practitioner, I have the opportunity to get to know my clients on deeper levels and learn to understand their needs and intentions for themselves. Very often, using intuition, I can thus pick a theme or word to focus on during my time with them. If I am massaging them, I can emulate my touch to convey the same intention. The results are powerful for the recipient. They feel the transference of energy. They feel and receive the shift. When I have coupled this exercise with asking the client what their intention is and having them state it out loud, it can be even more effective. At times I have believed that their faith and intent is more important than what I am doing.

When working in a group dynamic, the collective intention can feel even more powerful than one-on-one and can amplify our individual intuitive abilities. The example that comes to mind is the difference between congregating in church or even for a common cause versus praying alone or picketing alone. We all know this feeling and can imagine the power of connecting with others. And in that, I have experienced that transformation happens more easily en masse—more than one!

Facilitating a group to transform, whether an employee group or in a workshop environment, is very different than a one-on-one process. When working with a group, there is a more expansive group energy that becomes the collective process and a collective intention. I believe that if the group has come together in the moment, then there is a collective message or unspoken contract that each member of the group is there because of the mirroring and learning effect that is needed for the collective growth. The group energy is bigger than each individual, and tapping into what is necessary for the group requires a degree of presence and awareness that surpasses the one-on-one experience. With my individual clients, I am also acutely aware that they have come into my life for a purpose. We have an unspoken agreement that I have something for them that they need in this moment and that they have something to teach me. For myself, the one-on-one format is more fluid simply because my present moment awareness is more easily focused.

In the organizational or workshop environment, I recommend setting aside time for the individuals first, before working with them as a group. Although this is not a viable option when bringing people together for a transformational workshop, it is a most effective method for transforming a company that has more longevity than people spending a short period of time in each other's midst.

The advantage to a group environment is the collective energy. With that energy, all of the participants reap the benefits of a heightened experience. People have the opportunity to mirror and play off each other's energies. Sometimes this can support us in moving through triggers and moments of discomfort or see our own magnificence mirrored back at us from an unknown soul. The group environment presents an opportunity for growth that isn't always available when we are completely encapsulated in an environment that offers us more certainty.

One of the exercises I like to introduce at the end of my advanced workshops requires that one person sit in the middle of the group circle. The person in the middle faces each individual in the outer circle one at a time. The person they are facing then has to say something truthful and positive about their experience with this individual. The person receiving this love then breathes the truth into the heart and continues making eye contact until the truth is absorbed into their heart. It is very powerful for us as humans to hear how we affect the people around us in positive ways. Unfortunately, we rarely express our positive feelings for each other in the real world. We walk through life expressing much more of our discontent than focusing on the beauty.

In summary, this section has talked about the inner qualities of a transformation facilitator. As the facilitator, mastering the art of presence is essential for our effectiveness. We have to be willing to show up, surrender to what is, and be willing to change our perspective when necessary. When we allow our intuition to guide us and remain open to any possibility, we embody the desirable inner qualities to facilitate transformation.

Core Principles of Transformation

There are seven core principles of transformation that seem as relevant to the recipient as to the facilitator. I have found that as a facilitator, the embodiment of these principles within myself enabled me to be more proficient as a facilitator and teacher (Fig. 2.2).

If we think of ourselves as the infinity sign, with no beginning and no end, then we can embrace the idea that whether one is receiving or holding space, we are all on a transformational growth path in our own level of awareness. In this paradigm, we are all in it together, coming together for a connected experience of spirit. These principles of transformation include the ability to receive, showing up, expectation, faith, compassion, structure, and boundaries. As a facilitator, one cannot lead transformation without understanding and integrating these principles into their system. These qualities can define the effectiveness of our understanding of others and our leadership abilities. You will find that incorporating these principles and teaching their application with your group will enhance the entire transformation experience.

These core principles of transformation are as follows:

1. The ability to receive
2. Showing up
3. Expectation
4. Faith
5. Compassion
6. Structure
7. Boundaries

The Ability to Receive

I have had many memorable experiences, but one that comes up for me as I think about the ability to receive was after my husband Bill was in that motorcycle

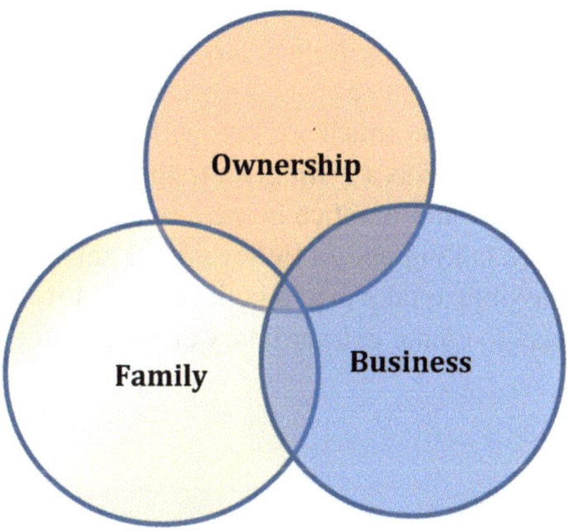

Fig. 2.2 The classic systemic view showing the interrelatedness of family, business and ownership systems

accident. Several of my close women friends organized a benefit for us a few months after the accident. When Bill and I showed up at the benefit, it was overwhelming. There must have been over 400 people packed in a restaurant with a generous silent auction, entertainment in the parking lot, a band, and both local massage schools showed up to do chair massage.

We set Bill up in a chair in the middle of the mayhem, so people could visit with him, and I proceeded to greet each of the people who had graced us with their presence. It was like speed dating. I had about 30 s with each person, and in that time, I felt the need to impart how thankful I was for their love and support and how much we loved them all the while being completely present and giving my undivided attention to each person. In the beginning of the evening, I struggled with this, but as the night progressed, I felt myself relaxing into and being willing to receive the gifts. I accepted their love by being more gracious through my willingness to receive. It was difficult and challenging for me to have so many show up and give freely. I didn't feel deserving even though I wanted to feel that deserving and was so thrilled for the community and the financial support that was much needed at the time. I had to ground myself, quiet my critical inside voice, and find a space to rejoice. I had to allow myself to receive a gift like no other I had ever received. It was like opening up a Christmas present in front of 400 people, and the experience was completely uncomfortable on many levels. I had to get comfortable with my discomfort, recognize and acknowledge how I felt inside, and breathe into the experience. In the end I found myself much more at ease and in a place of joy and appreciation. I found myself moving and shifting into a place of more grace and love, and that evening was transformational on many levels.

The ability to receive speaks to our own self-judgment and sense of worth. Receiving whole-heartedly requires us to be able to be aware and present with ourselves. And when we are self-critical, and judgmental, we are unable to be present and welcome the gifts of receiving. On a social level, so many times have I heard from others or out of my own mouth, "you didn't have to do that for me," or "Oh no, that is too much, I cannot accept this gift from you." These are words that I had been telling myself over and over early at the benefit party. Once I recognized and changed my critical thinking, I was able to accept and feel loved. One of the keys to grace is to receive and say thank you! When we are able to receive from others, we give them the gift of grace. We are able to celebrate them for their offering. I was once told years ago, in a workshop, that the amount one can give is in direct proportion to how much we are willing to receive. At the time, I poo-pooed this idea because I was a *great* giver to the point of self-exhaustion. It was not until I was able to hone and practice being a really generous recipient that I understood what they were talking about. Believe me; I am still a work in progress. I practice as much as possible to take in and believe in the love and joy in my life, and practice is the only way to create extraordinary change in one's life.

Showing Up

In order to help others transform, we have to show up completely as our powerful yet imperfect selves. Bring your magic, your spirituality, your imperfections, and your whole self and listen, see, and feel what is happening around you. Show up as your vulnerable and authentic self. When we show up for another person or group, we not only give them permission to also show up and transform; we bring the necessary elements to the table for people to transcend their own personal smallness. We give them permission to feel differently, to change their perspective, and to invite life into their being in a transcendent way. We do not know the effects we will have on someone or what impact we will make on each other's lives in any moment. Sometimes transformation is not a big move or a large surge. It can be as simple as a kind word to the hot dog stand vendor letting him know that he is the most important thing happening for you right in the moment…as you buy your hotdog.

I had one such experience today. I have not eaten a hot dog in 20 years, but there was this guy sitting out in the hot sun. He was leathered, tan, and bearded probably about 70 years of age, selling hotdogs. I asked him how he was and he kind of snorted. I said "living the dream?" I engaged as much as he would allow with kindness. And I tipped him more than I would usually, knowing that his need was greater than mine. I told him to have a good day and stay cool. By the end of our 5-min exchange, he smiled and thanked me for my grace. I do not know if I made any big transformative change in this man's life, but I know that I transformed his day with presence and kindness. I listened and was aware enough to see him as a kind, hard workingman and a fellow human. Sometimes being seen is all it takes to make someone's day a little brighter. Transformation happens all the time in the little moments. It is not change in the sense that change is inevitable. It is change in the sense of perspective and the willingness to see our perspective of a moment in a different light. Sometimes this is a large rejuvenating moment, and sometimes it is a series of whispers that accumulate into a new life.

My husband, many years ago when he was still in his 20 s, was tree planting in Louisiana. He had to ask a farmer permission to drive through his field to arrive at a site that his crew was working in. During the day the rains came, and he got stuck on his way out of the field. He went to the farmer's door with apologies that he needed help getting his truck unstuck. The farmer was thrilled. He said, "You have made my day son. I thought I was going to get through this day without being able to help someone. And I do my best to not let a day go by when I am blessed with helping."

That was a transformative moment for my husband, Bill. He has never let a day or week go by without reaching out and lending a hand to someone less fortunate or in need. Helping someone transform is an act of service. We will not always know the full brevity of our actions and how they translate for other people, but showing up as your best self and being present with people is part of creating a safe container of awareness for transformation to be possible. It truly is the container of grace and love.

Every engagement counts. Every person counts. And transformation starts with seeing, listening, and being present with people. That is just the beginning, and when we practice, whether in public, our work environments, our families and friends, or perfect strangers, we start a whole new dynamic of healing and change the vibration of our existence. We also affect those around us that are receptive to a shift in their own perspective.

Another vitally important aspect of holding space for another's transformation is to not project our own ideology onto that person. It is of utmost importance to ask versus tell. Don't assume that the person in front of you feels, thinks, and sees life in the same way or has the same priorities. One of my favorite teachers was teaching an NLP certification class that I took. He gave an example of the differences in peoples' values systems. As much as we are the same, we are also strangely different as people and are motivated by extremely different value systems. He described the difference between someone who values integrity versus someone whose highest value may be family. Let us say the person who values family is part of a gang. That person is willing to kill and die for family because their highest value is community and family, and they are willing to do anything for that to remain intact. On the other hand, the person whose highest value is integrity may not be able to conceive of such a horrifying act. With this kind of divisiveness, it is a wonder we can communicate and come together at all. When one is committed to the transformation of that person in front of us, it is imperative that we hold a space that is safe. Safe spaces are created through listening, being present, showing up and not projecting our ideology onto the person we are there for, and asking questions versus telling a person how to feel. Otherwise we are fueling our judgments and our need to be self-validated.

As facilitators, mindfulness and awareness are at the forefront of our minds. We need to check in with ourselves to make sure we are grounded and taken care of before entering a space to facilitate another's transformative moment. It's important to be aware and present of our own needs first. This grounds us in a place inside of ourselves that transmits to the person we are working with. This concept has been challenging for me to teach to people over the years. I continually have to pull from the plethora of tools I have learned from the workshops that I have participated in, my own transformative experiences, and the wealth of wisdom that my clients have so graciously shared with me through their own experiences, in my care and beyond.

As you are working with a client, stay in a place of consciousness versus unconsciousness. The person that you are holding space for needs to know that you are completely focused on their well-being and that you are able to provide a safe haven for them in order to support their experience. In a session, I may start out by inquiring about a client's mental and physical state and focusing entirely on their needs. I might share a story about myself to make them feel comfortable and not alone, or I might pull from an author and share that story in order to create and maintain a sense of rapport. As an NLP Master Practitioner, I may also incorporate mirroring body language and verbal language in order to help the person I am working with to relax and feel understood. I maintain a soft and compassionate tone of voice and stay very aware and focused on what my client is saying. I listen to them speak before I formulate any kind of response. This can be very powerful for clients, especially when one considers that most of us do not enjoy the satisfaction of being heard and seen as we move throughout our daily tasks. I ask questions to glean information and understand their desires and needs instead of telling the client what I think he or she feels or wants out of the experience. I may ask, "what do you want out of this experience today?" If they are unsure, I suggest in a light-hearted way, "complete nirvana?" The power of sweet suggestion and encouragement can be vital to the clients' sense of possibility!

Suggestions and guidance through language are also powerful ways for someone to integrate what has or is happening to them when they are on the precipice of a transformative shift. One evening I was working with a client that had experienced chronic arm pain for several years after recovering from breast cancer. She had been working with a physical therapist for years that had finally told her that she would live with this discomfort and nerve pain probably forever. A powerful suggestion, yes? On this particular evening, she allowed me to work more intensively on her arm, upper chest, and shoulder girdle regions where she had the tumor removed and had the scars that surgeries often leave—not visible scars mind you, but tissue degeneration and surgical trauma. After the session, as she was leaving, I laid a gentle hand on her arm and said, "I would like you to consider that the physical therapist didn't have all the information and that you absolutely do not have to live with this for the rest of your life." She gave me a smile of appreciation with a hint of doubt and went on her way. The next month when she came in for her regularly scheduled appointment, she had been pain-free for the entire interim. She was amazed and animated with excitement. This was a complete transformation for her. Granted, she and I had years of trust, rapport, and success on other levels that always makes it easier for people to believe and receive. She may not have had faith in herself, but she had faith in me and is a person of faith. And the experience was a true testament that language in the form of a compassionate suggestion can instigate transformation. How we choose to use our power as facilitators can be damaging or inspirational, depending on how we choose to go about communicating our message.

Expectation

Expectation limits outcome. Some of the greatest inhibitors of transformation are our expectations.

As facilitators, our expectations of an outcome can be debilitating to any kind of present moment experience. In my clinical experience, I find that my clients view of the world and any expectations of outcomes can inhibit their ability to receive the gift that is awaiting them. It is no different for facilitators. When I expect a certain outcome, I rarely see it come to fruition, usually because it is based on my own sense of perfectionism instead of holding space of nonjudgment and allowing the recipient to have their own experience. When I work with a client, whether in a coaching environment or through bodywork, I understand that I am merely a vessel. My job is to hold space and be present so that the magic and energy of the moment can be filtered through me. When I put any kind of expectation of outcome on the session, I not only discount my own magnificence but also deplete my own energy. Expectations inevitably lead to let down. Rarely does the outcome mirror our imaginations. As facilitators, it is our honor and our duty to remain without judgment of a suitable outcome for another or for ourselves. We are simply there to witness and guide with wisdom and intuition that which is not ours to judge and has very little to do with us.

I have seen so many clients and students have great expectations of what they think they need for themselves. Many times when we set ourselves up with expectations, we end up feeling let down. One of the ideas I impart to students is the letting go of expectations. Most often when we arrive with expectations of our experience in hand, we miss the opportunities in the moment. We literally sabotage our experience and miss seeing the gift that is in front of us because we are so enthralled with the expected outcome. Performance anxiety is another way of expressing our expectations of ourselves. The perfect path only exists in the flow of life and letting go of the incredible weight of what we expect from ourselves.

Without preloading our daily life with expectation, we are more able to experience what is versus what we think we need, want, and have been preprogrammed to believe about ourselves and the world around us. By letting go of an expected outcome, we are capable of being present to this moment. This is the space where transformation can shine, the space where our perspective can get tweaked in delightful and surprising ways and we can move closer to the infinite wisdom of grace and love that resides in all of us. This is very different from having faith in a process or even an intention. Expectations are limitations.

Change is inevitable, but transformation requires a willingness to explore and invite those shifts that may otherwise never transpire. Transformation requires a willingness to not only embrace your experience but to recognize the shift and have the patience and discipline to fully integrate that shift without expectation of a desired outcome.

Faith

There is a difference in experience between the people that have faith in themselves, a higher power, and even me as the facilitator. It doesn't seem to matter which, as long as faith is a driving force. The transformation in the moment is reliable. Faith is bigger than trust. It is a knowing that doesn't need to have conscious proof. I have always understood and had faith that I would be taken care of in my life. Not necessarily by a man or a mother so to speak, but a greater sense that, no matter what, I would be ok—more of a universal faith in the collective and the homeostatic reality of energy and life. That no matter what happens or transpires in life, I would rise to the occasion and be taken care of. And although I believe that trusting any experience is essential, faith heightens that experience.

I had the opportunity to work with a client that I saw just occasionally over the years. She booked a session with me reporting that she had suffered from vertigo for many months and was getting to the point where she could not drive safely anymore. When she arrived at my office, she was suffering to the point of seeming almost drunk. During the session, unbeknownst to me at the time, she prayed. She knew that I was going to heal her, completely trusted, and had faith that all of her angels were showing up to help facilitate her healing. At the end of the session, she felt completely normal, and we shared our collective experience together. We discussed prayer and faith and how vital they are to the shift she experienced and her willingness and belief being a key factor in her transformation. She was hesitant but hopeful that the vertigo was actually gone. She left my office and the vertigo has never returned to this date.

My experiences demonstrate that, as a facilitator, I cannot achieve results without the clients' willingness and participation. The transformation is equal to the clients' ability to receive and believe in the process.

Compassion

Compassion comes when we show up with all of our being. It is the culmination of our own pain, fear, anger, joy, and a lifetime of experience. When we show up as our authentic self and from a place of understanding ourselves, we are more likely to be able to hold space with compassion for others. Compassion is free of judgment, and it embodies present moment awareness. Compassion requires that we do not take anything personally and hold a safe container for another to express and be heard. Compassion is not pity, but rather a space of understanding and support. It doesn't present like comforting someone crying in order to fix or assuage his or her discomfort. More often it looks like holding space and allowing the person to cry it out as if this is the moment that they can truly delve into the emotion, release and not have their emotions shut down, fixed or soothed before they lose the precious moment forever. When someone is at the brink of transformation, compassion holds them in a safe container and allows the full emotional experience.

In the classroom, I often encounter students who want to soothe the person having a transformational moment. They want to rub their back and speak softly words like "its ok." Most of us have learned from an early age that expressing emotion is not acceptable. Culturally we are taught to hug, hold, or even say "get over it, you're not hurt." This is so ingrained in our society; most of us don't even question the ramifications of trying to "fix" the situation by reenacting our own discomfort with someone crying, screaming, laughing uncontrollably, writhing, or in general expressing emotion that is out of the comfortable norms of social behavior. In reality, when do we believe that this opportunity is supposed to happen for any of us? When is it acceptable behavior to feel fully? What if we allowed the person to have their experience and totally move through the pain into another realm of being? What happens when we don't try to fix, shut down, or maintain some kind of control and allow for the transformation to take place by simply being witness to the greatness of being human without judgment or having to "do" anything other than create a space of grace and love?

We are so uncomfortable with that which is uncomfortable in life. The longevity of pain is not socially acceptable, whether from our childhood or in sickness and dying. I noticed this most profoundly after Bill's motorcycle accident. In the beginning, right after the event, everyone I was in contact with was immensely compassionate. But as the months past, Bill and I were still in the midst of our life being turned upside down, and we were still in the trauma of healing and finding solutions to our new reality. People became less compassionate. I cannot count the number of times that a friend asked me how it was going, and by answering honestly, I expressed my pain and frustration that Bill and I were still in the thickness of navigating the changes in our lives. More often than not the comment would be "well, at least he is alive." This is not compassion. Of course I am thrilled that I did not lose my husband on that day. But the experience of rebuilding was very challenging, and that struggle is lost on most if it is a prolonged process, unless one has had the opportunity to come from a place of empathy and understanding. The discomfort of life makes us feel uncomfortable after a time. Compassion is present, in the moment and without regret or comparison to past experience or future anticipation. It doesn't compare. It is "right now" with another person, listening and holding a nonjudgmental space of wonderment. We need to allow the other person to express and have their own experience, whether one agrees or understands. And if we are asked, then and only then, do we offer solutions while still holding the space of loving kindness.

Structure

I have learned the hard way how important structure is in any kind of transformational endeavor. Bill and I started hosting transformational workshops at our mini-retreat center in 2007. We invited Lomi Lomi teachers from all over the United States and Canada each year for a weeklong transformational experience where each participant would share their ideas and knowledge with the collective. I had never experienced a workshop that was not facilitated until we explored the idea that first summer in 2007. Even though the participants were all highly adept, mature leaders in their fields of expertise, and the workshop was a success, I noticed that the participants didn't expand or experience the same intensity that we had all enjoyed at previous facilitated events. I later spoke with one of my mentors about my interpretation of the workshop, and she shared a beautiful metaphor with me that defined the reason that structure (defined facilitation) is so essential.

Imagine yourself with a group of people on a rooftop of a tall building without any railings. Notice that none of the people walk to the edge of the building and look down. Now imagine that there is a strong metal railing all around the edge of the building. Notice that the people will not only go to the edge and look down, but some will step on the first rung and hang over the railing.

The railing is the structure necessary in facilitating a transformational experience. The more we define the space for people, the more willing they will be to let go of their own inhibitions and trust that they are being supported. When we feel trust and support, even as leaders, we are able to perform with abandon, and we are able to unleash the unknown that otherwise may not be explored.

The word "structure," when applied in an organizational context, may have different connotations. Structure, in this context, may need a different delivery system based on the jargon used in your construct. In the organizational context, I think that "a foundation" or a "system of support" may be a more appropriate language. My experience with organizational leaders has brought to light that "structure" can be interpreted as an overbearing and undesirable quality. I encourage you to take the idea and morph it into an appropriate language for your application.

Boundaries

In therapy and the healing arts, the word "boundaries" is thrown around a lot. Having "good, healthy" boundaries is an essential part of any practice. Boundaries are also important to leaders and employees. In any kind of situation, we have specific boundaries that we deal with on a daily basis. With the "Me Too" movement, some very obvious boundary issues have come to light. But there are also boundary issues that are not so obvious ranging from passive aggressive behavior to the more subtle nuances that aren't as easily recognized.

Once I was lying on a massage table receiving a Lomi Lomi session. The pressure was too deep too early in the session, and I asked twice for less pressure and more movement. The therapist stopped working and responded in a very stern voice, "would you like me to leave so that you can get what you want?" I had been completely trusting of the people I was working with that day, and the comment was so out of left field that I was not able to react with emotional intelligence. My initial feeling was "please don't leave me." I immediately connected to my feelings of abandonment in childhood and was incapable of standing up for myself in my adultness.

This is a perfect example in our exploration about healthy boundaries. Do we really know how to have good ones? Can we maintain healthy boundaries for ourselves when we get emotional and/or are triggered by something? The Lomi facilitator above was triggered by what she probably felt was criticism, but my response was to go against my intuition and say "please, no, it's ok" even though it wasn't. In a perfect world, I could have stood in my power and said "yes, leave" and ended the session. The therapist could have been focused on creating a present, compassionate, and sacred environment for the session by checking in with herself before the session began. In my opinion, the initial reactions of both the therapist and myself did not reflect healthy boundaries!

We aren't always able to control our emotions and reactions. As people, we walk around in our lives acting and reacting to stimuli constantly. Most, if not all, of our responses and actions are unconscious. We wake up feeling good without a specific reason why, or bad. Someone says something that hurts our feelings one day, but the next day those same words don't have an impact. We create drama, while others avoid it, or we avoid it, while others create it. We see and feel one way, while someone sees and feels another, consequently creating division. On many levels we walk through life filling our needs with very unconscious acts using old learned behaviors and coping mechanisms to navigate our day.

So if I am suggesting that we are totally out of control, careening down some unknown but very familiar highway, how do we create good boundaries and what do they look like? What are they?

We increase our self-love and our self-awareness. We learn how to hold space for ourselves first. To give ourselves a soft embrace when we are not perfect and give ourselves approval always. We choose our company wisely and don't invite negativity into our lives. This includes choosing not to hang out with that self-deprecating, critical person in our own head that tells us we aren't good enough. We give ourselves every opportunity for success. We strive to improve ourselves with anything from sticky notes with mantras on our bathroom mirror, to faking it until we make it, or transformational weekend workshops. We search and explore the depths of our being to come to that place of self-acceptance and love. We commit to being honest with our critical voice. For example, when we have a let-down or don't show up and perform in the way that we would like to, what does our internal critic say to this? "I'm such a loser"? Or "I perform well most often, but today I could have done better." We practice grace and a balanced approach to negative emotions.

Basically, when we can see ourselves as fully realized and worthy, and when we feel fully engaged, then words that used to hurt no longer touch us. We become more transparent and allow life to move through us. Our actions and reactions come from self-love, not self-consciousness. When we come from love, we are here to serve. When we come from self-consciousness, we come from a place of power. Power in this vein is the desire to overpower another's energy by trying to be good enough. The victim is no different from the bully. Both are feeling less than and trying to get their needs met in non-resourceful ways.

Positive boundaries come from deep inside our souls. Our ability to act consciously is directly related to our unconscious imprinting. What we believe about ourselves directly translates to how we walk in this world and how we affect ourselves and the people around us. What we believe about ourselves defines the quality of our boundaries for others and ourselves.

So, just for today, I am willing to accept myself. I apologize, I speak my truth from my heart as I know it, I strive to do my very best each day, I love, I laugh, I walk in grace, I screw up, and I repeat. Basically, I *practice* good, healthy boundaries to the best of my ability, each and every day.

So how do we achieve this? What can we do for ourselves this weekend to let some of our bound-up self melt away, and how can we embody more compassion and empathy? How can we create more space within ourselves in order to invite our authentic self to come out and play with more joy and fulfillment in our lives? More connection?

Remember that there are always boundaries involved. When one has clear and respected boundaries, the higher the level of empathy and compassion for others. If there are fewer clear boundaries, the less space is available for love and grace. It is very challenging to stay kind-hearted when one feels that people are taking advantage of you or you feel threatened.

Healthy boundaries require us to speak our truth, decide what is right for ourselves, and then express ourselves appropriately. Boundaries require us to get in touch with our value system and fulfill our daily emotional needs based on our values. They require us to be willing to either communicate these needs when issues arise or learn how to walk away when a situation is not appropriate. Finding our voice and setting boundaries can be challenging at first, and sometimes we are not very graceful within the initial process. Practice makes defining boundaries easier!

In summary, the key principles for facilitating transformation start with our ability to receive and our ability to help others discover what that looks and feels like for them. We need to show up as ourselves without expectations of the end result. Faith and compassion create an environment that is conducive to change, while structure and boundaries allow a foundation to support a safe and effective model for transformation to take place.

Skills for Facilitating Transformation

While there are many skills that support facilitating personal transformation, I have identified the following five skills as the most essential:

1. Listening
2. Mindfulness and meditation in motion
3. Creating trust
4. Building rapport
5. Holding space

Acquiring the skill set necessary to be an effective facilitator begins with learning to listen and practicing a mindful, balanced approach to critical thoughts. It requires us to learn how to build rapport with employees or clients and create a trusting environment for them to feel safe. When we incorporate these five tools into our transformational paradigm, we not only hold loving space; we increase our effectiveness (Fig. 2.3).

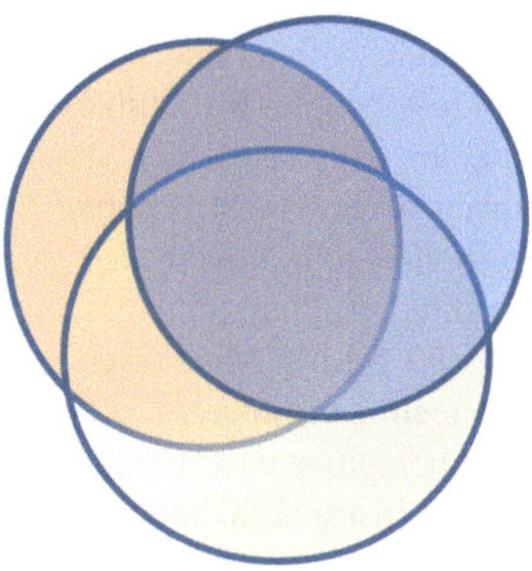

Fig. 2.3 Shows an enmeshed system, with the three primary systems ownership, business and individual systems deeply overlapped

Listening

Being a good listener is an art. However, being a good listener and being able to recognize our own reactive triggers is even a greater art, and the ultimate goal in listening skills. Listening requires that we stop the chatter in our own heads and turn our undivided attention to the speaker. It requires attention and the discipline of not thinking of a response before we have listened to the entire speech. In my sessions with clients, I find that asking a question instead of responding with opinion is a powerful way of communicating that you are listening. Listening requires that we quiet our own inner critic and show up with compassion, kindness, and willingness to hear and see the person in front of us without judgment. When we communicate to the person speaking that we have heard them, we convey an immediate sense of safety.

Compassion is at the core of creating real connection. It allows us to stretch beyond our perceived rightness and reach into the depths of our willingness to open our minds, open our hearts, and listen.

Most of us spend so much of our energy trying to be seen and heard that we lose the balance of seeing and listening. Growth comes from the mirror of another, not a reflection of our self. It is easy to stay in our comfort zone of politics, religion, moral codes, or the rightness of our own knowing and intuition. In Lomi, we stretch from a place of love, Aloha, and when we start from that space with an open heart, we have the opportunity to shift or transform from that place of love rather than the place of old ideologies that may not serve us as they once have.

Mindfulness and Meditation in Motion

Mindfulness not only involves being present with our daily habitual activities; it also requires a balanced approach to negative, critical thoughts. It requires us to be honest in our daily assessment of our inner critic and to change our language. Our judgments of others always come from our own inner critic of ourselves. As facilitators, it is essential that we stay mindful of ourselves, our surroundings, our language, tone, body language, and our clients' needs.

I have noticed that we as a society have a certain amount of catchy words that confuse people. Mindfulness is one of them. Meditation is another. I have clients that are expressing their frustrations weekly about not knowing what these words mean or how to incorporate them into our lives. They express all kinds of stress responses to not being able to accomplish this ethereal concept of mindfulness and meditation. They think "Is everyone else is doing it right? Am I the only one that doesn't get it?" Most often issues of performance and perfectionism overflow into the feeling of failure.

I not only try to help people lean into mindfulness and meditative practices with simple instruction, but I remind myself daily with the simplicity of my own routine. In fact, anytime we can keep our methods simple and give people workable tools, we create a permissive and accepting environment that is inclusive and achievable. One of the ways I motivate clients to achieve a mindful and meditative state is by encouraging them to be present in their actions and to take the time to pay attention to the little activities that we engage in each and every day. For example, when washing your hands, take the time to slow down and feel the water on your hands. Experience the temperature, the texture, and maybe even the smell if there is one. Feel the soap and look at the suds. Be completely present with the process as you intertwine your fingers with soap, rinse, and move toward the towel for drying. Don't stop…continue feeling the texture of the towel and notice when you know your hands are dry and the movement necessary to put the towel down. Focus in on this moment. Wipe off the counter and put things back the way you found them. We can translate this active meditation to all of thing activities we habitually do during each day by experiencing present moment awareness in everything from showering, getting into our car, washing dishes, and getting dressed.

Self-realization in the moment is the beginning of mindfulness. When I got to the point in life that I saw myself in my own judgment of others, I was able to say in each moment "there you are Michele!" in a laughing, and embracing way. I prefer to do it with humor simply because I long ago discovered that laughter is my best medicine for accepting my humanness.

Meditation is, for me, just another way to be present and mindful within myself, to transcend the monkey mind of worry, responsibility, and chaos that surrounds us in these times. When we take moments out of each day and reconnect with ourselves by just paying attention to our somatic responses to the simplest tasks, we allow ourselves moments of meditation and mindfulness throughout each day. Eventually, through practice, these habits will become our new way of being. These moments translate directly into being able to see, feel, and hear the subtle nuance of change or need while facilitating a transformational moment. It is a practice of self-awareness that leads to the successful facilitation of transformation. As my good friend and author, Laura Lander, once said, "It really is just this easy!".

Creating Trust

Trust is different than faith. Trust requires us to believe that someone has our back and will not let us fall. We can have faith in a process and not have trust in the people we are aligned with. We can have the faith that we are taken care of, but not trust a system. When we create a safe container and gain trust with our clients, our employees, and our friends and family, we allow people the lightness of personal liberty. Trust is the knowing that one is able to express and we can be ourselves without the ramifications of judgment or abandonment. When I sit back and close my eyes, ground myself into the comfy chair, and think about what trust feels like this is what comes up for me; someone is sitting in front of me, and they are completely accepting and nonjudgmental. I have an understanding that they can keep my secrets safe. They come from compassion and listen without interruption. They ask me questions relevant to what I am expressing, and because of this, I know they are listening and have my best interests at heart. They are honest and authentic with their sharing about themselves. They show a certain amount of vulnerability while still being solid and in control. They come from a place of compassion or empathy. They show up whole-heartedly. They are present and loyal in the sense that I know on an energetic level that they will not abandon me because of anything I say.

This is what I envision when I think of what trust means. I have tried to emulate this for my clients. My goal is to become the person that I can trust and then energetically, have the faith that the people who need these qualities will show up at my doorstep.

As a facilitator how do you create more trust? Nonjudgmental, safe, compassionate, listening, honest, authentic, relatable, empathetic, present, and available? When we show up and incorporate these attributes for another person, we manifest a trusting environment.

Building Rapport

One evening a friend called me up and asked if I would book a late evening session for a gentleman that was arriving from out of town for a much-needed mental health weekend. I agreed to meet with him. When he showed up, he wasn't sure what he wanted and seemed agitated. I like to talk with people for a time, especially new clients, before they lay down to receive massage. I like to build some trust and alleviate any concerns and set the stage for their safe container.

Early in the pre-talk, it became evident that this person was going to need more from me than my usual repertoire. He had been overseas and participated in several tours of duty. He was having a difficult time being home, controlling his bouts of rage and desperately wanted some insight into what he could do to help with his severe PTSD. I pulled out all of my tools in my Neuro-Linguistic Programming (NLP) training along with many more that I have learned over the years. My intuition told me that all I needed to create was a thread of trust for this man. He could shift in the way he needed if I could help him trust the situation and me. Nothing I tried was working, and after 45 min, I finally said, "I cannot imagine what you have been through, but I want to tell you a story about me." I proceeded to tell him, in detail, my story about watching Bill go down on a motorcycle. His energy immediately changed, and he moved forward in his seat listening intently. The look on his face was intensely present as he absorbed every word. The story literally was moving him from a place of distrust toward a place of being understood on some level, and his posture softened as did his tone. I was able to connect with him by sharing a story that was relatable trauma for him. In the bodywork session, we were able to get in touch with where he felt his anger and how to move those reactions from the belly of rage into his loving heart and other tools to help him diffuse and express these deep emotions he was grappling with.

I believe that sometimes rapport is as simple as finding the common denominator that binds us to each other. It isn't fancy tools that mirror body language and words, but just our humanness and connecting with our vulnerable selves by seeing those parts of us that we recognize in another person.

Holding Space

The culmination of all of these qualities, principles, and skills ends in one construct: holding space. What does this mean? How do we do it?

Well at first, we may not be very good at holding space. It takes practice.

Here are some integral guidelines for holding space (Plett 2015):

- *Keep your ego out of it! This is a big one.* As therapists, leaders, healers, or anyone in a place of power, we can have the tendency to think we know what is going on with a person and what ails them. We can ask ourselves, "Is it that our intervention is necessary or are we trying to 'fix' a person?" Intervening without someone's permission can do damage in ways unknown to us.
- *Give people permission to trust their own intuition and wisdom.* Listen into that wisdom. It is not for us to judge their issues; it is only for us to listen, share parts of ourselves when appropriate, and have empathy.
- *Only give people as much information as they can handle.* In many cases it is paramount that we listen in to see if they actually want your info or your opinion.
- *Don't take their power away.* This can be applied to many different kinds of situations from healing, to daily planning, to opinion and especially in dying.
- *Make them feel safe enough to fail. When people are learning, growing, and becoming more conscious and aware of themselves, they are bound to make mistakes along the way.* Once again, it is not for us to judge another's process, or shame them in anyway. Holding space includes allowing the people in front of you to evolve in their own time. And if we listen and witness, we may even learn something about ourselves within that paradigm.
- *Give guidance and help with humility and thoughtfulness.** If your guidance makes another feel foolish or inadequate…don't do it. When guidance is offered gently and it is invited, we are holding a beautiful space for another. Some warning signs that you are not holding space are "I think you should"; "If you changed (this), you would"; and so on. These statements are the perfect example of what I call the would have, could have, should have syndrome.
- *Create a container for complex emotions such as fear and trauma. When people are held in a deeper way than they are used to, they feel safe enough to allow complex emotions to surface that might normally remain hidden.* Culturally, we have the tendency to want to shut emotion down. For example, when someone cries, we comfort them, rub their back, and tell them that it will be ok. The end result is to make them feel better, or make them stop crying. I encourage us to allow the complex emotions to surface and be expressed versus soothed and shut down. When we allow people to express, we allow them to very possibly move on from the trauma instead of tucking it back into its hiding place.
- *Allow them to make different decisions and to have different experiences than you would.* We are different—different values, needs, religions, traumas, and cultural backgrounds. It is important to allow yourself the humility to understand that you may have an opinion, but it usually is wrong when it comes to another person's truth. This is a very powerful lesson to learn in life. When we project our own beliefs onto another person's actions, attitudes, and life, we can do irrepa-

rable damage to others and ourselves. We can make up stories that just are not true, and those stories can cause suffering for not only ourselves but for our clients, friends, and families.

When you hold space for another, you have to let go of you. You have to become a watcher or the witness of your own thoughts. This creates an opportunity to witness how much runs through our minds that is useless. And allows us to develop a deeper sense of stillness.

Summary of guidelines for holding space:

- Let go of judgment.
- Open your heart and have empathy.
- Allow another to have their experience.
- Give your complete undivided attention to the other person.

The signs that you are not holding space are self-consciousness, triggering, wanting to fix it, influence it, or affect any kind of outcome. Anytime you get upset by something, you are finding a nerve ending that is unhealed pain in yourself.

Holding space is not exclusive to facilitators. This is something powerful and engaging that one can practice and do for each other in every aspect of our lives.

Dr. Brene Brown (2012) reminds us that we can only create a genuine empathic connection if we are brave enough to really get in touch with our own fragilities.

Other Considerations for a Transformational Facilitator

In this next section, I describe the different avenues for transformation and the need to take the integration time necessary to see sustainable change. I also explore the need for self-care and what that looks like. In the end, as transformational facilitators, self-care is how we stay vibrant and creative and effective. Without it, we burn out for others and ourselves (Fig. 2.4).

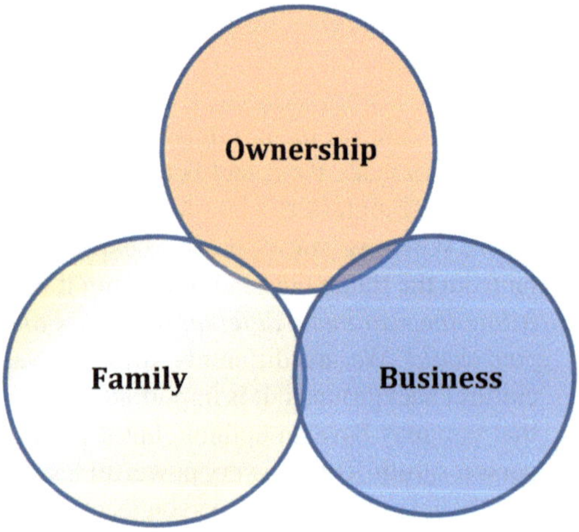

Fig. 2.4 Shows a deeply distant system, with the three primary systems ownership, business and individual systems barely intersecting

Integration

One of the core descriptions of transformation is that one may experience an extremely rejuvenating moment of revelation and transformation and think that it is done. The moment we open up our hearts to a transformative experience, it can feel like a huge adrenalin rush, and we believe that we are changed forever. However, when we experience a transformational moment, that is just the beginning. We have to take the time in subsequent weeks to integrate the moment into our lives. We have to roll it around on our tongues and be mindful to live in the new light of our expanded awareness. It is necessary to allow yourself enough space and compassion to implement the new ideas, the new vision, and the new way of operating whether in a personal way or in a group environment. Knowing, seeing, and feeling a new way of being is not enough. Integration is essential and takes mindfulness and self-compassion. This process can take weeks or even years depending on your circumstances and the weight of change. Listening in, taking care of oneself, and allowing yourself to screw up, fall down, dust yourself off, and try again are essential to allowing the space necessary for the new information and the new way of being to solidify.

One of my clients had been taking transformational workshops for years. She is an extremely talented and adept coach and consultant. She had studied under one gentleman for over 10 years and had created her life's work around those experiences. She shared with me that even though she had more than 500 h of training with her mentor, she never felt accepted or celebrated for her accomplishments in this field and had some residual pain and resentment because of it. We talked about other workshops where she had been seen and celebrated for her accomplished self. She admitted that she had taken a Shamanic Workshop at Esalen where the instructor had not only asked her to participate in a healing session with him but had gone on to invite her to an exclusive Shamanic training over the course of the next year. Yet she had declined. Recently, she decided to go back to her original mentor and take another advanced training with him. She expressed that after 5 years of being out of his workshop training, she saw it as an advantage to be able to walk back into the familiar workshop space as a barometer of her own growth and to be able to see her progression in life. When she signed up for the workshop, she was told that she was no longer invited and that some of the workshop attendants didn't feel safe. She was told her mentor had to consider the whole groups safety. This was a devastating blow to her. While we were talking about the contrast between the two instructors, she had an epiphany. She realized that she was attracted to the instructor that didn't see her because of old patterns of behavior and her beliefs about her own self-worth. She had been gravitating to the experience that supported how she felt about herself versus the experience that validated and celebrated her amazing skills as a healer and facilitator. With that knowledge, she has been able to change her life and say yes to opportunities when they are placed in front of her—invitations from people who see the value in what she brings to their lives. She integrated these transformational messages into her life by recognizing her own culpability in her experience. In the end, she agreed that she received her sense of a barometer without even having to spend the money on the workshop. In essence, she graduated and is integrating through mindfulness, awareness, and self-love.

Taking Care of Oneself as a Facilitator for Transformation

Leadership comes with challenges and immense responsibility. Being a good facilitator of change requires one to be aware, mindful, present, compassionate, and diligent about self-care. It also requires an immense amount of self-evaluation and ability to transcend one's own fear and uncertainty. Boundaries and self-care are essential parts of staving off exhaustion. When we are exhausted, we cannot be present with another person.

As a facilitator, I have to be very discriminating in my personal life. This includes whom I spend my time with and what kind of friend I choose to engage with in my free time. Being a good listener, present, and compassionate emanates a certain energetic vibe to the people in your life and even strangers. Often I find myself listening to someone I may have only just met, sharing their most intimate details in life to me. Sometimes I think they shock themselves with the immediate trust they feel in order to share with such depth. Everywhere I go, whether with close friends, going to receive a massage or people I have just met, I find that I end up holding space for people. This can be very exhausting in the sense that I never find myself being heard or having time off from the intensity of creating that safe container for other people. In the past, I have gone as far as booking a therapy appointment once a month so that I could enjoy an hour a month in my life to just sit and be heard. This is self-care. There needs to be a time for a facilitator to regroup and take extreme personal care. We are not machines and taking the time to reenergize is paramount. My favorite metaphor is to think of myself as a cup of cappuccino. When my cup is full and the foam is pouring out over the sides, this is when I have something to give others. When my cup is half full or empty, it is necessary to refuel myself through self-care. I cannot facilitate and hold space for others from a depleted state. As facilitators, this may be our biggest challenge. We need to create positive boundaries especially with our free time, understanding what we need to refill and be energized and we need to learn how to take time for ourselves.

I have had to practice saying no and being conscious and honest about my own needs. A dear friend, Laura Lander, once said to me, "Michele, when you say no to something, you are saying yes to something else. When you say yes to something, you say no to something else." At the time, this was profound, and I use this saying to help myself decide which way to turn for my self-care. Each moment of my personal care time, I have to ask myself "What am I trying to achieve? What is the outcome I need for myself in this moment?" When I take the time to be as present with my own needs as I am with the client or group I am facilitating, I maintain my energy and passion for my work. When I keep my cup full, I avoid exhaustion and burnout. My goal is to be sweet with myself and to allow myself a soft landing.

I have a friend that I adore. She has this habit of telling me how to feel and isn't particularly present in the moment. However, when it comes to buying a gift, she is always thoughtful and brings the right present that is relevant to my life, so in this sense, I believe that she pays attention even though it seems otherwise. She is *always* up and animated, and when we get together, she is telling me how great the day is and how awesome the experience is, and when she isn't saying that, she is explaining how the world works and how everyone should just feel better because everything is so great. There are days when I am not feeling receptive. Some days I do not have the patience for what seems like disingenuous in the moment because I am not in the mood to feel any other way than how I actually feel. Those days I know that I should pick another activity that is more suited to my own revival. On other days, she is perfect. She has the ability to catapult me into feeling like the most fun person in the universe. It just depends, and it is for me to figure out when I need to retreat for self-care and when I need my favorite extroverted friends. I have to embody the aforementioned attributes in this chapter and understand myself enough to set appropriate boundaries.

In the spirit of Aloha, if one is coming from a space of true compassion, it is impossible to dehumanize another. We need to allow ourselves the awareness of our bounded self-patterns, let go, and open our hearts to true compassion for all that surrounds us. We need to stop and listen to another's pain and joy with presence and mindfulness. We transcend the dominant paradigms of judgment and create a safe container for healing when we truly allow ourselves to leave our egos on the couch (Jim 2007) and be with inner essence and the experiential moment. We reach across the aisle, and our capacity for understanding, love, receiving, community, self-love, esteem, and fulfillment is available.

Summary: Transformation

This chapter has presented key qualities of a transformational facilitator, including the importance of presence. The ability to be present encapsulates many of the other key qualities of showing up and being willing to engage. Believing in ourselves enough to listen to our intuition and being willing to change and grow is essential to our success as facilitators. It has also discussed the key principles of transformation that help us understand our employees and clients and give us a road map to create a language that can be used as a basis for a group transformation. These principles include learning to receive, showing up without expectation, having faith in the process, and being compassionate to yourself and others. We create the foundation for safety and trust by creating enough structure and boundaries that people can shift their own awareness and experience effective change.

Additionally, this chapter has described some of the most important skills of transformational facilitation including our ability to practice mindfulness by balancing our critical thoughts, our ability to disengage from our own mental chatter and listen, and our proficiency at trust and rapport building. When we embody these skills, we are able to hold space for our clients and employees. Finally, it is important to allow yourself time for integration and self-care as a transformational facilitator. Without these, we cannot possibly sustain a life of service.

Transformation implies that a big moment is waiting and available for all of us. Transformation is a process that requires intention and the right connection in order to allow for the container of grace and love to arrive that is right for you. It is a road that never ends, intermixed with moments of excitement and the discipline of integration. When we stop growing, we start dying. Each and every moment that we shift toward our true selves is a celebration. It is like a death and rebirth that can happen over and over again on our journey to be whole.

I spoke with a new coaching client who was exploring what steps to take in her own transformation. I suggested that she listen to her gut. I told her that her intuition will tell her what modality is right for her in her journey of healing. As her mind twirled and she shared her apprehension about what path to take on her quest to change and transform the discomfort in her life, she came to the conclusion that she would try this new thing that I am offering. I am humbled by the people that come to me with their faith and their desire for a better way of existing. They stretch themselves beyond their imagined containers and give me the opportunity to not only facilitate their journey but to learn from them. It is an honor to serve, and in my life, it has been a large part of my own transformational journey. I thank these brave individuals that bring me their stories; their grief, anxiety, and stress; and their magnificence. Bless you all.

> In actuality, emotional unsafeness consists of dehumanizing behavior. The quintessential 'I am not enough.' Shame of what we believe about ourselves that is reflected upon us. (Brown 2012)

Creating a safe container for those that look up to and are relying on us for the tutelage of their growth is to serve on the highest level.

References

Brown B (2012) Daring greatly. Gotham Books, New York

Jim HU (2007) Wise secrets of Aloha. Weiser Books, San Francisco

Millman D (1980) The way of the peaceful warrior. H.J. Kramer

Plett H (2015) Art of hosting, circle, community, compassion, grace, grief, journey, leadership. HeatherPlett.com

Roth G (1998) Maps to ecstasy. Nataraj Publishing, Novato

Tolle E (1997) The power of now. Namaste Publishing, Vancouver

Cross-References

Daryl Conner, It's not what you do, it's who you are

Ginger Grant, The untapped power of imagination in the workplace

Nancy Kay, Self-awareness in personal transformation

Peggy O'Neal, Personal transformation: The next big risk

Alexis Racionero, The new leaders as spiritual hero: The way of awakening

Brian Gorman, The hero and the sherpa

Create the Future with a Transformation Model

3

Abraham M. Gutsioglou

Abstract

In this chapter, I take you on a journey that leads to the creation of a new version of yourself. I share my transformational journey and how it fuels me to help others live their life to the fullest. I challenge you to examine your own consciousness, and I teach you how to help others expand their self-awareness through practical tools that you can use to coach others as they create their own transformations.

Here are key ideas and principles that we will explore in our journey:

1. You will learn how the Transformation Model applies to three types of transformations.
   (a) Transformation of self
   (b) Transformation of others
   (c) Transformation of complex organizations
2. You will learn about the theories that inspired my work with the Transformation Model.
   (a) Maslow's theory of human motivation
   (b) Bandura's self-efficacy
   (c) Deci and Ryan's self-determination theory
   (d) Locke and Latham's goal setting theory

My hope is that you learn how to use the Transformation Model on yourself and to help people achieve their dreams. Welcome to the journey where you begin to think differently!

A. M. Gutsioglou (✉)
Think Differently LLC, Los Angeles, CA, USA
e-mail: abraham@thinkdiff-llc.com

J. Neal (ed.), *Personal, Educational and Organizational Transformation*, Future of Business and Finance, https://doi.org/10.1007/978-3-031-29253-8_3

Keywords

Personal transformation · Organizational transformation · Transformation Model · Goal attainment · Goal sustainment

Introduction

Personal transformation is the creation of a new version of yourself: a version that withstands cognitive and behavioral regression; a version that propels you to new levels and higher dimensions, as defined by your very own goals in life. The outcome of transformation is relative and personalized to your own journey. However, the process is universally applicable and simple to understand, albeit challenging to attain and sustain. Personal transformation requires tapping into one's consciousness, expanding self-awareness, reflecting actively, and possessing strong commitment.

This chapter opens with my very own transformational story, a story I call "Origins." It sets the foundation for my quest to help others create transformations. In this chapter, I highlight the differences and interdependency between change and transformation. This is followed by an exploration of common definitions of transformation and practical applications for transforming the self, others, and organizations. Then, I introduce you to a continuously evolving Transformation Model that you can use as a map on your journey toward success. I also share key ideas, templates, and techniques designed to help you create various types of transformations. Finally, I conclude the chapter with key theories that have inspired my work with the Transformation Model, which include Maslow's theory of motivation, Bandura's view on self-efficacy, Deci and Ryan's self-determination theory, and Locke and Latham's goal setting theory.

Origins

It was a beautiful, picturesque Friday in a forest in California; I must have been 16 at the time. If I close my eyes now, I can transport myself to that scene: the cool breeze caressing my face, the daylight shifting into night in the distance, all wrapped up in a feeling of freedom. My friends and I were up to no good, surrounded by the privacy of the surrounding trees. Without getting into details, I can tell you this – I did not surround myself with the best crowd. In fact, my life would have turned out very differently had it not been for the story I am about to share with you.

Two weeks prior, my school counselor had pulled me into her office to express her concern over the decisions I was making and the people I was surrounding myself with. In her eyes, I was living life on the fast lane, on a direct route to self-destruction. She feared my life would be wasted if I didn't get myself under control. However, her worry was something she couldn't fix. Rather, it would require me to go through a deep level of self-analysis and introspection. I was stuck in a world that only I could break free from. She said:

> Look at me! I know you are in there somewhere, but as of now you are just going through life, living like your future doesn't matter. Whether you believe me or not, you are destined for more and needed in this world. You need to see yourself and the world around you. No one can help you if you are not able to see yourself.

At the time, this made very little sense to me – I listened and heard what she said but had no clue what to do with the information or how to process it. So, I did what a typical 16-year-old would do – I brushed her off as "weird" and kept living my life.

Let us go back to that pre-evening in the forest. Surrounded by friends, laughing, and enjoying the world happening around us, we heard crackling noise in the distance. We went silent, looked at each other, and scanned the environment to see who was around. A few minutes went by in silence, but we didn't see anything or anyone. We dismissed it as wildlife and went back to having fun. Then we heard it again; this time closer and sounding much like human footsteps, crunching sticks and dry leaves on the ground with each step. We silently panicked, quickly packed our things, and prepared to take off running in different directions to make it difficult to be caught.

Then we heard a soft voice saying, "Hey, I'm friendly, don't worry. I am not here to bust you or get you in trouble." Although we couldn't fully make out facial features, the tone of voice was calming and put us at ease. We sat there quietly as the distant blurry figure sharpened to a tall, rugged man who must have been in his early to mid-20s. It turned out he was a backpacker and was hiking through the area when he heard us in the distance and wanted to approach us to make new friends.

He walked my way, shrugged his backpack from his shoulders, and sat next to me. Little did I know that my life was about to be transformed.

He turned to me, extended his hand, and said, "Hi, I am Jerimiah." I reciprocated, and he replied, "Wow, that's a strong name. It comes with great responsibility." I chuckled and shrugged my shoulders. He began to tell us the story of how he had been backpacking around the world, meeting new people, and creating new experiences. Given that none of us in the group had ever traveled, we were in awe of each word that came out of his mouth.

After a few stories and laughs, he turned to me and said, "This is going to sound weird, but something told me to sit next to you. I don't question my inner self, so here we are." I let out an awkward laugh. My initial thought was that he was a crazy hippie, but something told me to stay in the moment and listen. As he went on, he said, "There's more to you than meets the eye. It feels like you are lost and need help finding your path." That's where I stopped him and told him the story about my counselor and how she had said something similar. I kept going with how I felt like I didn't fit in with the people I surrounded myself with, but that they were all I knew and that I never thought about the future. I figured I would just follow in the footsteps of my friends or family. He said, "Now I know why I am sitting here with you. I have something for you."

He turned to the side to pick up his backpack from the ground. He dusted it off, reached into it, and pulled out a worn-out book. The cover barely kept the book together, the sides were torn, and what were once white pages had turned a yellowish-brown tint. He rummaged through his bag to find a pen and wrote something in the book. He handed it to me and said, "This book changed my life, and now it will change yours. Consider this a gift from the world. You are on a transformational journey and destined for more." He shook my hand and grabbed his backpack. Jerimiah grunted as he stood up, said goodbye to the crowd, and walked off into the distance, never to be seen again.

Before this day, I had never actively or willingly read a book. In all honesty, if I wasn't forced to do it for school, chances were that I would never do it at all. This time, with this book and this experience, something was different. I opened the book to read his note, but before I could read it, I was shocked to see many messages from people all over the world, some difficult to read because they had faded. I found his message in the bottom right-hand corner:

> This transformation is a gift, and now it is your responsibility to help others find theirs.

I started flipping through the pages to estimate how long it would take for me to read it, when something stopped me at a particular message:

> We meet people for a reason. Our paths cross because we are there to help them or they are there to help us. It is up to us to stop, pay attention, and listen to what the universe is telling us.

It was at this moment that I realized life would never be the same. My process of personal transformation began in the blink of an eye. I read that book within a few days, which was a record for me. When I finished, I was hungry for more – it was like my mind had been unlocked. The book answered some questions, but created more, putting me on a path of self-analysis.

The weeks following that night changed the course of my life. I immediately stopped wasting time with the people I called friends and began reading more and exploring the depths of my mind through active reflection and focused directive attention. Through this process, I realized that I had a choice in what my life could be – even more than that, I understood that I could have a positive impact on people and the world around me while traveling through the journey of life. Ever since, I have been on a mission to help people think differently about themselves and the world around them. Through this mission, I have created a map that helps people achieve their goals and transform themselves along the way. I call this "the Transformation Model," and today I will share it with you. My hope is that it will help you the way it has helped me.

Welcome to your transformation!

Let's Talk About Change and Transformation

Change in its simplest form is the difference between time, places, things, and events. Merriam-Webster's (n.d.-a) online dictionary defines change as follows:

> To make different in some particular (i.e., alter); to make radically different (i.e., transform); to give a different position, course, or direction; to replace with another; to make a shift from one to another (i.e., switch); to exchange; to undergo a modification.

What does change look like in a practical sense?

Let's say that you are sitting down while you read this, but then someone rings your doorbell, forcing you to get up to see who is at your doorstep. The act of shifting positions from sitting to standing is considered change. Your physical position in space changed, your focus and attention changed, and depending on who was at the door perhaps your mood changed.

Another way of looking at change is as the difference between the way things are right now (i.e., current state) and the way things can be (i.e., future state). According to Tim Creasy (2021), chief innovation officer of Prosci, an organization specialized in helping people through the process of change (i.e., change management):

> Change happens all around us: at home, in our community, and at work. Change can be internally motivated or externally motivated. The change can be a dramatic departure from what we know, or it can be minor. Change can be anticipated or unexpected.

This leads me to the question: Can one have change without changing?

Yes. Think about a time when you ran into someone who you had not seen or talked to in years. Perhaps they lost weight or have a new look or style; maybe everything about them from a physical perspective has changed. However, after you catch up with them, you realize that who they are at their core has not actually changed. They are still the same (rude or kindhearted) person you knew them to be back in the day. In this case, your friend has changed without changing. You might be asking yourself – how can someone change so much but not change at all? This occurs because we assign value, meaning, and purpose to the experiences we go through in life. In this situation, your view of this person remained constant and unchanged while everything about their physical appearance changed. The opposite can also occur, wherein the person's physical appearance remains constant while their personality becomes drastically different – you might even say they have transformed into an entirely different person. They look the same, but they make you feel different.

You might be asking yourself: Is change the same as transformation?

No, they are not the same. Think of it this way: You can have change without changing, and you can have change without transformation, but you cannot have a transformation without change. This is because change is part of the transformative journey. Think of change as a milestone along the path of transformation (see Fig. 3.1).

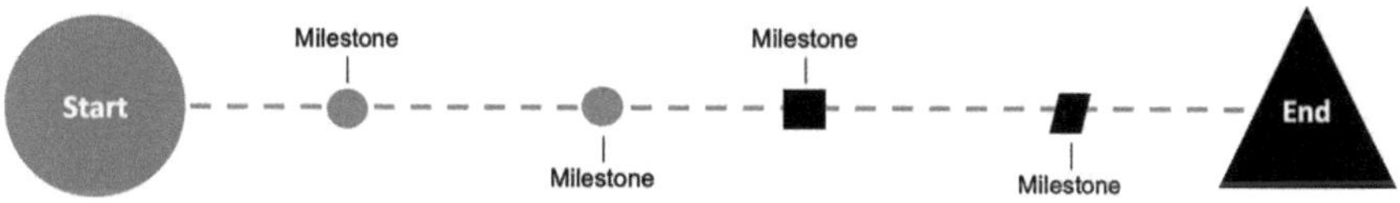

Fig. 3.1 Change as a milestone in the process of transformation

Transformation

If change is not the same as transformation, then what is it?

Transformation is a diverse and fluid concept that lends itself to a broad range of definitions. For example, Biology Online (2001) defines transformation as follows:

> The act, state or process of changing, such as in form or structure; the conversion from one form to another.

The last piece of that definition is key. "Conversion from one form to another" – think of the popular metaphor in which a caterpillar transforms into a butterfly, a biological process wherein something becomes another thing that is entirely new and different. Transformation can also take place within our minds and bodies. When talking about transformation, I refer to it as a process of tiny behavioral modifications combined with purpose, self-awareness, heightened consciousness, and directive intent that creates irreversible positive outcomes (i.e., change). Remember, change is a milestone along the way to transformation; it is the accumulative effect of tiny changes that create transformation.

When describing the difference between change and transformation, I like to use Judi Neal's (2018) explanation found in the *Handbook of Personal and Organizational Transformation*. Neal (2018, p. 5) explains it beautifully:

> Change is like water, which can take many forms. It can be heated up to become a vapor, but when it cools it will change back into liquid form. It can be frozen into ice, but when it melts, it will change back into liquid form, not so with transformation. The popular metaphor for transformation – a chrysalis transforming into a butterfly – is apt, in that the butterfly will never go back to being a caterpillar. It has transformed into something that is completely different and is a higher order of complexity…. So, when I and the authors in this Handbook of Personal and Organizational Transformation talk about transformation, we are talking about this kind of metamorphosis into something healthier, more evolved, more effective, and quantitatively different from what went before.

The Transformation Model

Imagine that you are preparing to go on a trip to a place that you have never been to before. One of the first things you do is look up directions for getting to your destination, which includes things like distance, arrival time, challenges along the way (i.e., traffic, accidents, etc.), and route complexity. Although you have directions for how to get there, the GPS itself will not transport you to your destination. But if you get lost along the way, your trusty map will help get you back on course. Much like a GPS providing you with step-by-step directions, I want you to think of the Transformation Model as a map to help you reach your destination. The Transformation Model includes steps to help you attain purposeful, long-lasting impact. It can be used for personal means or scaled to create organizational transformations. In this part of the chapter, you will learn how the Transformation Model came into existence. You will also acquire an illustrative overview of the model, learn about each step, and learn how it links to other established theories.

The Transformation Model: Beginnings

By trade, I am an international consultant specializing in transformations. My practice allows me to travel the world, helping organizations design, implement, and evaluate change and transformation interventions. I have helped thousands of people through the process and experience of change. In that process, I have seen some people regress to their old ways and others transform themselves and their lives into something entirely different. From a young age, I knew that I was put on this earth to help others find themselves and see the world around them in new ways. However, I never knew that I would do it by creating an entire map. My path to impact prior to the creation of the Transformation Model was through coaching people in group settings and one-on-one. With each client, I learned a new lesson, capturing it in my mind and in a journal. Over the course of time, I began to see patterns in the challenges people faced. I noticed that lack of clarity and purpose created similar roadblocks for my clients in the Philippines as for my clients in Mexico City. I worked with people all over the world, yet they all had very similar experiences – not identical, but similar enough to create patterns. Throughout my engagements, I took copious notes in my journals and used those observations as reference points when building solutions for the people I helped next. While forming solutions for others, I also tested the Transformation Model on myself and achieved consistently successful results.

The first time I extracted the model from my mind (onto a napkin), I was on a special assignment to fix a troubling situation with a client. I was brought onto the project because the client was pushing back, resisting change, and actively derailing the work the team was trying to implement. My ego took a hit when I was also unsuccessful. The client made it nearly impossible to work with them. Over the course of 2 days, I tried various tactics and techniques to bring them to a resolution, but nothing worked. Deep inside, I knew that something was getting in the way, but I could not figure out what it was or how to remove it. To make things more stressful, I was running out of time – I had to be back on the road by the sixth day, with a success or a failure on my record.

After the third day of trying and failing, I felt emotionally exhausted and frustrated. That evening, I sat alone in the hotel restaurant, feeling deflated by the day's work. While waiting for my meal to arrive, I observed the people around me – how they interacted, what they said to each other, and how they behaved. Nothing out of the ordinary, except for one server. He captivated people's attention, made people feel good about themselves, and in one instance, he quickly converted a hostile situation into a positive experience. I called him over and asked how he did it – his secret to converting a negative situation into a positive one. He looked at me and said:

Fig. 3.2 Early iteration of the Transformation Model

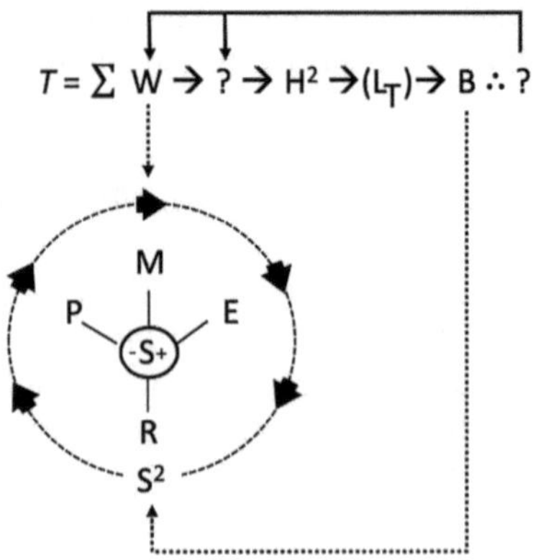

> Sir, I am not their server. I am their psychologist. I listen to my customers. I pay attention to their needs and dedicate my time to caring for them. People tell you what they want, not what they need.

This was my eureka moment! I realized I was approaching the situation as a consultant, which was the wrong approach. The client needed a coach – someone who listened and asked powerful questions. I was trying to "fix" my client's feelings instead of paying attention to and caring for them.

I dedicated the next few days to being a coach. I paid attention to my client's needs and was finally able to break through. It was this experience that inspired me to extract my mental models onto paper. In the process of extraction, patterns emerged with corresponding practical steps to break through each of the presenting challenges. This is when I realized that the cumulative effect of these steps would help my clients create the long-lasting impact they desired (i.e., personal and organizational transformations). The Transformation Model was born. The figure below is an early iteration of the model (Fig. 3.2).

The Transformation Model: A Birdseye View

Let's start by breaking down each element of the Transformation Model, which consists of seven key components: (1) what, (2) why, (3) how, (4) length of time, (5) barriers and blockers, (6) support system, and (7) now what. Although the elements are displayed in sequence (i.e., steps 1–7), they can be used in any order – the point of entry depends on the situation and intended outcome. The Transformation Model can be applied to various settings and used as a map for goal establishment, attainment, and sustainment.

The Transformation Model: A Map for Success

- *T* represents the total effect of the elements in the model; it is the accumulation of your entire approach and all your effort. Every action you take will add together to create the transformation you are looking to achieve. The greater your effort and resourcefulness, the higher the probability of success and the greater the impact of your transformation.
- *W* represents "What do you want to attain?"
  - It is critical for you to be specific and very clear regarding your "W" – in other words, what you want to attain. Ask yourself – what is my goal? What do I want? Be warned: A lack of clarity will significantly decrease your chances of success. You should always start with your end state in mind. You will not be able to create a plan of action if you are uncertain of what you want to attain (i.e., what your goal is). The single most important thing here is to have a crystal clear goal because it will allow you to define your outcome.
  - A common question here is as follows: Does goal type matter?
  - No, goal type is irrelevant. The Transformation Model is flexible and adaptive to any goal and situation. A goal can be personal, like increasing one's physical activity (i.e., working out). A goal can fall within a professional category, like starting a new business or building/expanding one's professional network. A goal can also be scaled to become part of a much larger organizational goal – for example, releasing new technology that employees must adopt or teaching employees' new ways of working.
- *?* represents "Why do you want this?"
  - Once you have identified the goal you want to attain, you can move on to this step, which is to align value with the level of importance. The degree of importance you assign to your goal will correspond to the priority with which you pursue it. Think of it this way: If something has low value, it will quickly drop from your list of priorities, which in turn leads to poor planning, weak execution, and minimal follow-through. For illustrative purposes, the matrix below describes the impact of value and priority on one's goals (see Fig. 3.3). The highest probability of success lives in the upper-right quadrant, where both value and priority are at their highest. As you move clockwise, you notice that goals can still be attained as long as there are no competing priorities. The moment a new priority steps into the situation, it puts the current goal at risk. The lower-left quadrant represents the goal with the lowest probability of success, in which there is low value and low priority. This is where new year's resolutions live. At face value, the resolution sounds like a good idea, and you may even try it out for a few weeks, but ultimately it lacks value and priority. When a goal has high value but low priority, it can also be bumped out (upper-left quadrant). However, when this goal drops, it makes you feel bad about yourself. Failure to succeed in this quadrant comes with negative self-talk and emotional baggage. It can create guilt and anxiety that will present itself as a psychological challenge the next time you attempt it. Having a clear reason for wanting your "what" will take you a long way. When things become dif-

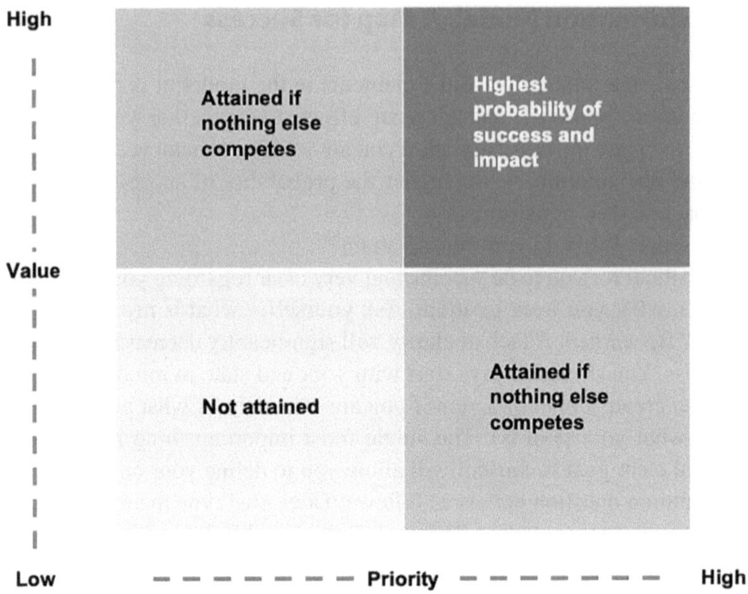

Fig. 3.3 The value-to-priority matrix

ficult, your "why" will serve as a motivational driver. This is a major reason why the Transformation Model starts with clarity in what you want to attain, followed by meaning and purpose (i.e., why you want to attain it).

- *H2* represents "*H*ow are you keeping track of your progress?" and "*H*ow will you know you have attained it?" It is squared because there are two "Hs" in the model.
  - Goal attainment is difficult and becomes nearly impossible if you don't know how to measure your progress or articulate what success looks like. This is the reason why you need a clear objective and a tangible way of measuring it. This step of the model is inspired by pilots and flight decks. A pilot is trained never to start the engine or take off without first going through multiple checklists. Pilots have an inspection checklist, a pre-engine start checklist, a taxi checklist, and a pre-takeoff checklist. Once they are in flight, they have several more checklists as well. As you can tell, pilots have a way of measuring the completion of each task. While in flight, they rely on their flight deck to help them measure progress. There are many instruments on the flight deck, but there are six specific instruments that they actively monitor. These instruments are collectively referred to as the pilot "six pack."
  - To quickly summarize, the six pack instruments are the following:
    1. Airspeed indicator (ASI), which measures speed
    2. Altimeter, which measures altitude above mean sea level
    3. Vertical speed indicator (VSI), which measures the speed of climb/descent
    4. Attitude indicator (AI), which measures the levelness of flight
    5. Heading indicator (HI), which helps provide direction
    6. Turn coordinator (TC), which measures turning/banking

- You might be asking yourself: How does a flight deck relate to personal goals and transformation?
- Think of your goal as a destination. Being clear about where you want to go is critical, but knowing how to measure your progress will make the difference between failure and success. Take the time to build your own six pack. Simplicity is key. I have seen clients overly complicate the process by coming up with multiple performance indicators. When people overcomplicate the process, it becomes a hassle to manage and sustain. My recommendation is to measure one thing at a time and not measure more than six items total. Here is an example of what a simple six pack can look like for a personal goal:
- The goal you are working on is to run a 5 k by specific date. For simplicity, we will say that you have never participated in any running events, so this will be your first one ever. Keep in mind that this is just one example of how you can measure progress, the point is for you to get a general idea of what it looks like, so that you can create a six pack of your own for any goal you want to attain.
- At this stage, we are not specifying what your running time will be or what place you will come in. This is because at this stage, it will add unnecessary pressure to your goal – the moment you have a bad day, the pressure will get into your mind and potentially push you into quitting. At this point, focus on building micro-habits and stacking them to a point where you can compare your performance against yourself and use it as motivation to get you to the next level (i.e., the "now what" of the Transformation Model).
- An example of a personal goal six pack: Run a 5 k by a specified date.
  1. Register for a 5 k event.
  2. Purchase proper running gear, like shoes and activewear.
  3. Create a walking schedule. For example, "I will walk for 10 min after work and before dinner on Monday, Wednesday, and Friday."
  4. Start walk-run schedule. For example, "I will run for 2-min intervals mixed with walking for 15 min a day on Tuesday and Thursday after work and before dinner."
  5. Run without stopping (not sprinting) for 5 min with walking intervals in between for 30 min on Saturday at 10:00 A.M.
  6. Run without stopping for 15 min with walking intervals in between for 40 min on Sunday at 10:00 A.M.
- As your goal evolves so should your measurements. The combined effort of the six pack will help you attain your goal. In later sections, we examine a few more examples for different types of goals. For now, just remember: If you can't measure it, you probably won't attain it.

• *LT* represents "length of time."
  - When you build a plan of action for your goal, you will need to consider how long it will take you to attain it. You can also think of it as the length of time you are giving yourself to reach your destination. The timeline you create will inform you how realistic your goal is to attain. A word of caution here: It is important that you don't fall into the trap of thinking that more time means a

higher chance of being successful. Too much time on your goal's horizon could be just as bad as a very short timeline. When the end time is near, you will notice "slippage," where priorities shift to accommodate for the time you have remaining. The less time you have, the harder you will have to work to stay on track. If you are not careful, "slippage" can quickly morph your desired end state into something entirely different. In the previous example, we did not specify when the 5 k would take place.

  - To illustrate how length of time impacts your success, consider the following:

    Very short timeline: You register for an event that is happening in 3 days. Given that you have never participated in this type of event, and you have not trained your body, the chances of you enjoying the process or participating in the race will drop significantly.

    Very long timeline: On the flipside, you register for a 5 k event that is scheduled to take place in 2 years. In this scenario, your brain will negotiate with you and win – it will say something like "You have time to prepare; we can start later." The lack of clarity and specificity is detrimental to goal attainment. This is how your brain wins the negotiation and tricks you into a false perception of goal commitment.

    Just right timeline: Although I would love to give you a very specific timeline that increases your success rate, I can't. This is because every goal is different and the effort, resources, and commitment individuals place on goals vary from person to person. However, I can say that your goal should be challenging enough to help you grow, but not so difficult that it will paralyze you from acting.

- *B* represents the "barriers and blockers" that *will* get in your way.
  - Goal attainment is filled with challenges, barriers, and blockers. I can tell you right now that you will encounter many of them along the way. These challenges are part of the process – the upside is that they contribute to your growth and development. The moment you feel that things are looking good is exactly when something will appear out of nowhere, reminding you that it won't be easy to reach your destination. These barriers hit hard and have the potential to halt your momentum; at times, they carry enough power to derail your plan. People who are unprepared to handle unplanned challenges are hit the hardest. Although it is impossible to prepare for every single event, you can mitigate total failure by anticipating common barriers and blockers. While helping people with personal transformations, I have found that, on average, there are four common barriers and blockers that people experience on their transformative journey (Fig. 3.4).

- Table 3.1 highlights some of the typical things you can expect to encounter with each of these barriers.
- Among these barriers and blockers are two that show up consistently: people and process.

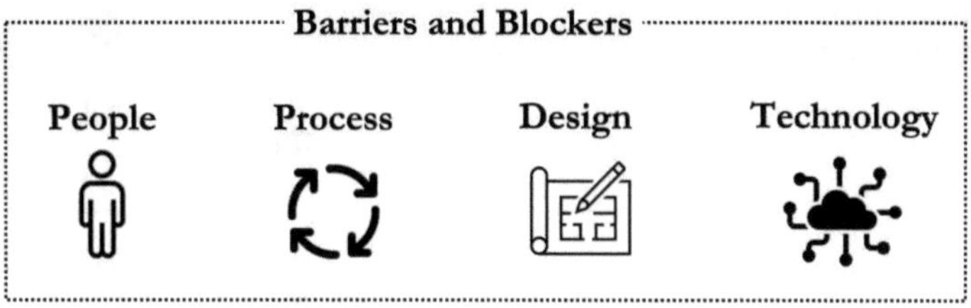

Fig. 3.4 Barriers and blockers

Table 3.1 Typical barriers and challenges

Barrier	Typical challenges
People	Will doubt you, put you down, and may even wish for you to fail
Process	Can distract you from your intended outcome
Design	May become overly complicated
Technology	Become a hassle and burden to manage and sustain

- At times, the people we love the most are also the ones who hurt us and hold us back from our potential success. The people we choose to surround ourselves with play a massive role in the outcomes we attain (or fail to attain) and the lives we lead. When it comes to people as barriers and blockers, you can expect things like emotions and behaviors to get in the way of attaining your goal. People will give you unsolicited opinions in the form of advice. They will go into detail on how you are not doing things the "right way" and go on to tell you what you should be doing instead. Ironically, these are the same people who have never done what they are telling you to do. They might not even have the courage to try like you have or get as far as you have. Here's something interesting to think about: 49% of the people in your life at this moment are worrying too much about themselves to care about your problems. Another 49% are happy that you have those problems, and not them. Then there is 1% who care about you and want you to succeed and 1% who can go in any direction at any point in time. I know this sounds like a jaded view of the world, but I call it like I see it based on what clients have told me. Don't get me wrong; there are plenty of people out there who truly care about you and want you to succeed, but you must proactively find them. Just be kind to yourself, have patience, and trust the process.
- When it comes to barriers and blockers with the process, you can expect factors like methods of doing things to get in your way. Our human brain loves automation, easy things, and big rewards in exchange for little effort. The moment you ask your brain to think, you slow it down because it is processing the information you are feeding it. The more complex your requests are, the more processing power your brain will use to generate an output, and if it ever has a choice to do something "easy," it will always choose that path. You will have to actively work on keeping your brain focused on the given task to achieve the outcome you are looking for. A process that requires little processing power from your brain will lead to increased success rates. My recommendation is for you to automate your

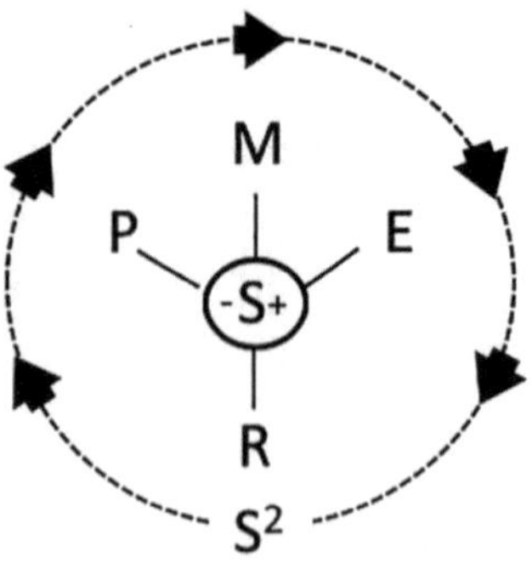

Fig. 3.5 Transformation Model support system

task-goal process as much as possible – build a process that strategically uses processing power. Automation is key!

- *S2* represents the "support system" you will need to help you succeed.
  - Interestingly, people and process show up as barriers and blockers, but they can also become your biggest support system in times of need. A support system will help you turn difficult situations around and can reinforce and sustain your growth. A support system can be a single person or a larger group of people. It can also be a place that helps you feel grounded and balanced.
  - A support system can also be a thing that functions as a symbolic reminder. I have seen clients wear bracelets, carry stones, or tokens. I have also had clients who write short messages on sticky notes which they place in the areas that they frequent the most throughout their day. For example, one person put motivational quotes next to the camera on their laptop, at eye level on the front door (so they read it before they leave their home), on the bathroom door, and on their refrigerator door. They even updated their phone's main screen to read "just breathe."
  - The Transformation Model is designed with a support system that surrounds you and your goal (as shown in Fig. 3.5), with the support system expressed as S2. The purpose of the support system is to provide you with stability, motivation, trust, and the confidence you need to keep going – especially when things get difficult.
- Let's take apart Fig. 3.5 and have a closer look. The support system is comprised of physical, mental, and emotional stimuli that operate as reinforcers. Figure 3.6 provides an illustration of these elements with examples provided in bullet points.
- When you think about your support system, I want you to imagine a music mixer like the one shown in Fig. 3.7.
- A music mixer plays a role like a support system in the Transformation Model. To explain: The function of the music mixer is to produce the best possible sound. To get the sound and quality you are looking for, you sometimes need to adjust specific levers and knobs to get more bass, while other times you adjust other levers and knobs to create more treble, and so on. This concept also applies to people, problems, and situations all around us. In the same way, you can adjust and modify physical, mental, and emotional levers in your support system to respond to various conditions and get the outcome you are looking for.

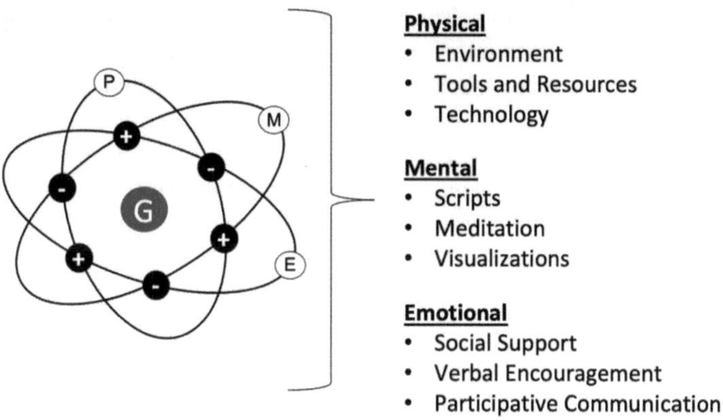

Fig. 3.6 The support system elements

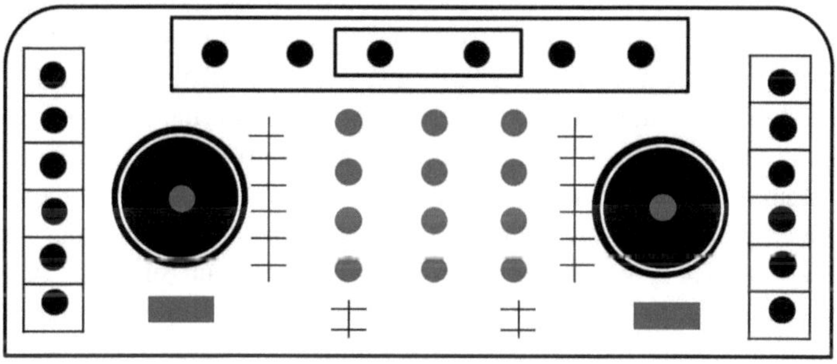

Fig. 3.7 The support system mixer

- Let's spend a few moments exploring each of the elements found within the Transformation Model's support system. We'll start with the physical reinforcers, which consist of things like the environment you are in, such as your office space or working conditions. Once, I had a client who did everything in one room, which made it extremely difficult for her to create a division between her work and her personal life. The blurred lines between work and personal space created stress and anxiety because she was consistently reminded of the things she was failing to do as the pile of overdue items kept rising. We had to sort through the physical mess before we could work through her priority list and get her business up and running. She cleaned and organized her working area, making it easier for her to focus. During her focus time, she chose to focus only on a single task at a time to minimize possible distractions.
- The physical element also means using tools, technology, and resources to increase efficiency. For example, when I wrote this section, I was on a trip and wouldn't be back in my home office for a few days, but I didn't let that stop me from using my time efficiently. While on a walk, I used my phone to dictate my thoughts. I just focused on speaking what was on my mind. I handled how it would look on the screen a few days later, when I knew I would be able to sit at

my desk with dual monitors. This is just one example of how any of us can use everyday items to augment the progress of our goals instead of allowing situations to get in the way and become an excuse for why we didn't do something.

- The next element of the support system is the mental reinforcers, which include things like cognitive scripts, visualization techniques, and meditation practice. The process of goal attainment and the journey of transformation is bumpy and lonely, which means you will spend many hours thinking and feeling things (mostly about your progress). Your mind will play tricks on you, causing impostor syndrome, self-doubt, and negative thoughts. Possessing mental strength will enable you to be resilient.
- I like to say to my clients:

  You are your best coach; the internal dialogue you have will make you or break you.

- I'd like to give you the same advice. Listen to the things you say to yourself throughout the day; I bet there will be quite a bit of self-criticism and judgement. It takes practice to be nice to yourself, as strange as it may seem. Why can't we just love ourselves and choose to be kind to our inner beings? Start by writing down a short mantra, something simple that you can remember and embrace. If it is too complicated, you won't use it, and it will go to waste. I like to use mantras that are three or four words; for example, "I am grateful," or "I am progressing." Once you have a few mental scripts that you can rely on, your next step is to fully leverage your imagination to visualize your success. Performance coaches, athletes, musicians, and artists use the visualization technique all the time. It is a way for them to train their minds and bodies to respond and work toward achieving that wonderful feeling of accomplishment. You can do this too! Give it a try – close your eyes and focus on your goal. Just imagine what it will feel like when you attain it, using all senses within your visualization. Teach your brain and your mind what it will be like to be at your best, as if you are already there. I promise you it will pay off in many ways, but you must practice this daily. This brings me to my next point: having a meditation practice.
- When I talk about meditating as part of your support system, I don't want you to misinterpret it as becoming a monk or changing your lifestyle to become someone or something else. That's not what meditation is. In fact, when I teach clients how to use meditation as a support system, they are amazed at how simple and unobtrusive it is. I am not a meditation expert, but I use what works for me and my clients, and I will now teach you so that you can use it in your journey of transformation. I want you to think of mediation as the act of pausing life and living within the brackets. You see, people tend to live their lives in the past, feeling depressed and sad because they can't go back to how things were. Others live in the future, experiencing constant anxiety about what could or should be. Both realms prevent people from being their best, right now at this very moment. Meditation teaches your body and your mind to pay attention to the present – with practice, you will learn to enjoy each moment. For now, here is a technique that you can add to your support system.

The 3-Minute Practice Technique

- *Mindset:* I suggest doing this at home or in a quiet place where you will not be disturbed for at least 5 min. Find a comfortable spot and begin.
- *Minute 1:* Take a deep breath through your nose. Hold it for 4 s, and then exhale through your mouth. Do this three times. On the third breath, close your eyes.
- *Minute 2:* Resume regular breathing. Focus your attention to one breath at a time. Feel your stomach go in and out. Repeat. This will help you stay in the moment.
- *Minute 3:* Bring your attention back to your body and surroundings. Allow your senses to connect with the world around you. Welcome back!

For those of you who want an extra challenge, practice this technique with your eyes open while dealing with daily life. You can start with something simple, like waiting in line for coffee or participating in a team meeting. Challenge yourself to simply be in the moment. Take things as they are, one breath at a time.

The next element of the support system is the emotional reinforcers, which include things like social support and encouragement. Emotions are huge drivers of behavior. People will make decisions and act in certain ways based on how they feel and how others around them make them feel. Time after time, I hear those clients want to change their goals or dream a little less because their friends and family have told them they are dreaming too big. Each time I hear this, I want to shake them and tell them to snap out of it! Having people around you who believe in you (no matter how crazy your goals may be) is huge! Whether we like it or not, the things people say to us or about us matter. Yes, some people are better at not allowing someone else's emotions to negatively influence their momentum, but it is very difficult to do if the direct support system is consistently creating a negative space.

Let's bring it all together – the Transformation Model's support system teaches you to (1) create a physical environment that will make it easier for you to build habits toward your goals. It reminds you to use technology to remove barriers and eliminate excuses; (2) train your brain and your mind to visualize the success you are looking for and build a mental script that pushes positive messages in your internal dialogue; and (3) surround yourself with people who want you to be great; the words they say will generate emotions that inspire and motivate you to keep driving in full force. It's really that simple! When you put your support system in place, you can use it like a music mixer, where some days you need more bass (i.e., emotional support) and other days you need more treble (i.e., physical support). Ultimately, you are in control of that mixer. You have the ability and strength to mix and amplify to create the music you want in life!

- ∴ represents "now what."
  - At this point, I want to remind you that change is not the same thing as transformation. Change can occur without transformation, but a transformation cannot take place without the process of change. This is because change is part of the transformative journey, a milestone along our transformation (Refer to Fig. 3.1).

- In the context of the Transformation Model, the "now what" step represents a much larger philosophical exploration of the self. This is where one's transformation takes place. It is the point of no return. It is the place where the caterpillar transforms into a butterfly; it is the place where one evolves into something completely different.
- In my work creating transformations, I've noticed that there are three types of people: (1) those who regress and go back to their old ways after attaining their goal; (2) those who are happy where they are and don't want anything more; and (3) those who want more from life and choose to continuously transform and propel themselves forward into higher levels.
- People start their journey by identifying what they want to attain and why they want to attain it. After going through each of the steps in the Transformation Model, they will reach a key milestone where they must ask themselves:

What happens next, now that I've attained my goal?

- The answer will depend on the reason they started in the first place. If it was tied to personal growth, they will need to spend some serious time reflecting on this, as it may indicate that they have more work to do. A decision must be made. Which person will I be? I've come this far; do I stop and turn back, or do I keep going?

Creative space: Use the box below to make some notes on what you've learned so far.

Application of the Transformation Model

Although transformations occur in different ways and for different reasons, they all have commonalities. In this section, I talk about three types of transformations: the transformation of self, the transformation of others, and the transformation of large, complex organizations. I will provide you with a practical "how to" approach so that you can use the Transformation Model in any of these areas.

The Transformation of Self: A Journey of Self-Discovery, Growth, and Development

I would like to start this section with two quotes that I share with my clients when we begin their personal transformations. The quotes are from Carl Jung. The first one reads as follows:

> We cannot change anything unless we accept it.

In my experience, people will say that they want things to be different, that they want to become someone or something else, and that they want a life of meaning and purpose, but they give up on their dream before they begin. I believe that their premature failure is because few of them are willing to look within themselves, to dig deep to make their unconscious conscious to achieve the results they want. It seems like not many people are interested in accepting that who they are today is not going to get them to where they want to be in the future. The journey of personal growth, development, and transformation begins with accepting that change must take place internally before it takes place in the physical world. Those who are willing to let go of irrational thinking and judgement and leave behind their psychological baggage are ready to move forward into their journey of personal transformation. Of course, it is easy for me to say that people must accept that change is necessary for growth, but I will be among the first to admit that it is not easy to explore the self. It is not easy to deconstruct one's feelings of regret, guilt, anxiety, and insecurity. This leads me to the second quote from Carl Jung, which reads as follows:

> No tree, it is said, can grow to heaven unless its roots reach down to hell.

I interpret this to mean that for us (as human beings) to fully grow and develop, we must do so with balance: a balance that can only be attained by exploring, deconstructing, understanding, and accepting our inner worlds. To be the architects and grand designers of our future, we must visit a dark world (i.e., our personal hell) comprised of our fears and taboos, along with a bright world (i.e., our personal heaven) comprised of our true kindness and radiant positive energy. I believe that most challenges we face in life are rooted in a lack of harmony and an inability to actualize. Too many people live their lives without paying attention to the experiences of their day and don't pay attention to why they feel the way they do. They don't realize that their life is on autopilot. This lack of intentionality forces them to recycle the same behaviors and wonder why they keep making the same mistakes.

To break free from autopilot, one must understand the basic human need to actualize. At any given moment, we can find ourselves living below the line, within the realms of our own personal hell. Ironically, within minutes we can then find ourselves basking in the glory of our personal heavens. This cycle never stops, even when we put our heads down to sleep. From the moment we are born until the moment we die; life is a continuous constant struggle to actualize.

What does it mean to actualize?

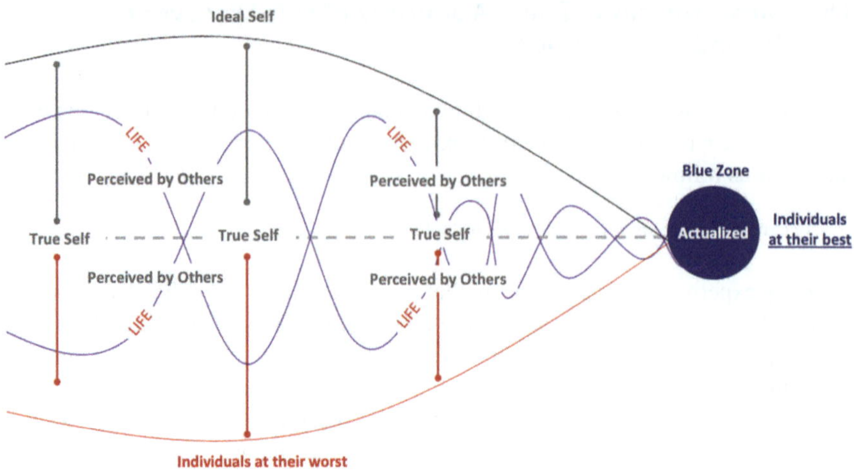

Fig. 3.8 Merging for actualization

We will explore this further in a later section, where I link the Transformation Model with Abraham Maslow's theory of human motivation. For now, I want you to think of actualization as being the best version of yourself. To actualize means to live the life you want, on your own terms. I believe that humans can actualize every day, multiple times per day. The difficult part is sustaining, prolonging, or consistently being able to experience it. To help you understand how this concept connects with personal transformation and the Transformation Model, I've created the illustration in Fig. 3.8, which I call merging for actualization.

Creative space: Use the box below to take some notes on what you think it means to actualize. What was your experience with actualization? Has it changed over your lifespan?

It is important for you to understand that the basic human need of actualization will be your foundation for the application of the Transformation Model. People who have gone through a personal transformation are able to live a life of meaning and purpose because they choose where to focus their energy. They choose to live in a place that I call the "blue zone" – a place of inner peace and well-being. This is where people are at their best (as shown in Fig. 3.8).

You can do this too!

Let's take this one piece at a time. Imagine that your life is a simple straight line, pictured as the dotted line in Fig. 3.8. This line represents you at your true self, nothing more and nothing less, in complete balance. Next is the version you wish you could be, shown on the top with a solid line labeled "ideal self." This is the highest version of you. This version of yourself is filled with hopes, dreams, fantasies, and wishes. Believe it or not, there are many people who have no clue what this is for them; they are living life aimlessly.

As you can see, there is a gap between your true self and your ideal self. Sometimes those two are closer together, and sometimes the two seem galaxies away. When the two are near each other is when we experience happiness and joy, because we are near proximity to the highest version of our self.

Life is an act of harmony and balance – this is where the worst version of self comes into play. This worst self is the exact opposite of our ideal self. We are at our worst when we are living below the line of our true self, far from our ideal self. When you find yourself at your lowest point, you will experience the most pain.

Now add other people's opinions. Whether we like it or not, others' words and opinions have an impact on us. It is possible to minimize the impact their opinions have on us, but it takes practice and conscious effort to do so. As you can see in Fig. 3.8, they are scattered throughout our lives, making themselves residents above and below the lines of our true self. Sometimes these opinions are positive and other times they are negative, but you can count on them always being present. It is up to you to decide which ones you will listen to and allow to impact your life.

The wavy lines represent our daily lives; sometimes they take us near our highest ideal self, and we feel like we are on top of the world, but that experience does not last forever, and it must balance itself by bringing us back down. In much the same way that we experience positivity, life will also find a way to give us negative experiences. Time spent in the negative space can sometimes feel like an eternity, but don't worry; these negative experiences and events won't last forever. They too must return to a balance state.

This gets us to the "blue zone," where people are at their best and living the life they want. Being in the blue zone means that you have found a way to merge your ideal self, true self, worst self, and others' perceptions of you with the waves that life throws at you. By merging them, you allow them to exist as they are while you live in the moment. With practice, you find yourself retaining a neutral mindset, which also allows you to take directive, focused action for the things you want in life. The more you practice, the more frequently you can visit those blue zones, as it is impossible to live in them full-time – something will always pull you out of them. Figure 3.9 depicts what it would look like to visit your blue zones across time.

Now that you understand the basic idea of merging for actualization, we can shift our thinking into its application with the Transformation Model. At this point, I

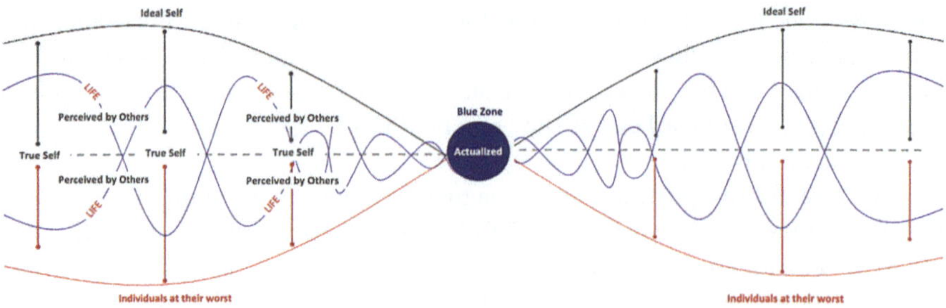

Fig. 3.9 Blue zone visits

want you to think about a time when you felt your best. Relive that moment in your mind – replay how you felt – see it vividly with all your senses. I want you to harness that feeling and practice visiting that place as often as you can. You will need that feeling when you practice creating your own transformation.

Creative space: Use the box below to take some notes on what it felt like to be in your blue zone – what it's like to be the best version of yourself. If you haven't had that feeling yet, that's what your imagination is for – create it!

To help you practice using the Transformation Model, I created a set of guided questions and dropped them into this section (see Tables 3.2 and 3.3) in the form of an easy-to-use table template. The table shows questions in the column on the left, with a few ideas to get you started in the column on the right. I recommend for you to print the template, invest time in actively writing out your responses to the questions, and when you are done, put them on the wall or somewhere that will force you to see them daily. I've had clients who make their responses on their computer screen; others print the sheet and place it in a picture frame on their desk. The bottom line is that you need to be consistently reminded of your goal. It is okay to change course along the way. You will need to adjust your path based on your challenges. However, your main goal and your "why" should remain stable.

Table 3.2 The Transformation Model as a guided questionnaire (*sample*)

The Transformation Model converted into a guided questionnaire		The Transformation Model serves as a mental model to think through a series of elements to leverage when creating a transformation
Best applied: At the onset of your idea – When you want your life to be different and you know that you are meant for more, but you are not sure how to do it *Instructions:* Make time to ask yourself the questions in the template below. Don't rush the process; dig deep within yourself		
What do I want to attain?		Be very specific and precise
Why do I want this? Why is this important to me?		Think of the meaning, value, and purpose. This is where you replay that amazing feeling of actualization. Remind yourself what it feels like to be the best version of yourself. Use that to keep you motivated and on track
How will I know I'm making progress? How will I know that I attained it?		Create a simple way to measure your progress and know what it will look like and feel when you have attained your goal
How long am I giving myself to attain my goal?		Careful with a short timeline, as you will have to be more aggressive with your dedication and focus. With a longer timeline, you have the risk of your goal being deprioritized
What will get in my way?		Many things will get in your way. The two most common barriers are the people you surround yourself with and the process you create (or neglect to create). Automate your process as much as you can

Note: Before you jump into the blank template to start your transformative journey, look at this sample I created for you. It is simple and designed to help you understand what you need to do for each question

Transformation of Others

After you use the Transformation Model on yourself and experiment with its core elements, it becomes easier to transition into helping others create their own transformation. A major difference between the transformation of self and the transformation of others is the focus of attention, energy, and resources. In the transformation of self, your entire focus is on you, your inner self, and your actualization. I argue that this is the most difficult of all three transformation types because you must be the coach and the one being coached at the same time. It requires you to get yourself unstuck, to be your own motivator, and to have enough awareness to be able to see your own blind spots. It is easier to help someone else transform because as an objective bystander, you can see when someone is headed for trouble far better than you can see it happening within yourself.

Transformation of others typically occurs through the process of coaching. This is not a requirement, but it is where it happens most commonly. The exciting part is that by now, you have learned all the elements of the Transformation Model and how they work together to create powerful outcomes. This means you don't have to spend much time relearning elements but can instead focus your attention and energy on helping others.

Table 3.3 Blank template: the Transformation Model as a guided questionnaire

The Transformation Model converted into a guided questionnaire	[redacted]	The Transformation Model serves as a mental model to think through a series of elements to leverage when creating a transformation
Best applied: At the onset of your idea – When you want your life to be different and you know that you are meant for more, but you are not sure how to do it *Instructions:* Make time to ask yourself these questions found in the template below. Don't rush the process; dig deep within yourself		
What do I want to attain?		
Why do I want this? Why is this important to me?		
How will I know I'm making progress? How will I know that I attained it?		
How long am I giving myself to attain my goal?		
What will get in my way?		

Note: Use this blank template to start your transformative journey. I care about you and your personal transformation. My email address is provided at the start of the chapter; stay in touch; I would love to hear about the progress you are making

Before we keep going forward, I want to talk about coaching. At some point in our lives, we have all experienced the feeling of being "stuck." Working with a coach can help us find clarity and overcome the barriers that hold us back.

What is a coach?

According to the International Coaching Federation (the gold standard in the coaching industry), coaching is defined as follows (ICF 2021):

> Partnering with clients in a thought-provoking and creative process that inspires them to maximize their personal and professional potential. The process of coaching often unlocks previously untapped sources of imagination, productivity, and leadership.

When coaching others, your job is to help them see their blind spots; you are not there to do the work for them. People will ask you to tell them what to do and give them the answers. You must refrain from doing so; your role as the coach is to ask powerful questions, so that the person you are coaching can do the work to experience their own transformation. The Transformation Model equips you to be their partner along their journey.

My advice is for you to begin your coaching engagements by understanding where the person you are working with is mentally and emotionally. Knowing where they spend their energy and mental resources will help you anticipate when and where they are most likely to get stuck. People spend most of their day thinking about two areas of their lives: the past or the future. The amount of time they spend ruminating over the past or future will give you a sense of how much regret (past) or anxiety (future) they will experience throughout the coaching agreement. Knowing the narrative they play in their minds will help you anticipate what they revert to when things get difficult, when they feel stressed, or when barriers present themselves. Your goal as their transformational coach is to encourage them to spend

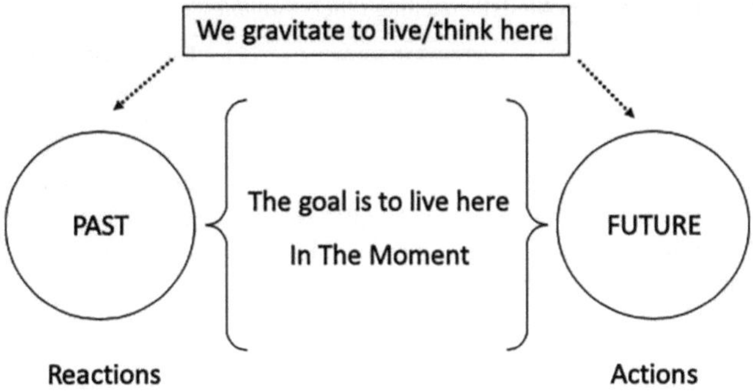

Fig. 3.10 Life within the brackets

more time within the brackets (see Fig. 3.10). To live within the brackets means to exist in the present moment. It means to understand that the past influences the future, but that that influence must travel through the present moment (Gutsioglou 2019). People have a choice in what parts of the past they allow to impact their future – they just don't realize it because it happens on autopilot (Gutsioglou 2020). That's where you come in as their transformational coach.

The average person will use what they know about the past to make decisions about the future. The decisions they make will be influenced by barriers and blockers in their lives, which means that identifying these things early will help keep them focused on the present moment and avoid getting stuck. As their coach, you can help them become more aware of what they can do to mitigate challenges by leveraging the support system element of the Transformation Model (Tables 3.4 and 3.5).

Reflection time: Use the box below to think about where you find yourself throughout the day. Are you the type of person who constantly thinks about the past, or are you the type of person who finds themselves in the future? If you were to capture your feelings in one word, what would that word be? Hint: you can use this activity when coaching others.

Table 3.4 The Transformation Model: coaching others (*sample*)

The Transformation Model converted into a guided questionnaire to coach others		The Transformation Model serves as a coaching map to help people think differently about how they see themselves and the world around them
Instructions: Use this template during the client intake process. Don't rush the process. Make sure to spend the time you need with each question. Move at the speed your client needs, not at the speed you want or think they should move		
What would you like to attain?	Have them describe in as much detail as they can. Get specific and precise responses	
Why is this important for you?	When the client gives you a response, keep digging into the question and ask them why in a different way. Have them dig deep into the meaning of their transformational goal. Don't be alarmed if they modify or change their goal. it is part of the discovery and growth process	
How will you know you attained it?	Have the focus on simple metrics. Keep them at a maximum of six metrics	
How long are you giving yourself to attain this?	Have them specify the exact date and time of completion. Be cautious of a very short or long timeline. Together you must sort out the proper duration	
What could get in the way?	Have the client reflect or tell a story of what prevented them from succeeding in the past. this will bring out potential future barriers/blockers. Remember, people and processes are the most common	
Are you willing to keep going when things get difficult?	Most people say yes, but quickly back out when things get difficult. Together, create a plan to prevent them from backing out	

Note: This sample is designed to help you understand what it looks like to use the Transformation Model when coaching others

Table 3.5 The Transformation Model: coaching others (*sample*)

The Transformation Model converted into a guided questionnaire to coach others		The Transformation Model serves as a coaching map to help people think differently about how they see themselves and the world around them
Instructions: Use this template during the client intake process. Don't rush the process. Make sure to spend the time you need with each question. Move at the speed your client needs, not at the speed you want or think they should move		
What would you like to attain?		
Why is this important for you?		
How will you know you attained it?		
How long are you giving yourself to attain this?		
What could get in the way?		
Are you willing to keep going when things get difficult?		

Note: Use this blank template to help others with their transformative journey

Transformation of Organizations

The next type of transformation we are talking about is known as organizational transformation or business transformation, which is a business strategy to move an organization from its current state into a desired future state.

Why would an organization need to transform?

The business world is filled with rapid, constant changes that force organizations to reimagine the way they work and how they go to market. Sometimes the changes are due to new technological advances, automation of old business processes, or shifting market conditions. Ultimately, it does not matter where the change stems from – in the end, it always requires people to think and behave in different ways. Without people doing things differently, there is no transformation, and the organization withers away. Senior business executives are paid to keep the organization alive and profitable for as long as possible. This requires organizational leaders to think of ways to keep the company ahead of its competitors. To accomplish this, they must go through a process called strategic planning, in which they analyze their current internal landscape and compare it to that of competitors, the industry, and the economy. The result is a multiyear strategic plan filled with decisions and target objectives that impact the organization at large. Fig. 3.11 depicts a simplified visualization of an organization's gap analysis (i.e., current state vs. future state) and transformative journey.

The transformation of organizations is nearly identical to the transformation of self (see Figs. 3.1 and 3.11) and the transformation of others. All transformations begin with the acceptance that change is needed. In organizations, key decision-makers must be willing to put the lives of many people through a treacherous journey to reach a desired future state. The biggest difference among the three types of transformations is that organizational transformations require many people to simultaneously agree to change. However, the path to achieving the desired future state can be accomplished using the Transformation Model.

Who would use the Transformation Model in these situations?

The most common types of people who utilize the Transformation Model are organizational leaders, management consultants, human resources professionals, or change management practitioners. They create the conditions to facilitate a mass

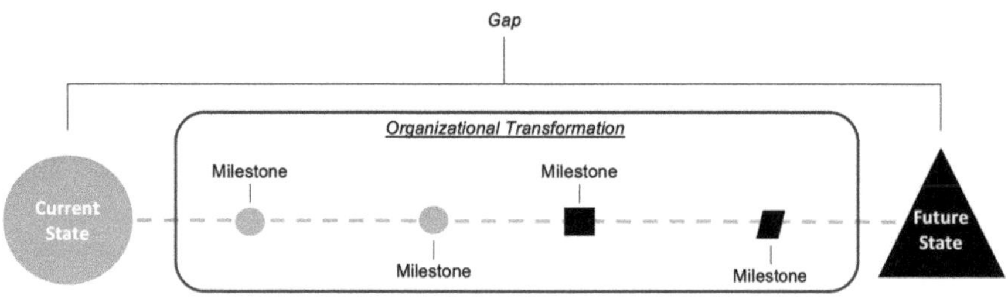

Fig. 3.11 Current state versus future state

transformative movement through many people, and they are the ones who must define and measure success along the way (i.e., the transformation).

A great way for you to learn how the Transformation Model applies to large, complex organizations is to see it through a short business case. Through the case, I will teach you about the specific levers you must use, the questions to ask when applying the Transformation Model, and the outcomes you can expect.

▶ Business Case: From Paper to the Cloud

Note

This case has been simplified with several assumptions to illustrate the process. A real situation can take months or years to move through each of the steps and phases mentioned in this case.

Your Avatar

To make the most of this example, you will play the role of the transformation consultant. I will be your ghost consultant, giving you advice on what to do and when and how to do it.

The Background

A newly appointed senior executive of a marketing agency has reached out to you personally to ask if you will help them with their transformation. After several back-and-forth conversations, you decide to accept the work.

The C-suite of this Fortune 500 company with a global presence has decided to make a bold move from archaic business processes into modern cloud-based processes. There are a minimum of 20 technology-related projects, but the project you are working on is one of the most critical. The leaders have tagged it as a digital transformation, and it will require everyone in the organization to change the ways they think and behave. If the project is successful, the organization will be entirely different – unlike anything it has ever known. To add to the complexity, there are three simultaneous transformations occurring within this organization: digital, process, and cultural transformation with a 5-year timeline.

Transformation projects		
Technology	Process	Cultural
Paper to cloud	Standard and global	Employee and customer centric
Years 1–2	*Years 3–4*	*Year 5*

The Transformation Model in Action

As the transformation consultant, you start with an intake conversation with your client the lead executive sponsor.

Your intake includes the items below:

1. What would you like to accomplish?
2. Why is this important for you (or the organizational leaders)?
3. How will you know you have accomplished this goal? In other words, how will you measure progress and ultimate success?
4. How much time do you project it will realistically take to reach the future state?
5. What are some of the barriers or blockers this project will experience along the way?

After your intake conversation, you think like a researcher and proceed with the following:

1. Reflect on your intake conversation and observations.
2. Form a hypothesis.
3. Create a testable approach using the Transformation Model.
4. Make a prediction based on your hypothesis.
5. Implement elements of the Transformation Model into your approach.
6. Gather feedback and iterate as needed.

Here are some of the challenges you learned about in this conversation:

- The company holds decentralized business processes all around the world.
- The goal is to standardize and globalize technology and business processes.
- They have been using an old system that was 100% customized.
- The developers of the system are expected to retire within 2 years.
- There was a failed attempt; you are the second consultant attempting this.

I am a visual thinker, so as your ghost consultant, I have an illustration to help you visualize what the process will look like from start to finish (see Fig. 3.12).

Keep in mind that this transformation will not be a clean linear approach. In fact, it will be ugly, hostile, and chaotic because you will be disrupting years of programmed behaviors in many people. The average person is on autopilot for most of their day. From the moment people wake up in the morning to the moment they fall asleep, they perform a set of autopilot behaviors that allow them to efficiently go about their day (Fig. 3.13). The moment they are asked to deviate from their routine and become aware/conscious of their actions, they slow down (Gutsioglou 2019). When the tasks they are asked to do are not in alignment with their routine, they resist and challenge the process.

Figure 3.14 shows how you as the transformation consultant need to explore what is hiding beneath the surface – your path to behavior modification is through

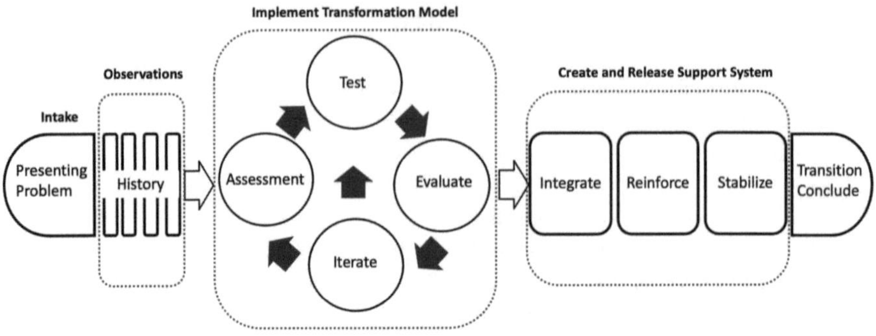

Fig. 3.12 From intake conversation to transition phase

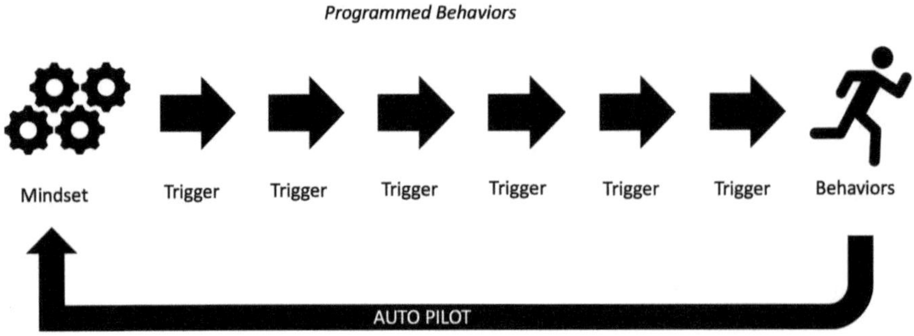

Fig. 3.13 Autopilot programmed behaviors

attitudes, beliefs, behaviors, and emotions. You can do this by obtaining a baseline of the patterns across the organization through focus groups, observations, and surveys. If you want to help people transform, you must understand them before you can help them become aware of their actions and how they align with the future (Gutsioglou 2019). Focus on creating alignment between their world and the transformative world you are trying to create.

At this point, you instruct your client to get senior executive involvement to cascade key messages throughout the organization. It is important for the top of the organization to direct the rest of the organization regarding which way to go. You must ensure that the messaging pushes downward as strategic objectives and enterprise priority. This will create clarity surrounding the fact that each business function must align with this transformation. The purpose is to get the rest of the organization involved, as it is critical for every person to be aware of what is happening and know what is expected of them throughout the journey. Expectation setting is typically achieved when initiative owners build roles, responsibilities, and key performance indicators that are shared through a communication plan. Remember: If progress can't be measured, then it will not take place. It would be terrible if everyone moved in different/opposite directions – or, worse, if they didn't make any progress. The last action lever you want to utilize is training and

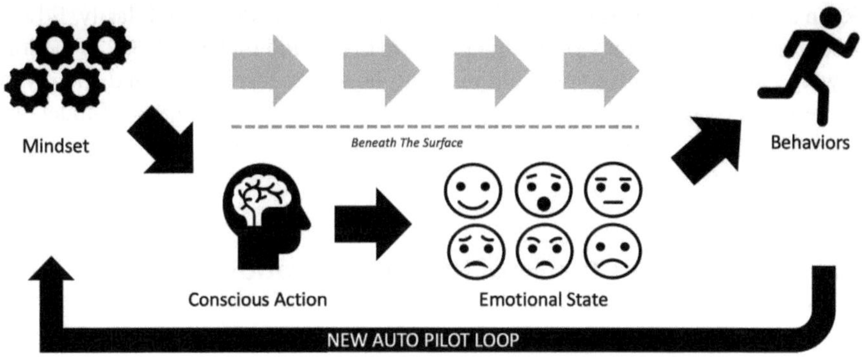

Fig. 3.14 New autopilot loop

Table 3.6 Transformation Model for complex transformations

Activity levers	Ask	Outcome
Executive involvement	What do you want to accomplish? Why do you want it?	Clarity, purpose, and alignment with strategy
Community involvement	How can people rally around this? What challenges might the community experience? How can they support each other?	Engagement from the community
Communication plan	How can we use the community to spread awareness?	A support system is created
Measuring progress	How will we keep track?	Ensuring you are on track
Knowledge transfer behavior sustainment	What can be done to maintain momentum?	Ways to reinforce desired behaviors

knowledge transfer, which is crucial for behavior sustainment. To help you see how specific activity levers and the Transformation Model work together, I have consolidated them into a simple view (see Table 3.6).

Congratulations! You have helped your client reach a transformative milestone. From your Transformation Model training, you know that a transformation is ongoing and requires a continuous evolution, so your next challenge is to help your client find an answer to the next question they will ask themselves: we've gotten this far, and we are no longer the same organization – what do we do next?

Theories That Inspired the Transformation Model

There are four theories that inspired my work on the Transformation Model, starting with Abraham Maslow's theory of human motivation (Maslow 1943), followed by Albert Bandura's view on self-efficacy (Bandura 1977), Edward Deci and Richard

Ryan's (SDT) self-determination theory (Deci and Ryan 1985), and, lastly, Edwin Locke and Gary Latham's goal setting theory (Locke and Latham 1990). In the following pages, I will give you a glimpse into how they inspired me and show you some of the ways in which I integrated them into the Transformation Model. To keep this short, I will share them as high-level overviews.

Let's begin with…

Abraham Maslow's Theory of Human Motivation

The reason I created the Transformation Model is because I believe that people are destined for more, and that if they apply themselves, they can achieve many great things. The first time I read Abraham Maslow's *A Theory of Human Motivation*, my world was rocked; my view on life and the potential for human capabilities completely changed. I attribute my inspiration and worldview on human potential to two specific passages from Maslow's paper.

The first passage that inspired my philosophy on human potential states the following:

> A musician must make music, an artist must paint, a poet must write, if he is to be ultimately happy. What a man can be, he must be. This need we may call self-actualization. (Maslow 1943, p. 382)

This is when I realized that as humans, we have an innate programmed need for more. There is something within us all that drives and fuels us to keep pushing forward until we achieve a state of happiness, but happiness is not a state of permanence. Which means that we will forever chase it, and with luck, some of us will lead a life that truly matters to our inner core.

The next passage helped me see why some people want more in life, while others settle when their basic needs are satisfied.

The passage reads as follows:

> People who have never experienced chronic hunger are apt to underestimate its effects and to look upon food as a rather unimportant thing. If they are dominated by a higher need, this higher need will seem to be the most important of all. (Maslow 1943, p. 387)

My mind exploded (figuratively, of course) when I understood that satisfaction of needs is a huge driver of animal motivation. Every animal will do what it must until its needs are fulfilled; only then will they be able to focus their energy and attention on the next need in the hierarchy. I spent subsequent days, months, and years studying myself, family, friends, colleagues, and strangers – all of which has brought me to the conclusion that I was put on this earth to help others find their way. I have been chasing that need to create transformations ever since. As an artist must paint, a transformer must transform.

Maslow's ideas gave me a perpetual energy to see the greatness in others. It set me on a path of self-discovery, self-expression, and actualization. While on this

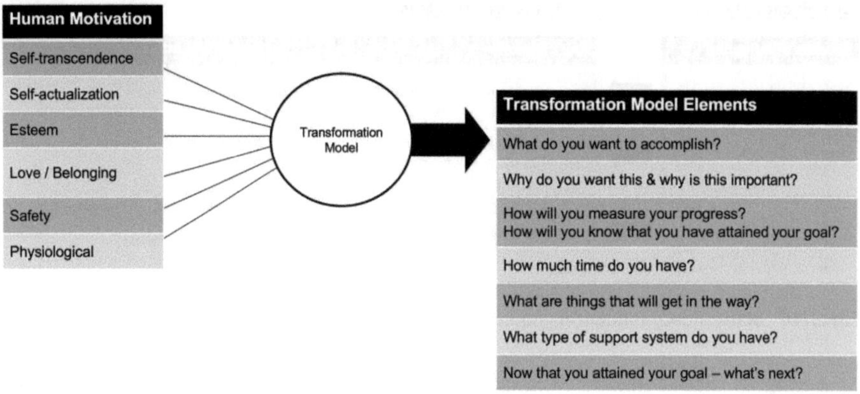

Fig. 3.15 Maslow's theory of human motivation and the Transformation Model

path, I have seen firsthand that people's needs monopolize their thoughts and behaviors. The only way that they can surpass their arrested development is by satisfying each need and actualizing what hides beneath the surface. When a person lacks the resources, capability, or tools to satisfy their needs, they will live a dissatisfied life.

I created the Transformation Model to give people a tool that shows them the way they must walk to find their inner greatness, their actualized life – their blue zone (refer to Fig. 3.8). The link between Maslow's theory of human motivation and the Transformation Model is simple. To illustrate this point, see Fig. 3.15, in which I demonstrate that a person can select a need as shown in Maslow's work and take it into the Transformation Model.

Any person who wants more and knows they are meant for more in life can use the Transformation Model to achieve it; they just need to be clear on the need or goal they are working on. I believe that anyone can start with any need (from Maslow's theory) and move into the Transformation Model to achieve what they are looking for. With the Transformation Model, people are better prepared in their journey to fully utilize their talents and abilities for a fulfilling life.

Albert Bandura's Unifying Theory of Behavioral Change

Studying Maslow's ideas helped me to see that a person's drive and motivation for behavioral change are rooted in a cognitive state (i.e., "I need food," "I need a promotion," "I need someone to love," etc.). The need to fulfill something begins as a thought, but it is a person's actions that lead to physical expression of that fulfillment. A major driving force in this process is a person's belief that they can achieve a desired outcome. It is this belief (i.e., self-efficacy) that fuels the behaviors that grant people access to goal attainment and ultimate success. Bandura said it best with the following quote:

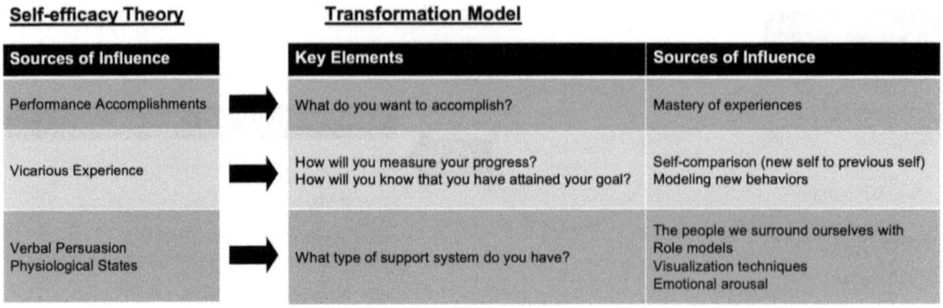

Fig. 3.16 Self-efficacy influencers on key elements of the Transformation Model

> Among the mechanisms of human agency, none is more central or pervasive than people's beliefs in their efficacy to influence events that affect their lives. This core belief is the foundation of human inspiration, motivation, performance accomplishments, and emotional well-being. Unless people believe they can produce desired effects by their actions, they have little incentive to undertake activities or to persevere in the face of difficulties. (Bandura 2018)

Bandura (1977, 1994, 2000) argued that when a person thinks about a future goal, they start by assessing whether certain actions will help them attain or avoid a given outcome. Their expectations about the actions they must take will be influenced by four sources (i.e., performance accomplishments, vicarious experience, verbal persuasion, and physiological states). These sources will in turn influence future behaviors. When a person is thinking about their future and their goals, they will revisit past experiences (i.e., sources of influence), which function by creating confidence boosters (e.g., "I believe I can do this!") or self-limiting beliefs (e.g., "There's no way, why even try!").

When I began building the Transformation Model, I knew that I had to find a way to strengthen people's mindsets while they were on their transformative journey. In my design, I integrated Bandura's self-efficacy into key elements of the Transformation Model to help people believe in themselves and to create a support system that they could rely on when things got difficult. Figure 3.16 shows how I connected self-efficacy sources of influence to key elements of the Transformation Model and their sources of influence.

Deci and Ryan's Self-Determination Theory

Bandura's work unlocked a new dimension of thought for me – that the path to success begins in the form of a thought, and a person can achieve many great things when they believe in themselves. This means that each time a person succeeds and rises through the challenges they face along the way, their mindset strengthens, and they can tap into that strength the next time they need it. However, in my early days of building the Transformation Model and working with clients around the world, I noticed that the overall outcome was consistently and significantly influenced by more than just a person's belief system. When you believe you can achieve something, you will try your best to achieve it. And so, my internal dialogue kicked in with a few questions:

Will different types of goals influence a person's mindset and behaviors? What other forces influence a person's thoughts and actions? Allow me to introduce you to self-determination theory (Deci and Ryan 1985), or SDT for short. SDT is a working theory that examines socio-contextual factors influencing human motivation and behavior. Deci and Ryan proposed that motivation begins from within but is highly influenced by forces beyond the inner self. Given that SDT is a large body of work and spans many areas, I will be doing it a disservice by trying to explain it all to you here. Instead, I encourage you to visit the Center for Self-Determination Theory website (https://selfdeterminationtheory.org) to learn more about the framework and its six mini-theories. For this section, I direct your attention to two specific mini-theories within the SDT framework that influenced my design of the Transformation Model.

The first mini-theory I used when building the Transformation Model was the basic psychological needs theory, or BPNT for short. According to BPNT, there are three underlying factors (i.e., needs) that influence intrinsic motivation: (1) self-determination (sometimes seen as autonomy), (2) competence, and (3) relatedness (Deci and Ryan 1985). Although SDT is mainly psychological, it postulates that human behavior is largely influenced by "experiences" – these experiences will satisfy or frustrate the psychological factors (i.e., needs) that drive a person's future behavior.

Here's how I align key elements of the Transformation Model with the three factors of BPNT.

Key elements of the Transformation Model	BPNT
Why do you want this/why is this important?	Self-determination (autonomy)
How will you measure your progress? How will you know that you have attained your goal?	Competence
What are things that will get in the way?	Competence, autonomy
What type of support system do you have?	Relatedness
What happens after you attain your goal?	Autonomy and competence

When I work with a client on a transformation, I focus on helping them build a map and plan that will satisfy their basic psychological needs along the way (Gutsioglou 2021). Doing so increases the resiliency and persistence they will need when things get difficult on the way to their goal. When they experience a setback, it will only be momentary because they have a plan to get them through it.

The second mini-theory I used when designing the Transformation Model was the goal contents theory (GCT for short), which highlights that there is a difference and clear distinction between intrinsic goals, extrinsic goals, and the impact they have on motivation and the overall well-being of a person. To clarify, intrinsic goals relate to things like relationships, personal growth, family, partnerships, and community, while extrinsic goals relate to things like monetary success, physical

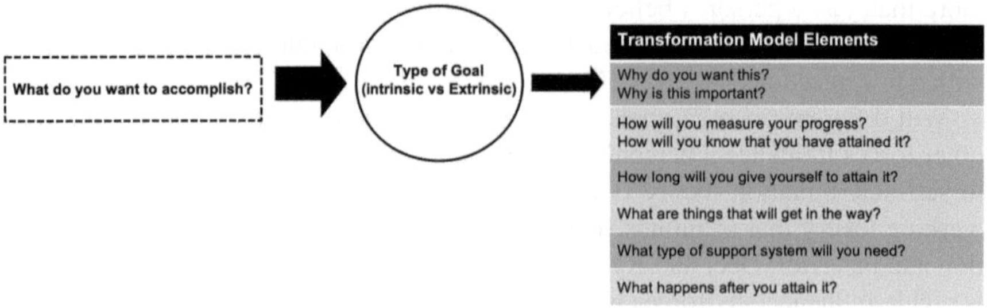

Fig. 3.17 Key elements of the Transformation Model with goal content theory

appearance, material goods, and fame or popularity. The premise of the theory is that a person will choose a type of goal (intrinsic or extrinsic) based on the things they value in life.

Here's how I aligned key elements of the Transformation Model with the goal contents theory.

As shown in Fig. 3.17, I begin engagements with the question, "What would you like to accomplish?" The response informs me what type of goal the person wants to work toward. Before jumping into solutions, I like to focus on understanding why the goal is important to the person. I find ways to ask the same question in multiple ways. I push the client to dig deep. This is important because it will help create alignment in the implementation strategy. To say it another way, someone interested in fulfilling a personal growth goal (e.g., building close relationships) will not perform well with extrinsic plans or strategies. It is imperative that there be alignment between you and what your client wants to accomplish (i.e., type of goal). This holds true if you are using the Transformation Model on yourself; I still recommend creating plans that align with the type of goal you want to accomplish. This increases your likelihood of sticking with the plan and accomplishing your goal.

As a word of caution, be careful with the types of clients you take and the types of goals you work on with them. I have found that people who focus solely on attaining extrinsic materialistic-type goals are perpetually unhappy and see the world in a negative way. They may reach their desired state and attain their goal, but they will consistently compare themselves to others and only see what they don't have. This sets them on a chase wherein they are always looking to find happiness from an object (or money or someone's approval). On the other hand, I have found that people who focus on achieving intrinsic personal growth-type goals are generally happier, more satisfied with life, and find ways to help others along their transformative journeys. Of course, I am making a general statement and would be foolish to tell you that everyone with an extrinsic- or intrinsic-type goal is the same – that's just wrong. However, understanding a person's goal type will tell you a great deal about the person, their story, and their commitment to the journey ahead.

Locke and Latham's Goal Setting Theory

Deci and Ryan's (1985) work on self-determination theory helped me see that people will focus their attention, energy, and resources on obtaining the things they see as valuable, whether that be financial success or a small number of close relationships. If I were to consolidate and simplify my view of SDT into a single simple sentence, it would be this:

People's views of the world will influence their goals and direct their behaviors.

This leads me to Edwin Locke and Gary Latham's (1990) goal setting theory (GST for short), the fourth theory that influenced my work on the Transformation Model. My research team and I had the honor of having Dr. Locke join our lab during one of our meetings, where we shared with him our ideas about the Transformation Model. He liked what we were building and how we were trying to help people in the process. During our conversation, he explained that a person's behavior is purposeful and fully regulated by the goals they set for themselves. Then he said something very simple that illuminated my view on GST and how we could use it to amplify our work with the Transformation Model.

Dr. Locke said:

> Life is a goal directed process. (Locke 2021, Personal Communication)

Then, he went on to say that goal setting theory started as a way for them to understand the reason why some people are more successful than others in achieving task performance goals. Locke and Latham were particularly interested in the following question: If people are the same in respect to knowledge, skills, and abilities, then what makes the successful ones different from the unsuccessful ones? He told us that it basically comes down to a person's conscious motivation. Motivation contributes to task performance and outcomes. Goal setting theory was created and expanded using an inductive approach, and it has been explored by many researchers from all over the world across several decades. Time after time, motivation shows up as a key contributor in task performance.

It is important to note that motivation is influenced by clarity, challenge, commitment, feedback, and task complexity. This is an excellent time to remind you about the support system mixer analogy I shared with you earlier in this chapter (refer to Fig. 3.7). Basically, if any of the motivation influencers are out of range for a person (e.g., too low/not challenging enough or too high/impossible to achieve), then motivation will dissipate. Alternatively, if a task or goal is too challenging or perceived as impossible to attain by the individual, then their motivation will drop to the point that they will not try. The same holds true for all other motivation characteristics. Having this knowledge of motivation, I started to think of ways to incorporate GST characteristics into the Transformation Model.

Here's how I aligned key elements of the Transformation Model with goal setting theory characteristics (Table 3.7).

Table 3.7 Key elements of the Transformation Model with goal setting theory

Key elements of the Transformation Model	Goal setting theory characteristics
What do you want to accomplish?	Clarity (specificity)
Why do you want this? Why is this important?	Commitment
How will you measure progress? How will you know you have attained it?	Clarity, feedback
How long will you give yourself to attain it?	Challenge, commitment
What are things that will get in the way?	Challenge, complexity
What type of support system will you need?	Clarity, feedback
What happens after you attain it?	Clarity, feedback, commitment

As you can see, I mapped key elements of the Transformation Model with the motivation characteristics found within goal setting theory. When I use the Transformation Model with my clients, I quickly get them to establish clarity, create a plan of action that nourishes commitment, and focus on tangible achievable actions and behaviors that build positive reinforcement throughout their journey (Gutsioglou 2020).

Conclusion

You and I began this journey talking about transformation and how it leads to the creation of a new version of yourself. I even shared my own transformational journey. I told you about a story I call "Origins" and how it sparked the fire that stills burns within me today to help others live the life they deserve. Then, throughout the chapter, I challenged you to closely examine your own level of consciousness, I showed you how to help others to expand their self-awareness, and I gave you some practical tools that you can use to coach others on how to create their very own transformations.

You and I have covered a lot during our time together. Just to recap what you have learned, I will provide you with a list of the key ideas and principles that we have covered in our journey together:

1. We began our journey with the "Origins" of my personal transformation.
2. We took a closer look at the concepts of change and transformation.
3. We examined the difference between change and transformation and examined how they work together.
4. I shared the story of how the Transformation Model came into existence.
5. I walked you through each element that makes up the Transformation Model.
6. You had the opportunity to learn how the Transformation Model applies to three different types of transformations.
   (a) Transformation of self
   (b) Transformation of others
   (c) Transformation of complex organizations

7. I told you about the four theories that inspired my work with the Transformation Model.
   (a) Maslow's theory of human motivation
   (b) Bandura's self-efficacy
   (c) Deci and Ryan's self-determination theory
   (d) Locke and Latham's goal setting theory

As I bring our time to a close, I want to thank you for reading my chapter. I hope you can use the Transformation Model on yourself or others. I truly believe it can help people achieve their dreams. I will leave you with this final piece of advice:

If you want to be different, you must think differently!

References

Bandura A (1977) Self-efficacy: toward a unifying theory of behavioral change. Psychol Rev 84:191–215

Bandura A (1994) Self-efficacy. In: Ramachaudran VS (ed) Encyclopedia of human behavior, vol 4. Academic, New York, pp 71–81

Bandura A (2000) Cultivate self-efficacy for personal and organizational effectiveness. In: Locke EA (ed) Handbook of principles of organization behavior. Blackwell, Oxford, pp 120–136

Bandura A (2018) Self-efficacy. https://albertbandura.com/albert-bandura-self-efficacy.html

Creasy T (2021) Change vs change management. Prosci. Retrieved June 6, 2021, from https://blog.prosci.com/Change-vs-Change-Management

Deci EL, Ryan RM (1985) Intrinsic motivation and self-determination in human behavior. Plenum, New York

Gutsioglou AM (2019) The round table: how to leverage the skills of multiple professions to revitalize a situation. Think Differently LLC, Los Angeles

Gutsioglou AM (2020) How to hack your brain and behavior to perform like a champion. LinkedIn Publishing. Retrieved from https://www.linkedin.com/pulse/how-hack-your-brain-behavior-perform-like-champion-gutsioglou-ph-d/

Gutsioglou AM (2021) Create your future: a plan based on meaning and purpose. Think Differently LLC. Retrieved from https://www.drabrahamgutsioglou.com/post/create-your-future-a-plan-based-on-meaning-purpose

ICF, the Gold Standard in Coaching | Read About ICF (2021) International Coaching Federation. Retrieved October 31, 2021, from https://coachfederation.org/about

Locke EA, Latham GP (1990) A theory of goal setting and task performance. Prentice Hall, Englewood Cliffs

Maslow A (1943) A theory of human motivation. Psychol Rev 50:370–396. https://doi.org/10.1037/h0054346

Merriam-Webster (n.d.-a) Change. In: Merriam-Webster.com dictionary. Retrieved May 22, 2021, from https://www.merriam-webster.com/dictionary/change

Neal J (2018) An overview of the field of transformation. In: Handbook of personal and organization. Springer. https://doi.org/10.1007/978-3-319-66893-2_26

Part II

Educational Transformation

A Return to Virtue: Embodiment, Chakras and Management Education

4

Kathryn Pavlovich

Abstract

This chapter explores the development of an innovative teaching method through integrating Eastern and Western philosophies that may create moral leaders. In a course, Self-Actualising Leadership, students are required to write two reflexive journals examining how their leadership is informed by virtues and are encouraged to examine this as an embodiment through the Eastern Vedic chakra system. The chapter describes the teaching innovation and the transformational learning that takes place, elucidated through student comments that are written in assignments. The chapter contributes to our understanding of transformation processes by demonstrating how virtues are stable and enduring through habitual practice; are multidimensional through integrating emotional, physical and spiritual perspectives; and may become the communal narrative for creating self-other awareness for a flourishing society.

Keywords

Chakra · Self-other awareness · Spirituality · Management education · Virtues

Introduction

Transforming management education from the more traditional practice of 'filling up' students with facts, knowledge and practices (Ramsey and Fitzgibbons 2005) to one of deep personal growth and awareness requires a shift in mindsets, attitudes and values. While Kuechler and Stedham (2018) posit that there is no standard

K. Pavlovich (✉)
Waikato Management School, Hamilton, New Zealand
e-mail: kathryn.pavlovich@waikato.ac.nz

J. Neal (ed.), *Personal, Educational and Organizational Transformation*, Future of Business and Finance, https://doi.org/10.1007/978-3-031-29253-8_4

method for improving transformational learning, there are many examples that demonstrate how shifting the focus to the student, their own experiences and resolution of unresolved feelings, thoughts and emotions can have a profound impact (Durant et al. 2017; Pavlovich 2010). Management education needs to place the student at the centre of the transformational inquiry, requiring experiential and engaged practices where students can reshape their thinking and develop new perspectives. Taylor and Cranton (2013) highlight that the student experience is central to transformational learning as it is the closest medium for reshaping patterns, and thus is the starting point for dialogue.

Critiquing the more common path of empirical science, Nisker (1998) stated that they reinforced that 'we live inside the bubble of the "self" as though we are "in here" and everything else is "out there"' (cited in Jotin Khisty 2006, p. 296). There is, therefore, increasing evidence that we need an alternative narrative that returns the focus to ourselves and how we act, as knowing our inner world is not possible by only observing the exterior world around us (Manz 2015; Scharmer 2009).

A focus on the inner world highlights that we humans are predisposed to virtuous behaviour (Sadler-Smith 2012) and advances a moral awareness of how we act. This awareness again attends to critique that business schools are too busy maximising shareholder value and economic self-interest rather than developing moral responsibility in students (Ghoshal 2005). Yet as MacIntyre (1981) explained there is a crisis in modern society, one that he calls 'emotivism', where morality is not based on community values, but on ideologically bound goals and values in which 'all moral judgments are nothing but expressions of preferences' (p. 12). Aristotle considered that the ultimate goal of human existence was the pursuit of excellences (arête), translated as virtues (Morales-Sánchez and Cabello-Medina 2015). Striving for excellence of character was deemed a necessary activity so that we humans could live in and collectively create a 'good society'. Bright et al. (2014, p. 452) concurred that 'a virtuous person cultivates habits of mind, intention, and behaviour that align with one's understanding of goodness, concern for achieving meaningful life, and creating positive human impact'. This may be achieved through the habitual internalisation and implementation of moral virtue that Aristotle (2009) claimed is the most ennobling of human behaviours. Living a life of moral virtue therefore means 'focusing on what a person is, including a person's dispositions to act in ways appropriate…, and to emphasise the unity and continuity of life' (Weaver 2006, p. 344).

The teachability of virtue, however, comes under scrutiny in management education. The development of moral character has been largely ignored, and some even question whether virtues are teachable (Crossan et al. 2013a; Hartman 2006). Indeed, Giacalone and Promislo (2013, p. 90) suggest that there is a stigmatisation of goodness, where 'students are taught to believe that being virtuous is dangerous and can undermine the materialist values that our culture has come to accept'. However, while teaching goodness may be difficult (Mintz 1996), Crossan et al. (2013b, p. 291) suggest that there is no empirical evidence to suggest that virtue is 'unteachable'.

Yet we may need to go beyond conventional Western methods to assist in the facilitation of such a transformation process. Many Eastern traditions continue to emphasise the importance of teaching goodness that emerges from the inner self rather than only teaching subjects. Weick and Putnam (2006), for instance, note that Western learning is concerned with creating knowledge as externalised objects, whereas Eastern learning focuses more on the internal processes of the mind that form awareness of the subjective self. This shift is important, as a central factor in the teachability of virtues is that they are more than a cognitive theoretical exercise, and developing appropriate ways of acting comes from an embodied living-in of experience. Mintz (1996, p. 829) explains that 'we become just by the practice of just actions, courageous by performing acts of courage. [These] characteristics develop from corresponding activities'. This 'learning-from-living shapes our personal notions of what is good and bad, right or wrong' (Klimoski 2006, p. 66). Eastern philosophies extend this understanding by claiming that the body (through the breath and the senses) is an important pathway to wisdom (Sinclair 2014).

The concept of embodiment, however, has not been widely examined in management education. Sutherland and Ladkin (2013) argue that the influence of the body ought to be given more attention in education because 'It is through our bodies that we most profoundly communicate our intentions and through our bodies we comprehend the impact of our classroom actions. Our bodies tell us most directly how an engagement is going' (p. 106). Marshall (2015, p. 260) too explains 'The body itself is not merely an object among other objects, but is itself the phenomenal body or "the situation from which our world and experience flows"'. The body is therefore the vehicle through which we connect the environment that we experience and the individual's sense-making of that experience (Merleau-Ponty 1964).

To integrate these two concepts – the cultivation of virtue and embodiment – I developed a teaching innovation using an eastern philosophy, the ancient Vedic chakra system, and reflexive practice intended to shift cognitive processing and rehabituate transformational behaviours. Engagement with the chakra system is intended to extend awareness of others; thus it offers an important lens for supporting students awareness of their own experience within a broader landscape that includes issues such as climate change, inequity and other grand challenges. Integrating these two concepts – broadening awareness of the self-other relationship through reflexive practice regarding virtuous action – may empower students to create positive action in organisations.

The following sections thus discuss the chakra system, the teaching innovation, student applications for learning and finally the chapter concludes with theoretical contributions.

Virtues and Chakras

First mentioned in the Vedic texts of the seventeenth century BC, chakras link the human body and mind into a single system to expand our conscious awareness. Chakra means 'wheel' in Sanskrit and refers to seven major wheel-like energy

Fig. 4.1 Chakra and anatomy. (Source: Vivekananda 2005, p. 38)

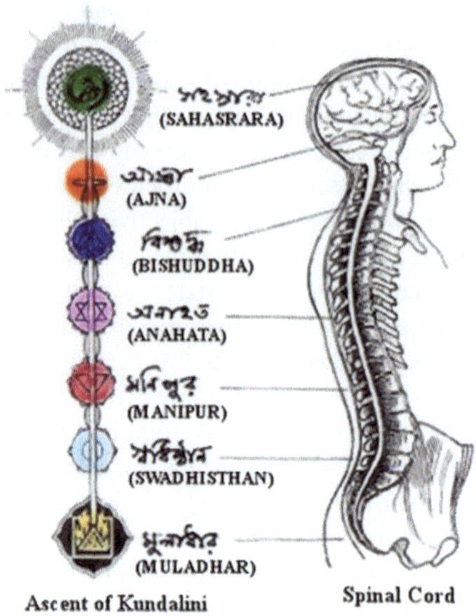

Source: Vivekananda (2005, p. 38)

vortexes in the body. Each of these vortexes is a discrete energy centre and is located along the spinal axis (see Fig. 4.1). It is claimed that through balancing these centres, one can become more harmonic with life, which may open us up to goodness through our direct experience (Hayashi 2015). Two features need special mention as they link the chakras with virtues. The first is that both require balancing. Like the chakra system, Bright et al. (2014) observe that virtues similarly require moderation as at the extremes they can be deficient or excessive (e.g. the virtue of compassion is cold-heartedness as a weakness and indulgence as an excess). Hence, virtues and the chakra energy points both have an ideal point for the optimal expression. Second, the chakra system has similarities with Maslow's (1943) hierarchy of needs system, suggesting that Maslow may have been greatly influenced by these ancient Vedic texts (Scandurra 1999; Beshara 2013). The familial elements of physiological, safety, belonging, esteem and self-actualisation correspond with the chakra energy vortexes (described below). Both models (Maslow's hierarchy of needs and the chakra system) suggest that evolvement is an upward spiral and that the categories fall into physical, intellectual and spiritual domains. However, Wilber (1981) argues that Maslow's lowest need (physiological) does not equate with the lowest level in the chakra structure as it is not so much a developmental process, as it is an ongoing survival activity. This, he argues, is the only significant difference. This difference is also noted by Barrett (2015) who too suggested that this lowest layer was about finding stability in life rather than being part of a growth trajectory. In his later years, Maslow amended his model to add self-transcendence at the top of his hierarchy. This final step acknowledges that engaging in goodness through service to others can assist in social change, akin to religious and Eastern traditions of transcendence and mysticism (Koltko-Rivera 2006). Hence, the chakra system has a deep lineage and offers complexity as a transformational learning tool through its integration of emotional, physiological and philosophical elements.

Vivekananda (2005, p. 38) notes that awareness and practice of chakra purification has physical, emotional and mental impacts, all of which enhance spiritual enlightenment. The interdependency of these body/energy/mind energy systems enable the expansion of human vitality through the practice of finding balance and harmonisation. Yet, the practice of chakra harmonisation is claimed to have significant positive physical, mental and emotional impacts (Vivekananda 2005). The physical impacts include strengthening of the nerve plexuses, endocrine glands and muscles and joints; mental impacts are developed though increasing neuroplasticity from flexible connections and pathways; and emotional impacts through reducing cortisol levels indicating lower impacts from stress and trauma through purification and revitalisation via the breath. While these assertions are significant, the student comments as a result of their reflexive practices integrating the mind, body and emotions did confirm a number of these claims.

As I explain the chakra system and its teaching application in the following section, I first explain the individual chakra points and their specific attributes as described in Table 4.1. The chakras are identified by number, with 1 (base) having the lowest vibration to 7 (head) the highest (columns one and two). More commonly, they are known by their Sanskrit names (column three), with Maslow's corresponding levels noted in column four. The meaning of each energy vortex is briefly described in column five, suggesting that focus on this chakra can purify this energy vortex. Columns six and seven outline the qualities of each chakra in their positive and negative expressions.

Purification of these chakras, as it is said, can occur through intentional focus and meditation and also through virtuous behaviour and actions. Hence, column eight in the table notes virtues associated with each chakra. Over the years, as I experimented with the chakra system in the classroom (described in detail in the following section), it became clear that the balancing of these chakras often had a direct relationship with specific virtues.

The mooladhara (base) chakra relates to security issues and thus can be balanced through gratitude; knowing that one's needs are provided by universal forces when one sees the world through grace. The second chakra, swadhisthana, concerns emotional balance. When unbalanced, emotional dramas can be experienced and pursued. A balanced spleen chakra neutralises emotion within relationships and is related to the virtue of forgiveness. The manipura chakra relates to power through both overuse and underuse. It is easy to see those who abuse power, but equally significant are those who are too shy to fully stand up for themselves. As Williamson (1992) noted, and popularised by Nelson Mandela, 'our deepest fear is that we are powerful beyond measure. It is our light, not our darkness that most frightens us'. Thus, this chakra is related to the balance by acknowledging self-worth with humility. The fourth chakra, anahata, is the heart centre and relates to finding compassion. This chakra is also the bridge between the lower physical chakras and the more

Table 4.1 The chakra system, attributes and related virtues

Number	Location	Sanskrit	Maslow	Meaning	Positive	Negative	Virtue
7	Head	Sahasrara	Self-transcendence	Enlightenment	Live for higher purpose	–	Service
6	Third eye	Anja	Self-actualisation	Truth	Pursuit of truth	Self-absorbed; action without wisdom	Intuition/wisdom
	Throat	Vishuddhi	Esteem	Communication	Speak higher truths	Complaining, shallow life (cocktail set)	Courage
4	Heart	Anahata	Love	Love	Warm hearted	Cold hearted	Compassion
3	Solar plexus	Manipura	Belonging	Power	Let go; let God	Too little or too much ego	Balance (humility/self-worth)
2	Spleen	Swadhisthana	Belonging	Emotions	Joy	Depression/hedonism	Forgiveness
1	Base	Mooladhara	Safety (Physiological) ↓	Security	KNOW security comes from within; physical needs will be looked after	Finding security through money	Gratitude

spiritual chakras above. The throat (vishuddhi) relates to truthful communication, and the related virtue is courage which is often needed to speak kindly and truthfully. The sixth chakra is anja and is located between on the forehead between the eyes and thus called the 'third eye'. The virtue connected with this is sourcing one's inner wisdom through intuition. Finally, sahasrara is the chakra at the top of the head and conveys enlightenment. Expression of this is through the virtue of service to others, without ego. Barrett (2015) too acknowledges this shift through the chakra system from a focus on self-transformation to a shift towards serving and making a contribution to others at the level of sahasrara.

Teaching System

This teaching innovation takes place in an elective fourth year undergraduate course – Self-Actualising Leadership – in a university management school in New Zealand, with sustainable management being a distinctive feature of the school for 20 years. Hence innovative teaching methods that may develop ethical and socially conscious corporate citizens are welcomed. This leadership course is offered once a year and generally attracts about 50 students, most of whom are undergraduate 20–23 year olds; however it also attracts a number of mature students wanting non-traditional approaches to deep transformational learning. The purpose of the course is to develop self-leadership skills in the students, more formally stated to

> *Align one's inner and outer worlds in a journey of discovering what energises and guides purpose. We explore strategies to enhance this self-actualisation for inner leadership, using mindfulness practices from neuroscience, theology and psychology. These practices can develop self-regulation and clarity of insight that may enhance energy, presencing and interpersonal skills. These skills may then be applied in the organisational context through case studies involving ethics, conscious enterprise and leadership.*

Leadership is therefore defined as a journey of finding purpose and meaning through an inner guidance of self-mastery. The course places the student's values at the centre of the learning journey as they seek to align their inner and outer worlds. The course is intensive, requiring students to examine their own moral compass. The course has three learning segments: the first segment asks the students to explore their individual value system. They are asked to write reflexive journals on an experience that has shaped them, to analyse and deconstruct their actions, and to identify future learning possibilities that may emerge from this process. These journals are often personal, and students have the option to hand them in during class to ensure confidentiality. The second segment examines these values within a leadership setting. In groups, the students interviewed leaders regarding the leaders' values and their impact in an organizational context. The report and presentation of these 'conscious' leader case studies allow the students to experience how these values shape organizational culture, social responsibility and purpose, making this a values-in-action activity rather than the values remaining theoretical and abstract. Students are often surprised how often these leaders draw on their virtues to guide their leadership and decision-making. This section is important in moving from their own experience to seeing how virtues are developed through 'learning from living' (Klimoski 2006). The third and final segment focuses on interconnection – examining self-other relationships through the United Nations Sustainable Development Goals, deep ecology, quantum physics, social enterprise and spirituality. This segment focuses on reflexive thinking – that we live in an interconnected and intersubjective world. The final assessment for this segment, and for the course itself, explores their overall learning through the creation of an artform and an associated presentation in the classroom of the learning experienced in the course.

This chapter, however, focuses more specifically on how virtuous leadership is developed through the everyday living-in of experiences, assisted through methods such as the chakra system to develop cumulative and processual perspectives of self-transcendence (Kempster 2006). Hence, the chakra system has been incorporated into the course as an option and is particularly related to learning objectives 1, 2 and 4 through reflexive journals. These learning objectives and associated assessments for the course are as follows:

1. To identify and apply tools for leader development (*reflexive journals*; *test*).
2. To develop self-awareness and reflexive practice (*reflexive journals*).
3. To evaluate the qualities of transcendental purpose (*purpose assignment and case studies*).
4. To understand the role of ethical and holistic leadership in an interconnected world (*presentation of the art assignment – course summary*).

Students have the opportunity to apply the chakra system in two reflexive journals and in a more limited capacity in their final assignment. I purposely use the word reflexive rather than reflective as while students are asked to reflectively step back and reassess a situation to bring unconscious experience, often uncomfortable, to the fore (Booth et al. 2009; Kisfalvi and Oliver 2015), they are also asked to think about their own reshaping of the world they live in through virtuous action. This reshaping is a critical aspect of reflexivity (Cunliffe 2004).

The topic for the first journal is self-selected as students become familiar with the practice of reflexivity (bending back the inquiry on self and other) through the personal questioning and honesty that such a process requires. The topic is deliberately open-ended to enable students the opportunity to deliberate on any troublesome issue. The second topic relates to a previous leadership experience. As noted earlier, leadership is defined as an activity of self-responsibility and self-mastery rather than the more common definition as leadership as authoritarian and heroic. In the 2000 word journals, students are asked to respond to four key processes (see Pavlovich 2010, for more details on this course):

1. Description: What happened? Describe the experience.
2. Embodiment: What did you feel? What were the emotions felt? Label and describe them. Did you feel a physical sensation in the body? What was your body telling you? Connect with the chakra system.

3. Analysis: Link this experience with literature to help analyse what was happening.
4. Learning: What story was being constructed? Where there distortions of facts? What virtue did you need to develop? What insights did you gain so that you can handle such a situation differently in the future?

Using the chakra practice is optional, as such an alternative learning system can challenge some students, but for others it provided a powerful lens for breaking through conventional management techniques. As one student noted, '*It was the class on the chakra system that changed my attitude. It inspired me and from this point I found myself thoroughly enjoying the course*' (Jon). Students also have the opportunity to comment on the effectiveness of the chakra system in their last assignment, which is a reflexive account on their overall learning experience through virtuous action.

The grading rubric encourages engagement with both embodiment and the chakra system and has been refined over the years (see Appendix). Of course, grading such personal and deep learning is always challenging, but, as noted above, years of teaching have fined-tuned the grading rubric to ensure consistency. In the classroom, I regularly remind the students that I am grading the development of a skill – not the experience itself – to ensure that they know that it is not a sad story that gets the high marks. Each component of the rubric demonstrates how the standard of work aligns with specific sections. The following are examples of what would be expected for an A grade. Please refer to the Appendix for the other grade outcomes. The five equal components consist of the following:

1. Reflective voice. For an A grade, students are expected to use 'I' statements in their reframing of beliefs and assumptions. This requires a deep inquiry that questions previous actions, while also including evidence of the self as relational. That is, circumstances develop through relationships, asking the student to unravel 'what happened'.
2. Analysis. For an A grade, the student is expected to discuss how the situation effected their mind, body and emotions. Certainly, a lot of the males had more difficulty discussing their emotions – which is why identifying the chakras made it easier for them. For example, if they stated that they felt the emotion in the stomach, they were able to connect the experience more with a sense of their personal power being under attack. It is important to also note that while males found this challenging, many of the top grades were from the males in the class. This reflection on embodiment thus became important in their understanding of the experience.
3. Reading analysis. Strangely, despite strongly encouraging students to use literature to unpick the experience, many do not. However, for an A grade, students were expected to (a) choose appropriate readings that helped explain their experience and (b) use this literature to analyse the experience rather than just describe it.

4. Learning described. This section asked the student to demonstrate their learning – thus while it was descriptive, there needed to be clear evidence of significant reframing of their assumptions for transformative learning. This meant that they demonstrated that they understand the notion of virtue as a framework for learning.
5. Professional report. Finally, marks are given for a professional report. For an A grade, this included an excellent academic writing style and grammar, appropriate structure to the report and accurate APA referencing.

While only 30% of students chose to analyse embodiment through the chakras, these students consistently did better and achieved higher grades for both their analysis and transformational learning, possibly because the chakra system provides a system for them to more precisely identify underlying hidden patterns of experience. They seem to have a deeper understanding and stronger sense of self following this analysis. Thus, these new interpretations of past experiences can result in transformative behaviour. Indeed, Vivekananda (2005) reminds us that engagement with the chakra system can help resolve emotional pain that, if not attended to, can cripple us until it is addressed; further it also enhances cognition through more flexible neuroplasticity.

The following discussion illustrates the developmental processes that can take place over the course from this reflexive practice. It should be noted that these chakras are not a bounded system, and while each represents a specific quality, there is overlay. For example, the seventh chakra of selfless service may also be felt in the sixth chakra of wisdom through an awareness of higher purpose. To exemplify this personal transformational learning practice, commentary from student work is used to highlight the virtue-based learning processes and the attributes of the associated chakra. It is important to note that these students have given permission for these quotes to be referenced in research work, as well as pseudonyms being used. Through an ethics approval process, the students are asked at the beginning of the course if they agree for their work to be used for research. After I have analysed their reports at the end of the course, I also ask follow-up with the students individually to ensure they still agree. I have rarely had anyone say no at the end of the course, and most students feel flattered that their ideas, thoughts, interpretations and new understandings can contribute to research findings.

Student Experiences Through the Chakra System

Mooladhara (Base): Gratitude

The virtue developed for this chakra is gratitude. Through focusing on gratitude, the students found that many of their fears related to survival subsided, illustrated in the following:

> *Since completing the journals, I have been expressing gratitude when I wake up in the morning, before I go to sleep at night and many times throughout the day. When I start to have bad thoughts to do with something or someone, I take a minute and think of all the good things in my life. Since doing this, I am happier, more optimistic and more satisfied with my life. I try not to see the bad things, only the good. It also takes a lot to get me stressed now, which is amazing considering the work load I have had in the past 2 months with full-time university and full-time work. I have even been told by staff members that they cannot believe how calm and relaxed I am. I put this down to learning how to show gratitude for the good in life and through enjoying my busy work rather than stressing about it* (Sam).

Many students express similar sentiments and note that through acknowledging gratitude, they experience less stress and a larger openness towards life. They note that their fears have decreased as they acknowledge greater personal fulfilment as they balance insecurities (related to mooladhara) with gratitude and positivity. These actions demonstrate both a change in character and behaviour, indicative in the development of virtue noted by Bright et al. (2014). The disposition to be thankful and to act in a positive way has created a more gracious and serene self, characteristic of both moral goodness and a more purposeful impact (Cameron et al. 2004).

Swadhisthna (Spleen): Forgiveness

The second virtue is forgiveness, and students get significant respite from being able to self-dialogue on deep issues that concern them. One student noted his experience of forgiveness. *This reflection has enabled me to evaluate the virtue of forgiveness, the lack of which has weakened my sense of divinity and disabled my ability to heal. I am now beginning the journey of freeing myself from self-limitations that involved revenge, anger and guilt, things that I felt in my lower stomach. Having learnt this, I have improved my ability to deal with my emotions* (Aaron).

The above comment illustrates Smedes (1996) observation that forgiveness is like setting a prisoner free and then discovering that the prisoner was you. Another student also gave this account on finding a way to handle his emotions: *Forgiveness has been a very useful virtue that I have picked up from this course, especially when making creative decisions in my band. When making music I get emotionally invested in my creations, but because it is a band other members like to add their input. My sense of control has been something I have struggled with and I have had to learn to let go. In doing so, I have been able to gain more enjoyment out of making music rather than fighting pointless battles with my band mates. The chakra model has helped me detach my emotions in order to use them in a way that is more constructive and progressive* (Pete).

Worthington et al. (2010) identify two forms of forgiveness, decisional and emotional. The latter involves replacing negative emotions with positive other-oriented emotions (e.g. empathy, sympathy and love), while decisional forgiveness involves positively changing behaviour. The first student example illustrates decisional forgiveness in that he had made a conscious choice to reprogramme his thinking; the latter is an example of emotional change through positive action. These quotes both show behavioural changes and action that support emotional regulation. This is in line with the significant amount of research emerging from neuroscience regarding the positive outcomes from decentering through self-regulation that result from a controlled response rather than an automatic reactive response (e.g. Gardner et al. 2005). The student statements therefore highlight the importance of how chakra purification impacts on emotional well-being. Barrett (2015) too calls this the relationship chakra.

Manipura (Solar Plexus): Self-Worth

This is the self-worth centre and focuses on personal power. It is located in the solar plexus centre which is where we feel threatened if our use of power is unbalanced (e.g. feeling sick in the stomach). Negative feelings associated with the solar plexus chakra are low self-esteem, fear of bullying, fear of rejection, oversensitivity to criticism, self-image fears and indecisiveness.

Carol explained a situation involving self-worth and the reactions in her body: *It was during our preparation for a student report, and Tom and I were agreeing on who would do what. But I felt as though what I had to say was inferior. Although I didn't identify with the feeling at the time but I can now see that I felt intimidated and bullied – my heart rate increased and a nervous feeling crept into my stomach. I felt as if my power was being taken away.*

Another student also commented on self-worth: *I can often relate to this negative emotion, but it has diminished over the course as I have learnt to be confident in my abilities. I know that I am not perfect, but that I also now have the skills to change things if I am unhappy with them. This, in turn, will help me to understand and better balance my self-worth, and therefore help me to create better relationships with others* (Alice).

Hence, this chakra relates to self-awareness through acknowledging one's strengths and weaknesses. Lack of self-confidence can be developed through decentering, acceptance of weaknesses and positive action for change. This inner work helps to balance a distorted or biased sense of self creating a stronger moral character regarding one's relation to others, events and the external world (Vago and Silbersweig 2012). The student quotes highlight how self-awareness can break habitual patterns and create more positive future actions. They also acknowledge the physical and psychological impacts that experiences have and how they can be held unwittingly in the body. Reflexivity helps reframe those experiences.

Anahata (Heart): Compassion

The centre chakra is the anahata centre which links both the lower (more physical) and upper (more spiritual) chakras through compassion towards oneself and towards others. The learning for students included the following:

Understanding the heart is essential to learning the reasons of its pain. I felt hate, anger, fear and jealousy when I was informed that I was no longer a candidate for the job. I was angry at myself as I felt I had disappointed myself. I was jealous of the other candidates who were offered the position over me and I was scared that I would not get a graduate position. However, I needed to learn to trust that there was another path for me. I needed to open my heart up to other opportunities (Daniel).

My learning in this course was about compassion. I finally recognised it in myself. I found myself acting compassionately at work without ever identifying or labelling it. I also learnt how much energy it took for me to even say, 'yes I am a compassionate person' (James).

These comments illustrate the power of compassion for oneself, and how this awareness enables connection with something greater than oneself. Compassion improves our relatedness to others and acts as a healing mechanism. These quotes therefore illustrate the shift from self to other as we strengthen our shared values of connectedness (Atkins and Parker 2012). Hence, compassion acts as a link from self into the intersubjective shared space of otherness. These quotes illustrate Cameron et al.'s (2004) qualities of moral goodness and positive impacts that are related to virtuous action.

Vishuddhi (Throat): Courage

The fifth chakra is located at the throat and relates to communication and eternal truths. The virtue most aligned to balancing this chakra is courage which is required to speak in the right way at the right time. This means saying things that others may not want to hear and also choosing words carefully to convey the right message. It also includes withdrawal from gossip. Students noted the following:

Of all the chakras I have the most problems with my throat chakra. I often feel a tight constricted feeling in my throat and I think it is the result of years of keeping my feelings and thoughts in. As a child I always felt that I had to be strong and that if I spoke my mind it would just upset people. Telling people how I really feel is something that I still find really difficult because I would rather suffer in silence than upset someone (Sarah).

When going to job interviews I get nervous and my communication is weaker than usual. Taking time to meditate and focus on my breathing has really helped unblock this (Lucy).

Courage is the strength to accomplish our goals in the face of opposition, involving genuineness and bravery. Hence, these comments demonstrate that relationships are important and that courage is needed to carefully construct and act in ways that are truthful and yet are gracious towards the other. Our communications are a visible witness into the state of our virtuousness, or as Bright et al. (2014) note, our ability to moderate our deficiencies and excesses. These quotes illustrate a shift in habits towards a moral code of courage, with Barrett (2015) calling this the alignment chakra.

Anja (Third Eye): Wisdom

The third eye is known to bring insight, self-knowledge, intuitive understanding and the ability to 'see' beyond the physical world. Thus, it is related to wisdom and living to one's highest purpose through questioning the day-to-day assumptions and values. A student recalled, *You can choose to tell different stories about what happened depending on how willing you are to reflect on your part on the story.... I was willing to fabricate a number of stories until I had the chilling realisation that I could act in a similar way again if I choose not to take full responsibility for this action now* (Taylor).

Another student noted that *Before doing this course, my purpose was to make money. I understand now that I was too young to judge what a path of real meaning was and so I trusted the judgement of others. Because it was the norm, I never questioned it.... Then during the course I got it. My purpose is now to develop my consciousness to the highest level attainable, and to help others do the same* (Adam).

Both these comments illustrate the insight that the students have gained regarding their own deeper meaning for life through the acquiring and application of wisdom. These quotes also demonstrate a shift in awareness from individualistic physical and emotional needs to spiritual self-other awareness. This chakra has a higher level of awareness that includes awareness of the impacts on the self-other relationship. Hence, these students acknowledge a deeper purpose within a broader, interconnected world that gives fulfilment and meaning to both themselves and to others – a moral code by which they are guided in life's actions.

Sahasrara (Head): Selfless Service

The highest virtue and that which sits at the centre of the head is that of selfless service. Over the course, students engage in conversations and tasks to discover their individual purpose: some find it; others recognise that it is a lifetime journey of discovery:

> *I have come to the realisation that my purpose in life is to help and touch the lives of as many people as I can. To help, care, support, service those many people who come into my life through listening, giving advice, offering solutions and remaining positive. Service is a virtue that means doing things for others, sharing a load, making a difference, doing what you can to assist other people* (Sally).

> *I have found that my purpose is not something that I should look for but rather it is something that already lies within me and it will find me. Throughout my life I have placed more importance on where I want to be and how I want my life to end up, but through learning about purpose I have come to realise that the destination is not what I should be focusing on but rather the journey* (Pat).

> *My first interview was with a sought-after corporation in a new and exciting building and I was very much looking forward to it. But something was missing. The interview was aggressive and mainly based on an online personality test. Because of this course, I knew immediately that I was looking for a job that goes beyond the corporation, one that has a higher sense of purpose for why people are here. I had a revelation that I can*

> *do anything. I have the power to be courageous, kind and extraordinary. I want to help change the world!* (Kesh).

Realisation within this chakra acknowledges the integration of self within a co-created and intersubjective world – that our purpose on earth is to assist in societal benefits through virtuous living. Service to others is the highest form of virtuous action, noted by both Eastern and Western traditions, and becomes a significant shift in transformation when students recognise this. Connection with this chakra also supports Cameron et al.'s (2004) claim that virtues can lead to unconditional societal benefit, and Barrett (2015) too calls this chakra the 'contribution' chakra.

Discussion

This chapter has highlighted the development of virtue and identifies a number of actions that emerge from such a study that may help seed more humanistic and moral leaders. The use of the chakra system is one way to develop virtuous action because of its venerable history that includes physical, emotional, mental and spiritual impacts. As these energy bodies are interconnected, this practice can enhance students' spiritual awareness of the sacredness of life and hence awaken a more moral leader through placing the student experience as the focus of inquiry.

There are a number of theoretical contributions that this chapter sheds light on. This chapter highlights the importance of virtues as stable and enduring qualities that Aristotle (2009) and many others have noted (e.g. MacIntyre 1981) as the foundation of living a 'good' life through a communal moral narrative of a society. Through the data, illustrations have been made regarding how this study extends Cameron et al.'s (2004) identification of three outcomes from virtuous living: moral goodness, human impact and unconditional societal benefits. However, this study also offers its own contributions. The first is in exposing students to these virtues as a *practice of habituation*. Han (2015) noted that virtues are a disposition; hence they are continually being constructed positively and negatively through daily activities. That is, they are not static but are always in a state of development. By writing reflexive journals, the students deepen their awareness of these virtues over the duration of the course so that the practice of virtue dispositions may become internalised to guide their future actions. The student quotes demonstrated how they identified, internalised and implemented actions around these virtues related to their own experiences, with many students commenting that they had given little thought to these virtues before the course. This process brings their experience to the fore in a quest to reshape and develop new perspectives. Experience is the starting point for the inner dialogue (Taylor and Cranton 2013). Such awareness reinforces Weaver's (2006), p. 344) comment that virtues enable us 'to act in ways appropriate… [for] the unity and continuity of life'. Application of the chakra system provides a visible and active representation for students to remember after the course to guide their future leadership.

A second contribution is that through awareness and practice, the multidimensional and durable qualities of virtues can become part of the students' *self-concept*. That is, the students better understand virtuous action, and when they stray from their recognised moral code, they know they are betraying their own self-hood (Han 2015), emotionally, physically and spiritually. This contribution demonstrates how moral virtue is more than a cognitive attribute and reinforces the need for more holistic teaching approaches that integrate embodied and multidimensional aspects of learning. The student quotes demonstrated how they felt at odds with their bodies when they strayed from their moral code. Not only does this highlight the importance of the chakra system in identifying the emotional, physical and spiritual self, it also reinforces Merleau-Ponty's (1964) claim that it is through being present with our body that we can more fully experience our world. One student summed up this paradox of selfhood by noting that *Discovering the chakra system has been both a blessing and a curse. The blessing is that I can now feel when things are out of kilter, but the curse is that I now have a responsibility to actively do something about it* (Keyla).

A third contribution relates to the application of the chakra system itself as a method for self-transcendence through its focus on *higher levels of consciousness*. As noted previously, the chakra system adds multidimensionality to developing virtuous leaders because it works on subtle energy systems. As students consider the virtues related to these chakra vortexes, this focus can assist in harmonising and revitalising physical, emotional, mental and spiritual energy systems that include neural, adrenal, and endocrine pathways in the physical body, stress reduction in the emotional body and broadening the self-other awareness in the spiritual body (Vivekananda 2005). Importantly, this reflexive activity may indicate why those students engaging with the chakra system noted less stress and improved well-being towards the end of the course (see earlier quotes). It also highlights the importance of experiential learning for transformation, particularly bringing the practice of embodiment into the classroom in order to feel and experience what can be tacit, hidden and uncomfortable (Kisfalvi and Oliver 2015).

The development of a higher level of consciousness leads to a final contribution related to leadership. As noted earlier, the purpose of this course is to develop the student's inner landscape for *virtuous leadership*. Imbued in this awareness is that moral action is purposeful and experienced through a reflexive self-other relationship that reflects the moral narrative of the society. In using the chakra system, students become aware of the difference between the lower chakras which are self-centred (ego-awareness) and the upper chakras (eco-awareness) that are more concerned with otherness. Hence, as Collins (2001, p. 75) notes, true leaders 'subjugate their own needs to the greater ambition of something larger and more lasting than themselves'. A similar conviction was evident in the student quotes related to higher levels of awareness – wisdom and service – where they repeatedly acknowledged the importance of doing purposeful 'good' work. This went beyond a theoretical interest and is reflected in many students' later choices of employment. Such 'practice' confirms a shift in our understanding of leadership, where purpose embraces a form of meta-level social good that impacts positively in the world

(Kempster et al. 2011; Pavlovich and Corner 2014). These contributions highlight the importance of incorporating such a teaching innovation in management education due to its integrated and multidimensional nature. It challenges the 'stigmatisation of goodness' that Giacalone and Promislo (2013) suggest permeate current approaches to management education and becomes a vital component in personal transformational learning.

Conclusion

Some commentators may claim that these virtue attributes can be developed without linking with the chakra system. However, the chakra system has an ancient lineage that works multidimensionally on subtle energy levels, giving the students a deeper system to work with. It also provides a more comprehensive structure for the students to 'hang' the virtues on. The chakra system has its own set of ancient traditions, and this introduction exposes students to a vast array of ancient texts to be explored and studied for transformational learning. It also sheds more light on Maslow's important hierarchy of needs, with its focus on deficits in the lower levels and more spiritual aesthetics in the upper levels. Linking this with the Vedic system enables a more integrated conversation on the multidimensionality of cognitive, emotional, physical and spiritual attributes for developing goodness.

The strength of this system is the integration of Eastern and Western philosophies, and its purpose is to deepen the insight provided by each. The journey over the duration of the course brings significant self-awareness, self-actualisation and self-transcendence to many students. This is enhanced by the system that synthesises their learning into a coherent structure that they will remember after they have left the course due to the habitualisation of self-identity that has occurred through the experiential approach.

The purpose of this system is to increase personal transformational learning for self-other awareness in business students. In a world currently facing much uncertainty through economic, climatic and social change, such an approach strengthens a reflexive 'other-orientation' as boundaries between fixed structures are softened. Educating students to be moral leaders may assist the improvement of society as these students can develop a skill set that for acting in ways that are more morally appropriate for collective benefits, which moral philosophers have argued is the common narrative of a flourishing society.

Appendix: Marking Schedule: Reflexive Journals (100%)

	Expectations	Unacceptable 0 (E)	Weak 5–9 (D)	Adequate 10–12 (C…B-)	Very good 13–15 (B…A-)	Outstanding 16–20 (A…A+)
Reflective Voice	Extent of 'I' – Questioning of actions Deep inquiry	No reflection	Externalised; about 'out there'; no I statements	Some questioning and I statements	Strong questioning; evidence of self as relational	Deep inquiry Reframing of assumptions, evidence of self as relational
Analysis – physical, emotional, mental, spiritual and chakras	Description and impact of feelings on the mind, body and spirit Consequences of the actions as a result	No mention of emotions, feelings and effect on the body	Limited mention of emotions, feelings and effect on the body	Some analysis of physical and emotional self	Analysis includes effects on the body and emotions Effect of embodiment noted	Analysis includes effects on the body, mind, emotions and chakras; Reflection on embodiment
Readings analysis	Appropriateness of readings chosen Links with topic Analysis rather than description	No readings	Few readings; mostly descriptive and not from reputable journals	Some readings noted; described rather than analysed	Good choice of readings and appropriate application; some analysis	Excellent choice and application of multiple sources; good analysis
Learning journey	The process of how you have learnt What you have learnt/ virtues noted What you do with this new knowledge in the future	No learning	Little learning; blaming others	Some learning noted; still focused on 'out there; virtue identified	Very good learning demonstrated; questioning of assumptions; virtue described	Outstanding learning demonstrated; strong reframing of assumptions Virtue understood as a learning concept
Professional image	Grammar, spelling, full paragraphs, punctuation, writing style, and APA referencing	Inadequate at this level Poor writing style Poor spelling, grammar Poor structure Poor APA references	Too many errors Writing style journalistic rather than academic Poor structure Some grammar and spelling errors Poor APA referencing	Adequate writing style Academically written Adequate structure Good grammar Good APA referencing	Very good writing style Comprehensive structure Very good grammar Academically written Good APA referencing	Excellent academic writing style Comprehensive structure to review Excellent grammar Excellent APA referencing

References

Aristotle (2009) Nicomachean ethics. http://classics.mit.edu/Aristotle/nichomachean.html

Atkins P, Parker S (2012) Understanding individual compassion in organizations: the role of appraisals and psychological flexibility. Acad Manag Rev 37(4):524–546

Barrett R (2015) The metrics of human consciousness. Lulu Press

Beshara R (2013) The chakra system as a bio-psycho-spiritual model of consciousness: Anahata as heart-centred consciousness. Int J Yoga 1:29–33

Booth A, Mclean M, Walker M (2009) Self, others and society: a case study of university integrative learning. Stud High Educ 34(8):929–939

Bright D, Winn B, Kanov J (2014) Reconsidering virtue: differences of perspective in virtue ethics and the positive social sciences. J Bus Ethics 119:445–460

Cameron K, Bright D, Caza A (2004) Exploring the relationships between organizational virtuousness and performance. Am Behav Sci 47(6):766–790

Collins J (2001) Level 5 leadership: the triumph of humility and fierce resolve. Harv Bus Rev 79(1):67–76

Crossan M, Mazutis D, Seijts G (2013a) In search of virtue: the role of virtues, values and character strengths in ethical decision making. J Bus Ethics 113(4):567–581

Crossan M, Mazutis D, Seijts G, Gandz J (2013b) Developing leadership character in business programs. Aca Manag Learn Educ 12(2):285–305

Cunliffe A (2004) On becoming a critically reflexive practitioner. J Manag Educ 28(4):407–426

Durant R, Carlon D, Downs A (2017) The efficiency challenge: creating a transformative learning experience in a principles of management course. J Manag Educ 41(6):852–872

Gardner W, Avolio B, Luthans F, May D, Walumbwa F (2005) "Can you see the real me?" a self-based model of authentic leader and follower development. Leadersh Q 16:343–372

Ghoshal S (2005) Bad management theories are destroying good management practices. Acad Manag Learn Educ 4:75–91

Giacalone R, Promislo M (2013) Broken when entering: the stigmatization of goodness and business ethics education. Acad Manag Learn Edu 12(1):86–101

Han H (2015) Virtue ethics, positive psychology, and a new model of science and engineering ethics education. Sci Eng Ethics 21:441–460

Hartman E (2006) Can we teach character? An Aristotelian answer. Acad Manag Learn Edu 5(1):68–81

Hayashi P (2015) Tattvabodha and the hierarchical necessity of Abraham Maslow. J Manag Spiritual Relig. https://doi.org/10.1080/14766086.2015.1076735

Jotin Khisty C (2006) Meditations on systems thinking, spiritual systems, and deep ecology. Syst Pract Action Res 19:295–307

Kempster S (2006) Leadership learning through lived experience: a process of apprenticeship? J Manag Org 12(1):4–22

Kempster S, Jackson B, Conroy M (2011) Leadership as purpose: exploring the role of purpose in leadership practice. Leadership 7(3):317–334

Kisfalvi V, Oliver D (2015) Creating and maintaining a safe space in experiential learning. J Manag Educ:1–28. https://doi.org/10.1177/1052562915574724

Klimoski R (2006) Introduction: Aristotle as a business ethics professor. Acad Manag Learn Educ 5(1):66–67

Koltko-Rivera M (2006) Rediscovering the later version of Maslow's hierarchy of needs: self-transcendence and opportunities for theory, research, and unification. Rev Gen Psychol 10(4):302–317

Kuechler W, Stedham Y (2018) Management education and transformational learning: the integration of mindfulness in an MBA course. J Manag Educ 42(1):8–33

MacIntyre A (1981) After virtue? A study in moral theory. University of Notre Dame Press, Notre Dame

Manz C (2015) Taking the self-leadership high road: smooth surface or potholes ahead? Acad Manag Perspect 29(1):132–151
Marshall P (2015) Neuroscience, embodiment and development. In: Lerner R (ed) Handbook of child psychology and developmental science, pp 244–283
Maslow A (1943) Hierarchy of needs: a theory of human motivation. Psychol Rev 50(4):370–396
Merleau-Ponty M (1964) Signs (McCleary RC, Trans). Northwestern University Press, Evanston
Mintz SM (1996) Aristotelian virtue and business ethics education. J Bus Ethics 15(8):827–838
Morales-Sánchez R, Cabello-Medina C (2015) Integrating character in management: virtues, character strengths, and competencies. Bus Ethics Eur Rev 24(S2):S156–S174
Nisker W (1998) Buddha's nature: Evolution as a practical guide to enlightenment. Bantam Books
Pavlovich K (2010) Educating for conscious awareness. J Manag Spiritual Relig 7(3):193–208
Pavlovich K, Corner PD (2014) Conscious enterprise emergence: shared value creation through expanded conscious awareness. J Bus Ethics 121(3):341–351
Ramsey V, Fitzgibbons D (2005) Being in the classroom. J Manag Educ 29(2):333–356
Sadler-Smith E (2012) Before virtue: biology, brain, behaviour, and the "moral sense". Bus Ethics Q 22(2):351–376
Scandurra AJ (1999) Everyday spirituality: a core unit in health education and lifetime wellness. J Health Educ 30:104–109
Scharmer O (2009) Theory U: leading from the future as it emerges. Berrett-Koehler Publishers, San Francisco
Sinclair A (2014) In: Ladkin D, Taylor S (eds) On knees, breasts and being fully human in leadership: the physicality of leadership: gesture, entanglement, taboo, possibilities. Emerald, pp 175–195
Smedes L (1996) The art of forgiveness: when you need to forgive and don't know how. Ballantine Books, New York
Sutherland I, Ladkin D (2013) Creating engaged executive learning spaces: the role of aesthetic agency. Org Aesthet 2(1):105–124
Taylor EW, Cranton P (2013) Handbook of transformative learning: theory, research, and practice. Jossey-Bass, San Francisco
Vago D, Silbersweig DA (2012) Self-awareness, self-regulation, and self-transcendence (S-ART): a system for understanding the neurobiological mechanisms of mindfulness. Front Hum Neurosci 6:296. https://doi.org/10.3389/fnhum.2012.00296
Vivekananda R (2005) Practical yoga psychology. Yoga Publications Trust, Mungar
Weaver G (2006) Virtue in organizations: moral identity as a foundation for moral agency. Organ Stud 27(3):341–368
Weick K, Putnam T (2006) Organizing for mindfulness: eastern wisdom and western knowledge. J Manag Inq 15(3):275–287
Wilber K (1981) Ontogenetic development: two fundamental patterns. J Transpers Psychol 13(1):33–58
Williamson M (1992) A return to love: reflections on the principles of a course in miracles. Harper Perenniel, New York
Worthington E Jr et al (2010) Forgiveness and spirituality in organizational life: theory, status of research, and new ideas for discovery. J Manag Spiritual Relig 7(2):119–134

Cross References

Corey Stanford and George Stanford, The Neurobiology of Personal Transformation
Satinder Dhiman, Self-Knowledge: Master Key to Personal Transformation and Fulfillment
Denise Frizzell and David Banner, Leader Self-Development, Maturation, and Meditation: Elements of a Transformative Journey
Eleftheria Egel and Louis Fry, Cultivating a Global Mindset Through "Being-Centered" Leadership

Lis DeAngelis, Clarifying the Relationship Between Transformative Teaching and Transformative Learning
Michael London and Bill Van Buskirk, The Co-created Classroom: From Teacher/Student to Mentor/Apprentice
Michelle French-Holloway, Teaching Creativity and Spiritual Meaning Using Insights from Neurobiology
Kathryn Goldman Schuyler, Michelle Olsen Taylor and Orit Wolberger, Bringing Mindful and Joy to Work: Action Research on Organizational Change
Mahhulika Sagaram and Prasad Kaipa, Personal and Organizational Transformation: Indian and American Perspectives and Experiences

A Journey to Transform Students into Implementing the Sustainability Mindset: A Case of Sekolah Tinggi Manajemen Ipmi (Ipmi International Business School)

5

Amelia Naim Indrajaya

Abstract

One of the objectives to develop the Center for Sustainability Mindset and Social Responsibility (CSMSR) of Sekolah Tinggi Manajemen Ipmi or popularly known as Ipmi International Business School is to transform students into implementing the sustainability mindset. This chapter is about developing the sustainability mindset by practicing several forms of experiential learning discovery journey programs. The sustainability mindset is introduced through different approaches such as presenting award-winning business supporting SDGs (Sustainable Development Goals), understanding the web of life, Aim2Flourish projects, eco-literacy campaign, detective challenge (understanding biospheric orientation), green projects, respecting diversity through virtual reality cardboard, designing life journeys, awareness campaign, developing life commitments to answer the global trend, conducting community engagement impacting people and planet, conducting business as an agent of world benefit, and writing a contemplative paper in the form of a letter to my unborn child. The 17 SDGs (Sustainable Development Goals) of the United Nations are embedded in the learning process.

The endeavors to transform students' perspective into having a sustainability mindset was designed to contribute to the personal transformation discussions. The results have shown that students were engaged after going through the four frameworks of system perspective, ecological worldview, and emotional and spiritual Intelligence, each through the thinking, heart (being), and hand (doing) approach and had shown a new transformed mindset through their acts and commitments as seen through interviews, observations, their campaigns' program to the communities, their writings, and life commitments/plans.

A. N. Indrajaya (✉)
Sekolah Tinggi Manajemen Ipmi, Jakarta, Indonesia
e-mail: amelia.naim@ipmi.ac.id

J. Neal (ed.), *Personal, Educational and Organizational Transformation*, Future of Business and Finance, https://doi.org/10.1007/978-3-031-29253-8_5

Keywords

Personal transformation · Experiential learning · Sustainability mindset · Social responsibility · Sustainable Development Goals

Introduction

Business schools all around the world are going through an awakening call. The focus toward growth and maximizing shareholder's value in the business school curriculums has resulted in business graduates who are pursuing profit by causing negative externalities both toward people and the planet. Globally, more and more business and management educators around the world are realizing that this trend needs to be transformed into a way of achieving a triple bottom line of people, planet, and then profit. Students need to understand the philosophy of business as fulfilling a real need with a positive social and environmental impact and by doing so will get long-term support from the stakeholders which ensures a sustainable profit (Urip 2010).

Businesses should be conducted with a corporate shared values approach. The company's stakeholder, management, policies, and actions should be considered in order to simultaneously achieve social and environmental performance. These would eventually support a long-term economic gain by implementing the Sustainable Development Goals in response to sustainable development issues (Indrajaya 2018). By implementing corporate shared values, corporations can collectively address global issues in the 17 Sustainable Development Goals (SDGs). The United Nations with its 181 member countries had made a pledge to achieve these 17 Sustainable Development Goals by 2030. This includes poverty and hunger eradication and improvements in health, education, employment, and the environment and a commitment to collaborate and partnership (www.un.org).

In order to achieve these Sustainable Development Goals, a new mindset of sustainability development as an important benchmark to anything that we do on a daily basis becomes very important. Kassel et al. (2016) posited that mindset is related to the concepts of paradigm and the way we look at the world's situation. We may see mindsets as something that appear rigid and according to the daily cultural habits evolved to be a fixed way of looking at the worldly situation. But in the situation of an anomaly, there is a good chance that individuals and societies could go through a transformation in mindset. In order to have a transformed mindset, students have to go through all the spiritual, emotional, and intellectually touching natural experiences (Indrajaya et al. 2017). Then humanity is awakened to the fact that we are interconnected. The newest COVID-19 virus spread all over the world is a taunting fact of how we are so interconnected. Humanity has started to realize there is this strong interconnection between the planet, people, and prosperity (Urip 2010). We have caused so much damage to the ecosystem and have caused climate change, the enormous gap between the rich and the poor, and social unrest. As society is concerned about our humankind's sustainability through the way the planet has been exploited, we also have seen the necessity to change the way we live, which also means a change in the educational paradigms. The mindset is seen through three indicators, (1) on the knowledge and how it can be related to a specific context, (2) on the being aspect and how these values may close the gap and lead to certain conducts, and (3) the doing part on how it is designed into a set of real action. Kassel et al. (2016) are using the approach of a mindset that measures sustainability through the knowledge, the values, and how it is translated into a set of real activities impacting the community.

The knowledge part is gained from understanding the ecosystem and how humanity has the power to orchestrate all the ecosystem in a way that does not sacrifice the well-being of future generations. This is also a result of contemplation focusing on the gap between personal values and a higher purpose. The understanding of how nature works, and how human beings have created so much harm, could simultaneously become an awakening experience and encourage a deep self-commitment for a better future (Indrajaya 2018). In order to transform the mindset into having sustainability as the key point, business schools need to transform the minds of young business school students.

It is generally known that the rank of business schools was seen through the numbers of salary and bonus reaped by the graduates after they become professional managers, focusing on growth and profit (https://grli.org/initiatives/the-5020-vision/). In the endeavor to support the 17 Sustainable Development Goals (SDGs), it is necessary to transform and have an alternative way of thinking which is not to the direction of growth and profit but more into the flourishing sustainability mindset. We need to develop business graduates who can be pioneers to develop a new concept of business as an agent of world benefit (Cooperrider and Zhexembayeva 2007). This is completely transforming the old way of focusing only on growth and profit. The transformed mindset will focus on whether the business is implementing a business model, where the more they do business, the more they do good. The concept has shifted the paradigm of thinking from "becoming the best in the world, to become to be the best for the world" (www.aim2flourish.com, 2020). Research has shown that this transformation to a higher purpose and a company with a spiritual culture, in the long run, increases employee satisfaction and commitment, which enables the company to become more profitable (Indrajaya et al. 2019).

Research has shown that businesses adopting corporate shared values will tend to be supported by the stakeholders (Urip 2010). The shift in thinking is happening. The focus is not toward the short-term gain, but it is now toward the long-term prosperity for all (Hermes and Rimanoczy 2018). The shift is also in the way of thinking. It is not either/or where businesses need to choose whether they will profit, or they will lose because of the giving and helping process. Google, for example, has proven that the more they give, the more they receive. There go so many other freemium business formats which defy the traditional belief of either/or and moves toward both giving and flourishing paradigm thinking. Business people can transform their business models to both giving and flourishing and at the same time, profiting from long-term sustainability.

This transformation of awareness and practicing sustainability mindset certainly needs a paradigm shift toward the common good (Daloz 2000). Students in business schools and many of their professors are not aware of this new transformed mindset. The vision of 50 + 20 reported that some students in the USA walked out of their classrooms. The students were fed up with being taught that free-market capitalism is the only economic system. When the professors teach economics, they teach capitalism by default. The curriculum is deemed fundamentally flawed. The 50 + 20 vision makes a sinister metaphor: "Simply adding business ethics and sustainability to a flawed curriculum would be just like putting lipstick on a pig" (50 + 20 Management Education for the World). So a theoretical class of business ethics and sustainability would not make any difference. The business school needs transformative mind-shifting programs to change the students' mindset.

This chapter shares a case of an experiential learning discovery journey designed to enable the personal transformation of students' mindset in a business school setting. The model of sustainability mindset is implemented and embedded in several subjects such as business ethics, outstanding values, and good corporate governance.

The next section will be the context of this case study. Readers will get the story of a movement on the sustainability mindset across the archipelago and the feel of the students' situation in Sekolah Tinggi Manajemen Ipmi, Jakarta, Indonesia. After the context, I will share the overview of the sustainability mindset framework. In order to elaborate more on the meaning of each of the frameworks, there will be a discussion of key concepts used in the sustainability mindset framework followed by the experiential learnings and the school projects designed and implemented for the frameworks.

The Context of This Case Study

This section will share the timeline of a sustainability mindset movement across the archipelago through the LEAP team and how it developed into setting up a Center for Sustainability Mindset and Social Responsibility (CSMSR) in Sekolah Tinggi Manajemen Ipmi. To give a clearer context, I will share the situation of the students prior to the programs.

Dr. Rimanoczy, the convener of the LEAP (Leverage, Expand, Accelerate, and Partnership) movement, paid a visit to me in 2013 as part of her effort to develop the LEAP movement. LEAP is described as leverage resources, expand awareness, accelerate change, and partner with forward-thinking individuals, to develop a generation of sustainability-minded leaders.

What started as a high dream to transform the world into a better place through business school students and professionals had manifested into her dissertation on sustainability mindset (written into a book with the title of *Big, Bang, and Being*; Rimanoczy 2017) and later to a development of an international group of professors around the world encouraging and sharing with each other on how to develop the sustainability mindset. I joined the movement, and it becomes a working group to support the sustainability mindset under UNPRME (United Nation Principle of

Responsible Management Education). This movement had encouraged the development of CSMSR (Center for Sustainability Mindset and Social Responsibility) in Sekolah Tinggi Manajemen Ipmi or internationally known as Ipmi International Business School.

The LEAP Movement in Implementing Sustainability Mindset

Sustainability has been a magic word used by scholars from different backgrounds of expertise. Nevertheless, on the aspects of the mindset and the transformation of the paradigm, it needs more real-life case studies and research. This is especially true when it comes to a spiritually and emotionally engaging real-life experience that opens up a new way of looking at the ecological worldview and the new systems perspectives. As part of the LEAP movement, I become actively involved in all of the LEAP programs and activities. The dream of LEAP is uniting all the professors from all corners of the world to share and create positive influence through the learning experience while developing the sustainability mindset with the students. The first LEAP group retreat was conducted during the Academy of Management Conference in Philadelphia in 2014. Professors from around the world gathered for a retreat before the event of the Academy of Management (AOM). During the AOM 2014, LEAP also had a professional development workshop on sustainability mindset. Since then, LEAP has an annual meeting usually conducted before the AOM, some sessions in the middle of the AOM, and sometimes LEAP has more than two meetings in a year in different parts of the world. The meeting of professors around the world does not only happen offline during or on special events, but it is managed through regular meetings through Zoom. Each of the professors' meetings, be it online or offline, are designed to inspire each other on new ways to implement the sustainability mindset.

In May 2015, LEAP members joined the Global Compact Discussion in the United Nations, New York City. The professors of LEAP are also the pioneering professor supporting the emerging movements of Aim2Flourish with a vision of transforming the business model from becoming the best in the world, to become the best for the world. The LEAP network as of November 2019 has 128 academic members from 112 universities in 42 countries (unprme.org).

The Contextual Background

Sekolah Tinggi Manajemen Ipmi is a pioneering international business school inspired by Harvard Business School and INSEAD and was established back in 1984, in Jakarta, Indonesia. The graduates of Ipmi MBA program have become leaders in quite a number of big companies in Indonesia. As a boutique business and management school, Ipmi remains a small school only providing business and management majors both in the undergraduate and graduate degrees. We also have an executive MBA program for professionals, entrepreneurs, and businessmen.

Before I explore the programs aimed to transform the students' mindset, I will share vivid observations of the students before CSMSR started the awareness program on the global goals (SDGs) and sustainability issues. The phenomenon of the students' mindset could be seen from the way they acted. Students had an attitude of indifference. As long as it did not impact their lifestyle, they did not make any attempt toward energy conservation, nor supporting sustainability issues, let alone supporting the global goals. For example, the following are several snapshots of observations taken from the students' activities while spending their time in the business school:

Scene One

Students would leave the class with the computer still on and the light still on. They would assume there is no hazard to them, as they are not paying for the electricity, so it is not part of their responsibility to turn the light off. This act of indifference had been going on for a while. Students were using all electrical equipment without any consideration that the electricity means more CO_2 which contaminated and worsened global warming. Even to go to the second floor from the first floor, they would use the elevator. They were not aware of the concept of energy conservation nor global warming or climate change issues.

After the sustainability mindset program was introduced, students were made aware of how electricity usage is impacting global warming and other environmental issues. Watching videos and statistical facts on the impact of lavish energy usage has given them a new perspective.

Scene Two

Students would mostly buy convenient-branded mineral water, and they did not realize that plastic bottle is a big problem for the earth. Everyone happily used several plastic bottles and tossed it to the garbage without feeling any guilt. Students were not aware of the concept to reduce, reuse, and recycle. They come from the medium- to high-income-level family, and the lifestyle is not encouraging them to recycle or preserve the energy/water or any other resources/scarce resources. An introduction to the Story of Stuff movement on YouTube has given them a new perspective on their daily consumption habits (www.storyofstuff.org).

Scene Three

Most students drove their cars; they rarely took public transportation even though the traffic is impossible in Jakarta, due to the heavy traffic. They are not familiar with the concept of carpooling. Some even have drivers. It is normal to have each car for each student for the middle-high level of society. Now, surprisingly, as seen through the commitment form they filled up after the awareness program (Attachment 1), more and more students decided to use their bikes and take advantage of public transportation.

Scene Four

Students were surprised to learn the concept of business as an agent of world benefit. Students only knew that some companies are doing philanthropic acts. This is merely about spending money for a social cause. They had never realized that it is possible to do business while doing good. The learning experiences and class activities have opened up their eyes that by changing the business model, you can earn money while supporting the global goals of the United Nations.

Scene Five

Being the students of a boutique business school, students never had exposure to the other side of life. For example, when asked about poverty, there is an anecdote saying a student would relate it to a family who can only afford one car, one house, and one maid. Of course, this is far from the truth because in Indonesia some people have to survive with only 2 USD a day. The students never had the experience of life at the bottom of the pyramid, therefore have little or no initiative to solve the poverty problem. The community engagement project visiting the communities from the bottom of the pyramids was an eye-opener and a mind-blowing experience to them and transformed their way of thinking.

Scene Six

The students were raised in a family with maids and nannies who took care of all their needs. This dampened their problem-solving skills and life skills. The habits of being taken care of have impacted them in an egocentric way of living. Priorities were given to self-gratification and hedonistic activities such as playing games, watching movies, spending time in cafés and restaurants, and hanging out in prestigious hangout places. Paying attention to the biospheric orientation was not a familiar concept to them. After the community program which brings them closer to nature and by participating through the experiential learning programs, they started to have pride in becoming an independent and influential person. Some even started their campaign program for a good cause. Some started their micro and small businesses for a good cause.

Faced with the indifference and the negligence atmosphere of the students, I was inspired by the LEAP team to do a transformation process in Ipmi by implementing the sustainability mindset through real-life experiences, community engagements, and projects conducted together with the business school students both in the undergraduate and graduate degree programs.

The Center for Sustainability Mindset and Social Responsibility of Sekolah Tinggi Manajemen Ipmi

The Center for Sustainability Mindset and Social Responsibility in Sekolah Tinggi Manajemen Ipmi is designed to facilitate the implementation of a syllabus, programs, research, community engagements, and experiential learning activities in supporting the transformation toward the sustainability mindset.

Overview of the Sustainability Mindset Framework and the Role of the CSMSR

The sustainability mindset is developed to support the global goals and locally embedded to make it relevant to all the local perspectives of professors from all corners of the world. The following is the big vision and mission of implementing the sustainability mindset by supporting the Sustainable Development Goals (SDG) of the United Nations.

SDGs as global goals are urgently needed to make sure that educators make their teaching relevant and focused on actions for a better world. Professors from around the world are sharing creative ways to make SDGs embedded into their business class's curriculum and engaging students to explore and find creative ways to transform student's mindset into supporting the global goals. The CSMSR (Center for Sustainability Mindset and Social Responsibility) has been quick to respond by implementing a local touch in the experiential learning programs designed to transform the mindset of the students toward implementing sustainability.

The ripple of influence started with the academic team members as the accelerators. The academic team, in turn, impacted the business school's students and through the professors' forum also inspired other colleagues around the world to join the movement. Students have been engaged in conducting empowering programs for their community and neighborhoods and implemented the quadruple helix between educational institutions, government, corporations, and communities to create an impact. The idea was to create a hands-on total immersion projects and to create a lot of noise in social media to develop an awareness of the SDGs in the general public. After graduation, students will also transfer the transformed mindset to work, and the executive students and the regular class students might readily become influencers in their workplace.

The CSMSR is also engaged in collaborative research on the implementation of the transformational sustainability mindset and produces the results through papers and materials presented at international conferences.

The mission of the Center for Sustainability Mindset and Social Responsibility is as follows:

- To develop an impactful learning experience by creating documents, tools, and exercises to develop the sustainability mindset
- To work on SDGs-based community projects and document the whole process from proposals to report including videos and pictures
- To produce chapters, books, and papers and present at national and international conferences
- To produce papers and present at academic settings
- To connect with other departments and/or faculty in their respective institutions, to promote a sustainability focus and create synergy
- To share ideas with other professors and develop a support group to share resources between collaborating institutions
- To disseminate the ideas of supporting the Sustainable Development Goals to a greater scale and share the success story through chapters and papers in international publications

The sustainability mindset focuses on transformative learning through both visible aspects and the internal way of thinking. The experiential transformative learning aspects are focused on innovations, new benchmarks, best practices, state-of-the-art technologies, radical innovation, and other approaches to solve the social and environmental challenges. The highlight of the mindset is connected to the internal dimension, be it in the individual or in a group level. The impact of the mindset is transforming the way the students look at the big pictures, the long-term values, the new assumptions, beliefs, and sense of purposes. And the most important thing, in the end, is that they implement the new mindset, commit to it, and leave a legacy through implementing it by working with the community.

Overview of the Sustainability Mindset Framework

In this section, I will present the four frameworks including the thinking, being, and doing aspects for each of the frameworks. At the end of the section, I developed a set of activities from my perspective of understanding after gathering all the relevant references and information. To ease understanding, the explanation of the frameworks below will be described through each of the components of thinking, being, and doing.

Figure 5.1 is used as the framework for designing students' activities. These elements are used to develop the form of innovative and collaborative action between students, faculty, and academia.

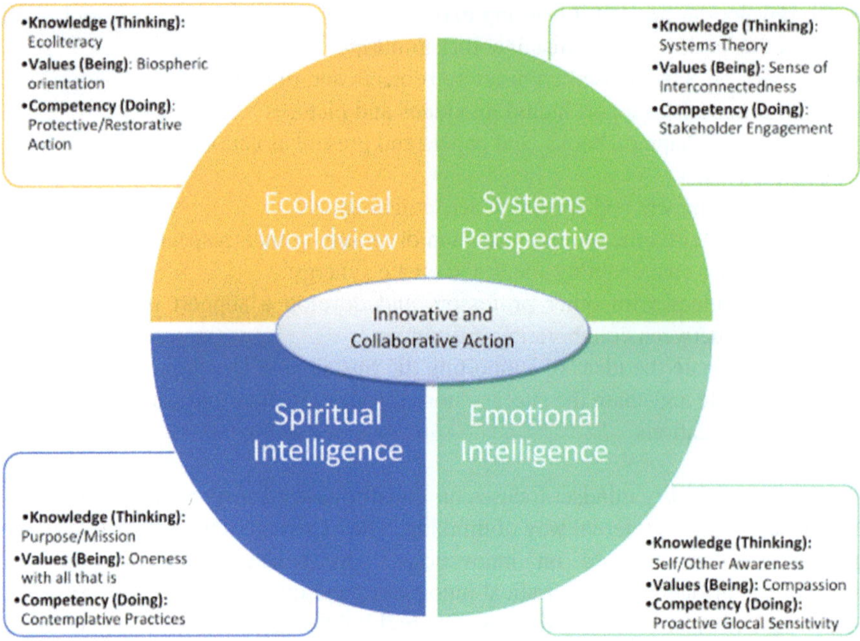

Fig. 5.1 Sustainability mindset framework. (Kassel et al. 2016)

Key Concepts of the Sustainability Mindset Framework and the Experiential Learning Practices

The sustainability mindset is focusing on the triple bottom line approach and the endeavors to support the global goals (Sustainable Development Goals of the United Nations).

The 2030 SDGs are new hopes and milestones for new perspectives of our inclusive world, based on peace, prosperity, and well-being. This is also a commitment to preserve our planet (www.undp.org). Through a closer examination of the ecological pressures, social, health, and economic challenge, Laszlo and Zhexembayeva (2011) proposed that there are three interconnected trends in the form of declining natural resources, increasing expectation by the stakeholder, and the high degree of transparencies made possible by communication through the Internet. And all these need to be addressed by the business leaders. Leaders need to mitigate the risk by redefining the way the companies operate (Laszlo and Zhexembayeva 2011). A shift in paradigm is required to act on these new forces. Businesses must develop an inclusive and flourishing business model, beneficial not just for their own sake but also make a positive impact on their sphere of influence (Urip 2010) and therefore will be supported by the stakeholders.

The Content Area of System Perspective

It is crucial in every strategic management decision to take into account the whole integrated system perspective and take into consideration the need and interests of all stakeholders influenced by the system. This also applies to the faculty and researchers while conducting their research and analyzing their strategy in transforming the students (Senge et al. 2008).

One of the important shifts in a system perspective is to move toward a long-term perspective as opposed to short-term system thinking. In the effort to increase efficiency and speed, it becomes a habit to make decisions based on a short-term horizon. Every action however also has consequences that are not immediately visible. While analyzing the possible impact, it is necessary to consider the long-term situations. Furthermore, making long-term decisions has a positive impact on global sustainability (Stachowicz Stanusch and Amann 2017).

Other important shifts in a systems perspective are to move from either/or thinking toward both/and thinking. Rational thinking and logic operate under the either/or logic, and when decisions are made solely from that perspective, they tend to create exclusion of key stakeholders, prioritizing one over the other and creating zero-sum solutions. Both/and thinking allows us to understand the paradox and calls for creative solutions that are inclusive of all stakeholders. These inclusive solutions are important for the healthy ecosystem and in the end, create fair and peaceful societies.

The third important concept is cyclical flow thinking. There are no linear processes in nature: All flows in cycles of birth, growth, death, and rebirth, and it goes on and on in a cycle. Many aspects of man-created unsustainability of the planet are a result of the linear thinking and forgetting the cyclical flow, which is a fundamental fact of nature's law.

Systems Perspectives: The Knowledge (Thinking) Aspects

The systems perspective requires a helicopter view of thinking related to the system theory as presented by Capra (1997). For the sustainability mindset implementation, particularly to the systems perspective, the concepts of both/and logic, cyclical flow, and long-term thinking are the best approach to broadened one's perspective (Rimanoczy 2010). Instead of the usual approach of either/or, the students need to train their paradoxical thinking using both/and logic. The either/or approach calls for a rigid way of thinking of only one interpretation, a right or wrong approach. On the other hand, both/and thinking encourages the students to see and respect different paradoxes and contradictions as the beauty of synergy from different perspectives. Instead of being exclusive, this both/and logic invites an inclusive approach of different perspectives to fulfill the needs of the stakeholders.

As we have mentioned above, another important systems perspective concept is cyclical flow. Humans just like all the other living creatures experience a cyclical flow – birth, life, and death. Even organizations go through a similar cycle just like the living creatures' cyclical flow. The usual way of rational thinking facilitates logic and linear cause-effect relationships. Business and management education is developed around linear and logical rational thinking, based on a set of hard data. The dependent variable is a function of several independent variables, based on the linear cause-effect approach. The problem of this linear thinking lies in the inability to picture the complex cyclical flow in a complex situation. Using cyclical flow understanding requires different perspectives, acknowledging the possibilities of multiple patterns and the existence of unknown variables.

Long-term thinking is the other important concept in systems perspectives. How very often we see case studies where management makes decisions based on a short-term target, to meet their urgent need to fulfill their quantitative bottom line. The reward system emphasizes the target which often means short-term achievements. Sometimes this shortsighted approach in the long-term becomes a menace, especially for the issue of sustainability. Pursuing sustainability requires the managers to see the long-term perspective instead of the shortsighted time horizon approach. This long-term view uses past history to learn from past mistakes and take into consideration the long-term impact of decision-making. All these paradigms of thinking need to be transformed into the mind of the business school students.

Systems Perspectives: The Being Aspects

To nurture the being aspects, students need to feel the value of being part of a great web of life, where everything is interconnected. By understanding and being part of the interconnections through experiential learning, students will understand the full picture. They will feel that everything is interconnected to sub-systems, and in turn, all sub-systems form an interlock and connected to the larger system including the local communities, governments, businesses, nations, and the environment and ecosystem.

Systems Perspectives: The Doing Aspects

The knowledge and the values aspect mentioned above will lead to the doing aspect. Students need to show their competencies in conducting real action. In the following section, I will share the detailed experiential learning in conducting these stakeholder engagement activities.

Experiential Learning for Developing Systems Perspectives: Some Suggestions

The classroom settings in our approach are designed to promote active learning where every student in the classroom will be the center of attention. The faculty take a role as facilitators. Real examples, story-telling, and other persuasive communications are used to keep the students engaged. If possible stay away from the "death by PowerPoint syndrome." This is how we picture the boredom of having to listen to a faculty explaining the classic power points.

In our class we encourage participative methods and take advantage of possible online tools, for example, we use www.mentimeter.com to make sure all the students' perspective counts and can be shown in the form of the word cloud, for example, in real-time immediate survey result. We also use online methods such as kahoot.it for competitions/quiz and other excitements for the classroom. We are lucky that now all these apps are available and the instructions to use it are available in a very user-friendly way. A bigger scale of interactive learnings was also conducted. The following are some of the active learning activities conducted to promote understanding of systems perspectives.

1. Award winner for innovative business model. The pre-requirement of this game is that the students are aware of the Sustainable Development Goals and the 2030 targets of the United Nations.

   In this game, students will understand the basic knowledge of a systems perspective. Students are introduced to successful business models that have implemented the radical innovation where the systems perspectives show the both/and approach rather than the either/or approach. For example, one of the popular Indonesian soy sauces produced by Unilever becomes a market leader through this approach. The sweet Soy Sauce of Kecap Bango was developed as a collaboration between the soy farmers as the soy suppliers with Unilever as the brand owner and Universitas Gadjah Mada as the research center producing high-quality soy seeds. This project has successfully transformed the farmers from being the poor uneducated farmers into highly skilled farmers using the research-based Malika (black soy seeds) as a result of the distinctive research of Universitas Gadjah Mada. In this program, Unilever has conducted a successful community engagement program with a triple-helix approach (orchestrating corporation, communities, and academicians/researchers) while ensuring high-quality supplies of soy seeds from the farmers. Unilever guarantees buying the soy from the farmer for a higher price than the market, and their successful community engagement program became the word of mouth which led to *Kecap Bango* becoming the market leader for soy sauce. In this example, the successful community engagement with the poor farmers in Central Java has led to a big promotional campaign, free of charge, for the soy sauce products and at the same time built a guaranteed high-quality value chain. It has now become a legend among the successful flourishing business stories.

Some business models are using the zero-waste cyclical flow approach where the waste in one business becomes the resources of the other business model owned by the same group. For example, there is the case of the Great Giant Pineapple business in South Sumatera. The pineapple skin's waste becomes the feedlot for the cow's farm. The cow's manure becomes the fertilizer for the pineapple farm. Zero-waste cyclical flow has guaranteed a high efficiency of the business, and the company enjoys competitive advantages through implementing the cyclical flow framework of thinking.

The main focus of these businesses, in the long run, is aiming at holy and sacred greater purposes. Research has shown that in some cases these corporations with a purpose and spiritual culture have created a higher satisfaction and commitment, and in some cases, these companies outperformed other companies who are not implementing the spiritual values and purpose in terms of net earnings, return on investment, and shareholder value by 400–500% in the long run (Garcia-Zamor 2003).

After the discussion on the successful innovative highly profitable business ideas for a greater purpose, the students are challenged in a team setting, to discuss an out-of-the-box dream business model, with the aim of supporting the global goals, but at the same time have to be profitable in order to be sustainable in the long run. A reward will be given to groups who convincingly present a business idea that makes a great impact. To make it interesting, the format is set up like an "award"-winning event. Each group has to present as if their business model were chosen as the winner of a business supporting at least one of the 17 Global Goals of the United Nations.

This becomes very amusing because the students can use their wildest fantasy of creating a business which defies the traditional thinking of either/or, linear, and short-term gain but rather uses the innovative both/and, cyclical flow, and long-term orientation and support a greater purpose to at least one of the Sustainable Development Goals of the United Nations. They will have to draw their business model posters and convincingly explain why they were chosen as the recipient of the winner award.

I have used several modifications of this game with different approaches accordingly. If the time is short, then we will use the award-winning approach. But if we have ample time, then it will be more like a competition of a start-up business ideas.

My colleagues from the entrepreneurship class successfully brought the idea to another level. They did it step by step purposefully until they could show a prototype of the product and have a whole scale of real business incubation-like process.

2. Interconnectedness: web of life. There is no pre-requirement prior to this game. In order to understand transformative learning richly, we need to recognize the extraordinary power and webs of relationships where we are invariably entangled somewhere maybe as a consumer, or a bypasser who evaluates and posts some influencing comments in the social media. We are constantly evaluating everything around us. We need to understand the interconnections to appreciate

the diversity which has provided such a rich synergy. When we appreciate diversity and interconnectedness, we can have more inclusive decisions supporting sustainability.

We introduce this "interconnectedness: web of life" exercise by choosing one item that touches almost everyone's life. For example, we use "the story of a cup of coffee." Students are divided into small teams. In a relatively short time, we ask the students to "find everything that matters" to produce a cup of coffee. This is a game to understand interconnectedness. The student will have to play as detectives to name the list of who plays a role for all of us to be able to drink a cup of coffee. Once they delve deeper into the discussion, they realize that there are so many things that are interconnected. For example, it includes the cup to hold the coffee, the fertilizers used by the farmers, the devices in the coffee plantation, the export/import companies, the trading companies, and the loan shark perhaps who have bought the coffee well before harvesting time with a very low price to cover the farmer's loan (caused by lending money to the farmers who has to buy the fertilizers from the loan shark in the first place), which is why lots of the farmers in the developing country do not enjoy a good profit from their margin during harvesting time.

Groups who came up with the longest and most relevant findings win. Students realize that everything is interconnected, and we live in this giant spider web of supply and demand, be it as a producer, a middleman, or just as consumers. So everything that we do matters. This helps us to make sure we only consume products with a good purpose and a good process respecting the earth and mankind. Sometimes simply trusting the label is not sufficient. We need to be aware of our surroundings, go to the farm and listen to the coffee farmers and try to understand the real facts of life. This helps us to better understand the web of life.

At the end of the game, facilitators can share some shocking pieces of information, for example, "Slavery in the Chocolate Industry" (https://youtu.be/ZNpwIzeyjKQ) or "Sweat Shops Behind Branded Items" (https://youtu.bc/exD6tc-wI0o). These case studies show the facts of unethical business conduct. After some shocking realities of life which show how greed has tempted business people into exploitation and unethical conduct, students are asked to do a self-reflection.

For the reflection, I use background subliminal message music, or stress-free relaxation music, and invite them all from the beta awareness thinking wave mode to the alpha thinking mode for mindfulness and relaxation. This is the frequency where the students are ready to absorb like a sponge and will be open to suggestions. I will use my low-tone persuasive voice and ask the students to see themselves as agents of change and that they have the power as an enabler/accelerator and influencer. I invite them to contemplate what and how they would do things differently to leave a legacy. This activity can be a good predecessor to the life journey exercise, which will be explained in the spiritual intelligence framework.

3. Aim2Flourish movements. Pre-requirements: Students with ample information on knowledge and being experience from the systems perspective are ready to move to the action module. Aim2Flourish is an inspiring platform showcasing businesses around the world that support at least one of the Sustainable Development Goals of the United Nations (www.aim2flourish.com).

   The beautiful part is that the whole process is done by students coming from all parts of the world. The students interview the business founders and/or key person to unravel the greater purpose behind every innovative business model through the appreciative inquiry approach. Unlike the problem-based approach, where students are focusing on the problem, in this appreciative inquiry approach, students are eager to focus on their appreciation toward the business model. This creates a positive atmosphere and, in lots of situations, is a life-changing experience (Cooperrider and Whitney 2005). I have had students who went on a boat to an island to interview a business owner, for example, and had a life-changing experience. Some of the experience was so moving and touching that they decide to change their life perspectives forever. Through the exposure with the inspirational idea creators, the students gained a sense of self-confidence. My students had convincingly said, "In the future, I will be the one interviewed by the students for this Aim2Flourish platform because now I have found my calling. This is the only way I would run my business. I am convinced that by supporting the Global Goals my business will be supported by the whole stakeholders and flourish."

   The strength of the Aim2Flourish platform is the implementation of the appreciative inquiry approach as we have mentioned above. The students interview business leaders by appreciating and celebrating their achievements. This appreciative approach gives the best chance to get motivated by interviewing the founder behind the innovations. Students have shared strong comments on how they were transformed through the whole process. One of the comments from Ipmi students was featured by AIM2Flourish as an example of student's feedback after joining the Aim2Flourish platform (as shared by Roberta Baskin, Director of Aim2Flourish).

   > Being a participant in this initiative (AIM2Flourish) is already a great achievement. Having an opportunity to conduct an interview and probe a particular innovation and flourishing story is a great learning experience for us. Our paradigms somehow shifted toward a sustainable direction of conducting business (in the future) wherein social innovation will form the nuclei of our business models. Writing the story highly inspired us. That in itself is already a huge reward for us. And, this was made possible through our enthusiastic and unselfish friend, mentor, and guru, Ms. Amelia Naim Indrajaya. We hope that you persistently continue your initiatives, sowing the seeds for future generations to nurture, grow and reap for the betterment of the earth and the universe we live. (Kassel and Rimanoczy 2018)

   Appreciative inquiry (AI) methodology is a wonderful methodology transforming a mindset from focusing on problems and shifting that mindset toward appreciation. This creates more positive energy, and the process sparks more enthusiasm on how to make it even better. This methodology is supported by Rimanoczy (2017) who posit that when we focus on strengths, we will unleash the potential power from within as a result of shifting our paradigm toward positive appreciation.

The Content Area of Ecological Worldview

A broad understanding of ecosystems is needed to bring about awareness and respect for the interconnections between all the attributes of the ecosystems, be it abiotic or biotic. Students need to see how humans interact with the natural world in performing their daily activities.

Ecological Worldview: The Knowledge Aspects

Eco-literacy is an important area within the sustainability mindset framework. We need to understand the principles of ecology which include systems thinking in terms of relationships, connectedness, and the context toward the big picture. Our challenge is to encourage the students of business schools who will be the future leaders to guard and make sure that nature's ability to sustain life is not in any danger. To achieve this we need to preserve our common home for creating a sustainable world, and this has become an urgent task (Capra and Mattei 2015). Sustainability mindset literacy especially in terms of eco-literacy becomes an important subject to understand especially among future business leaders.

The Ecological World: The Being Aspect

The ecological world needs to be respected and appreciated. The utilitarian approach studied in business school tends to focus on how to utilize the resources to maximize the shareholders' value, which is a menace for the long-term sustainability of scarce resources. Students need to demonstrate a good understanding of this biospheric value to be able to see from a different perspective. This value could be seen through the personal level, the community level, the enterprise, or the governmental level. Students got a chance to immerse themselves in a community project in nature to enhance their biosphere orientation. After the experience, students will understand how important it is to be inclusive, responsible, and implement sustainability mindset. These experiential learnings will support a new way of thinking toward practicing good corporate governance once they become part of the business people (Daniri 2014; Urip 2010).

Ecological Worldview: The Doing Aspect

The action part of the ecological worldview naturally will be in the endeavor to protect and restore the ecological equilibrium. This is imperative because so many places have degraded the environment so badly that it might not be possible to restore it back to its natural form. Even the loss of one species will make the ecosystem more fragile which forces the system to adapt accordingly or fail (Eisenstein 2013).

Programs to Improve Ecological Worldview

The knowledge part of ecological worldview requires eco-literacy. Students need to understand the challenges and the complexity of how all of the biotic and abiotic are linked to each other. The best program of understanding the ecological worldview is through a walk of nature in the wilderness. But being a part of the business school, we find ourselves among concrete buildings, trapped in the middle of a metropolitan city. I have tried to outsmart these circumstances by bringing the ambiance of nature into the classroom. We talk about the *Global Trends* book by Adrian Done (2011), with a focus on the chapter about ecosystems and biodiversity. And the activity can be based also on other books as long as they are inspiring and improving our eco-literacy. The name of the activity is "express your eco-literacy findings in the most out of the box approach showing threats and opportunities."

1. Express your eco-literacy findings in the most out of the box approach showing threats and opportunities. Pre- requirement: Read Chapter 10 on Ecosystem and Biodiversity from *Global Trends* (Done 2011) or other books that may improve eco-literacy. A week before class, each group of students is challenged to read and improve their eco-literacy and prepare an out-of-the-box presentation on their findings of ecosystems and biodiversity on both point of views: threats and opportunities. The target of this challenge is to increase their eco-literacy as much as possible and share it with the whole class in an inspiring out-of-the-box performance.

   The first time I assigned this challenge, I thought they would come up with the usual PowerPoint presentation about ecosystems and biodiversity. I had shared the rubric of evaluation, and I put a big portion of the grade on the inspiring, innovative, and creative criteria in addition to the content. To give a sense of competition, every group would evaluate all the other groups, and there would be a prize for the best group performance.

   I was not expecting much. But I was in for a big surprise. They took it seriously! One group set up a tent. They turned on the chirping sound of the woods as the background. They dimmed the light. And to my surprise, they started the scene by running around in "sarong" (this is a traditional skirt for men, usually for informal leisure time) in an act of panic. They had a video on the screen about a calamity in the jungle. The students were wearing a "sarong" to simulate exactly what would happen in the forest. I was surprised. All the students were so engaged, and this is even better than the usual students' play. They put extra effort to use the sound system to the max.

In the next scene, the students acted as the local champion discussing with the whole community. From the scene, the audience got a clearer picture of what had happened when the giant investors started to open up new businesses by creating a disaster in the communities' beloved forest and how it was impacting their well-being. In the end, they also prepared videos of their messages on their eco-literacy understanding both on the threats and opportunities. In the end, all the students committed to what they would do differently upon the discovery of this new fact.

I was speechless, this was much better than what I had expected. And they poured their hearts into doing this, because of the group competition and my enthusiasm for their performance. The beauty of it is that they are their own jury. So everyone in the classroom evaluated each other honestly on how much they learned, how creative, and how inspiring the groups' performance was.

These activities have become such a fun thing to do. My students were using all kinds of different costumes and wigs according to their roles, and some guys are playing female roles just for the fun of it.

I make sure that they learned something from the performance, by assigning the students to develop their commitment. This is based on what they learned and all the inspiration they got from the day's performance and how they would respond to it and leave a legacy (Fig. 5.2).

2. Detective challenge activities. In the endeavor to understand the value of ecological worldview through having the biospheric orientation, we use these detective challenge activities. Pre-requirement: Understanding carbon footprint and the issues of climate change and global warming.

Fig. 5.2 Express your eco-literacy finding in the out-of-the-box approach

Students are asked to be a detective and find out how much carbon footprint they make. Every person plays a role in contributing to the planetary challenges, mostly unintentionally and frequently without realizing it. Once we successfully identify how we are contributing to the problems, we have a chance to do something about it. The students were asked to detect and notice habits that require a transformation from each of their daily rituals. To make this diverse and fun, we do this in pairs. Each student would interview their partner in their rituals and habits. This is interesting because in Ipmi we have a great deal of diversity. Some are foreigners, some are Chinese Indonesian, some are Arabic Indonesian, Indian Indonesian, and of course, lots of them are Malay Indonesian. All of them have different beliefs, different cultures, and different rituals. They interview each other on how much of an ecological footprint they made and compared it to their grandma and grandpa, by interviewing them as well. It is interesting to see how the youngsters are using up the planet much faster than the elderly. It is a fact that the younger generations are more wasteful. One of the apps that we can use is https://www.footprintcalculator.org/.

At the end of this challenge, each group comes up with their detective findings in the form of noticing how many planets do we need if we continue to live like this, and they come up with a commitment to some transformative way of life, more suitable to preserve nature.

3. Environmental impact project. Pre-requirement: Understanding the global goals (17 UN SDGs) and awareness of global warming and climate change issues. In addition to the "thinking and being" activities mentioned above, we also need some hands-on total immersion learning opportunities, and we need to use the principles of eco-friendly activities in the form of protective/restorative action. Students are given an overview of the issues in the environmentally friendly model such as clean production, waste reduction through the 3R approach (reduce, reuse, recycle), clean energy, environmentally friendly offices, zero-waste cycle system, fair trade, life cycle assessment, carbon/ecological footprints, and other sustainable environmental issues. In our business school, we use a lot of case studies, and we focus on the case studies of businesses, implementing an environmentally friendly model that has utilized innovation for ecological sustainability. This exercise is conducted as a total immersion project, and we call it the environmental impact projects.

The main message of these hands-on activities is that the students should not focus on how to reduce cost by doing a green approach, but instead focus on developing an innovative (radical innovation) business model where the more they do business, the more they do good for the environment and society (Reinhardt 1998).

Students are assigned to report green innovations that have shown positive results and profitability. Through this detective work, students investigate a specific green innovative business model, and how the model might inspire. One of the firms investigated by the students was a micro-enterprise producing a "biopori" device, a tool to create small holes in the ground for storing water (Figs. 5.3 and 5.4). The holes become an organic waste dumpster and a flood

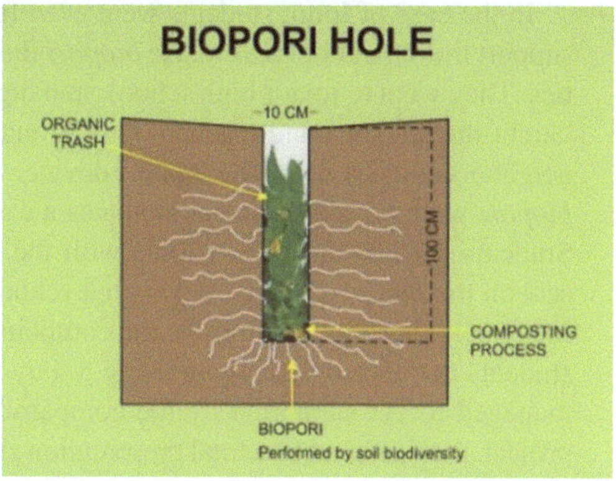

Fig. 5.3 Biopori hole

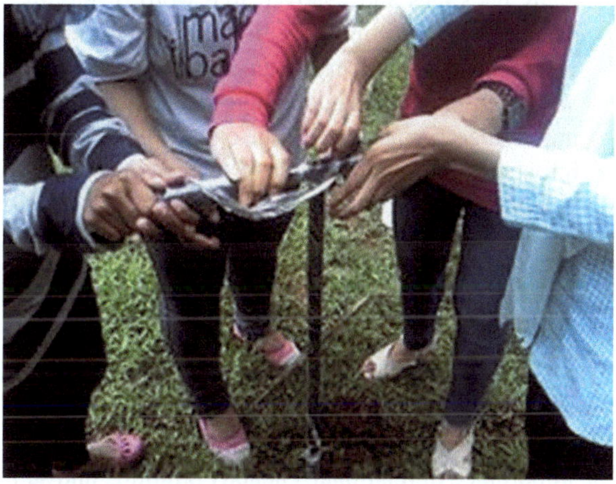

Fig. 5.4 The making of the biopori hole

prevention system as well. The *biopori* simple tool enables everyone to become a change-maker in their area. People build their own absorption holes with a multipurpose function using the *biopori* device. Rainwater is easily absorbed into the soil with *biopori* holes. With the *biopori* (absorption hole), the land will have enough water reserves, during the dry season. Worms make their own version of *biopori* in the soil; by providing additional absorption holes, we can help the worms to aerate and condition the soil, forming additional soil support and water reserves in the areas over time. The food waste and organic waste such as vegetables, food scraps, leftover fruits, grass cuttings, or dry leaves can be filled up in the absorption hole. Organic waste in the *biopori* hole turns into compost. This compost can be harvested from the hole every 3 months. After harvesting the compost, the hole is refilled with new organic waste to feed the microbes in the soil. Thus, the *biopori*, in the form of a small hole 10-cm wide, offers many benefits: saving water, preventing flooding, making compost, conditioning the soil, and reducing the waste stream. So the business model of a *biopori* device is a good example of a flourishing business model. The more you do business by selling more *biopori* devices, the more you do good!

In the case of Ipmi, students went even further by initiating a competition to support the spread of ideas to use *biopori* through a campaign in their communities. They went to junior high schools and high schools in the neighborhoods and taught the students and teachers how to make their own *biopori* holes in their neighborhoods by using the *biopori* device. The story and process of making the *biopori* were posted on social media as a campaign to promote green activities. Students gave away *biopori* tools with the Sekolah Tinggi Manajemen Ipmi's seal on the *biopori's* cover and visited schools, offices, and community housing in the neighborhood to promote the competition and the benefit of *bioporis*. The students conducted their fundraising to buy the *biopori* packages. Other groups managed to get supported by the company's CSR program. At the end of the project, they performed a final presentation showing how deeply they had learned about green innovation. First, the start-up entrepreneur producing *biopori* sold many packages and received free word-of-mouth advertising. Second, *biopori* became a tool to conduct a green campaign, promote awareness of ways to prevent flooding, and to create an organic dumpster/composter. Third, by using *biopori*, students became change-makers and conducted a campaign on the importance of installing your own *biopori* in your backyard. Fourth, students initiated a competition, where they invited high school students to send their video on *biopori*-related activities through YouTube and the highest Likes received rewards. Through this competition, the students were able to create more change-makers.

The Content Area of Emotional Intelligence

The emotional intelligence content area is concerned about interpersonal skills and the importance of relational, capacity building, and self-awareness. The challenge is to nurture relationships and maintain high resilience in social interactions be it in the individual, team, organizational, or the general social interaction level (Goleman et al. 2003; Senge et al. 2008).

Emotional Intelligence: The Knowing Aspects

People are the main orchestrator of equilibrium; in the spiritual belief, a human being is the vicegerent of God to take good care of the universe (Indrajaya 2017). Therefore the intrapersonal and interpersonal skills are very much needed to motivate all the intercorrelated relationships. Emotional intelligence is a way to ensure a smooth collaboration between people with different backgrounds, and this unity in diversity is a good way to support a sustainability mindset.

Emotional intelligence is an important factor for leaders to be able to form and develop relationships. With emotional intelligence, the leaders can form a high-resilience emotional bonding, which enables them to focus on the problem, even in a crisis or when facing uncertainty, volatility, change, and ambiguity. Emotionally intelligent leaders can work with a diverse background of people, and by respecting differences, they create broader options and bring people collaboratively and appreciatively through crises, problems, and complications. Empathy and respecting diversity is required for a deeper relationship and for building trust. Compassion is an important value, especially in building a long-term relationship.

Emotional Intelligence: The Being Aspects

In the endeavor to transform the students, efforts should be focused on creating transformative change through enthusiasm, follow-through, and tenacity. It is hard for someone without these qualities to strive among differences and prejudices.

Self-awareness is a fundamental beginning in order to understand one's self. This should be achieved before we work to understand others. We need to train the "ability" to decide through a positive rational neo-cortex modern way of thinking rather than the sympathetic nervous system reactions which ignite our prehistoric brains with the fight or flight options (Indrajaya 2020). Moods and emotions should be channeled into positive actions which will build trust and develop collaboration.

Emotional Intelligence: The Doing Aspects

The knowledge and value of emotional intelligence are most effectively implemented in an action learning program. The program should be a mixture of locally embedded values, interconnected to global issues. We use the term "glocal" to picture this globally connected and locally embedded approach. The emotional intelligence aspect is nurtured when we are faced with the hard facts of life which will touch sensitivity and form empathy and compassion of a human being into conducting the real action of helping. Competency on social skills, self-control, and empathy builds rapport and trust. The *glocal* approach gives the flexibility to react and decide in any level of social settings, be it a small local team or an intercultural global team. It is again not either/or but both globally connected and at the same time locally embedded. This inclusivity further supports sustainability.

Students need to train their sensitivity. They also need to exercise their empathy. They need to learn to adjust their emotional state to understand and accept differences, but not having to agree. One of the programs to develop this emotional intelligence is in the form of understanding and respecting each other's values.

The Programs to Improve Emotional Intelligence

The program we have used to develop the knowledge part of emotional intelligence is by conducting an awareness exercise. In order to be aware of diversity, we need to understand that humankind was made equal. It is like the different cells in our body, and together they make a beautiful synergy of a living body, each with their

Fig. 5.5 Google cardboard virtual headset

own unique role and differences. We need to understand our own traditions, beliefs, and cultures and also respect other people's diverse cultural backgrounds. When we explore our personal values, beliefs, assumptions, and motivations, we gain greater control over our own actions and can see new alternative behaviors.

The awareness program is done through the Google virtual reality device (Fig. 5.5). Pre-requirements of this activity include reading relevant literature on their own religious beliefs and on awareness of different beliefs, diverse cultures, and traditions.

1. Appreciating diverse cultures program. Pre-requirement: reading on each different belief and tradition system

   This program is conducted by using a virtual reality gadget. Thanks to technology, everyone can enjoy and experience the global world without physically being there. The virtual reality Google is used through a low-cost Google Virtual Reality Cardboard. Google was giving it away for free. With a simple step, in no time, the pieces of cardboard are turned into a virtual reality headset (Fig. 5.5). Once you put in your handphone and the program with the virtual reality app, you will be transported to any ancient place that the online virtual reality provides. With this simple gadget, you can see a three-dimensional perspective. You can have a 360-degree vision. Looking around you, it is as if you are now virtually in your chosen place.

   To appreciate the diverse cultural and traditional backgrounds, students are invited to set up in pairs, preferably two people from different backgrounds, different beliefs. To respect each other's beliefs, students experience the virtual reality of a spiritual sacred place. There are six different religious traditions recognized in Indonesia – first Islam and then Christianity, Catholicism, Buddhism, Hinduism, and Kong Hu Chu. Through this virtual reality headset, what seems impossible (e.g., visiting Mecca is forbidden for the non-Moslem believer), through this Google virtual reality, everyone can experience any part of the world including the sacred spiritual place like Kaaba, the house of Allah (God) in Mecca (Makkah). Everyone can witness the swirling movement encircling the Ka'ba. The movement is counterclockwise. If the pilgrim dares to take a clockwise movement, he or she would crash with the counterclockwise mass movement and would be certainly looking for trouble. The Ka'ba is a simulation of the movement of the universe. Every star, planet, and galaxy is in its respective orbit, all moving counterclockwise. And any attempt to defy the law of nature would cause a fatal collision – even creating a doomsday scenario. This simulation is designed to train humankind that following the call of nature and performing a flourishing act would mean creating a beautiful synergy. But violating the law of the universe would for sure create fatalities even to the point of creating your doomsday as you are not listening to your conscience by breaking the law of balance and nature.

The understanding of the symbols and simulation will support the importance of self-control and balance. On the other hand, the Muslim students can go and visit the sacred place of Catholics in the Vatican, for example. And both students can explore their different beliefs to be able to respect each other's beliefs. The understanding of different cultures and beliefs will create respect and harmony in diversity.

Students could explore their similarities in terms of the greater purpose of serving a good cause. By inviting each other to different places and understanding the substance behind traditions and rituals, students can discover unity in diversity. Students will learn to appreciate differences and look for ways to synergize and collaborate.

2. Community engagement project. Pre-requirement: Students should understand the global goals and the framework for the community engagement program.

   For the being aspect of developing emotional intelligence, students need to discover compassion, and this is done through the community engagement program where the students can choose the experience of supporting/helping marginalized people. In this program, students are invited to develop a voluntary community empowerment program. In the planning stage, they have to come up with a proposal for the program. The community program is evaluated through four different key point criteria. The first is how impactful. Therefore they should plan on how to measure the impact through a pre- and post-test, through surveys, focused group discussion, or other measurement forms for evaluating the program. Second is the scalability. Is it possible to enhance this project to a higher level? Is the framework applicable to a bigger scale? Third, the program is evaluated through the degree of innovation. How innovative is the idea? Is it a genuinely new form of community engagement? Is it a breakthrough, something that has not been done before? The last criteria are sustainability. Is there any capacity building and knowledge transfer while empowering the local champions? The students' projects are evaluated by the four criteria and also by direct observation of the process.

   One of the groups in our program decided to transfer the knowledge of upcycling used magazine papers to a group of women scavengers (Fig. 5.6). The

Fig. 5.6 Coco (**Co**llaboration **Co**operative) used magazine wallet business model. Madam PKK (women scavengers)

students taught the women how to make a wallet from used magazine paper. This project was flourishing to everyone involved in the business model because the students collaborated with the scavengers, and in the end, everyone earned additional incomes.

Now, this is beyond what I expected, this had led to the entrepreneurship ideas where the students were able to create a business model by supporting the global goals. In this case, it supported SDG number 1, "no poverty," because now the women scavengers can earn extra income. Later this became a new program in the outstanding values class, where I challenge the group of students to start a business model with just 30 USD or around Rp 400.000 (IDR) and at the same time supporting at least one of the SDGs. This extended version was also very successful. In 2 months my students made ten times the initial investment and decided to return my 30 USD. They made a lot of noise by offering their business model through social media and by promoting the story about the community that they are collaborating with. The invitation to the undergraduate students to start up a business with only 30 USD, with a sustainability mindset embedded in the model, was at first a surprising challenge for them. In the beginning, they were not sure what and how to start. But as they began designing the business model, the higher purpose of achieving and supporting the global goals give them a booster effect. Never had they dreamed of playing such an important role in their life, directly contributing to the Sustainable Development Goals of the United Nations! Their enthusiasm grew! The school acknowledged the effort and the impact made by the students, by promoting and also becoming the consumer of their products, and this appreciative approach created more energy,

Fig. 5.7 Beber puppet (an old classic art tradition)

promoting collaboration among the students and the faculty. Each team had to go through several presentation phases. At the very start when they developed their business model idea, they were illustrating their ability to think out of the box, and they came up with their genuinely innovative ideas.

One example of a business model launched by a student was focused on saving and preserving the cultural heritage in the form of "Save the *Beber* Puppet Art," a traditional art heritage of Javanese culture (see Fig. 5.7). The students designed and facilitated a social campaign to develop awareness about the importance of preserving this national and cultural art heritage. This art and tradition is a traditional heirloom dated back to 1244 AD. The students, as modern and millennials as they are, fight to support this ancient art from being lost forever. Most of the youngsters nowadays are not even aware of this traditional cultural art tradition. Through the campaign, the students raised the awareness of the local wisdom and tradition, and the fact that without support, all these traditional arts soon could only be found in history books.

In the endeavor to save the tradition, the students sold miniatures of the *Wayang Beber* to raise the funds. The video campaign, social media exposure, and the viral impact of patriotism of preserving the local wisdom created a successful emotional and spiritual awareness campaign. Even though the hype of selling these miniatures might be temporary, the students get the message of "doing well by doing good." The more they do business selling the artwork, the more they are helping the traditional artists to make an income while preserving the traditional art culture. In the process, they made a handsome amount of commission as well. These experiences are convincing them more that it is very much possible to do well by doing good.

Students have also developed a business model that does not require any start-up investment. They are implementing the partnership for the Sustainable Development Goals (SDG 17) by setting up a collaboration between a corporation, Unilever; the local communities; and the Rumah Pelangi Foundation, an

NGO working on sustainability issues, and the government, in this case, the Ministry of Environment. Ipmi serves as the facilitating educational institution. This is a good example of cooperation between corporations, NGOs, communities, government, and educational institutions. The first step was to set up an awareness campaign. Local champions from the communities were invited from the surrounding neighborhoods to participate in the awareness campaign. Speakers were invited from the Ministry of Environment, Energy Conservation, and NGO green activists. The local champions were divided into smaller groups based on their respective areas. Every group had to go through a brainstorming session on their current environmental challenges and explore the possibilities to improve these conditions. The awareness presentations opened up their paradigm to look for a solution for their social/environmental problem. The NGO provided the answers to their quest by facilitating and supporting the community to build their waste bank system.

Waste bank operations simulate the model of a bank, but instead of saving money, in this model, homeowners save their waste at the waste bank (see Fig. 5.6). The challenge is to introduce and implement the system to classify every home's garbage and waste. Organic waste should be processed into compost with a simple composting method using the composting liquid. Plastics, cans, and paper should all be classified and submitted to the waste bank. Unilever as the corporate sponsor helped by providing the ledger manual book and the logbook for each client of the waste bank. The logbook has a record of how much waste each client submitted to the waste bank. For example, plastic, paper, and other forms of waste have their value per kg. Hence, every client has a waste saving account book. The NGO experts became a partner to facilitate the process and help the community to set up their waste bank system and to teach them how to manage the whole process: from weighing the waste, connecting them to the garbage collector who paid for the waste, and teaching them how to do bookkeeping. The waste is sold daily to the garbage collector who pays cash to the waste bank. The clients usually save their money in the waste bank account until it reaches a substantial amount. Each waste bank also has its composting facilities and upcycle product shop where they sell upcycled products. The margin between the price paid by the garbage collector buyers and the price paid to the client plus the income from compost and upcycle products is the source of income of the waste bank. The amount might not be much, but as the volume increases, the amount becomes more significant. And most importantly, the waste bank system has successfully reduced the amount of trash sent to the landfill. This business model is beneficial for everyone involved in the process (Fig. 5.8). The students gained from the experience in developing a business model. Unilever together with its NGO collaborators gained by achieving its target on reducing waste. For each amount of growth, Unilever had committed to reduce the same amount of waste. By sponsoring this waste bank, they successfully taught the communities to collect their sachets, and other packaging waste into an upcycle product, and/or collecting it to the waste bank to add up to their waste saving account. The communities certainly gained by earning extra income

Fig. 5.8 A waste bank model

and managing their waste efficiently. The government also gained by achieving its goals in reducing waste to the landfill. The target was that the community would minimize their waste that goes to the landfill, since as a metropolitan city, Jakarta hardly has enough space for waste landfill. This is a tremendous help since in a large city like Jakarta, with a population of more than ten million, one of the most pressing problems is the waste handling system.

The students learned a lot about triple bottom line impact through the hands-on experiential learning of running an innovative start-up business with a social and environmental impact. They no longer talk only about reducing harm or complying with regulations, or what they would get from making a social impact or a green investment. Now they can transform the way they look at the business model. In the process, they are nurtured emotionally and spiritually through a whole new concept of business as an agent of world benefit (https://weatherhead.case.edu/centers/fowler/). This said, there were several challenges to be addressed. For example, first is the legal consideration. Some of the students are still minors younger than 17 years old and are not allowed to have their tax to report their business. Another issue is the tax obligations of these new enterprises. This problem has been addressed by setting up a cooperative system on the campus. The cooperative has its tax system, and the businesses created by the students are part of the cooperative activities. Even though there are still some challenges to solve, the output of the project is highly motivating.

Our community engagement project does not have to be profit-oriented. Other groups were also visiting scavengers, but they were focusing on giving health awareness programs, where the students shared the importance of cleanliness, washing hands, and personal hygiene. What makes this group transformed their mindset is their shocking fact-finding process. During the final report on the community engagement program, they were in tears telling stories on how they found out that these scavengers had to share one toothbrush for all of the scavengers in the compound (22 people). And how they barely made their commitment to follow the scavengers, because they had to walk for 3 h to follow the scavengers who collected the plastic rubbish and at the end, sold it with such a low price of 7 cents/kg. Sometimes they only got 10.000 IDR not even a dollar for all this trouble. The students found out that these scavengers do not use soap or shampoo, simply because they could not afford it. Even though they are not engaging the scavengers in any new business model activities, this community engagement program was still deemed to be successful in changing mindset. In the eye of the students, they would never see life the way they used to. Now they realize they have a big responsibility to proactively help to reduce poverty and become aware of the real social problems in Indonesia. In the eye of the scavengers, now they understand more about hygiene and health issues, and they received information on how to access the free health facilities and other important information.

The day of the final presentations was usually one of the most heartfelt touching programs. We had a group of students who invited the street kids they had been working with for the community program, to sing in the classroom as part of the final project. Other groups had invited students from the foundation of marginalized kids with disabilities to perform a show during the final presentation. Everyone shed a tear. The students realized whatever they are giving to these marginalized people, they are receiving even much more in terms of learning real-life values, endurance, perseverance, and the beauty of giving. I have received messages from the students that they feel blessed by doing these community engagement programs. They feel like going through a spiritual vacation. They are witnessing a "heaven-on-earth" feeling. And some of them made an effort to keep doing it, even though the class is over.

3. From millennials to millennials. Pre-requirements: Completion of the being and thinking aspects from the systems perspective, ecological worldview, and emotional intelligence. To exercise the competency or the doing aspect, students conduct a proactive glocal sensitivity campaign program. It is proactive because it is an awareness that helps to prevent a bigger problem in the future. It is glocal because it is supporting the global goals, yet it is embedded and modified to the local needs. At the same time, this program also increases sensitivity and awareness of the current situations. Students were assigned to conduct a campaign to support one or more issues in the global goals. For example, one group took the energy conservation campaign. The other group chose to conduct an anti-corruption campaign. In any topic that they choose, the challenge is to develop a plan to conduct an awareness workshop on one of the issues to support the global goal. The students need to experience the process of becoming the enabler,

Fig. 5.9 College students' brochure to attract high school students through Zoom

accelerator, and change-maker to their high school alma mater, by conducting an awareness program. They do it full scale, from designing the proposal, the brochure through to the detailed information of the campaign rundown. Figure 5.9 shows one of the brochures they created to attract high school participants. The beauty of this program is that these efforts were done by millennials for millennials. They were doing it in the language of the millennials, the millennials' way, very different compared to the traditional boring seminar format. Our students challenged the high school students to show the results of the awareness program by sharing their commitment and campaigns through the platform of TikTok, Instagram, and other popular online platforms. And without any hesitance, they gave away prizes to the high school students in the form of an online balance. In Indonesia, everyone is using their online balance to pay for almost everything – food, groceries, taxis, and motorbike taxis which are called *Gojek*. There are several popular payment platforms through online apps. Even the street hawkers take online payments. That is why the prizes in the form of the online balance are very popular among the millennials. From the evaluation form, I can see that the high school students enjoyed their college students' campaign very much, both in the offline and online formats. And through these "fun, experiential learning-the-millennial way," the college students have recruited high school militant students ready to safeguard the earth. This can be seen through the posting they made on social media.

The Content Area of Spiritual Intelligence

Spiritual intelligence is a form of intelligence that supports human beings in seeing themselves as part of the interconnectedness, a part of nature thoroughly embedded in it and nurtured by it in a whole web of life. Endangering the balance of life would mean an intervention in nature which may cause the whole system to adapt or fail (Eisenstein 2013). We humans are blended in the interconnection of life, and the spiritual intelligence in the human being will help us to see that humanity needs to restore the balance. We need to move from the utilitarian "take-make-waste" habits to a more sustainable "borrow-use-return" habit (Rimanoczy 2014). This means a new collaborative, sharing network, reusing, restoring, and recycling whenever possible. Spirituality will give the sense of stewardship to take care of the balance of life, not only by leading oneself but also leading the community, balancing the ecosystem, and preserving the environment. Spiritual intelligence will bring the belief of a holy purpose which will create a feeling of heaven on earth when you follow your conscience and do the right thing (Neal 2012).

Spiritual Intelligence: The Knowledge Aspect

Everyone needs to find his/her purpose in life. Having a sense of purpose for the greater good creates a meaningful life. Social contribution provides meaning to our life. When we practice mindfulness, we can use our reflective self-talk to discover "What is my purpose in life?" This motivates us to analyze our habits and make sure they follow the norms toward preserving nature and sustainability.

Spiritual Intelligence: The Being Aspects

Scharmer and Kaufer (2013) posited that we should see beyond a purely rational and factual way. They propose a transition from a self-egocentrism approach into a diverse cross-sector innovative way in the form of a co-creation to benefit all stakeholders. With spirituality and a sense of purpose, leaders and students are aiming for their higher purposes and for developing a higher engagement to support the communities and the environments.

Spiritual Intelligence: The Doing Aspects

The concept of mindfulness originates from Eastern traditions. It can be practiced by faculty by focusing on the present moment, feeling gratitude, and giving meaning to the surrounding. Indonesia is the country with the biggest Muslim population. Moslems perform prayer five times a day, and the concept of prayer is to move from the beta full alert thinking mode into the Alpha relaxation mode. Through rituals, a person can access their inner peace and often open up to new inspiration, sometimes experiencing something like a revelation. The state of mind of calmness supports the long-term, inclusive, nurturing, and flourishing way of thinking and therefore transforms the mind into supporting the sustainability mindset.

The Programs to Improve Spiritual Intelligence

Spiritual intelligence requires holistic thinking toward a greater purpose (Ibrahim 2004). One of the most powerful questions we can ask ourselves is "what is the purpose of life?"

The life journey. Pre-requirement: Understanding the triple heaven-on-earth questions. The materialistic economic paradigm focuses on consumption and profit, neglecting the higher self of the individual and our spiritual well-being. Incorporating into our life the concept of purpose helps to identify what matters to us personally, and what difference we want to make in the world. This is a powerful motivator to drive actions for the greater good and to shape a flourishing world. The life journey framework asks the student to plan their life according to their life's purpose (Ibrahim 2004).

- Creating your life's purpose identity. Students are asked to make their life's plan inspired by the life journey's template, starting with the life's purpose identity. They can make a Microsoft word document or a PowerPoint to explain their life plans in detail. A student can make a life's purpose identity; for example: on the 12th of December 2000, I was born to a proud couple: Bambang and Ita. I believe that my existence is for a noble purpose, which will be stated throughout the life journey map (see Fig. 5.10; the map has all the years of life up to 70 and can be expanded). My spiritual belief is to be an agent of change in serving the community, specifically in helping the farmers of Indonesia to be free of loan sharks by setting up an online system connecting the farmers and the consumers. To exercise my spiritual value, I will engage in spiritual practices to guide me in my commitment toward achieving my noble purpose. The spiritual practice will be according to my spiritual belief in Islam/Christian and joining Friday/Sunday activities in the mosque/church.
- The school supports the facilities for spiritual practices for the six religious beliefs acknowledged by the government. The Indonesian Basic Foundation

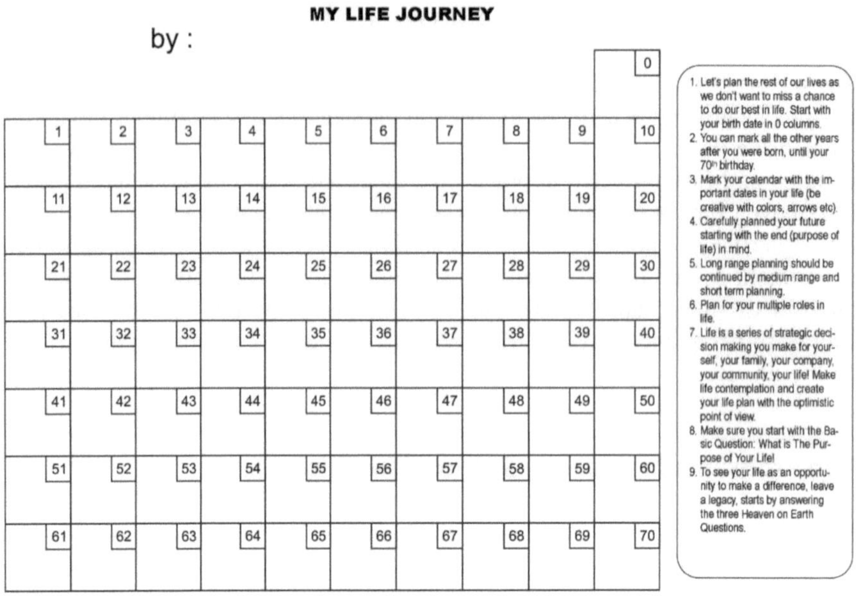

Fig. 5.10 Life journey's template

is Pancasila (five principles foundation) and the first principle is believing in one and only God. Students are encouraged to practice their religious beliefs and respect each other's different beliefs. For the Moslem students, each day they will have a mindfulness prayer scheduled for five times (usually the three schedules will be done in school time), which can be done individually or in a form of congregation prayer. And once a week, there will be a Friday mass prayer. These rituals serve a function as a continuous reminder of life's purpose, supporting people to be more pious, having high self-endurance, showing service-orientation, and commitment (Indrajaya 2019).

- Achieving one's dream is possible if you are committed and have a high level of resilience (Yeager and Dweck 2012). I have been using the Rutte (2012) approach of asking students the three heaven-on-earth questions. These questions ask you to recall a holy experience when you were doing something good. This heaven-on-earth feeling is when you feel goosebumps after doing something that touches your heart. Usually, this heaven-on-earth feeling comes when you serve and listen to the deepest conscience of your heart.
- First, we ask students to recall the vivid picture of these moments. In this exercise, we assume that we have a magic wand and that you can have your wishes come true. This enables you to design and plan anything you want to do, to make sure you can create your heaven on earth.
- Second, we ask everyone to write down their concrete actions in the next 24 h on how they will continue creating and enjoying heaven on earth. They can move

from the short term to medium term and long term, or vice versa. The most important thing is that this exercise challenges the students to think differently to leave a legacy and make a difference in life.

1. Mindfulness exercise. Pre-requirement: Watch a 19-min movie of the universe, taken from outer space (http://www.planetarycollective.com/overview/). There is also another good piece of watching the zoom-in zoom-out YouTube video, to understand how everything in this universe is interconnected (https://www.youtube.com/watch?v=Ww4gYNrOkkg). All the galaxies, stars, and planets are moving in their orbits in a very precise movement.

   This exercise helps to develop the mindset of becoming one with all that is/and to experience mindfulness through the reflective practice. This activity is about noticing when we need to pause, to think and observe, and noticing our speed and efficiency in creating automated actions. Sometimes these automated reactions may create unwanted consequences. Reflective practices help us to pause and to ponder the situation before jumping into action. Reflection is about noticing when we pause to think and observe. Learning is also enhanced when individuals regularly pause and reflect on what happened, how this matched the expectation, and how behaviors may have impacted the results.

   To do this exercise, students are challenged to go into nature, preferably where they will not meet people, because they will do the exercise (at least 40 min) in total silence. The students may not bring any gadgets, even a pen, a notebook, or any device to play music whatsoever. For 40 min, they just observe, ponder, contemplate, have an intrapersonal conversation with one's self. We ask them to give themselves a chance to just pause and reflect and discover what they experience after the 40 min of silence in nature.

   Our pace of life is increasingly fast, aided by technology and the growing urban concentration. This promotes reactive and automated, thoughtless behaviors. Processing information to understand what it means requires slowing down and creating spaces to observe, notice, and connect with our feelings. This nonthinking practice integrates our spiritual dimension and helps us develop mindfulness, an ancestral approach to expanding consciousness. Students write about their experiences and contemplations, and we invite them to come up with an out-of-the-box idea to show how they can play a good part in life.
2. Letter to the unborn babies. Pre-requirements: Understanding the impact of the materialistic world. Understanding the global trend, and the challenge to achieve and support the global goals

   Students are assigned to write a letter to their unborn babies. This letter addresses the facts of the materialistic life that we are now facing. The materialistic, consumption-oriented society has placed nature as something to be exploited to amuse the human being as the ruler of the universe. The philosophy is "take, make, and discard." We take even more and use even more resources in the name of business growth. This has resulted in a myriad of problems for our planet. We have to understand that we are one with nature, that we are a species within species, and that we were chosen by the Almighty to be the creature with the highest level of intelligence. A human with the neo-cortex ability of high-order thinking, therefore, can control one's self as the guardian of the universe. Students are asked to contemplate and picture how the planet would be like in the future if everyone does not realize their role to be the vicegerent of God to take care of the universe. The understanding of spiritual connection can shape behaviors and decisions that lead to more satisfying lives and a more harmonic relationship with each other and all beings.

To my surprise, the students came up with very moving and touching letters for their unborn babies. They went through reflective and contemplative learning and realize that now is the time to transform for the sake of the unborn future generations.

Conclusion

This chapter presented examples of activities and initiatives introduced by the author to the graduate and undergraduate students at the Ipmi International Business School – formally called Sekolah Tinggi Manajemen Ipmi. The programs are designed to transform the mindset of the students toward a sustainability mindset. Inspired by the framework of systems perspectives, ecological worldview, and emotional and spiritual intelligence of the sustainability mindset model, programs were developed through the thinking, being, and doing approach. After the programs, students were asked to post their commitments toward supporting the global goals (Attachment 1). The college students also developed more change-makers through their "raising awareness" campaign to high school students. The results show a highly promising output. I am seeing a transformed mindset through the daily observations, the conversations, their commitments, the concern they are showing through their letters for the unborn baby (Attachment 2), and the way they conducted their global goals campaign to the public. I am glad that Sekolah Tinggi Manajemen Ipmi is giving a chance to conduct these new experiential learning opportunities supporting the SDGs and a new model of business as an agent of world benefit in the curriculum and has become a part of the research conducted by the Center for Sustainability Mindset and Social Responsibility (CSMSR) of Sekolah Tinggi Manajemen Ipmi.

The limitations of our approach lie in the narrow context of just one business school. In the future, we hope that the CSMSR will collaborate with other business schools around the world to find out the best ways to encourage and develop the future leaders of the business school students to have a solid sustainability mindset, ready to develop the best business FOR the world!

Attachment 1: The Commitment of David Angga (Student of Business Ethics' Class)

What I will do which is fully under my control?
I will * I will use tumbler. * I will use public transportation. * I will bring my own bag when buying something. * I will never use plastic as possible as I can. * I will reduce electricity consumption. * I will use environmentally friendly products. * I will use lunch box. * I will turn-off unneeded electronic devices. * try to apply reduce, reuse, and recycle whenever possible. *
How would I create a circle of influence?
I will * make environmentally friendly products * make no plastic campaign * will recycle rubbish and influence others on this * will make a campaign to save the earth * will engage people to protect the environment * I will engage people to always maintain cleanliness * I will invite people not to use plastics

Attachment 2

Dear my unborn child,
As I write this, the earth is spinning, the stars are shining, and the whole galaxy is rotating, the same way as when you read this. Although, I could only imagine how different everything else must be, because the only *constant* in life is *change*. And change is exactly what I hope the majority of the human race has managed to achieve by the time you're old enough to roam the world on your own.

The planet is still mostly green and blue. I wake up, still, to the sounds of birds chirping, the 500 kg Amazonian green Anacondas still live and breathe outside of captivity, and more dangerous than any snakes. I'm sharing a living platform with greedy rich men in expensive suits who don't mind to immortalize any horrible ideas to get money, and fatten up their bellies and bank accounts.

Now, dear Child, I hope time has changed things when you come around. Today, kids are afraid of the world outside of their own. They live in a bubble of rising questions and pressure, as the media portrays and directs their every measure. The friends they make online are nothing more than illusions, all the communities, companionship, just for the sense of inclusion. Their morals and values are no longer planted by parents, they're confused by the constant addition of online information.

Adults cease to remember how to simply smile, they've forgotten the essence of life that is worthwhile. They work hard from 9 to 5 every single day. At the dinner table with family no one knows what to say. They all share the same exact genes, but they're nothing more than strangers it seems.

What is right? What is acceptable?

I am in no way eligible to create the perfect human, nor should there be perfection in appearance of any man. But a good heart takes you further in life, it'll grant you more than just the perfect husband or wife.

So here's a list of qualities I'll pray you'll possess, inhale it and let shine bright through your eyes.

First, let your heart be cleansed and your intention pure, every step you take, with love you'll endure.

The thing with humans is that we're born with a heart, however to value it, all begins with a start. But the big men still sit on their thrones, their hearts are uneasy; they scream, whine and groan.

They stay awake at night on a million-dollar bed, thinking of ways to double the money they've managed to collect. Their thoughts are cluttered, they begin to wonder, when they've fallen and suffered, who's going to be there?

Second, don't you let your thoughts dwell in hatred, for it ruins anything that was sacred. If anyone treats you unkindly, treat them with nothing but kindness, it's perhaps because the world hasn't shown them enough love and interest.

A heart full of abhorrence shuts the lights within you, it rots inside and bothers everything you do.

Third, remember that your presence and thoughts matter, your simple act could genuinely help those who suffer. Fight for those who feel mistreated, where unfairness is often repeated.

In you, I planted the strongest of strengths, through the pledge of courage that I sang.

With you, I have dreamed long before you were introduced, that by money and power you won't be seduced.

Fourth, forget not the ground you're attached to, all the beautiful colours that inhabit it; white, green, red and black too. Be the guard to all of God's creatures around you, be the voice to those who can't speak nor value.

As humans we're granted with tremendous blessings. We use our voices to protest, cry and sing. We use our power to break, hurt and destroy. We choose to ignore abuse, blind to the earth we destroy.

To be functional, you don't need to be 'activist', treat all beings with respect and learn to coexist.

Fifth, forget not the land you're bound to come back to, the red of your blood, and white of your bones, the spirit of those who fought for it too. Value the history of your motherland dear child, because with identity you'll stand strong even if all else failed.

Sixth, share your knowledge with the less fortunate, whether they can't afford it or are simply inconsiderate. Share your passion with gleaming desire, watch with patience as it slowly transpires.

Break boundaries that separate mankind, we've come way too far to press rewind. Racism, sexism, homophobia should no longer have a place; sexual preferences, gender, colour and others should all be embraced.

Seventh, the universe is a pole of countless uncertainty, even when you doubt one thing should guaranty. The dream you kept could turn to reality, when you put your faith in God's conservancy.

Dear my sunshine, whether I'm a corpse rattled with earthworms, or a wise mother dealing with heartburn, keep me in your prayers and I shall be close, to see the seven and the many other great traits you'll host.

Remember these aren't a way to pressure you,
For it's inevitable what you're born to do,
With endless love and possibility,
Through words we part in divinity,
Love,

Mum

References

Capra F (1997) The web of life: a new scientific understanding of living systems. Anchor, New York

Capra F, Mattei U (2015) The ecology of law: toward a legal system in tune with nature and community. Berrett-Koehler Publishers, San Francisco

Cooperrider D, Whitney DD (2005) Appreciative inquiry: a positive revolution in change. Berrett-Koehler Publishers, San Francisco

Cooperrider DAVID, Zhexembayeva N (2007) Business as an agent of world benefit. Kosmos 6(2), 2–33

Daloz LAP (2000) Transformative learning for the common good. In: Learning as transformation: critical perspectives on a theory in progress. Jossey-Bass, San Francisco, pp 103–123

Daniri MA (2014) Lead by GCG. Gagas Bisnis Indonesia, Jakarta

Done A (2011) Global trends: facing up to a changing world. Palgrave Macmillan, London

Eisenstein C (2013) The more beautiful world our hearts know is possible, vol 2. North Atlantic Books, Berkely

Garcia-Zamor JC (2003) Workplace spirituality and organizational performance. Public Adm Rev 63(3):355–363

Goleman D, Boyatzis RE, McKee A (2003) The new leaders: transforming the art of leadership into the science of results. Time Warner Books, London

Hermes J, Rimanoczy I (2018) Deep learning for a sustainability mindset. Int J Manag Educ 16(3):460–467

Ibrahim MD (2004) Mengelola hidup dan merencanakan masa depan. MHMMD Production, Jakarta

Indrajaya AN (2017) The role of spirituality as a strategy toward competitive advantage in the telecommunication industry model. Adv Sci Lett 23(9):8822–8826

Indrajaya AN (2018) Spiritual development programs, individual spirituality and sustainability mindset toward higher commitment to social and environmental impact. Int J Bus Stud 2(3):150–163

Indrajaya AN (2019) Spirit at work: the Telkom experience of great spirit grand strategy. PMN Publishing, Jakarta
Indrajaya AN (2020) Kiat Menjadi Pembicara yang Menginspirasi. Amna Foundation
Indrajaya AN, Afiff AZ, Balqiah TE, Rachmawati R (2017) The importance of spiritual leadership and spirit at work as intangible resource capabilities in the service industry: a resource-based view framework. In: 3rd Asia International Conference (AIC 2017)
Indrajaya AN, Daryanto WM, Sjahrifa C, Yeung S (2019) The interaction of spiritual leadership and individual spirituality impacting spirit at work toward enhancing organizational commitment and job satisfaction: a conceptual proposition. J Law Soc Manag 6(1):16–22
Kassel K, Rimanoczy I (eds) (2018) Developing a sustainability mindset in management education. Routledge, New York
Kassel K, Rimanoczy I, Mitchell SF (2016) The sustainability mindset: connecting being, thinking, and doing in management education. In: Academy of management proceedings, vol 2016, No. 1. Academy of Management, Briarcliff Manor, p 16659
Laszlo C, Zhexembayeva N (2011) Embedded sustainability: the next big competitive advantage. Routledge, New York
Neal J (2012) The Handbook of Faith and Spirituality in the Workplace. Springer
Reinhardt FL (1998) Environmental product differentiation: implications for corporate strategy. Calif Manag Rev 40(4):43–73
Rimanoczy IB (2010) Business leaders committing to and fostering sustainability initiatives. Teachers College, Columbia University, New York, NY
Rimanoczy I (2014) A matter of being: developing sustainability-minded leaders. J Manag Glob Sustain 2(1):95–122
Rimanoczy I (2017) Big bang being: developing the sustainability mindset. Routledge, New York
Rutte M (2012) Twelve arenas of leverage to take spirituality and work to its next level globally. In: Neal J (ed) Handbook of faith and spirituality in the workplace: emerging research and practice. Springer Nature, New York
Scharmer CO, Kaufer K (2013) Leading from the emerging future: from ego – system to ecosystem economies. Berrett-Koehler Publishers, San Francisco
Senge PM, Smith B, Kruschwitz N, Laur J, Schley S (2008) The necessary revolution: how individuals and organizations are working together to create a sustainable world. Crown Business, New York
Stachowicz Stanusch A, Amann W (eds) (2017) Fostering sustainability by management education. IAP, Charlotte
Urip S (2010) CSR strategies for a competitive edge in emerging markets. Wiley, New York
Yeager DS, Dweck CS (2012) Mindsets that promote resilience: when students believe that personal characteristics can be developed. Educ Psychol 47(4):302–314

Cross-References

The truth about transformation.: One person can change the world. Peggy O'Neal
Self-Awareness in. personal transformation. Nancy Kay
Self-Knowledge: Master key. to personal transformation and fulfillment. Satinder Dhiman
Leader self-development, maturation, and. meditation: Elements of a transformative journey. Denise Frizzell & David Banner
Enabling innovation with. human values: A recipe for transformation. William Miller & Debra Miller
Cultivating a global. mindset through "being-centered" leadership. Eleftheria Egel and Louis W. Fry
Teaching creativity. and spiritual meaning using insights from neurobiology. Michelle French

Part III

Organizational Transformation

Personal and Organizational Transformation: Indian and American Perspectives and Experiences

6

Madhulika Sagaram and Prasad Kaipa

Abstract

The chapter outlines and describes transformation from various perspectives and levels of engagement using various elements of transformation that are discussed from both the Indian and the US perspectives. Models of transformation from the Indian paradigm of oneness or non-duality are used to interpret the elements, process, and knowing of transformation. Personal and organizational transformation merges into lived experience facilitating a mental shift from understanding to presence in the now. Various and diverse points of view and their energies merge into one experience of transformation and beauty bringing together and synthesizing transformation as an experience of presence rather than a mere tool or concept.

Keywords

Learning · Synthesis · Narrative · Wisdom traditions · Leadership · Personal transformation · Organizational transformation · Accelerated learning

M. Sagaram
Ajahn Center for Pedagogy, Hyderabad, India

P. Kaipa (✉)
Kaipa Group, Campbell, CA, USA
e-mail: prasad@kaipagroup.com

J. Neal (ed.), *Personal, Educational and Organizational Transformation*, Future of Business and Finance, https://doi.org/10.1007/978-3-031-29253-8_6

Introduction

In this chapter, we write about personal and organizational transformation frameworks, narratives, and lived experiences, and we reflect on how they are similar and different in the United States and India. Our experience is that there are many similarities with important differences in how transformation efforts are initiated, supported, and managed in the context of both an individual and an organization.

Is organizational transformation sustainable without personal transformation of leaders? Change agents all over the world are well versed with this conundrum. We call it a conundrum because often organizational transformation projects are initiated without any thoughtful attention on personal transformation of people involved in those projects. In our experience, in order to see positive change manifest in the external world, it is required that we as individuals shift our actions and our consciousness to a higher level of thinking, feeling, and being. To sustain such a shift in consciousness, it is imperative that we build systems or approaches that facilitate transformation at the collective level. We have seen that in India personal transformation precedes organizational transformation in many cases, whereas in the United States, we have seen the reverse—in the context of transforming the organization, people are transformed. We will discuss the mental models, frameworks, and share narratives of many executives who have been interviewed exclusively to gather data for writing this chapter.

What Is Transformation?

Much has been said and written about transformation in various contexts and domains. Transformation is not a change process involving continuous improvement. It is beyond the form (hence called trans-form) and is a fundamental change in attitude or perspective and guides a different set of actions and results. According to Adams (1984), transformation refers to profound fundamental changes in thought and action, which are a direct result of profound changes in belief systems or paradigms. This train of thought can be further cemented by Kwiecinski (2018: 603) who states:

> Transformation is the evolution or revolution of an operating paradigm to one that is more encompassing of realities not allowed, considered, accounted for, or contained in the previous frame of reference. It generally occurs when we bump up against the limitations of our current frame of reference. Things are happening that we can't explain, or we see that we are consistently re-creating events and situations that we don't like because of the decisions we make.

Transformational learners create a vision for themselves, whereas leaders create a shared vision involving buy-in. O'Neal (2017a) states "Transformation requires a commitment beyond the usual"; there are no ways to plan or know when it can occur, and it is a substantiated change in context or way of being. Transformation occurs when an individual experiences themselves, their relationships, and the world they exist in alignment with the calling that brought them to the path to begin with.

The work of transformation includes surrender to the calling and applying chosen thought, knowledge, and emotion, intuitively using the whole brain and sensory perception in leading with honesty about being compassionate with self. The elements required for transformation include trust, patience, sitting with uncertainty, and self-awareness (O'Neal 2017b). It is important to note that these perspectives from the United States are, generally, grounded in the Western approach to consciousness rooted in thought, mind, brain, emotion, and self-awareness of personality. In contrast, Indian approaches to transformation involve awareness of self and surroundings to include body, mind, emotion, energy, and a higher order awareness that is a witness to both the awareness of self and the context. From the Indian perspective, transformation shifts understanding of reality. We begin with perspectives from the United States.

Models of Transformation: Perspectives from the United States

Neal (2018) identifies and outlines five different models of transformation, namely, transformation, transformational leadership, transformational learning, spirituality, and consciousness. We touch upon all the five categories of transformation throughout the chapter. Sometimes, there are clear demarcations in narratives between the categories while other instances point to an overlap.

Transformational Leadership

Transformational leadership has been described as an evolving process in which leaders influence followers and are in turn influenced by followers leading to modification of leadership behavior as a result of the interaction (Burns 1978). Such leadership behavior was first described as charismatic leadership (House 1977) and then evolved into transformational leadership (House and Shamir 1993; Hunt 1999). Charisma was included and integrated as a part of transformational leadership in the form of idealized influence (Bass 1985, 1995; Bass and Avolio 1994). Transformational leadership has been described as an evolving process in which leaders and followers influence each other leading to the modification of their behavior (Burns 1978).

Leaders have the ability to transform followers by making them aware and conscious about transcending self-interest for greater good of the organization (Bass 1985). The theory of transformational leadership proposed by Bass has been adapted to suit different scenarios and working environments in every field possible. Transformational leaders create and develop an inspirational vision, ooze confidence, and set high expectations for followers (Northouse 1997). At the same time, they set an example through appropriate role modeling by empowering others and encouraging followers by "walking the talk." Transformational leaders progressively help their followers transcend from ideas about mere survival to ideas about growth and professional development. They motivate others with their determination and confidence. Such leadership helps followers achieve difficult tasks with great ease and confidence (Yammarino et al. 1998).

Transformational leadership can be described at a micro level (individual level) and also at the macro level of power mobilization for institutional or organizational and social systems reform (Yukl 1989). It can further be a result of any of the four components of transformational leadership described below (Bass 1985). Transformational leadership has a major focus on idealized influence or charisma, intellectual stimulation, inspirational motivation, and individual consideration (Bass 1985; Northouse 1997).

Several researchers have used charisma as a basis to develop and propose new ideas and theories (Bass 1985; Burns 1978). Empirical results indicate that charismatic leaders make use of a set of consistent communication strategies for effecting social change by motivating, breaking down, and rearranging the standards of their followers. Idealized influence/charisma is often an important factor in inspirational motivation (Yammarino et al. 1998).

Inspirational motivation is a result of the interaction between the leader and followers; the followers are oriented toward higher-order thinking as well as tasks and are also trustful and respectful of their leader. This leads to greater motivation, and the followers accomplish more than the expectations set for them (Yukl 1989). Inspirational motivation is the step leading to intellectual stimulation and development of a vision (Yammarino et al. 1998).

Intellectual stimulation happens when transformational leaders stimulate their followers toward a higher order of thinking. Leaders can be the agents who confront their students to take up challenges and also provide them required support in the endeavor leading to individualized consideration. Individualized consideration is an important component of transformational leadership, and an effective leader is able to incorporate individualized consideration by including all the learners in the process. Such an inclusion enables the followers to rise above mundane issues and think about social change and greater good (Yammarino et al. 1998).

Transformational leadership can be described at an individual level (micro level) and also at the macro level of mobilization of power to change organizations, systems, and institution reform (Yukl 1989). Transformational leaders inspire their followers by appealing to higher ethical principles and moral values such as liberty, justice, equality, peace, and humanitarianism (Burns 1978). Leaders have the ability to transform followers by making them aware and conscious about transcending self-interest for greater good of the organization (Bass 1985). Hence, as a result of this interaction, the followers are geared toward higher-order tasks and are trustful and respectful of their leader. This leads to greater motivation, and the followers accomplish more than they are originally expected to do (Yukl 1989). However, transformational leadership cannot be possible without an involvement of learning in a state of altered consciousness.

Transformational Learning

According to Merriam et al. (2007), transformative learning is where change is quite dramatic and fundamentally changes the way we see ourselves and the world we live in. Of the many aspects of transformational or transformative learning, Mezirow talks about frame of reference being the meaning perspective with two dimensions to it. The two components of frame of reference are known to be a habit of mind and a point of view (Mezirow 2000). The habit of mind is described as the set of pre-oriented dispositions that act as a filter for interpreting meaning of experiences (Mezirow 2000). Point of view consists of meaning schemes that can be described as sets of beliefs, feelings, attitudes, and value judgments that can be changed easily in comparison to the habits of the mind (Mezirow 2000). Greater awareness has been associated and attributed to points of view more than habits of mind and the relative ease of transforming points of view than the latter (Mezirow 2000). Transformational learning occurs when there is transformation in beliefs or attitudes, that is, the meaning scheme or the entire perspective meaning habit of mind shifts (Mezirow 1997, 2000). Such shifts in learning, points of view, and habits of the mind allow for leadership to emerge to facilitate large-scale transformation often involving spirituality and consciousness.

Transformation, Spirituality, and Consciousness

Neal (2018) describes transformation in the Western paradigm as a feature emanating from social sciences. Spirituality is defined as an outcome of religion and theology; consciousness is explained in reference to quantum physics and allied sciences. When these three domains overlap with each other, it leads to the emergence of transformational learning and leadership (Neal 2018). While the mainstream work in transformation has been focused on leadership or learning, researchers in contemporary times have been charting a new path. The new age psychology movement in contemporary times has focused on many variations of personal transformation within the gamut of spirituality and consciousness. One of those points of view proposed by Eckhart Tolle (1997) emanates from the angle that no one can transform anyone, only space for transformation can be created, so grace and love can enter. Then, there is a plethora of points of view in the phenomenological paradigm from Maurice Merlau Ponty to Carl Jung, all situated in the external manifestation of internal experience. Apart from these constructs, there are those that believe that a catastrophic event is a primary trigger for transformation. Some consider a combination of suffering and evolution as the path for transformation.

Paths for Transformation

According to Neal (2018), transformation can happen in one of three ways:

1. As an evolutionary process such as a caterpillar turning into a butterfly.
2. Shift in worldview due to unintended consequences.
3. Intentional interventions.

Personal transformation can occur due to any of the above sources; however, intentional interventions are a major source of transformation at the organizational level. Individuals tend to operate at three different levels, namely, conscious level (words and actions), subconscious (thoughts, feelings, and experience), and unconscious (deep fears and assumptions, values, insecurities, attitudes, etc.). Typically, what we act and say from conscious state to include our actions and practices are driven or dominated by subconscious and unconscious states.

Making small changes in action and practice does not amount to transformational change. However, creating a discipline of small changes that are repeated regularly to become a habit in the unconscious state can support development of new behaviors, and new structures lead to the discipline required for transformation.

Nature of Selection of Candidates for Narratives

Candidates were chosen based on their engagement and expertise in the field of transformation. All candidates chosen for interviews to build narratives have demonstrated great felicity in facilitating transformation and transformational environments for individuals and organizations, at the collective level or system level. Their stories have been collected and presented as short narratives. Hence, the type of sampling was purposive sampling with a fixed agenda to obtain narratives of lived experiences from the candidates, so the chapter could include stories of transformation from various contexts to include personal, organizational, and social level change.

A social change model developed by the Higher Education Research Institute (1996) was designed for college students and promotes leadership development based on transformation, social responsibility, and the common good. This model is also applicable to many different areas of leadership development. The social model of leadership describes the values necessary for a leader at different levels, namely, individual, group, and community or society level (Komives et al. 2007) on the same lines of emerging patterns in the narratives in the chapter.

Individual values consist of commitment, congruence, and self-consciousness as its cornerstones (Komives et al. 2007). Individual values are important as they form the foundation of the leadership paradigm at the micro level. Group values include the component that is focused on cooperation, group work, and collaborations for effective social change (Komives et al. 2007). The major components of this feature include collaboration, common purpose, and solving controversy with civility (Higher Education Research Institute 1996). Society or community values are described as a focus on social ends to which the leadership development activity or process is directed (Komives et al. 2007). Citizenship involves individual responsibility and individual rights in tandem with the individual in a group or community (Komives et al. 2007).

The following narratives have been included here as purposive samples in the chapter. Since the chapter involves various models of transformation involving varied narratives from diverse contexts, we have specifically chosen narratives from people who have perspectives relevant to the United States and India and a larger global perspective. We have highlighted three narratives and provided brief bios for other leaders who have inspired our thinking.

Narrative of the Coauthor: Madhulika Sagaram

Dr. Madhulika Sagaram is the coauthor of this chapter and an independent researcher, facilitator, educator, and artist working in the areas of consciousness and learning, transformation, and Indigenous applied psychology pedagogies of India and constructivist pedagogy. She has done considerable work in transformation of learning environments for children in India. Notable among the work is the transformational work Dr. Sagaram has facilitated in underserved environments in India in the domain of Indigenous critical pedagogy in India involving arts and place-based learning.

In 1999, I wrote a handwritten note from Hyderabad to Dr. Ron Thomason at West Texas A&M University, Canyon, Texas (WTAMU). I wrote to him about my dreams, aspirations and about how I wanted to learn, study, do research and was only facing humiliation and lack of opportunity during my bachelor's degree studies in Agriculture in India. I went to study MS with a full research assistantship! Dr. Bob Stewart, who was my Academic advisor and mentor, provided me all the support and freedom I needed to reach my potential and Dr. Clay Robinson helped me understand I could do Mathematics and Statistics and helped me let go of the fears I was harboring regarding the discipline. I went on to study for my PhD at Texas A&M University, College Station, Texas (TAMU) and I was supported with assistantship as well as scholarship; it was and it remains the space that allowed me to be my best and reach my potential. I am who I am because I am a fighting Texas Aggie. I live my life on Aggie principles and when I pass on to the next realm, my name will be called along with all those Aggies that have passed on all across the world in Aggie Musters. Held across the world and The US army will give us a 21-gun salute for what we have given back to society and the world. This is a privilege and the awareness of the privilege has provided my life a remarkable North star as a guiding principle.

I did not go to TAMU to get a degree; it was a transformational experience of learning, service, excellence, respect, leadership, integrity and commitment. I met and learned from extraordinary faculty and from all my friends who continue to support me and encourage me. I went from a human being that was constantly drubbed with cynicism and toxic environments in India to a phenomenal learning environment that nurtured every capability I possessed. I am a creative individual and a resourceful professional today because of the love, respect and nurturing from all my teachers and professors in the US. My experience of higher education was a sublime lived experience that provided the foundation for sustained behaviors and attitudes that allowed me to contribute my gifts to the world.

As a graduate student, for the four years or more that I was engaged in becoming a researcher, I developed a certain bond with my professors that has turned into transformational learning for me! Dr. Leo Lombardini, my PhD advisor showed me a jacket the first day I joined him and said "This jacket is important. I wore it when I got married and I am going to wear it when my kids and each of my students does something remarkable." One day he wore the jacket when he attended a banquet for the Graduate Teaching Academy I had invited him to as I was presiding as its director. It has been 15 years since then but even today if I am faced with a difficult situation, I remember Leo in that jacket and that is what pushes me through. Another source of constant silent support and inspiration has been Dr. Bob Webb and he was The VP for Research and I an ordinary grad student; I remember how he treated every suggestion of mine with respect and consideration. That is a behavior that I emulated with my own employees later in life and that kind of egalitarian attitude is what I picked up to create a very flat structured non-profit organization after I returned to India. I faced grave issues and extenuating circumstances and I strongly believe my transformation at Texas A&M University was the foundation to face life with great courage and strength in the face of calamity. The importance of personal transformation cannot be stressed enough as a foundation for organizational transformation.

The above narrative describes a medley of an evolutionary process, such as a caterpillar turning into a butterfly, and shift in worldview due to unintended consequences for personal transformation. In contrast, the following narrative involves planned interventions in the case of organizational development.

It was in 2011, that I was called to this very old school in Secunderabad, India. It was originally a Montessori school but run by the daughter of the founder now who distanced herself from the Montessori method of teaching. As a result, the learning environment was solely based in memorization, teachers were quite demotivated as they did not know what was expected of them and children were suffering due to existent confusion. I set out to do a needs assessment and interviewed all the teachers to identify pain points and challenges along with their vision for the school and how they could contribute to the mission. Then I involved all the children in needs assessment disguised as games and activities identifying their learning needs. What I found was that the teachers were involved in petty politics because of favoritism from the management. A detailed discussion with management indicated it was only a perception among the teachers and there was a need to change that. Three plans were devised and all of them included feedback from teachers, children and management.

The management and teachers reached consensus and chose a weekend integrated learning plan that would get all the teachers to work with each other thereby showing teachers that their voice was heard and valued. Teachers were trained in innovative pedagogy and on every Saturday, they would engage the children in participatory integrated learning. This enabled cross talk between teachers as all of them had to work with each other to facilitate the approach. The children were happy because they had one day solely dedicated for hands on learning and slowly over the period of a year, the school shifted from memorization as the only device for learning towards a medley of learning approaches, collaborative engagement by the teachers and an overall conducive and joyful environment for learning.

Narrative of the Coauthor: Prasad Kaipa

Dr. Prasad Kaipa is the coauthor of this chapter and is an author, educator, executive coach, and researcher. Prasad strives to bring Indian Vedantic wisdom into management theory and practice. Just like the Japanese contribution to management and manufacturing, Indian wisdom can contribute to change management, leadership development, employee engagement, and motivation. Prasad has worked on personal transformation with over 135 C-suite executives and has conducted over 80 transformational leadership programs for executives in the United States, the UK, Denmark, Belgium, India, and Singapore.

It was in 1989, I attended a "Business of Business is Learning" conference in Goa, India. I represented Apple; where I was working on designing tools to augment human intelligence. I had a certain sense of clarity and confidence (bordering on arrogance) about my work and myself and was looking forward to this conference to learn and add to my perspective. Unfortunately, on the first day of conference, I was disappointed that participants were sharing stories of established positions and egoistic perspectives. I began to wonder whether it was a mistake for me to have gone to the conference. During closing session of the first day, I spoke about how I was feeling and openly wondered whether I was learning anything at all. Other participants became very quiet, but no one got defensive. When we returned the following day, we started at a much deeper place and people had dropped their façade and were open and receptive. The rest of the conference was deeply engaging, and we literally spent the entire five days digging deeper into both the topic at hand and who we are and what is happening in our lives. By the end of the conference, several of us made life changing decisions. Several books came out of that conference. Half a dozen of us quit our jobs in following two months. New companies got started and eight or nine of the original 35 still maintain deep friendship and are in regular communication with each other. I unintentionally became the catalyst for the transformation of entire group. The process that Harrison Owen (1997) used during that week became Open Space Technology and spread far and wide as a large-scale change and transformation enabler.

I felt wonderful making so many new friends and one of the organizers, Srinivas, introduced me to his friend who is a mystic. Mohan Rao, the mystic who later became my mentor and teacher, challenged what I learned in my life and my work. While I was talking about brain research and what I have learned about brain-based learning, he stopped me, asking questions about the pineal and pituitary glands and their role in learning and insight. Then he asked me "Have you learned about unlearning? Where does that come from in the brain? What does unlearning open up?" His questions really made me realize that not only I did not have any answers to many of his questions but also that I was not asking right questions in my research if I want to design tools that augments human learning or discover new ways of learning with the help of technology. Then he asked me to look into Yoga principles and Kundalini chakras and he basically helped me to understand that the brain is an organ that does not have awareness of itself. From his perspective, and that of Indian spirituality perspective, the brain is not where transformation takes place. The brain focuses more on pattern matching and survival and mostly operates from past memories.

That conversation with Dr. Mohan Rao got me thinking about what I know and how much I really know about learning, brain and thinking. I realized deeply that knowing sometimes does not lead to understanding let alone transformation. I understood the role of vulnerability and beginner's mind; I asked myself whether I could truly start at the beginning and approach my work with a fresh perspective. I had a lot of new thoughts bubbling through my head and when I read *Autobiography of a Yogi* (Yogananda 1946) on the way back from India, I was in a different realm. I had heard about that book from my friends in Apple and from my uncle, but I did not expect the impact it had on me. First the conference, then meeting with Mohan Rao prepared the ground for me to drop my ego and identity completely and within a month of returning from India, I left Apple without knowing what I would do next. It took me a year or more before I started focusing on what to do next and how to find another job that could put food on the table. Except that I was no longer interested in computers and tool design and was interested in experimenting with how people learn, think and create. It took me awhile but I ended up becoming a researcher and consultant in the area of organizational learning and leadership with no psychology degree or MBA education. So, in my case, I became a catalyst in a group transformation and that led to a personal transformation and that led to complete change in my career that I followed for next 30 years.

The above narrative describes a medley of an evolutionary process such as a caterpillar turning into a butterfly for personal and community transformation, but the narrative shifts toward planned interventions in case of organizational development as described in the following segment.

What Is the True Nature of Individual and Organizational Transformation?

Mr. Arun Jain is the founder and CEO of Intellect Design Arena and was also the founder of Polaris Software Labs, Mission Samriddhi, and a co-founder of Nucleus Software. He is well known for his passion for design thinking and leadership and is a regular meditator.

This change agent is the founder and CEO of a 200 million-dollar business and shares his journey through his own transformations and the transformation of the organizations he built and nurtured over the years.

Transformation is change in worldview; there are many facets to it. It can be looked at the individual, organization or community level and can also be an extension of an organized community level like a residential complex or a village or a city. At a personal level, every 5–6 years a new world view has emerged for me.

In 1985, when I visited my brother in the US, initially I did not want to go but when I went, I saw the software industry between August to December 1985. I returned and by April 1986 we set up Nucleus and went all ahead.

In 1991, I met Prasad Kaipa at the behest of Yogesh who was my business partner. I was shaken at first because he exposed me to myself and I was in denial. Then, slowly I understood it was an opportunity to learn. Then, I went through a process of self-transformation. I started focusing on what people like Peter Senge and Stephen Covey were saying and made much progress.

My third transformation was in Dharamshala in India where coaches Anil Sachdev, Dinesh Chandra and some others invited 15 CEO's, many of those were people I looked up to! During the program, we engaged in a certain activity by the fire in the evening. As we engaged with the process, silence in the group of learners was so intense, tears started pouring out. It created a certain reverberation, guilt came out and I asked myself, what is the true gift that I received from nature? I understood that my gift is entrepreneurial zeal. My vision guided me in building an organization that had high potential and a software services company named Polaris Labs was born and within 3 years was listed on stock exchange reaching multiple milestones later on.

My fourth transformation was in 2006 when my wife was diagnosed with cancer. It was a sudden crisis and silence entered my life; it was an opportunity to calm down. I immersed myself in Vedanta, historical knowledge, Jainism, anything where humanity and principles meet. I was searching for principles of nature. I engaged in swadhyay (self-study-reflection and praxis) and the program Unmukt was born based in boundaryless thinking. This later turned into design thinking, design thought and finally large-scale transformation between 2006 and 2015. 2015 was defined by the demerger of Polaris into 2 companies—Polaris as a software services company and Intellect as software product company. I kept myself to where my heart was, the difficult journey of building global software product brand out of India. That given me new energy by being vulnerable. I believe human mind learns ten times faster when vulnerable.

It was the toughest and most difficult emotional decision for me. My identity was linked to Polaris and I had to let go of it. In November of 2015, there were floods in Chennai and we got engaged in flood relief. Following that, we engaged in discovery of social impact programs until April 2016 when it dawned on me that we should celebrate what others are doing; when they are doing very good work it should be given support and encouragement and Mission Samriddhi was born.

What I understood from my personal transformation is that "crisis is a way for transformation; it showed me a new world view"—"celebrate the crisis, connect with others, catalyze transformation" was born out of it. Mission Samriddhi is about helping people who are doing great work in social development. The support system we have created for

Mission Samriddhi is providing a sense of purpose and it is bringing together village presidents, entrepreneurs, teachers, consultants, writers and innovators. Now, I am inspired by their great work and their purpose. Together, we are transforming the communities that we live in.

Organizational change is an improvement process that streamlines something whereas transformation is a root level change related to redesigning the system. The impact of organizational change and transformation is very different. I would say if organizational change is a 10 gm weight then transformation is 1000 gm weight. At the organization level, personal transformation has to link to performance management. Change has to lead to inspiration and then inspiration has to connect to performance management.

I would say the elements of transformation are 80% listening; to sustain transformation in the organization, it is important to listen so natural gifts of the person speaking can be identified. The rest is 20% communicating back with compassion and personal composure. Unfortunately, most organizations measure progress in business in terms of financial gains. Intellectual ability, compassion, personal composure etc. are not taken into consideration but they are essential for transforming the culture of the organization. Personal composure allows one to reflect and then respond to the situation. Resilience of the organization allows it to discover and rediscover itself as it goes through crisis after crisis!

The above narrative is a descriptive and a medley of metamorphosis, unintended consequences, and planned interventions for self and at a collective level. Overall, all the above narratives include individual values consisting of commitment, congruence, and self-awareness along with group values to include cooperation, group work, and collaborations for effective social change (Komives et al. 2007).

Section Summary and Insights

The above narratives helped in constructing certain patterns about personal and organizational transformation. Whether it is through personal lived experience or a study of the literature, the common element is that personal transformation occurs through tacit lived experience and organizational development mostly through planned interventions. Our observations are in line with what can be deciphered repeatedly from review of literature in the field of transformation. The patterns emerging out of the narratives also connect us to various elements of Indian philosophy and models of transformation pulled out from constructs of Indigenous applied psychology in Indian contexts.

It is quite clear from the above reflections that each person goes through transformation in a very individualized manner with a very specific lesson or set of lessons that arrive in patterns in space-time constructs to reach alignment of action, intention or desire, and word or reason (Albuquerque 2012). This alignment is called *Trikarana suddhi* in Indian wisdom traditions. If there is misalignment between what one says and does, that is, between word and action, then a credibility gap appears. If there is a gap between intention and word, a commitment gap appears; if there is a gap between intention and action, a courage gap appears. Essentially, personal transformation, which is the bedrock of organizational transformation, requires that we are authentic, vulnerable, and transform ourselves to a new playing field in consciousness.

Models of Transformation from Indian Contexts

In contrast, in the knowledge traditions, learning systems, and wisdom paradigms of India, the understanding of these facets is quite different from what has been described in the earlier sections. Quantum physics provides a foundation for shifts in energy to determine thoughts, feelings, mental consciousness, ego, attitudes, and behavior (Katz 2011). In psychology, conscious refers to being aware of self and the environment, and consciousness is considered to be such awareness (Chalmers 1996). This definition links consciousness to sense perception and awareness of environment but not beyond. In learning systems and knowledge traditions of India, consciousness is a higher-order awareness and intelligence that goes beyond the intellect defined in the psychological domain. In traditions of India, transformation is the ultimate goal of all human pursuits. Spirituality is a way of life, and consciousness is a heightened choice, free awareness capable of witnessing awareness.

Sri Aurobindo describes consciousness as the principle of our being, our existence. Whatsoever exists has consciousness and force or energy; it is to be understood that force and consciousness are interchangeable. It is the nature of the force or energy to be either at rest or at motion, and consciousness follows suit based on what it inherits (Albuquerque 2012).

Creation and Consciousness Model

In the classical non-dual paradigm of Indigenous Indian traditions of learning, there are three main theories or viewpoints of reality: creation of consciousness (*sristi-dristi vada*), creation through consciousness (*dristi-sristi vada*), and lastly, non-creation theory (*ajata vada*). It may be helpful to note that "vada" means theory or viewpoint, "*sristi*" means the world or creation, "*dristi*" literally means sight but in this context refers to consciousness, and "*jata*" means birth. Adding "a" as a prefix to "*jata*" negates the meaning, so "*ajata*" becomes unborn or no creation.

Creation of consciousness (*sristi-dristi vada*) is the view that the world is primary and gives rise to consciousness, which is the most commonplace model of the universe, that is, that first there was a universe in which life gradually evolved on planet earth and eventually human life and human consciousness evolved with fine tuning of sophistication of emotional balance. In Western philosophy, this is known as the realist paradigm of reality.

Creation through consciousness (*dristi-sristi vada*) is the view that consciousness is primary and the world is cocreated, that is, like in a dream through perception. If consciousness is all pervading and is primary, then consciousness manifests the apparent dream-world and dream-subject or object duality. In Western philosophy, this is known as the idealist paradigm of reality. *Ajata vada* is the radical view that there never was any creation at all and that there is only the absolute truth.

Transformation in non-dual paradigm often starts with the realist framework, which is the default conceptual framework of reality for most learners at the beginning of their journey. Then, the idealist conceptual framework is introduced, and later the non-creation viewpoint is brought in when the learner is ready. This is done in stepwise progression depending on how the learner is progressing with the process of transformation. The nature, context, and content for transformation differ depending on the framework of reality being used. The purpose of the non-dual paradigms or theories used for transformational learning is not that they are the only truth. A particular viewpoint paradigm or theory is to be adopted in order to remove ignorance and reveal that which cannot be taught, explained, or expressed in words, that which is beyond words.

Transformation Model of Knowledge Paths

There is a very interesting narrative of the play of consciousness and energy in Indian traditions. "One day, *Siva* (the masculine or consciousness) and *Shakti* (feminine or energy) had a disagreement and Siva decided he had enough. He told *Shakti*; he was leaving; *Shakti* in turn tried to stop him with a play of energy. Wherever *Siva* looked, he only saw *Shakti! Shakti* was space, time, beauty, transformation, including his consciousness. When he realized *Shakti* was present in every aspect of his reality and is inseparable, Siva understood the role his consciousness played in the manifestation of creation in ten different knowledge forms." These ten aspects of creation are called *Dasamahavidya* (Fig. 6.1) or the "ten great knowledge paths." In this section, we look at the various elements of transformation, namely, space, time, energy, beauty (feminine manifestations), and consciousness (masculine manifestation) in the process of transformation (growth and evolution) and the role of knowledge paths facilitating the same.

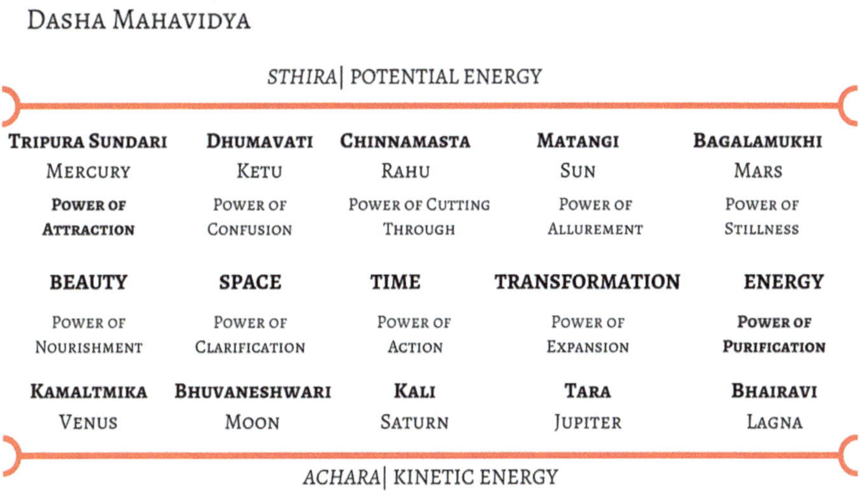

Fig. 6.1 Ten forms of knowledge paths (Dashamahavidya) and their aspects

Aspects of Transformation and Knowledge Paths

The space aspect of transformation appears as the power of confusion (*Dhumavati*) in its potential energy state and as the power of clarification (*Bhuvaneshwari*) in the kinetic state. Time appears as the power of cutting through (*Chinnamasta*) and as the power of action (*Kali*) in potential and kinetic states, respectively (Fig. 6.1). Likewise, energy manifests as *Bharaivi* (power of purification) and as *Bagalamukhi* (power of stillness) in kinetic and potential states, respectively. Transformation is understood through the knowledge path of *Matangi* (power of allurement) in potential form and as *Tara* (power of expansion) in kinetic form (Fig. 6.1). Finally, the power of attraction manifests as *Tripura Sundari* (the most beautiful in three dimensions) in the potential state and as the power of nourishment (*Kamaltamika*) in the kinetic state for the aspect of beauty (Fig. 6.1).

Culturally, the unfolding of these knowledge paths has a certain order in the larger process of transformation at the level of cosmos; *Bhairavi*, the power of purification in kinetic form of energy, initiates the process of purification. Then, *Dhumavati* represented by potential energy absorbs space into herself. Following this, *Kali* as the kinetic energy aspect of power of time initiates action, and *Tara* as the power of transformation expands in kinetic state. *Bagalamukhi*, who is the power of stillness in the potential state, creates the stage for energy transformation. *Chinnamasta* cuts through with her ability to act in the potential state of time. *Kamalatmika* arrives in kinetic state to provide nourishment as beauty, and *Bhuvaneshwari* as the power of clarification in kinetic state of space provides required impetus for transformation to turn into beauty. Finally, *Tripura Sundari* arrives as the potential state of beauty to create equilibrium.

The knowledge paths in their energy states remind us that whatsoever exists in kinetic state has the power of clarification, action, purification, expansion, and nourishment. Whatever remains latent in potential remains hidden, in confusion and masked, yet the same potential also holds the key to stillness, allurement, and attraction. Hence, *essentially what binds us is what releases us*! If a certain mindset binds us, then a shift of values, attitudes, and beliefs of the same mindset will release us.

What these knowledge paths allude to is the emergence of consciousness; an awareness of awareness in the form and name of human evolution. Plants, invertebrates, and other vertebrates are not known to have the ability to witness their own awareness, and even if it is present, it is subtle. This faculty of consciousness that can be described as an awareness of awareness is solely present in a conscious form in humans according to Indian systems of learning and transformation.

Aspects of Transformation in the Knowledge Path Model

Transformation has five different aspects in Indian learning systems: space, time, energy, transformation, and beauty in relation to consciousness (Fig. 6.1). Transformation manifests in five aspects as kinetic (*chara*) or potential (*sthira*) states of energy (Fig. 6.1).

Space

In Indian traditions, space refers to ether and surrounds all creation. Space plays a significant role, as one of the five primordial elements, in creating the form of all living and nonliving beings. For humans, this form represents their body and the space inside and outside the body; we are defined by the space that contains us. Universal consciousness from which everything gets created is endless, limitless in its expanse. When a part of this universal space takes some form with a certain name, it encloses a subsection of this universal space within itself; every form, including planets, an animal body, or a human body, exists in its own subspace. For any creation, it is impossible to exist in three dimensions without the space element being involved.

Space can be divided into three categories, namely, physical space (external), mental space (dream), and pure consciousness. An infinite amount of mental space simultaneously exists in the single point of being in pure consciousness. An infinite amount of physical space exists in mental space (Timalsina 2020). One point in space can encompass all the realms; what is it then that makes it possible? It is about the power of consciousness to create its own reality. It is about the power of consciousness to have own narratives and the rediscovery of the self in these narratives (Timalsina 2020). The Western psychology paradigm proposed by Viktor Frankl (1962) states that space exists between stimulus and response. Such space gives us power to choose our response and ultimately our growth and our freedom. Frankl's concept of space between stimulus and response is a construct that aligns with the understanding of space in Indian traditions. Thus, essentially, if space exists between stimulus and response, then time should exist between memory and anticipation.

Time: What Is Temporality?

In India, time is characterized by a historically discovered subjectivity and is cyclical, whereas in the West, time has a linear progression. According to Indian traditions, time is succession; if there is succession, it constitutes temporality. When particles cross from one space point to other, it is time. Time is inferred on the basis of action and succession. Therefore, time and space are both potencies in the mind. Whatever is the extent of potency in the mind, that scale is proportional to expansion of space and extension of time. There can be multiverses, parallel realties, and multiple subjectivities manifesting their egos in space-time constructs. The extension of time and expansion of space is an expression of mind. Time is elastic; one point in time can encompass all possible times (Timalsina 2020).

Energy: Power and Energy

Energy is power; the world is simply pulsating and vibrating in multitudes of forms that emerge and dissolve as we desire and wish. The freedom to desire and wish is the power embedded in us and inherent within us. If we actualize the power of freedom within us, we become free. So essentially, energy leads to transformation only when it is dynamic, action oriented, and kinetic. Such power and energy facilitate the actualization of freedom. In freedom, we first experience our temporality being in space and time; we also acknowledge how we are not determined by time and space. Freedom is considered power embedded in consciousness (Timalsina 2020). Learning is considered the foundational reality of pure consciousness.

Transformation

Both energy and transformation of conditioning and borrowed ideas are essential in facilitating large-scale transformation. Organizational and systems transformation builds upon personal transformation, and the connections are made explicit later in the chapter through autobiographical and experiential narratives. There is great beauty in transformation, freedom, reconceptualization, and reconstitution.

Beauty

Beauty is an amalgamation of space, time, energy, and transformation. It is the most sublime element of the process of transformation. Beauty manifests with transformation into love and truth in universal order. Beauty has nothing to do with sight or seeing; it is an intrinsic quality that is pervasive through all life and central to transformational processes.

The following section utilizes the various paths of transformation as described in the perspectives from the United States and weaves them through the models of transformation from Indian traditions to create two different kinds of frameworks: *with structure and without structure.*

The insights from the earlier narratives also tie in with the models discussed in that all the five aspects of transformation, namely, space, time, energy, transformation, and beauty, can be found in perspectives of personal and organizational transformation in varied ways. There is exceptional beauty when someone breaks open due to a loss or transforms from a caterpillar into a butterfly and space is created for time to manifest in a different manner transforming, transformation itself! The evolution of consciousness from the perspective of creation of consciousness or creation through consciousness as well as non-creation of consciousness are all relevant based on perception and perspective. Frameworks with structure described in the next section focus mainly on creation of consciousness, whereas frameworks without structure focus on creation through consciousness and the experience of being nothing in everything, non-creation of consciousness.

Frameworks of Transformation

In this section of the chapter, we are presenting our experiences working in the United States and India, and sharing our perspectives, experiences, and outcomes. Here, we share our frameworks of transformation for individuals and organizations and how we facilitated coaching (individuals) and workshops or executive education programs (organizations) in the United States and India. What participants took away and what they did with it comes across through narratives presented in this chapter. Our frameworks of transformation propose that *people mostly operate from conditioned mind on autopilot and do not leverage their potential.* The frameworks that emerged then provide a framework with structure and one without structure.

Framework with Structure

The framework begins by creating conditions in which participants feel secure and trusted but are given a challenge to dig deeper and unlearn their assumptions and mindsets. People fall into a gap or space through a designed experience where they question their beliefs, reexamine their stories, and reframe their perspectives. Once they do that, time dimension shifts for them, and they learn in an accelerated way and manifest higher skillsets and outcomes. While this can be a temporary change in their behavior, if the unlearning and letting go of old mindsets is deep and meaningful to them, they are permanently altered and operate out of the gap and expand their new skillset and live a transformed life. If they take up the chance to coach other people and help others to live out of this gap, then transformation not only becomes sustainable but also expands to their teams, families, and organizations. This is the transformational learning model that we describe as a discontinuous learning perspective. When transformation takes place, it is discontinuous in a gap.

This is a framework for personal transformation. The Indian models of *sristi-dristi*, *dristi-sristi*, and *ajatavada* connect to the above framework. For example, when people have a certain *dristi* or vision, it allows them to create *sristi* or conditions to manifest that vision. For personal transformation, *dristi-sristi* would work as a model resulting in creation through consciousness at the subconscious level.

On the other hand, the paradigm that is suitable for organizational development is *sristi-dristi*. This can be implemented by anthropomorphizing an organization and look at it as a human body with sensory organs. How does this organism see, hear, feel, and learn? This approach fits in with the paradigm of creation of consciousness.

The role of structure created in the workshops and executive education courses is with a focus on ground rules, boundary conditions for creating a safe space with minimum restrictions and maximum freedom. The first day of the program is all about structure. It bores the audience, but we create groups. Based on what they came to get out of the program, wc talk about resistance to change; discuss about what happens at the conscious, subconscious, and unconscious levels; and work with them on creating clarity, commitment, and outcomes for them and their organizations. Participants talk about one personal project and one organizational project that they want to apply based on what they learn. They are taught about taking notes in a way that clarifies what has been said, what their insights are, and what their action steps are in a delineated way. It looks very simplistic, but what is being created is a space for deeper intention and clear intention to emerge in their minds. They also create and present visionary collages and paste them on the walls so their visions and dreams are all around them.

Then, they are taken into the "heart" of the program from the body level and focus on culture. We try to create an appreciative culture in the room. We bring in brain concepts and do a simulation with the Heartmath biofeedback probe (emwave Pro), and show them how heart/brain coherence is like *Trikarana Suddhi*. With the focus on appreciative inquiry, we work with them on how happiness, play, and appreciative inquiry produce an empowering and nurturing culture and how "what you appreciate appreciates in magnitude" versus "what you depreciate (or put down makes interest, skill or capability) disappears." I ask them to connect with people who used to be important or who are still important but neglected because they are busy with their work or just forgot or lost the connection to their heart. This is where energy and beauty play an important role.

When they rethink about old friends, the context in which they got married to their sweethearts but are now living a routine boring married life, they get reignited with passion and energy and connect to each other. That opens up a huge space and a huge possibility in their lives, and they come alive in the program. It is about awakening and reconnecting the heart to the body. The program is about how they experience transformation in them right then and there. This is when time and space get altered as energy and transformation takes place. Beauty is experienced in great magnitude and intensity.

When incidents of reunion with lost family members or friends are reported in class, it triggers a new thought process in people. They start unlearning and seeing possibilities that they have never considered before. They begin to dream again, hope again, and envision living a life or learning music or serving people in their community selflessly. That is what third stage is about.

The third day is to get them to think for themselves. Another way of saying it is that after the body is safe, the heart is awakened. This allows the brain/head to think from first principles without being a slave to their beliefs, wounds, and trauma to shape their thinking. It is about coming back to "beginners mind" and to suddenly start thinking freshly and for themselves. Instead of shaped beliefs from and by parents, traditions, and old experiences, an ushering in a new emergence happens. This is what I call "igniting the natural genius."

In this stage, they tap into their creativity and innovation. Groups help each other by reinforcing and operating out of an appreciative stance and culture. This is what allows them to deal with their fears and they re-own their identity, personality, and genius. I challenge them on that day to revisit their collages (or vision boards that they brought to class). I ask them to expand their vision and think about a larger purpose: their North Star for themselves and others. They connect to their larger selves and operate out of that larger place at the level of collective consciousness.

That is when I have guest speakers to help them connect to larger possibilities of consciousness. After the body, heart, and mind are addressed, I then bring in the concept of the spirit of the organization. *The body is connected to structure; the heart is connected to culture. The mind is connected to creativity and innovation (the gap of creation). The spirit is connected with purpose, values, and contribution of organization to the larger vision of the country and the world.* Therefore, on the last day, I work with them on an enlightened self-interest approach to growing their business, building their brand, becoming part of a larger ecosystem to support the entire industry instead of a narrow competitive approach that they normally take. In this third stage, individual and organization transformation takes place simultaneously.

In the United States, people are interested in structure and process because it addresses the body and process. For example, Peter Block (1993) focuses on appropriate structure and right invitation to allow for transformation in large groups. Harrison Owen's Open Space Technology (1997) is a structure for the creation of space for people to be open and for magic to happen in the large group. The key is *to create that tipping point for individuals*. What that means is creating the right structure and process that invites people to step into open space.

Transformation is about changing from a "fixed mindset" to "growth mindset" (Dweck 2006). Transformation cannot be brought to business and management without facilitating it at the individual or personal level because lack of ownership does not make it sustainable. Transformation is possible only when new ideas are generated and passionately owned by the individual first before the transference happens at the group or organization or system level.

Transformation in Personal Development

This section engages with narratives from several change agents and identifies the aspects of transformation hidden within their stories. This subsection focuses on conscious space and transformation in the personal domain, whereas the following subsection is focused on organizational transformation. Personal transformation is often linked to creation of space and time along with a shift in worldview. A deep sense of loss or grief or a sudden shift can all facilitate such transformation. As described in the narratives from the previous segment, sometimes, a metamorphosis happens due to opportunity, coincidence, or a sudden event or a chance meeting with someone.

Narrative of Mr. Dinesh Chandra's Personal Transformation

Mr. Dinesh Chandra is skilled in developing authentic dialogue with the self, team, and other stakeholders whose ownership is the key to the successful implementation of a program.

After working as Director of Productivity/Quality at Beckman-Coulter in Miami, Florida, for 15 years, he left to work in 15 other countries, acquiring a global skill set and working with leading organizations such as American Express, Cisco, Eicher-Mitsubishi, Fujitsu, Harley-Davidson, Larsen & Toubro, Oracle, Port of Singapore Authority, and Tata Group. He has led many workshops on transformational leadership with business leaders around the globe.

He describes his transformation through suffering and personal loss.

> Losing a loved one was the source of personal transformation. Empathy and vulnerable feelings led me to write poetry and I developed more capability to understand pain. I came to realize and understand that pain is a gift. It led me to the awareness that we are all one! It made me think about how I can see divine in others. I experienced that when we are present in the moment, we create space and energy. Through my personal transformation, I understood that when an idea appears and I accept it in one instance, there is a need to reflect and apply it in all aspects of life.

It is important to ask good questions. They lead us to higher truth. For example, the question: "What does it mean to be a global citizen?" led me to new places and transformational experiences.

I had been working with Coulter Corporation (now Beckman Coulter) for over 15 years in Miami, Florida in a challenging role as Director of Productivity with the usual fringe benefits and a vision of a comfortable retirement.

On a normal day, while on a business trip somewhere in Europe, a question popped up in my mind and would not go away, "What does it mean to be a global citizen?" Initially, I thought I needed to travel to different countries to find the answer, however, after deeper reflection, I felt that working in different countries might be better. I decided to quit my highly sought-after job for the adventure of working in different countries, starting with my native country, India, where I was born and did my schooling. I felt indebted to Mother India and wanted to pay back in some way. I had the time of my life by sharing what I learned about Productivity with Quality and participated in the creation of a few unique quality and productivity-based showcases. The persistent question, "What does it mean to be a global citizen?" then took me to work in fifteen countries and gave me an opportunity to rub shoulders with some wonderful people around the globe.

I began observing commonalities among all humans, in spite of different skin colors, languages, prosperity levels and other differentiators we keep hearing about. Unsurprisingly, I discovered that most humans are passionate about something and want to receive authentic appreciation for their genuine desires and an opportunity to contribute. I also observed that we are caught up in our basic survival and can be xenophobic when fearful, yet deep in our core we are curious about others and feel the human connection. We are able to care for others, especially in their hour of need. Along with many global citizens around the world who are connected with us on our social networks, we continue to explore the practical ways to create business and work environments where people feel appreciated for their unique contributions and live a meaningful life, while caring for the whole.

Transformation is nothing but understanding higher truth and sharing of love. Transformation happens at various levels; physical, emotional, intellectual, occupational, social and spiritual. We move from a victim mentality to empowerment and then to acceptance finally leading to surrender in the present moment and oneness. Ultimately, transformation is about truth, love and beauty and transformations happen in aha moments! Everyone has a different truth and understanding, this itself is transformation.

This narrative highlighted the elements of space, time, energy, beauty, and transformation.

Narrative of Mr. Anil Sachdev's Personal Transformation

Mr. Anil Sachdev's career spans in manufacturing industry, management consulting, and education.

He is the founder and chairman of the School of Inspired Leadership that has the vision of developing leaders with character, competence, and enthusiasm. He is the managing trustee of Chinmaya Mission in Delhi and serves on the Global Board of Shizenkan University in Tokyo, The World Compassion Council in Seattle, and the Academic Council of CEDEP in the INSEAD campus at Fontainebleau. He has also been an executive coach for several decades.

Transformation is improvement in yourself or a system. It is turning your current reality into your vision through conscious facilitation; it can also be change in attitude through appreciative inquiry. Transformation causes vision, values and ultimately culture to

> change. Transformation is about finding yourself, communication with others, emotional resolution, better decisions, finding meaning in the gap, identifying purpose and wellbeing. Transformation is about identifying your fundamental capacity to learn, understanding who you are and shutting out noise. Transformation happens when you tap into the source. My story of transformation begins in my childhood when I used to meet Swami Chinmayananda that had a great impact on my life.
>
> The next transformational experience was during the India Pakistan war in 1971 when I was in college. Most of my family was in the Army so we used to dread the ringing of the phone. What if it was bad news! I wanted to show my support of the army and was thinking of how to do so. I wrote the script of a play in Hindi and requested students from the Film Institute of India in Pune to act in the play with a commitment to donate the proceeds to the families of the soldiers who were killed or injured in action. When they performed, luckily, it was a full house and we managed to raise five thousand rupees and donate to the Army wife's welfare association. I have done a lot of work with large systems and large-scale transformation throughout my life but this experience from my youth stands out for me. It was monumental for me because we were able to pull it off! We had several challenges and we still did it; that journey was remarkable, it prepared me for many other bigger things in life. I would say that experience of transformation stands out for me in my life.

This narrative highlighted the element of transformation.

Narrative of Mr. Kunal Sanghavi's Personal Transformation

Mr. Kunal Sanghavi is a chartered accountant (CA) from ICA, India, and a management graduate from the Indian School of Business (ISB) with varied experience in asset management businesses and wealth management products. Currently, he is the chief financial officer for HDFC securities and is a dynamic and creative team player with energy and keen learning ability with 16 years in all facets of financial services and capital markets. He has diverse experience from brokering and project management to risk management, production, and operations as well as managing a profit center for proprietary strategies, quantitative fund management, and commodities business.

He was a learner in a transformational leadership course for executives taught by the author Dr. Kaipa in 2018 at The Indian School of Business in Hyderabad, India.

> It was remarkable how Dr. Kaipa led us and channelized us! Depth did matter a lot; I saw myself in larger scheme of things. By the end of the program, I realized that my North Star has to continuously evolve towards my purpose. The very boring and mundane session on the first day turned into subtle deep insightful messages by the second day leading to introspection and figuring out how to act on the reflections. By the end of the program, I understood that career and job is not the end and that I also value social, charitable, religious aspects of my life. My job was important but equally important was what I could offer and give back to the society. His book *From Smart to Wise* had a profound impact on me, the journey from intellect to wisdom validated my belief system and that I am on the right track in life and that I have to be aware and conscious to charter my path. I was greatly inspired by the story of transformation at the State Bank of India. After, the program I was able to connect regular functioning to spirituality; I found a bridge to connect my spiritual journey to everyday life.
>
> Over the last few years, my journey shifted from money to time then time to energy and finally energy to health and wellbeing and I feel as if I have reached a balance in life

> now. I have become aware of my thought process and how I allocate my time and energy. This shift has helped me identify what I want to pursue other than my job, so my life is peaceful. I have understood that not all challenges are related to me directly. As a result of transforming my outlook about life, I was able to courageously take a lot of organizational challenges. As I started running with my purpose, and developed my purpose statement, something remarkable happened! I was able to reach out to eminent people who backed my candidature for a leadership position. Earlier, I never had such aspirations and never focused on leadership positions but that changed. I was able to take the organization out of a crisis; I dealt with regular issues, stakeholders, structural issues, financial issues at the same time. So, basically the transformation was this that I understood, I need to draw inspiration and build my confidence, be guided by purpose-led actions and engage in introspection.

This narrative highlighted the elements of time, energy, and transformation.

Personal transformation is possible through freedom and allowing the mind to remain in the present moment without oscillating between the past and the future. Presence in the now allows conscious space, time, beauty, and energy to manifest. Narratives in personal development are aligned with individual values consisting of commitment, congruence, and self-consciousness, and the narratives for organizational development described below align with group values to include cooperation, group work, and collaborations for effective organizational transformation (Komives et al. 2007).

Transformation in Organizational Development

This section highlights various facets of organizational development to include conscious leadership along with elements of transformation. By raising their consciousness, leaders can deepen and expand their awareness, stay connected with a larger purpose, and engage their whole being, that is, body, mind, heart, and soul, to build a healthier, equitable, and sustainable world. When the leader evolves in consciousness, his/her heightened self-awareness and witness consciousness can influence his/her ability to lead effectively when combined with contextual awareness. Conscious leaders who are themselves change agents have been described below through their own narratives.

Narrative of Mr. Dinesh Chandra on Organizational Transformation

Mr. Dinesh has been a coach for executives for several decades in the United States and India and is describing his lived experiences with transformation in organizational development.

> Executives function from their head and typically there is a transformation after a crisis when founders change, or an acquisition, or a crisis or reflection happens, or they lose a loved one and shift from mind to heart. I went from a production focus in my career to a new attitude and belief system about leadership. Then I worked on quality and organizational transformation. Personal transformation happened along the side. I worked with Eicher Consulting, focusing on respect for workers, at L&T which was top down orthodox but basically a learning organization. The Heavy Engineering division went against main-

> stream towards a collaborative model. Then at Blackman Cotton, transformational learning improved quality followed by Port of Singapore which was heavily entrenched in government bureaucracy, yet reached the number one stage in just 3 years. Transformation is nothing but change of form like water can change from liquid water to ice to steam or like how a butterfly metamorphosizes from a caterpillar. It is a shift in identity, values and beliefs. It goes from a victim mentality towards an awakening moment. Once the right questions are asked and the person understands their role in creation of problem, transformation happens. Once a shift towards ownership of responsibility happens, the person has control over his/her behavior. Intellectual transformation happens very fast then. The right attitude sets in and the person acts from a place of choice.

This narrative highlighted the elements of space, energy, and transformation.

Narrative of Mr. Deepak Raj on Organizational Transformation

Mr. Deepak Raj is an executive leader with over 15 years of multicultural leadership experience across Asian markets. Currently, he is the managing director of Keller Group Plc's ASEAN Business unit and based out of Singapore. He led the turnaround of the business unit. A civil engineer by training and alumni of IIT Madras and ISB, Deepak was featured in the CEO Magazine on "Turnaround Leadership." He was also selected as one of finalists for the British Chamber of Commerce Singapore's Individual Contribution of the Year 2020 Annual Business Award.

> I was already in a leadership position leading 500 employees for a decade when I joined ISB for the EMBA program. I realized that I was leading my organization intuitively and applying all that I was learning there. What the time at ISB gave me was structure in my thought process. I was influenced by smart and personal leadership in Dr. Kaipa's class. It was interesting to see how spiritual leadership, wise leadership and personal leadership could align at one point. When we are faced with adversity, perspective becomes important. Immediately after my EMBA at ISB in early 2018, there were structural changes within the organization, and I was trusted to turn around South East Asia business unit. The business unit was underperforming for the last few years and was dragging the whole Plc group down. I had to make some radical changes in a short time and was compelled to apply all that was learned. We had world class people—energetic, committed, experienced and had impressive qualifications from premium institutes, yet something hadn't been working in the old ways of management. I took time working side by side with the leadership team without getting into their personal domain and looked closely into our decision making. This was tough in a relationship-oriented culture in South East Asia. We changed our business model and made hard decisions of restructure. I had to ensure that while, I was letting go of some people, I had to ensure rest of the organization remains motivated and engaged! We conducted regular cultural building workshops across all the markets and when the quality of business started improving by means of making profits month on month and reduced attrition rate, the whole piece came together. Even today, I cannot tell which part was most useful, but it manifested perfectly just as it had tested my perspectives. As a whole, it came out better within a short span of less than 1 year!

> I would say 'action orientation' was what helped me. To be an "Authentic" leader and building "Trust", these traits closely resonates with me. I started focusing on finding my North Star or noble purpose, making decisions that support stakeholders' interests, focus on livelihoods. I became more aware that a thousand families were dependent on my decisions along with vendors, suppliers. My perception of Leadership role has changed somewhat after the program at ISB and Dr.Kaipa's program. I have come to

realize and understand that my thought process and decision-making impact other larger things and people's lives. I have embraced other's perspectives; I listen more and connect the whole and the community now.

This narrative highlighted the elements of space, time, energy, and transformation.

Narrative of Change Mr. Om Prakash Bhatt on Organizational Transformation

Mr. Om Prakash Bhatt served as Chairman of State Bank Group. Mr. Bhatt led State Bank of India (SBI) during challenging times. Under his leadership, SBI rose on the global list rankings of Fortune 500. He was also the Chairman of Indian Banks' Association, the apex body of Indian banks, and has served as India's economic diplomacy as government's nominee on the India–US CEO Forum, Indo–French CEO Forum, and Indo–Russia CEO Forum, forging links with a cross section of the world's business leaders. He is a governor on the Board of the Centre for Creative Leadership, USA. He was nominated Banker of the Year by Business Standard and Indian of the Year for Business in 2007 by CNN-IBN.

State Bank of India is the largest bank in India with over 210,000 employees, with about 20,000 branches and managing 25% of Indian economy. It was a 200+ year old organization with over 50% owned by Indian Government. It was known for slow and bad customer service, declining market share and drop in share price before this gentleman became the chairman of the bank. In 5 years, morale was up, market share increased significantly, share prize more than doubled, and customer service became exemplary. This is what he said about organizational transformation of the State Bank of India:

Transformation is a mental shift of values, thoughts, behavior, action and outcomes. It is a shift that happens from internal to external over time. My story of transformation was like a river, very little method in the madness. It is not a textbook case at all, it was based purely in if it can be done, it will be done and we can do it! Most of times, we are not conscious; we only know about something after it is done. I cannot think of one moment of transformation in my personal journey. Partly, because of sensibility, values cemented during childhood. A very subconscious part of growing up, it determines what you will do. A bank has a huge contact-connect, this became clear to me after I joined. SBI is a large organization that meets all kinds of people, the range is huge and the opportunity was huge. You realize that you are there to help these people and there are roadblocks. Some people are reveling in power, they enjoy what they can stop.

From childhood, I was reading Vivekananda, Paramahansa Yogananada and slowly a gentle acceptance and subliminal way got cemented through idealism. Every role became streamlined, and began to align in one direction. When, I was the branch manager, everything was manual and unless books are balanced, one did not go home. The customer transaction closed at 2 pm but one had to work as long as it took to balance everything and go home. I decided to allow flexibility and help customers after hours since everyone was working anyway. I introduced facilitation, we helped thousands of people with faster processing of demand drafts before examinations. 800 drafts were stamped ahead; what used to tale 5–10 min per draft took 5–10 s per draft. Stamping drafts ahead was not a part of existing process but we got a different qualitative response and buy-in from people.

Then I became the regional manager and had 34 branches under my jurisdiction. Bank managers had weekly reimbursements to be processed and I allowed faster and timely reimbursement on a weekly basis without any questions asked. I decided I will not allow the indignity of questioning the manager over small amounts of reimbursement for transport and miscellaneous matters that did not amount to anything. My region became the best in country because of the trust I placed in people and process. The bulk of loans in India are schematic, based in number of loans and the assets like land, cattle etc. I cut down unnecessary assessment of factors and there was a loan disbursement surge, it engaged the power of function. I did not do anything new but the way I could get people to produce results with small changes in process and more trust in people—instilled within me a certain bent of mind and a certain style of leadership.

Everyone would become my friend including union leaders. I would say our frameworks are different, can we work from both frameworks or via media or agree that this cannot be done. From 1988 onwards, there was branch computerization going on and I was the AGM (Assistant General Manager). People worked overtime, late into the evening hours and it was inconvenient. I allowed them to book a flight ticket and travel instead of customary train ticket which cut down their time on the train. Women employees were sent home with escorts assuring their safety at night. It was not to impress or incentivize anyone, it was appropriate, necessary and the right thing to do!

India had 14 circles then for banking and the Northeast circle was 14th, the last ranked. At the end of the same year I became the head of that Circle, it became ranked at number one. Later, as the Managing Director of State Bank of Travancore, I used the right language, behavior and connect towards an experience of success.

My journey towards the Chairmanship was unexpected. I was the least favorite to be picked because everyone else who was being considered was my senior. I was eligible for consideration, but the other four had a higher chance to get the job. My wife was the only one who was not surprised. Even in the US she would tell everyone, 'we have to go back because he has to become the chairman of SBI'. So, I was an accidental chairman and I did not have an agenda. I was impatient with complex things, instinctive, and too strong forward measures. SBI, was faring the worst when I became Chairman, morale was down and image was down as foreign banks entered the market and so did domestic private players. SBI suffered the most and the common talk was that it was natural, that the chunk of customers would go from SBI. I was uncomfortable with the slide. Earlier, there was great pride in being with SBI. A bank agent was given a lot of respect but that had taken a beating. I started asking questions. Changes come and go, they can be superficial; but in transformation, the psyche of people, organization, empowerment, enablement and mind shift happens. I did not change a single physical thing at SBI but in 5 years entire bank was transformed.

My personal triggers for transformation have been deep desire to do the right thing, live up to ideals and questioning myself, reflection. If I have to be banker to every Indian, how should I be? What should I do? *When we explain the context to people, meaning shifts*. When you contextualize in society, you arrive at deeper and deeper shades of meaning and there is a shift and balance appears.

Section Summary and Highlights

What emerges out of the narratives is that the framework with structure was in alignment with the creation of consciousness model where the change agent or facilitator of change was able to create space, and in that shift, the cycle of time transforms into a different pattern. As a result, the individual or group of individuals going through the experience of transformation of energy could perceive a shift in beauty of their being, existence, and contributions to the world.

While the above narratives for structured transformation at the individual and organization level are quite compelling, there are other examples for transformation that manifest without a structure. As we will see in the next segment, these narratives are compelling in a very different manner. Structured transformation creates space, but when transformation is facilitated without a structure, space emerges as there are no conditions set for time to manifest. Energy gets released based on the individual's capacity to expand into consciousness. Creation occurs through consciousness, and finally, all experience culminates into beauty via transformation of energy.

Framework Without Structure

Dr. Madhulika Sagaram, coauthor of this chapter, works with children accelerating several years of learning in short periods of time. The transformation that happens in the process of acceleration is described in a dialogue narrative between her and her student Nikhil (19-year-old) reminiscing about his experience between 2012 and 2015 when he was a part of an accelerated learning program.

Nikhil: I have been thinking akka (sister)…when you taught us, you did not exist! We thought we did everything but actually you did it…you were like air; you were there but you were not there …so we could find ourselves in that freedom. You are always there but you do not exist; you are nothing!

Madhu: Yes, I worked on myself for many years to be totally transparent so my students can walk through me and in doing that find themselves…that is the secret of my work; I shed my ego and become empty but when I tell others the same thing, they think I am lying. I am only shedding my ego and dissolving my personality so you can see your own reflection in me.

Nikhil: It is like a blackhole … entering a blackhole you go on to the other side. You think you are entering darkness, but by the time you come out, you are a different person because you leave your darkness inside the black hole…it must be like that only.

Madhu: Yes, actually a worm hole…I dissolved my magnetic field, I made myself empty so all of you could walk through me and in that you dissolved your own magnetic field and emotions. So, time got dissolved and space expanded and when you came out of the worm hole, you entered a new space time continuum and that is how I accelerated 7–8 years of learning in one year.

Nikhil: So, then you are nothing! We should live our life as nothing in everything. I understood this when I was teaching children last year. They could not learn if I was myself, I tried being like you, like air and I was able to do what you are able to do. That is the difference, at school, our teachers are everything, full of so many things… so we think they are teaching but we are not learning because they are giving us more conditioning. With you, you are air, space…flexible, porous and nothing and we grow in that!

Madhu: Yes, that is the secret…be flexible according to situation and flow. Earlier, I was like that only with my students … now, I am like that in everything and with everyone. Magnanimous, free flowing and in surrender to life…in acceptance of all lessons as they are, in acceptance of everything and everyone!

Nikhil: Be flexible but do not lose yourself…if you become like others, then you lose yourself!! All those students that left the program early, did they learn it?

Madhu: All those that left early also have the experience. When a similar experience or situation or person arrives again, they will resolve their emotion and magnetic field then!

> You are creating a new electromagnetic field for yourself right now...they will do it in a different space time continuum. The experience is there, it will mature in a different space time construct with a different person and interaction.
>
> Nikhil: I am going to be nothing in everything like you...in freedom!

Such an approach that is quite fluid without a set structure is often based in the understanding that transformation cannot be created, and suitable conditions can be facilitated so that transformation may manifest in space-time continuum based on emergence of energy and beauty as grace. It involves the knowledge paths or *Dasamahavidya* as described below.

(i) The situation of the facilitator in nothingness or *ajatavada* throughout the program.
(ii) The cycle of creation of consciousness or *sristi-dristi* for the facilitator.

Bhairavi, the power of purification in kinetic form of energy, initiates the process of purification for the facilitator. Following this, *Kali* as the kinetic energy aspect of power of time initiates action dissolving time, and *Chinnamasta* cuts through with her ability to act in the potential state of time. *Tara* as the power of transformation of transformation expands in kinetic state. *Bagalamukhi* who is the power of stillness in potential state creates a stage for energy transformation. *Kamalatmika* arrives in kinetic state to provide nourishment as beauty, and *Bhuvaneshwari* as the power of clarification in kinetic state of space expands providing required impetus for transformation to turn into beauty. Finally, *Tripura Sundari* arrives as the potential state of beauty to create equilibrium.

(iii) The cycle of creation through consciousness or *dristi-sristi* for the learner.

The learners situate themselves in the expanded space created by the facilitator in the knowledge path *Bhuvaneshwari* phase and dissolve the time element involving the *Kali* phase in order to expand in space. The collective consciousness created by the dissolution of time by the *Kali* knowledge path facilitates acceleration through expansion of space, and appropriate pedagogy is implemented. Learners are nurtured by the beauty of the *Kamaltmika* knowledge path and an equilibrium in beauty is created by *Tripura Sundari*. Then, *Dhumavati,* represented by potential energy, absorbs space into herself to return to the regular normalized state.

What this means in terms of transformation is that the facilitator in the above scenario creates space within herself so the learners can reconstitute their ego based on the collective consciousness that opportunities and learning environments were provided to them instead of being formed by the conditioning from family alone. In this fluid space that is created, all cause and effect cease to exist, and instead, correlations develop between one cause and many effects. This framework allows the child multiple possibilities to engage with themselves and the world.

The transformation that is described above is at the level of quantum potential and supports the emergence of beauty, love, truth, and freedom. Transformation unfolds as the learner engages with various possibilities and then enfolds back again in myriad ways to create patterns similar to those that emerge in origami, the Japanese art of paper folding, or the ancient science and art of mandalas in India and neighboring geographical areas. These patterns allow the learner to fold, unfold, and enfold, creating an infinite number of possibilities for themselves and others making the transformation authentic, continuous, and long lasting but allowing each individual to blossom and emerge into beauty in their own space-time continuum.

Narrative from Ms. Anne Stadler on Transformation Without Structure

Ms. Anne Stadler has spent decades doing good work both professionally and as a volunteer to seek solutions to world issues through nonviolence and alternative methods of conflict resolution. She creates open space for inspired practical action to create a world that works for all. She has worked locally, nationally, and internationally supporting high-performing inclusive teams building a beloved community where they live and work. Her professional life has been in three stages: (1) community organizing for nonviolent initiatives to end war; (2) KING TV television producer working with People Power (a broad regional coalition) to do programming on issues of racial justice, social and economic equity, and community thriving; and (3) leadership and organizational consultant supporting similar goals.

Anne is a veteran of the field of transformation and has spent the last 50 years or so experiencing quantum shifts of energy and resulting changes in herself and the community around her. She begins her narrative with a definition of transformation:

> The qualitative and quantum shift in a person or situation. The shift occurs in the quantum field, the mental form of reality. In a subjective perspective, it is not serial, it is an immediate presence. At an Open Space Technology conference, I once remarked, 'transformational learning occurs at the speed of light.' It can be a kind of gestalt! A metaphor that is commonly used is butterfly, turning from a caterpillar into butterfly. That is an effort to talk about it. It is not transformation, I would say. Transformation involves the death of identity, and the presence of a different form of identity. But that is how we tell ourselves the story, we talk about it; maybe we do not know how to presence it. It is important to presence transformation and bring ourselves into relationship with patterns that act on us at different levels so we are experiencing it. It took me a couple of months to come into my body when I first had a spiritual emergence experience. We look for safety for our story but the actual event is not a story. For example, if I am dealing with a sudden death, then I am telling the story of somebody's death; I am telling myself after the transformation what happened to me in relation to that! It is just a story; transformation is in the moment and in presence.
>
> I think the species is actively engaged in transformation and the planetary environment is engaged too, and my take is we'll keep transforming. I have a commitment for life to manifest all love all the time. In 1994 or 1996, I was in a meditation with The Dalai Lama and what appeared to us was 'live as if all life depends on you!' I think love is transforming us, we are essentially being burnished by love. What appears to be chaos, calamitous and frightening is simply the full presence of dissolution of love, so we can more fully be in love and manifest it in all relations and life. Systems have distorted and literally burnt up in their own fury. Those are the fires of love transforming us.
>
> 'Love is a spurt, all compact of fire'- William Shakespeare

> *Love isn't just sweetness, it is fire*. It is not destructive, it is clearing and burnishing, it is an essential quality. The fact is all aspects of transformation are just one, it is our specific focus on I or you and I or the community. That is the illusion again, a way to speak. You can hear across the barriers and you can hear common unity, diversity of form is still expressing in unity. A kaleidoscope reminds me that light is refracting through our form, to create different things. We do not separate or segregate, it interferes with the capacity to experience useful transformation. Transformation is deep resonance, a quality of your own capacity for ease and internal clarity. It is a change in physical form or surroundings. Transformation is the quantum quality of unexpectedness at the heart of knowing and naming 'transformation' rather than calling any change subjective awareness.

Narrative from Nipun Mehta on Transformation Without Structure

Mr. Nipun Mehta is the founder of ServiceSpace, an incubator of projects that work at the intersection of volunteerism, technology, and gift-economy. Nipun has received many awards, including the Jefferson Award for Public Service, Dalai Lama's Unsung Hero of Compassion, and Goi Peace Award. A few years ago, President Barack Obama appointed him to a council on poverty and inequality. He serves on the advisory boards of the Seva Foundation, the Dalai Lama Foundation, and the Good Science Center.

Nipun Mehta is essentially a change agent working on creating community spaces and gift economy.

> Transformation is not understudied but definitely under-understood. It is difficult to define it. We cannot create transformation, we can however, create conditions for transformation. When you put a time bound limit, it may create it in some instances when you do casual stuff, but it will not be a lasting transformation. There is always a timeline; a habit to make things time bound. Transformation is fundamentally averse to a timeline, yet it is something we can work towards.
>
> I have been through a remarkable transformation; in any moment kindness can shift us from me centeredness to we centeredness. Micro transformations through small acts of kindness can take us from 'me' to 'we.' Over time such micro transformations stick around leading to reformation of ego. In that time gap, we can experience more micro transformations for a multiplier effect. There is a role that serendipity has to play! One day I was running late at night and suddenly realized that there was someone possibly trying to mug me; it appeared to me he had a gun under a newspaper. Suddenly, I felt a connection and asked myself what if this was my brother? And I looked him straight in the eye and suddenly fear transformed into love. The question to ponder over is how does this micro transformation turn into behavioral change and how do you make it last? The question starts to beg as you create...How much is controlled by you and how much by the community? What I have understood through experience is this, that micro moments accumulate to turn into events, that act as tipping points leading to behavior change.
>
> The greatest predictor is the connection in the community, the collective effect, inner transformation that leads to external transformation and shift and modification in behavior. Transformation seems sudden because we don't know the context, time is a construct of our mind. However, if you are invested in understanding time, it may seem like many micro moments. The metaphor of farming is what seems most relevant in relation to transformation...when you plant a seed, planting a seed alone is not sufficient, nutrients, water etc. are not in control. One cannot predict the time for transformation; still we try to superimpose a timeline for transformation. Money, power and fame superimpose authority to create a short-term cycle of transformation. The influence of market, media and government requirements impose several end outcomes that are time bound. As a

result, we have this incredibly biased narrative of transformation as quantifiable, measurable and time bound change.

Inclusion of alternate forms of wealth without time limits and horizons allows latitude to have a nuanced insight and trust in the natural process of transformation. How do we collectively transform? How do you create a change of culture? It is possible if we have aligned incentives, but we have mixed incentives. We cannot do anything other than transforming ourselves. We are mixed ourselves, several elements playing together. You take two steps forward and one step backward. Finding a coherence of these incentives allows greater transformation. We have been doing this as a part of Service space in the form of retreats. In our Gandhi 1.0 format, we connected one to many; In the 2.0 version, we connected one to one network. But, in the 3.0 version, we connected many to many. We invited forty remarkable leaders for a retreat, in a collectivistic space for a five-day immersion into local culture followed by a five-day retreat. Forty participants along with thirty volunteers; an ecology of seventy where everyone is supporting everyone. What you have is a complete suspension of cause and effect. We do not superimpose any microcosm, so millions of connections got created while we were just holding collective space. Inner and outer transformation is as coherent as possible and we trust this field of emergence. Having hosted over a hundred retreats, I can say we cannot create transformation and we tell all participants there might be nothing, no shift after the event. We are coming together with many too many connections while fully understanding when and how it is going to blossom can only be found out when someone gets there. And there is a possibility nothing might happen. Still people who have calendars full for the next 3 years arrive creating space for the event. What that means is that trust is built first because someone can arrive without a predetermined outcome only if they have trust. A precondition for holding such a field of emergence of transformation is trust; only in the field of trust do you get a collective transformation. Micro-moments of other centeredness and small acts of kindness add up towards it. For transformation to happen, one has to set the right conditions; do your part and trust in conditions. There are a lot of preconditions that allow for coherence of incentives and intention. Transformation is hard and neither market, media or might give you transformation; perhaps something short term is possible, but I don't expect a genuine lasting transformation from it. Let it emerge.

Transformation in an open format based in facilitation of suitable conditions and learning environments tend to be largely society or community values described with focus on the social end to which the transformation is beneficial (Komives et al. 2007). Such transformation and its narratives involve individual responsibility and individual focus in accordance with the individual in a group or community (Komives et al. 2007).

Conclusion

The journey through this chapter reveals several layers of transformation from varied perspectives. Transformation is largely looked upon at the level of personal or group or organizational and social levels. In terms of perspectives from the United States, transformation is understood largely as leadership, learning, consciousness, or lately, as spirituality. However, what emerges out of this chapter that is of great importance is the various models and frameworks of transformation from Indian traditions and their applicability and relevance in contexts of human development.

Whether transformation is at the individual or group or organizational level, it boils down to human development. Humans get molded into the trap of doing due to conditioning and accumulated impressions through lived experience. The transformation of humans from the doing to the being paradigm involving consciousness and creation of space is the central emergence from this chapter. While this revelation is not new and work in this domain has been done by others in the West, the context of the models discussed in this chapter and application of the same through two different frameworks should be of real interest to both researchers and practitioners.

The emergence of transformation through perspectives of human development informs us of several aspects of layering that transformation manifests in and through lived experience. When transformation happens at the personal level, it manifests through evolution through serendipity or grief and suffering or gradual growth through interventions. As it has emerged from literature and narratives, there seem to be several avenues for personal development, and it can manifest at superficial short-term or lasting long-term temporal shifts. Organizational development on the other hand is heavily dependent on planned interventions, and transformation is valued in the immediate future, often measured in financial returns and monetary benefits. Finally, the narratives that emerged out in the perspectives of human development potential manifested at a greater depth and were spread out over a space-time continuum rather than fragmented spaces and time frames.

All the modes of transformation that have been discussed in various perspectives whether in the United States or India are valid. The relevance and validity of the mode of emergent transformation depends on the task that is to be accomplished and the type of transformation that is desired. What is of great value is to acknowledge and understand that each type of transformation must be facilitated based on sociocultural situations, resources available, problem at hand, and the possibility of application to real-life situations.

While creation of space was central to each framework of transformation, other aspects of transformation were involved in different capacities based on the framework used for transformation. When structure was used, various aspects of transformation from the knowledge paths model of transformation were facilitated in a designed approach in a series of steps. When structure was absent, whether in the framework or the narratives, aspects of transformation emerged in relation to an expansion of space. Awareness of self is facilitated when structure is involved, whereas it emerges naturally in a tacit manner when structure is absent in the facilitation of transformation.

At this juncture, within the scope of this chapter, we can conclude that there are varied people, diverse cultural contexts and different requirements of transformation in situations whether personal or organizational or collective domains. Further research and understanding over multiple transformation contexts would be required to deepen the understanding in different domains and paradigms to understand if transformation can be looked upon as a shift in human potential rather than as an individual or organizational or collectivistic shift in values and belief systems. A deeper understanding of human development and potential definitely will bring a much-required impetus to develop new matrices to understand, facilitate, and assess transformation from different perspectives.

References

Adams J (ed) (1984) Transforming work: a collection of organizational transformation readings. Miles River Press, Alexandria

Albuquerque D (2012) Mentoring management leadership on the principles of consciousness. Consciousness in corporate corridors. IBA Publications, Bangalore

Bass BM (1985) Leadership and performance beyond expectations. Free Press, New York

Bass BM (1995) Theory of transformational leadership redux. Leadersh Q 6:463–478

Bass BM, Avolio BJ (1994) Transformational leadership and organizational culture. Int J Public Adm 17:541–554

Block P (1993) Stewardship: choosing service over self-interest. Berrett-Koehler, San Francisco

Burns JM (1978) Leadership. Harper & Row, New York

Chalmers DJ (1996) The conscious mind: in search of a fundamental theory. Oxford University Press, Oxford

Dweck CS (2006) Mindset: the new psychology of success. Random House, New York

Frankl VE (1962) Man's search for meaning; an introduction to logotherapy. Beacon Press, Boston

Higher Education Research Institute (1996) A social change model of leadership development: guidebook version III. National Clearinghouse for Leadership Programs, College Park

House RJ (1977) A 1976 theory of charismatic leadership. In: Hunt JG, Larson LL (eds) Leadership: the cutting edge. Southern Illinois University Press, Carbondale, pp 189–207

House RJ, Shamir B (1993) Toward the integration of transformational, charismatic, and visionary theories. In: Chemers MM, Ayman R (eds) Leadership theory and research: perspectives and directions. Academic, Cambridge, MA, pp 81–107

Hunt JG (1999) Transformational/charismatic leadership's transformation of the field: an historical essay. Leadersh Q 10(2):129–144

Katz V (2011) Conversations with Maharishi: Maharishi Mahesh Yogi speaks about the full development of human consciousness, 2 vols. Maharishi University of Management Press, Fairfield

Komives SR, Lucas N, McMohan TR (2007) Exploring leadership: for college students who want to make a difference. Jossey-Bass, San Francisco

Kwiecinski P (2018) Whole system transformation with music. In: Handbook of personal and organizational transformation. Springer, New York

Merriam SB, Caffarella RS, Baumgartner LM (2007) Learning in adulthood: a comprehensive guide, 3rd edn. Jossey-Bass, San Francisco

Mezirow J (1997) Transformative theory out of context. Adult Educ Q 48(1):60–62

Mezirow J (2000) Learning to think like an adult: core concepts of transformation theory. In: Associates JM (ed) Learning as transformation: critical perspectives on a theory in progress. Jossey-Bass, San Francisco, pp 3–33

Neal J (2018) An overview of the field of transformation. In: Handbook of personal and organizational transformation. Springer, New York

Northouse PG (1997) Theory and practice. Sage Publications, Inc., San Francisco

O'Neal P (2017a) Transformation: the next big risk. In: Neal J (ed) Handbook of personal and organizational transformation. Springer, New York

O'Neal P (2017b) The truth about transformation: one person can change the world. In: Neal J (ed) Handbook of personal and organizational transformation. Springer, New York

Owen H (1997) Open space technology: a user's guide, 2nd edn. Berrett-Koehler, San Francisco

Timalsina S (2020) Yoga Vashista course content. https://www.facebook.com/groups/322374965425993/

Tolle E (1997) The power of now: a guide to spiritual enlightenment. Namaste Publications, Vancouver
Yammarino FJ, Spangler WD, Dubinsky AJ (1998) Transformational and contingent award leadership: individual, dyad, and group levels of analysis. Leadersh Q 9(1):27–54
Yogananda P (1946) Autobiography of a Yogi. The Philosophical Library, New York
Yukl G (1989) Managerial leadership: a review of theory and research. J Manag 15(2):251–289

Cross References

A Return to Virtue: Embodiment, Chakras, and Management Education
Creating Space for Personal Transformation
From Individual to Organizational Transformation: A Foucauldian Perspective on Transformational Leadership
The Metamanagement Model as a Framework for Organizational Transformation

The Metamanagement Model as a Framework for Organizational Transformation

7

Marcelo Cardoso

Abstract

Today's world is becoming increasingly more complex, fast in its changes, and, thus, obstinate in seeing to that human projections do not become a reality. Thought systems, which for centuries provided satisfactory expectations for the future of companies and humanity, have become obsolete and even prejudicial for their inefficiency, waste of energy and time, and for creating habits. This chapter aims to present the foundations and process for an alternative thought system (or metamap)—the Metamanagement Model—which, based on the Integral Metatheory (Wilber); theory of complex systems, Cynefin Framework (Snowden); and concepts such as antifragile (Taleb), sociocracy (Comte, Boeke, Buck, and Endenburg), holacracy (Koestler), deep democracy (Mindell), vulnerability (Brown), psychological safety (Edmondson and Kahn), and verbal human development (Kegan, Cook-Greuter, and Tolbert), dynamically and simultaneously act in three key dimensions of organizations, individuals, relationships, and systems, to promote evolutive transformations in systems for companies to pursue a desired direction. This text was based on bibliographic research, case studies of Consultoria Chie clients (Eileen Fisher, Kunumi, and Fazenda da Toca, among others), and author's personal experience as an executive at DBM do Brasil, Natura Cosméticos, and Fleury Medicina Diagnóstica. The result is that the Metamanagement Model can help build companies that transcend the limits of organizations as we see them today toward more collaborative models, with ecosystems of multiple interactions that lead to the emergence of a fairer and more inclusive society.

M. Cardoso (✉)
Chie Integrates, São Paulo, SP, Brazil
e-mail: marcelo@chieintegrates.com

J. Neal (ed.), *Personal, Educational and Organizational Transformation*, Future of Business and Finance, https://doi.org/10.1007/978-3-031-29253-8_7

Keywords

Metamodel · Management · Integral approach · Complex systems · Antifragile · Holacracy · Deep democracy · Human development · Organizational culture · Purpose · Identity

Introduction

Mapping *Terra Incognita*

One of the biggest issues about today's management models is the ability of organizations to move away from a mindset exclusively focused on command and control. Those systems were developed in the early twentieth century to account for increases in production volume demands. They do not include a logic in their processes that embraces the rapid dynamics of complexity and emergence of the unexpected that today's organizations experience. This transition process does not occur in an easy and swift manner. It is first necessary to identify, understand, become aware, and accept the origins of mindsets currently in effect in order to develop possible paths to evolve this model to a logic capable of providing the most appropriate answers to the challenges that many times seem unsurmountable and fatal for companies today.

As such, in order to jointly facilitate this transition in organizations, I developed the *Metamanagement Model*, a map based on different levels of awareness found in an organizational system that aims to expand the mindsets of individuals that comprise it and promote greater maturity and confidence in the ties that promote relations between them in order to transform the internal culture, giving it a more conscious, protagonist, and responsible role in relation to its individual and collective results, considering their impacts on our society and environment.

It is important to point out that there is no magical formula for pursuing this path, much less ready-made recipes, like many consulting firms still offer. The *Metamanagement Model* proposes to analyze the intrinsic characteristics of each organization (without forgetting to identify the biases that invariably, due to human nature, are brought by our own facilitators); recognize its history and the construction of its identity since its creation per the vision of its founders; and, based on these idiosyncratic elements, promote prototypes for specific development and engagement plans and actions that update the psychological contract between people in the company and the organizational strategy itself. In the Final Considerations presented at the end of this chapter, you will find a summary table that presents in more detail the roles and methods for conducting interventions in the *Metamanagement Model*.

Through this dynamic, we intend to shed light on aspects that may be acting invisibly inside systems and, with this new awareness, develop, with organizations and ourselves, an identity that acknowledges its deepest values and, at the same time, is sufficiently fluid to adapt and evolve in face of the different challenges that will undoubtedly be faced in its trajectory through reality.

A long time ago, European cartographers used to name regions not yet explored as *Terra Incognita* in their maps and, in the case of oceans, *Mare Incognitum*. They included in these uncharted territories the warning that "Here be dragons," in Latin *Hic sunt dracones*, to alert explorers about the possibility of coming face to face with these fantastic creatures in unknown lands, at least it's what appears in one of the oldest known world maps: the Hunt-Lenox Globe from ca. 1510. The metaphor is still valid today. Organizations that intend to exceed themselves and their own horizons must seek to exorcise the ghosts and monsters that at times they envision in their path (and that many times they will have to face in order to exorcise) to best navigate without drowning in the unknown and turbulent waters of the future, knowing specially that there will be no more safe havens and that this will no longer be a problem.

Part One: Current Context

Visions of the World, Visions of Business

The management models developed and adopted by organizations are intrinsically related to visions of the world shared by society and how these organizations adhere (or not) to the predominant technical- economic foundations of a given period.

These visions of the world determine not only how businesses are administrated and led, but also the values that guide their strategies and the purpose they serve society. Therefore, the more it adheres to the social and economic macroenvironment of the period, in thesis, the greater the ease to associate people (such as coworkers, partners, consumers, etc.) and promote interfaces favorable to the organization existence and prosperity.

In a quick retrospect, businesses, as we know them today, were born in the industrial revolution that began in the eigthteenth century. In turn, the professional managing of companies occurred in the beginning of the twentieth century, having as precursors Frederick W. Taylor and Henry Ford in the United States and Henri Fayol in Europe.

Taylor, Fayol, and Ford were White men born in the nineteenth century and, in their 50–60 s, prepared proposals to resolve the problem of transferring labor from the field to the new industrial model, gaining momentum in large cities. They were also responsible for significantly increasing the production rate of these people by structuring assembly or production lines, and for this historical reason, we still call workers as "human resources." The Industrial Revolution era, leveraged by the invention of steam engines, led to a major productivity leap worldwide. Management was born precisely to solve the productivity problems of this new scale.

If we put things into perspective, management has evolved very little in the last 100 years. A good part of what we do today in companies still carries that mechanical planning and control logic from last century. A lot of people believed, especially after World War II, when large management consulting firms underwent major growth and created the human resources industry, that organizations would envision their strategies, business, and people in a more integrated, systemic, and humanistic way.

However, what happens is that the United States set up a program with the biggest companies in the country to employ the main Armed Forces officials that were returning from World War II. These individuals left the warfront to become the main leaders in companies like General Motors and Ford, for example. With them came that military logic of dealing with management aspects through planning and control, of treating everything simply as a resource. So much so that, to this day, we continue to call people "human resources," and in addition to "retaining," "recruiting," and "selecting" individuals, we also prepare career "plans" and action "strategies.".Similarly, the entire organizational logic is structured based on well-defined hierarchies.

From the Industrial Revolution to now, organizations have found a reasonably solid and stable technical-economic foundation for their growth and expansion. We have witnessed during this time the tremendous inventiveness of business for generating prosperity, knowledge, technology, products, and services; we have also seen the nefarious consequences that this enlarged capacity, when submitted to intentions of little consciousness, has caused environmentally and socially. However, it appears that we are experiencing a major transition as mankind, probably much bigger than the Industrial Revolution itself, and this significant change inevitably implies profound changes in the way organizations work and do business.

Many factors have contributed to the growing landscape of uncertainty in organizations, such as the successive financial market crises and their impacts on the global economy, political polarizations and the risk of wars and terrorism, the environmental and natural resources crises, post-Internet behavioral and cultural changes, and the increase in people being guided by more evolved and complex visions of the world, among other factors. What's certain, however, is that many of the factors point to the impossibility of sustaining old standards, while others, such as emergence of the new economy with values based on flexibility, virtuality, organization in networks and fluidity, point to new possibilities for the future of business and organizations.

We do not exactly know what direction business will take moving forward since we are in the "eye of the storm" of global uncertainties, but we can say that the approach we use can point to consistent paths and base the co-creation of business models for the next generations. These models are based on complexities that are much deeper, encompassing, flexible, and responsible. They are capable of combining the needs of individuals, relationships, and systems, targeting sustainable results guided by visions of the future aligned with the integral development of mankind and the cosmos.

Complex Systems

Today, the first thing we must have in mind when talking about management quality is to identify the dynamic of contexts in which they are inserted. It is necessary to acknowledge the internal and external variables inherent to a given organization in order to be able to recognize the main elements involved in its management process. This perspective should provide a more encompassing logic, related to complex systems, and mirror natural nonlinear systems. In order to have this vision, this logic that seeks an appropriate management system for high complexity environments, we have developed what we call the *Metamanagement Model*, a map (and not a piece of land) based on perspectives of different awareness levels, and the theory of complex systems through which organizations can navigate through unknown and immediate territories that uninterruptedly surface in the future horizon. Through the *Metamanagement Model*, we acknowledge with greater amplitude the reality experienced by organizations to then execute evolutions, changes, and adaptations to their systems for the various, and many times unpredictable, possibilities that can come next. It is important to point out that the map does not provide ready responses of what to do in each situation but offers a checklist of what to take into account and what should not be forgotten. It also provides pointers for evaluating the key dynamics present in the system.

The current need of organizations to find other ways to manage is happening all over the world not because managers think it is cool or simply because they want to innovate. It is because organizations have serious pain points and, for this reason, makes it absolutely urgent. Today, most industries are suffering with disruptions that are continuously killing big companies at an astounding pace. Further, as said by consultant Alan Watkins, who wrote *Wicked & Wise: How to Solve the World's Toughest Problems* (2015) together with American philosopher and social thinker Ken Wilber, problems are not natural. They are created by human beings and their systems, nothing more.

It is very important to keep this insight of Watkins in mind, since the world will never be so calm and peaceful as it is now (at least from the perspective of who looks from the future toward the past). Contrary to what many believe, it will only increase in volatility and complexity. There will be no lack of problems. Based on this awareness, when we look at the various industries that are disruptively evolving today (for example, technology, nanotechnology, artificial intelligence, exponential medicine, and genetics), we see that to keep an organization alive it is necessary to always look for new maps. The *Metamanagement Model* is designed to be able to navigate through these new territories that keep popping up in front of us.

On the other hand, the idea of complexity and ambiguity, not having clear right answers, has always been present in our history, since the beginning of human culture. After all, every time we look at reality, we must deal with paradoxes, and the best way to deal with them is not trying to find the right and wrong polarities and solve them, but rather, sustain them while seeking the best balance for the different situations we will experience. One of the ways to transform volatility into vision clarity occurs when we move away from the reality we wish to analyze and, thus, expand our field of understanding and put into more perspective a greater part of the scenario involved, like when we look at a map. The same applies to the gains in clarity that emotional distance also confers. From a distance, we become aware that we do not have control and certainty over the situation and must develop the ability to better understand this environment and navigate in it.

This is how we are able to understand the dynamics of a complex system and gain more clarity on how it functions. However, upon acknowledging a system's characteristics, that is, its agility, its polarities, and paradoxes, we run the risk of getting paralyzed and losing agility and responsiveness. Further ahead, we will discuss why we generally become paralyzed when faced by these situations and how to keep them from happening.

When absolutely unexpected scenarios occur, we seek reverse engineering, that is, we track facts of the present in the direction of the past, to try and explain what happened, but nobody can state that someone, however more alert he/she was to movements and events at the time, had the faintest idea that a given fact could happen. The opposite is also true. Every time we anticipate an important change in the system, which we foresee with great certainty that something is going to happen, these projections end up not happening. This occurs because the system, for being complex and affecting directly and continuously the context and mindsets of people, somehow prepares itself.

A good example of this was "Y2K." It occurred at the turn of 1999 to 2000. As the new millennium approached, several IT specialists pointed out that computers at the time, programmed only to register dates in the 19XX format, would not be able to "understand" year 2000 and would begin registering that we were in the year 1900 or would simply stop working. With major repercussion in the media, the consequences of Y2K would be catastrophic. They said, among many other calamities, that we would go without electricity and that we even ran the risk of nuclear bombs being detonated. Everything that was under the control of computers could collapse if their systems were not updated. People from all over the world, especially the United States, stocked food and water because systems were not going to work, and there would be no more money, since bank records were going to disappear. But, as we know, this was a case of collective panic that resulted in nothing. People anticipated and prepared for the disaster with such intensity and amplitude, and it simply ended up not happening.

In order for a complex system, such as of a company, to adapt and survive all the constant changes, the best characteristic it should have is not resilience. A resilient system conveys the idea that, in view of a chaotic situation or a storm, it will bend, not break, and return to what it was before it was challenged. However, even though many believe that resilience is the best characteristic of adaptability that a system can have, in fact, it is its potential to be "antifragile" that will make it even stronger after the unforeseen variations that it invariably will face. In the book *Antifragile: Things That Gain from Disorder*, (2014), Nassim Nicholas Taleb, also author of the international bestseller *The Black Swan,* introduces the concept of "antigragile" and explains that it happens when a system learns to strengthen itself in face of disruption or disorder. One of the examples of antifragile systems he provides in the book is Silicon Valley, where tech companies continuously start up, become a global phenomenon, and soon need to adapt and self-renovate, in order to not become fragile and cease to exist.

The system of restaurants in São Paulo, Brazil, is another example of an anti-fragile system. We always see new spaces opening up and many closing down every week, but the large number of eating options in the city remains because the system has this ability to self-renovate, even in face of serious economic crises.

The Cynefin Framework

Still regarding organizational systems, we have the interesting Cynefin framework idea, which offers decision-makers a "sense of place" from where to view more appropriately the situations and challenges that arise in the day-to-day. Cynefin is a Welsh word that means "habitat" or "space of belonging." Dave Snowden, creator of the framework, is founder of Cognitive Edge and one of top experts on complexity in the world. He uses the term to refer to the idea that we all have connections (cultural, religious, geographic, etc.), which we might not be aware of.

The Cynefin framework offers four contexts for decision-making or "domains": Simple, Complicated, Complex, Chaotic, and a center named Disorder (Fig. 7.1).

The domains offer a "sense of place" from where we can analyze behaviors and the factors at hand and make better decisions. The domains on the right, Simple and Complicated, are "ordered": cause and effect are known or can be discovered. The domains on the left, Complex and Chaotic, are "unordered": cause and effect can only be deduced in hindsight or not at all.

We highlight here the Complex domain, in which cause and effect can only be deduced in hindsight, and there are no clear answers. The Cynefin framework calls this process "probe-sense-respond." Battle fields, markets, ecosystems, and corporate cultures are complex systems that are immune to a reductionist approach, since their own acts change the situation in unpredictable manners.

Agents are the most important thing in a complex system. Who are the agents in an organizational system? They are people, obviously, but within a role that the system gives them. This is an important concept. Individuals have several roles in

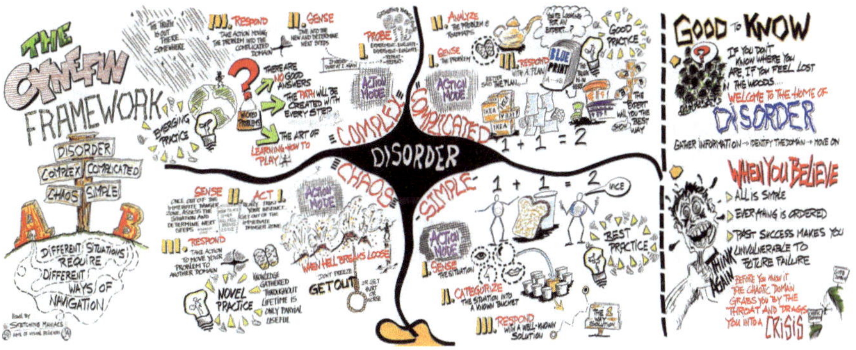

Fig. 7.1 The Cynefin framework. (Source: By Edwin Stoop (User:Marillion!!62)—[1], CC BY-SA 4.0, https://commons.wikimedia.org/w/index.php?curid=53810658, accessed Dec/2018)

their life, depending on the moment they are in. At work, they play a professional role. At home, they play a personal role of father, husband, son, and so forth. The manner in which they perform and express themselves in a role directly interferes in the organizational context and system, and the context and the system, in turn, interfere back on the individuals and the way they execute their roles.

It is very important to understand that within a complex system this dynamic of influences happens the entire time, different from the traditional way of looking at an organization, as if it were in engineering artifact and we were not part of it. In fact, we are always a part. The moment someone changes their mindset, he/she already starts to affect the system. Likewise, the moment an organization creates a new model that alters something, it affects our relationship with the system, which, in turn, can affect our mindset. This happens all the time in an implicit, subjective, and tacit manner, always influencing the system.

And this is why most interventions in an organization fail. Because they assume that, if an off-the-shelf model typical of consulting firms is installed in the organization, they will be able to alter the system as projected. "You are here and should be here," which is what consulting firms generally say. However, in complex systems, information should come before the model and not the other way around. What happens is we are always making an exotic (non-native) intervention in the system which, without a doubt, will generate unexpected consequences impossible to be mapped. This happens because what is being interpreted is at the subjective, tacit, and implicit level of how people and factors operate, not on the objective, expressed, and explicit.

Everyone who works in an organization has seen this happen several times. They also notice how these interventions create unexpected consequences. Therefore, when we think about an intervention, we must take into account the complexity of an organization, its culture, strategy, leadership development level, relationship between peers and coworkers, and so forth. All these fall under the complexity domain.

What falls under the simple domain? A production line is simple because there is the inflow of inputs, the production process, and the output. All perfectly planable. Hence, we should seek the best practices for a simple system. Let's purchase the best equipment to have the most appropriate assembly line for a particular production. Let's train employees to be the most productive possible for what the production line was designed for, and let's begin to plan and control. What falls under the Complicated domain in an organization? Supply chain and logistics are generally complicated. They have multiple entries and multiple exits. But, it is well planned and structured. The airplane is another complicated system because you have a million cables flowing to the pilot's cabin and several subsystems, everything duplicated. In this case, we need experts. Here, we do not need the best practice, but rather an expert to design the best solution. In the Chaotic domain, is a social mobilization, for example. We do not even know how it started, but see its major impulse of energy. The difference between chaotic and complex is that Chaotic has no boundaries and Complex has very clear boundaries.

This is how we should be navigating the entire time in organizations, in a continuously adaptive manner within complicated and complex domains. The ideal actions in an organization should first involve, when faced with a challenge or change, the launching of a prototype. If this prototype makes sense, let's increase its scale. Obviously, when we talk about escalating something in large organizations, everything becomes complicated, so you need to have multiple prototypes functioning. The intervention in the system must be coherent in the sense of one prototype making sense for a given context. The prototype is safe in case of failures. It's important to note that there's a difference between prototype and pilot. The pilot is to do something in a smaller scale of what would already be the perfect design. It's to take a ready and finished product and introduce it in a smaller market that, if something goes wrong, does not cause much damage to the brand. In turn, a prototype allows different experimentations and adaptations to be made. In this model, we can work with the Minimum Viable Product (MVP) concept, that is, we create the simplest product possible within the original concept, sufficiently perfect just to be launched. Once it's launched, we begin to receive information from the entire system, which allows us to have the data necessary to improve the prototype or quickly remove it from circulation. The prototype must be sufficiently granular so as to be scattered in the system in order to have a good quantity of distributed cognition. In other words, within a system, we have several types of mindsets scattered, so when we scatter the prototypes, we begin to see what works and what doesn't. This way, we will always be in a more reliable and safe laboratory environment, always in beta, and always in an imperfect scenario by definition. The old mindset says that all you need to do is plan, and 1 day everything will be perfect, everything will function, and all targets will be met. This planning and control logic no longer works for managing complex systems.

Part Two: The Metamanagement Model and Its Dimensions

In order for strategic and/or structural changes in an organization to truly take place, they must undergo a cultural evolution or transformation of their system. However, in general, consultancies and most organizational-culture analyses see cultural changes from what we believe to be the wrong perspective. They seek to understand the current culture in a given company, what's the desired culture, and design indicators for where they want to go. The problem we see here is that they are using the wrong science to address the issue, that is, they're trying to apply engineering methodologies to solve an issue that should be addressed by anthropology, which is precisely the discipline that studies human cultures. The solution that anthropology suggests for cultural issues is different. Consultants with an anthropology background arrive in a given place, observe behaviors, understand why things are where they are, and help people until they can understand why they behave in a given way and actions that even they cannot explain. These interventions should be done from inside the system out or run a serious risk of not having any effect due to a lack of legitimacy.

Companies interact and are affected the entire time by internal and external elements. They are a group composed of people who, through their relationships, symbols, and systems, share purposes and values that generate tangible and intangible products for society's development. Every company begins with a social (and not a private) contract because every company should ultimately generate some benefit for society.

If we imagine the internal and external elements of an organization (even though this is just a fiction of the traditional vision of planning, since there aren't such highly defined boundaries in open systems), we understand that the internal part is composed of employees, the company, and the limits of its walls, whereas the external part are the clients and everything that happens outside the organization. When we put this segmented vision aside, we can see multiple and different stakeholders at the service of a same organizational purpose.

Organizational Identity

But if we do not take into account the limits of an organization, what would distinguish it from the others? This is one of the fundamental points for the *Metamanagement Model* proposal: the identity of companies. What we call organizational identity, some companies call mission, values, and purpose. It is what explains why companies do what they do. It is something that transcends the products offered and the services provided. It is that dimension that gives the organization the possibility to perpetuate and exist over time: its *raison d'être*. What we have seen in working with several companies and in studying the theme is that organizations that remain alive for a long period of time are those that are able to have an identity that touches a philosophical dimension, in an existential, transcendental, and spiritual relationship. It is in the possibility it gives people to engage based on a common cause. A strong, long-lasting corporate identity that engages the greatest number of people should be supported by perennial and philosophical ideals, which connect people to something beyond making money from their products and brand. It is a more meaningful identity that asks for management to simultaneously include in their minds individuals, relationships and systems dimensions. This kind of identity invites people to engage and give meaning to their work. This has been recognized in works such as Jim Collins' *Built to Last: Successful Habits of Visionary Companies* (2004) to, more recently, the Golden Circle concept, originally presented by Simon Sinek in the book *Start with Why: How Great Leaders Inspire Everyone to Take Action* (2009) and developed in *Find Your Why: A Practical Guide for Discovering Purpose for You and Your Team* (2017), by the same author. These are just a few examples of works that address why people connect more at work than others and why certain brands are more recognized. It is this kind of identity that, despite being more complex, allows individuals, teams, and systems to engage and connect more with organizational challenges.

Every time a new reality emerges on an organization's horizon, it is filtered by its identity. Not in an explicit and concrete manner, but rather implicitly. At the same time that new facts occur externally, they unfold internally through the individuals, relationships, and organizational systems. From the perspective of many consulting firms, they perceive that they are dealing with closed, linear, and predictable systems in which everything can be planned and controlled.

However, reality has shown that such pretension is impossible to be true. This happens because companies want to believe that it's possible to create, in highly complex and volatile scenarios such as the ones they are in, the futures they would like to see happen. This is an unrealistic posture that ends up causing more entropy than solutions. From our perspective, the more efficient idea is the concept of dynamic management, which provides a realistic perspective of planning, controlling, and substituting strategies by managing through constant attention to facts as they emerge. That is, the only thing an organization can be certain when defining a strategy is that it will not occur in the manner it was designed. This does not mean that preparing strategies is not a good thing. Planning is important even for discussing and changing direction if and when necessary. But it's only through dynamic management that we free the organization's attention from the goals established in old scenarios for the continuous and adapted construction of a direction and a strategy that will work as a guide, allowing us to dynamically navigate in all sorts of unexpected waters.

Organization Dimensions

Every organization can be understood through three perspectives, or dimensions, which coexist and emerge simultaneously: individuals, relationships established between individuals, and the organization of management processes and procedures (systems). These three dimensions have particular characteristics and a development of their own but are inseparable and mutually influence each other.

Today, we see leaders giving unfair treatment in the three dimensions. Emphasis is normally given to the collective dimension of the organization, to systems, and to financial results. The individuals and relationships dimensions are perceived as a "means" for obtaining impersonal organizational results and objectives. This stems from a mechanistic and rational vision of the world (Fig. 7.2).

For the *Metamanagement Model*, all three dimensions are of fundamental importance and should receive full attention.

In the *Individuals* dimension, the bond of a given person with the organization occurs, before any other factor, through a psychological contract. This contract, which we will further address in Part Three of this chapter, connects the individual's purpose in life with that of the organization and occurs by sharing *Meaning*, allowing the individual to learn and evolve its *Mindset*. Just as important as meaning is to have a broad mindset, capable of recognizing meaning-making. Therefore, the independent and collaborative vertical development of individuals, as conceptualized by human development researchers, c.f. Kegan and Lahey (2009), Cook-Greuter (2010), and Torbert (2004), is strategic for organizations. With this, individuals activate their *Intrinsic Motivation*. Motivation is the quality of engagement of an

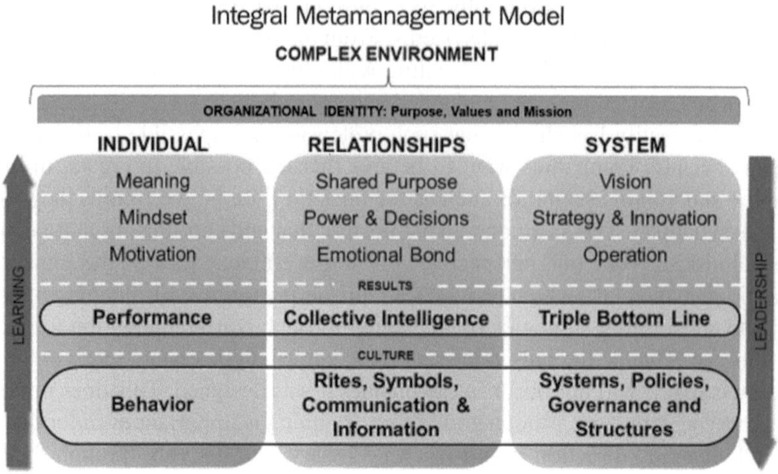

Fig. 7.2 Integral metamanagement model. (© Marcelo Cardoso)

individual with its function; the greater the motivation, the better the energy, and the result of the individual's action in his/her organizational and personal activities tends to be better.

Relationships make up the interpersonal dimension of an organization, probably the most neglected of the three dimensions by today's organizations. This dimension refers to the ability of individuals to interact and come together toward a shared purpose or task, regulating relationships of power and building emotional bonds.

The subtle aspect of organizational relationships is dictated by the shared purpose, which allows the synergy generated by relations between individuals to be targeted toward a common purpose or task. Many modern organizations suffer serious internal competition and organizational climate problems for not promoting an integration between individuals in areas, guiding them through shared purposes, which depends on, among other factors, being guided by high values, active and responsible leadership, and thorough training work in the individual dimension.

The purposes are governed by *relationships of power*, which are political divisions that regulate the organization's decision-making processes, varying by level of flexibility, reliability, and divergence capacity from one organization to another. If poorly managed, they can corrode relationships due to a pathological hierarchy of dominance, many times stemming from individual and group issues when relating to the role of authority. On the other hand, flaccid relationships of power can mean disengagement and disorganization due to a lack of clarity in roles within the group.

Lastly, the Relationships dimension is based on *emotional bonds* between the organization's individuals, which express the level of trust, respect, and mutual valuing that, if well-established, allow for the emergence of healthy divergences that improve learning, generate cohesion, and foster intimacy. Thus, they impact on evolving to higher levels of complexity and interdependence. Emotional bonds are highly desirable by more elaborate organizations and are perceived as a consequence of well-aligned work between organizational objectives and development of individuals and relationships.

The third dimension of organizations corresponds to inter-objective processes and structures, which we call *Systems*. It is the set of procedures that aims to achieve the purpose, based on a vision, transformed into strategies and controlled actions.

This is certainly the most valued and developed dimension in business today. Most bibliographies and disciplines dedicated to business emphasize the function dynamics of an organization in its objective aspects. This phenomenon would be mainly linked to the mechanistic vision of modern reality, with a strong reductionist bias both for subjectivity ("the ghost in the machine") and for the individual dimension ("a gear in the system"). Most business problems and challenges come from this reductionist vision that distorts the individuals and relationships dimensions, treating them merely as a means or resources for obtaining objective operational results (profits and other organizational results objectively measurable). On the other hand, emerging with a lot of consistency is new literature on ways to manage systems based on complexity, such as books that talk about dynamic management and permanent beta.

This dimension, however, is fundamental for maintaining and developing a healthy organization. Without a set of processes, systems, standards, and parameters for working, mankind would still live in rudimentary tribes. Right or wrong, social systems are essential for humanity (and human organizations) to solve the growing problems of complexity that are inherent in development.

The subtle aspect of the organization dimension is focused by the organizational *Vision* (already mentioned above in Organization Identity). This vision guides the organization's mission toward plausible future scenarios (considering, for such, the macroenvironment's level of uncertainty) and serves as a subtle connector for individual purposes and purposes shared between members.

The Vision, hence, activates the global *Strategy* of the business, which comprises a set of choices articulated by the decision process (governance), to transform the organization's vision into real results. In an organization with more perennial values, the strategic plan is potentially much more elaborate, as it is formulated based on a much more complex, deep (vertical reach), and broad (horizontal reach) vision of reality, which considers many more critical factors in its formulations.

The strategy is physically articulated by the *Execution* of strategic projects, by the set of guidelines, tools, and tasks stipulated by governance to achieve the strategies and make the vision real.

The biggest challenge of organizations is probably efficiency in the execution of highly complex strategic plans in a macroenvironment where the predominant level of awareness is not that great, including a considerable portion of coworkers and/or stakeholders directly involved in the tasks, systems, and technologies available. Inevitably, these organizations will impact their environments with a huge amount of tension stemming from the difference between reality and level of awareness of the current moment and the reality that guides the vision of the future and strategic plan.

Organizational Results

The limited and everyday vision of organizational results points, in general, only to return on investments (in the form of financial profits). Alternatively, the expanded vision of business sustainability focuses on the Triple Bottom Line (TBL) of economic, social, and environmental results.

For more conscious organizations, however, the results to be measured and cultivated go beyond the Triple Bottom Line. Just as important as the TBL are results in the Individual dimension, such as *Performance*, and results in the Relationships dimension, like *Collective Intelligence*.

Performance is generated by the intrinsic motivation based on the mindset and significance attributed by an individual and its relationship with the organization. It can be measured by the quality of performance in relation to commitments assumed. For an organization, this measure is not only convenient for pointing out how efficient and engaged an employee is, but is also important for checking the level of commitment of an individual.

Results in the relationships dimension are recognized as *Collective Intelligence*, a potential field of knowledge and transformation derived from relationships formed, from which the group's intelligence emerges from, where the whole is greater than the sum of the parts, as long as there is a positive alignment in the dimensions (individual, relationships, and systems) and the levels in each one of them. In fact, every company result is a fruit of a collective effort. Even though it serves individual and organizational results, collective intelligence has its own tacit and intrinsic value, in the beauty and complicity that only emerges in the inter-subjectivity dimension, one of the factors that has the most value in an organization and practically never is captured.

Lastly, we have *organizational results*. The Triple Bottom Line concept is without a doubt an important advancement toward business sustainability, measuring the impact of an organization's activities in a broader manner; however, we observe that for less philosophical organizations, the motivation for sustainability is limited to complying with laws or an institutional commitment, but only organizations that possess a more comprehensive vision of the world consider the theme of Triple Bottom Line a key aspect of the strategy or, better yet, a source for innovating and transforming the macroenvironment.

This transition is the same as saying that the impacts of an organization on society, considering its broad spectrum of influence, should not only stop harming society but also become factors of sustainable development capable of positively influencing the entire greater system.

Part Three: Metamodel Implementation Forms

Organizational Identity in Movement

To exemplify and deep dive a bit more into the concept of *Organizational Identity*, addressed in the previous section, let's consider, as an example, a transition in which we originally have a centralizing model, of the command and control type, that started out with a visionary founder. Let's imagine that this organization must change to a shared leadership model. How can we maintain and nurture an identity if the entrepreneur who generated the original model is not the one who will be managing the new system? When we have a company that is still living under the management of its owners and the founder wants to make a transition to a first professional generation, how can we guarantee that the identity, the essence of the identity, will remain in the organization and not be corrupted, diluted, or dogmatized?

This is the most difficult transition that every organization based on a founder experiences. Most companies do not survive the founder. This happens for two reasons: the first is the one we mentioned in the previous paragraph; the potential corruption, dilution, or dogmatization of the organizational identity's essence in a professionalization process. The second reason resides in the founder's difficulty to let go of the business and let it be run by other people.

The fact is that, when reality emerges, it brings with it elements from the past and freshness of the future, in both the individual and organizational perspectives (Fig. 7.3). We can imagine the dimension of this ambivalence when we think of a company with 500 or 2000 employees. It's the nervous system of each one that builds and has built this company. This dynamic between past and future is happening all the time, simultaneously. The challenge is to identify in this movement where we belong more and, based on this place, what we can transform the most. For

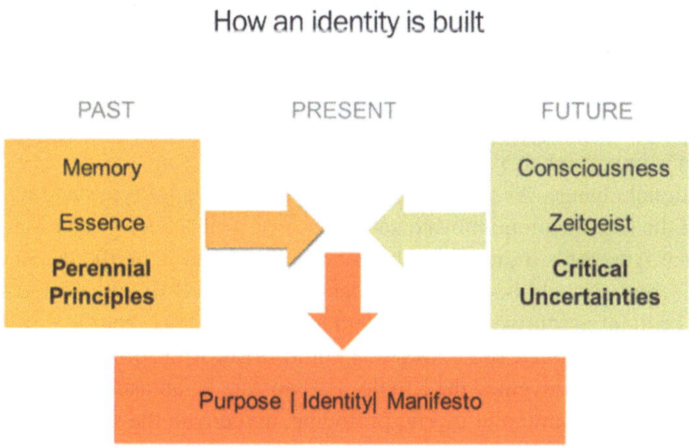

Fig. 7.3 Building an organizational identity includes elements from the past and also the future. (© Marcelo Cardoso)

example, moment by moment, to belong more, should I integrate more? And, to integrate more, what should I integrate? Therefore, the ideal reflection we should open ourselves up to based on the past should encompass two questions: "what is essential?" and "what should I take to the future?"

Our past should fit in a backpack, in something light that we can take with us, not a shipping container. If it's bigger than a backpack, it becomes dead weight. Therefore, we must identify what is essential in an organizational identity, what travels across time, and what is more perennial. The more ethereal elements, the more they are related to values and philosophy and the better for the perennity of a corporate identity's essence. What generally happens is that founders define these elements naturally. They do not think about this when creating an organization. They undertake because, somehow, this value was implicit and tacit. The founder dealt with this value as a market opportunity, like something that was happening.

As such, we must be aware of an organizational need to update its identity based on the identification of a new Zeitgeist, so we must separate what is essential from what is specific to the market and update the interpretation of concepts and values. At the same time, we must do the therapeutic and emotional work of separating the many nuances that comprise an organizational identity. One of them refers to a blessing and a curse for the founder. It is because the founder confuses his or her purpose and personal identity with those of the organization. This occurs for some time. Adizes (1990) says that, in its initial phase, an organization has these two elements in a jumbled manner. Later on, comes a moment when the organization becomes bigger than the founder itself. In this stage, many times, the founder kills the company so it doesn't become bigger than him or her. For this not to happen, there is some emotional, therapeutic, and spiritual work to be done to let go. Regardless of how many times the founder says he or she is ready, many times things are more complex than they seem. Because when we begin to deal with the future, he or she is still not there, but rather in this space of choosing the now. Therefore, the job has to do with co-creating its emergence. To co-create this future that is emerging, the idea is to try and go beyond the past or how we got out of the grooves of what we have been in so far, take a step into the emptiness, and experiment with an existence beyond everything we have experienced. The challenge is one of practice and experimentation.

And it's important to remember that were talking from the perspective of an organizational change. As such, how will it create new prototypes and innovation? How will the organization innovate and reinvent itself? A very good example is the story about Amazon's digital book reader Kindle. At the time the device was created, Amazon only sold books. Its founder and CEO, Jeff Bezos, selected a few of his most brilliant executives and sent them to California, and he told them to return only when they invented something that could break Amazon's current business.. Thus, the executives invented the Kindle. This posture is fantastic: to have the vision and, why not, the courage to invent, prototype, and create the seeds that can make your own business cease to exist as it is now.

Emerging Self-Management Models

Organization models that utilize all the diverse potential of its members have evolved to self-managed models.

For a model like this to work, there are two key premises:

1. For the person with the most power in the system be willing to distribute power.
2. For the person receiving the power be mature to deal with the consequences (rights and obligations) of sustaining power.

How do we distribute power in the system? What happens when people begin to make decisions that differ from those of the founder? Will he or she ultimately resist and end up having the last say? This, as we all know, is quite common. It is not an easy transition, but this is the first prerequisite: to allow power to flow out of the "boss's hands." The second prerequisite is that the person receiving the power be capable of dealing with the power he or she is receiving; since very often we project our early childhood experiences with the authority of our parents and later of our school teachers, in our current relationship with authority. Thus we become more submissive or more authoritarian. Remember the Milgram Experiment (1963) by famed social psychologist Stanley Milgram? The experiment looked into how individuals tend to obey authorities, even when going against common sense, like ordering people in white lab coats to give electric shocks to other people. As a result, 65% of the participants obeyed the orders and gave shocks up to the maximum level (450 volts). It is important to remember that the victims in this experiment were actors pretending to be shocked (the participants did not know this) (Milgram, 2009).

This issue of authority is the main challenge for evolving from an "owner" organizational model for both the person distributing power as well as was the one receiving the power. In general, who receives power, when time comes to making an important decision, he/she consults only with those who had power before him/her in the organization. People have a lot of difficulty making decisions in a collective and circular manner because this is not in our experience with reality. From a very young age, our experience with authority has been vertical, it's in our system. To make this transition, there is a lot of coming and going. It is not something quick or spontaneous.

However, once the company and the people enter this process, there is no going back. It is like someone who is illiterate, learns how to read and write, and wants to go back being illiterate. It is almost impossible. The organizational culture begins to live this way, with collective intelligence and never goes back.

Businesses, particularly in the technology sector, like startups, are based on this management model. Companies like Uber and Airbnb, for example, are businesses that were conceived within this circular model but ended up going back to a more vertical model. They continue having a "boss" who orders things and wants to increase market share. As such, they dropped a more advanced idea due to very poor execution. It is necessary to have a management repertoire because, otherwise, when leaders go to run very innovative businesses they end up resorting to very conventional management models. Without noticing that, when they do this, they collapse the business. For us, this is one of the main challenges of businesses today: to produce management models and organizational models that are reciprocal and symmetrical with the business models being proposed.

Zappos, an online shoe and clothing retailer based in Las Vegas, is one of the companies that implemented holacracy (Robertson, 2015), that is, it removed the exercising of power from a hierarchical structure, substituting it for an authority distribution system. This happened 2 years ago. Today, they have 300 management circles in a universe of 1200 employees. All employees participate in several circles, and the people choose the circles they want to participate in. In this process, 30% of Zappos' employees left the firm after it implemented holacracy. At Vagas.com in Brazil, which has 120 employees, things were no different, as I could verify from personal experience. In this company, all decisions are also based on consensus. Everyone can raise their hand and vote. At Vagas.com, 40 people also left the firm, alleging that "they only wanted a job that paid a good salary, without having to participate in decision circles."

This happens with holacracy because there isn't a fixed organizational design. In this system, people's responsibilities change according to how the business comes into contact with reality. The circuit's internal logics evolve according to what emerges. Another thing that differs from traditional systems and may scare some people away is the way meetings are held. In holacracy, it is necessary to ensure that everyone speaks and decides in a quick manner. Therefore, meetings do not last more than 10 or 15 min. Everyone speaks and decisions are made very quickly. People have autonomy, but they have autonomy within the limits of the structure they are in and the format of meetings and decision processes.

It is important to point out that implementation of a circle-based management system, that is, holacracy, is a journey that does not occur from one moment to the next. It starts out small, like a circle and then begins to increase its scope little by little. It is no use trying to change the entire company from 1 min to the other to this model. We must take one step at a time. If we try to transition too quickly, we run the risk of being left by the wayside. In order to introduce this model structure in an organization, the ideal is to substitute the traditional architecture for circles starting with a general company circle, composed of the CEO and Vice Presidents (VPs) of Development, Operations and Sales, for example (Fig. 7.4). These individuals, who have more power, select what other employees should also be in this circle to begin with. With these representatives, new circles are successively formed in the organization. Then, the process is inverted: people from the new circles elect a representative to be in the circle of highest power. With this, another win aspect is that communication in the organization becomes much easier. These representatives act like a hub; they are responsible for transmitting what happens between one circle and another, reporting the decisions made. The roles of each one change as the business evolves; there are no more "positions" or "job descriptions."

However, each circle has its own scope. There's the leadership circle, the marketing circle, the development circle, the sales circle, and so forth. This differs from some other companies where everything is done through meetings. In these

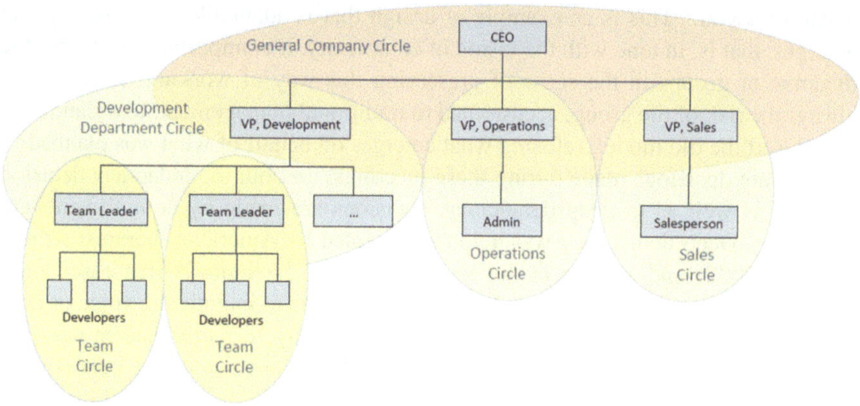

Fig. 7.4 Circle model

organizations, there are meetings for everything, and they occur the entire time. There are always several people in the meeting room who, simply, should not or did not have to be there, but if the person is not invited, he or she may feel excluded. Additionally, everyone feels the right to give their opinion on everything, at any time, and no one decides anything. What is decided at the end of these meetings is when the next one will be held. What we present here with holacracy is a very different model, because people only meet when there is a defined scope for discussion.

The leadership circle, or general circle, serves the organization's purpose. The objective of the other circles is to always contribute to the general company circle. With this, the organization's objectives are deployed among the purposes of the other circles, which determines the scope of each one of them. These scopes are guided by a permanent agenda and an emerging agenda, which is built in each meeting. These meetings can be held in three ways: (1) *the strategy meeting*, which occurs every 3 months or so, when people gather to check if the strategic direction continues being the same or whether the organization should make changes. This is where strategic implementation is discussed; (2) *the governance meeting*, one of the most important moments of our Metamodel, which is when accountability is attributed and new policies and processes are developed. This meeting occurs every 15 days and is where new development paths or product/service launchings are discussed by redefining new policies and procedures. This is where the owner of the new policy is defined; (3) *the tactical-operational meetings* can take place once or twice a day, or even weekly, depending on the type of business. This is where operational indicators are measured and actions resulting from them are defined.

As already mentioned, the agenda of these meetings can be permanent or emergent. For example, the leadership circle has an emerging agenda, which look into the strategy, results, culture, people development, and other factors that vary. This agenda is built on the spot. If, during the meeting, someone raises an unscheduled topic to be discussed, there should be no censorship. Since, in reality, the premise is "if this theme is relevant to you, if it's causing tension, the circle should resolve this tension for you." This is an example of design that is adaptable to the reality that emerges, that is, in tune with the vision of complexity. It is important to observe the dynamic of groups in the sense of preserving this way of working, since there's always the risk of the group, accustomed to traditional management, to try and subtly reinsert the old model, refusing what emerges on behalf of what was planned.

How are decisions made during these meetings? In both the holacracy decision process, as well as in deep democracy, decisions are made by commitment, not consensus. Deep democracy was a concept created by American therapist Arnold Mindell (2002) and applied at the end of apartheid in South Africa based on a Jungian approach. The urgent need of that context was to include the voice of people who were marginal and never had the opportunity to participate in decision processes. For such, they created a process by which the voice of the least counts. Traditional democracy, where the simple majority decides, became the last step in the decision process. In deep democracy, a decision is not reached by a simple majority of votes. If in a group of six people, four decide on a path and two disagree, a decision cannot yet be made. Instead of saying you two lost because the majority wishes to follow this other path, we must encourage discussion to reach a mutual commitment. We should try and understand the reasons of these two people for not being in agreement with the majority, and after listening to them, we must acknowledge the points of disagreement and question what would be the elements that would get the two people to agree with the decision. We should ask: "what would you need to commit to the majority's decision?" Based on the answers, we should try to include these new elements in the original decision and create a new proposal. Then, the group votes again until obtaining everyone's commitment, that is, everyone onboard with the final decision. This means that differences are acknowledged and accepted, in order for a decision to then be reached that everyone is willing to assume. This means that, when people leave the room after the decision is made, they won't say: "Did you see what they decided? I'm against it!", which is very typical in organizations. This attitude generates a lot of entropy at the moment a decision is implemented. In deep democracy, there is everyone's commitment, since they participated in coming up with the decision and, for this reason, will help make it happen. As such, decisions are made by commitment, not consensus.

In the figure below (Fig. 7.5), we have the top level structure of American clothing company Eileen Fisher, Inc., one of our clients. We see that the entire structure is designed in circles. We have the board, which is the guardian of the purpose, and the executive committee, which is called Facilitating Leadership Team (FLT). It is important to point out that Eileen Fisher, Inc. does not have a CEO. The company's executive leadership is composed of eight people, including the founder, Eileen Fisher. We then have the three main processes: creative (marketing), business (sales), and operations. They are structured in circles, are cross-functional, and are composed of people from different functions. On the sides of the dotted line, which acts as a support network for key processes, we have the support functions: Finance, IT, Social Consciousness, and human resource (HR). In addition to these circles in the illustration, they also have several project circles that exist to execute specific plans; they are circles that are born and end in the life cycle of a project.

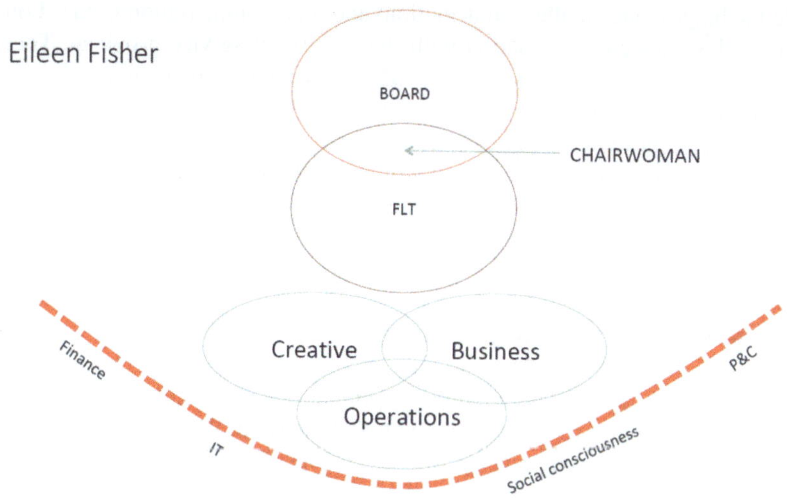

Fig. 7.5 Circle structure at Eileen Fisher, Inc.

Inside this circle-based system, there is a major issue related to employee compensation. In traditional systems, with well-defined job positions and hierarchies, positions are "weighed" according to their complexity and responsibility, and people receive compensation according to the weight of their job compared to other job positions in the market. Alternatively, with systems designed in circles, compensation is still an unresolved issue. However, there is one point that has already been well-defined in this aspect: there is no variable compensation based on performance. The key point here is to determine how to measure people's contribution to define their compensation. This has not yet been resolved and is one of the biggest conflicts in companies that have migrated to the system of circles because, in them, traditional compensation models still continue to be active. As such, we are still stepping in a new territory that needs to be mapped.

However, there is a successful compensation example in the system of circles at a psychology institute in São Paulo, Brazil called Instituto Evoluir. One of the aspects resolved at the institute refers to the myth that when there isn't the possibility of standing out or an individual contribution being recognized, people simply cross their arms, do not do their best and do not put in the effort, since the group will solve the issue on its own. This mindset, from our perspective, is associated to a school work dynamic: two or three do the activity and the rest include their name in the group, receiving a grade and not doing much work. We agree this is not a mature way of looking at work relations. At Evoluir, this quickly became old news. Individual contributions exist, but they are always evaluated by perception and always by the perception of who does things together. At the Institute, its group of 12 professionals makes a subjective evaluation every month of who contributed more or less to the final result. Additionally, the direct result is also taken into account, that is, the volume of service. Everyone talks to identify who in the month made the biggest and smallest contribution; and their compensation is based on the result of this subjective evaluation with the volume of service provided. There is zero standard deviation in the process. The convergence of opinions about who contributed the most and who contributed the least has always been very high.

We highly believe in the circle-based management model, but, obviously, we are still at the very beginning of the methodology, and the tools that will enable these concepts are still being developed. We must continue trying, making errors and adjustments, and learning.

Evolution of the Psychological Contract

When we talk about motivation and engagement, we are talking about where the people's energy comes from, in its individual dimension. What produces results in organizations is energy, our psychic energy. In spite of treating people as resources, we know we are talking about what makes them get up early in the morning or go to sleep late because of work, that is, the level of each person's engagement with the organization.

Every decision is filtered by a feeling, and our thoughts come from what we believe and value. People cannot think about what they do not know; they can only think about things that, somehow, relate to their environment.When we treat people like resources, we want pieces of people, but in order for them to engage at work, it is necessary to look at them in their entirety, and their various roles in life and in all of its dimensions. When we create a "Human Resources" area, we are simply discarding the entire subtle side of people's experience and creating a "human resource," an automaton or a gear. Then, we want to measure engagement from this perspective because, after all, in the traditional HR vision people belong to the organization. This way of measuring engagement is totally wrong because it stems from the idea that a person is a resource. In the same outdated logic, in addition to engaging, organizations want to "retain" individuals, which is crazy, because people are free; they cannot be retained.

A much more realistic and healthy path is to think about a psychological contract between people and organizations, a contract that defines the type and form of how this relationship will take place. This concept comes from Harvard Business School professor Chris Argyris (1960) and says that we only give meaning to work if we are able to come up with a psychological contract for it. This concept has been evolving for some time (Fig. 7.6). The first version appeared more or less after World War II and presented as main clause the condition that if I am loyal to the organization I work for, I will have job security. In spite of many people still believing this, this type of contract no longer is possible for any organization, even though there still are people who would like this to be true. This type of contract held true in the United States up to the 1970s and in Brazil until the 1990s.

More recently, this contract became more flexible, where long-term "arrangements" are substituted by more transactional and instrumental relationships, where there is practically no bond. Today, an employee offers his or her best performance,

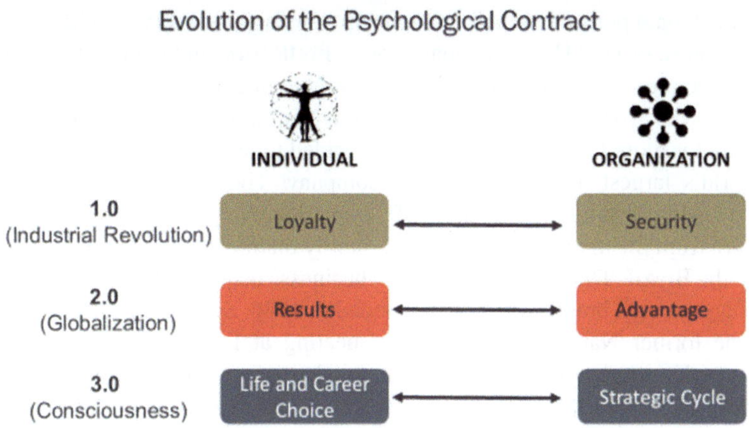

Fig. 7.6 Evolution of the psychological contract. (© Marcelo Cardoso/DBM do Brasil)

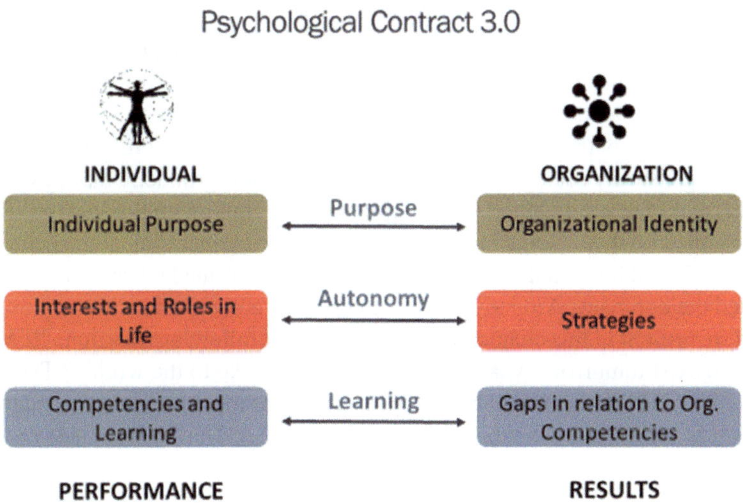

Fig. 7.7 Psychological contract 3.0. (© Marcelo Cardoso/DBM do Brasil)

and the organization gives this person a bonus, status, company car, advantages, and so forth, that is, a very short-term instrumental exchange relationship contract is formalized.

Today, we no longer talk about careers where employees are thinking about staying 25 years in the same company. We talk about cycles no longer than 3 years. Which means individuals can look at a given organization and reflect: "I could start another cycle in this same organization or is it time for me to change companies?" The nature of this 3.0 psychological contract is that it is born from the sharing of purposes between individuals and organizations (Fig. 7.7), that is, people's reflections about their cycles in companies undergo the possibility of manifesting aspects of their personal purpose in their relationship of being at the service of the organization's purpose or not. This is the main point of reflection and the point of entry.

An example we can mention of a 3.0 psychological contract had to do with an executive who worked at cosmetics company Natura. He had been working at the company for more than 10 years when he decided to leave and go work for Diageo, the world's largest distilled beverages company. The purpose/vision of Diageo weighed in his decision: "celebrating life, every day, everywhere." In reality, Diageo was born from the merger of two Scottish-family distillers that, later on, created this vision. In Brazil, Diageo, to expand its business, acquired Ypióca, a traditional Brazilian *cachaça* brand, which was founded in 1846. Some time after the acquisition, the former Natura executive, in a meeting at Diageo, was discussing the *cachaça* sales strategy that involved, among other issues, this beverage's consumption peak in the Northeast: 6:30 and 10:30 a.m. At this moment, he came to the conclusion that there was an imbalance between what he believed and wanted for life and what the company wanted. It is very important to always reflect on this: "Is where I am and what I'm doing in harmony with what I believe and want for my life and of others?"

We can also mention cases where organizations do not want to work with certain clients due to a lack of identification with values and purposes. Mercur is also an example of a holacracy company. Mercur was founded in 1924 in Santa Cruz do Sul, RS, Brazil, with the objective of fixing tires and producing rubber objects. Many people surely remember having used one of their products: the red eraser on one side and blue on the other, or the light green one, both with the Mercury Roman God stamped on them. Jorge Hoelzel Neto is the third-generation at the helm of the company. It was his grandfather, together with his great-uncle, Carlos Hoezel, who founded the company. Around 7 years ago, Mercur conducted an identity exercise, which we present in this chapter that begins with the following question: "If Mercur ceases to exist tomorrow, what difference will this make to the world?" They came to the conclusion that it would make no difference. At the time, one of its main businesses was selling rubber lining for tobacco planting. During the workshop, they made two decisions: to stop selling to Souza Cruz, the main tobacco company in the region, due to the harm caused by smoking and to stop selling licensed products (with references to cartoon characters), since they created exclusion. They were more expensive erasers or more expensive products that differentiated children in the classroom. They decided to stop the two businesses from 1 month to the next. Today, the company only manufactures products for health and education. One of Mercur's main product lines are items that promote inclusion, such as school equipment that allows children with disabilities to feel more included, and this is the company's main business today (click here to watch a TEDx Talks with Jorge Hoelzel Neto: https://www.youtube.com/watch?v=DpGpx4QgUbw).

It is important to point out that these actions are very necessary, but we should keep in mind that each one of us expresses our life purpose in all our roles in life. Purpose is not something that only guides a person's professional role. Therefore, it is possible for people to share an organization's purpose and, even so, have a conflict of roles. Many women who work in multinationals and have young children, for example, are invited for positions outside the country at the peak of their career. They end up having to choose between their social role of mother and their professional role. This becomes a major dilemma for women, because they face social pressures to be perfect in their various roles: be the best wife, the best mother, and the best professional. Here, the idea of making choices is very important: "Now, for the next few years, my choice is to follow this path." As such, it is fundamental to understand where the organization is going, that is, how one's choice harmonizes (or not) with the organization's strategic choice. Because when we do this, we select a learning path, since every time an organization establishes a strategy, it declares itself incompetent to execute. If in 3 years the company wants to be in a given place, it must do something it has not yet done. It must build new organizational competencies. This means that people need to learn new things collectively for the organization to acquire the competencies necessary to execute the new strategy established. On our side, if we believe that this is not our path, we must make choices.

This is why most competence management models in today's human resources areas are a big mistake. In general, companies design a competence management model based on the past and, with it, wish to build a future, leveraged by what people did in the past. It can't be like that. It is necessary to look at what people have in terms of potential to build this future. This is what produces performance and results, which we remind you are different things. Mixing up these two things can be a major source of suffering in organizations, since the only thing an individual can have is performance. An individual on his or her own cannot ensure results. A good metaphor for this is a collective sport. A player may have played his best match ever, but even so the team lost, the end result was bad. Still, the player will leave the field with a feeling of integrity. Performance ensures integrity, it does not guarantee results. A result is the fruit of collective effort, and even if the collective does everything right, it is possible that the result does not come. Results are not controlled.

We have successful experiences with projects already executed at companies like Natura, Fleury, and Eileen Fisher, at times involving more than 1000 workers. The projects focus on building bridges between individuals and organizations in the purpose, autonomy, and learning dimensions, as seen in Fig. 7.6 above regarding the Psychological Contract 3.0. We offer a 2-day workshop focused on helping people find their personal purpose and, based on it, build a new "contract," or bridge to the future, with the organization. Through tools that rescue individual history and self-awareness, people come out of this workshop with a draft of their career development plan. Then, on the third day, we bring in the organization dimension, which is to explain the company's identity and strategy for people to begin to understand, from the individual reflection cycle conducted before, what aligns with the company's purpose and strategy.

Another important part in the process described above is to prepare individuals to have this "recontracting" talk with the organization. Most people in an organization are not prepared to have this conversation, so we need to prepare the people and their respective managers to have a career talk with one fundamental premise: to develop people according to their talents, leverage what they do well and not tell them what their gaps are, and build an action plan for them to resolve them. Every time we try to be better at something we have some difficulty at, with a lot of effort, the maximum we are able to improve is from 5 to 6. Again, we will continue receiving feedback that we have a gap. On the other hand, assessment methodologies provide the clarity necessary for us to see what we do well to continue practicing what we do well and even improve things we do not do well because we gain more energy. Assessment methodologies can also guide us to be able to work with people who can help us in some specific aspect we do not excel at.

This is a completely different vision from what we see in most human resources areas. We propose building development by leveraging talents and not trying to fill gaps. What's interesting to us is to highlight that the things we do well are the things that energize us, and that, when facing them, our energy naturally grows. Nobody needs to ask us for more motivation because it's already there, natural and strong, to the point of even tolerating other things just because we have it. The logic of traditional development plans is the opposite of this. They ask that we waive what we do well to try and better things that aren't our strength. In this process, our vital energy dissipates.

In a different direction, what we propose is the creation of a development plan that is born in consonance with the life history of each individual, reinforced by its strengths, to build its life purpose and identify its personal values. Through this construction, we align the individual's purpose with that of the organization, that is, the career plan. The process also takes into account the individual and its relationship with different stakeholders. As such, what we have proposed is to include a 360-degree analysis with inputs from the organization, from the individual's circle of friends, from his or her family, and so forth. The result has always been very positive for the employee's development, including the insights that can surface from the confluence of aspects that comes from the family and work to help build a more meaningful development.

Development Plan and Engagement

When employees prepare their development plan in the company, they generally think about a course: "I'm going to take a course at Fundação Dom Cabral, a course at Harvard, etc." In fact, the main development path that should be considered is how to be sure you're occupying a job position that asks more from you than it can offer at that moment. How can you be sure that you will feel "butterflies in the stomach"? How can you be sure you will be responsible for a set of things over which you do not have the slightest idea of how to resolve? This is what will truly produce development in people. It is to be continuously challenged by your role in the organization. When you understand how you will build your succession and begin to think about your next cycle, that's when we can build a plan. When we do this type of reflection with a group of 300 or 400 people, for example, this becomes a fundamental input for building the model and development plan for the human resources area, that is, information emerges from the individuals and, obviously, from what the company needs to build. This combination is perfect for building a real plan for the HR area.

The best way to engage employees beyond their financial bonuses and material rewards for achieving or exceeding targets that, as already mentioned, many times no longer makes sense for the organization, is through the meaning that people see in their relationship with the company's identity. A major part of HR professionals know that roughly 87% of employees are not engaged with the company, and it's not because of the Millennials (youngsters that reached adulthood around the turn of the twenty-first century) who are more restless but rather because organizations have proven not to be a very motivating place and are unable to offer contexts with meaning to people. Therefore, individuals opt for one company after another and one challenge after the other. This differs from previous generations that tended to stay a long time in the same job, even if unsatisfied and unhappy, simply for the compensation. When we find meaning in what we do, we continuously learn and expand our mindset, allowing us to find the necessary motivation, which is something always intrinsic to our individual nature.

The idea of motivation in the workplace is much more than what companies work with today like "engagement actions," that is, giving questionnaires to identify if people are unsatisfied in relation to their career and toward the organization to see whether they are engaged or not and, based on this, prepare action plans that are never fully executed. In fact, real motivation is more related to the construction of an employee's psychological contract with its work. It is a proposal of the employee sharing a common purpose with the company, for him or her to be able to learn and have autonomy. This trident "Purpose, Learning, and Autonomy" represents the foundation for building engagement.

Enabling Teams That Function

As we know, there isn't a company that can exist without engagement, but believe it or not, when we enter a bookstore or Amazon.com, in the section earmarked for success-in-business books, you will see that almost all books talk about increasing market share, deploying strategies and financial results. A small portion of the books will talk about leadership development, one the most important dimensions for people and organizations because every execution occurs through a relationship. Nobody executes on their own. Every execution occurs in a collective space. After all, as we have already seen before, in order to operate with efficiency in a complex environment, it is necessary to have a wide variety of visions and repertoires to obtain a real solution. By including multiple perspectives, we can find several alternatives of prototypes that allow testing, adapting, and building a good solution. We generally think that to have good execution, all we need is planning. Obviously, planning is important (keep in mind the difference between improvisation and unpreparedness). We should always prepare ourselves, but also know that when we enter the field of action, everything will happen in accordance with what reality presents us, and always through its contexts, always in the collective.

It is in the field of relations that people share a purpose, a task, or an objective. It is in it that they regulate relationships of power and create emotional bonds. In actuality, groups that function are those that are capable of combining a feeling of people inclusion while also considering their opinions and perspectives when decisions are made. It is almost a system of simultaneous inclusion of opposite ends (or as coined by American consultant Barry Johnson: Polarity Management, 2014).

On the other hand, many times, in order to feel included, we give up on our opinion because we are scared: "If I say what I think, I will no longer be part of the group." It is the opposite of those indiscriminately sincere people that truly have difficulty being included: "I don't care! I speak my mind." In fact, the difficulty in sustaining the polarity between respectful and frank is in the entire relationship dynamic. If I am 100% of the time respectful with others, at some point, I will not be frank and honest. If I am 100% honest, at some point in time I will be disrespectful to others. It is necessary to dynamically identify what is the place of integrity that, at a given moment, best supports this polarity and in which context a group creates this possibility of balance, allowing people to be transparent and honest in an environment of respect, trust, care, and affection.

With this, we identify that the quality of the team has to do with the way individuals deal with divergence (Fig. 7.8). In order for the results of a group to be effective, people need to feel included and know that divergence, when it occurs, will also be accepted. Many times, we disguise divergences by shouting to others our point of view, without admitting we are diverging. For many, it is easier to do this than simply say "Even though I like you, I disagree with your point of view." This healthy way of dealing with conflicts only happens when there is trust among people. For trust to happen, it is necessary for people to be close with one another. We are not talking about big friendships, but know each one closely, entirely, in relationships. This integrity is conquered through vulnerability, that is, it reveals itself without the corporate masks of perfection and infallibility. Different from weakness, vulnerability reveals strength. The strongest are those who have the courage to show their imperfections.

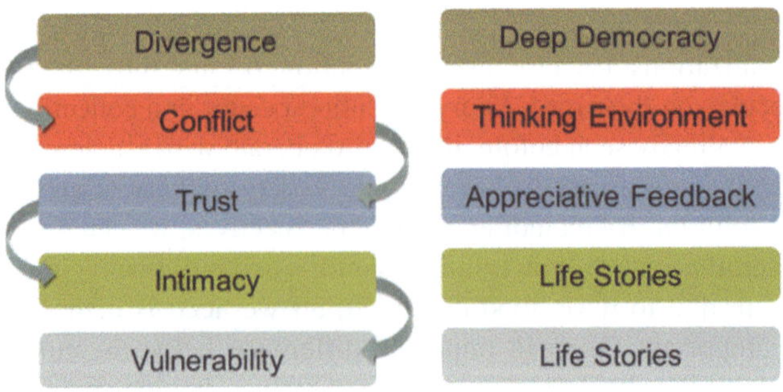

Fig. 7.8 Movements to promote healthy divergences. (© Marcelo Cardoso)

Organizational Culture

In the individual dimension, performance; in the relationships dimension, collective intelligence; and in the systems dimension, financial, environmental and social results.

In these conditions, what the group produces is the fruit of collective intelligence, building results and increasing performance. The expression of an organization's identity on individuals, relationships, and the systems that integrate these results, that is, its culture, takes place through the behavior of people, rituals, and symbols that the values, which come from the identity, emanate from the internal systems it possesses (e.g., promotion, contracting, reward, compensation, strategy preparation systems). A value that comes from the identity reflects in a ritual, which can be the way how people come together, for example. If everyone arrives late, how do we deal with tardiness? Meetings between the organization's leaders, company symbols, prizes, the manner how people dress to work, all these determine an organization's culture. In the design of its systems also, for example, if a given company holds collaboration/collective effort as a value and if the design of its bonus model reinforces individual targets, it will not be expressing this value in its day-to-day systems. People will act in an egotistical manner, not collectively. If another company holds openness and transparency as a value, but when it prepares its strategy and budget only a few people participate, what it will have is cynicism and people trying until the last moment to add some specific value of its area in the budget. Thus, the design of systems must reflect the organization's values, otherwise the result can be the opposite of what the organization aspires.

This dynamic and continuous relationship between behaviors, symbols, and systems is what we call organizational culture. As such, we like to see a company more like a school, in a permanent environment of learning that's continually being fed and nurtured. Various tensions that occur here are released and create energy for the system to feed and support itself, and company leadership is responsible for seasoning and flavoring the food. It is not the leadership of a single person but more and more the collective leadership of groups that, given their diverse nature, are able to sustain the most complex tasks in the organization.

Final Considerations

Based on what has been presented, we can see that there exists an essential difference between traditional management models and the *Metamanagement Model*. This difference stems from how the world is viewed. In general, consulting firms present a traditional mechanistic logic of viewing the world, that is, they perceive the issues they face in a linear and non-integrated manner. For them, things happen on a Cartesian plane, with well-defined coordinates and abscisses and, as a result, propose a well-determined (and, at times, unique) strategic plan to make corporate targets happen. In this understanding, it seems right that employees necessarily need to have a clear individual target, because if they don't, they will not perform.

Within the traditional model, it is through leadership's individual targets that the individual employee strategies are born, that is, leadership's strategic objectives are deployed into guidelines to define targets for their subordinates. Everyone must have clarity of what they have to do and, on top of that, to not have any doubt that targets will be achieved; a variable compensation program is linked to them (bonuses for results achieved). This way of perceiving the world does not take into consideration that each employee has his or her own personal characteristics and interests, and each person works in a certain way with one colleague and a different way with another. It does not take into account changes in the broader context that, as seen in the previous section, will certainly happen in a practically unpredictable manner. It does not include in its processes the "human" factor and its countless variables, many times even creating strategic plans as if human beings did not exist, as if they are going to be fulfilled on their own. This way of designing management models is done through a mechanistic and closed logic. Their sources of information basically come just from the market, based on a given period of time. They do not reflect the dynamism and volatility of today's markets. Companies want to increase market share and, based on this, define their strategies that are then deployed into unique and invariable guidelines for the entire company. Some strategies become process improvements, whereas others become projects that need to be standardized and transformed into a routine. In this vision, for them to happen, people just need to be trained and informed about them.

As already mentioned, in our *Metamanagement Model* process we have a different vision of reality. Our understanding of scenarios passes through the concept of open nonlinear systems, which we presented in the first part of this chapter. Our logic is systemic, open, and integrative. We look at the organizational management process through metacycles. Each metacycle corresponds to a complexity level of understanding reality and is interconnected with the previous through its integration. With this, each metacycle contains the perspectives of the previous cycle and takes them to a new dimension of complexity.

In practice, and different from the traditional model used by most management consulting firms, the metacycle concept is applied from the inside out in companies rather than from the outside in. First of all, to conduct a diagnostic based on the notion of metacycles, it is necessary to enter the system. Only after understanding from an internal perspective—immersed in the organization—how a given company and its employees operate is it possible to begin to prepare a strategic proposal for it. To obtain this more realistic, deep, and specific understanding of the organization, we developed a canvas to apply the Metamodel diagnostic. It presents the various stages of the process to be analyzed: Macroenvironment, Organizational Identity, Mission, Proposal, Values, and Brand, in the first sheet; Individuals, Relationships, and Organization, in the second; and Results, Culture, and Management Dynamic in the third.

An important perspective in the Metamanagement Model is that it should be used as a map. It functions like a rug of knots. During our analyses, we must pay attention to the point of the iceberg that will appear when people begin to make their testimonies. They will begin to share things that we can begin to pull like a ball of yarn, like someone undoing a knot. And it is important to remember that when we pull this string, this knot, there is an entire rug coming with it. It is based on this diagnostic, our sensibility and our personal and professional experiences that we will prepare our proposal for the company.

If the Metamanagement Model is capable of undoing a rug of knots, the question to be asked to conclude the diagnostic of an organization is: "Where is the leverage point? Where is the thread unraveling?" Based on everything that was seen and heard in an organizational system, we must discover what interference we can make to produce the most leverage possible in the system. The second point translates in the idea of making an intervention that possesses sufficient energy and attention to produce transformations, real changes in the system.

This mapping of knots present in the fabric of corporate environments and processes begins to help us understand what the first step should be to release energy, that is, to free the context in order to promote evolutive transformations in the system. This is something to always keep in mind, especially when we begin to use the *Metamanagement Model*. When looking at the multiple perspectives present in systems, we should ask: What is the next small step we can take to release energy from the system and help it advance in the desired direction?

In this path, we must remember that the combination of organizational value factors with emotional issues is always very strong. In general, it's the moral and emotional elements that will make the system deviate from the intended direction, and this deviation will cause very strong discomfort for everyone involved in the process. It is what we call "organizational schizophrenia." The organization has an official discourse, a speech, but the day-to-day experience shows something else. It's like the father who says to his young daughter: "Tell daddy that you love him," and the girl responds: "I love you daddy." Then, the father complains: "You only said it because I asked you to, right?" He causes a cognitive division in the child because she can't understand the paradox: "The person I love the most, when I express my love in a certain way, he punishes me." Unfortunately, these behaviors are also very common in the world of work.

Another important point to keep in mind when pulling the yarn in our process of preparing a proposal in the *Metamanagement Model* is to understand how we identify the different systems the organization is inserted in and their levels of consciousness in order to only then began to design the eventual interventions possible. We must be careful to not propose solutions at the continuous improvement level but rather proposals that truly provoke change and evolution. For such, we must also take one step backwards in relation to the situation that presents itself in the company and try to understand the mindset that produced that process. We should ask ourselves: "What is the field or culture that produces this mindset that leads to this process?" We should continue asking until we are able to understand the systemic dynamic of organizational values that the field or culture in question produces.

Invariably, if we ask employees what is the company's main problem, they will say that the organization's core problems are two: defining roles and responsibilities, and communication. Phrases like "we have a communication problem" and "we need to define roles and responsibilities" are typical, and, believe it or not, there are people who present solutions like: "we are going to increase communication" and "we are going to better define roles and responsibilities, this way we will get out of this impasse." Another phrase we might see is "we have a cash problem." All these answers refer to a single thing: symptoms. Cash flow problem is a symptom. Poor communication is a symptom. Undefined roles and responsibilities are a symptom. These are the traps we face when an employee says he or she has these problems in a diagnostic interview. In the Metamanagement Model, we must capture the information and put them into scale, into perspective; take a step backwards to understand what these people are saying and what they are really trying to say.

This is one of the main challenges in the process we propose, and this is why we call our experts Transformation Facilitators or Integrators. Our main issue when we kick off a new process is how we will shape and give mass to the elements we collected in our interviews.

Naturally, when our consultants look at something that is emerging from reality, we critically listen to the perspectives presented and pay attention to the words that people choose when speaking (or writing). We understand what level of consciousness they are operating in, and this way of operating is a characteristic of people who work with the Metamanagement Model. It cannot be done through questionnaires. Additionally, we maintain the fundamental consciousness that, every time we enter client-companies, we become part of their system, with all the entanglements that the system we are entering has.

This broader way of understanding is of extreme importance because to maintain this distancing that is necessary to acknowledge existing standards in companies, we must understand our own entanglements. In spite of also being part of the system, our point of view must always occur from the most distant point. This is important because, at times, we are contracted to resolve entanglements that the people responsible for it do not have capacity to solve, so they contract a consultant and put this person in the place of the company CEO, vice president, or director. If the consultant, many times due to vanity, takes on these roles that are not his, he will simply become a new "fuse" in the old fuse box, and will end up "burning" himself, the consulting firm he is part of, and the project result.

To make things clear, every time we enter a space, we become part of it, carrying our biases and unconsciously taking them inside. Upon entering the front door and beginning to talk to people as a consultant, we already are part of the system. In some cases, clients will ask for solutions that we probably have not entirely resolved within ourselves. Therefore, we must always remember that it is important for the consultant to live the role with humbleness, in order to allow for honest openness toward each other, allowing us to practice and integrate our issues and those of the company and not treat organizations as something separate. We must acknowledge ourselves as part of the system and as the last in the system. As such, we should always ask ourselves "How can I be of service to the system?" We always understand that the system is always right, in its own way and time. All organizational systems have their idiosyncrasies, their incoherences, and their confusions.

But do not be fooled, systems can always change and they do change. They always have the potential to transform themselves, maintaining something from their previous way of being. They always seek to preserve their essence. For such, it is fundamental to focus on the discovery that the system is revealing, both explicit and implicitly. We need to focus on whether, based on our own entanglement, from our poorly resolved stories, we run any risk of taking on a role that is not our role. We should ask, among seven billion people in the world, why we have to experience a given situation in an organization, since we always have something to learn. We are never isolated in the situations we experience. We must always—somehow—pursue the limits of our learning. This should continually happen so that we can always learn more and more.

In summary:

The Metamanagement Model Process—Summary

The Metamanagement Model process includes different players (which, by tradition, we coin "internal and external") to ensure that multiple perspectives and narratives form the transformation agenda. Since the Metamanagement Model is based on the perspective oriented at the ecosystem in which the company is part of, it seeks to transcend the "inside out" concept and involve in its journey coworkers, leaders, shareholders, suppliers, clients, surrounding community, NGOs, civil society entities, and so forth. Everyone is welcome to be active voices in the process. A typical journey of the Metamanagement Model process, considering that each organization is unique and lives a specific moment, takes anywhere between 6 and 9 months. During this time, every 2 or 3 months, thorough workshops are held: Identity (with multiple stakeholders), Strategy (executive committee and/or key leaders, as well as internal and external guests), and Management Model (entire team). Between one workshop and the next, biweekly meetings are promoted with the team involved in the project (the company's executive committee or leadership team, for example) for it to gain psychological assurance and execution capacity of what was discussed. These meetings are permeated by individual coaching sessions so participants can deep dive and incorporate, at their own pace, the lessons learned. Members of the project team are also invited to undergo experiences outside the organization, visiting other companies, spaces, and initiatives that can inspire the overall result. After the last workshop, when the new organizational management model is designed, follow-up meetings are held to check if what was designed and agreed to is truly being carried out. For such, among the workshops' participants, process guardians are chosen: internal coworkers that can come from different areas, such as human resources, management, culture, sales, and so forth, to act as agents of influence and transformation in the organization. In Dave Snowden and Boone (2007) perspective, the Metamanagement Model should be perceived as scaffolding, that is, a temporary structure that will sustain and support the system until it can maintain itself on its own with the new discoveries and challenges.

Considering the role that organizations played over the last century in conquering productivity increases and, with this new scale, better business management, we must recognize, from the perspective that we live an unprecedented complexity never seen before in our civilization, at every instant emergencies occur of challenges that we have never seen before as society, we are in a certain way also pioneers of our time, and we are only at the beginning of our journey. As such, we must remain alert to envision what will be the role of organizations and of labor relations in order to develop a fairer and more inclusive society. In this future, we will probably be able to see the limits transcend organizations as we see them today to more collaborative models of ecosystems with multiple interactions, which we do not yet fully understand what they mean. However, we strongly believe that the idea of having a map such as the *Metamanagement Model* can contribute to the creation and emergence of this new society.

References

Adizes I (1990) Corporate lifecycles: how and why corporations grow and die and what to do about it. Adizes Institute Publications, Santa Barbara County, California
Argyris C (1960) Understanding organizational behavior. Dorsey Press, Homewood
Cook-Greuter S (2010) Postautonomous ego development: a study of its nature and measurement. Integral Publishers, California
Johnson B (2014) Polarity management: identifying and managing unsolvable problems. HRD Press, Amherst
Kegan R, Lahey L (2009) Immunity to change: how to overcome it and unlock potential in yourself and your organization. Harvard Business Press, Boston
Milgram S (2009) Obedience to authority: an experimental view. Harper Perennial, New York
Mindell A (2002) The deep democracy of open forums: practical steps to conflict prevention and resolution for the family, workplace, and world. Hampton Roads Publishing Company, Charlottesville
Robertson B (2015) Holacracy: the new management system for a rapidly changing world. Henry Holt and Company, New York
Snowden DJ, Boone ME (2007) A leader's framework for decision making. Harv Bus Rev 85:69–76. PMID 18159787
Torbert W (2004) Action inquiry: the secret of timely and transforming leadership. Berrett-Koehler Publishers, San Francisco
Watkins A, Wilber K (2015) Wicked & wise: how to solve the world's toughest problems. Urbane Publications, Rochester

Cross-References

An Overview of the Field of Transformation, by Judi Neal
Whole Systems Transformation with Music, by Paul Kwiecinski
Activitating the Corporate Soul, by Ruediger Fox

Creating a Flow Organization to Lead into the Future, by Ruediger Fox
Organizational Transformation, by Mel Toomey
Cultivating a Global Mindset Through "Being-Centered" Leadership by Eleftheria Egel and Louis Fry
Global Transformation: Visions of an Imminent Future, by Karin Jironet
A New World Is Already Here: Lessons from Radically Different Organizations, by Lenette Schuijt

Family Business Transformation: A Systems View

8

Marc A. Silverman

Abstract

This chapter addresses the issue of family businesses' need for transformation from a systemic view. A systemic perspective is utilized to analyze the most common issues inherent in family businesses. The author illustrates key transformative challenges that most family businesses face and must resolve if the core systems are going to meet developmental and systemic challenges. Suggestions are offered for several kinds of interventions that help sustain the family, the family business, and its wealth over generations. The author utilizes cases that show how the issues impact the different family business systems with successes and failures. The author also suggests consultative competencies that are needed by the consultant wishing to assist thc transformation process.

Keywords

Family business · Transformation · Family business governance · Conflict resolution in family business · Succession planning · Systems approach · Enmeshment in family business systems · Family fracturing · Family protocols and constitution · Family business consultant competencies

Why Family Businesses Need Transformation?

Asking why family businesses need transformation is a little like asking why systems need to grow. Systems that do not evolve, die. Whether we are talking about plant life, technical systems, or human systems, if a system is not actively adapting

M. A. Silverman (✉)
Strategic Initiatives Inc., Miami, FL, USA
e-mail: marc@sii-inc.net

J. Neal (ed.), *Personal, Educational and Organizational Transformation*, Future of Business and Finance, https://doi.org/10.1007/978-3-031-29253-8_8

and growing in the process of evolutionary change it will soon not be able to meet the need of its individual parts and community and will cease to function. In the world of family business, sadly, we see this happening all the time in the fracturing of families and the loss of financial wealth. It is particularly seen in times of generational transition or succession planning.

When family businesses choose the path of transformation, they focus on proactively understanding the wounds of the present and the past, creating a vehicle and environment to heal past wounds. Once healed or transformed, all systems (individual, family, and family business) will most likely begin to flourish in a variety of ways. Transformation allows the system to confront past and present challenges in ways that strengthen the resilience of all the systems in alignment with their core values. This flourishing may be in business success, family cohesion, and togetherness, as well as in individual happiness, self-esteem, and alignment.

I offer three perspectives. First, I worked in my family's business for over 20 years. The family business was a family therapy office that included my father, mother, sister, and one of my brothers as well as non-family psychologists and social workers. I was second generation and expected to eventually run the business. This life experience combined with training and practice both in family therapy and organization development form the roots of my thinking.

Some Typical Cases

I want to begin with some short typical cases to highlight for the reader some of the classic and unique issues confronting family business owners.

A father and three sons work in a manufacturing business that the dad created. Dad is 75 and the kids are 48, 44, and 34. Who will take over when Dad retires or becomes unable to run this business? It is relatively well known that the great majority of family businesses do not succeed into the next generation (Carlock and Ward 2001). Currently, two of the sons are hopeful to become the CEO, and their wives are already practically at war with each other over who will be chosen as the next CEO. In fact, due to the conflict between the two in-laws, the family now cannot meet all together for holidays. Currently, in the business, Dad makes all the ultimate decisions. How should he choose the successor? In my view, this family and family business is facing a deep need to transform.

In another case, the CEO/Chairman of the Board is in his 90 s and still makes all decisions. His brothers (four of whom have also worked in the family business for over 50 years) and children of the nine siblings surround him are hoping to be crowned the next King of this famous retail chain. The CEO has not named a successor, and no governance structure is in place beyond the CEO/Board Chairman's authority. Although the CEO's advisors have all strongly recommended to the CEO that he get help in creating a succession plan, he has refused. This is a disaster about to happen.

In a third case, another patriarch, also in his 90 s, has succumbed to Alzheimer's. Two of the four children have worked in the family business for the majority of their life. The older son has been declared CEO, and the younger son, who is in charge of one of the major divisions, is deeply unhappy and hostile. The younger son deeply believes that his brother is not fit to be CEO and makes his view clear in practically every meeting. Board meetings are filled with anger, blame, and conflict. In this case, there were three external board members who recently all resigned together saying, "This is not a Board Meeting, it is a family war and we are not going to waste our time."

A Systems Approach

Holding a systems view means that the consultant views behavior, attitudes, and decisions are made in the context of a system(s), and each system impacts the other systems in which they overlap, just like a family influences the attitudes and behaviors of individuals and vice versa. Hence, a systems view is a lens in which to view events. As has been documented, (Jaffe 1991; Lansberg 1999) family business success over time has to do with addressing the needs in each system and between each system. We begin by looking at the three most basic systems: the family, business, and individual systems (see Fig. 8.1).

Health demands that there is reasonable balance between the various systems. Without balance in the system, disease or difficulty will occur somewhere. If a family member spends all his time at work, the marriage will likely suffer. If family or personal needs dominate the family member at work, their performance (and the organization as a whole) will most likely suffer. Sons may "want to work" in the business not out of personal desire or of love for the business but because it is the only way they can get close to their Dad. Family unhappiness can be expressed at work. Work unhappiness may be expressed in the family and so forth.

A systems view is a lens in which to view the various components of a family business. The basic diagram suggests that each family should be independent and with a little overlap. Of course, each person belongs in some degree to each system (if they are part of the business). This can get quite confusing. The model suggests

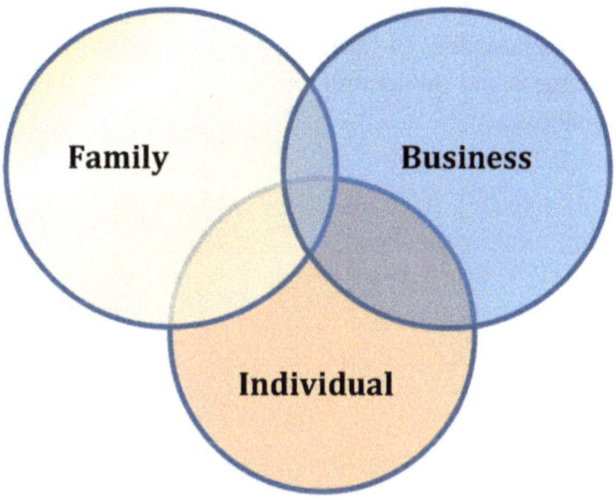

Fig. 8.1 The interrelatedness of family, business, and individual systems

that each system can be independent, that is, a family is still a family regardless of ownership and/or working in a family business. Each system has its own needs and challenges, and each system must address their own growth needs.

As each person ages, then each individual must face psychological developmental tasks. If a person is not able to face these developmental needs, other parts of the family or family business will suffer. Perhaps the patriarch fears retirement and continues in his role as CEO far beyond what should happen for the good of the business or family business members. It is rare that family members will say, "I do not have the competence to fill this growing position." Perhaps a family member who is Operations Manager has the competence to manage a 100 person manufacturing plant but not a 250-person manufacturing plant.

Here are the key systems. Of course, there are many subsystems particularly as the family and business mature, but this is the classic Family Business Systems model as developed by Davis and Tagliere (Gersick et al. 1997) (Fig. 8.2).

In these three systems, we have the management, the family, and the ownership. By definition, each system operates independently. The overlapping of the circles shows that each system impacts the other. Depending on the particular family, the amount of overlap may be quite severe or less severe.

In this case (Fig. 8.3), the systems are deeply overlapped.

Here, there is practically no differentiation between the systems (see Fig. 8.4).

In this case (Fig. 8.4), the systems are extremely distant, just barely connected.

For example, in an interview with a 55-year-old family business executive who expressed great unhappiness in working as the CEO for the family business, I asked "Why do you stay in this position": He responded, "It would deeply disturb my Dad if I left. I think he would never get over it, he would probably hate me and the business would also suffer deeply." There was some clear evidence to support what he was saying. His father although charismatic did not have the right skill set to lead the business at this time, and the CEO's brother who worked in the business was fairly incompetent in business. Meanwhile, this CEO had been in therapy for years for clinical depression and was on antidepressant medication. In this case, the older son was sacrificing his individual desires and needs for the family business.

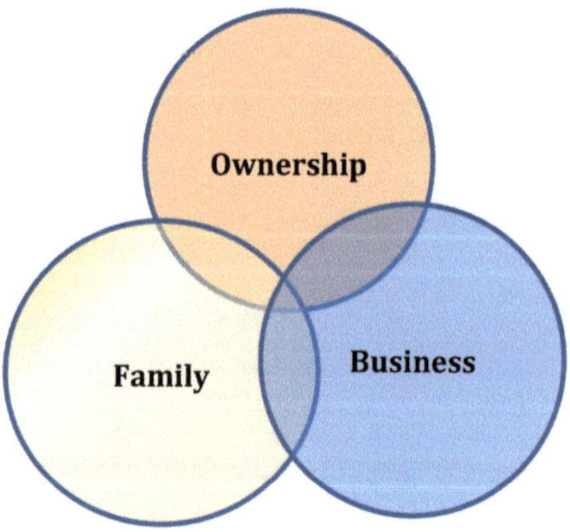

Fig. 8.2 The classic systemic view showing the interrelatedness of family, business and ownership systems

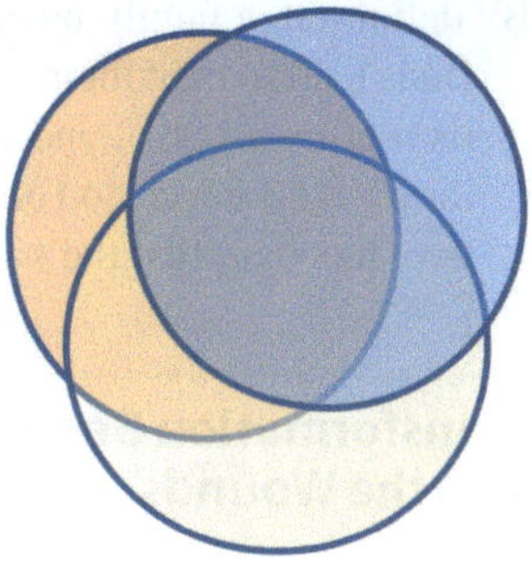

Fig. 8.3 Shows an enmeshed system, with the three primary systems ownership, business and individual systems deeply overlapped

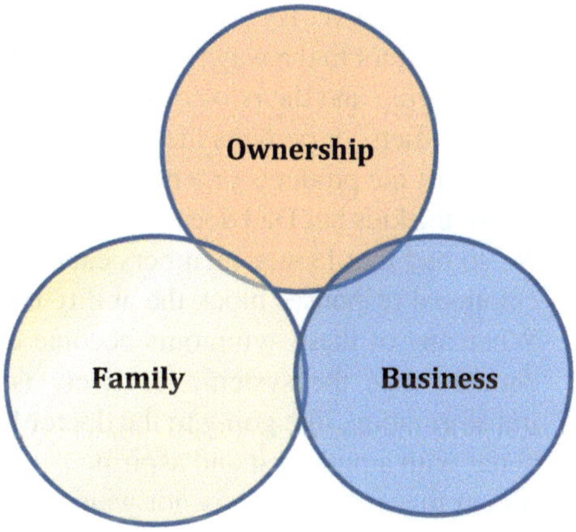

Fig. 8.4 Shows a deeply distant system, with the three primary systems ownership, business and individual systems barely intersecting

Most entrepreneurs will tell you they put in enormous hours in the building of their business. Often, the marriage suffers, and the kids suffer as well from Dad's absence. "I'm building this business for you," Dad usually exclaims. Even if true, it's often done at the expense of the family time and relationship needed inside the family, and his response is not acknowledging most likely narcissistic needs. The father–son bond may be extremely damaged; the kids may not even want the business; or the kids may feel the only way to gain Dad's love and attention or respect is through success in the family firm.

Let's take a personal growth need. In another family, the father was a very successful entrepreneur. Although not a micromanager, the father was clearly an autocratic leader. All business decisions ended up on his desk. In this family, there were several sons who at one time or another worked for the Dad in the family business. In this case, the fourth child who had worked in the family business for 20 years was telling Dad of his resignation. The father exclaimed, "Son I have done everything for you." The son replied, "Dad, that is true. My problem is that I am like a small tree trying to grow under the shade of a large and established tree. The only way I can get sunlight is if I move away from you and the family business so that I can get sunshine and create my own deep roots and blossom."

By definition, a family business is mixing the core systems of business and family. Dads tend to treat their sons more like sons than like nonfamily executives (nepotism at its worst!), and children often pull on their Dad's heartstrings in ways they would never do (or be allowed to do) if working for a professional executive. It is here that the seeds of narcissism and entitlement are born.

Transformation Begins with Identifying the Needs and the Wounds

In a general sense, there are two primary drivers for change; one is reactive and the other is proactive. By reactive, the system is reacting to external stimuli, and the system cannot find a way to move forward without confronting the issue such as: Dad is aging and the two sons in the business have deep and apparently unsolvable conflicts, or perhaps the sales of a company are in deep decline due to poor quality of the products or a poorly functioning sales department, which is run by one of the kids but Dad does not want to fire his son. Perhaps family relationships are so bad that family members cannot have dinner together, or an individual's emotional responses block the ability to receive feedback on work performance. When any of these symptoms become debilitating enough and the pain is high enough, then the system, reactively is ready for intervention and hopefully transformation, like going to the doctor because the body is sick after not getting better with simple rest and aspirin.

A system that is proactive is not waiting for external stimuli or pain to determine how best to adapt to evolutionary change. Being proactive is about setting positive goals or vision to create the ideal. Keeping with the health analogy, it is like taking care of one's health before one gets ill or pursuing education and training for expansion of competence. If we want our family business to strengthen our family bonds and create wealth for all of us and match personal passions then what obstacles do we need to face? We say we want to have long and happy personal life with family cohesion– what do we need to do to accomplish this?

Most family businesses are reactive. Like seeing a doctor, most family businesses look for assistance in transformation when deep difficulties have arisen and been present for some time. The key is not waiting too long. Deep hurt and anger is not usually healed just with time. Most often, the hurts and angers grow and fester.

Here is an example. At my first meeting with two brothers (one was about 72 and the other was 68) who had taken over their Dad's farm 40 years ago and built a multimillion dollar company, they explained the problem:

> *We are aging and both of us want to retire soon. Our concern is that the next generation does not get along, in fact they seem to hate each other. Yes* the younger brother continued—*we will all lose this fortune, given to us by our Dad and built by us. Selling it is not a very good option. Even if we bring an external CEO, in the future our kids will own the business and form the basis of the board. How can we get our children to become professionals and learn how to work together as a team? We will all be much happier and wealthier if they can.*

Other examples as mentioned before show such a high level of conflict that the feeling of enjoyment and satisfaction is far overshadowed by the anger and unhappiness that take place seemingly without end or resolution.

As mentioned, a proactive response is not waiting for external stimuli. It is similar to developing a healthy regime of exercise and diet to bring the body into top health as preventive medicine. These kinds of leaders are visualizing the future and asking, "How can we best prepare for the future?" Planning and actions come from anticipated growth needs. "What kinds of skills and competencies will my children and grandchildren need to benefit and maybe manage this fortune?"

What is needed for transformation? It is clear any of these systems (individual, family, and business) can get into trouble. Because they are deeply overlapped, difficulty and transformation (or the lack thereof) in one system will deeply impact the other. If a father and son improve their family relationship, it will also improve their family business relationship and vice versa. If an individual improves his emotional intelligence, this will impact his family and family business relationships. If the business soars under a son's or daughter's leadership, their family relationships and self-esteem will be positively affected.

Sometimes what needs transforming is the degree of overlap between the systems. Sometimes two or all three of the systems have so much overlap they lose their identity and need "to breathe" (what family therapists call enmeshed family systems. One family business owner explained his success with his brother and other family members this way: "I see my brother eight hours a day, six days a week. The last thing I want is to socialize with him on Sunday. This is how we maintain our good working relationship and a good family relationship." In another conversation between two deeply unhappy brothers, when probed as to the problem in their business relationship, one said "When my son suddenly died five years ago my brother never gave me heartfelt condolences. This hurt me enormously. I basically have wanted nothing to do with him since then." In the end, the goal is for the family to be and act like a family, a business to be, and act like a business.

The transformational needs of the family business are often different than the deeper wounds that must be healed in order for transformation to occur. Here are some typical "needs" as expressed by family business owners that are the external manifestation of the wounds.

- Succession planning can no longer be postponed due to illness, death, or inability to perform one's role.
- Departure of planned—or expected or successors.
- Significant conflict between siblings who work in the business.
- One family member insists on selling his/her shares.
- Due to death, ownership is transferred to spouse, children, or cousins who have little knowledge or the business.
- A family member's work performance is poor or his/her work behavior is breaking ethical or professional boundaries.
- Key family business executives are deeply unhappy and are threatening to quit or do resign.

- Ethical or conflict of interest violations; for example, a family member tries to secretly sell his/her shares either to another family member or nonfamily individual or utilizes the family business for personal gain such as providing special favors for certain suppliers.

These Are Systemic Issues!

Once the "need" is identified, the next challenge is seeing if it is related to a current or old wound as well as context and maturity of the family business. When the hurt and anger is deep, there are usually unhealed wounds underneath.

If the family business is obviously "late" in planning for succession, there may be several "wounds" driving this behavior including: lack of trust in planned-for successors, the patriarch's or matriarch's narcissistic needs, lack of competence in successors, conflict in the next generation, fear of retirement and death, the current successor's anger at his father's inability to empower him or her, him when he took over the business, and so on.

As the baton passes from one generation to the next, all family members need to address some common critical issues if they are to survive and thrive. These include determining who makes what decisions, deciding how conflicts are resolved, creating healthy separation of the ownership and management spheres of life, and developing plans for the evolution of each individual, the business, and the family.

All transformative change requires a level of emotional and spiritual intelligence. This includes the desire and willingness to change, a deep knowledge about what makes the business successful, and leadership skills. On an individual level, this may require the person to change some deeply held beliefs and attitudes, to receive feedback which the individual would rather not hear, and to learn ways of being in their family that are new and unfamiliar. In the family, it may mean to discuss painful incidents in that past that were never healed and that are impacting today's family communication and relationships. In the family business, it may mean making some difficult decisions about competence and empowerment of family members working in the business or facing corporate challenges of new markets and business models that are needed for growth.

Of course the wounds are different in each family or business system. You can usually identify wounds easily in that they are often talked about with great affect, usually with a lot of hurt and anger. In many families, a wound is often not one incident, but rather a sequence of incidents that have happened in the family, and the wound is often defined in many ways and crosses all the systems. Most often these wounds are related to failures of love or justice. Different family members may have quite different views on what happened, why, and the consequences. There may be many unresolved questions such as:

Is success at work the qualification to receive Dad's love?

What part of the family wealth will go to family members who have nothing or very little to do with the family business?

How will salaries and inheritance be set?

What is the role of money in this family?

Does more money equal more success?

How does Mom or Dad deal with their children's poor performance or behavior at work?

How is deeply inappropriate behavior (like aggression, drinking, taking drugs) dealt with in the family business?

How do these decisions honor, the family's history and legacy?

A Case of Competition and Jealousy

In this beautiful family with six children, the father, a very successful entrepreneur who owned and built several large businesses in different business sectors had passed away many years earlier. Of course, he wanted all of his children to prosper. He was survived by his wife and six children—two brothers and four sisters. The eldest son had been the "right-hand" of the father, and the youngest son had been a rebel as a teenager. When I met this family, the eldest son was about 63, and the youngest son was about 55. The daughters were all middle children between these two sons. Both sons were enormously bright and capable businessmen but deeply competitive with each other. Board meetings usually focused around hostile conflicts between the brothers with the sisters in the middle trying to help them find a solution.

When unable to find a solution, the decision ended up in the Mother's hands—she was over 90 years old at this time and unfamiliar with this 100 million-dollar business.

This was quite an unhappy family. Countless hours and tremendous emotional energy were consumed in these conflicts. Neither brother was particularly happy. What was the wound? How did this family get so stuck in this dynamic? One day, the younger brother shared with me this memory:

One day about 30 years ago, the family, as was our custom, were all going to my parents' vacation house. As is typical in many families over time our vacation home was short of space. We were originally a family of six, but then we all grew up, most got married, had children. At this moment I was not married but I had a fiancé. My fiancé and I arrived for the family weekend on Friday afternoon and my Dad greeted us and asked me if my fiancé and I would sleep in the garage as the bedrooms were already taken. We said "Yes."

My older brother with his wife arrived a few hours later in his new and shiny Porsche. He spoke to my Dad and said indignantly "I must have the garage for this vehicle." Dad agreed. The younger brother exclaimed to me "Imagine, I was displaced by my brother's car!" There were many examples of this kind of memory.

In this sad family dynamic, the younger brother felt he could never be on an equal footing with his older brother even though he became quite a successful businessman himself. He felt he could never measure up to his older brother in his father's eyes. This unhealed wound was about 40 years old.

Father Knows Best

This next story focuses on a father and his children both of whom worked in the family business. This father had two children, a son and a daughter. The son had a long history of drug abuse in his teenage years and 20 s. He was able to end his addiction but maintained a quite aggressive and hostile persona, particularly in the company.

At the time of my meeting the family, the father was CEO and Chairman of the Board, and his son was the Director of Sales. The daughter, who was Director of Marketing, had a "sweetheart deal"—she worked less than half time and was paid the same as the son. The father had made a deal with his children that when he passed away, the son would become CEO, get 51% of the shares, and the daughter would get 49%. The son and daughter were at war with each other constantly blaming each other for not meeting business goals. The Chief Financial Officer (CFO) was not a family member and had earned the trust of the father. At this point in time, the father was in his 80 s and was in early stages of dementia but still had final decision-making power in all aspects of the business.

The daughter was furious and untrusting of her brother and worried that when Dad passed, her brother would treat her even worse. With her husband, they came up with a plan. She became friendly with the CFO and convinced him that her brother's deeply aggressive leadership style would ruin the company. They decided that it would be best if the CFO became the next CEO, not her brother. Over about a year of secret conversations between the daughter and Dad, she convinced him of her plan.

One day, the son came to work and was called into his father's office The father said in essence "Son, the deal we made 30 years ago about your becoming the next CEO, I now see will ruin the company. I have asked the CFO to become the next CEO when I pass. Thankfully, he has agreed. After all," Dad continued, "(the CFO) is a great leader and everyone will benefit from the business success. I will give him controlling power in the company. Have a good day."

As one might imagine the relationship between the brother and sister became a full war, the board meetings were now attended by three attorneys (Dad's, Son's, and Daughter's), the son stopped attending any family gatherings, some of the grandchildren (children of the son and daughter who worked in the company) maintained a great distance from each other. The mother became clinically depressed, cried daily, rarely left the house, and was on strong medication. The mother was known to say things like "Why can't we be like a normal family where everyone gets together for the holidays and enjoys each other?"

Impact of the Wound on the Family and the Family Business

These examples are typical of what happens when family businesses do not transform. Deep wounds in any of the systems make a deep impact on the other systems. Whenever there are deep wounds that are not healed, these can become places of transformational needs and opportunities. These wounds will affect all the various systems (individual, family, business). If there is no transformation, the individual may show chronic low self-esteem/depression, cynicism, anger, helplessness, hopelessness and a carry a deep sense of victimhood. The family may fracture for generations, and the culture of the business or the family feels like a kind of "war."

In these cases, the business is often sold either to family or nonfamily shareholders, and the business often becomes an organization focused purely on financial success, but without heart. These next examples show families who end up deeply fractured, with great loss of self-esteem and a business solely focused on money.

The Fracturing of Family Relationships

This is a story of a quite enlightened family business of ten siblings who jointly owned a very successful retail business started by their Dad. The family with the help of several consultants over the years had a clear Family protocol in place with agreed upon rules about decision-making, conflict resolution, succession, and governance (family council, board of directors, and family office). The CEO, one of the siblings, had done an outstanding job, and there was no competition for his position. Several of the siblings worked with good results in the business, and others were just shareholders.

At a point in time, one of the siblings wished to sell his shares and, as guided by the protocol, made the proper announcements. The other siblings, particularly the one that was the CEO responded to him—"You have every right to do this and we have the money to pay you. But we strongly urge you not to do this. We are planning to go public as a company in a few years. Your share will be worth three to four times as much as they are worth today! So, I urge you to reconsider. Of course, if you do wish to cash out, again, we do have the cash on hand you have that right and we will honor your wish."

Discussion with many of the siblings took place, but this shareholder insisted on selling his shares. The transaction occurred, and the shareholder was happy. As was planned the company went public in about 3 years, and each person's shares went up in value enormously. The shareholder who sold his shares early became furious and did not talk to family members for at least 20 years following that event.

In this case, where all the rules were clear and agreed upon, there were no secrets, and the shareholder who wanted to leave was paid the agreed upon amount—the family fractured. Imagine the impact of those many families where the rules are not so clear and/or there are strong feelings of favoritism.

Common Wound Themes

In this section, common wounds are described and methods of intervention used by the author to transform the culture of the family and family business.

Sometimes, identifying the wound is relatively apparent once family members begin to share stories surrounding their legacy. These stories are the critical events in the entrepreneur's and business's development as in the case of the younger brother who was displaced by his brother's Porsche. Often, family business members, with very little prodding, will share "stories" that illustrate the wounds of the particular family.

It is helpful for the consultant to spend some time with various family members both individually and together where they tell the story of the birth of the business and critical factors in its growth. Some families keep the roots of the wounds quite secret. Positive or negative, the "stories" exist, sometimes called the "legacy." These stories are what make the family and the family business unique and in a sense define its soul.

As one can see from the examples above, certain themes begin to emerge. Most often one finds either in the family or the family business system:

- Deep unresolved hurt/anger.
- Perceived (and often actual) deep injustice or unfairness.
- Perceived (and often actual) real and assumed betrayal regarding agreements about compensation, inheritance, roles, and power in the business.
- Deep lack of empathy.

For some family members, even the telling the story of the wound is quite painful, and there may be great differences and discrepancies! In one family, the siblings' sharing of different versions of their history caused such great uproar between them that they had to be physically restrained. Regardless of the feeling tone of the participants, a critical part of the transformation is the ability of the consultant and family members to hear empathically the family members' telling and perception of various events that were experienced as deeply wounding. This is a first step in a transformation process.

This empathic listening by the consultant is best done in first in private interviews with all family members. It is usually helpful to also interview several nonfamily members who know the family or family business quite well. These nonfamily members may be board members, top-level executives, and advisors such as accountant, attorney strategic planner, or financial planner. Questionnaires are also often helpful in this diagnostic stage (Hubler 2020).

This is the diagnostic phase of the consulting process.

Typical Blocks to Healing and Transformation

Reflecting on these cases and others, the question emerges what themes appear to surface in the family and family businesses who appear not able to heal or transform themselves. From a holistic perspective in the psychological world, common blocks can be grouped in the cognitive, emotional, and/or spiritual arenas.

In the cognitive arena, what occurs most often when a person "thinks" they are thinking through a problem objectively but, in fact, they are not. Usually, there are faulty assumptions and unconscious projections built into their process that are unexamined or it could simply be that the person is not thinking well about how to solve an issue. There are numerous cognitive difficulties that can arise such magnifying or minimizing others' emotions, determining others' intent without checking with them directly, perceiving others in terms of one's own needs rather than with their own intent.

Emotional blocks occur when the person's emotions override their cognitive or spiritual abilities. Most often, the deep level of hurt and anger an individual is feeling may be blocking their ability to heal and move forward. In one case where a brother was furious at his brother at work, he yelled and exploded at his brother before even finding out if his assumptions that were fueling his rage were in fact true.

When a person is blocked from their spiritual core, traditional or nontraditional, this will also block the person's ability to transcend the blockage to transformation. On the other hand, when the spiritual core is sound, the family business will tend to act from their highest altruistic values. For example, one patriarch shared, "My Grandfather was in the mining business—it did not work out (late 1800s)—went bankrupt. Some people advised him to declare bankruptcy so he could avoid paying his very high debts—he did not. He paid his debts. This gave me a very important lesson—always maintain one's business integrity."

Here are some other common blocks to family business transformation. They include (1) blaming others, (2) denial of personal need to heal, (3) hopelessness, (4) inability to forgive, (5) assumption of other's not changing or being able to change, (6) and lack of an internal model of healing.

Blaming Others

When an individual's primary coping defense is to blame another—whether externally or internally—this will block their own ability for introspection and learning. In one case where an individual was describing the demise of his family's business, he consistently blamed either his brother or his father for its demise. Although many of his allegations toward his family members were true, his focus on blaming them blocked his own ability to learn from the situation, and it blocked the family and the family business's ability to transform.

Denial of Personal Need to Heal

For many people, denial is the first line of defense. Whether we are talking about addiction, a grief issue, or the hurt and anger one feels in a family or family business situation, by denying one's own pain and experience leads to a shutting down of authentic communication and relationship. Over time, the person may not feel their own feelings, making them even more difficult reach. "Everything is fine" said a family business member who hoped to become CEO and was passed over. His unconscious anger and rage led to more and more isolation from his family and to his own depression.

Hopelessness: Inflaming of One's Own or Other's Hurt and Anger

Some individuals when they reflect or discuss past hurtful episodes reignite their pain and suffering. Like giving oxygen to a small flame, some individuals fan this flame by recounting the story in a way where they see themselves as the victim with no hope for recovery. In fact, what they are doing psychologically is like standing in a hole with a shovel and deepening the hole with each expression of their feelings. The key is that their expression is not helping to release their emotions but rather to stay enclosed in a web of despair and hopelessness. They are holding the concept of "Life is terrible, and then you die."

Inability to Forgive

When a wrong has been committed, if the individual wants to move forward in their lives, it often requires the ability to forgive one's self and the perpetrator. The act of forgiveness frees the individual from the psychological and spiritual chains of the harm that was received. By not finding a way to forgive, the individual is held in a psychological confinement. One individual said:

> *I know I need to forgive my Dad for not appreciating and respecting my business acumen. But I cannot. My father was so narcissistic and aggressive with me he even tried to screw me in business. So I beat him at his game. I made much more money than he did. I was civil to him but never warm or loving. He never thanked me and I never thanked him. He died a lonely man.*

Sadly, this individual was unable to heal the great wounds he felt in his relationship with his father. His wounds are now impacting the destructive relationships with his generation as well.

Assumption of Other's Not Changing or Being Able to Change

Family members often hold an assumption that others in their family do not and will not change. By definition, we know our family members our whole lives and we develop over the years a perspective on each family member. Some individuals then make the assumption that the other will never change. At a bare minimum, this becomes like blinders blocking the ability to see small changes in others' behavior and attitudes. It is like putting a box around a person and not letting them get out of it. As a sibling once said "My brother was an autocratic leader for 20 years. He is not going to change now." In fact, the brother had been making changes for years that the sister did not see. Unlike this sister, most of his management team did not see him as a deep autocratic leader.

Lack of an Internal Model of Healing

Many people lack an internal model of healing. Most people understand that even with the best of intentions they often make mistakes. Perhaps a parent says to themselves and later the child, "I was too harsh with you today, I'm sorry." Or a child says to his/her parent, "I know I was too aggressive with you today, I'm sorry." However, not all people have this ability. Some people when they get into a conflict do not have an internal compass on how to resolve the issue in such a way that both they and the other person find a way to genuinely move forward in the relationship in a win–win kind of way. Having an internal model of healing requires a kind of emotional maturity or intelligence where one accepts the limitations of the other and/or one's self and finds a way to go forward in the relationship with dignity. A son said, "I know it is so difficult for my Dad to say 'I love you' but I know the love is there in the way he looks at me and the way he trusts me with some of his deepest fears and needs."

Not having an internal model of healing keeps one's relationships stuck, as if frozen in time. These individuals cannot find a way to see how issues can be healed and resolved, and it becomes a self-fulfilling prophecy. In one family business, the parents had divorced 20 years before I met with them. The two children worked with their Dad and maintained a close relationship with their Mom. The children were quite unhappy at work and quite critical of their Dad. When I probed the roots of their unhappiness, they quickly stated how awful their Dad had been to their Mom at the time of their divorce. Knowing the father, I had no reason to doubt their Dad's misbehavior.

But why was this causing difficulty in the present? Although they could acknowledge he had changed, they appeared to have no way of healing from the damage from their parents' painful divorce. In fact, neither of the children nor the father had any idea of how to improve their relationship in the present. In the children's judgment, like their Mother's judgment, their Dad's misbehavior could never be forgiven or healed.

What Happens When Healing/Transformation Does Not Occur?

When healing and transformation do not occur, the individual, the family, and the family business will all suffer. On an individual basis, the person's self-esteem and emotional intelligence often decreases, and their feelings of victimhood, hopelessness, and powerlessness increase. Defenses toward change and growth often strengthen as the psychological wound remains "stuck" as detailed in the section above. In essence, the individual's emotional intelligence, personal, and family well-being all suffer. The family often fractures as suggested by the case where one sibling sold his shares and then became financially poorer than his siblings. Lastly and interestingly, the family and the family business will often unconsciously repeat the trauma in the next generation. In a way, this is positive as it allows the system to transform itself if it is psychologically ready.

Case of Business over Family

This is a complex case where the trauma and its consequences in the first generation were repeated in the second generation.

The patriarch of this family spent an enormous amount of time building with his brother one of the most successful international businesses in their market sector. He and his brother had an extraordinary difficult and hostile relationship. In fact, they were unable to talk with each other at all. Their only communication took place in the board room where they would often scream at each other and the external board members attempted to resolve the differences. After fifty years they decided they were no longer able to stay together and one brother bought out the other brother's shares.

This story is about the brother who left that family business and used the funds to begin a new business. He was in his late 70s at the time. This new business was quite successful and several of his children and grandchildren worked with him in it. Upon his passing he left the controlling share (and decision-making power) to his wife. His wife was a strong and loyal partner to him his whole life and had never been involved with her husband's business(es). Upon the patriarch's death, she became Chairman of the Board. As he wanted all of his children to benefit from the company, shares were given equally to each of the three children.

The patriarch and his wife had three daughters. Each was married and had several children. One of the daughters was integrally involved in running the business as well as several of the grandchildren. One of the grandsons was married, and was a very able, but somewhat impulsive man in his early 40s. He wanted and was chosen as CEO. He appeared to be doing a quite reasonable job but one day it was alleged that he got involved intimately with one of the women who worked in the company. He denied this vehemently and was furious about the accusation.

As Chair of the Board the grandmother to this CEO was furious about this accusation of his unethical behavior, which she believed, and fired him. The grandson felt he never received a "fair hearing." The mother of the CEO (one of the three daughters) then refused any and all social visits between any members of her immediate family and the grandmother. Meanwhile, as shareholders, each of the three daughters maintained their seat on the board. The daughter, who was the mother of the CEO, decided with her children that her "fired" son could best represent their family branch at Board Meetings.

The Board Meetings are now full of hostility. The family is fractured. Family members cannot speak to each other just like it was between the two brothers of the first generation. The grandson (the fired CEO) says at the board meetings, "We all just have to be professional here." They have duplicated the relationship their father had with his brother both personally and in the board room—a deeply hostile and unhappy family relationship, a non-functioning work relationship while tied together as owners of a significant company and wealth.

Can this family business transform?

Case of Repeating Mom's Role

In this family, the second generation had recently taken over the reins of this company. In the second generation are four children, two boys and two girls. As had been designed by the father many years ago, the eldest son became CEO, the younger son his right-hand man, one daughter led her own division, and the other daughter who had been living in another country was welcome to join but had no particular role. As the parents faced health issues common for people their age, the conflict between the four children was becoming explosive.

The business was well-known in the country not only for being a good corporate citizen but also was known for the large number of projects to help the employees in their community. For example, they built a hospital that provided very inexpensive medical care for their employees. These kinds of projects were led by the wife of the founder. They were held in the highest esteem in the community and represented a way for the mother to be involved in the business without interfering with her husband or the business directly. The husband maintained ultimate control and decision-making in the business, and his wife (within a budget) was given full autonomy over decisions about community social work projects. This agreement appeared to work very well for the parents for many years. However, now with the couple in their later years (late 80 s and early 90 s) a lot of unhappiness with this "deal" was being expressed by the entrepreneur's wife for being kept out of the central part of the business.

Meanwhile, in the present, the four children were practically at war with one female sibling who is in a similar position as her Mom was to her Dad. Her brothers loudly proclaimed she had no role in the business and was not entitled to much of a voice in decision-making (even though she was now a 25% shareholder). They disliked all of her suggestions for innovations in the business. They continually proposed that she take on a project, separate from the main business, where she could have some autonomy and not bother the core business. In short, they insisted she take a secondary role in the business like their mom had done.

Strategies for Healing and Transformation

Often, a family business transition from one generation to the next requires a paradigm change of going from one owner to several owners. This paradigm shift requires the learning of new skills in going from an autocratic-based organization to a collaborative one. Most family businesses are built by an entrepreneur who had a business idea, worked like crazy, had a little luck, and was successful over time (Danco 1990). Decisions usually were made by the entrepreneur. The organization chart most resembled a spider web, with all decisions going to one person. If the business was large enough and the kids, or some of the kids, were interested and worked hard, they joined the business. Many family businesses get stuck in an autocratic culture where even when the children are in their sixties, Dad is still making all the critical decisions.

Often, more than one child of the entrepreneur works in the business. Even if only one child is working in the business, upon passing, many owners transfer part of their ownership to children who may not even work in the business. Governance, decision-making will most likely move from an autocratic model to a collaborative one particularly in the ownership system If not on the management level, then certainly on the ownership level. Of course, there must be a CEO with the power to make operational decisions. But if ownership of the company is shared among several children, then they will need to learn how to become at least a functional team, and, optimally, a high-functioning team!

If several of the kids work in the family business, then they need to learn how to become an excellent executive team with clear authority, boundaries, competencies, and deeply held shared vision, values, and mission.

Therefore, the paradigm must shift. In a case of five children, the eldest being the CEO (and a competent one), he felt that he could make all the decisions regarding the direction of the company. At a point in time, he was shocked to learn of his siblings' unhappiness and that they were not going along with some critical strategic decisions that he had made unilaterally. He lamented, "Dad never had this problem." He was correct! The difference was that Dad was 100% owner, and this son, although CEO, was a 20% owner. In this case, the transformative need was how to become a collaborative team of owners.

Sometimes, the third generation can play a pivotal role in the transformation process. With one large business that had three mature generations, it was the relationship between the third and first generation that allowed the financial transition between the first and second generation. In this case, the first generation patriarch trusted the third generation with his financial affairs, (not his wife and not the second generation). Therefore, by building the future family finances around the third generation, this allowed the transition to go relatively smoothly.

The need for organization development principles and values is high in helping families become effective teams of owners and/or executives and in how to adapt well to change. The field of organization development is particularly well equipped in this endeavor as on a fundamental level the participants must heal past wounds and develop a democratic culture with a shared vision, mission, and a statement of core values. Organization development principles provide a foundation from which the family can develop their own transformative process.

Getting help is not mandatory, but in the great majority of the cases, the results will be much better with an expert who has guided many family businesses in transformation. One does not need to be a surgeon to amputate someone's leg but is sure is better to have a professional on board!

Systemic Intervention Strategies

The problem most often is that the family's or individual's advisors stay within too narrow a focus, ignoring the impact of the change they make on the other systems. As mentioned earlier, a change in any one part of the system will impact all the systems. The most classic example is the estate planner working only with the patriarch and not seeking the impact on other family members or the financial planner who recommends business growth strategies without realizing the impact on various family executives. Other examples would be the organization development consultant ignoring the family dynamics present or the family therapist not understanding the family business dynamics.

How can the consultant intervene in a way that creates the environment and container for systemic change? This is perhaps the key question for transformation!

There are five basic steps that I recommend families and family businesses follow:

1. Create collective intention or shared mission, vision, and values.
2. Review the family's legacy as a group.
3. Identify your core values.
4. Define the values that will guide your future.
5. Develop a vision for all three systems (personal, family, business).
6. Specify the governance structure and all major policies needed to govern the family's role, responsibilities, and relationship with the family business.

This next section describes each of these interventions in greater detail.

Create Collective Intention or Shared Mission, Vision, and Values

The key to long-term sustainability in both the family and the business or wealth begins with the concept of collective intention. As the family business transitions to successive generations almost all want to find a way to maintain individual happiness, the love in the family, the success of the business, and the growth of financial wealth. Part of the great question is how to move the answer to this question from the patriarch to the family as a whole. This is often referred to as creating a shared mission, vision, and statements of core values, or what some call creating "collective intention." The mission, vision, and values must be formed by the generations together.

A good place to start is the exercise of first developing a family mission statement and family business mission statement. Some wonderful material has been written about this. The reader is suggested to look at Hughes (2004) and Covey (2007). It is important to begin differentiating these two systems in the consciousness of the family members. Mission is about purpose. What is the main purpose of the family? What is the main purpose of the family business? The differentiation process begins by answering these initial questions together as a group. Of course, underlying feelings may begin to emerge such as: *If this family's main purpose is about love, why are we fighting so much? Why don't I feel a deeper level of love in my family?* With the family business different feelings usually emerge. *Is this Dad's business or our business? How much control does the second generation really have? Are we really about making money or helping our community or employing workers?* Differentiating the purpose of these two basic systems of family and family business is key starting place and shows the amount of overlap or enmeshment in some of the critical family business systems.

Deep resistance to the process often begins here. As the family begins to proactively articulate the family mission, family business mission, and so on, family members often begin to feel deeply uncomfortable. They might say something with great sarcasm like, “Yes, we are just one big happy family here.” The key to success is for the consultant to stop the process here and help the family open the dialogue on their failure to have authentic happiness in the family and the business. By creating a safe space and facilitating deeply empathic dialogue, the healing takes place. Without this, the family may do the exercise of creating the mission statements, values statements, and vision only on a surface level.

Here is one family’s mission statement:

> *Our family at our best has a foundation of love and inspirational beliefs on making a better world. Our family rests on the pillars of unity, love, tolerance and respect, striving to resist the test of time and adversity. We are committed to maintaining the beauty of our legacy and to grow it together. Focusing first on guaranteeing the wellbeing and security of each family member, present and future, through unconditional support. The bonds of our connection will continue to be strengthened although we as a family may be geographically dispersed. We deeply value our family and we believe that the spirit of reciprocity is critical to our growth and evolution. We strive to be a family of affinity.*

Here is a family business mission statement that one family drafted:

> *We are committed to growing our family business, that began in 1975. We have great pride in our Legacy, which includes such Core Values as maintaining Customer Loyalty through a focus on providing highest quality products and service with a commitment to long-term satisfaction. We pride ourselves in our innovation and a corporate culture of deep caring and support in individual excellence and development.*
>
> *Our Business has been the glue in our family. We feel blessed in being able to work together as a Family Team. Part of our commitment is to continue to build our success in a way that welcomes family members into appropriate roles. We consider ourselves as stewards to this beautiful company that can facilitate “good lives” for us and all who are working with us. We are committed to continuing our corporate culture with development of continuous innovation towards meeting societal needs.*

As mentioned earlier, the legacy of the family and the family business is of great importance and value. Time should be spent where together the family reviews their development going back at least two generations. It is here that a great depth is often illuminated of the values of hard, hard work in the family business evolution. Usually, everyone already knows of much of this legacy, still the hearing of it in the total family group has a power as it brings each one closer to their personal purpose and desire of continuation. Many family legacies are full of unhappiness, struggle, and overcoming great obstacles. Most families do this verbally, but it can be a wonderful sharing to do this in video with pictures of key places and people or even a book.

From this base of the family legacy and the family business legacy, it is quite helpful to identify the core values. This can be done with the whole family drafting a statement of core values. I recommend that this is best done separately for the family and for the family business. After hearing the stories of struggle and success the family asks themselves, "What were the core values that drove the success of this family in the past? What were the core values that drove the success of this family business in the past?"

Upon completion of the above exercises, the family and family business group are then asked what values they wish to be guided by in the present and the future. Describing each value with specificity is important! Saying "Good Communication" or "Love" is not sufficient. For example, one family business wrote:

Openness to change—Part of our success comes from our ability to adapt to market, societal and economic change reasonably well. We strive to be an agile organization, open and able to change smartly and quickly. This requires being aware of our strengths and weaknesses, the trends in the market and an ability to predict future needs.

Advancement of knowledge—Because the world and market are in constant change, advancing our business knowledge is a requirement of success. Without continuous learning and advancement of our business knowledge, we will fall behind. We believe knowledge is easily accumulated both through formal and informal channels. This knowledge spans from industrial to marketing to organizational structure, leadership theory, emotional intelligence and decision-making.

Of course, having a clear sense of your mission is not the same as vision! What kind of family is desired in the future? What kind of family business (or businesses) is desired in the future? How will family members interact with the business? Is it the hope that children and grandchildren will work in the family business if they desire that or will they be restricted to ownership roles? Is it hoped the family will maintain a deep sense of closeness and cohesion or is it expected that family members will be living in several continents and different countries? A visioning process should be undertaken on all of the core systems (personal, family, executive, and ownership).

What if one's personal vision does not align with others, like in the case mentioned of the son who really did not want to be CEO of the company but stayed there unhappily for his father and the sake of the business. Or the lack of alignment in another case where three sons who were second generation owners of a reasonably well-functioning family business decided to sell the business. After the transaction, in discussions with the third generation, the second generation learned that the third generation wanted to run the business and were deeply disappointed that their parents had sold it.

Here is an excerpt of one family's business vision. The reader can see the full family business vision statement in Appendix 1.

We will become an international company—doing more and more business in other countries. We expect to grow our satellite companies and enter additional markets internationally.

We expect to reach growth rate of 20% annually while maintaining a minimum profit rate of 10%. We are investing in the development of new products—focusing on innovation and emerging customer needs.

Our success in part will be determined by our increasing ability to become more and more proficient at anticipating where the market is moving in order to deepen our brand and market penetration and serving these markets well, while maintaining our commitment to our values and our people.

What helps is not the flowery words but rather the act as a group creating what is sometimes called "Collective Intention." In all of these cases, by working together to define their mission, vision, and core values, the family forms a unique and powerful understanding and commitment to their goals.

Creating the Strategy/Rules of the Game

Having completed creation of a shared mission, vision, and values, the next question is how to implement it. The mission, vision, and values set the framework for where we want to go and why and under what set of operating principles or values. The next great issue is creation of policies or rules to which the family business will be run. This should be created with at least two generations participating and delineates creation of a governance structure, conflict resolution policies, employment policies, conflict of interest policies, and the succession plan. Most importantly, it becomes a model for the family together working as a team in creation of policies and procedures. The written document they create is usually titled a Family Constitution or Family Protocol.

By governance structure I mean agreeing on how decisions are made. In most family businesses, decisions are initially made by the founder. As the family business evolves, a governance structure is needed as the business, wealth, and next generation matures. Many families will benefit greatly from creating a board of directors, family council, and a family office. The governance structure determines who (or what body) makes what decisions. Here is a sample governance structure that a family created. In this case, the business was in the hands of the second generation. The patriarch had passed away about 15 years ago, and his spouse was not active in the business. The second generation ranged in age from about 40 to 60. The third generation of about 20 individuals ranged in age from 5 to 33 (Fig. 8.5).

Each governing body must have a clear set of rules to operate from. Some of the rules can be about the number of meetings per year, who takes notes, setting of agenda, the role of Chair, the role of Secretary, the power in relation to other governing bodies, the responsibilities of members, and the consequences if responsibilities are not fulfilled. These rules specify what decisions the shareholders can make, the

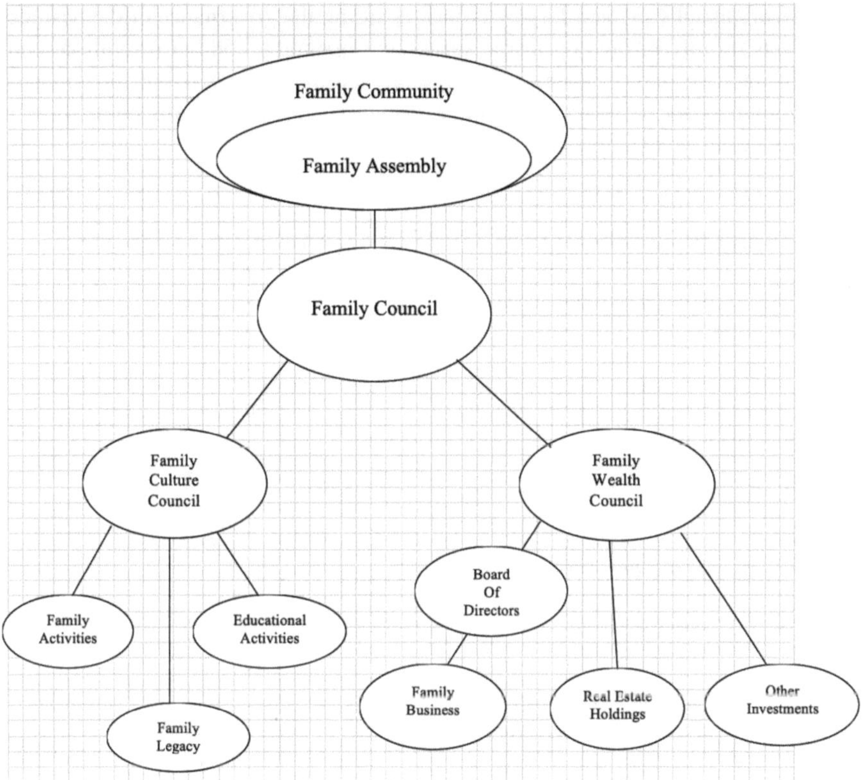

Fig. 8.5 Family business governance structure

board of directors can make, the family council can make, and the family office can make.

The key of course is that the creation of the governance structure is done collaboratively. Rather than imposed by the patriarch or someone else (for example, an attorney), this governing structure must be created by the family themselves with the guidance of the consultant. Many families hire an attorney to do this for them with quite poor results.

Creating the Rulebook, Family Protocol, or Family Constitution

Mission, vision, and core values are not enough! Families need to articulate and agree to all critical policies related to family participation in the family business, succession planning, conflict resolution, entry, and exit from the business, all relevant policies needed to maintain clarity and agreement dealing with these issues. Here are a few excerpts of actual policies developed by some families that I have worked with to give you an idea of the kinds of policies that are often needed.

Policies are usually created for any issues regarding the governance of the business and assets, family hiring and firing, succession planning, conflict resolution, conflicts of interest, performance review system, setting of expectation for youngest generation to work in the business, and expectations of future family owners.

More extensive examples are given in Appendix 3.

Philosophy of Family Employment (This Generation and Next)

Business needs dictate positions/competencies need to fulfill strategic plans. If family members—who have those skills— want to apply for that position—wonderful.

All family members are encouraged to follow their personal passions and dreams. If they are interested in working in the company, then they are encouraged to bring their ideas forward and to interview for an open position. If a family member has a particular skill but we do not have that kind of position, they can still apply and Family Wealth Council (FWC)/ Board and Human Resources will consider the possibility.

Supervision of direct descendants will be avoided whenever possible. Parents should not be direct supervisors of their children.

Standards of performance are expected to increase annually as defined by the industry and Strategic Plan

Project positions can be considered—that is, 6- month promotion campaign—family member can interview for this if they wish. This is the kind of position that we do not believe is a 12-month full-time.

Employment Policies for Family Members (This Generation and Future Generations)

Entrance Policies and Processes

Clear job description and responsibilities must be ritten.

Open positions are shared within family community. If any family member is interested, then they should talk to their branch and head of the family council (Godfather). If reasonable, then they should talk with human resources. Whenever possible, several candidates should be considered for each position.

Through intergenerational dialogue, the family protocol or constitution should include all policies regarding family conflict, family wealth, and family business. It can include any family business issues that have been or could become deeply conflictive. Some families include policies on spouses working in the business, conflicts of interest, how to leave the employ and ownership of the business, performance review of family members, and so on. This is where “the rubber meets the road!” The key is that the policies are formed as a team. This paves the way for future collaborative decision-making when there is more than one majority owner.

Competencies Transformative Family Business Consultants Need

Family business consulting is a very specialized field, and the knowledge and skills required to create successful change are unique to this form of consulting. In general, the transformative consultant needs a high degree of understanding in consulting skills and a fairly broad range of knowledge, which will be specified in this next section. As one might expect, competencies come from the various fields of family business, family dynamics, organization development, individual development, and business. This section describes some of the unique skills needed such as communication, empathy, conflict resolution, and family dynamics as well as business competencies, succession planning, governance, and group facilitation.

Knowledge Needed

Those who wish to act as a catalyst and guide for systemic transformation of family business systems will need an array of knowledge and skills. As this is a relatively new field, most advisors come from other fields, many of which can be enormously helpful. You are strongly encouraged to read Daryl Connor's (2019) chapter in this *Handbook,* particularly the sections on High Impact Consulting, Presence, and Authenticity. In general, it is most helpful have at least a basic knowledge and understanding of the following:

Communication, empathy, and conflict resolution skills—consultants should have a firm grasp of effective communication, empathy, and win–win conflict resolution skills as these are part of the foundation pieces of any healthy relationship (Stone et al. 1999). From my perspective, the consultant needs to be able to model open and effective communication, empathic regard for all members of the family, and the ability to resolved conflicts from a win–win perspective.

Family dynamics and legacy—Consultants should have at least a basic understanding of various models of family therapy such as Satir (1972), Framo (1992), and with particular attention to Bowen's work (Bowen 2004). Understanding the family's particular and unique history is of great importance as it sets a number of the norms that judge acceptable and unacceptable behavior and attitudes. An exploration with the older generation, their family background sets the context, which may be unconscious in younger generations.

Family business dynamics and legacy—Embedded in the life history of the family will be the life history of the business. The consultant, like a good investigative reporter, should raise questions in how the family business came to be. Looking at critical incidents in the development of the family business allows the family and the consultant to build an in-depth understanding of the particular strengths and learning the business leaders had to do in order not only to survive but also to thrive. By understanding how the business overcame key obstacles helps both the family and consultant to understand the soul and character of the family business. This sets the foundation for understanding the values that the family business was built on and whether they believe the same values or other ones serves the goals of the family business today and in the future.

Organization development, team development, and change theory—The field of organization development has a number of tools that can be very helpful for the consultant as they facilitate a proactive approach not only in strategy but also in creating a collaborative culture and team-building. If there are several family participants in the next generation working in the business, then their ability to become an effective team is crucial. In order to thrive, all systems will need to evolve or change. The form of leadership often shifts from autocratic to collaborative. The family ownership moves from perhaps one majority person to a second-generation team of owners/future owners. Individual growth needs also shift as family members age. There is a wealth of literature on Change Theory—see Recommended Reading at the end of this chapter.

Business and leadership—Consultants must have a reasonable understanding of business in general and at least a basic understanding of the industry and its business challenges. The distribution industry finds much different challenges than the restaurant industry. The consultant should have the knowledge that one acquires in any Masters of Business Administration (MBA) program in order to understand the business challenges their client(s) are facing, also practical business knowledge. The consultant should have a good grasp of leadership style and its impact on family and organizational culture such as (Block 1991) and (Covey 2007). More references are provided in the Recommended Reading List.

Governance, protocols, and board(s) of directors—Most family businesses particularly as they face moving from one generation to the next must carefully determine how decisions will be made. This is usually referred to as "Governance Structure." Most family businesses for legal and other reasons create a board of directors; however, many of these are deeply ineffective (Silverman 2011). The family business consultant must have an understanding of governance structures of family businesses and whether or not they are effective. Most family business find that they need much more than just a board of directors (Ward 1987) and (Gersick et al. 1997). The family business consultant needs a clear understanding of both formal and informal decision-making processes and the ability to help the family business set up the appropriate structures for their situation. Helping the family understand their own governance needs and structures that are in alignment with their values is a critical area of knowledge that the consultant can provide. Besides the academic knowledge in governance structures, the consultant should have a strong understanding in family protocols and constitution and the ability to help the family determine their own governance and conflict resolution mechanisms.

As mentioned earlier, family protocols typically include mission, vision, and values statements plus policies on all relevant family business issues. The consultant will need the skill to facilitate the family dialogue and to write or help the family write certain kinds of documents.

Individual development and emotional intelligence—An understanding of developmental psychology (Erikson 1980; Levinson 1978) and emotional intelligence (Goleman 1995) is quite helpful. Developmental psychology theory posits that all individuals face different critical challenges at different stages of their life cycle. The concept that emotional intelligence is teachable and learnable is quite important in dealing with the stress or working simultaneously in the various systems' (individual, family, and business) goals. Also, because family and critical developmental issues are faced in the family business, the emotional issues tend to be deeply magnified. For example, it is hard enough to get fired, but to get fired by your father is probably at least ten times more difficult!

Other Competencies

Besides the abovementioned cognitive skills, transformative consultants must have a deep self-knowledge. Cognitive understanding must be coupled with the individual's own inner work and understanding of his or her own individual character, family history, and family business history (if there is one). It is difficult to understand and intervene in a family system without deep self-knowledge. This is the same rationale used by psychotherapists to undergo their own personal therapy before helping others.

The following competencies are also of great importance:

Understanding expert versus *process models of consultation*—There are many forms of consultation that the client is often unaware. The major distinction is between the "Expert Model" and the "Process Model." Although the expert model may be transformation in the sense that the expert recommends certain policies or processes, at the same time, it is reinforcing the autocratic mode of intervention. Much more powerful, I believe, is the "Process Model" where the consultant sets up experiences and processes for the client to participate in and to develop their own policy. For example, there might be an issue of conflict of interest, perhaps the son of a food distributor wants to set up a restaurant utilizing his father's food. Is this a good idea? Is it fair to his brothers and sisters? Is his success maintaining a dependency on his father? The expert could intervene and say, "This is the right way to manage this issue." The process consultant would help the family to determine what governing policies are best for them.

Group facilitation skills—It will be difficult for the consultants to help the next generation to collaborate if they, themselves, do not know how to do it. Consultants must be skillful at group facilitation, have the ability to be a good team-player, and know how to collaborate with various family business teams as needed—empowering them in making decisions and actions that are in alignment with the clients' highest values and goals. A skilled consultant consciously models for the family the ability to dialogue constructively to sensitive and emotional issues, and he or she builds trust and hope in the family's confidence in completing this process.

Presentation, contracting, and synthesizing skills—The consultant will need reasonably strong presentation, contract, and synthesizing skills. Presentation skills are the ability to present research and knowledge in the various areas they are working on such as succession, core values, protocol policies, leadership, and so on. All consultation requires a contract between the consultant and the client. The consultant must be able to contract the work and fees in a way that is clear and fair. Many times the consultant will be facilitating discussion and development of policies on wide range of topics. The consultant must be able to synthesize discussion of family members in ways that all feel understood and, if possible, affirmed.

Trust building and ability to form therapeutic alliance with the clients—The consultant is in a very special role with the client. In order to work effectively, the consultant must gain the trust of the family members. The consultant will be working with extremely delicate and emotional material of some of the most important issues in the clients' lives. In order for the family members to share openly, they must have a high amount of trust in the consultant and feel that the consultant will act in the best interest of the client. In psychological terms, the consultant must build a therapeutic alliance with the client.

Ethics—The consultant must act in accordance with high moral values and ethics as defined by the field and in no way utilize privileged information for personal gain or to take advantage of any family member. The industry standard code of ethics for family business consultants can be found at the Family Firm Institute's webpage www.ffi.org.

Ability to facilitate conflict resolution between family members—All families have differences and will have conflict with each other at various times. The critical question is how the family members resolve conflicts. The consultant will need skills and knowledge in how to help the family resolve conflicts in a way that both parties feel understood, acknowledged, and that a reasonable process has been set in place for the resolution of conflicts. This is key for the long-term success of the family business.

Summary—The family business transformative consultant needs a to earn the trust of the whole family and family business system—no small feat! By avoiding a technician perspective, pursuing the primary issues, and creating a safe environment where deeply sensitive issues can be brought up and confronted in alignment with the family's highest values, the consultant will facilitate the building of deeper trust and hope within the system. As the trust between the family members increases, the need for consultation will decrease. Great consultants transfer their knowledge in such a way that they are no longer needed.

Family Businesses Need Transformative Consultants

In this chapter, we have looked at the need for transformation in the family business. Utilizing a systemic lens, we looked at particular difficulties family businesses often face and the kinds of interventions that can bring healing and transformation. The author then specified the kinds of skills and knowledge that would be most helpful to the consultant.

The transformative family business consultant must provide an environment that allows for deep confrontation and resolution of the deeper wounds in all the major systems so that all systems can evolve to their next level of beauty and maturity and adapt to the evolutionary growth challenges confronting them. In many cases, this is done best by a team of advisors who work together in the client's best interest.

The need is great! Consultants who help the family business transform are able to facilitate individual maturity and resilience in the family, as well as enhance family and wealth sustainability to present family members and to future generations.

References

Block P (1991) The empowered manager. Jossey-Bass, San Francisco

Bowen M (2004) Family therapy in clinical practice. Rowman & Littleton Publishers, Oxford

Carlock RS, Ward JL (2001) Strategic planning for the family business: parallel planning to unify the family and business. Palgrave Books, New York

Connor D (2019) It's not what you do, it's who you are. In: Neal J (ed) Handbook of personal and organizational transformation. Springer Publishers

Covey S (2007) How to develop your family mission statement. Simon & Schuster Audio, New York

Danco L (1990) Someday it'll all be … who's? The lighter side of the family business. University Press and Jamieson Press, Cleveland

Erikson EH (1980) Identity and the life cycle. W.W. Norton & Co, New York

Framo JL (1992) Family of origin therapy: an intergenerational approach. Routledge, New York

Gersick KE, Davis JA, Hampton MMC, Lansberg I (1997) Generation to generation: life cycles of the family business. Harvard Business School Press, Boston

Goleman D (1995) Emotional intelligence: why it can matter more then IQ. Bantam Books, New York

Hubler T (2020) Family's preparedness and effectiveness. https://www.hublerfamilybusiness.com/free-assessment.html

Hughes JJ (2004) Family wealth: keeping it in the family. Bloomberg Press, Princeton

Jaffe D (1991) Working with the ones you love: strategies for a successful family business. Conari Press, Berkeley

Lansberg I (1999) Succeeding generations: realizing the dream of families in business. Harvard Business School Press, Boston

Levinson DJ (1978) The seasons of a man's life. Random House Publishing Group, New York

Satir V (1972) People making. Science & Behavior Books, New York

Silverman MA (2011) An evolutionary model of family business boards. Family Business of Family Firm Institute

Stone D, Patton BP, Heen S, Fisher R (1999) Difficult conversations: how to discuss what matters most. Penguin Books, New York

Ward JL (1987) Keeping the family business healthy: how to plan for continuity, growth, profitability, and family leadership. Jossey-Bass, San Francisco

Company Rituals: A Valid Management Tool in the Organizational Field

9

Roberta Sferrazzo and Renato Ruffini

Abstract

Interpersonal relationships are fundamental both in the private and in the organizational sphere. They must be managed with a strong respect since people can remain wounded and blessed by the other. In companies, there are specific organizational tools that can contribute to transform personal wounds into relational blessings, that is, the organizational rituals. Rituals, indeed, are able to strengthen relational bonds and increase the sense of cohesion among people belonging to the same organization. However, companies are not always aware of rituals' presence or are not able to adequately manage their own rituals. This could happen when—rather than facilitating the transformation of a wound into blessing—control mechanisms exercised within companies generate manipulation practices that ruin relationships. Given this picture, we think that recognizing spontaneous rituals within an organization—through specific managerial leverages—could help to overcome relational wounds and to create an environment favorable to people's well-being.

Keywords

Blessings · Control · Docility · Interpersonal relationships · Learning · Manipulation · Rites · Rituals · Teaching · Wounds

R. Sferrazzo (✉)
Department of Organization Studies & Ethics, Nantes, France
e-mail: rsferrazzo@audencia.com

R. Ruffini
Department of Juridical Sciences "Cesare Beccaria", Università degli Studi di Milano, Milan, Italy
e-mail: renato.ruffini@unimi.it

J. Neal (ed.), *Personal, Educational and Organizational Transformation*, Future of Business and Finance, https://doi.org/10.1007/978-3-031-29253-8_9

Introduction

In the book of Genesis' (Gen 32), Jacob was both wounded and blessed by the angel at the same time. After the blessing, the angel said to him: "Your name will no longer be Jacob, but it will be Israel" (he fights with El—God). A new man is born after the fight, taking on the name of a people. This famous Bible episode is important as it stresses the relational problem among people and highlights the dynamic nature of relations, a constant oscillation between encounter and clash, aggression and trusting abandonment, where there are not any winners nor losers. Furthermore, it highlights how, in every relationship, we can find some mysterious zones that are part of the other person whom we have to accept and respect. Substantially, this episode shows how in every relationship both relational wounds (disappointment, frustration, rage, and rancor) and blessings are created.

The interpersonal relations theme is fundamental both in the economic and in the managerial field. In economic studies, starting from Smith's publication of *The Theory of Moral Sentiments in 1759* (Smith 1976), interpersonal relations have been included within the concept of "exchange," which leads people not to get contaminated by the others, creating a culture of immunity (Bruni 2020). In the fundamental formulation that was given by Smith, the exchange allows the absence of moral intentions in economic relations and has a dual utility: It makes the subjects equal and free from one another and creates wealth among individuals and nations. However, at the same time, it implies that interpersonal relations are irrelevant for economic activity. According to Smith (1976), the correctness of these relations is given as implicit and necessary, as it is based on moral sentiments of "sympathy" among people.

The interpersonal relations theme is central also in managerial and organizational activity, but management activity has been strongly influenced by the logic background of classical economics, relegating much of managerial thought to techniques and rational economic tools that are oriented to create incentive systems and interest alignment in the organizational field and to develop leadership logics. However, the technicalization of human relations, within the current managerial logic, represents a reductionist simplification that dilutes and disperses the complexity and the relational wealth among people. In particular, despite the importance of managerial techniques, they are not able to manage the equilibrium between the organization and its people, inducing in employees' situations of psychological and personal sufferance, making them feel manipulated, forced into a position they dislike, exploiting their potentialities, not recognizing their contribution. This feeling has negative effects also in business activity, especially in the current period, where the immaterial and increasingly sophisticated forms of production require strong participation on behalf of individuals, so far as to reach self-organization forms. In other words, using the biblical metaphor of Jacob, organizations, which are relational places, continuously create "wounds" to individuals that are not adequately managed and balanced by those "blessings" that are fundamental for the professional and personal growth of people.

Considering these observations, our main research question is the following: Why cannot relational wounds that are created in organizations become blessings? Out of metaphor, the question can also be formulated in this way: How can interpersonal relations be managed in the organizational context maintaining the equilibrium between individual and organization? Through this work, we would like to try to set up a research path that can advance the knowledge about the dynamics of interpersonal processes in institutions. In particular, all through the chapter, we will analyze the role that the management of rituals plays in coping with the interpersonal relationship phenomenon within organizations.

Theoretical Background

The Interpersonal Relations Phenomenon

Interpersonal relations are a set of moral, political, and social norms and customs based on individual and group behaviors. They constitute the microfoundation of institutional theory through which the relationship between individual and organization can be read (Powell and Colyvas 2008). Within this theoretical framework, the managerial techniques (such as budgeting processes, evaluation systems, and programming and control activities) constitute a privileged field where the cognitive foundations of institutional logics of the firm are created and on which the link between individual level and organizational level is based. The different contributions related to interpersonal relations, understood as microfoundations of the institutional analysis, highlight that individual behaviors tend toward forms of conformism to organizational praxis and that anxiety control constitutes the more generalized motivation of human conduct. Indeed, one of the reasons why, here, we have decided to rediscover the ritual dynamics in the organizational context is related to this anxiety factor. In particular, in the article "Don't stop believing: Rituals improve performance by decreasing anxiety" (Brooks et al. 2016) the authors demonstrated that rituals emerge when people experience anxiety and that rituals, that are connected to a broader belief system (such as religious rituals), reduce anxiety for those who subscribe to that belief system. According to the authors, there are four reasons that explain why rituals reduce anxiety:

(a) As the repetitive actions may satisfy the need for order
(b) As rituals could serve as a form of distraction, blocking negative thoughts
(c) As the symbolic value of a ritual may provide a buffer against threat and anxiety
(d) As rituals function as a type of placebo

Furthermore, one of the characteristic features of interpersonal relations is that their development is linked to a "ritual interaction" (Goffman 1967), that is through "face games" that have the aim to save face by avoiding embarrassing situations. Every interlocutor is interested in saving his own face and others' faces, and in this sense, a tacit collaboration toward the same goal may arise, even though everyone has different interests to achieve. If on the one hand ritual interactions can create equilibrium between individuals and the organization, at the same time, they can easily generate a culture of immunity (Bruni 2020), by creating a false and formal organizational environment.

Moved by this puzzle, we assume that managerial techniques, which tend to regulate and to control the production processes, favor forms of ritual interactions and could have an imposed ritual content through the internal bureaucracy. Starting from this assumption, we propose these two hypotheses:

(a) Managerial practices can easily create "wounds" in companies when they are imposed through formal procedures and control.
(b) Spontaneous rituals in companies are useful to foster interpersonal relationships at work, by creating a sense of cohesion and community among people belonging to the same organization.

To find some common points between managerial practices and rituals, we must necessarily talk about the origin of rites and rituals in the human history. Within this theoretical framework, we will try to answer our research question and our propositions, borrowing from sociological and theological analysis and from elaborations that constitute the organizational action of people also in secular contexts.

Rituals Studies in Different Fields

Etymologically, the term "rite" derives from the Sanskrit "Rta," that is a fundamental concept for the Vedic religion, as it means that all the individuals, the society, the sacred action, and the cosmos must conform to a specific order. If these things deviate from the rite, they risk breaking the order itself. Therefore, the rite represents what conforms to the order. This conception of the rite is not limited to indigenous people. We find it in all religions. The efficacy of a sacred action depends on the inexpensive execution of the rite. An important argument of discussion for scholars concerns the distinction and the link between rites and myths. Indeed, we know that the rites and the myths are present in the culture and religion of various populations, but it is the rite that marks their cultures.

The study of the rite was analyzed in depth by anthropologists, sociologists, and psychologists, as it concerns collective processes and exchange relations. Below, we resume the main rituals' analyses in the different disciplines.

Psychological Field From a psychological point of view, Freud identified the totem with the father figure, and he believed that through rites there is an emergence into the consciousness of some dynamics sedimented into the unconscious (2001: 116–187). Despite differences of thought between Freud and Jung, in this context, they had the same opinion. In a second phase, psychoanalytic studies moved through a relational paradigm, as we can see in other studies.

Anthropological Field Talking about the anthropological studies related to rites, we can affirm that much research has been conducted, especially if we take into consideration the social function and the cultural valence of the rite itself within various populations. The anthropologist Malinowski, through his research, discovered that people tend to satisfy, beyond their primary needs (biological needs and needs shared with other species), also the needs related to the transmission of information and abilities generated in a population. He also recognized the presence of a third type of need, that is, a higher need that is related to the emotional sphere, based on sentiments and relations of trust with other people. According to Malinowski (1948), the religion, through its rites, tries to satisfy these higher needs. Therefore, if religion responds to the need for social cohesion, it appears obvious that it uses public ceremonies and rites.

According to Durkheim in *The Elementary Forms of the Religious Life*, we can understand religion only starting from its origins and its primitive forms. For this reason, he started his studies in Australian tribes and discovered a strong link between religion and society (Durkheim 1961). In Durkheim's thought, there are no specific reasons for the creation of a rite, but it rises in a spontaneous way; in addition, at the center of a rite, there are no specific motivations or references to specific contents, but there is the need to gather and do an action together (Durkheim 1961).

Anthropologist Van Gennep's research demonstrated how many human societies have faced change through rites that have accompanied the passage from a situation to another—"rites of passage" (Van Gennep 1961). Anthropologist Turner evaluated Van Gennep's studies and found in the rites of passage the fundamental model of rituality. Turner (1988) stated that in modern conscience cognition, idea and rationality were dominant, but with postmodern turning, cognition was at the same level of volition and affection.

The concept of "limen" is fundamental in rites, and Turner, adding to Van Gennep's work, recognized in the rites of passage the separation game between the society and the following rehabilitation in it. More specifically, the rites of passage imply three main phases: (a) the separation from the social structure; (b) the entrance in the anti-structure, defined by Turner as the "communitas"; and (c) the rehabilitation in the ordinary social context (Turner 1991: 94–95). If on the one hand in the social structure relations are managed by some impersonal norms, in the communitas, that is, in the anti-structural phase, people live relations in a more direct way.

According to this conception, the rite leads again to the original process of civil cohabitation, reinforcing social relationships. This particular phenomenon underlines the fact that the rite reinforces the social structure and acts in the communitas' anti-structure. Thus, in case of a crisis that can undermine the social context, the human communities react by applying some rites as strategies to overcome a disaggregation danger. These strategies require a liminal phase based on the exit from the social life to solve problems and contradictions (Turner 1991). Trice and Beyer in their research did a comparison between Van Gennep's rites of passage and changes in role and status that happen in organizations, such as: persons entering occupations, supervisory selection and training, retirement ceremonials, and so on (1984: 657–658).

Sociological Studies Moving on to sociological studies, we find that they are similar to the anthropological ones. The most famous study of religion and rituals is that of Weber, in particular, *The Sociology of Religion* (Weber 1963). Both the study of religion and the study of rituals have been conducted by Weber in a sociological manner, considering collective relations born in old and modern cultures. Weber pointed out that the power of structure is based on stability and contrasts with the charisma that tends to subvert this functional plan; he described the relationship between charisma and institutions as that of a power that can subvert orders and that concerns every vital field. The charismatic momentum is neither controllable nor predictable, it is an extraordinary puissance, so necessarily extra-economic, but threatened for its virulence and threatening in its virulence as soon as the interests of daily economic life prevail. In the long run, the institution would not survive if it was not revitalized by the individuality of the charisma, and it would lose its humanity by crushing its members; "wounds" would just be wounds and would not take on any form of blessing. Charisma puissance can also lead to mortal wounds, and the revitalization of the institution can leave a death trail behind. As when a new charismatic leader comes to the forefront of the organization, sure it revitalizes it but at a high price when the consequences, such as factory closure, transfer or elimination of production lines, or reduction of staff, are taken into consideration. According to Weber, the tension between charisma and institutions is the tension that is created between ideal and real, both necessary, albeit opposite, to maintain the vitality of every community.

In the social studies field, rites have also been studied independently from their religious referent, considering ritual behaviors, the involvement of corporeality, and the logic of exchange as very important ritual features in social relations and interpersonal ones. We can think, for example, of Goffman's research related to face games (mentioned above) and to those microsocial dynamics that cross the daily life of the members of a community (Goffman 1967).

Neuroscientific Field Going to the neuroscientific field, some neuroscientists (c.f., Rappaport 1999) discovered that ritual behavior has some effects on:

(a) The central nervous system, in the sense that it tends to diminish the dominion of the left hemisphere, linked to rationality, and to valorize the right hemisphere, linked to emotionality.
(b) The entire central nervous system, through other parts of the body.

In other terms, the repetitive and rhythmic nature of rituals seems to be very important, because the rhythm of rituals enters into the biological rhythm of people. The rite, through the prevalence of the right hemisphere, linked to the emotional sphere, suspends the analytical and descriptive modality of reality (related to rationality) and favors a modality that is linked to a sense of belonging to reality, that is a holistic modality (related to sacred).

Cognitive Field In the cognitive approach, attention is especially posed on the relation between the rite and the ability of the mind. Burkert claimed that rites are religious strategies with the aim to control body behavior and decrease anxiety through biological schemes of actions, reactions, and sentiments (Burkert 1996). Deepening the relation between rite and culture through rituals, people interlace their body (linked to biological processes) with the collective body that we can identify with society and that is linked to cultural processes. Bell highlights that this intersection between the individual and the community is possible as the rite manages the body and makes people able to share values and group behaviors (Bell 2009).

Given this literature analysis, in the next paragraph, we will explore why managing rituals in organizations is so difficult and how to overcome the related problems. In particular, we will examine the managerial control aspect more in depth, so as to distinguish between a negative form of control and a positive one, to which rituals are strongly connected.

Discovering Wounds

Why Wounds in Organizations?

Corporate organizations are places where there is a continuous creation of wounds that, if not adequately tackled, do not have the balancing of "blessings" which are useful for the professional and personal development of people. For organizational "wounds," we mean all those manipulative and coercive forms exercised toward workers by their bosses. Specifically, wounds are created by wrong control practices perpetuated by managers. Control practices, indeed, are directed to correct any distorted behavior that the subject does compared to the pursued aim. They can constitute a "violent" action if they intervene in the spontaneous practice of a person, so against the freedom of the person itself. As the person establishes some personal aims, a control operation is such to induce a practice which does not correspond to the purposes that were set by the person.

There are many cases where controls that are exercised through procedures, rules, and relations are not clear in their purpose or limit individual's actions in situations where "entrepreneurship" and "autonomy" are required. A possible cause of the creation of relational "wounds" can derive from some phenomena of "double level of communication" (Watzlavick 1967) within the organization. There is the activation of a double communication when the subjects, who relate to each other, develop simultaneous transactions that are composed by a "social" level that is explicitly visible for those who are part of the transaction or for those who assist to it. At the same time, a slimmer transaction is fed, less evident, and partially implicit but perceptible and of a psychological nature (Berne 1964). This transaction transmits the real meaning of the communication. Paradoxically, the level of awareness of the two levels of communication for the two involved parties can be very high, and even though the psychological level is not apparently considered, it is that which determines the result of the communication. If courtship is the virtuous version, the critical allusion is what in the company usually produces major wounds.

Another source of wounds could be the organizational culture adopted within a company. Trice and Beyer said that culture "has two basic components: (1) its substance or the networks of meanings contained in its ideologies, norms, and values; and (2) its forms or the practices whereby these meanings are expressed, affirmed, and communicated to members" (1984: 654). Furthermore, they said that "several analysts [...] have argued that strong organizational cultures help to produce effective organizations. Strong cultures, they explain, give meaning and direction to organizational members' efforts" (1984: 665). Agreeing with this vision, we think that organizational culture can be a source of wounds as well if it is not homogeneous within the organizational context. What is a virtuous behavior in a company, in others can become a source of strong discomfort. Different organizational cultures can produce wounds but can also constitute a favorable ground for blessings.

Finally, the phenomenon of the relational wound can derive from the personal features of individuals. Psychology helps us identify personality features and visions of the world that make an individual more fragile compared to another and more sensitive to wounds. Different visions of the world, influenced by the culture where a person has grown, can be confirmed, amplified, or contained by the organizational culture in which a person works. People with a personality structure that always tends to self-relieve and that tends to project outside negative components can act as wound inflictors, without being able to grasp the teachings and the blessings that their wounds could have produced. Managerial discipline has always put a great deal of confidence and hope in the psychological investigation, through different schools of thought, to face wounds inflicted by organizational dynamics, analyzing case by case. We must not forget that this bipolar or multipolar relationship between people and organizations always takes place within a culture, which can change direction, transforming a wound into a blessing or a wound into vengeance. Wound creation mechanisms are a very complex phenomenon, widespread and connected to relational action, in particular in organizations. Therefore, the problem does not derive from the fact that there is the creation of "wounds," but from the fact that these often do not generate "blessings," which means that the organizational environment does not help people to generate blessings from wounds. In such cases, the organization becomes a source of discomfort for lots of people. Thus, it is very important to understand how to create an organizational environment that can facilitate the creation of "blessings" from wounds. To generate this environment that is favorable to employee well-being and to overcome relational wounds, we think that recognizing spontaneous rites and rituals in organizations could be a possible way. In the next paragraph, we will explain some of the reasons why we have this opinion, starting from the overcoming of manipulative control practices within companies.

The Distorted Effects of Control Systems

When negative events happen to a person and the internal relational processes listed above (control, interpersonal communication processes, culture, and personal weaknesses) are not able to support the person, giving meaning to his/her situation, then the wound happens. In brief, the wound consists of a situation in which the subjects, for objective or subjective reasons, feel injured or their dignity threatened without having any particular means of defense. All in all, the main common factor among the aforementioned causes of relational wounds within the organizational context is strongly connected to the control factor, which we will analyze in further depth in what follows.

In economics, we can find a strong emphasis on control. Menger (1963) attributes three main goals to economics: explanation, prediction, and control. This means that economists intend to interpret past events, to anticipate future events and to provide recipes for favorable interventions in the economy. This way of thinking is not so different from that of those who run companies. In human resource management practices, control is the main tool for managing organizations, as it "aligns employee capabilities, activities and performance with organizational goals and aspirations" (Sitkin et al. 2010: 3). Different controls and human resource management practices are used to reach these objectives: (a) outcome/output control, focused on reaching goals; (b) process controls, concerned with compliance with procedures; and (c) normative controls, oriented toward congruence among employees. However, nowadays it is possible to observe an increasing of impositions in the workplace. In a sense, we can talk about forms of violence, to be considered not as physical attacks toward somebody, but as psychological problems inflicted on somebody. In particular, we can observe violence in control systems when they rely on manipulative or coercive tactics. Indeed, process controls can be coercive insofar as they constrain behavior according to standardized rules and procedures.

In the organizational context, this attitude can be associated to what Alvesson and Spicer (2012) call "functional stupidity," that is, "the inability and/or unwillingness to use cognitive and reflective capacities in anything other than narrow and circumspect ways. It involves a lack of reflexivity, a disinclination to require or provide justification, and avoidance of substantive reasoning" (1201). Sometimes, tactics of "symbolic manipulation" (based on persuasion and seduction) are adopted to reach functional stupidity within organizations (Alvesson and Spicer 2012).

Through the rituals' lens, we can look for alternative forms to reach a specific end in organizations through learning processes rather than through control instruments. In what follows, we put the accent especially on the docility factor, which is strongly related to organizational rituals. Indeed, an alternative way to align companies' objectives and employees' ones consists of enhancing learning practices through the development of docility.

Today, in managerial practices, we can find some problems related to control systems insofar as they are exercised in a violent way. Starting from the past, it was possible to observe violent actions toward employees when the worker was considered "so stupid that the word 'percentage' has no meaning to him" (Taylor 1911:

59). Subsequently, in the mid-1960s, employees' management moved from punishment schemes to rewarding criteria. This happened when theory Y, based on carrot and reward, substituted for theory X, related to punishment and stick (McGregor 1960). After, following a positivist track, the same regimes used for natural science were transferred to management studies. Finally, by the late 1980s, when the management field was fully established, a new field—called critical management studies (CMS)—emerged, in order to critique the traditional management logics (Klikauer 2015). Although CMS approves of the capitalist profit system and is occupied with for-profit organizations, it criticizes the misuse of people inside organizations. Moreover, several scholars highlighted that CMS's telos is "micro-emancipation, the production of better managers, good management, shaping organisations to become fairer, and the idea that management's social engineering can be balanced" (Klikauer 2015: 207).

Managerial control is the main practice of manipulation exercised by managers. Indeed, control practices are created with the intent to correct distorted behavior. As mentioned before, some scholars (Alvesson and Spicer 2012) talk about forms of "symbolic manipulation" concerning managers which try to shape employees' psychological, emotional, and moral orientations. In particular, Fox (1974) distinguished between spontaneous and manipulated forms of "consensus." If, on the one hand, spontaneous forms of consensus originate when all individuals are moved by a common aim, on the other hand, manipulated consensus arises when one group has the institutional power to achieve its own interest.

Recent CMS studies prove how management is manipulative and how managers have the tendency to manipulate employees, especially in managing their emotions and behaviors, generating an alteration of their authenticity, culture, identity, heart, mind, and soul (Cunliffe 2014) or privileging some groups over others (Kunda 1992). In a sense, culture can become a strategic tool for control and manipulation. This can happen: (a) by using language, for example, by attaching several labels to specific occupations or grades; (b) through the use of symbols, such as expensive logos or big companies' headquarters; (c) by using rituals, such as ceremonies; and finally d) through sponsored myths.

But to what extent is it morally acceptable to limit employees' freedom asking them to behave in a certain way? Cunliffe (2014) argues that to overcome the problem of manipulation, managers should be relational and reflexive. Relational managers understand that we live not in an isolated way but in relation to others, and we try to adapt our identity to others through dialogical relationships. Reflexivity is based on the interconnection between dialogue and action, so reflexive managers should question how they relate to others and should be open to different vision of the world and to dialogue. In summary, according to Cunliffe (2014), relational and reflective managers question organizational and control practices and look for the arising of new forms of collaborative and inclusive realities.

Bardon and Borzillo (2016) showed, through their qualitative research, that employees can experience autonomy and control both in negative and/or positive ways, for different reasons. On the one hand, employees are happy when they are free to take actions they want without asking management for permission. On the other hand, the lack of control on participation and engagement is risky when individuals do not carry off their part of work. Furthermore, some people feel safe insofar as they rest in their comfort zone; conversely, autonomy can be destabilizing for the organization.

For what concerns control, on the one hand, some individuals feel grateful to their managers insofar as, for example, they monitor if their rhythm of work proceeds well, so exercising a reassuring function; on the other hand, other people can feel censored in developing their initiatives by their coaches, so generating demotivation in employees.

Looking at these studies, we can say that a good way to exercise a nonviolent control in organizations could be to find a good balance between control practices and autonomy. In this way, employees are guaranteed with the sufficient freedom and space they need to spread their innovative potential within organizations, and this can be a good occasion to them to grow both as people and as workers. We will treat this balance mechanism in control practices in the next section, introducing also a different tool of alignment, the teaching one.

Alternative Forms of Control and Teaching Practices

In the attempt to look for new forms of control within organizations, we must put our attention on the "New Forms of Work Organization" (NFWO) (Longoni et al. 2014) that are widespread in our days as a post-bureaucratic phenomenon. In the NFWO, we can observe a decreasing of control practices and an increasing of trust among employer and employees, such as in the participatory model of management, the third type of company, the ad-hocracy and the mission organization models, the model of agile management, the holacracy model, and liberated companies.

According to Bains (2007), individuality and authenticity should be fostered and encouraged within companies as "when people are happy and have the freedom to be themselves, they are more productive and give more of themselves" (241). In relation to this, new forms of normative control strategies emerged to overcome the dysfunctions of conventional organizational controls. This happened, for example, in call centers, where an overt control could impede the "just be yourself" approach, necessary to personalize customer service interaction (Fleming and Sturdy 2011). Indeed, in call centers, conventional forms of control can undermine individuals' personal touches and authenticity, because they are based on regimentation (technical control), standardization (bureaucratic control), and normalization (cultural controls) (Fleming and Sturdy 2011). Deepening the dysfunctions of these three forms of conventional controls, respectively: (a) technical control generates alienating effect; (b) normative control produces anti-authoritarian gestures; and (c) cultural control develops inauthenticity insofar as individuals feel forced to recognize themselves with the company's beliefs and values.

Some studies highlight the positive outcomes of "soft" normative controls, rather than of "hard" coercive control, insofar as employees can move in a "friendly environment" (Kinnie et al. 2000) and are guaranteed with opportunities for creativity and augmented well-being and satisfaction. For example, Fleming and Sturdy (2011), through their qualitative research in a call center, described an organizational environment able to overcome control dysfunctions applying the "just be yourself" philosophy. This approach allowed employees to freely release their social and emotional skills, leaving them the possibility to personalize their conversations with the clients, and obtaining, in this way, good results. Indeed, in this context, other forms of control could be counterproductive.

Looking at these studies, we can affirm that, on the one hand, control is necessary to guarantee the good functioning of the organization, but, on the other hand, it must be exercised assuring freedom's spaces to employees, that is, leaving them autonomy and giving them trust.

Trying to answer to our initial question, we identify also an alternative form, different from control practices, to align the ideal end and the fixed end of a company, that is, teaching practices. This system can arise insofar as people are willing to learn and are inserted in a teaching dynamic that leads them to autonomy.

There is a small grey area between control practices and the teaching's ones that is the training area. If the emphasis is bigger on the output to obtain, then the result will be control. Conversely, if there is a major emphasis for what concerns the status, then the result will be teaching. In comparison to control practices, the teaching system never risks becoming violent. Therefore, managers and leaders should consider it as a potential instrument of alignment within organizations, both for the good of employees and of the organization itself.

If leaders and managers enhance organizational rituals through a docility factor, they allow people to learn in a collective way. Moreover, in this case, a reciprocal mechanism of learning can arise. Indeed, docility allows the development of people's skill to be ready to be taught, both in the case of bosses and workers. Indeed, an alternative way to align companies' objectives and employees' ones consists of enhancing learning practices through the development of docility. In the management literature, there are not so many studies related to docility, but this concept has a very long tradition.

Etymologically, the meaning of docility is related to the Latin *docere*—to teach—which differs from the colloquial use of the adjective "docile," used to denote a passive, submissive, obedient educable, and easily taught person. Indeed, Aquinas (1947) talked about docility as the virtue of *studiositas*, related to the willingness to learn from others, claiming that "the term 'studiousness,' which properly regards knowledge, is applied to all the virtues" (Summa Theologiae, II-II, q. 166, a. 2, ad. 1).

Several authors have discussed docility in literature. Simon (1976), in particular, identified docility as one of the psychological elements of organizational learning. Indeed, he defined docility as "the human propensity for accepting information and advice that comes through social channels" (Simon 1976: 95). His definition is similar to Secchi and Bardone's ones, who studied docility through an experimental investigation. From the results obtained, they modified Simon's definition as follows: "Docility is the tendency to depend on suggestions, perceptions, comments, and to gather information from other individuals on the one hand, and to 'provide' information on the other" (2009, p. 8). In such a kind of relationship, the freedom factor plays a fundamental role and deserves a particular attention.

Freedom and Control Practices In the managerial and business ethics literature, there are many conceptualizations regarding the freedom topic. Focusing on the concept of negative freedom and positive freedom (Dierksmeier and Pirson 2010) allows us to better explain the connection between freedom and control practices within organizations. The concept of negative freedom consists in the maximum possible reduction of limits or constraints placed on a subject, another individual, group, or society. In this case, freedom is that area of action that an individual can take without being deliberately and legally obstructed by others. Practically, this concept of freedom is related not so much to the legal structure of the company but rather to the area of exercise of the ways in which individuals are controlled.

Starting from these premises, in many cases, the concept of negative freedom tends to be confused with the operational modalities of dialectical conflict management, such as forms of industrial democracy, participation, emancipation of workers, and similar initiatives. These connections between people and organization, even if positive in themselves, can still hide manipulative if not coercive forms of control. However, individuals may respond differently to manipulative practices, as well as to the presence of constraints. As we will see in a moment, only a qualitative and positive vision of freedom can consider these aspects because it focuses on individual development and self-empowerment. Indeed, freedom conceived in positive terms implies individuals' desire to be masters of themselves. Therefore, it is a question of the quality of freedom and not of mere quantity (reduction of constraints). This idea of freedom is closely linked to subjects' ability to exercise critical reason, which allows them to distinguish between what is necessary and what is contingent. This vision of freedom is qualitative, in as much as it fosters the development of people "capabilities" who are free to be what they really want to be in their lives (Sferrazzo and Ruffini 2021).

In management and organizational literature, the topic of freedom is not clearly practically defined. However, it seems that the model treated by academics and practitioners of the organizational context implies only the vision of negative freedom, that is, oriented toward removing the maximum of constraints. For example, we can see this phenomenon in the companies' attempt to reduce the bureaucratic elements, without considering why several bureaucratic structures are necessary for the well-functioning of companies (Parker 2002).

The vision of positive freedom, in which finalism is focused only on the development of the person, is in our opinion the only one that can really solve the manipulation and control problem. In other words, we are talking about such a kind of humanization of managerial practices as an alternative to the mechanistic approaches of management. In brief, we think that through the construction of a mutual benefit dynamics between the company and the worker, people could freely choose to submit themselves even to several hierarchical constraints, in as much as related to the construction of a mutual relationship of growth.

Moved by this puzzle, in the following paragraph, we will go more in depth in the organizational rituals topic. In particular, we will show the best mode through which organizational rituals should be managed within companies, in order to avoid manipulative or coercive control forms, taking inspiration from the notion of liturgy.

Favoring Spontaneous Rites in Organizations

Rituals in Organizations

Although there is a relative lack of work on rituals in organizations studies, some authors have already written about rituals in organizations. Islam and Zyphur consider rituals as a form of symbolic expression that takes place in organizations (Islam and Zyphur 2009). In particular, they define a ritual action as "a form of social action in which a group's values and identity are publicly demonstrated or enacted in a stylized manner, within the context of a specific occasion or event" (2009: 116). Some examples of this phenomenon include a graduation ceremony, a formal speech, or a dinner for new employees (in all these cases we face conventionalized enactments rather than spontaneous behaviors). Furthermore, according to these authors, rituals are structured to promote both stability and change and to allow individuals or groups to transition among organizational roles, to maintain organizational status, or to build solidarity within the organization. They also sustain that ritual events may originate from group members or may be management driven. In relation to this last case, Trice and Beyer said that managers:

> could profit from learning how to evaluate their rites and ceremonials in order to determine the degree to which they are achieving both desired and other consequences. Effective managers will be those who are good at making such assessments and using them to continue, modify, or discontinue ceremonial activities. A caution is in order, however. Because they arise so frequently and universally in human societies, it is doubtful that managers can be effective in suppressing popular rites and ceremonials when they want to. A better strategy would seem to be to try to domesticate them […] in such a way that their conservative consequences can be minimized. (1984: 666)

However, Trice and Beyer described in their research two types of organizational rites, that we consider close to our second research hypothesis, to reestablish equilibrium in social relations: (a) the rites of integration (such as carnival, Christmas parties, and picnics) and (b) conflict reduction rites (developed through organizational techniques, such as brainstorming, nominal groups, and the Delphi technique) (1984: 661–663).

The originality of this chapter, compared to what has been already done in literature, concerns the reasons why an organization does not recognize its rituals and does not favor the emergence of spontaneous ritual forms that can help to manage the individual–organization relation. To answer this question, we have considered the managerial practices as liturgies; rituals, in organizations, are often inserted within "liturgies" that are used to manage them.

Etymologically liturgy means "action for the populace" (from the Greek word *leitourgia*, composed by *laos*, that means "populace" and *ergon*, that means "action"). In particular, the philosopher Agamben highlighted that, in classical Greece, it indicated the obligation that the city imposed to its citizens (with a certain income) to provide for benefits of common interest, from the organization of gyms to the setting up of a choir for city parties and so on (2013: 1). Focusing on the religious field, liturgies, indicated in Latin with the word *munera*, developed in Imperial Rome starting from the third century after Christ and they refer to the service of people to god. Nowadays, liturgy is a fundamental pillar of the life of every church, as through it, the religious practice is highlighted daily and allows to institutionalize it; furthermore, through the liturgy, the history of the religious community is constantly revitalized, represented, and narrated.

Now, considering the common anthropological bases between religion and management and recognizing the appropriate differences between the two fields of human action, we can read the problem of managerial relations in business contexts through some research conducted on the liturgical theme in the field of different religions. Obviously, we easily perceive the scientific limits of operating in different disciplinary fields, but we think this could be a possible path to improve the comprehension of the dynamics of interpersonal relations in the corporate context.

In order to find a link between the religious liturgies and manipulated or spontaneous rituals that can be created in organizations, firstly we have introduced the Whitehouse's scheme, in which the religious experience is organized into two fundamental modes: the doctrinal mode and the imagistic mode (Whitehouse 2002). These modes are not types of religion, but organizational principles for the experience and the religious action; it follows that it is common for both modes to be put in practice within a single religious tradition. Secondly, we have provided a description of the characteristic elements of Christian liturgy.

The Doctrinal Versus Imagistic Mode In the doctrinal mode, the transmission of knowledge and religious practices are rationalized through the transmission of doctrines, both with the ecclesiastical hierarchy and through scientific research that transmits some cultural models that become an implicit memory of religious rituals. Practically, in the doctrinal mode, rationality becomes a religion and not its opponent. The instruments of this modality are the frequent repetition of concepts, the semantic clarity, the mediation of religious leaders, the verification of orthodoxy, and the centralization of the religious discourse. The doctrinal mode can be easily associated with the traditional control practices enacted within companies; therefore, it can easily lead to manipulative control practices, as we explained above.

The second mode is the imagistic and magic one, in which the religious experience has not got orthodoxies and does not affirm some revealed truth like in the doctrinal modality, but in the performative language of the lived experience. In this second case, the ritual experience is lived with intensity. This second mode is more close to the docility factor that we showed in the previous paragraphs. Indeed, this mode could lead people to a spontaneous reciprocal learning mechanism, overcoming the risk to exercise manipulative or coercive control forms. The liturgical element can help us to better understand the managerial and organizational implications of these two different ritual modes.

Managerial Practices as Liturgies

Concerning the Catholic Church, the Vatican Council II was interested in the reform and in the promotion of liturgy; however, today some people think that the problem is not yet solved. According to the theologian Tagliaferri, the liturgy, within the Catholic Church, assumes rationalistic and doctrinal features that are the cause of a "liturgical problem" regarding efficacy of faithful participation to the rite. Indeed, in the Catholic liturgy, the sacrament is strongly emphasized in the dogmatic assertion of its theological importance but is kept to a minimum in its ritual mediation, in order to preserve the specific Christological form from ritual dictates, which are likely to reduce liturgical practice to superstition (Tagliaferri 2006).

The liturgical reform was developed by these assumptions of anti-ritual suspicion, with undeniable rationalistic accents in the sequence of rites and the emphasis of faithful participation. The rationalistic vision tends to activate immunizing relational strategies with low emotional intensity. The critical hypothesis is that this "rationalistic" view empties the ritual paths, removing their transformational magic; it functionalizes the rite to revelation and develops a ritual communication process based on mere participation and proximity, forgetting that ritual communication is symbolic and with magical accents, as it transforms people and activates the passage of the liminal between rational understanding of religious experience and its practical experience. However, some religious liturgies, both Christian and of other faiths, emphasize ritual dynamics more in the imaginative forms of religiosity. In the Christian sphere, the Byzantine rites can be identified more in the imaginary model rather than in the doctrinal one. Indeed, the Byzantine liturgical system was characterized by the sumptuousness of the ceremonial and liturgical symbolism. Byzantine liturgies developed in the orthodox patriarchy of Constantinople, and they were gradually adopted during the Middle Age by the other orthodox Chalcedonian patriarchies of Alexandria, Antioch, and Jerusalem. We can place the origins of the "Byzantine Church" between the years 381 and 451, when the bishops, Gregorio di Nazianzo and Giovanni Crisostomo, started talking about eves, stations, litanies, preaching, psalmodies, songs, and so on. One of the main features of the Byzantine rite is its spontaneity, as it rises directly from the populace, and we can find this feature in a phrase of the Russian priest Schmemann, who wrote that liturgy "is not grace that comes down; it is the Church that enters into grace […]" (1973: 31).

Doing parallelism between liturgies and managerial practices, we can affirm that they operate through models of a rationalistic type. Practically, they are developed through liturgies of the budget, of conformity controls, of performance systems, operating rationally, based on doctrines with a strong ideological and practical value (that is the object of intensive training of individuals), on hierarchical mediation and centralized. In this painting, "managerial liturgies" have the aim to create shared semantics based on repetitions and rituals that guarantee the corporate orthodoxy, in the sense of controllability of the system for the pursued purposes. In this context, it is easy to understand how the managerial logics become mere rituals of control and sharing, with low emotional intensity and useful to manage and control everyone's anxiety. In this model, rituals are conformed to "dogmatic" needs of managerial action, but they are not able, deliberately, to exploit the ability to create a people transformation through experiences and paths that allow an individual development that is at the same time original and congruent with being in a corporate, individual, and collective environment.

In organizations, the emptying of the shared emotional dynamics creates an action field that can easily generate wounds that are difficult to interpret for the injured person and that are difficult to find by the organization. Therefore, together with the creation of wounds, the elements to give also blessings are absent. On the contrary, in our opinion, recognizing rites and rituals and their strengthening also in an antidogmatic, spontaneous, and imagistic key could contribute to create useful situations in order to build clear and effective relations. This would help generate an organizational culture that integrates people within the organization, generating relations that give "blessings"; the budget is fundamental, but people come before the budget.

One of the managerial leverages that could be useful for increasing the arising of the aforementioned blessings consists of introducing a liminal dimension. Van Gennep (1961) and Turner (1991) introduced the liminal concept in their anthropological studies, to indicate a period of time/space in between, occurring especially during transitory rites of passage. In management and organization literature, several authors have already analyzed the liminality topic in depth (see, for example, Söderlund and Borg 2018). In the organizational context, the liminal tool, somehow, allows people to exit from the classic, traditional, bureaucratic formal structures, to enter within an extraordinary time/space, within which there is the reinforcing relational aspect with colleagues. For example, some companies' sharing and collaboration spaces—promoted by leaders—could be defined as liminal spaces, such as plenaries, meetings, workshops, and lunches. Liminal and ritual moments are useful to build collective meaning. Furthermore, these moments help to foster a spirit of gratuitousness, in which it is possible to share power, belonging, knowledge, information, talent, and time. In other words, liminal spaces reinforce interpersonal bonds between people working within the organization.

Rituals enacted through liminal spaces serve as emotional anchors for social solidarity, allowing the affirmation of collective values and group. In this case, we can talk about "collective rituals." Workplaces are full of social and cultural contradictions, especially when there is a lumbering bureaucracy. Rituals allow participants to work within ambiguity and uncertainty. By deepening the relation between rite and culture through rituals, people interlace their body with the collective body of society. The rite, indeed, manages the body and allows people to share beliefs and group behaviors.

In companies, rituals help to construct a shared meaning and cohesion between people and provide a useful managerial leverage for leaders to strengthen social identification. However, the managerial organization, in addition to failing to recognize these rites, also tends not to enhance them. Furthermore, in some cases, companies try to take possession of rituals and manipulate them, reducing their beneficial effects. Rites are, in fact, powerful and delicate instruments because they act deeply on people and also work on an emotional level. It is possible to recognize three main elements of the "collective" dimension of rituals: (1) organizational culture, (2) changes, and (3) conflicts.

Organizational Culture Rituals always reveal something of the culture of an organization. Indeed, rituals are a form of symbolic expression that takes place in organizations. These ritual actions allow individuals or groups to transition among organizational roles, maintain organizational status, and build solidarity within the organization. Islam and Zyphur (2009) also asserted that ritual events may originate from group members or management.

Changes Transitions are usually associated with rites of passage. Anthropologist Van Gennep's (1961) research demonstrated how many human societies have faced change through rites that have accompanied the passage from one situation to another: "rites of passage." The concept of rites of passage was evoked in the organizational context by Eriksson-Zetterquist (2008), who described a trainee program in a transnational company. If young trainees had been recruited directly from school, they were first separated from either their student life or their working life and colleagues (if they were already working). The period of training was the liminal phase, which ran parallel to the investiture phase, including becoming managers, which was the purpose of the training. According to Trice and Beyer (1984), rituals not only communicate a shared understanding of culture, but also favor its management and change. Indeed, rituals can underpin the emotional dimension of persuasion, which managers use during change initiatives.

Conflicts Rituals can permeate all organizational levels. For example, Ren and Gray (2009) described relationship restoration after conflict as a ritualistic process influenced by culture. Jassawalla and Sashittal (2002) found that an intensive schedule of formal meetings for sharing information and managing conflicts became embedded rituals. Furthermore, in relation to "embedded rituals," Sosis and Ruffle observed that symbolism differentiates ritual from empty routine, claiming: "Rituals are not empty routines; they are always embedded with symbolism and endorsed by cosmological explanations that provide significance, insight, and appreciation for the performers!" (2004: 111).

Discussion

Based on our literature review and our understanding of company rituals, we agree with Ferris' (1988) recommendation that leaders move from a "controlling, ordering, manipulating management style" to a "loving, respectful, team-oriented style." This does not mean necessarily that control operations must be eliminated but that they should be exercised while paying attention to the fact that the control practice is exercised toward human beings, not toward inanimate things. For example, leaders or managers who must motivate employees can operate in two ways. On the one hand, they can oblige employees, in a coercive way, to serve their purposes; here, we are in presence of a violent control operation. On the other hand, they can compare their goals with their employees, to verify if they are compatible, and leave the employees free to assume their leaders' or managers' goals. In this way, the employees can become motivated by this process and inspired by what they want, and not by what their superiors want.

So, motivation is that leverage on which people exercising control functions in companies must base their reasoning. Managers and leaders must work on what motivates individuals to do something, if they want to align people's purposes to those of the organization. Indeed, motivation is not an element present in inanimate things, but we sure find it in people. The problem arises when managers treat people in the same way they treat machines. This is well explained in Ferris's words (1988), when he claims that "under the control mechanism of the engineering paradigm' we automatically assume that the imagination or creative spirit of others is irrelevant; those others feel the limitation, and they eventually shut off" (46). Conversely, the important thing is that managers and leaders are careful to act on people's motivation by guaranteeing employees freedom of choice, hence, without using coercion. It is important to allow, rather than to command, to obtain an energy release from employees, considering that energy constitutes the more important feature of motivation. Moreover, in an organizational environment where people feel free and trustworthy, they increase both their creativity and their productivity (Ferris 1988).

The teaching option allows insisting on the importance of people's motivation, especially if the organizational environment fosters the development of docility. The act of docility includes, indeed, two main points: to be ready to be taught and to learn how to teach others. For managers and for leaders acting in a docile way means that they must be aware both that they can learn from their employees and that they can teach them. This signifies that employees may freely express themselves, having the opportunity to freely give suggestions to their managers or leaders. In the same way, docile employees must be open to learn from their managers or leaders' experiences and to listen to their advices. A potential risk of docility consists of a condition in which people accept being used because they have been trained to do so. In this case, docility becomes an instrument of oppression and manipulation, constituting a source of a strict bureaucratic control and of undesirable behavior (Alvesson and Spicer 2012). However, in organizations it is necessary to improve collaboration and learning mechanisms, for which docility from individuals is necessary.

All throughout the chapter, we have tried to analyze what can make the difference in an organization if it is able to create the conditions to transform wounds into blessings. Indeed, wounds can be just a representation of discomfort for people and an inefficiency at a corporate level, or they can also become a source of blessings, contributing to a higher level of awareness and personal evolution, and ultimately, even if indirectly, contributing to the organizational success. We have identified rituals and rites as those instruments that answer to the main research question of this chapter, which is how to manage the interpersonal relations in the organizational context maintaining the equilibrium between the individual and collective identity.

Furthermore, although there are many aspects that encourage the passage from wounds to blessings, we have chosen to focus on the influence that rites and liturgies have that encourage or hinder these dynamics. Our first conclusion is that discovering spontaneous rites and rituals in organizations could be decisive to create a favorable terrain to encourage the emergence of blessings, and this happens because rites allow the development of intense relations at emotional level. From a practical point of view, the idea to analyze rites to understand interpersonal relations in a company can have two positive effects, reducing suffering and facilitating the transformation into blessings.

Rituals Spontaneous Dynamics

Applying the spontaneous ritual dynamics to the organizational context allows organizations to reach some important results in overcoming relational wounds, transforming them into blessings. The rite serves to meet the sacred. Indeed, in the fight between Jacob and the angel, the ritual aspect manifests in the blessing's request, in the name's change (from Jacob to Israel), in the temporality in which the episode occurs. Morning is coming and the angel says, "I have to go." The fight has a temporal boundary within which it is inscribed. The "fight" between Jacob and the angel has a before and an after, which allows both to face the risk (the before) and to heal the wounds (the after). In the rite, people enter and exit; they cross a limen, without which the rite would no longer exist, it would become the norm, and the battle could not continue indefinitely. The sacred lies in the mystery of the angel whose identity is not clear. The encounter with the sacred transforms and leaves a sign forever, in the wound first, and subsequently in the blessing.

But what are the reasons why ritual is necessary to allow organizational wounds to become blessings? In the ritual episode, individuals reach a syntony with others, transforming themselves through the ritual experience's sharing. In particular, people share their emotions during the ritual episode, and, above all, rituals generate a new spiritual force that reinforces both social cohesion and mutual recognition among people. Through their symbolic power, rituals guarantee meaning to actions, overcome passivity and resignation, and allow people to face changes and crises (Van Gennep 1961; Turner 1988, 1991).

Rituals foster the arising of blessings if they reinforce the aspect of identity within companies. The corporeality aspect in ritual is fundamental, the physical presence in a place, indeed, communicates strongly. In the current society, where the conceptual prevalence prevails, the ritual allows the action to resume its body, and that is why Jacob's struggle and physical wounding, which becomes a transformative blessing, is a metaphor for the struggles and wounds of individuals in organizations. Put simply, the definition of space, the movements of the body, and the rituals' performance lead to a system of meaning that cannot be underestimated. Rituals are endowed with a symbolic value that must be acknowledged by leaders of every organization.

A relevant aspect of each ritual is the identity status of those who take part to it and it can be identified as a representation of that status with the aim to establish borders because it underlines differences. For example: If a business meeting is a rite, having received an invitation or not and having a certain role or another in the meeting communicates the differences and identifies the hierarchies. This rite says a series of things about the organization/company to which people belong, for example, about its values, its divisions, the exercise of its powers, and its accepted and prohibited practices. But if this rite is not explicit and is a masked expression of power, if it just serves to affirm a certain hierarchical line, official or not, it loses its rite power. In this case, it can generate a series of counter-rites, to balance or modify power balances expressed through it. Indeed, a problematic aspect in organizations is the absence of clarity in the identification of a rite, and so indistinguishing it from the other forms of interaction in the company. If a certain type of action is a ritual but is not explicated, it will generate suffering and insolence, because the "negative" elements, such as the absence of productivity, slowness, uselessness, and redundancy, will play a role which jeopardizes a productive meeting.

Another important ritual element in organizations is the power to generate tension between charisma and institution that we have already mentioned above (Weber 1963). This tension between charisma and institution is the tension that is created between ideal and real, both necessary, albeit opposed, to maintain the vitality of every community. Rite could represent the way out to articulate the two levels without making them coincide or contrast. Indeed, according to Durkheim (1961), a ritual is a social phenomenon that activates the Mana transcendence, that is, a spiritual power/energy which in the culture of the Melanesians permeates the universe. A ritual, in particular, concerns the individual and allows the social group to reread the forces and to regenerate the mental states that are corroded by time. In brief, when rituals are called with their real name, they can dissolve the toxins of the institution, placing them in the Mana effervescence state (Durkheim 1961). Therefore, a rite does not oppose charisma, but it institutionally articulates it. When a rite is called with its name, and other things do not mask it, it creates that form within which it can express itself without destroying the institution. In this case, the inevitable wounds in the relationship between the individual and the institution can be contained in their consequences and can be hopefully accompanied by a positive transformation.

In the organizational context, blessings emerge even insofar as rituals allow people to be "seen" in the work activities they do. As Bruni (2020) highlighted:

> In modern large organizations the theory and practice of management makes more and more managers unable to see the work because they are "forced" to spend their time in the midst of paperwork and computers, to produce charts, indicators, controls; or to do "institutional" evaluation interviews, in which they have half an hour to consider work that is not seen in the daily routine of the 12 months of the year. These sophisticated tools do not allow managers to see the whole human-spiritual experience of the worker.

Rituals allow to both see and recognize people's work through ceremonies, debriefing meetings, or simply coffee breaks which constitute moments of mutual recognition through which the individuals' identity element can be strengthened.

The Limits of Rituals

Looking for the limits of rituals in organizations, we can affirm that on the one hand, the ritual praxis creates a shared order and articulates institution and charisma. On the other hand, rites (which Tagliaferri identifies as those of the Catholic Church but that can be the same for every institution) can become the transmission belt of authoritarianism and social conservatism, and this happens when there is the attempt to eliminate from them some constituent aspects of danger and to sublimate them, inserting them in an ethical framework. For example, it can happen that the attempt to eliminate conflict and to optimize decision-making strategies through bureaucratization and a capillary control of the process, based on "objective" criteria, disassociates interpersonal relations and cannot actually avoid wounds but instead deprives people of their energy and reduces performance.

Some aspects are very important and cannot be neglected, such as transparency, communicative "intimacy," the absence of double levels of communication, the importance of calling rites with their name and not masking them through productive activities, and so on. Rites should not be finalized to serve one doctrine rather than another one, but they should be autotelic and should constitute an act of gratuitousness, as we mentioned in the theoretical background referring to Durkheim's thought.

Scope of Rituals

Summarizing the results obtained from our reasoning, we claim that in companies, rituals and rites seem to have an important valence, in particular in some scopes:

(a) The first one is to manage the delicate balance between charismatic leadership and the institution.
(b) The second one is to manage changes where the presence of rituals could exercise a facilitating action.
(c) The third one is to manage relations among collaborators, through the fostering of the docility factor.

In companies, merger and acquisition situations are especially interesting: Here, ritual detection allows predicting "taboo" areas that will manifest a strong resistance to change if they are not sufficiently understood and respected, sometimes in a counterintuitive way, for example, by intervening on "ritualized" forms of inefficiency. In these cases, it could be useful to map the hidden rites and rituals to take notice of them and to adopt a therapeutic action. Furthermore, awareness allows an organization to recover the significance and the effectiveness of the rite by proposing it in its pure habit that means that the ritual is not nested within unnecessary procedures, in a compatible way with the specific corporate culture. In this path, the entire organization can work on one part not to nest the ritual within unnecessary procedures, and the other part inevitably rests in the charge of each individual working for the same organization. Thus, interventions can be on three levels:

(a) The first level is managerial and organizational, and can also be done through rituals.
(b) The second level tends to encourage awareness and the enhancement of personal resources.
(c) The third level consists in developing only "positive" control practices which lead people to acquire the docile factor, necessary to reach the learning process.

A punctual mapping of rites in different companies, also in the absence of specific needs, could serve to validate the expressed hypothesis by building a "database," which could be useful for further exploration and insights. Surely, we do not think that discovering rites and rituals in organizations is the resolutive path to face conflict, but a clear and explicit recovery of it could contribute to limit falsehood, that is always a dysfunctional dual form of communication.

In order to map rituals within the organizational context, it is necessary to distinguish them from the manipulative to the spontaneous ones. Therefore, it becomes necessary to question if control within the organization constitutes an approach to manipulative leverage or if it constitutes an approach that allows employees to flourish.

Conclusions

In this chapter, we showed the importance of joining rational and irrational elements in an organizational context, through a specific analysis focused on organizational rituals enacted within companies. To achieve this, an effort toward a balanced rethinking of both management tools and their use should be done. Introducing an ethical dimension in managerial leverages leads to deal with the habits—hence the customs—of the organizational community. We claim that rituals are effective managerial leverages to both identify and to better manage emotional aspects within companies and to incorporate an ethical factor in managerial practices.

Nowadays, companies are modifying their organizational structure in order to increase employee well-being. For example, some new forms of work organization are emerging in different countries to guarantee a greater degree of freedom and responsibility for people. In our view, these new managerial models should encourage emotional elements by recognizing ritualistic forms and by looking for a form of leadership that is ethically and economically more qualified to face the current challenges of our complex, volatile, and turbulent business environment.

Considering these observations, we invite leaders both to recognize and map the presence of rituals within organizations. This could be the way in which rituals might obtain a major consideration within organizations. To foster the arising of blessings within the organizational sphere, leaders are also called to both accompany and listen to people, so as to facilitate their human flourishing.

References

Agamben G (2013) Opus Dei: an archaeology of duty. Stanford University Press, Stanford
Alvesson M, Spicer A (2012) A stupidity-based theory of organizations. J Manag Stud 49(7):1194–1220
Aquinas ST (1947) Summa theologica. Benzinger Brothers, New York
Bains G (2007) Meaning Inc: the blueprint for business success in the 21st century. Profile Books, London
Bardon T, Borzillo S (2016) Communities of practice: control or autonomy? J Bus Strateg 37(1):11–18
Bell CM (2009) Ritual theory, ritual practice. Oxford University Press, New York
Berne E (1964) Games people play: the psychology of human relationships. Grove Press, New York
Brooks AW, Schroeder J, Risen JL et al (2016) Don't stop believing: rituals improve performance by decreasing anxiety. Organ Behav Hum Decis Process 137:71–85
Bruni L (2020) Critique of managerial reason. Human Manag J 6:5. https://doi.org/10.1007/s41463-020-00100-y
Burkert W (1996) Creation of the sacred: tracks of biology in early religions. Harvard University Press, Cambridge, MA
Cunliffe AL (2014) A very short, fairly interesting and reasonably cheap book about management. Sage, London
Dierksmeier C, Pirson MA (2010) The modern corporation and the idea of freedom. Philos Manag 9(2):5–25
Durkheim E (1961) The elementary forms of the religious life. Collier Books, New York
Eriksson-Zetterquist U (2008) Gendered role modelling—a paradoxical construction process. Scand J Manag 24(3):259–270
Ferris R (1988) How organizational love can improve leadership. Organ Dyn 16(4):41–51
Fleming P, Sturdy A (2011) 'Being yourself' in the electronic sweatshop: new forms of normative control. Hum Relat 64(2):177–200
Fox A (1974) Beyond contract. Faber, London
Freud S, Freud A (2001) Totem and taboo and other works. Random House, New York
Goffman E (1967) Interaction ritual. Essays in face-to-face behavior. Double Day Anchor Books, New York
Islam G, Zyphur MJ (2009) Rituals in organizations: a review and expansion of current theory. Group Org Manag 34(1):114–139
Jassawalla AR, Sashittal HC (2002) Cultures that support product-innovation processes. Acad Manag Perspect 16(3):42–54
Kinnie N, Hutchinson S, Purcell J (2000) 'Fun and surveillance': the paradox of high commitment management in call centres. Int J Hum Resour Manag 11(5):967–985
Klikauer T (2015) Critical management studies and critical theory: a review. Cap Class 39(2):197–220

Kunda G (1992) Engineering culture: control and commitment in a high-tech corporation. Temple University Press, Philadelphia
Longoni A, Golini R, Cagliano R (2014) The role of new forms of work organization in developing sustainability strategies in operations. Int J Prod Econ 147:147–160
Malinowski B (1948) Magic, science and religion and other essays. The Free Press, Glencoe
McGregor D (1960) Theory X and theory Y. Org Theory 358:374
Menger C (1963) Problems of economics and sociology. University of Illinois Press, Urbana
Parker M (2002) Against management: organization in the age of managerialism. Polity Press, Cambridge
Powell WW, Colyvas JA (2008) Microfoundations of institutional theory. In: Greenwood ER, Oliver C, Suddaby R, Sahlin K (eds) Sage handbook of organizational institutionalism. Sage, Thousand Oaks, pp 276–298
Rappaport R (1999) Ritual and religion in the making of humanity. Cambridge University Press, New York
Ren H, Gray B (2009) Repairing relationship conflict: how violation types and culture influence the effectiveness of restoration rituals. Acad Manag Rev 34(1):105–126
Schmemann A (1973) For the life of the world: sacraments and orthodoxy. St Vladimir's Seminary Press, New York
Secchi D, Bardone E (2009) Super-docility in organizations: an evolutionary model. Int J Org Theory Behav 12(3):339–379
Sferrazzo R, Ruffini R (2021) Are liberated companies a concrete application of Sen's capability approach? J Bus Ethics 170(2):329–342
Simon HA (1947) Administrative behavior (republished in 1957, 1976, 1996). Macmillan, New York
Sitkin SB, Cardinal LB, Bijlsma-Frankema KM (2010) Introduction and history. In: Control in organizations: new directions in theory and research. Cambridge University Press, Cambridge
Smith A (1976[1759]) The theory of moral sentiments. Oxford University Press, Oxford
Söderlund J, Borg E (2018) Liminality in management and organization studies: process, position and place. Int J Manag Rev 20(4):880–902
Sosis R, Ruffle BJ (2004) Ideology, religion, and the evolution of cooperation: field experiments on Israeli Kibbutzim. Res Econ Anthropol 23:89–117
Tagliaferri R (2006) La "magia" del rito: saggi sulla questione rituale e liturgica. Messaggero Ed, Padua
Taylor FW (1911) The principles of scientific management. Harper & Brothers, New York
Trice HM, Beyer J (1984) Studying organizational cultures through rites and ceremonials. Acad Manag Rev 9:653–669
Turner V (1988) The anthropology of performance. PAJ Publications, New York
Turner V (1991) The ritual process: structure and anti-structure, 7th edn. Cornell University Press, Ithaca
Van Gennep A (1961) The rites of passage. University of Chicago Press, Chicago
Watzlavick P (1967) Pragmatics of human communication: a study of interactional patterns, pathologies, and paradoxes. W.W. Norton & Company, New York
Weber M (1963) The sociology of religion. Beacon Press, Boston
Whitehouse H (2002) Modes of religiosity: towards a cognitive explanation of the sociopolitical dynamics of religion. Method Theory Study Religion 14(3–4):293–315

Cross-References

Family Business Transformation: A Systems View
From Individual to Organizational Transformation: A Foucauldian Perspective on Transformational Leadership
The Journey of Career Resilience Among Females
The Metamanagement Model as a Framework for Organizational Transformation

From Individual to Organizational Transformation: A Foucauldian Perspective on the Transformational Leadership

10

Jamila Alaktif and Stephane Callens

Abstract

Leaders have always faced challenges that require profound transformations. The work of the philosopher Michel Foucault is a major reference for transformation both on a personal and on a organizational level, since he campaigned to contribute to a better society, even if it meant questioning ideas and proposing new approaches in a world that was changing rapidly. Considering that a society cannot improve and innovate without a profound transformation, it is advisable to reflect on the microprocesses that lead to such a transformation. How many managers have been able to shake up the hierarchy and thus replace old, dusty practices with innovative practices, thanks to their sense of leadership? What do we have to learn from Foucauldian philosophy on this subject? We argue that there can be no organizational transformation without individual transformation. We discuss a new transformation model first at the individual level, then at the organizational level, based on leadership from the rich Foucauldian literature.

Keywords

Foucault · Leadership · Managers · Organizations · Self · Transformational leadership · Weber

J. Alaktif (✉)
ISC Paris Business School, France-Stanford Center for Interdisciplinary Studies, Stanford, CA, USA

S. Callens
Université d'Artois (France), Arras, France
e-mail: stephane.callens@univ-artois.fr

J. Neal (ed.), *Personal, Educational and Organizational Transformation*, Future of Business and Finance, https://doi.org/10.1007/978-3-031-29253-8_10

Introduction

The work of the philosopher Michel Foucault constitutes a major reference for questions of personal and organizational transformations that he believed would constitute a better society. His contribution focused mainly on the relationships among self-techniques, forms of interpersonal relations, and the development of large cultural and institutional values. He was interested in the analysis of the present, renewing methodological approaches, particularly those relevant in leadership theories.

Assuming that a company can improve and innovate without self-transformation, Foucault was interested in the processes that can lead to such disruptions. However, there can be no organizational transformation without individual transformation, and this is provided by strong, creative, and innovative leadership. What do we have to learn from Foucauldian philosophy on this subject?

Regarding the theories about leadership, the first framework of analysis was established by the sociologist Max Weber, who identified three major sources of power: (1) a charismatic nature, (2) legal-rational power, and (3) power based on tradition. This Weberian tradition was still active in the early 1970s, a time when Foucault referred to the notion of domination, a characteristic of Weber's analysis of power. The 1970s were centered, for Foucault, on analyses of the installation of public policy in European states from the Renaissance, and on this occasion, the tools introduced by Weber were reworked and redefined.

This chapter explains the progressive evolution from Weber to Foucault on leadership and transformation. We continue with transformational leadership, with a focus on the Foucauldian philosophy (Foucault 1961, 1966, 1971, 1975, 1997, 2001a, b, 2008, 2009, 2011) which highlights self-transformation and the role of emotions in the leadership process. Following a distinction between transformational leadership and transactional leadership, this chapter discusses the self in both the individual and the organizational transformation considering modern corporations. The chapter concludes with a reflection on transformational leadership in the age of the coronavirus that turned 2020 upside down.

Leadership and Transformation from Weber to Foucault

Weber: A Disconnection Between Leadership and Transformation

Max Weber is credited with formulating the first theories of organizational leadership. The founding contribution to these theories is in the scientific organization of work proposed by Frederick Taylor in the USA and, later, in France by Henri Fayol and Joseph Wilbois (Wilbois 1926). The earliest references in North America appear as part of an assessment of organizational functioning. However, the emergence of leadership theories takes place in various ways throughout the world. For example, the French refer to a vitalist approach in opposition to the culture of the engineer-organizers. Vitalism refers to leadership where the dynamism of leaders is acquired naturally and in the absence of any evaluation by their teams. This "vital momentum" is defended in the precritical philosophy by Bergson (Wilbois 1926). "Precritical" means that the philosophical references used do not lie in the ethics of autonomy proposed by Kant. Therefore, they refer to philosophies before the Age of Enlightenment. The vitalist philosophies are based on explanations by "a vital impulse," which makes it possible not to have recourse to operations of evaluation and measurement. In particular, there is a very strong methodological opposition between the approaches based on assessments and measures proposed by the pioneers in North America and Bergsonian vitalism.

These first French-speaking works date from the First World War (1914–1918) and were dominated by Henri Fayol (1848–1925). In contrast, the vision of engineering culture is quite hierarchical, featuring an organizer and a planner-leader. Other French-speaking works, particularly those serving as a reference for the first management schools seeking to distinguish themselves from the engineering culture, were based on a typology of powers internal to the organization in the first French-speaking works. The figure of the creative entrepreneur is inserted in a polyarchy (i.e., in the presence of several leaders in the same organization), eventually dominated by a single command and with an attached figure of the engineer-organizer (Wilbois 1926). The first French-speaking literature on leadership is distinguished by this composition of the various management functions within the organization, and it joins Weber's sociology in a ternary typology of powers. For Weber, leadership is also defined in competition with managerial and economic approaches as one of the three primary forms of domination: the charismatic, the traditional, and the legal-rational. The approach in French-speaking literature is that of the composition of different types in the management of firms and organizations, seeking to reconcile the figure of the creative entrepreneur strongly put forward by economic thought, that of the engineer-organizer, in a hierarchical order. This French-speaking approach differs from that of Max Weber, who is more attached to a political science approach.

The major contributions of Max Weber are presented as follows: a theoretical construction of the main forms of power and a consideration of the role of asceticism (i.e., following religious precepts with the aim of an intimate relationship with God) in the emergence of the modern world. A first major contribution is that of Weber's general theory of powers, in which charisma represents a central element for Weberian sociology. Weber conceives of three types of power: (1) bureaucratic power, which he calls "legal-rational," (2) traditional power, and (3) charismatic power (Table 10.1).

A legal-rational model is a form of domination that recognizes the legitimacy of acts performed and leaders chosen according to legal procedures and based on regulations established according to the demands of reason. Individuals obey people less than often than they obey impersonal and general rules. Legal-rational domination is accompanied by the constitution of a powerful bureaucracy, the main vector of rationalization (Valluy 2020).

Traditional power of authority derives from traditions such as royalty or organizations that function as tribes, led by a chief, in which the power of rulers can be

Table 10.1 The three types of domination according to Weber

	Rational	Traditional	Charismatic
Characteristic	The goals pursued	Routines	The affects
Incarnation	Without	Patrician	Individual
Organization type	Bureaucracy	Family	Sect
Figures	Officials, priests	Patriarchs	Prophets, leaders
Historical function	Preservation of the rational order in place	Preservation of order	Subversion of the order in place
Relations among the three types of domination	Opposition to the other two types and to change Impersonal rules opposed to charisma and tradition	Opposition to change Fight against leaders (against charisma) and resistance to rules (opposition to universal rationality)	Opposition to orders in place Fight against traditional leaders Subversion of the rules

Source: Petit (2013, p. 67)

unlimited. The China of Weber's time, which he reduced to the philosophy of Confucius, was an example for him of traditional power.

As for charisma, it is a central element for Weber. Charismatic individuals influence others who see them as leaders with exceptional ability. It does not matter whether this exceptional ability exists, as long as others perceive it to be so. Napoleon Bonaparte, Steve Jobs, and Elon Musk are examples of charismatic leaders.

For Weber, leadership contributes to the emergence of organizations through the role of a master of life who will have disciples. The recent works of historians underline the relevance of Weberian approaches for precise historical sequences, but are quite varied, for example, the forms of social life in the period of the High Middle Ages or the analysis of conceptions of power in the Nazi era (Kershaw 1995). Regarding the history of political philosophy in China, it is not limited to Confucius alone. The absence of forms of power, not including leadership, seems much more difficult to support in historical works. The emergence of an empire in China, for example, undoubtedly supposes a charismatic dimension of the first emperors.

Weber's other major contribution is to the role of post-Reformation Puritan asceticism (Luther and Calvin) in the West in the emergence of modern capitalism. Imperial China and the cities of the Italian Renaissance bear witness to the development of trade techniques and the intensification of trade, without this major cultural transformation as a consequence of the Protestant Reformation in Europe. For Weber, companies and administrations share the principles of similar organizations and are essentially part of a legal-rational approach. Weber's diagnosis is that, in his day, organizations lacked leadership.

For Weber, the only way out of bureaucracy is through leadership. However, the legal-rational form of power has a significant hold on organizations, and the increasing bureaucratization of organizations is inevitable. This sociology is that of an analysis of all forms of power and covers many different institutions, whether family, economic, or public. This Weberian approach differs from other theories of leadership, including American and French, but is found in other sociological currents, in particular with Durkheim (1953). Weber declines power only in the extreme form of domination.

Sociologists who followed Weber consider that several types of power cannot be substituted for each other. This approach is not found in the first French-speaking leadership literature for whom "depending on the nature of the company, such functional heads will predominate, but without any ever missing" (Wilbois 1926, p. 125). In the first French-speaking literature on leadership, the relationships between powers are considered to include three types—instruction, command, and influence—with associations between an emitting power (a leader) and a receiving power (an employee). Of the three types of power in the organization, only the organizer lacks an active role in this first theory of leadership (Wilbois, ibidem). The European approaches of the early twentieth-century leadership share the following concept: The strictly organizational approaches (proposed by Taylorism, for example) are a major threat, and they should be controlled by hierarchy and charisma.

In Weber's analyses, the creation associated with leadership is separated from the functioning of the economy. The first theories of leadership in the Francophone field reasoned differently. In the nineteenth century, a theory of the entrepreneur was developed by economists. Entrepreneurs connect creation and invention, on the one hand, and the market for goods and services, on the other. They often must deal with industrial or administrative directors, then with a polyarchy that includes several directors, such as the head of accounting, the chief of gas pay, and the production manager. Not until the twentieth century did leadership theory develop a layer of new issues, including how to reconcile all of these different powers within the company and ensure productive cooperation among its various major functions.

From Weberian Domination to Foucauldian Outspokenness

Weber makes a major contribution to the development of leadership, which is revisited by the French philosopher Michel Foucault, whose lectures in the early 1970s spoke of "domination" to analyze power in a Weberian approach. Circa 1975, Foucault gradually broke away from Weber and offered a new synthesis of this analysis of powers. His last lessons focused on straight talk, the parrhesia of the ancient Greeks. Here, the analysis of powers is more clearly developed than that of Weber, since Foucault also considers the dialogues in the organizations and the forms of criticism employed. Charisma and outspokenness thus represent the two clearest contrasts between the approaches of Weber and Foucault.

Indeed, Weber's words remain focused on political science organizations that present the same types of power as those seen in the political world. The theory of the company depends on the political theory of Weber. Charisma is the missing element in the political scene of Weber's time, just as Foucault considers that outspokenness, as it may have existed, also became the hidden element in his time. Weber's views approach a business ethics perspective: An economic conception is brought by Protestant Puritanism, but this approach is so rational that it lacks humanity. With Weber, political organizations are based on violence, domination, and discipline. Weber still belongs to the German historical schools, which conceive of history as a succession of dominations. Very clearly, this is no longer the case with Foucault, who retraced in his lectures of the mid-1970s the genealogy of these historical schools that appeared in the eighteenth century. The leader, according to Weber, does not fit into a hierarchical pattern. This leadership is the one that is the engine of history in traditional societies. The leader is surrounded by brothers and is opposed to calculations of money or power. Tachseen Kazi (2017) makes the connection with, on the one hand, the philosophical heroes of the cynical sect of antiquity and, on the other hand, the Weberian conception of leadership. Foucault indicates, however, that philosophy disappears at the beginning of the nineteenth century, since philosophers become teachers in a generalization of educational institutions. This character of the philosophical hero then shifts toward revolutionary life. With Foucault, leadership is disruptive; it displaces conventions, and it self-creates its style. Leadership is based on the ability to renew oneself (on the style of conduct, the responses to the problems encountered).

The *parrèsiastes* (the truth teller)—that is to say, the one who associates frank talk and wisdom in ancient Greece—is the king of derision. Foucault sketches a history of criticism based on four "truths"—prophecy, wisdom, techniques, and outspokenness. The history of ancient philosophy indicates a rapprochement of outspokenness and wisdom. In the Middle Ages, preaching combined straight talk and prophecy. Unlike those ancient societies in which straight talk is a specialty, modern times no longer know this specialization of telling the truth through straight-talking, according to Foucault. Frank talk contributes to the formation of three critiques: political, scientific, and philosophical. The straight talk associated with prophecy is found in revolutionary political discourse, hence a critique of science.

Foucault overcomes the limits of the Weberian framework from different sides:

- From the Foucauldian perspective, the concept of power is redefined due to the limits of Weberian analysis, which conceives of power only through war, violence, and discipline. Weber remains in a historicist tradition, where war situations are illustrated, as a unique approach, to understand all social and historical situations, including in organizations. Unlike this approach, which is highly limited, Foucault considers that there are different forms of management practices in the organization and the state. For example, this is the case in the power of a pastor, who can lead a group without any reference to war.
- Weber's conceptions correspond to a situation of a society of the first industrialization, and his assertions can only be understood about the society of his time: an omnipresence of discipline, a political activity based on violence, and a context of elitist and nationalist politics, undemocratic, which was that of Germany's Second Reich. Weber does not draw a real distinction between organizational leadership and political leadership, arguing that companies and states use the

same resources of power techniques. Weber's writings coincided with the development of large industries while Foucault published when Europe was breaking away from them. At that time, institutions were transformed, as was the case with mental health care, which transitioned from huge psychiatric hospitals to drug treatments at home.

Weber thinks in terms of the eviction and the struggle between management and leadership: either leadership or bureaucracy, promoted to an end-state status of the dynamics of organizational systems. This organizational pessimism separates sociological approaches from those of the first promoters of leadership theories. They have a less restrictive conception than Weber's of intraorganizational power relations. Foucault's conceptions were transformed in the 1970s, gradually lifting the previous restrictions placed on the analysis of power relations by these first theories.

From charisma to straight talk, the 1970s marked a renewal of analytical frameworks adopting an ethic of dialogue, absent from the structure of Weberian approaches.

Successive Contributions of Foucault

Foucault's works follow one another in three periods: archaeological (where Foucault recognizes one of his references in Weber), then genealogical (an intermediate phase where he reassesses Weber's notions of power, discipline, and the role of self-labor), and, finally, ethics (where he renews and redefines the power relations and analysis of ascetics). This progression is relevant in the case of a rapprochement between criticism, transformation, and leadership (Table 10.2).

The latest works on the history of the outspoken are part of a continuing enterprise of exploration of the various forms of criticism present in Foucault's earliest works (Table 10.3).

The leadership theories are of two orders:

Table 10.2 The relation to Weber in Foucault's research programs

Period	Main works	What is analyzed as transformation	Relationship to Weber
Archaeological	*History of Madness in the Classical Age; Words and Things*	The great discontinuities in speeches	The notion of domination is still used
Genealogical	*Monitor and Punish; History of Sexuality (vol. 1)*	Hermeneutics of the subject based on the practices of powers	A renewed analysis of micropowers
Ethics	*History of Sexuality (vol. 2 to 4)*	Stylizations of behavior and transformations of oneself and others	A study of the relationship between government of self and others

Source: The authors

Table 10.3 Outline of a history of criticism

Main "Tell the truth"	Antiquity	Middle ages	Modern times
The prophecy	The prophecy	The university is a rapprochement between wisdom, techniques, and teaching	The sciences contain a critical part
Wisdom	Techniques and teaching	Preaching brings prophecy and straight talk	The critical philosophy is that of human limitations
Techniques and teaching	Ancient philosophy is based on the rapprochement between wisdom and frank speaking		The formulation of a shared destiny is done with a critical part
Straight talk			

Source: Foucault, *The Courage of the Truth,* pp. 29–30, 2011

- Weber's analysis is confined to the sole domination, whereas Foucault renews an analysis of the powers and refocuses on an examination of this from the history of discourses of critique. The waves of bureaucracies that followed one another during the Weberian era created pessimism. He broke with that atmosphere by opening new perspectives, such as "governmentality," a concept introduced by Foucault (Foucault 2008) for governance. The term "governance" has been widely developed through the 2000s, which opens the way for governance theories.
- "To break away from oneself" is a Foucauldian expression of the transformation of oneself to allow for self-analysis and internalization of social coercion. Foucault proceeded to a general reassessment of the role of ascetics, already put forward by Weber. Asceticism is a moral or philosophical doctrine aiming at spiritual perfection through a constant discipline of life. It can be a life in which individuals deny themselves material pleasures. "Max Weber asked this question: If you want to adopt a rational behaviour and regulate your action based on true principles, what part of yourself should you give up? What asceticism is the reason for? What type of asceticism should we submit to? For my part, I asked the opposite question: How did certain types of self-knowledge become the price to pay for certain forms of prohibition? What do we need to know about ourselves to accept renunciation?" (Foucault, *Dits et écrits*, II, p. 1603).

The Self-Transformation in the Leadership Process: A Focus on Foucault

The Self-Transformation

Weber and Foucault set up theoretical frameworks for charismatic (Weber) and transformational (Foucault) leadership. These have been used in studies relating to the succession of the various major forms of organization.

Foucault presents criticism in organizations under several dimensions. The relationship he establishes between a critical and profound transformation bears simple and strong logical links: "Criticism is essential for any transformation. Because a transformation that would remain in the same mode of thought would be [...] only superficial. [...] A work of transformation [...] can only be done in the open air and always agitated by permanent criticism" (Foucault, Dits et Écrits, II 2001a, pp. 999–1000). If the initial work of thinking is insufficient, then the transformation is as well. The only limitation of this relation between criticism and transformation is that of operational practice. Critical activity must "make these transformations urgent enough for us to want to do them, and difficult enough to do so that they fit deeply into reality" (Ibidem, p. 1000). Only possible clumsiness can render this strong link between criticism and transformation inoperative.

The critical activity concerns an "ontology of ourselves." This Foucault expression designates a work of self understanding, with a question of the type: Why am I that? From this perspective, the first work of thought is to change oneself first. In these strong connections between criticism and transformation, the transformation of oneself is inserted. "So many things can be changed, fragile as they are, linked to more contingencies than necessities, to more arbitrariness than evidence, to more complex but temporary historical contingencies than to true anthropological constants," if there is "at the disposal of the work that we can do on ourselves" the greater part "of what is presented to us as inaccessible" (ibidem, p. 1001). To make oneself "other" is necessary for the truth; this theme is the one developed in Foucault's last course, with the discussion around cynical philosophy, the first expression of a cosmopolitan through an "other life," which identifies the horizon of another world, the transformation of the present situation. "There is no establishment of truth without an essential position of otherness. The truth is never the same" (Foucault 2009:311).

Self-transformation appears both trivial and major. It is commonplace because it is part of everyday life, where it is natural to do what is possible to transform, such as through clothing. It is major because, to better adapt to a changing environment and to create meaning, it is imperative to transform what is most personal, namely ideas, habits, and practices.

The links between transformation and critical theory are simple: In precritical theory (i.e., before Kant), we consider that "everything is in the best of all possible worlds." Here, transformation cannot be improvised and requires critical preparation, which can mobilize tools whose relevance must be assessed. Literature reviews of studies that refer to Foucault's work indicate a rather "defensive" use of the

Foucauldian theoretical reference in management sciences (Bardon and Josserand 2018). Today, the Foucault-inspired management works are numerous and fall mainly in the line of new critical boundaries. This literature could be called "Weber–Foucauldian," indicating little consideration of the evolution of Foucault's work vis-à-vis Weber. These critical theory approaches open up the role of power in management theories. The articles indicate that the notion of asceticism (or work on oneself) is central to both Weber and Foucault, with a greater sensitivity to the elements of continuity than to those of rupture between these two very different approaches to charismatic leadership and transformational leadership (for example, Kazi 2017). Self-transformation has several axes of analysis for Foucault, without this being taken up in the managerial literature (Bardon and Josserand 2018) (Fig. 10.1).

The place of emotions strongly depends on the mode of organization. "Governmentality," a neologism formed by Foucault long before the appearance of the notion of governance, asserted itself with the policies of the Renaissance period and the disappearance of the Roman Empire; it replaced a history of techniques of self and organizations in several periods:

- A period when life is formed by emotional communities that Weber defines as a group of people who follow a charismatic leader. These communities have varied standards of expression: royal court codes, angry family vendettas, mourners or professionals recruited during ceremonies for the deceased, etc. The organization is limited to a single, standardized form of life. Later, Foucault defines the techniques of the self as an endless questioning of the practices of individuals in the perspective of an invention of the self. He states that these self-techniques allow "individuals to perform, alone or with the help of others, a certain number of operations on their body and soul, their thoughts, their behaviour, their way of being; to transform to reach a certain state of happiness, purity, wisdom, perfec-

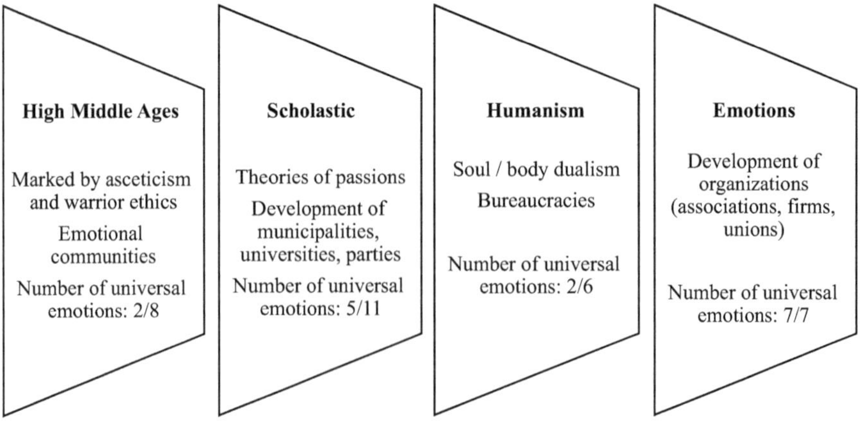

Fig. 10.1 Major periods in the history of organizations and number of universal emotions cited in the period/number of "passions" in the lists for the period concerned. (Source: The authors)

tion or immorality" (ibid., p. 1604). Employees wishing to tap into their full potential will be able to use personal development. In this case, the tracking makes it possible to measure the objectives to be reached (better time management, fewer fears, more positive thoughts, better self-confidence, etc.) to become the best version of oneself and to exercise better self-control. Self-techniques can be quite demanding.

- The development of administrative management under the impetus of the bureaucracies of the European states. Indeed, leadership, as evidenced in the French Revolution, is highly political. The question is: Who are the leaders? At the time, there was a strong will to place only political leaders in organizations, and there was only one type of organization. Critics rose up against the bureaucracies to demand much freer new forms of organization.
- However, we must wait for the Industrial Revolution to see new forms of organization such as firms, associations, and unions.

Importance of Emotions in Self-Transformation and Leadership

Emotions are governed by the charismatic personality in the Weberian model. There is a relationship between the governance of oneself, which one can call the management of oneself, and the governance of others, in the Foucauldian model. In this configuration, to think of power is to think about the governance of oneself and the governance of others.

Depending on the period of history, emotions are more or less taken into account in the functioning of the organization, depending on the hierarchical coordination. For example, in monasteries where the organization is linked to asceticism, emotions are less important. However, other organizations focus on more emotions and adapt their speech according to the chosen emotions. This is the case for political parties, for example, which instrumentalize the range of emotions of the voters, such as fear, sadness, anger, disarray, love, or even revenge. Gradually, as modern society advances, especially beginning in the twentieth century, organizations are attempting to understand and manage a range of emotions as the desired goals: to exhibit empathy, to detect fear and dread signals from their employees, to prevent and manage anger, and to anticipate depression.

An analysis of history over the past centuries to our modern times shows that functioning organizations often adopt one of the following strategies to generate emotions in their employees:

- Neutralization: At the beginning of the COVID-19 pandemic, directors at a retirement home in France asked nurses not to wear masks so as not to scare residents. Fear is considered an emotion that must be neutralized by pretending that everything is fine.
- Compartmentalization: Professional ethics differ according to specialization between situations. For example, the same nurse must welcome a bereaved family and perform precise technical protocols; these tasks are managed differently,

taking into account the emotions of each situation. For example, nurses must manage the emotions (sadness and anger) of a bereaved family with empathy. Then, they must complete the sanitation protocol of their tools; here, empathy is not required.
- Prescription: This is to say that scripts exist to manage emotions. For example, the smiles exhibited by salespeople in stores.
- Standardization: Emotions considered to be disturbing should be supervised.

This repertoire of emotion management, in Foucauldian reflection, comes from the governance of oneself as the basic technique. However, for a manager, this is insufficient. Truly transformational leaders must go above and beyond to identify other solutions that will apply to each situation they face.

Schematically, organizations would have been first prescriptive, then normative, and finally compartmentalized with a specialization of emotional work. Compartmentalization is employed in civil aviation and *not* in the railways, a mode of transport with rules dating back to the nineteenth century, suggesting that recent compartmentalization occurred during the twentieth century.

Indeed, the techniques of the self were highly developed from the first emotional communities, often animated by the charisma of a guru toward a few disciples. Neutralization practices are systematized in the political and moral treatises of Roman antiquity. Prescriptions and normalizations intervene; the sadness of young men is dispelled by dancing. Compartmentalization has arguably the fewest historical precedents in these four types of emotion regulations. The royal administrations of the Renaissance hardly had a complaints office.

How should organizations be characterized today? Highly hierarchical organizations (such as armies) remain, as well as universal services, while organizations are most often defined based on precise objectives, such as an increase in profits, investment in climate change, reduction of waste, the launch of new products, and so forth.

Organizations, Transactional, and Transformational Leadership

The Transactional Leadership

The distinction between the transactional leader and the transformational leader was introduced by Burns (1978; Plane 2015). The transactional leader practices compromise and establishes distributive justice, with a view to the proper functioning of the organization and the achievement of its objectives. The transformational leader has a vision, initiates projects, and provides real transformations. Whereas the transactional leaders care most about extrinsic motivation (financial incentives), the transformational leaders are characterized by intrinsic motivation.

Foucault's approaches take into account the conflicting dimensions and the impulses necessary for transformations. The approaches taught for the development and management of quality systems reconcile, for example, the transactional and transformational profiles through a principle of leadership. The quality system must not be bureaucratic and must respond to a principle of continuous improvement.

Change is seen today as the consequence of a transformation, with a great cultural change completing a process of transformation (Kotter 2015). Transactional and transformational approaches are rather complementary: Sustaining a quality system also presupposes a transactional approach that perpetuates the transformation achieved through appropriate incentives. A situation requiring rapid transformation due to an exceptional circumstance, such as the COVID-19 pandemic, catches health systems by surprise, and their many reforms around the world are based on impulses from transactional leaders. The European Union experienced a very serious public health crisis in the 1990s, with the epidemic of a new variant of Creutzfeldt-Jakob disease, which had appeared in the UK. The health security measures taken then were gradually eclipsed by "ordinary parliamentary procedures" that, since 2009, have appeared in Article 168 of the Constitutional Treaty of the European Union. A clear vision is widely shared around the world for sustainable development in the fight against climate change, yet modifications are slow to come, as transactional and transformational efforts of organizations and public agencies prove insufficient. Pure strategies placing all emphasis on the transactional (wait for a new, more ambitious agreement in the fight against climate change, limit public health to an ordinary parliamentary procedure) or, on the contrary, transformational (voluntary initiatives by organizations) efforts are less promising than the dynamic complementarities between the two approaches.

The Self in the Process of Individual Transformation

Historical studies indicate that small personal transformations underlie large transitions. The personal transformation has a real effect on organizational design, and these effects can be evaluated. In a contemporary context, systematic reviews of the literature highlight the need to strengthen the theoretical bases of transformational leadership. Comparative evaluations of leadership approaches highlight transformational leadership, despite its supposed theoretical weaknesses (Siangchokyoo et al. 2020).

According to Foucault, caring for oneself involves working on oneself. The intellectual context of the 1960s is that of a great diffusion of the theories of alienation: Colonization made us "other," and we have to come back to ourselves. The consumer society, the capitalist system, or modernity could be described in theoretical frameworks opposing another today's present, the destroyer of an authentic subject before a significant interruption in the chain of times, in a great episode of a past transformation of self. We would then be in need today of freeing ourselves from this straitjacket and the involuntary other that we are, the fruit of a lost battle.

In the 1970s, Foucault tended toward "optimism of action" (the expression is from Sartre) and in protecting the words of people directly concerned with a social issue: unskilled workers abandoned by their unions, prisoners, and the sick. The most important issues touch us directly through our bodies, and the protection of people, their speech, and their health must supplant all other considerations, usually carried by elements of national political speech. If Weber could provide any argument for the analysis of his time, it would be that of a leadership shortage both in organizations and in the political system. The audience of Michel Foucault at the Collège de France included many people with founding gestures for new organizations, as in the case of the French doctors. We were, therefore, in a situation contrary to the Weberian one of leadership shortage.

Transformational leadership necessarily involves transforming oneself. Foucault revalues a concern for oneself, a concern for personal development, so that the individual has an intrinsic strength to change things. Work on oneself can be that of a study anticipating the multiple and successive difficulties in the change (Kotter 2015). From the moment that individuals realize this fact and accept the need to question themselves, they can change and use their intrinsic resources for the benefit of transformation and of their environment. They draw from this construction the personal resources to contribute to the organization that employs them.

The 2020s are marked by profound institutional and organizational changes. In the UK, the lack of transformational leadership is advanced as an explanation for the difficulties of achieving the goal of Brexit—the UK's official exit from the European Union. The rhetoric employed by Brexit leaders and the press that supports them is that of the leadership of authenticity, in a rejection of former Prime Minister Theresa May's transactional leadership. In this rivalry, a planned break takes place in the most complete unpreparedness, in particular, in the absence of transformational leadership. The pro-Brexit press argues that the policy has become inauthentic. This distrust of political personnel spares leaders presented as "genuine," such as Nigel Farage, Boris Johnson, and Jeremy Corbyn. Brexit leaders travel by bicycle, have not changed their political beliefs from a young age, are sometimes thrown out of their homes by their partners, and deploy a dress code that eschews any form of elegance (Mueller et al. 2019). Brexit is thus presented as a large-scale experiment of the leadership of authenticity.

The Self in Organizational Transformation

The passage from self-transformation to organizational transformation is a characteristic often retained in the opposition between positive forms of leadership and simple rules of organizational management. The personal involvement of the project manager is a condition for the success of organizational transformation. How many of us have carried out a project under daunting circumstances because we believed in it, despite weak support or no support from our hierarchies?

A theme of commitment and personal accomplishment is transversal in the examination of leadership. Weber's observations of the differences in the economic relations of Asian and European societies seem obsolete today given the important role of Asia-Pacific in the world economy. Weber contrasted traditional Chinese Confucian leadership with the pursuit of personal achievement in the affairs of European merchants. The collapse of China in the nineteenth century is explained today by the imperial refusal of any transformation, unlike its Japanese neighbors. Weber's analysis rightly underlines the driving role of personal involvement, the situation in Asia during the Belle Époque and the operational difficulties in implementing a necessary change (Kotter 2015).

Coming back to our contemporary times, the standard is shaped by a set of people within organizations. Managers who can understand the ins and outs of this standard, from the moment they see a personal motivation in it, will adhere to this standard, not by obligation but with real interest (Alaktif and Callens 2020). In a comparative study of similar subsidiaries in Canada and France within the same telemarketing corporation, change is linked not only to personal interest and willingness to change but also to the respective forms of leadership in the organizations under study (Alaktif 2015). The team in Canada is more flexible thanks to transversal management open to change. The shared vision is that of customer service, customer satisfaction, and maintaining market share. This context gave way to leadership because of the openness of the human resources director, who accepts change on an individual basis and whose interpretation of headquarters standards is seen as a positive element, not necessarily as a constraint. On the contrary, the French team is endowed with a highly rigid bureaucratic system where it is important to respect the "great leader" and not create problems to satisfy the customer. The general attitude of the staff is desirable conformity. These two contrasting examples illustrate the decisive role of a leader, the Canadian executive, in the journey toward transformation.

The Weberian-inspired approaches are that of social criticism, with the idea that organizations tend toward a stable, organized state deemed dangerous. The different contemporary approaches—for example, those of quality systems—are based on the idea that organizations present dysfunctions and sources of possible improvement through a voluntary leadership approach. A quality approach supposes possible improvements to an organization. Growing problems often present themselves with organizational innovation present only in a small part of the organization. Clearly defined objectives on a global scale are not declined in certain parts of the organization, due to a lack of leadership from an intermediate scale. "If there are not enough leaders, the vision, communication and accountability that are at the heart of transformation are simply insufficient or too slow to meet our needs and expectations" (Kotter 2015, p. 192).

Conclusion: Transformational Leadership in the Era of Contemporary Issues, Reflection on the Management of the Coronavirus

Scholars in management sciences have widely studied leadership, which is paramount for any transition (Kotter 2015). The year 2020 is a useful demonstration of leadership, as it has been marked by the global coronavirus pandemic. Transformational leadership seeks to make the process of learning about this new disease as effective as possible. Recommendations include ensuring the best possible information flow, reducing anxiety felt by caregivers about taking supportive measures, organizing daily meetings with leaders to remain up to date on communications within the team, and making plans for any issues that develop: "Be prepared for the unexpected and respond in a calm and organized manner. Prepare a Plan B, Plan C and Plan D. Keep your answers simple and to the point. Don't overcomplicate any problem. Don't lie" (Grossman 2020).

Crisis medicine can be defined as the ability to deploy reactivity and innovation on a large scale. Thus, the response of a health system to a health crisis is a corollary of the organization, its mobilization of resources, and its relationship to innovation. The solution to this crisis lies in a transformation of health systems in the face of various challenges, whether they are changes of scale ranging from individual care to global coordination, management of innovation, and quick deployment of operations.

References

Alaktif J (2015) Diversity of origins and issues rising from standards: a case study in France and Canada (Doctoral dissertation). Retrieved from http://www.theses.fr/s18043

Alaktif J, Callens S (2020) Migration and climate change. Wiley, London

Bardon T, Josserand E (2018) Management innovations from a Foucauldian perspective: time to take action. Management 21:1244–1263

Burns JM (1978) Leadership. Harper & Row, New York

Durkheim E (1953) The rules of sociological method (trans: Solovay SA, Mueller JH). Free Press, New York

Foucault F (1997) Il faut défendre la société, Cours au Collège de France 1975–1976. Gallimard-Le Seuil, Paris

Foucault F (2001a) Dits et écrits, 2 volumes. Gallimard, Paris

Foucault F (2001b) L'Herméneutique du sujet, Cours au Collège de France 1981–1982. Gallimard-Le Seuil, Paris

Foucault F (2008) Le gouvernement de soi et des autres. Cours au Collège de France 1982–1983. Gallimard-Le Seuil, Paris

Foucault F (2009) Le courage de la vérité. Cours au Collège de France 1983–1984. Gallimard-Le Seuil, Paris

Foucault M (1961) Histoire de la folie à l'âge classique. Plon, Paris

Foucault M (1966) Les mots et les choses. Une archéologie des sciences humaines. Gallimard, Paris

Foucault M (1971) L'ordre du discours. Gallimard, Paris

Foucault M (1975) Surveiller et Punir. Naissance de la prison. Gallimard, Paris

Foucault M (2011) The courage of truth. The Government of self and others II. Lectures at the Collège de France 1983–1984. Palgrave Macmillan

Grossman VA (2020) Leadership essentials during a disaster. J Radiol Nurs 39(3):156-157

Kazi T (2017) Foucault and Weber on leadership and the modern subject. Foucault Stud 22:153–176

Kershaw I (1995) Essai sur le charisme en politique. Gallimard, Paris

Kotter J (2015) Conduire le changement. Feuille de route en huit étapes. Pearson, Paris. (First ed.: leading change, Harvard, Harvard Business Review Press, 1996)

Mueller F, Whittle A, Gadelshina G (2019) The discursive construction of authenticity: the case of Jeremy Corbyn. Discourse Context Media 31:100324

Petit V-C (2013) Leadership. L'art et la science de la direction d'entreprise. Pearson, Montreuil

Plane J-M (2015) Théories du leadership. Modèles classiques et contemporains. Dunod, Paris

Siangchokyoo N, Klinger RL, Campion ED (2020) Follower transformation as the linchpin of transformational leadership theory: a systematic review and future research agenda. Leadersh Q 31(1):Article 101341
Valluy J (2020) Segment – legal-rational legitimacy. In: Transformations of industrialized democratic states – TEDI – version on December 15, 2020, publication identifier in Web format: 38
Wilbois J (1926) Le chef d'entreprise. Sa Fonction et sa Personne. Alcan, Paris

Cross-References

A Return to Virtue: Embodiment, Chakras, and Management Education
Company Rituals: A Valid Management Tool in the Organizational Field
Personal and Organizational Transformation: Indian and American Perspectives and Experiences
The Metamanagement Model as a Framework for Organizational Transformation

The Journey of Career Resilience Among Women

11

Khadija Al Arkoubi and Geronda Wollack-Spiller

Abstract

Career resilience is the ability to bounce back and thrive in the face of workplace and life adversities. It plays a key role in enabling women to defeat hardships and create change in their lives. In this chapter, we explain why it is relevant to explore career resilience among females; we outline some strategies at the personal and organizational levels that have proven to assist women in enhancing their career resilience. Finally, we share stories of highly resilient women who transformed their careers and influenced other women around them.

Keywords

Career resilience · Women · Organizations · Transformation · Adversity · Stories · Gender

But that shadow has been serving you!
What hurts you, blesses you.
Darkness is your candle.
Your boundaries are your quest. You must have shadow and light source both.
Listen, and lay your head under the tree of awe.
Rumi (Enough Words) translated by Coleman Barks.

K. Al Arkoubi (✉)
Pompea College of Business, University of New Haven, West Haven, CT, USA
e-mail: kalarkoubi@newhaven.edu

G. Wollack-Spiller
thoughtbot, New York, NY, USA

J. Neal (ed.), *Personal, Educational and Organizational Transformation*, Future of Business and Finance, https://doi.org/10.1007/978-3-031-29253-8_11

Introduction

In a stormy world that is full of political, economic, social, cultural, and technological challenges, personal resilience among both men and women is increasingly considered as a significant coping strategy. Resilience is "a dynamic process encompassing positive adaptation within the context of significant adversity" (Coleman and Ganong 2002, p. 1). Adversity refers to stressful life events that cause disruptions in people's normal lives (Masten 1994). Examples include trauma, tragic events, bullying, harassment, discrimination, oppression, excessive workload, natural disasters, wars, serious health challenges, work-life conflict, stress, and burnout.

The conceptualization of resilience originated in developmental psychology in the 1970s and the following decades by Norm Garmezy when he was studying children and adolescents growing up with schizophrenic parents. He found out that thanks to resilience they defied the trauma and the adversities and emerged with positive developmental outcomes (Garmezy 1974, 1985).

According to him, determinants of resilience include a myriad of biological, psychological, social, and cultural factors that interact with one another to determine how one responds to stressful experiences. Hence, resilience is a dynamic and interactive concept (Rutter 2012) that has been examined at the individual, team, and the organizational levels using different conceptualizations. It has been perceived as a trait, state, and a process that may occur within or across career stages (Kossek and Perrigino 2016). The research on career resilience has been scant and fragmented, but it is gaining a momentum across multiple disciplines and occupations.

In this chapter, we are solely interested in women as they embrace resilience to influence their careers and their personal growth.

What makes some of them face the most challenging situations with courage and patience?

What makes them emerge stronger under the toughest circumstances be they professional or personal? How do they use their resilience to affect their lives and career success? What can organizations do to support them?

Before we dive deeper into career resilience and women's experiences, let us first provide an overview of women's most critical issues at work globally.

Women at Work: A Global Perspective

At a global level, 46.9% of women participated in the workforce in 2020 compared to men whose participation rate has reached 74% the same year (World Bank 2020). Women still suffer from discrimination in the workplace, in stereotyped occupations, and in families and societies. The gender pay inequality is still prevailing worldwide, and if persisting at the current rate, it will not be resolved in the medium term. The World Economic Forum (2021) revealed that women globally earn 37% less than men and that closing the gender gap in economic participation and opportunity may take 267.6 years. Besides, women still hold the major responsibility for the housework and care tasks resulting in an ongoing work-life conflict. In fact, millions of women worldwide are deprived of their legitimate right to paid maternity leave and other critical maternal and child health advantages. Furthermore, they are underrepresented in executive positions in the largest corporations of the world since 2.6% hold the position of chief executive officers, and all of them are white (Hinchliffe 2020). Similarly, their representation is low in leadership positions in business organizations and trade unions. In high-income countries, women engage in careers in health, education, and wholesale and retail trade. Conversely, most of them work in agriculture in low and lower middle-income countries.

The COVID-19 pandemic has put more pressure on working women and added to their challenges. According to McKinsey and Company (2021a, b), women mothers, black women, and women in senior positions have been largely affected. Therefore, one in every four women has considered leaving their job or changing their careers. Moreover, the pandemic has deepened the gender gaps globally and caused disproportionate losses in jobs and income with different regional and country variations (International Labor Organization 2021). "Globally, between 2019 and 2020, women's employment declined by 4.2 per cent, representing a drop of 54 million jobs, while men's employment declined by 3 per cent, or 60 million jobs" (ILO 2021, p. 1).

Currently, as the world prepares for the post-pandemic era, women are still taking the toughest hit in the most critical sectors such as health care, education, and other service-driven occupations.

Whether women are thriving in successful careers or suffering in miserable jobs and work conditions, they often benefit from their career resilience. In the following section, we explore the concept of career resilience and identify the key characteristics, emotions, and processes that enable individuals to develop it.

What Is Career Resilience?

The concept of "Career Resilience" or "Career Resiliency" emphasizes the meaning of resilience within the context of careers. Thus, people who are highly resilient will demonstrate a great ability to persist in the face of workplace adversities (Carson and Bedeian 1994) and will be successful in adapting to their working lives. It is also suggested that despite career disruptions, they will "maintain equilibrium, retain some sense of control over their environment, and continue to move on in a positive manner" (Jackson et al. 2007, p. 3). Similarly, Luthans (2002, p. 702) defines it as the "capacity to 'bounce back' from adversity, uncertainty, conflict, failure or even positive change, progress and increased responsibility." It is worth noting that this definition does not exclude positive changes in one's career. These could be a lateral or vertical promotion, a desired transfer to a new organization, embarking on a dream international career, and being in a context conducive to growth, creativity, and enhanced well-being.

Career resilience is a component of positive organizational behavior (Fredrickson 2001; Seligman and Csikszentmihalyi 2000) and a key dimension of "psychological capacity," which also encompasses self-efficacy, optimism, and hope (Luthans et al. 2006; Youssef and Luthans 2007). "It spans gender and diversity issues across occupations in that, for example, it can be a key resource for women in male-dominated professions" (Kossek and Perrigino 2016, p. 739).

Factors enabling career resilience include internal locus of control, flexibility and creativity, sense of hope and optimism, courage and determination, positive self-talk, and problem-solving skills (Borgen et al. 2004). Other sources of career resilience that have been recognized by researchers comprise resourcefulness, self-confidence, curiousness, self-discipline, sound judgment, and flexibility (Giordano 1997). In addition, other capabilities mentioned in the career scholarship include risk taking, independence, tolerance of uncertainty, and self-efficacy (Jiang et al. 2020).

To all these internal factors, we add spirituality and faith, drawing from Richardson's definition of resilience "the motivational force within everyone that drives them to pursue wisdom, self-actualization, and altruism and to be in harmony with a spiritual source of strength" (2002, p. 309).

In addition to the internal sources of resilience, there are external factors that help individuals to bounce back in the face of adversity. The most compelling include relationships, support systems in organizations and communities, and global connections (Masten 2005).

Relationships, especially the ones that are tied with caring members of the family and the community, have been considered as a main catalyst for personal and life transformations (Ledesma 2014). Social support systems and global connections, if used effectively, can ensure feelings of security and offer a sense of stability and purpose. Kossek and Perrigino (2016) confirm this view and place career resilience in its wider social context. They do not see it as a trait only. They coined the concept "Occupational Resilience" and believe in the role of the employee environment in building this capability. They also differentiate between cognitive, psychological, and physical resilience. The need for each type varies depending on the occupation. Women's career resilience is under-researched and requires a careful attention to shed light on the career experiences of women and identify the most effective coping strategies they can use to rise and thrive.

Why Do Women Need Career Resilience More Than Men?

In a highly turbulent world where the pace of change is fast and where organizations are forced to adapt, the current workforce needs career resilience more than ever.

As compared to men, women are compelled to embrace resilience to preserve balance and mitigate adversities for diverse reasons:

- First, women suffer from greater and increasing stress levels. In fact, the gender stress gap is widening according to the American Psychological Association (2015), and women continue to report a higher level of stress than men (5.2 vs. 4.5 on a 10-point scale in 2014). In fact, a recent study by Women's Health

Research at Yale conducted on stress in health care providers during the COVID-19 pandemic (Lowe et al. 2022) found that women are, in general, more exposed to life stress than men because of gender disparities in social position (e.g., occupation or profession) and psychosocial responsibilities (e.g., family duties, care-giving). In addition to exhaustion and stress, women engage in critical work that goes unnoticed and unrecognized by most organizations. They advocate, for instance, for diversity, equity, and inclusion. They also support individuals and teams without being rewarded (McKinsey & Company 2021a, b).

- Second, women enact multiple roles at the same time and feel obliged to make sacrifices. Being caregiver, breadwinner, and responsible for the family wellness leads to work–family conflicts. This situation has been observed across several occupations (physicians, nurses, surgeons, teachers, scientists, etc.) and has led to serious well-being problems including mental health symptoms and career withdrawals among women especially mothers (Frank et al. 2021).
- Third, women according to a survey of business leaders in 35 countries recognize gender bias as a barrier to advancement into leadership roles (Marston 2016). In addition, they most likely struggle to make their way to leadership in core business operations positions. Another study from the University of Exeter suggested that women have to face the *glass cliff* as an addition to the glass ceiling. This phenomenon implies that no change in a male leadership is needed when a company is performing well, yet when the same organization is going through a serious turmoil, a change to a female leader is preferred (Bruckmuller and Branscombe 2011).

Finally, while men and women perceive themselves as equally resilient, women, when asked, stated that they want to be even more resilient in the future (Bond and Shapiro 2014).

Considering women's willingness to continue learning how to enhance their resilience, the following section is a summary of what to do to get there.

Strategies for Developing Career Resilience at Individual Level: Tales of Resilient Females

Sticking to Faith and Accepting Adversity

Faith is a vital and central pillar in the lives of more than 80% of humans in this planet. In fact, a study by the Pew Research Center (2015) found that in 2010 only 16.4% of the globe's population was unaffiliated and that this percentage is expected to decrease to 13.2% in 2050. It is normal and expected that many women will lean on their spirituality during hard career times. Beaty and Pankake who conducted a study in 2016 that covered women leaders in education, mainly superintendents and principals, found out that spirituality and faith were fundamental in the way these women coped with adversity and how they even emerged stronger. For instance, one of them stated, "I've always been a Christian." Faith and spirituality provide these women with a value system that reinforces their perseverance, tenacity, hope, and optimism. It broadens their horizons and perspectives and makes them fearless. Several authors, including Giordano (1997, p. 1033), insist on the value of connectedness and having an "anchoring force" in life.

Accepting reality becomes a major step in having the courage to deal with it. Many women waste time in "denial attitudes" or they create and exaggerate stressors in their minds. This is true for men as well. According to Konnikova (2016), "Human beings are capable of worry and rumination: we can take a minor thing, blow it up in our heads, run through it over and over, and drive ourselves crazy until we feel like that minor thing is the biggest thing that ever happened."

This exaggerated perception of reality can only lead to passivity and inflexibility and is far from spiritual or faith-based attitudes.

Take, for instance, the example of Amani Al-Khatahtbeh, who chose to be resilient over being the victim of fear while growing up as a Muslim in America in post 9/11. She transformed herself and launched a meaningful career at the age of 17. As a writer, entrepreneur, and editor-in-chief of MuslimGirl.com, she has been inspiring many other women. Blumberg (2016) reports that Amani published her memoir "*Muslim Girl: A Coming of Age*" in 2016 where she describes growing up in a time of Islamophobia (post 9/11) and facing again in 2016 a political climate filled of hate, stereotyping, and bigotry. Her powerful message insists on giving voice to the voiceless. "One of the most important things for us to do to amplify [Muslim] voices is to pass the mic whenever we have it. If there's someone that can speak to a lived experience that you cannot, do not take up that space, do not speak on their behalf, let them speak for themselves" (Quoted by Blumberg 2016).

Searching for Meaning

When facing adversity, search for meaning and sense making become critical processes to reconstruct identity. Finding the most relevant cues to visualize a new future is an essential step toward an enhanced career and life. This search of meaning cannot occur without a belief system that offers existential interpretations of reality, "a cohesive life narrative and an appreciation of the uniqueness of oneself" (Tusaie and Dyer 2004, p. 4).

Coutu (2002, p. 7) shares the story of her friend Jackie, who over a period of 10 years suffered from multiple psychoses because of undiagnosed bipolar disorder. She writes that:

> Today, she holds down a big job in one of the top publishing companies in the country, has a family, and is a prominent member of her church community. When people ask her how she bounced back from her crises, she runs her hands through her hair. "People sometimes say, 'Why me?' But I've always said, 'Why not me?' True, I lost many things during my illness," she says, "but I found many more—incredible friends who saw me through the bleakest times and who will give meaning to my life forever."

People who do not accept to victimize themselves and find their own way to make sense of their crisis and restore their career and life are the ones who give us lessons on how resilience works.

Making sense of our career and assessing the challenges we face with wisdom will necessitate a deep *self-reflection.* The latter is the ability to analyze ourselves with honesty and authenticity to be able to clarify how to act differently and determine the coping strategies needed to overcome hardship with courage and strength. In other words, sense making and search for meaning will move us from the past and the present to a better future. The transition can only happen when we are also alert to our environment, its trends, and changes in terms of careers, occupations, industries, economic conditions, and so forth.

Turning Adversity into Opportunities

Stacy Copas, described as Australia's number one facilitator and coach on how to turn adversity into an opportunity, insists that being proactive is similar to "Learning to dig your well before you are thirsty" (Quoted in Kelleher 2015). She meant that women need to be tenacious about developing effective strategies to respond to disruption. Stacy's story is a great example of how she transformed hardship into significant achievements. She was 12 years old when she had a tragic accident that left her a quadriplegic and wheelchair dependent for the rest of her life. She has never given up. She continues to influence women and men through her talks, training, and coaching sessions as well as her writings. In 2015, she published her book titled *How to Be Resilient* based on her own life experiences. Stacy is not the only resilient woman who turned her adversity into a writing and coaching career. The story below describes how a group of women engineers who immigrated to the USA experienced high stress, disorientation, cultural shock, and disempowerment. Nevertheless, they displayed courage and high resilience skills and transformed themselves and their lives.

> My participants and I share several characteristics: we were middle class women in our countries of origin who came to the United States after having already completed undergraduate and even graduate studies, with two suitcases and the courage to face the unknown. By radically altering the spatial-temporal coordinates of our lives, we experienced cultural shock, poverty, and the effects of local immigration policies, such as visa entrapment. We can all point to mentors and fortunate encounters with people from the host culture who helped us along the way; we worked hard to achieve professional growth; we also had supportive spouses and families who were willing to change along with us. (Gabor 2014, pp. 115–116)

Seeking Mentors

Mentoring is a constructive long-term relationship developed between a senior experienced and skilled individual (mentor) and a less experienced person (protégé). The mentor's role is focal to providing psychological and career support and acting as a role model. Mentors enhance their mentees' self-awareness, instigate their self-efficacy, uncover their potential, and nurture the whole person (Megginson and Clutterbuck 2005). In addition, a study conducted in private and public organizations in North India covering 205 managers suggests that psychosocial mentoring acts as a significant predictor of career resilience (Arora and Rangnekar 2014).

The following is the story of Dr. Olga Jonasson, a pioneer woman in academic medicine and transplantation. She was the first woman to chair an academic surgery department in the USA. She passed away in 2006 at the age of 72. The following quotes are from her lecture on resilience, published by the American College of Surgeons.

> Another way we can help future generations, and help each other, is by simply giving each other a shot. In last year's Presidential Address for the Society of Vascular Surgery, I talked about chances. Giving chances to others and taking our own chances help us all bounce up. Giving chances demonstrates our humanity, and taking chances enhances our resilience and improves our ability to achieve our dreams. Giving and taking chances are essential leadership skills. The miracle of my being here is because many inspirational people took chances on me. The first was Norma Wagoner, PhD, Rush Medical School's dean of admissions and a professor of anatomy. A majority of my other early mentors were men, all of whom are tremendous role models for *helping* women succeed. I am extraordinarily grateful to those who helped me bounce up in my career, including Drs Robert E Condon, E Carmack Holmes, Edward Miller, and Wesley S Moore. Moore was the division chief at UCLA and he was a tremendous supporter. Twelve years after I finished my vascular fellowship, I returned to UCLA to take his role as division chief when he stepped down.
>
> And, last, I am grateful to those who did not take a chance on me. They, especially, sparked the fire that ignited my resilience. It is because of them that I learned how to adjust my sails and stay in the race. Each of us men and women will encounter challenges great and small in our careers. (Quoted in Freischlag and Silva 2015, pp. 5–6)

Olga's story is a powerful testimonial highlighting the role of mentors in strengthening the fabric of our resilience and enhancing our career outcomes.

Developing Nurturing Relationships and Asking for Help

Healthy connections and relationships are vital in everyone's life. However, women need to nurture a close social and professional network to go for guidance and professional support during rough career times. Bond and Shapiro (2014), who conducted a study in the UK on developing resilience for women's leadership success, discovered that career resilience is a relational behavior. They indicated that women thrive when they are socially and professionally supported by family, friends, and colleagues. Some, however, hesitate to ask for help. Below are excerpts from females' stories gathered from different research studies in different countries and contexts:

"I naturally don't like to ask for help, but I knew I had to. If you feel like you're doing it on your own, you'll crumble." Another said, "I can top it [resilience] up when I need to using my networks and asking for help." "The only way we women cope is through talking to a small group of trusted female colleagues. There is trust, empathy and a desire and willingness to help one another." (Bond and Shapiro 2014, p. 25)

Sonia from the UK describes herself as being from an African family and holds three qualifications at Masters level as well an undergraduate degree because: "For an African family, to progress in this society, you need education—that piece of paper!" After working as a scientist in various organizations for a number of years, she began to feel "limited" and enrolled on a part-time business development course. When her employer refused to support her study, she resigned and worked part-time elsewhere. During her varied transitions, she "networked like mad," finding that she was good both at connecting with people and helping people develop their own networks. She has been made redundant from two positions, but keeps going, believing that: "…if there is something you really want to do—if it's a passion—you don't give up!" Now she wants to set up her own business. (Bimrose and Hearne 2012, p. 341)

Ingrid, from Norway, quit her first job (in postal services) to study for a degree in international marketing. She then had a series of jobs in sales and marketing, moving expressly "for greater challenge—I was so young and fearless at the time!" Then she became a Human Relations Manager in the oil industry, while also studying part-time for a Masters qualification. She stayed in this job for nine years, partly because of the flexibility she needed to combine the care of her two children (then aged 11 and 13) with employment. With regard to her own future, Ingrid emphasized that looking for her next job: "I will use my networks to ensure that I take the right decision" and that you need "to find out what you really want." (Bimrose and Hearne 2012, p. 342)

Now that we have covered some strategies capable of helping women to foster career resilience in themselves, our attention will shift to organizations.

Strategies for Developing Career Resilience: The Organizational Level

Creating a Strong Value System

We have explained above that relying on faith and a strong value system is a key element in defying stress, misfortune, and other types of adversity at the individual level. The research conducted so far has shown that organizations with a strong value system are resilient and more successful. For instance, Coutu (2002) suggests that big corporations such as Johnson & Johnson and UPS have created cultures that are described according to her in "religious terms." They are formalized in documents called "Credo" and "Noble Purpose" and shared with the new employees at the orientation program. These strong and sustained value systems enable both organizations and their members, men and women, to be resilient during crisis times. She quotes the previous UPS Chairman and CEO, Mike Eskew, as he described the UPS workers strike in 1997:

> It was a hugely difficult time, like a family feud. Everyone had close friends on both sides of the fence, and it was tough for us to pick sides. But, what saved us was our Noble Purpose. Whatever side people were on, they all shared a common set of values. Those values are core to us and never change; they frame most of our important decisions. Our strategy and our mission may change, but our values never do. (p. 8)

It is clear that strong, shared values are the glue that keeps all employees stuck together during difficult individual and/or organizational times. As a result, organizations are expected to foster values of empathy, compassion, trust, and reciprocal support. However, this can never happen without creating an organizational climate where deep and meaningful social connections can flourish and where the value system is aligned with practice. A study by Ekiyor and Saro-Wiwa (2019) highlighted the role of empathic leadership in creating optimism, equanimity, and humor. These three outcomes positively affect the ability of workers to cope during challenging times.

Moreover, Solanki and Mandaviya (2021), who investigated gender differences in the perceived level of stress of university instructors in India, pointed out that organizations need to promote the values of equity and flexibility and prioritize women's well-being. In addition, enacting policies and practices that aim at reducing gender biases in the workplace, enhancing women's work conditions, and fostering support and collaboration are all key strategies that organizations can adopt to enhance women's resilience.

While this is true for both men and women, some organizations have realized the critical relevance of resilience specifically for women and have started building this capability among women through training.

Building Resilience as a Capability Through Training

Many academics pointed out that resilience training in the workplace enhances personal resilience and improves well-being. For instance, the Resilience Institute conducted a global study that analyzed whether resilience increased in 26,000 individuals who received resilience training. The findings clearly suggested that the training had a strong impact on reducing depression and the effects of stress, improving physical well-being and cognitive functioning (Hook 2017).

Similarly, another systematic review of workplace resilience training was undertaken on publications during the period from 2003 to 2014, which covered four countries: Australia, USA, UK, and Sweden (Robertson et al. 2015). The results indicated that resilience training can expand personal resilience and positively impact mental health and subjective well-being in employees. Other positive outcomes revealed by this study referred to enhanced psychosocial functioning and improved performance. This same study specified that most training programs covered in this research adopted a cognitive-behavioral approach to building resilience. Although the authors encouraged the inclusion of one-to-one training and support based on individual needs, they confirmed that there is no hard evidence for the most effective training content or format. The main training interventions being used comprise coaching, mindfulness and compassion-based practices, loving-kindness meditation, self-regulation of stress responses via technology (McCraty and Atkinson 2012), and multimodal cognitive behavioral techniques (e.g., attentional training, energy management, relaxation training, imagery, and self-talk).

It is worth noting that these aforementioned studies were concerned with resilience training for both men and women in different occupations (e.g., sales managers, police officers, administrative staff from a university, US Armed Forces personnel, public school teachers, human service professionals, nurses, physicians). It would be wise though to design training and leadership development programs in organizations from gender lens. In fact, devoting a particular attention to building and consolidating resilience in women is a major piece in reenergizing their careers and preventing gender biases such as glass ceiling, glass cliff, maternal wall, sticky floor, and so forth, hence, helping them to flourish as members of their families, organizations, societies, and global community.

Cultivating Strong and Deep Social Connections and Networks

As mentioned earlier, positive and deep relationships at work or derived from social networks have tremendous impact on women's career resilience. Nevertheless, how do we ensure that organizations are capable of cultivating meaningful social support systems?

Murphy (2017) reports that "people sit in an office full of coworkers, even in open-plan workspaces, but everyone is staring at a computer or attending task-oriented meetings where opportunities to connect on a human level are scarce" (p. 4). He also rang the bell that the rates of loneliness have doubled since the 1980s and that many employees and half of CEOs report feeling lonely in their roles although we live in the most technologically interconnected world.

Therefore, he calls "for companies to make fostering social connections a strategic priority" (p. 5).

To move from superficial and task-oriented relationships to deep connections, organizational members, men and women, have to recognize the need to know more about each other. For instance, Murphy (2017) shares the story of his team when he was at the Surgeon General's Office. While everyone was aware that they had to address critical public health issues, they created an "Inside Scoop" to share a portion of their lives every time they met. Listening mindfully to each other helped reduce stress and feelings of loneliness. It has given everyone a stronger sense of belonging and a deeper motivation to know each other better.

Now, just imagine women at work and the different adversities they may face. Take a few moments to think about the following selected hardships:

- A competent pregnant woman who is about to deliver her baby and is grappling with the idea of coming back to work after a short period of time because she is afraid of losing her job if she spends more time taking care of the baby

- A woman who is denied promotion because she is a woman and/or a mother of three
- A woman who is highly recognized as an achiever and is promoted to a leadership role during a time of turndown
- A woman who suddenly falls sick with a chronic disease and her situation requires her to drop everything to take care of her health first
- A woman who is getting divorced and needs to start a new life under new parameters
- A woman who had just been terminated because of a political incident at work

How can organizations create safe/relational spaces for these women to share their experiences with supportive colleagues? How can they foster meaningful professional and social networks?

The first step is to make sure that empathy, compassion, generosity, kindness, and mindful listening are all deeply rooted in the culture of the organization and espoused by everyone. Consequently, fostering professional and social networks will enable women to build resilience and overcome their struggles. This process has to be driven by leaders who have to enact the culture and lead by example.

Seibert et al. (2016) contend that owning a large professional network can enable women to be psychologically resilient. Their research concluded that women in such a situation could bounce back and develop a stronger professional identity. Nevertheless, helping women to build strong skills in creating and sustaining effective networks based on quality relationships is essential to career resilience and adaptability. It is not always how high the number of followers on our Twitter, LinkedIn, or Facebook that is relevant, but more importantly, it is the quality of the relationships we tie with members of our network at professional and personal levels that counts in times of shocks and struggles.

Creating a Solid Mentoring System

"When my long-time mentor left the company, it reinforced that the time was right for me to go too," stated a female participant in a research study by Seibert et al. on career resilience and adaptability (2016, p. 247). This is a clear example of how a solid and high-quality mentoring relationship can serve women's career development. Organizations that invest in building formal and effective mentoring systems are more prepared to assist women boost their resilience capability. Junior women mentees can learn from both male and female mentors' diverse sets of skills. These include, among others, navigating organizational politics, overcoming sex and gender stereotypes in organizations and societies, working their way toward career progression, sharing personal and professional stories of suffering and struggles with bravery, and achieving career psychological success.

Conclusion

Career resilience is pivotal in women's career adaptation and growth. Despite the intensity of adversities they may face at personal, career, social, or global levels, women can go the extra mile and enjoy the journey of individual transformation. They can use their internal and external resources combined with the personal and organizational strategies described above to beat hardships. The stories shared in this chapter translate women's drive to craft a transformative culture to themselves and to other women around them.

Since career resilience can be learned, organizations are expected to devote a greater attention to its development and to its benefits to organizational members.

We proposed four key initiatives that organizations could undertake to build women's career resilience.

1. Developing a strong culture based on values of compassion, care, reciprocal support, and respect of women's personal expectations will surely help females' hardiness and thriving.
2. Designing training programs tailored to individual needs and based on cognitive behavioral approaches has demonstrated satisfactory results in improving women's well-being and their psychosocial functioning.
3. Cultivating meaningful relationships and social networks in a healthy/safe climate at work has proven to assist women emotionally and cognitively to share their stories of resistance, resilience, and transformation. This step is fundamental for women to get beyond the vulnerability stigma, avoid social isolation, and build a higher self-efficacy.
4. Creating a formal and sustainable mentoring systems that women can access and use effectively is crucial in resolving their career problems and achieving long term personal and/or professional goals.

Finally, whether using individual or organizational resilience in building strategies, it is extremely relevant to recognize the key role of challenge, adversity, and crisis times in enabling women to rebound career disasters and transform their lives in and outside organizations.

References

American Psychological Association (2015) Stress in America: paying with our health Retrieved from https://www.apa.org/news/press/releases/stress/2014/stress-report.pdf

Arora A, Rangnekar S (2014) Workplace mentoring and career resilience: an empirical test. Psychol-Manager J 17(3):205–220

Beaty DM, Pankake A (2016) Women describe becoming resilient through adversity. Women in Higher Education. Retrieved from http://wihe.com/womendescribebecomingresilientthroughadversity/

Bimrose J, Hearne L (2012) Resilience and career adaptability: qualitative studies of adult career counseling. J Vocat Behav 81:338–344

Blumberg A (2016) 17 Muslim American women who made America Great in 2016. Huffpost. Retrieved from https://www.huffingtonpost.com/entry/17-muslim-american-women-who-made-america-great-in-2016_us_584204b7e4b09e21702ec3b1

Bond S, Shapiro G (2014) Touch at the top: new rules of resilience for women's leadership success. Retrieved from https://forbusinessake.files.wordpress.com/2014/11/tough_at_the_top.pdf

Borgen WA, Amundson NE, Reuter J (2004) Using portfolios to enhance career resilience. J Employ Couns 41(2):50–59. https://doi.org/10.1002/j.2161-1920.2004.tb00878.x

Bruckmuller S, Branscombe NR (2011) How women end up on the glass cliff. Harv Bus Rev. Retrieved from https://hbr.org/2011/01/how-women-end-up-on-the-glass-cliff

Carson KD, Bedeian AG (1994) Career commitment: construction of a measure and examination of its psychometric properties. J Vocat Behav 44:237–262. https://doi.org/10.1006/jvbe.1994.1017

Coleman M, Ganong L (2002) Resilience and families. Fam Relat 51:101

Coutu D (2002) How resilience works. Harv Bus Rev 80(5):1–13

Ekiyor R, Saro-Wiwa (2019) Worker's resilience: the exigency for empathic leadership. Eur J Bus Manag 11(17):96–99

Frank E, Zhao Z, Fang Y, Rotenstein LS, Sen S, Guille C (2021) Experiences of work-family conflict and mental health symptoms by gender among physician parents during the COVID-19 pandemic. JAMA Netw Open 4(11):e2134315. https://doi.org/10.1001/jamanetworkopen.2021.34315

Fredrickson BL (2001) The role of positive emotions in positive psychology: the broaden-and-build theory of positive emotions. Am Psychol 56(3):21–226

Freischlag AJ, Silva MM (2015) Bouncing up: resilience and women in academic medicine. Retrieved from Resilience and Women in Academic Medicine. https://doi.org/10.1016/j.jamcollsurg.2016.03.033

Gabor E (2014) Career as sensemaking for immigrant women engineers. J Ethnogr Qual Res 8:113–128

Garmezy N (1974) The study of competence in children at risk for severe psychopathology. In: Anthony EJ, Koupernik C (eds) The child in his family: children at psychiatric risk, vol 3. Wiley, New York, pp 77–97

Garmezy N (1985) Stress-resistant children: the search for protective factors. In: Davids A (ed) Recent research in developmental psychopathology. Pergamon Press, Elmsford, pp 213–233

Giordano B (1997) Resilience: a survival tool for the nineties. Assoc Perioperat Reg Nurs J 65:1032–1036

Hinchliffe E (2020) A new low for the global 500: no women of color run businesses on this year's list. Fortune, August 10

Hook B (2017) The benefits of learning resilience. Retrieved from https://resiliencei.com/2017/08/benefits-learning-resilience/

International Labor Organization (2021) Building forward fairer: women's rights to work and at work at the core of the COVID-19 recovery. Retrieved from: Policy Brief: Building Forward Fairer: Women's rights to work and at work at the core of the COVID-19 recovery (ilo.org)

Jackson D, Firtko A, Edenborough M (2007) Personal resilience as a strategy for surviving and thriving in the face of workplace adversity: a literature review. J Adv Nurs 60:1–9. https://doi.org/10.1111/j.1365-2648.2007.04412.x

Jiang Z, Yiqi J, Ingrid N (2020) Thriving and career outcomes: the roles of achievement orientation and resilience. Hum Resour Manag J 1–22. https://doi.org/10.1111/1748-8583.12287

Kelleher L (2015) The resilience factor in leadership: turning adversity into opportunities. Women's Agenda. Retrieved from www.womensagenda.com.au/career-agenda/leaders/itemlist/user/1083-LaurenKelleher

Konnikova M (2016) How people learn to become resilient. The New Yorker. Retrieved from https://www.newyorker.com/science/maria-konnikova/the-secret-formula-for-resilience

Kossek EE, Perrigino MB (2016) Resilience: a review using a grounded integrated occupational approach. Acad Manag Ann 10(1):729–797. https://doi.org/10.1080/19416520.2016.1159878

Ledesma J (2014) Conceptual frameworks and research models on resilience in leadership. SAGE Open July–September:1–8. https://doi.org/10.1177/2158244014545464

Lowe SR, Hennein R, Feingold JH et al (2022) Are women less psychologically resilient than men? Background stressors underlying gender differences in reports of stress-related psychological sequelae. J Clin Psychiatry 83(1):21br14098

Luthans F (2002) The need for and meaning of positive organizational behavior. J Organ Behav 23(6):695–706

Luthans F, Vogelgesang GR, Lester PB (2006) Developing the psychological capital of resiliency. Hum Resour Dev Rev 5(1):25–44

Marston A (2016) Transformative resilience: the way forward for women leaders. Retrieved from https://www.doublexeconomy.com/2016/04/22/transformative-resilience-the-way-forward-for-women-leaders/

Masten AS (1994) Resilience in individual development: successful adaptation despite risk and adversity. In: Wang MC, Gordon EW (eds) Educational resilience in inner-city America: challenges and prospects. Lawrence Erlbaum Associates, Mahwah, pp 3–26

Masten AS (2005) Ordinary magic: resilience processes in development. In: Annual progress in child psychiatry and child development, vol 56. Routledge, New York, pp 227–238

McCraty R, Atkinson M (2012) Resilience training programme reduces physiological and psychological stress in police officers. Glob Adv Health Med 1:44–66

McKinsey & Company (2021a) Seven Charts that show COVID-19's impact on women's employment, March 8. Retrieved from https://www.mckinsey.com/featured-insights/diversity-and-inclusion/seven-charts-that-show-covid-19s-impact-on-womens-employment

McKinsey & Company (2021b) Women in the workplace, September 27. Retrieved from https://www.mckinsey.com/featured-insights/diversity-and-inclusion/women-in-the-workplace

Megginson D, Clutterbuck D (2005) Techniques for coaching and mentoring. Routledge, New York

Murphy VH (2017) What do we know about loneliness and work? Harv Bus Rev. Retrieved from https://hbr.org/cover-story/2017/09/work-and-the-loneliness-epidemic

Pew Research Center (2015) The future of world religions: population growth projections, 2010–2050. Retrieved from https://www.pewresearch.org/religion/2015/04/02/religious-projections-2010-2050/

Richardson GE (2002) The metatheory of resilience and resiliency. J Clin Psychol 58(3):307–321

Robertson IT, Cooper CL, Sarkar M, Curran T (2015) Resilience training in the workplace from 2003 to 2014: a systematic review. J Occup Organ Psychol 88:533–562

Rutter M (2012) Resilience as a dynamic concept. Dev Psychopathol 24:335–344. https://doi.org/10.1017/S0954579412000028

Seibert SE, Kraimer ML, Heslin P (2016) Career resilience and adaptability. Organ Dyn 45:245–257

Seligman ME, Csikszentmihalyi M (2000) Positive psychology: an introduction. Am Psychol 55(1):5–14

Solanki S, Mandaviya M (2021) Does gender matter? Job stress, work-life balance, health and job satisfaction among university teachers in India. J Int Women's Stud 22(7):120–134. https://vc.bridgew.edu/jiws/vol22/iss7/10

The World Bank (2020) Labor force participation rate, female (% of female population ages 15+) (modeled ILO estimate), world [Data set]. The World Bank Databank

The World Economic Forum (2021) Global gender pay gap. Retrieved from https://www.weforum.org/reports/global-gender-gap-report-2021/digest

Tusaie K, Dyer J (2004) Resilience: a historical review of the construct. Holist Nurs Pract 18:3–10

Youssef CM, Luthans F (2007) Positive organizational behavior in the workplace: the impact of hope, optimism, and resilience. J Manag 33(5):774–800

Cross-References

From Individual to Organizational Transformation: A Foucauldian Perspective on Transformational Leadership
The Hero and the Sherpa: Your Guide Through Life's Challenges
The Metamanagement Model as a Framework for Organizational Transformation

Appendices

Appendix 1: One Family's Business Vision

We will become an international company – doing more and more business in other countries. We expect to grow our satellite companies and enter additional markets internationally.

We expect to reach growth rate of 20% annually while maintaining a minimum profit rate of 10%. We are investing in the development of new products – focusing on innovation and emerging customer needs.

Our success in part will be determined by our increasing ability to become more and more proficient at anticipating where the market is moving in order to deepen our brand and market penetration and serve these markets well, while maintaining our commitment to our values and our people.

A few of the keys to our success are honesty, vision, hard work, and perseverance. Our forefathers brought a determination to overcome obstacles and to reach goals. These goals included leaving a legacy that helps people and the community to reach a better life.

Our markets are changing at an exponential rate particularly in technology. Supply and demand is also changing as we witness a great increase in population. This change allows us to penetrate more markets. Investing in market studies is critical. We believe in planning for the best but always protecting and being prepared for business/investment failures. We must always preserve a safety net. Our businesses and assets currently are in a huge need of better organization and planning.

We view success as being based on the well-being of business owners and the amount of families that we impact positively. Strong business plans, clear market analysis, and analysis of competitor's success is important. There are always subjective and objective measures. Business growth evaluation should be done twice a year. Objective measures, such as standard business formulas both in market growth and financial measures, that is, return on investment (ROI), profit, capital growth, and so forth, will be utilized and also progress made on annual projections and goals.

We need to diversify as much as we can control. Now, 95% of our assets is in land. Our plan is to reduce this to be closer to 80%. The remaining 20% to 35%

J. Neal (ed.), *Personal, Educational and Organizational Transformation*, Future of Business and Finance, https://doi.org/10.1007/978-3-031-29253-8

needs to be different than our core business. This percentage can be both in businesses we control and in significant investments in others. We need to rebalance, otherwise we will suffer from not bringing in the level of revenue or capital growth that we could easily achieve.

Overall, we look for:

6–15% for return on investment
10–15% of growth in our businesses
3% of return on assets (ROA) in our businesses

In the future, we will invest in low-risk businesses with strong partners, hopefully making positive business decisions. It is our hope to give the best and to leave the best. By learning from others' and our own mistakes, setting clear business projections followed by hard work and a shared vision can guide a most positive future. We must be an agile and learning organization, embracing the ability to evolve and transform fast. We need a large vision that gives a clarity of ideas able to be articulated by all partners. Revenue growth starts here.

Overall, we see ourselves as macrodevelopers maximizing and giving value to land and being prepared for emerging and constantly changing markets. We may consider investment in tech industry and in financial markets.

We must guard against

1. *Not meeting our goals*
2. *Not seeing market needs and future*
3. *Not being prepared to face the needs that the city demands*
4. *Tax changes and increases that could seriously damage our core asset—land*

As we grow, we must continue to increase our entrepreneurship expertise and encourage each successive generation to excel at this endeavor! As we explore different businesses, we realize that we will need different kinds of business knowledge. We expect to bring in more expertise than within our family network. It is our goal to grow the family wealth and businesses consistent with our core values and mission in achieving personal, family, and business success.

Appendix B: Glossary of Family Business Terms

In this Glossary, I define the common family business terms typically used in family business transformation work. The reader is encouraged to look at various books in the Recommended Reading section (Appendix D), particularly (Jaffe, 2020), (Lansberg et al, 1997, Gersick et al, 1997).

Governance Structure is the structure that determines how different decisions are made and who has access to what information. The governance structure shown on Figure 4 is a fairly sophisticated family governance structure. In this family, the first generation had passed away, second generation had five people in their 50s and 60s, and the third generation ranged from teenagers to people in their 30s. Each family needs to create their own structure. Some families have both a family council and a family business council. Other have only one—the responsibilities differ depending on what is best for that particular family and family business.

Family Council this group is at the top of the hierarchy making sure all runs smoothly and reasonable progress is made in fulfilling the family and family business mission and vision under the values specified. The family council reports to the family community.

Family Office or Family Wealth Council or Family Business Council this group oversees the family wealth and often also serves as the investment arm of the family. Many families choose to hold much of their assets together (even after they have sold the business). This group often hires a manager such as a banker or investment professional. Family office reports to the family council.

Family Culture Council this is used in large families who want to have a committee that focuses on family issues only. Now that the family has a family vision, how do they create it? This is the responsibility of the family culture council.

Board of Directors or Advisors the reason to have a board of directors separate from owners is to bring in advisors who are not family members. This is usually a formal body driven by the laws of that state or country. Many family businesses create a board of advisors rather than a board of directors. Most countries assign liability to the board directors but NOT to boards of advisors. Like traditional boards this group's function is to oversee the business to make sure it is meeting shareholder needs and hires and fires the CEO and sometimes other critical officers.

Family Community this is usually all family members in all generations. Many families create both formal and informal family gatherings. The key here is to hold family gatherings solely for family enjoyment and not mixed in with business meetings.

Family Assembly usually is restricted to family shareholders or future family shareholders usually with a minimum age that requires, for example, at least 25 years old. Like a shareholder assembly, business is discussed, financial statements are reviewed, overall strategy is discussed, and hopefully approved. Information is usually held at a high level of confidentiality. Depending on the governance structure, they may need to approve major capital needs, profit distribution, concerns about board members, and overall functioning of the business and their financial returns.

Appendix C: Examples of Family Protocol Policies

Here are some examples of policies from some of the protocols that my family business clients have written, to give you a sense of different types of policies that families have created.

A. Philosophy of Family Employment

We appreciate that working in a family business is tricky. As we always want to preserve unconditional love and support for each individual's dream. If next generation's dreams are in connection with the company, we want them to participate in the company understanding that working in the company is based on competence and ongoing work performance. In short, they have opportunity to compete, realizing that their long-term employment is based on work performance and evaluation and that they bring the kinds of expertise that the company needs.

Job hiring is competitive. Family members have a "fair" shot to apply for any position where they meet the requirements.

For those who are interested in management jobs, it is most helpful if they have already worked in another company and received business education as that way they bring skills and knowledge. In short, the company is interested in individuals who help grow the company substantially. This makes them more competitive. If they do not have that then the other option is to join the company at entry level positions.

B. Employment Policies for Family Members

1. *Entrance Policies – family members may apply for positions as stipulated above. Family members are encouraged to apply for positions that they have the skills and knowledge to do. This may be entry level. Higher levels require more experience and knowledge.*
2. *Competitive Hiring – if there are two applicants with reasonably equal qualifications, bias will be for the family member. Family board members will not participate in the hiring process if possible (i.e., Management team positions must be hired by the CEO).*
3. *Roles, Responsibilities, and Performance Expectations – will be defined as clearly as possible in the job description and job profile. Family employees, like all employees, are subject to annual performance review. Expectations are for continuous learning, proficiency, improved performance, and company growth. Family compensation (including all benefits and vacation) is expected to be*

within market range. Performance review system is to be implemented by the end of 2020 for the whole company.

4. *Evaluation (Performance Review) and Development – family employee's performance will be reviewed like anyone else in the company with learning goals set and monitored on an annual basis.*

1. *Promotion is set through corporate policy. We are always looking for the "perfect fit" of personal aptitude, interest, and organizational needs.*
2. *Exit policies and severance pay will be paid as required by law. Proper notice must be given as required by law and/or corporate policy.*
3. *Retirement – when the individual reaches legal age for retirement, the company can decide on appropriate next steps.*

Another family put the following in their protocol:

Evaluation (Performance Review) and Development.
Family members understand that their work performance will be evaluated (as any other employee or manager). They must be open to criticism and feedback and make necessary changes to meet performance results as stipulated by superiors. Refusal or inability to do this may result in termination of their position.

Exit Policies (Executive Roles)

Individual's Choice
Proper notice must be given with enough time for human resource department to find an adequate replacement. It is expected that the higher the level of responsibility, the more time is needed.

An outgoing person may be asked to train a new person.

Company's Choice

If performance is inadequate and if after discussion and ample time to correct performance nothing changes, then, the person will either be put in a different position or asked to leave the company.

1. **Severance Pay –** *as required by law*
2. ***Health Issues –*** *if a family member or one of their family branch members is dealing with a health crisis, that is, cancer, and needs to not work for 6 or 12 months, then we will respond as a family that finds a way to meet with the individual's needs and the organizational needs. It is expected that family branch responds first, but general family will help financially, that is, as a loan. Level of crisis and amount of time is critical. It is agreed that all individuals have strong*

health insurance. Family Wealth Council (FWC) will review and coordinate health insurance for all family members. Responsibility is seen as held first by the individual, second by the branch, and lastly, by the Family Wealth Council. FWC will be responsible for determining amount of support given. The board will decide when replacement (if family executive) must be found. The business will work to supplement the individual – in need of income so that they are okay.

Appendix D: Recommended Reading

Beckhard, Richard, and Wendy Pritchard. (1992). *Changing the Essence: The Art of Creating and Leading Fundamental Change in Organizations.* San Francisco: Jossey-Bass.

Bowen, Murray. (2004). *Family Therapy in Clinical Practice.* Oxford, UK. Rowman & Littleton Publishers.

Covey, Stephen. (2013). *The 7 Habits of Highly Effective People: Powerful Lessons in Personal Change.* New York. Simon & Schuster Inc.

Dyer Jr., W.G. (1986.). *Cultural Change in Family Firms: Anticipating and Managing Business and Family Transitions.* San Francisco: Jossey-Bass.

Hughes, James Jr. (2007) *Family: The Compact Among Generations.* New York, NY: Bloomberg Press.

Jaffe, Dennis. (2020) *Borrowed From Your Grandchildren: The Evolution of 100 year old Family Enterprises.* Hoboken, NJ: John Wiley & Sons Inc.

McGregor, D. (1967). *The Human Side of Enterprise.* New York: McGraw Hill.

Miller, Danny and Breton-Miller, Isabel. (2005). *Managing for the Long Run.:Lessons in Competitive Advantage.* Boston: Harvard Business School Press.

Neal, J. and M. Vallejo. (2008). Family firms as incubators for spirituality in the workplace: Factors that nurture spiritual businesses, Journal of Management, Spirituality and Religion, Vol. 5, No. 2, 115–159.

Neubauer, Fred and Lank, Alden G. (1998) *The Family Business: Its Governance for Sustainability.* New York, NY: Routledge Press.

Ward, John L. (2011) *The Family Constitution: Agreements to Secure and Perpetuate Your Family Business.* New York, NY: Palgrave Macmillan.

Willams, Roy and Preisser, Vic. (2003). ***Preparing Heirs: Five Steps to a Successful Transition of Family Wealth and Values*** San Francisco, CA. Reed Publishers.

Index

J. Neal (ed.), *Personal, Educational and Organizational Transformation*, Future of Business and Finance, https://doi.org/10.1007/978-3-031-29253-8